DATE DUE

			PRINTED IN U.S.A.

ISBN 0-7876-2872-7

Kevin Hillstrom
Laurie Collier Hillstrom

ENCYCLOPEDIA *of*
Small Business

J-Z
VOLUME 2

ENCYCLOPEDIA *of*
Small Business

J-Z
VOLUME 2

...vin Hillstrom and Laurie Collier Hillstrom, *Editors*

Contributing Authors

...Paula M. Ard, Virginia L. Barnstorff, Christopher C. Barry, Laurence Barton, Bradley ...e Boyd, John Burnett, Robert Buttery, Boyd Childress, Amy Cooper, Raymond A. K. ...Richard C. Cuthie, Aldona Cytraus, Louis J. Drapeau, Sina Dubovoy, Art DuRivage, ...ham Gal, April Dougal Gasbarre, Edmund R. Gray, Susan Bard Hall, Heather Behn Hedden, Tona Henderson, Ned. C. Hill, Ronald M. Horwitz, Cynthia Ianarelli, Frederick C. Ingram, Clint Johnson, Kristin Kahrs, Susan M. Kasuba, Christine M. Kelley, Robert T. Kleiman, Jan Klisz, Michael Knes, David Kucera, John Lawler, Joan Leotta, John G. Maurer, Don Mayer, Bruce Meyer, Dave Mote, Matthew T. Pifer, Richard Rump, Anandi P. Sahu, Susan Salter, John Sarich, Arthur G. Sharp, John Simley, Kathryn Snavely, David Sprinkle, Paulette L. Stenzel, John E. Tropman, Karen Troshynski-Thomas, David E. Upton, David A. Victor, Etan Vlessing, Mark A. Vonderembse, Mark A. White, Roberta H. Winston, Charles Woelfel, Art Wojtowicz, Dave Zemens, and Judith A. Zimmerman

Gale Research Staff
Deborah M. Burek, *Managing Editor*

Eva M. Davis, Linda D. Hall, William H. Harmer, Kelly Hill, Sonya D. Hill, Yolanda A. Johnson, Karin E. Koek, and Julie A. Mitchell, *Contributing Editors*

Mary Beth Trimper, *Production Director*
Evi Seoud, *Assistant Production Manager*
Cindy Baldwin, *Product Design Manager*
Eric Johnson, *Art Director*

Jeff Chapman, *Programmer/Analyst*

Library of Congress Cataloging-in-Publication Data
Hillstrom, Kevin, 1963-
   Encyclopedia of small business / Kevin Hillstrom, Laurie Collier Hillstrom
      p. cm.
      Includes bibliographical references and index.
      ISBN 0-7876-1864-0 (set : alk. paper).—ISBN0-7876-2871-9 (vol.
1 : alk. paper).—ISBN 0-7876-2872-7 (vol. 2 :   alk. paper)
      1. Small business—Management—Encyclopedia.   2. Small business—
Finance—Encyclopedia.   I. Hillstrom, Laurie Collier, 1965-   .
II. Title.
   HD62.7.H553   1998   98-14862
   658.02'2—dc21   CIP

Copyright © 1998 by Gale Research
835 Penobscot Bldg.
645 Griswold St.
Detroit, MI 48226-4094

ISBN 0-7876-1864-0 (set), ISBN 0-7876-2871-9 (V1), ISBN 0-7876-2872-7 (V2)

Printed in the United States of America

CONTENTS

J

JOB DESCRIPTION

At the heart of the recruitment process lies the general concept that a company needs to hire people to complete certain tasks or group of tasks within the organization. The description of the various responsibilities of each position can usually be found within the "job description" or "job specification" that is typically put together by business owners or managers. Recruiters and personnel managers rely on clear and concise job descriptions to streamline the application and interviewing process and to judge work performance after a person has been hired. Job descriptions and specifications usually include known duties and responsibilities, required levels of education and work experience, salary and benefits provided to employees in exchange for their labor, and information regarding the work environment. Job descriptions also often include helpful details addressing other work-related issues, such as the position's travel obligations, normal work schedule, physical location where duties of position will be carried out, union status, supervisory relationships, bonuses, and any other information directly pertinent to the execution of any and all responsibilities associated with the job. In essence, wrote Philip B. Crosby in *The Eternally Successful Organization,* effective job descriptions simply let employees know what is expected of them: "If people are going to perform their assigned task, then they obviously have to know what it is, how to do it, and how to measure the results. Either someone has to explain it all to them or they have to figure it out themselves."

Researchers, executives, and small business owners all agree that job descriptions—if studied and created carefully and used appropriately as a **productivity** measurement tool—can help organizations, especially in the early stages of a worker's employment. "For purposes of learning and adaptation to one's role in an organizational setting, there is an axiom that states the clearer the role and various expectations that can be developed for employees, the better and faster success will be achieved," said Joseph D. Levesque, author of *The Human Resource Problem Solver's Handbook.* "Explicit, understandable, and agreeable roles and expectations are best, while ambiguity and inconsistency will lengthen and/or confuse adaptive learning. Structuring of the adaptation process for employees is important since most of our employees come to us from other organizational learning experiences where they may have developed some characteristics we're soon to find contrary to our organization's culture." One of the swiftest ways in which organizations can begin the process of employee adaptation is by clearly communicating their expectations via job descriptions.

JOB DESCRIPTIONS AND COMPANY CULTURE

The level of detail utilized in the creation of job descriptions and the monitoring of employee execution of the duties articulated therein can vary tremendously from organization to organization. A multinational corporation, for example, may have job descriptions that are far more formal and detailed in their contents than those used by a small local business. Companies in different industries tend to approach the issue of job descriptions differently as well (tool and die manufacturers, for example, are more likely to institute job definitions for various positions than are fishing charter services). And, finally, some business owners and management teams simply institute and nourish different company cultures that may have dramatically different conceptions of the need for and conceptions of job descriptions. As Meredith Belbin, Barrie Watson, and Cindy West observed in *People Management,* for instance, companies that operate in a flexible working environment in which employee roles are fluid and expectations change may find the quest to define various job parameters to be a daunting one. ''The essence of the problem is how clear directives, where these are needed, can be reconciled with flexible work systems,'' wrote Belbin, Watson, and West. ''One approach to this is for a manager to set up a job as a working hypothesis on how the work should be carried out. Added to this is a system of continuing feedback to check whether the job is proceeding as expected. Thus, the boundaries and content of the job can be defined through an interactive communication process.''

But researchers note that on the whole, larger organizations will often, out of either real or imagined necessity, institute more formalized job description/ monitoring procedures. Still, in many companies with detailed plans in this area, ''job descriptions are usually thought of as something for the lower-level people in an organization,'' said Crosby. ''Higher-ups have 'mission statements' which sound good but are hard to measure. So we have all these people doing things which we may or may not have agreed to do. It doesn't take very long before a great deal of the organization's work has very little to do with the main objectives of the business.'' He and other business consultants contend that job descriptions can help business enterprises maintain their focus at all job levels, including top management and ownership positions. Owners of family establishments or very small business enterprises, meanwhile, may simply decide that formal job descriptions are unnecessary. Ultimately, each small business owner needs to consider the unique aspects of his or her own business situation when deciding how to define and monitor the responsibilities of each work position.

JOB DESCRIPTIONS AND PERFORMANCE APPRAISALS

One major advantage associated with formal job descriptions is that it provides business owners and supervisors with a useful tool of performance measurement. ''Fundamentally, productivity means producing—getting the work done with the most advantageous results using the best possible methods,'' observed Levesque. ''Doing work and getting results is a measurement of *what* we do, while the methods used to carry out work is a measurement of *how* we

conduct ourselves and our work transactions. Therefore, each job is represented by what is within the defined scope of the position (job description) in relation to others we work with, and how each job function is carried out. . . . What does good communications of performance criteria constitute? At the very minimum it means giving employees copies of their job description and appraisal form, then explaining what kinds of job functions are evaluated against performance dimensions and standards.'' In addition, job descriptions are often used to provide potential job applicants with a sense of the various obligations and rewards of that position, to help businesses develop salary grades, and to help maintain a recognizable organizational structure.

But while the benefits that accrue to businesses that take the time and effort to devise and update job descriptions are numerous, consultants note that firms still need to be cognizant of what Allan Halcrow, editor of *Personnel Journal,* called the ''hidden traps in job descriptions.'' ''I'd be willing to wager that there's a potential legal nightmare lurking in your office. It's probably hiding where you would least expect it, tucked away in a file folder or notebook you haven't opened in months or years. It's called a job description,'' Halcrow said in *Folio: The Magazine for Magazine Management.* ''In today's litigious climate . . . those seemingly innocuous documents can come back to haunt you on issues such as overtime, performance reviews, and terminations.'' According to Halcrow, ''the fundamental problem is that the job descriptions you may consider merely guidelines about work tasks and expectations may be seen as much more definitive by attorneys and the courts.''

PERFORMANCE REVIEWS Annual or semi-annual performance reviews are fixtures in most establishments, and they are useful to both employee and employer for many reasons. But employers should know that they can also run into trouble here if they give an employee poor marks for their work on tasks that are not delineated in their official job description. ''You're at legal risk if you hold employees responsible for work that has not been defined in writing,'' Halcrow flatly stated. He noted that this problem is most likely to crop up in situations where a reorganization or attrition has prompted a reallocation of responsibilities within the organization. Of course, bestowing praise on an individual who takes on responsibilities not mentioned within his or her job description is unlikely to have unwanted repercussions. ''The key,'' said Halcrow, ''is to be careful not to tie negative outcomes (such as discipline or denial of a raise) to duties outside the job description'' or to unduly focus on those duties at the expense of those responsibilities that are specifically mentioned.

OVERTIME Practically all employers are aware of the differences in classifying employees as exempt or non-exempt in the area of **overtime** compensation. But Halcrow noted that many employers are not aware that overtime liability can be linked to an employee's duties *as they are described in his or her job description,* not according to what tasks the employee actually performs: ''For example, suppose you decide that one of your supervisors should be moved to a larger office, or to one closer to the production department. If the employee comes in over the weekend to pack or move boxes, you may be liable for overtime—even if the employee is exempt—because packing and moving are not part of the employee's usual job activities. . . . This principle applies to any tasks not normally performed by the employee, or to tasks that are not directly related to his or her normal job duties [such as going to the post office or addressing envelopes]. The important issue to consider isn't whether the activity is a one-time event, but whether the task relates to the employee's usual job duties.''

EMPLOYEE DISMISSALS Small business owners that decide to terminate an employee for poor performance have to make sure that they are doing so because of their dissatisfaction with the targeted employee's work on tasks that are discussed in the job description.

JOB DESCRIPTION "UPKEEP AND MAINTENANCE" Human resource management experts point out that there are a number of precautions that employers can take to help protect themselves from job description head-aches. These include updating, proper classification, and communication.

1) Continuous updating—According to Halcrow, ''each employee's job description should be amended when his or her duties change. Reassigning tasks or simply letting them drift until someone steps in to do them is not a good idea. It doesn't matter that everyone in the company know who's doing the work, and that the situation is 'understood.' '' He recommended that employers react quickly when an employee quits or is terminated, making sure that each task is formally reassigned in writing to another person's job description.

2) Proper classification—Employers who remain cognizant of job descriptions and classifications when assigning various tasks are far less likely to get tripped up on overtime hassles than businesses that are careless about such issues.

3) Communication—In addition to regularly scheduled performance reviews, employers should make sure that employees who find their duties and responsibilities undergoing change have the opportunity to ask questions—and even to raise objections.

FURTHER READING:

Arthur, Diane. *Recruiting, Interviewing, Selecting & Orienting New Employees.* New York: Amacom, 1991.

Belbin, Meredith, Barrie Watson, and Cindy West. ''True Colours.'' *People Management.* March 6, 1997.

Crosby, Philip B. *The Eternally Successful Corporation: The Art of Corporate Wellness.* New York: New American Library, 1990.

Degner, Jim. ''Writing Job Descriptions that Work.'' *Credit Union Executive.* November-December 1995.

Dorf, Paul, and Ethel P. Flanders. ''Classify Jobs Properly to Avoid Overtime Trap.'' *HRMagazine.* April 1994.

Halcrow, Allan. ''Hidden Traps in Job Descriptions.'' *Folio: The Magazine for Magazine Management.* December 1, 1992.

Levesque, Joseph D. *The Human Resource Problem-Solver's Handbook.* New York: McGraw-Hill, 1992.

Milkovich, George T., and John W. Boudreau. *Human Resource Management.* Boston, MA: Richard D. Irwin, 1991.

Shay, Tom. ''Job Descriptions Help You Manage.'' *Chilton's Hardware Age.* May 1990.

Wanous, John Parker. *Organizational Entry: Recruitment, Selection, Orientation and Socialization of Newcomers.* New York: Addison-Wesley, 1992.

Werther, William B., and Keith Davis. *Human Resources and Personnel Management.* New York: McGraw-Hill, 1993.

SEE ALSO: Employee Performance Appraisals; Employee Hiring; Employee Termination; Recruiting

JOINT VENTURES

A joint venture is a business enterprise undertaken by two or more persons or organizations to share the expense and (hopefully) profit of a particular business project. ''Joint ventures are not business organizations in the sense of proprietorships, partnerships or corporations,'' noted Charles P. Lickson in *A Legal Guide for Small Business.* ''They are agreements between parties or firms for a particular purpose or venture. Their formation may be very informal, such as a handshake and an agreement for two firms to share a booth at a trade show. Other arrangements can be extremely complex, such as the consortium of major U.S. electronics firms to develop new microchips. . . . A joint venture is, in effect, a form of partnership that is limited to a particular purpose.'' Joint ventures have grown in popularity in recent years, despite the relatively high failure rate of such efforts for one reason or another. Creative small business owners have been able to use this business strategy to good advantage over the years, although the practice remains one primarily associated with larger corporations.

Most joint ventures are formed for the ultimate purpose of saving money. This is as true of small neighborhood stores that agree to advertise jointly in the weekly paper as it is of international oil companies that agree to work together for purposes of oil and gas exploration or extraction. Joint ventures are attractive because they enable companies to share both risks and costs.

TYPES OF JOINT VENTURES Equity-based joint ventures benefit foreign and/or local private interests, groups of interests, or members of the general public. Under non-equity joint ventures (also known as cooperative agreements), meanwhile, the parties seek technical service arrangements, franchise and brand use agreements, management contracts, rental agreements, or one-time contracts, e.g., for construction projects. Participants do not always furnish capital as part of their joint venture commitments. There are, for example, non-equity arrangements in which some companies are more in need of technical services or technological expertise than they are capital. They may want to modernize operations or start new production operations. Thus, they limit partners' participation to technical assistance. Such arrangements often include some funding as well, albeit limited.

LEGAL STRUCTURE OF JOINT VENTURES

As Lickson observed in *A Legal Guide for Small Business,* joint ventures are governed entirely by the legal agreement that brought them into existence. ''Unless the joint venture is formalized by creation of a corporation or partnership, it never ripens into a tax-paying, legal entity on its own. Instead, the joint venture functions through the legal status of the venture participants, known as co-venturers or venture partners,'' Lickson wrote. ''Since the joint venture is not a legal entity on its own, it does not hire people, enter into contracts, or have its own tax liabilities. These matters are handled through the co-venturers. Corporate law, partnership law, and the law of sole proprietorship do not govern joint ventures; contract law governs joint ventures.'' And as Marc J. Lane noted in the *Legal Handbook for Small Business,* ''since the venture ends at the conclusion of a specific project, issues of continuity of life and free transferability become moot.''

WHY JOINT VENTURES FAIL

Small business owners should not engage in joint ventures without adequate planning and strategy. They cannot afford to, since the ultimate goal of joint ventures is the same as it is for any type of business operation: to make a profit. Experience dictates that both parties in a joint venture should know exactly what they wish to derive from their partnership. There must be an agreement before the partnership becomes a reality. There must also be a firm commitment on the part of each member to the project and to one another. One of the leading causes for the failure of joint ventures is that some participants do not reveal their true business agendas, or mislead their partners about their ability to uphold their end of the bargain.

Many small business consultants counsel clients to approach joint ventures cautiously. They acknowledge that such partnerships can be most valuable in nourishing a company's growth and stability, but also point out that smaller businesses usually have far less margin for error than do multinational corporations, or even mid-sized companies. Some experts recommend that business owners considering a joint venture with another establishment (or establishments) launch a small joint venture first. Such small projects allow companies to test the relationship without committing large amounts of money. This is especially true when companies with different structures, corporate cultures, and strategic plans work together. Such differences are difficult to overcome and frequently lead to failure. That is why a ''courtship'' is beneficial to joint venture participants.

Other factors that can have a debilitating impact on joint ventures include marketplace developments, lagging technology, partner's inability (rather than reluctance) to honor the contract, and regulatory uncertainties. Another problem with joint ventures concerns the issue of management. The managers of one company may be more adept and/or decisive with their decision-making than their counterparts at the other company. This can lead to friction and a lack of cooperation. Projects are doomed to failure if there is not a well-defined decision-making process in place that is predicated on mutual goals and strategies.

BENEFITS OF JOINT VENTURES

Among the most significant benefits derived from joint ventures is that partners save money and reduce their risks through capital and resource sharing. Joint ventures also give smaller companies the chance to work with larger ones to develop, manufacture, and market new products. They also give companies of all sizes the opportunity to increase sales, gain access to wider markets, and enhance technological capabilities through **research and development** (R&D) underwritten by more than one party. Until relatively recently, U.S. companies were often reluctant to engage in research and development partnerships, and government agencies tried not to become involved in business development. However, with the emergence of countries that feature technologically advanced industries (such as electronics or computer microchips) supported extensively by government funding, American companies have become more willing to participate in joint ventures in these areas. In addition, both federal and state agencies have become more generous with their financial support in these areas. Government's increased involvement in the private business environment has created more opportunities for companies to engage in domestic and international joint ventures, although they are still legally limited in what they can do and where they can operate.

FURTHER READING:

Harrigan, Kathryn Rudie, *Managing for Joint Venture Success.* Lexington, MA: Lexington Books, 1986.

Lane, Marc J. *Legal Handbook for Small Business.* Rev. ed. New York: AMACOM, 1989.

Lickson, Charles P. *A Legal Guide for Small Business.* Crisp Publications, 1994.

Lynch, Robert Porter, *The Practical Guide to Joint Ventures & Corporate Alliances.* New York: John Wiley and Sons, 1989.

SEE ALSO: Cost Sharing; Mergers and Acquisitions; Small Business/Large Business Relationships

K

A Keogh is an employer-funded, tax-deferred retirement plan designed for unincorporated businesses or self-employed persons, including those who earn only part of their income from self-employment. Covered under Section 401(c) of the tax code, Keogh plans are named after Eugene Keogh, the congressman who first came up with the idea. Keogh plans feature relatively high allowable contributions—25 percent of salary to a maximum of $30,000 annually, in some cases—which makes them popular among sole proprietors and small businesses with high incomes. In general, however, Keoghs are more costly to set up and administer than similar retirement programs, such as **Simplified Employee Pension (SEP)** plans, because they require annual preparation and filing of IRS Form 5500. This long and complicated document usually requires a small business to obtain the services of an accountant or financial advisor, plus the information reported becomes available to the public.

As is the case with other common types of retirement programs, Keogh contributions made on employees' behalf are tax-deductible for the employer, and the funds are allowed to grow tax-deferred until the employee withdraws them upon retirement. The funds held in a Keogh may be invested in certificates of deposit, mutual funds, stocks, bonds, annuities, or some combination thereof. Withdrawals are not permitted until after the employee has reached age 59 ½, or else the amount withdrawn is subject to a 10 percent penalty in addition to regular income taxes. Usually only the employer may contribute to a Keogh

plan. In addition, the employer can establish a vesting schedule through which employees gradually gain full rights to the funds in their accounts over a number of years. Keogh accounts must be opened by December 31 in order to qualify for tax deductions in a given year, but funds can be contributed until the company's tax deadline.

TYPES OF KEOGH PLANS

Keogh plans can be structured in a number of ways. Although it is possible to design a Keogh as a defined benefit plan (which determines a fixed amount of benefit to be paid upon retirement, then uses an actuarial formula to calculate the annual contribution required to provide that benefit), most Keoghs take the form of a defined contribution plan (which determines an amount of annual contribution without regard to the total benefit that will be available upon retirement). The three most common types of Keoghs are profit-sharing, money purchase, and combination plans—all of which fall under the category of defined contribution plans.

Profit sharing Keoghs are the most flexible, allowing the employer to make larger contributions in good financial years and skip contributions in lean years. This type of plan enables the employer to contribute a maximum of 15 percent of compensation, or $22,500 per employee, annually. In contrast, money purchase Keoghs are highly restrictive, requiring the employer to make a mandatory annual contribution of a predetermined percentage of compensation. For this reason, many smaller businesses or those with variable levels of income shy away from this type of plan. On the positive side, money purchase Keoghs allow the highest possible contribution—25 percent of compensation, to a maximum of $30,000 per employee, annually. Combination Keogh plans, as the name suggests, offer the best features of the other two primary types. Combination plans allow the employer to designate a fixed percentage of mandatory annual contribution, then supplement this amount with additional, discretionary contributions in years when profit levels are high. The total annual contributions in a combination plan cannot exceed 25 percent of compensation or $30,000.

Though Keoghs give small business owners valuable tax deductions and enable them to provide a valuable benefit to their employees, the plans also have some disadvantages. Business owners who employ other people are required to fund a retirement program for nonowner employees if they establish one for themselves. But because the owner's contributions to his or her own plan are based upon the net income of the business—from which self-employment taxes and contributions to employees' retirement accounts have already been deducted—the owner's allowable contributions are reduced. In the case of a money purchase or combination Keogh plan, for example, the business owner is only able to contribute 20 percent (rather than 25 percent) to his or her own retirement fund. But many companies find that the benefits of Keogh plans outweigh the drawbacks. Small businesses that offer such plans can use them to attract potential employees and deter current employees from leaving the company to work for a larger competitor. With their high allowable contribution levels, Keogh plans also give the business owner a good opportunity to achieve a financially secure retirement.

FURTHER READING:

Blakely, Stephen. "Pension Power." *Nation's Business.* July 1997.

Crouch, Holmes F. *Decisions When Retiring.* Allyear Tax Guides, 1995.

Nadel, Alan A. "Self-Employment Tax Treatment of Keogh and SEP Contributions and Unreimbursed Business Expenses." *The Tax Adviser.* November 1995.

Pedace, Frank Jr. "Keoghs: Unlocking the Key to Retirement Planning." *Air Conditioning, Heating and Refrigeration News.* September 16, 1996.

Weinstein, Grace W. "Financial Savvy for the Self-Employed: Planning Ahead for Your Retirement Can Reap High Rewards." *Black Enterprise.* September 1996.

SEE ALSO: Retirement Planning

L

LABOR SURPLUS AREA

A labor surplus area is an economic region in which the number of prospective—and qualified—employees for positions with a company or companies exceeds the number of jobs available. This state of affairs can be an important component in business success, for businesses operating in labor surplus areas can typically find the personnel they need to conduct their operations at lower payroll expense than can businesses that may have to offer more generous compensation packages to secure even mediocre employees. "Although many factors relating to labor are essential, with respect to location decisions, the primary factor is the availability of labor in the region," confirmed Howard Weiss and Mark Gershon in *Production and Operations Management.* "Typically, a company wants to see a high ratio between the number of potential employees and the number of jobs available. The reason for this is twofold. First, this gives the company a large pool of applicants to screen, allowing the company to be selective in hiring those it feels will best fits its needs, which leads to a productive work force. In addition, if there is competition for the positions due to the large labor pool, there will be less chance of the company's losing workers. Second, typically, a company does not want a region to be dependent on it. If most workers in the region depend on Company X and the company then moves or goes out of business, the entire region will be affected adversely, which reflects poorly on the company."

Business experts note, however, that a labor surplus does not truly exist unless there exists a surplus of prospective employees who possess the necessary skills and experience (educational or work) to handle the responsibilities of the jobs that need to be filled. While some companies engage in industries that require only semiskilled or unskilled labor, others—such as high technology companies—rely on a highly educated and skilled work force. Such a business may be located in a region in which large numbers of people are looking for employment, but unless those people also have the necessary training and skills to meet the company's needs, the business is not operating in a true labor surplus environment.

Many analysts and business consultants point out that the labor availability disparities that are evident in certain industries will continue to exist—and possibly widen—over the next few years. Some manufacturing and technology sectors, for example, are expected to operate with periodic shortages of labor talent for the next several years; this partially accounts for the high salary levels that skilled practitioners in these areas can currently command (the National Association of Colleges and Employers reported that starting salaries for computer science graduates rose nearly 8 percent from 1996 to 1997). But other geographic and industry sectors are expected to be able to take advantage of labor surpluses, and many observers contend that the current tight labor market that some industries are experiencing will ease in the coming years. "The labor force will grow in number in the next few years," predicted Anne Fisher in *Fortune.* "More people will be more highly educated than ever before. Market forces will kick in—albeit gradually—and guide people toward the growing number of high-skilled jobs that pay above-average wages. And, perhaps most important, employers will wake up" and recognize the importance of training their current work force. Fisher cited the growing number of "retirement-age" people staying in the work force, the dramatic growth in continuing education among adults, and the computer-literate character of today's youth as evidence of possible future labor surpluses in high-skilled industry areas.

FURTHER READING:

Edmondson, Brad. "Work Slowdown." *American Demographics.* March 1996.

Fisher, Anne. "What Labor Shortage?" *Fortune.* June 23, 1997.

Fullerton, Howard N., Jr. "Labor Force 2006: Slowing Down and Changing Composition." *Monthly Labor Review.* November 1997.

Lyne, Jack. "The Skills Gap: U.S. Work-Force Woes Complicate Business-Location Equation." *Site Selection.* August 1992.

"Scientists, Engineers—Shortage or Surplus?" *Research-Technology Management.* July-August 1996.

Weiss, Howard J., and Mark E. Gershon. *Production and Operations Management.* Boston, MA: Allyn and Bacon, 1989.

SEE ALSO: Employee Compensation; Employee Hiring; Work Force

LABOR UNIONS

A labor union is an organization of wage earners or salary workers established for the purpose of protecting their collective interests when dealing with employers. Though unions are prevalent in most industrialized countries, union representation of workers has generally declined in most countries over the past 30 to 40 years. In the United States, unions represented about one-third of all workers in the 1950s. Today, unions represent less than 15 percent of the labor force—and only about 10 percent of the labor force in the private sector (unions represented nearly 38 percent of public-sector workers in 1996). But although labor unions are not as strong a force in the United States economy as they have been in earlier decades, they continue to be an important factor in American business.

TYPES OF UNIONS

Unions can be categorized according to ideology and organizational forms. A distinction is often made between political unionism and business unionism. Although the goals and objectives of politically oriented unions may overlap those of business unions, political unions are primarily related to some larger working-class movement. Most political unions have some formal association with a working-class political party; these types of unions are more prevalent in Europe than they are in the United States. Contemporary American labor unions are best viewed as business unions. Business unions generally support the capitalist economic system and focus their attention on protecting and enhancing the economic welfare of the workers they represent, usually through some form of collective bargaining. According to U.S. law, unions can bargain with employers over wages, hours, and working conditions.

But while most American unions are classified as business rather than political unions, U.S. business unions often do have some involvement in the nation's politics. Most large national unions are involved in lobbying and electoral activities at various levels of government, including the federal level. However, such political efforts serve to supplement their principal economic goals. For example, many unions campaigned against passage of the **North American Free Trade Agreement (NAFTA)**. The labor movement feared that NAFTA would undercut jobs of union workers and weaken the ability of unions to negotiate favorable contracts with employers.

The earliest unions in the United States were known as craft unions. Craft unions represent employees, generally highly skilled, in a single occupation or group of closely related occupations. Craft unions are most common in occupations in which employees frequently switch employers and examples include the various skilled trades in the construction industry, such as carpentry, plumbing, and electrical work. A construction worker is usually hired to complete work at a specific job site and then moves on to work elsewhere (often for another employer). In addition to collective bargaining, craft unions often serve as a placement service for members. Employers contact the union's hiring hall and union members currently out of work are referred to jobs.

Closely related to craft unions, though distinct in many respects, are professional unions. A professional is generally understood to be an employee with advanced and highly specialized skills, often requiring some credentials, such as a college degree and/or a license. Professional unions are a much more recent development than craft unions and are most common in the public sector. Teacher's unions are one of the most visible examples of this type of union.

Most unionized workers in the United States belong to industrial unions. An industrial union represents workers across a wide range of occupations within one or more industries. A good example of an industrial union is the United Automobile Workers (UAW). It represents skilled craft workers, assembly-line workers, and unskilled workers in all of the major American automobile companies. The UAW negotiates separate contracts for workers with each of these companies. Although industrial unions began by organizing workers in a single industry or group of related industries, most have diversified over the past 30 to 40 years. For example, in addition to representing auto workers, the UAW represents workers in the tractor and earth-moving equipment industry (e.g., Caterpillar and John Deere) and in the aerospace industry (e.g., Boeing).

Another organizational form is the general union. General unions organize workers across all occupations and industries. Although some highly diversified unions, such as the Teamsters, may appear to be general unions at first glance, this form of organization does not really exist in the United States. Because they are typically politically oriented, general unions are more common in Europe and developing countries.

OPEN SHOP AND CLOSED SHOP The term '' open shop'' refers to a company policy that does not restrict the business's employee work force to union members. '' Closed shop,'' on the other hand, refers to a company that hires only union members. Under this latter arrangement, employees are required to join the existing union within a specified time after they have been hired.

UNION GROWTH AND DECLINE

Union membership in the United States has varied considerably throughout the country's history. Although unions have been in existence in some form in the United States for nearly 200 years, they did not attain any meaningful level of power and influence until the 1930s, when several factors combined to spur a dramatic rise in union growth (the unionization rate went from about 12 percent of the labor force in 1935 to between 32 percent and 35 percent in the mid-1950s):

1) The American economy shifted from an agricultural to an industrial base; industrial workers, who were concentrated in urban areas and increasingly shared the same language (English), were thus able to create a common culture that was absent among earlier generations of workers.

2) The Depression created a backlash against big business entities, who were viewed as the chief culprits for the country's economic difficulties.

3) Active support for organized labor was an integral part of Roosevelt's New Deal, and the passage of the National Labor Relations Act (NLRA) in 1935 was a potent new weapon for union organizers. The NLRA provided a means for official recognition of labor unions. Once recognized, an employer was legally bound to bargain with the union.

4) Economic growth during World War II and in the post-war era was an important facilitator of union growth.

By the mid-1950s, the most union-prone sectors of the American economy had largely been organized, and millions of workers saw improvements in their living standards as a direct result of union activity. Many economists observed that this rise in union fortunes helped non-union workers as well. ''Collective bargaining has significantly improved the wages and working conditions of unionized and nonunionized workers,'' contended Sar Levitan, Peter Carlson, and Isaac Shapiro in *Protecting America's Workers.* ''Other benefits of union representation include increased leisure, better medical coverage, and more secure pensions. . . . Finally, unions have helped non-union workers by lobbying for legislation that grants all workers such protections as equal employment, safe and healthy workplaces, and secure pensions.''

Unions maintained their strength at around one-third of the labor force until about 1960. Through the 1960s to mid-1970s, union membership declined gradually, decreasing to about 25 percent of the labor force. The rate of decline was much sharper in the 1980s, and by the mid-1990s union membership had declined to only 14 percent of the total labor force.

Factors often cited for the decline in union membership include the following:

1) The changing nature of the global economy. International competition has increased significantly over the past few generations, especially in sectors of the economy that were heavily unionized (e.g., automobiles, steel, and textiles). As these industries became more globally competitive, employer resistance to unions often increased. In addition, it became feasible for employers to relocate production facilities to areas of the country which have traditionally been less supportive of unionism (such as the southern and Mountain states) or overseas to less developed countries that have low wages and few unions. Finally, employment in traditionally nonunion industries expanded, while employment in heavily unionized sectors declined.

2) Shifting demographics of the **work force**. In the 1930s, ''blue collar'' workers represented a large proportion of the labor force. Now ''white collar'' workers (i.e., managers, professionals, and clericals) are a very large component of the labor force. In general, white collar workers have been difficult to organize (except in the public sector). Moreover, Levitan, Carlson, and Shapiro said that ''the growing numbers of women and youth in the labor force render unionization more difficult since these groups have traditionally displayed little interest in joining unions.''

3) Changing attitudes of government. As early as 1947, amendments were added to the NLRA that significantly expanded employer rights and limited the rights of unions. The best-known of these laws was the Labor Management Relations Act, also known as the Taft-Hartley Act. Moreover, appointees to the **National Labor Relations Board**, which enforces the NLRA, became increasingly pro-management in outlook during the 1970s and 1980s.

4) Increased management opposition to unions, in large part because of the perception that union demands and attitudes were unreasonable.

5) Ineffective union organization efforts. "The unions themselves have contributed to their declining fortunes," wrote Levitan, Carlson, and Shapiro. "Union organizing activity, measured by organizing expenditures and the number of elections held, has diminished during [the 1970s and 1980s]." Dwindling membership made some unions more vulnerable to the repercussions of strikes as well.

By the mid-1990s, however, there were indications that America's leading unions, which have been criticized in recent years as reactive and sluggish, had adopted more proactive measures in order to shore up existing membership and expand the presence of unions elsewhere. This "revival" of organized labor, as some observers have dubbed it, is being studied closely by all sectors of American business and academia.

INDUSTRIES FEATURING STRONG UNION PRESENCE

Unions have traditionally been strong in four sectors of the American economy: transportation, construction, mining, and manufacturing. They have lost substantial ground in all four of these sectors in the last 25 years. In the transportation sector, an important factor has been deregulation, particularly in the trucking and airline industries. Substantial increases in competition in those industries have made it difficult for unions to negotiate favorable contracts or organize new units. In construction, the growth of nonunion contractors, able to hire qualified workers outside of the union hiring hall system, undercut union contractors. At one time, more than 80 percent of all commercial construction in the United States had been unionized; today, however, the percentage of workers engaged in construction that belong to unions is a fraction of that. Foreign competition and technological change have weakened mining unions. In manufacturing, the whole range of factors previously discussed has been responsible for union decline. The only sector of the economy where unions have gained strength in recent years has

been public employment. In 1996, more than 37 percent of public employees at all levels of government—local, state, and federal—were unionized. The percentage of workers in unions in other industries, meanwhile, is as follows, according to 1996 U.S. Department of Labor statistics: Transportation (27 percent), Public Utilities (25 percent), Construction (18.5 percent), Manufacturing (17.2 percent), Mining (14 percent), Finance/Insurance/Services (5.7 percent), Wholesale/Retail (5.6 percent), Real Estate (2.4 percent), Agriculture (1.9 percent).

INTERNAL STRUCTURE AND ADMINISTRATION

Labor unions are complex and vary considerably with respect to internal structure and administrative processes. It is easiest to differentiate among three distinct levels within the labor movement: local unions, national unions, and federations.

LOCAL UNIONS Local unions are the building blocks of the labor movement. Although there are some free-standing local unions, the vast majority of locals are in some way affiliated with a national or international union. Most craft unions began as local unions, which then joined together to form national organizations. Some major industrial unions also began as amalgamations of local unions, though it was more common for national organizations to be formed first, with locals to be established later.

The duties of a local union almost always include the administration of a union contract, which means ensuring that the employer is honoring all of the provisions of the contract at the local level. In some instances, local unions might also negotiate contracts, although unions vary considerably in terms of the degree to which the parent union is involved in the negotiation process.

Another important function of the local union is servicing the needs of those represented by the union. If a worker represented by the union believes his or her rights under the union contract have been violated, then the union may intervene on that person's behalf. Examples of such situations include the discharge of an employee, failure to promote an employee according to a contract seniority clause, or failure to pay an employee for overtime. Virtually any provision of a contract can become a source of contention. The local union may try to settle the issue informally. If that effort is not successful, the union may file what is known as a *grievance*. This is a formal statement of the dispute with the employer; most contracts set forth a grievance procedure. In general, grievance procedures involve several different steps, with higher levels of management entering at each step. If the grievance cannot be settled through this mechanism, then the union may, if the contract allows, request a hearing before a neutral arbitrator, whose decision is final and binding.

Most craft unions have *apprenticeship programs* to train new workers in the craft. The local union, usually in cooperation with an employers' association, will be responsible for managing the apprenticeship program. In addition, local unions with hiring halls are responsible for making job referrals.

The jurisdiction of a local union depends to a large extent on the organizational form of the parent organization. Locals of industrial unions most often represent workers within a single plant or facility of a company (and thus are termed *plant locals*). For example, in the case of the UAW, each factory or production facility of each automobile manufacturer has a separate local union. In some rare cases, a factory may be so big that it requires more than a single local.

In contrast to plant locals, local craft unions (as well as some industrial unions) are best described as *area locals*. An area local represents all of a union's members in a particular geographical region and may deal with many different employers. Area locals are typically formed for one of two reasons. First, members may in the course of a year work for a number of different employers, as in the case of craft unions. Consequently, it would be difficult, if not impossible, to establish and maintain a separate local in each work location. Second, members may work continuously for a single employer, but each employer or location may be too small to justify a separate local union. The latter case is more typical of some industrial unions. The size of the region served by a local union depends on the number of members available. In large metropolitan areas, an area local might serve only members in a particular city. In less densely populated regions, an area local may cover an entire state.

Internal structures and administrative procedures differ between plant and area locals. In almost all local unions, the membership meeting represents the apex of power, as the officers of the union are accountable to the members much as the officers of a corporation are accountable to stockholders. However, in practice, membership participation in union affairs may be quite limited. In such instances, local union officers often enjoy considerable power.

Plant locals have a number of elected officials—usually a president, vice president, secretary, and treasurer. In most cases, the officers are full-time employees of the company the union represents, and the contract generally allows some release time for union affairs. In addition to the principal officers of the local, there are also a number of *stewards*. Stewards may be elected or appointed, depending upon the union. The steward serves as the everyday contact between the union and its rank-and-file members. If members have concerns about the affairs of the union,

these may be voiced to the steward. The steward's most important responsibility is handling grievances. Should a worker represented by the union have a dispute with the employer over his or her rights under the contract, the steward has the initial responsibility of representing the worker. Usually the steward will discuss the matter with the employee's supervisor to see if the dispute can be resolved. If not, a formal grievance may be filed, and it then proceeds through the grievance system. At higher levels in the grievance system the employee may be represented by a chief steward or union officers.

Area locals typically have more complex internal structures than plant locals. This is usually because of the large geographical region under the local's jurisdiction, along with the greater dispersion of members within the region. As in the case of plant locals, area locals hold periodic meetings in which the officials of the union are accountable to members. There are also elected officers in area locals, as well as stewards for the various work sites in the local's jurisdiction. The principal operating difference between a plant local and an area local is that the latter typically employs one or more full-time staff members to handle the affairs of the union on a daily basis. These staff members are usually called *business agents*. Given the dispersion of members over a large geographical area and the possibility that the local may be responsible for administering many different contracts, it is the business agent's responsibility to visit work sites regularly and deal with problems that may arise. The business agent may also be responsible for managing any apprenticeship programs and the union's hiring hall. Contracts are often negotiated directly by local unions and the business agents are usually responsible for these negotiations. In some unions, elected officers may serve as business agents, but normally business agents are separate staff members. Depending on the size of the local union, there may be a number of assistant business agents.

NATIONAL UNIONS In the mid-1990s, approximately 190 national unions conducted business in the United States, along with about 30 professional associations that carried on union activities. National unions are composed of the various local unions that they have chartered. Some unions have locals in Canada and therefore call themselves *international* unions. However, the terms *international union* and *national union* are generally used interchangeably in the United States.

As with local unions, the administrative structures of national unions vary considerably in complexity. One important factor is the size of the union: larger unions are structurally more complex. Structural complexity also differs between craft and industrial unions. Craft unions tend be smaller organizations that feature a decentralized decision-making structure. With craft unions, contracts usually have a limited geographical scope and are negotiated by local unions. The parent union can be of significant assistance, however. The national union pools the resources of local unions, thus helping out with things such as strike funds, and it may also provide research services and serve as the local union's voice in political matters at the national and state levels. In general, there are few intermediate units between the national office and the local craft unions. National officers, elected periodically, generally work on a full-time basis for the union. Such unions also hold national conventions, most often every couple of years. The officers of the national union are accountable to the convention, much as the officers of a local are accountable to membership meetings.

National industrial unions are typically more complex. They tend to be larger and have a more heterogeneous membership than craft unions (both in terms of skills and demographics). Although there are exceptions, contracts in industrial unions tend to be negotiated primarily by staff members from the national office. In many cases, the bargaining unit will include all locals from a particular company (across the entire country). Even if contracts are negotiated by locals, representatives from the national union will often participate in talks to assure that the contract conforms to patterns established by the national organization.

As with craft unions, national unions have periodic conventions and national officers. Depending on the union, the national officers may be elected directly by rank-and-file members or by some other body (such as convention delegates). National unions generally have a substantial paid staff who provide a variety of different services (e.g., research, legal representation, organizing new members, negotiating contracts, and servicing locals). National unions may also have one or more layers of hierarchy between the local unions and the national offices. For example, in the case of the UAW, there are different divisions responsible for the major industries in which that union represents workers. Within the automobile industry, there are divisions that correspond to each of the major manufacturers. There are other divisions that deal with the needs of special groups within the union (such as minority workers and skilled craft workers). Consequently, the structures of large industrial unions are often as complex as the companies with which they deal.

FEDERATIONS A federation is an association of unions. It is not a union in the usual sense of the term. Rather, it provides a range of services to affiliated unions, much as an organization such as the National Association of Manufacturers provides services to its member firms.

FURTHER READING:

Elkouri, F., and E. Elkouri. *How Arbitration Works*. Washington, D.C.: Bureau of National Affairs, 1985.

Lawler, J.J. *Unionization and Deunionization: Strategy, Tactics, and Outcomes*. Columbia, SC: University of South Carolina Press, 1990.

Levitan, Sar A., Peter E. Carlson, and Isaac Shapiro. *Protecting American Workers: An Assessment of Government Programs*. Washington, DC: Bureau of National Affairs, 1986.

Lipsky, D.B., and C.B. Donn. *Collective Bargaining in American Industry*. Lexington, MA: Lexington Books, 1987.

Mills, Daniel Quinn. *Labor-Management Relations*. 5th ed., New York: McGraw-Hill, 1994.

Sayles, Leonard, and George Strauss. *The Local Union*. New York: Harcourt, Brace, and World, 1967.

Taylor, B.J., and F. Witney. *Labor Relations Law*. Englewood Cliffs, NJ: Prentice-Hall, 1987.

Troy, Leo. ''Why Labor Unions are Declining.'' *Journal of Commerce and Commercial*. September 1, 1994.

''Unions and Strikers: A Huge Nonproblem.'' *Fortune*. May 31, 1993.

Worsham, James. ''Labor's New Assault.'' *Nation's Business*. June 1997.

SEE ALSO: Labor Unions and Small Business

LABOR UNIONS AND SMALL BUSINESS

Labor unions are commonly associated with big business and giant industries, but many small business owners find that unions are not limited to the government sector or to corporate behemoths such as General Motors, UPS, and Boeing. Labor unions are not as powerful or as plentiful as they were a few generations ago, but they remain a vital component of the American business landscape, and many small businesses rely on union employees for their operations. Indeed, all small business owners who employ workers should have a basic familiarity with the fundamentals of U.S. labor laws, since they offer protections to union and nonunion employees alike.

The likelihood that a small business will employ a unionized **work force** is predicated on a wide range of factors, including industry, geographic location, traditional strength of union presence, and the nature of the work involved. A Midwest-based business involved in the transportation industry, for example, is more likely to utilize union employees than a restaurant nestled in the heart of the traditionally non-union American south. But whether the business is unionized or not, owners must recognize that they and their employees are, to some degree, destined to exist in what Marc J. Lane, author of *Legal Handbook for Small Business,* characterized as a state of conflict. ''You and your co-owners . . . are dedicated to effecting cost economies wherever you can, and, as owners of capital, you may claim both the right and the obligation to decide how best to use that capital,'' wrote Lane. ''Your rank-and-file employees, on the other hand, are striving for the best compensation package and working conditions they can, and, since their jobs may be lost to business reverses, they may feel that they are entitled to have some influence on decisions.'' It is this desire for compensation and influence that are the underpinnings of labor unions' attraction, for as Lane noted, ''generally speaking, no one employee can usurp managerial authority, but a united organization of employees can effectively bargain with employers to gain a major role in business decision making.''

CORNERSTONES OF LABOR LAW

Hundreds of U.S. laws have some bearing on employee and employer rights and obligations in one area or another, but experts agree that six cornerstones of American labor law are the National Labor Relations Act of 1935(NLRA), the Labor Management Relations Act of 1947 (LMRA), the Fair Labor Standards Act of 1938 (FLSA), the Labor-Management Reporting and Disclosure Act of 1959 (LMRDA), the Civil Rights Act of 1964, and the Occupational Safety and Health Act of 1970.

THE NATIONAL LABOR RELATIONS ACT This act, which created the **National Labor Relations Board (NLRB)**, gives employees the right to organize and bargain collectively with their employers—in essence, it gives them the right to unionize. Importantly, it also confers legal protection on employees who try to organize their fellow workers into a union. It is worth noting, however, that this legislation also protects nonunion employees from being forced or otherwise coerced into joining a labor organization or engaging in collective bargaining. The act ensures that employees can choose their own representatives for the purpose of collective bargaining, establishes procedures for secret-ballot elections, and defines unfair labor practices, to which both employers and unions are subject. This law is also known as the Wagner Act.

LABOR MANAGEMENT RELATIONS ACT Also known as the Taft-Hartley Act, this legislation amended the National Labor Relations Act in ways that are generally thought to benefit business owners and management. While it forbade businesses from launching unwarranted or sudden lockouts of union employees, it also imposed restrictions on some union activities in the areas of organizing, picketing, striking, and other activities. It also outlawed the ''closed shop'' (which required that employers hire only union members) and gave the government the power to obtain injunctions against strikes that ''will imperil the national health or safety'' if they take place or continue.

FAIR LABOR STANDARDS ACT This act, also known as the Wage-Hour Act, ''establishes fair labor standards in employments in and affecting interstate commerce, and for other purposes,'' wrote Donald Weiss in *Fair, Square, and Legal.* ''It protects all workers, including children and women, by establishing minimum hourly wages and distinguishing between nonexempt employees (those to whom you must pay overtime for hours in excess of forty hours a week) and exempt (those to whom you do not have to pay overtime).'' Weiss noted that many employers view this law as pro-worker, but he added that the Act does provide employers with a significant freedom to shape ''specific forms of compensation or benefits not covered by the law,'' including gifts, special bonuses, travel and other reimbursable expenses, retirement/pension plans, and insurance plans.

LABOR-MANAGEMENT REPORTING AND DISCLOSURE ACT The Landrum-Griffin Act, as this legislation is sometimes known, was in large measure shaped to regulate the internal affairs of unions and to provide additional safeguards to ensure that the rules laid out in the Labor Management Relations Act of 1947 were adhered to.

CIVIL RIGHTS ACT OF 1964 This landmark legislation prohibited employers from discriminating in their hiring practices on the basis of race, religious beliefs, gender, or natural origin.

OCCUPATIONAL SAFETY AND HEALTH ACT OF 1970 This legislation, which created the **Occupational Safety and Health Administration (OSHA)** established guidelines and regulations to make workplaces safer and healthier for employees. ''Each employer shall furnish to each of his employees employment and a place of employment which are free from recognized hazards that are causing or are likely to cause death or serious physical harm to his [or her] employees,'' read one portion of the Act.

UNION ORGANIZATION EFFORTS AND THE SMALL BUSINESS OWNER

''If workers exercise their right to organize, employers should know what their rights are,'' wrote Harrison G. Darby and Margaret R. Bryant in *HRMagazine.* Indeed, some analysts believe that smaller business establishments may be more likely to encounter union organizing activities in the late 1990s than in previous years, given the AFL-CIO's stated intentions of approaching the work forces of smaller firms with greater zeal.

Historically, most business owners have not greeted unions with open arms because of concerns about their impact on bottom-line profitability and operational control. This viewpoint remains prevalent today, which has led consultants to make a number of recommendations to small- and mid-sized business owners hoping to ward off union organizers. ''Employers need to make preparations now—before there are any signs of union activity—and teach their managers how to immediately and lawfully respond to union organizing efforts,'' wrote Darby and Bryant. ''As union leaders commit serious money, time, and attention to organizing new members, employers should heed any warning signs and take steps to prepare for a union campaign. The best preparation is to anticipate issues that a union would be likely to raise and minimize the potential for union support. By identifying and correcting vulnerabilities, employers can blunt the edge of a union's strategy.''

Darby and Bryant also noted that there are certain solicitation and distribution rules that union organizers and supporters must adhere to, but they added that such rules ''must be promulgated before the start of union activity to avoid a charge of unlawful retaliation.'' These rules include bans on union literature, restrictions on internal efforts to convince employees to sign union authorization cards, and prohibitions expressly forbidding outside organizers from any activity on company property.

UNIONIZATION BIDS AND POSSIBLE MANAGEMENT RESPONSES If a union is able to garner sufficient interest from a business's employees (30 percent of the work force is the general rule), then it may petition the National Labor Relations Board for an election by secret ballot to determine whether the work force will join the union in question (a 50 percent response may result in union recognition even without the holding of an election). Writing in the *Legal Handbook for Small Business,* Lane indicated that ''if you [the small business owner] and your lawyer have any reasonable doubt that the union is the collective bargaining choice of a majority of the workers in a legally organizable bargaining unit, he will draft a refusal to recognize the union. Although your refusal to recognize a union that legitimately represents a majority can lead to later charges of unfair labor practices, recognizing a union that does not represent the majority is also illegal. When in doubt, opt for the refusal and let the NLRB conduct a secret election to determine the union's true status.''

In instances where an agreement is made to hold a union election, consultants note that anti-union business owners do have certain rights to make their case to the workers in their employ, provided that they do not violate any laws. ''Be careful to avoid any unfair tactics,'' wrote Lane. ''Improper conduct can induce the NLRB to set aside a management victory; and your repeated violations of the National Labor Relations Act can force union recognition even without an election.'' Darby and Bryant point out that according to U.S. labor law, ''management personnel have the right to express their views on unionization when answering questions or making statements about the union, its supporters, or its campaign communications. . . . [But] despite this broad right to free expres-

sion, managers and supervisors must never threaten or interrogate employees, promise them benefits or improved working conditions, or place employees' union activities under surveillance.'' Other tactics held to be unfair, said Lane, include the following:

- Polling employees about their attitudes toward the proposed union.
- Threatening or otherwise implying that a union victory will spell a loss of employment or benefits.
- Withholding of employee names and addresses from union organizers once an election agreement has been made.
- Visiting employees at their homes to lobby against the union.
- Unequal application of rules about solicitation on company grounds and company time (regarding pro- and anti-union forces).
- Favoritism toward antiunion employees.
- Discrimination against prounion workers.

In the weeks leading up to a union election, small business owners may also communicate the advantages of the current non-union arrangement with their employees, provided they do so in a lawful manner. Lane pointed to several tactics that might be used to the owner's advantage (provided, of course, that are factual):

- Delineate current benefits enjoyed by workers.
- Publicize the advantages of ''one-to-one'' interactions between employees and owners/managers.
- Highlight areas in which employees' wages, benefits, and working conditions are already above the norm.
- Highlight aspects of unions that might not be as palatable to some members of the work force, such as seniority systems that are sometimes interpreted as penalizing younger, ambitious employees.
- Explain that signing an authorization card does not mean that the employee has to vote for unionization.
- Explain the various difficulties associated with decertifying a union if the workers become unhappy with it.
- Maintain a high level of integrity in addressing various issues associated with unions.
- Correct any rumors, misrepresentations, or distortions with clear and accurate rebuttals.

DEALING WITH ELECTION OUTCOMES Once the NLRB-supervised election has been held, the small business owner is confronted with one of two outcomes, each of which come with their own unique challenges. The outcome most small businesses would prefer to deal with is a management victory in which the union organization effort is defeated. But even in this situation, management will likely have to deal with disappointed employees who had hoped for unionization and the lingering residue of what is almost always a stressful event. In addition, the election does not necessarily conclude the episode; the union may apply for a nullification of the results (based on allegations of unfair labor practices, etc.) or simply regroup and make another attempt down the line.

If the unionization drive is a successful one, the small business owner can proceed in one of four ways, according to Lane:

- File an unfair labor practices charge against the union and attempt to have the election set aside, provided the allegations have merit.

- Sell the business and subject the purchaser to the burdens of a union shop, as well as any liability for pending charges of unfair labor practices.

- Go out of business.

- Recognize the union and commence good-faith collective bargaining.

The collective bargaining agreement is basically a contract between the business and the union that explicitly states how workplace issues between management and employees will be handled.

UTILIZING LABOR UNIONS FOR BUSINESS SUCCESS

As indicated above, many businesses and industries try to avoid unions, convinced that their presence too often results in unwelcome sacrifices in the realms of profitability and control. But analysts point out that thousands and thousands of businesses that feature a unionized work force are tremendously successful. They note that the primary determinants of business success continue to be in the realms of business planning, marketing strategy, operational capabilities, technological advancement, and other areas, not in whether or not the business is unionized. In fact, some observers contend that labor unions can provide often-unappreciated benefits to both individual companies and larger economies.

"It may take some creative thinking and strategy, but unions can be a valuable ally when it comes to keeping top management aware of production issues," wrote Jim Treace in *Production*. "Outside the company, unions have political clout as well. At a time when state governors are delighted to shower tax breaks, training funds, and other goodies on anyone bringing a new factory into their state—even a direct competitor of yours—the unions' voting power can be a useful agent to make sure your existing plant gets its share. Second, union officials from the top down have an interest in some of the issues that can improve your operations: safety programs, ergonomics, and worker education."

The Economist concurred with this evaluation, noting that "by giving workers a collective voice, unions do not just push up wages. They can also improve a plant's, and hence an economy's, productivity and efficiency. They do this by establishing grievance procedures, helping to reduce staff turnover, and promoting stability in the work force. They can be an effective mechanism through which employers can consult workers, and can help to organize the training so crucial for honing the work force's skills."

FURTHER READING:

Black, John, Anne-Marie Greene, and Peter Ackers. "Size and Effectiveness: A Case Study of a Small Union." *Industrial Relations Journal.* June 1997.

Chapman, Elwood N. *Human Relations In Small Business.* Menlo Park, CA: Crisp Publications, 1994.

Darby, Harrison G., and Margaret R. Bryant. "When Unions Knock, How Should Employers Answer?" *HRMagazine.* July 1997.

Feldacker, Bruce. *Labor Guide to Labor Law.* 3rd ed. Prentice-Hall, 1990.

"The Future of Unions." *The Economist.* July 1, 1995.

Gould, William B., IV. *Agenda for Reform: The Future of Employment Relations and the Law.* The MIT Press, 1993.

J.K. Lasser Tax Institute. *How to Run a Small Business.* 6th ed. New York: McGraw-Hill, 1989.

Lane, Marc J. *Legal Handbook for Small Business.* Rev. ed. New York: Amacom, 1989.

Schupp, Robert W. "When Is a Union Not a Union? Good Faith Doubt and its Limitations in Collective Bargaining." *Labor Law Journal.* June 1997.

Sexton, Patricia Cayo. *The War on Labor and the Left.* Westview Press, 1991.

Sloane, Arthur A., and Fred Witney. *Labor Relations.* 6th ed. Englewood Cliffs, NJ: Prentice-Hall, 1988.

Townley, Barbara. *Labor Law Reform in U.S. Industrial Relations.* Gower Publishing Company Limited, 1986.

Treece, Jim. "On Unions." *Production.* April 1994.

Weiss, Donald H. *Fair, Square, and Legal: Safe Hiring, Managing & Firing Practices to Keep You & Your Company Out of Court.* New York: Amacom, 1991.

LAYOFFS

Layoffs are temporary or permanent reductions companies make in the number of employees on the payroll. Prior to the 1980s, layoffs were typically associated with business cycle downswings, with laid-off workers recalled as business conditions improved. Beginning in the 1980s, a greater proportion of layoffs resulted from plant and office closures and were, therefore, permanent. Many of these layoffs were associated with so-called re-engineering, restructuring, and **downsizing** efforts intended to make U.S. firms more profitable in the face of intensified global competition. As the U.S. economy improved in the early 1990s, large-scale layoffs continued even at highly profitable firms, indicating a break with historical patterns. Layoffs resulting from re-engineering and restructuring efforts were also unique in that a large proportion of managerial positions were affected.

PREVALENCE OF LAYOFFS IN THE 1990S

During the 1990s, many of the largest firms in the country underwent re-engineering or downsizing that resulted in massive layoffs. This constituted an important shift in the U.S. labor market in which even highly profitable firms laid off employees. At the end of 1993, Xerox showed consistent profitability; nonetheless, it announced the layoff of over 10,000 workers, nearly one-tenth of its work force. The layoffs disproportionately affected managerial rather than production employees. Also in 1993 Proctor & Gamble announced the layoff of 13,000 workers. Proctor & Gamble's chairman stated that the layoffs were necessary to improve the firm's position in the face of increasing price competition. These layoffs occurred despite an expansion in overall employment in the early 1990s, when openings were increasingly filled by part-time and temporary workers. A disproportionate number of layoffs occurred in the industrial sector while gains occurred in the service sector, accounting for 70 percent of new jobs in 1993.

A study published in *Fortune* magazine reported that 30 percent of all jobs existing in 1989 no longer existed at the end of 1993. More than 600,000 workers were permanently laid off in 1993—double the rate for 1989, when the economy was growing at a substantially slower rate. Fully two-thirds of the jobs lost resulted from plant or office closings, and thus were permanent layoffs. The study noted that layoffs were spread across all regions of the country and occurred in both large and small firms. Of the new jobs created since 1989, 70 percent were created by just 3 percent of firms.

An American Management Association survey of 870 companies revealed that one-half of these firms had laid off an average of 10 percent of their employees in 1992. Managerial employees accounted for nearly 60 percent of these layoffs—the first time this share exceeded 50 percent in the seven years the survey was conducted. Significantly, less than half of the firms that had laid off employees showed increased profitability, and only one-third showed increased labor productivity.

ALTERNATIVES TO LAYOFFS

Considering the mixed results large corporations have had with layoffs, some small businesses have adopted formal or informal no-layoff policies. In fact, the American Management Association reported that small firms (defined as those with less than 500 employees) are half as likely as large ones to lay off employees. According to Harvey Meyer in *Nation's Business,* avoiding layoffs can offer small businesses a number of benefits, including a loyal and motivated work force, improved **productivity** and **customer service**, reduced turnover, and less time and money spent recruiting and training new employees. By giving employees security and showing them that they are valued, no-layoff policies may enable small firms to pay lower wages than other companies in the same industry.

Such a policy can have pitfalls, however. It reduces the small business owner's ability to respond to a cash crunch, for example, and it may encourage employees who have been terminated to contest their firing in court. In addition, such a policy is unlikely to work for companies that have volatile sales levels or employ low-skilled workers who could be replaced easily. For small companies that must compete with larger ones to attract and retain a highly trained and skilled work force, however, a no-layoff policy can be a valuable tool. Some small businesses that promote no-layoff policies keep employees busy during slow periods with training sessions or painting, maintenance, and repair work. Others choose alternatives that cut costs and eliminate the need to downsize, such as hiring freezes, restrictions on **overtime**, pay reductions, job sharing, and shortened work weeks.

FURTHER READING:

Cameron, Kim. ''Downsizing Can Be Hazardous to Your Future.'' *HR Magazine.* July 1991.

Cross, Michael. *U.S. Corporate Personnel Reduction Policies: An Edited Collection of Manpower Layoff, Reduction and Termination Policies.* Brookfield, VT: Gower Publishing Co., 1981.

Deems, Richard S. *How to Fire Your Friends: A Win-Win Approach to Effective Termination.* Kansas City, MO: Media Publishing, 1989.

Eisen, Rebecca D. ''Devising a Layoff Contingency Plan.'' *HR Magazine.* June 1993.

"Job Insecurity," *Fortune*. May 30, 1994.

Meyer, Harvey. "Avoiding Pink Slips." *Nation's Business*. June 1997.

"Strong Companies Are Joining Trend to Eliminate Jobs." *New York Times*. July 26, 1993.

"Study: Layoffs Haven't Boosted Profits, Productivity." *Washington Post*. September 26, 1993.

"U.S. Companies Speed Pace of Downsizing." *Washington Post*. February 9, 1994.

LEADING ECONOMIC INDICATORS

A leading economic indicator is a statistic, such as housing starts, that is considered to signal the future direction of economic activity. Leading indicators tend to reach cyclical high and low points earlier than corresponding peaks and troughs in the overall economy, which makes them useful for predicting economic downturns or recoveries. In contrast, lagging indicators, such as the average prime interest rate charged by banks, generally trail behind changes in the business cycle. Coincident indicators, like manufacturing and trade sales, tend to rise and fall along with overall economic activity.

The most popular forecasting tool of this type is the Composite Index of Leading Economic Indicators (CLI), which is published monthly by the **U.S. Department of Commerce**. The CLI was created in the late 1950s by a group of economists led by Geoffrey Moore. It appears in numerous magazines and newspapers across the country and is monitored closely by government policy makers, financial analysts, and business leaders who seek to predict and prepare for the future direction of the economy. The CLI is composed of a series of 11 indicators from different segments of the economy selected specifically for their tendency to predict business cycles in the near future. The Commerce Department revises the data, definitions, and procedures used to construct the CLI periodically to ensure its accuracy.

The specific components of the CLI are: the average length of a work week for manufacturing employees; the average number of initial claims for unemployment insurance in state programs; the dollar value of new orders placed with manufacturers in the consumer goods and materials industries; the percentage of vendor deliveries that are slower, or require a longer lead time; the dollar value of contracts and orders for industrial plants and equipment; the number of new private housing units authorized by local building permits; the dollar change in manufacturers' unfilled orders in the durable goods industries; the percent change in sensitive materials prices; the average prices of 500 common stocks; the dollar change in the money supply M2; and the change in consumer expectations.

In order to successfully predict cyclical changes in economic activity, leading indicators must be interpreted using a filtering rule. One popular rule of thumb for interpreting the movement of leading indicators is that three successive periods of decline signal an imminent **recession**, while three successive periods of increase signal the beginning of a recovery. Economists apply much more sophisticated statistical models to interpret the performance of individual leading indicators or the CLI.

In an analysis for the *Journal of Forecasting*, Lahiri and Wang found that the CLI predicted turning points in the economy successfully, with a lead time of about 3 months using real-time data, but also sent some false signals of impending downturns. Koenig and Emery, in an article for *Contemporary Economic Policy*, found that the CLI predicted peaks in the business cycle an average of 8.2 months in advance and troughs an average of 4.2 months in advance. However, they still claimed that the CLI "failed to provide reliable advance warning of both recessions and recoveries" for several reasons: there is usually a one-month delay in publication of the CLI; the peaks and troughs are gradual and difficult to recognize in real time; and the index is subject to frequent revisions.

Still, the researchers emphasized that their results do not necessarily mean that the CLI is useless. Instead, the index may be relied upon to a great extent by government policy makers. These officials may respond to changes in the CLI by enacting policies to counteract the cyclical trends in the economy. For example, the Federal Reserve Board might raise **interest rates** in order to slow an economic expansion that is accompanied by **inflation**. Any successful counter-cyclical actions would make the CLI appear less reliable as a predictor.

FURTHER READING:

"Composite Indexes: Leading Index Components." *Survey of Current Business*. March 1995.

Koenig, Evan F., and Kenneth M. Emery. "Why the Composite Index of Leading Indicators Does Not Lead." *Contemporary Economic Policy*. January 1994.

Lahiri, K., and J. G. Wang. "Predicting Cyclical Turning Points with Leading Index in a Markov Switching Model." *Journal of Forecasting*. May 1994.

Linden, Dana Wechsler. "Sentinel on the Inflation Watch." *Forbes*. September 12, 1994.

LEASING PROPERTY

A lease is a contract between an owner and a user of property. In business lease agreements, the owner (commonly known in lease arrangements as the lessor) receives financial compensation and in exchange, the tenant (also known as lessee) is given the right to operate his or her business on the property. There are many different types of property lease arrangements that can be made, and many different considerations that business owners should weigh before entering into such a contract. But leasing is very popular with small business owners, in large measure because such arrangements allow new or financially-strapped businesses to divert their capital to other business needs. Indeed, many small businesses operate in leased facilities for their entire existence.

TYPES OF PROPERTY LEASES

FULL SERVICE LEASE This type of lease is used primarily in multi-tenant office buildings. In essence, lessees who agree to such arrangements pay a single lump sum for a wide range of supplementary services in addition to the lease payment. Under the terms of full service leases, the landlord is responsible for providing a number of different services for his or her tenants, including security, maintenance, janitorial, and various utilities (water, electricity, air, heat).

GROSS LEASE Under the terms of a gross lease contract, the lessee pays the lessor a gross amount for rent (as well as sales tax when applicable). Property costs such as property taxes, insurance, and maintenance are the responsibility of the landlord, while the tenant is responsible for utilities that it uses. Sometimes the lease contract will include provisions that require the tenant to cover property costs that go over a certain specified level.

Variations of this basic lease arrangement include the flat lease and the step lease. The flat lease is the most basic type of agreement, and generally the most popular with small businesses. It calls for the lessee to pay a flat set price for a specific period of time. The step lease, on the other hand, calls for a gradual escalation of the base rent payment over time in recognition of the likely rise in owner expenses in such areas as taxes, insurance premiums, and maintenance. A related lease contract, usually known as the cost-of-living lease, includes rent increases based on general inflation figures rather than increases in specific expenses.

NET LEASE The net lease is the most ubiquitous of the various lease contract types. Under the terms of a net lease, the tenant pays the landlord a base rent as well as an additional sum that covers the tenant's share of property taxes on the facility. When taxes increase, it is the responsibility of the tenants to cover those costs. The obligations of each tenant are figured by determining what percentage of the total facility is occupied by each tenant. If a business occupies 20 percent of a facility that has just been hit with a rise in property taxes, for example, that tenant is responsible for paying 20 percent of that increase.

Variations of the basic net lease include the ''double-net'' lease and the ''triple-net'' lease. Under the terms of a double-net lease, the terms of the contract are such that the tenant is responsible for picking up added insurance premiums as well as tax increases; under triple-net leases, tenants are responsible for covering insurance premiums, tax increases, *and* costs associated with maintenance and/or repairs of the building, the parking lot, and other areas used by the lessee. The triple-net lease is popular with landlords for obvious reasons, and small business owners should note that such arrangements sometimes make landlords less attentive to upkeep in these areas than they might be if they had to foot the bill themselves.

PERCENTAGE LEASE This arrangement calls for tenants to pay a base rent and/or a percentage of the lessee's gross revenue. This percentage, which can run as high as 10-12 percent in some contracts, is paid on an annual, semiannual, or quarterly basis (some malls and shopping centers, however, call for even more frequent payments). This lease arrangement is a favorite of lessors with property in coveted retail areas; the percentage lease is not favored by tenants, but the laws of supply and demand often make it possible for owners of desirable property to insist on it. For small business owners who sign such leases, it is important that they fully understand what the contract defines as ''gross revenue.'' ''Be specific in how you define gross sales,'' wrote Fred Steingold in *Legal Guide for Starting & Running a Small Business.* ''Depending on your type of business, certain items should be deducted from gross sales before the percentage rent is determined. Here are some possibilities:

- returned merchandise;

- charges you make for delivery and installation;

- sales from vending machines;

- refundable deposits;

- catalog or mail-order sales;

- sales tax.

In short, make sure your lease excludes all items that overstate your sales from the location you're renting.''

ADVANTAGES AND DISADVANTAGES OF LEASING

The Small Business Administration (SBA) counsels small business owners to consider a variety of factors when weighing whether to lease or buy property. These considerations include:

- Operating requirements—If the business's operating requirements are expected to change significantly over the next several years, leasing would probably be preferable, since it allows businesses to move more easily.

- Capital supply and capital needs—Leasing frees up a greater percentage of a small business's capital for other operating needs (advertising, production, equipment, payroll, etc.). If the business does not have a lot of extra cash on hand (and few small businesses do), then leasing may be the more sensible choice. This is probably the biggest reason why small companies lease.

- Financing and payment flexibility—It is generally easier to secure financing to lease rather than purchase a property. In addition, leases can be spread out over longer periods than loans and can be structured to compensate for cash flow variations (the latter can be an important factor for seasonal businesses).

- Resale value—Is the value of the property likely to increase? If so, how much? Many small business owners choose to purchase rather than lease—even if they have to accrue significant debt—if they decide that the asset is a worthwhile long-term investment.

- Equipment—Many lease agreements include stipulations that provide lessees with increased flexibility in terms of upgrading and/or maintaining equipment.

- Taxes—Property owners enjoy tax benefits such as depreciation and investment tax credits that are not open to tenants.

OTHER LEASE TERMS

In addition, there are other elements of a lease agreement that can weigh heavily on a contract's overall acceptability. Indeed, the details of lease contracts can vary enormously. "In theory," noted Steingold, "all terms of a lease are negotiable. Just how far you can negotiate, however, depends on economic conditions. If desirable properties are close to full occupancy in your city, landlords may not be willing to negotiate with you over price or other major lease terms. On the other hand, in many parts of the country where commercial space has been over-built, landlords are eager to bargain with small businesses to fill empty units."

LEASEHOLD IMPROVEMENTS Small business owners who find themselves in negotiations with property owners over lease terms should make sure that they pay attention to a variety of issues that, if overlooked, can be costly. For example, leases will usually cover any remodeling that needs to be done to the property and specify who will pay for it. Most of this remodeling falls under the category of "leasehold improvements": carpeting, insulation, plumbing and electrical wiring, lighting, windows, ceiling tiles, sprinkler and security systems, and heating and air conditioning systems all fall under this heading. Small business owners should try to ensure that the lease specifies each improvement that the landlord will make to the property and when those improvements will be made (ideally, they should be completed before the move-in date). The landlord's willingness to foot the bill for such improvements typically depends on several factors, among them the length of the lease agreement; the business's value to the landlord as a tenant ("anchor" tenants typically have more clout in these areas); and the likely long-term economic benefits harvested by the landlord from the improvements (in terms of property value and future rentals). However, as Steingold noted, "if you [the small business owner] have specialized needs—for example, you're running a photo lab or a dance studio—and your darkroom or hardwood floor would be of limited value to most future tenants, don't expect the landlord to willingly pick up the costs of the improvements. The landlord may even want to charge you something to cover the cost of remodeling the space after you leave." Some leases provide tenants with the option of making improvements themselves, provided that they adhere to certain guidelines and restrictions.

LENGTH OF LEASE Negotiations between tenants and landlords often snag on the question of lease length. As Craig Melby and Jane Utzman noted in their book *Site Smart,* "the length of the lease is usually a very important issue. Some landlords may want a long lease for financial stability, others may prefer a short lease because of hopes that rental rates may rise in the short term future. Tenants may want a short lease in case of a decline in their business, or if their business becomes more profitable and they need more space for expansion purposes. Other tenants may want a longer term lease because of their large investment in tenant improvements, amount of money spent advertising a new location, as well as moving costs if their lease isn't renewed. Depending on what the landlord wants, the length of the lease will effect all other concessions offered." Generally, small business owners try to secure leases with mid-range lengths. Leases of less than a year can leave them more vulnerable than they would like, but multi-year terms can be dangerous as well, especially if the business is new and unproven. A common compromise is to include an "option clause" in the contract so that the lessee can stay if he or she wishes at the conclusion of the original lease period.

EXCLUSIVITY Many small business owners quite reasonably insist that any lease agreement they sign contain what is commonly known as an "exclusivity clause." This clause provides the tenant with an exclusive right to sell his or her product or service on the property, "thus obligating the landlord to prevent other tenants from selling those same goods or services," wrote Melby and Utzman.

INSURANCE Landlords often ask lessees to secure insurance in the event that 1) the tenant damages the leased property, or 2) customers or others suffer injuries on the premises. "The landlord may specify the specific dollar amount of liability coverage required by the tenant," noted Melby and Utzman. "The landlord will also insure the building in respects to liability and property damage. While the landlord's and tenant's liability coverage may overlap, the property insurance covered by the landlord includes everything except the interior contents of the tenant's space. Most leases require [tenants] to provide the landlord with proof of insurance."

USE OF PREMISES Shopping center/strip mall landlords typically include language in the lease contract providing specific details on approved uses of the premises that is being rented. Such stipulations often serve to protect the businesses of other tenants. For example, the owner of a cafe in a strip mall may be quite unhappy if his neighbor, who formerly ran a quiet sports memorabilia shop, decides to change gears and launch a tattoo parlor. "The use of the space definitely affects the tenant mix of the [shopping center] and may directly affect the neighboring tenants as well," explained Melby and Utzman. "If the tenant changes their scope of business or products they sell, the image of the center might suffer. In many retail centers, landlords spend a significant amount of time and money attracting the right mix of tenants to the center that will attract a specific type of shopper. To maintain the center's value, the use must conform to the tenant mix that will most benefit the center."

In addition, lease contracts provide stipulations and regulations on a plethora of other issues of interest to both lessors and lessees. These include:

- Signage (regulates the size, style, and brightness of tenant advertising signs);
- Compliance with various **zoning ordinances**, permits, restrictions on use of space;

- Compliance with other local, state, and federal laws;
- Subletting or assigning the lease;
- Definition of the space being leased;
- Security deposit;
- Landlord's right to enter leased space;
- Relocation (wherein the landlord relocates a tenant to another space because of remodeling or expansion by a neighboring tenant);
- Default provisions;
- Hours of operation;
- Incidents of damage or destruction from natural causes;
- Repairs;
- Indemnification provisions;
- Abandonment (by the tenant, either through outright abandonment, diminished hours of operation, etc.);
- Condemnation (cases where all or part of the property is taken by city, county, state, or federal government for other use, such as road, right-of-way, or utility easement);
- Bailout clauses (in the event of catastrophic developments—tornadoes, riots, wars, floods, droughts, etc.);
- Cotenancy clauses (allows the business owner to break the lease if an anchor store closes or moves);
- Recapture clauses (also known as a cancellation clause, this allows landlords to evict tenants for breach of contract if the tenant is unable to meet minimum rent requirements).

CHOOSING BETWEEN EXISTING AND PLANNED BUILDINGS

Most start-up businesses move into already existing facilities. Many small business owners who have built up profitable, established enterprises, however, often have more options when they decide that the time is right to move. Indeed, some choose to arrange a lease in a building or facility (office center, shopping center, or industrial park) that is still in its planning stages. The savvy small business owner will consider the potential benefits and drawbacks of both choices before deciding. "Leasing in an existing building provides the Lessee . . . with more known at the time new space is occupied than any other facility option provides," said Wadman Daly in *Relocating Your Workplace.* "More so than in any other circumstances, the [lessee] is in a position to closely inspect both the facility and the terms of proposed leases in a number of competing locations. However, the nature of the lease in an existing building signifies minimum tenant control over the potential variables in either lease or facility. Rental rates, maintenance and escalation costs, utilities and building features are fixed or relatively non-negotiable. Landlords may vary in their abatements and finish-to-suit clauses, however their basic price structure, like that of the building and mechanical systems, remains unchanged. Of course, there are no investor implications with this option.'' But Daly cautions that leasing in a planned building contains its own mix of attractive features and uncertainties: ''Building features [in a planned building] will be new, up-to-date and, to a certain minimal extent, capable of adjustment to tenant need. If your lease is important enough to the developer, you may receive some attention when it comes to special requests for identification, parking, security, a prime location in the building, etc.'' Nonetheless, small business owners should be cautious when approaching such leases, for both the final appearance and utility of the building—as well as its costs—remain unseen and untested when the building is in its planning stages. ''Proposed rental rates must be examined in the light of comparable projects with similar advantages,'' Daly wrote. ''Descriptions of less obvious features like parking, air handling systems, security, maintenance, etc., should be clear and complete. The track record of the developer making the offer should be inspected carefully. Is there a history of quality construction at the rental rate asked, or one of build for quick re-sale? Is there a reputation for good maintenance or benign neglect? Regardless [of] the size of the lease or the duration of the proposed tenancy, these and related questions should be probed.''

FURTHER READING:

Daly, Wadman. *Relocating Your Workplace: A User's Guide to Acquiring & Preparing Business Facilities.* Crisp Publications.

Hill, David S. *Landlord and Tenant Law in a Nutshell.* West Publishing.

Melby, Craig, and Jane Utzman. *Site Smart.* West Palm Beach, FL: P.T. Publications.

Steingold, Fred S. *Legal Guide for Starting & Running a Small Business.* 3d ed. Berkeley, CA: Nolo Press, 1997.

Weber, Fred I. *Locating or Relocating Your Business.* Washington: U.S. Small Business Administration, n.d.

SEE ALSO: Business Site Selection

LEASING EQUIPMENT

A lease is in essence an extended rental agreement wherein the owner of the equipment (the lessor) allows the user (the lessee) to operate or otherwise make use of the equipment in exchange for periodic lease payments. ''There are a number of reasons that companies sometimes prefer to lease equipment rather than buying it,'' said Richard A. Brealey and Stewart C. Myers in *Principles of Corporate Finance.* ''For example, there may be good tax reasons. If the operator cannot use the depreciation tax shield, it makes sense to sell the equipment to someone who can. Also, the lessor may be better able to bear the risk of obsolescence, or be in a better position to resell second-hand assets. The lessor may be able to offer a very good deal on maintenance. Finally, it may be much less costly in time and effort to arrange a simple lease contract on a standard item of equipment than to arrange a normal loan.''

Equipment leasing is particularly favored by many small businesses, which often have future options because of limited capital. ''The practice of leasing equipment as a way to make the most efficient use of resources—particularly in times of tight credit—is found in a variety of industries,'' pointed out Jack Wynn in *Nation's Business.* ''One of the major categories of leased equipment consists of high-technology items such as computers, telecommunications equipment, and diagnostic tools. Another category is low-tech capital equipment, from office equipment and materials-handling machinery to marine cargo containers, trucks, trailers, rail cars, forklifts, and cranes.'' Finally, lease agreements are popular because they often contain provisions that allow the lessee to purchase the item at the end of the lease period if they so desire.

TYPES OF EQUIPMENT LEASES

The two primary types of leases are operating leases and long-term leases. Operating leases are characterized by short-term, cancelable terms, and the lessor bears the risk of obsolescence. These leases are generally preferable when the company needing the equipment needs it only for a short period of time. Under the usual terms of such agreements, a lessee can usually cancel an operating lease, assuming prior notice, without a major penalty. Long-term, noncancelable leases, which are also known as capital, full payout, or financial leases, are sources of financing for assets the lessee company wants to acquire and use for longer periods of time. Most financial leases are net leases, meaning that the lessee is responsible for maintaining and insuring the asset and paying all property taxes, if applicable. Financial leases are often used by businesses for expensive capital equipment.

In addition to these two basic leasing models, there are a considerable variety of other lease arrangements that are often used. These leases, each of which combine different financial and tax advantages, are actually hybrids of financial and operating leases that reflect the individual needs of lessor companies. For example, full-service leases are leases wherein the lessor is responsible for insurance and maintenance (these are commonplace with office equipment or vehicle leases). Net leases, on the other hand, are leases wherein the lessee is responsible for maintenance and insurance. Leveraged leases, meanwhile, are arrangements wherein the cost of the leased asset is financed by issuing debt and equity claims against the asset and future lease payments.

Small business experts caution prospective lessees to keep in mind that lease rates can vary considerably from lease company to lease company. Lease companies also may charge different rates for the same piece of equipment, depending on various characteristics of the business that is seeking the lease. Factors that can impact the lease rate include the credit history of the lessee, the nature of equipment wanted by the lessee, the length of the lease term, and whether the lessee or lessor is the primary beneficiary of tax credits associated with the transaction.

ELEMENTS OF EQUIPMENT LEASING CONTRACTS
Writing in *The Entrepreneur and Small Business Problem Solver*, William A. Cohen delineated ten major terms of most equipment leasing **contracts**:

- Duration of the lease
- Total rate or lease payment due the lessor
- Specific financial terms (date of the month that payment is due, penalties for late payment, etc.)
- Residual values and purchase options
- Market value of equipment (necessary for insurance purposes in the event of lost or damaged equipment)
- Tax responsibility
- Equipment updating or cancellation provisions
- Lessee renewal options
- Penalties for early cancellation without good cause
- Miscellaneous options (security deposits, warranties)

ADVANTAGES OF EQUIPMENT LEASING

There are several characteristics of equipment leasing that can be advantageous to small business owners. They include the following:

CONVENIENCE In instances where a company only needs a piece of equipment for a limited period of time, short-term leases can be most convenient. Rather than go to the trouble of negotiating purchase,

arranging insurance and registration, negotiating resale, and canceling insurance and registration, a business can simply rent the item for the duration of time needed. "Sometimes the cost of short term rentals may seem prohibitively high, or you may find it difficult to rent at any price," wrote Brealey and Myers. "This can happen for equipment that is easily damaged by careless use. The owner knows that short-term users are unlikely to take the same care they would with their own equipment."

FLEXIBLE FINANCING TERMS As Jack Wynn stated in *Nation's Business*, some lease arrangements are structured so that 100-percent financing is available. "Although payments for a lease may be somewhat higher than those for a conventional loan, there is no down payment, which helps preserve the lessee's operating capital and borrowing capacity. Similarly, leasing is an 'off the balance sheet' form of financing that is considered an operating expense, not a liability. This allows companies to acquire equipment without the acquisition affecting their capital budget. And lease payments usually can be spread over a longer period of time than the one to three years customary for bank loans."

CANCELLATION OPTIONS Some lease agreements provide lessees with cancellation options in the event that the equipment proves inadequate for the company's needs over the course of the agreement. Upgrades are sometimes available through these options. One vital category of equipment that often includes such an option is computer systems. "Computers are frequently leased on a short-term cancelable basis," stated Brealey and Myers. "It is difficult to estimate how rapidly such equipment will become obsolete, because the technology of computers is advancing rapidly and somewhat unpredictably. Leasing with an option to cancel passes the risk of premature obsolescence from the user to the lessor. Usually the lessor is a computer manufacturer or a computer leasing specialist, and therefore knows more about the risks of obsolescence than the user. Thus the lessor is better equipped than the user to bear these risks." A lease agreement equipped with a cancellation option may be more expensive than one that is not so adorned, but many small business consultants contend that the added security is well worth it. Brealey and Myers caution potential lessees to closely study lease agreements to see whether this option is included: "Some leases that *appear* expensive really are fairly priced once the option to cancel is recognized."

TAX BENEFITS Businesses that have equipment leasing expenses may be able to deduct the costs of those expenditures on their taxes. But monthly payments are tax-deductible only if the lease arrangement qualifies as a "true lease" in the eyes of the court. "This means the lease can last no longer than 80 percent of the useful life of the equipment, including lease renewals,'' said Wynn. Moreover, interest on lease payments is not deductible.

MAINTENANCE This option generally results in higher lease payments, but it is often money well-spent for small companies with limited financial and workforce resources. Under the terms of full-service leases, the lessor is responsible for all maintenance associated with the equipment being leased.

SPEED ''For businesses that need equipment and need it now, leases are a speedy alternative,'' stated Jill Amadio in *Entrepreneur.* ''While banks can take weeks to approve business loans, leases are often approved overnight, with far less paperwork and looser credit requirements.''

FINDING A LEASING COMPANY

Business consultants and long-time equipment lessees agree that leasing companies vary considerably in terms of product quality, leasing terms, and customer service. Small business owners should approach a number of lease companies if possible to inquire about lease terms. They should then carefully study the terms of each outfit's lease agreements, and check into the reputation of each company (present and former customers and agencies like the Better Business Bureau can be helpful in this regard). ''Be sure you ask a lot of questions,'' stated the *Entrepreneur Magazine Small Business Advisor.* ''Never assume anything. . . . Are there some terms you don't understand? When leasing different kinds of equipment or property, lessors might use a different term to describe something you're familiar with.''

FURTHER READING:

Amadio, Jill. ''To Lease or Not to Lease?'' *Entrepreneur.* February 1998.

Brealey, Richard A., and Stewart C. Myers. *Principles of Corporate Finance.* 4th ed. New York: McGraw-Hill, 1991.

Cohen, William A. *The Entrepreneur and Small Business Problem Solver.* 2d ed. New York: Wiley, 1990.

''Equipment Leasing: Business Vs. Rental Status.'' *Journal of Accountancy.* March 1993.

''Equipment Leasing Is a Wise Investment.'' *Office.* July, 1993.

Nevitt, P.K., and F.J. Fabozzi. *Equipment Leasing.* 3d ed. Dow Jones-Irwin, Inc., 1988.

Shapiro, Alan C. *Modern Corporate Finance.* New York: Macmillan, 1990.

Wynn, Jack. ''To Use but Not to Own.'' *Nation's Business.* January 1991.

SEE ALSO: Leasing Automobiles; Leasing Property

LEGAL SERVICES

Legal services are an important consideration for any business owner, but especially for small business owners, who often face a number of legal hurdles. Protecting the owner's personal assets from lawsuits against the business, ensuring protection for the business against discrimination lawsuits, wrongful termination and **sexual harassment**, employee **contracts**, **copyright** claims, and **incorporation** are just a few of the legal issues that commonly face small business owners. The high costs of retaining a lawyer often make it seem as if competent legal services are out of reach of most small business owners, but there are reasonably priced methods of obtaining such services.

PRE-PAID LEGAL SERVICES

Perhaps the most cost-effective way for small business owners to obtain legal advice is through a pre-paid legal services plan. These plans provide companies with affordable access to legal advice and attorney's services for one low, monthly fee. Pre-paid firms are being compared to health maintenance organizations (HMOs) because they offer a wide range of services at one low, set price.

''This concept is where health insurance was in the '50s or where HMOs were 15 years ago,'' said Nashville attorney Jack Bufkin in an article in the *Memphis Business Journal.* ''Prior to the '50s, people could go to the hospital and pay for it out of their pocket. You can't do that anymore. Today, people are expected to pay for the cost of a lawyer out of their pocket, but it's quickly getting to the point where most people can't afford the cost of going and getting a lawyer.''

This prepaid concept was pioneered by Caldwell Legal, U.S.A. in 1967. It is still one of the largest prepaid firms. It offers Caldwell's Business Protector Program, which is available in all 50 states. At each Caldwell field office, attorneys provide telephone consultation, document review, letter, and other services, all for $20 per month. The plan includes unlimited hours of toll-free telephone consultation. That seems like a lot of service for very little money, but research done by Caldwell shows that 73 percent of legal problems can be solved with a single phone call. If more extensive services are needed, additional fees are applied as they are accrued.

Another company that was founded in 1972 in Ada, Oklahoma, has become one of the largest prepaid legal firms, and perhaps the best known. PrePaid Legal Services, Inc. operates in 14 states and the District of Columbia as of 1997, with new offices planned every year. PrePaid has set up a program that essentially allows small business owners to purchase "legal insurance," much like they would purchase health insurance. The program is called the Pre-Paid Small Business Legal Defense Plan and is available only to for-profit companies that have fewer than 20 employees and $2 million or less in gross income.

PrePaid contracts with one law firm in each state that it does business, usually a very well regarded firm that might otherwise be inaccessible to small business owners. Just like with health insurance, the small businesses pay a monthly premium, usually less than $100 per month. For that fee, PrePaid clients are guaranteed many services, including 10 primary benefits. Other legal firms offering similar services typically provide a package that includes some combination of the following as well:

- Legal consultation services—Includes toll-free calls to an attorney and up to one hour of research.

- Legal correspondence services—The company will, on behalf of the business owner, write one letter per legal subject matter per year as part of the plan. Additional letters are available at a 25 percent discount.

- Designated consultations—An attorney will provide free telephone consultations for designated legal matters. Also included are two additional telephone consultations of up to 30 minutes each, for certain legal situations.

- Basic contract review—Includes up to three contracts of 15 pages or less reviewed each month before the business owner signs.

- Executed document review—An attorney will review one signed contract up to 10 pages in length each month and advise (by phone) what options the business owner has regarding the signed document.

- Legal document review—Attorney will review three business documents of up to 15 pages each month.

- Initial debt collection letters—Attorney will write up to 10 initial debt collection letters each month.

- Trial defense—Includes up to 60 hours of the attorney's time when the business is named as a defendant or respondent in a lawsuit. Every year that the business stays in the plan, an additional 60 hours are made available for free, with a maximum of 300 hours reached after five years in the plan.

- Reduced fee services—Provides a 25 percent discount off the attorney's normal corporate hourly rate for legal services.

- Reduced contingency fee services—Provides for a five percent discount off the attorney's corporate contingency fee for contingency-type cases.

"The greatest benefit of a pre-paid legal plan is that it provides a way to reduce the cost of legal services for small business owners while providing greater access to the legal system," said Bufkin. "Small business people are being hammered by legal issues. The time is right to offer a product like this."

PrePaid Legal Services, Inc. is one of the largest and oldest firms offering pre-paid legal coverage, but small business owners should shop around—there are other firms available, with new ones joining the industry each year. For example, the Lawyers Assurance Group of America maintains 20 franchises throughout the United States.

ADVANTAGES OF PRE-PAID SERVICES

The primary advantage associated with pre-paid legal services is savings. For example, a typical pre-paid plan might charge $125 per hour for attorney's fees, plus the monthly premium, which can range from $40 to $100 per month. Without the plan, the attorney's fees skyrocket to $180 to $350 per hour, with a retainer fee of several thousand dollars often demanded up front.

Quality service is another promise of most pre-paid plans. For example, one plan requires its attorneys to have a minimum of 15 years service, experience in business law, a favorable rating from Martindale-Hubbel (the rating service of the American Bar Association), and a clean record that shows no indication of ethical or malpractice claims against the attorney. Of course, these services vary in quality, just as attorneys as a group vary in quality. Small business owners should do their research before signing up with a service.

Another benefit of pre-paid plans is their size. Because they pool together hundreds of small businesses, they instantly become one of the largest clients of whatever firm handles the plan's account. This is a huge benefit for small business owners. One owner on his or her own will be a very small part of any law firm's business. As one business owner in Ohio said of his former legal firm, "I felt I wasn't important enough to them." As part of the pre-paid plan, however, the small business becomes one part of a very important client that the law firm wants to keep happy to ensure continued business. Like HMOs, pre-paid plans offer collective bargaining power, as lawyers find it worth their while to offer low cost services to plan members because of the high volume of business that is generated.

Pre-paid plans also make it easier for small businesses to practice preventive law instead of reacting to crises. Without the plan, a business owner is more likely to take his or her chances in any given situation and hope that no legal problems arise. This is because asking for legal advice can be so expensive. The plan, however, makes advice readily available and encourages owners to make use of it so that small problems do not become big problems.

HOW TO SELECT THE PLAN THAT IS RIGHT FOR YOU

The most important thing to look for is the number and type of services offered at a reduced rate as part of the plan. The number of services might be lower than what you expect, so make sure the plan has what you need. Also find out what the plan charges for services that are not covered as part of the basic plan. A set fee for additional work may be cheaper in the long run then receiving a discount on the firm's ''usual fee'' for such services.

Other factors to consider include:

- Deciding whether you would prefer to work with just one lawyer over the years, or whether the service can provide a different lawyer for each legal matter.

- Do your homework. Obtain a list of clients and ask them if they have been satisfied with the quality of the legal work they have received.

- Ask how the law firm handles conflicts of interest when the person or business with a case against you uses the same pre-paid plan.

SMALL BUSINESS LEGAL SOFTWARE

Small business owners can also gain expertise and reduce risks and costs by utilizing one of the legal software packages or print titles that are designed just for small businesses. There also are thousands of resources available on the Internet. Observers note that the demand for this subject, coupled with the ever-changing legal landscape and continued advances in computer technology, are likely to ensure that an expanded list of titles will be available to choose from for some time to come.

FURTHER READING:

Bahls, Steven C. and Jane Easter Bahls. ''Cover Charge: Prepaid Plans Put Routine Legal Services Within Your Budget.'' *Entrepreneur.* August 1996.

Perenson, Melissa J. ''Navigating the Law.'' *PC Magazine.* December 17, 1996.

''PrePaid Legal Services Announces New Venture to Benefit Small Business Owners.'' *PR Newswire.* May 21, 1997.

Sewell, Tom. ''Pre-Paid Legal Services Offered to Small Businesses.'' *Memphis Business Journal.* May 26, 1997.

Taylor, Dennis. ''Hear Ye! These Legal Services Won't Leave Firms Bankrupt.'' *The Business Journal.* September 30, 1996.

SEE ALSO: Certified Public Accountants; Financial Planners

LETTER OF INTENT

A letter of intent is essentially a document that summarizes the major ingredients of a proposed transaction, including the price, payment method, and important target dates (for contract signing and closing). In most cases, the letter of intent is not legally binding, but it is nonetheless regarded as a useful tool. As Charles F. Claeys observed in *Small Business Reports,* ''the non-binding letter confirms that the buyer and seller have reached a sufficient 'meeting of the minds' to justify the time and expense of executing a final purchase and sale agreement.'' A letter of intent is most often utilized in situations in which one party is selling a business or facility to another, but the document may also be used to delineate the relationship in a supplier/customer agreement.

Although letters of intent are nominally non-binding, business and legal experts still counsel business owners to be careful in crafting and using them. Claeys noted that ''the case law of every state is replete with disputes over the meaning of letters of intent. Most of these disputes stem from misperceptions about whether or not the letter binds one side or the other to complete the deal. In some cases, the courts have deemed the documents to be binding due to mistakes in their execution, forcing sellers to sell and buyers to buy when they wanted to back out of the deal.''

CONTENTS OF A STANDARD LETTER OF INTENT

Given the danger of accidentally signing off on a binding letter of intent, then, experts urge small business owners to secure the services of an attorney before signing on the dotted line. There are a few basic steps that small business owners should make sure when putting together a letter of intent to make sure that the document is not a legally binding one. First of all, you should make certain that the letter of intent specifically states that the letter will eventually be superseded by a definitive purchase-and-sale contract that will be legally binding, and that the letter also includes a explicit statement that the letter itself is not legally binding. ''If you neglect to state in the letter that you will not be bound legally until you sign a contract, the seller possibly could hold you against your will to the terms of the letter of intent,'' wrote

Mark Pestronk in *Travel Weekly.* Another big mistake that small business owners sometimes make in fashioning letters of intent is to agree to a statement that says that they will negotiate toward a purchase and sale agreement "in good faith." According to Claeys, "it's virtually impossible to get out of a deal once you've included this language, since the seller need only ask for reasonable terms to meet the 'good faith' criteria. Therefore, the letter should never include the good faith provision in any form."

Non-binding letters of intent may also include most or all of the following elements:

- Total compensation offered, including breakdown (size of security deposit, down payment, seller-financed debt, bank debt)

- Warranties of clear and marketable title

- Detailed list of all liabilities and assets to be purchased

- Assurances of the validity and assumability of contracts (if applicable)

- Tax liability limitations

- Operating condition of all equipment and machinery at time of purchase

- Stipulations allowing buyer to adjust the purchase price in the event that: 1) undisclosed liabilities come due after settlement, and 2) actual inventory purchased does not match amount specified in sale agreement

- Provisions that the business passes any and all necessary inspections

- Provisions that final sale is contingent on verification of financial statements, license and lease transfers

- Provisions that final sale is contingent on obtaining financing for purchase

- Restrictions on business operations until final settlement

- Non-competition and advisory clauses (these are sometimes arranged in a separate document)

- Allocation of purchase price

- Date for settlement (may also include "drop dead" date at which both sides agree to discontinue negotiations).

Business experts say, however, that most letters of intent are primarily concerned with delineating only the major terms of the transaction. Claeys pointed out that most letters of intent should consist of no more than half a dozen pages. "It defeats the purpose if you negotiate a lot of details about the transaction, such as the seller's representations and warranties and covenants regarding ongoing opera-

tions," he said. "You may as well proceed directly to a binding purchase and sale agreement if you're ready to settle these details."

Major terms that should be include in a letter of intent, however, include total price to be paid, including down payment and installment payments; description of assets or stock to be sold; tax allocation of the price among fixed assets, goodwill, noncompete covenants, and consulting fees; and target dates for contract signing and closing. Claeys noted that price and payment terms are easily the most important elements of the letter. "These key points are rarely, if ever, open to further negotiation as the deal moves forward, so you must negotiate them carefully . . . before the letter is signed," he stated. "If either party were to suggest changing these terms later in the process, the sale would undoubtedly fall apart."

ADVANTAGES AND DISADVANTAGES OF LETTERS OF INTENT

Letters of intent are, on the whole, more popular with buyers than sellers. "Sellers tend to make an emotional commitment to the deal once they sign the letter, even though they have no legal commitment to follow through," stated Claeys. "Thus, the letter helps you [the buyer] reduce the risk that the seller will bail out at a later date."

There are certain advantages associated with signing letters of intent for sellers. After all, a signed letter—even if legally non-binding—does signal that the prospective buyer is truly interested in making a deal, thus saving the seller from incurring unnecessary expenses to accountants and attorneys. Indeed, if a seller consents to sign a letter of intent, he or she can take comfort in the fact that it gives the prospective buyer a better chance of securing financing for the purchase (lenders tend to be favorably inclined toward borrowers who arrive armed with letters of intent).

But according to Claeys, "the disadvantages of the letter [for the seller] usually outweigh the advantages." He pointed out that once a prospective buyer has a signed letter in hand, he or she "tends to terminate its 'courtship' of the seller and toughen its stance on the details that remain to be worked out, including the seller's representations and warranties about how the business is doing, the indemnities for a breach of these representations, and covenants about how the business will be run prior to the change of ownership." Of course, the above-mentioned factors also tend to make letters of intent popular with buyers.

Some prospective buyers request that a "no-shop clause" be inserted into the language of the letter of intent. This clause, when implemented, basically means that the seller agree not to offer the assets or stocks that are for sale to anyone else for a set period of time. Sellers often refuse to include such a clause, because it means that they are turning away other potential buyers for the duration of the agreed-upon period (usually 60 or 90 days) even though the buyer making the no-shop request is not yet obligated to make the purchase (remember the letter of intent, when constructed correctly, is nonbinding).

One option for sellers who face this type of request is to ask the buyer for a deposit in return. This money can be used by the seller to cover his or her legal and accounting expenses if the deal ultimately fails to come together. Buyers may balk at this condition, however, reasoning that, as Claeys wrote, ''each party should bear its own risk of losing the pre-transaction costs.''

LETTERS OF INTENT FOR SUPPLIERS AND CUSTOMERS

Although letters of intent are primarily associated with purchases of entire businesses, they can also be used to delineate expectations between business **suppliers** and customers. These can be especially useful to businesses that have suppliers upon which they are particularly reliant. Such a letter is ''a guide rather than a contract,'' admitted Ernest L. Anderson Jr. in *Purchasing,* ''but it does make clear the outlines of the partnership. Anderson and other business consultants note that customer/supplier letters of intent can discuss all aspects of the relationship, including:

- Supplier and purchasing obligations associated with maintaining adequate inventories of goods and materials

- Order-handling, billing, and delivery procedures

- Handling of price changes

- Allocation of responsibilities in such areas as material quality and acceptance

- Efforts to reduce costs (of materials purchased, for instance)

- Treatment of gifts, gratuities, and other perks to and from suppliers (most are rejected outright)

- Duration of agreement.

FURTHER READING:

Anderson, Ernest L., Jr. ''A Sample Letter of Intent.'' *Purchasing.* October 6, 1994.

Claeys, Charles F. ''The Intent to Buy.'' *Small Business Reports.* May 1994.

Johansen, John A. *How to Buy or Sell a Business.* Washington: Small Business Administration, n.a.

Pestronk, Mark. ''Get It in Writing.'' *Travel Weekly.* May 6, 1996.

Tuller, Lawrence W. *Buying In: A Complete Guide to Acquiring a Business or Professional Practice.* Liberty Hall, 1990.

TullerYegge, Wilbur M. *A Basic Guide for Buying and Selling a Company.* New York: John Wiley, 1996.

SEE ALSO: Sales Contracts

LEVERAGED BUYOUTS

The term leveraged buyout (LBO) describes an acquisition or purchase of a company financed through substantial use of borrowed funds or debt. In fact, in a typical LBO, up to 90 percent of the purchase price may be funded with debt. During the 1980s, LBOs became very common and increased substantially in size, so that they normally occurred in large companies with more than $100 million in annual revenues. But many of these deals subsequently failed due to the low quality of debt used, and thus the movement in the 1990s has been toward smaller deals (featuring small-to medium-sized companies, with about $20 million in annual revenues) using less leverage.

The most common LBO arrangement among small businesses is for management to buy the outstanding shares of the company's stock, using company assets as **collateral** for a loan to fund the purchase. The loan is later repaid through the company's future cash flow or the sale of company **assets**. A management-led LBO is sometimes referred to as ''going private,'' because in contrast to ''going public''—or selling shares of stock to the public—LBOs involve gathering the outstanding shares into private hands. Subsequently, once the debt is paid down, the organizers of the buyout may attempt to take the firm public again. Many management-led, small business LBOs also include employees of the company in the purchase, which may help increase productivity and increase employee commitment to the company's goals. In other cases, LBOs are orchestrated by individual or institutional investors, or by another company.

According to Jennifer Lindsey in her book *The Entrepreneur's Guide to Capital,* the best candidate for a successful LBO will be in growing industry, have hard assets to act as collateral for large loans, and feature top-quality, entrepreneurial management talent. It is also vital that the LBO candidate post a strong historical cash flow and have low capital requirements, because the debt resulting from the LBO must be retired as quickly as possible. Ideally, the company should have at least twice as much cash flow as will be required for payments on the proposed debt. The LBO debt should be reduced to 50 percent of overall capitalization within one year, and should be completely repaid within five to seven years. Other factors improving the chances for a successful LBO include a strong market position and an established, unconcentrated customer base.

In order to improve the chances of success for an LBO, Lindsey noted that the deal should be undertaken when interest rates are low and the inflation rate is high (which will make assets more valuable). It is also vital that a management, employee, or outside investment group wants to own and control the company. Many LBOs involving small businesses take place because the owner wants to cash out or retire and does not want to sell to a larger company. LBOs can be very costly for the acquiring parties, with expenses including attorney fees, accounting evaluations, the printing of prospectus and proxy statements, and interest payments. In addition, if either the buyer or the seller is a public company, the LBO will involve strict disclosure and reporting requirements with both federal and state government agencies. Possible alternatives to an LBO include purchase of the company by employees through an **Employee Stock Ownership Plan (ESOP)**, or a merger with a compatible company.

ADVANTAGES AND DISADVANTAGES

A successful LBO can provide a small business with a number of advantages. For one thing, it can increase management commitment and effort because they have greater equity stake in the company. In a publicly traded company, managers typically own only a small percentage of the common shares, and therefore can participate in only a small fraction of the gains resulting from improved managerial performance. After an LBO, however, executives can realize substantial financial gains from enhanced performance. This improvement in financial incentives for the firm's managers should result in greater effort on the part of management. Similarly, when employees are involved in an LBO, their increased stake in the company's success tends to improve their productivity and loyalty. Another potential advantage is that LBOs can often act to revitalize a mature company. In addition, by increasing the company's capitalization, an LBO may enable it to improve its market position.

Successful LBOs also tend to create value for a variety of parties. For example, empirical studies indicate that the firms' shareholders can earn abnormally large positive returns from LBOs. Similarly, the post-buyout investors in these transactions often earn large excess returns over the period from the buyout completion date to the date of an initial public offering or resale. Some of the potential sources of value in LBO transactions include: 1) wealth transfers from old public shareholders to the buyout group; 2) wealth transfers from public bondholders to the investor group; 3) wealth creation from improved incentives for managerial decision making; and 4) wealth transfers from

the government via tax advantages. The increased levels of debt that the new company supports after the LBO decrease taxable income, leading to lower tax payments. Therefore, the interest tax shield resulting from the higher levels of debt should enhance the value of firm. Moreover, these motivations for LBO transactions are not mutually exclusive; it is possible that a combination of these may occur in a given LBO.

Not all LBOs are successful, however, so there are some potential disadvantages to consider. If the company's cash flow and the sale of assets are insufficient to meet the interest payments arising from its high levels of debt, the LBO is likely to fail and the company may go bankrupt. Attempting an LBO can be particularly dangerous for companies that are vulnerable to industry competition or volatility in the overall economy. If the company does fail following an LBO, this can cause significant problems for employees and suppliers, as lenders are usually in a better position to collect their money. Another disadvantage is that paying high interest rates on LBO debt can damage a company's credit rating. Finally, it is possible that management may propose an LBO only for short-term personal profit, resulting in long-term losses for others.

CRITICISM OF LBOS

Ever since the LBO craze of the 1980s—led by high-profile corporate raiders who financed takeovers with low-quality debt and then sold off pieces of the acquired companies for their own profit—LBOs have garnered negative publicity. Critics of LBOs argue that these transactions harm the long-term competitiveness of firms involved. First, these firms are unlikely to have replaced operating assets since their cash flow must be devoted to servicing the LBO-related debt. Thus, the property, plant, and equipment of LBO firms are likely to have aged considerably while the firm is privately held. In addition, expenditures for repair and maintenance may be curtailed as well. Finally, it is possible that research and development expenditures will be controlled. As a result, the future growth prospects of these firms may be significantly reduced.

Others argue that LBO transactions have a negative impact on the stakeholders of the firm. In many cases, LBOs lead to downsizing of operations, and employees may lose their jobs. In addition, some of the transactions have negative effects on the communities in which the firms are located.

Much of the controversy regarding LBOs has resulted from the concern that senior executives negotiating the sale of the company to themselves are engaged in self-dealing. On one hand, the managers have a fiduciary responsibility to their shareholders to sell the company at the highest possible price. On the other hand, they have an incentive to minimize what they pay for the shares. Accordingly, it has been suggested that management takes advantage of superior information about a firm's intrinsic value. The evidence, however, indicates that the premiums paid in LBOs compare favorably with those in inter-firm mergers that are characterized by arm's-length negotiations between the buyer and seller.

[Updated by Laurie Collier Hillstrom]

FURTHER READING:

Brealey, Richard A., and Stewart C. Myers. *Principles of Corporate Finance.* 4th ed. New York: McGraw Hill, 1991.

Fox, Isaac, and Alfred Marcus. ''The Causes and Consequences of Leveraged Management Buyouts.'' *Academy of Management Review.* January 1992.

Kaplan, Stephen. ''The Effect of Management Buyouts on Operating Performance and Value.'' *Journal of Financial Economics.* October 1989.

Latif, Yahya. ''What Ails the Leveraged Buyouts of the 1980s.'' *Secured Lender.* November/December 1990.

Lindsey, Jennifer. *The Entrepreneur's Guide to Capital: The Techniques for Capitalizing and Refinancing New and Growing Businesses.* Chicago: Probus, 1986.

SEE ALSO: Buying an Existing Business; Expansion

LIABILITIES

A liability is a debt assumed by a business entity as a result of its borrowing activities or other fiscal obligations (such as funding **pension plans** for its employees). Liabilities are paid off under either short-term or long-term arrangements. The amount of time allotted to pay off the liability is typically determined by the size of the debt; large amounts of money usually are borrowed under long-term plans.

Payment of a liability generally involves payment of the total sum of the amount borrowed. In addition, the business entity that provides the money to the borrowing institution typically charges interest, figured as a percentage of the amount that has been lent.

A company's liabilities are critical factors in understanding its status in any industry in which it is involved. As John Brozovsky noted in *Journal of Commercial Lending,* ''a basic understanding of accounting for liabilities is necessary to assess the viability of any company. Companies are required to follow certain accounting rules; however, the rules allow considerable flexibility in how a company accounts for liabilities.''

CURRENT LIABILITIES Current liabilities are short-term financial obligations that are paid off within one year or one current operating cycle, whichever is longer. (A normal operating cycle, while it varies from industry to industry, is the time from a company's initial investment in inventory to the time of collection of cash from sales of that inventory or of products created from that inventory.) Typical current liabilities include such accrued expenses as wages, taxes, and interest payments not yet paid; accounts payable; short-term notes; cash dividends; and revenues collected in advance of actual delivery of goods or services.

Economists, creditors, investors, and other members of the financial community all regard a business entity's current liabilities as an important indicator of its overall fiscal health. One financial indicator associated with liabilities that is often studied is known as working capital. Working capital refers to the dollar difference between a business's total current liabilities and its total current assets. Another financial barometer that examines a business's current liabilities is known as the current ratio. Creditors and others compute the current ratio by dividing total current assets by total current liabilities, which provides the company's ratio of assets to liabilities. For example, a company with $1.5 million in current assets and $500,000 in current liabilities would have a three-to-one ratio of assets to liabilities.

LONG-TERM LIABILITIES Liabilities that are not paid off within a year, or within a business's operating cycle, are known as long-term or noncurrent liabilities. Such liabilities often involve large sums of money necessary to undertake opening of a business, major expansion of a business, replace assets, or make a purchase of significant assets. Such debt typically requires a longer period of time to pay off. Examples of long-term liabilities include notes, mortgages, lease obligations, deferred income taxes payable, and pensions and other post-retirement benefits.

When debt that has been classified as long-term is paid off within the next year, the amount of that paid-off liability should be reported by the company as a current liability in order to reflect the expected drain on current assets. An exception to this rule, however, comes into effect if a company decides to pay off the liability through the transfer of noncurrent assets that have been previously accumulated for that very purpose.

CONTINGENT LIABILITIES A third kind of liability accrued by companies is known as a contingent liability. The term refers to instances in which a company reports that there is a possible liability for an event, transaction, or incident that has already taken place; the company, however, does not yet know whether a financial drain on its resources will result. It also is often uncertain of the size of the financial obligation or the exact time that the obligation might have to be paid.

Contingent liabilities often come into play when a lawsuit or other legal measure has been taken against a company. An as yet unresolved lawsuit concerning a business's products or service, for example, would qualify as a contingent liability. Environmental cleanup and/or protection responsibility sometimes falls under this classification as well, if the monetary impact of new regulations or penalties on a company is uncertain.

Companies are legally bound to report contingent liabilities. They are typically recorded in notes that are attached to a company's financial statement rather than as an actual part of the financial statement. If a loss due to a contingent liability is seen as probable, however, it should be included as part of the company's financial statement.

FURTHER READING:

Brozovsky, John. "A Review of Changes Affecting Accounting for Liabilities." *Journal of Commercial Lending*. March, 1994.

Smith, Jay M., Jr., and K. Fred Skousen. *Intermediate Accounting*. Cincinnati, OH: South-Western Publishing Co., 1987.

Williams, Georgina, and Thomas J. Phillips, Jr. "Cleaning Up Our Act: Accounting for Environmental Liabilities." *Management Accounting*. February 1994.

Winicur, Barbara. "Long Term Liabilities." *National Public Accountant*. January 1993.

SEE ALSO: Assets; Financial Ratios

LIFE INSURANCE

In general, life insurance is a type of coverage that pays benefits upon a person's death or disability. In exchange for relatively small premiums paid in the present, the policy holder receives the assurance that a larger amount of money will be available in the future to help his or her beneficiaries pay debts and funeral expenses. Some forms of life insurance can also be used as a tax-deferred investment to provide funds during a person's lifetime for retirement or everyday living expenses.

A small business might provide life insurance to its workers as a tax-deductible **employee benefit**—like health insurance and retirement programs—in order to compete with larger companies in attracting and retaining qualified employees. In addition, there are a number of specialized life insurance plans that allow small business owners to reduce the impact of **estate taxes** on their heirs and protect their businesses against the loss of a key employee, partner, or stockholder. Group life insurance is generally inexpensive and is often packaged with health insurance for a small additional fee. Companies that provide life in-

surance for their employees can deduct the cost of the policies for tax purposes, except when the company itself is named as the beneficiary.

Life insurance is important for individuals as well, particularly those who—like many entrepreneurs—are not covered by a company's group plan. Experts recommend that every adult purchase a minimum amount of life insurance, at least enough to cover their debts and burial expenses so that these costs do not fall upon their family members. The insurance industry uses a standard of five times annual income in estimating how much coverage an individual should purchase. In her book *Health Insurance: A Guide for Artists, Consultants, Entrepreneurs, and Other Self-Employed,* Lenore Janecek claims that entrepreneurs should determine the minimum amount of coverage they need by calculating how much they spend annually and how much debt they have, then adding the cost of funeral arrangements and, if applicable, college tuition for children.

The cost of life insurance policies depends upon the type of policy, the age and gender of the applicant, and the presence or absence of dangerous life-style habits. Insurance company actuaries use these statistics to determine an individual's mortality rate, or estimated number of years that person can be expected to live. Policies for women usually cost less than those for men, because women tend to live longer on average. This means that the insurance company will receive premiums and earn interest on them longer before it has to make a payment. Experts recommend that companies or individuals seeking life insurance coverage choose an insurance agent with a rating of A or better, and compare the costs of various options before settling on a policy.

TYPES OF LIFE INSURANCE POLICIES

TERM INSURANCE Term life insurance is the simplest and least expensive type, as it pays benefits only upon the policy holder's death. With annual renewable term insurance, the policy holder pays a low premium at first, which increases annually as he or she gets older. With level term insurance, the premium amount is set for a certain number of years, then increases at the end of each time period. Experts recommend that people who select term insurance make sure that their policies are convertible, so they can switch to a cash-value plan later if needed. They also should purchase a guaranteed renewable policy, so that their coverage cannot be terminated if they have health problems. Term insurance typically works best for younger people with children and limited funds who are not covered through an employer. This type of policy enables such a person's heirs to cover mortgage and college costs, estate taxes, and funeral expenses upon his or her death.

WHOLE LIFE INSURANCE With whole life insurance, the policy holder pays a level premium on an annual basis. The policy usually covers until the end of the person's life—age 90 or 100. In most cases, the policy holder is overcharged for the premium, and the extra amount goes into an interest-bearing dividend account known as a cash value account. The individual can use the money in this account to pay future premiums, or can withdraw it or borrow against it to cover living expenses. With a variable whole life policy, the individual controls the investments made with his or her cash value account. Selecting certain types of investments, such as mutual funds, may allow the policy holder to increase the balance in the account significantly. Regardless of the performance of the investments, however, the amount of the insurance benefit can never drop below its original value. When choosing a whole life policy, experts note, it is important to analyze the fund's past performance and inquire about commissions and hidden costs. Although whole life insurance can provide added security upon retirement, it should not be considered a replacement for retirement savings. In fact, Janecek revealed that, on the average, whole life policy holders only yielded between 2 and 4.5 percent on their investments over a twenty-year period.

UNIVERSAL LIFE INSURANCE Universal life insurance was introduced in the 1980s as a higher-interest alternative to whole life insurance. Universal life premiums are based not only on the cost of the insurance, but also on the interest rate offered on investments. Still, they are usually less expensive than whole life policies. Universal life policies provide individuals with a wider array of investment choices and higher projected interest rates. They are essentially similar to a term policy with a fixed rate of interest guaranteed for a year at a time.

CURRENT ASSUMPTION LIFE INSURANCE Current assumption life insurance features a fixed annual premium for the duration of the plan. This type of policy pays a set interest rate on premiums received, less the actual cost of the insurance. They can be useful as a tax-deferred investment vehicle, since they usually pay 2 to 4 percent more than banks. Policy holders may elect to overpay their premiums early in the plan period to accumulate cash value. They can withdraw or borrow from the funds later for any purpose, including retirement income, or can use the cash value to pay the premiums for the remainder of the plan period.

RIDERS AND OPTIONS Most types of life insurance policies give individuals the opportunity to add optional coverage, or riders. One popular option is accelerated benefits (also called living benefits), which pays up to 25 percent of the policy value to the holder prior to their death if they are struck by a serious illness. Another option, known as a waiver of premium, allows an individual to continue coverage without paying premiums if he or she becomes disabled. Many policies also provide an accidental death and dismemberment option, which pays twice the amount of the policy if the insured dies or loses the use of limbs as a result of an accident.

KEY PERSON PROTECTION

Small businesses tend to depend on a few key people, some of whom are likely to be owners or partners, to keep operations running smoothly. Even though it is unpleasant to think about the possibility of a key employee becoming disabled or dying, it is important to prepare so that the business may survive and the tax implications may be minimized. In the case of a partnership, the business is formally dissolved when one partner dies. In the case of a corporation, the death of a major stockholder can throw the business into disarray. In the absence of a specific agreement, the person's estate or heirs may choose to vote the shares or sell them. This uncertainty could undermine the company's management, impair its credit, cause the flight of customers, and damage employee morale.

Life insurance can help small businesses protect themselves against the loss of a key person by providing a source of income to keep business running in his or her absence. Partnership insurance basically involves each partner acting as beneficiary of a life insurance policy taken on the other partner. In this way, the surviving partner is protected against a financial loss when the business ends. Similarly, corporate plans can ensure the continuity of the business under the same management, and possibly fund a repurchase of stock, if a major stockholder dies. Although life insurance is not tax deductible when the business is named as beneficiary, the business may deduct premium costs if a partner or owner is the beneficiary.

FURTHER READING:

Anastasio, Susan. *Small Business Insurance and Risk Management Guide.* Washington: U.S. Small Business Administration, n.d.

Bury, Don. *The Buyer's Guide to Business Insurance.* Grants Pass, OR: Oasis Press, 1994.

Janecek, Lenore. *Health Insurance: A Guide for Artists, Consultants, Entrepreneurs, and Other Self-Employed.* New York: Allworth Press, 1993.

Lynn, Jacquelyn. ''A Quick Guide to Insurance.'' *Entrepreneur.* June 1997.

SEE ALSO: Business Insurance; Disability Insurance; Multiple Employer Trust

LIMITED LIABILITY COMPANY

The Limited Liability Company (LLC), a new hybrid of the **partnership** and the corporation, is becoming an increasingly popular legal alternative for business owners. Now available in almost all states, the LLC combines the benefits of limited liability and pass through taxation, much like an **S corporation**. But the LLC's legal structure is much looser, allowing many companies that find S corporation status too restrictive to take advantage of its benefits. Small business owners are taking advantage of the LLC because it is easier to set up and maintain than a corporation.

Because the LLC is a fairly new option in the United States (it first became available in Wyoming in 1977, but most other states did not follow suit until the 1990s), the laws governing this business form are very new and largely uninterpreted by court cases. In addition, each state has its own statutes concerning LLCs. Therefore, learning and keeping up with the laws that govern LLCs, which are still being fine-tuned, can be a tricky business. When considering the LLC option, consulting knowledgeable and up-to-date legal and tax advisors is a must.

ADVANTAGES OF FORMING AN LLC

LIMITED LIABILITY Like corporations, the LLC provides its members (owners) with protection from being personally responsible for the debt liabilities of the company. Members are only liable to the extent of their investments in the company. If a customer slips and is injured on company property, a law suit may still bankrupt the business, but it cannot touch the personal assets of the LLC's members. This limited liability, then, is a great advantage over partnerships because in general partnerships all members are liable for the company's debts, and in a limited partnership, at least one member must still be liable.

AVOIDING DOUBLE TAXATION Like S corporations, LLC's enjoy exemption from the **double taxation** required of **C corporations**. In other words, the LLC's profits pass through to the company's members, who report their share of the profits on their personal federal tax returns. The company itself does not pay a federal tax before the money is distributed to the members, as in the case of C corporations. But state and local taxes may still be levied against the LLC.

FLEXIBILITY OF INCOME DISTRIBUTION One of the biggest benefits that small businesses enjoy when choosing LLC status, according to Fred Steingold, author of *The Legal Guide for Starting and Running a Small Business*, is that it is "easier to allocate profits and losses for tax purposes." Whereas the amount of profits the S corporation's shareholders report on their federal tax returns must be proportional to their share of stock, an LLC's members can determine amongst themselves how to divide their income as long as they follow the Internal Revenue Service's rules on partnership income distribution.

SIMPLICITY Another great advantage of LLCs over corporations is the ease of setting up and running one. Whereas incorporation can be an involved and costly process, all that is required to start an LLC is the filing of an Articles of Organization and the drafting of an Operating Agreement defining the company's policies and procedures (a filing fee, though, will still be required of LLCs). And whereas a corporation requires a board of directors, officers, and regular shareholders' and directors' meetings, an LLC is not required to observe such formalities in its operation. An LLC can be run from day to day essentially as if it were a partnership.

NO OWNERSHIP RESTRICTIONS The biggest drawback of forming an S corporation—the restrictions on the type and number of shareholders the corporation may have—is avoided by forming an LLC. The members of an LLC may be foreign nationals or other companies, both of which are prohibited from owning stock in an S corporation. In addition, there is no limit on the number of members an LLC may have, as there is with an S corporation.

MEMBER INVOLVEMENT IN THE COMPANY One problem with limited partnerships is that those partners who wish to protect themselves with limited liability (which may be all but one of the members) are prohibited from direct involvement in running the company. These partners may have only a financial investment in the firm. All members of an LLC may be directly involved in the company's management without jeopardizing their limited liability.

ATTRACTIVE TO FOREIGN INVESTORS Because LLCs have been in existence in Europe and Latin America for over a century, investors from those parts of the world are particularly knowledgeable about this business form. According to *The Essential Limited Liability Handbook*, "LLCs often prove to be the most familiar and least imposing business structure for foreign entrepreneurs who wish to enter the American market."

DRAWBACKS OF FORMING AN LLC

NEWNESS LLCs are still a very new option in most states (only Wyoming and Florida have had LLC statutes on the books for over a decade). This means that the statutes governing the establishment of LLCs are still evolving. And there is virtually no case history in the courts to indicate how these laws will be interpreted. The **Internal Revenue Service** is also still working out its position concerning LLCs, so it will be imperative for small business owners to solicit legal and tax advice on the current laws before making a decision about whether or not to form an LLC. And because the laws may change while the LLC is in existence, it will be important to keep on top of the developments in LLC statutes to determine whether it remains in the company's best interests to operate as an LLC.

INTERSTATE BUSINESS MORE COMPLICATED Laws governing LLCs can vary widely from state to state, complicating the conduct of business across state lines. There are, as of yet, no uniform laws concerning LLCs, so an even greater knowledge of the state laws will be required of the company that does business in more than one state.

NO PERPETUAL EXISTENCE Most states require that an LLC's Operating Agreement set a limit to the company's existence (usually 30 years). And in the absence of a clause in the Operating Agreement providing for the continuance of the LLC in the event of the death or withdrawal of a member, the LLC will cease to exist when such events occur. The transfer of ownership is also more restricted for an LLC (like a partnership) than for a corporation.

CREATING AN LLC

It is important that the organizer(s) of a prospective LLC follow the ''enabling statutes'' or formation laws of the state in which the company will be formed in order to be designated as an LLC. Without this designation, the company will lack the protection of limited liability and will be treated as a general partnership. Therefore, the first step in creating an LLC is to find out your state's specific enabling statutes.

The organizer does not have to be one of the company's members. The organizer's function is to file the articles of organization, a task which can be accomplished by a lawyer, a hired agent from a service company specializing in such business, or a manager of the prospective company.

NAMING AN LLC Before forming an LLC, the company name must be reserved with the secretary of state or its equivalent. Most states require that the words ''Limited Liability Company'' or the abbreviation ''L.L.C.'' be included in the name of the company. In some states, ''Limited Company'' or ''L.C.'' is the preferred designation. In all states, though, the name of the LLC must not resemble the name of any other corporation, LLC, partnership, or sole proprietorship that is registered with the state.

THE ARTICLES OF ORGANIZATION This form, called the articles of organization or certificate of formation, must be obtained from the secretary of state's office or its equivalent, be filled out by the organizer(s), and be filed with the same office. A filing fee, which varies from state to state, will also be charged. This simple document requires, at minimum, the company name and address, a description of the business to be conducted, the name and address of the registered agent (the contact to whom notices of lawsuit or other official matters can be served), the names of the company's members and managers (usually the members themselves), and the dissolution date. Other information may be required, depending on which state the Articles of Organization are filed in. It is important that the Articles describe the business in a way that will allow the Internal Revenue Service to designate the company a partnership for tax purposes, and not a corporation. In order for the I.R.S. to do so, the Articles must show that the company possesses no more than two of the following four characteristics (which describe a corporation):

- Perpetual existence
- Centralized management
- Free transferability of ownership interest
- Limited liability.

One of the easiest ways to show that the LLC is not a corporation is to limit its existence. In fact, most states require that a dissolution date be determined in the Articles of Organization. On this date the LLC's assets will be liquidated and its business will cease (occurrences such as the mutual written agreement of the members or the death or retirement of a member may also terminate the LLC's existence before the dissolution date). If no date is specified, a default period of usually 30 years will be enacted. At a later date, though, the members may decide to continue the LLC's existence.

FEES Filing fees vary from state to state, from $50 to $500. In addition, some states require the LLC to publish an announcement of its creation to the public in a generally circulated newspaper. This latter requirement can be very expensive, ranging from $500 to $2,000.

THE OPERATING AGREEMENT At the first meeting of the members, called the organizational meeting, an Operating Agreement should be drafted. Although each state has laws governing how LLC's should be operated, the members should create their own Operating Agreement to document that all members agree on how the company should be run. It should be carefully constructed with an eye to preventing future disagreements and deadlocks. Most basically, the agreement should address the division of profits, members' voting rights, and company management. A good Operating Agreement will address the following issues:

- Who the members are and how they will be elected in the future.

- Grounds on which members may be terminated, and procedures to execute such terminations.

- Stipulations regarding allocation of business shares after the death of a member.

- If a member becomes disabled, how will the company provide for him/her (with disability insurance or out of its own funds)?

- How managers will be selected and what their duties, salaries, and grounds for dismissal will be.

- How major decisions will be made. (Which decisions will require unanimous approval of the members and which a simple majority vote? Which decisions can be delegated to the manager in charge of daily affairs?)

- How often meetings will be held and how much notice members must receive.

- Who will keep records and how they will be kept.

- How members will invest in the LLC: will only cash contributions be allowed, or can members contribute services as well? If so, which services will be accepted and how will they be valued?

- How profits and losses will be allocated to members.

- How compensation (salary) for actively participating members will be determined.

- How new capital should be acquired should the company need it.

- What procedures must be followed to transfer interests in the company.

- What banking procedures should be followed.

- Penalties, if any, if members or managers fail to act in accordance with the Operating Agreement.

FURTHER READING:

Damman, Gregory C. *How to Form and Operate a Limited Liability Company: A Do-it-Yourself Guide.* Bellingham, WA: Self-Counsel Press, 1995.

The Essential Limited Liability Handbook. Grants Pass: Oasis Press, 1995.

Friedman, Scott E. *How to Profit by Forming Your Own Limited Liability Company.* Chicago, IL: Upstart, 1995.

Handmaker, Stuart A. *Choosing a Legal Structure for Your Business.* Upper Saddle River, NJ: Prentice Hall, 1997.

Mancuso, Anthony. *Form Your Own Limited Liability Company.* Berkeley, CA: Nolo Press, 1996.

Shenkman, Martin M., Samuel Weiner, and Ivan Taback. *Starting a Limited Liability Company.* Wiley, 1996.

SEE ALSO: Professional Corporation

LOAN PROPOSALS

Loan proposals are formal, written documents that small businesses must prepare when they approach potential lenders or investors for funding. A complete loan proposal package should consist of completed loan application forms (if required), and a comprehensive **business plan** with complete **financial statements**. Ideally, the loan proposal should present information about the small business, its future prospects, and its financing needs in a straightforward manner. All the pertinent information the lender or investor might need in making a decision should be provided in a logical format. Loan proposals must be thorough yet concise, convincing yet honest. The aim is to answer all the questions that a lender or investor is likely to ask without overstating the facts and figures.

Preparing a solid loan proposal can be very time consuming, but it has proven to be the best way for a small business owner to demonstrate his or her understanding of the business and its financial demands to potential lenders and investors. Furthermore, the business plan portion of the loan proposal can serve as a sort of handbook for running the business. It presents criteria against which management's strategy and decisions can be continually evaluated. Overall, a formal loan proposal should illustrate why the small business is a good credit risk by placing it within the context of its market and competition, explaining any peaks and valleys in cash flow, and emphasizing the strengths of the management team.

ELEMENTS OF A LOAN PROPOSAL

The U.S. Small Business Administration publication *Handbook for Small Business* outlines some of the elements that should be included in a good loan proposal. It should begin with a summary page that provides contact information for the company, the amount of the loan request, the company's intended purpose for the funds, and the proposed repayment terms.

The next section should feature a description and summary of the business, including a brief history. The description should also include information on the size and potential for growth of the business's main markets, an analysis of the competition, and notes on any emerging industry trends. Other useful information might include an explanation of any unique aspects of the business's product or service, information on local advertising efforts, and a long-term growth plan.

The next major section of the loan proposal features information on the company's management team, including brief resumes outlining the experience of key employees. This section might also include notes on the business's current staffing level, along with an analysis of future staffing needs. The names and contact information for accountants and attorneys should also be provided.

The next section consists of the loan request itself. This section should provide the potential lender with details about the amount of funds needed, how they will be used, what collateral is available to secure the loan, the company's proposed repayment terms, and evidence of the small business's ability to repay the loan.

Another section should include supporting financial data, including a current balance sheet and income statement, three years of historical financial statements (for existing businesses), projections of cash flow for the next year, and personal financial statements for the business's primary owners or investors. Another important loan-related section should supply information on the business's current sources and uses of credit, including the names and contact information for lenders and trade creditors.

The final section of the loan proposal can include a variety of miscellaneous information that might help the lender to reach a favorable decision. For example, the small business owner could attach business licenses, copies of the partnership agreement or articles of incorporation, copies of tax returns, lease information if renting facilities, and information on insurance coverage.

MAKING THE PROPOSAL

In his book *Doing Business with Banks,* Gibson Heath recommended that the loan proposal be written using layman's terms, and illustrated with computer-generated graphics and charts that highlight key areas of the proposal and provide a visual representation of the ideas presented. Overall, the loan proposal must anticipate any objections the lender or investor might have to providing funds for the small business, and then provide the information needed to overcome the objections.

In an article for *Inc.,* Bruce G. Posner solicited comments from bankers regarding the most glaring weaknesses they saw in small business loan proposals. They all expressed a desire to see evidence that the business owner had thought the loan proposal all the way through. "Business owners come in with these beautiful three-ring binders. The numbers are in nice, straight columns, but a lot of these people haven't though about the assumptions they've made and what it will take to do what they say they'll do," said Jeffrey C. Gardner of U.S. Bancorp. "We need to know where the numbers come from. The sad part is that many people don't know what the projections are about because their accountant made all the assumptions."

Dev Strischek of Barnett Bank of Palm Beach County echoed these comments, noting that "The biggest weakness I see is a lack of specificity and a lack of preparation. A lot of people don't really know what they need the money for or how much they need. . . . We like to see a cash-flow analysis—how much they plan to sell, how much they spend on overhead, how much for inventory, and what's available for debt service. It's easier to do business with people who've thought things through."

After creating a formal, written loan proposal, the next step is to present the proposal to a potential lender. Heath recommended that the small business owner take one last look at the loan proposal before taking it to the bank, in order to verify the numbers and be ready to answer any questions with confidence. It is important that, rather than just dropping the loan proposal off, the small business owner meet with the lender to review the loan proposal in detail. The in-person presentation should focus on just a few key points of the proposal. It is intended to improve the lender's understanding of the business and the loan request, so that he or she will be able to defend the proposal to other decision makers. At the conclusion of the meeting, the small business owner should ask when a decision might be expected. It is also important for the small business owner to be available during that time period to answer any follow-up questions.

FURTHER READING:

Dawson, George M. *Borrowing for Your Business: Winning the Battle for the Banker's "Yes."* Dover, NH: Upstart Publishing, 1991.

Heath, Gibson. *Doing Business with Banks: A Common Sense Guide for Small Business Borrowers.* Denver: DBA/USA Press, 1991.

Posner, Bruce G. "Plugging Holes in Loan Proposals." *Inc.* April 1992.

Service Corps of Retired Executives. *Handbook for Small Business.* Washington: U.S. Small Business Administration, 1989.

Whittemore, Meg. "Creative Financing That Succeeds." *Nation's Business.* April 1995.

SEE ALSO: Loans

LOANS

A loan is the purchase of the present use of money with the promise to repay the amount in the future according to a pre-arranged schedule and at a specified rate of interest. Loan contracts formally spell out the terms and obligations between the lender and borrower. Loans are by far the most common type of **debt financing** used by small businesses. Loans can be classified as long-term (with a maturity longer than one year), short-term (with a maturity shorter than two years), or a credit line (for more immediate borrowing needs). They can be endorsed by co-signers, guaranteed by the government, or secured by **collateral**— such as real estate, accounts receivable, inventory, savings, life insurance, stocks and bonds, or the item purchased with the loan. The **interest rates** charged on the borrowed funds reflects the level of risk that the lender undertakes by providing the money. For example, a lender might charge a startup company a higher interest rate than it would a company that has shown a profit for several years.

CHARACTERISTICS OF LOANS

Loans have the following distinguishing characteristics:

1) *Time to maturity.* Time to maturity describes the length of the loan contract. Loans are classified according to their maturity into short-term debt, intermediate-term debt, and long-term debt. Revolving credit and perpetual debt have no fixed date for retirement. Banks provide revolving credit through extensions of a line of credit. Brokerage firms supply margin credit for qualified customers on certain securities. In these cases, the borrower constantly turns over the line of credit by paying it down and reborrowing the funds when needed. A perpetual loan requires only regular interest payments. The borrower, who usually issued such debt through a registered offering, determines the timing of the debt retirement.

2) *Repayment Schedule.* Payments may be required at the end of the contract or at set intervals, usually on a monthly or semi-annual basis. The payment generally comprises two parts: a portion of the outstanding principal and the interest costs. With the passage of time, the principal amount of the loan is amortized, or repaid little by little until it is completely retired. As the principal balance diminishes, the interest on the remaining balance also declines. Interest-only loans do not pay down the principal. The borrower pays interest on the principal loan amount and is expected to retire the principal at the end of the contract through a balloon payment or through refinancing.

3) *Interest.* Interest is the cost of borrowing money. The interest rate charged by lending institutions must be sufficient to cover operating costs, administrative costs, and an acceptable rate of return. Interest rates may be fixed for the term of the loan, or adjusted to reflect changing market conditions. A credit contract may adjust rates daily, annually, or at intervals of 3, 5, and 10 years. Floating rates are tied to some market index and are adjusted regularly.

4) *Security.* Assets pledged as security against loan loss are known as collateral. Credit backed by collateral is secured. In many cases, the asset purchased by the loan often serves as the only collateral. In other cases the borrower puts other assets, including cash, aside as collateral. Real estate or land collateralize mortgages. Unsecured debt relies on the earning power of the borrower.

COMMON TYPES OF LOANS

Consumers and small businesses obtain loans with varying maturity periods to fund purchases of real estate, transportation, equipment, supplies, and an array of other needs. According to W. Keith Schilit in *The Entrepreneur's Guide to Preparing a Winning Business Plan and Raising Venture Capital,* they receive these loans from a number of sources, including friends and relatives, banks, credit unions, finance companies, insurance companies, leasing companies, and trade credit. The state and federal governments sponsor a number of loan programs to support small businesses. Following are examples of some common types of loans.

SHORT-TERM LOANS A special commitment loan is a single-purpose loan with a maturity of less than one year. Its purpose is to cover cash shortages resulting from a one-time increase in current assets, such as a special inventory purchase, an unexpected decrease in accounts receivable, or a need for interim financing. Trade credit is another type of short-term loan. It is extended by a vendor who allows the purchaser up to three months to settle a bill. In the past it was common practice for vendors to discount trade bills by one or two percentage points as an incentive for quick payment.

A seasonal line of credit of less than one year may be used to finance inventory purchases or production. The successful sale of inventory repays the line of credit. A permanent working capital loan provides a business with financing from one to five years during times when cash flow from earnings does not coincide with the timing or volume of expenditures. Creditors expect future earnings to be sufficient to retire the loan.

INTERMEDIATE-TERM LOANS Term loans finance the purchase of furniture, fixtures, vehicles, and plant and office equipment. Maturity generally runs more than one year but less than five. Consumer loans for autos, boats, and home repairs and remodeling are also of intermediate term.

LONG-TERM LOANS Mortgage loans, or long-term loans, are used to purchase real estate and are secured by the asset itself. Mortgages generally run between ten and forty years. A bond is a contract held in trust with the obligation of repayment. An indenture is a legal document specifying the terms of a bond issue, including the principal, maturity date, interest rates, any qualifications and duties of the trustees, and the rights and obligations of the issuers and holders. Corporations and government entities issue bonds in a form attractive to both public and private investors. A debenture bond is unsecured, while a mortgage bond holds specific property in lien. A bond may contain safety measures to provide for repayment.

LOAN CONSIDERATIONS FOR SMALL BUSINESSES

When evaluating a small business for a loan, Jennifer Lindsey wrote in *The Entrepreneur's Guide to Capital,* lenders ideally like to see a two-year operating history, a stable management group, a desirable niche in the industry, a growth in market share, a strong cash flow, and an ability to obtain short-term financing from other sources as a supplement to the loan. Most lenders will require a small business owner to prepare a loan proposal or complete a loan application. The package of materials provided to a potential lender should include a comprehensive business plan, plus detailed company and personal financial statements. The lender will then evaluate the loan request by considering a variety of factors. For example, the lender will examine the small business's credit rating and look for evidence of its ability to repay the loan, in the form of past earnings or income projections. The lender will also inquire into the amount of equity in the business, as well as whether management has sufficient experience and competence to run the business effectively. Finally, the lender will try to ascertain whether the small business can provide a reasonable amount of collateral to secure the loan.

Experts indicate that borrowing can be a useful strategy, particularly for companies with good credit and a stable history of revenues, earnings, and cash flow. But small business owners should think carefully before committing to large loans in order to avoid cash flow problems and reduced flexibility. In general, a combination of loans and other types of financing is considered most desirable for small businesses.

In the Small Business Administration publication *Financing for the Small Business,* Brian Hamilton listed several factors entrepreneurs should consider when choosing between their various financing options. First, the entrepreneur must consider how much ownership and control he or she is willing to give up, not only at present but also in future financing rounds. Allowing the founders to retain ownership and control of the company is a major advantage of loans over equity financing, or selling stock to outside investors. Second, the entrepreneur should decide how leveraged the company can comfortably be, or its optimal ratio of debt to equity. Third, the entrepreneur should determine what types of financing are available to the company, given its stage of development and capital needs, and compare the costs and requirements of the different types. Finally, as a practical consideration, the entrepreneur should ascertain whether or not the company is in a position to make set monthly payments on a loan.

No matter what type of financing is chosen, careful planning is necessary to secure it. The entrepreneur should assess the business's financial needs, and then estimate what percentage of the total funds must be obtained from outside sources. A formal business plan, complete with cash flow projections, is an important tool in both planning for and obtaining financing. Lindsey noted that small businesses should consider loans as a financing option when federal interest rates are low, they have a good credit history or property to use as collateral, and they expect future growth in earnings as well as in the overall industry.

The main disadvantage of loans is that they require a small business to make regular monthly payments of principal and interest. Very young companies often experience shortages in cash flow that may make such regular payments difficult. Most lenders provide severe penalties for late or missed payments, which may include charging late fees, taking possession of collateral, or calling the loan due early. Failure to make payments on a loan, even temporarily, can adversely affect a small business's credit rating and its ability to obtain future financing. Another disadvantage associated with loans is that their availability is often restricted to established businesses. Since lenders primarily seek security for their funds, it can be difficult for unproven businesses to obtain loans. Finally, the amount of money small businesses may be able to obtain via loans is likely to be limited, so they may need to use other sources of financing as well.

FURTHER READING:

Guttman, Robert. *How Credit-Money Shapes the Economy.* M.E. Sharpe, 1994.

Hamilton, Brian. *Financing for the Small Business.* Washington: U.S. Small Business Administration, 1990.

Heath, Gibson. *Doing Business with Banks: A Common Sense Guide for Small Business Borrowers.* Lakewood, CO: DBA/ USA Press, 1991.

Lindsey, Jennifer. *The Entrepreneur's Guide to Capital.* Chicago: Probus, 1986.

McNeil, Jane H., and Edward T. O'Leary. *Introduction to Commercial Lending.* American Institute of Banking, 1983.

Rosenthal, James A., and Juan M. Ocampo. *Securitization of Credit.* New York: Wiley, 1988.

Schilit, W. Keith. *The Entrepreneur's Guide to Preparing a Winning Business Plan and Raising Venture Capital.* Englewood Cliffs, NJ: Prentice Hall, 1990.

Silver, A. David. *Up Front Financing: The Entrepreneur's Guide.* New York: Wiley, 1982.

Timmons, Jeffrey A. *Planning and Financing the New Venture.* Brick House Publishing Company, 1990.

Van Note, Mark. *ABCs of Borrowing.* Washington: U.S. Small Business Administration, 1990. Wray, L. Randall. *Money and Credit in Capitalist Economies.* Edward Elgar Publishing Company, 1990.

SEE ALSO: Loan Proposals

LOCAL AREA NETWORKS

In the modern office environment, each worker is equipped with a personal computer, containing its own disk drives and processor. Each of these PCs may be set up to communicate with other PCs over a local area network (LAN). In addition, the LAN may also connect the network of PCs with a series of printers, a mainframe computer, or file server, with even greater processing power and memory storage, and with other devices that can send messages from the network over telephone lines to another location.

As the name suggests, a LAN is local, meaning that it is a proprietary system limited to a finite number of users. It generally serves an area of less than one mile, and is usually confined to a single building. It is also a network, affording users both functional and communicative diversity through a distribution of resources. A LAN permits workers—isolated in separate offices—to operate off the same system, as if they were all sitting around a single computer.

One of the great attributes of a LAN is that it may be installed simply, upgraded or expanded with little difficulty, and moved or rearranged without disruption. Perhaps most importantly, anyone initiated in the use of a personal computer can be trained to communicate or perform work over a LAN. But despite their

great potential and capabilities, LANs have yet to demonstrate an increase in office productivity. They have certainly eliminated paper and speeded the flow of information, but in many cases they have also created additional work in terms of organization, maintenance, and trouble-shooting.

DEVELOPMENT OF LANS

The first distributed computing systems were introduced during the 1960s. Initially, they consisted of "dumb" terminals connected to a single mainframe processor via a wiring system. Instructions entered on the terminal keyboard were registered at the mainframe, where they were processed, and a visual representation of these instructions was sent back to the terminal for display on a screen. The first protocols for these distributed computer workstations were proprietary, meaning that they were designed specifically for equipment designed by a certain company. As a result, IBM equipment could not be mixed with DEC, Xerox, Wang, or any other manufacturer's machinery.

By the late 1970s, however, several companies proposed "open" standards under which equipment from one manufacturer could be made to emulate the operating system of another. This allowed manufacturers to compete for business in systems that had previously been closed to all but the system designer. The first of these standards was Ethernet, a "listen-and-transmit" protocol developed by Digital Equipment, Intel, and Xerox. Ethernet identified the type of instructions being generated and, if necessary, conditioned them so they could be read by the mainframe on a common terminal, or bus.

In 1980, the Institute of Electrical and Electronic Engineers (IEEE), determined that continued reluctance to open protocols would seriously retard the growth of distributed computer systems. It established a group called the 802 committee to establish networking standards for the entire industry. This would ensure that customers could migrate from one vendor to another without sacrificing their considerable investments in existing systems. The standards also compelled manufacturers to follow the standards, or risk being dealt out of the market.

Ethernet was offered to the 802 committee as a standard. Several manufacturers balked because Ethernet did not work well under heavy traffic. Instead, the Ethernet standard was adapted into three versions, corresponding to network designs. Still, these standards could support 1,024 workstations over an end-to-end distance of two kilometers. However, processor manufacturing technology had progressed so far that entire computers could be condensed into a single desktop unit. The first of these "personal computers" (PCs) was introduced by IBM in 1981. IBM's PC featured an open bus architecture, meaning that

IBM provided design specifications to other manufacturers in the hope that they would design compatible equipment and software for the system. IBM could impose this architecture on the market because it had very high market penetration and was the leading manufacturer in the industry.

The PC changed the type of information sent over office computer networks. Terminals were no longer "dumb," but contained the power to perform their own instructions and maintain their own memories. This took considerable pressure off the mainframe device, whose energies could now be devoted to more complex tasks. An analysis of common office tasks revealed that as much as 80 percent of the work performed by the average employee never left the room in which it was produced. This factor established demand characteristics for individual, worker-specific PCs. The remaining 20 percent of office tasks required transmission of data for access by other workers.

LANs enabled this shared data to be directed to a common printer, serving a dozen or more workers. This eliminated the need for each worker to have a printer and ensured that the one printer provided was not underutilized. In addition, LANs allowed data to be called up directly on other workers' computers, providing immediate communication and eliminating the need for paper. The most common application was in interoffice communications, or electronic mail (e-mail). Messages could be directed to one or several people and copied to several more over the LAN. As a result, an e-mail system became something of an official record of communications between workers. Addressees became obligated to respond to e-mail messages in a timely manner because their failure to answer could be documented for supervisors.

PCs transformed LANs from mere shared processors to fully integrated communication devices. In fact, developments in processing technology endowed some PCs with even greater capacity than the mainframe computers to which they were attached. For some applications, the need for a mainframe was completely eliminated. With processing power distributed among PCs, the mainframe's main role was eclipsed. While still useful for complex processing, administrative functions and data file storage became the job of a new device, the file server.

PHYSICAL COMPONENTS OF LANS

The physical properties of a LAN include interfaces, called network access units, which connect the PC to the network. These units are actually interface cards installed on PC motherboards. Their job is to provide a connection, monitor availability of access to the LAN, set or buffer the data transmission speed, ensure against transmission errors and collisions, and assemble data from the LAN into usable form for the PC.

The next part of a LAN is the wiring, which provides the physical connection from one PC to another, and to printers and file servers. The properties of the wiring determine transmission speeds. The first LANs were connected with coaxial cable, the type used to deliver cable television. These facilities are relatively inexpensive and simple to attach. More importantly, they provide great bandwidth (the system's rate of data transfer), enabling transmission speeds initially up to 20 megabits per second.

During the 1980s, however, AT&T introduced a LAN wiring system using ordinary twisted wire pair of the type used for telephones. The primary advantages of twisted wire pair are that it is very cheap, simpler to splice than coaxial, and is already installed in many buildings as obsolete or redundant wiring. In fact, many buildings were left with stranded 25-pair wiring once used for key telephone systems. But the downside of this simplicity is that its bandwidth is more limited. AT&T's first LAN product, StarLAN, had a capacity of only one megabit per second. Subsequent improvements expanded this capacity tenfold and eliminated the need for shielded, or conditioned, wiring.

A more recent development in LAN wiring is optical fiber cable. This type of wiring uses thin strands of glass to transmit pulses of light between terminals. Its advantages are that it provides tremendous bandwidth, allowing very high transmission speeds. And because it is optical rather than electronic, it is impervious to electromagnetic interference. Its main drawback, however, is that splicing is difficult and requires a high degree of skill. The primary application of fiber is not between terminals, but between LAN buses (terminals) located on different floors. As a result, fiber distributed data interface (FDDI) is used mainly in building risers. Within individual floors, LAN facilities remain coaxial or twisted wire pair.

Where a physical connection cannot be made, such as across a street or between buildings where easements for wiring cannot be secured, microwave radio may be used. However, it is often difficult to secure frequencies for this medium. Another alternative in this application is light transceivers, which project a beam of light similar to fiber optic cable, but through the air rather than over cable. These systems do not have the frequency allocation or radiation problems associated with microwave, but they are susceptible to interference from fog and other obstructions.

LAN TOPOLOGIES

LANs are designed in several different topologies, or physical patterns, connecting terminals. The most common topology is the bus, where several terminals are connected directly to each other over a single transmission path; it is analogous to a street with several driveways. Each terminal on the LAN contends with other terminals for access to the system. When it has secured access to the system, it broadcasts its message to all the terminals at once. The message is picked up by the one or group of terminal stations for which it is intended. The branching tree topology is an extension of the bus, providing a link between two or more buses. It may be likened to alleyways connecting several streets, each with many driveways. The connections between buses include impedance matching devices.

A third topology, the star network, also works like a bus in terms of contention and broadcast. But in the star, stations are connected to a single, central node that administers access. Several of these nodes may be connected to one another. For example, a bus serving six stations may be connected to another bus serving 10 stations and a third bus connecting 12 stations. The star topology is most often used where the connecting facilities are coaxial or twisted wire pair.

The ring topology connects each station to its own node, and these nodes are connected in a circular fashion. Node 1 is connected to node 2, which is connected to node 3, and so on, and the final node is connected back to node 1. Messages sent over the LAN are regenerated by each node, but retained only by the addressees. Eventually, the message circulates back to the sending node, which removes it from the stream.

TRANSMISSION METHODS USED BY LANS

LANs function because their transmission capacity is greater than any single terminal on the system. As a result, each station terminal can be offered a certain amount of time on the LAN, like a time-sharing arrangement. To economize on this window of opportunity, stations organize their messages into compact packets that can be quickly disseminated.

In contending for access, a station with something to send stores its data packet in a buffer until the LAN is clear. At that point the message is sent out. Sometimes, two stations may detect the opening at the same time and send their messages simultaneously. Unaware that another message has been sent out, the two signals will collide on the LAN. When this happens it is up to the network software to clear the wreckage, determine who should go first and ask both machines to try again.

In busy LANs, such collisions would occur all the time, slowing the system down considerably. To solve the problem, the LAN software circulates a token. This works like a ticket that is distributed only to one station at a time. Instead of waiting for the LAN to clear, the station waits to receive the token. When it has the token, the station sends its packet out over the LAN. When it is done, it returns the token to the stream for the next user. Tokens, used in ring and bus topologies, virtually eliminate the problem of collisions by providing orderly, non-contention access.

The transmission methods used on LANs are either baseband or broadband. The baseband medium uses a high-speed digital signal consisting of square wave DC voltage. While it is fast, it can accommodate only one message at a time. As a result it is suitable for smaller networks where contention is low. It also is very simple, requiring no tuning or frequency discretion circuits. As a result, the transmission medium may be connected directly to the network access unit and is suitable for use over twisted wire pair facilities.

By contrast, the broadband medium tunes signals to special frequencies, much like cable television. Stations are instructed by signaling information to tune to a specific channel to receive information. The information within each channel on a broadband medium may also be digital, but they are separated from other messages by frequency. As a result, the medium generally requires higher capacity facilities, such as coaxial cable. Suited for busier LANs, broadband systems require the use of tuning devices in the network access unit that can filter out all but the single channel it needs.

THE FILE SERVER

The heart of the LAN, the administrative software, resides either in a dedicated file server or, in a smaller, less busy LAN, in a PC acting as a file server. In addition to acting as a kind of traffic controller, the file server holds files for shared use in its hard drives, administers applications such as the operating system, and allocates functions.

Where a single PC is used as both a workstation and a file server, response times may lag because its processors are forced to perform several instructions at once. In addition, the system will store certain files on different PCs on the LAN. As a result, if one machine is down, the entire system may be crippled. And if the system were to crash due to undercapacity, some data may be lost or corrupted.

The addition of a dedicated file server may be costly, but it provides several advantages over a distributed system. In addition to ensuring access even when some machines are down, it is unencumbered by multiple duties. Its only jobs are to hold files and provide access.

The speed of the LAN is measured in terms of throughput, a figure different from transmission speed because it takes into account the capacity of the wiring and the distance between stations. The data rate, which most directly represents response time, is determined by throughput and other factors such as overhead bits and other signals, error and collision recovery, software and hardware efficiency, and the memory capacity of disk drives.

OTHER LAN EQUIPMENT

LANs are generally limited in size because of the physical properties of the network: distance, impedance, and load. Some equipment, such as repeaters, can extend the range of a LAN. Repeaters have no processing ability, but simply regenerate signals that are weakened by impedance. Other types of LAN equipment with processing ability include gateways, which enable LANs operating dissimilar protocols to pass information by translating it into a simpler code, such as ASCII. A bridge works like a gateway, but instead of using an intermediate code, it translates one protocol directly into another. A router performs essentially the same function as a bridge, except that it administers communications over alternate paths. Gateways, bridges, and routers can act as repeaters, boosting signals over greater distances. They also enable separate LANs located in different buildings to communicate with each other.

In some cases, separate LANs located in different cities—and even separate countries—may be linked over the public network. Whether these are ''nailed up'' dedicated links or switched services, the connection of two or more such LANs is referred to as a **wide area network (WAN)**. WANs require the use of special software programs in the operating system to enable dial-up connections that may be performed by a router. Unless limited to modem speeds, these connections may require special services such as ISDN (integrated services digital network) to ensure efficient transmission, particularly of large data files. Increasingly, companies employing LANs in separate locations also operate WANs. With the rise in use of the Internet as a business tool, WANs are expected to proliferate even further, as telephone carriers, cable television vendors, and even electrical power companies compete to provide companies with Internet access.

Another device different from, but related to, the LAN is the data PBX (private branch exchange). This is a device that works like an A/B switch, but routes messages to specific servers, rather than broadcasting to all stations. It is oblivious to operating systems and performs only circuit-switched connections. As a re-

sult, it is somewhat slower, and its applications are limited. Nonetheless, it is a suitable adjunct to many LANs because it can switch asynchronous terminals to a number of hosts or funnel several terminals into a single terminal port.

LAN DIFFICULTIES

LANs are susceptible to many kinds of transmission errors. Electromagnetic interference from motors, power lines, and sources of static, as well as shorts from corrosion, can corrupt data. Software bugs and hardware failures can also introduce errors, as can irregularities in wiring and connections.

LANs generally compensate for these errors by working off an uninterruptable power source, such as batteries, and using backup software to recall most recent activity and hold unsaved material. Some systems may be designed for redundancy, such as keeping two file servers and alternate wiring to route around failures.

PURCHASING A LAN

When purchasing a LAN, or even investigating the possibility of installing one, several considerations must be kept in mind. The costs involved and the administrative support needed often far exceed reasonable predictions. A complete accounting of potential costs should include such factors as purchase price of equipment, spare parts, and taxes, installation costs, labor and building modifications, and permits. Operating costs include forecasted public network traffic, diagnostics, and routine maintenance. In addition, the buyer should seek a schedule of potential costs associated with upgrades and expansion and engineering studies.

The vendor should agree to a contract expressly detailing the degree of support that will be provided in installing and turning up the system. In addition, the vendor should provide a maintenance contract that binds the company to make immediate, free repairs when performance of the system exceeds prescribed standards. All of these factors should be addressed in the buyer's request for proposal, or RFP, which is distributed to potential vendors.

A 1996 *Business Week* article estimated that only 70 percent of small businesses own PCs, and that of those, only 20 percent operate computer networks. But today, many companies offer products designed specifically to help small businesses install and use LANs simply and affordably. For example, 3Com offers a popular OfficeConnect kit that includes LAN setups for small businesses. Other major software and network providers, such as Microsoft and Novell, are planning products tailored toward the small business market as well. As a result, many more small businesses should soon be able to gain access to the advantages of LANs.

FURTHER READING:

Arnst, Catherine, et al. ''Wiring Small Business.'' *Business Week.* November 25, 1996.

Derfler, Frank J., and David Greenfield. ''Beyond the LAN.'' *PC Magazine.* December 20, 1994.

Feltman, Charles. ''A Reality Check on Virtual LANs.'' *Business Communications Review.* July 1996.

Green, Harry James. *The Business One Irwin Handbook of Telecommunications.* 2nd ed. Business One Irwin, 1991.

Seitel, Peter. ''Realistic Expectations Are Linchpins of Decent LAN.'' *Puget Sound Business Journal.* September 16, 1994.

SEE ALSO: Computers and Computer Systems; Management Information Systems; Telecommunications

LOSS LEADER PRICING

Loss leader pricing is an aggressive pricing strategy wherein a store sells certain goods below cost in order to attract customers who will, according to loss leader philosophy, make up for the losses on highlighted products with additional purchases of profitable goods. Loss leader pricing is employed by retail businesses; a somewhat similar strategy sometimes employed by manufacturers is known as **penetration pricing**. Loss leader pricing is, in essence, a bid to lure customer traffic away from the businesses of retail competitors. Retail stores employing this pricing strategy know that they will not make a profit on those goods that are earmarked as loss leaders. But such businesses reason that the use of such pricing mechanisms can sometimes attract large numbers of consumers who would otherwise make their purchases elsewhere.

In recent years, loss leader pricing has been practiced with considerable success, especially by large national discount retailers. The strategy is not without controversy, however. Indeed, many states have passed laws that severely limit—or explicitly forbid—selling products below cost. Lawsuits alleging that some loss leader pricing strategies amount to illegal business practices have increased in recent years, though the plaintiffs have not always been victorious. Opponents of loss leading pricing practices

argue that the strategy is basically predatory in nature, designed to ultimately force competitors out of business. Defenders of the practice contend that loss leader pricing is simply one of many measures that retail establishments take to increase in-store traffic and, ultimately, their financial well-being. They note that U.S. antitrust and trade regulation statutes are designed to protect competition, not individual competitors, and that legitimate marketplace competition inevitably results in economic winners and losers. The furor over the practice is not expected to subside any time soon, since many small businesses have been economically damaged over the past several years by larger competitors willing to take losses or razor-thin profit margins on some products in order to expand their customer bases.

Business experts note that suppliers sometimes object to loss leader pricing as well, despite the greater volume of sales that the practice often spurs within a given store. These increases may be offset by drops in sales at the stores of other clients. Such developments can strain relations between supplier and customer, and in worst case scenarios, bring pressure on the supplier to lower its price for the good(s) in question. Loss leader pricing has its greatest impact, though, in the retail community. It is there, noted *Super Marketing,* that ''retailers may find themselves caught up in a downward spiral on price when one of them breaks rank and loss-leads on a product.''

CHERRY PICKING In recent years, retail industries have acknowledged a side effect of loss leader pricing known as ''Cherry Picking.'' This is a practice wherein customers move from store to store, making purchases only on those products that are priced near or below acquisition cost. Such purchasing patterns effectively foil the strategy underlying loss leader pricing—to lure customers who will also buy products with healthier profit margins—but to date the practice is not deemed to be sufficiently widespread as to be of concern.

FURTHER READING:

Berry, Leonard L., and Manjit S. Yadav. ''Capture and Communicate Value in the Pricing of Services.'' *Sloan Management Review.* Summer 1996.

Harrison, Keely. ''Rebels Without a Cause?'' *Super Marketing.* February 10, 1995.

SEE ALSO: Pricing; Retail Trade

M

MAIL-ORDER BUSINESS

A mail-order business is one that receives and fulfills orders for merchandise through the mail. The terms ''mail-order,'' ''direct mail,'' and ''direct marketing'' are sometimes used as if they were synonymous, but in fact they have different meanings. While a mail-order business may solicit orders using a variety of direct mail packages and catalogs, there are also many businesses, organizations, and agencies that use direct mail that are not mail-order businesses. **Direct mail** is simply an advertising medium, just as television, radio, newspapers, and magazines are advertising media. With direct mail, a business attempts to sell its product through the mail by means of specifically addressed advertising.

Direct marketing, meanwhile, is actually an advertising/marketing methodology employed both by mail-order enterprises and other businesses. Direct marketing may be distinguished from other types of general advertising, noted Alexander Hiam and Charles D. Schewe, authors of *The Portable MBA in Marketing,* by ''the following characteristics: 1) A definite offer is made; 2) all the information necessary to make a decision is provided; and 3) a response mechanism is given—a toll-free telephone number or a mail-in coupon, for example.'' But while direct marketing makes heavy use of direct mail, it also employs a range of other advertising options—catalogs, coupons, periodicals, newspapers, telephone, radio, and television—to reach its target audiences.

A mail-order business, on the other hand, is simply a kind of commercial enterprise. A mail-order establishment is a business primarily engaged in soliciting sales via various media—often through direct marketing methodologies—and delivering, by mail, the merchandise that is ordered by customers (either via the mail or the telephone) as a result of those sales efforts. Mail-order businesses originally took orders primarily through the mail, but lower long-distance telephone rates and the advent of **toll-free telephone calls (800 numbers)** made it more convenient for customers to place orders over the telephone (the mail-in option is still generally offered, however).

Mail-order businesses represent a rapidly expanding segment of the U.S. economy. Estimates of the amount of consumer and business products purchased from mail-order firms vary, but some analysts estimate that consumers purchased approximately $100 billion of products by mail in the early 1990s on an annual basis. Moreover, according to a study sponsored by the Direct Marketing Association, revenue from catalogs—the principal marketing tool of many mail-order businesses—reached $53.4 billion in 1993, an average growth of nearly 7 percent annually since 1987.

MAIL-ORDER BUSINESSES TODAY

Mail-order businesses date back to pre-Revolutionary War days, when gardeners and farmers ordered seeds through catalogs. Indeed, several of America's largest modern-day retailers first established themselves as mail-order enterprises back in the nineteenth century. This trend, in which retail enterprises establish themselves via catalog sales before venturing into the nation's malls and other centers of commerce, is still evident today. Other businesses are primarily retail-oriented, and use mail-order campaigns to supplement store sales. But while some studies indicate that a mail-order establishment that also cultivates a presence in the retail world is more likely to be regarded as a viable enterprise by potential customers, many businesses exclusively engaged in mail-order sales enjoy fine reputations.

Mail-order shopping is popular in modern America for a variety of reasons. Historically, mail-order businesses became successful because they offered a wider variety of goods than could be found in local retail outlets. In addition, goods purchased through the mail were often less expensive than those available locally, in part because mail-order houses, blessed with the capacity to maintain far larger inventories than many of their retail competitors, could afford to offer more sizable discounts. Mail-order shopping also offered consumers more convenience than shopping at retail stores. Indeed, for consumers in remote rural sections of the country, their isolation from commercial centers made catalog or mail-order shopping a necessity. Finally, individuals pursuing a hobby or special interest were more likely to locate those hard-to-find items in a specialty catalog than in a store.

By the latter half of the twentieth century, several socioeconomic factors had further contributed to the growth of ''at-home shopping.'' Possibly the single most important factor was the dramatic increase in the number of women working outside the home. This change gave some families more discretionary income, but perhaps more tellingly, the trend also meant that women had less time to make purchases. Shopping convenience subsequently became a larger concern, and mail-order purchases that could be executed at home—without driving to a mall or other retail outlet—became more attractive. The emergence of credit cards and telephone-based ordering systems also helped mail-order businesses.

Mail-order businesses today offer consumers a wide array of products and services that they can order from their own home. Magazine subscription sales represent the largest segment of mail-order sales, while books and newspapers also account for a significant portion of mail-order business. The fastest-growing segment of the mail-order business, however, is that of specialty catalogs. Specialty catalogs are fast replacing the large general merchandise catalogs with which American consumers of earlier generations were familiar. In fact, several of the major merchandise catalogs have been discontinued and replaced with a series of specialty catalogs. The list of specialty goods sold through the mail is seemingly endless, encompassing hundreds of categories. Kitchenware, gourmet foods, outdoor clothing, health products, gardening products, sports equipment and apparel, music, collectibles, and computer software and equipment are but a few of the more popular categories of goods sold through specialty catalogs today.

CATALOG MARKETING A study conducted for the American Marketing Association in 1993 forecast that catalog sales would grow by an average of nearly 6.8 percent annually to reach $69.5 billion by 1997. There are three major categories of catalogs: business-to-business catalogs, consumer catalogs, and catalog showrooms. Business-to-business catalogs provide merchandise to be used in the course of business, including everything from office supplies to computers. In industrial settings, business-to-business catalogs are used to sell everything from heavy machinery to hand tools. Business-to-business catalogs are mailed to individuals at their place of business, with most purchases being made on behalf of the business rather than the individual.

Consumer catalogs are mailed to consumers at home. In her book *Catalog Marketing,* Katie Muldoon identified eight types of consumer catalogs. Unaffiliated catalogs are stand-alone ventures—not affiliated with any retailer or manufacturer—whose primary purpose is to sell merchandise by mail. The next type of consumer catalogs are retail catalogs, which include traffic generators, independent profit centers, and combination catalogs. Traffic generator catalogs are designed to build store traffic rather than to generate mail order sales. On the other hand, a retailer might set up a catalog as an independent direct mail operation that is expected to produce a profit on the basis of the sales it generates. Hybrids that are designed to generate store traffic as well as mail order sales combine the best of both worlds.

A third type of consumer catalog is the manufacturer-supported catalog. These may be designed to generate mail order sales, build store traffic, or simply create an image for the maker of a product. Incentive catalogs—which are often issued by credit card companies—offer consumers discounted name-brand merchandise with some proof of purchase of a particular product or use of a particular credit card. Catalogs issued by nonprofit organizations represent yet another type of consumer catalog. Museums have successfully used catalogs to increase sales of gift shop items, for example. Co-op catalogs are used to highlight merchandise from a variety of companies. These catalogs are relatively inexpensive to produce and are often found in non-traditional distribution channels such as bookstores and newsstands.

Syndicated consumer catalogs carry the name of a particular company, usually one that is well known and prestigious. However, the company whose name is on the catalog is not involved in its production and does not carry the merchandise listed in the catalog. Instead, the syndicator pays a commission to the company for use of its name and handles all of the aspects of the catalog business. Another category of consumer catalog is the international catalog. With improved telephone service, it is possible to order by telephone or fax from virtually anywhere in the world.

Catalog showrooms combine retail marketing with catalog marketing. A catalog showroom is essentially a retail outlet. The catalog, usually quite large, serves primarily to build traffic in the showroom. The trend in catalog showrooms has been to de-emphasize the mail order aspect of the catalog and present the showroom as a retail outlet with the added benefit of being able to place catalog orders from the showroom.

THE FUTURE OF MAIL-ORDER BUSINESS

Industry analysts forecast continued growth within the mail-order business, although they caution that competition has increased in the industry, in part because of the highly publicized success that some mail-order establishments have enjoyed. In addition, the growth in mail-order purchases has brought, perhaps inevitably, an attendant increase in concerns about a minority of establishments who engage in deceptive mailing practices or disregard commonly adhered to customer privacy parameters. Concerns over such issues have spurred discussion of increased regulation of mail-order businesses. Mail-order businesses, then, must remain aware of the constantly changing regulatory environment in which they operate.

STARTING A MAIL-ORDER BUSINESS

Mail-order's current popularity, as well as the almost uniformly positive assessments of its future prospects, have made it an attractive area for entrepreneurs. But while some entrepreneurs have been highly successful in mail order ventures, those who enter the business are not guaranteed to succeed. Indeed, the prospective mail-order business owner needs to consider a variety of factors before launching his or her enterprise.

The single most important factor to consider is whether the product or product line that would be featured in your mail-order business is a strong one. In assessing the strength of a product line, factors that should be weighed include the product's availability in other mediums (such as retail outlets), its intended demographic audience, and its unique qualities. Of course, just because a product is unique does not mean that it will be popular. A unique product that is of little use to customers will not be successful; conversely, some of the most profitable mail-order businesses concentrate on providing commonly available goods such as kitchen appliances. They are successful because they are able to convince customers that their products offer advantages in price, performance, or aesthetics. Still, some of the most spectacularly successful mail-order establishments have been ones that tap into previously unexplored customer groups by introducing products that are unique in one respect or another.

Another important consideration when weighing whether to launch a mail-order business is the cost of doing business. Catalogs are quite expensive to print and mail, and the nature of other direct mail advertising options, such as coupon mailings or newspaper advertising, precludes presentation of more than a couple products. This is not a deterrent if you are only selling one or two products, but if you have a sizable product line, such advertising avenues are far less attractive. The prospective mail-order business owner, then, must determine if he or she will sell sufficient quantities of their product(s) to compensate for marketing/ advertising costs and other expenditures. In addition, he or she also must gauge whether the product is suited for sale through mail order. If it is a delicate product, or one that might spoil or otherwise lose its attractiveness in a relatively short time span, then it might not be a good idea to subject it to the rigors and shipment schedule realities of mail order.

Finally, since many mail-order establishments rely on the mail to reach customers, it is vitally important for them to secure useful and reliable **mailing lists**. Good mailing lists can be secured from list brokers, magazine publishers, or trade associations. Of course, even the best mailing list is of little long-term use if the mail-order enterprise provides shoddy goods or customer service. ''Dissatisfaction with the product or a poorly conducted return program can cause enough bad will to ruin your business reputation or simply destroy your profit margin by the extra postage and handling charges involved,'' observed the editors of *How to Run a Small Business*.

Another business option for the prospective mail-order business owner is to sell goods that are actually manufactured by other establishments. Entrepreneurs who opt for this kind of mail-order business should make every effort to purchase the goods they are selling from the manufacturers themselves. Purchasing from secondary sources is significantly more expensive, for those establishments need to push up the price of the goods in order to realize a profit. Experts acknowledge, however, that in some instances—such as scenarios where an offered product dramatically exceeds estimated sales—it may be necessary to deal with secondary sources in order to meet customer orders.

Some mail-order businesses even arrange for their suppliers to ship the goods themselves. Under this system, mail-order outfits accept paid orders on behalf of the manufacturer, then pay the manufacturer to mail the product directly to the customer. Some mail-order houses shy away from this arrangement, however, for while such systems eliminate most inventory costs, they also compromise the independence of the mail-order house. If a manufacturer proves incompetent or engages in questionable business tactics—such as using the addresses supplied by the mail-order business to compile its own mailing list, thus cutting the mail-order house out of the action down the road—a mail-order enterprise can find its very existence threatened.

MARKETING AND ADVERTISING A MAIL-ORDER BUSINESS

Many mail-order establishments—and especially those that are relatively small and new—utilize other service companies to take care of various business needs. Advertising agencies are commonly used to handle that aspect of a company's business, while the mail-order industry's reliance on printed material (catalogs, brochures, advertising circulars, etc.) make securing a good printer a top priority for many mail-order houses.

Mail-order businesses, though, do have a wide range of media to choose from when advertising their products. Mail-order advertisements are commonly found in direct mail (including catalogs), classified ads, and display ads, but other media that can be used to advertise a mail-order business include television, radio, matchbooks, package stuffers, bill stuffers, transit advertising, daily newspapers, and freestanding inserts in Sunday newspapers. The sensible mail-order business owner, however, does not advertise indiscriminately. A mail-order business owner should instead determine which mediums will be most likely to reach his or her target audience. A mail-order house that specializes in deck furniture, for instance, would do well to concentrate its advertising expenditures in home improvement periodicals rather than late-night television spots.

REGULATIONS THAT AFFECT MAIL-ORDER BUSINESS

Mail-order businesses must comply with the regulations of the **Federal Trade Commission (FTC)** and the U.S. Postal Service (USPS). In addition, mail-order businesses may be subject to applicable state laws, especially concerning the collection of sales tax.

The FTC has issued several directives, guidelines, and advisory opinions concerning mail-order businesses. These and other relevant regulations are published in the Code of Federal Regulations (CFR), Title 16, Chapters 1 and 2, which is available in most large libraries or directly from the FTC. Among the most important of these FTC rules is the Mail-Order Merchandise Rule. This regulation, also known as the 30-Day Rule, is designed to protect consumers from unexpected delays in receiving merchandise ordered through the mail. It allows the customer to cancel any order not received within the time period advertised or, if none is stated, 30 days of order. According to the rule, in those instances in which shipment of goods is delayed, a customer must be notified within 15 days of placing his or her order. Moreover, if shipment is delayed past the agreed-upon delivery date (or 30 days), then the business must send a postage-paid return notice notifying the buyer that he or she may terminate the order for a full refund, which must be received within seven business days.

Another FTC rule requires all mail-order advertising to indicate the country of origin of the product being advertised if the product has a fabric as part of its content. This rule was designed to protect domestic textile and wool producers. Mail-order business are also subject to FTC guidelines concerning product guarantees and warranties that apply to all businesses.

Mail-order advertising frequently contains endorsements or testimonials. Under FTC guidelines, any endorsement must reflect the views of the endorser, and must not be reworded or taken out of context. In addition, the endorser must be a genuine user of the product. If the endorser has been paid, the ad must disclose that fact, unless they are celebrities or experts. Additional FTC rules apply specifically to endorsements by average consumers and expert endorsements.

The FTC has also issued guidelines to curb deceptive pricing by some mail-order businesses. These rules affect two-for-one offers, price comparisons, and other issues. The practice of advertising products that have yet to be manufactured, while legal, is subject to FTC requirements as well. FTC regulations call for this advertising practice, also called dry testing, to clearly state that sale of the product is only planned and that it is possible that consumers who order the product may not receive it. In addition, if the product is not manufactured, consumers who ordered it must be notified within four months of the original ad or mailing, and they must be given the opportunity to cancel their order without obligation.

In addition to FTC regulations, mail-order businesses must also be aware of USPS regulations. Lotteries, for example, are illegal under USPS regulations. As defined by the USPS, a lottery includes the element of chance, consideration—a term that means that one must make a purchase to enter—and a prize. In recognition of this definition, mail-order businesses instead organize sweepstakes that do not require any consideration, payment, or purchase on the part of the consumer. While sweepstakes have proved to be an effective method of advertising mail-order merchandise, many states have laws affecting their use.

Post office operations can impact on a mail-order enterprise in other ways as well. A mail-order house that presorts direct mailings by zip code can sometimes lower its **postal costs**, for example, while business-reply cards are subject to the approval of your postmaster. For complete information on postal rates, regulations, and requirements that could potentially impact a mail-order (or any other) business, contact your local post office or the Customer Programs Division of the U.S. Postal Service, Washington, DC 20260.

FURTHER READING:

Hiam, Alexander, and Charles D. Schewe. *The Portable MBA in Marketing.* Wiley, 1992.

J. K. Lasser Institute. *How to Run a Small Business.* 7th ed. New York: Simon and Schuster, 1994.

Keup, Erwin J. *Mail-Order Legal Guide.* Grants Pass, OR: Oasis Press, 1993.

Muldoon, Katie. *Catalog Marketing.* New York: American Management Association, 1988.

Simon, Julian L. *How to Start and Operate a Mail-Order Business.* 5th ed. New York: McGraw-Hill, 1993.

Small Business Administration. *Selling by Mail Order.* No. MT09. Washington: U.S. Small Business Administration, na.

Sroge, Maxwell. *Inside the Leading Mail-Order Houses.* 3rd ed. Lincolnwood, IL: NTC Business Books, 1989.

MAILING LISTS

Mailing lists are compilations of the names and addresses of actual and potential buyers of a product or service. These lists are created by companies for their own marketing initiatives (e.g., lists of all past and present customers), or they are purchased or rented from list brokers—companies that specialize in making list compilations. The importance of the list selection process is well documented. Indeed, business writer Murray Raphel claimed in *Direct Marketing* that the mailing list—not the contents of the mailer—is responsible for up to 60 percent of the success in a direct mailing.

Businesses rely on mailing lists to target the particular geographical or demographic market they are trying to reach. It is possible to rent or purchase mailing lists that include the names, addresses, and phone numbers of people in categories as specific as museum curators, tax shelter investors, or people who have recently moved. Current computer database technology makes it possible to build extremely selective mailing lists.

Obtaining and utilizing mailing lists for **direct mailing** campaigns is a favorite tactic of small business owners because of the relatively light expenses associated with it, but larger companies rely on direct mailings as well. Indeed, direct mail is used by more advertisers than any other medium, and more dollars are spent on it than on any other form of advertising. According to Nicholas Deihl of the Direct Marketing Association, direct mail accounted for 14 percent, or $34.6 billion, of advertising expenditures in the United States in the mid-1990s. Studies also indicated that sales figures for direct mail are continuing to expand at a healthy rate in both the consumer and business-to-business markets. This success is easily understood when one recognizes that direct mail allows a business to reach a precise target market, while personalizing the advertising to include the prospect's name. Further, direct mail supplies the customer with more advertising copy than could be included in a classified or display advertisement. Finally, although some consumers may be irritated by "junk mail," the continued widespread use of direct marketing is testimony to a predominately favorable consumer attitude. Indeed, researchers indicate that the majority of direct mail—even if unsolicited—is opened.

TYPES OF MAILING LISTS

There are three primary types of mailing lists, each of which are compiled in a different fashion:

RESPONSE LISTS Response lists consist of names and addresses of individuals at home or in the workplace who have responded to an offer of some kind (by mail, telephone, billing inserts, etc.). Because these people are known responders, their names are generally priced higher than those in lists compiled by other means. However, individuals on response lists may have responded to a media other than direct mail (e.g., telephone solicitation) and may not even open their "junk mail." Thus it is important for the small business owner to know what percentage of a list was direct-mail compiled. And always, the business owner's most valuable response list is the "house list" of current and past customers.

COMPILED LISTS Compiled lists contain names and addresses of individuals gleaned from the telephone directories, often enhanced with information gathered from public records (e.g., auto registrations, birth announcements, business start-ups). A very popular method of list compilation is through magazine subscriptions, since lists of readers provide an excellent means of targeting individuals in specific industries (e.g., *Institutional Investor*), or within distinct areas of interest (e.g., *Field and Stream*). Lists may also be compiled based on zip code when the small business owner seeks to reach consumers in a particular geographic area or income level (as dictated by the zip code). Credit card lists are also an effective means of list compilation.

COMPILED LISTS FROM RESPONSE MEDIA If a compiler creates a list from a professional association directory, this may be called a compiled list. However the association may well have brought in members via a mail solicitation. Thus an apparent compiled list is actually a compiled list of mail-responsive professionals.

THE LIST TEAM

Small business owners seeking to obtain and/or use a mailing list can turn to a variety of sources to help execute that task:

THE LIST BROKER Most small business owners utilize the services of a list broker when performing direct-mail marketing campaigns. In direct mail parlance, the broker is an agent who rents the prospect lists of one business to another. The broker is paid a commission, usually 20 percent, by the list owner each time a list is rented; the renter does not pay for the broker's service. It is important to note that the broker represents the renter and not the list owner. Since the broker researches, analyzes, and evaluates the tens of thousands of individual lists available, the broker is a marketing consultant—not just a source of list rentals.

THE LIST COMPILER The list compiler is usually a broker who rents a number of lists from published sources and combines them into composite lists, then rents them out. The compiler performs his or her own individual alchemy on a list, adding overlays and enhancements, and often refining it down to a manageable niche. Most compilers specialize in either consumer or business lists. Large compilers maintain large staffs to place literally millions of phone calls to verify data.

THE LIST MANAGER The list manager represents the list owner just as the broker represents the mailer. The primary job of the list manager is to maximize income for the list owner by promoting the lists to as many brokers and list users as possible.

THE SERVICE BUREAU The primary function of a service bureau is constantly improving the lists—a process called "list enhancement." A primary step in list enhancement is merge/purge, the elimination of duplicate names (which can be costly to the advertiser and annoying to the customer). Service bureaus are most commonly utilized in instances where large lists are involved.

THE LETTER SHOP Mechanically performing a mailing can be costly and time consuming. Thus small business owners often "farm out" their mailings to letter shops. These companies not only address the envelopes, but also mechanically insert the materials, seat and stamp the envelopes, and deliver them to the post office according to mailing requirements.

THE COST OF A LIST

The small business owner shops for a list that will provide the greatest number of responses at the lowest cost. Like most purchased items, lists vary in quality and price-generally, the more expensive the list, the better the quality. The least expensive lists are known as unqualified lists; these consist of a rundown of occupants in a specified geographic area. But many lists—such as a list of another establishment's identified customers—are much more expensive. Other factors can affect the cost of a list as well. For example, a list rented for a one-time mailing will often cost $50 to $75 per thousand names, while a multiple-use list may cost $25 per thousand names for each mailing.

THE MAILING PROCESS

Small business owners typically rent lists rather than purchase them outright. The reason for this is the efforts needed to keep lists current. Lists typically go bad at the rate of 2 percent per month—at the end of the year about a quarter of most lists are out of date. Further, the more often a list is used, the less effective it becomes. Thus assuring that a list is current and "fresh" is normally left to the expertise of an experienced list compiler.

Many list brokers prefer not to actually give out a rented list, but instead will arrange to have the pieces mailed through an independent mailing house. According to *Agency Sales Magazine*, when dealing with a reputable broker there is no need to fear—the broker provides receipts from the letter house assuring that the mailing was handled as agreed.

According to *Nation's Business* contributor Howard Scott, successfully using a mailing list is a three-step process:

DEVELOPING A CUSTOMER PROFILE The process begins with developing a profile of the ideal customer. Important questions include: What motivates the customer to buy? What is the customer's income level? Age? Profession? A precise profile allows the broker to provide a list tailored to the needs of the small business owner. This customization helps assure the highest possible response rate.

SHOPPING FOR THE LIST Small business owners can locate list brokers through telephone directories under the keyword "Mailing Lists," or by searching the World Wide Web. Additionally, owners may research lists directly through the catalogue *Direct Mail List Rates and Data*, published by Standard Rate and Data Service. Available in local libraries, this publication presents a comprehensive listing of mailing lists, arranged by subject in three categories: consumer, business, and farm.

Since the list broker fulfills the crucial role of marketing consultant to the small business, owners should choose a broker carefully. The broker should have experience in the owner's product line and customer base. Discussing options with several brokers before making a choice is considered wise. Further, the life of the list is to be considered carefully. Most reputable list brokers will provide the list pedigree, which states when the list was last purged, who else used the list, and the success rate of previous mailings.

A typical first-time mailing for a small business can be 3,000 to 5,000 names. A response rate of 2 to 3 percent on a direct-mail offer is considered good, while 1 percent is average. Although certain limited situations may dictate purchasing a list, first-time users are advised to "get their feet wet" by renting the list.

CREATING THE MAILER The mailer material should make an impact, but it need not necessarily be a pricey blockbuster. Small business owners are advised not to sell a product or service, but sell a specific deal. Successful mailer materials get right to the point, giving the prospective customer a reason to respond, and simple directions for doing so. Books on developing direct-mail marketing material are available at public libraries.

OTHER TIPS ON LISTS

In addition to the above considerations, small business owners should weigh the following when purchasing mailing lists:

Look ahead—Mailing houses typically schedule runs months in advance. For introducing a new product or service, improper planning can be disastrous. Thus small business owners are advised to plan ahead, taking into account the list broker's billing cycle: brokers typically bill their customer with 30 days to pay, and will not put out a piece of mail before receiving payment.

Utilize technology—Pioneering list brokers are establishing World Wide Web sites to provide information about their products and services. Many sites offer as many as 30,000 "data cards" for the prospective list user to view online. Although many web sites are merely electronic versions of the broker's printed catalog, some sites actually enable a small business owner to generate and purchase a mailing lists of up to 10,000 names while online.

Guarantees of Satisfaction—Some list brokers guarantee a small refund (e.g., 5 cents per piece) for any undelivered mail. But small business owners view such "hollow" agreements with skepticism: getting back undeliverable items requires mailing first class (which is prohibitively expensive), or putting "Address Correction Requested" on third class mailing envelopes (which involves a prohibitive expense per returned piece). According to Denny Hatch in *Target Marketing*, the only valuable guarantee is "If you don't like our list, you get your money back . . . period."

EXPANDING A CURRENT CUSTOMER LIST

While a rented list can pay handsome dividends, the small business owner's most valuable resource is usually its list of existing customers-this serves as a starting point for any mailing. But business enterprises that are content to rely solely on such a list are courting trouble, say business experts. Indeed, list updating is a relatively inexpensive way of shoring up a company's marketing efforts. The cost of expanding a list can be offset by renting the list to non-competing businesses. An owner may choose to manage the list in-house, or hire an outside list management company. The small business owner also has the option of securing a list brokerage firm to handle the renting, at the cost of a 20 percent commission.

FURTHER READING:

Bond, Cathy. "They've Got Their Little Lists." *Marketing.* May 2, 1991.

Burnett, Ed. *The Complete Direct Mail List Handbook.* Englewood Cliffs, NJ: Prentice Hall, 1988.

Cohen, William. *The Entrepreneur and Small Business Marketing Problem Solver.* New York: Wiley, 1991.

"Entrepreneur's Guide to Direct Mail Advertising." *Entrepreneur.* February 1994.

Fallek, Max. *How to Set Up Your Own Small Business.* American Institute of Small Business, 1995.

Hatch, Denny. "The Business of Business Lists: A Look at this Incredibly Unbelievably Complex World." *Target Marketing.* January 1997.

"How to Get and Use Mailing Lists." *Agency Sales Magazine.* March 1991.

Mummert, Hallie. "Free Money! (Renting of Mailing Lists)." *Target Marketing.* July 1993.

Raphel, Murray. "The Name of the Game Is the Name." *Direct Marketing.* August 1989.

Scott, Howard. "Targeting Prospects with Direct Mail." *Nation's Business.* September 1997.

"The MIN Top 100 (Largest Mailing Lists)." *Target Marketing.* January 1997.

Yoegel, Rob. "List Marketers Head to Cyberspace." *Target Marketing.* August 1997.

SEE ALSO: Advertising Strategy

MANAGEMENT BY OBJECTIVES

Management by Objectives (MBO) is a process in which a manager and an employee agree upon a set of specific performance goals, or objectives, and jointly develop a plan for reaching them. The objectives must be clear and achievable, and the plan must include a time frame and evaluation criteria. For example, a salesperson might set a goal of increasing customer orders by 15 percent in dollar terms over the course of a year.

MBO is primarily used as a tool for strategic planning, **employee motivation**, and performance enhancement. It is intended to improve communication between employees and management, increase employee understanding of company goals, focus employee efforts upon organizational objectives, and provide a concrete link between pay and performance. An important factor in an MBO system is its emphasis on the results achieved by employees rather than the activities performed in their jobs.

IMPLEMENTING AN MBO PROGRAM

To be successful, an MBO program should be part of a small business's overall system of planning and goal setting. The first step in implementing MBO is to establish long-range company goals in areas such as sales, competitive positioning, and human resource development. A small business owner may find it helpful to begin by defining the company's current business and looking for emerging customer needs or market trends that may require adaptation. Such long-range planning provides a framework for charting the company's future staffing levels, marketing approaches, financing needs, product development focus, and facility and equipment usage.

The next step in establishing an MBO system is to use these long-range plans to determine company-wide goals for the current year. Then the company goals can be broken down further into goals for different departments, and eventually into goals for individual employees. As goal-setting filters down through the organization, special care must be taken to ensure that individual and departmental goals all support the long-range objectives of the business. Ideally, a small business's managers should be involved in formulating the company's long-range goals. This approach may increase their commitment to achieving the goals, allow them to communicate the goals clearly to employees, and help them to create their own short-range goals to support the company goals.

At a minimum, a successful MBO program requires each employee to produce five to ten specific, measurable goals. In addition to a statement of the goal itself, each goal should be supported with a means of measurement and a series of steps toward completion. These goals should be proposed to the employee's manager in writing, discussed, and approved. It is the manager's responsibility to make sure that all employee goals are consistent with the department and company goals. The manager also must compare the employee's performance with his or her goals on a regular basis in order to identify any problems and take corrective action as needed.

Formulating goals is not an easy task for employees, and most people do not master it immediately. Small business owners may find it helpful to begin the process by asking employees and managers to define their jobs and list their major responsibilities. Then the employees and managers can create a goal or goals based upon each responsibility and decide how to measure their own performance in terms of results. In the Small Business Administration publication *Planning and Goal Setting for Small Business,* Raymond F. Pelissier recommended having employees create a miniature work plan for each goal. A work plan would include the goal itself, the measurement terms, any major problems anticipated in meeting the goal, a series of work steps toward meeting the goal (with completion dates), and the company goal to which the personal goal relates.

Small business owners may also find it helpful to break down employee goal setting into categories. The first category, regular goals, would include objectives related to the activities that make up an employee's major responsibilities. Examples of regular goals might include improving efficiency or the amount and quality of work produced. The second category, problem-solving goals, should define and eliminate any major problems the employee encounters in performing his or her job. Another category is innovation, which should include goals that apply original ideas to company problems. The final category is development goals, which should include those goals related to personal growth or the development of employees. Dividing goal setting into categories often helps employees think about their jobs in new ways and acts to release them from the tendency to create activity-based goals.

Another requirement for any successful MBO program is that it provide for a regular review of employee progress toward meeting goals. This review can take place either monthly or quarterly. When the review uncovers employee performance that is below expectations, managers should try to identify the problem, assign responsibility for correcting it, and make a note in the MBO files.

SMALL BUSINESS OWNER INVOLVEMENT

Given that MBO represents a relatively new and unusual way of thinking about job performance for many employees, small business owners may find it best to introduce MBO programs gradually and to include a formal training component. A small business's managers can be introduced to MBO through a classroom seminar taught by the small business owner or by an outside consultant. Either way, it is important that the managers be allowed to express any doubts and reservations they may have, and that the training include preparation of an actual goal by each participant. When MBO is brought back to the small business, it may be best to start slowly, with each employee only preparing a few goals. This approach will allow employees to learn to prepare goals that are achievable, develop ways to measure their own performance, and anticipate problems that will prevent them from attaining their goals.

Another factor determining the success of MBO programs is the direct involvement of the small business owner. Pelissier noted that the small business owner needs to champion the MBO system from the beginning, as well as set an example for the company's managers, in order for it to succeed. Since managers have a natural tendency to focus their attention upon their own functions rather than on the goals of the overall organization, it can be difficult to educate them about MBO. It is also important for the small business owner to remain patient during the implementation phase: in fact, Pelissier claimed that it may take three to four years before an MBO program creates quantifiable results in a small business.

Implemented correctly, however, MBO can provide a number of benefits to a small business. For example, MBO may help employees understand how their performance will be evaluated and measured. In addition, by allowing them to contribute to goal setting, it may increase the motivation and productivity of a small business's employees. MBO also stands to provide a small business's employees with the means to prioritize their work on a daily basis. Although employee performance evaluation is still a complex task under an MBO system, MBO can also provide an objective basis for evaluation. However, it is important to note that an employee's failure to meet pre-established goals can be attributed to many things besides personal failure. For example, the failure to meet goals could result from setting the wrong objectives, not taking into account company restrictions that may impinge upon performance, establishing improper measures of progress, or a combination of all of these factors.

Overall, establishing an MBO system in a small business may be difficult, but it is usually worth it. The most difficult aspect of implementing MBO may be simply getting people to think in terms of results rather than activities. Even when an MBO system is implemented well, a small business may encounter problems. For example, employees may set low goals to ensure attainment. Similarly, managers' objectives may focus on the attainment of short-term rather than long-term goals. Finally, employees and managers alike may fall victim to confusion and frustration. Some of the most common reasons for the failure of an MBO program include a lack of involvement among the top management of a small business, inadequate goal setting on a company-wide basis, implementation of an MBO system that occurs too rapidly, or the failure to instruct a company's managers and employees in the basics of MBO. Even though establishing an MBO program may be problematic, it can also offer significant rewards to small businesses.

FURTHER READING:

Bateman, Thomas S., and Carl P. Zeithaml. *Management: Function and Strategy.* Homewood, IL: Irwin, 1990.

Pelissier, Raymond F. *Planning and Goal Setting for Small Business.* Washington: U.S. Small Business Administration.

SEE ALSO: Business Planning; Employee Performance Appraisal

MANAGEMENT INFORMATION SYSTEMS

According to Kenneth C. Laudon and Jane Price Laudon in their book *Management Information Systems: A Contemporary Perspective,* an information system is "a set of procedures that collects (or retrieves), processes, stores, and disseminates information to support decision making and control." In most cases, information systems are formal, computer-based systems that play an integral role in organizations. Although information systems are computer-based, it is important to note that any old computer or software program is not necessarily an information system. "Electronic computers and related software programs are the technical foundation, the tools and materials, of modern information systems," Laudon and Laudon wrote. "Understanding information systems, however, requires one to understand the problems they are designed to solve, the architectural and design solutions, and the organizational processes that lead to these solutions."

Though it is sometimes applied to all types of information systems used in businesses, the term "management information systems," or MIS, actually describes specific systems that "provide managers with reports and, in some cases, on-line access to the organization's current performance and historical records," Laudon and Laudon noted. "MIS primarily serve the functions of planning, controlling, and decision making at the management level." MIS are one of a number of different types of information systems that can serve the needs of different levels in an organization. For example, information systems might be developed to support upper management in planning the company's strategic direction or to help manufacturing in controlling a plant's operations. Some of the other types of information systems include: transaction processing systems, which simply record the routine transactions needed to conduct business, like payroll, shipping, or sales orders; and office automation systems, which are intended to increase the productivity of office workers and include such systems as word processing, electronic mail, and digital filing. Ideally, the various types of information systems in an organization are interconnected to allow for information sharing.

SYSTEMS DEVELOPMENT

The development of effective information systems holds a number of challenges for small businesses. "Despite, or perhaps because of, the rapid development of computer technology, there is nothing easy or mechanical about building workable information systems," Laudon and Laudon stated. "Building, operating, and maintaining information systems are challenging for a number of reasons." For example, some information cannot be captured and put into a system. Computers often cannot be programmed to take into account competitor responses to marketing tactics or changes in economic conditions, among other things. In addition, the value of information erodes over time, and rapid changes in technology can make systems become obsolete very quickly. Finally, many companies find systems development to be problematic because the services of skilled programmers are at a premium.

Despite the challenges inherent in systems development, however, MIS also offer businesses a number of advantages. "Today, leading companies and organizations are using information technology as a competitive tool to develop new products and services, forge new relationships with suppliers, edge out competitors, and radically change their internal operations and organizations," Laudon and Laudon explained. For example, using MIS strategically can help a company to become a market innovator. By providing a unique product or service to meet the needs of customers, a company can raise the cost of market entry for potential competitors and thus gain a competitive advantage. Another strategic use of MIS involves forging electronic linkages to customers and suppliers. This can help companies to lock in business and increase switching costs. Finally, it is possible to use MIS to change the overall basis of competition in an industry. In an industry characterized by price wars, a business with a new means of processing customer data may be able to create unique product features that change the basis of competition to differentiation.

The impetus to develop a new information system can grow out of end-user demands, the availability of new technology, or management strategy. A variety of tools exist for analyzing a company's information needs and designing systems to support them. The basic process of systems development involves defining the project, creating a model of the current system, deriving a model for the new system, measuring the costs and benefits of all alternatives, selecting the best option, designing the new system, completing the specific programming functions, installing and testing the new system, and completing a post-implementation audit.

Information systems designers, whether internal to the company or part of an outside firm, are generally responsible for assuring the technical quality of the new system and the ease of the user interface. They also oversee the process of system design and implementation, assess the impact of the new system on the organization, and develop ways to protect the system from abuse after it is installed. But it is the responsibility of small business owners and managers to plan what systems to implement and to ensure that the underlying data are accurate and useful. "The organization must develop a technique for ensuring that the most important systems are attended to first, that unnecessary systems are not built, and that end users have a full and meaningful role in determining which new systems will be built and how," according to Laudon and Laudon.

FURTHER READING:

Laudon, Kenneth C., and Jane Price Laudon. *Management Information Systems: A Contemporary Perspective.* 2nd ed. New York: Macmillan, 1991.

McLeod, Raymond, Jr. *Information Systems: A Problem-Solving Approach.* New York: Macmillan, 1989.

SEE ALSO: Computers and Computer Systems

MANAGEMENT TEAM GROWTH

Nearly every successful small business starts out the same way—with a hardworking business owner who has a dream that he or she believes in and the work ethic to make that dream become a reality. If everything goes according to plan, that owner founds a business, the business grows, and new employees are hired. Even as those first employees are hired, however, the owner is still the decision-maker, the person who maintains power over the company. An article in the *Canadian Business Review* summed it up best: "As the company grows, many [owners] are still leading their organizations alone and continue to take hands-on control of all areas of the operation. This leads to a strangling effect on the development of the company." The savvy small business owner is the one who knows when to stop trying to do it all and when to expand his or her management team, especially with employees from outside the company.

In every growing business, the owner will reach the point where he or she has to go outside the company to hire a new addition to the management team.

This is an inevitable development once a business reaches a size in which responsibilities become fragmented and specialized. In the early days of a small business, it might be easy for the owner and one or two other people to manage everything, from the hiring to the manufacturing. Growth, especially rapid growth, makes that "do it all" approach unworkable—handling hiring and firing on the fly might be manageable when there are six employees in the whole company, but not when there are 60.

Proponents of hiring management personnel from outside the organization contend that such practices help to provide diversity at the company's highest level. Often, the business owner and the employees who help start the business will share the same vision and rarely disagree with each other. According to an article in the *Journal of Small Business Management,* having a variety of voices on the management team leads to an atmosphere that fosters constructive criticism and reduces complacency. The different perspectives foster company growth and "produces better decision making because whereas members with many years in a particular industry can offer insights based on rich experience, newcomers can provide fresh perspectives."

Different voices also create a system of checks and balances on the management team. A team comprised of long-time company insiders might suffer because the owner still views the company as being in the start-up phase and might be reluctant to delegate authority, which increases the likelihood that a single person will exert too much influence over the strategic direction of the entire company. Many business experts believe that outsiders, once they are acclimated to the company, are more likely to challenge the status quo and act as a balancing influence to the existing management team. In addition, people hired from the outside are usually specialists in the area that they were hired to oversee. This knowledge base often means that their opinion carries more weight than that of a longtime employee who is not a specialist in that field.

The *Journal of Small Business Management* article used a statistical analysis to show that small businesses that adapted larger management teams that featured members from many functional backgrounds experienced greater growth, concluding that "if managers of small businesses are trying to position their firms to realize growth, they should make sure that the top management team is comprised of individuals with different functional backgrounds."

FURTHER READING:

Beech, Wendy M. "Choosing the Team: the Management Plan Can Help Outline and Define the Duties of Your Key Personnel." *Black Enterprise.* Jan. 1998.

Candalino, Alexis W., and Mike Knowlton. "Small Companies as Business Laboratories." *Canadian Business Review.* Spring 1994.

Nelson, Robert B. "Empowering Employees Through Delegation." *Small Business Reports.* June 1994.

Weinzimmer, Lawrence G. "Top Management Team Correlates of Organizational Growth in a Small Business Context: A Comparative Study." *Journal of Small Business Management.* July 1997.

SEE ALSO: Business Expansion; Employee Hiring; Managing Organizational Change

MANAGING ORGANIZATIONAL CHANGE

Organizational change occurs when a company makes a transition from its current state to some desired future state. Managing organizational change is the process of planning and implementing change in organizations in such a way as to minimize employee resistance and cost to the organization, while also maximizing the effectiveness of the change effort.

Today's business environment requires companies to undergo changes almost constantly if they are to remain competitive. Such changes may be relatively minor—as in the case of installing a new software program—or quite major—as in the case of refocusing an overall **marketing** strategy. "Organizations must change because their environments change," according to Thomas S. Bateman and Carl P. Zeithaml in their book *Management: Function and Strategy.* "Today, businesses are bombarded by incredibly high rates of change from a frustratingly large number of sources.... Inside pressures come from top managers and lower-level employees who push for change. Outside pressures come from changes in the legal, competitive, technological, and economic environments."

Organizational change initiatives often arise out of problems faced by a company. In some cases, however, companies are encouraged to change for other, more positive reasons. "Change commonly occurs because the organization experiences some difficulty," Bateman and Zeithaml wrote. "But sometimes the most constructive change takes place not because of problems but because of opportunities." The authors used the term "performance gap" to describe the difference between a company's actual performance and the performance of which it is capable. Recognition of a performance gap often provides the impetus for change, as companies strive to improve their performance to expected levels. This sort of gap is also where many entrepreneurs find opportunities to begin new businesses.

Unfortunately, as Rick Mauer noted in an article for *HR Focus,* statistics show that many organizational change efforts fail. For example, 50 percent of quality improvement programs fail to meet their goals, and 30 percent of process reengineering efforts are unsuccessful. The most common reason that change efforts fail is that they encounter resistance from employees. Change appears threatening to many people, which makes it difficult to gain their support and commitment to implementing changes. Consequently, the ability to manage change effectively is a highly sought-after skill in managers. Companies need people who can contribute positively to their inevitable change efforts.

AREAS OF ORGANIZATIONAL CHANGE

Bateman and Zeithaml identified four major areas of organizational change: **strategy**, technology, structure, and people. All four areas are related, and companies often must institute changes in the other areas when they attempt to change one area. The first area, strategy changes, can take place on a large scale—for example, when a company shifts its resources to enter a new line of business—or on a small scale—for example, when a company makes productivity improvements in order to reduce costs. There are three basic stages for a company making a strategic change: 1) realizing that the current strategy is no longer suitable for the company's situation; 2) establishing a vision for the company's future direction; and 3) implementing the change and setting up new systems to support it.

Technological changes are often introduced as components of larger strategic changes, although they sometimes take place on their own. An important aspect of changing technology is determining who in the organization will be threatened by the change. To be successful, a technology change must be incorporated into the company's overall systems, and a management structure must be created to support it. Structural changes can also occur due to strategic changes—as in the case where a company decides to acquire another business and must integrate it—as well as due to operational changes or changes in managerial style. For example, a company that wished to implement more participative decision making might need to change its hierarchical structure.

People changes can become necessary due to other changes, or sometimes companies simply seek to change workers' attitudes and behaviors in order to increase their effectiveness. "Attempting a strategic change, introducing a new technology, and other changes in the work environment may affect people's attitudes (sometimes in a negative way)," Bateman and Zeithaml wrote. "But management frequently initiates programs with a conscious goal of directly and positively changing the people themselves." In any case, people changes can be the most difficult and important part of the overall change process. The science of **organizational development** was created to deal with changing people on the job through techniques such as education and training, team building, and career planning.

RESISTANCE TO CHANGE

A manager trying to implement a change, no matter how small, should expect to encounter some resistance from within the organization. Resistance to change is a normal reaction from people who have become accustomed to a certain way of doing things. Of course, certain situations or tactics can increase resistance. "Individuals, groups, and organizations must be motivated to change. But if people perceive no performance gap or if they consider the gap unimportant, they will not have this motivation. Moreover, they will resist changes that others try to introduce," Bateman and Zeithaml explained.

The authors outlined a number of common reasons that people tend to resist change. These include: inertia, or the tendency of people to become comfortable with the status quo; timing, as when change efforts are introduced at a time when workers are busy or have a bad relationship with management; surprise, because people's reflex is to resist when they must deal with a sudden, radical change; or peer pressure, which may cause a group to resist due to anti-management feelings even if individual members do not oppose the change. Resistance can also grow out of people's perceptions of how the change will affect them personally. They may resist because they fear that they will lose their jobs or their status, because they do not understand the purpose of the change, or simply because they have a different perspective on the change than management.

Fortunately, Bateman and Zeithaml noted, there are a number of steps managers can take to help overcome resistance to change. One proven method is education and communication. Employees can be informed about both the nature of the change and the logic behind it before it takes place through reports, memos, group presentations, or individual discussions. Another important component of overcoming resistance is inviting employee participation and involvement in both the design and implementation phases of the change effort. "People who are involved in decisions understand them better and are more committed to them," Bateman and Zeithaml explained. Another possible approach to managing resistance to change is through facilitation and support. Managers should be sure to provide employees with the resources they need to make the change, be supportive of their efforts, listen to their problems with empathy, and accept that their performance level may drop initially.

Some companies manage to overcome resistance to change through negotiation and rewards. They offer employees concrete incentives to ensure their cooperation. Other companies resort to manipulation, or using subtle tactics such as giving a resistance leader a prominent position in the change effort. A final option is coercion, which involves punishing people who resist or using force to ensure their cooperation. Although this method can be useful when speed is of the essence, it can have lingering negative effects on the company. Of course, no method is appropriate to every situation, and a number of different methods may be combined as needed. As Bateman and Zeithaml stated, ''Effective change managers are familiar with the various approaches and capable of flexibly applying them according to the situation.''

TECHNIQUES FOR MANAGING CHANGE EFFECTIVELY

Managing change effectively requires moving the organization from its current state to a future desired state at minimal cost to the organization. Bateman and Zeithaml identified three steps for managers to follow in implementing organizational change:

1) Diagnose the current state of the organization. This involves identifying problems the company faces, assigning a level of importance to each one, and assessing the kinds of changes needed to solve the problems.

2) Design the desired future state of the organization. This involves picturing the ideal situation for the company after the change is implemented, conveying this vision clearly to everyone involved in the change effort, and designing a means of transition to the new state. An important part of the transition should be maintaining some sort of stability; some things—such as the company's overall mission or key personnel—should remain constant in the midst of turmoil to help reduce people's anxiety.

3) Implement the change. This involves managing the transition effectively. It might be helpful to draw up a plan, allocate resources, and appoint a key person to take charge of the change process. The company's leaders should try to generate enthusiasm for the change by sharing their goals and vision and acting as role models. In some cases, it may be useful to try for small victories first in order to pave the way for later successes.

FURTHER READING:

Adebanjo, Dotun. ''Corporate Restructuring: Managing the Change Problem from Within.'' *Leadership and Organization Development Journal.* September 1996.

Austin, Mary Ruth. ''Managing Change.'' *Manage.* August 1997.

Bateman, Thomas S., and Carl P. Zeithaml. *Management: Function and Strategy.* Homewood, IL: Irwin, 1990.

''Becoming a Change Master.'' *Supervisory Management.* August 1994.

Dove, Rick. ''The Principles of Change.'' *Automotive Manufacturing and Production.* March 1997.

Maurer, Rick. ''Transforming Resistance.'' *HR Focus.* October 1997.

Recardo, Ronald J. ''Overcoming Resistance to Change.'' *National Productivity Review.* Spring 1995.

Schwartz, Andrew E. ''Eight Guidelines for Managing Change.'' *Supervisory Management.* July 1994.

Trahant, Bill, W. Warner Burke, and Richard Koonce. ''Twelve Principles of Organizational Transformation.'' *Management Review.* September 1997.

SEE ALSO: Business Expansion; Organizational Growth; Organizational Structure; Training and Development

MANUFACTURERS' AGENTS

Manufacturers' agents or representatives are independent contractors who work on commission to sell products for more than one manufacturer. They are not under the immediate supervision of the manufacturers—typically called principals—who they sell for, so their relationship generally falls into client-customer patterns.

Manufacturers' agent firms range from businesses operated by one sole entrepreneur to considerably more extensive organizations armed with numerous sales persons covering specific territories. In the mid-1990s, the typical agency was a corporation that employed six people (including both sales personnel and office personnel), according to the Manufacturers' Agents National Association (MANA). These firms, which are concentrated in major metropolitan areas but can be found in all 50 states, represent every conceivable product line, including goods produced in the automotive, plastics, electronics, food and beverage processing, apparel, lumber and wood, paper, chemical, and metals industries. Virtually any product that is made and sold can be handled by a manufacturers' agent.

Manufacturers' agents generally represent several different companies that offer compatible—but not competing—products to the same industry. This method reduces the cost of sales by spreading the agent's costs over the different products that he or she pitches. Consequently, manufacturers' agents view themselves as a cost-effective alternative to full-time salaried sales forces, and this is an evaluation that is shared by thousands of small- and medium-size manufacturers in the United States. Indeed, manufacturers' agents are particularly popular among companies that do not have the financial resources to launch their own sales team. In addition, since manufacturers' agents are generally paid by commission, the small manufacturer incurs no cost until a sale is made.

SMALL BUSINESSES AND MANUFACTURERS' AGENTS

ADVANTAGES In addition to the above-mentioned financial benefits that manufacturers' agents offer to small business owners, they also provide relocating or start-up firms with immediate front-line information on marketplace trends and **demographics**. By contracting with a manufacturers' agent, a company gains instant access to industry expertise or knowledge of a particular country or region.

There are other distinct advantages as well. For manufacturers with a narrow product line, agencies offer one of the best ways to access the market. Because they normally sell compatible products to a single market, the manufacturers' agent firms usually are well-connected with the manufacturers' principal market targets. This offers manufacturers immediate entry to markets that may be hard to reach with a direct sales force. In addition, rep firms can provide new firms with ideas of where to advertise, comment on what the competition is doing, and give estimates of a given territory's potential.

DISADVANTAGES Consultants and business owners note, however, that while using manufacturers' agents may make a lot of sense to the small company that needs to allocate its financial resources carefully and quickly learn about the marketplace, there are drawbacks associated with the practice as well. Lack of control over the agent is easily the most frequently mentioned complaint that business owners cite when discussing rep firms. Since the manufacturers' agent is not an employee of the company, the company's ownership can not dictate how he or she goes about business. Certainly, the small business owner can negotiate for certain things in his or her business dealings with the agent, just as any client can do with any vendor. But in the final analysis, the agent has far greater freedom to operate as he or she feels fit than do salespeople that are actual employees of the company.

Some critics also claim that since manufacturers' agents conduct business on behalf of more than one manufacturer, they are not always able to devote the necessary time to one single product line. Finally, some agents also may be reluctant or unable to provide service beyond the point of sale. Fundamental elements of customer service, such as start-up assistance and service often must be supplied by the manufacturer even if the goods were sold through a manufacturers' agent.

SELECTING A MANUFACTURERS' AGENT

Manufacturers have many factors to consider when they are in the process of selecting a manufacturers' representative. Small business owners should look for someone who shows an ability and a willingness to quickly become knowledgeable about their products and applications, as well as someone who will respond quickly to calls, present the product in terms of how it will meet customer needs, and represent the various product lines he or she markets in a just fashion, giving each line the attention it deserves, regardless of how much income it accounts for (this latter concern is especially acute for small and start-up businesses). The best rule of thumb for manufacturers is to be patient and do plenty of preliminary research. After all, the choice is going to be the primary link between the company and its target audience. A poor selection can ruin a company; conversely, a good choice can help launch a new manufacturer to long-term financial stability. Given the stakes involved in this choice, then, MANA suggested in its *Directory of Manufacturers' Sales Agencies* that business owners consider doing the following when weighing their choices:

1) Create a profile of the ideal agency—Make the profile clear, but also be flexible and realistic. Perfect agencies are nonexistent, but there are many that will do a good job if given the opportunity.

2) Create a profile of the manufacturing firm—Manufacturers are encouraged to compile a profile of their target customers, a rundown of the business's needs, and a summary of the governing philosophy of the business. Many agencies can be selective in terms of who they will add to their client list, so it makes sense to inform them about the business and its goals and prospects. The profile should be honest and touch on growth plans, real advantages of the product(s) it manufacturers, and previous history.

3) Secure referrals from other agencies—Manufacturers' representatives are a close-knit fraternity in the United States, and many can provide the names of several agencies that would be a good fit for the line.

4) Get referrals from other manufacturers—Companies in the same area that sell similar but noncompetitive products can be a good source of information in locating potential

representatives. Some may even recommend their own agencies, although others may be reluctant to have their agents take on additional product lines and responsibilities.

5) Be patient—While manufacturers often do not have the luxury of waiting forever when filling rep openings, doing preliminary research usually is a good idea. Many manufacturers who have been burned in this regard later admit that they did not devote sufficient time to exploring their options and learning about the agent they did select. It is better to take the needed time to select the right prospect than to rush into a bad situation and have to rectify it later.

6) Be flexible in setting up territories—Agents must have exclusive rights within a territory, but rather than assign arbitrary territories based on geography, it is often preferable to select the agents that best fit your line and let their coverage determine the territories.

DEALING WITH AGENTS

Manufacturers must remember that their rep firms are independent sales agencies that are not employees of any of its principals, but business partners with each of them. As such, the manufacturers can't have the same type of direct control as they do over their own personnel. From a legal standpoint, it is important to remember that the manufacturers pay nothing to a rep until a sale is made. They also pay no withholding taxes or Social Security. Using manufacturers' agents also means that some of the manufacturer's bookkeeping needs will be taken care of by non-employees. This is an important distinction for the **Internal Revenue Service**, which frowns mightily upon arrangements in which companies disguise employees under the veil of independent agencies or contractors. When judging this, the IRS typically uses as one of its tests the amount of direct control exercised over sales reps. If regular reports are demanded of independent agents, the IRS can declare the rep an employee and require the various withholding taxes that apply.

Communication remains an integral part of the relationship between agents and their clients. Both parties need to keep the other appraised about what the other is doing with respect to their operations. Agents should let their principals know what they are doing for them in the field, regardless of the level of sales at that particular moment, while agents need updated information on matters such as product specifications and pricing. Ultimately, both parties simply need to recognize that a cohesive working relationship is in their shared best interests. In their dealings with representatives, manufacturers expect loyalty; knowledge of the territory and/or industry; knowledge of product lines after a reasonable amount of exposure; quick response to suggestions; regular follow-up; and a fair share of the agent's time. Agents, meanwhile, have every right to expect: a fair contract that recognizes performance and rewards success and longevity; access to customer service, training, and technical back-up; a quality product; timely delivery; and a true commitment to build business in their territory.

FURTHER READING:

"How to Work Successfully with Manufacturers' Agencies." Special Report in *Directory of Manufacturers' Sales Agencies.* Laguna Hills, CA: Manufacturers' Agents National Association, 1994.

Gibbons, James J. "Recruiting Agents: Do it Right and You'll Never Have to Settle for Second Best." *Directory of Manufacturers' Sales Agencies.* Laguna Hills, CA: Manufacturers' Agents National Association, 1993.

Marshall, Michael, and Frank Siegler. "Selecting the Right Rep Firm." *Sales and Marketing Management.* January 1994.

"What Makes for a Long and Rewarding Relationship." *The American Salesman.* November 1992.

SEE ALSO: Free-lance Employment/Independent Contractors; Sales Commissions

MARKET ANALYSIS

Market analysis is a tool companies use in order to better understand the environment in which they operate. It is one of the main steps in the development of a **marketing** plan. The first step is to conduct **market research**—or gather information through **direct mail**, **telemarketing**, **focus groups**, etc. Then comes market analysis, which involves critically reviewing and organizing the data collected so that it can be used in making strategic marketing decisions. "Just as one would not build a house on sand, one should never undertake a marketing program that is not built on a firm foundation of market knowledge," David J. Freiman stated in his book *What Every Manager Needs to Know about Marketing.* "It is remarkable and alarming how little managers of businesses really know about their markets and the other elements of their outside environments."

A good market analysis should include information on industry trends, an assessment of major competitors and their strategies, a review of the channels of distribution, and a wide variety of data on current and potential customers. The market analysis provides the input for the next step in developing a marketing plan—market segmentation, or dividing an overall market into key customer subsets, or segments, whose members share similar characteristics and needs. The company then selects from among these segments the particular markets it wishes to target, and creates a marketing plan that will appeal to the target customers. ''Small businesses that identify the needs of specific target markets—existing and potential customers who are the focus of marketing efforts—and work to satisfy those needs, are more effective marketers,'' according to Gloria Green and Jeffrey Williams in *Marketing: Mastering Your Small Business.*

Most market analyses begin with a broad study of the overall industry and conclude with a narrow definition of the company's **target market**. Some of the industry factors that might be mentioned in a market analysis include the relative market share held by various competitors, the rate of new product introductions, the technological environment, and the impact of significant laws or regulations. A market analysis would also include overall market information such as sales history, current demand, and expected future trends. It is particularly important to know whether demand is increasing, decreasing, or remaining constant.

The next area of a market analysis involves creating an in-depth portrait of customers. Through market research, the company tries to answer such questions as: who are the primary decision makers and purchasers; what are their main motivating factors; and when and where do they tend to buy? The key is to understand how customers make their purchasing decisions in order to be able to influence those decisions. Market research might assess such demographic features as age, gender, income level, educational background, financial situation, marital status, household size, and ethnic or religious background. Once this information has been broken down through market analysis, the company then creates a detailed description of the most desirable segment of the market to be included in the marketing plan. The market analysis should demonstrate why the target market chosen is more favorable than other segments, since the company will be investing its limited resources in marketing to that target market.

In addition to its role in developing the marketing plan, market analysis has numerous other implications for company **strategy**. ''Once we understand the phenomena that underlie the behavior of our markets, we can assess our strengths and weaknesses relative to those phenomena. External threats and opportunities need to be carefully examined so that we can apply our strengths to areas with high potential and avoid major environmental pitfalls. Finally, we must link the resulting diagnosis to our corporate capabilities, strategies, and constraints in order to ensure a good fit between our marketing strategy and major corporate goals and objectives,'' Glen L. Urban and Steven H. Star explained in their book *Advanced Marketing Strategy.*

FURTHER READING:

Freiman, David J., ed. *What Every Manager Needs to Know about Marketing.* New York: AMACOM, 1986.

Sherman, Andrew J. *The Complete Guide to Running and Growing Your Business.* New York: Random House, 1997.

Urban, Glen L., and Steven H. Star. *Advanced Marketing Strategy.* Englewood Cliffs, NJ: Prentice Hall, 1991.

SEE ALSO: Competitive Analysis; Industry Analysis; Market Research

MARKET QUESTIONNAIRE

Market questionnaires are a form of quantitative, primary **market research** that can provide small business owners with specific information about their customers' needs. Whether conducted over the telephone, through the mail, or in person, market questionnaires are designed to survey a sample group of respondents whose opinions reflect those of the business's target customers.

Like other forms of market research, questionnaires are designed to connect marketers to consumers through information gathering and evaluation. Market research is commonly used to identify marketing problems and opportunities, as well as to develop and evaluate the effectiveness of marketing strategies. Small business owners, because of their usually limited financial resources, have a particular need for adequate, accurate, and current information to aid them in making decisions. Market research can help entrepreneurs evaluate the feasibility of a start-up venture before investing a great deal of time and capital, for example, as well as assist them in effectively marketing their goods and services.

''Questionnaire construction is one of the most difficult steps in marketing research,'' Gloria Green and Jeffrey Williams noted in their book *Marketing: Mastering Your Small Business.* ''Yet, many people seem to think putting together a good questionnaire is easy. That's why there are so many terrible questionnaires—full of confusing or incomprehensible questions all but guaranteed to produce worthless results.''

In general, a good market questionnaire will consist of a screening or qualifying question, an introduction, demographic questions, closed-ended questions, and open-ended questions. Each of these elements serves a particular purpose. The screening question, which should usually be posed first, makes sure that the respondent is a member of the target group and thus is qualified to participate in the survey. For example, a home remodeling and repair company might ask whether the person has had any work done in the previous six months. The introduction then informs qualified respondents what company is conducting the survey and why, and explains the benefits answering might have on their future business relationship with that company. Demographic questions—which cover such basic information as age, gender, marital status, education level, and income level—allow the business to categorize responses. Since some respondents may be hesitant to answer such personal questions, demographics should usually be addressed near the end of the questionnaire.

Closed-ended questions ask respondents to select from a limited set of answers. This enables businesses to collate responses and analyze results more easily. Closed-ended questions may require a ''yes'' or ''no,'' or ''true'' or ''false'' answer. They may also be set up as a multiple-choice question, so that respondents choose one possible answer from a list. Finally, closed-ended questions may involve a scaled response, such as rating a product or service on a scale of one to ten or on the basis of categories such as ''strongly like,'' ''like,'' ''neither like nor dislike,'' etc. In contrast, open-ended questions enable respondents to provide a more lengthy response in their own words. Although open-ended questions can provide valuable information, the results can also be difficult for companies to analyze and categorize.

According to Green and Williams, there are a number of guidelines small business owners should follow in order to create good market questionnaires that are likely to produce meaningful responses. First, the survey should be as short as possible and collect only necessary information. Second, questions should be clearly worded and concise, without excessive technical jargon. Third, questions should be objective, so that they do not imply a correct answer. Fourth, questions should be limited so that they only seek one piece of information, and answers should fall into distinct categories. Finally, questionnaires should be arranged so that they begin with easier questions and progress into more difficult ones after a measure of trust has been achieved. It may be helpful to test a market questionnaire on a small group and then make any necessary refinements before using it in a large-scale market research effort.

FURTHER READING:

Green, Gloria, and Jeffrey Williams. *Marketing: Mastering Your Small Business*. Chicago, IL: Upstart, 1996.

MARKET RESEARCH

The term market research encompasses a number of activities that are designed to connect marketers to consumers through information gathering and evaluation. Market research provides businesses with information about their customers, their competitors, and their overall industry. It is commonly used to identify **marketing** problems and opportunities, as well as to develop and evaluate the effectiveness of marketing strategies. Small business owners, because of their usually limited financial resources, have a particular need for adequate, accurate, and current information to aid them in making decisions. Market research can help entrepreneurs evaluate the feasibility of a start-up venture before investing a great deal of time and capital, for example, as well as assist them in effectively marketing their goods and services. Employing such marketing strategies as **market segmentation** and product differentiation would be nearly impossible without first conducting market research.

Although market research can be costly, it is often even more costly to make erroneous decisions based upon bad or inadequate information. In fact, an average business spends between 25 and 50 percent of its annual marketing budget on research activities. Conducting large-scale market research in-house is not possible for many small businesses, since it requires a comprehensive understanding of the problem to be addressed, the market, and the application of research procedures. But there is a great deal of helpful information available to entrepreneurs who know where to look, and there are many consultants, advertising firms, and market research specialists who offer their services to small businesses for a fee.

The information gathered through market research can be divided into two main categories. The first category—primary information—generally does not exist in a coherent form before the marketer gathers it in response to a particular question or problem. The most common methods of gathering primary market research information are through **direct mail**, **telemarketing**, and personal interviews. The other category—secondary information—has already been compiled and organized by a source other than the marketer. Rather than looking at a specific marketing problem faced by an individual company, secondary information generally tracks trends within a market, an industry, a demographic group, or a geographic region. A great deal of valuable secondary information is available to small business owners at little or no cost. Some possible sources of secondary market research information include government reports, trade association records, newspaper and magazine surveys, university-sponsored research, local chamber of commerce records, on-line services, and competitors' annual reports.

Market research can provide small business owners with the information they need to answer a wide range of questions, including: Who are my customers? Where are they located? How much and how often will they buy? and What product attributes do they prefer? Given the importance of market research—and its potential cost—experts recommend that businesses follow a step-by-step approach in order to gain the most benefits from their research activities. The first step in the market research process is to define the marketing problem to be addressed. Next, a marketer should determine what information is needed to solve the problem, as well as what sources should be used to acquire the information. Many businesses make a preliminary investigation at this early stage in order to give their definition of the problem more focus and to develop tentative answers that can be tested during the next stage of the process. The third step involves planning the research. This step includes selecting the techniques to be used for gathering data and deciding on an appropriate group, or sample, to be included in the research. Fourth, a marketer actually gathers the necessary data. The fifth step involves analyzing and interpreting the information that has been gathered. Finally, the marketer reaches a conclusion about the marketing problem and translates the findings into changes in the firm's overall marketing strategy.

There are three general types of market research suppliers that can assist small businesses with one or more steps in the above process. Some firms specialize in conducting overall market research that they release to a variety of clients for a fee. This type of firm includes syndicated services such as A.C. Nielsen and Company, which provides viewership ratings for national television programs. There are also custom market research firms that handle all aspects of the process, from defining the marketing problem and designing research techniques to evaluating results and formulating new marketing strategies. In contrast, smaller, specialty line suppliers usually concentrate on one aspect of the process. Marketers who wish to secure the services of a market research firm usually obtain bids from a number of suppliers. The following sections provide more information about the various types of market research that such suppliers perform.

TYPES OF MARKET RESEARCH

AUDIENCE RESEARCH Research on who is listening, watching, and reading is important to marketers of television and radio programs and print publications—as well as to advertisers who wish to reach a certain target audience with their message. Television and radio ratings demonstrate the popularity of shows and determine how much stations can charge for advertising spots during broadcasts. Publication subscription lists, which are audited by tabulating companies to ensure their veracity, are important in determining the per page rate for advertising.

PRODUCT RESEARCH Product research includes simple, in-person research such as taste tests con-

ducted in malls and in the aisles of grocery stores, as well as elaborate, long-term "beta testing" of high-tech products by selected, experienced users. The objective of product research can be simple; for example, a company may tweak the taste of an existing product, then measure consumers' reactions to see if there is room in the market for a variation. It can also be more extensive, as when a company develops prototypes of proposed new products that may be intended for market introduction months down the road.

In product research, as in all market research, there is a danger to paying too much attention to the wrong things. For instance, the introduction of New Coke was based on the outcome of taste tests that showed the public wanted a sweeter product. But later an angry public, outraged that Coca-Cola was planning to change the familiar formula, forced the company to ignore its taste tests and leave the original Coke on the market. The company had put too much stock in the results of the taste test studies, and had failed to factor in research that showed consumers were happy with the product as it was.

BRAND RESEARCH Brands, the named products that advertising pushes and for which manufacturers can charge consumers the most money, are always being studied. Advertisers want to know if consumers have strong brand loyalty (''I'd never buy another brand, even if they gave me a coupon''); if the brand has any emotional appeal (''My dear mother used only that brand''); and what the consumer thinks could be improved about the brand (''If only it came in a refillable container'').

Brand research, too, has its perils. Campbell's Soup once convened a focus group comprised of its best soup customers. One of the findings was that those customers saw no need for a low-salt alternative soup Campbell's wanted to market. Concerned that the general public seemed to want low-sodium products, Campbell's retested groups other than their best customers. This research found a market interested in a low-sodium soup. The loyal Campbell's customers loved the saltier product, while a larger group of potential customers preferred the low-salt alternative.

PSYCHOLOGICAL RESEARCH Perhaps the most controversial type of market research is psychological research. This type of research tries to determine why people buy certain products based on a profile of the way the consumers live their lives. One company has divided all Americans into more than 60 psychological profiles. This company contends the lifestyles these people have established, based upon their past buying habits and their cultural upbringing, influences their buying decisions so strongly that individual differences can sometimes be negated.

Psychological research is controversial because it measures attitudes about buying rather than the buying itself. Critics point to conflicting information uncovered through other market research studies. In one series of research projects, researchers asked people what they were planning to buy before they entered a store. After the people surveyed left the store, the same researcher examined what was actually in their shopping carts. Only 30 percent of the people bought what they had said they planned to buy just a half hour earlier.

SCANNER RESEARCH In contrast, there is no fooling the checkout scanner at the supermarket or the department store: it records what was actually purchased. This is valuable information an advertiser can use to help plan an ongoing marketing strategy. Scanner technology has changed the way advertisers track the sale of consumer products. Before scanners, advertisers received sales information only when retailers reordered stock, generally every two weeks. This meant that the advertisers had no way to quickly measure the effect of national advertising, in-store **sales promotions**, or the couponing of similar products by their competitors. Now, computer technology can send scanner information to advertisers within days or even hours.

DATABASE RESEARCH Virtually every type of consumer—credit card holders, smokers, drinkers, car buyers, video buyers—shows up on thousands of lists and databases that are regularly cross-referenced to mine nuggets of marketing research. Database research is growing in popularity among marketers because the raw data has already been contributed by the purchaser. All the marketer has to do is develop a computer program to look for common buying patterns.

Database research can be thought of as the ultimate tool in **market segmentation** research. For example, from zip code lists, marketers may determine where the wealthy people live in a city. That list can be merged with a list of licensed drivers. The resulting list can be merged with another list of owners of cars of a certain make older than a certain year. The resulting list can be merged with another list of subscribers to car enthusiast magazines. The final list will deliver a potential market for a new luxury car soon to be introduced and profiled in the car magazines. The people on the potential buyers' list could then be mailed an invitation to come see the new car.

Database research also allows companies to build personal relationships with people who have proven from past purchases that they are potential customers. For example, a motorcycle manufacturer such as Harley Davidson may discover from database research that a family with a motorcycle has a teenage son. That son is a potential new customer for everything from clothes to a new motorcycle of his own. Maintaining a personal relationship with customers also provides businesses with a basis for more detailed and economical market research than might be possible through random sampling.

POST-SALES OR CUSTOMER SATISFACTION RESEARCH Most companies no longer believe that a sale ends their relationship with a customer. Nearly one-third of the research revenues generated by the leading American market research firms concern customer satisfaction. Many companies now wait a few days or weeks, then contact customers with survey questionnaires or telephone calls. Companies want reassurance that the customer enjoyed the buying experience and that the product or service has met the buyer's expectations.

The reason behind post-sales research is to ensure that current customers are happy, will consider themselves future customers, and will spread positive word-of-mouth messages about the product and company. One study found that 70 percent of customers believed it was important for companies to stay in contact with them, but less than one-third of those same customers reported that they had heard from companies whose products they purchased. Nearly 90 percent of those surveyed said they would be more likely to choose a company's products if it stayed in touch with them and sought their satisfaction.

PERSONAL RESEARCH METHODS

CLOSED-END QUESTIONNAIRE A closed-end questionnaire is the type of market research most people have experienced. It includes such common activities as filling out a comment card at a restaurant or responding to a telephone survey. In closed-end questionnaires, the person being surveyed cannot expound on their answers. Such surveys usually ask for ''yes'' or ''no'' responses or for measures of multiple choice opinion (e.g., ''extremely interested,'' ''somewhat interested,'' ''not interested''). This type of market research is generally conducted to elicit the opinions and beliefs of the public. It is commonly used for political polling and to determine the awareness or popularity of a product or service.

The inherent problem with multiple-choice questionnaires that ask for clear-cut answers is that many people do not think in a clear-cut fashion. If not carefully prepared, closed-ended questions may elicit answers that do not provide a clear view of the person being surveyed. Sometimes, the company conducting the survey may intentionally or inadvertently write questions that elicit the answers it wants to receive, rather than answers that provide a true picture of what is happening in the marketplace.

OPEN-ENDED QUESTIONNAIRE Over time, market researchers have grown increasingly aware that people often have opinions that do not fit into a multiple-choice questionnaire. To capture these opinions and try to analyze them, researchers are shifting toward open-ended research—asking people to say exactly what is on their minds. For example, manufacturers are giving customers plenty of space on questionnaires to explain their likes and dislikes about products and services, and telephone researchers will frequently mix closed-end and open-end questions on the same survey to try to delve deeper. A ''no'' response to whether a person watches a particular cable television station may trigger a follow-up question of ''Why not?,'' for instance, and the answer will be taken down word for word.

A problem with both closed- and open-ended questionnaire research, particularly when conducted over the telephone, is that people gradually become bored or annoyed and stop providing their true opinions. In addition, some studies have shown that a large percentage of Americans refuse to answer marketing research surveys.

FOCUS GROUPS In-person, sit-down discussions around a table with groups of consumers, would-be consumers, never-buyers, or any other demographic group a company wishes to bring together are called **focus groups**. This can be the least expensive type of market research when handled on a local basis by a small business wanting to get a handle on its customers. Or, it can be one of the most expensive if a major corporation wants to test its plans in various sections of the country. Small, local businesses may invite a focus group to a neighborhood home to sit around the dinner table and discuss how the company can develop new markets. In contrast, most major corporations conduct their focus groups in a controlled environment, usually with a one-way mirror at one end of the room. This allows executives to observe the proceedings unobtrusively or to videotape the session for further study.

The key to gathering good information from a focus group is for the moderator to keep the conversation flowing freely without taking a side. The moderator's job is to involve everyone in the discussion and prevent any individuals from dominating the conversation. Most market research experts agree that focus group research should be accompanied by other types of research and not be the sole basis for launching new products. The reason is that opinions expressed among strangers may not always reflect the way people would react when alone. For example, a focus group discussing low-fat foods may garner an enthusiastic response from people who want to be publicly perceived as being concerned about their health. The same people, however, might say they never buy low-fat products if questioned during an anonymous phone interview.

FURTHER READING:

The Entrepreneur Magazine Small Business Advisor. Wiley, 1995.

Haim, Alexander, and Charles D. Schewe. *The Portable MBA in Marketing.* Wiley, 1992.

Lehmann, Donald R. *Marketing Research and Analysis.* 3rd Ed. Irwin, 1988.

Stevens, Mark. *The Macmillan Small Business Handbook.* Macmillan, 1988.

SEE ALSO: Brands and Brand Names; Market Questionnaires; Point-of-Sale Systems

MARKET SEGMENTATION

Market segmentation is the science of dividing an overall market into key customer subsets, or segments, whose members share similar characteristics and needs. Because it involves significant **market research**, market segmentation can be costly. But it is particularly important for small businesses, which often lack the resources to target large aggregate markets or to maintain a wide range of differentiated products for varied markets. Market segmentation allows a small business to develop a product and a marketing mix that fit a relatively homogenous part of the total market. By focusing its resources on a specific customer base in this way, a small business may be able to carve out a market niche that it can serve better than its larger competitors.

Market segmentation lies somewhere near the middle of a continuum of marketing strategies that range from mass marketing—in which a single product is offered to all customers in a market—to one-to-one marketing—in which a different product is specifically designed for each individual customer in a market. Most businesses realize that since no two people are exactly alike, it is unlikely that they will be able to please all customers in a market with a single product. They also realize that it is rarely feasible to create a distinct product for every customer. Instead, most businesses attempt to improve their odds of attracting a significant base of customers by dividing the overall market into segments, then trying to match their product and marketing mix more closely to the needs of one or more segments. A number of customer characteristics, known as segmentation bases, can be used to define market segments. Some commonly used bases include age, gender, income, geographical area, and buying behavior.

MARKETING STRATEGIES

Though mass marketing (also known as market aggregation or undifferentiated marketing) cannot fully satisfy every customer in a market, many companies still employ this strategy. It is commonly used in the marketing of standardized goods and services—

including sugar, gasoline, rubber bands, or dry cleaning services—when large numbers of people have similar needs and they perceive the product or service as largely the same regardless of the provider. Mass marketing offers some advantages to businesses, such as reduced production and marketing costs. Due to the efficiency of large production runs and a single marketing program, businesses that mass market their goods or services may be able to provide consumers with more value for their money.

Some producers of mass market goods employ a marketing strategy known as product differentiation to make their offering seem distinct from that of competitors, even though the products are largely the same. For example, a producer of bath towels might embroider its brand name on its towels and sell them only through upscale department stores as a form of product differentiation. Consumers might tend to perceive these towels as somehow better than other brands, and thus worthy of a premium price. But changing consumer perceptions in this way can be very expensive in terms of promotion and packaging. A product differentiation strategy is most likely to be effective when consumers care about the product and there are identifiable differences between brands.

Despite the cost advantages mass marketing offers to businesses, this strategy has several drawbacks. A single product offering cannot fully satisfy the diverse needs of all consumers in a market, and consumers with unsatisfied needs expose businesses to challenges by competitors who are able to identify and fulfill consumer needs more precisely. In fact, markets for new products typically begin with one competitor offering a single product, then gradually splinter into segments as competitors enter the market with products and marketing messages targeted at groups of consumers the original producer may have missed. These new competitors are able to enter a market ostensibly controlled by an established competitor because they can identify and meet the needs of unsatisfied customer segments. In recent times, the proliferation of computerized customer databases has worked to drive marketing toward ever-more-narrowly focused market segments.

Applying a market segmentation strategy is most effective when an overall market consists of many smaller segments whose members have certain characteristics or needs in common. Through segmentation, businesses can divide such a market into several homogeneous groups and develop a separate product and marketing program to more exactly fit the needs of one or more segments. Though this approach can provide significant benefits to consumers and a profitable sales volume (rather than a maximum sales volume) to businesses, it can be costly to implement. For example, identifying homogeneous market segments requires significant amounts of market research,

which can be expensive. Also, businesses may experience a rise in production costs as they forfeit the efficiency of mass production in favor of smaller production runs that meet the needs of a subset of the market. Finally, a company may find that sales of a product developed for one segment encroach upon the sales of another product intended for another segment. Nonetheless, market segmentation is vital to success in many industries where consumers have diverse and specific needs, such as homebuilding, furniture upholstery, and tailoring.

SEGMENTATION BASES

In order to successfully implement a market segmentation strategy, a business must employ market research techniques to find patterns of similarity among customer preferences in a market. Ideally, customer preferences will fall into distinct clusters based upon identifiable characteristics of the population. This means that if customer requirements were plotted on a graph using certain characteristics, or segmentation bases, along the axes, the points would tend to form clusters.

To be pursued by a marketer, according to Alexander Hiam and Charles D. Schewe in *The Portable MBA in Marketing,* the customer segments should be: 1) identifiable and measurable; 2) large enough to be profitable; 3) reached effectively (for example, its members must tend to view the same television programs, read the same publications, or shop in the same places); 4) responsive to marketing; and 5) stable and not expected to change quickly. A company might elect to serve a single market segment or attempt to meet the needs of several segments.

Determining how to segment a market is one of the most important questions a marketer must face. Creative and effective market segmentation can lead to the development of popular new products, but unsuccessful segmentation can cost a great deal of money and still not yield the desired results. There are three main types of segmentation bases for businesses to consider—descriptive bases, behavioral bases, and benefit bases—each of which breaks down into numerous potential customer traits.

Descriptive bases for market segmentation include a variety of factors that describe the demographic and geographic situation of the customers in a market. They are the most commonly used segmentation bases because they are easy to measure, and because they often serve as strong indicators of consumer needs and preferences. Some of the demographic variables that are used as descriptive bases in market segmentation might include age, gender, religion, income, and family size, while some of the geographic variables might include region of the country, climate, and population of the surrounding area.

Behavioral bases for market segmentation are generally more difficult to measure than descriptive bases, but they are often considered to be more powerful determinants of consumer purchases. They include those underlying factors that help motivate consumers to make certain buying decisions, such as personality, lifestyle, and social class. Behavioral bases also include factors that are directly related to consumer purchases of certain goods, such as their degree of brand loyalty, the rate at which they use the product and need to replace it, and their readiness to buy at a particular time.

Businesses that segment a market based on benefits hope to identify the primary benefit that consumers seek in buying a certain product, then supply a product that provides that benefit. This segmentation approach is based upon the idea that market segments exist primarily because consumers seek different benefits from products, rather than because of various other differences between consumers. One potential pitfall to this approach is that consumers do not always know or cannot always identify a single benefit that influences them to make a purchase decision. Many marketers use a combination of bases that seem most appropriate when segmenting a market. Using a single variable is undoubtedly easier, but it often turns out to be less precise.

THE SEGMENTATION PROCESS

Hiam and Schewe have identified six steps that companies should take in the market segmentation process. The first step is to determine the boundaries of the market. In completing this step, a marketer should use a formal business plan to develop a broad definition of their business, and then consider the offerings of both direct and indirect competitors to gain information about the basic needs of consumers in the market. The second step in the process is to decide which variables to use in segmenting the market. Many companies fall into the trap of collecting data on as many variables as possible and then attempting to sort through it later to draw meaningful conclusions. Instead, Hiam and Schewe recommend that marketers use their knowledge of the market to select a few relevant variables in advance. This approach is generally less expensive and will likely provide more useful results.

The third step in the market segmentation process is actually collecting and analyzing data, which involves applying market research tools. The goal in analyzing the data is to identify market segments that are internally homogeneous, yet are distinctly heterogeneous with respect to other segments. The fourth step is to develop a detailed profile of each market segment, which involves selecting those variables that are most closely related to consumers' actual buying behavior.

The fifth step in the market segmentation process is to decide which segment or segments to serve. In targeting a particular segment, a marketer should look for opportunities (i.e., customers with unsatisfied wants and needs) that provide a good match for the organization and its resources. It is important that the marketer consider not only the size and potential profitability of a market segment, but also whether the company's skills, technologies, and objectives would enable it to meet the needs of that segment better than its competitors. The sixth and final step is to develop a product and marketing plan that will appeal to the selected market segment. This involves identifying the product attributes that are most important to consumers in the segment, and developing a marketing strategy that will attract their attention. In fact, market segmentation can be usefully applied during the earliest stages of product design, when a company first identifies who its target customer will be in terms of demographic, geographic, and behavioral characteristics.

In general, customers are willing to pay a premium for a product that meets their needs more specifically than does a competing product. Thus marketers who successfully segment the overall market and adapt their products to the needs of one or more smaller segments stand to gain in terms of increased profit margins and reduced competitive pressures. Small businesses, in particular, may find market segmentation to be a key in enabling them to compete with larger firms. Many management consulting firms offer assistance with market segmentation to small businesses. But the potential gains offered by market segmentation must be measured against the costs, which—in addition to the market research required to segment a market—may include increased production and marketing expenses.

FURTHER READING:

Dickson, Peter R., and James L. Ginter. "Market Segmentation, Product Differentiation, and Marketing Strategy." *Journal of Marketing* 51: 1-10.

Hiam, Alexander, and Charles D. Schewe. *The Portable MBA in Marketing.* Wiley, 1992.

Sandhusen, Richard L. *Barron's Business Review Series, Marketing.* 2nd Ed. Hauppauge, NY: Barron's Educational Series, Inc., 1993.

SEE ALSO: Marketing; Product Positioning; Target Markets

MARKET SHARE

Market share refers to the percentage of the overall volume of business in a given market that is controlled by one company in relation to its competitors. For example, if the total sales of a certain product in a market is $100,000, and the company in question sold

$20,000 worth of that product, then the company had 20 percent market share. Market share is most meaningful in a relative sense; that is, when a company compares the market share it commands to the percentage held by its largest competitors. "The important factor in computing relative market share is not the exact number associated with the sales volume," Kenneth J. Cook wrote in his book *The AMA Complete Guide to Strategic Planning for Small Business.* "Your position relative to the competition is more important. You want to know basically if they dominate you, if you are relatively equal in size, or if you dominate them."

To calculate market share, a small business owner first needs to determine the total sales of a product in a **target market** over a specific time period, usually one year. Then the small business owner needs to calculate the total sales achieved by his or her company in that market over the same time period. It may also be useful to find out the sales level achieved by the company's largest competitors and then use that information to compute relative market share. Information on the overall size of markets is usually available through industry associations, which commonly track both sales and growth rates. If competing firms happen to be publicly owned, their sales figures can usually be gleaned from their annual reports. Otherwise, the small business owner may be need to make an educated guess based on his or her knowledge of each competitor and on information provided by the company's customers and sales staff.

APPLICATIONS OF MARKET SHARE INFORMATION

Many companies use market share as a managerial objective—i.e., a company might try to gain a specified share of the market by a certain time. Market share can be a useful objective in that it forces small business owners to pay attention to the overall market and to the actions of competitors. It is also easier to measure than some other common objectives, such as maximizing profits. But there are some potential pitfalls associated with setting a company objective of increasing market share. For example, a company may be tempted to set too low a price to achieve this goal, even though a larger sales volume does not always lead to higher profits.

Another application of market share information is in evaluating a company's competitive position in an industry in order to formulate an effective strategy. Information on a firm's relative market share—which indicates its competitive position—can be combined with information on the growth rate and attractiveness of the industry to determine the best future positioning of the firm. The attractiveness of an industry can be determined through an industry analysis, which points

out the threats and opportunities facing competitors. The growth rate of an industry can be determined by measuring trends in customer spending levels. As Michael E. Porter outlined in his book *Competitive Strategy: Techniques for Analyzing Industries and Competitors,* the results of these measurements can be plotted on a quadrant diagram. The horizontal side of the matrix represents the firm's competitive position and the vertical side represents the growth rate and attractiveness of the industry, both ranging from weak to strong.

If both the company's competitive position and the industry's attractiveness and growth rate are strong, then the company occupies a fortunate position and is known as a "star." The most appropriate strategy for star companies is to exploit their competitive advantage and protect themselves against new competitors entering the industry. If both the company's competitive position and the industry's attractiveness and growth rate are weak, then the company is in an unfortunate position and is known as a "dog." The potential for market growth is limited, and the company's future prospects in the industry do not appear promising. The most appropriate strategy for a dog company is to limit spending, generate as much cash as possible in the short term, and consider exiting the industry.

If a company holds a strong position in a weak industry, it is known as a "cash cow." The best strategy for companies in this situation is to milk the market for cash while not expending too many resources. Finally, if a company occupies a weak competitive position in a strong industry, it is known as a "question mark." The business owners have important strategic decisions to make. Although there is strong future potential in the industry, the company's weak position means that it will have to make a significant investment to take advantage of the opportunity presented. In this case, it is particularly important for the business owner to understand his or her customers and competitors to determine whether it will be possible for the company to develop a competitive advantage.

FURTHER READING:

Cook, Kenneth J. *The AMA Complete Guide to Strategic Planning for Small Business.* Chicago, IL: American Marketing Association, 1995.

Green, Gloria, and Jeffrey Williams. *Marketing: Mastering Your Small Business.* Chicago, IL: Upstart Publishing, 1996.

Porter, Michael E. *Competitive Strategy: Techniques for Analyzing Industries and Competitors.* New York: Free Press, 1980.

Urban, Glen L., and Steven H. Star. *Advanced Marketing Strategy.* Englewood Cliffs, NJ: Prentice Hall, 1991.

SEE ALSO: Competitive Analysis

MARKETING

Marketing is a general term used to describe all the various activities involved in transferring goods and services from producers to consumers. In addition to the functions commonly associated with it, such as advertising and **sales promotion**, marketing also encompasses product development, **packaging**, **distribution channels**, **pricing**, and many other functions. The modern marketing concept, which is applied by most successful small businesses, is intended to focus all of a company's activities upon uncovering and satisfying customer needs. After all, an entrepreneur may come up with a great product and use the most efficient production methods to make it, but all the effort will have been wasted if he or she is unable to consummate the sale of the product to consumers.

The importance of marketing in the modern business climate cannot be overstated. In fact, management guru Peter F. Drucker has claimed that marketing "is so basic it cannot be considered a separate function. . . . It is the whole business seen from the point of view of its final result, that is, from the customer's point of view." Marketing is the source of many important new ideas in management thought and practice—such as flexible manufacturing systems, flat organizational structures, and an increased emphasis on service—all of which are designed to make businesses more responsive to customer needs and preferences. This suggests that small business owners must master the basics of marketing in order to succeed.

In the *Macmillan Small Business Handbook,* Mark Stevens discussed four main areas of marketing in which entrepreneurs should concentrate their efforts: 1) determining the needs of customers through **market research**; 2) analyzing their own competitive advantages and developing an appropriate market strategy; 3) selecting specific target markets to serve; and 4) determining the best marketing mix to satisfy customer needs. The first three tasks are most appropriately performed when a start-up business is preparing to enter a market, or when an existing business is considering entering a new market or promoting a new product. The marketing mix, on the other hand, includes the main decision areas that an entrepreneur must consider on an ongoing basis. Some elements of the market environment, such as the general economic conditions, are beyond a small business owner's control. But he or she can adjust elements of the company's marketing mix—which consists of the "four Ps": product, place, price, and promotion—to better fit the market environment.

BACKGROUND

The term "marketing" is derived from the word "market," which refers to a group of sellers and buyers that cooperate to exchange goods and services. The modern concept of marketing evolved during and after the industrial revolution in the 19th and 20th centuries. During that period, the proliferation of goods and services, increased worker specialization, and technological advances in transportation, refrigeration, and other factors that facilitated the transfer of goods over long distances resulted in the need for more advanced market mechanisms and selling techniques. But it was not until the 1930s that companies began to place a greater emphasis on advertising and promoting their products and began striving to tailor their goods to specific consumer needs. By the 1950s, many larger companies were sporting entire marketing departments charged with devising and implementing marketing strategies that would complement, and even direct, overall operations. Since the 1970s, and particularly during the 1980s, the primary marketing trend has been a greater focus on providing benefits, rather than products, to customers.

MACRO-MARKETING AND MICRO-MARKETING

Macro-marketing refers to the overall social process that directs the flow of goods and services from producer to consumer. It is the economic system that determines what and how much is to be produced and distributed by whom, when, and to whom. E. Jerome McCarthy and William D. Perreault, Jr. identified eight universal macro-marketing functions that make up the economic process: 1) buying, which refers to consumers seeking and evaluating goods and services; 2) selling, which involves promoting the offering; 3) transporting, which refers to the movement of goods from one place to another; 4) storing, which involves holding goods until customers need them; 5) standardization and grading, which entails sorting products according to size and quality; 6) financing, which delivers the cash and credit needed to perform the first five functions; 7) risk taking, which involves bearing the uncertainties that are part of the marketing process; and 8) market information, which refers to the gathering, analysis, and distribution of the data necessary to execute these marketing functions.

In contrast, micro-marketing refers to the activities performed by the individual providers of goods and services within a macro-marketing system. Such organizations or businesses use various marketing techniques to accomplish objectives related to profits, market share, cash flow, and other economic factors that can enhance their well being and position in the marketplace. The micro-marketing function within an entity is commonly referred to as marketing management. Marketing managers strive to get their organizations to anticipate and accurately determine the needs and wants of customer groups. Afterward they seek to respond effectively with a flow of need-satisfying goods and services. They are typically charged with planning, implementing, and then measuring the effectiveness of all marketing activities.

THE TARGET MARKETING CONCEPT

Micro-marketing encompasses a number of related activities and responsibilities. Marketing managers must carefully design their marketing plans to ensure that they complement related production, distribution, and financial constraints. They must also allow for constant adaptation to changing markets and economic conditions. Perhaps the core function of a marketing manager, however, is to identify a specific market, or group of consumers, and then deliver products and promotions that ultimately maximize the profit potential of that **target market**. This is particularly important for small businesses, which more than likely lack the resources to target large aggregate markets. Often, it is only by carefully selecting and wooing a specific group that a small firm can attain profit margins sufficient to allow it to continue to compete in the marketplace.

For instance, a manufacturer of fishing equipment would not randomly market its product to the entire U.S. population. Instead, it would likely conduct market research—using such tools as demographic reports, market surveys, or **focus groups**—to determine which customers would be most likely to purchase its offerings. It could then more efficiently spend its limited resources in an effort to persuade members of its target group(s) to buy its products. Perhaps it would target males in the Midwest between the ages of 18 and 35. The company may even strive to further maximize the profitability of its target market through **market segmentation**, whereby the group is further broken down by age, income, zip code, or other factors indicative of buying patterns. Advertisements and promotions could then be tailored for each segment of the target market.

There are infinite ways to address the wants and needs of a target market. For example, product packaging can be designed in different sizes and colors, or the product itself can be altered to appeal to different personality types or age groups. Producers can also change the warranty or durability of the good or provide different levels of follow-up service. Other influences, such as distribution and sales methods, licensing strategies, and **advertising media** also play an important role. It is the responsibility of the marketing manager to take all of these factors into account and to devise a cohesive marketing program that will appeal to the target customer.

THE FOUR PS

The different elements of a company's marketing mix can be divided into four basic decision areas—known as the ''four Ps'': product, place, promotion, and price—which marketing managers can use to devise an overall marketing strategy for a product or group of goods. These four decision groups represent all of the variables that a company can control. But those decisions must be made within the context of outside variables that are not entirely under the control of the company, such as competition, economic and technological changes, the political and legal environment, and cultural and social factors.

Marketing decisions related to the product (or service) involve creating the right product for the selected target group. This typically encompasses research and data analysis, as well as the use of tools such as focus groups, to determine how well the product meets the wants and needs of the target group. Numerous determinants factor into the final choice of a product and its presentation. A completely new product, for example, will entail much higher promotional costs to raise consumer awareness, whereas a product that is simply an improved version of an existing item likely will make use of its predecessor's image. A pivotal consideration in product planning and development is branding, whereby the good or service is positioned in the market according to its brand name. Other important elements of the complex product planning and management process may include selection of features, warranty, related product lines, and post-sale service levels.

Considerations about place, the second major decision group, relate to actually getting the good or service to the target market at the right time and in the proper quantity. Strategies related to place may utilize middlemen and facilitators with expertise in joining buyers and sellers, and they may also encompass various distribution channels, including retail, wholesale, catalog, and others. Marketing managers must also devise a means of transporting the goods to the selected sales channels, and they may need to maintain an inventory of items to meet demand. Decisions related to place typically play an important role in determining the degree of vertical integration in a company, or how many activities in the distribution chain are owned and operated by the manufacturer. For example, some larger companies elect to own their trucks, the stores in which their goods are sold, and perhaps even the raw resources used to manufacture their goods.

Decisions about promotion, the third marketing mix decision area, relate to sales, advertising, **public relations**, and other activities that communicate information intended to influence consumer behavior. Often promotions are also necessary to influence the behavior of retailers and others who resell or distribute the product. Three major types of promotion typically integrated into a market strategy are personal selling, mass selling, and sales promotions. **Personal selling**, which refers to face-to-face or telephone sales, usually provides immediate feedback for the company about the product and instills greater confidence in customers. Mass selling encompasses advertising on traditional mass media, such as television, radio, direct mail, and newspapers, and is beneficial because of its broad scope. Publicity entails the use of free media, such as feature articles about a company or product in a magazine or related interviews on television talk shows, to spread the word to the target audience. Finally, sales promotion efforts include free samples, coupons, contests, rebates, and other miscellaneous marketing tactics.

Determination of price, the fourth major activity related to target marketing, entails the use of discounts and long-term pricing goals, as well as the consideration of demographic and geographic influences. The price of a product or service generally must at least meet some minimum level that will cover a company's cost of producing and delivering its offering. Also a firm would logically price a product at the level that would maximize profits. The price that a company selects for its products, however, will vary according to its long-term marketing strategy. For example, a company may underprice its product in the hopes of increasing market share and ensuring its competitive presence, or simply to generate a desired level of cash flow. Another producer may price a good extremely high in the hopes of eventually conveying to the consumer that it is a premium product. Another reason a firm might offer a product at a very high price is to discount the good slowly in an effort to maximize the dollars available from consumers willing to pay different prices for the good. In any case, price is used as a tool to achieve comprehensive marketing goals.

COMPETITIVE STRATEGIES

Often times, decisions about product, place, promotion, and price will be dictated by the competitive stance that a firm assumes in its target market. According to Michael Porter's book *Competitive Strategy,* the three most common competitive strategies are low-cost supplier, differentiation, and niche. Companies that adopt a low-cost supplier strategy are usually characterized by a vigorous pursuit of efficiency and cost controls. A company that manufactures a low-tech or commodity product, such as wood paneling, would likely adopt this approach. Such firms compete by offering a better value than their competitors, accumulating market share, and focusing on high-volume and fast inventory turnover.

Companies that adhere to a differentiation strategy achieve market success by offering a unique prod-

uct or service. They often rely on brand loyalty, specialized distribution channels or service offerings, or patent protection to insulate them from competitors. Because of their uniqueness, they are able to achieve higher-than-average profit margins, making them less reliant on high sales volume and extreme efficiency. For example, a company that markets proprietary medical devices would likely assume a differentiation strategy.

Firms that pursue a niche market strategy succeed by focusing all of their efforts on a very narrow segment of an overall target market. They strive to prosper by dominating their selected niche. Such companies are able to overcome competition by aggressively protecting market share and by orienting every action and decision toward the service of its select group. An example of a company that might employ a niche strategy would be a firm that produced floor coverings only for extremely upscale commercial applications.

BUSINESS VERSUS CONSUMER MARKETS

An important micro-marketing delineation is that between industrial and consumer markets. Marketing strategies and activities related to transferring goods and services to industrial and business customers are generally very different from those used to lure other consumers. The industrial, or intermediate, market is made up of buyers who purchase for the purpose of creating other goods and services. Thus, their needs are different from general consumers. Buyers in this group include manufacturers and service firms, wholesalers and retailers, governments, and nonprofit organizations.

In many ways, it is often easier to market to a target group of intermediate customers. They typically have clearly defined needs and are buying the product for a very specific purpose. They are also usually less sensitive to price and are more willing to take the time to absorb information about goods that may help them do their job better. On the other hand, marketing to industrial customers can be complicated. For instance, members of an organization usually must purchase goods through a multi-step process involving several decision makers. Importantly, business buyers will often be extremely cautious about trying a new product or a new company because they do not want to be responsible for supporting what could be construed as a poor decision if the good or service does not live up to the organization's expectations.

A chief difference between marketing to intermediate and consumer markets is that members of the latter are typically considering purchasing goods and services that they might enjoy but are not absolutely necessary. As a result, they are more difficult to sell to than are business buyers. Consumers are generally less sophisticated than intermediate buyers, are less willing to spend time absorbing individual marketing messages of interest to them, and are more sensitive to the price of a good or service. Consumers typically make a buying decision on their own, however (or, for larger purchases, with the help of a friend or family member), and are much more likely to buy on impulse than are industrial customers.

Despite the differences, a dominant similarity between marketing to intermediate buyers and consumers is that both groups ultimately make purchases based on personal needs. Consumers typically act on their desires to belong, have security, feel high self-esteem, and enjoy freedom and status. Business and industrial consumers react more strongly to motivators such as fear of loss, fear of the unknown, the desire to avoid stress or hardship, and security in their organizational role.

MARKETING FOR SMALL BUSINESSES

In the early stages of forming a small business, a business plan is a vital tool to help an entrepreneur chart the future direction of the enterprise. A well-prepared business plan should include an extensive marketing component that explores the needs of the target market and lays out a marketing program to meet them. In fact, some experts claim that entrepreneurs should actually design their organizations in a way that gives the marketing function prominence. Once the needs of the target customers have been identified, these experts say, every aspect of the company's marketing program, as well as the basic image that the company develops, should be oriented toward satisfying these needs. For example, the company's selection of advertising, channels of distribution, packaging, price, and even vehicles and dress codes should all be coordinated to appeal to the target market.

As a small business grows, it may be helpful to create a separate marketing plan. While similar in format to the general business plan, a marketing plan focuses on expanding a certain product line or service rather than on the overall business. According to the *Entrepreneur Magazine Small Business Advisor,* creating a marketing plan helps a small business to define its markets, review its competitive position, develop goals and objectives, and determine the marketing tactics and financial resources needed to achieve its goals.

A number of resources are available to assist small businesses in marketing their products and services. It may be prudent to seek legal advice before implementing a marketing plan, for example. A firm with experience in consumer law could review the small business's product, packaging, labeling, advertising, sales agreements, and price policies to be sure that they meet all relevant regulations to prevent prob-

lems from arising later. In addition, many advertising agencies and market research firms offer a variety of means of testing the individual elements of marketing programs. Although such testing can be expensive, it can significantly increase the effectiveness of a company's marketing efforts.

FURTHER READING:

Bly, Robert W. *Business to Business Direct Marketing.* Lincolnwood, IL: NTC Business Books, 1992.

Boyd, Harper W., Jr. and Orville C. Walker, Jr. *Marketing Management: A Strategic Approach.* Irwin, 1990.

Debelak, Don. *Total Marketing.* Irwin, 1989.

The Entrepreneur Magazine Small Business Advisor. Wiley, 1995.

McCarthy, E. Jerome and William D. Perreault, Jr. *Basic Marketing.* Irwin, 1990.

Porter, Michael E. *Competitive Strategy.* Free Press, 1980.

Stevens, Mark. *The Macmillan Small Business Handbook.* Macmillan, 1988.

SEE ALSO: Brands and Brand Names; Market Analysis; Product Positioning

MARKUP

Markup is the amount that a seller of goods or services charges over and above the total cost of delivering its product or service to make a desired profit. For example, if the total cost of a manufacturer's product is $20, but its selling price is $29, then the extra $9 is understood to be the "markup." Markup is utilized by wholesalers, retailers, and manufacturers alike.

For entrepreneurs in the process of starting a business, establishing markup is one of the most important parts of **pricing** strategy. Markups must be sizable enough to cover all anticipated business expenses and reductions (markdowns, stock shortages, employee and customer discounts) and still provide the business with a good profit. The informed small business owner, then, is far more likely to arrive at a good markup price than the business owner who has a flawed understanding of the company's likely sales, its total operating expenses—including material, labor, and overhead costs—and its place in larger economic trends.

Entrepreneurs should also recognize that a flat markup percentage should not be blindly stamped on all its products or services regardless of the frequency with which customers purchase those goods or services. As the Small Business Administration noted in its brochure *Pricing Your Products,* small business owners "should seriously consider different markup figures when some lines have very different characteristics. For instance, a clothing retailer might logically have different initial markup figures for suits, shirts, pants, and accessories. [The small business owner] may want those items with the highest turnover rates to carry the lowest initial markup.'' Indeed, a small business may be able to realize a hefty profit even when it attaches a considerably smaller markup to one line of products, provided that the sales volume for that product line is high. For example, if company A and company B are selling the same $5 product, but company A insists on attaching a $4 markup on the product while company B limits itself to a $2 markup, the disparity in retail price may allow company B to register sales three or four times greater than the sales posted by company A. Company B thus realizes greater profits from the product than company A, even though the latter business had a higher markup.

MARKUPS IN SPECIFIC INDUSTRIES Markups vary enormously from industry to industry. In some industries, the markup is only a small percentage of the total cost of the product or service. Others, however, are able to attach a far higher markup. Small appliance manufacturers can sometimes assign markups of 30% or more, while clothing is often marked up by as much as 100%. Even within industries, markups can vary widely. The automotive industry, for example, is usually limited to a 5–10% markup on new cars, but it realizes a far higher profit on the hugely popular sports utility vehicle market, where markups of 25% or more are not uncommon.

FURTHER READING:

Berry, Leonard L., and Manjit S. Yadav. ''Capture and Communicate Value in the Pricing of Services.'' *Sloan Management Review.* Summer 1996.

Pricing Your Products. Washington: U.S. Small Business Administration, n.a.

Rugledge, John. ''Pricing for Growth.'' *Forbes.* October 7, 1996.

Service Corps of Retired Executives (SCORE), Chapter 225. *Handbook for Small Business.* Washington: U.S. Small Business Administration, 1989.

Sinanoglu, Elif. ''Want a Markdown? Learn the Markup.'' *Money.* February 1996.

SEE ALSO: Costs; Profit Margin

MEDICARE AND MEDICAID

Medicare and Medicaid are health insurance programs sponsored by the federal government that cover medical expenses for elderly, disabled, and low-income Americans. Both programs took effect in 1965 and are administered by the Health Care Finance Administration (HCFA) of the Department of Health and Human Services. The U.S. government provides health care coverage to a variety of groups—including federal employees, military personnel, veterans, and Native Americans—but the Medicare and Medicaid programs account for the largest proportion of health care expenditures.

The cost of administering the programs has increased dramatically over the years with the rapid escalation in health care costs. In fact, the portion of overall government spending that went toward Medicare and Medicaid increased from 5 percent in 1970 to 12 percent in 1990 and, barring significant changes, was projected to reach 23 percent by 2000. As a result, many experts predict that Americans will not be able to depend upon the programs for their long-term health care needs in the future. For self-employed persons and small business owners, who are less likely to be covered by an employer's health insurance program, these statistics make obtaining private health insurance policies that much more important.

MEDICARE

Medicare is the nation's largest health insurance program, providing coverage for 37 million Americans who are age 65 or older or who have a disability. Medicare coverage consists of two parts. Part A, which is financed largely through Social Security taxes, provides hospitalization insurance. Intended to assist people who need long-term medical treatment, Medicare Part A covers inpatient hospital services, skilled nursing facilities, home health services, and hospice care. Part B, which is financed through premiums paid by those who choose to enroll in the program, provides supplemental insurance to help cover the cost of physician services, outpatient hospital services, and medical equipment and supplies.

Qualified people can enroll in the Medicare program by completing an application at their local Social Security Administration office. It is important to note that, once an employee becomes eligible for Medicare, a small business owner is no longer required to offer him or her **health insurance continuation coverage** under the provisions of the Consolidated Omnibus Budget Reconciliation Act (COBRA). Since Medicare does not cover all of an elderly or disabled person's health care costs, many insurance companies offer Medicare Supplemental Insurance (also known as Medigap coverage) to fill in the gaps. Medigap policies commonly take care of co-payments and over-limit expenses, for example, in exchange for a small premium. Due to past problems with disreputable Medigap providers, experts recommend that individuals shop carefully for this type of coverage.

MEDICAID

As the nation's second-largest health insurance program, Medicaid provides medical assistance to 36 million low-income Americans. It was established through Title XIX of the Social Security Act of 1965 to pay the health care costs for members of society who otherwise could not afford treatment. The program is jointly funded by the federal government and the state governments, but is administered separately by each state within broad federal guidelines. Medicaid recipients include adults, children, and families, as well as elderly, blind, and disabled persons, who have low or no income and receive other forms of public assistance. Medicaid also covers the ''medically needy,'' or those whose income is significantly reduced by large medical expenses.

Medicaid covers the full cost of a wide range of medical services, including inpatient and outpatient hospital care, doctor visits, lab tests, X-rays, nursing home and home health care, family planning services, and preventative medicine. A large proportion of the Medicaid population is elderly or disabled, and thus also qualifies for Medicare. In these cases, Medicaid usually pays for Medicare premiums, deductibles, and co-payments, in addition to some non-covered services.

THE FUTURE

Although many Americans plan to rely on Medicare to meet their health insurance needs later in life, the program as it stood in the mid-1990s actually covered less than half of an average elderly person's medical costs, according to Lenore Janecek in her book *Health Insurance: A Guide for Artists, Consultants, Entrepreneurs, and Other Self-Employed*. It does not provide funds for dental, vision, or hearing care, for example, and 97 percent of the time it does not cover nursing home care. In addition, Medicare deductibles more than doubled between 1983 and 1993, from $304 to $676, and seemed likely to continue to rise.

Even if the Medicare program remained basically the same beyond the year 2000, it would not provide adequate coverage for many Americans. But the program seemed likely to face significant changes to address the rising cost of health care and the increased need for coverage as the baby-boom generation neared retirement age. Both Medicare and Medicaid were featured prominently in discussions about the federal budget deficit, welfare reform, and health care reform in the mid-1990s. Various proposals to reduce the programs' budgets, introduce spending caps, and create new plans to cover children may be adopted in the near future. As a result, Janecek noted, entrepreneurs may face even greater challenges in ensuring their financial and physical well-being upon retirement.

FURTHER READING:

Anastasio, Susan. *Small Business Insurance and Risk Management Guide*. Washington: U.S. Small Business Administration, n.d.

Health Insurance. Arlington, VA: Council of Better Business Bureaus, 1995.

Janecek, Lenore. *Health Insurance: A Guide for Artists, Consultants, Entrepreneurs, and Other Self-Employed*. New York: Allworth Press, 1993.

SEE ALSO: Self-Employment Contributions Act (SECA)

MEETINGS

Meetings, while disliked by many, are an essential part of most business operations. They are often the best venue for communications to take place, for issues to be discussed, for priorities to be set, and for decisions to be made in various realms of business management. Because it is more common for responsibility to be spread out across an organization these days, and because cross-functional efforts are common at almost every business, meetings are the best method for achieving organizational participation.

Holding successful meetings, then, is essential. Poorly run meetings waste time and fail to generate ideas, and unfortunately, far too high a percentage of business meetings are characterized by ineffective processes. Indeed, some analysts estimate that up to 50 percent of meeting time is wasted. Entrepreneurs and small business managers should thus take the appropriate steps to ensure that the meetings that they call and lead are productive.

PLANNING A SUCCESSFUL BUSINESS MEETING

The most important step in holding a successful meeting is planning. This includes determining who should attend, who will run the meeting, and what will be discussed. Before the meeting, finalize a list of attendees. This is especially important for meetings where a quorum is needed to conduct official business. Without a quorum, it is usually best to simply postpone the meeting until more group members can attend.

When determining who to include in a meeting, several criteria should be weighed. Charlie Hawkins pointed out in *Public Relations Quarterly* that the most important personnel to invite are those people who can best achieve the objective of the meeting. This can be people who are affected by a problems, those who will be most affected by the outcome of the meeting, experts on the subject at hand, or people who are known to be good problem-solvers or idea generators. Inviting people solely for political reasons should be avoided if possible, although experts recognize that this may not always be possible. Avoid inviting disruptive people unless they absolutely have to be there. Finally, some meeting topics may benefit from the inclusion of an informed outsider who has no stake in the issue; sometimes a fresh, objective perspective can be most beneficial.

Once the meeting's moderator has determined who needs to be in attendance, he or she should develop an agenda and circulate it in advance of the meeting. There are two schools of thought on how to order the agenda. One school recommends starting the agenda with less-important items that can be handled quickly and easily. The theory is that this helps to build a positive atmosphere and makes it easier to move on to tougher issues later in the meeting. The other school of thought, however, feels that this is a waste of time and that the agenda should be prioritized, with the most important items coming first. This means jumping right into the most significant issue. Regularly-scheduled meetings, such as staff meetings, lend themselves to the ''most important first'' style.

Many consultants, managers, and business owners contend that the traditional agenda model of ''old minutes/old business/new business/adjournment'' does not really work anymore. Agendas need to be more fluid and dynamic, yet still need to be structured and effective. Adhering to the following tips can help ensure that the meeting agenda can be addressed effectively:

- State the purpose of the meeting and write it clearly at the top of the agenda. If no clear goal or topic comes to mind, then perhaps the meeting is not even necessary. Consider using a memo, e-mail, conference call, or series of one-to-one meetings to canvas participants about meeting topics prior to creating the agenda.

- Set priorities. Reading the minutes from a past meeting is a colossal waste of time. It is ok to hand out the minutes from the previous meeting, but reading them is just not needed.

- Less is more. One of the fundamental meeting mistakes is tackling too many issues. Keep the agenda focused on a few key items.

If other group members are to play a role at the meeting, call or visit them once the agenda is established so that they clearly understand their role. Assign a time limit to each of the agenda items. Having time limits helps keep a meeting on track and prevents rambling discussions. Never include the agenda item ''Any Other Business.'' It encourages time-wasting at the end of the meeting and also serves as a method for a savvy (or sneaky) meeting participant to exploit the

meeting by bringing up an item that is of importance to him or her alone.

Once an agenda has been established, many consultants recommend the appointment of a meeting facilitator in advance of the meeting itself. It is the facilitator's job to keep the meeting focused and on-schedule. He or she must remain ''issue neutral'' and encourage the free exchange of ideas without taking sides. The best facilitators are good listeners and communicators who successfully blend assertiveness with tact, discipline with humor, set a cooperative tone, and are achievement-oriented. The facilitator should remain focused and not allow side issues to distract from the agenda. Appointing a separate time-keeper who alerts the facilitator when agreed-upon time limits are approaching is recommended. Some professional meeting planners recommend using co-facilitators—this keeps one facilitator from falling in love with his or her own ideas. For small companies, this idea may not be feasible. However, if the company does hold a lot of meetings, perhaps several company members can be sent for formal training in meeting facilitation. This would make it easier to appoint co-facilitators.

For small companies, perhaps facilitators are not needed at every meeting. Indeed, small business owners often serve as facilitator, key information source, and chief strategist all in one. But some small businesses have successfully instituted systems in which meeting planning and leadership responsibilities are rotated among staff members.

CONDUCTING A SUCCESSFUL MEETING

Once the planning has been concluded, it is time to hold the meeting. Adhering to several simple rules can dramatically increase the likelihood that your meeting will be a productive one.

1) If you are facilitating the meeting, arrive early and be prepared. No exceptions to this rule are allowed. A late facilitator dampens the mood and gets the meeting off on the wrong foot because it makes it impossible for the meeting to start on time. Indeed, provided the facilitator is present, the meeting should begin at the time scheduled, even if other scheduled participants have not yet arrived. Waiting for latecomers rewards them for their behavior and implies that you value their time more than you value the time of those who showed up on time. If one of the latecomers is essential to the first agenda item, be flexible and move on to a later agenda item to keep things moving.

2) Facilitators interested in making certain that the meeting proceeds effectively should set

the appropriate tone from the outset. Chit-chat should be kept to a minimum, especially at the start of the meeting. Do not be a dictator—social interaction is an important part of building a cohesive team—but do not let valuable meeting time be wasted either. "Nothing saps the spirit like watching, powerless, as a meeting wanders into oblivion," observed Phaedra Hise in *Inc*.

3) Be sure to stick to the timed meeting agenda that was developed at the planning stage. This builds consensus for tabling discussions that are going nowhere. It also makes it easier to agree to send problems back to committees, and it keeps one long-winded group member from dominating the meeting. Using a phrase such as "We would like to hear what you have to say, but in order for the group to be out on time we have to move on," is a very successful tactic.

4) If some members of the group are not participating, actively seek out their opinion. Groups tend to be dominated by the most outgoing or opinionated members, but the quiet members often have great ideas of their own. Do not let one person or group dominate the floor.

5) Stay focused on the purpose of the meeting. If the group that is meeting is a large board that is primarily responsible for delegating tasks to smaller committees, make sure the larger group does not make the mistake of doing the work for the smaller groups instead of passing it on.

6) Schedule meetings for times that are likely to encourage concentrate on agenda items. For example, facilitators may want to consider holding short meetings before lunch and quitting time, when staff are less likely to dawdle over non-work related subjects. Conversely, many analysts believe that meetings that are held immediately after lunch, when people are often at their least energetic, are apt to be less effective.

7) Stand-up meetings are often touted as a great way to ensure that meeting participants stay focused. Another way to stay focused is to use what Hawkins termed the "parking lot" strategy. During the course of one discussion, it is not unusual for important ideas or concerns to arise that are not related to the topic at hand. When that happens, the facilitator can call "time out," identify the issue, and place it in a so-called "parking lot" so that it can be addressed at a later time. The group can then get back to the main focus of the meeting without losing topics or ideas that may be of importance to the firm.

8) Try to establish a consensus on business decisions that are arrived at in meetings. "Building consensus does not mean caving in to conform with what the boss wants," said Hawkins. "It does mean examining the plus and minus aspects of possible alternatives, and picking the one(s) that best meet the defined goals. The normal way of deciding—by voting—inevitably produces a win-lose situation. Those who are in the minority are liable to undermine the decision. Even if a voting process is used to pick the winners, a consensus process is recommended to isolate the concerns and address them. When this is done, the solution is refined to the point where everyone in the group can live with the recommendation and support it. A group that builds consensus in a constructive atmosphere is most likely a highly effective team."

9) Ensure that decisions that are made in meetings are adequately disseminated, especially to staff members who are personally impacted by the decision. Make sure that company resources are appropriately redistributed to enable execution of decisions.

MEETING PITFALLS

Despite the best efforts and the strongest facilitator, meetings can quickly spin out of control. Following are some common pitfalls that beset meetings, launching them into downward spirals of inaction and/or flawed decision making:

- The facilitator puts aside the meeting agenda for his or her own personal agenda

- The facilitator allows interruptions such as telephone calls

- Loud group members are allowed to dominate the meeting

- Decisions are made based on generalizations, exaggeration, guesswork, and assumptions

- Discussions consistently wander off the topic

- Key members of the group are not present

- Overly ambitious agendas

- Meetings that exceed previously agreed-upon time limits

- Minutes that are inaccurate or biased

- Too many participants

- Waiting for latecomers to arrive

- An unclear, or inappropriate, decision-making process. For example, taking a vote when leadership and unilateral action by a company's CEO is clearly needed.

MEETINGS IN A FAMILY-OWNED BUSINESS

Many small businesses are family-owned. While it might seem that a **family-owned business** might not need to worry about holding successful meetings, that is not true. Family meetings can be an important means of keeping the business fresh, generating new ideas, and keeping grievances to a minimum.

Family meetings, when run properly, can help ensure business success and its continued survival into the next generation. The meetings do not need to be formal, but they should be structured and should be held on a regular basis. Because a family business affects all family members—not just those who are an active part of the business—some analysts contend that everyone in the family should be invited to the meetings. If everyone takes the meeting seriously and is willing to participate, the meeting can lead to greater cohesion, communication, and long-range planning.

Business experts say that the agenda for such a meeting can combine business and pleasure. Serious topics—creating a mission statement, strategy planning, setting a clear path of succession, professional growth and development, market analysis, and estate planning are some examples—typically need to be addressed during these meetings, but the agenda should also reflect a recognition of the family environment in which it is taking place. Meetings that include a meal (dinner, picnic, etc.) as a centerpiece are among the most popular options.

As with any other meeting, the family meeting should have a facilitator. An outside facilitator can be brought in if family members are concerned that objectivity might otherwise be hard to achieve, but be forewarned that hiring a facilitator can be expensive. It is possible to use a family member as a facilitator as long as that person is able to remain unbiased in the face of emotional discussions. Steering clear of long-time family conflicts is also a must if the facilitator is to succeed at his or her job, although admittedly this can sometimes be difficult. "Facilitating one's own family meeting can seem daunting because of the potential emotional intensity of family discussions," wrote John Ward and Sharon Krone in *Nation's Business*. "To be effective, a family member acting as a facilitator must overcome emotional barriers, dispel longtime family stereotypes, and curtail long-standing conflicts among family members. All are tough to do."

Ward and Krone provided several other tips for holding successful family meetings, including the following:

- Consider using co-facilitators as a safeguard to prevent one family member from wielding undue influence over the meeting's direction and tone.

- The facilitator must keep other involved. Assign jobs—keeping notes, creating charts or overheads, keying and distributing minutes, or chairing committees—and avoid the impression that one person is dominating the meeting.

- Provide formal training for the facilitator. While the person selected may have strong interpersonal and leadership skills, formal training in communications, conflict resolution, active listening, decision making, and group management can prove invaluable.

- Each person attending the meeting should reflect on his or her own strengths and weaknesses and personality style.

- Recognize when professional help *is* needed. Intense conflicts and domination by one person or a small group of people are examples of when it might be time to bring in a professional facilitator.

- Avoid surprises. Distribute agendas and notes in advance if possible.

- Set ground rules for the meeting.

- Have fun. Even if the business at hand is very serious, set aside some time for relaxation or fun.

- Use a well-lit meeting room with comfortable furniture. Make sure refreshments are provided and provide ample breaks.

- Do not rush things, and do not overload the agenda with too many heavy topics if at all possible.

FURTHER READING:

"Advanced Agenda Writing: Tactics to Use Before You Call the Meeting to Order." *Oregon Business*. December 1996.

Brokaw, Leslie. "The Model Meetings Agenda." *Inc.* July 1994.

Butler, Ava S. "Taking Meetings by Storm." *Management Review*. October 1996.

Gorup, Sharon R. "Conducting Productive Meetings: How to Stay on Track." *Association Management*. January 1997.

Hawkins, Charlie. "First Aid for Meetings." *Public Relations Quarterly*. Fall 1997.

Hise, Phaedra. "Keeping Meetings Brief." *Inc.* September 1994.

Jones, Becky, Midge Wilker, and Judy Stoner. ''A Meeting Primer.'' *Management Review.* January 1995.

Krone, Sharon P., and John L. Ward. ''Do-It-Yourself Family Meetings.'' *Nation's Business.* November 1997.

Morgan, Chris. ''The Basics of Brainstorming.'' *Folio: The Magazine for Magazine Management.* November 1, 1997.

Peterson, Meg Cieply. ''Brainstorm: People and Pizza aren't the only Components.'' *The Business Journal.* June 2, 1997.

''Time's Up.'' *Industry Week.* June 9, 1997.

Wyatt, Stuart. ''How to Make Your Meetings More Effective.'' *Management Accounting.* April 1996.

MENTORING

Mentoring denotes a relationship between a more experienced person—the mentor—and a less experienced person—the protégé. The mentor's role is to guide, instruct, encourage, and correct the protégé. The protégé should be willing to listen to instruction and constructive criticism, and should also feel as though the mentor is concerned with his/her welfare. Mentor/ protégé relationships are less structured and more personal than traditional teacher/student situations.

HOW MENTORING WORKS IN SMALL BUSINESSES In many large corporations, formal systems of mentoring are being established. They are designed to quickly involve new employees in the work at hand, and to strengthen the work force in much the same way that other teambuilding strategies are designed to do. These systems pair experienced workers exhibiting (or needing to hone) strong leadership skills with new employees not yet acquainted with the nuances of the corporation, the work at hand, and their potential within the framework of the company.

While mentoring is perhaps most closely associated with large corporate settings, the practice can be effectively utilized by small businesses as well. Small business owners themselves can become involved in mentoring relationships, on either the mentor or the protégé side. Entrepreneurs may seek out business owners or executives with more experience in certain areas, and approach them about beginning a mentoring relationship. Because this kind of approach acknowledges success, experience, and market savvy, a potential mentor will likely be flattered and appreciate the drive and initiative of the potential protégé. In other instances, more experienced small business owners may wish to initiate mentor/protégé relationships from the mentor angle, spurred by philanthropic instincts or a wish to strengthen the skills and knowledge of other people within his or her organization. These mentoring systems can be loosely or formally structured, either determined by the owner or simply encouraged by the owner and initiated by employees.

In either case, attempts should be made to insure both diversity in the workplace, which can be strengthened by mentoring relationships, and a reasonable fit.

Proteges and mentors should feel relatively comfortable together, as the relationship ideally is one of trust and mutual growth. Mentors should not be expected to become drill sergeants or police; the mentor relationship is not intended to be one of management exerting its will over young or inexperienced employees. Rather, the relationship should reduce anxiety by clearly defining goals and boundaries, and should increase productivity as a result.

Small business owners seeking mentors have several structured alternatives to choose from. The **U.S. Small Business Administration** can put potential proteges into contact with some groups, and there is an internet mentoring service, maintained by the **Service Core of Retired Executives (SCORE)**, which provides e-mail counseling.

BENEFITS OF MENTORING

Mentoring relationships can be beneficial to all parties. Any mentoring situation requires an investment of time, experience, and trust. But these investments will be rewarded in a strong tie between colleagues and the deepened experience of not just the protégé, but also the mentor.

BENEFITS FOR THE MENTOR Mentors may receive great satisfaction from their experience with proteges. They feel respected and appreciated for their knowledge and skill. And mentors can become more invested in their work as a result: they have personal relationships to foster in the business setting, and they feel that the owner trusts and respects their judgment and talents. And as role models, mentors may even more closely evaluate their own performances and become more productive in their own business dealings and duties.

BENEFITS FOR THE PROTÉGÉ The protégé, whether a new employee of a business or a new entrepreneur, will benefit from the transfer of knowledge and know-how that can be passed on by a mentor of greater experience. Perhaps the greatest benefit is being able to learn from other people's mistakes; a mentor can warn of pitfalls as yet unforeseen by the protégé, saving the time and the pain of having to make those mistakes in order to know they exist.

An employee who is a protégé also benefits by having a mentor trained in the management of a business, who can pass along the true meanings behind policy decisions, and the unwritten rules of the workplace. The mentoring relationship can make the transition into productive, comfortable employee a much smoother one; the protégés will quickly learn what is expected from them, their place within the framework of the business, and what other people in the business are responsible for. Career opportunities and areas of improvement can both be sensitively illustrated by a mentor, and transitions within the company and changes of business practice can be made less stressful by having someone trusted to explain them.

BENEFITS FOR THE BUSINESS OWNER The business owner benefits from the mentor/protégé relationship within their business in some very real ways. New employees can be thoroughly trained in technical aspects of the work by a mentor, resulting in employees who move quickly through the learning curve and into productive work. Business owners are able to practice more hands-off management of companies which have strong, capable mentors; and mentoring relationships have also been shown to promote employee satisfaction, leading to decreased turnover in the workforce and higher production rates.

FURTHER READING:

Boyett, Joseph H. and Henry P. Conn. *Workplace 2000.* Penguin, 1991.

Eddy, Sandra E., ''Computer Ease: Virtual Mentors,'' *Entrepreneur Online*, November 1997.

Godshalk, Veronica, and John J. Sosick. "The Role of Leadership Styles and Mentoring Relationships in Influencing Follower Job-Related Stress." *Journal of Management Systems*, n.a.

Kennedy, Danielle. ''Guiding Light.'' *Entrepreneur.* July 1997.

MERCHANDISE DISPLAYS

Merchandise displays are special presentations of a store's products or services to the buying public. The nature of these displays may range somewhat from industry to industry, but all merchandise displays are predicated on basic principles designed to increase product purchases. Indeed, merchandise displays are an integral element of the overall merchandising concept, which seeks to promote product sales by coordinating **marketing**, **advertising**, and sales strategies.

Many business consultants believe that small business owners are among the leaders in innovative merchandise display strategies. W. Rae Cowan noted in *Chain Store Age Executive,* for example, that ''in many instances, smaller specialty chains are leading the way in store ambience supporting their overall marketing strategy in a broad range of categories from fashion through hardware and housewares and building supplies areas. By their very nature, specialty stores depend on their fixturing to generate a differentiation or niche in the marketplace. And being physi-

cally smaller in some cases allows for faster response to market trends and conditions. . . . Successful retailers today are using their fixturing to productively dispense their merchandise and communicate an appropriate environment on the retail floor.''

Merchandise displays generally take one of several basic forms:

- Storefront Window Displays—These typically open on to a street or shopping mall walk or courtyard and are intended to attract passerby that might not otherwise enter the store.

- Showcase Displays—These typically feature items that: 1) are deemed to be too valuable for display in storefront set-ups; or 2) are niche items of high interest to the business's primary clientele. These display centers are usually located in high traffic areas and typically feature multiple tiers for product display and a sliding door on the clerk's side for access.

- ''Found-Space'' Displays—This term refers to product presentations that utilize small but nonetheless usable areas of the store, such as the tops of product carousels or available wall space.

Storefront window displays and ''found space'' displays are particularly popular tools for publicizing and selling sale items.

KEYS TO SUCCESSFUL MERCHANDISE DISPLAY

Trudy Ralston and Eric Foster, authors of *How to Display It: A Practical Guide to Professional Merchandise Display,* cited several key components of successful merchandise display that are particularly relevant for small business owners. First, displays should be economical, utilizing only space, materials, and products that are already available. Second, displays should be versatile, able to ''fit almost anywhere, exhibit almost any merchandise, and convey almost any message.'' Finally, displays have to be effective. The ideal display, said Ralston and Foster, ''is readily visible to any passer-by and [should be arranged so that] there is no time or space lag between when a potential buyer sees the design and when he or she can react to it. [The ideal display] also shows the customer what the product actually looks like, not some flat and intangible picture of it. Few other forms of promotion can give such a vivid presentation of both the merchandise and character of a store.''

The effectiveness of these cornerstones of merchandising display strategy can be increased by remembering several other tips as well, including the following:

- Allocate merchandise display space and expenditures appropriately in recognition of customer demographics. If the bulk of your business's customers are males between the ages of 20 and 40, the bulk of your displays should probably be shaped to catch their interest.

- Be careful of pursuing merchandise display designs that sacrifice effectiveness for the sake of originality.

- Make certain that the cleanliness and neatness of the display is maintained.

- Do not overcrowd a display. Customers tend to pass over messy, busy-looking displays. Instead, Ralston and Foster affirm that "a display should feature a single item or point of interest. . . . Every primary article [in a display] must interact with every other so that they all come together as a group. If they don't it will look as if there is not one design, but several."

- Combine products that are used together in displays. For example, pairing ski goggles with other outdoor apparel is apt to be more effective than placing it alone or with some other product that is only tangentially related to skiing.

- Small items should be displayed so that would-be customers can get a good look at them without having to solicit the help of a member of the staff.

- Pay attention to details when constructing and arranging display backgrounds. For example, Foster and Ralston counsel business owners to "avoid dark backgrounds when customers will be looking through a window, since this makes the glass behave as a giant mirror."

- Merchandise displays can sometimes be utilized to educate customers. A well-conceived display could, for example, illustrate a product use that may not have occurred to most customers. "In addition to selling actual merchandise, display can be used to introduce a new product, a fashion trend, and a new 'look' or idea," explained Martin Pegler in *Visual Merchandising and Display*. "Display can be used to educate the consumer concerning what the new item is, how it can be worn or used, and how it can be accessorized. The display may also supply pertinent information, the price, and other special features."

All of these considerations need to be weighed when putting together a merchandise display. But ultimately, the final barometer of a display's worthiness is its ability to sell products. As Martin Pegler bluntly stated, "the test of a good display today is: *Does it sell?*"

FURTHER READING:

Cowan, W. Rae. "Store Fixturing and Display—Retailer's Strategic Tool for Product Positioning and Productivity in the '90s." *Chain Store Age Executive.* December 1993.

Fox, Bruce. "Brand Erosion Potential." *Chain Store Age Executive.* February 1994.

Pegler, Martin M. *Visual Merchandising and Display.* New York: Fairchild Publications, 1983.

Ralston, Trudy, and Eric Foster. *How to Display It: A Practical Guide to Professional Merchandise Display.* New York: Art Direction Book Co., 1985.

Ray, Susan. "Merchandising Concepts are Solid as Rock." *Amusement Business.* September 27, 1993.

Reese, Shelly. "Congestion, Distractions Weaken Sales Value of Endcap Displays." *Stores.* February 1997.

Urban, Glen L., and Steven H. Star. *Advanced Marketing Strategy: Phenomena, Analysis, Decisions.* Englewood Cliffs, NJ: Prentice Hall, 1991.

MERGERS AND ACQUISITIONS

A merger occurs when one firm assumes all the assets and liabilities of another. The acquiring firm retains its identity, while the acquired firm ceases to exist. A majority vote of shareholders is generally required to approve a merger. A merger is just one type of acquisition. One company can acquire another in several other ways, including purchasing some or all of the company's assets or buying up its outstanding shares of stock.

In general, mergers and other types of acquisitions are performed in the hopes of realizing an economic gain. For such a transaction to be justified, the two firms involved must be worth more together than they were apart. Some of the potential advantages of mergers and acquisitions include achieving economies of scale, combining complementary resources, garnering tax advantages, and eliminating inefficiencies. Other reasons for considering growth through acquisitions include obtaining proprietary rights to products or services, increasing market power by purchasing competitors, shoring up weaknesses in key business areas, penetrating new geographic regions, or providing managers with new opportunities for career growth and advancement. Since mergers and acquisitions are so complex, however, it can be very difficult to evaluate the transaction, define the associated costs and benefits, and handle the resulting tax and legal issues.

"In today's global business environment, companies may have to grow to survive, and one of the best ways to grow is by merging with another company or acquiring other companies," consultant Jacalyn Sherriton told Robert McGarvey in an interview for *Entrepreneur*. "Massive, multibillion-dollar corporations are becoming the norm, leaving an entrepreneur to wonder whether a merger ought to be in his or her plans, too," McGarvey continued.

When a small business owner chooses to merge with or sell out to another company, it is sometimes called "harvesting" the small business. In this situation, the transaction is intended to release the value locked up in the small business for the benefit of its owners and investors. The impetus for a small business owner to pursue a sale or merger may involve estate planning, a need to diversify his or her investments, an inability to finance growth independently, or a simple need for change. In addition, some small businesses find that the best way to grow and compete against larger firms is to merge with or acquire other small businesses.

In principle, the decision to merge with or acquire another firm is a capital budgeting decision much like any other. But mergers differ from ordinary investment decisions in at least five ways. First, the value of a merger may depend on such things as strategic fits that are difficult to measure. Second, the accounting, tax, and legal aspects of a merger can be complex. Third, mergers often involve issues of corporate control and are a means of replacing existing management. Fourth, mergers obviously affect the value of the firm, but they also affect the relative value of the stocks and bonds. Finally, mergers are often "unfriendly."

TYPES OF ACQUISITIONS

In general, acquisitions can be horizontal, vertical, or conglomerate. A horizontal acquisition takes place between two firms in the same line of business. For example, one tool and die company might purchase another. In contrast, a vertical merger entails expanding forward or backward in the chain of distribution, toward the source of raw materials or toward the ultimate consumer. For example, an auto parts manufacturer might purchase a retail auto parts store. A conglomerate is formed through the combination of unrelated businesses.

Another type of combination of two companies is a consolidation. In a consolidation, an entirely new firm is created, and the two previous entities cease to exist. Consolidated financial statements are prepared under the assumption that two or more corporate entities are in actuality only one. The consolidated statements are prepared by combining the account balances of the individual firms after certain adjusting and eliminating entries are made.

Another way to acquire a firm is to buy the voting stock. This can be done by agreement of management or by tender offer. In a tender offer, the acquiring firm makes the offer to buy stock directly to the shareholders, thereby bypassing management. In contrast to a merger, a stock acquisition requires no stockholder voting. Shareholders wishing to keep their stock can simply do so. Also, a minority of shareholders may hold out in a tender offer.

A bidding firm can also buy another simply by purchasing all its **assets**. This involves a costly legal transfer of title and must be approved by the shareholders of the selling firm. A takeover is the transfer of control from one group to another. Normally, the acquiring firm (the bidder) makes an offer for the target firm. In a proxy contest, a group of dissident shareholders will seek to obtain enough votes to gain control of the board of directors.

TAXABLE VERSUS TAX-FREE TRANSACTIONS

Mergers and acquisitions can be either tax-free or taxable events. The tax status of a transaction may affect its value from both the buyer's and the seller's viewpoints. In a taxable acquisition, the assets of the selling firm are revalued or "written up." Therefore, the depreciation deduction will rise (assets are not revalued in a tax-free acquisition). But the selling shareholders will have to pay capital gains taxes and thus will want more for their shares to compensate. This is known as the capital gains effect. The capital gains and write-up effects tend to cancel each other out.

Certain exchanges of stock are considered tax-free reorganizations, which permit the owners of one company to exchange their shares for the stock of the acquirer without paying taxes. There are three basic types of tax-free reorganizations. In order for a transaction to qualify as a type A tax-free reorganization, it must be structured in certain ways. In contrast to a type B reorganization, the type A transaction allows the buyer to use either voting or nonvoting stock. It also permits the buyer to use more cash in the total consideration since the law does not stipulate a maximum amount of cash that can be used. At least 50 percent of the consideration, however, must be stock in the acquiring corporation. In addition, in a type A reorganization, the acquiring corporation may choose not to purchase all the target's assets.

In instances where at least 50 percent of the bidder's stock is used as the consideration—but other considerations such as cash, debt, or nonequity securities are also used—the transaction may be partially taxable. Capital gains taxes must be paid on those shares that were exchanged for nonequity consideration.

A type B reorganization requires that the acquiring corporation use mainly its own voting common stock as the consideration for purchase of the target corporation's common stock. Cash must comprise no more than 20 percent of the total consideration, and at least 80 percent of the target's stock must be paid for by voting stock by the bidder.

Target stockholders who receive the stock of the acquiring corporation in exchange for their common stock are not immediately taxed on the consideration they receive. Taxes will have to be paid only if the stock is eventually sold. If cash is included in the transaction, this cash may be taxed to the extent that it represents a gain on the sale of stock.

In a type C reorganization, the acquiring corporation must purchase 80 percent of the fair market value of the target's assets. In this type of reorganization, a tax liability results when the acquiring corporation purchases the assets of the target using consideration other than stock in the acquiring corporation. The tax liability is measured by comparing the purchase price of the assets with the adjusted basis of these assets.

FINANCIAL ACCOUNTING FOR MERGERS AND ACQUISITIONS

The two principal accounting methods used in mergers and acquisitions are the pooling of interests method and the purchase method. The main difference between them is the value that the combined firm's balance sheet places on the assets of the acquired firm, as well as the depreciation allowances and charges against income following the merger.

The pooling of interests method assumes that the transaction is simply an exchange of equity securities. Therefore, the capital stock account of the target firm is eliminated, and the acquirer issues new stock to replace it. The two firms' assets and liabilities are combined at their historical book values as of the acquisition date. The end result of a pooling of interests transaction is that the total assets of the combined firm are equal to the sum of the assets of the individual firms. No goodwill is generated, and there are no charges against earnings. A tax-free acquisition would normally be reported as a pooling of interests.

Under the purchase method, assets and liabilities are shown on the merged firm's books at their market (not book) values as of the acquisition date. This method is based on the idea that the resulting values should reflect the market values established during the bargaining process. The total liabilities of the combined firm equal the sum of the two firms' individual liabilities. The equity of the acquiring firm is increased by the amount of the purchase price.

Accounting for the excess of cost over the aggregate of the fair market values of the identifiable net assets acquired applies only in purchase accounting. The excess is called goodwill, an asset which is charged against income and amortized over a period that cannot exceed 40 years. Although the amortization "expense" is deducted from reported income, it cannot be deducted for tax purposes.

Purchase accounting usually results in increased depreciation charges because the book value of most assets is usually less than fair value because of inflation. For tax purposes, however, depreciation does not increase because the tax basis of the assets remains the same. Since depreciation under pooling accounting is based on the old book values of the assets, accounting income is usually higher under the pooling method. The accounting treatment has no cash flow consequences. Thus, value should be unaffected by accounting procedure. However, some firms may dislike the purchase method because of the goodwill created and the necessity of amortizing it over a period of years.

HOW TO VALUE AN ACQUISITION CANDIDATE

Valuing an acquisition candidate is similar to valuing any investment. The analyst estimates the incremental cash flows, determine an appropriate risk-adjusted discount rate, and the computes the net present value (NPV). If firm A is acquiring firm B, for example, then the acquisition makes economic sense if the value of the combined firm is greater than the value of firm A plus the value of firm B. Synergy is said to exist when the cash flow of the combined firm is greater than the sum of the cash flows for the two firms as separate companies. The gain from the merger is the present value of this difference in cash flows.

SOURCES OF GAINS FROM ACQUISITIONS The gains from an acquisition may result from one or more of the following five categories: 1) revenue enhancement; 2) cost reductions; 3) lower taxes; 4) changing **capital** requirements; or 5) a lower cost of capital. Increased revenues may come from marketing gains, strategic benefits, and market power. **Marketing** gains arise from more effective advertising, economies of distribution, and a better mix of products. Strategic benefits represent opportunities to enter new lines of business. Finally, a merger may reduce competition, thereby increasing market power. Such mergers, of course, may run afoul of antitrust legislation.

A larger firm may be able to operate more efficiently than two smaller firms, thereby reducing costs. Horizontal mergers may generate economies of scale. This means that the average production cost will fall as production volume increases. A vertical merger may allow a firm to decrease costs by more closely coordinating production and distribution. Finally, economies may be achieved when firms have complementary resources—for example, when one firm has excess production capacity and another has insufficient capacity.

Tax gains in mergers may arise because of unused tax losses, unused debt capacity, surplus funds, and the write-up of depreciable assets. The tax losses of target corporations can be used to offset the acquiring corporation's future income. These tax losses can be used to offset income for a maximum of 15 years or until the tax loss is exhausted. Only tax losses for the previous three years can be used to offset future income.

Tax loss carry-forwards can motivate mergers and acquisitions. A company that has earned profits may find value in the tax losses of a target corporation that can be used to offset the income it plans to earn. A merger may not, however, be structured solely for tax purposes. In addition, the acquirer must continue to operate the pre-acquisition business of the company in a net loss position. The tax benefits may be less than their "face value," not only because of the time value of money, but also because the tax loss carry-forwards might expire without being fully utilized.

Tax advantages can also arise in an acquisition when a target firm carries assets on its books with basis, for tax purposes, below their market value. These assets could be more valuable, for tax purposes, if they were owned by another corporation that could increase their tax basis following the acquisition. The acquirer would then depreciate the assets based on the higher market values, in turn, gaining additional depreciation benefits.

Interest payments on debt are a tax-deductible expense, whereas dividend payments from equity ownership are not. The existence of a tax advantage for debt is an incentive to have greater use of debt, as opposed to equity, as the means of financing merger and acquisition transactions. Also, a firm that borrows much less than it could may be an acquisition target because of its unused debt capacity. While the use of financial leverage produces tax benefits, debt also increases the likelihood of financial distress in the event that the acquiring firm cannot meet its interest payments on the acquisition debt.

Finally, a firm with surplus funds may wish to acquire another firm. The reason is that distributing the money as a dividend or using it to repurchase shares will increase income taxes for shareholders. With an acquisition, no income taxes are paid by shareholders.

Acquiring firms may be able to more efficiently utilize working capital and fixed assets in the target firm, thereby reducing capital requirements and en-hancing profitability. This is particularly true if the target firm has redundant assets that may be divested.

The cost of debt can often be reduced when two firms merge. The combined firm will generally have reduced variability in its cash flows. Therefore, there may be circumstances under which one or the other of the firms would have defaulted on its debt, but the combined firm will not. This makes the debt safer, and the cost of borrowing may decline as a result. This is termed the coinsurance effect.

Diversification is often cited as a benefit in mergers. Diversification by itself, however, does not create any value because stockholders can accomplish the same thing as the merger by buying stock in both firms.

VALUATION PROCEDURES The procedure for valuing an acquisition candidate depends on the source of the estimated gains. Different sources of synergy have different risks. Tax gains can be estimated fairly accurately and should be discounted at the cost of debt. Cost reductions through operating efficiencies can also be determined with some confidence. Such savings should be discounted at a normal weighted average cost of capital. Gains from strategic benefits are difficult to estimate and are often highly uncertain. A discount rate greater than the overall cost of capital would thus be appropriate.

The net present value (NPV) of the acquisition is equal to the gains less the cost of the acquisition. The cost depends on whether cash or stock is used as payment. The cost of an acquisition when cash is used is just the amount paid. The cost of the merger when common stock is used as the consideration (the payment) is equal to the percentage of the new firm that is owned by the previous shareholders in the acquired firm multiplied by the value of the new firm. In a cash merger the benefits go entirely to the acquiring firm, whereas in a stock-for-stock exchange the benefits are shared by the acquiring and acquired firms.

Whether to use cash or stock depends on three considerations. First, if the acquiring firm's management believes that its stock is overvalued, then a stock acquisition may be cheaper. Second, a cash acquisition is usually taxable, which may result in a higher price. Third, the use of stock means that the acquired firm will share in any gains from merger; if the merger has a negative NPV, however, then the acquired firm will share in the loss.

In valuing acquisitions, the following factors should be kept in mind. First, market values must not be ignored. Thus, there is no need to estimate the value of a publicly traded firm as a separate entity. Second, only those cash flows that are incremental are relevant to the analysis. Third, the discount rate used should reflect the risk associated with the incremental cash flows. Therefore, the acquiring firm should not use its own cost of capital to value the cash flows of another firm. Finally, acquisition may involve significant investment banking fees and costs.

HOSTILE ACQUISITIONS

The replacement of poor management is a potential source of gain from acquisition. Changing technological and competitive factors may lead to a need for corporate restructuring. If incumbent management is unable to adapt, then a hostile acquisition is one method for accomplishing change.

Hostile acquisitions generally involve poorly performing firms in mature industries, and occur when the board of directors of the target is opposed to the sale of the company. In this case, the acquiring firm has two options to proceed with the acquisition—a tender offer or a proxy fight. A tender offer represents an offer to buy the stock of the target firm either directly from the firm's shareholders or through the secondary market. In a proxy fight, the acquirer solicits the shareholders of the target firm in an attempt to obtain the right to vote their shares. The acquiring firm hopes to secure enough proxies to gain control of the board of directors and, in turn, replace the incumbent management.

Management in target firms will typically resist takeover attempts either to get a higher price for the firm or to protect its own self-interest. This can be done a number of ways. Target companies can decrease the likelihood of a takeover though charter amendments. With the staggered board technique, the board of directors is classified into three groups, with only one group elected each year. Thus, the suitor cannot obtain control of the board immediately even though it may have acquired a majority ownership of the target via a tender offer. Under a supermajority amendment, a higher percentage than 50 percent—generally two-thirds or 80 percent—is required to approve a merger.

Other defensive tactics include poison pills and dual class recapitalizations. With poison pills, existing shareholders are issued rights which, if a bidder acquires a certain percentage of the outstanding shares, can be used to purchase additional shares at a bargain price, usually half the market price. Dual class recapitalizations distribute a new class of equity with superior voting rights. This enables the target firm's managers to obtain majority control even though they do not own a majority of the shares.

Other preventative measures occur after an unsolicited offer is made to the target firm. The target may file suit against the bidder alleging violations of antitrust or securities laws. Alternatively, the target may engage in asset and liability restructuring to make it an unattractive target. With asset restructuring, the target purchases assets that the bidder does not want or that will create antitrust problems, or sells off the assets that the suitor desires to obtain. Liability restructuring maneuvers include issuing shares to a friendly third party to dilute the bidder's ownership position or leveraging up the firm through a leveraged recapitalization making it difficult for the suitor to finance the transaction.

Other postoffer tactics involve targeted share repurchases (often termed ''greenmail'')—in which the target repurchases the shares of an unfriendly suitor at a premium over the current market price—and golden parachutes—which are lucrative supplemental compensation packages for the target firm's management. These packages are activated in the case of a takeover and the subsequent resignations of the senior executives. Finally, the target may employ an exclusionary self-tender. With this tactic, the target firm offers to buy back its own stock at a premium from everyone except the bidder.

A privately owned firm is not subject to unfriendly takeovers. A publicly traded firm ''goes private'' when a group, usually involving existing management, buys up all the publicly held stock. Such transactions are typically structured as **leveraged buyouts (LBOs)**. LBOs are financed primarily with debt secured by the assets of the target firm.

DO ACQUISITIONS BENEFIT SHAREHOLDERS?

There is substantial empirical evidence that the shareholders in acquired firms benefit substantially. Gains for this group typically amount to 20 percent in mergers and 30 percent in tender offers above the market prices prevailing a month prior to the merger announcement.

The gains to acquiring firms are difficult to measure. The best evidence suggests that shareholders in bidding firms gain little. Losses in value subsequent to merger announcements are not unusual. This seems to suggest that overvaluation by bidding firms is common. Managers may also have incentives to increase firm size at the potential expense of shareholder wealth. If so, merger activity may happen for noneconomic reasons, to the detriment of shareholders.

FURTHER READING:

Auerbach, Alan J. *Corporate Takeovers: Causes and Consequences.* Chicago, IL: University of Chicago Press, 1988.

Brealey, Richard A., and Stewart C. Myers. *Principles of Corporate Finance.* 4th ed. New York: McGraw-Hill, 1991.

Coffee, John C., Jr., Louis Lowenstein, and Susan Rose-Ackerman. *Knights, Raiders, and Targets: The Impact of the Hostile Takeover.* New York: Oxford University Press, 1988.

Gaughan, Patrick A. *Mergers and Acquisitions*. New York: HarperCollins, 1991.

McGarvey, Robert. "Merge Ahead: Before You Go Full-Speed into a Merger, Read This." *Entrepreneur*. October 1997.

Sherman, Andrew J. *Running and Growing Your Business*. New York: Random House, 1997.

SEE ALSO: Buying an Existing Business; Investor Relations and Reporting; Stocks; Tax Planning

METROPOLITAN STATISTICAL AREA

A Metropolitan Statistical Area (MSA) is a designation the U.S. government uses to refer to a region that, broadly speaking, consists of a city and its suburbs, plus any surrounding communities that are closely linked to the city because of social and/or economical factors. MSAs were known as Standard Metropolitan Statistical Areas (SMSAs) from 1959 to 1983 and, before that, as Standard Metropolitan Areas (SMAs).

Familiarity with MSAs can be most useful to small business owners, for statistical data about the demographic character of these regions can be helpful in devising marketing strategies, delineating sales territories, and determining the appropriate locations of operating facilities. Such information can be invaluable not only for the entrepreneur seeking to launch a new business, but for the established small business owner seeking to expand operations or anticipate marketplace trends.

The government uses the designation MSA for the purpose of applying uniform and consistent standards to the wealth of data collected, analyzed, and published by its myriad departments and agencies. Official definitions for what constitutes an MSA are developed, issued, and periodically revised by the federal Office of Management and Budget (OMB), following public commentary and hearings. These revisions are made in conjunction with the Federal Executive Committee on Metropolitan Areas. In fact, since the MSA and similar designations figure prominently in the compilation of statistics for the national census, the U.S. Department of Commerce's Bureau of the Census also has a voice in determining MSA definitions.

Although the OMB's official standards for defining these regions are highly complex, detailed, and marked by qualifications, MSAs are commonly defined as regions composed of one or more counties containing either: 1) a city with a population of at least 50,000 people, or 2) a Census Bureau-defined "urbanized area" with a population that, when combined with that of its component county or counties, totals at least 100,000 people. An important exception to how MSAs are defined exists in the New England states, however. In that region of the country, towns and cities rather than counties are used to designate regions as MSAs, and the total metropolitan population of the previously-mentioned "urbanized area" need only be 75,000 people. The Office of Management and Budget also notes that the MSA may include other "central" counties (any county with at least half of its population within the 'urbanized' area) and "outlying" counties that satisfy specific criteria of metropolitan character and integration with the central counties, as indicated by population density, growth, urbanization, and levels of commuting.

A region that meets these requirements for recognition as an MSA and also has a population of one million inhabitants or more may be recognized as a Consolidated Metropolitan Statistical Area (CMSA) under the following conditions: 1) separate component areas can be identified within the entire area according to specific statistical criteria, and 2) local public opinion supports the idea of the component areas. If recognized, these component areas are designated as Primary Metropolitan Statistical Areas (PMSAs). As with the CMSAs, PMSAs are composed of one or more counties (except in New England). If no PMSAs are formally recognized, however, the entire area is designated as an MSA.

The largest city in each MSA or CMSA is formally designated a "central city." Additional cities qualify if specified requirements are met in areas such as population and commuting patterns. The title of each MSA consists of the names of up to three of its central cities and the name of each state into which the MSA extends. There is an exception to this, however. Unless local public opinion voices support for including the name in the MSA title, cities with fewer than 250,000 inhabitants and less than one-third of the population of the MSA's largest city will not be included in the title.

As of June 30, 1996, there were 255 Metropolitan Statistical Areas in the United States. There were also 18 Consolidated Metropolitan Statistical Areas comprising 73 Primary Metropolitan Statistical Areas. In addition, there were 1 CMSA, 3 PMSAs, and 3 MSAs in Puerto Rico.

Information on the OMB's standards for defining MSAs and other such designations can be obtained from the Statistical Policy Office of the Office of Information and Regulatory Affairs, Office of Management and Budget in Washington, D.C. Information on the Census Bureau's application of these standards is available from the Secretary of the Federal Executive Committee on Metropolitan Areas, Population Division, U.S. Bureau of the Census, also in Washington, D.C.

SEE ALSO: Business Site Selection; Census Data

MEZZANINE FINANCING

Mezzanine financing, also sometimes referred to as subordinated debt or financing, is a rarely used but viable financing option for small businesses in search of **capital** for rapid growth. Under this arrangement, an entrepreneur borrows some of the money that he or she requires to execute the next stage of company growth (whether through acquisition, expansion of existing operations, etc.), then raises additional funds by selling stock in the company to the same lenders. Mezzanine debt is usually unsecured or junior debt that is subordinate to traditional loans or senior debt. "Subordinated debt is an extremely flexible form of financing," wrote Lawrence M. Levine in *Business Credit.* "Because they are more concerned than senior lenders about their overall yield, mezzanine lenders are very liberal in tailoring their investment to meet the financial, operating, and long-term cash flow needs of the borrower. As long as the subordinated lender's anticipated yield is satisfied, they can be flexible as to the amortization of the loan and the interest rate." Major sources of mezzanine financing include private investors, insurance companies, mutual funds, pension funds, and banks.

Business experts point to mezzanine financing as a particularly provocative financing option for some companies that have moved beyond start-up status but do not yet have the wherewithal to finance big growth moves themselves or via traditional lending arrangements. Indeed, Juan Hovey observed in *Nation's Business* that mezzanine financing owes its very name to the fact that "it raises growth capital for firms that are well beyond the start-up stage but not yet far enough off the ground to go public." Entrepreneurs launching start-up businesses, though, should be aware that this method is not viable for them; lenders willing to make this kind of deal will require prospective borrowers to show a proven record of substantial cash flow before they will even entertain the idea.

But for growing companies with a strong cash flow, mezzanine financing may be the answer. Certainly, the amounts that can be raised via mezzanine financing are substantial. According to *Private Placement Letter,* mezzanine financing raised more than $820 million in 1996 for companies of all sizes, and other sources place the amount considerably higher. Larger companies account for some of this activity, but analysts indicate that even modest-sized companies ($10-12 million in revenues) can expect to raise as much as $15-$20 million through this route. As one investment executive told *Nation's Business,* "a company can leverage two to three times its cash flow in senior secured debt. It can raise total debt to four to five times cash flow with a mezzanine deal. So if the company is doing $2 million in cash flow, it can probably raise $4 million to $6 million in senior debt and $4 million to $5 million more in mezzanine financing, for a total debt of $10 million, or five times cash flow."

Most experts believe that the use of mezzanine financing will continue to grow among both small and large companies. "More and more U.S. companies are committed to financial restructuring in order to create the incentives to maximize business value," stated mezzanine investment executive Robert F. Perille in *Corporate Cashflow Magazine.* "In addition, as our economy has become increasingly service-oriented and entrepreneurial, thousands of excellent companies no longer meet the asset-based formulas of commercial banks. These companies need financing to grow or facilitate a change in ownership, but they do not want to issue relatively expensive equity. This growing demand, coupled with an increasing supply of mezzanine capital from a diverse base of institutional investors, will assure mezzanine financing a place in future capital structures."

HOW MEZZANINE FINANCING WORKS

In a mezzanine financing arrangement, the borrower negotiates an arrangement with a lender wherein the necessary capital is secured by combining a loan with a stock purchase to the lender.

"As a rule, you pay only interest on the money you borrow (at prime plus two to four points) for five years or so," explained Hovey. "At that point, you [the business owner] cash out your investors by going public or by recapitalizing your business in a new round of financing. Your investors, meanwhile, have earned interest on their loans, and if the value of your business has increased, they realize capital gains by selling their stock in your company."

Lenders that review mezzanine financing requests closely examine several facets of the prospective borrower's business when weighing the deal. The most important consideration examined by a mezzanine lender is the company's capacity to generate cash flow. As Levine stated, "because the primary concern of a subordinated lender is a company's ability to generate cash, if it is anticipated that the business' cash flow is sufficient to repay the loan, it is quite likely subordinated debt can be used." In addition to cash flow, lenders also examine ownership flexibility, company history, growth strategy, and acquisition targets (when applicable). Business owners in need of capital, meanwhile, should do some comparison shopping of their own. "In selecting a source for mezzanine financing, companies should pay attention to personnel turnover, commitment to the business, track record, and flexibility in structuring," indicated Perille. "Low turnover and commitment to the business are key because businesses rarely perform exactly according to plan. Therefore, you need an investor who understands the business and will respond consistently and appropriately.''

ADVANTAGES AND DISADVANTAGES

As with most other types of financing, mezzanine financing includes both benefits and drawbacks for the small business owner.

ADVANTAGES

1) Even though the owner loses some independence, he or she rarely loses outright control of the company or its direction. Provided the company continues to grow and prosper, its owners are unlikely to encounter any interference from their lender.

2) The flexibility of the arrangement is often a big plus; ''[mezzanine financing] offers considerably more flexibility to structure coupon, amortization and covenants to accommodate the specific cash flow requirements of the business,'' wrote Perille.

3) Lenders who are willing to enter into the world of mezzanine financing tend to be long-term investors rather than people looking to make a quick killing.

4) Mezzanine lenders can provide valuable strategic assistance. ''Subordinated debt advisors often bring fresh insights to businesses because they are financially sophisticated and have a great deal of experience developing strategies to maximize long-term value,'' said Levine.

5) Mezzanine financing increases the value of stock held by existing shareholders, even though they will not have as great an ownership stake. Levine noted, for example, that a $10-million company that added $3 million of subordinated debt would be worth $13 million: ''If the shareholders' ownership interests decrease from 100 percent of $10 million to 90 percent of $13 million, the shareholder has seen the value of his holding increase by $1.7 million ($11.7 million vs. $10 million).

6) Most importantly, mezzanine financing provides business owners with the capital they need to acquire another business or expand into another production or market area.

DISADVANTAGES

1) Mezzanine financing does require the business owner to relinquish some measure of control over the firm. This can be difficult for entrepreneurs who have built a promising business in no small measure because of decision making styles that run heavily toward independence and daring. Moreover, Perille pointed out that ''mezzanine investors with long-term incentives like co-investment plans or carried-interest plans, which provide their professionals with a meaningful stake in the business, are more likely to be there for the long term and take a partnership perspective,'' and Levine added that the lender will have a vote on the company's board of directors and significant abilities to take decisive action if the company does not meet its financial projections.

2) Subordinated debt agreements may include restrictive covenants. Writing in *Journal of Business Strategy,* Kent Gross and Amin Amiri pointed out that since mezzanine lenders usually do not have any direct security interest in the assets of the borrower, lenders typically incorporate restrictive covenants into the loans that the borrower has to abide by; these include agreements by the lender not to borrow more money, refinance senior debt from traditional loans, or create additional security interests in the assets, as well as the various financial ratios that the borrower must meet.

3) Similarly, business owners who agree to mezzanine financing may be forced to accept restrictions in how they spend their money in certain areas, such as compensation of important personnel (in such instances, a business owner may not be able to offer above-market packages to current or prospective employees). In some cases, business owners have even been asked to take pay cuts themselves and/or limit dividend payouts.

4) Mezzanine financing is more expensive than traditional or senior debt arrangements.

5) Arranging for mezzanine financing can be an arduous, lengthy process. Most mezzanine deals will take at least three months to arrange, and many will take twice that long to complete.

FURTHER READING:

Brooks, Rory, and Jim Read. ''Mezzanine Gains Ground.'' *Investors Chronicle.* October 21, 1994.

Campbell, Katharine. ''Development Capital is Industrial Strength.'' *Financial Times.* December 2, 1997.

Conder, Martin. ''Management's Flexible Friend.'' *Acquisitions Monthly.* October 1994.

Gross, Kent, and Amin Amiri. ''Flexible Financing with Mezzanine Debt.'' *Journal of Business Strategy.* March-April 1990.

Hovey, Juan. ''A Little-Known Pathway to Growth.'' *Nation's Business.* March 1998.

Levine, Lawrence M. ''The Role of Subordinated Debt in Financing.'' *Business Credit.* May 1995.

Penman, Angus. ''Direct Financing Arrives.'' *Acquisitions Monthly.* October 1995.

Perille, Robert F. ''Mezzanine: Efficient Financing for Recapitalization or Rapid Growth.'' *Corporate Cashflow Magazine.* May 1996.

Wheatley, Simon. ''Alive and Kicking?'' *Acquisitions Monthly.* October 1996.

SEE ALSO: Business Expansion

MINIMUM WAGE

For small business owners employing those other than themselves, **employee compensation** can be a complex issue. Increasingly, creative compensation packages, such as performance-based compensation and others, are gaining acceptance and changing the way businesses pay their workers. One mode of compensation, though, is still ubiquitous: minimum wage.

Minimum wage regulations, enacted by the federal government, set the lowest level at which workers may be compensated by their employers. Changes in the minimum wage affect a large portion of the U.S. workforce. According to the *Wall Street Journal*, an estimated 10 million workers will be affected by recent changes in wage legislation. The overwhelming majority of minimum wage workers—90 percent—are employed in the private sector. Retail outlets, restaurants and hotels, and private households (which may employ housekeepers, gardeners, etc.) most often pay minimum wage. According to the Labor Department, of those likely to be affected by the increase in the minimum wage, only about one-third are youths ages 16 to 19, and just over half are part-time workers.

THE WAGE BILL AND SMALL BUSINESS JOB PROTECTION ACTS

Two recent enactments will affect the way small business owners compensate their minimum wage workers. Passed concurrently and often jointly referred to as the **Small Business Job Protection Act (SBJA) of 1996** (H.R. 3448), the acts misleadingly impact a much greater range of issues than simply wages. For instance, SBJA increases incrementally the amount a small business can deduct for equipment purchases from $17,500 currently to $25,000 in 2003. The bill also makes it easier for companies to avoid the problem of misclassifying an independent contractor as an employee, simplifies and liberalizes S corporation procedures, and makes it easier for small business owners to provide pension and retirement plans and spousal IRAs for their employees.

Most importantly however, it sets the new minimum wage rate. The rate is now $5.15 per hour, replacing the previous minimum, which was 4.75, effective as of October 1996. That rate boosted the minimum wage from $4.25, where it had been for five years. Although the new change means an average increase in yearly earnings of nearly $2,000 for full time minimum wage workers, some estimates have suggested that the minimum wage needs to be increased to $7.25 by the year 2002 to get families over the poverty line. At $5.15, annual income for a full time workers will be about $10,300 (mid-1990s government estimates indicated that the poverty level for a family of four was about $15,600). Bills are already being debated in Congress that would gradually increase the minimum wage to $7.25, but the prospects for passage of such a bill are uncertain at best.

WEATHERING THE CHANGES

As a small business owner, it is important to build in budgetary adjustments in advance of wage changes, as one might for any planned raises. Keeping abreast of legislative trends may help keep accounting procedures flexible.

Of course, not all small business owners are impacted by changes in minimum wage to the same degree. Some businesses rely heavily on a minimum wage work force, while others utilize workers who make significantly more than that base wage. The industry in which a business operates is usually the most important factor in determining wages paid, but geographic location can also be a key component. As one McDonald's corporation franchisee in Vail, Colorado, noted in the *Wall Street Journal*, ''Supply and demand matter more than minimum wage.'' This Vail franchise operator paid his employees some seven dollars per hour, higher than the typical McDonald's wage, because area skiing venues, hotels, and retailers all compete for the same limited employment pool. Some businesses are limited in their ability to make up for this reality in other parts of their operation, such as passing along higher workforce costs to the consumer in the form of higher prices. While this is an option for some companies, others operating in a competitive environment may simply have to accept diminished profit margin as a fact of life, at least for the near term, or cast about for savings elsewhere in the operation.

Still, some business analysts indicate that there are tangible advantages associated with paying employees above the minimum wage. In fact, according to a recent survey of small businesses conducted by National Small Business United and Arthur Andersen's Enterprise Group (in which 22 percent of respondents indicated that they paid at least a portion of their work force a minimum wage), higher-than-minimum wage structures have their advantages:

1) Fluctuations in the base wage, which is controlled by the federal government, will not impact a business that pays higher-than-minimum nearly as much as one that holds tightly to minimum wage to determine its payroll.

2) Employers that pay higher wages have better choices for new hires. Higher salaries mean better people because a larger group of candidates will be attracted to the open position(s).

3) Competitive salaries curb turnover. Workers are less tempted by other employers because they already make more than they would elsewhere. A stable workforce translated into fewer hours training and higher productivity.

OTHER STRATEGIES

Paying above the minimum wage is not the only way to cope, of course. The *Wall Street Journal* cites several other strategies that businesses use. They include:

1) Slash hours, but not jobs. This offsets the payroll impact, keeps workers' salaries stable, and perhaps most importantly prevents businesses from laying off workers they otherwise would not be able to afford.

2) Increase prices, but selectively. Businesses offering a variety of products or services can increase prices on a few, without giving customers the impression that they are getting hit at every turn.

3) Hire more carefully. Because wages comprise a very high proportion of a businesses budget, every dollar counts. For instance, the *Wall Street Journal* noted that one businessman, Edward R. Tinsey III, president of K-Bob's Steakhouses, prepared for the minimum wage increase by selectively raising menu prices and giving potential hires assessment profiles that are analyzed by a third party to make sure that his increased work force expenditures are well spent.

CONCLUSION

The recent increase in the minimum wage will have a widely varying impact on businesses. This is due to the fact that the majority already pay more than minimum wage. Those who do pay minimum wage, however, will have to shift their resources creatively in order to offset shortfalls. In any case, small business consultants—and even many small business owners—have indicated that the minimum wage issue, while it does have an impact on some small business operations, is not the most important issue confronting the small business entrepreneur. A recent survey by the National Federation of Independent Businesses, for instance, indicated that although 82 percent of their members were against the minimum wage hike, they ranked a minimum wage increase as 62nd in importance on a list of 72 issues that concerned them.

FURTHER READING:

Boulton, Guy. ''Small Businesses Fear, Workers Eager for Coming Rise in Minimum Wage.'' *The Wichita Eagle.* August 11, 1996.

Carroll, Rick. ''Minimum-Wage Hike: A Small Part of New Legislation.'' *Dallas Business Journal*, September 6, 1996.

Duff, Christina. ''New Minimum Wage Makes Few Waves.'' *Wall Street Journal*, November 20, 1996.

Evanson, David R. ''Blue Skies?'' *Entrepreneur.* November 1996.

''Federal Minimum Wage Increases to $5.15 an Hour.'' *Wall Street Journal*, September 2, 1997.

''Minimum Wage Debate May Escalate, with Bid to Boost Pay to $7.25 by 2002.'' *Wall Street Journal*, August 5, 1997.

Mehta, Stephanie N., and Michael Selz. ''New Proposals to Raise Minimum Wage Worry Some Small Employers.'' *Wall Street Journal*, Aug. 23, 1995.

Schmitt, Eric. ''Labor and Business Fight For Senate Vote on Wage.'' *The New York Times*, July 8, 1996.

MINORITY BUSINESS DEVELOPMENT AGENCY

Established in 1969 by executive order, the Minority Business Development Agency (MBDA) works to foster the creation, growth, and expansion of minority-owned businesses in the United States as a part of the **U.S. Department of Commerce**. The agency was originally called the Office of Minority Business Enterprise (OMBE), but its name was changed to its current incarnation in 1979.

The MBDA describes its mission as one of several facets, including: 1) coordination of federal government plans, programs, and operations that affect minority business enterprises; 2) promotion and coordination of activities of government and private organizations that help minority businesses grow; 3) collection and dissemination of information that will help those interested in establishing or expanding a successful **minority-owned business**; and 4) funding organizations to provide management and technical assistance to minority entrepreneurs. A wide range of individuals are eligible for MBDA assistance, including Hispanic Americans, Asian and Pacific Island Americans, Alaska Natives and Native Americans, African Americans, and Hasidic Jews.

The Minority Business Development Agency's primary headquarters are located in Washington, D.C., but it also maintains five regional offices (in Atlanta, Chicago, Dallas, New York, and San Francisco) and four district offices (in Miami, Boston, Philadelphia, and Los Angeles), as well as a group of local community-based outreach centers across the country. The centers are generally ensconced in regions that feature a large concentration of minority populations and large numbers of minority-owned businesses. These facilities include Minority Business Development Centers (MBDC), Native American Business Development Centers (NABDC), Business Resource Centers (BRC), and Minority Business Opportunity Committees (MBOC) that offer a variety of programs to assist minority entrepreneurs, including providing one-on-one assistance in writing business plans, marketing, management assistance, technical assistance, financial planning, and securing financing for business ventures. While these centers provide minority entrepreneurs with help in locating sources of financing and preparing loan proposals, they do not have any authority to make grants, loans, or loan guarantees to any qualified businessperson who wishes to purchase, start, or expand a small business. These centers are operated by private firms, government agencies (both state and local), educational institutions, and Native American tribes.

In recent years, the MBDA has also shown an increased emphasis on making certain that minority entrepreneurs are able to compete in the international marketplace. In 1992, for instance, it entered into an agreement with the International Trade Administration (ITA) to assist American minority entrepreneurs in their efforts to negotiate **exporting** hurdles and compete in foreign markets. Shortly after consummating this agreement, the MBDA launched its International Trade Initiative, which, according to *Business America*'s Linda L. Richardson, "closes the information gap for minority-owned firms having no direct knowledge or experience of exporting. The Agency's services initiatives provide basic data—export marketing plans, potential markets, trade leads, and technical assistance—to assist minority-owned firms in becoming 'export-ready' and to profit from the export assistance services provided by the U.S. Commercial Service." In addition, the MBDA has organized several "Development Matchmakers" delegations of minority business owners to foreign destinations. Minority-owned firms participating in the trade delegations have hailed from a wide range of industries, from medical supplies and waste management to retail, clothing manufacturing, engineering,

and architecture sectors. "In addition to practical information on how to do business overseas, the program puts Matchmaker participants in direct contact with prospective business partners, prescreened by the Commerce Department's overseas commercial staff," noted *Business America* contributor Judy Riendeau. "Matchmakers are extremely cost competitive, and offer an excellent way to develop contacts with others in the minority business community. The synergies created by being part of a 30-member delegation make Matchmaker an ideal vehicle for companies to exchange information about business opportunities in the United States, as well as other overseas markets of interest."

For more information on MBDA programs, minority entrepreneurs can contact the agency via e-mail (mbda@doc.gov), the telephone (202-482-4547), or on the Internet (http://www.doc.gov/agencies/mbda/index.html).

FURTHER READING:

"Frequently Asked Questions About the MBDA." Washington: Minority Business Development Agency.

Jones, Joyce. "Second Time Around: The MBDA Gets Its Second New Director for the Year." *Black Enterprise.* September 1995.

Richardson, Linda L. "Minority Business Development Agency Helps Minority-Owned Firms Overcome Export Hurdles and Compete in the International Marketplace." *Business America.* September 1995.

Riendeau, Judy. "Matchmaker Events Planned for Minority Companies." *Business America.* June 1994.

MINORITY-OWNED BUSINESSES

Minority-owned businesses are among the most important elements in the unprecedented growth, in both number and stature, of small business enterprises in the United States over the past several years. Indeed, during the 1980s and 1990s, the African-American, Hispanic, Asian, and Native American communities have all seen significant surges in small business start-ups and growth. This success has been attributed both to generally positive economic trends and advances in the realms of education and access to capital. Most observers agree, however, that minority entrepreneurs—like **women entrepreneurs** of all races—still face challenges that their white male counterparts are able to avoid. Racism remains a sad reality in some communities, industries, and corporate environments. In addition, many minority entrepreneurs believe that affirmative action programs and "set-asides," which have become a subject of considerable debate in the 1990s, remain an important factor in the success of many minority-owned businesses, and they worry that if such programs are eliminated, countless minority-owned companies will be devastated. Despite lingering racism and the uncertainty surrounding affirmative action, however, minority entrepreneurs have carved out significant business niches for themselves across the nation in both ethnic neighborhoods and majority-white communities.

Indeed, members of African American, Hispanic, Asian, Native American, Arab, and other minority groups have pursued entrepreneurial dreams in record numbers, despite the challenges and pitfalls that lurk with any new small business venture. "A number of challenges confront the courageous souls who aspire to be in business for themselves," wrote Suzanne Caplan, author of *A Piece of the Action.* "The work is hard, the hours long, the pressures are great, and the rewards are sometimes elusive. When racism and sexism are added, an additional hurdle must be jumped. But even with these daunting obstacles, most [minority entrepreneurs] who have done it would do it again if they were asked. The desire to be creative and independent outweighs the prejudice and misconceptions."

GROWTH OF MINORITY-OWNED ENTERPRISES

In the 1980s and 1990s, various surveys showed a pronounced increase in the number of minority business enterprises. This rapid growth, suggested *American Demographics,* "is changing the profile of America's business owners." The magazine noted, for example, that the number of minority-owned businesses rose from less than 750,000 in 1982 to more than 1.2 million in 1987, nearly one-tenth of all of the nation's businesses. This marked an increase of 66 percent during a period when the total number of all American businesses grew by only 14 percent. "The mid-1980s were good years for minority business owners," wrote *American Demographics* contributor William O'Hara. "Every significant minority group experienced an increase in the number of businesses owned and in rates of business ownership. But some minority groups have much higher rates of business ownership than others, and the increases of the mid-1980s were not evenly shared."

Indeed, studies indicated that Asians experienced the biggest increase in small business success. The number of companies owned by Asians (including people of Japanese, Korean, Vietnamese, and Chinese descent) grew by 89 percent from 1982 to 1987. "The popular image of Asians as industrious immigrants is true," said O'Hara. "Asians own 57 businesses for every 1,000 people, by far the highest business ownership rate of the four major [ethnic groups in America]. . . . The high rate of business ownership among Asians is due to several factors. First is their high level of

educational attainment. In 1990, about 40 percent of adult Asian Americans had completed college, compared with only 23 percent of non-Hispanic whites. Asian Americans also have relatively high incomes, which provide them with more capital to launch small businesses." Finally, *American Demographics* pointed out that many recent immigrants from Asian countries come to the United States specifically to establish themselves in the business world, either as part of a larger company or as an entrepreneur. American government statistics indicated that whereas nearly 40 percent of immigrants from Asia and the Pacific Islands were engaged in professional or executive career areas, only 17 percent of immigrants from other parts of the world claimed such occupations. In addition, statistics have indicated that Asians—in large part because of their education and financial resources—tend to own larger companies with more employees than do other minorities. Finally, O'Hara noted that some Asian subgroups, such as Koreans—which have enjoyed perhaps the highest level of entrepreneurial success of any ethnic group—have shown a "willingness to pool their resources to help other Koreans start or expand a business."

Hispanic-owned businesses have also enjoyed significant increases in numbers and stature over the past several years. The number of Hispanic-owned firms grew by 81 percent from 1982 to 1987, due in large part to the tremendous success that entrepreneurs of Cuban descent have enjoyed. For that same period, business growth was comparatively weak among black-owned businesses (38 percent). And in the early 1990s statistics indicated that African Americans owned fewer than five percent of U.S. businesses even though they comprise about 12 percent of the nation's population. Nonetheless, business experts and economists have noted that black and Hispanic entrepreneurs have been among the biggest beneficiaries of America's sustained economic growth in the 1990s. Indeed, *Hispanic Business* magazine estimated that the number of Hispanic-owned businesses in the United States increased from about 420,000 in 1987 to approximately 585,000 in the mid-1990s. *Black Enterprise* magazine, meanwhile, pointed out that when it published its first list of the top 100 black-owned industrial businesses in 1973, their combined annual sales totaled $473 million; conversely, the total from its 1995 listing of black-owned businesses was more than $6.7 billion.

The last major ethnic group in the United States are Native Americans. American Indians are less likely than any other major American racial and ethnic group to own their own business. However, researchers contend that the relative scarcity of Native American small business owners can be traced in large part to the fact that many Indians live on remote, sparsely populated reservations in states that are themselves relatively lightly populated.

FACTORS IN MINORITY BUSINESS GROWTH

Analysts cite several reasons for the explosive growth in minority-owned businesses in the United States over the past two decades. Certainly, affirmative action programs and general economic trends have been significant influences. But observers also cite several other factors, including community support, increased networking, efforts to revitalize inner cities, increased levels of education and business experience, and improved access to capital.

- Community Support—Many entrepreneurial ethnic minorities benefit by instituting businesses within their communities that meet needs of that community. When these businesses succeed, the individual communities gain a greater measure of autonomy and financial health, thus laying the groundwork for additional businesses. Community banks have been among the most visible supporters of minority entrepreneurs seeking to revitalize moribund neighborhood and business districts. Finally, many immigrant groups have done a laudable job of supporting entrepreneurs within their communities.

- Increased **Networking**—As the number of minority entrepreneurs has grown, so too has the number of organizations, associations, and other groups that have formed to provide assistance and information to minority-owned businesses. In addition, minority entrepreneurs have become adept at taking advantage of established business practices such as networking to assist them in opening their own firms. Networking—interactions among business people for the purpose of discussing mutual problems, solutions, and opportunities—is extremely important to minority business owners.

- Programs—In addition to federal set-aside programs, a variety of local, state, and federal agencies have extended help—whether in the form of legal expertise, grants, loans, or some other type of assistance—to encourage the establishment of minority-owned businesses.

- Corporate Acceptance—Observers point to increased corporate acceptance of minority-owned businesses as a key factor in the successes that minority-owned enterprises have registered over the past two decades. "Well-established companies are buying from minority businesses as never before," wrote Nolton. "Corporations that are members of the National Minority Supplier Development Council now purchase more than $23 billion in goods and services annually from minority firms—compared with $86 million in 1972, when the council was chartered."

- Urban Revitalization—Many minority entrepreneurs have established themselves as business owners in urban areas at a time when several large cities have experienced heartening signs of rebirth. Moreover, state and federal agencies have shown increased willingness to provide greater assistance to business owners and others who are intent on reversing declines in urban areas, which typically contain large minority populations. "The breakthroughs being made in minority-business development could lead to solutions for breaking the cycles of poverty that so deeply affect minority communities," said *Nation's Business* writer Sharon Nolton.

- Higher Levels of Education and Business Experience—As one executive with the National Minority Supplier Development Council told *Nation's Business,* modern-day minority-owned businesses are significantly stronger than they used to be in several important respects: "They're stronger, they're better financed, they're owners are better prepared, they're better business people in general than were their predecessors. They're better positioned to take advantage of any opportunities that are out there." Other analysts agree, noting that business schools and entrepreneurship programs have seen increases in minority enrollment.

- Access to Financing—Minority-owned businesses have benefited from several economic trends. Perhaps most importantly, black, Hispanic, Arab, Asian and other minority businesspeople have benefited from the financial community's belated recognition that small businesses are powering much of the nation's current economic growth, and that small companies will likely become an even more important component of the U.S. economy in the coming years. Moreover, the emergence of alternative financing sources friendly to minority entrepreneurs has made it easier for minority-owned businesses to secure funds for start-up costs or expansions. Finally, agencies such as the **U.S. Small Business Administration (SBA)** have increased the volume of loans to minorities (in fiscal year 1994, for example, the SBA increased the amount it loaned to minority business owners by nearly 60 percent over the previous year).

- Expansion into Emerging Markets— Traditionally, minority business owners have been primarily involved in small-scale retailing and service industries such as restaurants, beauty parlors, dry cleaners, laundromats, and grocery stores. But increasing number of minority entrepreneurs have successfully ventured out into realms where minority owners had previously been less commonplace, such as manufacturing and high-technology industries. "Minority entrepreneurs are also targeting larger markets, increasing their chances of success," wrote Nolton. "Coupled with minority business owners' increased individual power is their greater sophistication in the use of group power and technology to accomplish economic goals."

AFFIRMATIVE ACTION AND "SET-ASIDE" PROGRAMS

Affirmative Action and "set-aside" programs, which were first instituted more than 20 years ago to help minority-owned businesses survive in an economic world that was all too often colored by racial prejudice, have become subjects of fierce, sometimes impassioned debate across much of the United States over the past several years.

Set-asides were first created in 1953, when the U.S. government passed a law that set aside five percent of all procurement contracts for small businesses owned by socially and economically disadvantaged people. The SBA has defined and redefined the term "socially and economically disadvantaged" many times since then by adding different groups and deleting others. The core group under the original law included African Americans, Hispanic Americans, Native Americans, Asian Pacific Americans, and other minorities. By the early 1970s, the U.S. government passed a series of regulations and laws designed to ensure that private contractors with lucrative government contracts, set aside a small percentage of their work for assignment to subcontractors owned by individuals from "socially and economically disadvantaged" backgrounds. "The regulations in some government agencies were written specifically for minorities, and in some instances required a specific percentage of participation," wrote Caplan. "The theory behind these laws was that when public (tax) money was being spent, all citizens should have an equal right to compete for contracts, and that minority-and women-owned companies needed special assistance to secure a fair share of the opportunities." In

ensuing years, it became clear that such programs were a tremendous boon to many minority-owned businesses.

By the 1980s and 1990s, though, critics of affirmative action and set-aside policies argued that minority-owned businesses were coming of age and could compete in the mainstream economy. In fact, they said, "set-asides" impede minority-owned businesses' chances of success, because companies came to depend on them to the detriment of seeking contracts through competition. Finally, some critics contended that such policies discriminated against white business owners. "Once seen as a redress for past discrimination, many now characterize affirmative action programs as reverse discrimination," summarized the *Pittsburgh Business Times*.

Many researchers and minority entrepreneurs reject these arguments, however. They point out that revenues of minority-owned businesses still fall short of those found in comparable white-owned firms, and as Rhonda Johnson noted, the combined revenues of *Black Enterprise*'s top 100 industrial and service companies still does not match the revenue of one Fortune 100 company. Finally, many supporters of affirmative action programs contend that "public policy drives private behavior," and that any government decision to tear down programs designed to help minority-owned businesses would serve as a sort of tacit approval for companies to return to discriminatory behavior that they engaged in in the past.

SOURCES OF ASSISTANCE

Minority entrepreneurs have several sources of assistance that they can pursue in building and expanding their businesses. The U.S. Small Business Administration, for example, has provided billions of dollars in contracts, grants, and loans to minority businesses. In 1993 alone, the SBA guaranteed nearly 27,000 loans totaling more than $6.4 billion to small- and women-owned businesses. The number reached $7 billion in 1994 and $9 billion in 1995. In addition, the agency provides valuable information and assistance through programs like SCORE and its 8(a) contract program.

Several organizations have also been developed to help minorities in the world of business, including the National Black Chamber of Commerce (2000 L St. NW, Suite 200, Washington, DC 20036, phone 202-416-1622), the U.S. Pan Asian American Chamber of Commerce(1329 18th St. NW, Washington, DC 20036, phone 202-296-5221), the U.S. Hispanic Chamber of Commerce (1030 15th St. NW, Suite 206, Washington, DC 20005, phone 202-842-1212), the National Indian Business Association (1605 Carlisle NE, Suite A1, Albuquerque, NM 87110, phone 505-256-0589), the National Association of Minority Contractors (806 15th St. NW, Suite 240, Washington, DC 20005, phone 212-347-8259), the National Association of Black Women Entrepreneurs(P.O. Box 1373, Detroit, MI 48231, phone 313-559-9255), and the National Minority Supplier Development Council(15 W. 39th St., New York, NY 10019, phone 212-944-2430).

FURTHER READING:

Caplan, Suzanne. *A Piece of the Action: How Women and Minorities Can Launch Their Own Successful Businesses.* New York: AMACOM, 1994.

Fraser, George. *Success Runs in Our Race.* New York: William Morrow & Co., 1995.

Green, Shelley, and Paul Pryde. *Black Entrepreneurship in America.* New Brunswick, CT: Transaction Publishers, 1990.

Holdron, Don P. "Perspectives on Minority Business." *The Review of Black Political Economy.* Fall 1993.

Judd, Richard J., William T. Greenwood, and Fred W. Becker, eds. *Small Business in A Regulated Economy.* New York: Quorum Books, 1988.

Light, Ivan, and Edna Bonacich. *Immigrant Entrepreneurs: Koreans in Los Angeles, 1965-1982.* Berkeley CA: University of California Press, 1988.

Nolton, Sharon. "Minority Business: The New Wave." *Nation's Business.* October 1995.

O'Hara, William. "Reaching for the Dream." *American Demographics.* January 1992.

"Pushed to the Margins." *Pittsburgh Business Times.* April 15, 1996.

Whittemore, Mary. "Expanding Opportunities for Minorities and Women." *Nation's Business.* December 1990.

Willie, Charles Vert. *Black and White Families.* Bayside, NY: General Hall Inc., 1985.

SEE ALSO: Community Relations; Government Procurement

MISSION STATEMENT

Mission statements are documents that are intended to serve as a summary of a business's goals and values. Their contents often reflect the fact that they are utilized both as an internal performance enhancer and as a **public relations** tool.

Mission statements serve several purposes, but at their core, they are usually intended as a means by which a business's ownership or management attempt to attach meaning to an organization's operations beyond profit and loss statements. Indeed, Jay A. Conger, writing in *The Charismatic Leader,* indicated that one of the primary means by which the effectiveness of business leadership can be measured is by "their ability to make the organization's work *meaningful* for employees. . . . To accomplish this, the leader must not only be able to sense meaningful

opportunities in the environment but also to describe them in ways that maximize their significance."

The value of the mission statement is also sometimes thought to increase with the size of an organization. *Fortune* contributor Andrew Serwer, for instance, contended that whereas entrepreneurial companies of relatively small size can get by without a mission statement, since the leader can communicate personally with each staff member. Expansion, however, can make it more difficult for entrepreneurs to communicate efficiently with individual staff members about their future plans, their vision of the company's goals, and the values that will guide the company's operation. "A mission statement not only provides that information, but it's also the foundation for any performance-enhancement initiative," wrote Karen Adler and Paul Swiercz in *Training & Development.*

When produced in a thoughtful and careful manner, mission statements can be superb vehicles for communicating the importance of an organization's activities and the overarching reasons why employees should value their work there. Unfortunately, many critics agree with *InfoWorld's* Bob Lewis, who contended that many of today's mission statements are produced in a formulaic, jargon-heavy manner that renders them bereft of vitality and meaning. Lewis and others argue that all too often, businesses of all shapes and sizes attach far greater weight to the mission statement's public relations function than to its value as a potential touchstone that can help the business maintain a steady course through the many obstacles and challenges of the modern business world.

CHARACTERISTICS OF EFFECTIVE MISSION STATEMENTS Small business owners, consultants, and researchers all agree that effective mission statements generally feature most of the following characteristics:

1) Simple, declarative statements—Mission statements that are cluttered with trendy buzz words and jargon rather than basic declarations of organizational goals and values tend to fall flat. Conversely, a mission that can be easily articulated is more likely to be remembered and to have resonance.

2) Honest and realistic—Observers agree that it is pointless—or worse, that it can actually turn into a negative—for a business enterprise to create and publicize a mission statement if it is at odds with its known operating philosophy. A company may espouse an abiding concern for the environment in its statement of mission, but if its everyday operations reflect a callous disregard for or outright hostility to established environmental protections, the statement may merely

engender or deepen employee cynicism about management and generate negative public response (hypocrisy often attracts greater attention than silence).

3) Communicates Expectations and Ethics— As Sharon Nelton noted in *Nation's Business,* a thoughtfully rendered mission statement can define not only what a company's business goals are, but also the methodologies it chooses to get there. A good mission statement often includes general principles to which a business's workers are expected to adhere, and in return, includes declarations of the business's obligations to its employees, its customers, and the community in which it operates.

4) Periodically Updated—Just like other business documents, mission statements can lose their vitality and relevance over time if they are not reexamined on a regular basis. As Lewis noted in *InfoWorld,* mission statements should undergo continual redefinition and refinement to ensure that they remain fresh and useful.

FURTHER READING:

Adler, Karen, and Paul Swiercz. ''Taming the Performance Bell Curve.'' *Training & Development.* October 1997.

Conger, Jay A. *The Charismatic Leader: Behind the Mystique of Exceptional Leadership.* San Francisco: Jossey-Bass, 1989.

Lancaster, Hal. ''Getting Your Goals for Life and Work Down in Writing.'' *Wall Street Journal.* October 14, 1997.

Lewis, Bob. ''Mission Statements: Don't Write a Word Until Your Ideas are Clear to All.'' *InfoWorld.* January 29, 1996.

Nelton, Sharon. ''Put Your Purpose in Writing: A Mission Statement Can Give Your Company the Focus It Needs for Survival and Growth.'' *Nation's Business.* February 1994.

Quigley, Joseph V. ''Vision: How Leaders Develop It, Share It, and Sustain It.'' *Business Horizons.* September-October 1994.

Serwer, Andrew. ''Lessons from America's Fastest Growing Companies.'' *Fortune.* August 8, 1994.

Vander Weyer, Martin. ''Mission Improvable.'' *Management Today.* September 1994.

MOBILE OFFICE

Advances in communication technology, entrepreneurial creativity, and the increasingly hectic pace of modern life have all combined to encourage the development and refinement of mobile business offices. Indeed, entrepreneurs have been a driving force in the creation of computers, telephones, and other office equipment that are both effective and portable. ''The goal of providing portability and adequate power to meet business people's needs also has led to a substantial degree of convergence among mobile computing, organizing, and communications technologies,'' wrote Tim McCollum and Albert Holzinger in *Nation's Business.* ''This convergence now enables small-business people to compute and coordinate wherever they are, using one of a few coordinated devices and either traditional wired or new wireless telephone networks.''

Mobile office technology allows entrepreneurs and other businesspeople to access data or information from their place of business in any location. This versatility can be vital in closing a deal, delivering a report, or saving a presentation. Of course, many businesspeople rely on portable office equipment primarily during transitional periods—at the airport, in hotel rooms or during business trips—but observers have noted that mobile office technology has also become an essential performance tool for sales representatives, business planners, and busy entrepreneurs. Moreover, some enterprising small business owners have learned to synthesize communication technology with today's system of roadways to create truly mobile businesses that do not rely on a central office.

MOBILE BUSINESSES In recent years, increasing numbers of small businesses—both start-ups and established ventures—have devised systems wherein they can successfully deliver their products or services through a mobile facility or office. ''Many entrepreneurs find that packaging a business in a van, truck, bus, or car is a way to rejuvenate an existing firm or launch a new one,'' confirmed Carol Dilks in *Nation's Business.* Dilks noted that enterprises that are conducive to mobile office treatment are numerous, including optical services, maid services, lawn maintenance, veterinary services, and a host of others. Indeed, many observers suggest that any limitations in mobile businesses that currently exist are present only because the right entrepreneur has not yet come along to figure out how to deliver the product or service ''on wheels'' in a profitable way.

Entrepreneurs with mobile businesses also point to several major advantages associated with such arrangements. Mobile businesses do not have the expense of maintaining a store, which—with rent, furniture, utilities, and other **overhead** costs—can be a very expensive part of operations. In addition, owners of mobile businesses report that they register savings because of reduced rates of theft and insurance. Finally, these business owners contend that by going to the customer's home or business, they: 1) immediately establish their interest in satisfying the client; and 2) create a dynamic wherein both the businessperson and the customer can concentrate on one another rather than peripheral distractions such as other customers. Business consultants warn, however, that mobile businesses need to adhere to a very high standard of professionalism to calm possible customer fears about legitimacy and quality. ''People like to know there's an 'entity,' one executive admitted to *BC Business*. ''It makes them more comfortable and confident to know a business has a real office, not just a phone and a computer somewhere.''

FURTHER READING:

Baker, Dean. ''Desks on Wheels.'' *Oregon Business*. September 1997.

Bianchi, Alessandra. ''Wheeling and Dealing.'' *Inc.* January 1995.

Dilks, Carol. ''Business on the Move.'' *Nation's Business*. March 1984.

Findley, Nigel D. ''The Great Communicators: Making the Most of the Mobile Office.'' *BC Business*. March 1993.

Kerven, Anne. ''The Mobile Office.'' *Colorado Business Magazine*. December 1997.

McCollum, Tim, and Albert G. Holzinger. ''Making a Move to Portability.'' *Nation's Business*. September 1997.

Nussbaum, Debra. ''Taking the Office to the Highway.'' *New York Times*. September 14, 1997.

SEE ALSO: Business Travel; Communication Systems; Customer Service

MONEY MARKET INSTRUMENTS

The money market is the arena in which financial institutions make available to a broad range of borrowers and investors the opportunity to buy and sell various forms of short-term securities. The money market is not a physical place, but an informal network of banks and traders linked by telephones, fax machines, and computers. Money markets exist both in the United States and abroad.

The short-term debts and securities sold on the money markets, which are known as money market instruments, have maturities ranging from one day to one year and are extremely liquid. Some examples of common money market instruments include: treasury bills, federal agency notes, **certificates of deposit (CDs)**, eurodollar deposits, commercial paper, bankers' acceptances, and purchase agreements. The suppliers of funds for money market instruments are institutions and individuals with a preference for the highest liquidity and the lowest risk.

The money market is important for businesses because it allows companies with a temporary cash surplus to invest in short-term securities, and it also allows companies with a temporary cash shortfall to sell securities or borrow funds on a short-term basis. In essence, it acts as a repository for short-term funds. Large corporations generally handle their own short-term financial transactions, participating in the money market through dealers. Small businesses, on the other hand, often choose to invest in money-market funds, which are professionally managed mutual funds consisting only of short-term securities.

Although securities purchased on the money market carry less risk than long-term debt, they are still not entirely risk free. After all, banks do sometimes fail, and the fortunes of companies can change rather rapidly. But, as Richard A. Brealey and Stewart C. Myers explained in their book *Principles of Corporate Finance,* ''the range of possible outcomes is less for short-term investments. Even though the distant future may be clouded, you can usually be confident that a particular company will survive for at least the next month. Second, only well-established companies can borrow in the money market. If you are going to lend money for only one day, you can't afford to spend too much time in evaluating the loan. Thus you will consider only blue-chip borrowers.''

TYPES OF MONEY MARKET INSTRUMENTS

TREASURY BILLS Treasury bills (T-bills) are short-term notes issued by the U.S. government. They come in three different lengths to maturity: 90, 180, and 360 days. The two shorter types are auctioned on a weekly basis, while the annual types are auctioned monthly. T-bills can be purchased directly through the auctions or indirectly through the secondary market. Purchasers of T-bills at auction can enter a competitive bid (although this method entails a risk that the bills may not be made available at the bid price) or a noncompetitive bid. T-bills for noncompetitive bids are supplied at the average price of all successful competitive bids.

FEDERAL AGENCY NOTES Some agencies of the federal government issue both short-term and long-term obligations, including the loan agencies Fannie Mae and Sallie Mae. These obligations are not generally backed by the government, so they offer a slightly higher yield than T-bills, but the risk of default is still very small. Agency securities are actively traded, but are not quite as marketable as T-bills. Corporations are major purchasers of this type of money market instrument.

SHORT-TERM TAX EXEMPTS These instruments are short-term notes issued by state and municipal governments. Although they carry somewhat more risk than T-bills and tend to be less negotiable, they feature the added benefit that the interest is not subject to federal income tax. For this reason, corporations find that the lower yield is worthwhile on this type of short-term investment.

CERTIFICATES OF DEPOSIT Certificates of deposit (CDs) are certificates issued by a federally chartered bank against deposited funds that earn a specified return for a definite period of time. They are one of several types of interest-bearing "time deposits" offered by banks. An individual or company lends the bank a certain amount of money for a fixed period of time, and in exchange the bank agrees to repay the money with specified interest at the end of the time period. The certificate constitutes the bank's agreement to repay the loan. The maturity rates on CDs range from 30 days to six months or longer, and the amount of the face value can vary greatly as well. There is usually a penalty for early withdrawal of funds, but some types of CDs can be sold to another investor if the original purchaser needs access to the money before the maturity date.

Large denomination (jumbo) CDs of $100,000 or more are generally negotiable and pay higher interest than smaller denominations. However, such certificates are insured by the Federal Deposit Insurance Corporation (FDIC) only up to $100,000. There are also eurodollar CDs, which are negotiable certificates issued against U.S. dollar obligations in a foreign branch of a domestic bank. Brokerage firms have a nationwide pool of bank CDs and receive a fee for selling them. Since brokers deal in large sums, brokered CDs generally pay higher interest rates and offer greater liquidity than CDs purchased directly from a bank.

COMMERCIAL PAPER Commercial paper refers to unsecured short-term promissory notes issued by financial and nonfinancial corporations. Commercial paper has maturities of up to 270 days (the maximum allowed without Securities and Exchange Commission (SEC) registration requirement). Dollar volume for commercial paper exceeds the amount of any money market instrument other than T-bills. It is typically issued by large, credit-worthy corporations with unused lines of bank credit and therefore carries low default risk.

Standard & Poor's and *Moody's* provide ratings regarding the quality of commercial paper. The highest ratings are A1 and P1, respectively. A2 and P2 paper is considered high quality, but usually indicates that the issuing corporation is smaller or more debt burdened than A1 and P1 companies. Issuers earning the lowest ratings find few willing investors.

Unlike some other types of money-market instruments, in which banks act as intermediaries between buyers and sellers, commercial paper is issued directly by well-established companies, as well as by financial institutions. "By cutting out the intermediary, major companies are able to borrow at rates that may be one to one and a half percent below the prime rate charged by banks," according to Brealey and Myers. Banks may act as agents in the transaction, but they assume no principal position and are in no way obligated with respect to repayment of the commercial paper. Companies may also sell commercial paper through dealers who charge a fee and arrange for the transfer of the funds from the lender to the borrower.

BANKERS' ACCEPTANCES "A banker's acceptance begins life as a written demand for the bank to pay a given sum at a future date," Brealey and Myers noted. "The bank then agrees to this demand by writing 'accepted' on it. Once accepted, the draft becomes the bank's IOU and is a negotiable security. This security can then be bought or sold at a discount slightly greater than the discount on Treasury bills of the same maturity." Bankers' acceptances are generally used to finance foreign trade, although they also arise when companies purchase goods on credit or need to finance inventory. The maturity of acceptances ranges from one to six months.

REPURCHASE AGREEMENTS Repurchase agreements, also known as repos or buybacks, are Treasury securities that are purchased from a dealer with the agreement that they will be sold back at a future date for a higher price. These agreements are the most liquid of all money market investments, ranging from 24 hours to several months. In fact, they are very similar to bank deposit accounts, and many corporations arrange for their banks to transfer excess cash to such funds automatically.

FURTHER READING:

Black, Pam. "CDs That Try a Little Harder." *Business Week*, September 5, 1994.

Brealey, Richard A., and Stewart C. Myers. *Principles of Corporate Finance.* 4th ed. New York: McGraw-Hill, 1991.

Dunnan, Nancy. *Dunn and Bradstreet Guide to Your Investments.* New York: Harper Collines, 1991.

Munn, Glen G., I. Garcia, and Charles J. Woelfel, eds. *Encyclopedia of Banking and Finance.* 9th ed. Pasadena, CA: Salem Press, 1991.

Nayar, Nandkumar and Michael S. Rozeff. "Commercial Paper and the Cost of Capital, Rating, Commercial Paper, and Equity Returns." *Journal of Finance.* September 1994.

Retkwa, Rosalyn. "New CP-Funded Loans Broaden Market but Aren't Always Cheap." *Corporate Cashflow Magazine.* August 1993.

MONEY SUPPLY

The supply or stock of money consists of all the money held by the nonbank public at any point of time. But the definition of money is applied broadly here. People recognize currency (consisting of notes and coins) as money, since currency in one form or another has been used as a medium of exchange since ancient times. In modern day advanced societies, cash is still "king," but another key component of money has emerged in the form of checkable deposits in the banking system, as people can write checks on their accounts (deposits) to pay for goods and services or to repay debt. A third, relatively minor, component of the money supply is the amount of outstanding traveler's checks. The sum of currency held by the nonbank public, checkable deposits, and traveler's checks yield a measure of money supply officially known as the M1 (or money aggregate) measure of money supply in the United States. In the mid-1990s, nearly 30 percent of the M1 measure of money supply was in currency; while about 70 percent was in checkable deposits (an additional 1 percent was in traveler's checks).

It should be noted that credit cards are not regarded as part of the money supply. Individuals do use credit cards for numerous transactions. Indeed, their ubiquitous presence in stores across North America and many international lands, along with their utility in making purchases, has led many to refer to credit cards as "plastic money." But credit cards are essentially a means of buying goods or services on credit, whereas payment by cash or checks is a transaction in which money changes hands at the actual time of the purchase.

FEDERAL RESERVE MEASUREMENTS OF MONEY SUPPLY

Every nation has a central bank that monitors the money supply and almost always determines the level of money supply in the economy. In the United States, the Federal Reserve System serves as the central bank of the country. The Federal Reserve, commonly referred to as the Fed, uses three different measures of money supply—M1, M2, and M3. M2 and M3 measures of money supply built on the narrowly defined M1 measure by successively broadening the money supply measure.

In order to understand why the Federal Reserve System uses successively broader measures of money supply, one has to go back to the ordinary definition of money and then consider what else can be converted into ordinary money with minimum difficulty. The example of savings account deposits can be used to demonstrate why the M1 measure of money supply is broadened. Remember, the narrow M1 definition of money supply includes checkable deposits, but not savings account deposits. Savings account deposits are excluded from that definition because of the inability of a savings account to be directly used in making payments, unlike a checking account. However, with just a phone call to one's bank, one can transfer money from savings into checking and then make the payment by writing checks on the checking account. Similarly, an individual could go to the bank

and withdraw money in cash from his or her savings account, thus converting resources in the savings account into ordinary money. In recognition of this admittedly minor difference in status, savings account deposits are sometimes referred to as near-money. Since the M1 definition of money supply does not properly reflect the extent of true money supply in the economy, The Federal Reserve coined broader measures of money supply (M2 and M3) to capture the characteristics of money in items other than those included in the M1 definition.

M2 AND M3 MEASURES OF MONEY SUPPLY In addition to currency, checkable deposits, and traveler's checks, the M2 definition of money supply includes the following, all of which can be classified as "near money":

- Savings deposits
- Small-denomination time deposits
- Money market deposit accounts
- Money market mutual fund shares (noninstitutional)
- Overnight repurchase agreements
- Overnight Eurodollars
- Consolidation adjustment (this latter item is merely an accounting adjustment applied to the M2 measure to avoid double counting of assets; for example, an M2 consolidation adjustment would subtract short-term repurchase agreements and Eurodollars being held by money market mutual funds, since they are already included in the balances of those funds).

The so-called M3 definition of money supply, meanwhile, includes not only all the assets defined within the M1 and M2 measures, but also the following:

- Large-denomination time deposits
- Money market mutual fund shares (institutional)
- Long-term repurchase agreements
- Term Eurodollars
- Consolidation adjustment.

To monitor the supply of money in the economy, the Federal Reserve looks at all three measures of the money supply but tends to focus on the M2 measure. Historically, there has been considerable debate among economists regarding the value of the Fed's emphasis on the M2 monetary aggregate.

While growth rates of all three measures of money supply do have a tendency to move together, economists and business executives also have pointed to some notable periods of economic activity in which there have been glaring discrepancies in the movements of these monetary aggregates. For example, according to the M1 measure, the growth rate of money supply did not accelerate between 1968 and 1971. However, if the M2 and M3 measures are used as the guide, a different story emerges—they show a significant acceleration in the growth rate of money supply. Because of this kind of divergent behavior, the battle to find the true measure of money supply continues.

CONTROLLING THE NATION'S MONEY SUPPLY

In every free market economy the money supply is controlled by the nation's central bank, the chief monetary authority for the country. A central bank is known by different names in different countries. For example, in the United States the central bank is known as the Federal Reserve System; in England, it is known as the Bank of England; and in Germany, it is called the Bundesbank.

The Federal Reserve System in the United States uses three different methods to control and manipulate the nation's money supply. Its efforts in this regard are inextricably intertwined with the American banking system. After all, all definitions of money supply underscore the fact that deposits at commercial banks, savings and loan associations (S&Ls), credit unions, and mutual savings banks (collectively known as depository institutions) are an integral part of the money supply. Why are depository institutions involved in the money supply process? Depository institutions profit by taking deposits from individuals and businesses and making loans to a variety of borrowers. The difference between what they earn from the loans made and the amount paid to depositors (in additional to the operating costs) constitutes the basis for profits to the depository institutions. This arrangement encourages banks and other depository institutions to loan out as much of depositors' funds as possible (provided that they receive sufficient assurances that the loans will be paid back). However, the Federal Reserve has put a restriction on this behavior—the depository institutions are required to keep a fraction of the deposits in reserves at the Federal Reserve. Thus, the depository financial institutions can only lend out the excess reserves—(vault cash and cash deposits at the Federal Reserve)—over and above the reserves required by law to be kept at the Federal Reserve Bank.

In manipulating the money supply, it is the level of the excess reserves that the Federal Reserve attempts to influence to affect the growth rate of the nation's money supply. To illustrate this, let us assume that through some mechanism the Fed is able to increase the amount of excess reserves in the banking system. Banks armed with the subsequent extra resources want to lend those resources prudently in order to earn interest on loans made. Further, assume that loans are made by simply creating deposits (which are part of the money supply) in borrowers' names. Creating additional deposits results in an increase in the money supply. While the preceding logic may appear like an academic concoction, this is what happens in the real world. The only question that remains to be answered is as to how the Federal Reserve manipulates the level of excess reserves in the banking system.

There are three instruments available to the Federal Reserve Bank that it can use to manipulate the excess reserves in the banking system and thus the level of money supply—the reserve requirement ratio, the discount rate, and open market operations.

THE RESERVE REQUIREMENT RATIO The reserve requirement ratio is the legal ratio determined by the Federal Reserve (within limits established by the Congress) that it requires of the depository institutions in calculating the minimum reserves they must keep to conform to the federal banking law. Thus, if the Fed increases the reserve requirement ratio, it automatically reduces the amount of excess reserves in the banking system. For example, a bank with $100 million in deposits, $18 million in reserves, and a reserve requirement ratio of 10 percent will be required to keep a minimum of $10 million in required reserves (the 10 percent reserve requirement ratio applied to $100 million in deposits), thus giving it an excess reserve of $8 million. If the Federal Reserve increases the reserve requirement ratio from 10 percent to 15 percent, the institution would then have to keep $15 million in legal reserves. This leads to a decrease in the level of excess reserves from $8 million to $3 million. A decrease in the amount of excess reserves reduces the ability of the bank to make loans, to create additional deposits, and, ultimately, to increase the money supply. In this example, the bank started from positive excess reserves and then increased the reserve requirement ratio. If it had started from zero excess reserves and then increased the reserve requirement ratio, the levels of deposits and money supply would be forced to fall—banks caught with deficient minimum legal reserves would have to reduce the level of deposits, consistent with available reserves.

The Federal Reserve can both lower and raise the reserve requirement ratio to affect money supply. However, raising the legal reserve ratio is especially powerful when the banking system has no excess reserves. Despite the apparent potency of the reserve requirement ratio as an instrument of money supply manipulations, it is seldom utilized by the Federal Reserve in influencing money supply. A change in the reserve requirement ratio is a legal change and it is not advisable to change the rules of the game frequently. Thus, while the reserve requirement ratio may be utilized in a financial emergency, the Federal Reserve does not use the ratio to manipulate the nation's money supply on a regular basis.

THE DISCOUNT RATE The discount rate is the interest rate the Federal Reserve Bank charges banking institutions for the loans it makes to them. The Federal Reserve was initially created as a lender of last resort—its function was to lend to banks in need of funds through discounting banks' holdings of Treasury bills and other financial units. Essentially, the Fed made loans to banks with Treasury bills serving as collateral. Of course, if banks can borrow from the Federal Reserve at a low rate of interest and lend to its borrowers at higher interest rates, it will be clearly profitable for them. By lowering the discount rate, the Federal Reserve lowers the cost of borrowing and increases banks' willingness to borrow. This can potentially increase the level of excess reserves in the banking system, which in turn sparks an increase in the overall money supply. Raising the discount rate, on the other hand, can have the opposite effect on the level of excess reserves and the money supply.

While the discount rate can potentially be used to influence the levels of excess reserves and money supply in the economy, the Federal Reserve does not use this method to induce increased borrowing by banks. The Federal Reserve dislikes profit-based borrowing by the depository institutions; it looks far more kindly on so-called ''need-based'' borrowing by banks. Such borrowing may take place when banks, due to some unanticipated factors, fall short of funds. Even then, Federal Reserve closely monitors any bank that borrows from the Fed too frequently.

The preceding discussion suggests that the Federal Reserve does not like to use the discount rate as an instrument to manipulate the level of money supply in the economy on a regular basis (by manipulating the level of excess reserves in the banking system). The Fed, however, does utilize this instrument in an indirect way in manipulating money supply—it uses the discount rate as a signaling device. When the Federal Reserve Bank lowers the discount rate, it signals to the banking system and the financial market that it is in favor of increasing money supply. When the Fed increases the discount rate, it sends out the opposite message. In fact, banks often take the Fed's announcement of the discount rate change quite seriously—if the Federal Reserve raises the discount rate, for example, major banks follow up by raising their prime rates (the rate a bank charges its best customers). As homeowners and other borrowers are well aware, such decisions by the Fed can have quite a ripple effect throughout the U.S. economy.

OPEN MARKET OPERATIONS Open market operations are the third and the most frequently used instrument by the Federal Reserve in manipulating the money supply. In open market operations, the Federal Reserve Bank uses market forces to manipulate the level of the excess reserves and thus the money supply in the economy. In open market operations, the Federal Reserve either buys Treasury securities (bills and bonds) from banks or sells Treasury securities to them. When the Federal Reserve sells Treasury bonds to banks, the Fed receives cash in exchange for bonds. When this occurs, the excess reserves in the banking system go down, which in turn puts downward pressure on the money supply. Again, the opposite effect can be achieved if the Federal Reserve sells Treasury securities to the banking system.

The Federal Reserve uses open market operations to manipulate the nation's money supply on a regular basis. Indeed, open market operations are considered the main instrument of monetary policy available to it.

MONEY SUPPLY UNCERTAINTIES The Federal Reserve is fairly adept at manipulating America's money supply. Nonetheless, there are some uncertainties regarding the magnitude of a monetary aggregate or the exact time when the increase in the money supply materializes after the Fed initiates the process of expanding the money supply. For example, the Federal Reserve increases the level of excess reserves in the banking system to increase the money supply. However, banks may be reluctant to loan (and thus to increase the money supply) because of lack of creditworthy borrowers or their desire to wait for better opportunities. Thus, the Federal Reserve's attempt to increase money supply is frustrated. Despite this uncertainty, the Fed is able to determine changes in the money supply since banks have to report periodically to the Federal Reserve.

FURTHER READING:

Froyen, Richard T. *Macroeconomics: Theories and Policies*, 4th ed. New York: Macmillan Publishing, 1993.

Mishkin, Frederic S. *The Economics of Money, Banking and Financial Markets*, 4th ed. New York: Harper Collins, 1995.

Ritter, Lawrence S., and William L. Silber. *Principles of Money, Banking and Financial Markets*. 6th ed. New York: Basic Books, 1989.

MULTICULTURAL WORK FORCE

A multicultural work force is one wherein a company's employees include members of a variety of ethnic, racial, religious, and gender backgrounds. Whereas past eras in American business saw few examples of multiculturalism, most of today's small business owners and corporate executives recognize that attention to the challenges and opportunities associated with the growing trend toward culturally diverse work forces can be a key factor in overall business success.

"A combination of work force demographic trends and increasing globalization of business has placed the management of cultural differences on the agenda of most corporate leaders," wrote Taylor Cox, Jr. "Organizations' work forces will be increasingly heterogeneous on dimensions such as gender, race, ethnicity, and nationality. Potential benefits of this diversity include better decision making, higher creativity and innovation, greater success in marketing to foreign and ethnic minority communities, and a better distribution of economic opportunity. Conversely, cultural differences can also increase costs through higher turnover rates, interpersonal conflict, and communication breakdowns."

TRENDS IN CULTURAL DIVERSITY IN AMERICA

The United States has always been an immigrant culture. Aside from Native Americans, the entire population has immigrant origins. The traditional view toward immigrants was that they would wish to assimilate to the dominant Anglo-Saxon population of the nation's earliest colonial settlers. The assimilation process, according to the traditional view, however, was never expected to be total. Each group would add a distinguishing contribution to the overall national culture so that in time the myriad immigrant groups would alter the cultural norms of the rest of the nation in subtle ways. This philosophy was summed up in the notion of the country as the "American melting pot." But this conception of the nation was predicated on the willingness of the immigrant—and the demands of the dominant culture—that unfamiliar cultural practices and attitudes be discarded or at the very least sublimated, especially in work place settings. Additionally, during some periods, certain groups were deemed to be unable to assimilate no matter how much they were willing to bury their cultural differences with the dominant culture. A variety of peoples have been victimized by this attitude over the years, including African Americans, Asian Americans, and Jews.

The Civil Rights movement of the 1960s, however, had a direct effect on the assimilationist norm of the melting pot. It changed the view of the United States as a single culture welcoming those different from the dominant norm only if they would only drop their ethnic or cultural distinctiveness. The double standard as applied to certain groups of Americans came under scrutiny; the belief in integration into a dominant norm was questioned. Assuredly, such re-examination took place within the long-dominant na-

tive-born, white, non-Hispanic community. But perhaps the most significant impact of the Civil Rights movement was that immigrants and distinctive native-born minority groups began, as Stephen Steinberg argued in *The Ethnic Myth,* "to affirm their right to a separate identity within the framework of a pluralist nation."

The re-examination of the desirability of the domination of the work force by a culturally monolithic norm led to laws that required businesses to provide culturally diverse groups with greater opportunities to enter the work place. Title VII of the Civil Rights Act of 1964, for example, made it unlawful to discriminate on the basis of race, color, national origin, or religion. Equal opportunity for employment, in turn, allowed for the entry into the American work force of increasing numbers of individuals from cultural groups that had historically been victims of discrimination. This, in turn, led groups that had attempted to assimilate to question their decision to subsume their own cultural values to the dominant norm. Thus, even within the historically favored white community, ethnic groups began to see benefits in returning to—or at least not hiding—their own cultural differences. Finally, as longstanding barriers to integrated work forces crumbled, increasing numbers of companies came to recognize both the business value of multicultural work forces and the negative repercussions associated with an inability or unwillingness to accommodate such demographic changes.

TODAY'S CHALLENGES Not all people in organizations value diversity. As a rule, people are most comfortable with those like themselves and emphasizing diversity may undermine that comfort level. Diversity tends to breed new approaches to old practices and long-standing problems. Individuals in organizations may find such change troubling. Moreover, individuals with strong prejudices against certain groups may find rapidly changing demographics in the work force threatening either because they find change itself disquieting or because they hold a position they feel they might not be able to maintain if groups historically excluded from their workplace are allowed to compete in an unhindered way for their positions.

Given such realities, R. Roosevelt Thomas, Jr. wrote in *Beyond Race and Gender* that companies need to go beyond simple recognition of cultural diversity to active diversity management: "Managing diversity is a comprehensive managerial process for developing an environment that works for all employees." Diversity management is an inclusive process since all employees belong to a culture, including those from the organization's traditionally dominant cultural group. Thomas indicated that diversity management must not be viewed as "an us/them kind of problem to be solved but as a resource to be managed." Anthony Carnevale and Susan Carol Stone, authors of *The American Mosaic,* emphasized that valuing diversity involves "recognizing that other people's standards and values are as valid as one's own," and note that for most organizations, valuing and managing diversity requires nothing less than cultural transformation. This is a prodigious task, for it requires people—especially those of the dominant culture—to let go of their assumptions about the universal rightness of their own values and customary ways of doing things and to become receptive to other cultures.

In this regard, cultural diversity in the work place mirrors many of the same issues at play in the realm of international business. In international business interactions, people who have learned differing conceptions of normative behavior are forced to suspend judgment of one another. Cultural norms shift relative to language, technological expectations, social organization, face-saving, authority conception, nonverbal behavior and the perception of time.

ORGANIZATION TYPES

Taylor Cox, Jr., an expert in the field of organization behavior, cited three primary organization types in the realm of cultural diversity development. Most U.S. businesses, he indicated, generally fall within one of the three models. The first of these types, called the monolithic organization, is characterized by a homogeneous work force composed primarily of while males with few women or minority men in management positions (although he contended that this type of organization can exist in any situation where one "identity group"—blacks, Hispanics, etc.—is dominant). Moreover, many of these organizations feature high levels of occupational segregation, with women and minority men concentrated in lower-paying occupations. This environment, noted Cox, makes it a practical necessity for women, minority men, and foreign nationals who do enter the organization to accept the organizational norms already in place (which were put together by the dominant group). Cox pointed out that, ironically, "one positive note [of the monolithic organization] is that intergroup conflict based on culture-group identity is minimized by the relative homogeneity of the work force." But he also noted that since this organization type generally places little importance on the integration of cultural minorities, discrimination and prejudice is likely to be prevalent. "Aside from the rather obvious downside implications of the monolithic model in terms of under-utilization of human resources and social equality, the monolithic organization is not a realistic option for most large employers in the 1990s." But Barbara Jorgensen observed in *Electronic Business Buyer* that it can be difficult for owners and managers to turn such organizations around, especially if they are big and their work force is entrenched: "Manag-

ing diversity is a lot like implementing quality: it's tough to define and it requires a massive culture change. You can't even apply statistical process control to it."

The second type of organizational type is the plural organization. Cox contended that this model is an improvement over the monolithic organization in several important respects: "It has a more heterogeneous membership than the monolithic organization and takes steps to be more inclusive of persons from cultural backgrounds that differ from the dominant group." Examples of such initiatives include hiring and promotion policies that may give preference to minorities, training on equal opportunity issues, and reviews of compensation systems to ensure fair treatment of all workers. These improvements also spur greater levels of social interaction between members of different backgrounds, and greater identification with the organization among minority members. But many companies that have such measures in place maintain management teams with little minority representation, an indication that principles of multicultural management have not infiltrated all levels of the company. And Cox suggested that this "affirmative action approach to managing diversity" has spurred charges from white males that such policies "discriminate against white males and therefore perpetuate the practice of using racioethnicity, nationality, or gender as a basis for making personnel decisions. . . . This backlash effect, coupled with the increased number of minorities in the organization, often creates greater inter-group conflict in the plural organization than was present in the monolithic organization."

The third type of organization described by Cox is the multicultural organization. Primary characteristics of this kind of organization include integration of minorities into all structural levels of the company, including management/executive positions; integration of informal/social networks of the business; absence of prejudice and discrimination; and a mindset that not only accommodates diversity (a hallmark of the plural organization) but also *values* that diversity.

KEYS TO EFFECTIVE CREATION AND MANAGEMENT OF A MULTICULTURAL WORK FORCE

Experts indicate that business owners and managers who hope to create and manage an effective, harmonious multicultural work force should remember the importance of the following:

- Setting a good example—This basic tool can be particularly valuable for small business owners who hope to establish a healthy environment for people of different cultural backgrounds, since they are generally able to wield significant control over the business's basic outlook and atmosphere.

- Communicate in writing—Company policies that explicitly forbid prejudice and discriminatory behavior should be included in **employee manuals**, **mission statements**, and other forms of **written communication**. Jorgensen referred to this and similar practices as ''internal broadcasting of the diversity message in order to create a common language for all members of the organization.''

- Training programs—Training programs designed to engender appreciation and knowledge of the characteristics and benefits of multicultural work forces have become ubiquitous in recent years. ''Two types of training are most popular: awareness and skill-building,'' wrote Cox. ''The former introduces the topic of managing diversity and generally includes information on work force demographics, the meaning of diversity, and exercises to get participants thinking about relevant issues and raising their own self-awareness. The skill-building training provides more specific information on cultural norms of different groups and how they may affect work behavior.'' New employee orientation programs are also ideal for introducing workers to the company's expectations regarding treatment of fellow workers, whatever their cultural or ethnic background.

- Recognize individual differences—Writing in *The Complete MBA Companion*, contributor Rob Goffee stated that ''there are various dimensions around which differences in human relationships may be understood. These include such factors as orientation towards authority; acceptance of power inequalities; desire for orderliness and structure; the need to belong to a wider social group and so on. Around these dimensions researchers have demonstrated systematic differences between national, ethnic, and religious groups.'' Yet Goffee also cautioned business owners, managers, and executives to recognize that differences between individuals can not always be traced back to easily understood differences in cultural background: ''Do not assume differences are always 'cultural.' There are several sources of difference. Some relate to factors such as personality, aptitude, or competence. It is a mistake to assume that all perceived differences are cultural in origin. Too many managers tend to fall back on the easy 'ex-

planation' that individual behavior or performance can be attributed to the fact that someone is 'Italian' or 'a Catholic' or 'a woman.' Such conclusions are more likely to reflect intellectually lazy rather than culturally sensitive managers.''

- Actively seek input from minority groups— Soliciting the opinions and involvement of minority groups on important work committees, etc., is beneficial not only because of the contributions that they can make, but also because such overtures confirm that they are valued by the company. Serving on relevant committees and task forces can increase their feelings of belonging to the organization. Conversely, relegating minority members to superfluous committees or projects can trigger a downward spiral in relations between different cultural groups.

- Revamp reward systems—An organization's performance appraisal and reward systems should reinforce the importance of effective diversity management, according to Cox. This includes assuring that minorities are provided with adequate opportunities for career development.

- Make room for social events—Company-sponsored social events—picnics, softball games, volleyball leagues, bowling leagues, Christmas parties, etc.—can be tremendously useful in getting members of different ethnic and cultural backgrounds together and providing them with opportunities to learn about one another.

- Flexible work environment—Cox indicated that flexible work environments—which he characterized as a positive development for all workers—could be particularly ''beneficial to people from nontraditional cultural backgrounds because their approaches to problems are more likely to be different from past norms.''

- Don't assume similar values and opinions— Goffee noted that ''in the absence of reliable information there is a well-documented tendency for individuals to assume that others are 'like them.' In any setting this is likely to be an inappropriate assumption; for those who manage diverse work forces this tendency towards 'cultural assimilation' can prove particularly damaging.''

- Continuous monitoring—Experts recommend that business owners and managers establish and maintain systems that can continually monitor the organization's policies and practices to ensure that it continues to be a good environment for all employees. This, wrote Jorgensen, should include "research into employees' needs through periodic attitude surveys."

"Increased diversity presents challenges to business leaders who must maximize the opportunities that it presents while minimizing its costs," summarized Cox. "The multicultural organization is characterized by pluralism, full integration of minority-culture members both formally and informally, an absence of prejudice and discrimination, and low levels of inter-group conflict. . . . The organization that achieves these conditions will create an environment in which all members can contribute to their maximum potential, and in which the 'value in diversity' can be fully realized."

FURTHER READING:

Amott, Teresa L., and Julie A. Matthaei. *Race, Gender, and Work*. Boston: South End Press, 1991.

Carnevale, Anthony Patrick, and Susan Carol Stone. *The American Mosaic*. New York: McGraw-Hill, 1995.

Copeland, Lennie. "Valuing Workplace Diversity." *Personnel Administrator*. November 1988.

Cox, Taylor, Jr. *Cultural Diversity in Organizations*. San Francisco: Berrett-Koehler Publishers, 1993.

Cox, Taylor, Jr. "The Multicultural Organization." *Academy of Management Executive*. Vol. 5, No. 2, 1991.

Faird, Elashmawia, and Philip Harris. *Multicultural Management*. Houston, TX: Gulf Publishing Company, 1993.

Fernandez, John P. *Managing a Diverse Work Force*. Lexington, MA: Lexington Books, 1991.

Foster, Badi, et al. "Workforce Diversity and Business." *Training and Development Journal*. April 1988.

Goffee, Rob. "Cultural Diversity." *The Complete MBA Companion*. Lanham, MD: Pitman Publishing, 1997.

Jorgensen, Barbara. "Diversity: Managing a Multicultural Work Force." *Electronic Business Buyer*. September 1993.

Pollar, Odette, and Rafael Gonzalez. *Dynamic of Diversity: Strategic Programs for your Organization*. Menlo Park, CA: Crisp Publications, 1994.

Simons, George, Philip Harris, and Carmen Vasquez. *Transcultural Leadership: Empowering the Diverse Workforce*. Houston, TX: Gulf Publishing Company, 1993.

Steinberg, Stephen. *The Ethnic Myth: Race, Ethnicity, and Class in America*. New York: Atheneum, 1981.

Thomas, R. Roosevelt, Jr. *Beyond Race and Gender*. New York: Amacom, 1991.

Victor, David A. *International Business Communication*. New York: Harper Collins, 1992.

SEE ALSO: Alien Employees; Training and Development

A Multiple Employer Trust (MET) is a group of ten or more employers who form a trust in order to minimize the tax implications of providing certain types of benefits for their employees, particularly **life insurance**. The U.S. Congress authorized the formation of METs in 1984 under Section 419(A) of the Internal Revenue Code. The rules set forth for METs are stringent and require that no single employer contribute more than 10 percent of total funding for the benefit plan purchased by the MET. In addition, the MET must be an indivisible entity, with all participating employers sharing equally in the benefits forfeited by other members of the group.

The main purpose of a MET is to give entrepreneurs and small business owners a tax-friendly way to provide life insurance benefits for themselves and their key employees. Under ordinary circumstances, life insurance is tax deductible for the employer in the current year, but any amounts that could be considered "bonus" life insurance must be reported as taxable income by the employee. Larger businesses are often able to get around this problem by funding life insurance benefits as part of a qualified retirement or profit-sharing plan. Although the benefits provided through such plans are usually tax free, there are a number of restrictions and complicated paperwork requirements associated with them that reduce the attractiveness of life insurance for smaller businesses. For example, the government requires companies that set up qualified plans to establish eligibility and vesting rules and then offer the benefits to all employees who meet them.

THE IMPORTANCE OF LIFE INSURANCE

It may seem odd for small businesses to go to the trouble of forming a MET just for the sake of providing life insurance for employees. But life insurance has a variety of uses that make it a very attractive benefit, particularly for key employees. A small business might need to provide life insurance to its workers in order to compete with larger companies in attracting and retaining qualified employees. For example, in addition to providing benefits upon the death or disability of the insured, some forms of life insurance can be used as a tax-deferred investment to provide funds during a person's lifetime for retirement or everyday living expenses. There are also a number of specialized life insurance plans that allow small business owners to reduce the impact of estate taxes on their heirs and protect their businesses against the loss of a key employee, partner, or stockholder.

Small businesses tend to depend on a few key people, some of whom are likely to be owners or partners, to keep operations running smoothly. Even though it is unpleasant to think about the possibility of a key employee becoming disabled or dying, it is important to prepare so that the business may survive and the tax implications may be minimized. In the case of a partnership, the business is formally dissolved when one partner dies. In the case of a corporation, the death of a major stockholder can throw the business into disarray. In the absence of a specific agreement, the person's estate or heirs may choose to vote the shares or sell them. This uncertainty could undermine the company's management, impair its credit, cause the flight of customers, and damage employee morale.

Life insurance can help small businesses protect themselves against the loss of a key person by providing a source of income to keep business running in his or her absence. Partnership insurance basically involves each partner acting as beneficiary of a life insurance policy taken on the other partner. In this way, the surviving partner is protected against a financial loss when the business ends. Similarly, corporate plans can ensure the continuity of the business under the same management, and possibly fund a repurchase of stock, if a major stockholder dies. Although life insurance is not tax deductible when the business is named as beneficiary, the business may deduct premium costs if a partner or owner is the beneficiary.

MET REQUIREMENTS

Participating in a MET enables a small business to provide life insurance to its key employees without subjecting them to negative tax implications. It does this by allowing tax-deductible contributions to a life insurance plan, made by the employer on behalf of employees, to be used for severance benefits. Basically, the cash value of the life insurance is available for severance benefits, while the mortality portion of the life insurance is payable to the beneficiary named by insured. A MET must be structured properly in order to comply with the tax laws, but the rules are significantly less extensive than with qualified pension and profit-sharing plans.

The rules that a MET must follow in order to gain tax benefits are laid out in IRS Notice 95-34. This notice states that severance benefits can only be paid when the termination of employment is beyond an employee's control. Otherwise, if the severance arrangements appear to be providing deferred compensation benefits to an employee, the employer's tax deduction will be denied. The notice also states that the deduction will not be allowed for ''nondeductible prepaid expenses,'' which may include contributions to the plan that are made as lump sums or using accelerated funding techniques.

FURTHER READING:

Anastasio, Susan. *Small Business Insurance and Risk Management Guide.* Washington: U.S. Small Business Administration, n.d.

Budihas, John S. ''Multiple Employer Trust Used for Fringe Benefits.'' *National Underwriter Life and Health.* September 4, 1995.

White, Jane, and Bruce Pyenson. *Employee Benefits for Small Business.* Englewood Cliffs, NJ: Prentice-Hall, 1991.

SEE ALSO: Employee Benefits

N

NATIONAL ASSOCIATION OF SMALL BUSINESS INVESTMENT COMPANIES

The National Association of Small Business Investment Companies (NASBIC) is an organization of **Small Business Investment Companies (SBICs)** that have been specially licensed under the Small Business Investment Act of 1958, overseen by the **U.S. Small Business Administration (SBA)**, to provide funding to start-up companies. NASBIC's primary concern, however, is with providing representation before government on behalf of the SBIC industry. The association is located at 1199 N. Fairfax St., Ste. 200, Alexandria, Virginia, 22314. Phone: (703) 683-1601.

SMALL BUSINESS INVESTMENT COMPANIES According to NASBIC, the 282 SBICs operating in the United States and Puerto Rico are privately organized and managed financial institutions that invest **capital** in small independent businesses. They differ from venture capital firms in that they are licensed by the Small Business Administration. In exchange for investing only in small businesses, the SBA helps SBICs qualify for government-insured long-term **loans**. SBICs have complete control over their own lending policies and investment choices and are not bound by government regulation to make capital available to any particular type of business or business owner.

SSBICs, or Special Small Business Investment Companies, are identical to SBICs except in the respect that they tend to concentrate their lending in the area of socially and economically disadvantaged entrepreneurs. However, all SBICs may consider applicants from all backgrounds.

According to NASBIC, "since 1958, the SBIC program has provided approximately $13 billion of long-term debt and equity capital to approximately 80,000 small U.S. companies, with more than $1.6 billion invested in 1996." The SBICs currently operating hold a combined $6 billion in assets under management. Among the companies that began with funding from an SBIC are Apple Computer, Federal Express, Outback Steakhouse, America Online, and Intel.

CONSIDERATIONS NASBIC reports that small business owners contemplating a pitch to an SBIC should be mindful of the following considerations:

1) Amount of capital needed—SBIC policies differ and many have specific ranges they are willing to lend within.

2) Decide whether your business will be better served by a straight loan, an equity investment, or another kind of financing—SBICs offer different options, but these are not often found under the same roof.

3) Your business's industry—Some SBICs choose to lend only to businesses in a particular area, due to the expertise of the SBIC's officers or directors.

4) Geography—Although SBICs may operate regionally or even nationally, it is wise to look into the closest suitable SBIC, because they tend to lend to businesses in their general locale.

Seekers of financing should also note that SBICs may consider working in conjunction with one another to provide pooled capital if a special case merits a departure from standard policy, so no one company should be immediately ruled out.

REQUIREMENTS Your business qualifies as a "small business" if it has a "net worth under $18 million and average after-tax earnings of less than $6 million for the past two years," according to NASBIC. If your business fails these tests, it may qualify under employment or annual sales parameters.

When presenting a business to an SBIC for consideration, business owners must provide a business plan that includes information on every aspect of the operation, including detailed descriptions of the product or service and the facilities; an explanation of the customer base and distribution system; a description of the business's competition; an account of all key personnel and their qualifications; and financial statements, such as balance sheets and revenue projections. The ultimate acceptance or denial process will take a few weeks, although an indication will be made immediately of general interest or lack thereof.

When considering all sources of funding, a small business owner should weigh the appropriateness of each source with his or her needs. The wide variety of funding options provide many choices, with only a small number, perhaps, that will be suitable. SBICs provide a unique offering in that they have the security of the government behind them, but the flexibility of a private firm. This will prove to be the best choice for some.

FURTHER READING:

Beltz, Cynthia A. *Financing Entrepreneurs*. Aei Press, 1994.

Entrepreneur Magazine. *Entrepreneur Magazine Guide to Raising Money*. John Wiley & Sons, 1997.

Flanagan, Lawrence. *Raising Capital: How to Write a Financing Proposal*. Psi Research - Oasis Press, 1994.

Gillis, Tom S. *Guts & Borrowed Money: Straight Talk for Starting & Growing Your Small Business*. Bard Press, 1997.

Ross, Duncan M., and Andrew Godley. *Banks, Networks, and Small Firm Finance*. Frank Cass & Co., 1996.

NATIONAL ASSOCIATION OF WOMEN BUSINESS OWNERS

As of 1996, there were nearly 8 million women-owned businesses in the United States. As the number of women-owned businesses grows, representation and support for this group becomes more and more critical. The National Association of Women Business Owners (NAWBO), based in Washington D.C., provides women-owned businesses with a resource for such support and representation. Covering the many faceted interests of **women entrepreneurs** in all areas of business, the NAWBO has over 50 chapters in the United States and maintains affiliate chapters around the world. Membership is available through annual dues paid to both the national organization and to a local chapter.

HISTORY The NAWBO began as a small group of Washington, D.C., businesswomen who started meeting in 1974. They began as a networking group, meeting to discuss mutual experiences, exchange information, and help develop business skills for group members. They incorporated as the NAWBO on December 19, 1974. The first members in the newly formed organization were recruited in 1976, and in 1978, the first national chapters were formed.

MISSION The NAWBO's vision and mission statement states that the organization hopes to propel women entrepreneurs into "economic, social and political spheres of power worldwide." Principle aims of the organization, as articulated in their mission statement, include:

- Strengthen the wealth creating capacity of members and promote economic development;

- Create innovative and effective changes in the business culture;

- Build strategic alliances, coalitions, and affiliations;

- Transform public policy and influence opinion makers.

PROGRAMS The goal of the NAWBO is to provide women-owned businesses with visibility in the political, economic, and social spheres of business, and to provide women entrepreneurs with assistance in gaining access to financial opportunities. NAWBO programs reflect these priorities. For example, the NAWBO has allied itself with organizations such as Wells Fargo Bank and AT&T to offer programs that provide financial assistance to new women-owned businesses. This assistance takes the form of special loans, discount prices on certain equipment and services, and other opportunities which may translate into substantial savings on the start-up costs of business.

Chapter, regional, national and international contacts provide **networking** opportunities that may be otherwise unavailable to small businesses. The NAWBO also provides educational experiences and leadership training, and sponsors a wide range of special conferences, workshops, seminars, and counseling services.

In addition to its position as "helping hand," the NAWBO has established a strong political presence, emerging as a strong voice of advocacy for small women-owned businesses. For example, the group was instrumental in supporting and helping to pass the 1988 Women's Business Ownership Act, which expanded women entrepreneurs' access to credit markets; instituted a three-year, $10 million training and technical support initiative for women business owners; and created a National Women's Business Council. A regular presence on Capitol Hill, members of the NAWBO work to make sure that the needs of women-owned businesses are represented.

AFFILIATIONS The NAWBO is the United States' representative in Les Femmes Chefs d'Entreprises Mondiales (FCEM, or The World Association of Women Entrepreneurs) with chapters in 33 countries, representing almost 30,000 businesses. This affiliation allows NAWBO members access to international business ideas and trends and provides networking opportunities throughout the world.

The National Foundation for Women Business Owners (NFWBO) is a nonprofit research and leadership development foundation established by NAWBO. This offshoot of the NAWBO gathers information about women-owned businesses and makes that information available to organizations around the globe.

NAWBO is also affiliated with the Small Business Technology Coalition (SBTC) and with the Women Business Owners Corporation (WBOC), which helps small women-owned businesses compete for government contracts. This organization helps women entrepreneurs and business owners to meet professional certification and training needs.

FURTHER READING:

Crowley, Lyle. "There's No Business Like Small Business." *Working Woman.* October 1996.

Reynolds, Rhonda. "On Our Own." *Black Enterprise.* July 1995.

Reynolds, Rhonda. "Wells Fargo Woos Women Entrepreneurs." *Black Enterprise.* February 1996.

Seglin, Jeffrey L. "The Best Little Advocacy Group in America." *Inc.* May 1994.

SEE ALSO: Business Associations

NATIONAL BUSINESS INCUBATION ASSOCIATION

The National Business Incubation Association (NBIA), founded in 1985, is a nonprofit organization comprising incubator developers and managers, corporate joint venture partners, venture capital investors, and economic development professionals. The association seeks to promote the growth of new business and educate the business and investor community about the benefits of **business incubators**. NBIA offers information and training on how to form and manage incubators; conducts statistical research; provides a referral service; and publishes a newsletter, membership directory, various reports and monographs, and a state-of-the-industry analysis. The NBIA also hosts an annual convention where it bestows a number of industry awards, including the Randall M. Whaley Incubator of the Year Award, the Graduate of the Year Award, and the Tenant of the Year Award. The association is located at 20 E. Circle Dr., Suite 190, Athens, OH 45701. Phone: (614) 593-4331.

BUSINESS INCUBATORS Business incubators are facilities that provide shared resources for young businesses, such as office space, consultants, and personnel. They may also provide access to financing and technical support. These services provide the new businesses with a somewhat protected environment in which to grow before they becomes self-sustaining. The ultimate goal of any business incubator is to produce viable businesses, called "graduates" of the incubator. The NBIA reports that there are 550 incubators currently operating in North America, with a new program opening about once per week on average.

A business qualifying for incubator assistance must meet certain criteria, in much the same way it would for a venture capital firm. Some incubators have diversified interests, accepting different types of start-ups into the fold, whereas others concentrate in one particular area or industry. For instance, some special interest incubators exclusively support women and minority-owned businesses and others choose to focus on innovative software or medical applications. According to the NBIA, incubator clients may be categorized as follows: 40 percent service, 23 percent light manufacturing, 22 percent technology, and 7 percent research; an additional 8 percent are classified as "other." More than 13,000 clients are currently being assisted by incubators providing services in rural, urban, and suburban settings.

A variety of sponsors support incubators. Some incubators are supported by government and nonprofit bodies. These incubators' main goals are job creation, tax base expansion, and economic diversification. Other incubators are affiliated with universities and provide faculty, alumni, and related groups with research and business opportunities. In addition, a number of incubators are hybrids combining resources from both government and the private sector. Finally, a relatively small percentage of incubators are privately run. These incubators are operated by various types of investment groups and maintained to provide returns on funds invested by the group. Their main focus is usually on innovative applications for new technology and the development of commercial real estate. The remainder of incubators are sponsored by a variety of non-traditional organizations, such as Native American tribes, chambers of commerce, church groups, and others. Entrepreneurs seeking assistance from an incubator would be wise to seek out those most likely to support their business goals.

MEMBERSHIP Membership in the NBIA conveys a variety of benefits. They include a subscription to the *NBIA Review*, the association's newsletter; access to BatorLink, the NBIA's Internet discussion group; research, documentation, and dissemination services; support from NBIA staff for information and referrals; legislative and government program updates; and discounts on publications, educational materials, Microsoft (tm) products, insurance products from Biddle Insurance Services, and Paychex payroll services. Contact the organization by mail or phone for information on how to apply for membership.

FURTHER READING:

Hayhow, Sally. *Business Incubation: Building Companies, Jobs and Wealth.* National Business Incubation Association, 1997.

Hayhow, Sally. *A Comprehensive Guide to Business Incubation.* National Business Incubation Association, 1996.

Information Tools for Industry. Southern Technology Council, 1996.

Lichtenstein, Gregg A. and Thomas S. Lyons. *Incubating New Enterprises: A Guide to Successful Practice.* Aspen Institute, 1996.

Rice, Mark P., and Jana Matthews. *Growing New Ventures, Creating New Jobs: Principles and Practices of Successful Business Incubation.* Quorum Books, 1995.

Tornatzky, Dr. Louis G., et al. *The Art and Craft of Technology Business Incubation: Best Practices, Strategies, and Tools from 50 Programs.* National Business Incubation Association and Institute for Local Government Administration and Rural Development, 1996.

NATIONAL LABOR RELATIONS BOARD

The National Labor Relations Board (NLRB) is a federal organization that oversees the establishment and conduct of union organizations as well as the conduct of businesses involved with unions.

HISTORY AND PURPOSE OF THE NLRB The NLRB was created in 1935 by Congress to administer the National Labor Relations Act (NLRA). The NLRA is the law that governs relations between **labor unions** and employers whose operations involve interstate commerce. Though there are other federal and state laws which also protect the rights of employees, such as the Fair Labor Standards Act (FLSA), the NLRA is the Act specifically tied to the NLRB and to union organization.

The Act itself gives employees the right to organize and bargain collectively with their employers, as well as the right not to organize. In short, employees may join a union or not, as they so choose. Coverage of the law is relatively exclusive, covering only employees working for employers involved in interstate commerce with a few exceptions (airlines, railroads, agriculture and government). The act ensures that employees can choose their own representatives for the purpose of collective bargaining, establishes procedures for secret-ballot elections, and defines unfair labor practices, to which both employers and unions are subject.

The NLRB conducts elections and prevents and remedies unfair labor practices. It is made up of two different "arms." The Board is a group of five persons based in Washington, D.C., who act in a judicial capacity, though they are not judges. This group decides whether improper labor practices have actually occurred, either during an election campaign or during management-union bargaining sessions. The General Counsel is the prosecutorial side of the Board. It has offices throughout the country and is charged with the investigation and prosecution of those who engage in unfair labor practices. The NLRB is designed to be completely equitable, taking sides for neither management nor union, acting as a sort of "referee" in what is usually an emotionally charged action between employees and employers.

IMPACT ON BUSINESS The employees of any business may seek representation by filing a petition with the NLRB requesting an election. The NLRA requires that representation must be by a "labor organization," as defined by the NLRA. The definition of a labor organization is fairly liberal, and entrepreneurs should always be familiar with both large and smaller unions that might seek to organize a business' employees. The larger ones, such as the **AFL-CIO** or the United Auto Workers (UAW), are well known, but there are many smaller organizations as well.

Once an election has been held and employees have determined that they want representation by a union for the purposes of collective bargaining, the employer is required by law to bargain with no other organization for the workers in that business. All workers are covered by the decision, whether they become members of the union or not. Generally, such employment concerns such as wages, hours, and working conditions are included in the collective bargaining agreement, which is set up during meetings between the employer and the union representatives.

UNFAIR LABOR PRACTICES The judicial arm of the NLRB becomes involved when there is a dispute about the conduct of the employer or the union during a union election campaign or during bargaining. The General Counsel investigates the charge to determine if it is valid and should be pursued. The charge can become a local level complaint at this stage, or can be dismissed. The great majority of charges filed with the NLRB are settled or withdrawn at the stage when investigation has been completed, before a complaint has been issued.

If a complaint is filed, the case is heard before an Administrative Law Judge, part of the judicial arm of the NLRB. The Administrative Law Judge's decision on the case is adopted by the Board. If exceptions are made, the transcript, briefs, and other documentation of the case is sent to the Board in Washington for a decision. The NLRB rarely hears oral arguments; it usually making decisions based on the documentation from the Administrative Law Judge.

The NLRB decisions do not have the impact of law because the NLRB is an administrative agency. Their decisions are recommendations, but NLRB opinions carry a great deal of weight in courts of law. If either the union or employer is unwilling to follow the guidelines set down in the decision, the NLRB files a petition in the Court of Appeals—the level directly below the Supreme Court—for the district where the case arose. If this decision is contested, the Board will request that the U.S. Supreme Court hear the case.

FURTHER READING:

Gould, William B, IV. *A Primer on American Labor Law*, 2d ed. Cambridge, MA: MIT Press, 1986.

A Guide to Basic Law and Procedures Under the National Labor Relations Act. Revised ed. Washington: U.S. National Labor Relations Board, 1991.

"Managing American Labor." *Financial World.* June 25, 1991.

Miller, Edward B. *An Administrative Appraisal of the NLRB.* Labor Relations and Public Policy Series no. 16. Philadelphia, PA: University of Pennsylvania, 1977.

Weiler, Paul C. *Governing the Workplace: The Future of Labor and Employment Law.* Cambridge, MA: Harvard University Press, 1990.

SEE ALSO: Labor Unions and Small Business

NATIONAL VENTURE CAPITAL ASSOCIATION

The National Venture Capital Association (NVCA), founded in 1973, is an organization of **venture capital** firms, corporate backers, and individuals dedicated to professionally investing private capital in new companies. In their own words, they exist to "define, serve, and represent the interests of the venture capital and private equity industries" by, among other things, promoting the public policy interests of the venture capital and entrepreneurial communities. The group seeks to foster greater understanding of the necessity of investing in young companies and their role in the overall health of the United States economy. To that end, it works to stimulate the flow of risk equity capital to emerging and developing companies. It also aims to promote communication between venturing bodies throughout the United States and strives to improve the level of knowledge of the venturing process in government, universities, and the general business community. In support of these activities, the NVCA conducts research, hosts educational and networking programs, and serves as an information clearinghouse for its members. It makes available the results of its research in various publications, such as its *Annual Economic Impact of Venture Capital Study, Job Creation Survey, Expert Analysis of Legislative and Regulatory Issues,* and other scholarly works. The organization is located at 1655 N. Fort Myer Dr., Suite 700, Arlington, Virginia 22209. Phone: (703) 351-5269.

VENTURE CAPITAL Because new business owners often lack the collateral and experience to garner traditional bank (debt) financing, the start-up often must seek funds elsewhere. Many entrepreneurs seek "venture capital" informally, obtaining seed money from friends and family or wealthy individuals willing to risk an investment. Others, of course, seek funding by professional firms. In these cases, the firm assesses any number of business plans to determine which holds the greatest potential for success and then finances its construction. The venture capital firm will have an ongoing relationship with the start-up, providing coaching, training, management expertise, and other services, and often holding a seat on the young company's board of directors. Should your business be accepted for funding by a venture capital firm, expect the organization to take an active part in shaping your business.

According to the NVCA, funds used by venture capital firms come from a variety of sources, including institutional investors such as pension funds, foundations and endowments, insurance companies, wealthy individuals, professional money managers, foreign investors, and the venture capitalists themselves.

NVCA MEMBERSHIP Benefits and services accorded the NVCA member include, among other things, a voice in public policy. Venture PAC (political action committee), which is managed by the NVCA, advocates public policies that would be beneficial to the entrepreneurial and venture communities. The association also provides educational programs accessible throughout the United States. Programs are conducted by industry scholars, practitioners, and analysts. In addition, the NVCA offers a director and officer insurance program intended for both members and their portfolio companies that provides risk management and loss control protection.

The Regional Member Committee program, a network of liaison groups that represents members from across the United States, works with the NVCA Board of Directors and staff to design and enhance the programs offered by the association. The committees, which are composed of members from each of the six regions, include Education, Public Relations, Research, Tax Policy and others. Finally, the NVCA's affiliate organization, the American Entrepreneurs for Economic Growth (AEEG), seeks to ''serve as a united voice on public policy issues for entrepreneurs'' and represents nearly 10,000 emerging growth company executives employing some one million workers.

MEMBERSHIP REQUIREMENTS AND ADMISSION PROCEDURES NVCA has several requirements of potential members. Those seeking membership (by invitation) must be capital organizations, investment advisors, corporate investors, or buyout funds. Members need not be full time venture capitalists, but they must have as their primary business the deployment of venture capital. They also must represent capital funds and utilize a professional approach before and after they make an investment, including the maintenance of a continuing interest in companies they sponsor. The managers of the business must be American citizens or resident aliens and operate from an office located in the United States. In addition, members must invest from a dedicated U.S.-based venture capital pool of funds of at least one million dollars. Finally, the members' business must be subject to U.S. taxation and laws. Should a company be interested in membership, it would need to fill out and submit an application. Membership applications are available online at http://www.nvca.org/become.html. Dues are scalable and depend on the amount of capital under management.

FURTHER READING:

Flanagan, Lawrence. *Raising Capital: How to Write a Financing Proposal.* Psi Research - Oasis Press, 1994.

Gillis, Tom S. *Guts & Borrowed Money: Straight Talk for Starting & Growing Your Small Business.* Bard Press, 1997.

Lister, Kate, Tom Harnish, and Catherine E. Lister. *Directory of Venture Capital.* John Wiley & Sons, 1996.

Lundgren, Douglas A. *Venture Capital: An Authoritative Guide for Investors, Entrepreneurs, and Managers.* McGraw-Hill, 1998.

Paul, Philip C. *Where to Find Venture Capital.* Rainbow Books, 1995.

Ross, Duncan M., and Andrew Godley. *Banks, Networks, and Small Firm Finance.* Frank Cass & Co., 1996.

NEGOTIATION

Negotiation describes any communication process between individuals that is intended to reach a compromise or agreement to the satisfaction of both parties. Negotiation involves examining the facts of a situation, exposing both the common and opposing interests of the parties involved, and bargaining to resolve as many issues as possible. Negotiation takes place every day in nearly every facet of life—from national governments negotiating border disputes, to companies negotiating work agreements with labor unions, to real estate agents negotiating the sale of property, to former spouses negotiating the terms of a divorce. Small business owners are likely to face negotiations on a daily basis when dealing with customers, suppliers, employees, investors, creditors, government agencies, and even family members. Many companies train members of their sales forces in negotiation techniques, and many others hire professional negotiators to represent them in business dealings. Good negotiation requires advance preparation, a knowledge of negotiating techniques, and practice.

Regardless of the type of negotiation, experts recommend entering into it with a cooperative rather than a competitive attitude. They stress that the point of negotiating is to reach agreement rather than to achieve victory. ''Any method of negotiation may be fairly judged by three criteria,'' Roger Fisher and William Ury wrote in their book *Getting to Yes: Negotiating Agreement without Giving In.* ''It should produce a wise agreement if agreement is possible. It should be efficient. And it should improve or at least not damage the relationship between the parties.'' When one of the parties uses ''hard'' negotiating techniques—or bullies and intimidates the other side in order to obtain a more favorable arrangement—it only creates resentment and poisons future negotiations. Instead, the idea should be to find a win/win solution that satisfies the needs and interests of both parties.

PREPARING FOR A NEGOTIATION

Good negotiation requires advance preparation, an understanding of the underlying assumptions and needs to be satisfied on both sides, a basic knowledge of human behavior, and mastery of a range of negotiating techniques, strategies, and tactics. In his book *Fundamentals of Negotiating,* Gerard I. Nierenberg outlined a number of steps toward adequately preparing for a negotiation. The first step is to ''do your homework'' about the other side. In nearly every negotiation, this will entail research to uncover their underlying motivations. In negotiating a business property lease, for example, it may be useful to find out the cost to the landlord of keeping the building vacant. The next step is to assess your own side's needs and establish objectives for the negotiation. It is important that the objectives remain relatively fluid, however, so as not to hinder the negotiation.

Another element of preparing for a negotiation involves deciding whether to use an individual or a team as your representative. This decision needs to be considered separately for every negotiation, and will always depend to some extent on what the other side is doing. A negotiating team offers a number of potential advantages. For example, it enables a small business to involve people with different areas of expertise in order to avoid misstatements of fact. Teams can also play into negotiating strategies and help gain concessions through consultation among team members. However, it is important to note that bringing extra people can be harmful to a negotiation when they do not have a distinct function. Using a single negotiator also offers some advantages. It prevents the weakening of positions that often occurs through differences of opinion within a team, and it also may help gain concessions through the negotiator's ability to make on-the-spot decisions.

The next step in preparing for a negotiation involves choosing a chief negotiator. Ideally, this person should have experience and training in negotiations, as well as a strong background in the area of the issue to be negotiated. Another important element of negotiation is selecting the meeting site. For a small business, holding the meeting on its own premises may provide a psychological advantage, plus will save on travel time and expense. It may also be helpful in enabling the negotiators to obtain approval from managers or use their own facilities to check facts and find additional information as needed. Holding a negotiation at the other side's offices, however, may help the negotiators devote their full attention to the task at hand without distractions. It may also play into negotiating strategy by enabling the negotiators to temporarily withhold information by claiming a need to speak to higher level people or gather more information. A third alternative for a meeting site is a neutral location. Whatever site is chosen, it should be large enough to accommodate all parties and feature a telephone, comfortable chairs, and visual aids, and the availability of refreshments.

THE NEGOTIATION PROCESS

Fisher and Ury recommend conducting negotiations according to the process of "principled negotiation." Their method has four main tenets:

1) Separate the people from the problem. The idea should be for both sides to work together to attack a problem, rather than attacking each other. To achieve this goal, it is necessary to overcome emotional responses and set aside egos.

2) Focus on interests rather than positions. The natural tendency in many negotiations—for example, dickering over the price to be paid for an antique—is for both sides to state a position and then move toward middle ground. Fisher and Ury warn against confus-

ing people's stated positions with their underlying interests, and claim that positions often tend to obscure what people truly hope to gain through negotiation.

3) Generate a variety of options before deciding what to do. The pressure involved in any type of negotiation tends to narrow people's vision and inhibit their creativity, making it difficult to find optimal solutions to problems. Instead, Fisher and Ury suggest developing a wide range of possible solutions as part of the negotiating process. These possible solutions should attempt to advance shared interests and reconcile differences.

4) Base the result on objective criteria. No one will be happy with the result of a negotiation if they feel that they have been taken advantage of. The solution is to find and apply some fair standard to the problem in order to guarantee a mutually beneficial result.

Fisher and Ury's principles provide a good overall guide for the actual negotiation process. In his book, Nierenberg offered a number of other tips and strategies that may be effective in promoting successful negotiations. For example, it may be helpful to ask questions in order to form a better understanding of the needs and interests of the other side. The questions must be phrased diplomatically and timed correctly in order to avoid an antagonistic response. The idea is to gain information and uncover basic assumptions without immediately taking positions. Nierenberg stressed the importance of listening carefully to the other side's responses, as well as studying their facial expressions and body language, in order to gain quality information.

Nierenberg noted that good negotiators will employ a variety of means to accomplish their objectives. Small business owners should be aware of some of the more common strategies and techniques that they may see others apply or may wish to apply themselves. One common strategy is forbarance, or "patience pays," which covers any sort of wait or delay in negotiations. If one side wishes to confer in private, or adjourn briefly, they are employing a strategy of forbearance. Another common strategy is to present a *fait accompli,* or come to a final offer and leave it up to the other side to decide whether to accept it. In a simple example, a small business owner may scratch out one provision in a contract that he or she finds unacceptable, then sign it and send it back. The other party to the contract then must decide whether to accept the revised agreement. Nierenberg warns that this strategy can be risky, and encourages those who employ it to carefully appraise the consequences first.

Another possible negotiating strategy is reversal, which involves taking a position that seems opposed to the original one. Similarly, feinting involves apparently moving in one direction in order to divert attention from the true goal. For example, a negotiator may give in on a point that is not very important in order to make the real objective more attainable. Another strategy involves setting limits on the negotiation, whether with regards to time, the people involved, or other factors. It is also possible to change the participation in the negotiation if it seems to be at an impasse. For example, a neutral third party may be enlisted to help, or one or two people from each side may be sent off to continue the negotiation separately. It may also be helpful to break down the problem into small pieces and tackle them one by one. Another strategy might be to trade sides for a short time and try to view the situation from each other's perspective. All of these techniques may be applied either to gain advantage or to push forward a negotiation that has apparently reached an impasse.

FURTHER READING:

Fisher, Roger, and William Ury. *Getting to Yes: Negotiating Agreement without Giving In.* 2nd ed. New York: Penguin, 1991.

Nierenberg, Gerard I. *Fundamentals of Negotiating.* New York: Hawthorn Books, 1977.

NEPOTISM

In the business world, nepotism is the practice of showing favoritism toward one's family members or friends in economic or employment terms. For example, granting favors or jobs to friends and relatives, without regard to merit, might be considered nepotism. These practices can have damaging effects on businesses—such as eroding the support of non-favored employees or reducing the quality and creativity of management. In response, some larger companies have instituted "antinepotism" policies, which prevent relatives (by blood or marriage) from working in the same department or firm. But in many smaller, **family-owned businesses**, nepotism is viewed in more positive terms. Family members are trained in various aspects of management to ensure the continuity of the company when members of the earlier generation retire or die. In fact, in many small businesses nepotism is considered a synonym for "succession."

One of the most common arguments against nepotism is that the emotional ties between people who are related may negatively affect their **decision making** and growth at the office. In the past, many businesses sought to avoid even the appearance of nepotism by forbidding relatives from working closely together. As women entered the work force in greater numbers and took on more significant jobs, however, rules regarding nepotism began to change. Both the man and the woman in a married couple were often too valuable for a company to lose. Instead of instituting strict antinepotism rules, many businesses decided that family members could be accommodated within a merit system, especially if there was no direct supervisory link between the positions of related employees.

In their book *The Best Companies for Women*, Baila Zeitz and Lorraine Dusky compared the results of surveys taken in the early and late 1980s to demonstrate these changes of policy. While 17 percent of surveyed companies had antinepotism rules in 1980, the number dropped to 2 percent by 1987. Similarly, 72 percent of the companies forbade married couples from working in the same department or function in 1980, compared to 37 percent in 1987.

NEPOTISM IN SMALL BUSINESSES

Nepotism can be useful in smaller, family-owned businesses. The emotional bonds between family members can actually have a positive effect on individual performance and company results. In addition, hiring family members can fill staffing requirements with dedicated employees. But in order to avoid potential pitfalls and ensure that relatives work together effectively, the company should establish formal guidelines regarding hiring, reporting structure, training, and succession. These guidelines will be different depending on the family's size, culture, history, and line of business, in addition to other factors. "How strict or liberal the rules . . . are is less important than clear communication of the rules before they are needed and fair application of the rules when timely," Craig E. Aronoff and John L. Ward wrote in *Nation's Business*.

Regarding hiring, Aronoff and Ward recommend that family members meet three qualifications before they are allowed to join the family business on a permanent basis: an appropriate educational background; three to five years of outside work experience; and an open, existing position in the firm that matches their background. Of these qualifications, Aronoff and Ward stress that outside work experience is the most important for both the business and the individual. They claim that it gives future managers a wider experience base that makes them better equipped to deal with challenges, lets them learn and make mistakes before coming under the watchful eye of the family, makes them realize what other options exist and thus appreciate the family firm, and provides them with an idea of their market value.

Aronoff and Ward also suggest that family members begin their association with the business by working part-time during their school years or participating in internships. In addition, they stress that companies who hire family members should make it clear to the individuals that they will be fired for illegal or unethical behavior, regardless of their family ties. Finally, they recommend that family businesses encourage their employees to maintain outside associations in order to avoid problems associated with a lack of creativity or accountability in management. For example, future managers could participate in industry or civic groups, enroll in night school classes or attend seminars, take responsibility for a division or profit center, and have their job performance reviewed by outside consultants or directors. Such steps can improve the employee's self-confidence and preparation for an eventual leadership role in the business.

FURTHER READING:

Aronoff, Craig E., and John L. Ward. *Family Business Succession: The Final Test of Greatness.* Marietta, GA: Business Owner Resources, 1992.

Aronoff and Ward. "Rules for Nepotism." *Nation's Business.* January 1993.

Ford, Robert, and Frank McLaughlin. "Nepotism." *Personnel Journal.* September 1985.

Frieswick, Kris. "Successful Succession." *Industrial Distribution.* April 1996.

Turpin, Joanna R. "Succession Planning Requires Long-Term Strategy, Implementation." *Air Conditioning, Heating, and Refrigeration News.* April 28, 1997.

Zeitz, Baila, and Lorraine Dusky. *The Best Companies for Women.* New York: Simon and Schuster, 1988.

SEE ALSO: Succession Plans

NET INCOME

Net income is an **accounting** term that can be defined as the difference between a company's total revenues (money earned from sales or investments) and total expenses (money paid to produce goods or services, plus salaries, rent, depreciation, etc.) for a given period of time. Also known as net earnings, after-tax income, or profit, net income is the "bottom line" of the formal accounting report known as the income statement. If a company's total expenses exceed its total revenues for a certain period, it can be said to have experienced a net loss. If revenues and expenses should turn out to be equal, the company will have broken even.

Net income is one of the most important indicators of the financial health of a business. "Some people view the **income statement** as the most important of the three required financial statements [the others are the **balance sheet** and the statement of changes in financial position] because it is designed to report the amount of net income and the details of how that amount was earned," according to Glenn A. Welsch, Robert N. Anthony, and Daniel G. Short in their book *Fundamentals of Financial Accounting.* "The amount of net income for the period represents a net increase in resources (or a net decrease if a loss) that flowed into the business entity during that period as a result of operational activities."

Most income statements will show three separate income figures. The first is pretax income, which is the amount the company earned before taxes. Reporting of this figure is optional. The second is income before extraordinary items, which is equal to ordinary revenues less ordinary expenses. Extraordinary items include any nonoperating gains or losses that are unusual in nature and infrequent in occurrence. They are separated from ordinary income in order to avoid confusing the readers of income statements. Reporting of this figure is mandatory whenever there are extraordinary items to be included.

The third and final income figure shown on an income statement is net income. It is the difference between total revenues and total expenses for the period, including taxes and extraordinary items. Net income always appears as the last figure in the body of the income statement, and its reporting is mandatory. Corporations (but not sole proprietorships or partnerships) are also required to divide the net income figure by the number of shares of stock outstanding in order to report the earnings per share (EPS) for the period.

In addition to providing information on its own, net income is also frequently compared to other figures in **financial ratios** in order to provide further information about a company's overall health. For example, financial analysts often divide net income by total sales in order to find a company's rate of return on sales. This figure provides a good indication of the amount of profit the company is able to earn for every dollar of sales. Another common ratio examined by financial analysts is return on stockholders' equity, which can be found by dividing net income by the average equity for the period. As Charles T. Horngren and Gary L. Sundem wrote in their book *Fundamentals of Financial Accounting,* "This ratio is widely regarded as the ultimate measure of overall accomplishment."

FURTHER READING:

Hilton, Ronald W. *Managerial Accounting.* New York: McGraw-Hill, 1991.

Horngren, Charles T., and Gary L. Sundem. *Introduction to Financial Accounting.* 4th ed. Englewood Cliffs, NJ: Prentice Hall, 1990.

Welsch, Glenn A., Robert N. Anthony, and Daniel G. Short. *Fundamentals of Financial Accounting.* 4th ed. Homewood, IL: Irwin, 1984.

NET WORTH

Net worth is a basic measure of the value of a business. It can be defined as the difference between a company's assets and liabilities, as they are recorded on the balance sheet. Net worth is one of many terms used to describe the value of the equity held by owners of a business. As Glenn A. Welsch, Robert N. Anthony, and Daniel G. Short explained in their book *Fundamentals of Financial Accounting,* "Owners' equity sometimes is called net worth, **capital**, or proprietorship. However, the preferable designations are a) owner's equity for a sole proprietorship; b) partners' equity for a partnership; and c) stockholders' or shareholders' equity for a corporation." In contrast to these more specific terms, net worth can be used to describe the value of any business, as well as the financial position of an individual.

It is important to note that net worth measures only the book, or accounting, value of a business. This amount is not usually the same as the market value of a business, which is the amount an informed buyer would pay to acquire the business in an arm's-length transaction. Improving net worth is a matter of increasing **assets** or decreasing **liabilities**. If a business has liabilities in excess of its assets, it is said to have a negative net worth. This condition is considered detrimental for a business, and often prevents it from acquiring new funds through bank loans.

ELEMENTS OF THE BALANCE SHEET

Determination of a company's net worth comes from its **balance sheet**. The balance sheet outlines the financial and physical resources that a company has available for business activities at a particular point in time. It is important to note, however, that the balance sheet only lists these resources and makes no judgment about how well they will be used by management. For this reason, the balance sheet is more useful in analyzing a company's current financial position than its expected performance.

The main elements of the balance sheet are assets, liabilities, and owners' equity. Assets generally include both current assets (cash or equivalents that will be converted to cash within one year, such as accounts receivable, inventory, and prepaid expenses) and noncurrent assets (assets that are held for more than one year and are used in running the business, including fixed assets like property, plant, and equip-

ment; long-term investments; and intangible assets like patents, copyrights, and goodwill). The balance sheet also includes two categories of liabilities, current liabilities (debts that will come due within one year, such as accounts payable, short-term loans, and taxes) and long-term debts (debts that are due more than one year from the date of the statement).

The difference between assets and liabilities as reported on the balance sheet is recorded in owners' equity accounts. These accounts detail the permanent capital of the business, also known as its net worth. The total equity usually consists of two parts: 1) contributed capital, or the money that has been invested by shareholders; and 2) retained earnings, or the money that has been accumulated from profits and reinvested in the business. In general, the higher the net worth of a business, the better the ability of the business to borrow additional funds.

FURTHER READING:

Bangs, David H., Jr. *Managing by the Numbers: Financial Essentials for the Growing Business.* Dover, NH: Upstart Publishing, 1992.

Welsch, Glenn A., Robert N. Anthony, and Daniel G. Short. *Fundamentals of Financial Accounting.* 4th ed. Homewood, IL: Irwin, 1984.

NETWORKING

Networking is the process of intentionally meeting people, making contacts, and forming relationships in hopes of gaining access to such business-related benefits as career advice, job leads, business referrals, useful information and ideas, and emotional support. For example, a small business owner's network might include clients, vendors, fellow members of trade or professional associations, bankers, accountants, professors at a local business school, friends who are employed in similar industries, and other small business owners. Each person that a small business owner adds to his or her network is at the center of their own network, so in actuality the network is expanded considerably with every new member. Ideally, networks serve both social and business functions and are mutually beneficial for their members. The relationships formed in networking help people create a larger world for themselves, with a variety of new relationships, opportunities, and resources.

BENEFITS OF NETWORKING

In an article for the *Training and Development Journal,* Frank K. Sonnenberg identified three main benefits that accrue to those who practice effective networking: referrals, relationships, and leads. Referrals, which are particularly important in growing a small business, take many forms. For example, a satisfied client might suggest others who may need the company's products or services. Similarly, a network member who is familiar with the company's offerings might provide an endorsement or allow the small business owner to mention his or her name in marketing efforts. It is good networking practice and a matter of professional courtesy to thank the person who provided the referral and to keep them informed of the results of the new contact. In addition, it is important never to use someone as a referral without first securing their permission. If a referral does result in a new client relationship, care should be taken to provide the new client with the same level of product or service quality that was enjoyed by the one that gave the referral. Otherwise, the small business risks ruining both client relationships.

Another benefit of networking is establishing relationships, which can have a number of positive outcomes for small businesses. Forming a close relationship with a client, for example, might provide invaluable insight into their needs. In addition to giving the small business a good opportunity to promote or develop products and services to meet those needs, this insight might also help the small business owner to fix small problems before they escalate into large ones. The insights gained from one client can often be applied to other clients in order to improve those relationships. Close client relationships can also provide information about competitors, their relative strengths and weaknesses, and what it takes to stay ahead of them.

Finally, networking can be an excellent source of leads, whether on new business opportunities, new career options, or further networking possibilities. For example, the head of a construction company that is erecting an office building might share a network with an interior designer. When the building is close to completion, the head of the construction company might provide the interior designer with leads on the occupants of the building and their furnishing needs. In turn, the interior designer might alert a network contact who sells office supplies when the new occupants are preparing to move into the building.

FINDING NETWORKING OPPORTUNITIES

Opportunities for networking abound. One well-known example of a possible contact is the person occupying the next seat on an airplane. But it is possible to take a more organized approach. In an article for *Entrepreneur,* Leann Anderson outlined several strategies for finding networking opportunities. First, she suggested making a list of specific groups of people that would be helpful to know for business purposes, from potential customers to other small businesses that offer complementary products or services. Then it is necessary to identify where best to find them. Perhaps they are likely to participate in certain activities, belong to certain organizations, or frequent certain places or events. The final step is to become involved in those organizations or activities. Another possibility to explore is organizations that are dedicated to providing business networking opportunities, like **chambers of commerce**.

GUIDELINES FOR ESTABLISHING AND MAINTAINING A SUCCESSFUL NETWORK

Successful networking involves making it a personal practice to view every situation—both inside and outside of the business environment—as an opportunity to meet new people. In an article for *Manage,* Anna Boe suggested several key points in adding a new acquaintance to the network. First, when meeting people, it is important not to be afraid of rejection, and not to take it personally when it occurs. Second, it is helpful to exchange names, occupations, and other pertinent information shortly after meeting someone new. The best way to strike up a conversation is usually to ask questions to draw people out and get them talking about themselves.

But simply meeting and exchanging information with another person is not enough. Networking is a long-term strategy—not one that should be pursued only when contacts are urgently needed—and networks must be continually formed and improved upon over time. It is important to keep in touch with new acquaintances and nurture the relationships. It is also helpful to grant favors warmly when they are requested, and to be flexible when asking others for their time, information, advice, or a referral. In addition, merely attending conferences or meetings is not enough to establish and maintain a strong network. Instead, it requires one-on-one time with other people. Another factor in establishing networks is to become an active rather than passive participant in **business associations**, clubs, or groups.

Networking has its own rules of etiquette that must be followed if it is to be practiced successfully. Most importantly, networking should consist of give-and-take relationships. People who only want to do one or the other quickly lose members from their networks. Boe noted that giving should be its own reward, and that people who grant favors should avoid the temptation to keep score or expect an immediate favor in return. On the other hand, it is important to allow others an occasional opportunity to reciprocate, or else they will become hesitant to ask for help.

The other common-sense rules of etiquette for successful networking include not smothering people or wasting their time, calling on contacts at convenient times, being reasonable and considerate with requests, spreading requests around among various contacts, not making promises that cannot be kept, and not revealing sensitive information that may be acquired through network contacts. Finally, networking should not be equated with sales. Instead, it should be considered an information-gathering exercise that can eventually lead to new business opportunities.

FURTHER READING:

Anderson, Leann. "Make the Connection: Networking Opportunities Are Everywhere. Don't Let Them Pass You By." *Entrepreneur.* July 1997.

Boe, Anna. "Making Networking Work for You." *Manage.* July 1993.

Sonnenberg, Frank K. "The Professional (and Personal) Profits of Networking." *Training and Development Journal.* September 1990.

NON-COMPETITION AGREEMENTS

Non-competition agreements are restrictive **contracts** between employers and employees that 1) prohibit workers from revealing proprietary information about the company to competitors or other outsiders, or 2) forbid workers from themselves competing with their ex-employer for a certain period of time after leaving the company. These agreements, which are also sometimes called confidentiality or nondisclosure agreements, typically defines confidential information, identifies ownership rights, and details employee obligations to ensure that confidentiality is maintained.

Proprietary information, which is more commonly referred to under the heading of "trade secrets," is information that a company wishes to keep confidential or protect from those outside the company. Proprietary information can cover just about any aspect of a business's operation, including production formulas, processes, and methods; business and marketing plans; salary structure; customer lists, contracts; **intellectual property**; and computer systems.

EMPLOYEE AND EMPLOYER RIGHTS "The employee does owe the owner a duty of loyalty while employed," observed the *Entrepreneur Magazine Small Business Advisor.* "This means that if the employer finds the employee calling about another job while still employed, or trying to solicit coworkers to work somewhere else, the employer has a right to damages if it can prove its case." But workers have rights as well, including the one to establish a competing business. "The day after the employee leaves, he or she can call coworkers on the phone and solicit them."

While employees generally have every right to make use of skills and experiences gained in one company when they set off on the next stage of their lives, it is illegal for them to make off with trade secrets of their former place of employment. Still, business owners do not always win court cases against ex-employees who pilfer in this area for the simple reason that the business owner "never identified the company's confidential or trade secret information," noted the *Small Business Advisor.* "An ex-employee does not have the right to steal company confidential information or trade secrets that are identified as such; however, the ownership of information developed through company procedures must clearly differentiate what belongs to the employee and what to the company. The easiest way to accomplish this is through nondisclosure agreements."

ENFORCING NON-COMPETITION AGREEMENTS Non-competition agreements are an important tool that small business owners may wield to ensure that key personnel do not walk off and establish a competing business on the strength of knowledge and contacts that they gained during their stint at the small business in question. These documents have significant deterrent value in many situations, and they should be signed by any employees who have access to sensitive company information (many consultants recommend that business owners insist on one as a condition of employment). But as *Profit-Building Strategies for Business Owners* observed, "many employees have signed a noncompete agreement and then broken it. In such a case, you'll have to decide whether to bring suit."

Non-competition covenants are usually enforced by the courts if they are reasonable with respect to time and place and do not unreasonably restrict the former employee's right to employment. Of course, different parties have different conceptions of what constitutes a "reasonable" restriction. Business attorney Morgan Chu told *Small Business Reports* that the courts are far more likely to side with the business owner if he or she does not go overboard on imposing restrictions in the following areas:

- Nature of prohibition—"What work is the employee prohibited from engaging in?" queried *Small Business Reports.* "A salesperson of heart pacemakers who starts selling medical staples would probably not violate a non-compete agreement."

- Duration of agreement—Non-competition agreements are less likely to be enforced if they go beyond one year or so.

- Geographic area—While it is generally recognized that small business owners have a right to request competition protection from ex-employees in the immediate area in which they operate, stipulations that forbid ex-workers from setting up a similar business in some distant geographic area or region are likely to be overturned.

- Restrictions on Solicitation—"Who is the employee prohibited from soliciting?" asked *Small Business Reports*. "Is it customers whom the employee personally acquired or any or your company's customers? The narrower your restriction, the more likely a court will enforce it."

In some cases the covenants are enforced only if the employee has gained proprietary information during the course of his or her employment. In addition, the courts generally consider it unfair competition for one company to induce employees of another company who have acquired unique technical skills and secret knowledge during their employment to terminate their employment and use their skills and knowledge for the benefit of the competing firm. In such a case the plaintiff company could seek an injunction to prevent its former employees and the competing company from using the proprietary information.

FURTHER READING:

"How to Protect Yourself from Employees Who Become Competitors." *Profit-Building Strategies for Business Owners.* April 1993.

"Keeping Secrets Secret." *Small Business Reports.* February 1994.

NONPROFIT ORGANIZATIONS

Nonprofit organizations are institutions that are conduct their affairs for the purpose of assisting other individuals, groups, or causes rather than garnering profits for themselves. Nonprofit groups have no shareholders; do not distribute profits in a way that benefits members, directors, or other individuals in their private capacity; and (often) receive exemption from various taxes in recognition of their contributions to bettering the general social fabric of the community.

Nonprofit organizations are far more important to the overall U.S. economy than is generally recognized. Indeed, some sources indicate that the sum total of nonprofit groups comprise a third sector of the American economy, along with the private (business) and public (government) sectors. The Society of Non-

profit Organizations (SNPO), for instance, notes that 983,000 nonprofit organizations were in operation in the U.S. in 1990. The SNPO claims that 8.6 million people (more than 6 percent of the total adult population in the country) held paid positions in nonprofit organizations at that time, and that nonprofits generated more than $535 billion in 1990 revenues. Of these revenues, the Society of Nonprofit Organizations estimated that approximately $126 billion came as a direct result of gifts from individuals ($102 billion), bequests ($8.5 billion), foundations ($9.2 billion), and corporations ($5.9 billion). Moreover, the estimated 89 million volunteers that contributed their services to nonprofit organizations provided a staggering total of 19.5 billion hours of assistance in 1993, according to SNPO (an equivalent of 8.8. million full-time employees).

TYPES OF NONPROFIT ORGANIZATIONS

A wide range of charitable and other institutions are classified as nonprofit organizations under the Internal Revenue Code. Many of these qualify under the definition provided in Section 501(c)(3) of the Code, which stipulates that all of the following qualify for tax-exempt status: "Corporations, and any community chest, fund or foundation, organized and operated exclusively for religious, charitable, scientific, testing for public safety, literary or educational purposes, to foster certain national or international amateur sports competition, or for the prevention of cruelty to children or animals," provided that the institutions adhere to basic standards of behavior and requirements of net earnings allocation.

CHARITABLE ORGANIZATIONS Charitable institutions comprise the bulk of America's nonprofit organizations. These include a wide variety of institutions involved in the realms of poverty assistance (soup kitchens, counseling centers, homeless shelters, etc.); religion (churches and their ancillary possessions, such as cemeteries, radio stations, etc.); science (independent research institutions, universities); health (hospitals, clinics, nursing homes, treatment centers); education (libraries, museums, schools, universities, and other institutions); promotion of social welfare; preservation of natural resources; and promotion of theatre, music, and other fine arts.

ADVOCACY ORGANIZATIONS Advocacy organizations are groups that "attempt to influence the legislative process and/or the political process, or otherwise champion particular positions," explained Hopkins. "They may call themselves 'social welfare organizations' or perhaps 'political action committees.' Not all advocacy is lobbying and not all political activity is political campaign activity. Some of this type of program can be accomplished through a charitable organization, but that outcome is rare where advocacy is the organization's primary undertaking.''

MEMBERSHIP GROUPS This kind of nonprofit organization includes **business associations**, veterans' groups, and fraternal organizations.

SOCIAL/RECREATIONAL ORGANIZATIONS Social and recreational organizations such as country clubs, hobby and garden clubs, college and university fraternity and sorority organizations, and sports tournament organizations all can qualify as nonprofit organizations, provided that they adhere to basic guidelines of net earnings distribution, etc. Unlike other tax-exempt organizations, however, their investment income is taxable.

"SATELLITE" ORGANIZATIONS Hopkins pointed out that ''some nonprofit organizations are deliberately organized as auxiliaries or subsidiaries of other organizations.'' Such organizations include cooperatives, retirement and other employee benefit funds, and title-holding companies.

EMPLOYEE BENEFIT FUNDS Some profit-sharing and retirement programs can qualify for tax-exempt status.

ADVANTAGES AND DISADVANTAGES OF INCORPORATING

All nonprofit organizations are faced with the decision of whether or not to incorporate. ''There are many benefits'' associated with **incorporation**, as Ted Nicholas noted in *The Complete Guide to Non-profit Corporations.* ''Some are the same as those commonly enjoyed by *for-profit* business corporations. Others are unique to the nonprofit corporation. Perhaps the greatest advantages of all—granted exclusively to organizations with bona fide nonprofit status—is exemption from taxes at federal, state, and local levels.'' In addition to tax exemption, Nicholas cited the following as principle advantages of forming a nonprofit corporation:

- Permission to solicit funds—Many nonprofit organizations depend on their ability to solicit funds (in the form of gifts, donations, bequests, etc.) for their very existence. Nicholas noted that whereas some states bestow a fund-raising privilege on nonprofit corporations as soon as their articles of incorporation are filed, other states require groups to fulfill additional obligations before granting permission to solicit funds.

- Low postage rates—Many nonprofit corporations are able to use the U.S. mail system at considerably lower rates than private individuals or for-profit businesses. To secure these lower rates, nonprofits must apply to the Postal Service for a permit, but this is generally not a major hurdle, provided that the nonprofit group has its affairs in order. ''The importance of the mailing rate advantage is directly proportional to the volume of mail the nonprofit corporation generates in the course of its business,'' said Nicholas. ''Membership solicitations are usually mailed third class. Nonprofit corporations that rely on membership income can use the mail even more extensively to service their members. So potential savings from a special mailing permit are considerable.''

- Exemption from labor rules—Nonprofit organizations enjoy exemption from the various rules and guidelines of union collective bargaining, even if their work force is represented by a union.

- Immunity from tort liability—This advantage is not available in all states, but Nicholas observed that some states still provide nonprofit charitable organizations with immunity to tort liability. ''It is important to recognize, however, that where it exists, the immunity protects only the nonprofit corporation—not the agent or employee where negligence injures someone.''

In addition, nonprofit corporations enjoy certain advantages that are also bestowed on for-profit corporations. These include legal life (nonprofit corporations are guaranteed the same rights and powers of individuals), limited personal liability, continued existence beyond the involvement of original founders, increased public recognition, readily available information on operations, ability to establish employee benefits programs, and flexibility in financial recordkeeping.

But there are also certain disadvantages associated with incorporating. Nicholas cited the following as principle drawbacks:

- Costs associated with incorporation—Although these costs are usually not too excessive, especially for organizations of any size, incorporation does generally involve some extra costs.

- Additional bureaucracy—''An unincorporated nonprofit organization can be structured so informally that its operators could keep whatever records they chose on the backs of envelopes or as scribbled notes on paper napkins,'' said Nicholas. ''Not so in a nonprofit corporation. As a legal entity, the corporation is subject to some specific recordkeeping obligations set down by the state in which it is incorporated.'' In addition, there are certain activity guidelines to which incorporated organizations must adhere.

- Sacrifice of personal control—Depending on where incorporation takes place, the organization may have to appoint a board of directors to oversee operations (although founders of nonprofit groups can often exercise considerable control in influencing the composition of the board and the flavor of corporate bylaws and articles of incorporation). Founders and directors of unincorporated groups are under no such obligation.

''Generally, the advantages far outweigh the disadvantages,'' summarized Hopkins. ''The disadvantages stem from the fact that incorporation entails an affirmative act of the state government: It 'charters' the entity. In exchange for the grant of corporate status, the state usually expects certain forms of compliance by the organization, such as adherence to rules of operation, an initial filing fee, annual reports, and annual fees. However, these costs are frequently nominal and the reporting requirements are usually not extensive.''

ORGANIZING A NONPROFIT ORGANIZATION

''Being enthusiastic, imaginative, and creative about establishing a nonprofit organization is one thing,'' observed Hopkins. ''Actually forming the entity and making it operational is another. For better or worse, the exercise is much like establishing one's own business. It is a big and important undertaking, and it should be done carefully and properly. The label 'nonprofit' does not mean 'no planning.' Forming a nonprofit organization is as serious as starting up a new company,'' he claimed. ''The first question for an individual interested in establishing a nonprofit organization should be: What is the nonprofit organization going to do? Just like starting a business, the first step is to determine the organization's functions, then match the category of tax-exempt status (if any) to the organization's purposes and functions.'' From there, would-be founders need to study a wide range of issues, many of which are also basic considerations for small business owners and other individuals involved in for-profit endeavors. Often, the counsel of a good attorney and/or accountant can be valuable at this stage. Primary issues include the following:

- Decide what legal form the organization will take (public charity or private foundation, incorporated or unincorporated, etc.)

- If incorporating, take necessary legal steps to make that decision a reality (devise bylaws, submit articles of incorporation, etc.)

- Investigate options and decide on principal organization programs and emphases

- Determine the leadership of the organization (directors, officers, primary staff positions)

- Define compensation for such positions

- Find a physical location for the organization (factors here can range from variations in state law to availability of reasonable office space)

- Put together a strategic plan for achieving organization goals at both community and larger levels

- Decide how to go about funding those goals (gifts, grants, unrelated income, etc.?)

- Determine which media avenues will be best for publicizing the organization's goals and securing volunteers

- Devise an ongoing business plan that 1) serves as a blueprint for institution goals and development, and 2) can be periodically reviewed and adjusted as appropriate

FUNDRAISING

Nonprofit institutions can turn to several different methodologies to raise funds designed to support their mission. This is especially true for nonprofits that have tax-exempt status, because it permits donors to deduct their gifts from their own personal income tax liability. Major avenues of fundraising used by nonprofit organizations include the following: Fundraising events (dinners, dances, charity auctions, etc.); direct mail solicitation; foundation grant solicitation; in-person solicitation (door-to-door canvassing, etc.); telemarketing; and planned giving (this includes bequests, which are given to the organization after the donor's death, and gifts made during the donor's lifetime through trusts or other agreements).

EFFECTIVE SOLICITATION AND REVENUE MANAGEMENT In order to prosper, nonprofit institutions not only need to know where the sources of funding are, they also need to know how to solicit those funds and how to effectively manage that revenue when it comes into their possession.

Certainly, solicitation of donors (whether they take the form of individuals, corporations, or foundations) is a vital component of many organization's operations. After all, most activities can only be executed with funding. But many nonprofit institutions are not accomplished in this area, either because they do not allocate adequate resources or because of problems with execution. Writing in *Fund Raising Management*, Robert Hartsook listed the following as common solicitation errors that nonprofit groups make:

- Not listening to donor expectations
- Unwarranted assumption of a donor's willingness to contribute
- Lack of follow-up after initial contact
- Inadequate research on potential donors and their ability to contribute
- Inability to close presentation with donor commitment
- Neglecting to establish rapport with potential donors prior to solicitation
- Framing solicitation as ''begging'' rather than as a reasonable request for help with a worthy cause
- Neglecting to tailor solicitation to individual donors
- Approaching potential donors without knowledge of how donations impact them in the realms of tax deductions, etc.

Of course, even the most effective solicitation campaigns will wither if the organization proves unable to allocate its financial and other resources wisely. ''Fundraising begins by determining exactly what financial and human resources are needed to accomplish the mission [of the organization],'' wrote Larry W. Kennedy in *Quality Management in the Nonprofit World.* ''In the short run, money can be raised on the organization's vision and the promises it makes to help its clients and, therefore, its community. It will not take long, though, for contributors to want to see results. . . . Performance is what counts.'' Indeed, an organization may be devoted to addressing a perfectly worthwhile cause, and its membership may be enthusiastic and dedicated, but most nonprofit organizations—and especially charitable ones—rely on funds from outside sources. And poorly run nonprofits will find that their revenue streams will dry up quickly if they do not leverage their funds wisely.

TRENDS IN THE NONPROFIT WORLD

Observers have pointed to several trends in the nonprofit community that are expected to continue or develop in the next few years. These range from changes in fundraising targets to expanded competition between nonprofit organizations to regulatory developments. The following is a listing of some issues that nonprofit organizations will be tracking in the coming years:

1) Increased emphasis on retaining donors— According to Robert F. Hartsook of *Fund Raising Management,* ''non-profit organizations will focus on the renewal of donors rather than on the acquisition of new ones. As our country's population growth begins to plateau, it will be necessary for non-profits to more keenly target their marketing efforts.''

2) Corporate giving—Corporate giving to philanthropic causes has emerged as a major marketing tool for corporations in recent years, and this source of funds is expected to assume even greater importance as federal and state governments pare back their spending on various social programs.

3) Increased reliance on volunteerism—Reduced government expenditures on social programs is also expected to spur increased demand for volunteers who can meet the expected growth in organization activity. This need will be especially acute for nonprofit organizations primarily involved in charitable activities.

4) Competition with for-profit enterprises— Many analysts believe that this issue could have tremendous implications for nonprofit organizations in the future. Spurred by representatives of the for-profit small business community, regulatory agencies have undertaken more extensive reviews of ways in which some activities of tax-exempt groups allegedly damage the fortunes of for-profit businesses (who, of course, are subject to local, state, and federal taxes). Much of the controversy in this area centers around the definition and treatment of unrelated business income (income generated by tax-exempt organizations from ventures that are unrelated to their primary mission). ''There is a potential that all of this will lead to nothing,'' wrote Hopkins, ''or it could bring an in-depth inquiry into the federal and state law distinctions between for-profit and nonprofit organizations, the rationale for the tax exemption of certain types of nonprofit organizations, and whether some existing tax exemptions are outmoded and some new forms of tax exemption are required.''

5) Continued emphasis on planned giving— ''Nonprofit organizations will enjoy a significant increase in realized bequests,'' said Hartsook. ''This will happen as a result of planned giving programs put in place 10 to 15 years ago. With the evidence at hand of how successful planned giving can be, many institutions will increase their dependence on this methodology.''

6) Continued dominance of women in nonprofit community—According to *Fund Raising Management,* women occupied approximately two-thirds of all staff positions

in nonprofit organizations in the mid-1990s, a percentage that may increase even more in the coming years.

7) Increase in government regulation among nonprofits—Government oversight of fund-raising activities may continue to increase at both the state and federal levels, at least in part because of the solicitation practices of some "fringe philanthropic groups," said Hartsook. "Unfortunately, telemarketing for nonprofit organizations has received a bad name because of fringe philanthropic organizations that solicit and collect large sums of money—while dedicating most of those funds to the costs of fund raising and salaries." According to Hopkins, this increase in government regulation may be especially evident at the state level: "States that have formerly foregone the desire for a fund-raising law have suddenly decided that their citizens now need one. States with fund-raising regulation laws are making them tougher. Those who administer these laws—the state regulators—are applying them with new vigor."

8) Growth in self-regulation within the nonprofit community—Self-regulation within various sectors of nonprofit operation underwent a noticeable increase in the late 1980s and early 1990s, and this trend is expected to continue with the introduction of new certification systems, codes of ethics, and watchdog groups.

9) Major donors will maximize benefits from contributions—According to Hartsook, major donors will increasingly incorporate aspects of planned giving into their philanthropic efforts in order to maximize their tax deductions. "Significant gift giving will incorporate an aspect of planned gifts in order to afford the donor maximum tax deductions," he stated. "As the level of tax recognition diminishes, major donors will turn to this methodology in order to maximize tax advantages."

FURTHER READING:

Drucker, Peter F. Managing the Non-profit Organization: Principles and Practices. New York: HarperBusiness, 1990.

Hartsook, Robert F. "Predictions for 1997." Fund Raising Management. January 1997.

Hartsook, Robert F. "Top Ten Solicitation Mistakes." Fund Raising Management. March 1997.

Hopkins, Bruce R. The Law of Tax-Exempt Organizations. New York: John Wiley & Sons.

Hopkins, Bruce R. A Legal Guide to Starting and Managing a Nonprofit Organization. 2d ed. New York: John Wiley & Sons, 1993.

Kennedy, Larry W. Quality Management in the Nonprofit World: Combining Compassion and Performance to Meet Client Needs and Improve Finances. San Francisco: Jossey-Bass, 1991.

Krit, Robert L. The Fund-Raising Handbook. Glenview, IL: Scott Foresman, 1991.

Listro, John P. Accounting & Reporting for Nonprofit Organizations. Dubuque, IA: Kendall/Hunt Publishing, 1992.

Nicholas, Ted. The Complete Guide to Nonprofit Corporations. Enterprise Dearborn, 1993.

Nichols, Judith E. "Philanthropic Trends for the 1990s." Fund Raising Management. August 1990.

Overton, G.W., ed. Guidebook for Directors of Nonprofit Corporations. Chicago, IL: American Bar Association, 1993.

Schoenhals, G. Roger. On My Way in Planned Giving. Seattle, WA: Planned Giving Today, 1995.

Warwick, Mal. "Outsider-In Marketing: A New Way to Look at Marketing for Nonprofits." Nonprofit World. September/October 1997.

NONPROFIT ORGANIZATIONS AND HUMAN RESOURCES MANAGEMENT

Staffing decisions are among the most important decisions that **nonprofit organizations** make. Just as for-profit businesses of all different sizes and areas of operation rely on their personnel to execute their strategies and advance their goals, so too do nonprofit groups. It follows, then, that nonprofit organizations need to attend to the same tasks as profit-seeking companies do when they turn to the challenges of establishing and maintaining a solid work force. To accomplish this, nonprofit organizations have to address the following six personnel issues, as delineated in the Small Business Administration publication *Human Resources Management:*

- Assessing personnel needs

- Recruiting personnel

- Screening personnel

- Selecting and hiring personnel

- Orienting new employees to the organization

- Deciding compensation issues.

"An effective non-profit manager *must* try to get more out of the people he or she has," wrote Peter F. Drucker in *Managing the Non-Profit Organization.* "The yield from the human resource really determines the organization's performance. And that's decided by the basic people decisions: whom we hire and whom we fire; where we place people, and whom we promote. The quality of these human decisions largely determines whether the organization is being run seriously, whether its mission, its values, and its objectives are real and meaningful to people rather than just public relations and rhetoric.''

ASSESSING ORGANIZATION NEEDS

A key component of any endeavor to build a quality core of personnel is an honest assessment of current and future internal needs and external influences. Leaders and managers of nonprofit organizations should study workload history, trends in the larger philanthropic community, pertinent changes in the environment in which they operate (layoffs, plant closings, introduction of a new organization with a similar mission, legislative developments, etc.), personnel demands associated with current and planned initiatives, operating budget and costs, and the quality and quantity of the area worker pool, both for volunteer and staff positions. Moreover, all of these factors need to be studied within the framework of the organization's overarching mission statement. For as many nonprofit leaders have noted, adherence to other general business principles (sound fiscal management, retention of good employees through good compensation packages, etc.) is of little solace if the organization loses sight of its mission—it's reason for being—in the process.

Writing in *Human Resources Management,* Gary Roberts, Carlotta Roberts, and Gary Seldon noted several fundamental business principles concerning assessment of personnel needs that apply to nonprofits as well. These principles include:

- Fill positions with people who are willing and able to take on the job.

- Providing accurate and realistic job and skill specifications for each position helps ensure that it is filled by someone capable of handling the responsibilities associated with that position.

- Written job descriptions are essential to communicating job expectations.

- Employees that are chosen because they are the best available candidate are far more likely to have a positive impact than those that are chosen on the basis of friendship or expediency.

- Performance appraisals, when coupled with specific job expectations, help boost performance.

''The process of selecting a competent person for each position is best accomplished through a systematic definition of the requirements for each job, including the skills, knowledge and other qualifications that employees must possess to perform each task,''

they concluded. ''To guarantee that personnel needs are adequately specified, 1) conduct a job analysis, 2) develop a written job description, and 3) prepare a job specification.''

RECRUITING, SCREENING, AND SELECTING ORGANIZATION WORK FORCE

RECRUITING For many nonprofit organizations, publicizing its very existence is the most important step that it can take in its efforts in **recruiting** staff and volunteers alike. This is especially true of the latter element of the nonprofit organization work force. Volunteers are the life-blood of countless nonprofit organizations, for they attend to the basic tasks that need performing, from paperwork to transportation of goods and/or services to maintenance. Writing in *Quality Management in the Nonprofit World,* Larry W. Kennedy noted that ''they supply valuable human resources which, when properly engaged, can be worth tens of thousands of dollars in conserved personnel costs to even the smallest organizations.''

Nonprofit groups rely on two basic avenues to publicize their work and their staffing needs: local media (newspapers, newsletters, radio advertising, billboards, etc.) and other community organizations (municipal governments, churches, civic groups, other nonprofit organizations, etc.) Many nonprofit groups have found that contact with some community organizations, particularly churches and civic groups, can be particularly rewarding since these organizations already have members that may be predisposed toward lending a hand.

SCREENING AND SELECTION The interviewing process is another essential component of successful staffing for nonprofit groups. This holds true for volunteers as well as for officers, directors, and paid staff. Indeed, Larry W. Kennedy remarked in his book *Quality Management in the Nonprofit World* that ''volunteers should be recruited and interviewed systematically the same way you would recruit paid staff. An orderly and professional approach to volunteer management will pay off handsomely for your organization. What you do in the recruitment phase of your work will set the standard for volunteer performance. If you are disciplined and well organized, you will often attract more qualified volunteers.''

Managers of nonprofit organizations should make sure that they do the following when engaged in the process of staffing screening and selection:

- Recognize that *all* personnel, whether they are heading up your organization's annual fundraising drive or lending a hand for a few hours every other Saturday, have an impact on the group's performance. Certainly, some positions are more important than others, but countless nonprofit managers can attest that an underperforming, unethical, or unpleasant individual can have a disproportionate negative impact on organization morale and/or organization reputation in the community. This can be true of the occasional volunteer as well as the full-time staff member.

- Use an application form that covers all pertinent areas of the applicant's background.

- Ensure that your screening process provides information about an individual's skills, attitudes, and knowledge.

- Try to determine if the applicant or would-be volunteer is interested in the organization for legitimate reasons (professional development and/or advancement, genuine interest in your group's mission) or primarily for reasons that may not advance your organization's cause (loneliness, corporate burnout, etc.).

- Objectively evaluate prospective employees and volunteers based on criteria established in the organization's job specifications.

- Be realistic in putting together your volunteer work force. "Managers cause most of the problems with volunteers by making unreasonable assumptions about their intentions and capabilities," wrote Kennedy. An organization that sets the bar too high in its expectations of volunteers (in terms of services provided, hours volunteered, etc.) may find itself with a severe shortage of this potential valuable resource.

- Recognizing that would-be volunteers and employees bring both assets and negative attributes to your organization, nonprofit groups should be flexible in accommodating those strengths and weaknesses. "If you want people to perform in an organization, you have to use their strengths—not emphasize their weaknesses," said Drucker.

Organizations that pay attention to these guidelines will be far more likely to enjoy positive and lasting relationships with their volunteers and staff than those who fill their human resource needs in haphazard fashion. As Kennedy said, "the time to begin evaluating the probably reliability of human resources is prior to their insertion into your internal structure."

ORIENTING STAFF AND VOLUNTEERS TO THE ORGANIZATION

Training is a vital component of successful nonprofit organization management. But many nonprofit managers fail to recognize that training initiatives should be built for all members of the organization, not just those who are salaried employees. "Specialized training should be designed for every person in the organization, including board members and volunteers," contended Kennedy. "The principles of quality management should be reinforced in each phase of training, with generous opportunities given to the trainees to talk about their questions and concerns. . . . If we select and train people with well-established and consistently implemented guidelines, we greatly increase the potential for team building. Beyond that, a common objective, a commitment to quality, a sincere concern for the team members, and a dedicated leader can cause wonderful things to happen. When those factors are not present, things can occur that are not so pleasant. . . . Volunteers who are shoddily intruded into an organization's processes or who are not well managed can create chaotic inconsistency in services. The additional, time, energy, and money needed to clean up well-intentioned but off-target volunteer efforts can quickly offset any gains provided by their services."

POOR PERFORMERS Many nonprofit organizations find that at one point or another, they must address poor performance by a member of the organization. When that person is a paid member of the staff, dealing with the issue is in many respects no different than it would be in the for-profit world. Organizations of all types have a right to assume certain standards of performance from paid employees, and if that standard is not met, they should by all means take the steps necessary to ensure that they receive the necessary level of performance from that position, even if that means **employee termination**.

The situation becomes more complex when the person is a volunteer, however. The volunteer worker is an essential element of many nonprofit organizations, and the primary characteristics of volunteerism—selfless service—make it difficult to remove poor performers. In addition, insensitive handling of one volunteer can have a negative impact on other volunteers upon which your organization relies. Nonetheless, Kennedy stated that "volunteers should be held accountable just as though they were being paid top dollar to work. This does not mean that you can be careless about people's feelings. Even-for-profit managers have learned that managing and supervising requires certain social graces and sensitivity to every individual. However, the reluctance of nonprofit managers to hold volunteers accountable to reasonable levels of performance or to terminate bad volunteer relationships can be their downfall."

Drucker noted that most nonprofits will sooner or later have to deal with people "who volunteer because they are profoundly lonely. When it works, these volunteers can do a great deal for the organization—and the organization, by giving them a community, gives even more back to them. But sometimes these people for psychological or emotional reasons simply cannot work with other people; they are noisy, intrusive, abrasive, rude. Non-profit executives have to face up to that reality.'' If all else fails, such disruptive volunteers should be asked to leave. Otherwise, other members of the organization, including the executive, will find that their capacity to contribute is diminished.

Drucker agreed that dismissing an underperforming or otherwise undesirable volunteer can be a difficult task. ''The non-profit executive is always inclined to be reluctant to let a non-producer go. You feel he or she is a comrade-in-arms and make all kinds of excuses,'' he granted. He contended that nonprofit managers should adhere to a basic guideline in such instances: ''If they try, they deserve another chance. If they don't try, make *sure* they leave. . . . An effective non-profit executive owes it to the organization to have a competent staff wherever performance is needed. To allow non-performers to stay on means letting down both the organization and the cause.''

COMPENSATING THE ORGANIZATION'S EMPLOYEES AND VOLUNTEERS

TANGIBLE BENEFITS As Ted Nicholas noted in *The Complete Guide to Nonprofit Corporations,* nonprofit corporations may establish fringe benefits programs for their employees. People that can be covered under these programs include not only staff personnel, but also directors and officers. ''The benefits,'' wrote Nicholas, ''can be as attractive as those provided by for-profit business corporations. In addition, the benefits can be far more economical for the corporation and beneficial to the employees than any program that could be offered by unincorporated organizations. The non profit corporation can establish an employee pension and retirement income plan. It can provide for sick pay and vacation pay. It may arrange for group life, accident and health insurance coverage for its officers and employees. It can elect to cover its employees' personal medical expenses that are not covered by the group insurance plans, provided that the corporation can pay all or part of the cost of the various employee benefits it sets up. It can require some contribution from the employees covered by the fringes.''

Bruce Hopkins observed in his *Legal Guide to Starting and Managing a Nonprofit Organization* that ''there is a tendency in our society to expect employees of nonprofit organizations to work for levels and types of compensation that are less than those paid to employees of for-profit organizations. Somehow, the nonprofit characteristics of the organization become transferred to the 'nonprofit' employee.'' Hopkins goes on to note that while this perception may indeed

be a reality because of the budgetary constraints under which many nonprofit organizations operate, in other instances employees do not feel entitled to compensation levels that are offered to employees of for-profit businesses. In other cases, meanwhile, nonprofit groups feel no obligation to provide comparable levels of compensation in terms of salary, benefits, etc., relying instead on the altruistic leanings of some people. Organizations that operate under the assumption that their workers should accept compensation packages that are dramatically smaller than those offered by the corporate world simply because of the nature of their mission, however, run the risk of losing out on many talented people. Indeed, Hopkins pointed out that ''many nonprofit organizations, particularly the larger ones (universities, hospitals, major charities, and trade associations), require sophisticated and talented employees. Because these individuals are not likely to want to be 'nonprofit' employees, nonprofit and for-profit organizations compete for the same pool of talented persons. This competition extends not only to salaries but also to benefits and retirement programs.''

Experts indicate that although the compensation packages that are offered by nonprofit organizations are constrained by the so-called private inurement doctrine, which holds that the profits realized by a nonprofit organization can not be passed along to private individuals (as dividends are passed along to shareholders in a for-profit enterprise), they can still offer attractive compensation packages to employees provided that they are judged to be ''reasonable.'' When weighing whether it considers compensation to be reasonable, the Internal Revenue Service studies whether compensation arrangements exceed a certain percentage of the organization's gross revenues. Excessive compensation can be penalized by imposition of additional taxes and fines, but the most damage to organizations who do this can often be found in the realm of reputation; few allegations are more damaging to a nonprofit organization's community standing than the charge that it is bestowing excessive compensation (in the form of salary, country club memberships, etc.) to top executives or others.

INTANGIBLE BENEFITS Successful managers of nonprofit organizations recognize that the people who compose their organizations—volunteers, employees, officers, and directors alike—are often participating in the group at least in part for altruistic reasons. Indeed, Drucker noted that ''although successful business executives have learned that workers are not entirely motivated by paychecks or promotions—they need more—the need is even greater in non-profit institutions. Even paid staff in these organizations need achievement, the satisfaction of service, or they become alienated and even hostile. After all, what's the point of working in a non-profit institution if one doesn't make a clear contribution?''

Leaders of nonprofit organizations, then, need to always be on the look out for ways in which they can show their paid staff, their volunteers, and their leadership how their involvement in the organization is making a difference, whether the group is involved with ministering to the economically disadvantaged or devoted to protecting a beloved natural resource. As Father Leo Bartel, Vicar for Social Ministry of the Catholic Diocese of Rockford, Illinois, told Drucker, ''We give [volunteers] opportunities to deepen in themselves and in each other the sense of how important the things are that they are doing.''

FURTHER READING:

Bateman, Thomas S., and Carl P. Zeithaml. *Management: Function and Strategy.* Homewood, IL: Richard D. Irwin, 1990.

Drucker, Peter F. *Managing the Non-profit Organization: Principles and Practices.* New York: HarperBusiness, 1990.

Hartsook, Robert F. ''Predictions for 1997.'' *Fund Raising Management.* January 1997.

Hopkins, Bruce R. *A Legal Guide to Starting and Managing a Nonprofit Organization.* 2d ed. New York: John Wiley & Sons, 1993.

Kennedy, Larry W. *Quality Management in the Nonprofit World: Combining Compassion and Performance to Meet Client Needs and Improve Finances.* San Francisco: Jossey-Bass, 1991.

Nicholas, Ted. *The Complete Guide to Nonprofit Corporations.* Enterprise Dearborn, 1993.

Nichols, Judith E. ''Philanthropic Trends for the 1990s.'' *Fund Raising Management.* August 1990.

Roberts, Gary, Gary Seldon, and Carlotta Roberts. *Human Resources Management.* Washington, D.C.: U.S. Small Business Administration, n.a.

SEE ALSO: Employee Compensation; Employee Hiring; Employee Screening; Human Resource Management; Nonprofit Organizations; Work Force

NONPROFIT ORGANIZATIONS AND TAXES

In recognition of the ''public good''-oriented goals and objectives of **nonprofit organizations**, U.S. law grants these groups a number of special privileges. Of these, perhaps none is more valuable than the bestowal of tax-exempt status. Such status basically means that the organization's income and assets are not subject to federal taxes, and federal exemptions often (though not always) pave the way for state and local tax exemptions as well. For-profit enterprises, on the other hand, are subject to local, state, and federal taxation.

Writing in his book *Quality Management in the Nonprofit World,* Larry W. Kennedy explained that ''the pursuit of profit for personal or individual gain is called private enterprise. Profits gained through private enterprise are taxable. Enterprise by tax-exempt organizations has as its goal for attaining profits the continued provision of services for the public good. Profits earned from public enterprise related to our tax-exempt mission are not taxable. Nonprofit organizations can engage in virtually any business enterprise in the fulfillment of their mission objectives and remain comfortably within the purposes of their tax-exempt status. Where the enterprise is *unrelated* to the stated mission, *only* that income that is generated by the unrelated enterprise is taxable. Gifts, contributions, and income generated by another enterprise related to the organization's mission statement would remain tax exempt.'' It should be noted, however, that complete exemption from federal taxation does not *automatically* mean that the organization avoids other kinds of taxation, such as state and/or local income taxes, sales taxes, and property taxes.

In addition, Bruce R. Hopkins noted in his *Legal Guide to Starting and Managing a Nonprofit Organization* that not all nonprofit organizations qualify as tax-exempt organizations: ''Nearly every tax-exempt organization is a non-profit organization, but not all nonprofit organizations are eligible to be tax-exempt,'' he said. ''The concept of a nonprofit organization is broader than that of a tax-exempt organization. Some types of non-profit organizations (such as mutual, self-help type entities) do not, as a matter of federal law, qualify for tax-exempt status.'' Ted Nicholas, author of *The Complete Guide to Nonprofit Corporations,* offered a similar assessment. He stated that ''while the great bulk of nonprofit organizations are presumed to be tax-exempt in nature, there are exceptions to that premise.'' But he also went on to note that ''the terms *nonprofit* and *charitable* are not interchangeable. A nonprofit organization is not necessarily charitably motivated, and, likewise, an organization that is truly charitable in nature may be a profit-making enterprise. And both kinds of organizations may be entitled to tax-exempt status from the IRS. For example, a religious and apostolic association or corporation, even if it is organized for profit, and a teacher's retirement fund association, which is operated to produce profits for its beneficiaries, are both eligible for tax exemptions.''

DEVELOPMENT OF NONPROFIT TAX-EXEMPT STATUS

Until the end of the 19th century, all U.S. entities—whether they were private individuals or businesses—were exempt from taxation unless they were subject to a particular tax levy. The Tariff Act of 1894, however, changed that situation irrevocably.

That legislation imposed a flat 2 percent tax rate on all U.S. corporations, but in recognition of the fundamentally different goals and objectives of for-profit businesses and charitable and educational groups, the bill exempted the latter organizations from the tax. "The important aspect of this legislation is that organizations involved in enterprise and whose profits would be used for altruistic purposes were specifically excluded from the requirement to share the profits of their work through taxation," wrote Kennedy. "The initial emphasis of tax exemption was to protect the enterprises of nonprofit organizations from taxation, and it has remained as the central function of tax-exempt law to this day."

In recent years, the United States has seen a dramatic increase in the number of tax-exempt organizations operating around the country. Indeed, the rise in the number of churches, nursing homes, hospitals, chambers of commerce, charitable organizations, and social service agencies in many community has led some observers to voice concern about the tax-base stability of some areas. "In some cities and towns, a substantial portion of the entire lot of privately held real estate is owned by tax-exempt organizations," wrote Nicholas. "This means there isn't any revenue flowing into local tax coffers from this sector." This state of affairs has led some corporate and individual taxpayers to register complaints about the "free ride" that some exempt organizations enjoy. "Even the tax-exempt status of churches, protected from the very beginning of the tax code, has been questioned in recent years, particularly in reference to church investments in secular properties," Nicholas said.

NONPROFITS AND PROFITABILITY

Many people operate under a fundamental misconception about nonprofit organizations and revenue. As Kennedy stated, "the word 'nonprofit' may carry with it an inference about profit that causes some people to think profitability by a nonprofit organization is illegal. To the contrary, we are free to do anything a for-profit company might do as we pursue our goals, *including making profits*. The law is designed to provide all the benefits of a free-market system plus the special favor of tax incentives for individuals and corporations who want to contribute financially to our efforts. Not only can we operate enterprises profitably as tax-exempt organizations but we can also prosper through the patronage of others."

But there are significant stipulations in place concerning the *distribution* of those profits that must be met for an organization to claim tax-exempt status. These are delineated in Section 501 of the Internal Revenue Code:

1) The organization must be organized and operated exclusively for one or more of the following purposes: for religious, educational, charitable, scientific, or literary purposes; to test for public safety; to encourage amateur sports competition (either national or international); to prevent cruelty to children or animals; to lessen the burdens of government (through creation and/or maintenance of public buildings, monuments, parks, natural attractions, etc.); and to maintain public confidence in the legal system. Naturally, the organization may be involved in more than one of the above areas.

2) Net earnings garnered by the organization may not, under any circumstances, be distributed for the private benefit of individuals.

3) The organization may not participate in any way in any political campaigns, directly or indirectly (although it can use a political action committee or PAC to engage in political activities that are not political campaign activities.

4) The organization may not spend "excessive" time or energy on efforts to influence legislation. It is a common misconception that nonprofits may not engage in legislative activities, but as Hopkins stated "a charity is permitted to engage in far more lobbying efforts than most people realize. Indeed, under some circumstances, a charitable organization can spend more than one-fifth of its funds for legislative ends."

FILING FOR TAX-EXEMPT STATUS

A wide variety of organizations are eligible for tax-exempt status because of their goals and activities. These include the following:

- Corporations organized under an Act of Congress (includes federal credit unions)

- Title-holding corporations for exempt organizations

- Religious organizations

- Educational organizations

- Charitable organizations

- Scientific organizations

- Literary organizations

- Public safety organizations

- Organizations devoted to national or international amateur sports competitions

- Organizations devoted to preventing cruelty to children

- Organizations devoted to preventing cruelty to animals
- Civic leagues
- Social welfare organizations
- Local associations
- Labor organizations
- Agricultural and horticultural organizations
- Business leagues, chambers of commerce, and real estate boards
- Social and recreational clubs
- Fraternal beneficiary societies and associations
- Voluntary employees' beneficiary associations
- Domestic fraternal societies and associations
- Teachers' retirement fund associations
- Benevolent life insurance associations
- Mutual irrigation or ditch companies
- Mutual or cooperative telephone companies
- Cemetery companies
- State-chartered credit unions and mutual reserve funds
- Mutual insurance companies or associations
- Cooperative agricultural organizations
- Supplemental unemployment benefit trusts
- Employee funded pension trusts (provided they were created prior to June 25, 1959)
- Organizations of past or present Armed Forces members
- Group legal services organizations
- Black lung benefit trusts
- Withdrawal liability payment funds
- Veteran's organizations (provided they were created prior to 1880)
- Religious and apostolic associations
- Cooperative hospital service organizations
- Cooperating service groups of operating educational organizations
- Farmer's cooperatives
- Political organizations (parties, committees, etc.)
- Homeowners' associations

Nicholas pointed out that "some organizations such as churches, associations of churches, and auxiliary agencies of churches—mission societies and youth groups, for instance—are generally considered automatically tax-exempt. They are not required to request this status from the government taxing agencies. However, virtually all other kinds of organizations that fit legal definitions of eligibility for tax-exempt status due to their special benevolent purposes and goals cannot assume that status. They must ask the Internal Revenue Service to officially recognize their tax-exempt status."

To do so, organizations have to file an application for tax exemption with the IRS (nonprofit organizations may also have to make separate applications to state and local tax agencies if they wish to secure exemptions from taxes imposed by those jurisdictions). In most instances, this filing step is a mere formality; approval of tax exemption is almost always based on the IRS's ruling on the organization's exemption application (the primary legal basis for all tax exemptions is Section 501 of the Internal Revenue Code of 1954). Organizations who have their exemption application approved, then, will often find that they are free from tax obligations at the local and state levels as well.

Experts note that while some nonprofit organizations are exempted from paying certain taxes, that does not mean that they have no filing obligations. "Despite the favoritisms the law frequently bestows on nonprofit organizations, the reporting requirements are not one of them, particularly when the organization is tax-exempt," said Hopkins. "The annual information return that most tax-exempt organizations have to file with the IRS is far more extensive than the tax returns most commercial businesses must file. Then, there may be several state annual reports (if the organization is doing business in more than one state) and the state annual charitable solicitation act reports (perhaps over 40 of them)." Given this reality, most nonprofit organizations choose to use the services of professionals attorneys and accountants in compiling and delivering these reports.

UNRELATED BUSINESS INCOME

United States law has long differentiated between the activities of tax-exempt organizations that are related to the performance of tax-exempt functions and those that are not. Income garnered from these latter activities is subject to taxation. For incorporated organizations, net revenue from unrelated activities is subject to federal corporate income tax law, while for organizations that are not incorporated, this revenue—commonly referred to as "unrelated business income"—is subject to the canon of federal tax law on individuals. "The objective of the unrelated business income tax is to prevent unfair competition between tax-exempt organizations and for-profit, commercial enterprises," explained Hopkins. "The rules are intended to place the unrelated business activities of an exempt organization on the same tax basis as those of a nonexempt business with which it competes.... An organization's tax exemption will be denied or revoked if an inappropriate portion of its activities is not promoting one or more of its exempt purposes."

This area of tax law, noted Hopkins, has been one marked by upheaval and change in recent years. "As tax-exempt organizations struggle to generate additional income in these days of declining governmental support, proposed adverse tax reform, more sophisticated management, and greater pressure for more services, [tax-exempt organizations] are increasingly drawn to service-provider activities, some of which may be unrelated to their exempt purposes. The growth of service-provider activities, the increasing tendencies of the courts to find activities unrelated because they are 'commercial,' and the unrest over 'unfair competition' between tax-exempt organizations and for-profit entities—all of these are clear evidence that this aspect of the law of tax-exempt organizations is constantly evolving and will be reshaped."

FURTHER READING:

Drucker, Peter F. *Managing the Non-profit Organization: Principles and Practices.* New York: HarperBusiness, 1990.

Hartsook, Robert F. "Predictions for 1997." *Fund Raising Management.* January 1997.

Hopkins, Bruce R. *The Law of Tax-Exempt Organizations.* New York: John Wiley & Sons.

Hopkins, Bruce R. *A Legal Guide to Starting and Managing a Nonprofit Organization.* 2d ed. New York: John Wiley & Sons, 1993.

Kennedy, Larry W. *Quality Management in the Nonprofit World: Combining Compassion and Performance to Meet Client Needs and Improve Finances.* San Francisco: Jossey-Bass, 1991.

Moses, Nancy. "The Nonprofit Motive." *Wall Street Journal.* March 17, 1997.

Nicholas, Ted. *The Complete Guide to Nonprofit Corporations.* Enterprise Dearborn, 1993.

SEE ALSO: Nonprofit Organizations; Tax Planning

NONQUALIFIED DEFERRED COMPENSATION PLANS

Nonqualified deferred compensation plans are used by businesses to supplement existing qualified plans. As Lawrence Bader and Yale Tauber noted in *Compensation & Benefits Management,* deferred compensation arrangements are proliferating in today's business and regulatory environment, and they are extending deeper into organizations. Small business owners, in particular, have made greater use of these deferred compensation plans in recent years, utilizing them to reward top executives and directors and woo top outside personnel. Another factor contributing to firms' efforts to defer compensation when possible, added Bader and Tauber, is the current limitations on deductible current compensation.

Companies have recognized other pluses associated with nonqualified deferred compensation plans as well. "One big advantage to [nonqualified] deferred compensation plans is that they escape the non-discrimination rules imposed on qualified plans," explained John B. Connor Jr. in *Small Business Reports.* "That means [small business owners] can offer the plan to a select group of employees, making it a more cost-effective benefit than a qualified plan. Administrative costs are lower as well because the plans are exempt from the U.S. Department of Labor's reporting requirements. All that's required is a one-time letter to the DOL stating that your plan is in place and has a given number of participants. In addition, small companies are discovering that deferred compensation plans can help them court executives from larger firms. In essence, your company can level the recruitment playing field by tailoring a benefits package comparable to that of big companies."

There are two main types of nonqualified deferred compensation plans from which small business owners may choose: supplemental executive retirement plans (SERPs) and deferred savings plans. These two options share several common characteristics, but there are also important differences between the two. For example, eligibility for both plans may be based on the executive's salary, position, or both. But whereas deferred savings plans require employees to contribute their own earnings, executives that are placed in SERPs receive their compensation from their employers.

SUPPLEMENTAL EXECUTIVE RETIREMENT PLANS (SERPS)

"Executives consider SERPs to be an especially attractive plan because the company foots the bill for the benefits," wrote Connor. "SERPs generally are structured to mirror defined-benefit pension plans that promise a stated benefit from the employer at retirement." SERP benefits, which can be allocated in conjunction with other benefit plans like qualified-plan savings and Social Security benefits, may be calculated in any number of ways. Employers may choose to pay their executives a flat dollar amount for an agreed-upon number of years; a percentage of their salary at retirement multiplied by their years with the company; or a fixed percentage of their salary at retirement for a given number of years.

Connor noted that "by their very nature, SERPs require more formal funding arrangements than deferred savings plans because [employers] must pay out the promised benefits at a future date. Many companies still use a pay as you go approach to meeting these obligations—supplying an executive's retirement benefits from general assets—but this method puts the pay-out burden on future managers." Other businesses, however, have chosen to fund their SERPs via sinking funds or corporate-owned life insurance (COLI).

SINKING FUNDS Businesses that utilize the sinking fund method allocate money on an annual basis to a fund that will cover benefit payments as they come due. This money can be invested by the company as it sees fit, but it is nonetheless earmarked for retirement payments.

CORPORATE-OWNED LIFE INSURANCE (COLI) The COLI funding method, noted Connor, "generally is used to recover the cost of providing the benefits." Under this option, businesses buy **life insurance** plans on those directors and executives that they wish to compensate. Each company pays the premiums on the purchased policies, and as each executive retires, the firm pays out his or her benefits from operating assets for a previously established period of time. The key benefit for the small business owner, however, is that his or her business would be "designated the sole beneficiary of the insurance policy proceeds, which it would receive tax-free," explained Connor. "At the executive's death, then, your company is reimbursed for some or all of the costs of the plan, including the actual benefits paid, the insurance premiums, and the loss of the use of your company's money for other purposes." Entrepreneurs should note, however, that their firm will not receive a tax deduction for its contributions to a SERP until the director or executive actually receives the benefit payments (businesses using qualified compensation plans, on the other hand, receive deductions in the current year).

DEFERRED SAVINGS PLANS

Deferred savings plans are similar to 401(k) plans in that affected employees are allowed to set aside a portion of their salary (usually up to 25 percent) and bonuses (as much as 100 percent) to put into the plan. This money is directly deducted from employee paychecks, and taxes are not levied on the money until the employee receives it. "Over the years, the executive contributions accumulate earnings in one of two ways," stated Connor. "Most commonly, the company simply guarantees a fixed rate of return on the deferrals, which would come from its general operating assets at the time of payout. A second option, which is becoming more popular, is to tie each executive's savings to the performance of a particular mutual fund; he or she would select the fund from among several offered by your plan." For those companies that set up a fixed rate of return on the deferrals, they may invest the monies in question however they wish, provided they ultimately meet their payout obligations. In addition, consultants note that some small businesses (and large ones as well) have established a policy wherein they will offer matching funds on employee deferrals or add profit-sharing or incentive-based contributions.

Experts point out that executives with deferred savings plans have a variety of payout options to choose from. They may choose to set up regular post-retirement payouts for five to ten years after retirement, but they also have the option of arranging for short-term deferrals to help them pay for a new house, college education for children, and other expenses. If an executive enrolled in this type of plan dies or is fired from the company prior to retirement, he or she (or their family) receives a lump-sum payout of their benefits. It should be noted, however, that nonqualified deferred compensation plans will not be protected from creditors if the company that created them files for **bankruptcy**.

PLANS FOR TAX-EXEMPT ORGANIZATIONS

Nonqualified deferred compensation plans may also be utilized by tax-exempt organizations, but managers of these entities should be aware that for tax-exempt organizations, such plans are subject to considerably more stringent Internal Revenue Service (IRS) regulations. Still, Janet Den Uyl stated in *Healthcare Financial Management* that "alternatives are available to tax-exempt organizations seeking to set up such plans. By subjecting employer-paid, tax-deferred compensation to risk of forfeiture or by paying the required taxes, tax-exempt organizations can develop workable alternatives for funding nonqualified deferred compensation plans."

Den Uyl pointed out that, unlike organizations that operate to register profits, tax-exempt organizations trying to set up nonqualified deferred plans are subject to Internal Revenue Code Section 457. This extends to both nonelective (employer-paid) and voluntary (employee-paid) deferred compensation plans. "For-profit organizations pay taxes on the deferred compensation until it is paid to employees," she explained. "Tax-exempt organizations, by definition, are not subject to this taxation. In addition, assets held by tax-exempt organizations to fund nonqualified plans grow tax free because the organization itself is exempt from taxes. By subjecting nonqualified deferred compensation plans to strict forfeiture requirements, the IRS intends to discourage the provision of tax-sheltered deferred compensation to highly paid employees at the expense of all employees in tax-exempt organizations.''

This code allows for the existence of two types of deferred compensation plans: eligible and ineligible. According to *Healthcare Financial Management*, contributions to eligible plans are limited to the lesser of $7,500 (not indexed) or 25 percent of an employer's compensation, less contributions to 401(k) or 403(b) plans. ''In general, it is financial advantageous to highly compensated employees to maximize contributions to 403(b) and 401(k) plans,'' wrote Den Uyl. ''However, maximizing these contributions can be accomplished only at the expense of the 457 plan.'' Given this reality, ''employees who choose to maximize contributions to 403(b) and 401(k) plans can participate only in an ineligible 457 plan. With an ineligible plan, deferred compensation is taxed currently unless it is subject to a substantial risk of forfeiture.''

FUNDING OPTIONS Tax-exempt organizations seeking to fund employer-paid deferred compensation plans can choose from a number of options:

1) Unfunded benefits that vest at retirement. Under this strategy, employers provide supplemental retirement benefit plans with assets that are not dedicated to funding the plan. If the employer runs into financial trouble before the employee or employees covered under the plan retire, it can use those assets to pay off its creditors.

2) Unfunded benefits that vest during employment. Den Uyl noted that with this plan, ''vesting occurs according to plan objectives as defined by the employer and, as vesting occurs, the employer provides a cash distribution to cover taxes. The ultimate benefit at retirement is reduced to reflect the annual distribution of a portion of the benefit to pay taxes.''

3) Benefits funded with deferred annuities. Under this arrangement, the small business owner would acquire deferred annuities in the name of participating employees. Den Uyl pointed out that the employer that takes this tack usually provides cash distributions to cover the tax on both the contribution and the cash distribution, since contributions to the annuity are regarded by the IRS as taxable income.

Similarly, organizations looking to fund voluntary nonqualified deferred compensation plans may pursue the following funding alternatives:

1) Traditional deferred compensation plans with non-compete clauses. These do not pay out money until the end of a specified period of time. If an employee who is part of the plan leaves the company to join a competing business before that specified period of time elapses, then the employee forfeits the contributions. Analysts note, however, that this choice is often not a palatable one for employers, since employees will likely resent efforts to impose such restrictions.

2) Deferred annuities. Under this alternative, employees purchase deferred annuities with after-tax income, and they do not owe taxes on annuity earnings until payout.

3) Deferral using after-tax dollars. Under this plan, employees are immediately vested and taxed on the deferred compensation. After-tax compensation is subsequently placed in a mutual fund by the employer, but it is maintained for the benefit of the employee.

FURTHER READING:

Aisenbrey, Beverly W., and Michael A. Thompson. ''Setting the Terms of the Deal: Restructuring Compensation Plans for Initial Public Offerings and Spinoffs.'' *Compensation and Benefits Review.* September-October 1996.

Bader, Lawrence, and Yale Tauber. ''The High Cost (Sometimes) of Deferred Compensation.'' *Compensation & Benefits Management.* Summer 1997.

Brunetti, Frank L. ''Small Business Tax Solutions.'' *Journal of Accountancy.* June 1995.

Connor, John B., Jr. ''Pay Me Later.'' *Small Business Reports.* July 1994.

Den Uyl, Janet. ''Options for Nonqualified Deferred Compensation Plans.'' *Healthcare Financial Management.* September 1996.

Fundamentals of Employee Benefit Programs. Employee Benefit Research Institute, 1990.

Galloway, Wesley. ''Examining Reporting Standards Criteria: Many Deferred Compensation Plans Will Not Need to Be Reported.'' *American City & County.* February 1998.

Gomez-Mejia, Luis R., ed. *Compensation and Benefits.* The Bureau of National Affairs, Inc., 1989.

Hall, Steven E., and Claude E. Johnston. ''Designing State-of-the-Art Deferred Compensation Plans.'' *Compensation & Benefits Management.* Spring 1996.

''IRS Issues Long-Awaited Deferred Compensation Employment Tax Rules.'' *Tax Management Compensation Planning Journal.* March 1, 1996.

Jenks, James M., and Brian L.P. Zevnik. *Employee Benefits Plain and Simple.* Collier Books, 1993.

Morse, Charles T., William E. Hall Jr., and Brian J. Lake. ''More than Golden Handcuffs.'' *Journal of Accountancy.* November 1997.

SEE ALSO: Employee Benefits; Employee Compensation; Nonprofit Organizations

NONTRADITIONAL FINANCING SOURCES

Entrepreneurs can turn to a variety of sources to finance the establishment or expansion of their businesses. Common sources of business **capital** include personal savings, **loans** from friends and relatives, loans from financial institutions such as banks or credit unions, loans from commercial finance companies, assistance from **venture capital** firms or investment clubs, loans from the **U.S. Small Business Administration** and other government agencies, and personal or corporate credit cards. But for some businesspeople, these sources of financing are either unavailable, or available with restrictions or provisions that are either impossible for the company to meet or deemed excessive by the business owner. In such instances, the capital-hungry entrepreneur has the option of pursuing a number of nontraditional financing sources to secure the money that his or her company needs.

SELLING ASSETS Some entrepreneurs choose to sell some of their personal or business **assets** in order to finance the opening or continued existence of their enterprise. Generally, business owners that have already established the viability of their firm and are looking to expand their operations do not have to take this sometimes dramatic course of action, since their record will often allow them to secure capital from another source, either private or public. Whether selling personal or business assets, the small business owner should take a rational approach. Some entrepreneurs, desperate to secure money, end up selling business assets that are important to basic business operations. In such instances, the entrepreneur may end up accelerating rather than halting the demise of his or her business. Only nonessential equipment and inventory should be sold. Similarly, care should be taken in the selling of personal assets. Items like boats, antiques, etc. can fetch a pretty good price. But before embarking on this course of action, the entrepreneur should objectively study whether or not the resulting income will be sufficient, or whether the enterprise's financial straits are an indication of fundamental flaws.

BORROWING AGAINST THE CASH VALUE OF YOUR LIFE INSURANCE Entrepreneurs who have a whole **life insurance** policy have the option of borrowing against the policy (this is not an option for holders of term insurance). This can be an effective means of securing capital provided that the owner has held the policy for several years, thus giving it some cash value. Insurers may let policyholders borrow as much as 90 percent of the value of the policy. As long as the policyholder continues to meet his or her premium payment obligations, the policy will remain intact.

Interest rates on such loans are generally not outrageous, but if the policyholder dies during the period in which he or she has a loan on the policy, benefits are usually dramatically reduced.

SECOND MORTGAGE Some entrepreneurs secure financing by taking out a second mortgage on their home. This risky alternative does provide the homeowner with a couple of advantages: interest on the mortgage is tax deductible and is usually lower than what he or she would pay with a credit card or an unsecured loan. But if the business ultimately fails, this method of financing could result in the loss of your home. ''Second mortgages are best for people who want to borrow all the money they need at one time and secure fixed, equal payments,'' wrote Cynthia Griffin in *Entrepreneur.*

FURTHER READING:

Andresky Fraser, Jill. ''Show Me the Money: You Can Look for Money in All the Wrong Places.'' *Inc.* March 1997.

Entrepreneur Magazine Guide to Raising Money. New York: John Wiley & Sons, 1998.

Financing for the Small Business. Washington: U.S. Small Business Administration, 1990.

Griffin, Cynthia. ''Breaking the Bank.'' *Entrepreneur.* March 1998.

''Passing the Buck.'' *Entrepreneur.* May 1997.

Stolze, William J. *Start Up Financing: An Entrepreneur's Guide to Financing New or Growing Business.* Franklin Lakes, NJ: Career Press, 1997.

NONVERBAL COMMUNICATION

Nonverbal communication—such as facial expressions, gestures, posture, and tone of voice—is an important component of personal business interactions. Nonverbal communication can help a small business owner to get a message across, or to successfully interpret a message received from another person. On the other hand, nonverbal communication can also send signals that interfere with the effective presentation or reception of messages. ''Sometimes nonverbal messages contradict the verbal; often they express true feelings more accurately than the spoken or written language,'' Herta A. Murphy and Herbert W. Hildebrandt noted in their book *Effective Business Communications.* In fact, studies have shown that between 60 and 90 percent of a message's effect may come from nonverbal clues. Therefore, it is important for small business owners and managers to be aware of the nonverbal messages they send and to develop the skill of reading the nonverbal messages contained in the behavior of others. There are three main elements of nonverbal communication: appearance, body language, and sounds.

APPEARANCE In oral forms of communication, the appearance of both the speaker and the surroundings are vital to the successful conveyance of a message. ''Whether you are speaking to one person face to face or to a group in a meeting, personal appearance and the appearance of the surroundings convey nonverbal stimuli that affect attitudes—even emotions—toward the spoken words,'' according to Murphy and Hildebrandt. For example, a speaker's clothing, hairstyle, use of cosmetics, neatness, and stature may cause a listener to form impressions about her occupation, socioeconomic level, competence, etc. Similarly, such details of the surroundings as room size, furnishings, decorations, lighting, and windows can affect a listener's attitudes toward the speaker and the message being presented. The importance of nonverbal clues in surroundings can be seen in the desire of business managers to have a corner office with a view rather than a cubicle in a crowded work area.

Appearance also makes a difference in the effectiveness of written forms of communication. For example, the type of envelope used for a letter may either convey importance or cause it to be thrown away as junk mail. Similarly, overnight mail and telegrams may convey urgency and cause the recipient to respond more promptly.

BODY LANGUAGE Body language, and particularly facial expressions, can provide important information that may not be contained in the verbal portion of the communication. Facial expressions are especially helpful as they may show hidden emotions that contradict verbal statements. For example, an employee may deny having knowledge of a problem, but also have a fearful expression and glance around guiltily. Other forms of body language that may provide communication clues include posture and gestures. For example, a manager who puts his feet up on the desk may convey an impression of status and confidence, while an employee who leans forward to listen may convey interest. Gestures can add emphasis and improve understanding when used sparingly, but the continual use of gestures can distract listeners and convey nervousness.

SOUNDS Finally, the tone, rate, and volume of a speaker's voice can convey different meanings, as can sounds like laughing, throat clearing, or humming. It is also important to note that perfume or other odors contribute to a listener's impressions, as does physical contact between the speaker and the listener. Silence, or the lack of sound, is a form of nonverbal communication as well. Silence can communicate a lack of understanding or even hard feelings in a face-to-face discussion. As a response to written communication, silence can indicate a lack of interest or even disrespect for the sender.

FURTHER READING:

Golen, Steven. *Effective Business Communication.* Washington: U.S. Small Business Administration, 1989.

Murphy, Herta A., and Herbert W. Hildebrandt. *Effective Business Communications.* 6th ed. New York: McGraw-Hill, 1991.

Townsend, Robert. *Up the Organization.* New York: Knopf, 1984.

SEE ALSO: Oral Communication

NORTH AMERICAN FREE TRADE AGREEMENT

The North American Free Trade Agreement (NAFTA) is a treaty that was signed on August 12, 1991 by the United States, Canada, and Mexico; it went into effect on January 1, 1994. (Free trade had existed between the U.S. and Canada since 1989; NAFTA broadened that arrangement.) On that day, the three countries became the largest free market in the world—the economies of the three nations at that time was more than $6 trillion and directly affected more than 365 million people. NAFTA was created to eliminate tariff barriers to agricultural, manufacturing, and services trade, remove investment restrictions, and protect intellectual property rights, all while addressing environmental and labor concerns (although many observers charge that the three governments have been lax in ensuring environmental and labor safeguards since the agreement went into effect). Small businesses were among those that were expected to benefit the most from the lowering of trade barriers since it would make doing business in Mexico and Canada less expensive and would reduce the red tape needed to import or export goods.

Highlights of NAFTA included:

- **Tariff** elimination for qualifying products. Before NAFTA, tariffs of 30 percent or higher on export goods to Mexico were common, as were long delays caused by paperwork. Additionally, Mexican tariffs on U.S.-made products were, on average, 250 percent higher than U.S. duties on Mexican products. NAFTA addressed this imbalance by phasing out tariffs over 15 years. Approximately 50 percent of the tariffs were abolished immediately when the agreement took affect, and the expensive Mexican customs-users fees are scheduled to be totally eliminated by 1999. Among the areas specifically covered by NAFTA are construction, engineering, accounting, advertising, consulting/management, architecture, healthcare management, commercial education, and tourism.

- Elimination of nontariff barriers by 2008. This includes opening the border and interior of Mexico to U.S. truckers and streamlining border processing and licensing requirements. Nontariff barriers were the biggest obstacle to conducting business in Mexico that small exporters faced. However, in 1997, the United States government delayed full implementation of the NAFTA provision that would have allowed Mexican trucks to travel throughout the four states bordering Mexico and permitted U.S. trucks to travel through Mexican border states. This delay was due in large measure to the vocal opposition of organized labor in the U.S., which raised concerns about the safety of Mexican trucks. Trucks from both sides are still permitted to travel in a commercial zone on either side of the border, but the full elimination of this barrier, which observers indicate would be beneficial to small businesses, has not occurred yet.

- Establishment of standards. The three NAFTA countries agreed to toughen health, safety, and industrial standards to the highest existing standards among the three countries (which were always U.S. or Canadian). Also, national standards could no longer be used as a barrier to free trade. The speed of export-product inspections and certifications was also improved.

- Supplemental agreements. To ease concerns that Mexico's low wage scale would cause U.S. companies to shift production to that country, and to ensure that Mexico's increasing industrialization would not lead to rampant pollution, special side agreements were included in NAFTA. Under those agreements, the three countries agreed to establish commissions to handle labor and environmental issues. The commissions have the power to impose steep fines against any of the three governments that failed to impose its laws consistently. Environmental and labor groups from both the United States and Canada, however, have repeatedly charged that the regulations and guidelines detailed in these supplemental agreements have not been enforced.

- Tariff reduction for motor vehicles and auto parts and automobile rules of origin.

- Expanded telecommunications trade.

- Reduced textile and apparel barriers. The textile industry, which has many small businesses, has been one of the biggest success stories of NAFTA. The agreement has cre-

ated a shift in the growth of textile and apparel trade from the Far East to North America. A study ordered by the U.S. Congress in 1997 showed that U.S. textile and apparel exports to Mexico rose 79 percent over the three years from 1994 through 1996 to $2.8 billion. Meanwhile, Mexico's textile and apparel exports to the U.S. rose from $1.4 billion in 1993 to $4.2 billion in 1996.

- More free trade in agriculture. Mexican import licenses were immediately abolished, with most additional tariffs phased out over a 10-year period.

- Expanded trade in financial services.

- Opening of insurance markets.

- Increased investment opportunities.

- Liberalized regulation of land transportation.

- Increased protection of **intellectual property** rights. NAFTA stipulated that, for the first time, Mexico had to provide a very high level of protection for intellectual property rights. This is especially helpful in fields such as computer software and chemical production.

- Expanded the rights of American firms to make bids on Mexican and Canadian government procurement contracts.

One of the key provisions of NAFTA provided ''national goods'' status to products imported from other NAFTA countries. No state, provincial, or local governments could impose taxes or tariffs on those goods. In addition, customs duties were either eliminated at the time of the agreement or scheduled to be phased out in five or 10 equal stages. The one exception to the phase out was specified sensitive items, for which the phase out period would be 15 years.

Supporters love NAFTA because it opened up Mexican markets to U.S. companies like never before. The Mexican market is growing rapidly, which promises more export opportunities, which in turn means more jobs. Supporters, though, had a difficult time convincing the American public that NAFTA would do more good than harm. Their main effort centered on convincing people that all consumers benefit from the widest possible choice of products at the lowest possible price—which means that consumers would be the biggest beneficiaries of lowered trade barriers. Special interest and ''consumer'' groups who had the most to lose with NAFTA tried to convince legislators and the voting public otherwise.

The U.S. Chamber of Commerce, which represents the interests of small businesses, was one of the most active supporters of NAFTA, organizing the owners and employees of small and mid-size businesses to support the agreement. This support was key in countering the efforts of organized labor to stop the agreement.

NAFTA AND SMALL BUSINESS

So what do all the changes implemented by NAFTA mean to small business owners? There are many opinions on that topic, although most agree that NAFTA has opened up new opportunities for small and mid-size businesses. Mexican consumers spend more each year on U.S. products than their counterparts in Japan and Europe, so the stakes for business owners are high. (Most of the studies of NAFTA concentrate on the effects of U.S. business with Mexico. Trade with Canada has also been enhanced, but the passage of the trade agreement did not have as great an impact on the already liberal trade practices that America and its northern neighbor abided by.

Some small businesses were affected directly by NAFTA. In the past, larger firms always had an advantage over small ones because the large companies could afford to build and maintain offices and/or manufacturing plants in Mexico, thereby avoiding many of the old trade restrictions on exports. In addition, pre-NAFTA laws stipulated that U.S. service providers that wanted to do business in Mexico had to establish a physical presence there, which was simply too expensive for small firms to do. Small firms were stuck—they could not afford to build, nor could they afford the export tariffs. NAFTA leveled the playing field by letting small firms export to Mexico at the same cost as the large firms and by eliminating the requirement that a business establish a physical presence in Mexico in order to do business there. The lifting of these restrictions meant that vast new markets were suddenly open to small businesses that had previously conducted business only in the United States. This was regarded as especially important for small businesses that produced goods or services that had matured in U.S. markets.

Many other small businesses were affected indirectly by NAFTA. For example, examine a large telecommunications company that exports goods to Mexico. It would not be uncommon for up to 80 percent of the suppliers to that large company to be small businesses. When trade barriers were dissolved, the large telecommunications company began to rapidly expand into Mexico, which is in desperate need of telecommunications improvements. As a result, the small firms benefit greatly from the large firm's new business markets.

None of this is to say that American companies can go in and magically take control of the Mexican market for their product. There is a saying in Mexico that states, ''Mexicans for the Mexicans,'' and Mexi-

can businesses live by it. What this means to U.S. companies is that any firm that hopes to do business there better plan on forming alliances and partnerships with Mexican firms, or form a Mexican subsidiary if possible.

Additionally, small firms also must plan on learning just how to do business in Mexico, where things operate very differently than in the United States. Mexican business regulations, hiring practices, employee benefit requirements, taxation schedules, accounting principles—all this and much more must be studied before conducting business in Mexico. The best way to make your way through the myriad rules for doing business in Mexico is to hire a consulting firm that does business there.

OPPOSITION TO NAFTA

Organized labor and firms that have a vested interest in keeping trade barriers in place (i.e., older companies that are unable to compete on a global scale or are most damaged by import competition) are the most vocal opponents of the agreement. Many argue that the abolishment of trade barriers will make it easy for U.S. firms to pack up and move to Mexico to take advantage of cheap labor. Without middle-class factory workers making products and earning wages, middle-class entrepreneurs will have no one to sell their goods and services to, which will put them out of business.

Some businessmen (large and small alike) also believe that, despite the side agreement on environmental issues, U.S. companies will be at a large disadvantage to Mexican firms when it comes to pollution control and clean-up. The argument goes that while U.S. firms will have to comply with U.S. **Environmental Protection Agency** and Department of Natural Resources regulations, Mexican firms will be able to cheaply and quickly produce goods since they do not have to follow those regulations until all environmental standards are hammered out by the three participating countries. Additionally, the fear is that Mexico does not possess the manpower, the money, or the political will to effectively regulate pollution even after the standards are agreed upon. Three years after NAFTA was signed, many of these fears had been realized. The side agreement on the environment remains one of the biggest problems. Canada and Mexico accepted it only grudgingly, and enforcement of any of the provisions has been nonexistent.

Some opposition to NAFTA is on the grounds that some business owners think it is unethical to take advantage of Mexican workers, who may be paid poor wages. Others think that better-paying manufacturing jobs in the United States will slip across the border to Mexico, thus depriving U.S. workers of these jobs. Observers who criticize the pact on these grounds also contend that, to compete with those companies that do take advantage of cheap labor in Mexico, U.S. companies that keep their facilities in America will be forced to lower wages or cut the number of employees.

THREE YEARS LATER: THE EFFECTS OF NAFTA

In 1997, supporters and critics of NAFTA took a long, hard look at what the treaty had done to U.S. trade. Both sides tried to claim victory for their point of view, but the consensus was that NAFTA was a success. Generally speaking, it was not as big a triumph as supporters would have you believe, but on the other hand, neither were the job losses as bad as critics had predicted. Overall, U.S. employment increased by five percent and U.S. output by eight percent during the first three years of NAFTA, although analysts point out that these increases can be attributed to myriad factors, of which NAFTA is only one. Job losses in the U.S. that can be attributed to NAFTA have been minimal. The U.S. Labor Department reported in 1997 that 128,303 U.S. workers lost their jobs because of competition with Mexico and Canada, but 2.2 million jobs were created annually since NAFTA took effect. As of 1997, only 117,000 Americans had signed up for the benefits offered to workers displaced by NAFTA.

Change has been most dramatic in Mexico. U.S. firms are setting up joint ventures in Mexico that, for the first time, use local firms for materials and parts. The quality of goods produced in Mexico has gone up, and the biggest beneficiaries are Mexican consumers. After putting up with decades of shoddy products and nonexistent customer service, Mexicans are finding quality products at reasonable prices (either made in Mexico or imported from the U.S. or Canada without tariffs). Wages and working conditions have improved in many areas also.

Still, despite seemingly positive effects, there is still a great deal of squabbling over NAFTA in American political circles. While there is almost no chance that NAFTA will be repealed, U.S. trade is stuck in a kind of holding pattern while the debate over extending free trade goes on. Other nations remain wary of doing business in the United States, concerned that they will not get the same treatment as Mexico and Canada. The next step of NAFTA is supposed to be the ''fast-track'' inclusion of Chile and Latin America into the treaty, but even that is stalled. The best advice for small businesspersons hoping to take advantage of free trade is to strongly explore new markets in Mexico and Canada while monitoring slow international trade developments on other fronts.

FURTHER READING:

Allen, Mike. ''NAFTA Is a Good Treaty, But Could Be Better.'' *San Diego Business Journal.* July 21, 1997.

Banker, John. ''On the 'Wrong' Side of Free Trade: Why Some Firms Side with Labor Against NAFTA.'' *The Business Journal-Milwaukee.* November 13, 1993.

Edmond Jr., Alfred. ''Making the Most of NAFTA: Here's What to Do when the Barriers to Mexico's Markets Come Down.'' *Black Enterprise.* February 1994.

Hiatt, Roger L. ''The NAFTA Spells Opportunity for Business.'' *The Kansas City Business Journal.* February 26, 1993.

Holzinger, Albert G. ''Why Small Firms Back NAFTA.'' *Nation's Business.* November 1993.

Magnusson, Paul. ''NAFTA: Where's that 'Giant Sucking Sound'?'' *Business Week.* July 7, 1997.

Maynard, Roberta. ''A Good Time to Export.'' *Nation's Business.* May 1994.

Ostroff, Jim. ''Report: NAFTA Helped Both U.S. and Mexico.'' *WWD.* July 14, 1997.

Reynolds, Alan. ''The Politics of NAFTA.'' *National Review.* October 18, 1993.

''Small Businessman Expects a Lift-Up from NAFTA.'' *San Diego Business Journal.* February 15, 1993.

''What NAFTA Means to Small Businesses: Mexico Is an Important Market for Small and Medium Sized U.S. Businesses.'' *Arkansas Business.* November 15, 1993.

''When Neighbours Embrace: the NAFTA Effect.'' *The Economist.* July 5, 1997.

SEE ALSO: Exporting; General Agreement on Tariffs and Trade; International Marketing

O

OCCUPATIONAL SAFETY AND HEALTH ADMINISTRATION

The Occupational Safety and Health Administration (OSHA) was established by the Williams-Steiger Occupational Safety and Health Act (OSH Act) of 1970, which took effect in 1971. OSHA's mission is to "assure, in so far as possible, every working man and woman in the nation safe and healthful working conditions." Nearly every employee in the United States comes under OSHA's jurisdiction. The only exceptions are people who are self-employed, workers in mining and transportation industries (which are covered by other agencies), and most public employees. Thus, nearly every private employer in the United States needs to be cognizant of OSHA rules and regulations. Because OSHA is an administrative agency within the U.S. Department of Labor, it is administered by an assistant secretary of labor.

OSHA OBJECTIVES AND STANDARDS

OSHA seeks to make workplaces safer and healthier by making and enforcing regulations, which the OSH Act calls "standards." The OSH Act itself establishes only one workplace standard, which is called the "general duty standard." The general duty standard states: "Each employer shall furnish to each of his employees employment and a place of employment which are free from recognized hazards that are causing or are likely to cause death or serious physical harm to his [or her] employees." In the OSH Act, Congress delegated authority to OSHA to make rules further implementing the general duty standard.

Standards made by OSHA are published in the *Code of Federal Regulations* (*CFR*). The three types of regulations are called interim, temporary emergency, and permanent. Interim standards were applicable for two years after OSH Act was passed. For this purpose, OSHA was authorized to use the standards of any nationally recognized "standards setting" organization such as those of professional engineering groups. Such privately developed standards are called "national consensus standards." Temporary emergency standards last only six months and are designed to protect workers while OSHA goes through the processes required by law to develop a permanent standard. Permanent standards are made through the same processes as the regulations made by other federal administrative agencies. As OSHA drafts a proposal for a permanent standard, it consults with representatives of industry and labor and collects whatever scientific, medical, and engineering data is necessary to ensure that the standard adequately reflects workplace realities. Proposed standards are published in the *Federal Register*. A comment period is then held, during which input is received from interested parties including, but not limited to, representatives of industry and labor. At the close of the comment period, the proposal may be withdrawn and set aside, withdrawn and re-proposed with modifications, or approved as a final standard that is legally enforceable. All standards that become legally binding are first published in the *Federal Register* and then compiled and published in the *Code of Federal Regulations*. It is important to note that many of OSHA's permanent standards originated as national consensus standards developed by private professional organizations such as the National Fire Protection Association and the American National Standards Institute. Examples of permanent

OSHA standards include limits for exposure of employees to hazardous substances such as asbestos, benzene, vinyl chloride, and cotton dust.

NATIONAL INSTITUTE OF OCCUPATIONAL SAFETY AND HEALTH The OSH Act of 1970 also established a research institute called the National Institute of Occupational Safety and Health (NIOSH). Since 1973, NIOSH has been a division of the U.S. government's Centers for Disease Control (CDC). The purpose of NIOSH is to gather data documenting incidences of occupational exposure, injury, illness and death in the United States. This information, which is highly valued by OSHA, is gathered from a wide variety of sources, ranging from industry groups to labor unions, as well as independent organizations.

OSHA RECORD-KEEPING REQUIREMENTS

OSHA requires all companies subject to its workplace standards to abide by a variety of occupational regulations. One of OSHA's major requirements is that companies keep records on facets of their operations relevant to employee safety and health. All employers covered by the OSH Act are required to keep four kinds of records:

- Records regarding enforcement of OSHA standards

- Research records

- Job-related injury, illness, and death records

- Job hazard records.

OSHA ENFORCEMENT OF STANDARDS

OSHA inspectors conduct planned or surprise inspections of work sites covered by the OSH Act to verify compliance with the OSH Act and standards promulgated by OSHA. The OSH Act allows the employer *and* an employee representative to accompany OSHA's representative during the inspection. It should also be noted that in 1978, in *Marshall v. Barlow*, the United States Supreme Court declared that in most industries, employers have a right to bar an OSHA inspector from his/her premises if the inspector has not first obtained a search warrant.

If violations are found during an inspection, an OSHA citation may be issued in which alleged violations are listed, notices of penalties for each violation are given, and an abatement period is established. The abatement period is the amount of time the employer has to correct any violation(s). Penalties for a violation can be civil or criminal and vary depending on the nature of the violation (minor or serious, willful or nonwillful, or repeated). Penalties are naturally more severe for serious, repeated, willful violations. Since OSHA must refer cases to the United States Justice Department for criminal enforcement, it has not made extensive use of criminal prosecution as an enforcement mechanism. Instead, the agency has historically relied on civil penalties.

An employer has 15 days to contest an OSHA citation, and any challenge is heard by an Administrative Law Judge (ALJ) within OSHA. The ALJ receives oral and written evidence, decides issues of fact and law, and enters an order. If the employer is dissatisfied with that order, it can be appealed to the Occupational Safety and Health Review Commission, which will, in turn, enter an order. Finally, within 30 days of the issuance of that order, the employer or the Secretary of Labor can take the case to the United States federal court system by filing an appeal with a United States court of appeals.

OSHA AND ITS STATE COUNTERPARTS

Pursuant to the OSH Act, an individual state can pass its own worker health and safety laws and standards. Indeed, the 1970 legislation encouraged individual states to develop and operate their own job safety and health programs. If the state can show that its job safety and health standards are ''at least as effective as'' comparable federal standards, the state can be certified to assume OSH Act administration and enforcement in that state. OSHA approves and monitors state plans, and provides up to 50 percent of operating costs for approved plans. As of the mid-1990s, 23 states and jurisdictions operated complete state plans covering not only the private sector, but also state and local government employees).

To gain OSHA approval for a 'developmental plan,' the first step in the process of instituting a state plan for job safety and health, the applying state must first assure OSHA that it will, within three years, have in place all the structural elements necessary for an effective occupational safety and health program. These elements include: 1) appropriate legislation; 2) regulations and procedures for standards setting, enforcement, appeal of citations, and penalties; 3) adequate resources (both in number and qualifications of inspectors and other personnel) for enforcement of standards.

Once a state has completed and documented all its developmental requirements, it is eligible for certification. Certification is basically an acknowledgment that the state has put together a complete plan. Once the state has reached a point where it is deemed capable of independently enforcing job safety and health standards, OSHA may enter into an 'operational status' agreement with the state. Once this occurs, OSHA in effect steps aside and allows the state to enforce its laws.

The ultimate accreditation of a state plan is known as ''final approval.'' When OSHA grants final approval, it relinquishes its authority to cover occupational safety and health matters that are addressed by the state's rules and regulations. Final approval can not be given until at least one year after certification, and it is predicated on OSHA's judgment that worker protection is at least as effective under the state's standards as it is under the federal program. The state must meet all required staffing levels and agree to participate in OSHA's computerized inspection data system before being allowed to operate without OSHA supervision.

HISTORY OF THE RELATIONSHIP BETWEEN OSHA AND BUSINESS

OSHA has traditionally used "command and control" kinds of regulation to protect workers. "Command and control" regulations are those which set requirements for job safety (such as requirements for guard rails on stairs) or limits on exposure to a hazardous substance (such as a given number of fibers of asbestos per cubic milliliter of air breathed per hour). They are enforced through citations issued to violators.

In 1984 OSHA promulgated the Hazard Communication Standard (HCS), which was viewed as a new kind of regulation differing from "command and control." The HCS gives workers access to information about long-term health risks resulting from workplace exposure to toxic or hazardous substances, and requires manufacturers, importers, and distributors to provide employers with evaluations of all toxic or hazardous materials sold or distributed to those employers. This information is compiled in a form known as a Material Safety Data Sheet (MSDS). The MSDS describes the chemical's physical hazards such as ignitability and reactivity, gives associated health hazards, and states the exposure limits established by OSHA. In turn, the employer must make these documents available to employees, and requires employers to establish hazard communication education programs. The employer must also label all containers with the identities of hazardous substances and appropriate warnings. Worker "Right-to-Know," as implemented on the federal level through the HCS, is designed to give workers access to information so that they can make informed decisions about their exposure to toxic chemicals.

OSHA has been criticized by businesses and industry groups throughout its history. In the 1970s, it was criticized for making job-safety regulations that businesses considered to be vague or unnecessarily costly. For example, a 1977 OSHA regulation contained detailed specifications regarding irregularities in western hemlock trees used to construct ladders. In the Appropriations Act of 1977, Congress directed OSHA to get rid of certain standards that it described as "trivial." As a result, in 1978 OSHA revoked 928 job-safety standards and increased its efforts to deal with health hazards.

On the other hand, OSHA has also been criticized by unions and other pro-worker groups throughout its history for doing too little to protect employees. Throughout its existence, OSHA has been criticized for issuing too few new standards, for failing to protect workers who report violations, for failing to adequately protect workers involved in the clean up of toxic-waste sites, and for failing to enforce existing standards. The latter charge has been a particularly frustrating one for OSHA. Funding for enforcement has dwindled in recent years, and over the last 20 years, both Congress and various presidential administrations have publicly supported efforts to keep OSHA and other agencies "off the backs" of business.

OSHA REFORMS

In recent years, critics of OSHA have become even more vocal in their complaints. They contend that American workplace safety and health regulations are too often excessively burdensome on businesses of all shapes and sizes. Some of these critics call for fundamental changes in the regulatory environment, insisting that changes should be made to encourage voluntary industry compliance on worker safety issues and reductions of penalties for nonserious violators of standards. Even some defenders of OSHA acknowledge that the agency has tended toward excessive bureaucracy and imposition of penalties that make no allowances for extenuating circumstances. OSHA itself has acknowledged that "in the public's view, OSHA has been driven too often by numbers and rules, not by smart enforcement and results. Business complains about overzealous enforcement and burdensome rules. . . . And too often, a "one-size-fits-all" regulatory approach has treated conscientious employers no differently from those who put workers needlessly at risk." Worker advocates and others, however, point out that OSHA standards have been an important factor in the dramatic decline of injury and illness rates in many industries over the past few decades, and they express concern that reforms could put workers in a variety of businesses at greater risk.

OSHA's recent reform initiatives, then, have sought to address those issues raised by its critics while simultaneously ensuring that American workers receive adequate health and safety protection in the workplace. In 1995 OSHA announced a new emphasis on treating employers with aggressive health and safety programs differently from employers who lack such efforts. "At its core," said OSHA, "this new approach seeks to encourage the development of worksite health and safety programs. . . . OSHA will be looking for programs with these features: management commitment, meaningful participation of employees, a systematic effort to find safety and health hazards whether they are covered by existing standards or not, documentation that the identified hazards are fixed, training for employees and supervisors, and ultimately a reduction in injuries and illnesses." Those firms armed with good safety programs will receive special recognition that will include: the lowest priority for enforcement inspections, the highest priority for assistance, appropriate regulatory relief, and major penalty reductions. Businesses that do not adequately provide for their workers' health and safety, however, will be subject to "strong and traditional OSHA enforcement procedures. . . . In short, for those who have a history of endangering their employees and are unwilling to change, OSHA will rigorously enforce the law without compromise to assure that there are serious consequences for serious violators."

OSHA announced its intention to pursue several initiatives to make the above changes possible. These include nationwide implementation of the "Maine 200" program, a highly successful initiative wherein 198 out of 200 Maine companies, when provided with a choice between stepped up enforcement or partnerships with government to realize workplace safety goals, chose partnerships. "The Maine program is extremely promising," said OSHA. "In two years, the employers self-identified more than fourteen times as many hazards as could have been cited by OSHA inspectors (in part, because OSHA's small staff could never have visited all 1,300 worksites involved). Nearly six out of ten employers in the program have already reduced their injury and illness rates, even as inspections and fines are significantly diminished. OSHA will expand the most successful features of this program nationwide."

OSHA also announced its plans to make more tightly focused inspections on companies that have effective safety and health programs. If a company with a strong record meets selected safety/health criteria, the OSHA inspector will conduct an abbreviated inspection. Conversely, in situations where a safety and health program is nonexistent or inadequate, a complete site inspection, including full citations, will be undertaken. OSHA also indicated that it planned to: target inspections at employers with poor worker safety and health records; conduct more inspections in industries with higher injury and illness rates; introduce additional incentives for employers with safety and health programs; promote greater worker participation in creating and maintaining workplace safety and health programs; streamline OSHA regulations; increase use of technologies to streamline work; and adjust the criteria by which it evaluates inspectors ("inspectors have been told clearly that there are no numeric inspection goals and that their performance will not be judged by the number of citations and fines they issue but by their success in finding and reducing hazards associated with injuries and illnesses"). Finally, OSHA has expressed satisfaction with a pilot "quick-fix" program. "Using this model," noted OSHA, "compliance officers reduce penalties for violations that are abated—during the inspection. This policy encouraged employers to increase employee protection immediately, while freeing OSHA employees from monitoring abatement and follow-up paperwork."

OSHA AND SMALL BUSINESS

In recognition of the special challenges that often face small businesses—and the limited financial resources that they often have—the Occupational Safety and Health Administration administers a number of special programs specifically designed to help entrepreneurs and small business owners provide a productive yet safe environment for their employees. In addition, there are a number of situations in which OSHA has the discretion to reduce penalties for small businesses.

Among the special programs that OSHA has instituted for small businesses are the following:

- Penalty Reduction—OSHA may grant reductions of up to 60 percent for businesses that qualify as small firms.

- Penalty Reductions for Good Faith—OSHA has the option of granting a 25 percent penalty reduction if a small business has instituted an effective safety and health program for its employees.

- Flexible Requirements—OSHA gives smaller firms greater flexibility in certain safety areas in recognition of their limited resources (i.e., lead in construction, emergency evacuation plans, process safety management).

- Consultation Program—While not limited to small businesses, OSHA on-site consultation program has been particularly helpful to smaller companies (small firms accounted for about 40 percent of the program during the mid-1990s). This service, which is run by state agencies, provides businesses with the option of requesting a free on-site consultation with a state representative who helps them identify potential workplace hazards and improve or implement effective workplace safety and health programs.

- Training Grants—OSHA awards grant money to non-profit groups for the development of programs designed to help entrepreneurs and small business owners establish safety and health guidelines for their companies.

- Mentoring—OSHA and the Voluntary Protection Programs Participants Association (VPPA) operate a mentoring program to help small firms applying for entry into VPP refine their health and safety programs. The VPP is an OSHA program that is intended to recognize a firm's safety and health achievements. This mentoring program matches applicants with VPP members (often in the same or a related industry) who can help by sharing their experience with and knowledge about workplace safety and health programs.

In addition, many states with their own federally approved safety and health standards offer additional programs of assistance to small businesses.

THE VALUE OF CONSULTATION PROGRAMS OSHA and business consultants alike encourage small business owners to take advantage of available consultation programs. A comprehensive consultation can provide small business owners with a wide variety of information that can help ensure that they are in compliance with regulatory requirements.

Consultations will typically include appraisal of all mechanical and environmental hazards and physical work practices; appraisal of the firm's present job safety and health program; conference with management on findings; written report of recommendations and agreements; and training and assistance with implementing recommendations. ''The consultant will then review detailed findings with you in a closing conference,'' noted OSHA. ''You [the business owner] will learn not only what you need to improve, but also what you are doing right. At that time you can discuss problems, possible solutions and abatement periods to eliminate or control any serious hazards identified during the walk-through. . . . The consultant can help you establish or strengthen an employee safety and health program, making safety and health activities routine considerations rather than crisis-oriented responses.''

FURTHER READING:

Bodwin, Amy. ''Work-Safety System Clogged: State Audit.'' *Crain's Business Detroit.* April 12-18, 1993.

Boggs, Richard F. ''OSHA Can't Do It All.'' *Safety & Health.* April 5, 1992.

Kerrigan, Karen. ''OSHA Reforms Winding through Congress.'' *Washington Business Journal.* February 23, 1996.

''The New OSHA—Reinventing Worker Safety and Health.'' Washington: Occupational Safety and Health Administration, 1995.

Stenzel, Paulette L. ''Right to Act: Advancing the Common Interests of Labor and Environmentalists,'' *Albany Law Review.* Vol. 57, no. 1, 1993.

Yohay, Stephen C. ''Recent Court Decisions on Important OSHA Enforcement Issues.'' *Employee Relations Law Journal.* Spring 1997.

SEE ALSO: Environmental Law and Business; Workplace Safety

OFFICE AUTOMATION

Office automation refers to the varied computer machinery and software used to digitally create, collect, store, manipulate, and relay office information needed for accomplishing basic tasks and goals. Raw data storage, electronic transfer, and the management of electronic business information comprise the basic activities of an office automation system.

The history of modern office automation began with the typewriter and the copy machine, which mechanized previously manual tasks. In the 1990s, however, office automation is increasingly understood as a term that refers not just to the mechanization of tasks but to the conversion of information to electronic form as well. The advent of the personal computer in the early 1980s revolutionized office automation, and today, popular operating systems like DOS (Disk Operating System) and user interfaces like Microsoft Windows dominate office computer systems. This revolution has been so complete, and has infiltrated so many areas of business, that almost all businesses use at least one commercial computer business application in the course of daily activity. Even the smallest companies commonly utilize computer technology to maintain financial records, inventory information, payroll records, and other pertinent business information.

THE BASICS OF OFFICE AUTOMATION

Generally, there are three basic activities of an office automation system: data storage of raw data, data exchange, and data management. Within each broad application area, hardware and software combine to fulfill basic functions.

Data storage usually includes office records and other primary office forms and documents. Data applications involve the capture and editing of files, images, or spreadsheets. Word processing and desktop presentation packages accommodate raw textual and graphical data, while spreadsheet applications provide users with the capacity to engage in the easy manipulation and output of numbers. Image applications allow the capture and editing of visual images.

Text handling software and systems cover the whole field of word processing and desktop publishing. Word processing is the inputting (usually via keyboard) and manipulation of text on a computer. Word processing is frequently the most basic and common office automation activity. Popular commercial word processing applications include Novell's

WordPerfect and Microsoft Word. Each provides the office user with a sophisticated set of commands to format, edit, and print text documents. One of the most popular features of word processing packages are their preformatted document templates. Templates automatically set up such things as font size, paragraph styles, headers and footers, and page numbers so that the user does not have to reset document characteristics every time they create a new record.

Desktop publishing adds another dimension to text manipulation. By combining the features of a word processor with advanced page design and layout features, desktop publishing packages have emerged as valuable tools in the creation of newsletters, brochures, and other documents that combine text and photographs, charts, drawings and other graphic images.

Image handling software and systems are another facet of office automation. Examples of visual information include pictures of documents, photographs, and graphics such as tables and charts. These images are converted into digital files, which cannot be edited the same way that text files can. In a word processor or desktop publishing application, each word or character is treated individually. In an imaging system, the entire picture or document is treated as one whole object. One of the most popular uses of computerized images is in corporate presentations or speeches. Presentation software packages simplify the creation of multimedia presentations that use computer video, images, sound, and text in an integrated information package.

Spreadsheet programs allow the manipulation of numeric data. Early popular spreadsheet programs such as VisiCalc and Lotus 123 greatly simplified common business financial record keeping. Particularly useful among the many spreadsheet options is the ability to use variables in pro forma statements. The pro forma option allows the user to change a variable and have a complex formula automatically recalculated based on the new numbers. Many businesses use spreadsheets for financial management, financial projection, and accounting.

DATA EXCHANGE

While data storage and manipulation is one component of an office automation system, the exchange of that information is another equally important component. Electronic transfer is a general application area that highlights the exchange of information between more than one user or participant. **Electronic mail**, voice mail, and facsimile are examples of electronic transfer applications. Systems that allow instantaneous or "real time" transfer of information (i.e. online conversations via computer or audio exchange with video capture) are considered electronic sharing systems. Electronic sharing software illustrates the collaborative nature of many office automation systems.

Office automation systems that include the ability to electronically share information between more than one user simultaneously are sometimes referred to as groupware systems. One type of groupware is an electronic meeting system. Electronic meeting systems allow geographically dispersed participants to exchange information in real time. Participants in such electronic meetings may be within the same office or building, or thousands of miles apart. Long-distance electronic sharing systems usually use a telephone line connection to transfer data, while sharing in the same often involves just a local area network of computers (no outside phone line is needed). The functional effectiveness of such electronic sharing systems has been one factor in the growth of **telecommuting** as an option for workers. Telecommuters work at home, maintaining their ties to the office via computer.

Electronic transfer software and systems allow for electronic, voice, and **facsimile transmission** of office information. Electronic mail uses computer-based storage and a common set of network communication standards to forward electronic messages from one user to another. Most of these systems allow users to relay electronic mail to more than one recipient. Additionally, many electronic mail systems provide security features, automatic messaging, and mail management systems like electronic folders or notebooks. Voice mail offers essentially the same applications, but for telephones, not computers. Facsimile transmissions are limited to image relay, and while usage of this communication option has declined somewhat with the emergence of electronic mail, fax machines remain standard in almost all business offices in America. In addition, new technologies continue to transform fax use, just as they have influenced other modes of corporate communication. For example, facsimile converters for the personal computer that allow remote printing of "faxed" information via the computer rather than through a dedicated facsimile machine are now available. Indeed, these facsimile circuit boards for the microcomputer are slowly replacing stand-alone fax machines.

DATA MANAGEMENT

Office automation systems are also often used to track both short-term and long-term data in the realms of financial plans, workforce allocation plans, marketing expenditures, inventory purchases, and other aspects of business. Task management or scheduling systems monitor and control various projects and activities within the office. Electronic management systems monitor and control office activities and tasks through timelines, resource equations, and electronic scheduling. As in data exchange, groupware and network computer systems are gaining in popularity for data management. Under such arrangements, multiple members of the office environment are provided with access to a variety of information at a central electronic location.

OFFICE AUTOMATION CONSIDERATIONS: PEOPLE, TOOLS, AND THE WORKPLACE

Businesses engaged in launching or upgrading office automation systems must consider a wide variety of factors that can influence the effectiveness of those systems. These factors include employee attitudes toward computers and electronic information, proliferating office automation choices, budgetary and physical space considerations, changes in communication infrastructure, and other considerations.

- Training—People involved with office automation basically include all users of the automation and all providers of the automation systems and tools. A wide range of people—including software and hardware engineers, management information scientists, executives, mid-level workers, and secretaries—are just a few of the people that use office automation on a daily basis. As a result, training of personnel on these office automation systems has become an essential part of many companies' planning. After all, the office automation system is only as good as the people who make it and use it, and smart business owners and managers recognize that workplace resistance to these systems can dramatically lessen their benefits.

- Choice—A dizzying array of office automation alternatives are available to businesses of all shapes, sizes, and subject areas. Such systems typically involve a sizable investment of funds, so it is wise for managers and business owners to undertake a careful course of study before making a purchase. Primary factors that should be considered include: cost of the system, length of time involved in introducing the system, physical condition of the facility into which the system will be introduced, level of technical support, compatibility with other systems, complexity of system (a key factor in determining allocations of time and money for training), and compatibility of the system with the business area in which the company is involved.

FURTHER READING:

Carter, Leon. "Office Machines Meet LAN's In The Digital Office of the Future." *Purchasing.* November 25, 1993.

Dykeman, John. B. "The State of Office Applications Software." *Managing Office Technology.* June 1993.

Laudon, Kenneth C., and Jane P. Laudon. *Management Information Systems: Organization and Technology.* Macmillan, 1994.

Martin, E. Wainright, et al. *Managing Information Technology: What Managers Need To Know.* Macmillan, 1991.

Page, Heather. "Branching Out: Network Computers Offer a Low-Cost Solution to Your Growing High-Tech Needs." *Entrepreneur.* September 1997.

Stevens, Tim. "The Smart Office." *Industry Management.* January 17, 1994.

SEE ALSO: Computers and Computer Systems

OFFICE ROMANCE

Office romances are situations in which two members of a business establishment—whether coworkers in an office or on a shop floor—become romantically involved with one another. For businesses of all sizes, such developments can complicate business operations. After all, office romances that go awry can not only result in emotional pain for one or both of the principals involved, but can also trigger losses of workplace **productivity** that directly impact on the business. Indeed, office romances that go fabulously well can have the same bottom-line impact on a company if the couple spends an inordinate amount of work time courting one another. These concerns are often heightened in small business establishments, which often feel losses of personnel and productivity more acutely than do larger companies.

But most companies operating today recognize that attempts to neutralize or forbid office romances are probably doomed to failure. "Some would go so far as to suggest that office romance began the day men and women began working under the same roof," stated Ann Brocklehurst in *Maclean's.* "And the current consensus is that it is becoming even more common as men and women spend more time on the job and less time in traditional settings such as churches and community social groups." And many observers—experts, small business owners, and CEOs alike—contend that most office romances do not have an appreciable negative impact on business operations. In fact, defenders of office romance sometimes argue that the practice can actually improve workplace performance in such areas as morale, cooperation, and work force stability. They argue that the ultimate impact of an office romance on a business is often predicated on the fundamental nature of the relationship.

CONDITIONS THAT CONTRIBUTE TO OFFICE ROMANCE

The workplace's status as fertile territory for office romance is well-entrenched in American society, particularly in today's business and social climate, and for good reason. "Social scientists and human resource professionals have long recognized that the workplace is probably the most social, active, challenging, energetic, and, yes, even sexy places that people gather," wrote Joseph D. Levesque in *The Human Resource Problem-Solver's Handbook.* "And they do so under unique, varying, and unassuming conditions, all of which make romantic attraction not only normal, but sometimes even fostered. Many employment environments, especially the formal office setting, establish fashionable dress standards or expectations. Even if this is inadvertent, it sets up a certain type of sexuality by encouraging employees to look their best—to look professionally attractive." Levesque noted that the nature of workplace activities also contribute to feelings of attraction: "Work related interaction gives people the rather unsuspecting opportunity to get acquainted with another's ideas, feelings, ambitions, interests, mannerisms, values, preferences, and personal habits—the very things we examine on a more conscious level when engaged in such mating rituals as dating. When people's work bring them together in close association with each other, the stage can easily become set for unconscious development of attraction, whether it becomes the product of a lengthy and involved project, a singular business trip, or sporadic but intense contact with each other." Social scientist Marcy Crary, writing in *Organizational Dynamics,* concurred that the workplace is often festooned with conditions that foster intimacy: "Most of us have been socialized into thinking of intimacy and work as two separate compartments in our lives; intimacy takes place at home and work takes place at our place of employment. But for many people the realities of day-to-day experiences belie these rational arrangements of our worlds. Working closely together can create a sense of intimacy between people, or the creation of intimate relationships may be essential to performing the task itself."

Lisa A. Mainiero, author of *Office Romance: Love, Power, and Sex in the Workplace,* noted that larger societal factors also have come into play. One reason for the increase in workplace romance, she contended, "concerns security, old-fashioned comfort, and safety. With the difficulties involved in meeting people of kindred spirit, and the rampant fear of sexually transmitted disease, we are more comfortable establishing relationships with those whom we already know well. We feel safer, more secure, and more knowledgeable about dating a coworker than, say, someone we meet at the local bar on a Saturday night.... Another reason in propinquity. The modern-day office has taken the place of church, neighborhood, and family networks in bringing people together. We choose employers today not only because we are challenged by a new and exciting job opportu-

nity, but also because we genuinely will like the culture of the company and the people with whom we will work." Indeed, academic studies indicate that future spouses are more likely to meet at work than in school, neighborhood, or other social settings.

Finally, feelings of attraction between coworkers are inevitable because of human nature. As one executive told Mainiero, "You don't turn off your feelings of sexual attraction just because you're walking through an office door. We are all human, and our hormones don't shut off between nine and five."

KINDS OF OFFICE ROMANCE

Each office romance is unique, but in general, business consultants and social scientists point to several basic types, each of which have are likely to have a different impact on business operations.

RELATIONSHIPS BETWEEN MENTORS/SUPERVISORS AND SUBORDINATES These kinds of office romances, which are often cited as among the most potentially damaging of workplace relationships, are also more likely to involve small business owners—who, after all, are usually the ultimate boss of a business enterprise. "The most difficult problems that tend to result from workplace romance—that is, those liaisons where there evolves the most pronounced kinds of adverse effects—are the romantic involvements between those in the management ranks and those between managers and subordinate employees," stated Levesque. "Why? Simply because they inherently have the capacity to do more damage to the structural integrity of the organization, their own credibility as objective decision-makers, and those that rely on their judgment and guidance. These conditions and their effect rarely develop to a level of significant impact on the organization when romance takes shape between non-management co-workers. In these cases, the worst effect is typically minor productivity problems within their work unit," which can be corrected through supervisory action." Mainiero agreed, writing that "boss-subordinate relationships bring out the worst of the risks associated with office romance. . . . Hierarchical relationships—or any relationship where there is power inequity—can be exploited or manipulated. Sex can be traded for promotion. But it is only those with power who can recommend career assignments, promotions, raises, and favorable projects; peers cannot do so. It is for this reason that boss-subordinate or mentor relationships should be strictly avoided." She also pointed out that such relationships can cause morale problems among other employees in the small business, who may feel that the relationship is creating unequal treatment in terms of tasks, opportunities, etc. Small business owners should thus exercise caution when pondering such a relationship, and they should be aware of the potential problems that can arise if their manager(s) engage in such a relationship.

RELATIONSHIPS BETWEEN PEERS Office romances between peers in a business—whether they are partners in a business or entry-level employees—do not have the same perils as do boss/subordinate relationships, but they are obviously not without risk. Romances that end badly can result in a strained office atmosphere, loss of productivity, and even, in some cases, the departure of valued employees.

FLINGS Flings are basically short-lived romantic entanglements. The repercussions of such behavior can vary tremendously within a business, depending on the emotions and goals of the principals involved, their "post-fling" attitudes, and the degree to which the fling becomes common knowledge, either within the office or in their personal lives (especially if a spouse is involved). Some flings may transpire with no ill effects, while others—especially if the small business owner is involved—can wreak heavy damage on a business.

LONG-TERM RELATIONSHIPS Most people—small business owners, managers, and employees alike—enter into office romances in the hopes of building a long-term relationship with the other individual, and in some instances this can actually take place. "This relationship," wrote Levesque, is "the one everyone admires and hopes . . . will flourish into a permanent, meaningful bond."

EXTRAMARITAL AFFAIRS The above-mentioned types of office romances can have a significant impact on the workplace, but the fallout from extramarital affairs is often most deeply felt in the homes of those involved (although they can often take a big toll in the office as well). Extramarital affairs, when discovered, often result in the dissolution of marriages, which in turn can cause significant havoc in a worker's (or an owner's) relationship with children, living arrangements, and state of mind. Within the office, meanwhile, such affairs can cause considerable problems in terms of morale and productivity. Once again, the impact of this kind of office romance can vary considerably, depending on the identities and goals of those involved. A business enterprise is far more likely to be damaged by an extramarital affair between the owner and a key employee than one in which the principals are two part-time employees.

DISPARATE VIEWS OF OFFICE ROMANCE

Assessments of the dangers of office romance vary dramatically. Some observers view it as a wholly undesirable condition that should be avoided by business owners and managers if at all possible, while others view it as a potential positive development, provided that the relationship lies within certain parameters. After all, a relationship that is marked by nepotism concerns or features a married person who is committing adultery is far more likely to raise eyebrows than one between two single people who have no reporting relationship with one another.

Some analysts, business owners, and managers view office romances in almost entirely negative terms. "While there may be a small percentage of workplace romance liaisons that have pleasant and fulfilling culminations (usually marriage), these situations are typically infrequent to those that become painful and end that way," claimed Levesque. "For the organization there is loss too. Inevitably there is a decline in performance, be it productivity, decisions, objectivity, or morale. There also evolves the disruption of working relationships, the emergence of rivalries, inappropriate disclosure of organizational information, damage to the company reputation, and all too frequently having to release an otherwise valued employee."

Other observers, however, are far less critical of the practice, and suggest that many such relationships can actually improve a company's performance. Management consultant Kaleel Jamison, for example, indicated in *Personnel Administrator* that "[sexual attraction] may be disruptive, but . . . if properly managed, it can be not disruptive but actually energizing and productive within the organization." Mainiero agreed, although she noted that "it is true, as popular opinion suggests, that there are a number of risks and disadvantages to a poorly conducted, unprofessional, [or exploitative] office romance. This cannot be denied. But it is equally true that some romances, under certain limited conditions, can be quite beneficial—in terms of corporate morale, employee motivation, and departmental productivity."

DEALING WITH OFFICE ROMANCES

Most experts believe that banning dating among employees is not a reasonable solution, although exceptions can certainly be made in instances where one of the principals involved has a supervisory role over the other. Restrictions against inter-office dating can be particularly hard to enforce in small business establishments, where the environment may be more relaxed and work-related interdependencies may be more pronounced, thus encouraging an atmosphere of social interaction.

But companies can still take steps to minimize the risk that an office romance will have a deleterious impact on workplace productivity or morale. Small business owners are encouraged to explore the following:

1) Recognize that employees follow your lead. If you are prone to becoming involved with employees or partners, you can hardly blame

your employees if they interpret such behavior as a green light to engage in office romances of their own.

2) Use good judgement. Entrepreneurs who have established their own business may have more opportunities to enter into workplace romances, given their economic status and authority. Self-discipline may be necessary, especially if you are not looking for any long-term commitment (that may not be the case with the other person in the relationship)

3) Establish basic parameters of behavior through written policy guidelines. Policies specifically highlighting the unacceptableness of extramarital affairs and abuses of mentor/subordinate relationships are particularly common.

4) Do not overstep boundaries of employee privacy. Businesses that are overzealous in attempts to sever, repair, or otherwise react to office romances run the risk of attracting a lawsuit.

5) On the other hand, business owners have a right to intervene in situations where a workplace relationship—either in full blossom or on the rocks—is having a detrimental effect on business productivity. Such intervention can range from informal discussions of performance problems to formal warnings and other disciplinary actions (including termination if serious violations of workplace professionalism have taken place). Consultants note that in many instances, prompt response to workplace issues that arise from an office romance gone sour can go far toward addressing the problem. Unfortunately, many managers and business owners wait until it is too late. "Management typically feels inept or inappropriate in stepping in, and consequently avoids addressing the issue until complications occur—and then it's usually handled by a termination or forced resignation," wrote Levesque. Sometimes, office romances turn so sour that the company faces the unpleasant prospect of removing one of the people from the work area. But whereas larger companies often have the option of transferring a person to another office location, smaller enterprises typically do not have this option; instead, they can only reassign one of the affected people to another project or area of the office, and adopt some sort of monitoring process to ensure that both people behave in a professional manner so as not to damage the business in any way. Basically, business owners need to make it abundantly

clear that workplace performance is their primary concern.

DISTINGUISHING BETWEEN FLIRTING AND SEXUAL HARASSMENT

Given the increase in **sexual harassment** lawsuits that have been brought against companies in recent years, it is not surprising that small business owners have expressed concern about the sometimes blurry boundaries between office flirtations—which may lead to full-fledged office romances—and ugly instances of sexual harassment. "Aside from behavior that is clearly offensive, how can anyone know what another person will find improper?" wrote Catherine Dold in *Cosmopolitan*. "What's more, how can you be a little flirtatious and sexy and let a coworker know you might be interested in dating? There is no magic formula to distinguish proper from inappropriate office demeanor, experts say. It all has to be looked at in context."

While businesses can take certain steps to define inappropriate office conduct, many of them quite effective, stopping sexual harassment is often a more complicated issue if the two people involved were formerly romantically involved. "Suppose you decide that you want to break off the affair, and your lover disagrees?" queried Mainiero. "You may find yourself dealing with a very serious problem. Breakups bring out the worst in people." Indeed, some people resort to harassment in the wake of a breakup, while others have been known to level false harassment charges after being jilted. If an office relationship degenerates to such a point, it is important for the business owner to maintain an impartial stance and make sure that decisions are made on the basis of the evidence at hand.

FURTHER READING:

Anderson, C., and P. Hunsaker. "Why There's Romancing at the Office and Why It's Everyone's Problem." *Personnel*. February 1985.

Brocklehurst, Ann. "When Two is Company: Some Bosses Disapprove, but Romance at the Office Seems to be on the Rise." *Maclean's*. November 6, 1995.

Crary, Marcy. "Managing Attraction and Intimacy at Work." *Organizational Dynamics*. Spring 1987.

Dold, Catherine. "Office Romance in the Age of Sexual Harassment." *Cosmopolitan*. March 1996.

Harris, Lynn. "New Rules for Office Romance." *Glamour*. December 1996.

Hymowitz, Carol. "Drawing the Line on Budding Romances in Your Workplace." *Wall Street Journal*. November 18, 1997.

Jamison, K. "Managing Sexual Attraction in the Workplace." *Personnel Administrator*. August 1983.

Kantrowitz, Barbara. "Those Cheatin' Hearts: It's Not Just the Military; Sex and Adultery can Roil Any Office—and Raise Questions About What the Rules Are." *Newsweek*. June 16, 1997.

Levesque, Joseph D. *The Human Resource Problem-Solver's Handbook*. New York: McGraw-Hill, 1992.

Loftus, Mary. ''Frisky Business.'' *Psychology Today*. March/April 1995.

Mainiero, Lisa A. *Office Romance: Love, Power, and Sex in the Workplace*. New York: Rawson Associates, 1989.

Michaels, James W. ''Sex and Work.'' *Forbes*. May 6, 1996.

''Romance in the Workplace: Corporate Rules for the Game of Love.'' *Business Week*. June 18, 1984.

SEE ALSO: Employee Privacy; Employee Rights; Liabilities

OFFICE SECURITY

According to a survey by the U.S. Department of Justice, businesses lose between $100 billion and $300 billion annually due to crime. Office security has grown in importance in the last 10 to 15 years as more and more people resort to violence or sabotage to settle a score, either real or imagined, with a company or one of its employees. Well-publicized instances of disgruntled employees wreaking havoc in the workplace have brought security to the forefront for every office building manager and business owner.

Office security can be broken down into two main areas: 1) protecting your office and employees from vandalism, theft, and personal attacks; and 2) protecting your office from corporate sabotage, both from inside the company and out. The first area deals more with the actual office itself—its layout, the use of security guards, alarm systems, and so on. The second area is primarily concerned with protecting a firm's **intellectual property** through the introduction and utilization of such measures as shredders, computer security, and employee surveillance.

PHYSICAL SECURITY: PROTECTING THE OFFICE AND EMPLOYEES

Office security is an issue for every business, no matter the size. ''There is not a business that's too small to consider the security issues that may effect them,'' contended one commercial security consultant in an interview with *Business First of Buffalo*. There are many steps that can be taken to improve security, steps that can cost a few dollars or a few hundred thousand dollars. To find out what is best for his or her company, a small business owner should hire a security consultant to visit the business premises and conduct a thorough security analysis. This can identify weak spots and provide a clear plan for upgrading security.

The best place to start when examining office security is the physical layout of the office itself, or the layout of the larger building of which the office is a part. Office design should stress wide, open areas with clear sight lines. Hallways and offices should be open and have no nooks or crannies where an intruder could hide in the shadows. All areas should be well lit, especially after hours when employees might be working alone or in small groups. Mirrors in stairwells and inside and outside of elevators allow employees to see around corners or past obstructions.

Doors and windows are the most obvious access points to an office and should be secure. Avoid double doors because they are easily hinged open. Ideally, entranceway doors—particularly those used for deliveries—should be steel, or steel sheathed. This helps with security and also aids in fire prevention. Door hinges should face inward whenever possible; use nonremovable pins and screws if it is not possible. Simply upgrading hinges and door locks is one of the cheapest and most effective security steps a business can take. Deadbolt locks are best, whether they are electronically controlled or manual. Combination locks on washrooms and other common areas are also an excellent option. Employees don't have to carry keys and the combination can be changed frequently. All windows should use key locks, and windows near the ground level or fire escapes should have steel bars or lockable gates that meet local fire codes.

INCREASED USE OF ELECTRONICS

Improvements in electronics, computers, and other high-tech security features have given business owners new tools to fight crime in recent years. Perhaps the most common electronic tools are closed circuit surveillance systems and access control systems.

Closed circuit surveillance systems use television cameras to monitor specific areas of a company's work space. Signals from the cameras are fed back to a central monitoring post, where a security guard or company employee watches for signs of unusual activity. These systems are effective both during business hours and after hours. Videos are one of the best way to identify and convict criminals, but a closed circuit system only works as well as the people monitoring it. The guard or employee must give the video monitors his or her complete attention.

Access control systems start with establishing point of control access over an office. That means that all tenants and guests are routed through a control area before admittance is authorized. The control point can be as low tech as a sign-in sheet or as high tech as an elaborate system to scan the fingerprints or retinas of visitors. Most common is the use of access cards, or ''swipe'' cards. These cards are electronic ''keys''— the user passes a part of the card through an electronic reader stationed outside a door, and, if the person is authorized to enter, the door is unlocked. Newer versions of the swipe cards include video imaging. A central computer stores a photo of the employee and as much pertinent information as the company desires, including work hours, emergency contact numbers, license plate numbers and make of car, and other information. Electronic cards are preferable to metal keys because an electronic key can be deactivated at a moment's notice if an employee is fired or deemed a security risk. If metal keys are used, every lock in the building has to be replaced if a security breach is suspected.

Other electronic systems that are being used by security-conscious firms include tiny hidden cameras, panic buttons that summon security when pressed, and electronic door chimes that make it easy to tell when someone has entered a work space. The tiny cameras are perhaps the most popular innovation. They are small enough to be hidden in a clock face or a heating vent, yet provide a powerful tool for monitoring employees in areas where employee theft is suspected. Use of the cameras only works if their existence is kept a secret from the employees that are under suspicion.

ALARM SYSTEMS

Alarm systems are another popular office security tool. There are two primary types of alarm systems: those that sound a loud siren or other noise when a break-in is detected, and those that send a silent alarm directly to a security company or to the police, who then respond to the alarm. The type of alarm chosen depends in large part where the business is located. Loud alarms work well in small towns or in low-crime areas, but businesses located in urban or high-crime areas have found that nearby residents have often become so used to alarms going off that they ignore them. In that case, a silent system linked directly to the police may be preferable.

Systems can range in complexity and price. However, any alarm system must cover at least all the doors and windows into a business to be effective. Most common are motion sensors that detect movement where it is not supposed to be occurring, or window glass bugs that detect the sound of breaking glass and trigger the alarm. Examples of advanced systems include combined audio and video alert systems that are triggered by noise. When the sounds of a break-in are detected, the security company is alerted and can listen in to what is occurring at the site. The security company can then activate video monitors to see what is happening at the site, or the cameras can be set up to begin recording automatically when the first sound is detected.

As with the closed circuit television systems, the key to a good alarm system is that it must be monitored at all times. If an alarm goes off and no one is there to notice, or if it is ignored, then office security has not been enhanced at all. In fact, the alarm may have provided a false sense of security that kept a company from pursuing other security measures.

SECURITY GUARDS

Using security guards is an increasingly popular form of office security. Guards can be used in two ways: to monitor the front desk of a company or building and serve as the access control point determining who is allowed into the building; or, to patrol the grounds of a larger company or office complex.

The old image of the security guard—an elderly gentleman who slept as much as he monitored the grounds—is a thing of the past. Today's guards, especially those who monitor building access, should have good communication skills and be able to handle many roles. Guards often act as concierges and goodwill ambassadors, greeting the public as they come into a company and answering questions and providing directions. They help market the building and provide a positive presence that people remember. Traditional uniforms have given way to a "soft look" of blazers and trousers at many security firms. Guards are almost never armed—the practice has come to be regarded as just too dangerous—and they are primarily expected to do four things at all times: deter, detect, observe, and report. Today's guards can also be expected to help out by arranging for building maintenance or even assisting in life-threatening situations.

The other type of security guard—the type that patrols the grounds of a larger company or an office park—receive conflicting marks from security experts. Some feel that simply driving or walking by each part of a office complex every hour or half-hour does little to prevent crime, that it still leaves a large window of time for criminal activity to occur. Others argue the very presence of the guards is enough to deter all but the most professional or determined criminals. The question of whether to use such guards is one that each company will have to answer for itself.

Small business owners should know that using security guards is not cheap. Round-the-clock coverage by a team of guards can cost upwards of $100,000 annually. Additionally, theft by the guards themselves has been a problem for some businesses. Many security firms pay minimum wage, so turnover is high, and background checks are sometimes marked by carelessness or indifference. To ensure that you are really hiring the best firm possible, screen prospective choices carefully. Look for firms that perform thorough background checks, pay better than minimum wage, and have low turnover.

THE ROLE OF EMPLOYEES

It is common knowledge that a security system is only as secure as its weakest link. In many cases, that weak link is the company's employees. Untrained in security measures and prone to the attitude that "it can't happen to me," many employees are their own worst enemies when it comes to security. When a company installs a new security system, it should take the time to bring in a security consultant to speak to employees about what they can do to increase their own safety and improve the company's security. Among the measures the consultant will advise are:

- Do not leave valuables unattended.

- Lock doors after hours.

- Do not go into poorly lighted areas after dark.

- Bolt down or secure equipment if possible.

- Engrave social security or other number on office equipment and keep a list of serial numbers to give to the police and insurance companies in case of theft.

- Provide each employee with a drawer that locks.

- Verify identification and purpose of visit before letting non-employees into office space.

- Deposit checks and cash daily.

- Never leave visitors unsupervised.

- Try to leave with at least one other employee if working late.

- Do not advertise vacation plans.

- Keep emergency numbers posted at every phone.

- Make sure confidential files are secured when the office is closed.

CORPORATE SABOTAGE AND PROTECTING INTELLECTUAL PROPERTY

As computers have become an everyday part of almost every business, companies have found it harder and harder to protect their proprietary information and their money. The *Los Angeles Times* reported that the FBI estimates that commercial espionage, or the theft of information, costs U.S. companies and government agencies nearly $100 billion annually. Much of that theft is occurring electronically. The Computer Security Institution surveyed 536 corporations, banks, and government agencies and found that 75 percent reported suffering large online money losses. Fearing bad publicity, only 17 percent of those companies reported the theft. In its estimates of corporate theft, the FBI estimates that cyber theft accounts for $10 billion of the total each year, with the average electronic bank theft averaging $250,000. Perpetrators are rarely caught.

Unfortunately for most companies, the greatest risk of theft or sabotage (conventional or computer), often comes from the firm's employees themselves. Edwin C. Bliss, the author of *Are Your Employees Stealing You Blind?* estimates that fully one-third of

small business failures can be blamed on internal theft of money, property, information, and time. Employers need to take steps to monitor employees to cut down on theft and sabotage. "Few occurrences are as potentially destructive to a business as the theft, embezzlement, or misappropriation of company funds or other assets by its employees," said one Coopers and Lybrand executive in a *San Antonio Business Journal* article.

Business security experts warn that employee theft can take many forms. Examples include:

- Forgery of company checks for personal gain.

- Using a "ghost payroll," which occurs when one or more employees create "phantom" employees, submit time cards for those employees, and then cash their paychecks themselves.

- Outright theft of cash from a register drawer.

- "Sweethearting," at the cash register, which can mean granting a friend or other person a discount at the register when they pay, undercharging them, or ringing up fewer items than the person has actually bought.

Internal computer theft has become one of the most common forms of **employee theft** now that computers have become more common in nearly every industry sector. Indeed, employees often are more computer literate than their bosses, which may strengthen the temptation to abscond with proprietary information or otherwise engage in illicit activities. Indeed, computer theft can take many forms, including false data entry, which is almost impossible to track; slicing off small amounts of data or money that add up over time; superzapping, which occurs when a computer network security bypass code falls into the wrong hands; and scanning, or using a high-speed computer to locate data that would be impossible to find by hand, then using that data for illegal purposes.

Sabotage, which can also cost millions, almost always involves disgruntled current or former employees and can take almost any form, from ruining mahogany panels in an elevator to squirting silicone gel in every computer that a company owns. As mentioned above, using access control cards for employees that can be easily deactivated makes it easier to keep ex-employees out of the workplace and track the activities of current employees.

STOPPING EMPLOYEE THEFT

Because employee theft is so prevalent and so costly to businesses, a business owner needs to take every precaution and use every means possible to stop employee theft. Some of the steps that can be taken include:

- Making sure that security starts at the top. Executives must set a good and honest example. Establish a clear policy on theft and security and distribute it to all employees.

- Follow up on references provided by prospective new hires.

- Keep checkbooks locked up.

- Control cash flow and have good documentation on where money is spent.

- Do not leave bookkeeping to just one person without checks and balances.

- Audit internal financial documents frequently using independent auditors.

- Only allow a few people to have authority to sign checks.

- Check all invoices to make sure they match what was delivered.

- As mentioned, use monitoring cameras and monitor phone use.

BEYOND EMPLOYEE THEFT

Theft of information and money does occur from the outside too. Increased reliance on the Internet and on opening up computer networks to remote users has left companies wide open for hackers, or computer thieves. Hackers penetrate computer networks and steal either information, which they sell, or use computers to manipulate bank accounts and steal cash. Companies can protect their data by conducting frequent audits, by setting strict password standards, and by using technology to block unwanted users by setting up a ''firewall.'' No network is impenetrable, but firewalls make it difficult for all but the best hackers to break into a computer system. Until recent years, firewalls were only available for large corporations that had large networks, but now they are available for the small business owner. That is important, since many small businesses conduct business by PC and must leave their computers on 24-hours-a-day to receive or send data or faxes.

On the opposite end of the technological spectrum from firewalls are paper shredders. No matter how computerized an office is, there are still reams of paper and sensitive documents that could cause trouble if they fell into the wrong hands. Paper shredders solve that problem and are now considered to be a basic part of office security, especially since the Supreme Court ruled that anything put out in the trash is public property.

There are three kinds of shredders—strip-cut, particle or cross-cut, and disintegrator. Strip-cut cuts documents into long strips of paper, usually 1/4-inch wide or less. Particle, or cross-cut, also cut papers into 1/4-wide strips, but they also cut them into short pieces instead of leaving long strips. Disintegrators do just what you think they would: cut and shred the paper into fine confetti. Some companies that deal with securities information or government data are required to use the latter type of shredder. Shredders range in price from under $100 to over $10,000 for industrial machines. In addition to paper, industrial models can shred floppy disks, metal-reinforced folders, metal-bound computer data, paper clips, and tape files.

When purchasing a shredder, choose one that meets your corporate needs and budget. Place the machine in a central location that makes it easy for employees to use. If the money is there, purchase personal shredders for top employees who routinely deal with sensitive documents.

FURTHER READING:

Bliss, Edwin C., with Isamu S. Aoki. *Are Your Employees Robbing You Blind?* Pfeiffer and Co. 1993.

Chanen, Jill Shachner. ''Securing the Premises: Simple Changes in Office Policy, Setup Can Safeguard a Small Practice.'' *ABA Journal.* April 1997.

De Siena, Robert. ''Safety and Security Challenges for the Nineties.'' *Real Estate Weekly.* June 22, 1994.

Di Dio, Laura. ''Networks Need Defense Against Hacker Attacks.'' *Computerworld.* November 24, 1997.

Jaffe, Susan Biddle. ''Office Building Security Grows More Sophisticated.'' *Philadelphia Business Journal.* April 6, 1992.

Lombardi, John H. ''Office and Office Building Security.'' *Security Management.* Nov. 1994.

Manis, Robert A. ''Discouraging the Inside Job.'' *Inc.* April 1994.

Mitchell, Gabrielle C. ''Firewalls Help Protect Home Systems from Poison Applets.'' *Computer Retail Week.* April 28, 1997.

Nelson, Jack. ''Grappling With Crime Wave on the Web.'' *Los Angeles Times.* Nov. 30, 1997.

Parent, Tawn. ''Is Your Office Safe?'' *Indianapolis Business Journal.* January 6, 1992.

Poling, Travis E. ''A Thief Among Us: Employee Sabotage and Theft Leave Businesses Holding Hefty Tab.'' *San Antonio Business Journal.* January 2, 1993.

Rodriguez, Karen. ''Virtual Office Raises Risks in Security.'' *Communications Week.* May 13, 1996.

Rosenthal, Tracy. ''Keep Your Building and Your Employees Secure.'' *Business First of Buffalo.* July 25, 1994.

''Tighten Office Security for Yourself and Your Employees.'' *Profit-Building Strategies for Business Owners.* November 1992.

Tyler, Geoff. ''Ringing the Changes for Office Security.'' *Estates Gazette.* May 18, 1996.

Vollmart, Sara. ''Shredders: A Powerful Office Security Tool.'' *The Office.* February 1993.

SEE ALSO: Computer Crime; Facility Layout and Design; Violence in the Workplace; Workplace Safety

OFFICE SUPPLIES

Office supplies encompass a wide range of materials that are used on a regular, everyday basis by business owners and/or employees. Staple office supply items that are often utilized by even the smallest company or home office include pens, writing paper, notebooks, Post-It notes, scissors, erasers, computer diskettes, binders, slides, file folders, labels, basic reference materials (dictionaries, etc.), file cabinets, fax paper, envelopes, and a host of other items. In addition, equipment that is used in most office environments—printers, copy machines, fax machines—is sometimes included under this umbrella term, but most definitions of office supplies include the materials—paper, ink—that are used in these machines, but not the machines themselves.

Indeed, despite the growth of technologies that supposedly herald the impending arrival of the ''paperless office,'' in today's business environment most offices would be decidedly incomplete without paper, pencils, pens, and notebooks that are necessary for the operation of today's offices. Although their cost is small when purchased separately, in the aggregate they amount to a substantial portion of office expense. Small business owners should thus make sure that they pay attention to office supply costs and keep all receipts of such purchases, since office supplies are a legitimate business deduction for tax purposes.

Managing Office Technology reports that office superstores and catalogue supply houses are fast becoming the most efficient and inexpensive way to purchase various types of supplies. The average client of these superstores is the small- to medium-sized business, as well as the home office market. The convenience of being able to find virtually any item at one location is one of the primary reasons for the increased popularity of the superstores. In addition to convenience, these stores and catalogues offer merchandise that is very competitively priced since they are able to purchase their goods at bulk rates. Some of these savings are usually passed along to small business customers, especially if these stores are operating in a competitive environment.

The proliferation of Internet shopping has also opened up a new source for office supply purchases. According to *Computerworld,* various office supply businesses—including some of the giant retail companies—are hurriedly establishing their presence on the World Wide Web. Office supply superstore Office Depot, for example, is building an Internet-based electronic commerce system. In addition, Boise Cascade Office Products Co. is also turning the Internet into a source for office supplies; by August 1997 approximately 650 corporate customers were using the Boise Cascade online system. Boise Cascade expects to reduce their costs by about 45 cents for each line item purchased from their Web site. Hopefully, these savings will be passed on to the customer.

FURTHER READING:

Malik, Mary S. ''New Ways of Getting What You Need.'' *Managing Office Technology.* August 1994.

''Pitney Bowes Survey Shows Fax Usage is on the Rise.'' *PC Week*, September 22, 1997.

Prata, Kathleen. ''Office Products Update.'' *Indiana Business Magazine,* September 1994.

Reynolds, Rhonda. ''Setting Up at Home: To Get the Job Done, You Need the Right Space and Tools.'' *Black Enterprise*, July 1994.

OPERATIONS MANAGEMENT

Operations management is a multi-discipline field that focuses on managing an organization's operations. ''The typical organization consists of the integration of many different functions,'' wrote Howard J. Weiss and Mark E. Gershon in *Production and Operations Management.* ''The two most obvious functions are to provide the product or service and to sell the product or service. Operations management focuses on the function of providing the product or service. It is concerned with the planning and controlling of all activities necessary for the provision of the firm's product or service.'' The scope of operations management, then, is a vast one, including decision making processes at all stages of the life of a product or service. Decisions include: what products to produce, how large a facility to build, where to locate the facility with respect to customers and suppliers, what techniques and equipment to use to make the goods or to provide the services, how many units to produce during a given period, how employees should be trained, and what methods should be utilized to enhance product quality. Operations managers apply ideas and technologies to increase productivity and reduce costs, improve flexibility to meet rapidly changing customer needs, enhance product quality, and improve customer service.

KEY ISSUES IN OPERATIONS

As an organization develops plans and strategies to deal with the opportunities and challenges that arise in its particular operating environment, it should consider issues related to: designing a system that is capable of producing the services and goods in demanded quantities; planning how to use the system effectively; and managing key elements of the operations. Each of these topics is described briefly in the following sections.

DESIGNING THE SYSTEM Designing the system begins with **product development**. Product development involves determining the characteristics and features of the product. It should begin with an assessment of customer needs and eventually grow into a detailed product design. The facilities and equipment that will produce the service or good, as well as the information systems needed to monitor and control performance, are part of this system design process. In fact, manufacturing process decisions are integral to a system's ultimate success or failure. ''Of all the structural decisions that the operations manager faces, the one with the greatest impact on the manufacturing operation's success is the process/ technology choice,'' said Thomas S. Bateman and Carl P. Zeithaml in *Management: Function and Strategy.* ''This decision addresses the question 'How will the product be made?' '' Product development should be a cross-functional decisionmaking process that relies on teamwork and communication to install the marketing, financial, and operating plans needed to successfully launch a product.

Product design is a critical task because it determines the characteristics and features of the product, as well as how the product functions. Product design determines a product's cost and quality, as well as its features and performance. These are important factors on which customers make purchasing decisions. Techniques such as Design for Manufacturing and Assembly (DFMA) are being implemented to improve product quality and lower costs. DFMA focuses on operating issues during product design. This can be critical even though design costs are a small part of the total cost of a product. Design is important because it may fix up to 90 percent of the total production costs. After all, procedures that waste raw materials or duplicate effort can have a substantial negative impact on a business's operating profitability.

Quality Functional Deployment (QFD) is also being used to improve product design by focusing design efforts on customer needs. QFD is a set of planning and communication routines that focuses attention on customer wants and coordinates actions.

Process design describes how the product will be made. The process design decision has two major components: a technical (or engineering) component and a scale economy (or business) component. The technical component includes selecting equipment and sequences for production. Decisions must also be made about the sequence of operations. For example, should a car rental agency inspect a car that has been returned by the customer first or send it to be cleaned and washed by maintenance? Most likely, the car should be inspected first so the damage that might occur in the cleaning process would not be counted against the customer.

The scale economy or business component involves applying the proper amount of mechanization (tools and equipment) to make the organization's work force more productive. This includes determining: 1) If the demand for a product is large enough to justify mass production, such as a fast food restaurant that purchases specialized equipment to make a large volume quickly; 2) If there is sufficient variety in customer demand so that flexible production systems are required, such as a full-service restaurant that purchases general purpose equipment to produce its diverse menu; and 3) If demand for a product is so small or seasonal that it cannot support a dedicated production facility.

Facility design involves determining the capacity, location, and layout for the facility. Capacity is a measure of an organization's ability to provide the demanded services or goods in the quantity requested by the customer and in a timely manner. Capacity planning involves estimating demand, determining the capacity of facilities, and deciding how to change the organization's capacity to respond to demand.

Facility location is the placement of a facility with respect to its customers and suppliers. Facility location is a strategic decision because it is a long-term commitment of resources that cannot easily or inexpensively be changed. When evaluating a location, management should consider: customer convenience, initial investment for land and facilities, government incentives, and operating transportation costs. In addition, qualitative factors may be important, such as recreational activities for employees, an adequate transportation infrastructure, and a favorable labor environment.

Facility layout is the arrangement of the work space within a facility. It considers which departments or work areas should be adjacent to one another so that the flow of product, information, and people can move quickly and efficiently through the production system.

Job design specifies the tasks, responsibilities, and methods used in performing a job. For example, the job design for a word processing specialist at a publishing company would describe needed equipment and would explain the standard operating procedures.

PLANNING THE SYSTEM Planning the system describes how management expects to utilize the existing resource base created as a result of the production system design. One of the outcomes of this planning process may be to change the system design to cope with environmental changes. For example, management may decide to increase or decrease capacity to cope with changing demand, or rearrange layout to enhance efficiency.

Decisions made by production planners depend on the time horizon. Long-range decisions could include the number of facilities required to meet customer needs, or how technological change might affect the methods used to produce services and goods. The time horizon for long-term planning varies with the industry and depends on how long it would take an organization to build new facilities or make major technological changes. For example, in the aircraft industry it may take five to ten years to design a new aircraft and build a facility to produce it. A farm equipment manufacturer, on the other hand, may be able to operate with a much shorter time horizon for production planning because changes in its operations can be made more quickly.

In medium-range production planning, which is normally about one year, organizations find it difficult to make major changes in facilities. At most, modest expansion may be achieved or limited new equipment installed. Here, production planning may involve determining work force size, developing training programs, working with suppliers to improve product quality and improve delivery systems, and determining the amount of material to order on an aggregate basis.

Scheduling has the shortest planning horizon. As production planning proceeds from long-range to short-range, the decisions become more detailed. In scheduling, management decides what products will be made, who will do the work, what equipment will be used, which materials will be consumed, when the work will begin, and what will happen to the product when it is complete. All aspects of production come together to make the product a reality.

Writing in *The Complete MBA Companion,* Thomas E. Vollman stated that ''companies should never be content with their manufacturing planning and control systems (MPCS).'' Indeed, he pointed out that larger companies that had historically relied on ''informal'' planning and control systems—long characterized by a lack of computers, long production periods, and low inventory accuracy—have either fallen by the wayside or changed their ways in order to compete. Other observers, meanwhile, note that while smaller businesses may not always be facing the same mandate to change (depending on the particular industry and competitive niche in which they operate), the overwhelming majority of small business enterprises are either in the midst of grappling with such changes or destined to face a different operating environment sometime in the near future.

''The first step towards acquiring a modern MPCS is a basic materials requirements planning (MRP) system,'' said Vollman. ''This allows a company to know whether it can achieve particular objectives. . . . The efficacy of a company's detailed planning, however, goes beyond lining up the schedules of component parts with those of the assembly of finished goods. Enhancements can also be made to the master production schedule at the 'front end'—in areas like demand management and production planning—and to detailed shop floor execution at the 'back end.' ''

MANAGING THE SYSTEM Managing the system involves working with people to encourage participation and improve organizational performance. Participative management and teamwork are becoming an essential part of successful operations. Motivation, leadership, and training are receiving new impetus. In addition, material management and quality are two key areas of concern.

Material management includes decisions regarding the procurement, control, handling, storage, and distribution of materials. Material management is becoming more important because, in many organizations, the costs of purchased materials are over 50 percent of the total product cost. Questions regarding quantities and timing of material orders need to be addressed here. In addition, companies have to make decisions about which materials vendors they will use.

Quality management programs and high product quality are essential to compete in today's business environment. Quality is increasingly becoming customer-driven with emphasis put on obtaining a product design that builds quality into the product. Then, the process is designed to transform the product design into a quality product and the employees are trained to execute it.

BUILDING SUCCESS WITH OPERATIONS

To understand operations and how they contribute to the success of an organization, it is important to understand the strategic nature of operations, the value-added nature of operations, the impact technology can have on performance, and the globally competitive marketplace.

Organizations can use operations as an important way to gain an advantage over competition. What factors influence buying decisions for most consumers? For most services and goods, price, quality, product performance and features, product variety, and availability of the product are critical. All these factors are substantially influenced by actions taken in operations. For example, when productivity increases, product costs decline and product price can be reduced. Similarly, as better production methods are developed, quality and variety may increase.

By linking operations and operating strategies with the overall strategy of the organization (including engineering, financial, marketing, and information system strategy) synergy can result. Operations become a positive factor when facilities, equipment, and employee training are viewed as a means to achieve organizational objectives, rather than as narrowly focused departmental objectives. The criteria for judging operations is changing from cost control, which is a narrowly defined operating objective, to more global performance measurements in such areas as product performance and variety, product quality, delivery time, and customer service. When flexibility is designed into operations, an organization is able to rapidly and inexpensively respond to changing customer needs.

In today's business environment, a key component of operational flexibility in many industries is technological know-how. Technology is the application of knowledge, usually in the form of recently developed tools, processes, or procedures, to solve problems. Advances in technology make it possible to build better products using fewer resources. As technology fundamentally changes a product, its performance and quality often increases dramatically. For example, an electronic watch is cheaper, more reliable, and takes less care than a traditional mechanical watch. Customers value the product more and will pay more for it, but with many electronic products today, the costs of production have declined substantially. However, new competitors have emerged as well, making it important for businesses to try to register advantages in any and all areas of operations management.

Over time, operations management has grown in scope and increased in importance. Today, it has elements that are strategic, it relies on behavioral and engineering concepts, and it utilizes management science/operations research tools and techniques for systematic decisionmaking and problem-solving. As operations management continues to develop, it will increasingly interact with other functional areas within the organization to develop integrated answers to complex interdisciplinary problems. Indeed, such interaction is widely regarded as essential to long-term business success for small business establishments and multinational corporations alike. "In many companies, corporate strategy is developed as a series of independent statements," warned Terry Hill, Alastair Nicholson, and Roy Westbrook in The Complete MBA Companion. "Lacking essential integration, the result is a compilation of distinct, functional strategies that sit side by side, layer by layer, in the same corporate binder. Integration is not provided if, in fact, it was ever intended." They suggest that "in many companies major strategic decisions are made covering the markets and customers that are to be grown without any attempt to embrace the perspectives of operations as to its ability to support those requirements and to make anticipated profits. This failure is further compounded by the fact that operations investments are large (in terms of asset size) and fixed (in terms of the timescale to undertake change)." Given this reality, then, Hill, Nicholson, and Westbrook state that operations strategy starts "with an agreement about markets—how a company competes in them, the operations tasks that follow, and the priority investments and developments that operations needs then to undertake."

FURTHER READING:

Andrews, Katherine Zoe. "Learning How to Learn." Harvard Business Review. March/April 1996.

Bateman, Thomas S., and Carl P. Zeithaml. Management: Function and Strategy. Homewood, IL: Richard D. Irwin, 1990.

Blackstone, J.H. Capacity Management. Cincinnati, OH: South-Western Publishing Co., 1989.

Chase, R.B., and D.A. Garvin. "The Service Factory." Harvard Business Review. Vol. 67, no. 4, 1989.

"First Steps." Inc. May 1995.

Hill, Terry, Alastair Nicholson, and Roy Westbrook. "Strategic Management of the Operations Function." In The Complete MBA Companion. Lanham, MD: Pitman Publishing, 1997.

Krajewski, L. J., and L. P. Ritzman. Operations Management: Strategy and Analysis. Reading, MA: Addison-Wesley Publishing Company, 1993.

Stevens, Tim. "Converting Ideas into Profits: Strategic Management of the Innovation Process Pays Big Dividends at the Bottom Line." Industry Week. June 3, 1996.

Sule, D. R. Manufacturing Facilities: Location, Planning, and Design. Boston, MA: PWS-KENT Publishing Company, 1988.

Suzaki, K. The New Manufacturing Challenge: Techniques for Continuous Improvement. New York: The Free Press, 1987.

Umble, M. M., and M. L. Srikanth. Synchronous Manufacturing. Cincinnati, OH: South-Western Publishing Co., 1990.

Vollman, Thomas E. "Systems are Never Good Enough." In The Complete MBA Companion. Lanham, MD: Pitman Publishing, 1997.

Vonderembse, M. A., and G. P. White. Operations Management: Concepts, Methods, Strategies. St. Paul, MN: West Publishing Company, 1991.

Weiss, Howard J., and Mark E. Gershon. Production and Operations Management. Boston, MA: Allyn and Bacon, 1989.

SEE ALSO: Business Planning; Business Site Selection; Facility Layout and Design

OPPORTUNITY COST

Simply stated, an opportunity cost is the cost of a missed opportunity. Applied to a business decision, opportunity cost might refer to the profit a company could have earned from its capital, equipment, and real estate if these assets had been used in a different way. The concept of opportunity cost may be applied to many different situations. It should be considered whenever circumstances are such that scarcity necessitates the election of one option over another. Opportunity cost is usually defined in terms of money, but it may also be considered in terms of time, person-hours, mechanical output, or any other finite, limited resource.

Although opportunity costs are not generally considered by accountants—**financial statements** only include explicit costs, or actual outlays—they should be considered by managers. Small business owners should factor in opportunity costs when computing their operating expenses in order to provide a bid or estimate on the price of a job. Opportunity costs increase the cost of doing business, and thus should be recovered as a portion of the **overhead** expense charged to every job. Ignoring opportunity costs may lead small business owners to undercharge for their services and overestimate their profits.

EXAMPLES OF OPPORTUNITY COSTS

One way to demonstrate opportunity cost lies in the employment of investment capital. For example, a private investor purchases $10,000 in a certain security, such as shares in a corporation, and after one year the investment has appreciated in value to $10,500. The investor's return is 5 percent. The investor considers other ways the $10,000 could have been invested, and discovers a bank certificate with an annual yield of 6 percent and a government bond that carries an annual yield of 7.5 percent. After a year, the bank certificate would have appreciated in value to $10,600, and the government bond would have appreciated to $10,750. The opportunity cost of purchasing shares is $100 relative to the bank certificate, and $250 relative to the government bond. The investor's decision to purchase shares with a 5 percent return comes at the cost of a lost opportunity to earn 6 or 7.5 percent.

Expressed in terms of time, consider a commuter who chooses to drive to work, rather than using public transportation. Because of heavy traffic and a lack of parking, it takes the commuter 90 minutes to get to work. If the same commute on public transportation would have taken only 40 minutes, the opportunity cost of driving would be 50 minutes. The commuter might naturally have chosen driving over public transportation because he could not have anticipated traffic delays in driving. Once the choice has been made to drive, it is not possible to change one's mind, thus the choice itself becomes irrelevant. Experience can create a basis for future decisions, however: the commuter may be less inclined to drive next time, now knowing the consequences of traffic congestion.

In another example, a small business owns the building in which it operates, and thus pays no rent for office space. But this does not mean that the company's cost for office space is zero, even though an accountant might treat it that way. Instead, the small business owner must consider the opportunity cost associated with reserving the building for its current use. Perhaps the building could have been rented out to another company, or demolished in order to make room for a strip mall. The foregone money from these alternative uses of the property is an opportunity cost of using the office space, and thus should be considered in calculations of the small business's expenses.

FURTHER READING:

Baumol, William J., and Alan S. Blinder. *Economics, Principles and Policy.* 2d ed. Orlando, FL: Harcourt Brace Jovanovich, 1982.

Fischer, Stanley, and Rudiger Hornbusch. *Economics.* New York: McGraw-Hill, 1983.

Miller, Bruce L., and A. G. Buckman. "Cost Allocation and Opportunity Costs." *Management Science.* May 1987.

Primeaux, Patrick, and John Stieber. "Managing Business Ethics and Opportunity Costs." *Journal of Business Ethics.* June 1997.

Silver, Gerald A. "When Opportunity Knocks, It Costs." *Graphic Arts Monthly.* June 1990.

Sonfield, Matthew C. "The Contingency Plan—How to Profit from Opportunities Created by Others." *American Journal of Small Business.* Summer 1984.

OPTIMAL FIRM SIZE

Optimal firm size refers to the speed and extent of growth that is ideal for a specific small business. The optimal size is particular to a certain business and depends on a variety of internal and external factors. For some **home-based businesses**, the optimal size may be the two founding partners—a husband and wife. For some companies trying to compete in rapidly changing industries, however, growth may be necessary for survival. As James A. Schriner explained in an article for *Industry Week,* "Growing a company is like blowing up a balloon. Your first few breaths, though difficult, produce immediate results. Subsequent breaths expand the balloon proportionally until it nears capacity. Stop too soon and the balloon never reaches its potential. Stop too late and it bursts."

Very large companies do stand to gain some advantages due to their size—such as increased **market share**, access to low-cost **capital**, brand recognition, and **advertising** reach—but size does not guarantee success in most industries. Remaining small can offer businesses a number of advantages as well, such as greater responsiveness to market changes and closer contact with customer groups. In fact, some experts suggest that large companies should reorganize so that they behave as a group of small companies in order to adapt to a wider range of business situations.

In an article for *Nation's Business,* Michael Barrier described ''a classic small-business pattern: An entrepreneur has a good idea, makes it successful, and expands it, perhaps to many locations. It's a pattern that appeals to many small business people—but not to all—because . . . growth has its costs.'' For one thing, growth tends to change the entrepreneur's role in the business. Instead of concentrating on the nuts and bolts of the particular business, which may be what the entrepreneur does best, he or she may end up managing a staff and working in an office-type environment, without regular contact with customers. Of course, growth of at least the rate of inflation is necessary if the business hopes to be able to retain key employees and keep up with market changes. ''However wary a small business owner may be of the risks involved in expansion, growth of some kind—in revenues, profits, number of employees, or size of facilities—is essential for almost every business,'' Barrier stated.

The key to finding the optimal firm size is to grow in a controlled way. In some cases, restraining growth is simply a matter of saying ''no,'' or turning down new business. This is particularly true for service businesses that depend on the personal attention of the founder. When turning down business becomes necessary, the entrepreneur may wish to provide referrals in order to maintain good relations with potential customers. Another strategy in restraining growth involves hiring employees who like working in a small company atmosphere. These people tend to enjoy the diversity of challenges they encounter in a small business, and they often have a strong interest in the product and can provide their expertise to customers. It is important to note, however, that restraining growth does not mean refusing to change. Small businesses are not likely to remain in business long if they cannot be creative and adapt to changes in customer tastes and competitors' tactics.

Schriner noted that one factor influencing the optimal size of a business is the availability of workers and other resources in the surrounding community. In fact, he suggested that it is possible for businesses to outgrow the communities in which they operate, particularly when they are located in a remote area. In this case, it may be difficult to attract talented workers from outside the immediate area, forcing the company to pay sharply higher wages to compete for labor. In addition, sometimes communities cannot afford to provide services to growing businesses, and companies may need to help by paying for school expansions or new fire engines, for example. Finally, Schriner claimed that being too integral a part of a community can make it difficult for a growing company to adapt to a changing business environment. Some factors that may indicate a company has outgrown its community include: employing more than ten percent of the local work force; growing at a faster rate than the community's labor force; providing more than one-third of the local government's funding through taxes; and being responsible for the death of the community if the company should shut down.

FURTHER READING:

Barrier, Michael. ''Can You Stay Small Forever?'' *Nation's Business.* October 1996.

Lawler, Edward E. III. ''Rethinking Organization Size.'' *Organizational Dynamics.* Autumn 1997.

Koretz, Gene. ''Little Guys Are Making Plans: Small Businesses Are Set to Expand.'' *Business Week.* June 2, 1997.

Schriner, James A. ''How Big Is Too Big?'' *Industry Week.* May 6, 1996.

SEE ALSO: Business Expansion; Organizational Growth

ORAL COMMUNICATION

Oral communication describes any type of interaction that makes use of spoken words. It is one of the two main types of communication, along with **written communication**. Oral communication is a vital part of the business world. ''The ability to communicate effectively through speaking as well as in writing is highly valued, and demanded, in business,'' Herta A. Murphy and Herbert W. Hildebrandt wrote in their book *Effective Business Communications.* ''Knowing the content of the functional areas of business is important, but to give life to those ideas—in meetings or in solo presentations—demands an effective oral presentation.'' The types of oral communication commonly used within an organization include staff **meetings**, personal discussions, presentations, telephone calls, or the informal employee grapevine. Oral communication with those outside of the organization might take the form of face-to-face meetings, telephone calls, speeches, teleconferences, or videoconferences.

Small business owners and managers are frequently called upon to make presentations, conduct interviews, or lead meetings, so oral communication skills are an important area for development. Presentations might be made to employees for training purposes, or to potential customers for sales purposes. In either case, good presentation techniques can generate interest and create confidence. Interviewing skills might be needed for hiring new employees, conducting performance appraisals, or doing market research. Meetings or conferences can be important tools for relating to employees or to interested parties outside of the organization in order to solve problems or set goals. In order to understand the principles of effective oral communication, it is helpful to look at the basic process of communication.

THE COMMUNICATION PROCESS

The communication process begins when a fact or idea is observed by one person. That person (the sender) may decide to translate the observation into a message, and then transmit the message through some communication medium to another person (the receiver). The receiver then must interpret the message and provide feedback to the sender indicating that the message has been understood and appropriate action taken.

According to Murphy and Hildebrandt, good communication should be complete, concise, clear, concrete, correct, considerate, and courteous. More specifically, this means that communication should: answer basic questions like who, what, when, where; be relevant and not overly wordy; focus on the receiver and his or her interests; use specific facts and figures and active verbs; use a conversational tone for readability; include examples and visual aids when needed; be tactful and good natured; and be accurate and nondiscriminatory. Unclear, inaccurate, or inconsiderate business communication can waste valuable time, alienate employees or customers, and destroy goodwill toward management or the overall business.

Perhaps the most important part of business communication is taking the time to prepare an effective and understandable message. According to Murphy and Hildebrandt, the first step is to know the main purpose of the message. For example, a message to a supplier might have the purpose of obtaining a replacement for a defective part. The next step is to analyze the audience so that the message can be adapted to fit their views and needs. It may be helpful to picture the recipient and think about which areas of the message they might find positive or negative, interesting or boring, pleasing or displeasing. After that, the sender needs to choose the ideas to include and collect all the necessary facts. The next step involves organizing the message, since a poorly organized message will fail to elicit the required response. It may be helpful to prepare an outline or draft beforehand, paying particular attention to the beginning and ending portions. Finally, before transmitting the message it is important to edit and rehearse.

PREPARING ORAL PRESENTATIONS

As is true of all sorts of communication, the first step in preparing for oral communication involves determining the purpose of the talk. According to Hildebrandt and Murphy, business presentations tend to have one of three general purposes: to persuade, to inform or instruct, or to entertain. Good speeches also have a more specific purpose of achieving a desired result. Out of the purpose will come the main ideas to be included in the presentation. These ideas should be researched thoroughly and adapted to the needs of the audience.

The ideas should then be organized to include an introduction, a main body or text, and a summary or conclusion. Or, as the old adage about giving speeches goes, "Tell them what you're going to tell them, tell them, and tell them what you told them." The introduction should grab the listener's interest and establish the direction for the remainder of the presentation. The main body should include one to three main points, each supported by facts. The conclusion should restate the key points and emphasize the desired action.

Visual aids are an important component of oral presentations. Whether they are displayed on chalkboards, dry-erase boards, or flip charts, or presented using a slide projector, overhead projector, or computer program, visual aids should be meaningful, creative, and interesting in order to help the speaker get a message across. Visual aids should also be adapted to the size of the audience. It is important to avoid spending too much time referring to a visual aid, since that usually leaves the audience looking at the speaker's back.

Once the presentation has been organized and the visual aids have been selected, the speaker should rehearse out loud and revise as needed. It may help to practice in front of a mirror or in front of a friend in order to gain confidence. A good oral presentation will include transitional phrases to help listeners move through the material, and will not be overly long or technical. It is also important for the speaker to anticipate questions the audience might have and either include that information in the presentation or be prepared to answer afterward.

According to Murphy and Hildebrandt, oral presentations can be delivered in four ways: extemporaneously (from an outline or notes); by reading from a manuscript; from memory; or impromptu. The extemporaneous approach is usually preferred, as it allows the speaker to make eye contact and develop a rapport with the audience. Reading from a manuscript is sometimes necessary during very long speeches, but it is still important to look up at the audience often. Memorization should be used only for short talks, and then only the main topics and ideas should be memorized—rather than the entire text—to give a more natural feel to the presentation. When impromptu comments are required, it helps to be prepared as much as possible through careful listening and taking down notes.

The delivery of effective oral presentations also requires a speaker to consider his or her vocal pitch, rate, and volume, as well as nonverbal elements such as posture, gestures, and facial expression. It is important to incorporate changes in vocal pitch to add emphasis and avoid monotony. It is also helpful to vary the rate of speaking—although it should never be too fast, over 160 words per minute—and incorporate pauses to allow the listener to reflect upon the message. Finding the appropriate volume is crucial to the success of a presentation. It may be helpful to practice ahead of time in the room where the speech will be delivered, and to breathe deeply and expel air from the diaphragm. Finally, speakers should be careful not to add extraneous words or sounds—such as ''um,'' ''you know,'' or ''okay''—between words or sentences in a presentation.

''Your outward appearance mirrors your inner mood,'' Murphy and Hildebrandt said of the importance of nonverbal elements in effective oral presentations. ''Thus good posture suggests poise and confidence; stand neither at rigid attention nor with sloppy casualness draped over the podium, but erect with your weight about equally distributed on each foot.'' Some movement may be helpful to hold listeners' attention or to increase emphasis, but constant shifting or pacing should be avoided. Likewise, hand and arm gestures can be used to point, describe, or emphasize, but they should be varied, carefully timed, and adapted to the audience. Finally, good speakers should make frequent eye contact with the audience, let their facial expression show their interest in the ideas they are presenting, and dress in a way that is appropriate for the occasion.

OTHER TYPES OF ORAL COMMUNICATION

The same principles that apply to other forms of oral communication also apply to telephone calling. It is important to plan business calls by determining the purpose, considering the audience (including the best time to call), and deciding the ideas to be included and the questions to be asked. When answering the telephone in a business setting, it is important to answer promptly and state your name and department in a clear, pleasant voice. Communication over the telephone can create impressions that are vital to small business success.

An often overlooked element of oral communication is listening. Good listening skills can be vital in finding a solution to grievances or even in making sales calls. Listening involves showing an interest in the speaker, concentrating on the message, and asking questions to ensure understanding. It helps to be prepared for the discussion, to avoid arguing or interrupting, to take notes as needed, and to summarize the speaker's statements.

FURTHER READING:

Golen, Steven. *Effective Business Communication.* Washington: U.S. Small Business Administration, 1989.

Murphy, Herta A., and Herbert W. Hildebrandt. *Effective Business Communications.* 6th ed. New York: McGraw-Hill, 1991.

Townsend, Robert. *Up the Organization.* New York: Knopf, 1984.

SEE ALSO: Nonverbal Communication

ORGANIZATION STRUCTURE

An organizational structure is the pattern or arrangement of jobs and groups of jobs within an organization. This pattern pertains to both reporting and operational relationships. In addition, structures only qualify as such if they have some degree of permanence. ''The concept of structure . . . implies a configuration of activities that is characteristically enduring and persistent,'' confirmed Stewart Ranson, Bob Hinings, and Royston Greenwood in *Administrative Science Quarterly.* The individual elements of an organization structure typically include a variety of components that *Portable MBA in Management* contributors Phyllis and Leonard Schlesinger termed organizational ''building blocks'': 1) departments or divisions; 2) management hierarchy; 3) rules, procedures, and goals; and 4) temporary building blocks such as task forces or committees.

Ideally, organizational structures should be shaped and implemented for the primary purpose of facilitating the achievement of organizational goals. Indeed, having a suitable organizational structure in place—one that recognizes and addresses the various human and business realities of the firm in question— is a prerequisite for long-term success. But as Gibson, Ivancevich, and Donnelly noted in *Organizations: Behavior, Structure, Processes,* ''It is entirely reasonable to acknowledge that in many instances, organization structures do not contribute positively to organizational performance because managers are unable by training or intellect to design a structure that guides the behavior of individuals and groups to achieve high levels of production, efficiency, satisfaction, quality, flexibility, and development.'' Small business owners seeking to establish a beneficial organizational structure for their enterprise, then, need to recognize that the process is a complex one that usually requires considerable planning and research.

KEYS TO ERECTING AN EFFECTIVE ORGANIZATIONAL STRUCTURE

All sorts of different organizational structures have been proven effective in contributing to business success. Some firms choose highly centralized, rigidly maintained structures, while others—perhaps even in the same industry sector—settle on decentralized, loose arrangements, and in some instances, both types can survive and even thrive. "There is no one best way to design an organization," stated Phyllis and Leonard Schlesinger in *The Portable MBA in Management*. "Organizational research has shown that the more we know about particular types of organizations, the less we can generalize about the optimal design for an effective organization. Generally, organizational theorists believe that no one structure, set of systems, or method of staffing is appropriate for every organization. Organizations operate in different environments with different products, strategies, constraints, and opportunities."

But despite the wide variety of organizational structures that can be found in the business world, the successful ones tend to share certain characteristics. Bateman and Zeithaml cited several characteristics that separate effective architects of organizational structure from ineffective designers. Utilizing these tools is especially important for entrepreneurs and established small business owners, since these individuals play such a pivotal role in determining the final design.

When weighing possible organizational structures, the small business owner should be able to:

1) Understand the growth patterns of the organization, as well as the unwelcome baggage that such growth may bring.

2) Have a command of the authority relationships in the organization.

3) Maintain a working knowledge of the **organization chart** (if applicable).

4) Institute effective "span of control" (the number of subordinates who report directly to a supervisor). Bateman and Zeithaml contended that "the span should be wider when the work is routine; subordinates are highly trained, the supervisor is highly capable; the jobs are similar, and performance is measurable and comparable; subordinates prefer autonomy to close supervisory control; and the organization is large. If the opposite conditions exist, then a narrow span of control is more appropriate."

5) Understand strengths and weaknesses of various organizational forms.

6) Understand pros and cons of departmentalization options.

7) Design jobs for optimum productivity and worker satisfaction.

8) Delegate appropriately and effectively.

9) Understand the role of the owner and/or manager in the organization "and how dif-

ferent organizational roles can effectively interrelate."

FURTHER READING:

Bateman, Thomas S., and Carl P. Zeithaml. *Management: Function and Strategy.* Boston, MA: Richard D. Irwin, 1990.

Duncan, R. "What is the Right Organization Structure?" *Organizational Dynamics.* Winter 1979.

Gibson, James L., John M. Ivancevich, and James H. Donnelly Jr. *Organizations: Behavior, Structure, Processes.* 8th ed. Boston, MA: Richard D. Irwin, 1994.

Naisbitt, J., and P. Aburdene. *Re-Inventing the Corporation.* New York: Warner Books, 1985.

Ranson, Stewart, Bob Hinings, and Royston Greenwood. "The Structuring of Organizational Structures." *Administrative Science Quarterly.* March 1980.

Schlesinger, Phyllis F., and Leonard A. Schlesinger. "Designing Effective Organizations." *The Portable MBA in Management.* Allan R. Cohen, ed. New York: John Wiley & Sons, 1993.

Wilmott, Hugh C. "The Structuring of Organizational Structures." *Administrative Science Quarterly.* September 1981.

SEE ALSO: Organizational Growth

ORGANIZATION THEORY

An organization, by its most basic definition, is an assembly of people working together to achieve common objectives through a division of labor. An organization provides a means of using individual strengths within a group to achieve more than can be accomplished by the aggregate efforts of group members working individually. Business organizations (in market economies) are formed to deliver goods or services to consumers in such a manner that they can realize a profit at the conclusion of the transaction. Over the years, business analysts, economists, and academic researchers have pondered several theories that attempt to explain the dynamics of business organizations, including the ways in which they make decisions, distribute power and control, resolve conflict, and promote or resist organizational change. Indeed, thinkers from a variety of disciplines have made significant contributions to the study of organizations and their workings over the years.

Of the various organizational theories that have been studied over the years, the open-systems theory has emerged as perhaps the most widely known, but others have their proponents as well. Indeed, some researchers into organizational theory propound a blending of various theories, arguing that an enterprise will embrace different organizational strategies in reaction to changes in its competitive circumstances, structural design, and experiences.

BACKGROUND

Modern organization theory is rooted in concepts developed during the beginnings of the Industrial Revolution in the late 1800s and early 1900s. Of import during that period was the research of Max Weber (1864-1920), a German sociologist. Weber believed that bureaucracies, staffed by bureaucrats, represented the ideal organizational form. Weber based his model bureaucracy on legal and absolute authority, logic, and order. In Weber's idealized organizational structure, responsibilities for workers are clearly defined and behavior is tightly controlled by rules, policies, and procedures. In effect, Weber's bureaucracy was designed to function like a machine; the organization was arranged into specific functions, or parts, each of which worked in concert with the other parts to form a streamlined process.

Weber's theories of organizations, like others of the period, reflected an impersonal attitude toward the people in the organization. Indeed, the work force, with its personal frailties and imperfections, was regarded as a potential detriment to the efficiency of any system. Although his theories are now considered mechanistic and outdated, Weber's views on bureaucracy provided important insight into the period's conceptions of process efficiency, division of labor, and hierarchy of authority.

Another important contributor to organization theory in the early 1900s was Henri Fayol. He is credited with identifying strategic planning, staff recruitment, employee motivation, and employee guidance (via policies and procedures) as important management functions in creating and nourishing a successful organization.

Weber's and Fayol's theories found broad application in the early and mid-1900s, in part because of the influence of Frederick W. Taylor (1856-1915). In a 1911 book entitled *Principles of Scientific Management*, Taylor outlined his theories and eventually implemented them on American factory floors. Taylor's theory of scientific management mimicked the four basic managerial functions identified by Fayol, and adopted the same basic attitudes about process efficiency championed by Weber. Although elements of Taylor's research and findings have been criticized as being false, he is credited with helping to define the role of training, wage incentives, employee selection, and work standards in organizational performance.

Researchers began to adopt a less mechanical view of organizations and to pay more attention to human influences in the 1930s. This development was motivated by several studies that shed light on the function of human fulfillment in organizations. The best known of these was probably the so-called Hawthorn Studies. These studies, conducted primarily under the direction of Harvard University researcher Elton Mayo, were conducted in the mid-1920s and 1930s at a Western Electric Company plant known as the Hawthorn Works. The company wanted to determine the degree to which working conditions affected output.

Surprisingly, the studies failed to show any significant positive correlations between workplace conditions and productivity. In one study, for example, worker productivity escalated when lighting was increased, but it also increased when illumination was decreased. The results of the studies demonstrated that innate forces of human behavior may have a greater influence on organizations than do mechanistic incentive systems. The legacy of the Hawthorn studies and other organizational research efforts of that period was an emphasis on the importance of individual and group interaction, humanistic management skills, and social relationships in the workplace.

The focus on human influences in organizations was reflected most noticeably by the integration of Abraham Maslow's "hierarchy of human needs" into organization theory. Maslow's theories introduced two important implications into organization theory. The first was that people have different needs and therefore need to be motivated by different incentives to achieve organizational objectives. The second of Maslow's theories held that people's needs change over time, meaning that as the needs of people lower in the hierarchy are met, new needs arise. These assumptions led to the recognition, for example, that assembly-line workers could be more productive if more of their personal needs were met, whereas past theories suggested that monetary rewards were the sole, or primary, motivators.

Douglas McGregor contrasted the organization theory that emerged during the mid-1900s to previous views. In the 1950s, McGregor offered his renowned Theory X and Theory Y to explain the differences. Theory X encompassed the old view of workers, which held that employees preferred to be directed, wanted to avoid responsibility, and cherished financial security above all else.

McGregor believed that organizations that embraced Theory Y were generally more productive. Theory Y adopted a more optimistic view of human nature. Among other things, it theorized that: humans can learn to accept and seek responsibility; most people possess a high degree of imaginative and problem-solving ability; employees will self-govern, or direct themselves toward goals to which they are committed; and, importantly, satisfaction of ego and self-actualization are among the most important rewards that organizations can provide its workers.

OPEN-SYSTEMS THEORY

Traditional theories regarded organizations as closed systems—autonomous and isolated from the outside world. In the 1960s, these mechanistic organization theories, such as scientific management, were spurned in favor of more holistic and humanistic ideologies. Recognizing that traditional theory had failed to take into account many environmental influences that impacted the efficiency of organizations, most theorists and researchers embraced an open-systems view of organizations.

The term "open systems" reflected the new-found belief that all organizations are unique—in part because of the unique environment in which they operate—and that they should be structured to accommodate unique problems and opportunities. For example, research during the 1960s indicated that traditional bureaucratic organizations generally failed to succeed in environments where technologies or markets were rapidly changing. They also failed to realize the importance of regional cultural influences in motivating workers.

Environmental influences that affect open systems can be described as either specific or general. The specific environment refers to the network of suppliers, distributors, government agencies, and competitors with which a business enterprise interacts. The general environment encompasses four influences that emanate from the geographic area in which the organization operates. These are:

- Cultural values, which shape views about ethics and determine the relative importance of various issues. Individualism, democracy, and the puritan work ethic have all been cited as examples of cultural values that shape business organizations in the United States. In addition, regional and local values often affect organizations. For instance, a region beset with environmental woes as a result of a corporation's irresponsible disposal of waste materials might be more welcoming of waste-disposal regulatory proposals than an economically depressed region that is relatively free of such pollution.

- Economic conditions, which include economic upswings, recessions, regional unemployment, and many other regional factors that affect a company's ability to grow and prosper. Economic influences may also partially dictate an organization's role in the economy.

- Legal/political environment, which effectively helps to allocate power within a society and to enforce laws. The legal and political systems in which an open system operates can play a key role in determining the long-term stability and security of the organization's future. These systems engage in a sort of balancing act; they are responsible for creating a fertile environment for the business community, but they are also responsible for ensuring—via operating regulations, taxes, employee rights laws, and other rules—that the needs of the larger community are addressed.

- Quality of education, which is an important factor in high technology and other industries that require an educated work force. Businesses will be better able to fill such positions if they operate in geographic regions that feature a strong education system.

The open-systems theory also assumes that all large organizations are comprised of multiple subsystems, each of which receives inputs from other subsystems and turns them into outputs for use by other subsystems. The subsystems are not necessarily represented by departments in an organization, but might instead resemble patterns of activity.

An important distinction between open-systems theory and more traditional organization theories is that the former assumes a subsystem hierarchy, meaning that not all of the subsystems are equally essential. Furthermore, a failure in one subsystem will not necessarily thwart the entire system. By contrast, traditional mechanistic theories implied that a malfunction in any part of a system would have an equally debilitating impact.

BASIC ORGANIZATIONAL CHARACTERISTICS

Organizations differ greatly in size, function, and makeup. Nevertheless, the operations of nearly all organizations—from the multinational corporation to a a newly opened delicatessen—are based on a division of labor, a decision-making structure; and rules and policies. The degree of formality with which these aspects of business are approached vary tremendously within the business world, but these characteristics are inherent in any business enterprise that utilizes the talents of more than one person.

Organizations practice division of labor both vertically and horizontally. Vertical division includes three basic levels—top, middle, and bottom. The chief function of top managers, or executives, typically is to plan long-term **strategy** and oversee middle managers. Middle managers generally guide the day-to-day activities of the organization and administer top-level strategy. Low-level managers and laborers put strategy into action and perform the specific tasks necessary to keep the organization operating.

Organizations also divide labor horizontally by defining task groups, or departments, and assigning workers with applicable skills to those groups. Line units perform the basic functions of the business, while staff units support line units with expertise and services. In general, line units focus on supply, production, and distribution, while staff units deal mostly with internal operations and controls or public relations efforts.

Decision-making structures, the second basic organizational characteristic, are used to organize authority. These structures vary from operation to operation in their degree of centralization and decentralization. Centralized decision structures are referred to as ''tall'' organizations because important decisions usually emanate from a high level and are passed down through several channels until they reach the lower end of the hierarchy. Conversely, flat organizations, which have decentralized decision-making structures, employ only a few hierarchical levels. Such organizations are typically guided by a management philosophy that is favorably disposed toward some form of employee empowerment and individual autonomy. Decentralized structures are more representative of humanistic organization theories, while traditional tall organizational structures are more mechanistic.

A formalized system of rules and policies is the third standard organizational characteristic. Rules, policies, and procedures serve as templates of managerial guidance in all sectors of organizational production and behavior. They may document the most efficient means of accomplishing a task or provide standards for rewarding workers. Formalized rules provide managers with more time to spend on other problems and opportunities and help ensure that an organization's various subsystems are working in concert. Ill-conceived or poorly implemented rules, of course, can actually have a negative impact on an enterprise's efforts to produce its goods or services in a profitable or satisfactory manner.

Thus, organizations can be categorized as informal or formal, depending on the degree of formalization of rules within their structures. In formal organizations, say researchers, management has determined that a comparatively impersonal relationship between individuals and the company for which they work is viewed as the best environment for achieving organizational goals. Subordinates have less influence over the process in which they participate, with their duties more clearly defined.

Informal organizations, on the other hand, are less likely to adopt or adhere to a significant code of written rules or policies. Instead, individuals are more likely to adopt patterns of behavior that are influenced by a number of social and personal factors. Changes in the organization are less often the result of authoritative dictate and more often an outcome of collective agreement by members. Informal organizations tend to be more flexible and more reactive to outside influences. But some critics contend that such arrangements may also diminish the ability of top managers to effect rapid change.

ORGANIZATIONAL THEORY IN THE 1980S AND 1990S

By the 1980s several new organizational system theories received significant attention. These included Theory Z, a blending of American and Japanese management practices. This theory was a highly visible one, in part because of Japan's well-documented productivity improvements—and the United States' manufacturing difficulties—during that decade. Other theories, or adaptations of existing theories, emerged as well, which most observers saw as indicative of the ever-changing environment within business and industry.

The study of organizations and their management and production structures and philosophies shows no sign of abating in the 1990s. Indeed, an understanding of various organizational principles continues to be seen as vital to the success of all kinds of organizations—from government agencies to business—of all shapes and sizes, from conglomerates to small businesses. ''As we observe how different professionals working in different kinds of organizations and occupational communities make their case, we see we are still far from having a single 'theory' of organization development,'' wrote Jay R. Galbraith in *Competing with Flexible Lateral Organizations*. ''Yet, a set of common assumptions is surfacing. We are beginning to see patterns in what works and what does not work, and we are becoming more articulate about these patterns. We are also seeing the field increasingly connected to other organizational sciences and disciplines,'' such as information technology and coordination theory.

FURTHER READING:

Cherrington, David J. *Organizational Behavior: The Management of Individual and Organizational Performance.* Needham, MA: Allyn and Bacon, 1994.

Galbraith, Jay R. *Competing with Flexible Lateral Organizations.* 2d ed. Reading, MA: Addison-Wesley, 1994.

Gortner, Harold F., Julianne Mahler, and Jeanne Bell Nicholson. *Organization Theory: A Public Perspective.* 2d ed. Orlando, FL: Harcourt Brace & Co., 1997.

Gray, Jerry L., and Frederick A. Starke. *Organizational Behavior: Concepts and Applications.* 4th ed. Merrill, 1988.

Hatch, Mary Jo. *Organization Theory: Modern, Symbolic, and Postmodern Perspectives.* OUP-USA, 1997.

Ivancevich, John M., and Michael T. Matteson. *Organizational Behavior and Management.* Irwin, 1990.

Northcraft, Gregory B., and Margaret A. Neale. *Organizational Behavior: A Management Challenge*. The Dryden Press, 1990.

Schermerhorn, John R., Jr., James G. Hunt, and Richard N. Osborn. *Management Organizational Behavior*. Wiley, 1982.

SEE ALSO: Organization Structure

ORGANIZATIONAL BEHAVIOR

Organizational behavior is an academic discipline concerned with describing, understanding, predicting, and controlling human behavior in an organizational environment. Organizational behavior has evolved from early classical management theories into a complex school of thought—and it continues to change in response to the dynamic environment and proliferating corporate cultures in which today's businesses operate. "The task of getting organizations to function effectively is a difficult one," wrote David A. Nadler and Michael L. Tushman in Hackman, Lawler, and Porter's *Perspectives on Behaviors in Organizations*. "Understanding one individual's behavior is a challenging problem in and of itself. A group, made up of different individuals and multiple relationships among those individuals, is even more complex. . . . In the fact of this overwhelming complexity, organizational behavior must be managed. Ultimately the work of organizations gets done through the behavior of people, individually or collectively, on their own or in collaboration with technology. Thus, central to the management task is the management of organizational behavior. To do this, there must be the capacity to *understand* the patterns of behavior at individual, group, and organization levels, to *predict* what behavior responses will be elicited by different managerial actions, and finally to use understanding and prediction to achieve *control*."

THE BEHAVIORAL SCIENCES Organizational behavior scientists study four primary areas of behavioral science: individual behavior, group behavior, organizational structure, and organizational processes. They investigate many facets of these areas like personality and perception, attitudes and job satisfaction, group dynamics, politics and the role of leadership in the organization, job design, the impact of stress on work, decision-making processes, the communications chain, and company cultures and climates. They use a variety of techniques and approaches to evaluate each facet and its impact on individuals, groups, and organizational efficiency and effectiveness. "The behavior sciences," stated James Gibson, John Ivancevich, and James Donnelly in *Organizations: Behavior, Structure, Processes,* "have provided the basic framework and principles for the field of organizational behavior. Each behavioral science discipline

provides a slightly different focus, [and] analytical framework. . . . for helping managers answer questions about themselves, nonmanagers, and environmental forces."

In regard to individuals and groups, researchers try to ascertain why people behave the way they do. They have developed a variety of models designed to explain individuals' behavior. They investigate the factors that influence personality development, including genetic, situational, environmental, cultural, and social factors. Researchers also examine various personality types and their impact on business and other organizations. One of the primary tools utilized by organizational behavior researchers in these and other areas of study is the job satisfaction study. These tools are used not only to measure job satisfaction in such tangible areas as pay, benefits, promotional opportunities, and working conditions, but also to gauge how individual and group behavior patterns influence corporate culture, both positively and negatively.

ORGANIZATIONAL BEHAVIOR AND CORPORATE CULTURE

The terms "**corporate culture**" and "organizational behavior" are sometimes used interchangeably, but in reality, there are differences between the two. Corporate culture encompasses the shared values, attitudes, standards, and beliefs and other characteristics that define an organization's operating philosophy. Or, as Gibson, Ivancevich, and Donnelly indicated, "in straightforward terms, the organization's culture is its personality, atmosphere, or 'feel.' The culture of an organization defines appropriate behavior and bonds, it motivates individuals, and it governs the way a company processes information, internal relations and values." Organizational behavior, meanwhile, can be understood in some ways as the study of corporate culture and its various elements, as well as other important components of behavior such as organization structure and organization processes. Organizational behavior, said Gibson, Ivancevich, and Donnelly, is "the field of study that draws on theory, methods, and principles from various disciplines to learn about *individual* perceptions, values, learning capacities, and actions while working in *groups* and within the total *organization;* analyzing the external environment's effect on the organization and its human resources, missions, objectives, and strategies. . . . Effective managers know what to look for in terms of structure, process, and culture and how to understand what they find. Therefore, managers must develop diagnostic skills; they must be trained to identify conditions symptomatic of a problem requiring further attention. Problem indicators include declining profits, declining quantity or quality of work, increases in absenteeism or tardiness, and negative employee attitudes. Each of these problems is an issue of organizational behavior."

FURTHER READING:

Egan, Gerard. "Cultivate Your Culture." *Management Today.* April 1994.

Gibson, James L., John M. Ivancevich, and James H. Donnelly Jr. *Organizations: Behavior, Structure, Processes.* 8th ed. Boston: Richard D. Irwin, 1994.

Gordon, George G. "Industry Determinants of Organizational Culture." *Academy of Management Review.* April 1991.

Hodgetts, Richard M. *Organizational Behavior: Theory and Practice.* New York: Macmillan Publishing Company, 1991.

Phegan, Barry. *Developing Your Company Culture: The Joy of Leadership.* Context Press, 1996.

SEE ALSO: Organizational Development; Organization Theory

ORGANIZATIONAL CHART

Organizational charts are detailed representations of **organization structures** and hierarchies. They are typically used to provide both employees and individuals outside of the establishment with a "snap-shot" picture of the organization's reporting relationships, divisions of work, and levels of management. Obviously, smaller firms—whether they consist of a single owner of a home-based business, a modest shop of a few employees, or a family-owned business with a dozen or so workers—are less likely to utilize organization charts, since the information that is gleaned from chart representations is typically pretty self-evident with such businesses. "Small organizations can get along very well without them as long as everyone understands what they are to do and who they are to do it with," stated James Gibson, John Ivancevich, and James Donnelly in *Organizations: Behavior, Structure, Processes.* But many consultants and small business owners contend that an organization chart can be a useful tool for growing firms.

Business owners endeavoring to allocate responsibilities, activities, and management authority to various employees also have to make certain that they coordinate the activities of those employees to avoid both gaps and redundancies in operations and management. "It is helpful to think of organizational design elements as building blocks that can be used to create a structure to fulfill a particular purpose," stated Phyllis and Leonard Schlesinger in *The Portable MBA in Management.* "A structure is built by defining the requirements of each individual job and then grouping the individual jobs into units. These units are grouped into larger and larger units and coordinating (or integrating) mechanisms are estab-

lished for these units. In this way, the structure has been built to support organizational goals and achieve the key factors for success." Ideally, a detailed organizational chart will provide the business owner or manager with an accurate overview of the relationships of these units/responsibilities to one another and a reliable indication as to whether the firm is positioned to meet the business's fundamental goals. "The organization chart is an organizational skeleton," summarized Thomas S. Bateman and Carl P. Zeithaml in *Management: Function and Strategy.* "It is the framework that provides the bare bones of the organization. Through it, orders are given, decisions are made, and communications flow."

ADVANTAGES AND DISADVANTAGES ASSOCIATED WITH ORGANIZATION CHARTS

While organizational charts are commonly used by mid- and large-sized companies, as well as by significant numbers of smaller businesses with varied operations and employees that number in the dozens, their usefulness has been a subject of some debate. Gibson, Ivancevich, and Donnelly offered a comprehensive synopsis of the pros and cons associated with organization charts in *Organizations: Behavior, Structure, Processes.*

ADVANTAGES "Those who believe that organization charts are necessary to ensure effective management point out that confusion develops without them," wrote Gibson, Ivancevich, and Donnelly. "Individuals do not understand their jobs—what they must do, how they are to do it, and with whom they should work. Managers of different organizational subunits . . . do not understand how their work fits into the work of other subunits. In the absence of an organization chart to clarify relationships, illogical and confusing ones will develop. In fact, the very process of charting the organization is a good test of its soundness, because any relationship that cannot be charted is likely to be unsound and therefore confusing to those working in it." They went on to note that many proponents of organizational charts argue that even more benefits can accrue if the establishment takes the trouble to flesh out the various responsibilities of each part of the chart, including managers, departments, and same-task groups, and that supporters of chart use believe that organizations that have such structures in place will be more likely to make personnel decisions based on objective analysis. Gibson, Ivancevich, and Donnelly conclude by noting that "pro-chart" individuals believe that such representations can be useful to both small and large companies: "The argument that organization charts are necessary only when the organization becomes too big for any one individual to manage does not hold. In many instances, small firms that do rather well in the early stages of their development begin to fail when the founders can no longer manage in their personal styles. The transition from successful small firm to successful large firm is impaired because the employees are doing jobs that fit their personality and unique skills rather than jobs necessary for organizational performance. Organization charts and supporting documents are necessary from the very beginning of a firm's existence, not just when it gets too big for one person to manage.''

DISADVANTAGES Gibson, Ivancevich, and Donnelly also noted, however, that the above perspective is not universally accepted by business consultants, researchers, executives, and managers. Indeed, detractors contend that ''organization charts do not show the important relationships among individuals and units. In fact, what they do show may be misleading. For example, they do not show informal lines of communication and influence. The hierarchical drawing of a chart depicts an intended chain of communication and authority; but in practice, many channels of communication and authority exist,'' both horizontally and diagonally, and through a variety of communications means (telephone, computer, etc.). Writing in *Perspectives on Behaviors in Organizations,* contributors David A. Nadler and Michael L. Tushman characterized such models as ''narrow and static in perspective. . . . It excludes such factors as leader behavior, the impact of the environment, informal relations, power distribution, etc. Such a model can only capture a small part of what goes on in an organization.''

Critics of organization charts also charge that the diagrams sometimes paint a misleading picture of the importance and influence of various people within an organization. Charts are, out of necessity, somewhat streamlined representations that only provide so much detail to a user. In some instances, for example, an organization chart may depict two employees as being equal in power and influence, when in reality, despite the fact that, similarity of job titles aside, one of the individuals is rapidly ascending through the ranks and has the ear of the owner, while the other may be regarded as steady but unremarkable (or even worse, an individual whose position has deteriorated from a higher level over the previous years).

''Perhaps the most damaging criticism of organization charts is that they encourage individuals to take a very narrow view of their jobs,'' wrote Gibson, Ivancevich, and Donnelly. ''Job definitions imply what people will not do as well as clarifying what they will do. The result is an organization that is not responsive to change, that lacks flexibility. The organization chart and all the supporting documentation . . . become substitutes for action and creative responses. In fact, some managers adamantly oppose the creation of organization charts even when employees complain that they need some direction to understand what they should do. These managers respond by saying that it is better to go ahead and fail than to do nothing.''

USING ORGANIZATION CHARTS TO STUDY ORGANIZATION STRUCTURE

As alluded to earlier, the process of constructing an organization chart is sometimes cited as a valuable means by which a company can test its structural soundness. Proponents say that charts can be used to ensure that, as one executive told *Inc.*'s Teri Lammers, ''no one's productivity is constrained by the structure.''

Researchers, consultants, and executives note that this benefit can be even more pronounced in today's business world, which has seen dramatic changes in operating philosophies and management direction over the past few decades. Indeed, corporations are increasingly implementing innovative organizational redesigns in efforts to increase their productivity. The growth in cross-functional teams and reorganizations, for example, can easily blur both reporting and operational relationships between various segments of a business. It is important, then, for businesses that do rely on organizational charts to continually examine and update those diagrams to ensure that they reflect current business realities. In fact, the changes in organizational structures have spurred innovative changes in the format of many organizational charts. Whereas traditional models have been formatted along general ''up-down'' lines, newer models sometimes utilize flattened or ''spoke'' frameworks.

FURTHER READING:

Austin, Nancy K. ''Reorganizing the Organizational Chart.'' *Working Woman.* September 1993.

Bateman, Thomas S., and Carl P. Zeithaml. *Management: Function and Strategy.* Boston, MA: Richard D. Irwin, 1990.

Cherrington, David J. *Organizational Behavior: The Management of Individual and Organizational Performance.* Boston, MA: Allyn and Bacon, 1994.

Gibbons Paul, Lauren. ''Building a New IT Organizational Chart.'' *PC Week.* August 4, 1997.

Gibson, James L., John M. Ivancevich, and James H. Donnelly Jr. *Organizations: Behavior, Structure, Processes.* 8th ed. Boston, MA: Irwin, 1994.

Huse, E. F., and T. G. Cummings. *Organizational Development and Change.* St. Paul, MN: West, 1985.

Lammers, Teri. ''The New, Improved Organizational Chart.'' *Inc.* October 1992.

Schlesinger, Phyllis F., and Leonard A. Schlesinger. ''Designing Effective Organizations.'' In *The Portable MBA in Management.* Allan R. Cohen, ed. New York: John Wiley, 1993.

SEE ALSO: Job Descriptions; Organizational Growth

ORGANIZATIONAL DEVELOPMENT

Organizational development (OD) is an application of behavioral science to organizational change. It encompasses a wide array of theories, processes, and activities, all of which are oriented toward the goal of improving individual organizations. Generally speaking, however, OD differs from traditional organizational change techniques in that it typically embraces a more holistic approach that is aimed at transforming thought and behavior throughout an entity. Definitions of OD abound, but they are all predicated on the notion of improving organizational performance through proactive activities and techniques. A fairly representative definition of OD was offered by Gordon L. Lippitt, Peter Longseth, and Jack Mossop in *Implementing Organizational Change:* "Organization development is a planned, managed, systematic process to change the culture, systems and behavior of an organization, in order to improve the organization's effectiveness in solving its problems and achieving its objectives."

ORGANIZATIONAL DEVELOPMENT BASICS

Although the field of OD is broad, it can be differentiated from other systems of organizational change by its emphasis on process rather than problems. Indeed, traditional group change systems have focused on identifying problems in an organization and then trying to alter the behavior that creates the problem. But Margaret Neale and Gregory Northcraft observed in *Organizational Behavior: A Management Challenge* that OD initiatives, in contrast, focus on identifying the behavioral interactions and patterns that cause and sustain problems. Then, rather than simply changing isolated behaviors, OD efforts are aimed at creating a behaviorally healthy organization that will naturally anticipate and prevent (or quickly solve) problems.

OD programs usually share several basic characteristics. For instance, they are considered long-term efforts of at least one to three years in most cases. In addition, OD stresses collaborative management, whereby managers and workers at different levels of the hierarchy cooperate to solve problems. OD also recognizes that every organization is unique and that the same solutions cannot necessarily be applied at different companies—this assumption is reflected in an OD focus on research and feedback. Another common trait of OD programs is an emphasis on the value of teamwork and small groups. In fact, most OD systems implement broad organizational changes and overcome resistance largely through the efforts of small teams and/or individuals.

An integral feature of most OD programs is an individual known as the "change agent." This is the catalyst—either a group or individual—that facilitates the OD process. Change agents are often outside consultants with experience managing OD programs, although companies sometimes utilize inside managers. The advantage of bringing in outside OD consultants is that they often provide a different perspective and have a less biased view of the organization's problems and needs. The primary drawback associated with outside change agents is that they may lack an in-depth understanding of key issues particular to the company. In addition, outside change agents may have trouble securing the trust and cooperation of key players in the organization. For these reasons, some companies employ a external-internal team approach, which combines the advantages of internal and external change agents. "Are change agents necessary for organizational development to take place?" queried James Gibson, John Ivancevich, and James Donnelly, authors of *Organizations: Behavior, Structure, Processes.* "Once we recognize that organizational development involves substantial changes in how individuals think, believe, and act, we can appreciate the necessity of someone to play the role of change agent. But who should play the role? Existing managers? New managers? Or individuals hired specifically for that purpose? Depending upon the situation, any of these can be called upon to orchestrate the organizational development process. The point is that the role of the change agent is necessary for organizational development to occur."

CHARACTERISTICS OF ORGANIZATIONAL DEVELOPMENT

Gibson, Ivancevich, and Donnelly cited several distinguishing characteristics of organizational development practices. These included the following:

1) Planned and long-term—According to the authors, "OD is a data-based approach to change that involves all of the ingredients that go into managerial planning. It involves goal setting, action planning, implementation, monitoring, and taking corrective action when necessary. Because of the significance of the anticipated and desired change, no quick results are expected."

2) Problem-oriented—Organizational development practices are shaped specifically to address organizational problems.

3) Action-oriented—Whereas some approaches to change are primarily observational in character, "OD focuses on accomplishments and results."

4) Systems approach—"OD is both systemic and systematic," said Gibson, Ivancevich,

and Donnelly. "It's a way of more clearly linking the human resources and potential of an organization to its technology, structure, and management processes."

5) Uses change agents—Again, OD requires the presence of a facilitator/catalyst "to assist the organization in redirecting its functioning."

6) Learning principles—The cornerstone of all OD practices is re-educating individuals and organizations using basic learning principles.

IMPLEMENTING OD PROGRAMS

OD efforts basically entail two groups of activities: "action research" and "interventions." Action research is a process of systematically collecting data on a specific organization, feeding it back for action planning, and evaluating results by collecting and reflecting on more data. Data gathering techniques include everything from surveys and questionnaires to interviews, collages, drawings, and tests. The data is often evaluated and interpreted using advanced statistical analysis techniques. .

Action research can be thought of as the diagnostic component of the OD process. But it also encompasses the intervention component, whereby the change agent uses actions plans to intervene in the organization and make changes, as discussed below. In a continuous process, the results of actions are measured and evaluated and new action plans are devised to effect new changes. Thus, the intervention process can be considered a facet of action research.

OD interventions are plans or programs comprised of specific activities designed to effect change in some facet of an organization. Numerous interventions have been developed over the years to address different problems or create various results. However, they all are geared toward the goal of improving the entire organization through change. In general, organizations that wish to achieve a high degree of organizational change will employ a full range of interventions, including those designed to transform individual and group behavior and attitudes. Entities attempting smaller changes will stop short of those goals, applying interventions targeted primarily toward operating policies, management structures, worker skills, and personnel policies. Typically, organization development programs will simultaneously integrate more than one of these interventions. A few of the more popular interventions are briefly described below.

INTERPERSONAL INTERVENTIONS Interpersonal interventions in an OD program are designed to enhance individual skills, knowledge, and effectiveness. These types typically utilize a certain number of people (10 to 20 is common) in a group setting. The group usually meets at a specific time for one or two weeks. The meetings are unstructured, leaving the group to determine subject matter within the context of basic goals stipulated by a facilitator. As group members try to exert structure on fellow members, anxiety ensues and the group becomes more aware of their own and other's feelings and behaviors.

For example, a group of managers in a marketing department might participate in one of these groups (sometimes called a T-group) together. The members would then describe their perception of each member's behavior and the group might suggest improvements. Finally, each member would identify areas of personal improvement and then act to make changes. The end result would be that the team would become more proficient because of greater understanding and subsequent efforts to improve.

A second example of an interpersonal intervention is process consultation, which helps a company understand and alter processes by resolving interpersonal dilemmas. Although they are similar to T-groups, process consultations are more task-oriented and involve greater input by the change agent. For example, a change agent may observe an individual manager in meetings and conversations during a workday, and then make specific suggestions as to how the manager could alter his or her behavior to improve performance.

Other types of interpersonal interventions include those designed to improve the performance review process, create better training programs, help workers identify their true wants and set complementary career goals, and resolve conflict.

GROUP INTERVENTIONS OD group interventions are designed to help teams and groups within organizations become more effective. Such interventions usually assume that the most effective groups communicate well, facilitate a healthy balance between both personal and group needs, and function by consensus as opposed to autocracy or majority rule.

Group diagnostic interventions are simply meetings wherein members of a team analyze their unit's performance, ask questions about what the team needs to do to improve, and discuss potential solutions to problems. The benefit of such interventions is that members often communicate problems of which their co-workers were unaware. Ideally, such communication will spur problem-solving and improved group dynamics.

Team-building meetings sometimes involve getting the group away from the workplace for a few days. In addition, the group members go a step further than diagnosing problems by proposing, discussing, and evaluating solutions. The purpose of the meetings is to formulate specific procedures for addressing problems. The chief advantage of such interventions is that they help the team reach a consensus on solving problems (away from the pressures of the workplace), thus eliminating incongruent actions and goals that diminish the group's efficiency.

Role analysis technique (RAT) is used to help employees get a better grasp on their role in an organization. In the first step of a RAT intervention, people define their perception of their role and contribution to the overall company effort in front of a group of coworkers. Group members then provide feedback to more clearly define the role. In the second phase, the individual and the group examine ways in which the employee relies on others in the company, and how they define his or her expectations. RAT interventions help people to reduce role confusion, which can result in either conflict or the perception that some people are not doing their job. A popular intervention similar to RAT is responsibility charting, which utilizes a matrix system to assign decision and task responsibilities.

INTERGROUP INTERVENTIONS Intergroup interventions are integrated into OD programs to facilitate cooperation and efficiency between different groups within an organization. For instance, departmental interaction often deteriorates in larger organizations as different units battle for limited resources or become detached from the needs of other units.

Conflict resolution meetings are one common intergroup intervention. First, different group leaders are brought together to secure their commitment to the intervention. Next, the teams meet separately to make a list of their feelings about the other group(s). Then the groups meet and share their lists. Finally, the teams meet to discuss the problems and to try to develop solutions that will help both parties. This type of intervention, say supporters, helps to gradually diffuse tension between groups that has arisen because of faulty communication.

Rotating membership interventions are used by OD change agents to minimize the negative effects of intergroup rivalry that result from employee allegiances to groups or divisions. The intervention basically entails temporarily putting group members into their rival groups. As more people interact in the different groups, greater understanding results.

OD joint activity interventions serve the same basic function as the rotating membership approach, but these involve melding members of different groups to work together toward a common goal. Similarly, common enemy interventions achieve the same results by finding an adversary common to two or more groups and then getting members of the groups to work together to overcome the threat. Examples of common enemies utilized in such programs include

competitors, government regulation, and economic conditions.

COMPREHENSIVE INTERVENTIONS OD comprehensive interventions are used to directly create change throughout an entire organization, rather than focusing on organizational change through subgroup interventions. One of the most popular comprehensive interventions is survey feedback. This technique basically entails surveying employee attitudes at all levels of the company and then disseminating a report that details those findings. The employees then use the data in feedback sessions to create solutions to perceived problems. A number of questionnaires developed specifically for such interventions have been developed.

Structural change interventions are used by OD change agents to effect organizational alterations related to departmentalization, management hierarchy, work policies, compensation and benefit incentives programs, and other elements. Often, the implemented changes emanate from feedback from other interventions. One benefit of change interventions is that companies can often realize an immediate and very significant impact as a result of relatively minor modifications.

Sociotechnical system design interventions are similar to structural change techniques, but they typically emphasize the reorganization of work teams. The basic goal is to create independent groups throughout the company that supervise themselves. This administration may include such aspects as monitoring quality or disciplining team members. The theoretic benefit of sociotechnical system design interventions is that worker and group productivity and quality is increased because workers have more control over (and subsequent satisfaction from) the process in which they participate.

A fourth OD intervention that became extremely popular during the 1980s and early 1990s is **total quality management (TQM)**. TQM interventions utilize established quality techniques and programs that emphasize quality processes, rather than achieving quality by inspecting products and services after processes have been completed. The important concept of continuous improvement embodied by TQM has carried over into other OD interventions.

MANAGING CHANGE THROUGH ORGANIZATIONAL DEVELOPMENT

Organization development initiatives do not automatically succeed. The benefits of effective OD programs are myriad, as many executives, managers, and business owners will attest. But OD interventions that are pursued in a sloppy, half-hearted, or otherwise faulty manner are far less likely to bring about meaningful change than those that have the full support of the people involved. Writing in the *Academy of Management OD Newsletter,* consultant William G. Dyer stipulated several conditions that had to be present if an OD intervention could have any meaningful chance of bringing about the desired change:

- Ownership and all involved personnel needed to be genuinely and visibly committed to the effort.

- People involved in OD have to be informed in advance of the nature of the intervention and the nature of their involvement in it.

- The OD effort has to be connected to other parts of the organization; this is especially true of such areas as the evaluation and reward systems.

- The effort has to be directed by appropriate managers and guided by change agents (which, if used, must be competent).

- The intervention should be based on accurate diagnosis of organizational conditions.

- Owners and managers should show their commitment to OD at all stages of the effort, including the diagnosis, implementation, and evaluation.

- Evaluation is key to success, and should consist of more than asking people how they felt about the effort.

- Owners and managers need to show employees how the OD effort relates to the organization's goals and overriding mission.

FURTHER READING:

Burke, W. Warner. *Organization Development: A Normative View.* Reading, MA: Addison-Wesley Publishing, 1987.

Cherrington, David J. *Organizational Behavior: The Management of Individual and Organizational Performance.* Boston, MA: Allyn and Bacon, 1994.

Connor, Patrick E., and Linda K. Lake. *Managing Organizational Change.* New York: Praeger Publishers, 1988.

Dyer, William G. "Team Building: A Microcosm of the Past, Present, and Future of O.D." *Academy of Management OD Newsletter.* Winter 1989.

French, W. L. *Behavioral Science Interventions for Organization Improvement.* 3rd ed. New York: Prentice-Hall, 1983.

Gibson, James L., John M. Ivancevich, and James H. Donnelly Jr. *Organizations: Behavior, Structure, Processes.* 8th ed. Boston, MA: Richard D. Irwin, 1994.

Goodstein, Leonard D., and W. Warner Burke. "Creating Successful Organization Change." *Organizational Dynamics.* Spring 1991.

Gray, Jerry L., and Frederick A. Starke. *Organizational Behavior: Concepts and Applications*, 4th ed. Columbus, OH: Merrill Publishing Company, 1988.

Huse, E. F., and T. G. Cummings. *Organizational Development and Change.* St. Paul, MN: West, 1985.

Ivancevich, John M., and Michael T. Matteson. *Organizational Behavior and Management.* Homewood, IL: Richard D. Irwin, Inc., 1990.

Lippitt, Gordon L., Peter Longseth, and Jack Mossop. *Implementing Organizational Change.* San Francisco, CA: Jossey-Bass, 1985.

London, Manual. *Change Agents.* San Francisco, CA: Jossey-Bass, 1985.

Northcraft, Gregory B., and Margaret A. Neale. *Organizational Behavior: A Management Challenge.* Chicago, IL: The Dryden Press, 1990.

SEE ALSO: Managing Organizational Change; Organizational Growth; Organization Structure

ORGANIZATIONAL GROWTH

Most companies strive to grow: small firms want to get big, big firms want to get bigger. Indeed, companies have to grow, observed Philip B. Crosby, author of *The Eternally Successful Organization,* "if for no other reason than to accommodate the increased expenses that develop over the years. **Inflation** also raises the cost of everything, and retaliatory price increases are not always possible. Salaries rise as employees gain seniority. The costs of benefits rises because of their very structure, and it is difficult to take any back, particularly if the enterprise is profitable. Therefore cost eliminations and profit improvement must be conducted on a continuing basis, and the revenues of the organization must continue to increase in order to broaden the base."

Most firms, of course, desire growth in order to prosper, not just to survive. Organizational growth, however, means different things to different organizations. How, then, is growth defined? How is it achieved? How does a company survive it?

There are many parameters a company can select to measure its growth. The most meaningful yardstick is one that shows progress with respect to an organization's stated goals. The ultimate goal of most companies is profit, so net profit, revenue, and other financial data are often utilized as "bottom-line" indications of growth. Other business owners, meanwhile, may use sales figures, number of employees, physical expansion, or other criteria to judge organizational growth.

STAGES OF ORGANIZATIONAL GROWTH

Successful businesses typically go through several stages of organizational growth (small business failures often do not reach all these steps) that, despite differences in industry involvement, competition, geographic region, and other factors, are alike in some fairly fundamental respects. Thomas S. Bateman and

Carl P. Zeithaml, authors of *Management: Function and Strategy,* summarized this development as a five-stage process:

1) During the earliest stages of an organization's life, the firm generally expends most of its energy on making and/or selling a product or service. Internal structure is basic, and is often typified by relatively few employees.

2) Once the product or service has been established in the marketplace, the entrepreneur who founded the business begins to develop formal operating methodologies to handle the increasing numbers of people necessary to fulfill the firm's production obligations. Early manifestations of departmentalization often can be seen during this period. ''At this stage,'' said Bateman and Zeithaml, ''management introduces budgets, inventory systems, and work standards. As these control techniques are adopted, the organization becomes more formal and bureaucratic. A hierarchy of positions, job titles, and authority relationships is built.'' In all too many cases, the management hierarchy acquires negative attributes, such as bureaucracy, political intrigue, and diluted knowledge about products/services and customers.

3) In this stage, companies become increasingly decentralized, exchanging a structure wherein decisions were made at the top of a departmentalized company for a decentralized one organized by products or geography. ''Thus, operations become highly dispersed and diversified,'' commented Bateman and Zeithaml. ''That is, the organization has many different products, markets, territories, and manufacturing facilities. To complicate things, the firm may acquire new companies that add to its diversity. Top management may learn it is losing control over its operations.''

4) According to Bateman and Zeithaml, companies often react to cumbersome operations by adding new staff and/or initiating new programs designed to ''exert more control over operations,'' but in many cases these developments merely trigger another onslaught of red tape.

5) Companies react through ''greater collaboration through another organizational structure. Corporate staff is reduced, with personnel either terminated or reassigned.''

Of course, stages of growth vary significantly from business to business. Some firms, blessed with far-thinking leaders and competent managers and em-

ployees, are able to skirt most of the rocky shoals that lurk underneath the strong waves of organizational growth. It is not written in stone, for instance, that a company has to endure a period of poor communication between its various elements on the way to future well-being. Others, meanwhile, can trip up in areas that most businesses navigate easily (an entrepreneur who picks his or her first few managers on the basis of personal loyalties rather than organizational needs, for example). The presence of a detailed, well-conceived long-range business plan can be a great help to small business owners seeking to expand with a minimum of growing pains.

WAYS IN WHICH ORGANIZATIONS ACHIEVE GROWTH

Many academic models have been created that depict possible growth stages/directions of a company, but management consultant Tom Peters suggested that there are several ''real-world'' ways in which both large and small companies may pursue a course of organizational growth.

- Joint Venture/Alliance—This strategy is particularly effective for smaller firms with limited resources. Such partnerships can help small business secure the resources they need to grapple with rapid changes in demand, supply, competition, and other factors. Forming **joint ventures** or alliances gives all companies involved the flexibility to move on to different projects upon completion of the first, or restructure agreements to continue working together. Subcontracting, which allows firms to concentrate on those aspects of their business that they do best, is sometimes defined as a type of alliance arrangement (albeit one in which the parties involved generally wield differing levels of power). Joint ventures and other business alliances can inject partners with new ideas, access to new technologies, new approaches, and new markets, all of which can help the involved businesses to grow. Indeed, establishing joint ventures with overseas firms has been hailed as one of the most potentially rewarding ways for companies to expand their operations. Finally, some firms realize growth by acquiring other companies.

- Licensing—''License your most advanced technology,'' advised Peters, who argued that truly proprietary technologies are quickly becoming extinct. Peters and other consultants contend that competitors will soon copy whatever a company develops in the realm of technology (and other areas), so it may make good sense for a company to turn to licensing. This creates cash flow for the company to fund future research and development.

- Sell Off Old Winners—Some organizations engaged in a concerted effort to grow divest themselves of mature ''cash cow'' operations to focus on growing newer product or service lines. This option may sound contradictory, but analysts note that businesses can command top prices for such tried and true assets. An addendum to this line of thinking is the divestment of older technology or products. Emerging markets in Latin America and Eastern Europe, for instance, have been favorite places for companies to sell products or technology that no longer attract high levels of interest in the United States. These markets may not yet be able to afford large quantities of state-of-the-art goods, but they can still benefit from older models.

- New Markets—Some businesses are able to secure significant organizational growth by tapping into new markets. Creating additional demand for a firm's product or service, especially in a market where competition has yet to fully develop, can spur phenomenal growth for a small company (although the competitive vacuum will generally close very quickly in these instances).

- New Product Development—Creation of new products or services is a primary method by which companies grow. Indeed, new product development is the linchpin of most organizations' growth strategies.

- Outside Financing—Many small companies turn to outside financing sources to fund their expansion. Smaller private firms search for **capital** from banks, private investors, government agencies, or venture capital firms.

PROBLEMS ENCOUNTERED WITH ORGANIZATIONAL GROWTH

Small business owners seeking to guide their organizations through periods of growth—whether that growth is dramatic or incremental—often encounter difficulties. After all, when a firm is small in size, the entrepreneur who founded it usually serves as its primary strategic and operational leader and can often easily direct and monitor the various aspects of daily business. In such environments, added Theodore Caplow, author of *Managing an Organization,* the small business owner also can ''understand a larger proportion of the relationships subordinates have with

each other and with outsiders.'' Organizational growth, however, brings with it an inevitable dilution of that ''hands-on'' capability, while the complexity of various organizational tasks simultaneously increases. ''As the organization grows,'' said Caplow, ''control becomes more complex by the mere accretion of numbers. There are ways of reducing the complexity by delegating responsibility and installing better date systems but there is no way of avoiding it altogether.''

According to Caplow, organizational growth also triggers an almost inevitable ''diminution of consensus about organizational goals.'' He attributed this ''in part to the inherent difficulty of getting a larger number of people who know each other less well to agree about anything, in part to the importation of new people and ideas, but mostly to the brute fact that as an organization grows, its relationships to its members and to the environment necessarily change.'' Oftentimes, organizational growth has a transformational effect on the business, especially if the growth has been realized via dramatic rather than incremental means (such as opening of a second store, a new promotional blitz for a popular product, or major expansion of services). Caplow pointed out that such growth can be particularly disorienting for employee and owner alike: ''often the people involved may not realize that anything significant has occurred until they discover by experience that their familiar procedures no longer work and that their familiar routines have been bizarrely transformed.''

Small business owners, then, face a dizzying array of organizational elements that have to be revised in accordance with changing realities. Maintaining effective methods of communications with and between employees and departments, for example, become ever more important as the firm grows. Similarly, good **human resource management** practices—from hiring to training to empowerment—have to be implemented and maintained. Establishing and improving standard practices is often a key element of organizational growth as well. Indeed, a small business that undergoes a significant burst of growth will find its operations transformed in a number of ways. Often, it will be the owner's advance planning and management skills that will determine whether that growth is sustained, or whether internal constraints prematurely rein in that growth.

FURTHER READING:

Bateman, Thomas S., and Carl P. Zeithaml. *Management: Function and Strategy.* Boston: Richard D. Irwin, 1990.

Bildner, James L. ''Hitting the Wall.'' *Inc.* July 1995.

Caplow, Theodore. *Managing an Organization.* New York: Holt, Rinehart and Winston, 1983.

Churchill, Neil C., and Virginia A. Lewis. "The Five Stages of Small Business Growth." *Harvard Business Review.* May-June 1983.

Crosby, Philip B. *The Eternally Successful Organization: The Art of Corporate Wellness.* New York: New American Library, 1990.

Grousbeck, H. Irving, Michael J. Roberts, and Howard H. Stevenson. *New Business Ventures and the Entrepreneur.* 4th ed. Boston, MA: Richard D. Irwin, 1994.

Kotter, John P., Vijay Sathe, and Leonard A. Schlesinger. *Organization: Text, Cases, and Readings on the Management of Organizational Design and Change.* Boston: Richard D. Irwin, 1986.

Mintzberg, Henry, and James Brian Quinn. *The Strategy Process: Concepts and Contexts.* Englewood Cliffs, NJ: Prentice Hall, 1992.

Peters, Tom. "Get Innovative or Get Dead, Part 1." *California Business Review.* Fall 1990.

SEE ALSO: Business Expansion; Emerging Markets; Managing Organizational Change; Organizational Development

ORGANIZATIONAL LIFE CYCLE

The organizational life cycle (OLC) is a model which proposes that over the course of time, business firms move through a fairly predictable sequence of developmental stages. This model, which has been a subject of considerable study over the years, is linked to the study of organizational growth and development. It is based on a biological metaphor—that business firms resemble living organisms because they demonstrate a regular pattern of developmental process. Organizations that are said to pass through a recognizable life cycle, wrote Gibson, Ivancevich, and Donnelly in *Organizations: Behavior, Structure, Processes,* are fundamentally impacted by external environmental circumstances as well as internal factors: "We're all aware of the rise and fall of organizations and entire industries. . . . Marketing experts acknowledge the existence of product-market life cycles. It seems reasonable to conclude that organizations also have life cycles."

In a summary of OLC models, Quinn and Cameron wrote in *Management Science* that the models typically propose that "changes that occur in organizations follow a predictable pattern that can be characterized by developmental stages. These stages are sequential in nature; occur as a hierarchical progression that is not easily reversed; and involve a broad range of organizational activities and structures." The number of life cycle stages proposed in various works studying the phenomenon have varied considerably over the years. Some analysts have delineated as many as ten different stages of an organizational life cycle, while others have flattened it down to as few as three stages. Most models, however, tout the organizational life cycle as a period comprised of four or five stages that can be encapsulated as start-up, growth, maturity, decline, and death (or revival).

TRENDS IN OLC STUDY

While a number of business and management theorists alluded to developmental stages in the early to mid-1900s, Mason Haire's 1959 work *Modern Organization Theory* is generally recognized as one of the first studies that used a biological model for organizational growth and argued that organizational growth and development followed a regular sequence. The study of organizational life cycles intensified, and by the 1970s and 1980s it was well-established as a key component of overall organizational growth.

Organizational life cycle is an important model because of its premise and its prescription. The model's premise is that requirements, opportunities, and threats both inside and outside the business firm will vary depending on the stage of development in which the firm finds itself. For example, threats in the start-up stage differ from those in the maturity stage. As the firm moves through the developmental stages, changes in the nature and number of requirements, opportunities, and threats exert pressure for change on the business firm. Baird and Meshoulam stated in the *Academy of Management Review* that organizations move from one stage to another because the fit between the organization and its environment is so inadequate that either the organization's efficiency and/or effectiveness is seriously impaired or the organization's survival is threatened. The OLC model's prescription is that the firm's managers must change the goals, strategies and strategy implementation devices of the business to fit the new set of issues. Thus, different stages of the company's life cycle require alterations in the firm's objectives, strategies, managerial processes (planning, organizing, staffing, directing, controlling), technology, culture, and decision-making. For example, in a longitudinal study of 36 corporations published in *Management Science*, Miller and Friesen proposed five growth stages: birth, growth, maturity, decline, and revival. They traced changes in the organizational structure and managerial processes as the business firms proceeded through the stages. At birth, the firms exhibited a very simple organizational structure with authority centralized at the top of the hierarchy. As the firms grew, they adapted more sophisticated structures and decentralized authority to middle- and lower-level managers. At maturity, the firms demonstrated significantly more concern for internal efficiency and installed more control mechanisms and processes.

GROWTH PHASES Despite the increase in interest in OLC, though, most scholarly works focusing on organizational life cycles have been conceptual and hypothetical in content. Only a small minority have attempted to test empirically the organizational life cycle model. One widely-cited conceptual work, however, was published in the *Harvard Business Review* in 1972 by L. Greiner. He used five growth phases: growth through creativity; growth through direction; growth through delegation; growth through coordination; and growth through collaboration. Each growth stage encompassed an evolutionary phase (''prolonged periods of growth where no major upheaval occurs in organization practices''), and a revolutionary phase (''periods of substantial turmoil in organization life''). The evolutionary phases were hypothesized to be about four to eight years in length, while the revolutionary phases were characterized as the crisis phases. At the end of each one of the five growth stages listed above, Greiner hypothesized that an organizational crisis will occur, and that the business's ability to handle these crises will determine its future:

Phase 1—Growth through creativity eventually leads to a crisis of leadership. More sophisticated and more formalized management practices must be adopted. If the founders can't or won't take on this responsibility, they must hire someone who can, and give this person significant authority.

Phase 2—Growth through direction eventually leads to a crisis of autonomy. Lower level managers must be given more authority if the organization is to continue to grow. The crisis involves top-level managers' reluctance to delegate authority.

Phase 3—Growth through delegation eventually leads to a crisis of control. This occurs when autonomous employees who prefer to operate without interference from the rest of the organization clash with business owners and managers who perceive that they are losing control of a diversified company.

Phase 4—Growth through coordination eventually leads to a crisis of red tape. Coordination techniques like product groups, formal planning processes, and corporate staff become, over time, a bureaucratic system that causes delays in decision-making and a reduction in innovation.

Phase 5—Growth through collaboration, is characterized by the use of teams, a reduction in corporate staff, matrix-type structures, the simplification of formal systems, an increase in conferences and educational programs, and more sophisticated information systems. While Greiner did not formally delineate a crisis for this phase, he guessed that it might revolve around ''the psychological saturation of employees who grow emotionally and physically exhausted by the intensity of team work and the heavy pressure for innovative solutions.''

Finally, Greiner contended that managers must realize that solutions to a given crisis will cause a future crisis to emerge, and that not all companies survive each crisis point. Moreover, he argued that these stages can have beneficial repercussions for businesses: ''Each phase results in certain strengths and learning experiences in the organization that will be essential for success in subsequent phases. . . . [Crises] provide the pressure, ideas and awareness that afford a platform for change and the introduction of new practices.''

ORGANIZATION LIFE CYCLE AND THE SMALL BUSINESS OWNER

Entrepreneurs who are involved in the early stages of business creation are unlikely to become preoccupied with life cycle issues of decline and dissolution. Indeed, their concerns are apt to be in such areas as securing financing, establishing relationships with vendors and clients, preparing a physical location for business operations, and other aspects of business start-up that are integral to establishing and maintaining a viable firm. Basically, these firms are almost exclusively concerned with the very first stage of the organization life cycle. Small business enterprises that are well-established, on the other hand, may find OLC studies more relevant. Indeed, many recent examinations of organization life cycles have analyzed ways in which businesses can prolong desired stages (growth, maturity) and forestall negative stages (decline, death). Certainly, there exists no timeline that dictates that a company will begin to falter at a given point in time. ''Because every company develops at its own pace, characteristics, more than age, define the stages of the cycle,'' stated Karen Adler and Paul Swiercz in *Training & Development.*

Small business owners and other organization leaders may explore a variety of options designed to influence the enterprise's life cycle—from new products to new markets to new management philosophies. After all, once a business begins to enter a decline phase, it is not inevitable that the company will continue to plummet into ultimate failure; many companies are able to reverse such slides (a development that is sometimes referred to as turning the OLC bell curve into an ''S'' curve). But entrepreneurs and managers should recognize that their business is always somewhere along the life cycle continuum, and that business success is often predicated on recognizing where your business is situated along that measuring stick. ''During any given interval in an organization's history, it will be growing, stable, or declining,'' wrote Theodore Caplow in *Managing an Organization.* ''The task of management is easiest in a growing organization because growth itself—whatever its real cause—is usually viewed as a sign of managerial success and because the input of new resources occasioned by growth can be used to pay for mistakes. Managing a stable organization is a more difficult task and calls for a finer adjustment of means and ends, careful decision-making, and alertness to the external environment. The management of a declining organization may be easy or hard, depending upon whether the decline is regarded as inevitable.''

FURTHER READING:

Adler, Karen R., and Paul M. Swiercz. ''Taming the Performance Bell Curve.'' *Training & Development.* October 1997.

Baird, L., and I. Meshoulam. ''Managing Two Fits of Strategic Human Resource Management,'' *Academy of Management Review,* January 1988.

Caplow, Theodore. *Managing an Organization.* New York: Holt, Rinehart, and Winston, 1983.

Chandler, A. *Strategy and Structure: Chapters in the History of the Industrial Enterprise.* Cambridge, MA: MIT Press, 1962.

Churchill, N., and V. Lewis. ''The Five Stages of Small Business Growth.'' *Harvard Business Review.* May-June 1983.

Dodge, H. Robert, and John E. Robbins. ''An Empirical Investigation of the Organizational Life Cycle Model for Small Business Development and Survival,'' *Journal of Small Business Management.* January 1992.

Dodge, H. Robert, Sam Fullerton, and John E. Robbins. ''Stage of the Organizational Life cycle and Competition as Mediators of Problem Perception for Small Businesses.'' *Strategic Management Journal.* February 1994.

Gibson, James L, John M. Ivancevich, and James H. Donnelly, Jr. *Organizations: Behavior, Structure, Processes.* 8th ed. Boston, MA: Irwin, 1994.

Greiner, L. ''Evolution and Revolution as Organizations Grow,'' *Harvard Business Review.* July-August 1972.

Hanks, S., C. Watson, E. Jansen, and G. Chandler, ''Tightening the Life-Cycle Construct: A Taxonomic Study of Growth Stage Configurations in High-Technology Organizations,'' *Entrepreneurship Theory and Practice.* Winter 1993.

Kazanjian, R. ''Relation of Dominant Problems to Stages of Growth in Technology-Based New Ventures.'' *Academy of Management Journal.* June 1988.

Miller, D., and P. Friesen, ''A Longitudinal Study of the Corporate Life Cycle,'' *Management Science.* October 1984.

Quinn, R., and K. Cameron, ''Organizational Life Cycles and Shifting Criteria of Effectiveness: Some Preliminary Evidence.'' *Management Science.* January 1983.

Smith, K., T. Mitchell, and C. Summer, ''Top Level Management Priorities in Different Stages of the Organizational Life Cycle,'' *Academy of Management Journal.* December 1985.

Tyebjee, T., A. Bruno, and S. McIntyre, ''Growing Ventures Can Anticipate Marketing Stages,'' *Harvard Business Review.* January-February 1983.

SEE ALSO: Managing Organizational Change; Organization Theory

OUTSOURCING

Outsourcing occurs when a company purchases products or services from an outside supplier, rather than performing the same work within its own facilities, in order to cut costs. The decision to outsource is a major strategic one for most companies, since it involves weighing the potential cost savings against the consequences of a loss in control over the product or service. Some common examples of outsourcing include manufacturing of components, computer programming services, tax compliance and other accounting functions, and payroll and other human resource functions. A relatively new trend in outsourcing is employee leasing, in which specialized vendors recruit, hire, train, and pay their clients' employees, as well as arrange health care coverage and other benefits. According to research conducted by *CFO: The Magazine for Senior Financial Executives,* there were 146,000 outsourcers providing products or services to other companies in the United States as of December 1994, an increase of 65 percent from the 88,000 that existed in 1989.

The growth in outsourcing in recent years is partly the result of a general shift in business philosophy. Prior to the mid-1980s, many companies sought to acquire other companies and diversify their business interests in order to reduce risk. As more companies discovered that there were limited advantages to running a large group of unrelated businesses, however, many began to divest subsidiaries and refocus their efforts on one or a few closely related areas of business. Companies tried to identify or develop a ''core competence,'' a unique combination of experience and expertise that would provide a source of competitive advantage in a given industry. All aspects of the company's operations were aligned around the core competence, and any activities or functions that were not considered necessary to preserve it were then outsourced.

Successful outsourcing thus requires a strong understanding of the organization's capabilities and future direction. As William R. King explained in *Information Systems Management,* ''Decisions regarding outsourcing significant functions are among the most strategic that can be made by an organization, because they address the basic organizational choice of the functions for which internal expertise is developed and nurtured and those for which such expertise is purchased. These are basic decisions regarding organizational design.'' Outsourcing based only upon a comparison of costs can lead companies to miss opportunities to gain knowledge that might lead to the development of new products or technologies. *Business Week* called companies that had outsourced too many of their core functions "hollow corporations," and claimed that they had relinquished their reason for existence.

Outsourcing can be undertaken to varying degrees, ranging from total outsourcing to selective outsourcing. Total outsourcing may involve dismantling entire departments or divisions and transferring the employees, facilities, equipment, and complete responsibility for a product or function to an outside vendor. In contrast, selective outsourcing may target a single, time-consuming task within a department, such as preparing the payroll or manufacturing a minor component, that can be handled more efficiently by an outside specialist. The opposite of outsourcing is insourcing, when a staff function within a company markets its product or service to external as well as internal customers.

ADVANTAGES AND DISADVANTAGES OF OUTSOURCING

Companies that decide to outsource do so for a number of reasons. The primary reason is to achieve cost savings or better cost control over the outsourced function. Companies usually outsource to a vendor that specializes in a given function and performs that function more efficiently than the company could. Anticipated cost savings sometimes fail to materialize, however, because the vendor must make a profit and because the company incurs additional transaction costs when interacting with the vendor. Another common reason for outsourcing is to achieve headcount reductions or minimize the fluctuations in staffing that may occur due to changes in demand for a product or service. Companies also outsource in order to reduce the workload on their employees, or to provide more development opportunities for their employees by freeing them from tedious tasks.

Some companies outsource in order to eliminate distractions and force themselves to concentrate on their core competencies. Still others outsource to achieve greater financial flexibility, since the sale of assets that formerly supported an outsourced function can improve a company's cash flow. A possible pitfall in this reasoning is that many vendors demand long-term contracts, which may reduce flexibility. A common reason for outsourcing computer programming and other information technology functions is to gain access to new technology and outside expertise. Some experts claim, however, that companies are exposed to new technology by vendors anyway, and that they could simply hire people with the expertise they seek. But this is not true for small businesses, which often cannot afford to hire computer experts or develop the in-house expertise to maintain high-level technology. When such tasks are outsourced, the small business

gains access to new technology that may help it compete with larger companies.

Company politics is another common reason for outsourcing. For example, some companies might begin outsourcing initiatives after observing the successful efforts of a competitor. Others might be pushed toward outsourcing by managers seeking personal gain or by a desire to eliminate troublesome departments. Finally, outsourcing provides an attractive option for start-up firms as they grow. In these instances, outsourcing can free the entrepreneur from tedious and time-consuming tasks, such as payroll, so that he or she can concentrate on the marketing and sales activities that will enable the firm to make money.

Some of the major potential disadvantages to outsourcing include poor quality control, decreased company loyalty, a lengthy bid process, and a loss of strategic alignment. There may also be inherent advantages of maintaining certain functions internally. For example, company employees may have a better understanding of the industry, and their vested interests may mean they are more likely to make decisions in accordance with the company's goals. A general rule of thumb is that companies should never outsource any function that directly affects quality or service.

STEPS IN SUCCESSFUL OUTSOURCING

Once a company has made the decision to outsource, there are still a number of factors it must consider in making a successful transition and forming a partner relationship with the vendor. Ethel Scully recommended a series of steps for companies to follow in *National Underwriter*. First, the company should determine what sort of outsourcing relationship will best meet its needs. Some businesses share strategic decision-making with their vendors, while others only outsource on a limited, as-needed basis. Next, the company needs to obtain the support of key personnel for the decision to outsource. Many companies encounter resistance from employees who feel that their jobs are threatened by outsourcing. Scully suggested forming a team consisting of an outsourcing expert, representatives from senior management and human resources, and the managers of all affected areas of the company to help address employee concerns about the decision.

Then the company can begin contacting potential vendors, either formally or informally, and asking specific questions about the services provided and the terms of the contract. Ideally, the vendor will have experience in handling similar business and will be able to give the client's needs the priority they deserve. "Consider the service company's knowledge of the entirety of your business, its willingness to customize service, and its compatibility with your firm's business culture, as well as the long-run cost of its services and its financial strength,'' said service provider Carl Schwenker in *Money*.

Finally, the company should select a vendor it trusts in order to develop a mutually beneficial partner relationship. It is important for the company to develop tangible measures of job performance before entering into an agreement, as well as financial incentives to encourage the vendor to meet deadlines and control costs. The contract should clearly define responsibilities and performance criteria, outline confidentiality rules and ownership rights to new ideas or technology, and include a means of severing the relationship if necessary. Since the vendor is likely to have more experience in preparing outsourcing agreements than a small client company, it may also be helpful to consult with an attorney during contract negotiations.

FURTHER READING:

Elliot, Vince. ''Outsourcing without Risk.'' *Journal of Property Management.* January/February 1995.

Evans, David, Judy Feldman, and Anne Root. ''Smart New Ways to Manage Subcontractors.'' *Money.* March 15, 1994.

Foxman, Noah. ''Succeeding in Outsourcing.'' *Information Systems Management.* Winter 1994.

Groenfeldt, Tom. ''Outsourcing Hits the Desktop.'' *Journal of Business Strategy.* July-August 1996.

Hammond, Keith H. ''The New World of Work.'' *Business Week.* October 17, 1994.

King, William R. ''Strategic Outsourcing Decisions.'' *Information Systems Management.* Fall 1994.

Lacity, Mary, Rudy Hirschheim, and Leslie Willcocks. ''Realizing Outsourcing Expectations: Incredible Expectations, Credible Outcomes.'' *Information Systems Management.* Fall 1994.

Mello, John P. ''Outsource Taxes? Why Not?'' *CFO: The Magazine for Senior Financial Executives.* January 1995.

Meyer, N. Dean. ''A Sensible Approach to Outsourcing: The Economic Fundamentals.'' *Information Systems Management.* Fall 1994.

Scott, Miriam Basch. ''Outsourcing Affords Employers Improved Administration, Benefits.'' *Employee Benefit Plan Review.* November 1994.

Scully, Ethel. ''Many Factors to Weigh in Decision to Outsource.'' *National Underwriter.* January 16, 1995.

Springsteel, Ian. ''Outsourcing Is Everywhere.'' *CFO: The Magazine for Senior Financial Executives.* December 1994.

SEE ALSO: Free-lance Employment/Independent Contractors; Cost Control and Reduction; Organizational Development

OVERHEAD EXPENSE

Overhead expenses are those production and nonproduction costs not readily traceable to specific jobs or processes. Overhead expenses encompass three general areas: indirect materials, indirect labor, and all other miscellaneous production expenses, such as taxes, insurance, **depreciation**, supplies, utilities, and repairs. Therefore, overhead expense is part of the total costs of maintaining and staffing a facility.

Production overhead includes such items as factory supplies and materials that are used in the production process, supervisors' salaries, maintenance and repairs of machinery, and utilities. Nonproduction overhead includes salaries of building maintenance, medical, and security personnel, rent or depreciation on plant and equipment, insurance on plant and equipment, the costs of meeting government regulations, and administrative salaries and expenses.

DETERMINING OVERHEAD RATES

The accurate accounting and allocation of overhead expense are very important in calculating the cost of goods sold and in setting a profitable selling price for products. But since the exact amount of overhead expense that will need to be applied to products is not known at the time the products are manufactured, overhead expense must be estimated as part of the budget process. The manufacturer's accountant, with the help of production supervisors and decision-point managers, develops projections of the volume of sales, the volume of production, and the cost of production for the coming year.

If the company produces only one product, the accountant merely divides the total estimated overhead by the expected volume of output to derive the standard overhead rate, burden rate, or indirect cost rate (an overhead rate per unit). During the fiscal year, the accountant keeps track of the number of finished goods going into inventory and allocates overhead for these units by multiplying by the standard overhead rate. The finished goods are then said to have absorbed a portion of the total overhead costs.

In a company that produces more than one product, however, the procedure is much more complex. The accountant's allocation of overhead is complicated by the variations in the production processes for different products. One item may require a labor-intensive finishing process, for example, while another relies more on machinery. As a result, the same standard overhead rate cannot be applied accurately to all products. Instead, the accountant must choose an activity base upon which to calculate the allocation of overhead to finished products.

OVERHEAD EXPENSE

Commonly used activity bases include direct labor hours, direct labor costs, and machine hours. The formula for allocating overhead is as follows: Overhead Rate Per Unit Activity Base = Overhead to be Allocated (dollars of overhead)/Volume of Activity Base (direct labor-hours or machine hours). For example, a company that estimates it will incur $50,000 in overhead expense and 10,000 direct labor hours would apply an overhead rate of $5.00 per machine hour when costing its products.

ABSORPTION AND OVERHEAD VARIANCES

Since the company must estimate its total overhead expense, however, it may find that, in applying the predetermined rate, the allocation of overhead either exceeded or fell short of actual costs. This variance, termed the "burden variance," means that overhead was either: 1) overabsorbed (overapplied)—the application of the predetermined rate exceeded the actual overhead used; or 2) underabsorbed (underapplied)—the application of the predetermined rate fell short of the actual overhead used.

Burden variance can result from the following spending variations, or budget variance:

1) The total amount actually spent for production overhead varied from the budget.

2) The price paid for units of overhead factors varied from the budgeted prices.

3) The quantity of overhead factors per unit of finished product varied from the quantity per budgeted unit.

4) The mix of overhead factors used changed so that the average cost of overhead per unit of product varied from the amount budgeted.

Burden variance may also result from the following volume variances:

1) Actual volume varied from the volume used to set the predetermined overhead rates.

2) Seasonal fluctuations distorted the averages.

Underabsorbed overhead exists as a debit balance in the company's production overhead clearing account at the end of the year. Overabsorbed overhead is reflected as a credit balance in that account. To report these balances in the **financial statements**, the accountant examines the cause of the variance and chooses a method to satisfy the reporting objective. In reporting the variances the accountant considers at least three alternatives:

1) Divide the under- or overabsorption in any period between the income statement and the balance sheet in direct proportion to the distribution of the overhead absorbed during

the period. The objective of this method is to have inventory cost and the cost of goods sold approximate the average costs of production in the period.

2) Report the variance in full as a loss or a gain on the income statement for the period in which it arises. The purpose of this method is to measure the inventory at its normal cost, with the income statement accounting for all variances from the budget. Inefficiencies due to overspending or underproduction are costs of the period rather than costs of the products manufactured during the period. When plant utilization falls short of budget, there is a loss (or an expense for idle capacity) to be reported in the income statement for the period.

3) Carry all burden variances to the balance sheet for the end of the period to be added to or offset against similar amounts arising in preceding or succeeding periods. The company's management exercises this option when it expects that a portion of the burden variance may be offset. It does not extend this practice to the annual reporting, however, where it splits the burden variance between inventory and the cost of goods sold if the variance is either large enough to have a material effect on the financial statement and if it represents overabsorption, or likely to be recoverable from the sale of the inventory in later periods.

COST CLASSIFICATION PROBLEMS

In some instances, the cost of applying certain production costs to specific units may be prohibitive. Therefore, management recognizes these costs as part of the production overhead to be absorbed on a per-unit basis and may devise some arbitrary method of allocation. Some examples of these costs are:

- Glue, staples, nuts, bolts, nails, plastic wrap, tape, etc.—elements common to a variety of products without specific measurements.

- Shared time and travel expenses resulting from performing services at a number of customer sites.

- Overtime premiums, resulting from over-scheduling, are averaged over the entire production for the period.

SUMMARY

Overhead costs are of many different types and can be associated only indirectly with product units. The allocation of overhead is one of the most chal-

ENCYCLOPEDIA OF SMALL BUSINESS

739

lenging problems of accounting. Performed effectively, however, it provides a company's management with an accurate accounting of costs and with the ability to set profitable market prices.

Differences in production processes call for the use of activity bases in setting standard overhead rates. Production overhead variances, resulting from over- or underapplied overhead, often occur when using standard rates. But the accountant can make necessary adjustments in internal and external reporting.

FURTHER READING:

Black, Homer A., John E. Champion, and Gibbs U. Miller. *Accounting in Business Decisions: Theory, Method, and Use.* Upper Saddle River, NJ: Prentice Hall, 1973.

Hilton, Ronald W. *Managerial Accounting.* McGraw-Hill, 1991.

Meigs, Robert F., and Walter B. Meigs. *Accounting: The Basis for Business Decisions.* 8th ed. New York: McGraw-Hill, 1990.

Shillinglaw, Gordon, and Philip E. Meyer. *Accounting: A Management Approach.* 7th ed. Irwin, 1983.

Welsch, Glenn A. *Budgeting: Profit Planning and Control.* Upper Saddle River, NJ: Prentice Hall, 1976.

SEE ALSO: Costs

OVERTIME

Overtime is work done by hourly employees beyond the regular work hours per week. Any work over forty hours per week for an hourly worker is considered overtime. Overtime and overtime compensation are provided under the federal Fair Labor Standards Act of 1938. It is required under the FLSA that employers pay employees working more that forty hours per week time-and-a-half, or 150 percent of the worker's salary for those hours exceeding the weekly average.

EXEMPT AND NON-EXEMPT EMPLOYEES U.S. labor law distinguishes between ''exempt'' and ''non-exempt'' employees regarding overtime. Exempt employees do not have to be paid overtime if they work more than 40 hours a week. Members of this class of employee include executives, managers, and front-line supervisors, ''as well as employees whose jobs require making decisions and using personal judgment, creativity, or innovativeness but who are not classified as managers,'' wrote Donald Weiss in *Fair, Square, & Legal.* ''Teachers and educational administrators, salespeople, and other people working on commission or for tips for service, employees of service organizations in which more than 50 percent of the organization's gross income derives from *intra-state* as opposed to *interstate* commerce—these are all people to whom overtime need not be paid.''

DECIDING TO USE OVERTIME Businesses with seasonal peaks, with quotas and deadlines, or with the possibility of rush orders, will at some point probably not be able to meet staffing needs with the regular hours worked by employees. It is at these crisis points that overtime becomes an invaluable tool for the employer.

Overtime, though, should be used sparingly, and its use should not become routine. An employer should not rely on employees working many more hours per week to routinely make up for work not accomplished during the regular work week. If this is the case—if overtime becomes essential to the performance of a business, even during regular operating scenarios—there may be other factors, such as poor compensation, morale, or inadequate staffing levels, to be considered.

The ideal use of overtime is when employees are willing to work longer hours for increased pay, and the employer needs qualified, trained individuals who will not need excessive supervision while tackling an increased work load.

A serious drawback to be considered in the use of overtime is the effect it has on employees' regular production. Increased work hours during one period may lead to increased **absenteeism** during others, due to family commitments that were put off during ''crunch'' periods or to illness exacerbated by stress. Also, a lull in productivity sometimes occurs after periods of overtime, a result of employee burn-out.

All overtime should be authorized by a manager or supervisor, preferably in writing. Consideration should be given to tracking the work accomplished during overtime hours; this ensures that employees are continuing to be productive at the increased pay rate, even with the stress of longer hours and increased sales or other pressures. Tracking what work is done on overtime will also aid the owner or manager of a business to better plan for staffing needs in the future.

ALTERNATIVES TO OVERTIME Because overtime can become very expensive, and can sometimes be draining for regular employees, a business owner or manager may consider alternate plans of human resource management.

The first determination to be made is whether the amount of overtime used throughout the year is enough to justify the hiring of additional staff. This step should be very carefully considered, however, because while overtime is expensive, so are the hidden costs (payroll taxes, social security, benefits) associated with hiring additional employees.

If the overtime is strictly occasional, though, one alternative is hiring temporary workers. This can be done independently by the owner or manager, or through a temporary employment agency. Depending on the task (and how much training and supervision is required) the temporary employee can save businesses significant overtime expenses. This alternative can be particularly attractive if increased staffing needs are seasonal and predictable, so that temporary employees can be hired in advance.

EMPLOYEE REACTIONS TO OVERTIME Many employees welcome the opportunity to augment their regular salaries with overtime pay. Some businesses can effectively use overtime as a kind of voluntary bonus: if the employees are willing to put in the added hours, they will be rewarded with increased pay. Because of the strong positive feelings many employees have about the opportunity to earn overtime pay, employers should carefully weigh the pros and cons of hiring temporary help; regular employees will recognize the loss of overtime, and morale may suffer, particularly if overtime has become an integral part of the business cycle.

But the feeling in the business world is that many employees are placing ever greater value on leisure/ family time, even if that means making some sacrifices in the realm of compensation. In addition, analysts point out that families that have both parents in the work force may not value overtime as much as employees of the past. Employers should remain sensitive to employees' needs and responsibilities outside of the workplace, and should recognize that employees may not always be willing to volunteer for overtime.

FURTHER READING:

Boyett, Joseph H., and Henry P. Conn. *Workplace 2000.* New York: Penguin, 1991.

Employees: How to Find and Pay Them. U.S. Small Business Administration, n.a.

Mitchell, Daniel J. B., *Human Resource Management.* PWS-Kent, 1989.

Moeller, Karin, ''Paying for Keeps.'' *Entrepreneur Online*, n.a.

Weiss, Donald H. *Fair, Square, and Legal: Safe Hiring, Managing & Firing Practices to Keep You & Your Company Out of Court.* New York: AMACOM, 1991.

SEE ALSO: Employee Compensation

P

Packaging refers to the container or wrapper that holds a product or group of products. Most commercial packaging serves two basic functions: protecting the product from damage during shipping, and promoting the product to the ultimate consumer. Some common types of packaging include shipping cartons, containers for industrial goods, and bags, boxes, cans, and other holders for consumer products. Packaging is of great importance to both sellers and buyers of products. It can prevent spoiling, breakage, tampering, or theft; enhance convenience in use or storage; and make products easier to identify. A significant improvement in packaging can even create a ''new'' product by expanding the ways in which it can be used, and thus its potential markets. For example, a soup that is packaged in a microwavable bowl might suddenly increase its sales to working people.

Good package design can be particularly important for small businesses. In fact, packaging sometimes gives a product more **sales promotion** than its producer could afford through advertising. Since many potential customers first notice a new product after it has arrived on the shelves of a store, it is vital that the packaging provide consumers with the information they need and motivate them to make a purchase. But packaging decisions involve a number of tradeoffs. While making a product visible and distinctive may be the top priority, for example, small businesses must also comply with a variety of laws regarding product labeling and safety. Protecting products during transport is important, but small businesses also need to keep their shipping costs as low as possi-

ble. The following provides an overview of some of the factors to consider in packaging products for consumer markets.

BACKGROUND

Before World War II, packaging was used primarily to surround and protect products during storage, transportation, and distribution. Some packages were designed with aesthetic appeal and even for ease-of-use by the end consumer, but package design was typically left to technicians. After World War II, however, companies became more interested in marketing and promotion as a means of enticing customers to purchase their products. As a result, more manufacturers began to view packaging as a way to lure buyers.

During the mid-1900s, several influences combined to turn packaging into an integral part of most companies' marketing mix. Consumers became better educated, and their wealth and expectations generally increased. Consequently, consumers began to rely much more heavily on manufactured goods and processed food items. New technologies related to production, distribution, and preservatives led to a massive proliferation in the number and type of products and brands available in industrialized nations. Thus, packaging became a vital means of differentiating items and informing inundated consumers.

The importance of consumer packaging was elevated in the United States during the late 1970s and 1980s. Rapid post-war economic expansion and market growth waned during that period, forcing companies to focus increasingly on luring consumers to their product or brand at the expense of the competition. Package design became a marketing science. And, as a new corporate cost-consciousness developed in response to increased competition, companies began to alter packaging techniques as a way to cut production, storage, and distribution expenses. Furthermore, marketers began to view packaging as a tool to exploit existing product lines by adding new items and to pump new life into maturing products.

PACKAGE DESIGN

Consumer packaging serves to contain and communicate. A product's "packaging mix" is the result of several requirements that determine how a package accomplishes those two basic functions. Robert D. Hisrich identified eight major package requirements that dictate the mix. A package must: protect the product, be adaptable to production-line speeds, promote or sell the item, increase the product's density, help the consumer use the product, provide reusable value to the user, satisfy legal requirements, and keep packaging-related expenses low. Two classes of package design criteria are functional requirements and sales requirements.

FUNCTIONAL REQUIREMENTS Package design must meet five groups of functional criteria: in-home, in-store (or warehouse), production, distribution and safety, and legal. In-home requirements usually dictate that packaging be easy to use and store, remind users when and what to repurchase, reinforce consumers' expectations of the product, and tell them how to safely and effectively use the product. In addition, increasing numbers of consumers expect packaging to be recyclable and environmentally sensitive.

In-store criteria require that packaging attract attention on the shelf, instill confidence in the buyer, identify the product or brand and differentiate it from the competition, communicate benefits and uses, and entice customers to actually purchase the item. The product must also be easy for retailers to store and stock on the shelves or the floor, and simple to process at a check-out counter or other final point of distribution. For instance, packaging that is oddly shaped and takes up a large amount of space may draw attention, but it may also be shunned by mail-order sellers concerned about shipping costs or by space-conscious store retailers.

Production demands, the third group of functional criteria influencing packaging, are primarily based on cost. A designer may create a fantastic package that would perform excellently in the marketplace, but if the company cannot find a way to produce the package cost-effectively, the design is useless. Among the most important considerations is production line speed. If a container is too long, wide, or short, it could significantly slow the speed of the production machines. Or, if the top or spout of a container is too small or is oddly shaped, the product may not flow easily into the package.

Packaging considerations related to distribution and safety are important and numerous. If an unacceptable portion of the goods are damaged during storage, **transportation**, or distribution, the package has failed. Likewise, if the package injures the user, future sales could be lost or the company could be liable for damages. As a result, packaging engineers face numerous technical considerations that have a residual impact on the final look and feel of the package. For instance, packages must be able to withstand the pressure of several other crates stored on top of them. They must also be able to resist moisture, adapt to temperature changes, and withstand rough handling. From a cost standpoint, packages must also be designed to suit standardized transportation requirements related to weight, size, and durability.

Furthermore, packages should ideally be designed to handle normal use by consumers. For example, a vegetable oil container must be able to fall from a counter without breaking and to have very warm oil poured back into it without melting. Examples of packages that may result in harm to consumers include: those with sharp edges, such as some pull-top canisters; glass containers that hold products made for use in the shower, which could cause serious injury if dropped; and heavy item boxes which might break when the consumer is carrying them or cause strain or injury to the consumer when picked up or set down.

The fifth basic group of functional packaging requirements relate to laws and legislation. Various federal laws have been passed to protect consumers from misrepresentation and unsafe products. For instance, some laws require that potentially dangerous goods, such as gasoline or drugs, be stored in specially constructed containers. Other laws forbid producers from misrepresenting the quality or quantity of a product through misleading packaging. Perhaps the most influential class of laws that affect packaging, however, is that related to labeling.

PRODUCT LABELING The label is the text printed on a product package or, in the case of items like clothing, attached to the product itself. Legally, labels include all written, printed, or graphic material on the containers of products that are involved in interstate commerce or held for sale. The main body of legislation governing packaging and labeling is the Fair Packaging and Labeling Act of 1966. It mandates that every product package or label specify on its "principal display label" (the part of the label most likely to be seen by consumers) the following information: 1) the product type; 2) the producer or processor's name and location; 3) the quantity (if applicable); and 4) the number and size of servings (if applicable). Furthermore, several restrictions apply to the way that the label is displayed. For example, mandatory copy required by the act must be in boldface type. Also, if the company is not listed in the telephone book, the manufacturer's or importer's street address must be displayed.

Other information required by the act relates to specific foods, toys, drugs, cosmetics, furs, and textiles. For instance, under the act, labels for edible products must provide sodium content if other nutritional information is shown. They must also show ingredients, in descending order from the one of highest quantity to the one of least quantity. Certain food items, such as beef, may also be required to display qualitative ''grade labels'' or inspection labels. Likewise, ''informative labeling'' may be required for products such as home appliances. Informative label requirements mandate information about use, care, performance capability, life expectancy, safety precautions, gas mileage, or other factors. Certain major home appliances, for example, must provide the estimated cost of running each make and model for one year at average utility rates.

Congress passed significant new labeling legislation, the Nutrition Labeling and Education Act of 1990, that became effective in the mid-1990s. This act is intended primarily to discourage misleading labeling related to health benefits of food items. Specifically, many package labels subjectively claimed that their contents were ''low-fat,'' ''high-fiber,'' or possessed some other health virtue when the facts indicated otherwise. Basically, the new laws require most food labels to specify values such as calorie and cholesterol content, fat and saturated fat percentages, and sodium levels.

SALES REQUIREMENTS In additional to functional requirements, product packaging must be designed in a way that will appeal to buyers. The four principal merchandising requirement areas are: apparent size, attention drawing power, impression of quality, and brand-name readability.

Apparent size entails designing packaging to look as large as possible without misrepresenting the actual contents. This objective can be achieved by ensuring that the panels or dimensions of the package most likely to be viewed by the consumer are the largest, and that the product or brand name is shown on the most visible areas in large letters. In addition, the package can be made to look larger by using solid colors and simple, bold designs free of borders, superfluous art work, and unnecessary print. The pretense of largeness is particularly important for packages containing commodity items, such as rice, driveway salt, and canned fruit or vegetables.

Attention drawing power refers to the aesthetics and obtrusiveness of the package design. Depending on the product and the goals of the marketers, the package may be made to appear attractive, exciting, pure, soft, sexy, scary, intriguing, or to evoke some other emotion. In most cases, though, the product is displayed on the front of the package in the form of a picture, art, or see-through window. In addition, bright colors, glossy stock, obtrusive carton displays, and other elements can garner positive attention if used prudently.

A quality impression is an important sales requirement for packaging because items that are perceived to be of low quality are usually assumed to be a poor value, regardless of price. Examples of packaging mistakes that convey low quality or poor value include: faded lettering or colors, tacky designs or strange typeface, outdated pictures and designs, and cheap construction.

Readability, the fourth basic sales requirement for successful package design, means that the package must be extremely simple and easy to read. This is of paramount importance for products like breakfast cereal that are shelved next to several competing brands and products. If the package attempts to convey too many messages, it will likely fail to connect with the consumer. Because of the mass of buying choices, buyers typically do not take time to absorb messages on packaging, with the possible exception of high-priced specialty items. Among other guidelines, letters or logos should be large and printed in the same type style as that used in complementary print and television advertising. The requirement of readability contributes to the difficulty in packaging completely new products.

PACKAGING STRATEGY

One of the most critical roles for packaging is promoting products. Indeed, just as ease-of-use and readability are elements of the strategic packaging mix, packaging is an important part of a company's strategic marketing mix. Most packages for consumer products are designed for one of three purposes: 1) to improve the packaging of an existing product; 2) to add a new product to an existing product line; or 3) to contain an entirely new product.

Redesign of packaging for existing products may be prompted by several factors. Many times, a company may simply want to breathe new life into a maturing product by updating its image or adding a new feature to the package, such as an easy-pour spout. Or, a company may redesign the package to respond to a competitive threat, such as a new product that is more visible on the shelf. Other strategic reasons for package redesign are: changes in the product; economics, which may require less or more expensive packaging; product line restructuring; alterations in market strategy, such as aiming the product at a different age group; trying to promote new uses for a product; or legal or environmental factors that lead to new materials or technology. Even small packaging changes for established brands and products typically require careful consideration, since a great deal of money is often at risk if a company alienates or confuses customers.

A second reason for package design is to extend a product or brand line. An example of a product line extension is the Tide detergent brand line, which was extended to include Tide Free, a detergent without dyes or perfumes. In the case of product extensions, the packaging strategy is usually to closely mimic the established brand or product, but to integrate the benefits of the new feature into the existing package in such a way that customers will be able to easily differentiate it from other products in the line. The chief risks inherent in packaging for extensions are that the new package will confuse customers or frustrate retailers.

The third impetus for package design is the need to generate housing for an entirely new product. This is the most difficult type of packaging to create because it often requires the designer to instill consumer confidence in an unknown product or brand, and to inform the buyer about the product's uses and benefits. Packaging for products and brands that are entirely new to the marketplace require the most education, and are therefore the most challenging to develop. In contrast, packaging for goods that are entering established product categories require less education, but they must overcome established competition. A common packaging strategy for such products entails mimicking the packaging of leading products, which helps to assure the buyer that the product is "normal."

FURTHER READING:

Boyd, Harper W., Jr., and Orville C. Walker, Jr. *Marketing Management: A Strategic Approach.* Irwin, 1990.

Hisrich, Robert D. *Marketing.* Barron's Business Library, 1990.

Lusch, Robert F., and Virginia N. Lusch. *Principles of Marketing.* Kent, 1987.

McCarthy, E. Jerome, and William D. Perreault, Jr. *Basic Marketing.* Irwin, 1990.

Schoell, William F., and Joseph P. Guiltinan. *Marketing: Contemporary Concepts and Practices.* 5th ed. Needham, MA: Allyn and Bacon, 1992.

SEE ALSO: Brands and Brand Names; Marketing; Product Liability

PARTNERSHIPS

In the words of the Uniform Partnership Act, a partnership is "an association of two or more persons to carry on as Co-owners a business for profit." The essential characteristics of this business form, then, are the collaboration of two or more owners, the conduct of business for profit (a nonprofit cannot be designated as a partnership), and the sharing of profits, losses, and assets by the joint owners. A partnership is not a corporate or separate entity; rather it is viewed as an extension of its owners for legal and tax purposes, although a partnership may own property as a legal entity. While a partnership may be founded on a simple agreement, even a handshake between owners, a well-crafted and carefully worded partnership agreement is the best way to begin the business. In the absence of such an agreement, the Uniform Partnership Act, a set of laws pertaining to partnerships that has been adopted by most states, would govern the business.

There are two types of partnerships:

GENERAL PARTNERSHIPS In a general partnership, all of the partners are equally responsible for the business's debts and liabilities. In addition, all partners are allowed to be involved in the management of the company. In fact, in the absence of a statement to the contrary in the partnership agreement, each partner has equal rights to control and manage the business. Therefore, unanimous consent of the partners is required for all major actions undertaken. Be advised, though, that any obligation made by one partner is legally binding on all partners, whether or not they have been informed.

LIMITED PARTNERSHIPS In a limited partnership, one or more partners are general partners, and one or more are limited partners. General partners are personally liable for the business's debts and judgments against the business; they can also be directly involved in the management. Limited partners are essentially investors (silent partners, so to speak) who are not allowed to participate in the company's management and who are also not liable beyond their investment in the business. State laws determine how involved limited partners can be in the day-to-day business of the firm without jeopardizing their limited liability. This business form is especially attractive to real estate investors, who benefit from the tax incentives available to limited partners, such as being able to write off depreciating values.

ADVANTAGES OF FORMING A PARTNERSHIP

COLLABORATION As compared to a **sole proprietorship**, which is essentially the same business form but with only one owner, a partnership offers the advantage of allowing the owners to draw on the resources and expertise of the co-partners. Running a business on your own, while simpler, can also be a constant struggle. But with partners to share the responsibilities and lighten the workload, members of a partnership often find that they have more time for the other activities in their lives.

TAXATION The profits of a partnership pass through to its owners, who report their share on their individual tax returns. Therefore, the profits are only taxed once (at the personal level of its owners) rather than twice, as is the case with corporations, which are taxed at the corporate level and then again at the personal level when dividends are distributed to the shareholders. The benefits of single taxation can also be secured by forming an **S corporation** (although some ownership restrictions apply) or by forming a **limited liability company** (a new hybrid of corporations and partnerships that is still evolving).

EASY AND INEXPENSIVE A partnership, as opposed to a corporation, is fairly simple to establish and run. No forms need to be filed or formal agreements drafted (although it is advisable to write a partnership agreement in the event of future disagreements). The most that is ever required is perhaps filing a partnership certificate with a state office in order to register the business's name and securing a business license. As a result, the annual filing fees for corporations, which can sometimes be very expensive, are avoided when forming a partnership.

FLEXIBILITY OF MANAGEMENT Because the owners of a partnership are usually its managers, especially in the case of a small business, the company is fairly easy to manage, and decisions can be made quickly without a lot of bureaucracy. This is not the case with corporations, which must have shareholders, directors, and officers, all of whom have some degree of responsibility for making major decisions.

UNIFORM LAWS One of the drawbacks of owning a corporation or limited liability company is that the laws governing those business entities vary from state to state and are changing all the time. In contrast, the Uniform Partnership Act provides a consistent set of laws about forming and running partnerships that make it easy for small business owners to know the laws that affect them. And because these laws have been adopted in all states but Louisiana, interstate business is much easier for partnerships than it is for other forms of businesses.

EASE OF ACQUIRING CAPITAL Partnerships generally have an easier time acquiring capital than corporations because partners, who apply for loans as individuals, can usually get loans on better terms. This is because partners guarantee loans with their personal assets as well as those of the business. As a result, loans for a partnership are subject to state usury laws, which govern loans for individuals. Banks also perceive partners to be less of a risk than corporations, which are only required to pledge the business's as-

sets. In addition, by forming a limited partnership, the business can attract investors (who will not be actively involved in its management and who will enjoy limited liability) without having to form a corporation and sell stock.

DRAWBACKS OF FORMING A PARTNERSHIP

CONFLICT WITH PARTNERS While collaborating with partners can be a great advantage to a small business owner, having to actually run a business from day to day with one or more partners can be a nightmare. First of all, you have to give up absolute control of the business and learn to compromise. And when big decisions have to be made, such as whether and how to expand the business, partners often disagree on the best course and are left with a potentially explosive situation. The best way to deal with such predicaments is to anticipate them by drawing up a partnership agreement that details how such disagreements will be dealt with.

AUTHORITY OF PARTNERS When one partner signs a contract, each of the other partners is legally bound to fulfill it. For example, if Anthony orders $10,000 of computer equipment, it is as if his partners, Susan and Jacob, had also placed the order. And if their business cannot afford to pay the bill, then the personal assets of Susan and Jacob are on the line as well as those of Anthony. And this is true whether the other partners are aware of the contract or not. Even if a clause in the partnership agreement dictates that each partner must inform the other partners before any such deals are made, all of the partners are still responsible if the other party in the contract (the computer company) was not aware of such a stipulation in the partnership agreement. The only recourse the other partners have is to sue.

The Uniform Partnership Act does specify some instances in which full consent of all partners is required:

- Selling the business's **goodwill**;
- Decisions that would compromise the business's ability to function normally;
- Assign partnership property in trust for a creditor or to someone in exchange for the payment of the partnership's debts;
- Admission of liability in a lawsuit;
- Submission of a partnership claim or liability to arbitration.

UNLIMITED LIABILITY As the previous example illustrated, the personal assets of the partnership's members are vulnerable because there is no separation between the owners and the business. The primary reason many businesses choose to incorporate or form limited liability companies is to protect the owners from the unlimited liability that is the main drawback of partnerships or sole proprietorships. If an employee or customer is injured and decides to sue, or if the business runs up excessive debts, then the partners are personally responsible and in danger of losing all that they own. Therefore, if considering a partnership, determine your assets that will be put at risk. If you possess substantial personal assets that you will not invest in the company and do not want to put in jeopardy, a corporation or limited liability company may be a better choice. But if you are investing most of what you own in the business, then you don't stand to lose any more than if you incorporated. Then if your business is successful, and you find at a later date that you now possess extensive personal assets that you would like to protect, you can consider changing the legal status of your business to secure limited liability.

INSTABILITY OF BUSINESS Unlike corporations, which exist perpetually, regardless of ownership, general partnerships dissolve if one of the partners dies, retires, or withdraws. (In limited partnerships, the death or withdrawal of the limited partner does not affect the stability of the business.) Even though this is the law governing partnerships, the partnership agreement can contain provisions to continue the business. For example, a provision can be made allowing a buy out of a partner's share if he or she wants to withdraw or if the partner dies.

LIMITATIONS ON TRANSFER OF OWNERSHIP Unlike corporations, which exist independently of their owners, the existence of partnerships is dependent upon the owners. Therefore, the Uniform Partnership Act stipulates that ownership may not be transferred without the consent of all the other partners. (Once again, a limited partner is an exception: his or her interest in the company may be sold at will.)

CHOOSING A PARTNER

Because of the need for compromise and the dynamics of shared authority that come along with sharing a business, partnerships can be very difficult to maintain and run efficiently. Therefore, the single most important decision a small business owner has to make when forming a partnership is the choice of a partner. In fact, warns Edward A. Haman in *How to Write Your Own Partnership Agreement*, "you should only take on a partner if you absolutely need that person's money or expertise." As an alternative, he advises, you could try to "get the money as a loan, or hire the person as a consultant to get the expertise." But if you decide that forming a partnership is the best choice, consider the following when selecting a partner (anyone may become a partner, except minors and corporations):

ASSETS

- How much does your partner own in personal assets? If you own much more than your partner, then creditors will come after you in the event of extensive debts.

PERSONALITY

- Do you possess compatible personality types?

- How do you each deal with stress?

- How do you make decisions? Does your prospective partner tend to talk things through with others or make impulse decisions?

ROLES

- What role do each of you intend to take in the business? Are these roles compatible? Do you both hope to be in charge of the accounts or dealing with vendors, for example? Or can you split up the duties in a way that satisfies both of you?

SHARING RESPONSIBILITIES

- How much time will your partner contribute to the enterprise?

- Can you count on you partner to show up to work on time? Or you will be expected to cover for him?

- Is your prospective partner a hard worker, or will he or she routinely leave tasks for you to complete?

GOALS FOR THE BUSINESS

- How do each of you envision the future of the business? Do you hope to build up a solid business and then expand to other locations? Does your partner share that vision or does he or she hope only to be able to make a decent living out of one business with fewer responsibilities than would be required if running a chain of stores?

FORMING A PARTNERSHIP

RESERVING A NAME The first step in creating a partnership is reserving a name, which must be done with the secretary of state's office or its equivalent. Most states require that the words "Company" or "Associates" be included in the name to show that more than one partner is involved in the business. In all states, though, the name of the partnership must not resemble the name of any other corporation, limited liability company, partnership, or sole proprietorship that is registered with the state.

THE PARTNERSHIP AGREEMENT A partnership can be formed in essentially two ways: by verbal or written agreement. A partnership that is formed at will, or verbally, can also be dissolved at will. In the absence of a formal agreement, state laws (the Uniform Partnership Act, except in Louisiana) will govern the business. These laws specify that without an agreement, all partners share equally in the profits and losses of the partnership and that partners are not entitled to compensation for services. If you would like to structure your partnership differently, you will need to write a **partnership agreement**.

It may be advisable to consult a lawyer before drafting the agreement, but you should at least research the issue on your own. A thorough partnership agreement should generally cover the following areas:

- Name and address

- Duration of partnership—You can specify a finite date on which all business will terminate or you can include a general clause that explains the partnership will exist until all partners agree to dissolve it or a partner dies.

- Purpose of business.

- Partners' contributions—These may be in cash, property or services. Be sure to determine the value of all non-cash contributions.

- Partners' compensation—Determine how profits will be split up and how often. Also decide if any of the partners will receive a salary.

- Management Authority—Will partners be able to make some decisions on their own? Which decisions will require the unanimous consent of all partners?

- Work hours and vacation.

- Kinds of outside business activities that will be allowed for partners

- Partner withdrawal—Decide how the retirement, withdrawal, disability, or death of a partner will be handled through a buy-sell agreement. Also determine whether or not a partner who has simply withdrawn will be allowed to operate a competing business.

- Disposition of the partnership's name if a partner leaves.

- How to handle disputes—Decide whether or not mediation or arbitration will be provided for in the case of disputes that cannot be resolved amongst the partners. This is a way to avoid costly litigation.

RIGHTS AND RESPONSIBILITIES OF PARTNERS

The Uniform Partnership Act defines the basic rights and responsibilities of partners. Some of these can be changed by the partnership agreement, except, as a general rule, those laws that govern the partners' relationships with third parties. In the absence of a written agreement, then, the following rights and responsibilities apply:

RIGHTS

- All partners have an equal share in the profits of the partnership and are equally responsible for its losses.

- Any partner who makes a payment for the partnership beyond its capital, or makes a loan to the partnership, is entitled to receive interest on that money.

- All partners have equal property rights for property held in the partnership's name. This means that the use of the property is equally available to all partners for the purpose of the partnership's business.

- All partners have an equal interest in the partnership, or share of its profits and assets.

- All partners have an equal right in the management and conduct of the business.

- All partners have a right to access the books and records of the partnership's accounts and activities at all times. (This does not apply to limited partners.)

- No partner may be added without the consent of all other partners.

RESPONSIBILITIES Partners must report and turn over to the partnership any income they have derived from use of the partnership's property.

- Partners are not allowed to conduct business that competes with the partnership.

- Each partner is responsible for contributing his or her full time and energy to the success of the partnership.

- Any property that a partner acquires with the intention of it being the partnership's property must be turned over to the partnership.

- Any disputes shall be decided by a majority vote.

FURTHER READING:

Burton, Kermit. *The Non-Lawyers Partnership Kit.* Medina, OH: Alpha Publications, 1992.

Clifford, Denis. *The Partnership Book: How to Write a Partnership Agreement.* 5th ed. Berkely, CA: Nolo Press, 1997.

PARTNERSHIP AGREEMENTS

Edwards, Paul. *Teaming Up: The Small-Business Guide to Collaborating with Others to Boost Your Earnings and Expand Your Horizons.* G.P. Putnam's Sons, 1997.

Haman, Edward A. *How to Write Your Own Partnership Agreement.* Clearwater, FL: Sphinx Publishing, 1993.

Handmaker, Stuart A. *Choosing a Legal Structure for Your Business.* Upper Saddle River, NJ: Prentice Hall, 1997.

Selecting the Legal Structure for Your Business. Washington: U.S. Small Business Administration. n.a.

Steingold, Fred S. *The Legal Guide for Starting and Running a Small Business.* Second Edition. Berkeley, CA: Nolo Press, 1995.

PARTNERSHIP AGREEMENTS

Partnership agreements are written documents that explicitly detail the relationship between the business partners, as well as their individual obligations and contributions to the **partnership**. Since partnership agreements should cover all possible business situations that could arise during the life of the partnership, the documents are often complex, and legal counsel in drafting and reviewing the finished contract is generally recommended. If a partnership does not have a partnership agreement in place when it dissolves, the guidelines of the Uniform Partnership Act and various state laws will determine how the assets and debts of the partnership are distributed.

RECOMMENDED ELEMENTS OF THE PARTNERSHIP AGREEMENT

1) Name and address of partnership.

2) Duration of partnership—Partners can point to a specific termination date or include a general clause explaining that the partnership will exist until all partners agree to dissolve it or a partner dies.

3) Business purpose—Some consultants recommend that partners keep this section somewhat vague in case opportunities for expansion arise, while others, such as *Legal Handbook for Small Business* author Marc J. Lane, feel otherwise: "Avoid any conflict in entrepreneurial goals. Since a general partnership obligates you for the business acts and omissions of your copartners, it is wise to limit the scope of your business activities by contract."

4) Bank account information—This section should note which bank accounts are to be used for partnership purposes, and which partners have check-signing privileges.

5) Partners' contributions—Valuation of all contributions, whether in cash, property or services.

6) Partners' compensation—Determine how and when profits (and salaries, if applicable) will be distributed. "Spell out the profit-and-loss split in detail," counseled Lane, "as well as any rights to distributions. Beyond living expenses and personal tax liabilities, you may want to limit both income distributions and capital withdrawals and let the partnership use its money to grow."

7) Management authority—What are the operational responsibilities of each partner? Will partners be able to make some decisions on their own? Which decisions will require the unanimous consent of all partners? What are the voting rights of each partner? How will tie votes be resolved?

8) Circumstances under which new partners might be admitted into the partnership.

9) Work hours and vacation.

10) Kinds of outside business activities that will be allowed for partners.

11) Disposition of partnership's name if a partner leaves.

12) Dispute resolution—Stipulates what kinds mediation or arbitration will be utilized in the case of disputes that cannot be resolved amongst the partners. This is a way to avoid costly litigation.

13) Miscellaneous provisions—This portion of the agreement might delineate the circumstances under which the agreement could be amended, for example.

14) Buy-Sell Agreement.

THE BUY-SELL AGREEMENT The buy-sell agreement is one of the most important elements of any partnership agreement. It details what will happen to the partnership if one of its partners leave the business. In essence, it specifies the terms of a buyout in the event of death, divorce, disability, or retirement. "Having a buy/sell agreement in place makes a great deal of difference," commented Mary Rowland in *Nation's Business,* "to guarantee the smooth transition of a business and ensure that it need not be sold at an inopportune time." Indeed, the importance of this particular element of the partnership agreement is underlined by the fact that in recent years, loan institutions, companies that provide bonding for construction jobs, and other outside firms have begun to insist that small business clients have buy/sell agreements in place.

The two primary structures for buy/sell agreements are cross purchase agreements, in which the remaining partnership owners buy the departing partner's stock or partnership interest, and the stock redemption agreement, in which the company buys the stock of the departing owner. The advantage of the cross purchase agreement, wrote Rowland, is that ''the purchasers get a tax saving 'step up' in basis to the market value of that portion of the business. . . . With a cross purchase agreement, the owners typically buy life insurance policies on one another to finance the agreement. If there are just two owners, it's pretty straightforward,'' but with multiple shareholders, this arrangement can get confusing and expensive.

With stock redemption agreements, on the other hand, ''the company would own the life insurance policy and pay the premiums,'' said Rowland. ''An advantage to this type of agreement is that if there are a number of owners, only one policy on each is necessary.'' Disadvantages of this type of buy/sell agreement include absence of 'step up' savings and the fact that in cases where the life insurance used to finance the redemption agreement is owned by a business structured as a C Corporation, the company might be liable for the alternative minimum tax (AMT) on any proceeds.

FURTHER READING:

Jasper, Margaret C. *Law for the Small Business Owner.* Dobbs Ferry, NY: Oceana Publications, 1994.

Lane, Marc J. *Legal Handbook for Small Business.* Rev. ed. New York: Amacom, 1989.

Rowland, Mary. ''The Importance of Buy/Sell Agreements.'' *Nation's Business.* March 1995.

Shapiro, Mort. ''Get It in Writing.'' *CA Magazine.* August 1996.

Williford, Jerry S., and Robin L. Imrie. ''The Accountant's Role in Preparing and Amending Partnership or LLC Agreements.'' *Journal of Partnership Taxation.* Summer 1996.

PART-TIME BUSINESS

Thousands of American entrepreneurs supplement their income by starting and maintaining part-time small businesses. The circumstances and goals of these business owners run the gamut, but many are operated out of the home and are utilized to supplement income derived from other sources (a full-time job, retirement benefits, etc.).

As Thomas Amirault observed in *Occupational Outlook Quarterly,* people often establish part-time enterprises out of economic necessity. But statistics also indicate that many individuals—and especially people with higher levels of education—launch part-time entrepreneurial ventures to make use of skills that may not be tapped in their full-time work. Finally, the ability and desire to launch a business on a part-time basis is often impacted by family considerations; in some instances, the cost of raising children may serve as an incentive to start a business on the side, but in other cases, a parent may decide that the hours involved in looking after his or her children precludes the possibility of a part-time business.

Many owners of part-time businesses, however, contend that if the desire is there, a part-time venture can be managed by most people. ''Fact is, even if you have a full-time job, you probably have more spare hours at your disposal than you realize,'' wrote Greg Daugherty in *Writer's Digest.* ''Say you work 40 hours a week and spend another ten hours commuting. That's just 50 hours out of the 168 hours in any seven-day week. You've still got another 118 hours to do with as you please.''

Part-time businesses are also regarded by many entrepreneurs as a sensible option in situations where the ultimate success of the venture seems unclear. ''Part-time entrepreneurs can . . . limit their risks compared with those taken by individuals who plunge in full-time,'' wrote David E. Gumpert in *Working Woman.* ''For one thing, part-timers don't have the same pressure to produce cash flow, because they can hold down a job at the same time and operate out of their homes. For another, part-timers can go more slowly and learn the skills of running a business as they go along; they have the luxury of making errors and revising their business concept as they proceed.''

BALANCING OBLIGATIONS TO YOUR PART-TIME BUSINESS AND FULL-TIME EMPLOYER

It is vitally important for entrepreneurs who already have a full-time job to make sure that their part-time business does not interfere with their obligations to their employers. Moreover, it is important for part-time business owners to make sure that their employers do not begin to *perceive* that the side business is taking priority, for in the final analysis, your ability to meet the demands of both businesses is irrelevant if your employer begins to feel—fairly or not—that the arrangement is detracting from your job performance. For this reason, part-time business owners may want to weigh the likely reaction of their employer before even publicizing the existence of the part-time venture. Daugherty also noted that ''your employer may well have rules on outside work. . . . If you don't know, ask. And if you value your job, do your best to comply with them.''

Other factors can help an entrepreneur establish a part-time venture without unduly complicating regular job obligations, too. Gumpert noted, for example, that many successful part-time businesses share the following characteristics:

1) The very nature of the business lends itself to part-time, home-based work. "Service businesses often allow for this kind of flexibility," wrote Gumpert. "Men have for years carved out entrepreneurial opportunities as part-time plumbers, electricians, and carpenters. Women [are] discovering similar opportunities in such areas as consulting and teaching." Retail stores and manufacturing establishments, however, are far less conducive to part-time businesses.

2) The individual's full-time job is flexible enough to give him or her to take care of the entrepreneurial business's needs during normal business hours (9 a.m. to 5 p.m.). "Your full-time job should allow for development of the part-time business—for instance, by offering contacts and flexible hours and responsibilities. . . . Ideally, the job itself provides the basis for the new business."

OTHER KEYS TO PART-TIME SUCCESS Some customers, especially if they are other businesses, may be wary of contracting with part-timers. As Daugherty indicated, "the mere fact that you're a part-timer will sometimes be held against you." The most effective way to counter the perception held in some quarters that part-time business owners are less reliable and responsive (because of obligations to their full-time employer) than full-time entrepreneurs, according to Daugherty and others, is simply to not advertise your part-time status. Of course, you should also not lie about it if the issue comes up.

Entrepreneurs launching part-time business ventures should also be very wary of overextending themselves. Many individuals tend to take on more part-time work than they can easily handle, especially during the first few months of operation, when they have less experience in estimating the time involved in executing various tasks. While finances are often a factor in establishing a part-time business, most part-time entrepreneurs do not begin a venture with the expressed intention of turning their life into a chaotic rush of impending deadlines. Complications associated with underestimating the amount of time a given project or assignment will take are also typically compounded if the entrepreneur in question has significant family obligations (child or elder care, for instance).

Small business researchers also note that some of the most successful part-time businesses are those that were formerly full-time endeavors. Indeed, many full-time entrepreneurs choose to scale back their hours after a certain number of years. They may do this for any number of reasons; some simply reach retirement age and wish to relax a little more, others decide to start a family, and still others may decide that they wish to spend more of their time traveling or indulging other interests (including other promising entrepreneurial ventures). In many instances, switching a business from full-time status to part-time status can actually strengthen the enterprise's hourly productivity. For example, the entrepreneur who decides to turn his 50-hours-a-week venture into one that requires him to spend half that amount of time on the business each week will naturally do his best to maintain relations with his best clients, while letting less valuable or more problematic clients go. As many business owners will quickly attest, having greater freedom to pick and choose who you do business with can be a most valuable side benefit of going part-time.

LEGAL AND TAX CONSIDERATIONS

Owners of part-time businesses should also consider the potential legal and tax ramifications of their activities. "Taxes may be one of the last things anyone thinks about when starting a part-time business, but they out to be high on the priority list for anyone who is serious about making money in a part-time venture," said *Los Angeles Business Journal* contributor Bob Howard. "Additional income from a part-time business means additional taxes, but those who wait until the end of the year may wind up paying penalties or not being able to take deductions they had counted on." Part-time business owners should thus consider doing one of the following: 1) have their regular employers take out more withholding taxes, or 2) file quarterly estimated tax payments. Either approach can go far toward helping the part-time entrepreneur avoid tax penalties or a big end-of-the-year tax blow.

In addition, owners of part-time enterprises should make sure that they take full advantage of available tax deductions. Gumpert noted that "part-timers get the same tax advantages [as full-time entrepreneurs], including deductions for travel, entertainment, home office, and related expenses, plus deductible retirement plans." Howard noted, though, that home-based business tax deductions can vary significantly, often depending on whether the business is a full- or part-time venture. "The IRS now requires that a home office be used 'exclusively and regularly as a place of business to meet or deal with patients, clients, or customers' in the normal course of the business. The word 'exclusively' is very important because it means any room or space designated as a home office must be used 100 percent for business in order to qualify for the deduction."

FURTHER READING:

Adams, Bob. *Adams Streetwise Small Business Start-Up.* Holbrook, MA: Adams Media Corp., 1996.

Amirault, Thomas. "Multiple Jobholders: What Else Do I Want to Do When I Grow Up?" *Occupational Outlook Quarterly.* Winter 1996.

Attard, Janet. *The Home Office and Small Business Answer Book.* New York: Henry Holt, 1993.

Bowers, Brent. "Finding the Best Part-Time Job for You." *New Choices for Retirement Living.* November 1994.

Daugherty, Greg. "Part-Time Writing, Full-Time Success." *Writer's Digest.* July 1996.

Dunnan, Nancy. "The Part-Time Solution." *Parents Magazine.* May 1996.

Gumpert, David E. "Doing a Little Business on the Side: How Entrepreneurs Start Up a Business and Hold Down a Job." *Working Woman.* October 1986.

Howard, Bob. "Part-Time Business Income Can Cause Tax Trouble for Wage Earners." *Los Angeles Business Journal.* December 23, 1996.

"Nurturing Part-Timers to be Entrepreneurs." *Nation's Business.* March 1996.

Weinrauch, J. Donald. "Starting a Part-Time Small Business." *Journal of Small Business Management.* October 1982.

SEE ALSO: Career and Family; Home-based Business

PATENT AND TRADEMARK OFFICE

The Patent and Trademark Office (PTO) has, for the past 200 years, been responsible for administering all laws relating to trademarks and patents in the United States. It has thus been an important agency for several generations of entrepreneurs and small business owners, as well as for larger corporations and universities. The PTO describes itself thusly: "Through the issuance of patents, we encourage technological advancement by providing incentives to invent, invest in, and disclose new technology worldwide. Through the registration of trademarks, we assist businesses in protecting their investments, promoting goods and services and safeguarding consumers against confusion and deception in the marketplace. By disseminating both patent and trademark information, we promote an understanding of intellectual property protection and facilitate the developments and sharing of new technologies world wide."

In addition to handling the nation's patents and trademarks, the PTO also has a notable advisory function. It serves as both a developer of **intellectual property** policy and an advisor to the White House and the Department of Commerce on patent/trademark/copyright policies. In addition, the PTO provides information and guidance on intellectual property issues to international commerce offices such as the International Trade Commission and the Office of the U.S. Trade Representative.

By nearly all accounts, the PTO has historically done a laudable job of protecting the intellectual property rights of businesses and individuals while simultaneously encouraging the growth of business. "Since its inception, the patent system has encouraged the genius of millions of inventors," wrote *Inventor's Desktop Companion* author Richard C. Levy. "It has protected these creative individuals by allowing them an opportunity to profit from their labors, and has benefited society by systematically recording new inventions and releasing them to the public once the inventors' limited rights have expired. . . . Under the patent system, American industry has flourished. New products have been invented, new uses for old ones discovered, and employment given to millions."

LEGAL UNDERPINNINGS OF THE PTO

The fundamental principles of the modern American patent system were first codified into law in 1790. Guided by Secretary of State Thomas Jefferson in its early years, the patent office grew quickly, and in 1849 the Department of the Interior was given responsibility for maintaining it. In 1870 the powers of the patent office were expanded dramatically; the commissioner of patents was given jurisdiction to register and regulate trademarks. The office thus came to be responsible for all American trademarks, even though the word "trademark" would not appear in its name for another 105 years (the Patent Office became the Patent and Trademark Office on January 2, 1975). In 1926 responsibility for the Patent Office was handed over to the Department of Commerce, where it remains today.

The PTO currently touts the following laws as the primary statutory authorities guiding its programs:

- 15 U.S.C. 1051-1127—Contains provisions of the Trademark Act of 1946, a law that governs the office's trademark administration.

- 15 U.S.C. 1511—Establishes the PTO as a subordinate agency of the **U.S. Department of Commerce**.

- 35 U.S.C.—Provides the PTO with its basic authority to administrate patent laws.

- 44 U.S.C. 1337-1338—Gives the PTO authority to print trademarks, patents, and other material relevant to the business of the Office.

THE PTO IN THE 1990S

In 1991 the PTO underwent a significant change in operation. The Omnibus Budget Reconciliation Act (OBRA) of 1990 included provisions to make the Office a self-supporting government agency that would not receive federal funding. In order to provide the PTO with needed operating funds, Congress raised the PTO's patent application fees by 69 percent to cover operating costs and maintain services for inventors. This change was essential, given the huge volume of patent and trademark applications that pass through the PTO's doors every year (in 1994, for instance, the PTO received more than 200,000 patent applications).

By the mid-1990s, however, both Congressional leaders and the Clinton Administration were giving serious consideration to diverting much of the money brought in by the PTO to fund other government programs or balance the federal budget. If such proposals do occur, inventor groups and small business analysts contend that independent inventors and small business owners will bear the brunt of the blow. As Janean Chun indicated in *Entrepreneur,* many observers believe that such diversions ''will result in delays in patent approvals and an increase in the fees charged to maintain patents. . . . Industry insiders feel the PTO can scarcely afford to see that money dispersed.'' Indeed, leaders of such inventors' groups as the Inventors Awareness Group and the United Inventors Association of the USA contend that the PTO is actually in need of additional funding given the annual 10 percent growth in patent applications that the Office has seen in the 1990s.

FURTHER READING:

Chun, Janean. ''Patent Leather.'' *Entrepreneur.* June 1997.

Levy, Richard C. ''The Patent and Trademark Office.'' In *The Inventor's Desktop Companion.* Detroit, MI: Visible Ink, 1995.

SEE ALSO: Inventions and Patents; Trademarks and Copyrights

PAYROLL TAXES

Payroll taxes include a number of different taxes that must be withheld from wages by all businesses that have employees. Small businesses that employ persons other than the owner or partners are required to withhold payroll taxes from the wages paid to employees, remit these taxes to the **Internal Revenue Service (IRS)**, and make regularly scheduled reports to the IRS about the amount of payroll taxes owed and paid. Businesses are not required to withhold payroll taxes on wages paid to independent contractors. It is important to be aware of the distinctions between independent contractors and employees, however, because the penalties for misclassification can be severe.

Many small businesses fall behind in paying these taxes or filing the associated reports at some time during their existence. This is a very bad practice, however, because significant interest and penalties apply for late payment or nonpayment of payroll taxes. In fact, the Trust Fund Recovery Penalty allows the IRS to hold a small business owner or accountant personally liable for 100 percent of the amount owed, even in cases where the business has gone bankrupt.

TYPES OF PAYROLL TAXES

Three main types of taxes fall under the category of payroll taxes:

1) The regular income tax that must be withheld from employees' paychecks. Employees can adjust their income tax withholding by filing Form W-4 with their employer and designating the number of withholding allowances they wish to claim. Ideally, the total income tax withheld should come close to equaling their overall tax liability at the end of the year. By adjusting their withholding allowances properly, employees can avoid owing large amounts in taxes or providing the government with an interest-free loan.

2) Federal Insurance Contribution Act (FICA) taxes, which include contributions to federal Social Security and Medicare programs. Employers are required to withhold 7.65 percent of the first $62,700 of an employee's income for FICA taxes. Employers are also required to match that amount for every employee, so that the total FICA contribution is 15.3 percent. Self-employed persons are required to pay both the employer and employee portions of the FICA tax.

3) Federal Unemployment Tax (FUTA), which is approximately 1 percent of the first $7,000 in wages paid to an employee. This tax is paid in full by the employer.

PAYROLL TAX REMITTANCE AND REPORTING

In addition to withholding payroll taxes for employees, employers must remit these taxes to the IRS in a timely manner. The regular income taxes and the portion of the FICA taxes that are withheld from employees' wages each pay period must be remitted to the IRS monthly, along with a Federal Tax Deposit Coupon (Form 8109-B). If the total withheld is less than $500, however, the business is allowed to make the payments quarterly. In 1996, the IRS began requiring businesses that owed more than $47 million in payroll taxes annually to make their monthly payments via telephone or computer through the Electronic Federal Tax Payment System. The threshold for electronic filing was scheduled to drop to $50,000 in annual payroll taxes by January 1, 1997, but the deadline was pushed back to June 30, 1998. In addition, two bills were introduced in Congress that would make electronic payments of payroll taxes voluntary for small businesses with few employees.

Employers must also file four different reports regarding payroll taxes. The first report, Form 941, is the Employer's Quarterly Federal Tax Return. This report details the number of employees the business had, the amount of wages they were paid, and the amount of taxes that were withheld for the quarter. The other three reports are filed annually. Form W-2—the Annual Statement of Taxes Withheld—must be sent to all employees before January 31 of the following year. It details how much each employee received in wages and how much was withheld for taxes over the course of the year. Copies of the W-2 forms for all employees also must be sent to the Social Security Administration. The third report, Form W-3, must be sent to the IRS by February 28 of the following year. It provides a formal reconciliation of the quarterly tax payments made on Form 941 and the annual totals reported on Form W-2 for all employees. The final report is the Federal Unemployment Tax Return, Form 940, which outlines the total FUTA taxes owed and paid for the year.

Most states—as well as some large cities—have their own income tax that businesses must withhold from employees' wages and report to the appropriate authorities. States may also have other payroll taxes that must be collected from employees, as well as unemployment taxes that must be paid by the company. The payment schedules and reporting procedures for state and local payroll taxes are usually consistent with those applied to federal payroll taxes.

EXCEPTIONS TO PAYROLL TAX RULES

There are certain situations in which small businesses can avoid owing payroll taxes. For example, special rules apply to sole proprietorships and husband-and-wife partnerships that pay their minor (under 18) children for work performed in the business. These small businesses receive an exemption from withholding FICA taxes from their children's paychecks, and are also not required to pay the employer portion of the FICA taxes. In this way, the parent and child each save 7.65 percent, for a total of 15.3 percent. In addition, the child's wages can still be deducted from the parents' income taxes as a business expense. Children employed in small family businesses also usually qualify for an exemption from the FUTA tax until they reach age 21.

There is no limit on how much children can earn and still receive the FICA tax exemption. However, it is important that the wages paid to the child are reasonable for the job performed, and that the hours worked by the child are carefully documented, so it will be clear to the IRS that the child has not been paid

for nothing. In addition, parents should note that their child's financial aid for college may be reduced if they earn more than $1,750 per year.

Small businesses also are not required to withhold payroll taxes for persons who are employed as independent contractors. Using independent contractors rather than hiring employees can be a very attractive option for small businesses. By avoiding responsibility for payroll taxes and all the associated paperwork, as well as avoiding the need to pay benefits, businesses may find that using an independent contractors cost between 20 and 30 percent less than hiring an employee. But misclassifying an employee as an independent contractor can have dire consequences for a small business. The IRS examines such relationships very carefully, and in cases where an independent contractor must be reclassified as an employee, the business may be liable for back taxes plus a special penalty of 12 to 35 percent of the total tax bill.

The IRS uses a 20-step test to determine whether someone is an employee or an independent contractor. True independent contractors, according to the IRS definition, are in business for themselves with the intention of making a profit and are not under the direct control of the client company. To protect their companies from potential problems, small business owners should make sure that independent contractors are paid by the job rather than by the hour, set their own hours and rules, work on their own premises using their own equipment, sign a specific contract for each project, and make themselves available to multiple clients. Rather than withholding taxes, small businesses simply file an annual informational return—Form 1099, Statement of Miscellaneous Income—detailing the total amount paid to each contractor. No reporting is required for contractors that were paid less than $600 over the course of a year.

TRUST FUND RECOVERY PENALTY

''All too often in a small-business setting, the owner or executive finds himself/herself in a cash flow bind and must make a choice between paying essential suppliers and employees' salaries to stay in business or remitting employees' payroll taxes to the IRS on a timely basis,'' Ray A. Knight and Lee G. Knight explained in an article for *Management Accounting*. ''A typical scenario is that, for short-term survival, the business owner or executive decides to meet current creditors' requirements and forces the IRS to become a creditor with the hope that in the long term the business can pay the IRS the delinquent taxes plus interest and penalties. Often, however, the business becomes insolvent and declares **bankruptcy**. To avoid a significant erosion of tax revenue and to address this problem, in 1954 Congress enacted a penalty—equal to the unpaid payroll taxes—against all responsible persons who willfully fail to collect and turn over the money.''

This penalty for the failure to withhold or remit payroll taxes, known as the Trust Fund Recovery Penalty (TFRP), is included under Section 6672 of the Internal Revenue Code. It allows the IRS to hold individuals associated with a business personally liable for 100 percent of the unpaid amount when the business fails to meet its payroll tax obligations. The TFRP applies to employee funds that the employer holds in trust for the IRS—all of the regular income tax withheld and the employee half of the FICA tax—but not to the employer portions of payroll taxes. The penalty is particularly severe because the IRS considers an employer who fails to pay to be violating a trust. The TFRP can be applied in addition to civil and criminal penalties, including the seizure of business assets and forced closure of the business. And since it is a penalty rather than a tax, the TFRP is not erased by bankruptcy.

In order to apply the TFRP to an individual, the IRS must prove the person's responsibility (that he or she had the power to make the decision about whether or not to pay) and willfulness (that he or she knowingly failed to act rather than made an honest mistake) for the business's failure to remit payroll taxes. In making its determination about who to hold responsible, the IRS looks at who made the financial decisions in the business, who signed the checks, and who had the duty of tax reporting. Under these rules, a small business owner can be found personally liable even if a staff member or outside accountant was directly responsible for payroll tax compliance. In cases where both the business and the owner go bankrupt, the company's accountant may be tagged as the responsible party and held personally liable.

Because the law regarding payroll tax noncompliance is so sweeping, small business owners should pay particular attention to the trust fund taxes. It is vital to keep the taxes that are covered by the TFRP current, even when the business is experiencing cash flow problems. If it appears as if the small business is heading for bankruptcy, these taxes should be paid prior to filing, when management can still designate where the IRS should apply payments. After the company files for bankruptcy it loses this option, and the IRS will apply any payments elsewhere since they can collect the TFRP from individuals associated with the company. ''Obviously, if a company is experiencing cash flow problems, accountants and other responsible persons are tempted to pay creditors who cry loudest and whose nonpayment will have an immediate negative impact, such as vendors who will stop shipping necessary supplies,'' Knight and Knight noted. ''Not paying the IRS may solve short-term cash flow problems—but at the long-term personal expense of the responsible person who makes that decision.''

FURTHER READING:

Barlas, Stephen. ''Electronic Avenue: A New Deadline for Electronic Tax Filing Gives Small Businesses a Break—For Now.'' *Nation's Business.* October 1997.

Charles, Harry. ''Avoiding the 100 Percent Penalty.'' *National Public Accountant.* June 1991.

Dailey, Frederick W. *Tax Savvy for Small Business.* 2nd ed. Berkeley, CA: Nolo Press, 1997.

DeJong, David S., and Ann Gray Jakabcin. *J.K. Lasser's Year-Round Tax Strategies.* New York: Macmillan, 1997.

Ellentuck, Albert B. *Laventhol and Horwath Small Business Tax Planning Guide.* New York: Avon Books, 1988.

The Entrepreneur Magazine Small Business Advisor. New York: Wiley, 1995.

Knight, Ray A., and Lee G. Knight. ''Pay the IRS First, or Else!'' *Management Accounting.* December 1993.

Marullo, Gloria Gibbs. ''Hiring Your Child: Tax Breaks and Trade-Offs.'' *Nation's Business.* June 1997.

Robertson, Cliff. *The Small Business Tax Advisor: Understanding the New Tax Law.* Blue Ridge Summit, PA: Liberty House, 1987.

SEE ALSO: Outsourcing; Tax Planning; Tax Withholding

PENETRATION PRICING

Penetration pricing is a strategy employed by businesses introducing new goods or services into the marketplace. With this policy, the initial price of the good or service is set relatively low in hopes of ''penetrating'' into the marketplace quickly and securing significant market share. ''This pricing approach,'' wrote Ronald W. Hilton in *Managerial Accounting,* ''often is used for products that are of good quality, but do not stand out as vastly better than competing products.''

Writing in *Basic Marketing,* E. Jerome McCarthy and William Perreault Jr. observed that ''a penetration pricing policy tries to sell the whole market at one low price. Such an approach might be wise when the 'elite' market—those willing to pay a high price—is small. This is the case when the whole demand curve [for the product] is fairly elastic. A penetration policy is even more attractive if selling larger quantities results in lower costs because of economies of scale. Penetration pricing may be wise if the firm expects strong competition very soon after introduction. A low penetration price may be called a 'stay out' price. It discourages competitors from entering the market.'' Once the product has secured a desired market share, its producers can then review business conditions and decide whether to gradually increase the price.

Penetration pricing, however, is not the same as introductory price dealing, in which marketers attach temporary low prices to new products when they first hit the market. "These *temporary* price cuts should not be confused with low penetration prices," wrote McCarthy and Perreault Jr. "The plan [with introductory price dealing] is to raise prices as soon as the introductory offer is over."

SKIMMING VERSUS PENETRATION

Some manufacturers of new products, however, take a decidedly different tack when introducing their goods to the marketplace. Some choose to engage in skimming pricing, a strategy wherein the initial price for the product is set quite high for a relatively short time after introduction. Even though sales will likely be modest with skimming, the profit margin is great. "This pricing approach," remarked Hilton, "often is used for unique products, where there are people who 'must have it,' whatever the price. As the product gains acceptance and its appeal broadens, the price is lowered gradually. Eventually the product is priced in a range that appeals to a wide range of buyers." Hilton went on to use the introduction of video games as a prime example of skimming. Initially priced so that they were affordable only to a relatively small—though still meaningful—percentage of the market, the games became much in demand as prices were gradually lowered.

"The decision between skimming and penetration pricing," said Hilton, "depends on the type of product and involves trade-offs of price versus volume. Skimming pricing results in much slower acceptance of a new product, but higher unit profits. Penetration pricing results in greater initial sales volume, but lower unit profits."

FURTHER READING:

"Case Study: How to Price Your Products to Increase Profits." *Business Owner.* May-June 1995.

Cohen, William A. *The Entrepreneur and Small-Business Problem Solver.* 2d ed. Wiley, 1990.

Hilton, Ronald W. *Managerial Accounting.* New York: McGraw-Hill, 1991.

McCarthy, E. Jerome, and William D. Perreault, Jr. *Basic Marketing: A Managerial Approach.* 10th ed. Irwin, 1990.

SEE ALSO: Pricing

PENSION PLANS

The term "pension plan" is now used to describe a variety of retirement programs that companies establish as a benefit for their employees—including **401(k) plans**, **profit sharing** plans, **simplified employee pension (SEP)** plans, and **Keogh plans**. In the past, however, pension plans were differentiated from other types of retirement plans in that employers were committed to providing a certain monetary level of benefits to employees upon retirement. These "defined benefit" plans, which were common among large employers with a unionized work force, have fallen into disfavor in recent years.

Some individuals also choose to establish personal pension plans to supplement their retirement savings. Making sound decisions about retirement is particularly important for self-employed persons and small business owners. Unlike employees of large companies, who can simply participate in the pension plans and investment programs offered by their employers, entrepreneurs must set up and administer their own plans for themselves and for their employees.

Though establishing and funding pension plans can be both time-consuming and costly for small businesses, such programs also offer a number of advantages. In most cases, for example, employer contributions to retirement plans are tax deductible expenses. In addition, offering employees a comprehensive retirement program can help small businesses attract and retain qualified people who might otherwise seek the security of working for a larger company. The number of small firms establishing pension plans has grown during the 1990s, but small employers still lag far behind larger ones in providing this type of benefit for employees. According to Connecticut-based consulting firm Access Research Inc., 24 percent of small businesses (those with fewer than 100 employees) offered retirement plans in 1996, compared to 51 percent of medium-sized businesses (between 100 and 1,000 employees) and 98 percent of large businesses (more than 1,000 employees).

PENSION PLAN OPTIONS FOR SMALL BUSINESSES

Small business owners can set up a wide variety of pension plans by filling out the necessary forms at any financial institution (including a bank, mutual fund, insurance company, or brokerage firm). The fees vary depending on the plan's complexity and the number of participants. Some employer-sponsored plans are required to file Form 5500 annually to disclose plan activities to the IRS. The preparation and filing of this complicated document can increase the administrative costs associated with a plan, because the business owner may require help from a tax advisor or plan administration professional. In addition, all the information reported on Form 5500 is open to public inspection.

A number of different types of pension plans are available. The most popular plans for small businesses all fall under the category of defined contribution plans. Defined contribution plans use an allocation formula to specify a percentage of compensation to be contributed by each participant. For example, an individual can voluntarily deduct a certain portion of his or her salary, in many cases before taxes, and place the money into a qualified retirement plan, where it will grow tax-deferred. Likewise, an employer can contribute a percentage of each employee's salary to the plan on their behalf, or match the contributions employees make.

In contrast, defined benefit plans calculate a desired level of benefits to be paid upon retirement—using a fixed monthly payment or a percentage of compensation—and then the employer contributes to the plan annually according to a formula so that the benefits will be available when needed. The amount of annual contributions is determined by an actuary, based upon the age, salary levels, and years of service of employees, as well as prevailing interest and inflation rates. In defined benefit plans, the employer bears the risk of providing a specified level of benefits to employees when they retire. This is the traditional idea of a pension plan that has often been used by large employers with a unionized work force.

In nearly every type of qualified pension plan, withdrawals made before the age of 59 $\frac{1}{2}$ are subject to an IRS penalty in addition to ordinary income tax. The plans differ in terms of administrative costs, eligibility requirements, employee participation, degree of discretion in making contributions, and amount of allowable contributions. Free information on qualified retirement plans is available through the Department of Labor at 800-998-7542, or at their website at www.dol.gov on the Internet.

The most important thing to remember is that a small business owner who wants to establish a qualified plan for him or herself must also include all other company employees who meet minimum participation standards. As an employer, the small business owner can establish pension plans like any other business. As an employee, the small business owner can then make contributions to the plan he or she has established in order to set aside tax-deferred funds for retirement, like any other employee. The difference is that a small business owner must include all nonowner employees in any company-sponsored pension plans and make equivalent contributions to their accounts. Unfortunately, this requirement has the effect of reducing the allowable contributions that the owner of a proprietorship or partnership can make on his or her own behalf.

For self-employed individuals, contributions to a qualified pension plan are based upon the net earnings of their business. The net earnings consist of the company's gross income less deductions for business expenses, salaries paid to nonowner employees, the employer's 50 percent of the Social Security tax, and—significantly—the employer's contribution to retirement plans on behalf of employees. Therefore, rather than receiving pre-tax contributions to the retirement account as a percentage of gross salary, like nonowner employees, the small business owner receives contributions as a smaller percentage of net earnings. Employing other people thus detracts from the owner's ability to build up a sizeable before-tax retirement account of his or her own. For this reason, some experts recommend that the owners of proprietorships and partnerships who sponsor pension plans for their employees supplement their own retirement funds through a personal after-tax savings plan.

PERSONAL PENSION PLANS FOR INDIVIDUALS

For self-employed persons and small business owners, the tax laws that limit the amount of annual contributions individuals can make to qualified retirement plans, as well as the requirement that qualified plans established by an employer must cover all employees, may make these plans less desirable. "If you're relying on a tax-qualified plan to fund your retirement, it's time to rethink that strategy," Arthur D. Kraus wrote in an article for *Small Business Reports*. "You may want to use a non-qualified plan to supplement or even replace your qualified savings." Kraus recommended that small business owners consider setting up a personal pension plan to provide a source of income and security in their retirement. These plans have nearly unlimited annual contributions and do not have to be offered to employees. "You can sock away as much money as you want each year and use the plan just to cover yourself—as most small business owners do—or offer it to a few top managers," Kraus stated. "And that's not the best part. You can draw tax-free income in retirement from a personal pension plan."

Establishing a personal pension plan involves purchasing a variable life insurance policy and paying premiums, which basically take the place of annual contributions to a retirement plan. The amount paid in is invested and allowed to grow tax-free. Both the premiums paid and the investment earnings can be accessed to provide the individual with an annual income upon retirement. The only catch is that, unlike qualified retirement plans, the annual payments made on a personal pension plan are not tax-deductible. However, Kraus claimed that the tax savings in retirement often offset the loss of the tax deduction during the working years.

Although other types of insurance policies—such as whole life or universal life—can also be used for retirement savings, they tend to be less flexible in terms of investment choices. In contrast, most variable life insurance providers allow individuals to select from a variety of investment options and transfer funds from one account to another without penalty. Many policies also allow individuals to vary the amount of their annual contribution or even skip making a contribution in years when cash is tight. Another worthwhile provision in some policies pays the premium if the individual should become disabled. In addition, most policies have more liberal early withdrawal and loan provisions than qualified retirement plans. The size of the annual contributions allowed depends upon the size of the insurance policy purchased. "The bigger the policy, the higher the premiums—and thus, your plan contributions," according to Kraus. "The IRS also sets a maximum annual contribution level for each size policy, based on your age, gender, and other factors."

Upon reaching retirement age, an individual can begin to use the personal pension plan as a source of annual income. Withdrawals—which are not subject to income or Social Security taxes—first come from the premiums paid and earnings accumulated. After the total withdrawn equals the total contributed, however, the individual can continue to draw income in the form of a loan against the plan's cash value. This amount is repaid upon the individual's death out of the death benefit of the insurance. "Is a personal pension plan right for you? That depends on whether other savings will meet your retirement needs," Kraus noted. "But given the benefits of the plan—tax-free earnings, tax-free retirement income, protection for your heirs, and even disability benefits—it's clear that this savings strategy is well worth considering."

FURTHER READING:

Battle, Carl W. *Senior Counsel: Legal and Financial Strategies for Age 50 and Beyond.* Alworth Press, 1993.

Blakely, Stephen. "Pension Power." *Nation's Business.* July 1997.

Connor, John B., Jr. "Pay Me Later." *Small Business Reports.* July 1994.

Crouch, Holmes F. *Decisions When Retiring.* Allyear Tax Guides, 1995.

Gordon, Marcy. "Pensioners Go Underpaid." *Detroit Free Press.* June 17, 1997.

Hunnisett, Henry S. *Retirement Guide: An Overall Plan for a Comfortable Future.* Self-Counsel Press, 1990.

Kraus, Arthur D. "A Pension Plan of Your Own." *Small Business Reports.* March 1994.

Martin, Ray. *Your Financial Guide: Advice for Every Stage of Your Life.* Macmillan, 1996.

SEE ALSO: Health Insurance Options; Life Insurance; Retirement Planning

PER CAPITA INCOME

Per capita income is the average amount of money each person in a nation makes during the course of a year. It is calculated by dividing national income, which is the sum of all the individual and corporate income arising from a nation's production of goods and services, by the total population of the nation. Per capita real income is the same figure, but adjusted to eliminate changes in prices or purchasing power over time. Many economic terms are commonly divided by population and expressed as per capita, or per person, amounts. Examples might include per capita **gross national product (GNP)** and per capita savings.

It is important to remember that per capita income figures represent a national average; in reality, income is not distributed evenly among all members of the population. Income varies by geographical region, for example, because the primary source of income in one area might be industry while in another it might be agriculture. Another geographical difference is based on the fact that wages tend to be higher in large cities than in small towns or rural areas. Income also tends to differ between individuals with different educational backgrounds.

Due to the difficulties of interpreting per capita income figures within a nation, per capita income is most often used to compare the standard of living in different countries. Per capita income varies greatly around the world, and the gap between relatively poor and relatively rich countries is becoming larger all the time. According to Susan Dentzer in *U.S. News and World Report,* the top 20 percent of countries worldwide (based on annual national income) reported per capita income figures an average of 65 times greater than the bottom 20 percent of countries in 1988.

In the United States, per capita income nearly doubled from 1959 to 1993 to reach $20,864 in current dollars, as Ben Stein noted in *New York.* In fact, the annual growth rate of per capita income over the twenty-year period from 1973 to 1993 was 1.38 percent. In addition, there were many indications that Americans had more money and were living better than before. Three times as many newly constructed homes contained more than two bathrooms in 1992 than in 1970, for example, while the average square footage of new houses increased by one-third over the same period. Stein argued that such statistics are misleading, however. After adjusting for **inflation**, Stein found that per-hour private-sector earnings, excluding agricultural work, rose only .3 percent per year, or 10.6 percent over the past thirty-four years. In addition, he reported that inflation-adjusted weekly earnings had actually declined by 2 percent since 1959.

Stein attributed the decline in real income in part to the fact that the overall American labor force has increased by 12 percent from 1954 to 1993. An increase in the number of people working means that national and per capita income tends to rise, even though the average income per worker remains the same or declines because it is divided among more people. In addition, Stein noted that the government figures for per capita income growth include nonmonetary benefits received by workers, such as health care and retirement coverage. These payments, which have increased markedly in recent years, tend to inflate per capita income figures and hide underlying trends affecting wages. Other factors Stein found to reduce per capita income growth include fewer people pursuing higher education and companies keeping wages low in order to compete with foreign firms.

FURTHER READING:

Bureau of Economic Analysis. *Survey of Current Business.* March 1995.

Dentzer, Susan. ''The Wealth of Nations: A Growing Slice of the World Economy Is Now in the Hands of the Affluent.'' *U.S. News and World Report.* May 4, 1992.

Pomice, Eva, and Robert F. Black. ''Is Your Job Safe?'' *U.S. News and World Report.* January 13, 1992.

Stein, Ben. ''Whining and Dining: Why We're Richer and Poorer.'' *New York.* April 11, 1994.

PERSONAL SELLING

Personal selling is the process of communicating with a potential buyer (or buyers) face-to-face with the purpose of selling a product or service. The main thing that sets personal selling apart from other methods of selling is that the salesperson conducts business with the customer in person. Though personal selling is more likely to be effective with certain types of products or services, it has important applications for nearly all kinds of small businesses. In fact, most of history's successful entrepreneurs have been skilled salespeople, able to represent and promote their companies and products in the marketplace.

Personal selling is one part of a company's promotion mix, along with advertising, **sales promotion**, and **public relations**. Advertising is any form of paid sales presentation that is not done face-to-face. Television and radio commercials, newspaper and magazine advertisements, and **direct mail** inserts are well-known forms of advertising. Sales promotion is the use of incentives—such as **coupons**, discounts, rebates, contests, or special displays—to entice a customer to buy a product or service. Public relations is the act of building up a company's image in the eyes

of the community in the hopes of translating the feelings of goodwill into sales. An example of public relations might include a company sponsoring a charity event.

Personal selling offers entrepreneurs both advantages and disadvantages in comparison with the other elements of the promotion mix. On the positive side, personal selling allows the salesperson to target the message specifically to the audience and receive immediate feedback. In this way, it is more precise than other forms of promotion and often has a greater persuasive impact. Conversely, personal selling cannot reach as many potential customers as advertising, plus the cost of each contact is much higher. Another advantage is that personal selling can be an important source of marketing information. Salespeople may learn about competitors' products, for example, or about emerging customer needs that may lead to the development of a new product. If the sales force is well trained—acting as problem solvers and advisors for customers rather than using hard-sell tactics—personal selling may help a small business build loyal, long-term relationships with customers.

A small business may choose to use any or all of the promotion mix elements in selling its products. Deciding how to allocate resources for each component involves a number of factors. Some of the things entrepreneurs should consider when deciding on the ideal promotion mix include the type of product or service, the value of the product or service, and the budget allotted for marketing.

WHEN TO USE PERSONAL SELLING

In general, if a product has a high unit value and requires a demonstration of its benefits, it is well suited for personal sales. For example, an encyclopedia is a high-priced item and most people do not feel they need one. After a demonstration, however, most people agree it would be a useful item to have. Therefore, encyclopedias are well suited to a promotion mix that emphasizes personal selling. Highly technical products, such as computers and copiers, are also primarily sold through personal sales methods. Products that involve a trade-in, like automobiles, are usually handled through personal selling to help facilitate the trade-in process. Finally, a company that cannot afford a mass-advertising campaign might consider personal selling as an alternative to advertising. Since sales force compensation is largely based on actual sales, personal selling may require less money up front than other parts of the promotion mix.

SELLERS' AGENTS

One method that many small manufacturers and wholesalers use to reduce the costs of personal selling—which can be the most critical aspect of the promotion mix for these types of businesses—is to hire an experienced selling agent. Selling agents—sometimes known as **manufacturers' agents**—are independent salespeople who work under contract with one or more companies and are usually paid a straight commission on sales. Hiring a selling agent allows a small business to save the time and money it would have to invest in recruiting and training an in-house sales force. In addition, an agent with experience in selling similar products may provide ready-made customers and quick entry into a sales territory. Selling agents are particularly helpful for businesses whose products experience seasonal or fluctuating sales, since they are only paid for the sales they make.

The main disadvantages of selling agents are that they usually work for several different firms, so they are unable to devote 100 percent of their attention to any one client, and that it may be difficult to retain the customers gained in this way once the relationship with the agent is severed. It is also difficult to control the selling methods used by agents, and they may not be able to provide the service that some customers require.

TYPES OF SALES POSITIONS

There are many different types of personal sales jobs. A driver-salesperson merely delivers the product and has few selling responsibilities. An inside order taker—such as a sales clerk in a retail store or a telephone representative with a catalog sales company—takes orders from within a selling environment and requires some selling skills. In contrast, an outside order taker goes to the customer's place of business to take orders. Some selling skills are required in this position, especially to establish new accounts. A missionary sales person, rather than selling an actual product or service, instead tries to make a customer feel good about the company and products he or she represents. The pharmaceutical and liquor industries frequently employ missionary salespeople.

A sales engineer might be found in technical industries such as computers and copiers. Sales engineers provide technical support, explain the product, and help adapt the product to the customer's needs. Finally, a creative salesperson may attempt to sell goods (such as vacuum cleaners or encyclopedias), but more often represents ideas, such as services (insurance) or causes (charities). These salespeople usually deal with customers who are unaware of their need for the service or product, so they must possess the most developed selling skills of all the types of salespeople.

STEPS IN COMPLETING A SALE

The many different types of salespeople all go through the same basic steps when making a sale: prospecting and qualifying, preapproach, approach, presentation and demonstration, handling objections, closing, and follow-up. Although training for personal sales forces may vary from one organization to another, the majority of the training will include some version of these steps.

Prospecting and qualifying involve locating potential customers and finding out if they are in a position to buy. Prospecting, or lead-generation, can be as simple as asking current customers for names of acquaintances who may also be interested, or as sophisticated as using a database or mailing list. Often the company provides leads, but a truly successful salesperson will also be able to generate his or her own leads. Prospecting usually involves an element of cold-calling—that is, calling an unknown potential customer and introducing oneself and the product. After possible customers have been located through prospecting, a salesperson must qualify them. This entails assessing their readiness and ability to buy. Personal selling almost always requires a salesperson to contact many prospects before completing a sale.

The preapproach step involves researching the prospective customer—often another company. The salesperson may read up on the company, talk to other vendors, or study the overall industry. At this stage, the salesperson will also try to determine the best time to make the sales call and establish sales call objectives. During the next step, the approach, it is crucial for a salesperson to make a positive first impression while introducing himself or herself, the company represented, and the product or service being offered. It is also important that the salesperson listen carefully to the prospect and respond appropriately.

Once the approach has been made, the salesperson should be ready to launch into the demonstration or presentation. Depending on the company and the product or service, there are generally three types of presentations. The prepared or ''canned'' approach involves a tightly scripted talk that is either memorized or read. The formula approach is less rigid. Depending on the buyer's response to some carefully asked questions, the seller will go to a formula presentation that he or she hopes will meet the customer's needs. The third presentation style is the need-satisfaction approach, in which the seller tries to uncover the customer's needs, mostly by listening. Presentations and demonstrations may involve any number of visual aids, such as flip-charts, or samples of the products themselves. One of the keys to a successful presentation is product knowledge. The more the salesperson knows about the product or service, the more relaxed he or she will be, and the more able to answer questions, shape his or her presentation to address customer concerns and desires, and handle objections.

PHYSICAL DISTRIBUTION (vertical, left margin)

Handling objections is the next phase of selling. Almost every customer will present objections to making a purchase. A good salesperson is not flustered by these objections and handles them in a positive, confident manner. One approach to handling objections, used frequently with canned presentations, is simply to acknowledge the objection then continue with the presentation.

The next step in the process of completing a sale—closing, or asking the buyer to make a purchase—is often identified by novice salespeople as the toughest step. In fact, some new salespeople are so reluctant to be perceived as aggressive that they never try to close the sale. Consequently, the customer may become annoyed and decide not to purchase just for that reason. Customers must be given the opportunity to purchase. Salespeople need to learn to look for signals that a closing is appropriate. Common signals that customers give include asking questions, making comments, leaning forward or nodding, or asking about price or terms.

The last step in completing a sale—following up—is often neglected, but is important for many reasons. The follow-up, which can be done in person or by telephone, gives the customer the chance to ask questions and reinforce his or her buying decision. The salesperson can review how to use the product, go over instructions and payment arrangements, and make sure the product has arrived in proper working order. This step ensures repeat business, is a good opportunity to obtain referrals, and increases the chances that subsequent payments will be made.

IMPROVING THE REPUTATION OF PERSONAL SELLING

Personal selling involves specific steps, requires training and experience, and employs some highly talented people. Unfortunately, personal selling is also commonly perceived as being a less than reputable field of work. Unethical salespeople, aggressive or hard sell tactics, and misleading sales pitches have made many buyers wary of personal sellers. Fortunately, much has been done to address this issue. Selling associations such as the Direct Selling Association have adopted codes of ethics that dictate standards of behavior that all members are to follow. Most organizations with personal sales forces also adopt their own codes of ethics that provide guidelines regarding the type of sales pitch that can be made, and the hours during which a sales call may be made. Many companies also prohibit the use of misleading information or pressure tactics to make a sale.

FURTHER READING:

Armstrong, Gary, and Philip Kotler. *Principles of Marketing.* 4th ed. Upper Saddle River, NJ: Prentice-Hall, 1989.

Kimball, Bob. *AMA Handbook for Successful Selling.* Lincolnwood, IL: NTC Business Books, 1994.

Kotler, Philip. *Marketing Management.* 8th ed. Upper Saddle River, NJ: Prentice-Hall, 1994.

Kotler, Philip, and Gary Armstrong. *Marketing: An Introduction.* 3rd ed. Prentice-Hall, 1993.

McCarthy, E. Jerome, and William D. Perreault, Jr. *Basic Marketing.* 10th ed. Irwin, 1990.

Stair, Lila B. *Careers in Marketing.* Lincolnwood, IL: VGM Career Horizons, 1991.

Stanton, William J., Michael J. Etzel, and Bruce J. Walker. *Fundamentals in Marketing.* 10th ed. New York: McGraw-Hill, 1994.

SEE ALSO: Sales Management; Sales Force

PHYSICAL DISTRIBUTION

Physical distribution is the set of activities concerned with efficient movement of finished goods from the end of the production operation to the consumer. Physical distribution takes place within numerous wholesaling and retailing distribution channels, and includes such important decision areas such as **customer service**, inventory control, materials handling, protective **packaging**, order procession, **transportation**, warehouse site selection, and warehousing. Physical distribution is part of a larger process called "distribution," which includes wholesale and retail marketing, as well the physical movement of products.

IMPORTANCE OF PHYSICAL DISTRIBUTION

Physical distribution activities recently have received increasing attention from business managers, including small business owners. This is due in large part to the fact that these functions often represent almost half of the total marketing costs of a product. And not surprisingly, physical distribution costs nationally amount to approximately 20 percent of the country's total gross national product (GNP). And while small business cost-cutting efforts have historically focused on production, owners are increasingly looking to physical distribution activities for cost-cutting opportunities.

The importance of physical distribution is also based on its relevance to customer satisfaction. By storing goods in convenient locations for shipment to wholesalers and retailers, and by creating fast, reliable means of moving the goods, small business owners can help assure continued success in a rapidly changing, competitive global market.

A SYSTEM APPROACH

Physical distribution can be viewed as a system of components linked together for the efficient movement of products. Small business owners can ask the following questions in addressing these components:

- **Customer service**—What level of customer service should be provided?

- Transportation—How will the products be shipped?

- Warehousing—Where will the goods be located? How many warehouses should be utilized?

- Order processing—How should the orders be handled?

- Inventory control—How much inventory should be maintained at each location?

- Protective packaging and materials handling—How can efficient methods be developed for handling goods in the factory, warehouse, and transport terminals?

These components are interrelated: decisions made in one area affect the relative efficiency of others. For example, a small business that provides customized personal computers may transport finished products by air rather than by truck, as faster delivery times may allow lower inventory costs, which would more than offset the higher cost of air transport. Viewing physical distribution from a systems perspective can be the key to providing a defined level of customer service at the lowest possible cost.

CUSTOMER SERVICE

Customer service is a precisely-defined standard of customer satisfaction which a small business owner intends to provide for its customers. For example, a customer service standard for the above-mentioned provider of customized computers might be that 60 percent of all PCs reach the customer within 48 hours of ordering. It might further set a standard of delivering 90 percent of all of its units within 72 hours, and all 100 percent of its units within 96 hours. A physical distribution system is then set up to reach this goal at the lowest possible cost. In today's fast-paced, technologically advanced business environment, such systems often involve the use of specialized software that allows the owner to track inventory while simultaneously analyzing all the routes and transportation modes available to determine the fastest, most cost-effective way to deliver goods on time.

TRANSPORTATION

The United States' transportation system has long been a government-regulated industry, much like its telephone and electrical utilities. But in 1977 the deregulation of transportation began with the removal of federal regulations for cargo air carriers not engaged in passenger transportation. Deregulation has since expanded in ways that have fundamentally altered the transportation landscape for small business owners, large conglomerates and, ultimately, the consumer.

Transportation costs are largely based on the rates charged by carriers. There are two basic types of transportation rates: class and commodity. The class rate, which is the higher of the two rates, is the standard rate for every commodity moving between any two destinations. The commodity rate is sometimes called a special rate, since it is given by carriers to shippers as a reward for either regular use or large-quantity shipments. Unfortunately, many small business owners do not have the volume of shipping needed to take advantage of commodity rates. However, small businesses are increasingly utilizing a third type of rate that has emerged in recent years. This rate is known as a negotiated or contract rate. Popularized in the 1980s following transportation deregulation, contract rates allow a shipper and carrier to negotiate a rate for a particular service, with the terms of the rate, service, and other variables finalized in a contract between the two parties. Transportation costs vary by mode of shipping, as discussed below.

TRUCKING—FLEXIBLE AND GROWING The shipping method most favored by small business (and many large enterprises as well) is trucking. Carrying primarily manufactured products (as opposed to bulk materials), trucks offer faster and more frequent delivery to more destinations in the country than any other mode. Trucks are particularly useful for short-distance shipments, and they offer relatively fast, consistent service for both large and small shipments.

AIR FREIGHT—FAST BUT EXPENSIVE Because of the relatively high cost of air transport, small businesses typically use air only for the movement of valuable or highly-perishable products. However, goods that qualify for this treatment do represent a significant share of the small business market. Such disparate goods as computers, furs, fresh flowers, high-fashion clothing, and lobsters all may be shipped by small business owners who are conscious of time of delivery concerns. Owners can often offset the high cost of air freight transportation with reduced inventory-holding costs and the increased business that may accompany faster customer service.

WATER CARRIERS—SLOW BUT INEXPENSIVE There are two basic types of water carriers: inland or barge lines, and oceangoing deep-water ships. Barge lines are efficient transporters of bulky, low-unit-value commodities such as grain, gravel, lumber, sand, and steel. Barge lines typically do not serve small businesses. Oceangoing ships, on the other hand, operate in the Great Lakes, transporting goods among port cities, and in international commerce. Sea shipments are an important part of foreign trade, and thus are of vital importance to small businesses seeking an international market share.

RAILROADS—THE NATION'S LEADING TRANS-PORTER Railroads continue to control the largest share of the transportation market, and they represent the most efficient mode for the movement of bulky commodities over long distances. These commodities include coal, chemicals, grain, non-metallic minerals, and lumber and wood products. Like barge lines, railroads typically do not serve small businesses.

PIPELINES—SPECIALIZED TRANSPORTERS More than 200,000 miles of pipelines cross the United States in order to efficiently transport natural gas and oil products from mining sites to refineries and other destinations. In addition, so-called slurry pipelines transport products such as coal, which is ground to a powder, mixed with water, and moved as a suspension through the pipes. Although few if any small businesses move their goods by pipeline, the availability of affordable energy resources is vital to their success. Thus many owners belong to professional organizations maintaining a lobbying presence in Washington to represent their interests on energy issues (as well as other small business concerns).

INTERMODAL SERVICES Small business owners often take advantage of multi-mode deals offered by shipping companies. Under these arrangements, business owners can utilize a given transportation mode in the section of the trip in which it is most cost efficient, and use other modes for other segments of the transport. Overall costs are often significantly lower under this arrangement than with single-mode transport. The most widely used small business intermodal service is "birdyback," which combines motor pickup and delivery with air shipping over longer distances. Likewise, "fishyback" coordinates the efforts of motor carriers and water carriers. And "piggyback" service—although not popular with small businesses—combines truck and rail service, and is overall the most widely accepted intermodal service.

SERVICES FOR SMALL LOADS Of vital importance to small businesses are transporters specializing in small shipments. These include bus freight services, "next-day" or overnight delivery services, the United States Postal Service, and others. Since small businesses can be virtually paralyzed by transportation strikes or other disruptions in small shipment service, many owners choose to diversify to include numerous shippers, thus maintaining an established relationship with an alternate shipper should disruptions occur. Additionally, small businesses often rely on freight forwarders who act as transportation intermediaries:

these firms consolidate shipments from numerous customers to provide lower rates than are available without consolidation. Freight forwarding not only provides cost savings to small businesses, it provides entrepreneurial opportunities for start-up businesses as well.

WAREHOUSING

Small business owners who require warehousing facilities must decide whether to maintain their own strategically located depot(s), or resort to holding their goods in public warehouses. And those entrepreneurs who go with non-public warehousing must further decide between storage or distribution facilities. A storage warehouse holds products for moderate to long-term periods in an attempt to balance supply and demand for producers and purchasers. They are most often used by small businesses whose products' supply and demand are seasonal. On the other hand, a distribution warehouse assembles and redistributes products quickly, keeping them on the move as much as possible. Many distribution warehouses physically store goods for fewer than 24 hours before shipping them on to customers.

In contrast to the older, multi-story structures that dot cities around the country, modern warehouses are long, one-story buildings located in suburban and semi-rural settings where land costs are substantially less. These facilities are often located so that their users have easy access to major highways or other transportation options. Single-story construction eliminates the need for installing and maintaining freight elevators, and for accommodating floor load limits. Furthermore, the internal flow of stock runs a straight course rather than up and down multiple levels. The efficient movement of goods involves entry on one side of the building, central storage, and departure out the other end.

Computer technology for automating warehouses is dropping in price, and thus is increasingly available for small business applications. Sophisticated software translates orders into bar codes and determines the most efficient inventory picking sequence. Order information is keyboarded only once, while labels, bills, and shipping documents are generated automatically. Information reaches hand-held scanners, which warehouse staff members use to fill orders. The advantages of automation include low inventory error rates and high processing speeds.

INVENTORY CONTROL

Inventory control can be a major component of a small business physical distribution system. If an operation has an inventory-holding cost of 23 percent per year (a percentage which is realistic in many industries), then $1,000 of inventory held for a single year costs the owner $230. Costs include funds invested in inventory, depreciation, and possible obsolescence of the goods. Experts agree that small business inventory costs have dropped dramatically due to deregulation of the transportation industry.

Inventory control analysts have developed a number of techniques which can help small businesses control inventory effectively. The most basic is the **Economic Order Quantity (EOQ)** model. This involves a trade-off between the two fundamental components of an inventory control cost: inventory-carrying cost (which increases with the addition of more inventory), and order-processing cost (which decreases as the quantity ordered increases). These two cost items are traded off in determining the optimal warehouse inventory quantity to maintain for each product. The EOQ point is the one at which total cost is minimized. By maintaining product inventories as close to the EOQ point as possible, small business owners can minimize their inventory costs.

THE JUST-IN-TIME SYSTEM The Just-in-Time (JIT) inventory system, borrowed from the Japanese, has rapidly gained acceptance in American small businesses. Indeed, its underlying philosophy is ubiquitous in small and large companies alike. JIT involves minimizing the inventory-carrying costs of parts used in production, as well as finished products, by reducing the overall inventory levels of these items in warehouses. JIT requires efficient, well-trained employees who maintain precise schedules of incoming parts and outgoing products. JIT inventory systems are especially important in the food industry, where small businesses must guarantee product freshness.

ORDER PROCESSING

The small business owner is concerned with order processing—another physical distribution function—because it directly affects the ability to meet the customer service standards defined by the owner. If the order processing system is efficient, the owner can avoid the costs of premium transportation or high inventory levels. Order processing varies by industry, but often consists of four major activities: a credit check; recording of the sale, such as crediting a sales representative's commission account; making the appropriate accounting entries; and locating the item, shipping, and adjusting inventory records. An item not available for shipment is known as a stockout.

Technological innovations such as increased use of the Universal Product Code are contributing to greater efficiency in order processing. Bar codes systems give small businesses the ability to route customer orders efficiently and reduce the need for manual handling. The coded information includes all the data necessary to generate customer invoices, thus eliminating the need for repeated keypunching.

Another technological innovation affecting order processing is **Electronic Data Interchange**. EDI allows computers at two different locations to exchange business documents in machine-readable format, employing strictly-defined industry standards. Purchase orders, invoices, remittance slips, and the like are exchanged electronically, thereby eliminating duplication of data entry, dramatic reductions in data entry errors, and increased speed in procurement cycles.

PROTECTIVE PACKAGING AND MATERIALS HANDLING

An important component of a small business physical distribution system is material handling. This comprises all of the activities associated with moving products within a production facility, warehouse, and transportation terminals. One important innovation is known as unitizing—combining as many packages as possible into one load, preferably on a pallet. Unitizing is accomplished with steel bands or shrink wrapping to hold the unit in place. Advantages of this material handling methodology include reduced labor, rapid movement, and minimized damage and pilferage.

A second innovation is containerization—the combining of several unitized loads into one box. Containers that are presented in this manner are often unloaded in fewer than 24 hours, whereas the task could otherwise take days or weeks. This speed allows small export businesses adequate delivery schedules in competitive international markets. In-transit damage is also reduced because individual packages are not handled en route to the purchaser.

FURTHER READING:

Aizenman, Nurith C. "The Case for More Regulation." *Washington Monthly.* October 1997.

Artman Les. Clancy, David. "Distribution Follows Consumer Movement." *Transportation and Distribution.* June 1990.

Brenner, Gary, Joel Ewan, and Henry Custer. *The Complete Handbook for the Entrepreneur.* Englewood Cliffs, NJ: Prentice Hall, 1990.

Burstiner, Irving. *The Small Business Handbook.* Englewood Cliffs, NJ: Prentice Hall, 1989.

Cavinato, Joseph. "How to Keep Customers Coming Back for More." *Distribution.* December 1989.

Evans, James. *Production and Operations Management: Quality, Performance, and Value.* St. Paul, MN: West Publishing Company, 1997.

Johnson, James, and Donald Wood. *Contemporary Physical Distribution and Logistics.* 3d ed. New York: Macmillan, 1986.

Mulcahy, David. *Warehouse Distribution and Operations Handbook.* New York: McGraw-Hill, 1994.

Schmenner, Roger. *Production and Operations Management: From the Inside Out.* New York: Macmillan, 1993.

Wood, Donald, and James Johnson. *Contemporary Logistics.* Upper Saddle River, NJ: Prentice Hall, 1996.

SEE ALSO: Distribution Channels; Distribution Networks; Transportation

POINT OF SALE SYSTEMS

Point of sale (POS) systems are complicated electronic systems that provide businesses with the capability to retain and analyze a wide variety of inventory and transaction data on a continuous basis. POS systems have been touted as valuable tools for a wide variety of business purposes, including refining strategies for reaching **target markets**; tracking supplier purchases; determining customer purchasing patterns; analyzing sales (on a daily, monthly, or annual basis) of each **inventory** item, department, or supplier; and creating reports for use in **purchasing** decisions.

Basic point of sale systems currently in use include standalone electronic cash registers, also known as ECRs; ECR-based network systems; and controller-based systems. All function essentially as sales and **cash management** tools, but each has features that are unique.

STANDALONE ECRS These electronic registers operate independently of one another, and are thus the most limited of the three POS system types. They cannot provide their owners with storewide reporting or file sharing; they can merely report the business activity at that particular register. Given its limitations, ECRs are usually used by small independent retailers that feature a limited number of register sites. Indeed, these systems are often perfectly suited for small businesses, because they still do provide many helpful features, including: automatic sales and tax calculation ability; calculation of change owed to the customer; sales report generation capability; capacity to sort food stamps and trading stamps (through programming of function keys); and scanning. Perhaps most importantly, they are the least expensive POS option available.

NETWORK SYSTEMS "Surpassing the capabilities of its standalone cousins are ECR-based point-of-sale systems," stated *Chain Store Age Executive.* "With these systems, terminals are arranged into a primary/secondary configuration. One ECR in the store has more memory than the others; it serves as the primary terminal and receives data from the secondary terminals. This allows for easy storewide reporting and file sharing." In addition, these network systems, which have the same features as standalones, have the capacity to transmit data to mainframe systems.

CONTROLLER-BASED POS SYSTEMS The top POS systems are controller-based systems in which each terminal is connected to a computer—the "controller" of the system—which receives and stores all sales, merchandise, and credit data. "The controller checks all data from the terminals for transmission errors and reformats the data for use by the headquarters computer," according to *Chain Store Age Executive.* "It may also perform sales analysis and price look-up. By having a dual-controller arrangement in which the computers back each other up, the chance for a total system failure can be reduced. Because of the importance of accurate data capture in sophisticated point-of-sale systems, retailers are increasingly turning to scanning as an alternative to error-prone keypunch entry of sku or upc numbers." Indeed, scanning has become a ubiquitous feature in even the smallest retail outlets over the past several years.

Point of sale systems, like many other computer-based innovations, continue to change and develop at a rapid pace. In addition, the demand for POS systems has spawned many new manufacturers, each of which offer a dizzying array of standard and optional POS features to their customers. Given the expense involved and the proliferating number of POS software packages, small business owners should make sure that they adequately research both their current and future needs before making a purchase, so that they are able to acquire a customized POS system that best fills their operating requirements.

FURTHER READING:

Durocher, Joseph. "Point of Departure: Don't Think of Your POS System as Merely a Cashbox but Rather as a Management Tool." *Restaurant Business.* September 1, 1994.

Shulman, Richard S. "The Year of the POS Connection." *Supermarket Business.* February 1986.

"Systems to Keep the Checkout Counter Humming." *Chain Store Age Executive.* October 1990.

POSTAL COSTS

No business owner will escape postal costs entirely, no matter how small or technologically savvy his or her company is. From the occasional letter or invoice to large regular shipments, businesses continue to rely on some level of paper interaction to operate despite the ever-growing presence of e-mail and other high-tech modes of communication. The U.S. Postal Service remains the primary medium through which such paper communications go, and it provides a variety of services for businesses and individuals.

EXPRESS MAIL SERVICE The Postal Service's most competitive alternative to other private delivery services, such as FedEx and UPS, is Express Mail. This service provides next day delivery by 12 p.m. to most destinations, even on weekends and holidays. Express Mail costs several dollars less than the large private delivery services, making it the best option for frequent large shipments under 70 lbs., if cost is the only consideration. The cost for Express Mail is scaled up to 70 lbs., so business owners needing to send heavier packages for quick delivery should check with their local post office for details on larger shipments.

PRIORITY MAIL Priority Mail is similar to Express Mail, provides two-day service to most domestic destinations. If an item can wait for two days to be delivered, this is the least expensive option. Again, this alternative is less expensive than those offered by privately owned delivery companies. Both Priority Mail and Express Mail rates end at 70 lbs, and packages must measure 108 inches or less in combined length and girth.

STANDARD MAIL (A) AND FIRST-CLASS Standard Mail (A) is the primary option used by retailers, catalogers, and other advertisers to promote products and services. Items must weigh less than 1 lb. to qualify under this designation. Although the charge per ounce on the single-piece rate is the same as First-Class mail, Standard Mail (A) bulk mailings (i.e. not single pieces) can, if pre-sorted by ZIP Code, save money. Pre-sorting saves the post office some processing time and the payoff for the mailer is a reduced rate. However, if the bulk mailing contains errors, found by random sample checking by the postal staff, the charge increases. Then the mailer has the option of correcting the errors, or paying the additional fee. Standard Mail (B) is the same system, but it is applied to packages weighing more than 1 lb.

First-Class, on the other hand, allows the mailer the option of simply dropping mail into any mail drop box, provided it already has the correct amount of postage on each piece. Also, First-Class mail is the generally used option for post cards, regular mail such as bills or letters, and similar single items. The rates for both Standard Mail (A) and First-Class Mail in the late 1990s were 32 cents for the first ounce and 23 cents for each additional ounce, up to 11 ounces, but as users of the U.S. Mail are well aware, these rates tend to rise every few years.

POSTAGE METERS Personal postal metering has long been an option for businesses that make heavy use of the mail system. It allows the user to pre-stamp their mailings according to precise weight, while still at their business location. The convenience of this item has made it a perennially popular one with many small business owners.

According to *Business Journal*, though, electronic postal metering is the wave of the future. Electronic postal metering (sometimes referred to as E-postage), which will shortly replace mechanical postal metering systems currently purchased or leased from the post office, enables customers to download postage over the Internet. Customers will soon be able to purchase a hardware plug-in that connects to the printer port of their PCS. The software accompanying the device will enable the user to download postal credit to a chip stored inside the meter over the Internet from a vendor licensed by the Postal Service. The mailer then uses the electronic meter to print a postal bar code on packages and letters. This new technology should further ease mailings for small business owners, although some analysts claim that malfunctions that occur under this new system may prove troublesome to correct.

FURTHER READING:

''Applying Postage with a Keystroke.'' *Nation's Business.* December 1997.

Cole-Gomolski, Barb. ''Postage Due for E-mail.'' *Computerworld.* October 13, 1997.

Fernandes, Lorna. ''E-Stamp may Lick Problem.'' *The Business Journal.* October 20, 1997.

McCarthy, Shawn P. ''Snail Mail via the Internet?'' *Logistics Management.* October 1997.

Mull, Angela. ''Required Postage Meter Change-Out Better Deal.'' *The Business Journal.* October 17, 1997.

SEE ALSO: Delivery Services

PREGNANCY IN THE WORKPLACE

Nearly all small business owners that maintain a paid staff will, at one time or another, learn that one or more of their employees are pregnant. In fact, Bureau of Labor Statistics figures indicate that fully 80 percent of all working women will become pregnant at some point in their working lives. Historically, this news has not always been welcomed by employers, and while research and highly publicized episodes indicated that mid-sized and large companies have been more likely to behave in a discriminatory fashion against pregnant employees than small businesses, which on the whole are more likely to cultivate a more relaxed, family-friendly atmosphere, the latter have also been known to look unkindly on news of an employee's pregnancy. Indeed, researchers observed that attitudes toward pregnant employees have tended to be predicated more on company culture than on the size of the firm. For example, a small business headed by a driven entrepreneur who is determined to meet or exceed an ambitious agenda of growth may greet the news that his or her top salesperson is pregnant with far less equanimity than the leadership of a larger company that places greater weight on the long-term value of the salesperson.

For the most part, companies of all sizes have adopted more enlightened views of workplace pregnancy issues in recent years. This change can be traced in part to their need to comply with legal protections that have been established on behalf of pregnant workers, but it can also be attributed to increased recognition of the vital importance of women in the workplace and increased awareness of the negative impact that discriminatory practices can have on other women employees and on bottom-line performance. Nonetheless, unfair treatment of pregnant employees persists in some quarters. "Despite the laws designed to protect workers who become pregnant, female employees increasingly believe they are unfairly denied promotions, proper medical leave, and even their jobs because they have become pregnant, or because they might become pregnant," wrote Amy Oakes Wren, Roland E. Caldwell, and Linda Ache Caldwell in *Business Horizons*. Wren, Caldwell, and Caldwell blame this festering problem in large measure on management inability to recognize the fundamental demographic changes taking place in the American workplace: "The issue of pregnancy discrimination has become even more focused as women of childbearing age enter the work force at higher rates and corporate downsizing forces many managers to seek higher levels of productivity among remaining employees. Unfortunately, some managers have taken unlawful actions against pregnant workers because they perceive them as less productive, absent more often, or unable to perform their jobs. [But] with two-thirds of the net additions in the U.S. work force in the remainder of the 1990s projected to be female, the treatment of women at work is a crucial issue for organizations."

PREGNANCY DISCRIMINATION AND FEDERAL LAW

Over the past few decades, the United States has passed three federal laws that provide legal protections to pregnant employees as well as employees who might become pregnant. These are Title VII of the 1964 Civil Rights Act, the Pregnancy Discrimination Act of 1978, and the **Family and Medical Leave Act (FMLA)** of 1993.

TITLE VII OF THE CIVIL RIGHTS ACT This legislation expressly forbids employers with 15 of more workers on their payroll from refusing to hire, discharge, or otherwise discriminate against any person in any way, shape, or form because of that person's gender. However, this law left a giant loophole for employers, because the Supreme Court ruled in a mid-1970s case that discrimination based on pregnancy was not the same as discrimination based on sex. In other words, a disability plan that provided benefits to both men and *non-pregnant* women was found to meet the criteria of Title VII. Such plans, said the Court, were simply insurance policies that covered some risks and not others. Pregnancy was ruled to be one of those risks that was not covered.

PREGNANCY DISCRIMINATION ACT OF 1978 This law was drawn up to close the above-mentioned loophole. This legislation stipulated that all employers treat pregnant and non-pregnant employees in the same way, both in terms of benefits received and all other respects.

FAMILY AND MEDICAL LEAVE ACT OF 1993 When it passed in 1993, the Family and Medical Leave Act (FMLA) was hailed as a ground breaking law that provided important federal protections for both men and women faced with issues related to pregnancy, childbirth, adoption, placement for foster care, and family sickness. It was bitterly opposed by some segments of the business community, but family advocates ultimately prevailed. The FMLA stipulates that men and women can take as many as 12 weeks of unpaid leave annually for the birth or adoption of a child, care of a sick child, placement for foster care, or because of morning sickness or other illness (the illness does not have to be pregnancy-related). Employers and employees alike should note, however, that the FMLA does not impact businesses with fewer than 50 employees.

AVOIDING DISCRIMINATORY BEHAVIOR

Wren, Caldwell, and Caldwell cited a number of ways in which employers—either intentionally or unintentionally—can run afoul of the various antidiscrimination rules that have been erected to protect women employees who are or may become pregnant. "Examples range from intentionally eliminating pregnant applicants from the labor pool to unintentionally discriminating against a pregnant woman because of an apparently sex-neutral insurance policy," they wrote.

- Employers may not refuse to hire, refuse to promote, or fire a pregnant employee because of her pregnancy. Moreover, experts warn that the person's pregnancy can not be *any* factor in the action taken. If the pregnancy was a consideration in any way, shape, or form, then the employer is liable.

- Employers have to provide the same benefits to all employees, whether or not they are pregnant, although they do not have to provide additional benefits to pregnant workers.

- Employers may not refuse to adjust workloads for a pregnant employee if they do so for a worker who is not pregnant but claims some other disability or mitigating circumstance.

- Employers may not discriminate against staff members just because they might get pregnant.

- Employers may not discriminate against employees who 1) have had an abortion, or 2) are considering having an abortion.

- Employers may not forbid a pregnant employee from continuing to work if she wants to and is physically capable of doing all tasks associated with the work.

- Employers may not evaluate pregnant and non-pregnant employees differently. This is especially true, say Wren, Caldwell, and Caldwell, ''when the employer has unilaterally lessened the employee's work load in response to the pregnancy.''

- Employers have a responsibility to make sure that pregnant employees are not excluded from taking part in the normal office environment since such exclusions can have a detrimental impact on the employee's cognizance of important work-related issues.

- Employers may not threaten to fire an employee because of her pregnancy or potential pregnancy.

- Employers are not allowed to reassign employees to lower-paying positions because of pregnancy. Similarly, employers may not change a worker's job description and then eliminate the new job via reorganization.

- Employers may not engage in discriminatory practices against men whose wives or partners become pregnant. It should be noted, however, that application of this law may vary from state to state, since states have different views of the rights of married and unmarried couples.

- Employers can not demand medical notes from a pregnant woman's doctor concerning her work status if they do not require similar documentation from doctors of other employees who have short-term disabilities.

The above guidelines add up to a very simple mandate for employers: Treat your pregnant employees no differently than you would any other employees.

MANAGING THE LOSS OF EMPLOYEES DURING PREGNANCY AND MATERNITY LEAVE

Obviously, pregnant employees should not have to endure discrimination from their employers. Indeed, many researchers, executives, and business owners contend that employers that are understanding and treat their pregnant employees fairly can often count on a heightened level of loyalty from that employee upon their return from maternity leave. But businesses also have to recognize that employee pregnancy means the loss—sometimes temporary, sometimes permanent—of workers, some of whom may be quite valuable to the firm's operation.

Businesses, then, have to figure out ''how to balance the personal needs of a pregnant worker with the bottom-line imperatives of running a business,'' wrote Julia Lawlor in *Sales and Marketing Management.* She noted that effective management of this issue entails paying attention to the impact that pregnancy-related absences can have on important business areas, such as sales: ''In a fiercely competitive marketplace, governed by even fiercer laws protecting women against discrimination at work, managers must be prepared to handle a host of difficulties surrounding pregnancies and maternity leave: How to accommodate a rep [sales representative] who's having a difficult pregnancy—severe morning sickness, backaches, complications that require bed rest—without seeming unfair to other reps; deciding who should cover a rep's territory while she's out, and how that person should be compensated; determining who will visit out-of-town customers when the salesperson is unable to travel; navigating antidiscrimination laws.''

Not surprisingly, prior planning is often cited as an essential element of effectively managing the impact of pregnancies on business operations. Business owners and managers should figure out in advance how the pregnant person's responsibilities will be handled in her absence. Many experts encourage those owners and managers to talk openly with the pregnant employee about possible work dispersal options. The pregnant employee is often the person best equipped to make knowledgeable decisions about allocation of responsibilities. Moreover, opening and maintaining good communication with the pregnant employee can provide owners and managers with the information (anticipated length of maternity leave, restrictions on travel, etc.) they need to make informed decisions about business operations.

In addition, companies have to make sure that other employees that are impacted by a staffer's absence due to pregnancy are adequately compensated for the extra work that they take on. Employees that are asked to ''cover'' for a pregnant colleague for an extended period of time without receiving any parallel adjustment in compensation or recognition will quickly recognize that their employer is in essence trying to get something for nothing. Employers who do this may manage to keep all facets of the business running fairly smoothly, but it can also erode employee loyalty to the business and create needless friction between the pregnant employee and her co-workers.

FURTHER READING:

Armstrong, Michael. *A Handbook of Human Resource Management.* Kogan Page Limited, 1988.

Beer, Michael, Bert Specter, Paul R. Lawrence, D. Quinn Mills, and Richard E. Walton. *Human Resource Management.* New York: The Free Press, 1985.

Burstiner, Irving. *The Small Business Handbook.* Rev. ed. Prentice Hall, 1988.

Compliance Guide to the Family and Medical Leave Act. U.S. Department of Labor, 1996.

Lawlor, Julia. "Pregnant Pause." *Sales and Marketing Management.* February 1998.

"Managing a Salesperson's Pregnancy." *Sales and Marketing Management.* February 1998.

Oakes Wren, Amy, Roland E. Caldwell Jr., and Linda Ache Caldwell. "Managing Pregnancy in the Workplace." November-December 1996.

SEE ALSO: Career and Family; Employee Rights

PRESENT VALUE

Present value (PV) calculations determine how much $1 to be paid at a certain time in the future is worth today. The answer depends upon the length of time involved and the prevailing **interest rate**. In other words, the present value of an amount to be received in the future is the discounted face value considering the length of time the receipt is deferred and the required rate of return (or appropriate discount rate under the circumstances). Present value is the result of the time value of money concept, which recognizes that today's dollar is worth more than the same dollar received at a future point in time. This notion can be demonstrated by examining several common financial transactions:

- Money invested in bank certificates of deposit may earn interest at 5 percent. At that rate, $1,000 deposited on January 1 will accumulate $50 of interest by December 31, making the total available to the investor $1,050. Since this investor is willing to lend his money to the bank for 5 percent annual interest, that rate may be viewed as the required rate of return, or the discount rate. The $1,050 to be received on December 31

thus had a PV to that investor at January 1 of exactly $1,000 ($1,050/(1+.05)^1$).

- Annuity contracts can be bought from insurance companies whereby a single payment is made to the insurance company in exchange for a defined series of annual (or monthly) payments made back to the buyer. In these cases the simple sum of the periodic repayments from the insurance company to the buyer exceeds the original annuity purchase price, in absolute terms. However, when considering the deferred repayment and the implied rate of return on the money loaned, the amounts exactly equate, on a present value basis.

- Mortgage loans are basically the reverse of the above described annuity contract. Here, the individual borrows the money, promising to make scheduled repayments to the mortgage holder or lender. Again, due to the differential timing of cash flows, and the fact that the bank requires interest to be paid on the borrowed funds, the PVs equate. That is, the PV of the sum of the future mortgage payments is exactly equal to the amount borrowed (which by definition is at the PV on the date of the loan).

The formula for calculating the present value of a series of future receipts is:

$$PV = \frac{\text{cash flow 1}}{(1+\text{interest rate})^1} + \frac{\text{cash flow 2}}{(1+\text{interest rate})^2} + \cdots + \frac{\text{cash flow n}}{(1+\text{interest rate})^n}$$

Where cash flows 1 to n are the future receipts, the interest rate is the discount rate appropriate for the stated period, and n is the number of periods over which future receipts occur.

The interest, or discount, rate used in PV calculations is a key element in determining the PV. This importance is emphasized when the future amounts occur over an extended period of time, due to the power of compounding. For example, the final payment on a 30-year loan at 7 percent interest would be worth approximately 13.1 percent of its face amount on a present value basis at the date of loan origin $[1/(1+.07)^{30}]$. By contrast, the 30th payment on a loan with a 9 percent interest rate would be worth only 7.5 percent $[1/(1+.09)^{30}]$ of its face amount in present value terms at the origin. This simple example shows the power of compounding when time periods are long.

The discount rate used in a given circumstance must compensate the lender of funds for three elements of return:

1) **Inflation**: just to remain even in terms of buying power, the return of money at a future date must be appended by the Consumer Price Index rate. In other words, if a person lends an amount of money adequate to buy a loaf of bread at $t=0$, he will require repayment at $t=1$ of the original amount plus the fraction of that amount representing the CPI increase over the period. That way he will be able to buy the same loaf of bread at $t=1$.

2) Time value of money (TVM): beyond simply keeping even with inflation, the investor or lender has a basic preference for consumption sooner rather than later. The cost of compensating for this aspect of human nature has been found to be about 1 to 2 percent per year. That is, the real rates of return on riskless assets have averaged about 1.5 percent.

3) Risk: in addition to postponing the preferred immediate consumption and having to reimburse for inflation's erosion of buying power, many types of investment involve a risk of default. That is, the investor may never again see his funds, for example if the company goes bankrupt. Compensating for this element of required return can be considerably more expensive than the first two combined. For example, junk bonds may be paying interest at 12 percent, while anticipated inflation is only 4 percent and TVM is about 1.5 percent. This would mean that the risk premium component of the overall interest rate is 6.5 percent (12 percent − 4 percent − 1.5 percent).

FURTHER READING:

Brealey, Richard A., and Stewart C. Myers. *Principles of Corporate Finance.* 4th ed. New York: McGraw Hill, 1991.

Pindyck, Robert S., and Daniel L. Rubinfeld. *Microeconomics.* 2nd ed. New York: Macmillan, 1992.

PRESS KITS/NEWS RELEASES

Press kits are packets of printed background information that are provided to members of the media at a press conference. News releases, which can be included in press kits or distributed separately, are brief, printed statements that outline the major facts of a news story in journalistic style. As part of its overall **public relations** effort, a small business may need to prepare press kits or news releases in order to disseminate new information about its products, services, operations, or other activities to the public. A steady flow of news helps to make a small business more visible to the public and creates favorable interest in its activities.

In his book *Public Relations for the Entrepreneur and the Growing Business,* Norman Soderberg lists several possible types of news stories that a small business could generate. For example, a small business might announce the promotion, transfer, retirement, or hiring of personnel, or the negotiation of a new labor contract. Building new facilities, planning a major expansion, installing new equipment, or offering a new product are other newsworthy events that might occur in a small business. In addition, human interest stories might arise from the unusual hobbies or avocations of employees, the success of company-sponsored sports teams or events, or the company's participation in charity or community activities. If a small business received an award or a visit from a celebrity, these events might provide impetus for a news story as well. In general, a newsworthy story should be timely, of general or human interest, and somewhat unusual.

PREPARING A NEWS RELEASE

In order to attract the attention of the media to anything but a vitally important story, a small business will probably have to prepare and send out a news release. Ideally, the news release will generate enough interest that the media will choose to cover the story themselves. A news release may also be useful as a handout to provide basic information to reporters who come to cover a story.

Soderberg explains that a well-written news release should include "five Ws and an H": who, what, when, where, why, and how. The lead, or first few lines of the news release, should address all of these questions, though not necessarily all in one sentence. The remainder of the news release should provide supporting information—such as facts and figures or quotes from people involved—in most-important to least-important order. Overall, a news release should be crisp and concise, never exceeding two pages in length, and similar to a newspaper article in content and style. It is important that a small business owner find someone to write the news release who has a good command of language, grammar, and punctuation.

News releases should be typed on company letterhead and include the name and address of the company, its trademark or logo, the name and telephone number of a contact person (usually the small business owner, even if the job of preparing the news release is delegated to another person), the date, and the words "News Release." The importance and scope of the story determines where it should be sent. In most cases, it would be appropriate to send it to the business editors of the local print media. Sometimes sending it to local radio and television contacts might be appropriate as well. A small business can create a mailing list of relevant addresses, which can be found in media and trade journals and some reference books, to simplify the process. But small business owners should avoid the temptation to follow up a news release with a telephone call.

HOLDING A PRESS CONFERENCE

Soderberg cautions small business owners against arranging a press conference unless it concerns a major announcement, or the subject is so important that reporters will require the opportunity to ask questions, or a major dignitary or celebrity is involved. Otherwise, a news release or telephone call is the preferred method of disseminating information to the media. If the news warrants a press conference, it should be timed to accommodate the release of the local papers (morning for an afternoon paper, afternoon for a morning paper) and held at a centrally located site with sufficient seating. When television coverage is expected, it is important to provide a visual element for the cameras. For example, a scale model of a new plant, a demonstration of a new process, or a sample of a new product might provide strong visual support at a press conference. The small business should also provide press kits to the members of the media in attendance at a press conference. These packets of printed background materials might include a news release, data sheets, photographs, biographies of important persons, and other pertinent information.

FURTHER READING:

Marken, G.A. "Let's Do Away with Press Releases." *Public Relations Quarterly.* Spring 1994.

Morton, Linda P. "Do Public Relations Managers and Technicians Value News Releases Differently?" *Public Relations Review.* Winter 1996.

Ryan, Michael. "Models Help Writers Produce Publishable Releases." *Public Relations Quarterly.* Summer 1995.

Saltz, Linda Citroen. "How to Get Your News Releases Published." *Journal of Accountancy.* November 1996.

Soderberg, Norman R. *Public Relations for the Entrepreneur and the Growing Business.* Hinsdale, IL: Probus, 1986.

Zacek, Judith. "Using the Media: No News Isn't Good News." *Travel Weekly.* July 20, 1995.

PRICE/EARNINGS (P/E) RATIO

The price/earnings ratio (P/E ratio) provides a comparison of the current market price of a share of stock and that stock's earnings per share, or EPS (which is figured by dividing a company's net income by its number of shares of common stock outstanding). For example, if a company's stock sold for $30 per share and it posted earnings per share of $1.50, that company would have a P/E ratio of 15. A company's P/E ratio typically rises as a result of increases in its stock price, an indicator of the stock's popularity.

"The price-earnings ratio is part of the everyday vocabulary of investors in the stock market," noted Richard Brealey and Stewart Myers in *Principles of Corporate Finance,* because a company's P/E ratio is often viewed as an indicator of future stock performance. "The high P/E shows that investors think that the firm has good growth opportunities, that its earnings are relatively safe and deserve a low capitalization rate, or both."

John B. Thomas observed in the *Indianapolis Business Journal,* however, that "while accepting that a high P/E ratio is usually a sign of high expectations, analysts and brokers nonetheless are quick to caution that the ratios are only part of the puzzle." A company may post an artificially high P/E ratio as a result of factors that can either boost stock prices or diminish earnings per share. Restructuring charges, merger and acquisition rumors (whether true or false), and high dividend yields all have the capacity to push a company's P/E ratio upward. In other instances, legitimately high P/E ratios can be adversely impacted down the road by such factors as market conditions, technology, and increased competition from new rivals (who may, in fact, be drawn to the industry by the company's previously posted P/E ratios).

Conversely, while a low P/E ratio is often a good indication that a company is struggling, appearances can again be deceiving. In addition, different industry sectors often have diverse P/E ratio averages. A company may have a fairly low P/E ratio when compared with all other corporations; when compared with the other companies within its industry, however, it may be a leader.

Finally, a company that posts a loss has no earnings to compare with its stock price. As a result, no P/E ratio can be determined for the company. Still, these companies may remain viable choices for investment if an investor decides that the company under examination is headed toward future profitability.

Since so many factors can influence a company's P/E ratio, industry analysts caution against relying on it too heavily in making investment decisions. As one analyst remarked to the *Indianapolis Business Journal,* while a company's P/E ratio is a valuable and often accurate investment tool, "if you're going to buy and sell stocks based on a P/E ratio, you're not going to make money. You'd better look at why it is high or low."

EARNINGS PER SHARE (EPS)

Earnings per share is one of the two factors that determine a company's P/E ratio; the other is the price of the company's stock. EPS is derived by dividing a corporation's net income by the number of shares of common stock that are outstanding. A company with 30,000 outstanding shares of common stock and a net income of $270,000 would thus have an earnings per share of $9.

An essential part of determining the P/E ratio, earnings per share has also come to be regarded as an important piece of information for the investment community in and of itself. "A primary concern of investors is how profitable a company is relative to their investment in the company," wrote Jay M. Smith, Jr., and K. Fred Skousen in *Intermediate Accounting*. "The investor is concerned with how net income relates to shares held and to the market price of the stock.... Only by converting the total amounts to per share data can a meaningful evaluation be made," because EPS figures can illustrate the degree to which a company's net income is keeping pace with its capital structure. In recognition of the importance of this information, corporations are required to report EPS amounts on their income statement (the requirement was suspended for nonpublic entities in 1978).

FURTHER READING:

Bierman, Harold, Jr., and Seymour Smidt. *Financial Management for Decision Making.* New York: Macmillan Publishing Company, 1986.

Brealey, Richard, and Stewart Myers. *Principles of Corporate Finance.* 2d ed. New York: McGraw-Hill Book Company, 1984.

"Don't Get Burned by Hot Stocks," *Money.* October 1994.

Smith, Jay M., Jr., and K. Fred Skousen. *Intermediate Accounting.* Cincinnati: South-Western Publishing Co., 1987.

Thomas, John B. "P/E Ratios Driven by Variety of Factors, Carry Variety of Meanings," *Indianapolis Business Journal.* May 23, 1994.

Welsch, Glenn A., Robert N. Anthony, and Daniel G. Short. *Fundamentals of Financial Accounting.* Homewood, IL: Richard D. Irwin, Inc., 1984.

SEE ALSO: Stocks

PRICING

Intelligent pricing is one of the most important elements of any successful business venture. Yet many entrepreneurs fail to educate themselves adequately about various pricing components and strategies before launching a new business. Smart small business owners will weigh many marketplace factors before setting prices for their goods and services. As the Small Business Administration (SBA) indicated in *The Facts About Pricing Your Products and Services,* "you must understand your market, distribution costs, and competition. Remember, the marketplace responds rapidly to technological advances and international competition. You must keep abreast of the factors that affect pricing and be ready to adjust quickly."

COST FACTORS AND PRICING

There are three primary cost factors that need to be considered by small businesses when determining the prices that they charge for their goods or services. After all, price alone means little if it is not figured within the context of operating **costs**. A company may be able to command a hefty price for an item, only to find that the various costs of producing and delivering that item eliminate most or all of the profit that it realizes on the sale. It should also be noted that **service businesses** often find it more difficult to accurately gauge their costs, especially in the realm of employee hours. A freelance copyeditor may find that one 2,500-word article takes twice as long to complete as another article of the same size because of differences in quality that are often difficult to anticipate ahead of time.

LABOR COSTS Labor costs consist of the cost of the work that goes into the manufacturing of a product or the execution of a service. Direct labor costs can be figured by multiplying the cost of labor per hour by the number of employee-hours required to complete the job. Business owners, however, need to keep in mind that the "cost of labor per hour" includes not only hourly wage or salary of the relevant employees, but also the costs of the fringe benefits that those workers receive. These fringe benefits can include social security, retirement benefits, insurance, unemployment compensation, workers' compensation, and other benefits.

MATERIAL COSTS Material costs are the costs of all materials that are part of the final product offered by the business. As with labor, this expense can apply to both goods and services. In the case of goods, material costs refer to the costs of the various components that make up a product, while material costs associated with services rendered typically include replacement parts, building parts, etc. A deck builder, for example, would include such items as lumber, nails, and sealer as material costs.

OVERHEAD COSTS **Overhead expenses** are costs that can not be directly attributed to one particular product or service. Some business consultants simply refer to overhead costs as those business expenses that do not qualify as labor costs or material costs. These costs include indirect expenses such as general supplies, heating and lighting expenditures, **depreciation**, taxes, advertising, rental or leasing costs, transportation, employee discounts, damaged merchandise, business memberships, and insurance. A certain percentage of employees usually fit in this category as well. While the wages and benefits received by an assembly line worker involved in the production of a specific product might well qualify as a labor cost, the wages and benefits accrued by general support personnel—janitors, attorneys, accountants, clerks, human resource personnel, receptionists—are included as overhead.

Overhead expenses are typically divided into two categories—**fixed and variable expenses**. Fixed expenses are regular (usually monthly) expenses that will not change much, regardless of a company's business fortunes. Examples of fixed expenses include rent, utilities, insurance, membership dues, subscriptions, accounting costs, and depreciation on fixed assets. Variable expenses are those expenses that undergo greater fluctuation, depending on variables such as time of year (for seasonal businesses), competitor advertising, and sales. Expenses that are more heavily predicated on company revenues and business owner strategies include office supplies, mailing and advertising, communications (telephone and Fax bills), and employee bonuses.

COST OF GOODS SOLD One of the most important tools that accountants and entrepreneurs use to gauge the health of businesses is the "cost of goods sold." This figure is in essence the business's total cost of manufacturing the products it sells or—in the case of retail firms—its total expenditures to purchase products for resale. Delivery and freight charges are typically included within this equation. Cost of goods sold provides business owners with a rough measurement of their gross profit margin. The figure usually bears a close relationship to sales, but it may vary significantly if increases in the prices paid for merchandise cannot be offset by increases in sales prices, or if profit margins swell because of special purchase deals or sudden surges in product popularity.

PRICING STRATEGIES

Small businesses have many different pricing strategies from which they can choose, but they need to select carefully. An ill-considered decision can place a heavy burden on the business.

MANUFACTURER'S SUGGESTED RETAIL PRICE Many small businesses prefer to simply price their goods in accordance with the manufacturer's suggested retail price. They thus eliminate costs associated with making their own pricing decisions or pursuing more proactive pricing strategies. Critics note, however, that this strategy—such as it is—is utterly heedless of the competition, which may be able to offer a lower price for any number of reasons.

PRICE BUNDLING This is the practice of giving the customers the option of buying several items or services for one price. A furniture retailer, for example, might offer customers a sofa and love seat combination at a price that is somewhat lower than what the two goods would cost if bought separately. Similarly, a landscaper might lure customers by offering two free months of lawn maintenance with any major landscaping job. Leonard Berry and Manjit Yadav noted in *Sloan Management Review* that bundling has several advantages, especially for service-oriented businesses: "The cost structure of most service companies is such that providing an additional service costs less than providing the second service alone. . . . A second benefit of bundling that appeals to customers is purchasing related services from one service provider. They can save time and money by interacting with an paying one provider rather than multiple providers. Third, bundling effectively increases the number of connections a service company has with its customers."

MULTIPLE PRICING Similar to price bundling, multiple pricing is the practice of selling multiple units of an item for a single price. A grocery store that offers two boxes of macaroni and cheese at a single price, for instance, is engaged in multiple pricing. Whereas price bundling is more commonly employed for big-ticket items, multiple pricing is usually used to sell inexpensive consumable items such as razor blades, shampoo, household cleaning products, and food and beverages.

COST-PLUS PRICING This methodology, popular with manufacturers, involves adding together all labor, material, and overhead costs (the "cost") and then adding the desired profit (the "plus").

COMPETITIVE PRICING Some small business owners choose to base their own prices on the prices of their principal competitors. Business owners who choose to follow this course, however, should make sure that they look at competing businesses of similar size and strength. "It's very chancy to compete with a large store's prices," noted the SBA's *The Facts About Pricing Your Products and Services,* "because they can buy in larger volume and their cost per unit will be less. Instead, price products based on your local small-store analysis, then highlight other competitive factors, like personalized customer service and convenient location." Competitive pricing among service-oriented businesses, meanwhile, is a hazier proposition, since the nature and quality of services offered can vary so widely from business to business. Still, it is often employed, if only as a general pricing guideline.

PRICING ABOVE COMPETITION If a business is operating in a community in which low prices are most customers' primary concern, then this pricing strategy is obviously doomed to failure. In settings in which price is not the customer's most important consideration, however, some small businesses can do quite well employing this strategy. The key to making ''pricing above competition'' work, say experts, is to provide customers with added benefits that justify paying the higher price. These benefits can take the form of: 1) convenient or exclusive location; 2) social status; 3) exclusive merchandise; and 4) high level of service. The latter can take the form of home or office delivery of goods, service and/or product knowledge, speed of service, attractive return policies, and friendly atmosphere.

Some business owners also boost prices in markets that have few competitors, reasoning that the community has little choice but to buy from their businesses. Such prices rarely reach outrageous levels, but they can become sufficiently high that enterprising entrepreneurs will recognize an opportunity to undercut the business with more inexpensively priced goods or services.

PRICING BELOW COMPETITION Pricing below competition is the practice of setting one's prices below those of its competitors. Commonly employed by major discount chains such as Wal-Mart—which can do so because its purchasing power enables it to save on its costs per unit—this strategy can also be effectively used by smaller businesses in some instances (though not when competing directly with Wal-Mart and its ilk), provided they keep their operating costs down and do not spark a price war. Indeed, the smaller profit margins associated with this pricing strategy make it a practical necessity for participating companies to: exercise tight control over inventory; keep labor costs down; keep major operational expenses such as facility leases and equipment rental under control; obtain good prices from suppliers; and make effective use of its pricing strategy in all advertising.

PRICE LINING Companies that engage in this practice are basically hoping to attract a specific segment of the community by only carrying products within a specified price range. This strategy is often employed by businesses whose goods/services or location are likely to attract upscale buyers, though others use it as well. Advantages sometimes accrued through price lining practices include: reduced inventory and storage costs, ease of merchandise selection, and enhanced status. Analysts note, however, that this strategy frequently limits the company's freedom to react to competitors' pricing strategies, and that it can leave businesses particularly vulnerable to economic trends.

ODD PRICING Odd pricing is used in nearly all segments of the business world today. It is the practice of pricing goods and services at prices such as $9.95 (rather than $10) or $79.99 (rather than $80) because of the conviction that consumers will often round the price down rather than up when weighing whether to make a purchase. This little morsel of pricing psychology has become so universally employed that many observers question its value; still, the practice remains widespread across the United States (and elsewhere).

Other commonly used pricing policies include **penetration pricing** and skimming pricing (for manufacturers) and **loss leader pricing** (for retailers).

FACTORS IN ARRIVING AT A PRICING STRATEGY

Entrepreneurs encounter numerous considerations that should be weighed when assigning a price to their goods or services. These considerations range from the needs and desires of target consumers to general economic conditions. The SBA cited the following factors as among the most important to consider when arriving at a pricing strategy.

- Is the price of the good or service of significant importance to target consumers?

- How popular is the product or service being offered?

- What pricing and marketing strategies are compatible with the business's other characteristics (location, service reputation, promotions, etc.)

- Does the owner enjoy final pricing authority?

- Are there opportunities for special market promotions?

- What are competitors charging for similar goods or services?

- Should competitors' temporary price reductions be matched?

- What level of markup can be achieved for each product line or area of service?

- Will prices generate a satisfactory profit margin after calculating operating expenses and reductions?

- When reducing prices on goods or services, do you consider competitors' likely reactions?

- Are there legal factors to consider when establishing price?

- Should ''odd pricing'' or ''multiple pricing'' practices be introduced?

- Should marketing efforts highlight sales of selected high-profile products to attract customers?

- If coupons and other discount measures are offered, how will they impact on net profits?

- Will characteristics of the product sold (handling costs, installation requirements, alterations, etc.) meaningfully add to operating costs?

- Will product quantities be unduly reduced as a result of spoilage, breakage, employee theft, or shoplifting?

- Will services such as home/office delivery, gift wrapping, etc. be included in the purchase price?

- Are economic conditions in area of operation particularly good or bad?

- Will employees receive discounts on store items that they purchase?

- Will senior citizens or students receive discounts on goods or services?

- What markdown policies are in place?

REVISITING PRICING STRATEGIES

Since pricing is one of the single most important factors in determining whether a business will be successful, small business owners should continuously review their pricing policies to make certain that they remain in keeping with marketplace realities. Business environments can change quickly, and the successful entrepreneur will learn to change his or her pricing strategies accordingly. William Cohen, author of *The Entrepreneur and Small-Business Problem Solver,* described six different circumstances in which small business owners should review their pricing and make changes if necessary: 1) when introducing a new product or product line; 2) when testing for the best price; 3) when attempting to break into a new market; 4) when competitors change their prices; 5) when general economic conditions become inflationary or recessionary; 6) when weighing major changes in sales strategy. Indeed, any significant change in any aspect of a business's operations—from rising costs of raw materials to changing insurance premiums—should spark a review of company pricing strategies.

REAL PRICE AND NOMINAL PRICE

Economists, business owners, and other people engaged in the world of commerce have long recognized that historical events can help business owners evaluate current business plans and propose future strategies, including pricing strategies. Indeed, as Robert Pindyck and Daniel Rubinfeld observed in *Microeconomics,* "we often want to compare the price of a good today with what it was in the past or is likely to be in the future." Such comparisons are meaningless, however, unless those prices are measured "relative to the overall price level. In absolute terms, the price of a dozen eggs is many times higher today than it was 50 years ago, but relative to prices overall, it is actually lower. Therefore, we must be careful to correct for inflation when comparing prices across time. This means measuring prices in *real* rather than *nominal* terms." Pindyck and Rubinfeld go on to define the nominal price of a good (its "current dollar" price) as its absolute price, noting that the nominal price of a quart of milk was 40 cents in 1970 and about 80 cents in 1990. The real price, however, is defined as the price relative to an aggregate measure of prices (usually the Consumer Price Index-CPI). Percentage changes in the CPI measure the rate of inflation in the economy.

SURVIVING COMPETITORS' DISCOUNT PRICING STRATEGIES

Major discount stores such as Wal-Mart, Sam's Club, Target, K-Mart, Office Depot, Staples, Best Buy, and Circuit City have gained control of large blocs of the American business world over the last several years on the strength of their one-stop shopping and discount prices, the latter a result of their ability to buy goods at bulk rates. Many small business owners have felt the impact of these stores—indeed, cautionary tales concerning the impact that such stores can have on formerly vibrant downtown shopping areas have proliferated in recent years.

Many observers believe, however, that some small business failures that occurred in the wake of these titans' arrivals could have been avoided if small business owners had adopted different strategies to deal with the new competitive environment in which they were operating. Indeed, economists and business analysts agree that most small businesses cannot compete with large chains in the area of price; the bulk-rate buying power advantage that the big stores enjoy is simply too great to overcome. But they contend that many small businesses can still co-exist with these titans if their owners outmaneuver the big stores in other areas. Effective strategies that can be used to help negate the discount pricing strategy employed at the big chains include:

- Emphasize value and personal service rather than price.

- Offer attractive ancillary services (home and office delivery, generous return policies, etc.)

- Define your market segment or niche and devote energies accordingly.

- Control inventory.

- Streamline to eliminate less profitable areas of business.

- Target advertising and promotions to reach most likely customers.

- Steer customers to the most profitable aspects of your business.

- Establish your business's industry knowledge as an additional resource for customers.

- Maintain good relations with vendors. Add product to increase customer spending.

- Build strong relationships with vendors.

- Meet or beat prices of big discounters on selected lead items or services.

- Make intelligent use of price strategies such as price bundling.

Of course, pricing remains a very big component in determining a company's success or failure. "The key to success," concluded the SBA in its *Pricing Your Products* brochure, "is to have a well-planned strategy and established policies and to constantly monitor prices and operating costs to ensure a profit." Finally, the SBA cautioned entrepreneurs to "remember that the image of your business is crucial to obtaining and keeping the clientele and that your pricing structure and policies are a major component of your image."

FURTHER READING:

Berry, Leonard L., and Manjit S. Yadav. "Capture and Communicate Value in the Pricing of Services." *Sloan Management Review.* Summer 1996.

"Case Study: How to Price Your Products to Increase Profits." *Business Owner.* May-June 1995.

Cohen, William A. *The Entrepreneur and Small-Business Problem Solver.* 2d ed. Wiley, 1990.

The Facts About Pricing Your Products and Services. Washington: U.S. Small Business Administration, 1996.

Marn, M.V., and R.L. Rosiello. "Managing Price, Gaining Profit." *Harvard Business Review.* September-October 1992.

Pindyck, Robert S., and Daniel L. Rubinfeld. *Microeconomics.* 2d ed. Macmillan, 1992.

Pricing Your Products. Washington: U.S. Small Business Administration, n.a.

Smith, G. E., and T. T. Nagle. "Financial Analysis for Profit-Driven Pricing." *Sloan Management Review.* Spring 1994.

Walker, Bruce J. *A Pricing Checklist for Small Retailers.* Washington: U.S. Small Business Administration, n.a.

Winninger, Thomas J. *Price Wars: How to Win the Battle for Your Customer.* St. Thomas Press, 1994.

PRIVATE LABELING

Private labeling is when a retailer purchases products from various manufacturers and then markets those products under its own brand. Private label goods are often referred to as "store brands," as opposed to the "name brands" that are sold under the brand name of the manufacturer. For example, the consumer products giant Proctor and Gamble manufactures peanut butter and sells it under the brand name Jif, while the supermarket chain Kroger purchases peanut butter from smaller manufacturers and sells it as Kroger brand peanut butter. Private label products tend to be less expensive than competing name brands, largely because of reduced **advertising** expenditures.

Private labeling gained prominence during the recession of the late 1980s, when many consumers chose to give up expensive name brand products in an effort to save money, and many retailers began to market store brands in an attempt to increase sales. But when consumer confidence in the economy rebounded in the 1990s, consumer loyalty to name brands did not. Today, private labeling is a widespread business practice among supermarkets, drugstore chains, and mass merchandisers. These retailers sell hundreds of different items under their own brand names, from basic household items and food to specialty items and even clothing.

In the early days private label goods were essentially cheap imitations of the leading brands, even copying the colors and designs of the major competitors' **packaging**. Even though court rulings have supported right of private labelers to imitate the packaging of leading brands (unless there is documented confusion among consumers), private label retailers have now moved away from imitation and toward attractive packaging of their own design. Some retailers believe that they need eye-catching packaging because they do not do much advertising, and instead rely on consumers taking notice of their offerings as they walk through store aisles.

Another emerging trend concerns the type of products that are sold as store brands. Whereas the majority of private label products used to be the most basic household goods, the areas of growth in recent years have been in premium and super-premium goods. "The growth in premium brands shows that while today's consumers are value-conscious, they're still picky about product quality," Jenny McCune wrote in an article for *Small Business Reports.* "Inferior goods aren't attracting consumers at any price, which is why sales of generic goods—the no-name, no-frills varieties—are actually down."

The continued growth of private labels has encouraged retailers to devote significantly more attention to developing store brands. "Eager to satisfy these value-conscious consumers and make higher margins to boot, many retailers are promoting their house brands as never before," McCune noted. "They've focused on improving the quality of store brands to better compete with name brands and other private-label lines. They're also lavishing the brands with marketing attention, rather than simply tossing the goods on the shelves and leaving them to fend for themselves.''

McCune claimed that the recent growth of private labels has also provided new opportunities for small and medium-sized manufacturers in a whole spectrum of industries. Rather than competing directly with much larger companies and incurring the related advertising expenses, these small manufacturers can grow by marketing their products to retailers. ''Despite the competition, the trends in private labeling present opportunities for small and midsize manufacturers that can meet the demands of this market,'' McCune stated. In essence, the small businesses who create private label goods serve as the manufacturing arm for their retail customers.

FACTORS IN SUCCESSFUL PRIVATE LABEL MANUFACTURING

In her article, McCune outlined three main factors that determine the potential for success of small businesses that wish to manufacture private label goods: the right product, a competitive price, and a strong **marketing** program. For products to be considered for private labels, they must have a large sales potential, because retailers are not usually interested in branding low-demand items. In addition, the manufacturer must be able to assure that the product quality is as good or better than the leading brands. As McCune explained, ''A retailer puts its own name on the line when it private labels your product, and it won't want that name to be sullied by inferior or inconsistent quality.'' Small manufacturers may gain a marketing advantage if they are willing to assume responsibility for product quality, rather than leaving the retailer holding the bag. This might involve providing a toll-free number on product packaging for consumers to make complaints or suggestions, or giving the retailer a discount on future orders if the quality does not meet predetermined standards.

The type of manufacturing process involved is another important product-related aspect of private labeling. In general, private labels are most appropriate for products that can be manufactured on a tight schedule while maintaining high quality standards. Private label manufacturers must be able to assure their retail clients of reliable, on-time delivery. In addition, they must be flexible enough to ramp up production quickly to meet increases in demand or to change the product's formulation according to the retailer's wishes. ''Given these demands, private labeling generally isn't for industry newcomers,'' McCune noted. ''Retailers look for manufacturers, whether large or small, that are well-regarded in their fields. In a relatively young company, however, the

owners' own reputation can compensate for the firm's short track record.''

Pricing is another important component of successful private label manufacturing. The price must compare favorably to competing name brands while also enabling both the manufacturer and the retailer to make money. In general, private label sales provide high volume but tight margins, so price calculations are crucial. McCune claimed that private label goods are usually priced 20 percent or more below the market leader. In addition, the retailer generally expects to see a profit margin on private label goods that is 7 or 8 percent higher than it receives with name brands. When calculating the final sales price for private label items, manufacturers must be sure to consider any costs that are incurred especially for the private label line. These may include tailoring the product to meet retailer specifications, or designing special packaging for each retailer.

The third factor in successful private label manufacturing is a strong marketing program. The marketing program for private label goods consists of two parts: contracting with retailers to become their supplier for a certain product, and assisting the retailer in marketing that product to the final consumer. If a small business lacks expertise in dealing with retailers, it is possible to hire distributors or consultants who specialize in private-label selling. For small manufacturers who proceed on their own, however, McCune recommended getting all of the conditions of the contract in writing. It is particularly important to determine the amount of packaging that must be kept in stock, since extra packaging with a certain retailer's label becomes useless if the deal falls through. Manufacturers will want to keep the amount as low as possible and perhaps also include a clause that requires the retailer to reimburse them for unused packaging. It is also important that the contract specify realistic delivery dates, product design modifications, and the amount of notice required to terminate the contract. Finally, it may also be useful for private label manufacturers to contribute their product marketing expertise to their retail accounts. This may involve recommending specific promotions or even creating advertisements and writing ad copy.

Overall, McCune noted that private label manufacturing can present tremendous opportunities for small businesses, as well as significant challenges. For example, creating private label goods often requires developing a partnership with retail clients. ''Private label veterans . . . warn newcomers to be prepared for some hand-holding, since the relationship between retailer and private-label supplier tends to be especially close,'' McCune wrote. Still, she recommended that small businesses who manufacture private label goods not allow any one retailer to account for more than 15 percent of their sales. After all, most contracts in this area are open-ended, which enables retailers to change suppliers at any time. Another potential challenge is that name-brand manufacturers are increasingly being attracted by the growth of private labeling. It has encouraged many to reduce prices, improve value, and in some cases even set up private-label divisions of their own to take advantage of their excess manufacturing capacity.

FURTHER READING:

Doherty, Katherine. "Private Label's Staying Power." *U.S. Distribution Journal.* November 15, 1994.

Kaplan, Andrew. "A Name for Itself." *U.S. Distribution Journal.* March 15, 1995.

McAllister, Liane. "The Cachet of Private Labels." *Gifts and Decorative Accessories.* January 1997.

McCune, Jenny. "Catch a Growing Wave." *Small Business Reports.* June 1994.

"The Store Brand Challenges Ahead." *Supermarket Business.* January 1998.

SEE ALSO: Brands and Brand Names; Product Positioning; Quality Control

PRIVATE PLACEMENT OF SECURITIES

Private placement occurs when a company makes an offering of securities not to the public, but directly to an individual or a small group of investors. Such offerings do not need to be registered with the **Securities and Exchange Commission (SEC)** and are exempt from the usual reporting requirements. Private placements are generally considered a cost-effective way for small businesses to raise **capital** without "going public" through an initial public offering (IPO).

"Although most business owners dream of taking their company public someday, many have had to wait years for a traditional public offering," Gary D. Zeune and Timothy R. Baer explained in an article for *Corporate Cashflow Magazine.* "For them, a private placement of equity or debt has been a quicker, less expensive way to raise a limited amount of capital from a limited number of investors. A private placement has been appropriate when a company still lacks the financial strength or reputation to appeal to a broad base of investors and cannot afford the expense of a public offering."

ADVANTAGES AND DISADVANTAGES

Private placements offer small businesses a number of advantages over **initial public offerings** (IPOs). Since private placements do not require the assistance of brokers or underwriters, they are consid-erably less expensive and time consuming. In addition, private placements may be the only source of capital available to risky ventures or start-up firms. "With loan criteria for commercial bankers and investment criteria for venture capitalists both tightening, the private placement offering remains one of the most viable alternatives for capital formation available to companies," Andrew J. Sherman wrote in his book *The Complete Guide to Running and Growing Your Business.*

A private placement may also enable a small business owner to hand-pick investors with compatible goals and interests. Since the investors are likely to be sophisticated business people, it may be possible for the company to structure more complex and confidential transactions. If the investors are themselves entrepreneurs, they may be able to offer valuable assistance to the company's management. Finally, unlike public stock offerings, private placements enable small businesses to maintain their private status.

Of course, there are also a few disadvantages associated with private placements of securities. Suitable investors may be difficult to locate, for example, and may have limited funds to invest. In addition, privately placed securities are often sold at a deep discount below their market value. Companies that undertake a private placement may also have to relinquish more equity, because investors want compensation for taking a greater risk and assuming an illiquid position. Finally, it can be difficult to arrange private placement offerings in multiple states.

RESTRICTIONS AFFECTING PRIVATE PLACEMENT

The SEC formerly placed many restrictions on private placement transactions. For example, such offerings could only be made to a limited number of investors, and the company was required to establish strict criteria for each investor to meet. Furthermore, the SEC required private placement of securities to be made only to "sophisticated" investors—those capable of evaluating the merits and understanding the risks associated with the investment. Finally, stock sold through private offerings could not be advertised to the public and could only be resold under certain circumstances.

In 1992, however, the SEC eliminated many of these restrictions in order to make it easier for small companies to raise capital through private placements of securities. The rules now allow companies to promote their private placement offerings more broadly and to sell the stock to a greater number of buyers. It is also easier for investors to resell such securities. Although the SEC restrictions on private placements have been relaxed in recent years, it is nonetheless important for small business owners to understand the various federal and state laws affecting such transactions and to take the appropriate procedural steps. It may be helpful to assemble a team of qualified legal and accounting professionals before attempting to undertake a private placement.

Many of the rules affecting private placements are covered under Section 4(2) of the federal securities law. This section provides an exemption for companies wishing to sell up to $5 million in securities to a small number of accredited investors. Companies conducting an offering under Section 4(2) cannot solicit investors publicly, and the majority of investors are expected to be either insiders (company management) or sophisticated outsiders with a preexisting relationship with the company (professionals, suppliers, customers, etc.). At a minimum, the companies are expected to provide potential investors with recent financial statements, a list of risk factors associated with the investment, and an invitation to inspect their facilities. In most respects, the preparation and disclosure requirements for offerings under Section 4(2) are similar to Regulation D filings.

Regulation D—which was adopted in 1982 and has been revised several times since—consists of a set of rules numbered 501 through 508. Rules 504, 505, and 506 describe three different types of exempt offerings and set forth guidelines covering the amount of stock that can be sold and the number and type of investors that are allowed under each one. Rule 504 covers the Small Corporate Offering Registration, or SCOR. SCOR gives an exemption to private companies that raise no more than $1 million in any 12-month period through the sale of stock. There are no restrictions on the number or types of investors, and the stock may be freely traded. The SCOR process is easy enough for a small business owner to complete with the assistance of a knowledgeable accountant and attorney. It is available in all states except Delaware, Florida, Hawaii, and Nebraska.

Rule 505 enables a small business to sell up to $5 million in stock during a 12-month period to an unlimited number of investors, provided that no more than 35 of them are non-accredited. To be accredited, an investor must have sufficient assets or income to make such an investment. According to the SEC rules, individual investors must have either $1 million in assets (other than their home and car) or $200,000 in net annual personal income, while institutions must hold $5 million in assets. Finally, Rule 506 allows a company to sell unlimited securities to an unlimited number of investors, provided that no more than 35 of them are non-accredited. Under Rule 506, investors must be sophisticated. In both of these options, the securities cannot be freely traded.

DISCLOSURE

Although the 1992 SEC revisions eliminated the requirement for companies to prepare a Private Placement Memorandum for investors, experts suggest that it is still a good idea. The memorandum should describe the business, provide background information on management, discuss the terms of the offering (including the number of shares available, the price, and the intended use for the funds), outline the company's capital structure before and after the sale of securities, disclose the opportunities and risks involved in the investment, and provide copies of financial statements. Overall, the level of disclosure should be consistent with applicable state and federal securities laws, as well as with the sophistication of potential investors and the complexity of the terms of the offering.

A series of documents known as subscription materials should also be included with the information sent to potential investors in a private placement transaction. Subscription materials consist of two major documents that investors sign to indicate their desire to subscribe to purchase the securities offered. One of these documents is the offeree and purchaser questionnaire, which asks for background information about the investor to determine his or her level of sophistication. The second document is the subscription agreement, which is a contract showing that the investor has reviewed the offering information, is aware of the risks involved, and wants to invest.

FURTHER READING:

Saxlehner, Andrew C. "Equity Made Easy." *Inc.* July 1983.

Sherman, Andrew J. *The Complete Guide to Running and Growing Your Business.* New York: Random House, 1997.

Steinberg, Carol. "The DPO Revolution: Direct Public Offerings Turn Customers into Investors." *Success.* March 1997.

Stevens, M. "An Easier Way to Raise Business Capital." *Dun and Bradstreet Reports.* March-April 1984.

Stolze, William J. *Start Up Financing: An Entrepreneur's Guide to Financing a New or Growing Business.* Franklin Lakes, NJ: Career Press, 1997.

Sutton, David P., and M. William Benedetto. *Initial Public Offerings: A Strategic Planner for Raising Equity Capital.* Chicago: Probus, 1988.

Taylor, Lon W. "Raising Capital through Private Placements." *Journal of Business Strategy.* July-August 1988.

Zeune, Gary D., and Timothy R. Baer. "Floating a Stock Offering: New Buoyancy from the SEC." *Corporate Cashflow Magazine.* August 1993.

PRIVATIZATION

Defined in the strictest of terms, privatization means the sale of public utilities to private concerns.

But as *Public Works* magazine noted, "in the broader sense of the term . . . and the definition that applies to most contemporary discussions, privatization is the contract operation of a public utility or service by a private entity. It most often occurs in solid waste management, water/wastewater treatment, fleet maintenance, road/bridge building and maintenance, and municipal management." Small businesses that provide services in these and other areas have been among the biggest winners in the growing national trend toward privatization. As *Public Works* commented, "opportunities abound for private concerns to offer to manage public services with a close eye on cost and efficiency."

Privatization efforts in America today are in large part a reaction to dissatisfaction with government performance and/or unhappiness with the level of taxation that is levied on individuals and businesses by municipal, state, and federal governments to pay for services. (Privatization of public services has been largely a "bottom up" experience in the United States, with local governments in the forefront and state and federal levels of government trailing behind.) The purpose of privatization is to take advantage of the perceived cost efficiencies of private firms. Indeed, proponents of the practice say that privatization results in better performance of needed services at lesser cost. Even after privatization, however, government intervention is necessary in order to ensure that satisfactory services are provided to residents.

"Privatization in the 1990s has involved contracting out of government services and the sale of divestment of government assets," wrote Simon Hakim and Edwin Blackstone in *American City and County.* "The government usually allows the firm to choose how it will satisfy the contract. For example, a contract may specify trash removal services for the area residents a certain number of times per week. The firm is normally allowed to choose the methods it will use to perform the requirements of the contract, the trash trucks, used, and the number of workers on each trash truck. The profit motive will encourage the firm to produce the services efficiently at the least cost, a motive absent in government provision of services."

GROWTH OF PRIVATIZATION

"Privatization may be a popular buzzword today, but the concept has been around since the first municipality hired Joe and his wagon to pick up the trash instead of getting city employee Frank to do it," remarked *Public Works.* "The difference today is that privatization is encroaching into all areas of public administration. And governments are expecting public agencies to compete—dollar for dollar—with private operators or surrender management of services. For years, our country has supported the idea that a

public workforce was the best provider of essential services. Public employees would reliably and efficiently protect the public safety and deliver water and power; maintain roads and bridges; collect refuse and treat sewage. . . . In return, public employees enjoyed a certain job stability and a wide range of desirable benefits." But proliferating responsibilities, fiscal belt-tightening, sometimes lackluster performance by workers, and—in the cases of larger cities, especially—festering problems with infrastructure gradually led increasing numbers of city planners and public policy makers to look to privatization.

Today, several of the nation's largest cities, including New York, Indianapolis, Philadelphia, and Phoenix have contracted out a broad spectrum of services that were previously attended to exclusively by city employees. Indeed, New York City opened up bidding from private companies on 40 different municipal services in 1995 alone. Smaller cities and towns have instituted outsourcing philosophies as well, and many service businesses, both large and small, have garnered significant new contracts as a result. *American City and County* reported that various analyses indicate that this trend will likely continue. It noted that studies conducted by the Reason Foundation found that between 1987 and 1995, the percentage of local governments that contracted out services "grew substantially," while the Mercer Group reported that whereas slightly more than 50 percent of the 120 local governments surveyed contracted out janitorial services in 1987, by 1995 that percentage had increased to 70. Studies tracking other major services show similar privatization growth rates. "Cost pressures, both internal and external, are rated as the most important reasons that officials decided to privatize a service," stated a report on privatization conducted by a coalition of Illinois academic, business, and municipal groups. "The main obstacle is the lack of information or evidence of the benefits of privatization. Many officials also report they would like more information on certain aspects of privatization. It can be deduced that providing additional information on privatization to city officials will lead to increased acceptance."

VARIATIONS IN PRIVATIZATION

The term privatization has been applied to three different methods of increasing the activity of the private sector in providing public services: 1) private-sector choice, financing, and production of a service; 2) public-sector choice and financing with private-sector production of the service selected; 3) and deregulation of private firms providing services. In the first case, the entire responsibility for a service is transferred from the public sector to the private sector, and individual consumers select and purchase the amount of services they desire from private providers.

For example, solid-waste collection is provided by private firms in some communities. The third form of privatization means that government reduces or eliminates the regulatory restrictions imposed on private firms providing specific services.

The second version of privatization refers to joint activity of the public and private sectors in providing services. In this case, consumers select and pay for the quantity and type of service desired through government, which then contracts with private firms to produce the desired amount and category of service. Although the government provides for the service, a private firm carries out the actual execution of it. The government determines the service level and pays the amount specified in the contract, but leaves decisions about production decisions to the private firm.

ADVANTAGES AND DISADVANTAGES OF PRIVATIZATION

The merits and drawbacks of privatization have been subjects of considerable debate among businesspeople, city leaders, and public employees alike. Indeed, each element of privatization—from its apparent cost-saving properties to its possible negative impact on minority workers—provokes strong reaction. About the only thing that everyone can agree on is that the trend has been enormously beneficial to owners of small- and mid-sized businesses. Following are some privatization issues that communities, public providers, and private providers all need to consider:

COSTS AND PRODUCTIVITY Proponents of privatization argue that whereas government producers have no incentive to hold down production costs, private producers who contract with the government to provide the service have more at stake, thus encouraging them to perform a higher level at lower cost. The lower the cost incurred by the firm in satisfying the contract, the greater profit it makes. On the other hand, the absence of competition and profit incentives in the public sector is not likely to result in cost minimization. Of course, small- and mid-sized companies also need to make sure that they do not sacrifice an acceptable profit margin in the zeal to secure a contract.

Although private firms may pay lower wages and fringe benefits than local governments, the major cause of the cost differences between the private and governmental sectors is employee productivity. Lower labor costs may arise either from lower wages (which means that the government was paying wages higher than necessary for a given skill) or from less labor input (which means that the government was hiring unnecessary workers). Private firms have more flexibility than governmental units to use part-timers to meet peak periods of activity, to fire unsatisfactory workers, and to allocate workers across a variety of tasks. Moreover, critics of municipal governments argue that they are less likely to reward individual initiatives or punish aberrant behavior when compared with their private sector counterparts.

Finally, supporters of privatization argue that the trend has spurred improvements in performance by public service providers. ''Evidence shows that public agencies should be allowed to bid on contracts along with private operators,'' wrote Blackstone and Hakim, ''since this exposure to competition has led many public agencies to improve their service delivery and significantly reduce costs.''

SERVICE Expected quality of service varies from community to community, depending on a wide range of factors such as historical service levels, local taxation, and possible changes in service requirements. Moreover, *Public Works* observed that good service is sometimes defined differently by citizens, public service providers, and private service providers. ''Response time and public confidence need to be taken into account when judging the pros and cons of private/public,'' stated *Public Works*. ''Stability may be a concern in the eyes of the public; a government agency cannot walk away at the end of a contract period.''

OPERATING PHILOSOPHIES Proponents of privatization state that private firms may be more likely to experiment with different and creative approaches to service provision, whereas government tends to stick with the current approach since changes often create political difficulties for elected officials. In addition, private firms may use retained earnings to finance research or to purchase new capital equipment that lowers unit production costs. On the other hand, government may not be able or willing to allocate tax revenues to these purposes as easily, given the many competing demands on the government's budget.

REGULATORY REALITIES In some cases, local, state, and federal regulations may determine whether a service can even be handed over to a private provider. Moreover, ''the ultimate responsibility (in the eyes of the public, if not the courts) rests with the public agency that assigns operating rights to a private concern,'' stated *Public Works*. ''The local government will still be held responsible for the cost and quality of the service under contract.''

COMPETITION Supporters of privatization often cite the competitive environment that is nourished by the practice as a key to its success. Private owners have a strong incentive to operate efficiently, they argue, while this incentive is lacking under public ownership. If private firms spend more money and employ more people to do the same amount of work, competition will lead to lower margins, lost customers, and decreased profits. The disciplining effect of competition does not occur in the public sector. Still, even advocates of privatization agree that private ownership produces the public benefits of lower costs and high quality only in the presence of a competitive environment. Privatization cannot be expected to produce these same benefits if competition is absent. Given this reality, analysts strongly encourage municipal governments to make sure that the bidding process is an ethical one.

MONITORING AND ENFORCEMENT Critics of privatization of government services contend that problems sometimes arise in various aspects of the process, including the bidding process, the precise specification of the contract, and the monitoring and enforcement of the contract. For example, some observers have raised concerns that potential suppliers may initially offer a price to the government that is less than actual production costs to induce the government to transfer the service to the private sector or to win the contract. Subsequently, the contractor would then demand a higher price after the government has dismantled its own production system. Such ''low-balling'' in the bidding process may be reduced if the local government requires relatively long-term contracts, or constructs contracts that give them flexibility in hiring and firing outside firms.

Public Personnel Management magazine also noted that governments need to take several important precautions before handing out a contract in order to avoid litigation and legal liability. These precautions include detailed performance specifications for service providers, guidelines for the evaluation of competitive bids, and labor relations strategies. For their part, private bidders need to make certain that these precautions are reasonable ones that will not unduly impact their ability to perform both profitably and professionally.

Commonly utilized methods of contract monitoring, meanwhile, include performance appraisals, tracking complaints, citizen satisfaction surveys, reports from contractors, field observations, and ongoing cost comparisons.

EMPLOYMENT Privatization is understandably viewed as an alarming trend by some public employees. In some cases, privatization results in layoffs of public sector employees, although governments often reassign them to other government jobs, place them with private contractors, or offer them early retirement programs. These possibilities have been particularly upsetting to public employee unions, which have been at the forefront of efforts to block privatization. Indeed, one of the principal objections to privatization is that it replaces positions that featured compensation that could be used to support a family with private sector spots that offer modest compensation. This change, say detractors, is further evidence of the pinch

that working-class families are feeling in the otherwise robust economy of the mid-1990s. Indeed, critics such as the *Journal of Commerce and Commercial*'s David Morris contend that private companies are only able to promise meaningful financial savings over public agencies because of the comparatively low salaries they pay their workers. Another charge leveled at privatization initiatives is that they too often have a disproportionate impact on minorities. ''Governments often hire minorities in larger proportions than other workers,'' wrote Blackstone and Hakim. ''Thus, if government size is reduced, relatively more minority workers are likely to lose their jobs.'' In recognition of these fears, some service contracts now require private contractors to hire affected public employees or give them hiring preference.

DEMOGRAPHIC AND GEOGRAPHIC FACTORS Smaller municipalities may incur relatively high unit costs if they operate their own services as a result of not being able to achieve economies of scale. These localities may benefit from turning to a contractor that serves multiple communities. Privatization is also more acceptable in fast-growing communities. If services are being expanded to cover new residents, private contractors are less likely to displace existing public sector employees. Finally, contracting out varies with the number of services provided to residents. As the number of services increases, differences in the cost and effectiveness with which they are provided become more apparent. Therefore, municipalities providing diverse services may be more open to exploring private sector options than those localities where services are more limited.

FURTHER READING:

Blackstone, Edwin, and Simon Hakim. ''Private Ayes: A Tale of Four Cities.'' *American City and County.* February 1997.

Elam, L.B. ''Reinventing Government Privatization Style—Avoiding the Legal Pitfalls of Replacing Civil Servants with Contract Providers.'' *Public Personnel Management.* Spring 1997.

Henkoff, Ronald. ''Some Hope for Troubled Cities.'' *Fortune.* September 9, 1991.

Kodrzycki, Yolanda. ''Privatization of Local Government Services: Lessons for New England.'' *New England Economic Review.* May/June, 1994.

Lieberman, Ira W. ''Privatization: The Theme of the 1990s—An Overview.'' *Columbia Journal of World Business.* Spring 1993.

Morris, David. ''The Downside of Privatization.'' *Journal of Commerce and Commercial.* February 9, 1996.

''Private/Public Partnership: A Balancing Act.'' *Public Works.* September 1997.

Schine, Eric. ''America's New Watchword: If It Moves, Privatize It.'' *Business Week.* December 12, 1994.

Schriener, Judy, Stephen H. Daniels, and William J. Angelo. ''Gold in the Hills of Privatization.'' *ENR.* October 24, 1994.

Spengler, Jim. "Privatization: A Make or Buy Business Decision for Arlington, Texas." *Nation's Cities Weekly*. January 16, 1995.

Sturdivant, John N. "Privatization: It Often Doesn't Work, Increases Costs and Lacks Accountability." *Site Selection*. April 1996.

SEE ALSO: Government Procurement

PRO FORMA STATEMENTS

Pro forma, a Latin term meaning "as a matter of form," is applied to the process of presenting financial projections for a specific time period in a standardized format. Businesses use pro forma statements for decision-making in planning and control, and for external reporting to owners, investors, and creditors. Pro forma statements can be used as the basis of comparison and analysis to provide management, investment analysts, and credit officers with a feel for the particular nature of a business's financial structure under various conditions. Both the American Institute of Certified Public Accountants (AICPA) and the **Securities and Exchange Commission (SEC)** require standard formats for businesses in constructing and presenting pro forma statements.

"Anyone thinking of going into business should prepare pro forma statements, both income and cash flow, before investing time, money, and energy," James O. Gill wrote in his book *Financial Basics of Small Business Success.* As a vital part of the planning process, pro forma statements can help minimize the risks associated with starting and running a new business. They can also help convince lenders and investors to provide financing for a start-up firm. But Gill emphasized that pro forma statements must be based upon objective and reliable information in order to create an accurate projection of a small business's profits and financial needs for its first year and beyond. To ensure the credibility of underlying information, the entrepreneur must conduct careful research. Gill suggested speaking with owners of similar businesses, lawyers, accountants, customers, suppliers, and federal agencies during the information-gathering stage. After preparing initial pro forma statements and getting the business off the ground, the small business owner should update the projections monthly and annually.

USES OF PRO FORMA STATEMENTS

BUSINESS PLANNING A company uses pro forma statements in the process of **business planning** and control. Because pro forma statements are presented in a standardized, columnar format, management em-

ploys them to compare and contrast alternative **business plans**. By arranging the data for the operating and financial statements side-by-side, management analyzes the projected results of competing plans in order to decide which best serves the interests of the business.

In constructing pro forma statements, a company recognizes the uniqueness and distinct financial characteristics of each proposed plan or project. Pro forma statements allow management to:

1) Identify the assumptions about the financial and operating characteristics that generate the scenarios.

2) Develop the various sales and budget (revenue and expense) projections.

3) Assemble the results in profit and loss projections.

4) Translate this data into cash-flow projections.

5) Compare the resulting balance sheets.

6) Perform ratio analysis to compare projections against each other and against those of similar companies.

7) Review proposed decisions in marketing, production, research and development, etc., and assess their impact on profitability and liquidity.

Simulating competing plans can be quite useful in evaluating the financial effects of the different alternatives under consideration. Based on different sets of assumptions, these plans propose various scenarios of sales, production costs, profitability, and viability. Pro forma statements for each plan provide important information about future expectations, such as: sales and earnings forecasts; cash flows; balance sheets; proposed capitalization; and income statements.

Management also uses this procedure in choosing among budget alternatives. Planners present sales revenues, production expenses, **balance sheets**, and **cash flow statements** for competing plans with the underlying assumptions explained. Based on an analysis of these figures, management selects an annual budget. After choosing a course of action, it is common for management to examine variations within the plan.

If management considers a flexible budget most appropriate for its company, it would establish a range of possible outcomes generally categorized as *normal* (expected results), *above normal* (best case), and *below normal* (worst case). Management examines contingency plans for the possible outcomes at input/output levels specified within the operating range. Since these three budgets are projections appearing in a standardized, columnar format and for a specified time period, they are pro forma.

During the course of the fiscal period, management evaluates its performance by comparing actual results to the expectations of the accepted plan using a similar pro forma format. Management's appraisal tests and re-tests the assumptions upon which it based its plans. In this way pro forma statements are indispensable to the control process.

FINANCIAL MODELING Pro forma statements provide data for calculating **financial ratios** and for performing other mathematical calculations. Financial models built on pro forma projections contribute to the achievement of corporate goals if they 1) test the goals of the plans, 2) furnish findings that are readily understandable, and 3) provide time, quality, and cost advantages over other methods.

Financial modeling tests the assumptions and relationships of proposed plans by asking ''What If'' questions regarding the effect on company performance of: changes in the prices of labor, materials, and overhead; an increase or decrease in the cost of goods sold; a change in the cost of borrowing money; an increase or decrease in sales volume; or a change in inventory valuation. Computer-assisted modeling has made assumption testing more efficient. The use of powerful processors permits on-line, real-time decision making through immediate calculations of alternative cash-flow statements, balance sheets, and the income statements.

ASSESSING THE IMPACT OF CHANGES A company prepares pro forma financial statements when it expects to experience or has just experienced significant financial changes. The pro forma financial statements present the impact of these changes on the company's financial position as depicted in the income statement, balance sheet, and the cash-flow statement. For example, management might prepare pro forma statements to gauge the effects of a potential merger or joint venture. It also might prepare pro forma statements to evaluate the consequences of refinancing debt through issuance of preferred stock, common stock, or other debt.

EXTERNAL REPORTING Businesses also use pro forma statements in external reports prepared for owners (stockholders), creditors, and potential investors. For companies listed on the stock exchanges, the SEC requires pro forma statements with any filing, registration statements, or proxy statements. The SEC and organizations governing accounting practices require companies to prepare pro forma statements when essential changes in the character of a business's financial statements have occurred or will occur. Financial statements may change because of:

1) Changes in accounting principles due to adoption of a generally accepted accounting principle different from one used previously for financial accounting.

2) A change in accounting estimates dealing with the estimated economic life and net residual value of assets.

3) A change in the business entity resulting from the acquisition or disposition of an asset or investment, and/or the pooling of interests of two or more existing businesses.

4) A correction of an error made in report or filing of a previous period.

Management's decision to change accounting principles may be based on a) the issuance of a new accounting principle by the Financial Accounting Standards Board (FASB), b) internal considerations taking advantage of revised valuations or tax codes, or c) the accounting needs of a new business combination. By changing its accounting practices, a business might significantly affect the presentation of its financial position and the results of its operations. The change also might distort the earnings trend reported in the income statements for earlier years. Some examples of changes in accounting principles might include valuation of inventory via a first-in, first-out (FIFO) method or a last-in, first-out method (LIFO), or recording of **depreciation** via a straight-line method or an accelerated method.

When a company changes an accounting method, it uses pro forma financial statements to report the cumulative effect of the change for the period during which the change occurred. To enable comparison of the pro forma financial statements with previous financial statements, the company would present the financial statements for prior periods as originally reported, show the cumulative effect of the change on net income and retained earnings, and show net income on a pro forma basis as if the newly adopted accounting principle had been used in prior periods.

A change in accounting estimate may be required as new events occur and as better information becomes available about the probable outcome of future events. For example, an increase in the percentage used to estimate doubtful accounts, a major write-down of inventories, a change in the economic lives of plant assets, and a revision in the estimated liability for outstanding product warranties would require pro forma statements.

THE SEC FORMAT

The SEC prescribes the form and content of pro forma statements for companies subject to its jurisdiction in circumstances such as the above. Some of the form and content requirements are:

1) An introductory paragraph describing the proposed transaction, the entities involved, the periods covered by the pro forma information, and what the pro forma information shows.

2) A pro forma condensed balance sheet and a pro forma condensed income statement, in columnar form, showing the condensed historical amounts, the pro forma adjustments, and the pro forma amounts. Footnotes provide justification for the pro forma adjustments and explain other details pertinent to the changes.

3) The pro forma adjustments, directly attributable to the proposed change or transaction, which are expected to have a continuing impact on the financial statements. Explanatory notes provide the factual basis for adjustments.

PRO FORMA STATEMENTS FOR CHANGES IN ENTITY AND FOR BUSINESS COMBINATIONS The FASB, the AICPA, and the SEC have provided significant directives to the form, content, and necessity of pro forma financial statements in situations where there has been a change in the form of a business entity. Such a change in form may occur due to changes in financial structure resulting from the disposition of a long-term liability or asset, or due to a combination of two or more businesses.

The purpose of pro forma financial statements is to facilitate comparisons of historic data and projections of future performance. In these circumstances users of financial statements need to evaluate a new or proposed business entity on a basis comparable to the predecessor business in order to understand the impact of the change on cash flow, income, and financial position. *Pro forma adjustments* to accounting principles and accounting estimates reformat the statements of the new entity and the acquired business to conform with those of the predecessor.

Occasionally, a partnership or sole proprietorship will sell all or part of the business interest. Sometimes it is necessary, especially if the business is "going public," to reorganize into a corporation. The financial statements on a corporation with a very short history are not helpful in a thoughtful analysis of future potential. Similarly, because of the differences in federal income tax liabilities, a restatement of the predecessor business in historical terms only confuses the picture. Since the financial statements of the predecessor business do not contain some of the expense items applicable to a corporation, the pro forma financial statements make adjustments to restate certain expenses on a corporate basis. In particular these would include:

1) Stating the owners' salaries in terms of officers' salaries.

2) Calculating the applicable federal taxes on the predecessor business as though it were a corporation.

3) Including corporate state franchise taxes.

4) For partnerships acquired through the pooling of interests, adding the balance of the partners' capital to contributed capital in the combined company rather than to retained earnings.

Subchapter **S corporations** exercise the tax-option of the shareholders to individually assume the tax liability rather than have it assumed by the corporation as a whole. If the shareholders choose to go public or change their qualifications, the corporation loses the tax-option. Therefore, in addition to the pro forma statement showing historical earnings, the new company will make pro forma provision for the taxes that it would have paid had it been a regular corporation in the past. When acquisition of a Subchapter S corporation is accomplished through the pooling of interests, the pro forma financial statement may not include any of the retained earnings of the Subchapter S corporation in the pooled retained earnings.

When presenting the historical operations of a business previously operated as a partnership, the accountant would make adjustments to bring the statement in line with the acquiring corporation. Historical data listed would include net sales; cost of sales; gross profit on sales; selling, general, and administrative expenses; other income; other deductions; and income before taxes on income. Pro forma adjustments would restate partnership operations on a corporate basis, including estimated partnership salaries as officers and estimated federal and state taxes on income, as well as pro forma net income and pro forma net income per share. Accountants make similar adjustments to pro forma statements for businesses previously operated as sole proprietorships and Subchapter S corporations.

ACQUISITION OR DISPOSAL OF PART OF A BUSINESS For a company that decided to acquire part of a new business or dispose of part of its existing business, a meaningful pro forma statement would adjust the historical figures to demonstrate how the acquired part would have fared had it been a corporation. Pro forma statements would also set forth conventional financial statements of the acquiring company, and pro forma financial statements of the business to be acquired. Notes to the pro forma statements explain the adjustments reflected in the statements.

A pro forma income statement would combine the historical income statement of the acquiring company and a pro forma income statement of the business to be acquired for the previous five years, if possible. Pro forma adjustments would exclude overhead costs not applicable in the new business entity, such as division and head office expenses.

The purchase of a sole proprietorship, partnership, Sub-Chapter S corporation, or business segment requires pro forma statements for a series of years in order to reflect adjustments for such items as owners' or partners' salaries and income taxes. In this way, each year reflects the results of operations of a business organization comparable with that of the acquiring corporation. However, the pro forma statements giving effect to the business combination should be limited to the current and immediately preceding periods.

SUMMARY

Pro forma statements are an integral part of business planning and control. Managers use them in the decision-making process when constructing an annual budget, developing long-range plans, and choosing among capital expenditures. Pro forma statements are also valuable in external reporting. Public accounting firms find pro forma statements indispensable in assisting users of financial statements in understanding the impact on the financial structure of a business due to changes in the business entity, or in accounting principles or accounting estimates.

Although pro forma statements have a wide variety of applications for ongoing, mature businesses, they are also important for small businesses and start-up firms, which often lack the track record required for preparing conventional financial statements. As a planning tool, pro forma statements help small business owners minimize the risks associated with starting and running a new business. The data contained in pro forma statements can also help convince lenders and investors to provide financing for a start-up firm.

FURTHER READING:

Gill, James O. *Financial Basics of Small Business Success.* Menlo Park, CA: Crisp Publications, 1994.

Livingstone, John Leslie. *The Portable MBA in Finance and Accounting.* New York: Wiley, 1992.

Merrill, Ronald E., and Henry D. Sedgwick. *The New Venture Handbook: Everything You Need to Know to Start and Run Your Own Business.* AMACOM, 1987.

Mosich, A. N., and E. John. Larsen. *Intermediate Accounting.* McGraw-Hill Book Company, 1986.

Rappaport, Louis H. *SEC Accounting Practice and Procedure.* The Ronald Press Company, 1966.

SEE ALSO: Budgets and Budgeting; Decision Making; Incorporation

PROBATIONARY EMPLOYMENT PERIODS

When hiring new employees, many employers use probationary employment periods to ascertain whether the new workers will be able to handle the duties and challenges associated with their new job. "The essential purpose of a probationary period," wrote William E. Lissy in *Supervision,* is to allow management to observe a new hire's performance before granting permanent status."

TRIAL PERIODS AND SMALL BUSINESS Many consultants to small business owners believe that probationary employment periods—also sometimes known as trial periods—can be quite useful to both entrepreneurs hoping to get a start-up off the ground and established small business owners seeking to maintain or increase their current level of success. As countless small business owners and researchers will attest, the quality of a small company's work force can mean the difference between business success and business failure. Indeed, personnel costs (wages, benefits, etc.) are among the most expensive elements of business operations; this cost becomes multiplied if your business is saddled with a poor worker. Probationary periods are simply meant to give the small business owner the best possible chance of securing and retaining quality employees—and releasing substandard employees without legal penalty.

"A two-week or thirty-day probationary or trial period is recommended for all new employees," stated Elwood N. Chapman in *Human Relations in Small Business.* "This gives both parties a chance to size up the situation. The employee can test the work environment, skills required, and future possibilities. The employer can test how the new person will product and fit into the team. Up to the day the trial period is over, either party can cancel the arrangement."

Business experts state that small business owners should take the following steps when implementing a probationary period with a new hire:

- Make sure that the specifics of the probationary period (length of probation, for instance) are explicitly stated in company guidelines.

- Make certain that the new employee is aware that he or she will be "on probation" for the specified period.

- Monitor how well the new employee executes assigned tasks.

- Monitor the new employee's work habits; for example, a new worker who is consistently tardy in arriving at work or returning from lunch may well be a cause for concern.

- Monitor how well the new employee gets along with supervisors/managers.

- Monitor how well the new employee gets along with fellow staff.

- Determine whether the new hire is a "self-starter," or one who needs continued guidance.

- Provide the new hire with feedback that will help him or her shape performance to business expectations; this will not only improve the likelihood of securing a good worker, but also provide the employer with possible legal protection in the event of an unfair dismissal legal action (documentation indicating a pattern of poor performance carries significant legal weight).

Of course, not every employee will be a superior one, and shortcomings in one (or even more) of the above areas does not necessarily mean that the employee should be let go (factors such as availability of other workers, performance in critical areas, etc., usually have to be considered). But analysts indicate that new employees who perform poorly during probationary periods are rarely able to dramatically improve their performance after the trial period has ended. After all, if the worker did a bad job during a probationary period, when all parties were aware that performance would be monitored, why should the small business owner believe that the worker's performance would improve at the conclusion of that trial period, when pressure to "be on one's best behavior" would presumably be relieved somewhat. Ultimately, each business owner has to decide for him or herself whether the employee's performance during the trial period warrants continued employment.

FURTHER READING:

Aikin, Olga. "The Trials of Working Life." *Personnel Management.* December 1991.

Chapman, Elwood N. *Human Relations in Small Business.* Menlo Park, CA: Crisp Publications, 1994.

Lissy, William E. "Probationary Employees." *Supervision.* April 1995.

Loh, Eng Seng. "Employment Probation as a Sorting Mechanism." *Industrial and Labor Relations Review.* April 1994.

SEE ALSO: Employee Hiring

PRODUCT COSTING

Product costing is the process of tracking and studying all the various expenses that are accrued in the production and sale of a product, from raw materials purchases to expenses associated with transporting the final product to retail establishments. It is widely regarded as an extremely important component in evaluating and planning business strategies. As John A. Lessner indicated in the *Journal of Accountancy,* "in today's hotly competitive business environment, accurate product costing has become critically important to a business's survival."

Product costing has undergone a dramatic metamorphosis in America over the past 50 years, as *Textile World*'s Frank Wilson noted: "In the 1940s, cost estimates normally included nothing more than total manufacturing costs. In the late '50s direct costing was implemented to separate variable [cost of materials, cost of transportation] and fixed [interest payments on equipment and facilities, rent, property taxes, executive salaries] costs." Indeed, Lessner remarked that "fifty years ago, when manufacturing was far less automated than it is today, the costs of materials, labor and overhead were just about evenly divided. Now, production of a product's various components is often so synchronized on highly automated production lines that there is little or no need to maintain component inventories; thus, the old costing formulas, still used by many industries, are no longer applicable. . . . Further complicating the costing equation is the trend in manufacturing to focus more attention on quality, flexibility and responsiveness, to meet customer needs. This makes production-line cost analysis more difficult because each line requires small, but significant, changes in production techniques."

As a result, Wilson noted that today's managers have found that the limited information available through older job costing methods is wholly "inadequate for the requirements of today's marketplace." Instead, companies are increasingly turning to detailed and long-range examinations that provide a truer picture of a product's true costs and benefits. "Companies are discovering that their competitiveness is enhanced when purchasing, manufacturing, logistics, and product design groups begin using total life cycle costing," wrote Joseph Cavinato in *Chilton's Distribution.* "Total life cycle cost recognizes that the purchase price of an item is only part of its total cost, just the beginning of a series of costs to be accumulated by the firm, its downstream customers, and users until the end of the product's life."

COSTS ASSOCIATED WITH MANUFACTURED PRODUCTS

Cavinato noted that there are myriad potential **costs** associated with selling a product, and charged that many of these are not adequately examined by manufacturers. Possible costs include:

- Developing and maintaining supplier relationships.

- **Transportation** costs—This includes carrier payment terms; special charges in the realms of packaging, handling, and loading and unloading; and loss and damage expenses.

- Sales and freight terms—Conditions that define payment terms, sales, and title transfers.

- Payment terms—options here range from 15 days to as many as 90 days in some industries, and letter of credit terms provide additional options. These options, observed Cavinato,''often are not considered by managers in purchasing, traffic, and sales. Instead, most firms mandate these terms and they become 'boiler plate' in purchase orders, carrier contracts, and invoices. It can be mutually beneficial to negotiate these terms with suppliers and carriers.

- Costs to receive, process, or make ready—This includes unloading, counting, inspection, and inventory costs, as well as expenses associated with disposal of packaging and other product protection/transportation materials.

- Logistics costs—Many of these expenses (warehousing, loading, unloading, handling, inventory control) are typically lumped together under the catch-all title ''Overhead,'' despite the fact that costs for each of these can vary significantly depending on the arrangement.

- Production costs—Expenses accrued in actual manufacture of goods.

- Warranty costs.

- Quality costs—Includes costs associated with defective products (what percentage and how far down the production line), inspections, product returns, chargebacks, cooperage, and storage.

- Lot size costs—This transportation expense, noted Cavinato, covers inventory and cash flow costs associated with lots of varying size.

- Supplier inventory—Availability of raw materials—or lack thereof—can be an important cost factor.

- **Overhead expenses** of supplier and customer transactions—Includes billing, collection, payment preparation, and receiving processes. ''Logistics people,'' wrote Cavinato, ''can easily identify those customers that are easy to do business with, and those that cause hidden costs and create hassles that take people away from productive tasks.''

- Product improvement and modification—This includes cost of correcting defects and standardization of materials and packaging.

- Downstream service costs—Costs associated with repairing goods once they have been sold.

- Waste costs—Costs associated with meeting federal or state laws and community expectations on environmentally friendly production and packaging processes.

PRODUCT COSTING IN MULTI-PRODUCT ENVIRONMENTS

Some manufacturers distort true product costing results by evenly distributing costs for a certain aspect of production across all product lines, even though costs might vary with each specific product. In some instances, this practice might have little or no impact on a business's well being; a company that is enjoying record growth and profits on all three of its product lines, for instance, is unlikely to be seriously harmed by accounting practices that evenly divide transportation costs three ways, even though one of the product lines may account for, say, half of the firm's transportation expenses. Huge profits mask such inequities fairly well. But relatively few companies are in such a luxurious position. Most companies—and especially most small businesses, which typically have less margin for error than their larger cousins—need to work hard to arrive at true product costing figures. ''As national and global competition increase,'' wrote Lessner, ''even tiny costing disparities can have an overwhelming impact on whether a product—or an entire company, for that matter—survives.''

Lessner uses the example of scrap costs to point out the perils of not isolating each product's real production costs. In most instances, he notes, accounting for scrap generated in the manufacturing process is fairly straightforward. ''If scrap is an insignificant component in a product's production, managers generally ignore it as a cost factor,'' and conversely, if it is a big factor, managers endeavor to control it and factor its cost into product pricing. ''Things get more complicated, however, when producing many lines of a similar product,'' wrote Lessner. ''For example, a manufacturer may have a custom product line that requires frequent production line stops, adjustments, and start-ups; such a line often has high scrap costs. The company also may have a stock product line that runs nearly nonstop; as a result, its scrap costs are relatively low. Manufacturers still using the traditional cost-accounting approach typically collect scrap costs as overhead expenses and charge them to a single cost center. Cost center overhead, including scrap, is then applied to all product lines on the basis of direct labor costs. The result is scrap costs are charged to all products consuming direct labor, regardless of the scrap they actually generate.'' Lessner and other business experts warn that while such accounting practices may not immediately hamstring a company, these practices can have an adverse impact on the business's ability to accurately analyze job costs over time. ''Over the long term,'' said Lessner, ''product profitability analyses that use these distorted costs cause management to erroneously assume custom products generate better margins than they actually do,'' and top performing goods end up subsidizing other, less profitable, product lines.

An examination of these and other characteristics of product costing makes it clear that the practice is, as Lessner stated, ''surely one of the most important pieces of management information accountants provide. It affects the success of contract bidding and product pricing. As such, it ultimately determines the success of a company.''

PRODUCT COSTING IN NONMANUFACTURING FIRMS

Although product costing is primarily associated with manufacturing businesses, it also has applications in non-manufacturing industries. ''Merchandising companies include the costs of buying and transporting merchandise in their product costs,'' observed Ronald W. Hilton in *Managerial Accounting*. ''Producers of inventoriable goods, such as mining products, petroleum, and agricultural products, also record the costs of producing their goods. The role of product costs in these companies is identical to that in manufacturing firms.'' Business experts also note that while service-oriented companies (both service businesses and non-profit organizations) do not offer products that can be stored and sold in the manner of manufactured items, they nonetheless need to track the varied costs that they accrue in offering their services. After all, the services that they offer are in essence, their ''product'' line. ''Banks, insurance companies, restaurants, airlines, law firms, hospitals, and city governments all record the costs of producing various services for the purposes of planning, cost control, and decision making,'' wrote Hilton.

FURTHER READING:

Brealey, Richard A., and Stewart C. Myers. *Principles of Corporate Finance.* 4th ed. New York: McGraw-Hill, 1991.

Cavinato, Joseph. ''Product Costs From Cradle to Grave.'' *Chilton's Distribution.* January 1992.

Hilton, Ronald W. *Managerial Accounting.* New York: New York: McGraw-Hill, 1991.

Lessner. John A. ''Traps to Avoid in Product Costing.'' *Journal of Accountancy.* July 1991.

Wilson, Frank C. ''How Modern is Your Company's Costing System?'' *Textile World.* September 1991.

Product development is the process by which a company does one of two things: 1) creates an entirely new product that either adds to an existing product line or occupies an entirely new niche; 2) modifies or updates an existing product. Successful product development is essential for any business if it hopes to exist for any length of time.

NEW PRODUCT DEVELOPMENT

According to a study by the Product Development and Management Association, new products were defined as ''new applications, major product changes, and new-to-the-world products.'' Products that fit this definition have always been an important part of any company's success, but studies show that new products are becoming even more important. Customer demand for new products has increased. The PDMA recently surveyed 200 U.S. companies and found that new product accounted for 28 percent of total sales in the previous five years and that the number was expected to increase to 37 percent in the next five-year period. Additionally, the study revealed that new products were expected to account for 39 percent of total profits in the next five-year period, an increase of 12 percent from the previous five years.

What this means is that new products are essential to survival. ''Innovate or die'' has become a rallying cry at small and large businesses as increasingly savvy consumers demand the newest and the best products. Mike Sinyard, owner of Specialized Bicycles, the inventor of the mountain bike, was quoted in *Nation's Business* as saying that ''At trade shows, the first thing customers say is, 'What's new?' Every year you have to raise the ante. If you were not to do it, you'd be left in the dust.'' To prove his point, Sinyard admitted that he must revise the company's 37 products annually (from small changes to complete redesigns) and that fully 50 percent of a line of bike accessories the company also sells is totally replaced by new products each year.

NEW PRODUCT DEVELOPMENT FOR SMALL COMPANIES

It's easy to see that the market demands new products, but how is a small company to go about delivering them? Professor Kim Clark, the Harry E. Figgie Jr. Professor of Business Administration at Harvard Business School identified three key strategies in *Industry Week*.

FOCUS First, a small business needs to focus on its goals. Limited time and resources mean that hard decisions must be made and a strategic plan needs to be developed. Companies should "do the right things right" by using the best information available to choose the right technologies and decide on what new products to invest in. Small companies are often growing quickly and can pick and choose among many seemingly strong new product avenues, but the key is to decide what the company does very well and then concentrate on that area or areas.

Selecting the right focus can be a balancing act, however. A company needs to keep both short-term and long-term success in sight and needs to weigh rapid cash generation versus growth, **product life cycles**, and technology and market capabilities. All of these factors must come into play, and the risks associated with each must always be considered.

Clark says that one way a company can stay focused is to develop a "product-line architecture." Once a company creates its overall **strategy** and determines how it will reach its goal, it should map out exactly what product lines it will choose to achieve that goal. Says Clark in *Industry Week*, "Product-line architecture tells you how your product line will look, what types of products you will have in what markets, how they will be positioned, and in what sequence they will be introduced."

Defining a product-line architecture demands that correct decisions be made early in the product development process. Companies should be rigorous and quantitative when coming up with new product specifications or definitions. They should, as much as is possible, precisely define the product qualities and price points that a market will bear. Mistakes made early in the process will often not show up until it is far too late—either at the prototype or final product stage.

Customer feedback is essential at this stage and can eliminate mistakes in focus. As Mike Anthony, a director with Pittiglio Rabin Todd McGrath (PRTM), told *Industry Week*, companies should ask themselves a series of questions when creating a new product-line vision: "How would someone use this product? How would you articulate the benefit to the customer? Is this something a customer can really understand [as to] how it makes their life easier?"

FIND THE RESOURCES The second step in Clark's strategy for small businesses is locating the resources and skills needed to create and market the new product. Small companies may lack the in-house resources needed to create a new product, making it seem out of reach, but analysts note that small business owners have other avenues that they can often pursue. If the product idea is good enough, the company should look outside its own walls for partnership and outsourcing opportunities. **Outsourcing** may seem more expensive at first, but many companies have found that in the long run, outsourced projects often come in under budget.

By outsourcing key parts of a project—design, manufacturing, or even sales and marketing, for example—a small company can concentrate on what it does best—developing market-driven product ideas.

LEADERSHIP The third and final step a small company needs to follow is to find the leadership needed to bring a new product from the idea stage to completed product. Clark feels that any company can find product managers, but those that find leaders who are willing to take chances will be the ones that succeed. This leader will often take the form of a "product champion." A strong product champion will be able to balance all the issues associated with a product—economic, performance requirements, regulatory issues, management issues, and more—and create a winning new product.

The product champion has to guide the project through a predetermined series of viability tests—checkpoints in the development process at which a company evaluates a new product to determine if the product should proceed to the next development stage. Think of a series of gates. At each gate, the product is reevaluated and the market reexamined. If the product is still viable and still fits in with a company's long-range goals, it moves on to the next gate. If it is determined that the market has shifted, or technology has changed, or the project has become too expensive, then the product must be killed, no matter how much money has already been poured into it.

This is where a strong product champion makes the difference—he or she has to have the guts to make the call to kill the product and must be able to convey the reasons for that decision to the product development team. If goals were clearly defined, resources properly allocated, and leadership was strong, then the decision to kill a project should not be a difficult one.

LAUNCHING A NEW PRODUCT

Once the product-line architecture has been established and a new product is being developed, it is time for a company to think about how to successfully launch the product in it's target market. This is the stage where an advertising or public relations agency can come into play, especially for small businesses without the internal resources to handle such a job themselves. When using an outside agency to launch a product, a company should:

- Have a well-defined product concept (which is where product-line architecture comes into play).

- Provide the agency with background information on its products and goals.

- Conduct necessary patent research, applying for new patents as needed.

- Have the manufacturing process in place and ready to go, either internally or via outsourcing.

- Have a formal business plan in place that defines funding of the project

- Determine who will approve the marketing or advertising plan that the agency creates (the fewer people communicating with the agency, the better).

- Determine the proper timing for the launch.

Don't wait until the last minute to hire an agency. Plan ahead, even if the product is a year or two from being ready for the market. According to Bob Dorr of the New Jersey-based Gillespie marketing firm, as quoted in *Nation's Business,* ''One to two years is an ideal amount of time to plan the launch. At a minimum, a company should meet with its advertising or public relations firm six months ahead of the launch date.'' Anything less than that, and the agency may not be able to guarantee the proper editorial or advertising coverage of the launch in the media. Additionally, waiting until the last minute to plan a launch drastically increases the cost of the launch since everything associated with the job then becomes a rush request, which always cost more.

SPEED-TO-MARKET AND PRODUCT DEVELOPMENT

Most of what is outlined above has been a part of basic product development knowledge for many years. In that framework, speed to market was important, but it often was not the most critical factor in new product development. In the 1990s, that is no longer true—speed to market is perhaps the most crucial part of product development. Improved communication (especially the Internet), increased globalization, and rapid changes in technology have put tremendous pressure on companies to get their product to market first. ''If you can reduce one product process from three months to two weeks,'' said Jack Thorne, professor of entrepreneurship at Carnegie Mellon University, in *Nation's Business*, ''it gives you a stronger competitive position.''

To improve speed to market, a company should first make sure that it is making the best possible use of available technology. If it is, then there are other steps that can be taken to speed product development through efficient, market-oriented product planning that takes the customer into account:

DEVELOP A PRODUCT STRATEGY Set goals on how much of your company's business you want to come from new products over the next several years, establishing one-, three-, and five-year goals, for example. One method of establishing a product-line architec-

ture is through a system known as portfolio management. Much like establishing a stock portfolio, a company can establish a product portfolio that defines what its product mix will be over the course of the next several years. The portfolio should include both breakthrough products (innovative and groundbreaking new products) and derivative products (products which represent incremental changes to existing products.) Having a clearly defined product strategy increases speed to market by eliminating products that don't fit the strategy, freeing up money and time for products that do.

DEFINE AND DIFFERENTIATE THE PRODUCT According to a 1996 survey of new product managers by Group EFO Ltd., the main reason a new product failed was lack of competitive difference. What does that have to do with speed to market? If a company has not clearly defined its product strategy, it will waste time and money bringing products to market that are not innovative in any of five areas: formulation, positioning, packaging, technology, or creating a new market. Eliminating those products by identifying a market opening and jumping on it means that resources that might have been wasted on those products have now been freed up and can be used to get winning products to market faster.

TEST THE MARKET In a best-practice study conducted in 1996, the Product Development and Management Association found that two factors are most likely to predict product success: in-depth interviews with customers and observations of how people use a product. Such hands-on research early in the planning stage can seem time-consuming and costly, but in the long run, it can actually save both time and money by indicating which products will be winners, allowing a company to concentrate resources on those products.

Most companies today still pursue a mix of traditional customer interviews, surveys, and focus groups to gather data about potential new products, and in many cases, that mix works just fine. However, many cutting edge companies are unsatisfied with the old methods of gathering customer research and are experimenting with a new concept known as the ''lead user.'' Lead users are those highly advanced users who love to tinker or rebuild existing products to meet their needs. They are progressive thinkers who have identified a product that is not currently available to meet a need that they have and expect to reap large benefits from such a product when it is created.

Information can be gathered from lead users via conventional methods (e.g., questionnaires) or unconventional methods, such as videotaping customer use of the product or establishing a constant observatory presence at a representative customer outlet. Some measures are out of reach for small businesses, but the lead user concept works at all levels. Even without a lot of money, a creative company can find ways to gather data from its most important users. For example, RGT Enterprises, Inc. could not afford costly market research when it developed a new children's toothbrush, but the company was able to gather invaluable information by taking the toothbrush to local daycare centers and surveying parents.

While most product development experts still believe in the importance of **market research** and test markets, there is a growing segment that argues that customer research is too time-consuming and costly and can be cut back or even eliminated from the product development process. Far more important, say these critics, is to identify and monitor world trends, regardless of how they mesh with current products. Monitoring trends gives a company a better idea of how to meet not only a customer's expressed needs, but his or her unarticulated needs as well.

MAINTAIN DISCIPLINE AND FOCUS It is vital for small business enterprises to set schedules and stick to them. Many consultants urge businesses to resist the urge to tweak or redesign a product at every stage. Once an idea has reached the product stage, freeze the design of that product and resist the urge to change it if some new piece of information becomes available. Set up a cross-functional team involving all areas of the company that have a role in the product; this not only helps build a better product, but also helps assure that one functional area is unable to claim unfamiliarity with the product as a justification for asking for changes late in the process. This can drastically increase the speed to market.

SERVICE COMPANIES AND NEW PRODUCTS

While the above steps directly pertain to companies that produce products rather than those that offer services, companies in the service industry can essentially adopt the same approach to product development. Service companies should take a disciplined, analytical approach to developing new services, relying on targeted customer input just as companies outside the service sector do.

Companies in the service industry know that they are competing for customers based on perceived value as much as actual price. If a customer feels they are getting better treatment, or more service options, or more ''free'' services as part of their purchase, they are more likely to remain a client of that company. If, however, a company stops innovating and adding new services to its core business, then the service becomes a commodity and clients look at only one thing—price—when deciding on what company to choose.

Service companies should routinely ask themselves a series of questions:

- Could current services be presented in a different way?

- Could they be offered to new customer groups?

- Are their little things that can be tweaked to freshen or update a service?

- Could services be improved or changed?

Because by their very nature services are easy to copy (no materials or product knowledge is needed), service companies actually face more pressure to innovate and develop new products than manufacturers. By continually asking the above questions and by following the same models manufacturing companies follow when pursuing product development, service companies can stay ahead of their competitors and make their services clearly identifiable to consumers.

PITFALLS TO PRODUCT DEVELOPMENT

Finally, when embarking on the product development process, try to remember in advance what the obstacles to success are. According to *Industry Week*, there are pitfalls that a product champion (as well as a company's upper management) should be aware of when it comes to new product development. Among the mistakes that cause the wrong new product ideas to be funded are:

- Becoming too attached to the company's own technology and expertise and always going for large projects as a result, instead of being satisfied with incremental gains.

- Technical staff too attached to a project and too proud to admit defeat, even when a project can not be justified according to pre-established criteria.

- No real criteria for deciding if a project is good or bad.

- Changes in strategy at the corporate level are not conveyed to the product development team.

- Money and staff allocated to a project are hidden in the budget of another project.

- Company decision-makers blinded by the charisma or charm of the person presenting the new product idea.

- Project accepted on the basis of who gets it first.

FURTHER READING:

Berenson, Conrad, and Iris Mohr-Jackson. ''Product Rejuvenation: A Less Risky Alternative to Product Innovation.'' *Business Horizons*. November/December 1994.

De Young, Garrett. ''Listen, Then Design.'' *Industry Week*. Feb. 17, 1997.

Kinni, Theodore B. "Focus, Leverage, and Leadership: Kim Clark on New Product Development." *Industry Week.* March 28, 1995.

Maynard, Roberta. "The Heat is On." *Nation's Business.* October 1997.

Maynard, Roberta. "Launching Your Product." *Nation's Business.* August 1995.

Stevens, Tim. "Balancing Act: Product Development." *Industry Week.* March 17, 1997.

Stevens, Tim. "Tool Kit for Innovators." *Industry Week.* June 5, 1995.

Taninecz, George. "What Went Wrong?" *Industry Week.* Dec. 16, 1996.

SEE ALSO: Product Costing; Product Positioning

PRODUCT LIABILITY

Product liability comprises a number of laws and court rulings that apply to any business that makes or sells a product. Businesses that make or sell products are responsible for ensuring that those products are safe and do not pose a hazard to the public. Such businesses can be held liable for any damage or harm their products might cause.

According to Section 102(2) of the Uniform Product Liability Act, product liability includes "all claims or action brought for personal injury, death, or property damage caused by the manufacture, design, formula, preparation, assembly, installation, testing, warnings, instructions, marketing, packaging, or labeling of any product." Product liability issues have become increasingly important to manufacturers and marketing managers. In the last twenty years, the liability of manufacturers has been greatly expanded as a result of the spread of the doctrine of strict liability and the adoption of new theories that permit recovery in so-called "delayed manifestation" cases.

Because of their usually limited resources, small businesses must be particularly aware of their responsibilities under product liability laws. In addition to making safe products, this responsibility also extends to prominently displaying warnings of any potential hazards on products and **packaging**. Experts recommend that small business owners consult with legal counsel experienced in the product liability field. An attorney can help the small business owner sift through the numerous federal and state laws that apply to different types of products. Small businesses are also encouraged to purchase product liability insurance. Unfortunately, the increasing number of lawsuits and large damage awards in this area have made such insurance very expensive and reduced the amount of coverage available. In fact, the expense of insuring against prod-

uct liability has prevented small manufacturers from competing in certain product areas.

DEVELOPMENT OF PRODUCT LIABILITY LAWS

Product liability began to have meaning in the mid-1800s, when the American courts increasingly found that sellers of goods had a "duty" to use reasonable care in the production of those goods. Sellers were held liable to third parties for negligence in the manufacture or sale of goods "inherently dangerous" (the danger of injury arises from the product itself, rather than from a defect in the product) to human safety, ranging from food and beverages to drugs, firearms, and explosives. In 1962, tort principles were first applied to product liability. The landmark case of *MacPherson v. Buick Motor Co.* (1961) concerned liability of the auto manufacturer to the buyer of a car sold through a dealer. Although the concept of "inherently dangerous" goods was still held to be significant, there was a shift to negligence (tort) principles in this case—that is, the producer was required to apply "due care" in the marketing of goods to users.

The case had an immediate and widespread effect on product liability law. It established that because manufacturers knowingly market products which affect the interests of consumers, they owe a legal duty of caution and prudence to consumers. Since manufacturers may foresee potentially harmful product effects, they are responsible for attempting to minimize harm. Establishing this legal duty between the manufacturer and the consumer made it possible for plaintiffs to argue the negligent breach of that duty. The principles laid down in *MacPherson* are now accepted throughout the country and followed by all American courts. Eventually, the concept of "inherently dangerous" products fell into disuse and the concept of negligence was expanded beyond production to include labeling, installation, inspection, and design.

Four elements must be present for a product liability case to be considered under the negligent tort principles:

1) The particular defendant owes a duty to the particular plaintiff to act as a reasonably prudent person under the same or similar circumstances.

2) There is a breach of such a duty by the defendant—that is, a failure to act reasonably.

3) There is an injury, including personal injury or property damage.

4) There is a causal link between defendant's breach of duty and injuries sustained by the plaintiff.

The concept of negligence is applicable to every activity preceding a product's availability in the market. So everything from product design, the inspection and testing of materials, and the manufacture and assembly of the product to the packaging, the accompanying instructions and warnings, and the inspection and testing of the final product are all susceptible to negligence. Negligence can result from omission as well as commission—failure to discover a flaw is as negligent as creating one. Similarly, failing to provide adequate warnings about potential dangers in the use of a product is a violation of duty.

Still it may be difficult to prove negligence in product liability cases. Defendants only must meet the general standards of reasonable behavior as judged against the behavior of a reasonably careful competitor who demonstrates the standard skills and expertise of the industry. In reality, a manufacturer must only show that ''ordinary care under the circumstances'' was applied to avoid liability for negligence. This is easy compared to the task of consumers showing evidence to the contrary.

Many products, even the most ordinary, pose some level of risk, and the law recognizes that it is often not possible to design a totally safe product. However, manufacturers are legally obligated to warn consumers about known dangers. Manufacturers may be found negligent if:

1) They fail to warn users about recognized risk,

2) The warning is too vague to be adequate, or

3) The warning is not brought to the user's attention.

There is no duty to warn against misuse that is so rare or unusual that it cannot be foreseen. The obligation to warn consumers of potential dangers poses a unique difficulty for manufacturers who must not only provide warnings, but must communicate them such that a reasonable person will find and understand them. In some cases a warning buried in a product's instructions may be judged inadequate; in other situations, a warning sticker on the product itself may be considered sufficient.

STRICT PRODUCT LIABILITY

The most recent evolution in tort law, strict liability, has transformed the very nature of product liability because it eliminates the entire question of negligence. Strict liability only requires a plaintiff to demonstrate that a product caused an injury because it was defective; the reason for the defect is irrelevant. The product itself, not the defendant's use, is under investigation.

Under strict liability, the manufacturer is held liable for allowing a defective product to enter the marketplace. The issue is a matter of public policy, not the manufacturer's unreasonable or negligent conduct. The introduction of a defective product into the marketplace brings each member of the product's distribution channel into liability for negligence. The theory of strict liability holds that manufacturers:

1) Have the greatest control over the quality of their products;

2) Can distribute their costs by raising prices; and

3) Have special responsibilities in their role as sellers.

The tort of negligence at least provided the responsible person a standard by which to measure negligence, although it imposed the added burden of proving that the defendant was negligent. Although strict liability eases those burdens for the plaintiff and improves chances of recovery, it does not provide a universally accepted standard for measuring failure. Instead, it relies on what has become known as the ''consumer-expectation'' test: one who sells any product in a defective condition unreasonably dangerous to the user is subject to liability for physical harm caused to the user if 1) the seller is engaged in the business of selling such a product, and 2) the product is expected to and does reach the user without substantial change in the condition in which it is used. ''Unreasonably dangerous'' is defined as dangerous beyond the expectations of the ordinary consumer who purchases it. Despite its great influence, this definition has not been universally accepted.

Tort law does recognize that some products beneficial to society cannot be made entirely safe. Prescription drugs and vaccines are notorious examples. Such products are not considered defective simply because of their inevitable hazards; something else must be wrong with them as well. Therefore, drug companies are not held strictly liable for a properly manufactured product accompanied by appropriate directions and warnings. In sum, design defects are not the same as manufacturing defects.

One defense manufacturers have employed with controversy is called ''state of the art.'' This means that manufacturers should be held accountable only for information available to them at the time of manufacture. Flaws or defects which arose due to unavailable knowledge are not considered in questions of liability. The problem interpreting this defense concerns the variation of knowledge and its applications across the country.

FURTHER READING:

Clement, David E. "Human Factors, Instructions and Warnings, and Product Liability." *IEEE Transactions on Professional Communication.* September 1987.

Downs, Philip E. and Douglas N. Behrman, "The Product Liability Coordinator: A Partial Solution." *Journal of the Academy of Marketing Science.* Fall 1986.

Gooden, Randall. "Reduce the Potential Impact of Product Liability on Your Organization." *Quality Progress.* January 1995.

Lane, Marc J. *Legal Handbook for Small Business.* New York: Amacom, 1989.

Morgan, Fred W. "Tampered Goods: Legal Development and Marketing Guidelines." *Journal of Marketing.* April 1988.

Siomkos, George, and Paul Shrivastava. "Responding to Product Liability Crises." *Long Range Planning.* October 1993.

Spiro, George W. *Legal Environment of Business.* Upper Saddle River, NJ: Prentice Hall, 1993.

SEE ALSO: Consumer Product Safety Commission

PRODUCT LIFE CYCLE

The theory of a product life cycle was introduced more than four decades ago to explain the expected life cycle of a typical product from design to obsolescence. Writing in *Marketing Tools,* Carole Hedden observed that the cycle is represented by a curve that can be divided into four distinct phases: introduction, growth, maturity, and decline. The goal is to maximize the product's value and profitability at each stage. It is primarily considered a marketing theory.

INTRODUCTION

This is the stage where a product is conceptualized and first brought to market. The goal of any new product introduction is to meet consumer's needs with a quality product at the lowest possible cost in order to return the highest level of profit. The introduction of a new product can be broken down into five distinct parts:

- Idea validation, which is when a company studies a market, looks for areas where needs are not being met by current products, and tries to think of new products that could meet that need. The company's marketing department is responsible for identifying market opportunities and defining who will buy the product, what the primary benefits of the product will be, and how the product will be used.

- Conceptual design occurs when an idea has been approved and begins to take shape. The company has studied available materials, technology, and manufacturing capability and determined that the new product can be created. Once that is done, more thorough specifications are developed, including price and style. Marketing is responsible for minimum and maximum sales estimates, competition review, and market share estimates.

- Specification and design is when the product is nearing release. Final design questions are answered and final product specs are determined so that a prototype can be created.

- Prototype and testing occurs when the first version of a product is created and tested by engineers and by customers. A pilot production run might be made to ensure that engineering decisions made earlier in the process were correct, and to establish quality control. The marketing department is extremely important at this point. It is responsible for developing packaging for the product, conducting the consumer tests through focus groups and other feedback methods, and tracking customer responses to the product.

- Manufacturing ramp-up is the final stage of new product introduction. This is also known as commercialization. This is when the product goes into full production for release to the market. Final checks are made on product reliability and variability.

In the introduction phase, sales may be slow as the company builds awareness of its product among potential customers. Advertising is crucial at this stage, so the marketing budget is often substantial. The type of advertising depends on the product. If the product is intended to reach a mass audience, than an advertising campaign built around one theme may be in order. If a product is specialized, or if a company's resources are limited, than smaller advertising campaigns can be used that target very specific audiences. As a product matures, the advertising budget associated with it will most likely shrink since audiences are already aware of the product.

Author Philip Kotler has found that marketing departments can choose from four strategies at the commercialization stage. The first is known as "rapid skimming." The rapid refers to the speed with which the company recovers its development costs on the product—the strategy calls for the new product to be launched at a high price and high promotion level. High prices mean high initial profits (provided the product is purchased at acceptable levels of course), and high promotion means high market recognition. This works best when the new product is unknown in the marketplace.

The opposite method, "slow skimming," entails releasing the product at high price but with low promotion level. Again, the high price is designed to recover costs quickly, while the low promotion level keeps new costs down. This works best in a market that is made up of few major players or products—the small market means everyone already knows about the product when it is released.

The other two strategies involve low prices. The first is known as rapid penetration and involves low price combined with high promotion. This works best in large markets where competition is strong and consumers are price-conscious. The second is called slow penetration, and involves low price and low promotion. This would work in markets where price was an issue but the market was well-defined.

Besides the above marketing techniques, **sales promotion** is another important consideration when the product is in the introductory phase. According to Kotler and Armstrong in *Principles of Marketing,* ''Sales promotion consists of short-term incentives to encourage purchase or sales of a product or service. Whereas advertising offers reasons to buy a product or service, sales promotion offers reason to buy now.'' Promotions can include free samples, rebates, and coupons.

GROWTH

The growth phase occurs when a product has survived its introduction and is beginning to be noticed in the marketplace. At this stage, a company can decide if it wants to go for increased **market share** or increased profitability. This is the boom time for any product. Production increases, leading to lower unit costs. Sales momentum builds as advertising campaigns target mass media audiences instead of specialized markets (if the product merits this). Competition grows as awareness of the product builds. Minor changes are made as more feedback is gathered or as new markets are targeted. The goal for any company is to stay in this phase as long as possible.

It is possible that the product will not succeed at this stage and move immediately past decline and straight to cancellation. That is a call the marketing staff has to make. It needs to evaluate just what costs the company can bear and what the product's chances for survival are. Tough choices need to be made—sticking with a losing product can be disastrous.

If the product is doing well and killing it is out of the question, then the marketing department has other responsibilities. Instead of just building awareness of the product, the goal is to build brand loyalty by adding first-time buyers and retaining repeat buyers. Sales, discounts, and advertising all play an important role in that process. For products that are well-established and further along in the growth phase,

marketing options include creating variations of the initial product that appeal to additional audiences.

MATURITY

At the maturity stage, sales growth has started to slow and is approaching the point where the inevitable decline will begin. Defending market share becomes the chief concern, as marketing staffs have to spend more and more on promotion to entice customers to buy the product. Additionally, more competitors have stepped forward to challenge the product at this stage, some of which will inevitably offer a higher quality version of the product at a lower price, which makes it hard for the company at the mature stage to compete. This can touch off price wars, and lower prices mean lower profits, which will cause some companies to drop out of the market for that product altogether. The maturity stage is usually the longest of the four life cycle stages, and it is not uncommon for a product to be in the mature stage for several decades.

A savvy company will be looking to lower unit costs as much as possible at the maturity stage so that profits can be maximized. The money earned from the mature products should then be used in research and development to come up with new product ideas to replace the maturing products. Operations should be streamlined, cost efficiencies sought, and hard decisions made.

From a marketing standpoint, experts argue that the right promotion can make more of an impact at this stage than at any other. One popular theory argues that there are two primary marketing strategies to utilize at this stage—offensive and defensive. Defensive means doing whatever it takes to keep market share from slipping away. This can mean special sales and promotions—coming up with new colors for a longstanding product, for example. It can also mean quite literally defending the quality and integrity of your product versus your competition.

Marketing offensively means looking beyond current markets and attempting to gain brand new buyers. Relaunching the product is one option. Other offensive tactics include changing the price of a product (either higher or lower) to appeal to an entirely new audience or finding new applications for a product.

DECLINE

This occurs when the product peaks in the maturity stage and then begins a downward slide in sales. Eventually, revenues will drop to the point where it is no longer economically feasible to continue making the product. Investment is minimized. The product can simply be discontinued, or it can be sold to another company. A third option that combines those elements is also sometimes seen as viable, but comes to fruition only rarely. Under this scenario, the product is discontinued and stock is allowed to dwindle to zero, but the company sells the rights to supporting the product to another company, which then becomes responsible for servicing and maintaining the product.

It's important to note, however, that a product that enters decline can still be saved. In her article on product longevity and life cycles, Hedden singled out the Hallmark Company as an example of an organization that fought off decline. Faced with new competitors hitting niche card markets and declining sales, Hallmark reinvented itself. It developed specialized card lines that appealed to specific groups, such as young people or minorities. It fell back on its trademark brand by emphasizing it's "crown" logo in advertising campaigns, implying that the crown was an unmatched sign of quality. It used new technology to learn more about its customers and to lower production costs. In the end, these steps seem to have worked, as Hallmark is stronger than ever and no longer losing market share.

PROBLEMS WITH THE PRODUCT LIFE CYCLE THEORY

While the product life cycle theory is widely accepted, it does have critics who say that the theory has so many exceptions and so few rules that it is meaningless. Among the holes in the theory that these critics highlight:

- There is no set amount of time that a product must stay in any stage; each product is different and moves through the stages at different times. Also, the four stages are not the same time period in length, which is often overlooked.

- There is no real proof that all products must die. Some products have been seen to go from maturity back to a period of rapid growth thanks to some improvement or redesign. Some argue that by saying in advance that a product must reach the end of life stage, it becomes a self-fulfilling prophecy that companies subscribe to. Critics citing this charge say that some businesses interpret the first downturn in sales to mean that a product has reached decline and should be killed, thus terminating some still-viable products prematurely.

- The theory can lead to an over-emphasis on new product releases at the expense of mature products, when in fact the greater profits could possibly be derived from the mature product if a little work was done on revamping the product.

- The theory emphasizes individual products instead of taking larger brands into account.

- The theory does not adequately account for product redesign and/or reinvention.

FURTHER READING:

Grantham, Lisa Michelle. "The Validity of the Product Life Cycle in the High-tech Industry." *Marketing Intelligence and Planning.* June 1997.

Hedden, Carole. "From Launch to Relaunch: The Secret to Product Longevity Lies in Using the Right Strategy for Each Stage of the Life Cycle." *Marketing Tools.* September 1997.

Ryan, Chuck, and Walter E. Riggs. "Redefining the Product Life Cycle: the Five-Element Product Wave." *Business Horizons.* September/October 1996.

SEE ALSO: Advertising Strategy; Pricing; Product Costing; Product Development; Product Positioning

PRODUCT POSITIONING

Product positioning involves tailoring an entire **marketing** program—including product attributes, image, and price, as well as **packaging**, distribution, and service—to best meet the needs of consumers within a particular market segment. In this way, product positioning is part of the overall process of **market segmentation**, but involves a narrowing of focus. "Segmentation analysis tells us how the market is defined and allows us to target one or more opportunities," Glen L. Urban and Steven H. Star wrote in their book *Advanced Marketing Strategy.* "Product positioning takes place within a **target market** segment and tells us how we can compete most effectively in that market segment."

The key to product positioning is understanding the dimensions consumers use to evaluate competing marketing programs and make purchase decisions. It may be helpful for small business managers to create a graph in order to map consumer perceptions along several different dimensions. Once consumer perceptions are understood, the next step is to select the best positioning for the product and take steps to align the marketing program behind this positioning choice. Some examples of possible positioning choices include quality, reliability, and unique features or benefits. Before delving into product positioning further, it may be helpful to understand the process and goals of market segmentation.

MARKET SEGMENTATION

Market segmentation is the science of dividing an overall market into key customer subsets, or segments, whose members share similar characteristics and needs. Because it involves significant market research, market segmentation can be costly. But it is particularly important for small businesses, which often lack the resources to target large aggregate markets or to maintain a wide range of differentiated products for varied markets. Market segmentation allows a small business to develop a product and a marketing mix that fit a relatively homogenous part of the total market. By focusing its resources on a specific customer base in this way, a small business may be able to carve out a market niche that it can serve better than its larger competitors.

In general, customers are willing to pay a premium for a product that meets their needs more specifically than does a competing product. Thus marketers who successfully segment the overall market and adapt their products to the needs of one or more smaller segments stand to gain in terms of increased profit margins and reduced competitive pressures. But the potential gains offered by market segmentation must be measured against the **costs**, which—in addition to the market research required to segment a market—may include increased production and marketing expenses.

In their book *The Portable MBA in Marketing,* Alexander Hiam and Charles D. Schewe identified six steps that companies should take in the market segmentation process. The first step is to determine the boundaries of the market. In completing this step, a marketer should use a formal business plan to develop a broad definition of their business, and then consider the offerings of both direct and indirect competitors to gain information about the basic needs of consumers in the market. The second step in the process is to decide which variables to use in segmenting the market. Many companies fall into the trap of collecting data on as many variables as possible and then attempting to sort through it later to draw meaningful conclusions. Instead, Hiam and Schewe recommend that marketers use their knowledge of the market to select a few relevant variables in advance. This approach is generally less expensive and will likely provide more useful results.

The third step in the market segmentation process is actually collecting and analyzing data, which involves applying market research tools. The goal in analyzing the data is to identify market segments that are internally homogeneous, yet are distinctly heterogeneous with respect to other segments. The fourth step is to develop a detailed profile of each market segment, which involves selecting those variables that are most closely related to consumers' actual buying behavior.

The fifth step in the market segmentation process is to decide which segment or segments to serve. In targeting a particular segment, a marketer should look for opportunities (i.e., customers with unsatisfied wants and needs) that provide a good match for the organization and its resources. It is important that the marketer consider not only the size and potential profitability of a market segment, but also whether the company's skills, technologies, and objectives would enable it to meet the needs of that segment better than its competitors.

UNDERSTANDING CONSUMER PERCEPTIONS

Product positioning—which is the sixth and final step in the market segmentation process—involves developing a product and marketing plan that will appeal to the selected market segment. In order to position a product effectively, a small business must identify the attributes that are most important to consumers in the segment, and then develop an overall marketing strategy that will attract consumers' attention. Positioning can be usefully applied during the earliest stages of product design, when a company first identifies who its target customer will be in terms of demographic, geographic, and behavioral characteristics.

A number of tools exist to help marketers understand the consumer perceptions that underlie purchase decisions. One such tool, a perceptual map, is a graph that can portray various product positioning options in a visual manner. Marketers can create perceptual maps from market research data in order to identify consumer needs that are not being fulfilled. For example, say that consumers were asked to rate home computers on the following attributes: 1) ease of use, 2) availability of service, 3) processing speed, and 4) data storage capacity. These four attributes could be combined into two perceptual dimensions: 1) utility (consisting of ease of use and availability of service), which would appeal to non-experts who needed a basic computer for business or personal use; and 2) technical (consisting of processing speed and storage capacity), which would appeal to experienced computer users who wanted the latest in technology. Then each brand of home computer could be represented on the graph according to consumers' perceptions of the product. If most computer manufacturers touted their products' technical attributes, there might be an opportunity for a new market entrant who emphasized ease of use and service.

However, it is also important to understand the relative importance that consumers place upon the different dimensions. In the home computer market, for example, consumers ultimately want both utility and technical characteristics, but vary in the importance they place upon each product dimension. "The implications of these importances for positioning are significant," according to Urban and Star. "It is necessary to understand preference differences within the targeted market segments because they are important in selecting a position for a brand and in determining the competitive structure within the segment. When preferences vary within a segment, positions and physical product features may vary considerably. If preferences are relatively homogeneous within a segment, the positions of competing brands will be relatively similar, and the quantity of advertising and promotion will be the critical competitive weapons.''

It is also important to note that price is not represented in the home computer perceptual map, whereas price definitely has an effect on the final purchase decision made by consumers. Marketers can reflect the importance of price by adding a dimension to the perceptual map, so that it becomes a cube, or by dividing the dimensional coordinates of each brand by its average price. The resulting map would show ''utility per dollar'' and ''technical attributes per dollar,'' or the tradeoffs consumers make between the original dimensions and price. Finally, small business owners need to consider the fact that perceptual maps show ''overall dimensions of evaluation and not detailed features,'' as Urban and Star noted. ''Feature selection is critical in positioning, however, because features are an important determinant of overall perception and choice.'' In fact, product features influence both consumer perceptions and product pricing.

POSITIONING OPTIONS

Once marketers have mapped consumer perceptions of competing brands and gained an understanding of the target segment, the next step is to select a position for their products. In positioning a product within a market segment, marketers should try to maximize the share of consumer choices attained by their product in order to achieve long-run profitability for the firm. Strategies that can help marketers to maximize share include adding features desired by consumers or advertising to improve consumer perceptions. Both of these strategies can be costly, however, so it is important to ''balance the costs of positioning with price and share changes to identify the strategy that will achieve maximum long-run profitability,'' according to Urban and Star. ''The best position is the one that meets financial as well as marketing goals.''

One method of achieving a favorable position is to make strong advertising claims about product attributes that are preferred by consumers. The only catch is that the product must actually fulfill the claims, or else consumers will lower their perceptions and decide against repeat purchases. As Urban and Star stated, ''Good marketing is based on products that are advertised and sold honestly and generate real value by filling customer needs.''

Marketers have several different positioning options available to them. One positioning option is quality, which includes not only defect-free production but also product design and customer service that meets or exceeds customer expectations. ''The quality concept begins with design, carries through production, distribution, and service, and ends in total customer satisfaction,'' Urban and Star explained. Another positioning option available to marketers involves offering unique features or benefits that consumers are unable to find in competing products. Ideally, such features and benefits grow out of the company's unique sources of competitive advantage in the marketplace. This makes it difficult for competitors to match the features and benefits without incurring high costs. ''If we develop a unique competitive advantage on a dimension of importance to a significant portion of the market, we can enjoy a substantial share and high margins,'' Urban and Star noted. Of course, continued **market research** and **innovation** are necessary to maintain such a competitive advantage.

In some cases, rather than selecting a product position within the accepted structure of a market segment, a company may instead try to create a new dimension of importance to consumers. But creating a new dimension is difficult and usually results from major product innovations. ''The final result of innovation may be either a new positioning within the current structure or the creation of a new dimension or an additional segment,'' according to Urban and Star. Another option available to marketers is to position products across different, yet overlapping, market segments. It is important to note, however, that since some consumers may belong to both segments, positioning claims for a product should never conflict. To avoid confusing consumers, it may be necessary to use a different brand name for the product in each segment, or to make a broad appeal to both segments and then change the positioning slightly within each segment.

FURTHER READING:

Frank, R.E., W.F. Massy, and Y. Wind. *Market Segmentation.* Englewood Cliffs, NJ: Prentice-Hall, 1972.

Hiam, Alexander, and Charles D. Schewe. *The Portable MBA in Marketing.* New York: Wiley, 1992.

McCarthy, E. Jerome, and William D. Perreault, Jr. *Basic Marketing.* 10th ed. Homewood, IL: Irwin, 1990.

Urban, Glen L., and Steven H. Star. *Advanced Marketing Strategy.* Englewood Cliffs, NJ: Prentice Hall, 1991.

PRODUCTIVITY

Worker productivity is one of the key issues for any business, but for small businesses with limited resources, getting the most out of the least is an essential element in establishing and maintaining competitiveness. Small businesses need to have tools in place to measure productivity and must combine increased productivity with a commitment to quality and efficiency. Innovative goal setting, planning, and organizing are essential to improving productivity.

To improve productivity, a company first needs to be able to put meaningful methodologies of measurement in place to evaluate and monitor the performance of a business operation. To be meaningful, productivity measurements must show a linkage with profitability; after all, it is the bottom line that is the ultimate barometer of a company's success. Measurements should clearly demonstrate how efficiently (or inefficiently) a company is using its resources to produce quality goods and services. In the simplest terms, productivity is simply the ratio between the quantity of goods and services produced and the quantity of resources used to produce them. Economists have come up with a number of intricate ways to measure productivity, but any business owner can tell that if he or she is producing more of a product with the same number of resources, productivity has gone up. Of course, the opposite is true if fewer products are being produced.

In the past, productivity was a stand-alone issue—a company could either improve it, or it could not. For most small businesses, increasing productivity has meant one thing—improving the output rate. When this is the only goal, improving quality is seen as a very expensive proposition that does nothing to boost output. In other words, improved quality and increased output are seen as mutually exclusive ideas. This way of thinking is a mistake. In fact, small business owners need to realize that just the opposite is true. An increase in quality most often results in lower costs as rework is eliminated and unnecessary inspections are eliminated. Improved quality should be seen as a strategic tool that can increase efficiency by improving resource utilization and increasing customer satisfaction while lowering costs.

Another tool to increase productivity is to improve communications between workers and management. This may be easier in a small firm than a large one since the total number of employees is lower. Managers must sell employees on their obligation to make things work better at the company, both in the work environment and the work product. By gathering input from more and more workers, that job can be made easier.

A business owner or CEO can begin gathering input from workers by starting at the top and letting the process filter down. Off-site retreats with top managers to discuss the company's values and goals are a good place to start. From there, those values and goals can be communicated to the whole work force at the same time it is conveyed to them that their input matters and that direct communication is valued throughout the organization. If something goes wrong, any employee should feel safe in stepping forward and identifying the problem without fear of reprisals. If one person has a conflict with another employee, they should be encouraged to go directly to that other person instead of ignoring the problem or complaining about it to people who cannot solve it. A high-level manager, or even the CEO or owner, can step in to solve disputes if there is still a conflict after communications have been initiated.

This improved and open communication eases tension in the workplace and fosters a cooperative, growth-oriented atmosphere. Employees feel that their problems will be listened to and that their suggestions will be taken seriously, which means they are more likely to work harder and to think creatively when initiating production improvements.

Improved communication can also lead to another step known to enhance productivity in small businesses—enabling the **work force**. Once communication channels are open, upper management may find that employees are as committed to improving the business as they are. They also realize that front-line employees are quite often the best source of ideas on how to improve productivity and the best source for implementing those ideas. In small businesses, employees are often forced to perform a greater variety of tasks than employees at large firms—it is up to small business owners to take advantage of that fact by empowering employees. As Jay Nathan observed in the *Review of Business,* '' empowerment in the small business environment enables employees and management to learn and implement new ways of working, thus improving business operations for increased profits and productivity.''

True empowerment also requires employers to provide their workers with the skills and knowledge to perform their jobs, as well as the unquestioned support of management. Upper management must provide ongoing training and skills development, while managers should act as coaches and leaders who make needed resources available. Finally, a mutual trust and caring must develop between associates and managers—such trust is essential if positive changes are to occur.

INCREASED PRODUCTIVITY THROUGH INCENTIVES

Another way to get employees to work harder and improve productivity is to let them share in any gains that result from the productivity improvements. Pay-for-performance bonus systems, or gain sharing, has become a popular incentive in the 1990s with both large and small businesses. For example, one restaurant in Ohio offered to pay cash incentives to all employees if food costs dropped below 35 percent of total sales. The very first month, employees offered up several money-saving suggestions that resulted in a 1.7 percent drop in food costs and a $40 payout to everyone on staff. Payouts since then have gone as high as $95; in the two months where results did not meet the 35 percent goal, no payouts were made.

Gain sharing, and programs like it, have become successful because they increase employee awareness of the company's bottom line and their ability to have an impact on the firm's financial fortunes. From the employer's standpoint, gain sharing is a "win-win" proposition since employees work harder, feel more committed to the business, and profits (or some other measurable goal) improve.

How does a small business institute a gain-sharing program? First, keep things simple. Pick no more than five key business indicators that are important to the business's success. For example, a sales staff might focus on account growth, market penetration, and customer retention. Selecting more than five objectives complicates the issue and makes it harder for employees to understand. Likewise, it is important to select objectives that the employees have direct control over. Meeting goals that require actions outside their sphere of influence demoralizes employees and makes it far less likely that any improvements will be seen. The plan should be written in language that is easy to understand, with the bottom line goal clearly stated.

Once goals are determined, they have to be measured. Choose a realistic means of measuring progress, and, more importantly, choose realistic goals and performance targets that can be reached through productivity improvements. Employees have no problem spotting and ignoring unrealistic goals that they know they have no hopes of attaining. Goals should be both short-term (monthly) and long-range (annual). Also, it is important to note that goals will almost certainly change over time as employees become more efficient and meet the original goals.

Communication is an important part of the gain sharing process. Once management starts measuring productivity, it needs to share the data it gathers with employees so they can see the progress (or lack thereof) being made. This step—sharing financial or production data that was once considered confidential— might be new for many companies, but it must occur so that employees can make good decisions and sharpen their problem-solving skills. Communication should continue throughout the life of the program; business consultants counsel clients to use tools such as newsletters or memos to tell employees about success stories throughout the company. This lets employees know that their actions matter and provides other employees with examples of how to make improvements. Very visible means of communication such as large charts tracking progress against the goal are also very effective.

In addition to sharing information, management must enable employees to make decisions and act on them without too many layers of approval. Employees are the best source of ideas for improving productivity, and making them feel that they are in control of the program is a key part of making it work. Employees are sure to rebel against any program that they feel is being forced on them by upper management or by an outside consulting firm. One of the best ways to ensure employee buy-in is to form a cross-functional group made up of employees from throughout the company to help design and administer the plan.

Eventually, each department should come up with its own set of goals, but the initial plan must be a company-wide one with a big picture goal. Once that goal is stated, each department can look at its own operations and come up with a set of smaller goals that are all designed to help meet the larger goal. Departments should not set their smaller goals in a vacuum—quite often, the performance of one department is directly dependent on the performance of another department, so it is important that those two departments work together in establishing goals.

Once all the goals are set, the reward needs to be determined. The biggest caution that experts offer is to make sure the reward is worth the employee's efforts. If the incentive is too small, the plan might fail because employees simply do not care if they make the improvements needed to get what they view as inconsequential rewards. Experts recommend that employees be able to earn between four and eight percent of their annual salary as a reward for meeting gain sharing goals. Rewards can be paid as an increase in annual salary, or as a one-time bonus.

It should be noted that gain sharing can be an especially successful tool for a small business that is about to grow beyond the owner-several employee stage. When the company consists of the owner and just a few employees, the owner can control all operations and can rewards employees as he or she sees fit. As the company grows and is split into departments with managers who report to the owner, control is decentralized. The owner may step away from the day-to-day managerial responsibilities and therefore lose touch with the workflow. It is at that point that gain sharing can be an important tool to pull employees together and keep them working towards a common goal.

Finally, one note of caution about gain sharing or incentive-based pay. Managers must make sure that employees do not become so focused on the targets needed to achieve gain sharing that they neglect other parts of their work or let quality slip. This is the most common criticism of gain sharing, and it is one of the most important reasons that short-term goals must be combined with long-range goals if the plan is to work. That way, workers will be able to see that if they commit too much effort to the short-term goal, the long-term goal may be lost.

USING TECHNOLOGY TO IMPROVE PRODUCTIVITY

From the time of the first factory, using machines to assist or even replace humans and improve productivity has been the norm. Using machines to create interchangeable parts, the creation of the assembly line, the use of robots to take over manual tasks—these are just a few of the dramatic improvements in productivity that came about as a result of technology. Today, that practice continues unabated. The giant leaps made in computer and robotic technology in the last decade have given business owners tremendous new options for improving productivity.

What is different about this wave of better productivity through technology is that it is directly impacting small businesses. In the past, leaps in technological know-how most often benefited large corporations that had the money to invest in expensive new systems. Today, when the most inexpensive laptop computer is more powerful than some of the behemoth mainframe computers that existed in the 1960s, even the smallest business can afford to take advantage of technology to make his or her business grow. Computers, voice mail, fax machines, e-mail—most people today would not dream of starting a business without these technological aids by their side.

Computers and other advances have simply let small businesses get more done in less time—the very essence of increased productivity. *Entrepreneur* magazine noted that a 1996 survey by KeyCorp, a Cleveland-based banking firm, showed that 45 percent of those surveyed said technology "had allowed their small business to perform faster and more efficiently." Examples of technological gains include database management software that make it easy to manage inventory, fax-back and e-mail services used by customer service departments to disseminate information that previously had to go through the mail, bar-coding technology that can be used to track customer purchases in a computer database that automatically sends a message to reorder a particular product when in-stock levels drop below a preset point, and "home pages" on the World Wide Web which allow small companies to go global for very little cost.

All of the above are examples of how technology was used to help a company grow; technology can also increase productivity and cut expenses by helping a company "stay small" in other areas. For example, instead of having to outsource bookkeeping operations or hire more customer support people, a small business can now look to computers (easy-to-use accounting software, for example) and communications technology to register significant savings in both time and money.

Communications tools, in fact, are the next wave of technology. Desktop videoconferencing, company intranets which can be linked to manufacturers and suppliers, paging and wireless communications—all are in their infancy right now and are expected to explode in use in the near future. At the center of this boom is the Internet. As Jacques Clay of Hewlett Packard told *Entrepreneur,* "Small businesses will use it to communicate with customers, sell products via their web pages, and create very targeted advertising for local, regional, or international audiences."

Business-to-business communications will also increase as the Internet expands, making it easier to find partners to do business with.

While almost everyone concedes that small businesses must invest in technology to compete, there are still complaints about technology. The two most common are that it is still too expensive in many areas, and thus out of reach to many business owners. The second is that it is still too complicated and difficult to learn. About 23 percent of firms in the KeyCorp survey said that learning to use their new technology was a problem. The computer industry seems to be taking this complaint seriously and developing a new wave of "plug and play" products that are easy to install and easy to use. Computer networks designed just for small businesses are being marketed that have fewer bells and whistles, fewer set-up requirements, and more customized software.

FURTHER READING:

Aboganda, Wilfredo M. "Productivity Measurement Methodology." *Industrial Engineering.* November 1994.

DeMott, John S. "Smaller Is Better, Nimbler, Cheaper." *Nation's Business.* April 1994.

Fuller-Love, Nerys, and R.W. Scapens. "Performance Related Pay: A Case Study of a Small Business." *International Small Business Journal.* July-September 1997.

Ibielski, Dieter. "So What About Small Business Productivity?" *National Productivity Review.* Winter 1997.

Jasinowski, Jerry J. "The Path to Growth." *Chief Executive (U.S.).* March 1997.

Livingston, Abby. "Gain-Sharing Encourages Productivity." *Nation's Business.* January 1998.

Maynard, Roberta. "Are Your Employees Helping Your Company Grow?" *Nation's Business.* April 1994.

Maynard, Roberta. "Tapping Employee's Insights to Expand Productivity." *Nation's Business.* November 1996.

Nathan, Jay. "Empowerment As a Workplace Strategy in Small Business." *Review of Business.* Winter 1993.

Page, Heather. "Wired for Success: Entrepreneurs Reap the Rewards of the Technology Revolution." *Entrepreneur.* May 1997.

Wrennall, William. "Productivity: Reengineering for Competitiveness." *Industrial Engineering.* December 1994.

SEE ALSO: Corporate Culture; Delegation; Employee Motivation; Employee Reward Systems; Quality Control; Training and Development

PROFESSIONAL CORPORATIONS

A professional corporation is a variation of the corporate form of business organization that is available to entrepreneurs who provide professional services—such as doctors, lawyers, accountants, consultants, and architects. "Professionals," Frederick W. Dailey explained in his book *Tax Savvy for Small Business,* "are treated as small businesses under the tax code. Most of them operate as **sole proprietorships** or **partnerships**, and are subject to the same tax rules as other similar businesses. However, certain professionals who offer services may form and operate a special type of entity, called a professional corporation." Some states require professionals to form this type of entity if they wish to incorporate. In a professional corporation, the owners perform services for the business as employees.

The first laws that permitted the formation of professional corporations were intended to give professionals some of the tax advantages enjoyed by corporations without also giving them the benefit of limited liability. If a regular corporation—which is a distinct entity under the law—becomes insolvent, its creditors can only claim business **assets** for the repayment of debts, not the personal assets of its owners. This is in contrast to regular proprietorships and partnerships, which are not legally distinct from their owners or partners. Since personal responsibility is a key factor in being a professional, the law could not allow professionals to escape liability for their own actions by incorporating. The lines between different forms of business organization have been blurred in recent years, however, as more tax advantages have become available to sole proprietorships and partnerships, and more limited liability has been granted to professional corporations.

PERSONAL SERVICE CORPORATIONS

Most professional corporations qualify as personal service corporations (PSC) for federal tax purposes, provided that they also qualify under state law. To qualify as a PSC under Internal Revenue Service rules, a professional corporation must be organized under state law and then pass two federal tests: the function test and the ownership test. The function test requires that substantially all (95 percent) of the business activities of the professional corporation involve services within specific occupations in the fields of health, law, engineering, accounting, actuarial science, consulting, or performing arts. The ownership test requires that substantially all the professional corporation's outstanding stock be held directly or indirectly by qualified people, either: 1) employees who are currently performing professional services for the corporation; 2) retired employees who did so prior to their retirement; 3) or their heirs or estates. If a professional corporation organized under state law does not qualify as a PSC, then it is treated as a general partnership for federal tax purposes.

PSCs are taxed like regular **C corporations**, but with a flat corporate tax rate of 35 percent rather than a graduated rate depending on the level of income earned. The PSC files a corporate tax return and also issues Form K-1 to all shareholder/employees to show their individual shares of the corporation's profit or loss. Any income that is retained in the PSC is subject to the corporate tax rate, while any salaries paid to employees are considered tax-deductible business expenses. Like most small corporations, however, PSCs are likely to pay out all business income to shareholders in the form of salaries, bonuses, and fringe benefits, thus reducing corporate taxable income to zero. Of course, the shareholder/employees still must pay personal income taxes on the income they receive.

ADVANTAGES AND DISADVANTAGES

Organizing as a professional corporation offers many potential advantages to qualified small business owners. Some of the primary advantages involve tax breaks that are not available to unincorporated businesses. For example, professional corporations can create retirement plans and 401(k) plans for their employees that have higher contribution limits than plans available to individuals or unincorporated businesses. In addition, professional corporations can provide health and **life insurance** as a tax-free benefit to their employees by establishing a Voluntary Employees' Beneficiary Association (VEBA). They can also take tax deductions for disability insurance, dependent care, and other fringe benefits provided to employees. In most cases, such benefits are tax-deductible for the corporation, and also are not considered taxable income for the employees.

Another advantage available to professional corporations is perpetual existence. Unlike sole proprietorships and partnerships—which legally dissolve when an owner dies or leaves the company—professional corporations can continue operations without interruption if a shareholder/employee dies or withdraws. Another advantage is that professional corporations may enable shareholder/employees to avoid personal liability for another employee's negligence. In most cases, one owner is liable for another's actions only if he or she would have been liable as a shareholder of a regular corporation. In contrast, all members of a regular partnership are exposed to personal liability.

There are also a few potential disadvantages associated with the professional corporation form of organization. For example, passive loss limitations may apply that restrict the amount nonactive shareholders can deduct for tax purposes in the event of business losses. In the case of a partnership, all partners are able to deduct their share of business losses from their personal taxable income. Since most professional corporations have only active shareholders and do not experience losses, however, this tax liability is not usually an issue. The flat corporate tax rate that applies to professional corporations may be another source of disadvantage. Retaining earnings within the business will rarely make sense due to the higher tax bracket, and this may reduce the firm's flexibility in distributing income to shareholder/employees. In contrast, most regular corporations can ''split income''—or adjust the amount paid out to shareholder/employees—so that both the company and the individual can gain the most favorable tax bracket possible.

CHOOSING AMONG THE ALTERNATIVES

Many states now provide professionals with several options about how to organize their businesses. The main alternatives to forming a professional corporation or personal service corporation include organizing as a **limited liability company (LLC)** or as a limited liability partnership (LLP). These options differ in the costs and tax benefits involved, as well as in the amount of liability protection afforded. For example, limited liability companies combine the liability protection afforded by professional corporations with the taxation flexibility provided by partnerships. LLCs are taxed similar to S corporations, so the income flows through to the shareholder/employees rather than accruing to the business and then being distributed to owners and employees. Limited liability partnerships are similar to regular partnerships except that they provide additional protection for partnership assets against malpractice suits. However, the partners in an LLP are required to carry hefty insurance or guarantee deposits in exchange for this protection.

The main advantages of organizing as a professional corporation, as outlined above, include tax benefits and transferability of ownership. However, the flat corporate tax rate prevents shareholder/employees from retaining earnings in the professional corporation, which may limit opportunities for expansion and growth. In addition, professional corporation owners may face the problem of double taxation upon liquidation of the business. Income from the sale of real estate or equipment might accrue to the business, for example, where it would be taxed at the corporate rate. If this income were then distributed to shareholders as dividends (since the company was no longer in business and thus could not pay it out as salaries and benefits to employees), then it would be subject to taxation again as personal income.

According to Roberta Schmalz in an article for *Outlook,* a professional or group of professionals should choose the type of business organization best for them by considering the following criteria:

- Which type of organization costs the least to form?
- Which type provides the best tax results?
- Which type offers the best liability protection?
- Which type is best suited for multi-state operations (if applicable)?
- And finally, which type is best for the professionals and their clients?

Of course, state laws differ regarding the types of business organizations that are available to professionals, so it is important to consult with an accountant familiar with the states in which the company will do business.

FURTHER READING:

Dailey, Frederick W. *Tax Savvy for Small Business: Year-Round Tax Advice for Small Businesses.* Berkeley, CA: Nolo Press, 1997.

Malamud, Richard B. ''In Search of a Definition of a Personal Service Corporation.'' *Tax Notes.* May 26, 1997.

Samelson, Donald P., Gary M. Cavett, and James W. Clifton. ''Choosing the Form of Business for Professionals.'' *Taxation for Accountants.* January 1995.

Schmalz, Roberta. ''PC, LLC, or LP? The Choice Is Yours.'' *Outlook.* Fall 1995.

SEE ALSO: Incorporation; Succession Plans; Tax Planning

PROFIT MARGIN

The profit margin is an **accounting** measure designed to gauge the financial health of a business firm or industry. In general, it is defined as the ratio of profit earned to total sales receipts (or costs) over some defined period. The profit margin is a measure of the amount of profit accruing to a firm from the sale of a product or service. It also provides an indication of efficiency in that it captures the amount of surplus generated per unit of the product or service sold. In order to generate a sizeable profit margin, a company must operate efficiently enough to recover not only the costs of the product or service sold, operating expenses, and the costs of debt, but also to provide compensation for its owners in exchange for their acceptance of risk.

As an example of a profit margin calculation, suppose firm A, in July 1997, made a profit of $10 on the sale of a $100 television set. Dividing the dollar amount of earnings by the product cost, that firm's profit margin would be .10 or 10 percent, meaning that each dollar of sales generated an average of ten cents of profit. Thus, the profit margin is very important as a measure of the competitive success of a business, because it captures the firm's unit costs.

A low-cost producer in an industry would generally have a higher profit margin. Since firms tend to sell the same product at roughly the same price (adjusted for quality differences), lower costs would be reflected in a higher profit margin. Lower cost firms also have a strategic advantage in a competitive price war, because they have the ability to undercut their competitors by cutting prices in order to gain market share and potentially drive higher cost firms out of business.

Firms clearly exist to expand their profits. But while increasing the absolute amount of dollar profit is desirable, it has minimal significance unless it is related to its source. This is why firms use measures such as profit margin and profit rate. Profit margin measures the flow of profits over some period compared with the costs, or sales, incurred over the same period. Thus, one could compute the profit margin on costs (profits divided by costs), or the profit margin on sales (profit margin divided by sales).

Other specific profit margin measures often calculated by businesses include: 1) gross profit margin—gross profit divided by net sales, where gross profit is the total money left over after sales and net sales is total revenues; 2) net profit margin—net profit divided by net sales, where net profit (or net income) is profit after deducting costs such as advertising, marketing, interest payments, and rental payments.

Profit margin is related to other measures such as the rate of profit (sometimes called the rate of return), which comprises various measures of the amount of profit earned relative to the total amount of capital invested (or the stock of capital) required to generate that profit. Thus, while the profit margin measures the amount of profit per unit of sales, the rate of profit on total assets indicates the efficiency of the total investment. Or, put another way, while the profit margin measures the amount of profit per unit of capital (labor, working capital, and depreciation of plant and equipment) consumed over a particular period, the profit rate measures the amount of profit per unit of capital advanced (the entire stock of capital required for the production of the good).

Using our previous example, if a $1,000 investment in plant and equipment were required to produce the $100 television set, then a profit margin of 10 percent would translate into a profit rate on total investment of only 1 percent. Thus, in this scenario, firm A's unit costs are low enough to generate a 10 percent profit margin on the capital consumed (assuming some market price) to produce the TV set; but in order to achieve that margin, a total capital expenditure of $1,000 must be made.

The difference between the profit margin measure and the profit rate concept then lies in the rate at which the capital stock depreciates, and the rate at which the production process repeats itself, or turnover time. In the first case, if the entire capital stock for a particular firm or industry is completely used up during one production cycle, then the profit margin would be exactly the same as the profit rate. In the case of turnover, if a firm succeeds in doubling the amount of times the production process repeats itself in the same period, then twice as much profit would be made on the same capital invested, even though the profit margin might not change. More formally, the rate of return = profit margin × sales / average assets, where average assets is the total capital stock divided by the number of times the production process turns over. Thus, the rate of return can be increased by increasing the profit margin or by shortening the production cycle. Of course, this will largely depend on the conditions of production in particular industries or firms.

If costs rise and prices do not rise to keep up, then the profit margin will fall. In times of business cycle upturns, prices tend to rise; in business cycle downturns, prices tend to fall. Of course, many factors, and not only costs, will affect the profit margin—namely, industry-specific factors that relate to investment requirements, **pricing**, type of market, and conditions of production (including production turnover time).

It is important for small business owners to remember that generating a profit margin does not guarantee that their business is healthy, or that they will have money in the bank. Rather, a small business must have a positive cash flow in order to pay its bills and compensate its employees. To use a profit margin figure to determine whether a start-up firm is doing well, an entrepreneur might compare it to the return that would be available from a bank or another low-risk investment opportunity.

FURTHER READING:

Gill, James O. *Financial Basics of Small Business Success.* Menlo Park, CA: Crisp Publications, 1994.

Helfert, Erich A. *Techniques of Financial Analysis.* Homewood, IL: Irwin, 1987.

Raiborn, Cecily A., Jesse T. Barfield, and Michael R. Kinney. *Managerial Accounting.* West Publishing Company, 1993.

PROFIT SHARING

Profit sharing refers to the process whereby companies distribute a portion of their profits to their employees. Profit-sharing plans are well established in American business. The annual U.S. Chamber of Commerce Employee Benefits Survey indicates that somewhere between 19 and 23 percent of U.S. companies have offered some form of profit sharing since 1963. Other estimates place the number of companies offering profit-sharing plans in the 1990s somewhere between one-fourth and one-third of all U.S. firms. For small businesses, profit sharing provides an important means of increasing employee loyalty and tying **employee compensation** to company performance. Profit sharing is a particularly attractive option for newer small businesses with uncertain profit levels, as it allows business owners to share the wealth during good times without obligating them to do so during lean years.

Historically, profit-sharing plans have their roots in the nineteenth century, when companies such as General Foods and Pillsbury distributed a percentage of their profits to their employees as a bonus. The first deferred profit-sharing plan was developed in 1916 by Harris Trust and Savings Bank of Chicago. There was a sharp increase in profit-sharing plans during World War II, when wages were frozen. Deferred profit-sharing plans enabled wartime employers to provide additional compensation to their employees without actually raising their wages.

The Employee Retirement Income Security Act of 1974 (ERISA) provided a further boost in the use of profit-sharing plans. ERISA regulates and sets the standards for pension plans and other employee benefit plans. Many employers found that a simple profit-sharing plan avoided many of ERISA's rules and regulations that affected pension plans.

Many companies have turned to profit-sharing plans during hard economic times, when they are unable to provide guaranteed wage increases. Chrysler Corporation, for example, introduced profit-sharing for its union and nonunion employees in 1988 during an economic recession. Its profit-sharing plan was offered as part of its union contract in exchange for wage concessions made by its work force. Corporate earnings at the time were weak, so profit-sharing payouts were small. By 1994, however, Chrysler had recovered and was paying an average profit-sharing bonus of $4,300 per person to 81,000 workers, a total outlay of approximately $348 million.

TYPES OF PROFIT-SHARING PLANS

Companies may use any number of different formulas to calculate the distribution of profits to their employees and establish a variety of rules and regulations regarding eligibility, but there are essentially two basic types of profit-sharing plans. One type is a cash or bonus plan, under which employees receive their profit-sharing distribution in cash at the end of the year. The main drawback to cash distribution plans is that employee profit-sharing bonuses are then taxed as ordinary income. Even if distributions are made in the form of company stock or some other type of current payment, they become taxable as soon as employees receive them.

To avoid immediate taxation, companies are allowed by the **Internal Revenue Service (IRS)** to set up qualified deferred profit-sharing plans. Under a deferred plan, profit-sharing distributions are held in individual accounts for each employee. Employees are not allowed to withdraw from their profit-sharing accounts except under certain, well-defined conditions. As long as employees do not have easy access to the funds, money in the accounts is not taxed and may earn tax-deferred interest.

Under qualified deferred profit-sharing plans, employees may be given a range of investment choices for their accounts, including stocks or mutual funds. Such choices are common when the accounts are managed by outside investment firms. It is becoming less common for companies to manage their own profit-sharing plans due to the fiduciary duties and liabilities associated with them. A 401(k) account is a common type of deferred profit-sharing plan, with several unique features. For example, employees are allowed to voluntarily contribute a portion of their salary, before taxes, to their **401(k) plans**. The company may decide to match a certain percentage of such contributions. In addition, many 401(k) accounts have provisions that enable employees to borrow money under certain conditions.

OTHER ISSUES CONCERNING PROFIT-SHARING PLANS

Deferred profit-sharing plans are a type of defined contribution plan. Such employee benefit plans provide an individual account for each employee. Individual accounts grow as contributions are made to them. Funds in the accounts are invested and may earn interest or show capital appreciation. Depending on each employee's investment choices, their account balances may be subject to increases or decreases reflecting the current value of their investments.

The amount of future benefits that employees will receive from their profit-sharing accounts depends entirely on their account balance. The amount of their account balance will include the employer's contributions from profits, any interest earned, any capital gains or losses, and possibly forfeitures from other plan participants. Forfeitures result when employees leave the company before they are vested, and the funds in their accounts are distributed to the remaining plan participants.

Employees are said to be vested when they become eligible to receive the funds in their accounts. Immediate vesting means that they have the right to funds in their account as soon as their employer makes a profit-sharing distribution. Companies may establish different time requirements before employees become fully vested. Under some deferred profit-sharing plans employees may start out partially vested, perhaps being entitled to only 25 percent of their account, then gradually become fully vested over a period of years. A company's vesting policy is written into the plan document and is designed to motivate employees and reduce employee turnover.

In order for a deferred profit-sharing plan to gain qualified status from the IRS, it is important that funds in employee accounts not be readily accessible to employees. Establishing a vesting period is one way to limit access; employees have rights to the funds in their accounts only when they become partially or fully vested. Another way to limit access is to establish strict rules for making payments from employees accounts, such as upon retirement, death, permanent disability, or termination of employment. Less strict rules may allow for withdrawals under certain conditions, such as financial hardship or medical emergencies. Nevertheless, whatever rules a company may adopt for its profit-sharing plan, such rules are subject to IRS approval and must meet IRS guidelines.

The IRS also limits the amount that employers may contribute to their profit-sharing plans. The precise amount is subject to change by the IRS, but 1996 tax rules allowed companies to contribute a maximum of 15 percent of an employee's salary to his or her profit-sharing account. If a company contributed less than 15 percent in one year, it may exceed 15 percent by the difference in a subsequent year to a maximum of 25 percent of an employee's salary.

Companies may determine the amount of their profit-sharing contributions in one of two ways. One is by a set formula that is written into the plan document. Such formulas are typically based on the company's pre-tax net profits, earnings growth, or some other measure of profitability. Companies then plug the appropriate numbers into the formula and arrive at the amount of their contribution to the profit-sharing pool. Rather than using a set formula, companies may decide to contribute a discretionary amount each year. That is, the company's owners or directors—at their discretion—decide what an appropriate amount would be.

Once the amount of the company's contribution has been determined, different plans provide for different ways of allocating the funds among the company's employees. The employer's contribution may be translated into a percentage of the company's total payroll, with each employee receiving the same percentage of his or her annual pay. Other companies may use a sliding scale based on length of service or other factors. Profit-sharing plans also spell out precisely which employees are eligible to receive profit-sharing distributions. Some plans may require employees to reach a certain age or length of employment, for example, or to work a certain minimum number of hours during the year.

Although profit sharing offers some attractive benefits to small business owners, it also includes some potential pitfalls. It is important for small business owners who wish to share their success with employees to set up a formal profit sharing plan with the assistance of an accountant or financial advisor. Otherwise, both the employer and the employees may not receive the tax benefits they desire from the plan. Also, small business owners should avoid making mentions of profit sharing or stock ownership to motivate employees during the heat of battle. Such mentions could be construed as promises and lead to lawsuits if the employees do not receive the benefits they feel they deserved.

FURTHER READING:

Blakely, Stephen. "Pension Power." *Nation's Business.* July 1997.

Crouch, Holmes F. *Decisions When Retiring.* Allyear Tax Guides, 1995.

The Entrepreneur Magazine Small Business Advisor. Wiley, 1995.

SEE ALSO: Employee Benefits; Retirement Planning

PROPRIETARY INFORMATION

Proprietary information, also known as a trade secret, is information that a company wishes to keep confidential or protect from those outside the company. Proprietary information can include secret formulas, processes, and methods used in production. It can also include a company's business and marketing plans, salary structure, customer lists, contracts, and computer systems. In some cases the special knowledge and skills that an employee has learned on the job are considered to be a company's proprietary information.

Although legal protections exist for inventions (patents), creative works (copyrights), and distinctive names and symbols (trademarks), no specific form of legal protection is available for trade secrets. In fact, there is no single standard by which to determine whether or not information is proprietary—some 39 U.S. states have different laws that define a trade secret and the conditions under which it is considered to have been stolen. But there is a significant body of case law covering proprietary information and trade secrets that recognizes a company's right to have proprietary information and provides the company with remedies when its trade secrets have been misused or appropriated illegally. In some ways this lack of specific forms of protection makes it easier for small businesses to protect their proprietary information, since no complicated forms or formal registration are required. In other ways, however, the lack of specific forms of trade secret protection hurts small businesses because it makes it difficult to prove a violation of rights.

In general, for information to be considered proprietary, companies must treat it as confidential. Thus, information that is readily available in public sources will not be treated by the courts as proprietary. In addition, proprietary information should give the firm some sort of competitive advantage and should not be generally known outside of the firm. A company must be able to demonstrate that it has taken every reasonable step possible to keep the information private if it hopes to obtain court assistance in protecting its rights.

There are several steps a company can take to protect its proprietary information. Key employees with access to proprietary information may be required to sign restrictive covenants—also called confidentiality, nondisclosure, or **noncompetition agreements**—that prohibit them from revealing that information to outsiders or using it to compete with their employer for a certain period of time after leaving the company. These restrictive covenants are usually enforced by the courts if they are reasonable with respect to time and place and do not unreasonably restrict the former employee's right to employment. In some cases the covenants are enforced only if the employee has gained proprietary information during the course of his or her employment.

In addition, the courts generally consider it unfair competition for one company to induce employees of another company who have acquired unique technical skills and secret knowledge during their employment, to terminate their employment and use their skills and knowledge for the benefit of the competing firm. In such a case the plaintiff company could seek an injunction to prevent its former employees and the competing company from using the proprietary information.

Companies may also develop security systems to protect their proprietary information from being stolen by foreign or domestic competitors. Business and industrial espionage is an ongoing activity that clandestinely seeks to obtain trade secrets by illegal methods. A corporate system for protecting proprietary information would include a comprehensive plan ranging from restricting employee access, to data protection, to securing phone lines and meeting rooms. In some cases a chief information officer (CIO) would be responsible for implementing such a plan.

FURTHER READING:

"Keeping Secrets Secret." *Small Business Reports.* February 1994.

Lickson, Charles P. *Legal Guide for Small Business.* Menlo Park, CA: Crisp Publications, 1994.

"How to Protect Yourself from Employees Who Become Competitors." *Profit-Building Strategies for Business Owners.* April 1993.

SEE ALSO: Intellectual Property; Inventions and Patents; Office Security

PROTOTYPES

Prototypes are working models of entrepreneurial ideas for new products. "A prototype is defined an an original model on which something is patterned," wrote Richard C. Levy in *The Inventor's Desktop Companion.* "If you do not have the time, money, skills, or commitment to build a prototype of your idea, the odds of your ever licensing it are reduced to practically zero." An entrepreneur armed with a good prototype, on the other hand, is thus able to show potential investors and licensees how the proposed product will work without having to rely exclusively on diagrams and his/her powers of description.

TYPES OF PROTOTYPES There are three major types or stages of prototype creation, each of which can be used by the enterprising entrepreneur in securing financing and/or a licensee.

1) Breadboard—This is basically a working model of your idea, intended to serve the basic function of showing how the product will work, with less concern for aesthetics. "The breadboard doesn't have to look good or even work well," stated Jacquelyn Denalli in *Business Start-Ups.* "It simply

proves your idea can be reduced to practice.'' Tomima Edmark, writing in *Entrepreneur,* added that a breadboard ''is used in the early stages of product development to demonstrate functionality and communicate your idea to potential model makers or manufacturers so they can create a finished product for sale.''

2) Presentation Prototype—This type of prototype is a representation of the product as it will be manufacturered. Often used for promotional purposes, it should be able to demonstrate what the product can do, but it is not necessarily an exact copy of the final product. ''In building your model,'' said Denalli, ''consider these issues: the item's sale price, materials, manufacturing costs, marketing details, safety factors, how it will be sold and distributed, and the profit margin. If you plan to license your invention to a manufacturer, you can often do so with a model.''

3) Pre-Production Prototype—This type of prototype is for all practical purposes the final version of the product. It should be just like the finished product in every way, from how it is manufacturered to its appearance, packaging, and instructions. This final-stage prototype is typically expensive to produce—and far more expensive to make than the actual unit cost once the product is in full production—but the added cost is often well worth it. It is most valuable because it enables inventors and producers to go over every aspect of the product in fine detail, which can head off potential trouble spots prior to product launch. In addition, Denalli pointed out that ''you can make drawings or photographs of the sample to use in brochures, mailings, pamphlets, advertising, and so on. You can also use the prototype to show to potential buyers, whether manufacturers or buyers for department stores.''

PROTOTYPE CREATION CONSIDERATIONS Prospective entrepreneurs with a new product idea should make sure that they consider the following when putting together a prototype:

- Adequately research the requirements of the product prototype. Edmark recommended that entrepreneurs follow these basic steps: 1) Write down all the materials, supplies, and tools that might be needed in creating the prototype; 2) Identify and order the various steps necessary to assemble the prototype; 3) identify which parts can be easily purchased and/or found around the home, and which parts will need to be custom made (''In most cases, use standard parts. They're always easier to find than custom parts and will be easier to purchase in bulk when the product is manufacturered'').

- Make sure the prototype is well-constructed. ''Prototypes must be well made because often they take quite a beating at the hands of executives,'' warned Levy. ''Don't be surprised when prototypes come back broken because they were mishandled or poorly packed for shipment. It happens at the best of companies. It comes with the territory.''

- Do not shirk on presentation, even at the prototype stage. ''You must be as sophisticated and slick in your presentation to potential licensees as they will have to be in their pitch to the trade and/or the consumer,'' wrote Levy.

- Recognize that complex product ideas may require outside assistance from professional prototype makers. Universities, engineering schools, local inventor organizations, and invention marketing companies are all potential sources of information on finding a good person to help you make your prototype. But before hiring a prototype maker, entrepreneurs should make certain that they can meet your expectations. To help ensure that you are satisfied, conduct research on the maker's business reputation and make certain that you adequately communicate your concept.

- Consider making multiple submissions to potential licensees. Some inventors send prototypes to several manufacturers at the same time. Levy recommended, however, that ''if a company asks you to hold off further presentations until it has an opportunity to review the item at greater length, try to set guidelines. In all fairness, some products require a reasonable number of days to be properly considered. However, if you feel the company is asking for an unreasonable period of time, seek some earnest money to hold the product out of circulation.''

FURTHER READING:

Denalli, Jacquelyn. ''Inventor's Circle—Terms of Invention.'' *Business Start-Ups.* November 1993.

Edmark, Tomima. ''Model Approach: Creating a Prototype that will Wow Investors.'' *Entrepreneur.* October 1997.

Levy, Richard C. *The Inventor's Desktop Companion: The Guide to Successfully Marketing and Protecting Your Ideas.* Detroit, MI: Visible Ink Press, 1995.

SEE ALSO: Investor Presentation

PUBLIC RELATIONS

Public relations describes the various methods a company uses to disseminate messages about its products, services, or overall image to its customers, employees, stockholders, suppliers, or other interested members of the community. The point of public relations is to make the public think favorably about the company and its offerings. Commonly used tools of public relations include news releases, press conferences, speaking engagements, and community service programs.

Although advertising is closely related to public relations—as it too is concerned with promoting and gaining public acceptance for the company's products—the goal of advertising is generating sales, while the goal of public relations is generating good will. The effect of good public relations is to lessen the gap between how an organization sees itself and how others outside the organization perceive it.

Public relations involves two-way communication between an organization and its public. It requires listening to the constituencies on which an organization depends as well as analyzing and understanding the attitudes and behaviors of those audiences. Only then can an organization undertake an effective public relations campaign.

Many small business owners elect to handle the public relations activities for their own companies, while others choose to hire a public relations specialist. Managers of somewhat larger firms, on the other hand, frequently contract with external public relations or advertising agencies to enhance their corporate image. But whatever option is chosen, the head of a company is ultimately responsible for its public relations.

GOALS OF PUBLIC RELATIONS

Some of the main goals of public relations are to create, maintain, and protect the organization's reputation, enhance its prestige, and present a favorable image. Studies have shown that consumers often base their purchase decisions on a company's reputation, so public relations can have a definite impact on sales and revenue. Public relations can be an effective part of a company's overall **marketing** strategy. In the case of a for-profit company, public relations and marketing should be coordinated to be sure they are working to achieve the same objectives.

Another major public relations goal is to create good will for the organization. This involves such functions as employee relations, stockholder and **investor relations**, media relations, and **community**

relations. Public relations may function to educate certain audiences about many things relevant to the organization—including the business in general, new legislation, and how to use a particular product—as well as to overcome misconceptions and prejudices. For example, a nonprofit organization may attempt to educate the public regarding a certain point of view, while trade associations may undertake educational programs regarding particular industries and their products and practices.

STEPS IN A PUBLIC RELATIONS CAMPAIGN

Effective public relations requires a knowledge, based on analysis and understanding, of all the factors that influence public attitudes toward the organization. While a specific public relations project or campaign may be undertaken proactively or reactively (to manage some sort of image crisis), the first basic step in either case involves analysis and research to identify all the relevant factors of the situation. In this first step, the organization gains an understanding of its various constituencies and the key factors that are influencing their perceptions of the organization.

In the second step, the organization establishes an overall policy with respect to the campaign. This involves defining goals and desired outcomes, as well as the constraints under which the campaign will operate. It is necessary to establish such policy guidelines in order to evaluate proposed strategies and tactics as well as the overall success of the campaign.

In step three, the organization outlines its strategies and tactics. Using its knowledge of the target audiences and its own established policies, the organization develops specific programs to achieve the desired objectives. Finally, step four involves actual communication with the targeted public. The organization then employs specific public relations techniques, such as press conferences or special events, to reach the intended audience.

In step five the organization receives feedback from its public. How have they reacted to the public relations campaign? Are there some unexpected developments? In the final step, the organization assesses the program and makes any necessary adjustments.

AREAS OF PUBLIC RELATIONS

Public relations is a multifaceted activity involving different audiences as well as different types of organizations, all with different goals and objectives. As a result, there are several specific areas of public relations.

PRODUCT PUBLIC RELATIONS Public relations and marketing work together closely when it comes to promoting a new or existing product or service. Public relations plays an important role in new product introductions by creating awareness, differentiating the product from other similar products, and even changing consumer behavior. Public relations can help introduce new products through staging a variety of special events and handling sensitive situations. For example, when the Prince Matchabelli division of Chesebrough-Pond's USA introduced a new men's cologne, there were twenty-one other men's fragrances being introduced that year. To differentiate its new offering, called Hero, Prince Matchabelli created a National Hero Awards Program honoring authentic male heroes and enlisted the participation of Big Brothers/Big Sisters of America to lend credibility to the program. Similarly, when Coleco introduced its Cabbage Patch Kids dolls, public relations helped increase awareness through licensed tie-in products, trade show exhibits, press parties, and even window displays in Cartier jewelry stores.

Public relations is often called on to give existing products and services a boost by creating or renewing visibility. For example, the California Raisins Advisory Board organized a national tour featuring live performances by the California Dancing Raisins to maintain interest in raisins during a summer-long advertising hiatus. The tour generated national and local publicity through media events, advance publicity, trade promotions, and media interviews with performer Ray Charles. Other public relations programs for existing products involve stimulating secondary demand—as when Campbell Soup Co. increased overall demand for soup by publishing a recipe booklet—or identifying new uses for the product. Public relations can interest the media in familiar products and services in a number of ways, including holding seminars for journalists, staging a special media day, and supplying the media with printed materials ranging from ''backgrounders'' (in-depth news releases) to booklets and brochures. Changes in existing products offer additional public relations opportunities to focus consumers' attention. An effective public relations campaign can help to properly position a product and overcome negative perceptions on the part of the general public.

EMPLOYEE RELATIONS Employees are one of the most important audiences a company has, and an ongoing public relations program is necessary to maintain employee good will as well as to uphold the company's image and reputation among its employees. The essence of a good employee relations program is keeping employees informed and providing them with channels of communication to upper levels of management. Bechtel Group, a privately held complex of operating companies, published an annual report for its employees to keep them informed about the company's operations. The company used surveys to determine what information employees considered useful. A range of other communication devices were used, including a monthly tabloid and magazine, a quarterly video magazine, local newsletters, bulletin boards, a call-in telephone service, and ''brown bag'' lunches where live presentations were made about the company. Suggestion systems are another effective way to improve employee-management communications.

Other public relations programs focusing on employees include training them as company public relations representatives; explaining benefits programs to them; offering them educational, volunteer, and citizenship opportunities; and staging special events such as picnics or open houses for them. Other programs can improve performance and increase employee pride and motivation. Public relations can also play a role in recruiting new employees; handling reorganizations, relocations, and mergers; and resolving labor disputes.

FINANCIAL RELATIONS Financial relations involves communicating not only with a company's stockholders, but also with the wider community of financial analysts and potential investors. An effective investor relations plan can increase the value of a company's stock and make it easier to raise additional capital. In some cases special meetings with financial analysts are necessary to overcome adverse publicity, negative perceptions about a company, or investor indifference. Such meetings may take the form of full-day briefings, formal presentations, or luncheon meetings. A tour of a company's facilities may help generate interest among the financial community. Mailings and ongoing communications can help a company achieve visibility among potential investors and financial analysts.

Annual reports and stockholder meetings are the two most important public relations tools for maintaining good investor relations. Some companies hold regional or quarterly meetings in addition to the usual annual meeting. Other companies reach more stockholders by moving the location of their annual meeting from city to city. Annual reports can be complemented by quarterly reports and dividend check inserts. Companies that wish to provide additional communications with stockholders may send them a newsletter or company magazine. Personal letters to new stockholders and a quick response to inquiries insure an additional measure of good will.

COMMUNITY RELATIONS A comprehensive, ongoing community relations program can help virtually any organization achieve visibility as a good community citizen and gain the good will of the community in which it operates. Banks, utilities, radio and television stations, and major retailers are some of the types of organizations most likely to have ongoing programs that might include supporting urban renewal, performing arts programs, social and educational programs, children's programs, community organizations, and construction projects. On a more limited scale, small businesses may achieve community visibility by sponsoring local sports teams or other events. Support may be financial or take the form of employee participation.

Organizations have the opportunity to improve good will and demonstrate a commitment to their communities when they open new offices, expand facilities, and open new factories. One company increased community awareness of its presence by converting a vacant building into a permanent meeting place. Another company built its new headquarters in an abandoned high school that it renovated. One of the more sensitive areas of community relations involves plant closings. A well-planned public relations campaign, combined with appropriate actions, can alleviate the tensions that such closings cause. Some elements of such a campaign might include offering special programs to laid-off workers, informing employees directly about proposed closings, and controlling rumors through candid and direct communications to the community and employees.

Organizations conduct a variety of special programs to improve community relations, including providing employee volunteers to work on community projects, sponsoring educational and literacy programs, staging open houses and conducting plant tours, celebrating anniversaries, and mounting special exhibits. Organizations are recognized as good community citizens when they support programs that improve the quality of life in their community, including crime prevention, employment, environmental programs, clean-up and beautification, recycling, and restoration.

CRISIS COMMUNICATIONS Public relations practitioners become heavily involved in crisis communications whenever there is a major accident or natural disaster affecting an organization and its community. Other types of crises involve bankruptcy, product failures, and management wrongdoing. In some cases, crises call for an organization to become involved in helping potential victims; in other cases, the crisis may require rebuilding an organization's image. In any case, experts recommend that business owners prepare a **crisis management** plan in advance to deal with potential crises in an honest and forthright manner. The main objective of such a plan is to provide accurate information quickly in order to reduce uncertainty. After the San Francisco earthquake of 1989, for example, the Bank of America utilized its public relations department to quickly establish communications with customers, the financial community, the media, and offices in 45 countries to assure them the bank was still operating.

GOVERNMENT AND POLITICAL RELATIONS Public relations in the political arena covers a wide range of activities, including staging debates, holding seminars for government leaders, influencing proposed legislation, and testifying before a congressional committee. Political candidates engage in public relations, as do government agencies at the federal, state, and local levels.

Trade associations and other types of organizations attempt to block unfavorable legislation and support favorable legislation in a number of ways. The liquor industry in California helped defeat a proposed tax increase by taking charge of the debate early, winning endorsements, recruiting spokespersons, and cultivating grassroots support. A speakers bureau trained some 240 industry volunteers, and key messages were communicated to the public through printed materials and radio and television commercials.

PUBLIC RELATIONS IN THE PUBLIC INTEREST Organizations attempt to generate good will and position themselves as responsible citizens through a variety of programs conducted in the public interest. Some examples are environmental programs (including water and energy conservation) and antipollution programs. Health and medical programs are sponsored by a wide range of nonprofit organizations, healthcare providers, and other businesses and industries. These range from encouraging other companies to develop AIDS-in-the-workplace policies to the American Cancer Society's Great American Smokeout. Other programs offer political education, leadership and self-improvement, recreational activities, contests, and safety instruction.

CONSUMER EDUCATION Organizations have undertaken a variety of programs to educate consumers, building good will and helping avoid misunderstandings in the process. Opportunities for educating consumers might include sponsoring television and radio programs, producing manuals and other printed materials, producing materials for classroom use, and releasing the results of surveys. In addition to focusing on specific issues or industries, educational programs may seek to inform consumers about economic matters and business in general.

OTHER PUBLIC RELATIONS PROGRAMS Other types of programs that fall under the umbrella of public relations include corporate identity programs, ranging from name changes and new trademarks to changing a company's overall image. Special events may be held to call attention to an organization and focus the public's good will. These include anniversary celebrations, events related to trade shows, special exhibits, or fairs and festivals. Speakers bureaus and celebrity spokespersons are effective public relations tools for communicating an organization's point of view. Speakers bureaus may be organized by a trade association or an individual company. The face-to-face communication that speakers can deliver is often more effective than messages carried by printed materials, especially when the target audience is small and clearly defined.

PUBLIC RELATIONS FOR SMALL BUSINESSES

Like other types of organizations, small businesses can benefit from public relations in terms of their relationships with customers, employees, investors, suppliers, or other interested members of the community. Since small business owners are the most visible representatives of their own companies, they frequently handle many of the public relations functions themselves. But experts caution small business owners against taking on this responsibility if they are unqualified, or if they are unable to give public relations the attention it deserves. In these cases, entrepreneurs may choose to hire a public relations specialist or contract with an outside agency.

In his book *Public Relations for the Entrepreneur and the Growing Business,* Norman R. Soderberg outlines the main qualifications for public relations professionals. An ideal candidate would be creative and enterprising, possess good communication skills and solid news judgment, have a thorough knowledge of the business, be sincere and considerate in dealing with people, and make a good impression as a representative for the company. Some of the skills required in public relations work include writing and editing, public speaking, graphic arts, public opinion polling, and advertising. The responsibilities of a public relations executive include interpreting public opinion, advising management, generating opportunities to increase public awareness and acceptance, disseminating good publicity, and evaluating the results of campaigns. In order to perform these duties effectively, the public relations professional must know what is going on in the business, which means that he or she requires access to management.

There are a variety of reasons why a small business owner might decide to contract public relations work out to an external agency. For example, company personnel may be inexperienced in handling public relations; the company may be geographically distant from its main audiences; the company may not be able to afford to hire a full-time public relations executive with the needed skills; or the company may want the objective judgment of an outsider. A small business owner can locate reputable public relations firms through the Small Business Administration, the Public Relations Society of America, the trade press for their industry, or the recommendations of fellow business people or local news people. When choosing between several potential agencies, a small business

owner should consider those that have experience in the industry, clients in similar industries, financial stability, and a compatible overall philosophy. Contracting with an outside firm can be costly—some charge their clients a monthly retainer, while others charge straight hourly rates for limited services.

While communication is the essence of public relations, an effective public relations campaign is based on action as well as words. Whether it is practiced formally or informally, public relations is an essential function for the survival of any organization. Small business owners cannot afford to neglect public relations. But lavish parties and gifts are not necessary—it is possible to vastly improve a small business's image within its community while also controlling public relations expenditures. Sponsoring a local softball team, speaking at a chamber of commerce meeting, and volunteering at a neighborhood clean-up are among the wide variety of public relations activities readily available to small businesses.

FURTHER READING:

Bernays, Edward L. *The Later Years: Public Relations Insights, 1956-1986.* Rhinebeck, NY: H&M Publishers, 1986.

Bianco, David, ed. *PR News Casebook: 1000 Public Relations Case Studies.* Detroit, MI: Gale Research, 1993.

Lesly, Philip, ed. *Lesly's Handbook of Public Relations and Communications.* New York: Amacom, 1991.

Soderberg, Norman R. *Public Relations for the Entrepreneur and the Growing Business.* Hinsdale, NJ: Probus Publishing Co., 1986.

Weiner, Richard. *Professional's Guide to Public Relations Services.* New York: Amacom, 1988.

Young, Davis. *Building Your Company's Good Name.* New York: Amacom, 1996.

SEE ALSO: Corporate Image; Press Kits/Releases

PURCHASING

Purchasing is the act of buying the goods and services that a company needs to operate and/or manufacture products. It was estimated in 1996 that the purchasing department of the average company spent between 50 and 70 percent of every company revenue dollar on items ranging from raw materials to services. As a result, there has been greater focus on purchasing in recent years as firms look at ways to lower their operating costs. Purchasing is now seen as more of a strategic function that can be used to control bottom-line costs. Companies are also seeking to improve purchasing processes as a means of improving customer satisfaction.

THE TRADITIONAL PURCHASING PROCESS

The traditional purchasing process involved several steps—requisition, soliciting bids, purchase order, shipping advice, invoice, and payment—that have come to be increasingly regarded as unacceptably slow, expensive, and labor intensive. Each transaction generated its own paper trail, and the same process had to be followed whether the item being purchased was a box of paper clips or a new bulldozer.

In this traditional model, purchasing was seen as essentially a clerical function. It was focused on getting the right quantity and quality of goods to the right place at the right time at a decent cost. The typical buyer was a shrewd negotiator whose primary responsibility was to obtain the best possible price from **suppliers** and ensure that minimum quality standards were met. Instead of using one supplier, the purchaser would usually take a divide-and-conquer approach to purchasing—buying small amounts from many suppliers and playing one against the other to gain price concessions. Purchasing simply was not considered to be a high-profile or career fast-track position—when surveys were taken of organizational stature, purchasing routinely rated in the lowest quartile.

That attitude has changed in recent years, in part because of highly publicized cases wherein companies have achieved stunning bottom-line gains through revamped purchasing processes. In addition, increased competition on both the domestic and global levels has led many companies to recognize that purchasing can actually have important strategic functions. As a result, new strategies are being used in purchasing departments at companies of all size.

Analysts observe that in this new purchasing environment, a guideline known as the total cost of ownership (TCO) has come to be a paramount concern in purchasing decisions. Instead of buying the good or service that has the lowest price, the buyer instead weighs a series of additional factors when determining what the true cost of the good or service is to his or her company. According to Anne Millen Porter in *Purchasing* magazine, these factors can include ''price, freight, duty, tax, engineering costs, tooling costs, letter of credit costs, payment terms, inventory carrying costs, storage requirements, scrap rates, packaging, rebates or special incentive values, [and] warranty and disposal costs.'' To lower TCO, companies are taking a number of steps to improve purchasing.

STRATEGIC SOURCING

Strategic sourcing is one of the key methods that purchasing departments are using to lower costs and improve quality. Strategic sourcing involves analyzing what products the company buys in the highest volume, reviewing the marketplace for those products, understanding the economics and usage of the supplier of those products, developing a procurement strategy, and establishing working relationships with the suppliers that are much more integrated than such relationships were in the past. During this process, the team conducting the analysis should ask these questions:

- Why do we buy this product or service?

- What do we use it for?

- What market conditions do suppliers operate under?

- What profit margin do suppliers seek to obtain?

- What is the total price of purchasing from a particular vendor (in other words, the cost of the item plus the costs associated with quality problems)

- Where is the good or service produced?

- What does the production process look like?

The products that are purchased in the highest volume will be the best candidates for cost reductions. That is because once those products are identified, the company can then justify the time and expense needed to closely study the industry that supplies that product. It can look at the ways key suppliers operate, study their business practices to see where the most money is added to the final cost of the product, and then work with the supplier to redesign processes and lower production costs. This maximizes the contribution that suppliers make to the process.

By knowing the market and knowing how much it costs for a supplier to do business, the purchasing department can set ''target prices'' on goods. If the supplier protests that the price is far too low, the purchasing company can offer to visit the supplier's site and study the matter. As one purchasing executive explained in *Industry Week*: ''We have 15 to 20 people who study the cost of everything we purchase. We know what it costs for a supplier to make a part, including all the overhead and the profit. So if a supplier comes in once we've given him a target price and says, 'You guys are crazy,' we send one of our engineers to visit the company. They look at the supplier's production process to see if they can spot a problem that's causing the supplier's prices to be higher. If necessary, our engineer helps the supplier rearrange the production line to make it more efficient. Proponents argue that these ''supplier alliances'' can result in improved buyer/seller communication, improved planning, reductions in leadtime, concurrent engineering, decreased paperwork, and better customer service.

The alliances also can sometimes register significant improvements in product **quality control**.

Buyers can build clearly-defined quality targets into their target prices. It will then work with the supplier to improve the manufacturing process until that quality target is met. Such a process can yield enormous results. (For example, *Purchasing* magazine reported in January 1997 that since Allied Signal went to a strategic sourcing environment in 1992, it has seen the number of defective goods received from suppliers drop from 40,000 parts per million to 1,970 parts per million.) Other benefits for buyers include reduced inventory levels, faster time to market, significant cost savings, and reduced development costs.

Not all suppliers can meet the high standards demanded in this purchasing environment. Some studies indicate that companies that adapt strategic sourcing have lowered the number of suppliers they use by an average of nearly 40 percent. What characteristics makes a good supplier, then? If the supplier is willing to partner, then analysts have identified several traits that good suppliers share:

- Commitment to continuous improvement
- Cost-competitive
- Cost-conscious
- Customer-oriented
- Encourages employee involvement
- Flexible
- Financially stable
- Abe to provide technical assistance.

Analysts indicate that suppliers receive some benefits in the emerging purchasing dynamic as well. Reduced paperwork, lower overhead, faster payment, long-term agreements that lead to more accurate business forecasts, access to new designs, and input into future materials and product needs have all been cited as gains. Other observers, meanwhile, point out that some buyer-supplier relationships have become so close that suppliers have opened offices on the site of the buyer, an arrangement that can conceivably result in even greater improvements in productivity and savings. Of course, companies are not going to form such "partnerships" with all of their suppliers. Some form of the traditional purchasing process involving bidding and standard purchase orders and invoices will continue to exist at almost every company, and especially at smaller companies that do not have the financial weight to make large demands on their suppliers.

EMPOWERING TEAMS

In addition to strategic sourcing, there are other methods companies can use to improve purchasing. One is creating **cross-functional teams** that involve purchasing personnel in every stage of the product design process. In the past, purchasers were not in-volved at all in the design process. They were simply instructed to purchase the necessary materials once a new product had been created. Now, purchasers (and suppliers) are increasingly included from the start of the new product process to ensure that the products needed to create product are readily available and are not prone to quality problems. Suppliers tend to be experts in their field, so they bring a large knowledge base to the design process that would otherwise be missing. This can help prevent poor designs or manufacturing mistakes.

These teams have broken down barriers and helped abolish the old manufacturing method that was known as the "over the wall" method of productions—each business unit would work on a project until its portion of the job was completed. It would then "throw the product over the wall" to the next functional team that was waiting to perform its part of the manufacturing process. The new cross-functional teams often include personnel from purchasing, manufacturing, engineering, and sales and marketing.

Purchasing teaches other members of the team how to deal directly with suppliers, cutting the purchasing personnel out of the loop. This is important in that it eliminates much of the time-consuming work that buyers had to deal with (soliciting bids, creating purchase orders, etc.) and frees them to concentrate on the part of their job where their expertise most pays off: finding suppliers and negotiating prices and quality standards. As Ben Lapner, the director of materials and purchasing at Accuride Corp., told *Purchasing* magazine, "Purchasing should be concerned with the strategic planning aspects of procurement process. Buying itself deals with the daily transactions and replenishment actions that should be performed as close to the company's end user as possible."

JUST-IN-TIME PURCHASING

Just-in-time (JIT) manufacturing has become one of the biggest trends in all facets of industry in recent years. JIT companies maintain only enough inventory to manufacture the products they need in the very near future. Parts are ordered on a near-continuous basis and often go directly from the loading dock to the assembly line. The benefits of this system include reduced inventory, improved quality, reduced lead-time, reduced scrap and rework, and reduced equipment downtime. However, when a company shifts to JIT manufacturing, it must also shift to just-in-time purchasing.

JIT purchasing requires a nearly 180-degree change in purchasing philosophy. Traditional purchasing meant building a supplier list over time by constantly adding new suppliers, spreading purchases around, and maintaining higher inventory levels in case demand for a product soared or quality from a supplier dipped suddenly. JIT purchasing demands that buyers narrow their supplier list to a chosen few who can deliver high-quality products on-demand and in a timely fashion.

Writing in *Industrial Management.* Bernhard Hadeler stated that JIT purchasers must look for a minimum of three things in suppliers: 1) demonstrated excellent quality; 2) ability to make frequent, on-time deliveries; and 3) ability to provide very large volume commitments or single sourcing arrangements. Quality may be the toughest of these standards for suppliers to meet; the JIT purchaser should deal only with companies that utilize statistical analysis to verify the quality of their output. Failure to do so should eliminate the supplier from even being asked to submit a bid.

For frequent, on-time deliveries, it often helps if the supplier is located in the same geographic region as the buyer. That way, it is easier for the supplier to react to a sudden, unexpected demand for its product, and it costs far less to make the frequent deliveries that are needed. Those lower costs can in part be passed on to the buyer.

In single sourcing arrangements, it is not uncommon for the buyer to exert some influence over the supplier's business processes. The buyer has made such a significant commitment to the supplier and is such a large portion of the supplier's total business, that it has the right to expect some say in the supplier's business practices. For some suppliers, this is an uncomfortable arrangement.

PURCHASING CARDS

As transaction costs soar (some companies report spending as much as $300 per transaction in clerical and other costs), companies are looking to buy smarter and cut costs any way possible. One popular method is recent years is to supply certain employees with purchasing cards, or corporate procurement cards.

The cards are similar to credit cards; in fact the big three credit card companies—VISA, MasterCard, and American Express—are among the leaders in purchasing cards. In most cases, the cards are used to purchase small business items, and then a master bill is sent straight to the purchasing department. But Catherine Romano stated in *Management Review* that the cards do differ from true credit cards in key ways. In some cases, the cards work only between a buyer and suppliers identified in advance, eliminating the bank that is involved with credit cards. Additionally, the cards can be coded to include a variety of important transaction information that reduces the amount of paperwork needed to track the sale, including sales tax data, customer code (such as job number or cost center), taxpayer identification number, and more. This coding allows companies to receive valuable information about each transaction and greatly streamlines the purchasing process.

The cards are beneficial to suppliers as well. The most important advantage is that the vendor receives payment much more quickly than in the past—sometimes in as short a period as two or three days. Additionally, the supplier saves money by not having to issue and mail an invoice, and the supplier knows the credit worthiness of the customer before the transaction is even processed.

FURTHER READING:

Hadeler, Bernhard J. ''Supply Strategy: Capturing the Value.'' *Industrial Management.* July/August 1994.

Harrington, Lisa H. ''Buying Better: Strategic Sourcing Can Improve Suppliers' Productivity, Component and Product Quality—and Improve the Bottom Line.'' *Industry Week.* July 21, 1997.

Kulkarni, Shashank. ''A Supply-Side Strategy.'' *Journal of Business Strategy.* September/October 1997.

Minahan, Tim. ''Purchasing Rebuilds to Battle Poor Quality.'' *Purchasing.* Jan. 16, 1997.

Porter, Anne Millen. ''Purchasing Pros Insist They Buy On Far More than Price.'' *Purchasing.* May 1, 1997.

''Purchasing Cards Change Corporate Buying Practices.'' *Corporate Cashflow Magazine.* Nov. 1995.

Romano, Catherine. ''Purchasing Cards Save Money.'' *Management Review.* April 1994.

Stundza, Tom. ''Purchasing Evolves Into Supply Management.'' *Purchasing.* July 17, 1997.

SEE ALSO: Inventory Control Systems

Q

QUALITY CIRCLES

In their volume *Japanese Quality Circles and Productivity,* Joel E. Ross and William C. Ross defined a quality circle as "a small group of employees doing similar or related work who meet regularly to identify, analyze, and solve product-quality and production problems and to improve general operations. The circle is a relatively autonomous unit (ideally about ten workers), usually led by a supervisor or a senior worker and organized as a work unit." In other words, a quality circle is a participatory management technique that enlists the help of employees in solving problems related to their own jobs. Employees who participate in quality circles usually receive training in formal problem-solving methods—such as **brainstorming**, pareto analysis, and cause-and-effect diagrams—and then are encouraged to apply these methods to either specific or general company problems. After completing an analysis, they often present their findings to management and then handle implementation of approved solutions.

Although most commonly found in manufacturing environments, quality circles are applicable to a wide variety of business situations and problems. They are based on two ideas: that employees can often make better suggestions for improving work processes than management; and that employees are motivated by their participation in making such improvements. Thus, implemented correctly, quality circles can help a small business reduce costs, increase **productivity**, and improve employee morale. Other potential benefits that may be realized by a small business include greater operational efficiency, re- duced absenteeism, improved employee health and safety, and an overall better working climate. In their book *Production and Operations Management,* Howard J. Weiss and Mark E. Gershon called quality circles "the best means today for meeting the goal of designing quality into a product."

The interest of U.S. manufacturers in quality circles was sparked by dramatic improvements in the quality and economic competitiveness of Japanese goods in the post-World War II years. The emphasis of Japanese quality circles was on preventing defects from occurring rather than inspecting products for defects following a manufacturing process. Japanese quality circles also attempted to minimize the scrap and downtime that resulted from part and product defects. In the United States, the quality circle movement evolved to encompass the broader goals of cost reduction, productivity improvement, employee involvement, and problem-solving activities.

BACKGROUND

Quality circles were originally associated with Japanese management and manufacturing techniques. The introduction of quality circles in Japan in the postwar years was inspired by the lectures of W. Edwards Deming (1900-1993), a statistician for the U.S. government. Deming based his proposals on the experience of U.S. firms operating under wartime industrial standards. Noting that American management had typically given line managers and engineers about 85 percent of the responsibility for quality control and line workers only about 15 percent, Deming argued that these shares should be reversed. He suggested redesigning production processes to more fully account for quality control, and continuously educating all employees in a firm—from the top down—in quality control techniques and statistical control technologies. Quality circles were the means by which this continuous education was to take place for production workers.

Deming predicted that if Japanese firms adopted the system of quality controls he advocated, nations around the world would be imposing import quotas on Japanese products within five years. His prediction was vindicated. Deming's ideas became very influential in Japan, and he received several prestigious awards for his contributions to the Japanese economy.

The principles of Deming's quality circles simply moved quality control to an earlier position in the production process. Rather than relying upon post-production inspections to catch errors and defects, quality circles attempted to prevent defects from occurring in the first place. As an added bonus, machine downtime and scrap materials that formerly occurred due to product defects were minimized. Deming's idea that improving quality could increase productivity led to the development in Japan of the Total Quality Control (TQC) concept, in which quality and productivity are viewed as two sides of a coin. TQC also required that a manufacturer's suppliers make use of quality circles.

Quality circles in Japan were part of a system of relatively cooperative labor-management relations, involving company unions and lifetime employment guarantees for many full-time permanent employees. Consistent with this decentralized, enterprise-oriented system, quality circles provided a means by which production workers were encouraged to participate in company matters and by which management could benefit from production workers' intimate knowledge of the production process. In 1980 alone, changes resulting from employee suggestions resulted in savings of $10 billion for Japanese firms and bonuses of $4 billion for Japanese employees.

Active American interest in Japanese quality control began in the early-1970s, when the U.S. aerospace manufacturer Lockheed organized a tour of Japanese industrial plants. This trip marked a turning point in the previously established pattern, in which Japanese managers had made educational tours of industrial plants in the United States. Lockheed's visit resulted in the gradual establishment of quality circles in its factories beginning in 1974. Within two years, Lockheed estimated that its fifteen quality circles had saved nearly $3 million, with a ratio of savings to cost of six to one. As Lockheed's successes became known, other firms in the aerospace industry began adopting quality circles. Thereafter quality circles spread rapidly throughout the U.S. economy; by 1980, over one-half of firms in the Fortune 500 had implemented or were planning on implementing quality circles.

In the early-1990s, the U.S. **National Labor Relations Board (NLRB)** made several important rulings regarding the legality of certain forms of quality circles. These rulings were based on the 1935 Wagner Act, which prohibited company unions and management-dominated labor organizations. One NLRB ruling found quality programs unlawful that were established by the firm, that featured agendas dominated by the firm, and addressed the conditions of employment within the firm. Another ruling held that a company's labor-management committees were in effect labor organizations used to bypass negotiations with a labor union. As a result of these rulings, a number of employer representatives expressed their concern that quality circles, as well as other kinds of labor-management cooperation programs, would be hindered. However, the NLRB stated that these rulings were not general indictments against quality circles and labor-management cooperation programs, but were aimed specifically at the practices of the companies in question.

REQUIREMENTS FOR SUCCESSFUL QUALITY CIRCLES

In his book *Productivity Improvement: A Guide for Small Business,* Ira B. Gregerman outlined a number of requirements for a small business contemplating the use of quality circles. First, the small business owner should be comfortable with a participative management approach. It is also important that the small business have good, cooperative labor-management relations, as well as the support of middle managers for the quality circle program. The small business owner must be willing and able to commit the time and resources needed to train the employees who will participate in the program, particularly the quality circle leaders and facilitators. It may even be necessary to hire outside facilitators if the time and expertise does not exist in-house. Some small businesses may find it helpful to establish a steering committee to provide direction and guidance for quality circle activities. Even if all these requirements are met, the small business will only benefit from quality circles if employee participation is voluntary, and if employees are allowed some input into the selection of problems to be addressed. Finally, the small business owner must allow time for the quality circles to begin achieving desired results; in some cases, it can take more than a year for expectations to be met.

But successful quality circles offer a wide variety of benefits for small businesses. For example, they serve to increase management's awareness of employee ideas, as well as employee awareness of the need for innovation within the company. Quality circles also serve to facilitate communication and increase commitment among both labor and management. In enhancing employee satisfaction through participation in decision-making, such initiatives may also improve a small business's ability to recruit and retain qualified employees. In addition, many companies find that quality circles further teamwork and reduce employee resistance to change. Finally, quality circles can improve a small business's overall competitiveness by reducing costs, improving quality, and promoting innovation.

FURTHER READING:

Gregerman, Ira B. *Productivity Improvement: A Guide for Small Business.* New York: Van Nostrand Reinhold, 1984.

Gryna, Frank M., Jr. *Quality Circles: A Team Approach to Problem Solving.* AMACOM, 1981.

"New Rules on Employee Involvement." *Industry Week.* February 1, 1993.

McMillan, Charles J. *The Japanese Industrial System.* Walter de Gruyter, 1984.

Noble, Barbara Presley. "Worker-Participation Programs are Found Illegal." *New York Times.* June 8, 1993.

"Recent NLRB Decisions Shed Light on Employees Rights." *U.S. Glass, Metal and Glazing.* February 15, 1993.

Ross, Joel E., and William C. Ross. *Japanese Quality Circles and Productivity.* Reston Publishing Company, 1982.

Sasaki, Naoto, and David Hutchins. *The Japanese Approach to Product Quality.* Pergamon Press, 1984.

Uchitelle, Louis. "Workers Seek Executive Role, Study Says." *New York Times.* December 5, 1994.

Weiss, Howard J., and Mark E. Gershon. *Production and Operations Management.* Boston: Allyn and Bacon, 1989.

SEE ALSO: Quality Control; Training and Development

QUALITY CONTROL

Quality control refers to the process, most often implemented in manufacturing, of monitoring the quality of finished products through statistical measures and an overall corporate commitment to producing defect-free products. Quality control principles can also be utilized in service industries.

The term "quality control" came into common use in the 1950s thanks to W. Edward Deming, whose "Fourteen Points" have become the bible for quality control proponents. With the post-war world returning to normal manufacturing patterns, Deming preached that inspecting products for quality after they were manufactured was unacceptable. Instead, he proposed a process known as "statistical quality control" that would use closely monitored performance measures to gauge quality as a product was being manufactured. The goal of statistical quality control was to gather data that would allow for the constant improvement of manufacturing processes, which would in turn improve quality control. Introducing such statistical con-

trols could be expensive, but Deming argued that instituting quality measures ultimately saved companies money.

Another important tenet of Deming's beliefs was that upper management was largely to blame for quality failures. He firmly believed that, given the right tools and working environment, workers would strive to create the highest quality products possible. In Deming's own words, "the basic cause of sickness in American industry and resulting unemployment is failure of top management to manage." He believed that strong leadership led to an inspired work force that did not fear management and did not fear taking chances when seeking ways to improve quality.

If strong leadership is the buzzword for managers in a quality environment, then empowerment is the key concept for workers in Deming's system. Improved education and training are the key factors in reaching employees and making them believe that their increased participation in the work process is an essential part of improving quality. Involvement, participation, and teamwork are seen as absolute musts if a quality workplace is to be created.

The Japanese were the first to adopt Deming's Fourteen Points, and with great success. As an example, Deming learned of one Japanese factory that doubled production in just one year and was expecting to gain an additional 25 percent improvement the following year, with no increase in the amount of hours worked. All this occurred as a result of simply improving quality. What is most significant about this achievement is the year it happened—1951. Many American and European companies chose to ignore these dramatic results and nearly perished as a result. Critics contend that by the time American manufacturing plants realized that quality control was a significant issue, it was the late 1970s and Japanese firms such as Honda and Sony were taking over large portions of the American consumer market.

In the 1990s, most American firms have embraced quality control practices. Analysts indicate that when firms first began adopting these principles, many went too far, becoming bogged down in quality control charts and measurements of inconsequential operating factors. In too many cases, American industry went from ignoring statistical quality control to applying it to every single facet of a business, no matter how small. This overemphasis quickly disappeared, however, and has been replaced by a commitment to overall quality control that is unprecedented in the American workplace.

THE SCOPE OF JAPANESE INFLUENCE

Because they have been practicing quality management since the 1950s, the Japanese are still the leader in producing quality products in a number of industries and are still the role model for U.S. companies to emulate. For example, a study of the air conditioning industry in the early 1990s found that the worst Japanese air conditioning plant had an error rate that was less than one-half that of the *best* U.S. company.

This drastic difference is largely due to the Japanese adherence to one of Deming's most important ideas—that quality should be "designed in" to a product instead of "inspected out." Japanese firms treat suppliers as equals, sharing information with them as if the supplier was an internal department of the company. This ensures that quality is already a part of the product before it is even manufactured.

Another common practice in Japan that has found its way to the United States are " **quality circles**." Workers are brought together on a regular basis to brainstorm about quality and manufacturing processes, all with an eye towards improving quality. The circles are a success if management follows through on its end of the deal and incorporates the suggestions made in the quality circles into operations. When workers see their suggestions implemented, it increases their confidence in management and in the company as a whole, which in turn increases their commitment to the company and to producing high quality goods.

A highly trained work force is one of the keys to producing quality goods, and the training programs of many American companies reflect this recognition, for they are allocating more time and money to this area. Still, many U.S. companies lag behind in this respect. Researchers have stated that a higher commitment to training and lifelong learning are needed if the commitment to quality is to continue.

Today, the key components of quality control that were preached by Deming and practiced by the Japanese—including **benchmarking**, supplier partnering, and continuous improvement—have found their way into American industry. Each of these components demands a closer look.

BENCHMARKING

Benchmarking is a continuing process of measuring products, services, and practices against your strongest competitors. More simply stated, it means using the best companies as the yardstick against which your company measures itself. If your company comes up short, than improvements must be made to ensure that your products are just as high in quality as those of your competitor.

There are two types of benchmarking:

COMPETITIVE BENCHMARKING This entails benchmarking against direct competitors in the market-place. This can include comparing specific numerical or statistical measurements such as return on assets used or market share. The more detailed information that can be obtained about a competitor, the better.

NONCOMPETITIVE BENCHMARKING This method can take two forms. The first is measuring your company against the best companies in the world, regardless of industry. For instance, companies such as 3M, Coca-Cola, and General Electric are considered to be trendsetters and leaders in quality, so companies from nearly every industry study them and copy their best practices. Business analysts note that noncompetitive benchmarking is a broader—and sometimes more useful—instrument of quality control. By only benchmarking against competitors, a company only ensures it will be as good as that competitor. By benchmarking against the best companies in the world, a company can aspire to be as good as those companies and can surpass the competition in its own industry. Additionally, companies may find it easier to gain access to information about companies they do not compete with because they are not seen as a threat to the well-being of the company.

The second type of noncompetitive benchmarking is internal benchmarking, which involves comparing functions or processes in different departments within the same organization. Internal benchmarking is often seen as a logical starting point for a business that is attempting to use benchmarking for the first time.

To successfully benchmark, a company must first look closely at its own practices and conduct a rigorous self-assessment. Once that self-assessment is completed, the company has a good idea of where it stands on each quality issue and can successfully compare itself to other companies. The self-assessment must be honest and thorough. It should identify weaknesses, but should also highlight strengths. Improving weaknesses that are identified should be tied to stated company strategic aims.

SUPPLIER PARTNERING

Supplier partnering is an increasingly common practice in the United States. Simply put, it means that manufacturers work directly with their parts and components **suppliers** to improve quality at the supplier's location. This can involve direct participation in the supplier's operations—that is, staff from the manufacturer might work on-site at the supplier's office or provide technical assistance and equipment—or simply a very close working relationship that more resembles a partnership rather than a simple business transaction between two unrelated companies.

One of the biggest methods of partnering with suppliers involves sharing the use of statistical controls. This is an underdeveloped area in the United States that should grow in the coming years. Most manufacturers have switched to outsourcing as a means of cutting the costs of production. This increased emphasis on outsourcing means that the companies that supply the parts or components must place just as much emphasis on quality as the manufacturer if the finished product is to be high quality.

Among the quality issues that still need to be addressed in the manufacturer-supplier relationship are:

- Inconsistent quality levels from suppliers, even from different plants of the same supplier.

- While most first-level, or Tier 1 suppliers have made a commitment to quality control, that commitment has yet to be made by Tier 2 suppliers (those companies that supply smaller parts or raw material to the Tier 1 supplier). The importance of quality must trickle all the way down the supply chain to be meaningful.

- In many industries, mergers are occurring at a record pace. Whenever a merger of two suppliers occurs, there is the chance that quality will suffer while the details of the merger are hammered out.

In many industries, especially the auto industry, manufacturers are overcoming these supplier problems by helping the suppliers meet quality standards.

The other facet of supplier partnering means that the manufacturer also actively seeks out feedback from the supplier on how the former's operations can be improved. Suppliers often have a unique perspective on the industry they work in and on the companies they supply and can provide valuable advice on how to make changes for the better. When this happens, it is important that the two companies have a framework in place to manage the partnering system. This can mean that the manufacturer's purchasing department would be deemed as the intermediary between the two companies, passing information from the supplier back to the appropriate internal customers.

CONTINUOUS IMPROVEMENT

Continuous improvement (CI) is a method for improving every facet of a company's operations and increasing competitiveness by developing a company's resources. The improvement can involve many goals—producing products with zero defects or achieving 100 percent customer satisfaction—but CI has the same basic principles no matter what the goal:

- Involve the entire company at all levels

- Find savings by improving existing processes, not by investing more money

- Gather data about company operations and quantify that data, which becomes the baseline against which improvements will be measured

- Do not forget that common sense is perhaps the most important component of CI

- Do not just give lip service to improvement—implement or practice ideas

Continuous improvement most often involves creating a team that includes representatives from all areas of the company. The team first spends time learning—about the company they work for (looking at it in new ways) and about other companies (benchmarking is common during this phase). The necessary quantitative data is created. The team then proposes solutions to management and begins to implement those solutions. Once that is achieved, follow-up mechanisms must be put in place that seek additional improvements as time goes by. The team might change members with the passage of time, but hopefully it will become an established and accepted part of the company even as its roster changes. If the endeavor works as planned, the team will have improved quality to show as a result of its initial efforts. This can make even skeptical employees buy into the concept, which in turn leads to the continued search for even more improvements, Hence the term continuous improvement. Follow-up mechanisms can include regular audits or regularly scheduled meetings to evaluate progress.

OTHER QUALITY BUZZWORDS

Quality control and literature about it have become a huge cottage industry in the business world. In addition to the terms outlined in this article, there are several other popular concepts and terms associated with quality control that are actually offshoots of the larger issue, or separate issues altogether. Among the most popular are:

- **ISO 9000**—This is a series of international standards that set out requirements and recommendations that specify how management operations are to be conducted at a company to ensure that quality is the end-result. ISO 9000 is part of the "conformance to specifications" school of quality control that believes that, by setting standards for companies to follow that the consumer is aware of, and ensuring that those standards are never deviated from, then quality is achieved. Essentially, its goal is to prevent nonconformity. Companies must undergo a comprehensive program to apply for ISO 9000 certification, reviewing and documenting management procedures, creating job descriptions from the ground up, preparing a quality manual, and submitting to periodic standards checks by an external body. The process is not cheap, but it does give a company that qualifies for the certification a badge to demonstrate its commitment to quality.

- Six Sigma—This new defect-reduction program was pioneered by General Electric's Jack Welch. A sigma is a mark on a bell curve that measures standard deviation. In American industry today, most companies average between 35,000 and 50,000 defects per million operations; GE followed this trend by averaging 35,000, or 3.5 sigma. Welch determined that this was unacceptable—he wanted the error rate reduced to an almost nonexistent 3.4 errors per million operations, or ''Six Sigma,'' a concept first introduced by Motorola in the early 1990s. Motorola was able to achieve six sigma quality, but it took eight years to go from three to six. Welch has mandated that GE reach the mark in five years. More and more companies are expected to follow the lead of GE and Motorola, since both companies are considered world leaders.

- Quality Awards—As quality control grows in popularity, companies strive to prove to customers that quality is their most important concern. One way they do this is to compete for the plethora of quality awards that are now available. The most famous of these is the Malcolm Baldridge National Quality Award, but others such as the European Quality Award and the Deming Award also exist. Additionally, there are hundreds of state, regional, and local quality awards. The awards, which are given to both large and small companies, carry a rigorous set of quality standards that a company must meet or exceed before it can even be considered for an award. Some companies coincide the launch of new quality control programs with announcements that they will be seeking one of the awards as a means of giving employees an incentive to improve quality and as a means of demonstrating to customers their commitment to quality.

- Mistake-proofing, or poka-yoke—''Poka-yoke'' is a Japanese term that comes from two words that mean ''avoid error.'' The concept was created by a Toyota engineer who felt that workers should always strive to avoid making any mistakes. The concept most often refers to ''designing in'' methods of avoiding mistakes—for example, putting guards on drill presses that prevent the machine from drilling a hole too deep and ruining a part. As a result, poka-yoke has come to have a second meaning—in addition to referring to the broad concept, it refers to any tool or process used to prevent a mistakes. Mistake-proofing is one of the easiest ways for small companies to reduce errors. It is easy and relatively inexpensive to perform an audit of existing poka-yokes and to draw up a flow chart of a production process to identify where other poka-yokes might be installed. Once the initial work is done, adding new poka-yokes can be an ongoing and continuous process. One warning to business owners—using the terms ''mistake-proofing'' or ''fool-proofing'' can anger workers, who may view the terms as being disparaging.

Finally, there is one term associated with the quality control movement that is too broad and too important to cover here. **Total quality management**, or TQM, has become an important quality movement in its own right and is fully explained in a separate entry in this title.

THE FUTURE OF QUALITY CONTROL

Despite the growing importance of quality control in the United States, there is still room for improvement in many areas. One of the most important is the attitude towards teams, especially cross-functional ones. **Cross-functional teams** are recognized by quality experts as one of the best ways to increase speed to market and improve quality. Slowly, as American firms adopt other quality measures, they are also adopting the team philosophy. Still, improvements must be made. Too many firms still rely on the old styles of product development and production, handing off responsibility for a product from one department to the next with no interaction between the departments.

Another problem to be overcome in the future is **downsizing**. One of the key business principles of the 1990s, downsizing means improving technology and work processes so that the same amount of work can be done with fewer employees. While the move to downsize has improved the bottom line at many companies, it has also raised quality concerns. Some believe that there has been a marked reduction in the quality of some products because too many firms engaged in downsizing without making sure that their internal processes and infrastructure was adequately equipped to handle the loss of employees.

FURTHER READING:

Beard, Thomas L. "The Maturation of American Quality." *Modern Machine Shop.* April 1997.

Buttle, Francis. "ISO 9000: Marketing Motivations and Benefits." *International Journal of Quality & Reliability Management.* July 1997.

Calingo, Luis Maria R. "The Evolution of Strategic Quality Management." *International Journal of Quality & Reliability Management.* December 1996.

Conlin, Michelle. "Revealed at Last: The Secret of Jack Welch's Success." *Forbes.* January 26, 1998.

Davenport, Jerry Lee Jr., and Thomas Li-Ping Tang. "Learning from Japanese Companies and Japanese Transplants in the United States." *Employment Relations Today.* Spring 1996.

Heller, Robert. "Fourteen Points that the West Ignore at Its Peril." *Management Today.* March 1994.

Henricks, Mark. "Make No Mistake." *Entrepreneur.* October 1996.

Hinckley, C. Martin. "The Quality Question." *Assembly.* November 1997.

Joiner, Brian L. "The Future of Quality in the United States." *National Underwriter Property & Casualty-Risk & Benefits Management.* December 16, 1997.

Kinni, Theodore B. "Lofty Goals: Superstructuring With Quality Standards and Awards." *Industry Week.* September 4, 1995.

Morgan, James. "The New Look of Quality." *Purchasing.* January 11, 1996.

Murphy, Elana Epatko. "Communicate Quality Standards on Every Level." *Purchasing.* January 11, 1996.

Murphy, Elana Epatko. "Look to Production for Tips on Boosting Quality." *Purchasing.* November 27, 1997.

Porter, Anne Millen. "In Some Companies Quality Culture Is Tangible." *Purchasing.* January 16, 1997.

Prado, J. Carlos. "Increasing Competitiveness with Continuous Improvement." *Industrial Management.* July-August 1997.

"Quality Revolution Not Over Yet." *Purchasing.* March 6, 1997.

Songini, Marc. L. "Setting Sights on Perfection." *Industrial Distribution.* August 1997.

Van de Vliet, Anita. "To Beat the Best." *Management Today.* January 1996.

"What Is Benchmarking?" *Food Manufacture.* May 1996.

Wilkinson, Adrian and Hugh Willmott. "Quality Management, Problems and Pitfalls: A Critical Perspective." *International Journal of Quality & Reliability Management.* February 1996.

Wright, Richard B. "Why We Need ISO 9000." *Industrial Distribution.* January 1997.

SEE ALSO: Training and Development

R

REBATES

Rebates, widely known as refunds, are a popular tool used by businesses to promote their products and services. Rebates are distinct from **coupons** and other forms of **discount sales** in that they reimburse a customer for part of the purchase price following rather than at the time of sale. A relatively new method of **sales promotion**, rebating evolved from the **marketing** technique of offering coupons. They were initially offered by producers of grocery-store goods and subsequently by manufacturers of nonfood items. Currently, businesses making use of rebates are diverse and include the manufacturers of health and beauty aids, household supplies, and small and large appliances, as well as automakers, wine and liquor manufacturers, and segments of the computer industry. The cash amounts these companies offer their customers is similarly wide-ranging; some rebates of less than a dollar are offered, while other rebates on ''big ticket'' items such as automobiles have reached a couple thousand dollars. The size of the rebate offered basically depends on the base retail price, the nature of the product being promoted, and the number of goods backed up in the production pipeline.

The first step in rebating, as outlined by Susan J. Samtur in *Cashing in at the Checkout,* is for the manufacturer to issue an offer of a rebate to all who purchase its product; typically the offer carries an expiration date of six to eight months. The purchaser then completes a form provided by the manufacturer and mails it—along with any other items the manufacturer may require, such as a cash-register receipt or the Universal Product Code (UPC) snipped from the packaging—to the address specified on the form.

Most commonly, the purchaser sends the rebate form and related (''proof of purchase'') items not to the manufacturer but to one of several large clearinghouses hired by the manufacturer to handle these transactions—for instance, the Young America Corporation in Minnesota or the Nielson Clearing House in Texas. The clearinghouse then processes the form and sends the purchaser a check in the manufacturer's name, usually within four to eight weeks from the time the purchaser mails in the required information.

Companies use a number of means to get their rebate forms into the hands of customers. Many companies supply a pad of tear-off rebate forms to the stores selling their products; others print the form directly on the packaging or on a tag hanging from the merchandise. To announce the rebate offer and distribute the forms, companies may also place advertisements in newspapers and magazines, utilize home mailers, and/or place ads in the myriad refunders' newsletters developed by consumers to avail themselves of these offers. In addition, companies frequently use television and radio advertisements to publicize their rebate promotions.

Rebates are highly attractive to most consumers, for they provide a partial cash reimbursement for their purchases that is tax-free (the Internal Revenue Service views rebates as a reduction in the price paid for a product, rather than as income). And for manufacturers, rebating provides numerous advantages: it induces prospective customers to try their products; it boosts company sales and visibility; it relieves problems of excess inventory; and it attracts interest from retailers, who often help promote the offer and expand the shelf space allotted to the manufacturer's goods accordingly. Rebate promotions can thus help a company increase its leverage with retailers and develop brand loyalty and repeat business among consumers over the long run. Indeed, a study conducted by United Marketing Services (UMS) found that rebates are an effective means of establishing product awareness with consumers.

In the 1990s several innovative offshoots of rebating began to emerge. Among these were the linking of customer purchases to rebates in the form of contributions to retirement plans, tuition costs, and air-mileage credits. Other variations on rebate promotions include offers to refund a fixed percentage of the purchase price, rather than a set dollar amount; providing a ''bounceback coupon'' that can be redeemed on a later purchase; and making contributions to charitable causes based on customer participation in the promotion.

FURTHER READING:

''How Rebates Affect Purchases Behavior.'' *Adweek's Marketing Week.* January 16, 1989.

Samtur, Susan J., with Tad Tuleja. *Cashing in at the Checkout.* Stonesong Press/Grosset & Dunlap.

Smith, Anne Kates. ''Buying Shopper Loyalty.'' *U.S. News & World Report.* April 27, 1992.

RECESSION

A recession is a downturn in the business cycle that occurs when the real **gross national product (GNP)**—the total output of goods and services produced by the U.S. population—declines for two consecutive quarters, or six months. Recessions are usually characterized by a general decrease in output, income, employment, and trade lasting from six months to a year. A more severe and long-lasting economic crisis is known as a depression.

Virtually all advanced world economies that are not controlled centrally have experienced recurring cycles of slump and recovery in business activity since the Industrial Revolution. The United States suffered through four severe depressions in the 1800s, as well as the Great Depression in the 1930s. These crises cost a great deal in terms of national wealth and personal hardship. Since then, however, sophisticated analysis of economic trends has combined with increased government intervention to prevent such extreme fluctuations in economic activity. In fact, no depressions have occurred in industrialized nations since World War II, although many recessions have occurred. Governments monitor the **business cycle** closely and take various steps to stabilize the economy

before it reaches extreme peaks and troughs. Formerly, the typical stages in the business cycle were depression, recovery, prosperity, and recession. Today, the phases are usually defined using the more moderate terms upswing, peak, recession, and trough.

THE BUSINESS CYCLE

Prior to entering the recession phase of the business cycle, the economy reaches the peak of its expansion. When it nears the full-employment level of output, its rate of growth begins to slow. Prices are generally rising, so consumers demand fewer products and services. As a result, companies begin to hire fewer new workers, and demand falls even further with the reduction in incomes. Productivity and output begin to decline as costs increase, and companies respond by decreasing investment. Gradually, the overall economy contracts, as the decrease in investment reduces production and employment. Eventually, government intervention and the natural progression of the business cycle cause the recession to end, or reach a trough or turning point, and the upswing stage begins.

Though the general pattern of the business cycle is understood, in reality the situation is not usually so clearly defined. The economy progresses through the stages very gradually, and not all regions, sectors, or businesses are affected in the same way at the same time. In addition, there are many other patterns of economic activity that interact with and complicate the business cycle. For example, economists often observe seasonal variations in output and sales in some sectors of the economy. Retail sales tend to pick up around Christmas, while construction tends to increase during the summer months. Economists also describe independent cycles of investment in certain industries, such as shipbuilding or agriculture. Finally, the overall level of economic activity tends to expand every year. These factors combine to make recessions difficult to predict or define.

A number of changes have taken place or been instituted by the government to stabilize fluctuations in economic activity, and thus reduce the incidence and severity of recessions, over the years. For example, the growth of the service sector, with its relatively stable demand and its tendency to employ salaried personnel, has been a stabilizing influence. The corporate trend toward stable dividend policies has also helped, as has increased federal regulation of the stock market and the banking industry. Some experts claim that instituting a progressive income tax and an unemployment insurance program have also worked to moderate fluctuations in the business cycle. Finally, the government often intervenes directly with monetary or fiscal controls to prevent inflation, and with job training programs and public welfare to reduce the negative effects of unemployment.

THE U.S. RECESSION OF 1990-1991

Despite such measures, however, recessions still occur in the United States and worldwide. During the U.S. recession that lasted from July 1990 through March 1991, the economy showed the lowest growth rate since the Great Depression. *U.S. News and World Report* called the recession "unlike any the country has experienced in the post-World War II era, the result of years of profligacy and irresponsible government policies," and claimed it was responsible for the loss of 1.9 million jobs through early 1992. In fact, some analysts stated that this recession could have been as bad as the Great Depression if not for increased government spending—which represented 25 percent of GNP in 1991 as opposed to 3 percent in 1930—and federal deposit insurance for banks.

Still, economists disagreed on what caused the recession and the slow recovery, how long the recession officially lasted, and how a similar situation could best be prevented in the future. Some experts attributed the prolonged recession to industrial overcapacity, which led to falling asset values for many businesses. Others claimed that an overall decrease in consumption was responsible, whether in response to an increase in oil prices following the Persian Gulf War or due to a slowdown in the rate of population growth. Some analysts blamed technology, stating that the proliferation of electronically controlled credit cards led consumers to build up personal debt. Whatever the reasons for the recession, however, it seemed clear that the best course of action for individuals, businesses, and the government was to include the likelihood of another recession in their future plans.

FURTHER READING:

"America's Sluggish Recovery." *Economist.* June 5, 1993.

Blanchard, Oliver. "Consumption and the Recession of 1990-1991." *American Economic Review.* May 1993.

"Brightening Up: The Economy." *Economist.* December 11, 1993.

Caballero, Ricardo J., and Mohamad L. Hammour. "The Cleansing Effect of Recessions." *American Economic Review.* December 1994.

Hall, Robert E. "Macro Theory and the Recession of 1990-1991." *American Economic Review.* May 1993.

Hansen, Gary D., and Edward C. Prescott. "Did Technology Shocks Cause the 1990-1991 Recession?" *American Economic Review.* May 1993.

"On Understanding the History of Capitalism." *Monthly Review.* October 1992.

Pomice, Eva, and Robert F. Black. "Is Your Job Safe?" *U.S. News and World Report.* January 13, 1992.

Ulan, Michael. "Is the Current Business Cycle Different? Does How We Measure Matter?" *Business Economics.* April 1994.

SEE ALSO: Leading Economic Indicators

RECORD RETENTION

Record retention refers to the practice of retaining copies of business or personal records over time. It is important for small business owners not only to keep good records, but also to know which ones to retain and for how long. Some aspects of record retention are determined by **Internal Revenue Service** guidelines. Certain records that substantiate a small business's income, expenses, and withholding and payment of taxes must be retained for at least three years, or until the statute of limitations on an IRS audit expires. But good record retention is also in the best interest of companies. A poor system can not only prevent managers from retrieving the information they need to make sound business decisions, but can also pose a security risk.

The means chosen for record retention are also important for the simple reason that small businesses often suffer from a shortage of space. An article in *Purchasing* noted that paper records in an average business multiply at a rate of 7 percent per year, while electronic data stored on computer networks increases at a rate of 60 percent per year. Although some small businesses may find it adequate to keep their records in file folders, many find it helpful to use an electronic storage medium. The IRS issued new guidelines regarding electronic storage of business records in early 1997.

TYPES OF RECORDS

Businesses generate three main kinds of records: income, expenses, and capital expenditures. Income includes the revenue from sales of products or services, including both cash receipts and the collection of receivables. Expenses include cash disbursements and accounts payable that cover all operating expenses. These records should be maintained continuously. In the case of expenses, the records must not only prove that an expense was incurred, but also show how it was related to business. This is particularly important in the case of meals and entertainment expenses, for which the records must indicate the date, place, amount, and purpose of the expenses, as well as the type business relationship with the person entertained.

It is also important for small business owners to keep records for major capital purchases to determine depreciation for tax purposes. These records must include the date and place of purchase, a complete description of the item, the amount paid, how it was purchased, and the date when it was put into service for the business. Keeping these basic business records enables business owners to track their progress, identify problems, and take advantage of all possible tax deductions.

Small businesses that employ people other than the owner or partners are required by the IRS to keep detailed payroll records. In fact, there are a total of 20 different types of records that must be kept for income tax withholding, FICA (Social Security) tax withholding, and FUTA (federal unemployment) taxes. These records—which include employees' names, addresses, and Social Security numbers, the amount and date of wages paid and withheld, and the amount of each type of tax paid, among other things—must be retained for at least four years from the time the relevant taxes were due or were paid, whichever was later. Experts also recommend that small businesses keep careful records regarding any automobile, life, fire, health, and other insurance coverage they hold. These records should list policy numbers and carriers, amounts of premiums and dates paid, and information on claims.

HOW LONG TO RETAIN VARIOUS TYPES OF RECORDS

There are a number of different types of records that small business owners should retain indefinitely—for the life of the business. These include copies of federal income tax returns, annual financial statements, general ledgers, fixed asset records, and corporate documents (charter, bylaws, stock records, patent and trademark applications, labor contracts, pension records, etc.). Regular business documents that support financial statements and tax payments—such as canceled checks, payroll checks, bank statements, invoices, purchase orders, and personnel records—should be retained for at least six years. These time periods allow for a margin of safety in meeting the IRS rules, which also address the means that may be used in retaining records.

Most of the IRS guidelines for record retention are included in Section 6001 of the Internal Revenue Code. "Virtually all taxpayers are required to keep records sufficient to establish the amount of gross income, deductions, credits, or any other relevant matters concerning their tax liability," Noelle Allen explained in an article for *The Tax Advisor*. These records can take the form of paper files or computerized data. Further IRS guidelines for record retention were issued in 1997 through Procedure 97-22, which allows taxpayers to transfer their paper files or computerized records to an adequate electronic storage media. "The general requirements are that an electronic storage system must ensure an accurate and complete transfer of the hard copy or computerized books and records to an electronic storage media, and the system must also index, store, preserve, retrieve, and reproduce the electronically stored books and records," Allen wrote. The procedure allows the IRS to test the storage system periodically without actually conducting an audit, and

if it does not comply with the guidelines then the taxpayer may be subject to penalties.

More information about record retention is available in the IRS publications *Recordkeeping for Individuals* and *Guide to Record Retention Requirements*.

FURTHER READING:

Allen, Noelle. "New Revenue Procedure Outlines Electronic Record Retention Rules and Allows for Destruction of Originals." *The Tax Advisor*. July 1997.

Dailey, Frederick W. *Tax Savvy for Small Business: Year-Round Tax Advice for Small Businesses*. Berkeley, CA: Nolo Press, 1997.

"Don't Underestimate the Need for Recordkeeping." *Purchasing*. November 9, 1995.

The Entrepreneur Magazine Small Business Advisor. New York: Wiley, 1995.

Krumwiede, Tim, Raymond A. Zimmermann, and Patricia Eason. "Record Retention Needed to Avoid Tax Redeterminations." *Taxation for Accountants*. December 1995.

SEE ALSO: Recordkeeping; Tax Planning

RECRUITING

Recruiting describes the processes companies use to find qualified candidates to fill job openings. Some types of recruiting, such as college recruiting and **networking**, also serve to bolster the company's image among certain groups of potential employees. Effective recruiting is particularly important for small businesses, since finding and hiring talented employees is a key ingredient for growth. The Small Business Association publication *Human Resources Management* outlines three main steps in the recruiting process: assessing future personnel needs; developing a detailed description of the position to be filled and a corresponding profile of the person needed to fill it; and selecting the sources that will yield the best possible candidates. Throughout the recruiting process, small business owners must remain aware of the legal issues involved in hiring employees.

Assessing future personnel needs involves taking a close look at the company's expected workload, the capabilities of the current work force, the anticipated turnover, and the available labor supply. How the company stands in relation to these factors will help management to forecast future employment needs and develop a strategy to meet them. When a need has been identified, the next step is to perform a job analysis to collect information on all the tasks involved in the position and the types of skills, knowledge, and abilities required to do them. The job analysis leads directly to a **job description**, which defines all the duties and responsibilities of the position to be filled. Finally, the small business owner can use the job description to prepare a job specification—a written description of the person needed to fill the position. The job specification is the basis for recruiting, as it provides the standard against which applicants can be measured.

Next comes the actual search for candidates. In his book *Hiring Winners,* Richard J. Pinsker recommends that companies begin the search process as early as possible in order to generate a long list of candidates from which to choose. Even in the early stages of the hiring process, it is vital to consider the legal environment. The Civil Rights Act of 1964 and the Equal Employment Act of 1972 forbid discrimination based on race, color, national origin, sex, age, disability, veteran status, or religion. Therefore, it is illegal for recruiters to inquire about an applicant's age, marital status, children, nationality, or church, and employers must be careful to avoid any mention of such issues in employment ads. It is also illegal to require candidates to submit a picture along with their applications.

SOURCES OF QUALIFIED APPLICANTS

There are a wide variety of sources available for small business owners to use in finding qualified applicants to fill job openings. Some of the most common sources include:

- *Current employees.* Promoting someone from within the company helps keep employee morale high, but small business owners should take this approach only if the person meets the job specifications. In order to facilitate hiring from within, many companies maintain a skills bank on current employees, post notices about job openings and encourage employees to apply, and incorporate apprenticeship programs into employee training. Hiring from within may be difficult when there is a pressing need to fill a position and the required expertise does not exist in-house. Furthermore, Pinsker noted that it is a good idea for companies to fill at least 20 percent of job openings from outside, because outsiders tend to bring new ideas.

- *Employee referrals.* Many job openings in small businesses are best publicized by employees via word of mouth. Most employees will only recommend applicants with proven abilities. New hires can be an especially good source of referrals.

- *Networking.* Networking—developing a wide range of personal contacts within the industry and community—can provide a number of benefits to small business owners,

including job candidates or referrals. Sources of networking connections include trade shows, associations, committee memberships, and charity functions. Pinsker suggests that business owners also encourage their employees to develop their own networks of contacts and to contribute names to the company list.

- *Unsolicited applications.* Most businesses receive unsolicited resumes and job applications when they are not hiring. All applicants should be treated courteously, but the materials submitted by qualified candidates should be kept on file for future reference.

- *Schools and colleges.* Depending on the type of position to be filled, high schools, trade and vocational schools, colleges, and universities can be good sources of candidates. Students are particularly good candidates for part-time positions or those in which prior experience is not needed. College recruiting is generally handled through a placement office. Companies usually send a representative to campus twice per year to meet with and interview students. Pinsker emphasizes that business owners should consider college recruiting as an opportunity to promote their company to both students and faculty.

- *Alumni placement offices.* Many colleges keep resumes on file for alumni who are seeking job or career changes. Alumni files can be a good source for companies seeking educated candidates with more work experience than recent graduates generally have.

- *Job fairs.* Job fairs can be useful for companies that need to hire several employees in a given specialty, such as engineering or computer programming. At a job fair, companies usually pay a booth fee and send representatives to collect resumes and pre-screen candidates. Like college recruiting, job fairs provide small businesses with an opportunity to promote themselves to potential hires.

- *Associations.* Most trade associations maintain a central clearinghouse of candidates who wish to change jobs. Trade shows, conventions, and seminars sponsored by associations can also provide valuable opportunities to meet potential employees.

- *Public employment offices.* The U.S. Department of Labor offers job placement services to some categories of workers free of charge. In many cases, public employment offices will provide small businesses with lists of pre-screened applicants for a certain opening.

- *Private employment agencies.* These organizations match job seekers with potential employers for a fee, usually paid by the employer once a candidate is hired.

- *Outplacement agencies.* Outplacement firms are similar to private employment agencies, but their fees are usually paid by former employers who have laid off or downsized workers. Small businesses with job openings can usually be placed on a mailing list free of charge to receive information on candidates who need a new job.

- *Temporary services.* These firms offer employees to fill a wide range of needs, from clerical to manufacturing to professional services. Hiring temporary employees can be a valuable method for companies to screen people before hiring them on a permanent basis.

- *Advertising.* Employment advertising includes everything from a "help wanted" sign in the window, to print ads in local newspapers or specialized publications like trade magazines, to classified ads on cable television or the Internet. For a small business, publicizing the fact that job openings exist is key to gaining access to a pool of applicants. Advertising can be expensive, however, so it is important to evaluate media carefully. It may be helpful to ask other business owners about their experiences advertising in various media. Small business owners must also be sure that their employment ads comply with equal opportunity employment laws and do not expose the company to charges of discriminatory hiring practices. Ads should concentrate on the skills and responsibilities of the position, rather than on the traits of applicants. In print ads, it is important to avoid nuances that suggest a certain gender or age of applicant is preferred. For example, the word "salesman" should be replaced with "salesperson," "waitress" should be changed to "wait staff," and "young" should be deleted in favor of "energetic." In addition, the recruiter should make certain that all the qualifications listed are actually necessary for effective performance of the job.

Other possible sources of recruiting leads include bankers, accountants, consultants, customers, competitors, and other professionals with whom the small business has regular contact. If the recruiting process is successful, the small business owner will have a substantial list of qualified candidates from which to select the one person who best matches the job specifications. The selection should be made through a formal screening process that may include an employment application, employment tests, and a personal interview. Each step in the process serves to narrow the field of candidates until a final selection can be made.

FURTHER READING:

Pinsker, Richard J. *Hiring Winners.* New York: Amacom, 1991.

Roberts, Gary, Gary Seldon, and Carlotta Roberts. *Human Resources Management.* Washington: U.S. Small Business Administration, n.d.

Steingold, Fred S. *Legal Guide for Starting and Running a Small Business.* Berkely, CA: Nolo Press, 1992.

SEE ALSO: Employee Hiring; Employee Screening; Employment Interviewing; Temporary Services

RECYCLING

Over the past few decades, recycling has become a central component of many business operations in the United States, valued for the cost-savings associated with some programs as well as its general environment-friendly aspects. Recycling programs are comprised of three elements in a continuum represented by the well-known "chasing arrows" symbol that adorns recyclable products: 1) collection of recyclable materials from the waste stream; 2) processing of those materials into new products; and 3) purchasing of products containing recycled materials.

THE GROWTH OF RECYCLING IN THE BUSINESS WORLD

The importance of recycling programs in the business world to the environment can hardly be overstated. Businesses account for approximately one-third of the United States' total solid waste. In the early 1990s, for example, studies indicated that each office worker in America produced from one-half to one and one-half pounds of solid waste each day, of which 70 to 90 percent was paper. Not surprisingly, then, paper accounts for a higher percentage (an estimated 40 percent) of the American waste stream than any other material. Many corporate recycling programs reflect this reality, and even businesses with exceedingly modest recycling programs sometimes take steps to collect wastepaper for recycling.

Recycling first emerged as an ongoing component of business operations in the late 1960s and early 1970s, as concerns about the pace at which the United States and other nations were consuming natural resources became widespread. (Previous recycling campaigns, such as the ones introduced in America during World War II, were relatively short-term efforts that were not predicated on environmental concerns.) The first national Earth Day celebration in 1970 heralded anti-litter campaigns, the creation of the federal **Environmental Protection Agency (EPA)**, and the introduction of some of the first municipal and corporate recycling programs.

Legislation during that period provided an additional impetus for recycling programs, especially in the federal government. The Solid Waste Disposal Act had established resource recovery goals as a priority for U.S. environmental and energy conservation programs. The Resource Recovery Act of 1970 amended the previous legislation, mandating paper recycling and procurement of recycled products in federal agencies wherever economically feasible. The well-known Resource Conservation and Recovery Act of 1976 completely revised both acts, imposing requirements regarding hazardous waste disposal and mandating the recycling of non-hazardous waste in federal facilities. The legislation included the requirement that federal agencies "purchase items that contain the highest percentage of recovered materials practicable given their availability, price and quality." Around the same time, deposit laws that encouraged recycling of glass beverage bottles were passed in several states around the country.

The Environmental Protection Agency and the General Services Administration (GSA), which were jointly charged with administration of the program, launched "Use It Again, Sam," an earnest and widespread federal office paper recycling program, in 1976. Within two years, 90 federal agencies and their 115,000 employees were recycling, their efforts guided by a comprehensive, EPA-issued manual. The federal recycling program declined in the 1980s. Many state and local governments around the country stepped in to fill this void in the ensuing decade, but overall, low disposal costs relegated recycling to little more than an afterthought of solid waste management in the 1970s and early 1980s.

In the late 1980s, however, several factors converged to revive interest in recycling as an attractive alternative to traditional disposal. Growing concerns about both the proliferation and toxic characteristics of landfills around the country brought closures, increased regulation, higher costs, and public opposition to location and expansion of landfills. Other options, such as incinerators, were explored, but these proved controversial as well. Another important factor was a general increase in anxiety about the state of America's (and the world's) environment. Finally, growing numbers of companies came to see environmental friendliness as a viable means of attracting consumers.

By the late 1980s, a number of eastern states had adopted mandatory recycling legislation. This trend toward recycling legislation, combined with increasing consumer demand for environmental responsibility and corporate frustration with rising waste disposal expenses, prompted a modest revitalization of recycling programs in the 1990s.

DEFINING "RECYCLABLE" AND "RECYCLED CONTENT"

Given the popularity of recycled products and the various benefits that accrue from being known as a good corporate citizen, most businesses are eager to use terms like "recyclable" and "recycled content" on their **packaging** and in their advertising. But as J. Stephen Shi and Jane M. Kane pointed out in *Business Horizons,* the government has clearly defined those terms to prevent businesses from making misleading or fraudulent recycling claims. "For a product to be labeled recyclable," wrote Shi and Kane, "the product must be easily collected, separated, or otherwise recovered from what would generally be considered trash and then used for making a new package or product." They go on to note that companies also have a responsibility to qualify whether it is the product or the packaging (or both) that is recyclable, or to qualify claims of responsibility if the product is purchased in an area with limited recycling facilities.

"Recycled content," meanwhile, refers to goods made out of materials that would have otherwise been thrown out for good, relegated to a landfill or incinerator. "To qualify as having recycled content," wrote Shi and Kane, "the materials can come from waste produced in either the manufacturing process or post-consumer use [materials recycled by consumers]. . . . Again, manufacturers must be careful to indicate exactly what part—the product or the package—is made from recyclable material. If there is more than one component to the packaging, the manufacturer must indicate exactly which part of the packaging is made from recycled content. An example of this type of packaging is a paperboard box that is made of recycled materials covered by plastic shrink wrap that is not." Finally, they warn that manufacturers are guilty of misleading consumers if they claim that a product is composed of recycled content in instances where the company was merely following normal industry practice. "A manufacturer that routinely gathers spilled raw materials after trimming finished products and then adds the trimmings to virgin material for further production of the same product cannot claim that its product is made out of recycled content," they explained.

Business consultants, officials, and environmental groups all recognize that some of the regulations regarding permissible recycling/environmental claims are complex, but they urge business owners not to let this fact scare them off. Full descriptions of the rules governing recycling claims are available, and the potential benefits—both to the business and the environment—can often make the additional research an ultimately worthwhile endeavor.

INITIATING AND MAINTAINING EFFECTIVE RECYCLING PROGRAMS

The federal government's *Office Recycling Program Guide* notes five basic, interconnected components of a comprehensive recycling program: education, collection, marketing, procurement, and monitoring and evaluation.

EDUCATION Education encompasses training of both leaders and participants in recycling practices. Not surprisingly, the most successful recycling programs are ones that have the active involvement of business owners and managers and the full participation of employees. Observers of successful recycling initiatives note that this involvement is much more likely to occur if the company owners and work force are well-informed about the reasons for recycling and the ways in which recycling practices can be effectively instituted. There are a wide variety of resources available to businesses interested in organizing recycling programs. Regional Environmental Protection Agency (EPA) offices and state-affiliated natural resource departments throughout the country offer information packets and recycling kits.

After learning about recycling in general, business owners and managers should continue the education process by studying the operational factors that will be unique to their company's recycling efforts. One of the most effective ways in which this can be accomplished is through the use of a "waste audit." A waste audit should note the sources, amounts, and types of trash generated; the current methods and cost of disposal; and the volume of potentially recyclable trash. Based on these findings, leaders of recycling programs can determine which materials to target. Some experts advise beginning recyclers to limit their programs to one type of waste, usually high-quality bond and computer paper. Once participants have grown accustomed to recycling, the program can be expanded to include aluminum, newspaper, plastics, glass, cardboard and other materials. The types and volumes of materials to be recycled will govern the methods of collection employed.

COLLECTION Collection comprises the nuts-and-bolts logistics of separating, gathering, and storing recyclables from trash at their source. The most common methods of collection employed in the workplace are the desktop container, a series of designated containers, or a central collection area, but some businesses employ vendor sorting, where mixed recyclables are stored together and sorted off-site by the waste hauler. These containers are usually brought by

janitorial or mailroom staff to a storage area, where they are kept until they are picked up. Some companies dealing with sensitive, proprietary, or confidential information may also need to consider destruction (by shredding, for example) as part of this step.

Maintenance of quality standards is paramount to this facet of a successful recycling program. Similar materials, like white and colored paper, may have a market separately, but are nearly worthless when mixed. Processors of most types of paper discourage commingling of "stickies" (labels, stickers and tape), food, and other contaminants. Although source separation has proven to be the best collection method, new technological advances will almost certainly relieve some of this separation pressure in the future.

MARKETING Marketing recyclable materials to a processor involves research and contracting. Dealers in waste paper—the most commonly recycled material—can be found in local phone directories or through contact with the Paper Stock Institute of America. The *EI Environmental Services Directory,* "the nation's largest, most in-depth directory of environmental service providers," lists and describes over 2,000 vendors. There are many variables that entrepreneurs and small business owners should heed when seeking a buyer for their recyclable materials, however. Foremost among these is usually cost. "The quality of a particular collected material greatly affects the price that interested buyers are willing to pay," stated the *Encyclopedia of the Environment.* "Uncontaminated materials—for example, glass that is free of stones, ceramics, or other material—command prices substantially greater than contaminated materials. To help in evaluating the quality of a material, government and industry organizations have developed numerous quality standards. The actual price of a material depends on additional factors such as its relative abundance and the subsequent cost of transporting it to manufacturers."

PROCUREMENT Although it is sometimes overlooked, procurement is a vital component of recycling programs. Procurement helps "close the recycling loop," for it is the process whereby companies arrange to purchase and use supplies made from recycled materials. Most analysts of recycling programs contend that implementation of this stage of recycling often lags behind other stages. Recent studies indicate that while an overwhelming majority of businesses do have recycling collection systems of one kind or another in place, a far lower percentage of those businesses purchase recycling materials for use in their own operations.

This is due in part to the costs associated with developing additional capacity to use "secondary"—rather than virgin—materials. As the *Encyclopedia of the Environment* observed, "market conditions must be appropriate for companies to even consider new investments, credit must be available for financing projects, and sites have to be found and regulatory permits obtained.''

MONITORING AND EVALUATION Each aspect of the recycling program should be monitored and evaluated for efficiency and progress. This is especially important for smaller companies, where flawed practices can have a more pronounced impact on fundamental business health. A cost-benefit analysis of the program can strengthen management support and encourage expansion to other areas of the company and/or other products in the waste stream.

FURTHER READING:

Beverly, Dawn. *Business Recycling Manual.* New York: Inform, Inc. and Recourse Systems, Inc., 1991.

Cichonski, Thomas J., and Karen Hill. *Recycling Sourcebook.* Detroit, MI: Gale Research, Inc., 1993.

Curry, Gloria. ''Increasingly Cost-Effective, Recycling Programs Continue to Grow,'' *Office.* August 1993.

Eblen, Ruth A., and William R. Eblen, eds. *The Encyclopedia of the Environment.* Boston, MA: Houghton Mifflin, 1994.

Hart, Stuart L. ''How Green Production Might Save the World.'' *Northwest Environmental Journal.* 1994.

Kimball, Debi. *Recycling in America: A Reference Handbook.* Santa Barbara, CA: ABC-CLIO, 1992.

Office Recycling Program Guide. Office of Administrative and Management Services, 1993.

Ortbal, John. ''How to Cultivate an Office Recycling Program,'' *Modern Office Technology.* April 1991.

Shi, J. Stephen, and Jane M. Kane. ''Green Issues.'' *Business Horizons.* January-February 1996.

Steuteville, Robert. ''Corporate Recycling Reaps Savings,'' *BioCycle.* August 1993.

Stundza, Tom. ''Treat Scrap as Trash and You Throw Money Away,'' *Purchasing.* July 18, 1991.

Webb, Nan. ''Recycling Tasks Are Part of the Job,'' *Purchasing World,* March 1991.

SEE ALSO: Business Ethics; Environmental Law and Business

REFINANCING

Refinancing is the refunding or restructuring of debt with new debt, equity, or a combination of both. The refinancing of debt is most often undertaken during a period of declining interest rates in order to lower the average cost of a firm's debt. Sometimes refinancing involves the issuance of equity in order to decrease the proportion of debt in the borrower's **capital** structure. As a result of refinancing, the maturity of the debt may be extended or reduced, or the new debt may carry a lower **interest rate**, or some combination of these options.

Refinancing may be done by any issuer of debt, such as corporations and governmental bodies, as well as holders of real estate, including home owners. When a borrower retires a debt issue, the payment is in made in cash and no new security takes the place of the one being paid off. The term ''refunding'' is used when a borrower issues new debt to refinance an existing one.

CORPORATE OR GOVERNMENT DEBT REFINANCING

The most common incentive for corporations or governmental bodies to refinance their outstanding debt is to take advantage of a decline in interest rates from the time the original debt was issued. Another trigger for corporate debt refinancing is when the price of their common stock reaches a level which makes it attractive for a firm to replace its outstanding debt with equity. Aside from reducing interest costs, this latter move gives a firm additional flexibility for future financing; by retiring debt, the firm will have some unused debt capacity. Regardless of the reason for the refinancing, the issuer has to deal with two decisions: 1) Is the time right to refinance, and 2) What type of security should be issued to replace the one being refinanced?

If a corporation or governmental body wishes to refinance before the maturity date of the outstanding issue, they will need to exercise the call provision of the debt. The call provision gives the borrower the right to retire outstanding **bonds** at a stipulated price, usually at a premium over face amount, but never less than face. The specific price which an issuer will need to pay for a call appears in the bond's indenture. The existence of a call premium is designed to compensate the bond holder for the firm's right to pay off the debt earlier than the holder expected. Many bond issues have a deferred call, which means the firm cannot call in the bond until the expiration of the deferment period, usually between five and ten years.

The cash outlay required by exercising the call provision includes payment to the holder of the bond for any interest which has accrued to the date of the call, and the call price, including premium (if any). In addition, the firm will need to pay a variety of administrative costs, including a fee to the bond's trustee. Of course, there will also be flotation costs for any new debt or equity that is issued as part of the refinancing.

Sometimes an issuer may be prohibited from calling in the bonds (e.g., during the deferred call period). In these instances, the issuer always has the opportunity to purchase its bonds on the open market. This strategy may also be advantageous if the outstanding bond is selling in the market at a price lower than the call price.

Open market purchases involve few administrative costs. The corporation will recognize a gain on the repurchase if the market value is below the amount at which the corporation is carrying the bonds on its books (face value plus or minus unamortized premium or discount), or a loss on the repurchase if the market value is above the book value.

The major difficulty with open market purchases to effect a refinancing is that typically the market for bonds is "thin." This means that a relatively small percentage of an entire issue may be available on the market over any period of time. As a result, if a firm is intent on refinancing a bond issue, it almost always needs to resort to a call. This is why virtually every new bond that is issued contains a call provision. If an outstanding issue does not permit a call, another option available to the issuer is to seek tenders (offers to sell at a predetermined price) from current bond holders.

The new debt instrument issued in refinancing can be simple or complex. A corporation could replace an existing bond with traditional bonds, serial bonds (which have various maturity dates), zero-coupon bonds (which have no periodic interest payments), or corporate shares (which have no maturity date, but which may have associated dividend payments). One factor that a firm needs to consider is that the administrative and flotation costs of issuing either common or preferred shares are higher than for new debt. Furthermore, dividend payments, if any, are not tax deductible.

The decision to refinance is a very practical matter involving time and money. Over time the opportunity to refinance varies with changing interest rates and economic conditions. When a corporation anticipates an advantageous interest rate climate, it then analyzes the cash flows associated with the refinancing. Calculating the present value of all the cash outflows and the interest savings assists in comparing refinancing alternatives that have different maturity dates and capitalization schemes.

MORTGAGE REFINANCING

Owners of residential or commercial real estate use a similar method to analyze their refinancing decisions. In residential real estate the conventional wisdom applies the "2-2-2 rule": if interest rates have fallen two points below the existing mortgage, if the owner has already paid two years of the mortgage, and if the owner plans to live in the house another two years, then refinancing is feasible. However, this approach ignores the present value of the related cash flows and the effects of the tax deductibility of interest expense and any related points.

Therefore, a better analysis of a mortgage refinancing decision should be conducted as follows: 1) Calculate the present value of the after-tax cash flows of the existing mortgage; 2) Calculate the present value of the after-tax cash flows of the proposed mortgage; 3) Compare the outcomes and select the alternative with the lower present value. The interest rate to be used in steps one and two is the after-tax interest cost of the proposed mortgage.

FURTHER READING:

Arsan, Noyan, and Eugene Poindexter. "Revisiting the Economics of Mortgage Refinance." *Journal of Retail Banking.* Winter 1993-1994.

Bierman, Harold, Jr., and Seymour Smidt. *Financial Management for Decision Making.* New York: Macmillan, 1986.

Haugen, Robert A. *Introductory Investment Theory.* Prentice-Hall, 1987.

Sharpe, William, F., and Gordon J. Alexander. *Investments.* 4th ed. New York: Prentice-Hall, 1990.

Shillinglaw, Gordon, and Philip E. Meyer. *Accounting: A Management Approach.* 7th ed. Chicago: Irwin, 1983.

Tower, Jonathan. "Rate Plunge Ignites a Boom in Refinancing Market." *American Banker.* August 8, 1997.

Welsch, Glen A., Robert N. Anthony, and Daniel G. Short. *Fundamentals of Financial Accounting.* 4th ed. Chicago: Irwin, 1984.

SEE ALSO: Debt Financing

REGULATION D

Regulation D is a section of the U.S. federal securities law that provides the means for small businesses to sell stock through **direct public offerings** (DPOs). A DPO is a financial tool that enables a company to issue stock directly to investors—without using a broker or underwriter as an intermediary—and avoid many of the costs associated with "going public" through an **initial public offering** (IPO). Regulation D exempts companies choosing this form of offering from many of the registration and reporting requirements of the **Securities and Exchange Commission (SEC)**.

DPOs, private placements of stock, and other exempt offerings provide small businesses with a quicker, less expensive way to raise capital than IPOs. The primary advantage of DPOs over IPOs is a dramatic reduction in cost. IPO underwriters typically charge a commission of 13 percent of the proceeds of the sale of securities, whereas the costs associated with a DPO are closer to 3 percent. DPOs also can be completed within a shorter time frame and without extensive disclosure of confidential information. Finally, since the stock sold through a DPO goes to a limited number of investors who tend to have a long-term orientation, there is often less pressure on the company's management to deliver short-term results.

DPOs and other exempt offerings also involve disadvantages, however. For example, the amount that a company can raise through a DPO within any 12-month period is limited. In addition, the stock is usually sold at a lower price than it might command through an IPO. Stock sold through exempt offerings is not usually freely traded, so no market price is established for the shares or for the overall company. This lack of a market price may make it difficult for the company to use equity as loan collateral. Finally, DPO investors are likely to demand a larger share of ownership in the company to offset the lack of liquidity in their position. Investors eventually may pressure the company to go public through an IPO so that they can realize their profits.

RULES 504, 505, AND 506

Regulation D—which was adopted in 1982 and has been revised several times since—consists of a set of rules numbered 501 through 508. Rules 504, 505, and 506 describe three different types of exempt offerings and set forth guidelines covering the amount of stock that can be sold and the number and type of investors that are allowed under each one. The most common type of DPO is the Small Corporate Offering Registration, or SCOR, which is included in Rule 504. SCOR gives an exemption to private companies that raise no more than $1 million in any 12-month period through the sale of stock. There are no restrictions on the number or types of investors, and the stock may be freely traded. The SCOR process is easy enough for a small business owner to complete with the assistance of a knowledgeable accountant and attorney. It is available in all states except Delaware, Florida, Hawaii, and Nebraska.

A related type of DPO is outlined in Rule 505. This option enables a small business to sell up to $5 million in stock during a 12-month period to an unlimited number of investors, provided that no more than 35 of them are non-accredited. To be accredited, an investor must have sufficient assets or income to make such an investment. According to the SEC rules, individual investors must have either $1 million in assets (other than their home and car) or $200,000 in net annual personal income, while institutions must hold $5 million in assets. Finally, a DPO conducted under Rule 506 allows a company to sell unlimited securities to an unlimited number of investors, provided that no more than 35 of them are non-accredited. Under Rule 506, investors must be sophisticated, or able to evaluate the merits and understand the risks of the transaction. In both of these options, the securities cannot be freely traded.

FURTHER READING:

Donahue, Mark F. "New Exemptions from the Registration Requirements of the Securities Act of 1933: Regulation D." *Securities Regulation Law Journal.* Fall 1982.

Field, Drew. "Raising Equity through a Direct Public Offering." *Bankers Magazine.* March-April 1991.

"Going Private—Regulation D." *In Business.* July-August 1983.

Lowes, Robert L. "Try a Do-It-Yourself Public Offering." *Medical Economics.* April 14, 1997.

Saxlehner, Andrew C. "Equity Made Easy." *Inc.* July 1983.

Sherman, Andrew J. *The Complete Guide to Running and Growing Your Business.* New York: Random House, 1997.

Steinberg, Carol. "The DPO Revolution: Direct Public Offerings Turn Customers into Investors." *Success.* March 1997.

Stevens, M. "An Easier Way to Raise Business Capital." *Dun and Bradstreet Reports.* March-April 1984.

Sutton, David P., and M. William Benedetto. *Initial Public Offerings: A Strategic Planner for Raising Equity Capital.* Chicago, IL: Probus, 1988.

Taylor, Lon W. "Raising Capital through Private Placements." *Journal of Business Strategy.* July-August 1988.

Zeune, Gary D., and Timothy R. Baer. "Floating a Stock Offering: New Buoyancy from the SEC." *Corporate Cashflow Magazine.* August 1993.

REGULATORY FLEXIBILITY ACT

The Regulatory Flexibility Act (RFA) is a law, first enacted in 1980, designed to make government agencies review all regulations that it establishes to ensure that they not impose a disproportionate economic burden on small business owners and other small entities (non-profit organizations and small governmental jurisdictions). In the years following the enactment of the RFA, however, many small business owners contended that agencies too often ignored the law. Periodic attempts to revise the RFA failed until March 1996, when the Small Business Regulatory Enforcement Fairness Act (SBREFA) became law. This new legislation cast the Regulatory Flexibility Act in an entirely new light, for it amended the 1980 law to allow for judicial review of government agencies' compliance with it. Before the 1996 law was passed, small business owners had had no legal recourse when faced with regulations that they felt were unfair to smaller companies. "There was no statutory requirement that forces an agency to do an analysis," explained one spokesman for the Senate Committee on Small Business in *Nation's Restaurant News.* With the passage of the Small Business Regulatory Enforcement Fairness Act, however, "a small entity, including businesses—if an agency rule seems unfair—can challenge it in court. And if they prevail, they can modify it or strike it to reduce the impact on that entity."

LEGISLATIVE HISTORY OF THE RFA

Prior to 1980, American small businesses were forced to adhere to the same regulations as far larger companies, even though they did not have nearly the same resources to bring to bear. Entrepreneurs and directors of nonprofits repeatedly charged that when regulations put forth by the **Environmental Protection Agency (EPA)**, the **Occupational Safety and Health Administration (OSHA)**, and other agencies were applied evenly, without regard to the size of the enterprises affected, they sometimes did serious damage to smaller organizations. As the Small Business Administration noted in its *Guide to the Regulatory Flexibility Act,* "the costs of complying with a particular regulation . . . may be manageable for a business with 500 or more employees, or revenue in the millions of dollars. On the other hand, a smaller company may not have the ability to absorb the expenses as easily, to set competitive prices, to devise innovations or even to continue as a viable entity." The *Guide* added that as more businesspeople and politicians investigated the situation, "evidence indicated that uniform application of federal regulatory requirements imposed increases in the economies of scale and affected small entities' ability to compete effectively. Reports . . . cited these disproportionate economic burdens on small business as contributing to declines in productivity, competition, innovation, and the relative market shares of small business."

The passage of the RFA in 1980, then, was meant to blunt much of the burden that regulatory changes were laying on the shoulders of small businesses. According to the RFA, each agency was supposed to analyze how its regulations affected the ability of small businesses to compete. In addition, RFA directed agencies to balance the needs of small business with the benefits of the regulation being considered. The law called for agencies to propose regulatory alternatives for smaller companies that would be unduly hurt if forced to adhere to the original regulations. The Regulatory Flexibility Act still allowed agencies to put together needed regulatory measures in such realms as workplace safety and environmental protection, but it meant to give a greater voice to small businesses by encouraging agencies to listen to small business concerns and study ways in which regulations could be adjusted for them.

During the 1980s, however, many entrepreneurs and other members of the business community came to feel that the RFA was an unacceptably weak law. The law—which actually went into effect on January 1, 1981—included no legal penalties that could be imposed on agencies that did not follow the Act's guidelines, so some agencies paid little attention to the RFA. Observers felt that some agencies were simply recalcitrant, while others, burdened by inadequate budgets, did not have the resources to satisfactorily address the issues laid out in the RFA. Most observers granted that the Regulatory Flexibility Act was valuable in certain cases, but by the early 1990s there was a growing clamor in the small business community and Congress for an amended RFA.

In September 1993 President Clinton signed Executive Order 12866, which highlighted the responsibilities of government agencies to adhere to the principles of RFA. That same year, the Clinton administration's National Performance Review task force formally recommended that agency compliance with the RFA be subject to judicial review. Less than three years later, in March 1996, a number of major amendments to the RFA—including provisions adding judicial review—became law with the passage of the Small Business Regulatory Enforcement Fairness Act.

SMALL BUSINESS REGULATORY ENFORCEMENT FAIRNESS ACT

The 1996 act included several components that drew praise from small business owners. While the addition of judicial review of agency compliance with the RFA received the bulk of attention, the amendments also gave agencies additional responsibilities in the areas of policy review and outreach, and gave nonagency entities (small businesses, Congress) more influence in the regulatory process.

JUDICIAL REVIEW The Small Business Regulatory Enforcement Fairness Act amended the RFA so that small businesses finally had legal recourse when confronted with regulations that they felt did not adhere to the RFA. It created a complaint process whereby small businesses can seek review of the rule in court. Under the 1996 amendments, noted the SBA, "the court may review the final regulatory flexibility analysis, the agency's certification that the rule has no impact on small entities, and the agency's compliance with periodic reviews of current rules. Under the amendment, judicial review also applies to interpretative rulemakings promulgated by the IRS [Internal Revenue Service]." (Prior to the 1996 legislation, interpretative rulemakings of the IRS had been exempt from the RFA because of provisions of the Administrative Procedure Act.) In addition, the RFA now includes a provision that reimburses small business operators for legal fees incurred if it successfully challenges a regulation as overly harsh.

PERIODIC REVIEWS SBREFA reinforced RFA review guidelines for government agencies. Under the amended RFA, agencies are required to review all existing regulations to see if they have a significant economic impact on meaningful numbers of small entities (businesses, nonprofits, small government bodies). In situations where a "significant" impact is found, the agency in question is directed to review the regulations and determine whether they should remain in place, be revised, or be rescinded. Factors to be evaluated include: continued need for the regulation; impact of industry and economic trends on the regulation; public comments on the regulation's strengths and weaknesses; complexity of the regulation; and extent to which the regulation overlaps, duplicates, or conflicts with already existing federal, state, or local laws.

OUTREACH RFA now requires both OSHA and EPA to put together small business advocacy review panels every time they propose a regulation that is likely to have a big economic impact on a large number of small businesses. This information-gathering step is designed to solicit small business input on both the likely compliance costs of the regulations and possible mutually acceptable regulatory alternatives. A report reflecting the results of the review panel meetings is then prepared.

In addition, federal agencies are directed under RFA to publish a listing of all proposed or final regulations expected to be implemented during the following year. This requirement, say proponents, provides small business owners with more time to study the regulations and their likely impact on their establishments. Finally, the RFA now requires agencies to prepare easily understandable guide books to help businesses comply with regulations.

EXPANDED AUTHORITY FOR CHIEF COUNSEL FOR ADVOCACY The 1996 amendments to the RFA expanded the authority of the SBA's chief counsel for advocacy. The RFA now allows the chief counsel—who has been formally designated to monitor agency compliance with the law—to file amicus briefs in situations where regulations are being reviewed in court.

LEGISLATIVE REVIEW A provision of the 1996 legislation established a 60-day review period during which Congress will be able to reject any new regulations that are held to be unnecessary.

Despite these changes, however, some critics contend that SBREFA has not lived up to expectations in its first two years of existence. "The law was supposed to open up a new era of federal friendliness toward entrepreneurs," wrote Stephen Barlas in the December 1997 issue of *Entrepreneur.* "And while it's premature to call the law a bust, SBREFA's shortcomings are becoming readily apparent." Detractors argued that Congress showed little inclination to exercise its increased powers of legislative review, and they claimed that other review panels called for in SBREFA have been slow to take shape.

RFA COVERAGE

The Regulatory Flexibility Act was intended to extend protection to three different types of small entities in the United States:

- Small businesses (as defined by the SBA)

- Small organizations (nonprofit establishments that are independently owned and operated and not dominant in their field)

- Small governmental jurisdictions (defined as governments of cities, counties, towns, townships, villages, school districts, and other districts with populations of less than 50,000)

For further information on the Regulatory Enforcement Act, contact the Office of Advocacy of the Small Business Administration at 409 Third St., SW, Washington, DC 20416.

FURTHER READING:

Allen, Robin Lee. "Regulatory Bill Lets Small Operators Flex Muscles." *Nation's Restaurant News.* April 22, 1996.

Barlas, Stephen. "Regulatory Relief: A New Bill to Ease Small-Business Burdens Just May Make It through Congress." *Entrepreneur.* April 1996.

Barlas, Stephen. "In Limbo." *Entrepreneur.* December 1997.

SBA Advocacy—Guide to the Regulatory Flexibility Act. Washington: U.S. Small Business Administration, 1997.

Warner, David. "Putting the Brakes on Federal Rules." *Nation's Business.* March 1995.

RELOCATION

Relocation is the action of transferring a company's place of operation from one physical location to another. For small businesses, the act of relocating is often fraught with uncertainty, since the margin for error in companies with modest financial resources is so small. Indeed, the quality (or lack thereof) of a business relocation can be pivotal in determining the financial success or failure of all sorts of business ventures in a wide spectrum of industries, including retail, service, wholesale, and manufacturing efforts.

Small businesses look to relocation for many different reasons. Some business owners turn to relocation as a last resort, a final effort to reverse the fortunes of a floundering business. These efforts rarely succeed, though the reasons vary from business to business. In many cases, the source (or sources) of the business's financial difficulties lie in areas other than physical location. Inadequate capital, poor management, flawed marketing plans, wasteful production processes, lousy work habits, and a range of other maladies may be more directly responsible for a company's anemic performance than its physical location. Of course, some small businesses struggle despite the presence of competent and hardworking management/ownership and sound business practices. In such cases, physical location might be a significant factor in the company's disappointing performance, and relocation could go far toward turning the business's financial fortunes around.

But business experts note that relocation is generally an expensive process, and that small businesses that are struggling financially may find it difficult to stay afloat during this transition period. After all, companies that decide to relocate must absorb several financial blows simultaneously: 1) They have to pay for the expense of moving their people, office furniture, and equipment into their new facilities; 2) They have to pay for necessary changes to the new facility (these changes can range from relatively minor rewiring to extensive reshaping of the facility's physical layout); 3) Before relocation, business owners and/or staff have to devote time to relocation research, negotiation, etc. that would otherwise be spent on attending to money-making tasks; and 4) During relocation, many businesses have to basically stop their business until they are situated in their new place of business. This latter reality can cripple a fragile business, especially if the relocation process proves more problematic than anticipated (as it often is).

Of course, many successful businesses relocate as well, drawn by locales that feature high traffic, attractive physical attributes, proximity to needed transportation, advantageous financial terms, or, in some cases, community environment.

RELOCATION TRENDS

In recent years, business observers have pointed to a general trend in business relocations away from major metropolitan areas and toward small- and medium-sized communities. Certainly, some companies are limited in their relocation options by customer **demographics** and other factors, but many firms—especially those established by entrepreneurs—have forsaken large cities for smaller towns. Indeed, desires for quieter lifestyles away from pollution, crime, and other attributes often associated with large cities, coupled with the advances that have made **telecommuting** a reality, have led many entrepreneurs to relocate to more rural locations.

But although such settings have many positive aspects in terms of so-called "quality of life" considerations, entrepreneurs and other small business owners still need to weigh the potential drawbacks of making such a move on their livelihoods. As Brian Steinberg observed in *Entrepreneur,* "hurdles litter the track. [Entrepreneurs] must absorb the shock of adjusting to rural culture, navigate the difficulties of keeping family together, and discover new business practices necessitated by an out-of-the-way location." Steinberg went on to describe several obstacles that small business owners may face when trying to make a successful relocation to a small-town setting. "The struggle to find employees constitutes one concern for rural entrepreneurs; getting along with the neighbors is yet another. While the added tax dollars and employment opportunities a new company provides a small town are quite welcome, the success a firm might bring can also have some undesirable effects. A successful company may supersede existing firms in importance and influence, taking away employees and even driving up home prices. Towns sometimes offer economic incentives to lure new business owners—money local companies might view as ill-spent."

In addition, some entrepreneurs find that smaller communities do not provide the same level of services that can be found in larger cities. These inconveniences, noted Steinberg, can range from troublesome ones like unreliable electric service (perhaps necessitating the purchase of backup generators), lack of overnight delivery services (Federal Express, etc.), and an absence of local access numbers for Internet service (which can force businesses to pay exorbitant costs to access the Internet) to downright crippling ones, like a dearth of qualified workers. "Preparation is the key to a successful move to the hinterlands," concluded Steinberg. "Location, available work force, proximity to transportation, local attitudes, and culture shock are all factors to consider."

LOCATION NEEDS OF VARIOUS BUSINESS TYPES

Small businesses will have different site needs that need to be considered when relocating, depending on their industry—retail, service, wholesale, or manufacturing—and their own financial and cultural factors. Whatever their area of business, however, small business owners need to make sure that they take the time to adequately examine all facets of a move. "A well organized site selection process should include research, planning, developing the transaction structure, analyzing the proposal, documenting the transaction, and negotiating for government incentives," wrote John R. Frazier in *Los Angeles Business Journal.* When researching the merits and drawbacks of each potential relocation site, Frazier urged business owners to define each place by three primary measurements: specific location attributes, physical attributes, and occupancy cost parameters. "Specific location attributes might relate to transportation issues such as circulation patterns of surface streets and access to rail. Additional considerations would include corporate identity/image issues, attitudes regarding alternative government jurisdictions and any special utility needs for the proposed use," he wrote. "Physical attributes address structure and layout as they relate to form and function and include such on-site characteristics as topography, existing layout, ceiling heights and load bearing requirements. Goals with respect to occupancy costs will vary according to whether the firm plans to occupy on a fee ownership basis or as a tenant, but . . . could include special tenant improvement allowances, moving allowances, an option to purchase, a cash incentive, or even an ownership position as a tenant.''

Business consultants and small business owners who have successfully undertaken relocation efforts urge managers and owners of small enterprises to examine a long list of specific concerns before making any relocation decisions. A relocation based on knowledge, after all, is far more likely to succeed than one that is predicated on assumptions and hopes.

1) Determine if projected revenues will cover the cost of leasing or purchasing the site.

2) Research whether ancillary costs associated with the relocation can be absorbed by the company.

3) Honestly appraise the impact that relocation will have on the business's cash flow and productivity.

4) Determine whether it will be possible to secure lenders to help cover costs associated with moving into the new business site.

5) Investigate whether the targeted site is located in an area that has restrictive ordinances that will unduly interfere with your company's operations

6) Enlist the services of experts to determine if both the exterior and interior of the target building or facility are in good condition and adequately meet your business's layout and image requirements.

7) If refurbishment is necessary, find out how much it will cost and how long it will take.

8) Determine whether neighbor businesses complement your company, or whether they might detract from your company's image or its ability to attract its primary demographic audience.

9) Gauge the attitudes of your workforce—and especially the feelings of key personnel—about relocation

10) If in an environment where you share maintenance, housekeeping, and other service costs with other companies, investigate whether the set-up is a good one for your company.

11) Check into the safety and security aspects of the facility.

12) Determine whether the site will be able to accommodate your company if it needs to expand.

13) Find out if competitors are located nearby. If so, try to determine how successful they are, and whether the region will be able to support your business and those of competitors.

14) Gauge whether the site is customer-friendly in terms of layout, parking, etc.

15) Is the area immediately surrounding the building in a state of flux? Development of vacant buildings or lots, construction sites, and other landmarks can dramatically change the complexion of an area.

16) Determine if leasehold improvements will need to be made.

17) Research whether existing or proposed government regulations might have an impact on the value of the facility.

18) Learn about the regulatory and tax climate of the area in which you are considering relocating.

19) Determine whether suppliers of raw materials and other goods and services necessary to your operation will be readily available.

Small business owners who take the time to inform themselves in these areas are far more likely to relocate successfully than those who do not attend to such issues.

FURTHER READING:

Ady, Robert M. ''Discussion: How to Select an Ideal Business Site.'' *New England Economic Review*. March-April 1997.

Bahls, Jane Easter. ''Love Thy Neighbor?'' *Entrepreneur*. July 1995.

Daly, Wadman. *Relocating Your Workplace: A User's Guide to Acquiring and Preparing Business Facilities*. Crisp Publications, n.d.

Frazier, John R. ''Keeping Goals in Site.'' *Los Angeles Business Journal*. May 25, 1992.

Fusi, Deborah S. ''Site Selection Spotlights Superlatives in Business Park Occupancy, Space and Size.'' *Site Selection*. December 1989.

Mihaly, Mary. ''Smart Moves.'' *Industry Week*. June 5, 1995.

Schriner, Jim. ''Picking Your Neighborhood.'' *Industry Week*. July 3, 1995.

Schriner, Jim. ''Where Will Employees Want to Live?'' *Industry Week*. March 3, 1997.

Steinberg, Brian. ''Green Acres: Why Some Entrepreneurs are Saying 'Goodbye, City Life.' '' *Entrepreneur*. October 1997.

Steingold, Fred S. *Legal Guide for Starting and Running a Small Business*. 3d ed. Berkeley, CA: Nolo Press, 1997.

Venable, Tim. ''Getting Better Location Assistance: Here's How.'' *Site Selection*. April 1996.

Weber, Fred I., Jr. *Locating or Relocating Your Business*. Washington: U.S. Small Business Administration, n.d.

SEE ALSO: Business Site Selection; Optimal Firm Size; Rural Businesses

RENOVATION

Office and building renovation is a common undertaking in today's competitive business environment, as businesses endeavor to keep up with infrastructure needs (especially those sparked by technology use) and provide aesthetically pleasing settings for customers. Small business owners and consultants agree that a well-conceived and carefully planned renovation effort can revitalize a business and provide it with much-needed room to grow in the future. But they also note that renovation periods can have a negative impact on productivity and profitability. Often, the inconveniences associated with office and building renovation projects make it a practical impossibility for businesses to maintain the exact same level of operations that they met during non-renovation periods. However, experts indicate that small business owners—whether they are building tenants or building owners—can take several steps to ensure that the negative aspects of renovation are minimized.

SMALL BUSINESS TENANTS AND RENOVATION

Many small business owners are co-tenants of a building with other businesses. These entrepreneurs may well find themselves faced with an impending renovation. This is especially true if they are operating their businesses in older buildings. Sometimes these renovations take place within the physical space of the business itself; on other occasions, the renovation may be limited to common areas—such as lobbies, outer building areas, stairways, or elevator systems—that are shared by all the tenants. In either case, the impending arrival of a renovation crew should signal a period of preparation on the part of the small business owner.

"Tenants are usually very pleased with the modern conveniences and new environments that are created after a major office renovation project has been completed," wrote Lawrence Hearn in the *Journal of Property Management*. But during the period when the renovation is actually taking place, small business owners may find themselves feeling everything from anxiety to deep anger about the impact that it is (or seems to be) having on their company. The most effective way in which small business tenants can minimize these negative emotions is by establishing and maintaining good lines of communication with the building owner before and during the renovation process.

Hearn stated that good communication between building owners/managers and tenants is a priority whether the renovation is a minor capital improvement or a comprehensive rehabilitation project. "Almost any physical change in the work environ-ment can be disruptive and potentially threatening to the tenant's business," he added. "It is management's, and ultimately ownership's, responsibility to make sure tenants are kept informed every step of the way during construction."

Hearn noted that smart building managers will take the initiative in talking with their business tenants so that they are more likely to "feel as if they are part of the renovation process, instead of becoming victims of the procedure. Retail tenants are particularly sensitive to signage and good access to their space." But if you are a small business owner and you feel that the facility's ownership is doing an inadequate job of informing you of renovation issues and schedules, it is entirely within your rights to demand more information and input. Business owners should make sure that they thoroughly review their leasing contract, soliciting legal assistance if necessary, to make sure that they are being treated fairly.

Some business owners who inhabit facilities that are undergoing renovation adopt a fatalistic sort of attitude toward the process, surrendering meekly to renovation strategies without offering any workable alternatives to plans that might unnecessarily hinder their operations. Other entrepreneurs, meanwhile, err on the other end of the spectrum by making unreasonable demands that may ultimately drag out the renovation process for several extra days or weeks. Small business experts counsel owners to instead adopt a middle ground. They have to recognize that renovation efforts almost inevitably bring about some measure of inconvenience for tenants and their customers, but that they ultimately increase the value of the location for business operation. On the other hand, if a business owner spots a problem during a review of upcoming or ongoing renovation plans, he or she should bring it to the attention of building management. A renovation strategy that would render a key loading dock unavailable during a big delivery period, for example, should immediately be brought to the attention of the landlord. Small business owners should also recognize that many facility managers want to help tenants out in whatever way they reasonably can. After all, they do not want to lose tenants and go to the trouble of finding new ones. As Hearn pointed out to facility owners, "although it may cost more, it is sometimes wiser to schedule work in high service areas at night or on the weekends. The same holds true for heavy pounding or other work that requires large equipment. You will certainly make up the cost difference if you keep your tenants happy and away from the construction headache as much as possible."

RENOVATING PROFESSIONAL OFFICES

Office and facility renovations may also be undertaken by small business enterprises that either own or are the sole tenants of the building in which they operate. Business owners that provide professional services are especially likely to renovate to meet changing internal demands, attract new clients, and keep existing ones. Indeed, doctors, dentists, attorneys, architects, engineers, and the like recognize that the appearance of their offices can be a significant component in their overall success. "With competition up and reimbursements down, a medical office that's shabby, impedes productivity, or can't accommodate expansion plans can be a big liability," cautioned Laura Clark in *Medical Economics.*

Analysts note that professional offices are more likely to renovate rather than relocate for two fundamental reasons: cost and client retention. Even a major renovation of an existing facility is likely to be considerably less expensive than the total costs associated with relocating to another facility. Perhaps even more importantly, existing patients and clients are accustomed to finding the office at a given location. "If you move, they may not follow you," warned one consultant in *Medical Economics.*

Renovation strategies can vary considerably, depending on the needs and concerns of the office in question. A medical practice or architectural firm may be amply equipped to integrate new technology with existing operations, only to recognize that its growth has been hampered because it is saddled with an unattractive waiting area. In this situation, the renovation may amount to little more than some new carpeting, wallpaper, and furniture. Other firms, however, may find that only a major rehabilitation effort will be sufficient to correct long-standing problems with infrastructure such as an ineffective floor plan or cramped office space.

Clark pointed to several other concerns that professional service firms (and many other businesses) have to consider when weighing renovation plans as well. For example, businesses have to be in compliance with the Americans with Disabilities Act of 1990. Much of the renovation work that took place in the early 1990s was undertaken specifically to address this law, which required facilities to become fully accessible by widening hallways, installing ramps, and adapting drinking fountains and bathrooms for use by people in wheelchairs. Most buildings are now in compliance with the ADA, but building owners looking to renovate need to make sure that their new plans adhere to ADA parameters. Professional service firms also need to factor in their attractiveness to recent graduates when weighing their renovation strategies. For example, "Young [physicians] coming out of residencies are going to consider the attractiveness and efficiency of your office," one renovator told *Medical Economics.* "They're simply not going to want to come to work in a dingy, 1940s-style medical building."

Finally, before committing to a major renovation effort, professional service firms should discuss matters with appropriate experts, including architects, accountants, and lenders. Selecting a contractor should be done carefully as well; business owners are urged to check into the contractor's reputation for quality, timeliness, and financial soundness before making an agreement. Finally, firms should call in legal representation before signing a contract. As one renovation expert indicated in *Medical Economics,* "[attorneys] should write all kinds of ceilings and floors into your contract so you don't get burned. Believe it or not, you can force your contractors to stay on schedule and within budget—or pay a penalty—but you've got to show them you're very serious about that right up front."

FURTHER READING:

Clark, Laura. "Revitalize Your Practice with an Office Renovation." *Medical Economics.* June 3, 1991.

Hearn, Lawrence. "Retaining Tenants During Renovation." *Journal of Property Management.* July-August 1995.

Kaiser, Harvey H. *The Facilities Manager's Reference: Management, Planning, Building Audits, Estimating.* Kingston, MA: R.S. Means Co., 1989.

Konz, Stephen. *Facility Design.* New York: John Wiley and Sons, 1985.

Kruk, Leonard B. "Facilities Planning Supports Changing Office Technologies." *Managing Office Technology.* December 1996.

J. K. Lasser Institute. *How to Run a Small Business.* 7th ed. New York: McGraw-Hill, 1994.

Malpas, William. "Management: Minimizing Construction Risks." *Progressive Architecture.* June 1990.

Pelland, Dave. "Creating Buildings, Not Problems: Managing Construction Risk Effectively." *Risk Management.* November 1996.

"Re-Dressing Office Buildings for Success." *Building Design & Construction.* May 1993.

SEE ALSO: Facility Layout and Design; Leasing Property

REQUEST FOR PROPOSAL

Request for Proposal or RFP is the process by which a corporate department or government agency prepares bid documents to acquire equipment or services. RFPs are frequently published in the legal documents section of pertinent newspapers or in trade journals covering the industry in which the department operates. The RFP can also be distributed to a list of qualified potential bidders that have already been contacted and prequalified as eligible by the agency or department. "Qualified" is a key word in answering or preparing any RFP. Qualification frequently depends on follow-up investigation on the part of the hopeful bidder, and careful wording of the original RFP.

Although RFPs are primarily associated with government agencies since their responsibility to get equipment and consulting talent under the most beneficial circumstances possible is closely monitored by the press and tax watchdogs. Some private companies also employ RFPs, though, usually when purchasing commodities or services that do not bear directly on the company's own products or services.

ELEMENTS OF AN ATTRACTIVE RFP

Some RFP work requests are of a scale beyond the scope of small or mid-sized companies, but others provide such businesses with valuable opportunities to expand their client base and operations. Before bidding on an RFP, however, entrepreneurs and business owners should make sure they fully understand the nature of the work request.

For instance, some are RFPs are decidedly more informative than others. When scanning RFPs, vendors should make certain that it specifically describes what needs to be delivered or executed to fulfill the needs of the company or agency that posted the notice. In order to do so, it is often necessary for potential vendors to educate themselves about the nature of the agency or corporation that has submitted the RFP. Vendors should also inquire whether the work request could translate into additional work on associated projects down the line. For instance, if the equipment will eventually be networked to a building that is not yet built, but is in the long range plans of the agency or company, a vendor may decide that a low price on the initial RFP is viable if it advances its prospects for a more long-term arrangement down the line.

Before making any bid, vendors should also check the RFP for other factors that might influence their response. Will the asked-for equipment be subject to notable environmental conditions or regulations? If the equipment will be used in foreign countries, is the equipment compatible with the standards of those nations? Will ancillary costs associated with design, production, transportation, or some other aspect of delivery eat into the profit margin to an unacceptable extent? Are the RFP and the equipment or services it seeks legal under local, state, and federal laws? Is the RFP asking for both equipment and service? (Companies that sell equipment might not be able to adequately service it, yet that service performance may be written into the RFP in a separate section from the equipment specifications; responders must know they can fulfill the entire contract before answering it.) Are deadlines and performance clauses contained within the RFP reasonable? Will the RFP agency require the winning vendor to sign a perform-ance bond that guarantees delivery of goods or services by a certain date?

Most companies and agencies that submit work requests provide prospective bidders with ample time to study the RFP before the deadline. Some companies give vendors as much as one month from the time the RFP is published before the bids are due. This allows bidders time to tinker with their bids, possibly allowing them to seek out new vendors of their own to help meet the needs of the RFP.

STAYING ON THE BID LIST

Companies wishing to bid on RFPs should monitor the legal notices in local newspapers and trade magazines, and contact the purchasing departments of corporations and government agencies likely to request services and equipment. Then they should investigate the requirements to be added to the "bid list." Finally, once the company has fulfilled all obligations necessary to be added to the list, the company's leadership needs to make certain that it stays on that list.

Government agencies and corporate departments are sometimes reluctant to delete vendors from bid lists because of fears that such cuts will elicit favoritism charges. Nonetheless, establishments submitting RFPs do seek to keep bid lists to manageable size, since every bid requires scrutiny. One favored way to keep the bid list down is to require potential vendors to refile every few years. Another is to ask vendors to provide certain information about their companies, such as past sales and experience or number of employees available to service the account. Such requirements cull the number of bidders down, eliminating companies that are too disorganized or feeble to keep up. Conversely, a small business that meets all such requirements in a timely fashion is essentially serving notice that it has its act together.

Companies seeking RFP business should also be cognizant of the fact that winning bids are not always exclusively a matter of providing the lowest cost or the highest level of customer service. Some corporations and government agencies give special consideration on their bid lists to minority- and women-owned companies.

FURTHER READING:

Stein, Murry. "Don't Bomb Out When Preparing RFPs." *Computerworld.* February 15, 1993.

SEE ALSO: Business Proposals; Contracts

RESEARCH AND DEVELOPMENT

Research and development (R & D) is a process intended to create new or improved technology that can provide a competitive advantage at the business, industry, or national level. While the rewards can be very high, the process of technological innovation (of which R & D is the first phase) is complex and risky. The majority of R & D projects fail to provide the expected financial results, and the successful projects (25 to 50 percent) must also pay for the projects that are unsuccessful or terminated early by management. In addition, the originator of R & D cannot appropriate all the benefits of its innovations and must share them with customers, the public, and even competitors. For these reasons, a company's R & D efforts must be carefully organized, controlled, evaluated, and managed.

OBJECTIVES AND TYPES OF R & D

The objective of academic and institutional R & D is to obtain new knowledge, which may or may not be applied to practical uses. In contrast, the objective of industrial R & D is to obtain new knowledge, applicable to the company's business needs, that eventually will result in new or improved products, processes, systems, or services that can increase the company's sales and profits.

The National Science Foundation (NSF) defines three types of R & D: basic research, applied research, and development. Basic research has as its objectives a fuller knowledge or understanding of the subject under study, rather than a practical application thereof. As applied to the industrial sector, basic research is defined as research that advances scientific knowledge but does not have specific commercial objectives, although such investigation may be in the fields of present or potential interest to the company.

Applied research is directed towards gaining knowledge or understanding necessary for determining the means by which a recognized and specific need may be met. In industry, applied research includes investigations directed to the discovery of new knowledge having specific commercial objectives with respect to products, processes, or services. Development is the systematic utilization of the knowledge or understanding gained from research toward the production of useful materials, devices, systems, or methods, including design and development of prototypes and processes.

At this point, it is important to differentiate development from engineering, which can be defined as utilization of state-of-the-art knowledge for the design and production of marketable goods and services. In other words, research creates knowledge, and development designs and builds prototypes and proves their feasibility. Engineering then converts these prototypes into products or services that can be offered to the marketplace or into processes that can be used to produce commercial products and services.

R & D AND TECHNOLOGY ACQUISITION

In many cases, technology required for industrial purposes is available in the marketplace, usually for a price. Before embarking on the lengthy and risky process of performing its own R & D, a company should perform a "make or buy" analysis and decide whether or not the new R & D project is strategically and economically justified. The following influencing factors should be considered: proprietariness, timing, risk, and cost.

PROPRIETARINESS If a technology can be safeguarded as proprietary—and protected by patents, trade secrets, nondisclosure agreements, etc.—the technology becomes exclusive property of the company and its value is much higher. In fact, a valid patent grants a company a temporary monopoly for 17 years to use the technology as it sees fit, usually to maximize sales and profits. In this case, a high-level of R & D effort is justified for a relatively long period (up to 10 years) with an acceptable risk of failure.

On the contrary, if the technology cannot be protected, as is the case with certain software programs, expensive in-house R & D is not justified since the software may be copied by a competitor or "stolen" by a disloyal employee. In this case, the secret of commercial success is staying ahead of competition by developing continuously improved software packages, supported by a strong marketing effort.

TIMING If the market growth rate is slow or moderate, in-house or contracted R & D may be the best means to obtain the technology. On the other hand, if the market is growing very fast and competitors are rushing in, the "window of opportunity" may close before the technology has been developed by the new entrant. In this case, it is better to acquire the technology and related know-how, in order to enter the market before the competition.

RISK Inherently, technology development is always riskier than technology acquisition because the technical success of R & D cannot be guaranteed. There is always the risk that the planned performance specifications will not be met, that the time to project completion will be stretched out, and that the R & D and manufacturing costs will be higher than forecasted. On the other hand, acquiring technology entails a much lower risk, since the product, process, or service, can be seen and tested before the contract is signed.

Regardless of whether the technology is acquired or developed, there is always the risk that it will soon become obsolete and be displaced by a superior technology. This risk cannot be entirely removed, but it can be considerably reduced by careful technology forecasting and planning. If market growth is slow, and no winner has emerged among the various competing technologies, it may be wiser to monitor these technologies through ''technology gatekeepers'' and be ready to jump in as the winner emerges.

COST For a successful product line with relatively long life, acquisition of technology is more costly, but less risky, than technology development. Normally, royalties are paid in the form of a relatively low initial payment as ''earnest money,'' and as periodic payments tied to sales. These payments continue throughout the period of validity of the license agreement. Since these royalties may amount to 2 to 5 percent of sales, this creates an undue burden of continuing higher cost to the licensee, everything else being equal.

On the other hand, R & D requires a high front-end investment and therefore a longer period of negative cash flow. There are also intangible costs involved in acquiring technology—the license agreements may have restrictive geographic or application clauses, and other businesses may have access to the same technology and compete with lower prices or stronger marketing. Finally, the licensee is dependent upon the licensor for technological advances, or even for keeping up to date, and this may be dangerous.

MOVING AHEAD WITH R & D

Once the decision has been made to perform R & D, the company should decide where and how it should be carried out. There are various possibilities: in-house R & D in the company laboratories, externally contracted R & D, and joint R & D. In-house R & D commands a strategic advantage, since the company is the sole owner of the technology and can protect it from unauthorized uses. In addition, since R & D is basically a learning process, the company can develop a group of experienced scientists and engineers that can be employed in developing more advanced products and processes and in transferring the results of their R & D to operations and to customers. However, since R & D personnel do not like to work alone and are stimulated by peers, the laboratory should have a critical mass in the core technologies and support services; this critical mass may exceed the company resources.

External R & D is usually contracted out to specialized nonprofit research institutions or to universities. The advantages are that these institutions may already have experienced personnel in the disciplines to be researched, as well as the necessary laboratory and test equipment. This will save money and especially time with respect to in-house R & D. The disadvantages are that the company will not benefit from the learning experience, and may become overly dependent on the contractor. Also, the technology transfer may be difficult and there is always the possibility of leaks to competitors. In the case of universities, costs are usually lower and there is the additional benefit of identifying graduate students who may be hired later and researchers who may be employed as consultants when needed.

Joint R & D became popular in the United States after antitrust laws were relaxed and tax incentives were offered to R & D consortia. In a consortium, several companies with congruent interests join together to perform R & D, either in a separate organization or in a university. The advantages are lower costs, since each company does not have to invest in similar equipment; a critical mass of researchers; and interchange of information among the sponsors. The disadvantages are that all the sponsors have access to the same R & D results. However, because of antitrust considerations, the R & D performed must be precompetitive, and each participant in the joint R & D must apply separately the information obtained to its products, processes, and services.

R & D LABORATORY ORGANIZATION AND FUNDING

R & D is usually performed within R & D laboratories, also called R & D centers, for reasons of efficiency and control and to facilitate communications and synergy among researchers. The organizational positioning and the funding of these laboratories is often a controversial matter and is still evolving. An R & D laboratory can be organized internally according to three patterns: by functions, by projects, and matrix. In the functional organization, all researchers working in a specific discipline are grouped in a unit and report to a manager, who is a recognized expert in the field. This organization is similar to the various academic departments of a university. The advantages are close interaction with peers and competent evaluations of the scientific value of the researchers' work. The main disadvantage is that most industrial R & D projects require the contributions of different disciplines, and there is often nobody responsible for managing the project and integrating the work of the researchers.

In the project organization, all researchers working on a given project report to a project manager, who is usually not an expert in their specific disciplines. The project manager evaluates the researchers on the basis of practical results, time, and money, rather than on the value of their scientific and technical contributions. The advantages are that the project can be professionally managed and corrective actions taken if the results expected are not forthcoming or budgets are not met. The main disadvantage is that projects have, by definition, a limited life. A project team, as an organization, is disbanded as soon as the work has been completed. The researchers now have no "home" and must look for work on new projects, which may or may not be forthcoming.

The matrix organization attempts to combine the best features of the functional and project organizations, by assigning every researcher to two superiors: a functional manager and a project manager. The functional manager is responsible for evaluating the scientific value of the researcher's work, planning his/her career development, and providing a "home" between projects. The project manager is responsible for evaluating the researcher's contributions to the project and giving him/her the resources needed to get the job done. Obviously, the two managers must work closely together in assigning the duties of the researchers, integrating their evaluations, and reporting them to higher management.

In practice, small and shorter-term projects are generally run according to a functional organization, with one researcher taking on the project administration (not management) duties. Larger, longer-range projects are organized as independent projects with strong professional project management. When project responsibility is transferred to operations, some of the researchers move too, thereby ensuring an effective transfer of technology.

R & D PROJECT SELECTION, MANAGEMENT, AND TERMINATION

Industrial R & D is generally performed according to projects (i.e., separate work activities) with specific technical and business goals, assigned personnel, and time and money budgets. These projects can either originate "top down" (for instance, from a management decision to develop a new product) or "bottom up" (from an idea originated by an individual researcher). The size of a project may vary from a part-time effort of one researcher for a few months with a budget of thousands of dollars, to major five- or ten-year projects with large, multidisciplinary teams of researchers and budgets of millions of dollars. Therefore, project selection and evaluation is one of the more critical and difficult subjects of R & D management. Of equal importance, although less emphasized in practice, is the subject of project termination, particularly in the case of unsuccessful or marginal projects.

SELECTION OF R & D PROJECTS Normally, a company or a laboratory will have requests for a higher number of projects than can be effectively implemented. Therefore, R & D managers are faced with the problem of allocating scarce resources of personnel, equipment, laboratory space, and funds to a broad spectrum of competing projects. Since the decision to start on an R & D project is both a technical and a business decision, R & D managers should select projects on the basis of the following objectives, in order of importance:

1) Maximize the long-term return on investment

2) Make optimum use of the available human and physical resources

3) Maintain a balanced R & D portfolio and control risk

4) Foster a favorable climate for creativity and innovation.

Project selection is usually done once a year, by listing all ongoing projects and the proposals for new projects, evaluating and comparing all these projects according to quantitative and qualitative criteria, and prioritizing the projects in "totem pole" order. The funds requested by all the projects are compared with the laboratory budget for the following year and the project list is cut off at the budgeted amount. Projects above the line are funded, those below the line delayed to the following year or tabled indefinitely. Some experienced R & D managers do not allocate all the budgeted funds, but keep a small percentage on reserve to take care of new projects that may be proposed during the year, after the laboratory official budget has been approved.

EVALUATION OF R & D PROJECTS Since R & D projects are subject to the risk of failure, the expected value of a project can be evaluated ex ante according to the following statistical formula:

$$EV = P \times pt \times pc \times pf$$

where P is the payoff if the project is successful; that is, the stream of net income accruing to the company over the life of the new product (or process, or service) resulting from the project. The payoff P is then multiplied by the probability of success, which is the product of three separate probabilities:

1) "pt" is the probability of technical success, i.e., that the new product or process will meet the technical and functional specifications

2) "pc" is the probability of commercial success, i.e., that the new product will be accepted by the marketplace and will achieve the forecasted market share

3) "pf" is the probability of financial success, i.e., that the new product will achieve the forecasted financial goals, in terms of profits, return on investment, and cash flow.

Consequently, project evaluation must be performed along two separate orthogonal real dimensions: technical evaluation, to establish the probability of technical success; and business evaluation, to establish the payoff and the probabilities of commercial and financial success. Once the expected value of a project has been determined, it should be divided by the forecasted cost C of the project, in order to obtain a benefit/cost ratio R of the form R = EV/C. Obviously the higher this ratio, the more desirable the project.

For more advanced and longer term projects, leading to major (rather than incremental) innovation, it may be difficult to establish reliable values of P, C, pt, pc, and pf. In this case, a relative comparison of projects is made based on their respective technical quality and potential business value. Technical quality is evaluated by analyzing and rating the clarity of the project goals; the extent of the technical, institutional, and market penetration obstacles that must be overcome; the adequacy of the skills and facilities available in the laboratory for carrying out the work; and how easily can the project results be transferred to an operation. Potential business value of a project is defined in terms of the market share of an existing market that can be captured by the new product; or by the size of a new market that can be developed by the new product; or by the value of new technology that can be sold by the company or transferred to its customers.

After the first tentative list of projects has been established in order of priority, it is "matched" with the existing laboratory human and physical resources to make sure that these resources are well utilized. In fact, creative human resources are the laboratory's most valuable asset, and these should not be wasted by asking researchers to do work outside their disciplines and interests. Also, it is difficult to change in a short time the "mix" of available disciplines and equipment, and to hire and fire researchers. Thus, a shift towards new disciplines should be done gradually, avoiding the underutilization or overloading of the existing resources.

Once the tentative list of prospects has been modified according to the above, the entire project portfolio of the R & D laboratory should be balanced, in order to control risk, according to three types of probabilities listed above. Technical risk is controlled in two ways: 1) by having a spectrum of projects ranging from low to medium-high technical risk; 2) by avoiding "bunching" too many projects in the same technology, particularly if the technology could be replaced by a superior technology during the expected lifetime of the new product.

Commercial risk can be controlled by not having "too many eggs in one basket," that is, by targeting different market segments (government, capital equipment, consumer, industrial, international, etc.) and attacking different competitors, since directly targeting a major competitor may trigger a dangerous counter offensive and a price war. Financial risk is controlled by having a majority of small- and medium-size projects (in terms of R & D expense), a few large projects, and no projects that, in case of failure, could bankrupt the company. Financial risk, in terms of cash flow, is also controlled by having a spectrum (in time-to-payoff) of more short- and medium-term projects than long-term projects. This type of spectrum is also psychologically important to maintain the credibility of the R & D laboratory in the face of upper-level executives who keep asking "What have you done for me lately?"

By definition, R & D is a risky activity, and there are no "zero risk" R & D projects, since these would then be engineering projects. While the majority of the projects in an R & D portfolio should be categorized as low-risk, some medium-risk projects are justified, and even a few high-risk projects, provided their expected value is high.

Finally, project evaluation and selection should be made objectively, in order to develop and maintain a favorable climate for creativity and innovation. Researchers will be naturally disappointed when their projects are not approved. Some may even suspect that other projects were preferred for subjective reasons, such as the "halo" effect (the past track record and prestige of other, more senior, researchers), the reluctance of management to terminate less deserving projects, and especially political influences to select "pet" projects of executives. If there is a feeling that project selection is not done objectively, many researchers, particularly the junior ones, will lose their enthusiasm and renounce proposing new projects of a high potential value for the company. Eventually, if this situation persists, the laboratory will lose its creativity and concentrate on routine low-risk (but also low-payoff) or "political" projects, and it will have difficulty in keeping and attracting the best researchers. Therefore, it is desirable that the project evaluation and selection criteria be properly explained and that all researchers be asked to participate in the evaluation process. Also, the finalized project portfolio should be presented to, and discussed with, all the researchers.

MANAGEMENT OF R & D PROJECTS The management of R & D projects follows basically the principles and methods of project management. There is, however, one significant caveat in relation to normal engineering projects: R & D projects are risky, and it is difficult to develop an accurate budget, in terms of technical milestones, costs, and time to completion of the various tasks. Therefore, R & D budgets should be considered initially as tentative, and should be gradually refined as more information becomes available as a result of preliminary work and the learning process. Historically, many R & D projects have exceeded, sometimes with disastrous consequences, the forecasted and budgeted times to completion and funds to be expended. In the case of R & D, measuring technical progress and completion of milestones is generally more important than measuring expenditures over time.

TERMINATION OF R & D PROJECTS Termination of projects is a difficult subject because of the political repercussions on the laboratory. Theoretically, a project should be discontinued for one of the following three reasons:

1) There is a change in the environment—for instance, new government regulations, new competitive offerings, or price declines—that make the new product less attractive to the company;

2) Unforseen technical obstacles are encountered and the laboratory does not have the resources to overcome them; or

3) The project falls hopelessly behind schedule and corrective actions are not forthcoming.

Due to organizational inertia, and the fear of antagonizing senior researchers or executives with pet projects, there is often the tendency to let a project continue, hoping for a miraculous breakthrough that seldom happens.

In theory, an optimal number of projects should be initiated and this number should be gradually reduced over time to make room for more deserving projects. Also, the monthly cost of a project is much lower in the early stages than in the later stages, when more personnel and equipment have been committed. Thus, from a financial risk management viewpoint, it is better to waste money on several promising young projects than on a few maturing ''dogs'' with low payoff and high expense. In practice, in many laboratories it is difficult to start a new project because all the resources have already been committed and just as difficult to terminate a project, for the reasons given above. Thus, an able and astute R&D manager should continuously evaluate his/her project portfolio in relation to changes in company strategy, should continuously and objectively monitor the progress of each R&D project, and should not hesitate to terminate projects that have lost their value to the company in terms of payoff and probability of success.

In conclusion, by assuring a close coupling with the company's strategic goals and by maintaining close contacts with operations, the laboratory and the R & D function will maintain credibility and strengthen its strategic value for the company.

FURTHER READING:

Hampton, John J., ed. *AMA Management Handbook.* AMACOM, 1994.

Martin, Michael J.C. *Managing Technological Innovation and Entrepreneurship.* Reston, 1984.

Roussel, Philip. A., Kamal N. Saad, and Tamara J. Erikson. *Third Generation R & D.* Harvard Business School Press, 1991.

Twiss, Brian. *Managing Technological Innovation.* 3rd ed. Pitman, 1985.

SEE ALSO: Business Planning; Strategy

RESUMES

A résumé is a document presented by a job applicant to a prospective employer outlining and summarizing that person's qualifications for employment. A résumé generally includes data on education, previous work experience, and personal information, and well-crafted ones are composed in such a way as to maximize the applicant's attractiveness as a potential employee. A résumé is generally accompanied by a cover letter which introduces the applicant and the résumé to the employer. The purpose of a résumé is to obtain an interview, not to land a job. This is an important distinction. Whether or not a person is hired is largely determined by what transpires during the job interview, not by the résumé. A résumé is extremely important, however, because it provides the employer with a first impression of the job applicant. From this first impression a decision will be made as to whether or not an interview will be granted.

RÉSUMÉ APPEARANCE Résumés are read from two perspectives: the appearance of the physical document itself and the content of the résumé. Résumé appearance concerns the presence (or absence) of typographical errors, poor grammar usage, sloppy sentence structure, garish colors, unconventional typefaces, paper stains, etc.

RÉSUMÉ INFORMATION The content of the résumé, as indicated earlier, is the actual information included in the document. The content of most résumés falls into four broad categories: education, previous work experience, personal data, and social data. The first two are self-explanatory. Personal data includes such things as address and telephone number. Social data includes military status, club memberships, references, etc.

Handbooks that provide detailed advice on compiling résumés are available in most bookstores and libraries. These guides generally agree on the types of information to include on a résumé but sometimes differ on the format and hierarchical arrangement of the résumé. Some authors feel that educational information should be presented first while others feel previous work experience should be foremost. Other authors of such handbooks offer advice on tailoring a résumé to fit one's particular employment situation (looking for an entry-level position, re-entering the job market, or changing fields or vocations). Most of these handbooks, however, have one thing in common: they generally lack empirical data on what a prospective employer is looking for in a résumé. References in these handbooks to this aspect of the applicant, résumé, and employer scenario are often anecdotal.

EMPLOYERS AND RÉSUMÉS

When reading résumés, employers generally are looking for hard data and information. Functional résumés (résumés with no dates) are often viewed as indicators of excessive job movement or attempts to hide large gaps in one's career. Nebulous phraseology such as "exposure to" sometimes indicate a lack of depth of work experience, as does excess space devoted to education, personal, and social data. (Of course, recent college or high school graduates and other people relatively new to the work force often have little choice but to highlight such information, and the discerning employer will take this factor into account).

Many small business consultants urge their clients to study résumés closely, citing the unfortunate frequency with which some applicants include outright lies. A Massachusetts-based management consultant, for instance, told *Nation's Business* writer Peter Weaver that a résumé should only be used as a starting point for launching a thorough examination of an applicant's business, professional, and interpersonal skills. "Hiring someone based on false claims in a résumé not only weakens a firm's work force but also can lead to costly legal action," said Weaver, who noted that many businesses are held legally responsible for the actions of all employees—even those who may have been placed in positions on the basis of fraudulent information.

Some employers have turned to automated résumé banks or reference checking firms to help them fill their workforce needs. Banks will, for a fee, mail out copies of résumés to prospective employers. Using technical terminology and job-related phrases a computer will match the résumés it stores in its data bank with job descriptions supplied by its clients. Résumé banks, however, are not professional recruiters; the latter are compensated for their services in terms of a percentage of a recruit's salary. Résumé banks charge a sliding fee for their services.

FURTHER READING:

Roberts, Gary, Gary Seldon, and Carlotta Roberts. *Human Resources Management.* Washington: U.S. Small Business Administration, n.a.

Weaver, Peter. "Ignoring a Résumé Can Prove Costly." *Nation's Business.* September 1997.

SEE ALSO: Employee Hiring; Written Communication

RETAIL TRADE

Retailers are business firms engaged in offering goods and services directly to consumers. In most—but not all—cases, retail outlets are primarily concerned with selling merchandise. Typically, such businesses sell individual units or small groupings of products to large numbers of customers. A minority of retailers, however, also garner income through rentals rather than outright sales of goods (as in the case of enterprises that offer furniture or gardening tools for rent) or through a combination of products and services (as in the case of a clothing store that might offer free alterations with the purchase of a suit).

The retail industry is a massive part of the overall U.S. economy. In the mid-1990s, for example, retail establishments accounted for better than one out of five jobs in the country, and pulled in more than $2 trillion on an annual basis. Moreover, many retail niches are characterized by a healthy population of smaller enterprises; indeed, the vast majority of retail employees in the United States work at establishments with fewer than 20 employees.

Retail trade is widely known as a very competitive area of commercial endeavor, and observers note that many fledgling retail establishments do not survive for more than a few years. Indeed, competition for sales has become so great that consumers have seen a marked blurring of product lines among retailers. Increasingly, retailers have taken to stocking a much greater variety of goods than their basic industry classification would indicate (bookstores, for example, increasingly stock music products, while food, liquor, office supplies, automotive supplies, and other wares can all be found in contemporary drug stores). This development further complicates efforts to establish and maintain a healthy presence in the marketplace. But for the small business owner who launches a retail store on an adequate foundation of capital, business acumen, and attractive merchandise, involvement in the trade can be rewarding on both financial and personal fulfillment levels.

PRIMARY RETAIL TYPES Retail enterprises can be either independently owned and operated or part of a "chain," a group of two or more stores whose activities are determined and coordinated by a single management group. Stores that are part of a chain may all be owned by a single company, but in other cases, the stores may be franchises that are independently owned by a small businessperson.

Many different types of retail establishments exist, and, as noted above, the overall industry has seen a significant blurring of the boundaries that had long separated the wide range of companies operating under the retail umbrella. Nonetheless, retailing establishments still generally fall into one of the following general categories:

- Specialty Stores—These establishments typically concentrate their efforts on selling a single type or very limited range of merchandise. Clothing stores, musical instrument stores, sewing shops, and party supply stores all fall within this category.

- Department Stores—These establishments are comprised of a series of departments, each of which specializes in selling a particular grouping of products. Under this compartmentalized arrangement, consumers go to one area of the store to purchase tableware and another area to acquire bedding, for example.

- Supermarkets—These retail establishments, which are primarily involved in providing food to consumers but have increasingly ventured into other product areas in recent years, account for the vast majority of total food-store sales in America.

- Discount Stores—These retail outlets offer consumers a trade-off: lower prices (typically on a broad range of products) in exchange for lower levels of service. Indeed, many discount stores operate under a basic ''self-service'' philosophy.

- Mail-Order Businesses and other Nonstore Retailing Establishments—Mail-order sales have become an increasingly ubiquitous part of the American retail landscape; indeed, some retail establishments subsist entirely on mail order, forsaking traditional stores entirely, while other companies maintain operations on both levels. In addition, this category includes sales made to end consumers through telemarketing, vending machines, and other nonstore avenues.

FURTHER READING:

Buss, Dale D. ''The Little Guys Strike Back.'' *Nation's Business.* July 1996.

Dolber, Roslyn. *Opportunities in Retailing Careers.* Lincolnwood, IL: VGM Career Horizons, 1989.

Du, Fanglan, and Ira Apfel. ''The Future of Retailing.'' *American Demographics.* September 1995.

Occupational Outlook: 1994-95. Scottsdale, AZ: Associated Book Publishers, Inc., 1994.

RETIREMENT PLANNING

Retirement planning describes the financial strategies individuals employ during their working years to ensure that they will be able to meet their goals for financial security upon retirement. Making sound decisions about retirement is particularly important for self-employed persons and small business owners. Unlike employees of large companies, who can simply participate in the pension plans and investment programs offered by their employers, entrepreneurs must set up and administer their own plans for themselves and for their employees.

Though establishing and funding retirement plans can be costly for small businesses, such programs also offer a number of advantages. In most cases, for example, employer contributions to retirement plans are **tax deductible business expenses**. In addition, offering employees a comprehensive retirement plan can help small businesses attract and retain qualified people who might otherwise seek the security of working for a larger company. The number of small firms establishing retirement plans has grown during the 1990s, but small employers still lag far behind larger ones in providing this type of benefit for employees. According to Connecticut-based consulting firm Access Research Inc., 24 percent of small businesses (those with fewer than 100 employees) offered retirement plans in 1996, compared to 51 percent of medium-sized businesses (between 100 and 1,000 employees) and 98 percent of large businesses (more than 1,000 employees).

Retirement planning is a topic of interest not only to older small business owners, but to young entrepreneurs as well. The debate over whether Social Security will be available for the younger members of the current work force adds legitimacy to the need for early retirement planning. Longer life expectancies mean that more money must be set aside for retirement, while the uncertainty of investment returns and inflation rates makes careful planning essential. In fact, some experts recommend that individuals invest a minimum of 10 percent of their gross income from the time they enter the work force to guarantee a comfortable retirement.

LAWS GOVERNING RETIREMENT PLANS

The Social Security Administration was created in the 1930s as part of President Franklin Roosevelt's New Deal. Private **pension plans** mushroomed shortly thereafter, offering coverage to millions of employees. In 1962 the Self-Employed Individuals Retirement Act established tax-deferred retirement plans with withdrawals starting between the ages of 59 ½ and 70 ½. These plans—also known as **Keogh plans** after their originator, New York Congressman Eugene J. Keogh—were intended for the self-employed and for those who have income from self-employment on the side. Embezzlement from pension plans by trustees led to the passage of the Employee Retirement Income Security Act of 1974 (ERISA). One of the main provisions of ERISA was to set forth vesting requirements—time periods over which employees gain full rights to the money invested by employers on their behalf. ERISA governs most large-employer-sponsored pension plans, but does not apply to those sponsored by businesses with less than 25 employees.

TYPES OF RETIREMENT PLANS

The two main categories of retirement plans are defined contribution and defined benefit. Defined contribution plans use an allocation formula to specify a percentage of compensation to be contributed by each participant. For example, an individual can voluntarily deduct a certain portion of his or her salary, in many cases before taxes, and place the money into a qualified retirement plan, where it will grow tax-deferred. Likewise, an employer can contribute a percentage of each employee's salary to the plan on their behalf, or match the contributions employees make.

In contrast, defined benefit plans calculate a desired level of benefits to be paid upon retirement—using a fixed monthly payment or a percentage of compensation—and then the employer contributes to the plan annually according to a formula so that the benefits will be available when needed. The amount of annual contributions is determined by an actuary, based upon the age, salary levels, and years of service of employees, as well as prevailing interest and inflation rates. In defined benefit plans, the employer bears the risk of providing a specified level of benefits to employees when they retire. This is the traditional idea of a ''pension plan'' that has often been used by large employers with a unionized work force. But defined benefit plans can also be useful for small business owners who are nearing retirement age and wish to put away as much money as possible.

Perhaps the most significant difference between defined benefit and defined contribution plans is the voluntary nature of defined contribution plans. Such plans are fully voluntary, so that hourly or salaried employees elect to have a certain percentage of money deducted—before taxes—from their paychecks. Conversely, defined benefit plans involve automatic contributions made by the employer, with no active participation on the part of the employee.

In the 1980s, defined benefit plans declined in popularity in favor of defined contribution plans. Part of this decline can be attributed to the fact that the work force became more mobile, and fewer people were willing to commit their entire working lives to a single employer in order to gain a pension. Employers, too, began moving away from defined benefit plans because of the financial pressure involved in funding them. Such pressure increased for some categories of employers in 1996, when nondiscrimination rules took effect. These rules state that public sponsors must offer the same benefits to all employees regardless of their compensation. Many state and local municipalities have moved to defined contribution plans to avoid this new mandate.

One significant advantage of defined contribution plans is that the amount invested by employees can be rolled over into another account with another employer. Rollover activity into similar tax-deferred plans has continued to increase as tax laws require a 20 percent withholding tax to be paid on the lump sum if it is not rolled over. Another reason for the growth of defined contribution plans was the emergence of **401(k) plans**, in which employers can match contributions made by employees. But defined contribution plans continued to face scrutiny by many financial advisers for two reasons: 1) the investment decisions made by the company may be too restrictive for employees to meet individual goals; and 2) many times employees are not educated about the risk and returns associated with the investment vehicles available through the company plan. Similarly, the voluntary nature of defined contribution plans makes detractors wonder if ill-informed employees will have less money in their defined contribution accounts at retirement than they would have had under a defined benefit plan.

OPTIONS FOR SMALL BUSINESSES

Small business owners can set up a wide variety of retirement plans by filling out the necessary forms at any financial institution (a bank, mutual fund, insurance company, brokerage firm, etc.). The fees vary depending on the plan's complexity and the number of participants. Some employer-sponsored plans are required to file Form 5500 annually to disclose plan activities to the IRS. The preparation and filing of this complicated document can increase the administrative costs associated with a plan, as the business owner may require help from a tax advisor or plan administration professional. In addition, all the information reported on IRS Form 5500 is open to public inspection.

The most important thing to remember is that a small business owner who wants to establish a qualified plan for him or herself must also include all other company employees who meet minimum participation standards. As an employer, the small business owner can establish retirement plans like any other business. As an employee, the small business owner can then make contributions to the plan he or she has established in order to set aside tax-deferred funds for retirement, like any other employee. The difference is that a small business owner must include all nonowner employees in any company-sponsored retirement plans and make equivalent contributions to their accounts. Unfortunately, this requirement has the effect of reducing the allowable contributions that the owner of a proprietorship or partnership can make on his or her own behalf.

For self-employed individuals, contributions to a retirement plan are based upon the net earnings of their business. The net earnings consist of the company's gross income less deductions for business expenses, salaries paid to nonowner employees, the employer's 50 percent of the Social Security tax, and—significantly—the employer's contribution to retirement plans on behalf of employees. Therefore, rather than receiving pre-tax contributions to the retirement account as a percentage of gross salary, like nonowner employees, the small business owner receives contributions as a smaller percentage of net earnings. Employing other people thus detracts from the owner's ability to build up a sizeable before-tax retirement account of his or her own. For this reason, some experts recommend that the owners of proprietorships and partnerships who sponsor plans for their employees supplement their own retirement funds through a personal after-tax savings plan.

Nevertheless, many small businesses sponsor retirement plans in order to gain tax advantages and increase the loyalty of employees. A number of different types of plans are available. The most popular plans for small businesses all fall under the category of defined contribution plans. In nearly every case, withdrawals made before the age of 59 ½ are subject to an IRS penalty in addition to ordinary income tax. The plans differ in terms of administrative costs, eligibility requirements, employee participation, degree of discretion in making contributions, and amount of allowable contributions. Brief descriptions of some of the most common types of plans follow:

SIMPLIFIED EMPLOYEE PENSION (SEP) PLANS Simplified Employee Pension (SEP) plans are employer-funded retirement accounts that allow small businesses to direct at least 3 percent and up to 15 percent of each employee's annual salary into tax-deferred **individual retirement accounts (IRAs)** on a discretionary basis. SEP plans are easy to set up and inexpensive to administer, as the employer simply makes contributions to IRAs that are established by employees. The employees then take responsibility for making investment decisions regarding their own IRAs. Employers thus avoid the risk and cost involved in accounting for employee retirement funds. In addition, employers have the flexibility to make large percentage contributions during good financial years, and to reduce contributions during hard times. SEP plans are available to all types of business entities, including proprietorships, partnerships, and corporations. In general, eligibility is limited to employees 21 or older with at least three years of service to the company and a minimum level of compensation.

SAVINGS INCENTIVE MATCH PLAN FOR EMPLOYEES (SIMPLE) Savings Incentive Match Plan for Employees (SIMPLE) plans take two forms: a SIMPLE IRA and a SIMPLE 401(k). Both plans became available in January 1997 to businesses with less than 100 employees, replacing the discontinued Salary Reduction Simplified Employee Pension (SARSEP) plans. They were intended to provide an easy, low-cost way for small businesses and their employees to contribute jointly to tax-deferred retirement accounts. An IRA or 401(k) set up as a SIMPLE account requires the employer to match up to 3 percent of an employee's annual salary, up to $6,000 per year. Employees are also allowed to contribute up to $6,000 annually to their own accounts. Companies that establish SIMPLEs are not allowed to offer any other type of retirement plan. As of early 1997, most small businesses chose the SIMPLE IRA option, as the SIMPLE 401(k) proved more expensive than a regular 401(k) due to the company matching requirements. The main problem with the plans, according to Stephen Blakely in *Nation's Business,* was that "Congress is already drafting legislation that would make SIMPLE less simple and more costly for the very businesses the plans were created to serve."

PROFIT SHARING PLANS Profit sharing plans enable employers to make a discretionary, tax deductible contribution on behalf of employees each year, based on the level of profits achieved by the business. The total annual contribution is generally allocated among employees as a percentage of their compensation. Plan costs are tax deductible for the employer, and plan earnings are tax deferred for employees. Profit sharing plans are easy to implement, offer design flexibility, and provide a wide range of investment choices. Eligibility is typically limited to employees who are at least 21 years of age and who have at least one year of service. The employer's maximum deduction is 15 percent of the total annual salaries paid to nonowner employees (adjusted to 13.04 percent for the small business owner).

A common variation is the age-based profit sharing plan, in which contributions are based on an allocation formula that factors in the age or number of years to retirement of participants. Age-based profit sharing allows employers to reward valued older employees for their length of service. Another variation is the new comparability profit sharing plan, which allows employers to define classes of employees and set up the retirement plan so that certain classes benefit the most in terms of allocation. These types of profit sharing plans are similar to defined benefit plans, but the employer contributions are discretionary.

MONEY PURCHASE PENSION PLANS Money purchase pension plans are similar to regular profit sharing plans, but the employer contributions are mandatory rather than discretionary. The main advantage of money purchase plans is that they allow larger employer contributions than regular profit sharing plans. The employer determines a fixed percentage of profits that will be allocated to employee retirement accounts according to a formula. The maximum employer contribution jumps to 25 percent of payroll for nonowner employees (adjusted to 20 percent for the small business owner) or a total of $30,000 per employee. There are also combination money purchase-profit sharing plans that allow employers to select a fixed percentage for mandatory contribution and also retain the option of contributing additional funds on a discretionary basis when cash flow permits.

401(K) PROFIT SHARING PLANS The popular 401(k) plans are profit sharing plans that include a provision for employees to defer part of their salaries for retirement. The employer can make annual profit sharing contributions on behalf of employees, the employees can contribute up to $9,500 (as of 1996) of pre-tax income themselves, and the employer can choose to match some portion of employee contributions. 401(k) plans offer a number of advantages. First, they allow both employer and employee to make contributions and gain tax advantages. Second, they can be set up in such a way that employees can borrow money from the plan. Third, 401(k) plans enable employees to become active participants in saving and investing for their retirement, which raises the level of perceived benefits provided by the employer. The main disadvantages are relatively high set up and administrative costs. Eligibility for 401(k) plans is typically limited to employees at least 21 years of age who have at least one year of service with the company.

Small businesses that establish 401(k)s must be careful to avoid liability for losses employees might suffer due to fluctuations in the value of plan investments. Under ERISA, plan sponsors can avoid liability by ensuring that their 401(k) meets three criteria: offering a broad range of investment options to employees; communicating sufficient financial information to employees; and allowing employees to exercise independent control over their accounts.

WHICH PLAN TO CHOOSE

Small business owners must carefully examine their priorities when selecting a retirement plan for themselves and their employees. If the main priority is to minimize administrative costs, a SEP plan may be the best choice. If it is important to have the flexibility of discretionary contributions, a profit sharing plan might be the answer. A money purchase plan would enable a small business owner to maximize contributions, but it would require an assurance of stable income, since contributions are mandatory. If the small business counts upon key older employees, an age-based profit sharing plan or a defined benefit plan would help reward and retain them. Conversely, an employer with a long time horizon until retirement would probably do best with a defined contribution plan. Finally, a small business owner who wants employees to be able to fund part of their own retirement should select a SIMPLE or a 401(k) plan. There are also many possibilities for combination plans that might provide a closer fit with a small business's goals. Free information on retirement plans is available through the Department of Labor at 800-998-7542, or on the Internet at www.dol.gov.

FURTHER READING:

Battle, Carl W. *Senior Counsel: Legal and Financial Strategies for Age 50 and Beyond.* New York: Alworth Press, 1993.

Blakely, Stephen. ''Pension Power.'' *Nation's Business.* July 1997.

Connor, John B., Jr. ''Pay Me Later.'' *Small Business Reports.* July 1994.

Crouch, Holmes F. *Decisions When Retiring.* Allyear Tax Guides, 1995.

Hunnisett, Henry S. *Retirement Guide: An Overall Plan for a Comfortable Future.* Bellingham, MA: Self-Counsel Press, 1990.

Martin, Ray. *Your Financial Guide: Advice for Every Stage of Your Life.* Macmillan, 1996.

Philip, Christine. ''Value of Defined Contribution Plans Debated.'' *Pensions and Investments.* February 20, 1995.

RETURN ON ASSETS

Return on assets (ROA) is a financial ratio that shows the percentage of profit that a company earns in relation to its overall resources. It is commonly defined as net income (or pretax profit) / total assets. ROA is known as a profitability or productivity ratio, because it provides information about management's performance in using the assets of the small business to generate income. ROA and other **financial ratios** can provide small business owners and managers with a valuable tool to measure their progress against predetermined internal goals, a certain competitor, or the overall industry. ROA is also used by bankers, investors, and business analysts to assess a company's use of resources and financial strength.

As James O. Gill noted in his book *Financial Basics of Small Business Success,* most entrepreneurs decide to start their own businesses in order to earn a better return on their money than would be available through a bank or other low-risk investments. If the ROA and other profitability ratios demonstrate that this is not occurring—particularly once a small business has moved beyond the start-up phase—then the entrepreneur should consider selling the business and reinvesting his or her money elsewhere.

It is important to note, however, that many factors can influence ROA, including a firm's degree of capitalization. "ROA favors highly capitalized institutions," Steven Davidson noted in an article for *America's Community Banker.* "Especially for such institutions, the ROA measure treats equity capital as 'free funds'—there is no 'cost' associated with them. Financial theory as well as common sense tells us that this is certainly not the case." As a result of this and other limitations, it is advisable to combine ROA with other measures of profitability and performance.

USES FOR ROA

Unlike other profitability ratios, such as return on equity (ROE), ROA measurements include all of a business's assets—including those which arise out of liabilities to creditors as well as those which arise out of contributions by investors. For this reason, ROA is usually of less interest to shareholders than some other financial ratios. However, the inclusion of liabilities makes ROA even more valuable as an internal measurement tool, particularly in evaluating the performance of different departments or divisions of companies.

"ROA is a good internal management ratio because it measures profit against all of the **assets** a division uses to make those earnings. Hence, it is a way to evaluate the division's profitability and effectiveness. It's also more appropriate here because division managers seldom get involved in raising money or in deciding the mix between debt and equity," James A. Kristy and Susan Z. Diamond wrote in their book *Finance without Fear.* "One of the cardinal rules in managing business professionals is to hold them accountable for only those activities they control. ROA comes close to doing just that."

Another common internal use for ROA involves evaluating the benefits of investing in a new system versus expanding a current system. The best choice will ideally increase productivity and income as well as reduce asset costs, resulting in an improved ROA

ratio. For example, say that a small manufacturing company with a current sales volume of $50,000, average assets of $30,000, and a net profit of $6,000 (giving it an ROA of $6,000 / $30,000 or 20 percent) must decide whether to improve its current inventory management system or install a new one. Expanding the current system would allow an increase in sales volume to $65,000 and in net profit to $7,800, but would also increase average assets to $39,000. Even though sales would increase, the ROA of this option would be the same—20 percent. On the other hand, installing a new system would increase sales to $70,000 and net profit to $12,250. Because the new system would allow the company to manage its inventory more efficiently, the average assets would increase only to $35,000. As a result, the ROA for this option would increase to 35 percent, meaning that the company should choose to install the new system.

FURTHER READING:

Allred, James K. "Looking at the Return on Assets." *Modern Materials Handling.* May 1997.

Bangs, David H., Jr. *Managing by the Numbers: Financial Essentials for the Growing Business.* Dover, NH: Upstart Publishing, 1992.

Casteuble, Tracy. "Using Financial Ratios to Assess Performance." *Association Management.* July 1997.

Davidson, Steven. "Measuring Profitability." *America's Community Banker.* October 1997.

Gill, James O. *Financial Basics of Small Business Success.* Menlo Park, CA: Crisp Publications, 1994.

Kristy, James E., and Susan Z. Diamond. *Finance without Fear.* New York: American Management Association, 1984.

Larkin, Howard. "How to Read a Financial Statement." *American Medical News.* March 11, 1996.

RETURN ON INVESTMENT

Return on investment (ROI) is a financial ratio that compares the amount of income derived from an investment with the cost of the investment. ROI is known as a profitability ratio, because it provides information about management's performance in using the resources of the small business to generate income. ROI and other financial ratios can provide small business owners and managers with a valuable tool to measure their progress against predetermined internal goals, a certain competitor, or the overall industry. ROI is also used by bankers, investors, and business analysts to assess a company's use of resources and financial strength.

As James O. Gill noted in his book *Financial Basics of Small Business Success,* most entrepreneurs decide to start their own businesses in order to earn a better return on their money than would be available through a bank or other low-risk investments. If the ROI and other profitability ratios demonstrate that this is not occurring—particularly once a small business has moved beyond the start-up phase—then the entrepreneur should consider selling the business and reinvesting his or her money elsewhere. However, it is important to note that many factors can influence ROI, including changes in price, volume, or expenses, as well the purchase of assets or the borrowing of money. In addition, ROI is limited by the fact that it focuses on one period of time and thus should be considered a short-term performance measure. Ignoring the long-term effects of investments can cause poor decision-making, so it is advisable to combine ROI with other measures of profitability and performance.

USES OF ROI

The general formula for computing ROI is income / invested **capital**. ROI can be computed on a company-wide basis by dividing **net income** by owners' equity. This measure indicates how well the overall company is utilizing its equity investment. Calculated in this way, ROI provides a good indicator of profitability that can be compared against competitors or an industry average. Experts suggest that companies usually need at least 10–14 percent ROI in order to fund future growth. If this ratio is too low, it can indicate poor management performance or a highly conservative business approach. On the other hand, a high ROI can either mean that management is doing a good job, or that the firm is undercapitalized.

ROI can also be computed for various divisions, product lines, or profit centers within a small business. In this way, it gives management a basis for comparing the performance of different areas. One large division may generate much higher profits than another, smaller division, for example, which might encourage management to consider investing further in that division. But an ROI analysis might reveal that a great deal more capital investment was required by the large division than by the smaller one. The smaller division may have generated a lower dollar amount of profit, but a greater percentage of profit on every dollar of investment. As Ronald W. Hilton wrote in his book *Managerial Accounting,* "The important question is not how much profit each division earned, but rather how effectively each division used its invested capital to earn a profit."

ROI can also be used to evaluate a proposed investment in new equipment by dividing the increase in profit attributable to the new equipment by the increase in invested capital needed to acquire it. For example, a small business may be able to save $5,000 in operating expenses (and thus raise profit by the same amount) by spending $25,000 on a piece of new equipment. This yields an ROI of $5,000 / $25,000 or 20 percent. If this figure is higher than the company's cost of capital (the interest paid on debt and the dividends paid to investors) prior to the investment, and no better investment opportunities exist for those funds, it may make sense to purchase the equipment.

In addition to the various uses ROI holds for a small business managers, it can also be a useful measure for investors. For example, a stockholder might calculate the return of investing in a company by the following formula: dividends + stock price change / stock price paid. This calculation of ROI measures the gain (or loss) achieved by placing an investment over a period of time.

FURTHER READING:

Bangs, David H., Jr. *Managing by the Numbers: Financial Essentials for the Growing Business.* Dover, NH: Upstart Publishing, 1992.

Casteuble, Tracy. "Using Financial Ratios to Assess Performance." *Association Management.* July 1997.

Gill, James O. *Financial Basics of Small Business Success.* Menlo Park, CA: Crisp Publications, 1994.

Hilton, Ronald W. *Managerial Accounting.* New York: McGraw-Hill, 1991.

Larkin, Howard. "How to Read a Financial Statement." *American Medical News.* March 11, 1996.

SEE ALSO: Risk and Return

RISK MANAGEMENT

Risk management involves identifying, analyzing, and taking steps to reduce or eliminate the exposures to loss faced by an organization or individual. The practice of risk management utilizes many tools and techniques, including insurance, to manage a wide variety of risks. Every business encounters risks, some of which are predictable and under management's control, and others which are unpredictable and uncontrollable. Risk management is particularly vital for small businesses, since some common types of losses—such as theft, fire, flood, legal liability, injury, or disability—can destroy in a few minutes what may have taken an entrepreneur years to build. Such losses and liabilities can affect day-to-day operations, reduce profits, and cause financial hardship severe enough to cripple or bankrupt a small business. But while many large companies employ a full-time risk manager to identify risks and take the necessary steps to protect the firm against them, small companies rarely have that luxury. Instead, the responsibility for risk management is likely to fall on the small business owner.

The term risk management is a relatively recent (within the last 20 years) evolution of the term "insurance management." The concept of risk management encompasses a much broader scope of activities and responsibilities than does insurance management. Risk management is now a widely accepted description of a discipline within most large organizations. Basic risks such as fire, windstorm, employee injuries, and automobile accidents, as well as more sophisticated exposures such as product liability, environmental impairment, and employment practices, are the province of the risk management department in a typical corporation. Although risk management has usually pertained to property and casualty exposures to loss, it has recently been expanded to include financial risk management, such as interest rates, foreign exchange rates, and derivatives.

STEPS IN THE RISK MANAGEMENT PROCESS

According to C. Arthur Williams Jr. and Richard M. Heins in their book *Risk Management and Insurance,* the risk management process typically includes six steps. These steps are 1) determining the objectives of the organization, 2) identifying exposures to loss, 3) measuring those same exposures, 4) selecting alternatives, 5) implementing a solution, and 6) monitoring the results. The primary objective of an organization—growth, for example—will determine its strategy for managing various risks. Identification and measurement of risks are relatively straightforward concepts. Earthquake may be identified as a potential exposure to loss, for example, but if the exposed facility is in New York the probability of earthquake is slight and it will have a low priority as a risk to be managed.

Businesses have several alternatives for the management of risk, including avoiding, assuming, reducing, or transferring the risks. Avoiding risks, or loss prevention, involves taking steps to prevent a loss from occurring, via such methods as employee safety training. As another example, a pharmaceutical company may decide not to market a drug because of the potential liability. Assuming risks simply means accepting the possibility that a loss may occur and being prepared to pay the consequences. Reducing risks, or loss reduction, involves taking steps to reduce the probability or the severity of a loss, for example by installing fire sprinklers.

Transferring risk refers to the practice of placing responsibility for a loss on another party via a contract. The most common example of risk transference is insurance, which allows a company to pay a small monthly premium in exchange for protection against automobile accidents, theft or destruction of property, employee disability, or a variety of other risks. Because of its costs, the insurance option is usually chosen when the other options for managing risk do not provide sufficient protection. Awareness of, and familiarity with, various types of insurance policies is a necessary part of the risk management process. A final risk management tool is self-retention of risks—sometimes referred to as "self-insurance." Companies that choose this option set up a special account or fund to be used in the event of a loss.

Any combination of these risk management tools may be applied in the fifth step of the process, implementation. The final step, monitoring, involves a regular review of the company's risk management tools to determine if they have obtained the desired result or if they require modification. *Nation's Business* outlined some easy risk management tools for small businesses: maintain a high quality of work; train employees well and maintain equipment properly; install strong locks, smoke detectors, and fire extinguishers; keep the office clean and free of hazards; back up computer data often; and store records securely off-site.

FURTHER READING:

Anastasio, Susan. *Small Business Insurance and Risk Management Guide.* Washington: U.S. Small Business Administration, n.d.

Blakely, Stephen. "Finding Coverage for Small Offices." *Nation's Business.* June 1997.

Head, George L., and Stephen Horn II. *Essentials of Risk Management.* Malvern, PA: Insurance Institute of America, 1991.

Lynn, Jacquelyn. "A Quick Guide to Insurance." *Entrepreneur.* June 1997.

Williams, C. Arthur Jr., and Richard M. Heins. *Risk Management and Insurance.* New York: McGraw-Hill, 1989.

SEE ALSO: Business Insurance; Workplace Safety

RISK AND RETURN

The term "risk and return" refers to the potential financial loss or gain experienced through investments in securities. An investor who has registered a profit is said to have seen a "return" on his or her investment. The "risk" of the investment, meanwhile, denotes the possibility or likelihood that the investor could lose money. If an investor decides to invest in a security that has a relatively low risk, the potential return on that investment is typically fairly small. Conversely, an investment in a security that has a high risk factor also has the potential to garner higher returns. **Return on investment** can be measured by nominal rate or real rate (money earned after the impact of inflation has been figured into the value of the investment).

Different securities—including common **stocks**, corporate **bonds**, government bonds, and Treasury bills—offer varying rates of risk and return. As Richard Brealey and Stewart Myers noted in their book *Principles of Corporate Finance,* ''Treasury bills are about as safe an investment as you can get. There is no risk of default and their short maturity means that the prices of Treasury bills are relatively stable.'' Long-term government bonds, on the other hand, experience price fluctuations in accordance with changes in the nation's interest rates. Bond prices fall when interest rates rise, but they rise when interest rates drop. Government bonds typically offer a slightly higher rate of return than Treasury bills.

Another type of security is corporate bonds. Those who invest in corporate bonds have the potential to enjoy a higher return on their investment than those who stay with government bonds. The greater potential benefits, however, are available because the risk is greater. ''Investors know that there is a risk of default when they buy a corporate bond,'' commented Brealey and Myers. Those corporations that have this default option, though, ''sell at lower prices and therefore higher yields than government bonds.'' In the meantime, investors ''still want to make sure that the company plays fair. They don't want it to gamble with their money or to take any other unreasonable risks. Therefore, the bond agreement includes a number of restrictive covenants to prevent the company from purposely increasing the value of its default option.''

Investors can also put their money into common stock. Common stockholders are the owners of a corporation in a sense, for they have ultimate control of the company. Their votes—either in person or by proxy—on appointments to the corporation's board of directors and other business matters often determine the company's direction. Common stock carries greater risks than other types of securities, but can also prove extremely profitable. Earnings or loss of money from common stock is determined by the rise or fall in the stock price of the company.

There are other types of company stock offerings as well. Companies sometimes issue preferred stock to investors. While owners of preferred stock do not typically have full voting rights in the company, no dividends can be paid on the common stock until after the preferred dividends are paid.

RISK AND RISK AVERSION

Many types of risk loom for investors hoping to see a return on their money, noted Jae K. Shim and Joel G. Siegel in their *Handbook of Financial Analysis, Forecasting, & Modeling.* Business risk refers to the financial impact of basic operations of the company. Earnings variable in this area include product demand, selling price, and cost. Liquidity risk is the possibility that an asset may not be sold for its market value on short notice, while default risk is the risk that

a borrower company will be unable to pay all obligations associated with a debt. Market risk alludes to the impact that market-wide trends can have on individual stock prices, while interest rate risk concerns the fluctuation in the value of the asset as a result of changes in interest rate, capital market, and money market conditions.

Individual risk aversion is thus a significant factor in the dynamics of risk and return. Cautious investors naturally turn to low-risk options such as Treasury bills or government bonds, while bolder investors often investigate securities that have the potential to generate significant returns on their investment. Certain types of common stock that fit this description include speculative stocks and penny stocks.

Many factors can determine the degree to which an investor is risk-averse. William Riley and K. Victor Chow contended in *Financial Analysts Journal* that ''relative risk aversion decreases as one rises above the poverty level and decreases significantly for the very wealthy. It also decreases with age—but only up to a point. After age 65 (retirement), risk aversion increases with age.'' Riley and Chow note that decreases in risk aversion often parallel higher degrees of education as well, but speculate that ''education, income and wealth are all highly correlated, so the relationship may be a function of wealth rather than education.''

Economically disadvantaged families are, on the surface, often seen as risk-averse; in actuality, however, decisions by these households to avoid investment risk can be traced to a lack of discretionary income or wealth, rather than any true aversion. As Riley and Chow noted, ''risk aversion can . . . be expected to decrease as an individual's wealth increases, independent of income. Someone whose stock of wealth is growing can be expected to become less risk-averse, as her tolerance of downside risk increases.''

FURTHER READING:

Bierman, Harold, Jr., and Seymour Smidt. *Financial Management for Decision Making.* New York: Macmillan, 1986.

Brealey, Richard, and Stewart Myers. *Principles of Corporate Finance.* 2d ed. New York: McGraw-Hill, 1984.

Brigham, Eugene F. *Financial Management: Theory and Practice.* Fort Worth: Dryden Press, 1991.

Riley, William B., Jr., and *K. Victor Chow. ''Asset Allocation and Individual Risk Aversion.''* Financial Analysts Journal. December, 1992.

Shim, Jae K., and Joel G. Siegel. *Handbook of Financial Analysis, Forecasting, & Modeling.* Englewood Cliffs, NJ: Prentice Hall, 1988.

SEE ALSO: Investor Relations and Reporting; Stocks

ROBOTICS

The Robotic Industries Association defines *robot* as follows: "A robot is a reprogrammable, multifunctional manipulator designed to move material, parts, tools or specialized devices through variable programmed motions for the performance of a variety of tasks." Recently, however, the industry's current working definition of a robot has come to be understood as any piece of equipment that has three or more degrees of movement or freedom.

Robotics is an increasingly visible and important component of modern business, especially in certain industries. Robotics-oriented production processes are most obvious in factories and manufacturing facilities; in fact, approximately 90 percent of all robots in operation today can be found in such facilities. But although these robots, termed "industrial robots," were found almost exclusively in automobile manufacturing plants as little as 10 to 15 years ago, industrial robots are now being used in laboratories, research and development facilities, warehouses, hospitals, energy-oriented industries (petroleum, nuclear power, etc.), and other areas. The costs associated with establishing manufacturing processes that rely on industrial robots have thus far limited the number of companies that have been able to fully employ robotics, but many business experts expect that, as robotics technology develops and implementation costs drop, smaller companies will increasingly be able to make use of robotics in their production processes as well.

ROBOTICS TECHNOLOGY

Today's robotics systems operate by way of hydraulic, pneumatic, and electrical power. Electric motors have become increasingly small, with high power-to-weight ratios, enabling them to become the dominant means by which robots are powered.

Robots are, of course, comprised of several different elements, depending on their purpose. The hand of a robot, for instance, is referred to in the industry as an end effector. End effectors may be specialized tools, such as spot welders or spray guns, or more general-purpose grippers. Common grippers include fingered and vacuum types. Another central element of robotics control technology is the sensor. It is through sensors that a robotic system receives knowledge of its environment, to which subsequent actions of the robot can be adjusted. Sensors are used to enable a robot to adjust to variations in the position of objects to be picked up, to inspect objects, and to monitor proper operation (although some robots are able to adjust to variations in object placement with-

out the use of sensors, provided they have sufficient end effector flexibility). Important sensor types include visual, force and torque, speed and acceleration, tactile, and distance sensors. The majority of industrial robots use simple binary sensing, analogous to an on/off switch. This does not permit sophisticated feedback to the robot as to how successfully an operation was performed. Lack of adequate feedback also often requires the use of guides and fixtures to constrain the motions of a robot through an operation, which implies substantial inflexibility in changing operations.

Robots are programmed either by guiding or by off-line programming. Most industrial robots are programmed by the former method. This involves manually guiding a robot from point to point through the phases of an operation, with each point stored in the robotic control system. With off-line programming, the points of an operation are defined through computer commands. This is referred to as manipulator level off-line programming. An important area of research is the development of off-line programming that makes use of higher-level languages, in which robotic actions are defined by tasks or objectives.

Robots may be programmed to move through a specified continuous path instead of from point to point. Continuous path control is necessary for operations such as spray painting or arc welding a curved joint. Programming also requires that a robot be synchronized with the automated machine tools or other robots with which it is working. Thus robot control systems are generally interfaced with a more centralized control system.

COMMON USES OF ROBOTICS

Industrial robotics have emerged as a popular manufacturing methodology in several areas in recent years, including welding, materials transport, assembly, and spray finishing operations.

SPOT AND ELECTRIC ARC WELDING Welding guns are heavy and the speed of assembly lines requires precise movement, thus creating an ideal niche for robotics. Parts can be welded either through the movement of the robot or by keeping the robot relatively stationary and moving the part past the robot. The latter method has come into widespread use since it generally requires less expensive conveyor systems. The control system of the robot must synchronize the robot with the speed of the assembly line and with other robots working on the line. Control systems may also count the number of welds completed and derive productivity data.

PICK AND PLACE OPERATIONS Industrial robots also perform what are referred to as pick and place operations. Among the most common of these operations is loading and unloading pallets, used across a broad range of industries. This requires relatively complex programming, as the robot must sense how full a pallet is and adjust its placements or removals accordingly. Robots have been vital in pick and place operations in the casting of metals and plastics. In the die casting of metals, for instance, productivity using the same die-casting machinery has increased up to three times, the result of robots' greater speed, strength, and ability to withstand heat in parts removal operations.

ASSEMBLY Assembly is one of the most demanding operations for industrial robots. A number of conditions must be met for robotic assembly to be viable, among them that the overall production system be highly coordinated and that the product be designed with robotic assembly in mind. The sophistication of the control system required implies a large initial capital outlay, which generally requires production of 100,000 to one million units per year in order to be profitable. Robotic assembly has come to be used in the production of a wide range of goods, including circuit boards, electronic components and equipment, household appliances, and automotive subassemblies.

SPRAY FINISHING OPERATIONS Industrial robots are widely used in spray finishing operations, particularly in the automobile industry. One of the reasons these operations are cost-effective is that they minimize the need for environmental control to protect workers from fumes.

Robots are also used for quality control inspections, since they can be programmed to quantitatively measure various aspects of a product's creation, and the use of robots in environmental applications, such as the cleaning of contaminated sites and the handling and analysis of hazardous materials, represent important growth markets for robotics producers.

Non-industrial applications for robots in security, commercial cleaning, food service, and health care are also on the rise.

FUTURE OF ROBOTICS

Recent research and development has addressed a number of aspects of robotics. Robotic hands have been developed which offer greater dexterity and flexibility, and improvements have been made in visual sensors as well (earlier generations of visual sensors were designed for use with television and home video, and did not process information quickly for optimal performance in many robotics applications; as a consequence, solid-state vision sensors came into increased use, and developments were also made with fiber optics). The use of superconducting materials, meanwhile, offers the possibility of substantial improvements in the electric motors that drive robotic arms. Attempts have also been made to develop lighter robotic arms and increase their rigidity. Stan-

dardization of software and hardware to facilitate the centralization of control systems has also been an important area of development in recent years. Indeed, "robots are simply more programmable and flexible than ever before," wrote *Tooling & Production* contributor Katina Z. Jones. "Multiple cells can be more easily accommodated and cybernetic gadgetry such as virtual reality and computer simulation have added a new dimension to the sales and installation of robotics."

FURTHER READING:

"Accuracy is Only Relative on Robotics, Automation." *Tooling & Production.* November 1996.

Alkhafaji, Abbas F. "Strategic Applications of Robotics Technology." *Management Decision.* July 1991.

Bergstrom, Robin P. "Common Sense and Robot Use." *Production.* February 1993.

Breger, Bill, and Angela Charles. "Strong Sales Favor U.S. Robot Production." *Plastic News.* November 29, 1993.

Donleavy, G. D. "Evaluating the Potential of Office Robotics." *Long Range Planning.* April 1994.

Dorf, Richard, ed. *Concise International Encyclopedia of Robotics: Applications and Automation.* New York: John Wiley & Sons, 1990.

"The Droid Void Is Ending." *Ward's Auto World.* January 1994.

Durrant-Whyte, H. F. *Integration, Coordination and Control of Multi-Sensor Robot Systems.* Kluwer Academic Press, 1988.

Jasany, Leslie C. "Knowledge (and Power) to the People." *Automation.* July 1990.

Jones, Katina Z. "Robots Serve Up New Directions." *Tooling & Production.* April 1995.

Taylor, P. M. *Understanding Robotics.* Washington: CRC Press, 1990.

SEE ALSO: Automation

ROYALTY FINANCING

Royalty financing is a relatively new concept that offers an alternative to regular **debt financing** (loans and trade credit) and **equity financing** (venture capital and stock sales). In a royalty financing arrangement, a small business would receive a specific amount of funds from an investor or group of investors. This money might be put toward launching a new product or expanding the company's marketing efforts. In exchange, the investors would receive a percentage of the company's future revenues over a certain period of time, up to a specific amount. The investment can be considered an "advance" to the company, and the periodic percentage payments can be considered "royalties" to the investors.

Royalty financing arrangements offer a number of advantages to small businesses. Compared to equity financing, royalty financing enables entrepreneurs to obtain **capital** without giving up a significant ownership position in the company to outside investors. The founders of the company are thus able to preserve their equity position, which may help motivate them toward continued success. In addition, royalty financing arrangements—since they most resemble loans—are not subject to state and federal securities laws, as some equity financing deals are. Thus the company is able to save the time and money it might otherwise devote to complex filings and legal fees. Royalty financing also increases a company's ability to structure deals with individual investors, who might be attracted to the idea of receiving a monthly or quarterly yield over the life of their investment. In contrast, equity financing arrangements often show no yield until the stock is sold.

Compared to debt financing, royalty financing provides more convenient payback terms and less severe penalties for default. In addition, the infusion of cash may help the company increase sales, which may make it a better candidate to obtain more financing later. Finally, royalty financing enables a small business to keep its options open for later financing rounds. In contrast, a company that incurs significant debt or sells a great deal of equity in its early stages may find it difficult to attract investment later.

DETAILS OF ROYALTY FINANCING

As an example, suppose that a small business obtains an ''advance'' of $100,000 against future sales from individual investors or an economic development organization. In exchange, the investors would receive 3 percent of the company's total sales for a 10 year period, to a maximum of $300,000. If the company repaid the investment over 10 years, then the investors would earn a compound annual return of 11.6 percent. However, if the investors reached their maximum royalties of $300,000 in half that time, the initial investment would yield an annual return of 24.5 percent.

A small business interested in royalty financing may be able to negotiate a grace period, so that royalties will not begin to accrue for a quarter or more following the close of the deal. It may also be possible to establish a lag between the time revenues are realized by the company and the time royalties are paid to investors. This sort of arrangement can give the small business time to put the capital to work and increase sales before paying a percentage of sales as royalties. In most cases, these arrangements are acceptable to investors since they still offer a better deal than most equity financing arrangements, which only pay when the stock is sold.

In an article for *Entrepreneur,* David R. Evanson noted that royalty financing may tend to work best for small businesses that have some elasticity in pricing, so that they can raise prices to cover the percentage of royalties without losing customers. Royalty financing is also suitable for companies for which increased marketing efforts have an immediate impact on sales. However, royalty financing may not be a good option for companies with very tight profit margins. In summary, the capital gained through royalty financing can enable a fledgling business to launch a new product or expand its marketing efforts without having to give up too much equity in the early stages. In royalty financing, investors own a piece of the company's revenue stream rather than a piece of the company itself.

FURTHER READING:

Evanson, David R. ''Cash Is King: Royalty Financing Keeps Investors Happy—and Keeps Your Company in Your Own Hands.'' *Entrepreneur.* December 1997.

RURAL BUSINESSES

Rural businesses are those firms that are established and operate in rural settings, far from the metropolitan areas that have traditionally been the site of most non-agricultural business enterprises. Most businesses continue to conduct business in large cities or thriving suburbs, but analysts contend that technological advances, demographic changes, and increased attention to ''quality of life'' considerations have all combined to spur meaningful business growth in many rural areas as well.

Increased receptiveness to new businesses has also had an impact on the growth of commerce in some rural regions. As Brian Steinberg observed in *Entrepreneur* in 1997, ''many small towns in states such as Iowa and Indiana are crying out for new businesses. Dependent for generations on sagging agricultural or manufacturing economies, these towns need entrepreneurs and the jobs they supply to stay economically viable.''

CHARACTERISTICS OF RURAL BUSINESSES Commenting in the *OECD Observer,* Chantal Illouz-Winicki and Dennis Paillard discussed unique features of business creation in rural areas. For example, the majority of growth in rural economies comes from existing business enterprises rather than new ones, particularly in the industrial sector. This is by no means an indication that new businesses—industrial or otherwise—cannot survive in rural settings. It merely means that existing businesses are particularly well-equipped to continue once they have established themselves. Reasons for this include the higher percentage of family-owned businesses in smaller towns (which helps with issues of long-term continuity), less competition in local markets, and what Illouz-Winicki and Paillard described as "more determination when firms run into difficulties, through a genuine or perceived lack of alternatives."

Experts have also noted that businesses in rural areas tend to be characterized by their activities. Companies that specialize in providing personal services (such as propane delivery or rubbish removal) are commonplace, since there is a large and steady demand for these services, which in more metropolitan areas would be handled by companies armed with city contracts. Manufacturing establishments, on the other hand, are more scarce because of transportation and work force issues. "In isolated areas, business creation is usually aimed at local consumer markets (retailing, community services) or new market niches (products with a strong regional identity)," said Illouz-Winicki and Paillard. "In more accessible areas it is aimed more at services or intermediate goods (sub-contracting). It is notable that business services, from office maintenance to consulting, are still under-represented in rural areas because local markets are so small."

FACTORS IN RURAL BUSINESS GROWTH

The growing appetite for a simpler, more relaxed way of life has long been touted as a primary reason for the increase in rural businesses in recent years. Certainly, this has been a factor, but several other considerations warrant mention as well, including general economic conditions, **demographic** changes, and new modes of communication such as the Internet. Of course, not all rural regions experience business growth at the same rate; indeed, some rural areas continue to flounder even as others blossom with new business opportunities. "It is not easy to explain why an area is dynamic, or backward," admitted Illouz-Winicki and Paillard. "Complex forces are at work: specific local factors, structures and aspects that are hard to assess precisely, such as cultural traditions, business networks, and an attractive natural setting."

DEMOGRAPHIC CHANGES Business experts believe that demographic changes will likely continue to encourage growth in rural businesses over the next few decades. As more and more "baby boomers" enter into retirement age with disposable income, analysts point to rural businesses as some of that trend's chief beneficiaries. Moreover, this trend transcends national boundaries, for it can be seen not only in the United States, but in Canada, Europe, and other regions of the world. "Catering for senior citizens is a potential source of activity whose scale has to be assessed without delay," said Illouz-Winicki and Paillard. "This social group, more mobile than earlier genera-

tions, often with more disposable income than the rest of the population, is of growing demographic and economic importance. Rural areas are already benefiting from this trend in tourism, in high season and at other periods; and senior citizens are also becoming new residents, either temporary or permanent."

TRAVEL AND TOURISM The tremendous growth in the travel industry has been a significant source of income for many small towns in rural settings. Indeed, economists cite the travel and tourism industry as an engine of terrific economic growth in many rural areas that are blessed with notable natural or cultural surroundings. Many small towns located near national parks, sites of historical interest, and scenic areas have seen a surge in businesses aimed at nabbing tourist dollars, and many rural regions have ridden the growth in travel and tourism to new levels of economic prosperity. Of course, this is not a meaningful factor for many rural areas that are not situated in the vicinity of a national park or other popular tourist destination. Still, many rural city planners have successfully spurred new levels of economic activity by marketing attractive elements of the region (lakes and rivers, festivals, or historical sites) in order to draw tourists.

THE INTERNET AND OTHER TELECOMMUNICATIONS ADVANCES The amazing capacities of the Internet and other relatively new means of **telecommunications** have enabled business owners in even the most remote locations to dramatically expand their potential customer base. "Small remote communities are attempting to bridge their isolation by taking their businesses and even their local governments online," wrote David Goodman in *Inc.* "'Community networking,' as the phenomenon is known, brings the Internet to people in far-flung outposts. Rural businesses have seized the opportunity to play in the big leagues, with entrepreneurs of every stripe now hawking their wares in cyberspace." Goodman cited the following as key steps for any rural business community hoping to establish an online presence:

1) Organize—This step could take the form of arranging Internet training for local business owners and managers.

2) Outreach—"Talk to people and community organizations face-to-face to explain how the Internet can help their business.

3) Educate—According to Goodman, providing classes on Internet use to both employees and the larger community can help rural businesses "develop a critical mass of technoliterate citizens."

4) Target—Provide workshops and training seminars specifically tailored to individual business sectors so that their membership

can see how an Internet presence can benefit them.

5) Provide Access—Small towns should follow the lead of their larger brethren, which often provide the public with free access to the Internet at local libraries or community centers.

Finally, the rise of telecommuting and other communication advances has made it increasingly possible for software developers, freelance writers, graphic artists, and others who maintain home-based businesses to establish themselves wherever they wish, provided they have reliable computer and/or postal resources at their disposal.

COMMON OBSTACLES TO BUSINESS GROWTH IN RURAL AREAS

A significant percentage of new businesses in rural areas are established businesses that relocate. Indeed, many entrepreneurs have established their business ventures in rural regions of the country in recent years. This trend has been especially evident among small business owners who have decided to relocate for "quality of life" reasons. These entrepreneurs are sometimes limited in their relocation options by customer demographics and other factors, but the desire for quieter, less hectic lifestyles has proven to be a potent one, as families search for homes that are not bedeviled by traffic, crime, and other attributes often associated with large cities.

Nonetheless, small business owners are urged to weigh the obstacles that often confront businesses that decide to relocate in rural locations. These hurdles range from different cultural standards and finding new friends to negotiating new ways of transporting goods or finding quality employees. In addition, services in rural areas often do not match those that can be routinely relied upon in more metropolitan areas. Unreliable electrical service, skimpy or nonexistent overnight delivery options, and increased telecommunications costs (for regular telephone service as well as Internet connections) can all complicate the efforts of businesses in rural locations. These difficulties can be particularly problematic for businesses that are involved in high-tech areas. "For technology-dependent businesses to thrive in remote areas, connecting a computer to the Internet is the easy part," wrote Goodman. "Finding employees who have the savvy to use the technology or . . . finding someone to fix your computer can be far more challenging."

FURTHER READING:

Goodman, David. "Small Town, Big Connections: Community Networking Gives Rural Business a Chance to Play in the Big Leagues." *Inc.* June 18, 1996.

Illouz-Winicki, Chantal, and Dennis Paillard. "New Business in Rural Areas." *OECD Observer.* February-March 1998.

Pezzini, Mario. "Entrepreneurial Towns." *OECD Observer.* December 1995-January 1996.

Steinberg, Brian. "Green Acres: Why Some Entrepreneurs are Saying 'Goodbye, City Life.' " *Entrepreneur.* October 1997.

Steingold, Fred S. *Legal Guide for Starting and Running a Small Business.* 3d ed. Nolo Press, 1997.

Stickey, Marcia. "Home-Grown Businesses Find Rural Niche: Rural States Need to Break Out of the Urban Economic Development Mold." *Successful Farming.* February 1995.

Venable, Tim. "Getting Better Location Assistance: Here's How." *Site Selection.* April 1996.

Weber, Fred I., Jr. *Locating or Relocating Your Business.* U.S. Small Business Administration, n.d.

SEE ALSO: Business Site Selection; Target Markets

S

A small business has the option of incorporating at the beginning of its existence or after years of doing business. Once it incorporates, it has two choices: to be a regular **C corporation** by default or to elect S corporation status, a name derived from Subchapter S of the Internal Revenue Code. This status was derived in an effort to make incorporating more attractive to small businesses and allow them to enjoy some of the benefits of corporate status while avoiding some of the drawbacks. While most small businesses are eligible for S status, there are some requirements that must be met, such as limitations on the number and kind of stockholders the corporation may have.

In *Choosing a Legal Structure for Your Business*, Stuart Handmaker explains that "Essentially, there isn't any difference between a C corporation and an S corporation. Each of them is a corporation, and each one has the same characteristics, shareholders, directors, officers, records, minute books, problems, and the like. The only real difference is that the S corporation has filed a special form with the Internal Revenue Service stating that it wants to be an S corporation." What makes the S corporation different from the C corporation, then, is that it has special status in the eyes of the IRS. In short, the S corporation is viewed as a partnership or sole proprietorship for taxation purposes. This means that the corporation itself is not taxed, as C corporations are; rather the S corporation's profits are passed on to its shareholders, who pay income tax on that money. In nearly all other respects, though, the S corporation is essentially the same as the C corporation. Most importantly, S corporations re-

ceive the benefit of limited liability that goes along with being a corporation. The combined benefits of limited liability (the lack of which is the main drawback of partnerships or sole proprietorships) and avoidance of double taxation (the main drawback of C corporations) makes the S corporation the most popular legal structure amongst small business owners.

BECOMING AN S CORPORATION

FILING WITH THE INTERNAL REVENUE SERVICE Once a business has gone through the procedure of becoming a corporation by filing the **articles of incorporation**, etc., it can elect S corporation status by filing form 2553 with the IRS. All of the corporation's shareholders must sign this form or file special shareholder consent forms. These rules apply to anyone who has held stock in the company during the current tax year. To be eligible for S corporation status for the current tax year, a corporation must file the form by the fifteenth day of the third month of the corporation's tax year. Once the form has been filed, it is not necessary to file every year.

ELIGIBILITY For a corporation to be eligible for S corporation status, the following conditions must be met and maintained:

- The business must have become a corporation prior to filing for S corporation status. See **Incorporation** for more information on this process.

- The business must also have no more than 75 stockholders. Until the Small Business Job Protection Act of 1996 was passed, corporations with more than 35 shareholders were disqualified, but now the limit is 75, allowing most small businesses to fall within the guidelines.

- All of the business's stock must be owned by individuals who reside in or are citizens of the United States. Estates or trusts may be allowed as stockholders, but corporate or foreign investors are not allowed. This includes other businesses that are not corporations, such as partnerships or sole proprietorships. This provision, therefore, excludes corporate subsidiaries from claiming S corporation status.

- The business must issue only one class of stock. This means that with the purchase of stock must come the same economic rights, such as receiving dividends or compensation in the event of liquidation at the same time and in the same amount per share as all other shareholders. Voting rights may differ amongst the shareholders without being considered a sign of the possession of different classes of stock.

INELIGIBLE BUSINESSES Those businesses that are ineligible for S corporation status include:

- All financial institutions, such as banks and savings and loans;

- Insurance companies;

- Businesses that receive ninety-five percent or more of their gross income from exports (also known as DISCs, Domestic International Sales Corporations);

- Corporations that use the possessions tax credit;

- C Corporations that have been S corporations within the last five years.

BENEFITS OF S CORPORATION STATUS

LIMITED LIABILITY Like C corporations, S corporations are considered to be separate entities apart from their owners for all purposes except taxation. This means that debts incurred by the corporation are the responsibility of the corporation, not its shareholders, who can only be held accountable only up to the amount they invested in the corporation. If the corporation does not possess enough assets to pay its debts, the shareholders will not be required to make up the difference out of their own pockets. In addition, if the corporation is sued, liability rests on the shoulders of the corporation, not its shareholders.

AVOIDING DOUBLE TAXATION According to the Internal Revenue Service, an S corporation is not a separate taxable entity. Instead, the corporation's profits are considered to be the shareholders' income

(whether the money is distributed or not). Therefore, the corporation's earnings turn up on the shareholders' personal federal tax returns, the amount of which must be proportional to their share of stock. This can be a beneficial arrangement for many small businesses, because the money is taxed only once on the federal level. (State and local taxes may still be levied against the corporation.) C corporations, on the other hand, are required to pay a federal corporate tax on all profits, and then the shareholders must pay income taxes on their share of dividends that are distributed once the corporation tax has been deducted. In essence, then, that money has been taxed twice. In the case of businesses that intend to leave most of the profits in the corporation or reinvest significant portions of the profits back into the business, though, C corporation status may be preferential if the corporate tax bracket is lower that your personal tax rate. But for companies that plan to pay shareholders all or most of the profits, S corporation status helps them avoid **double taxation**. **Professional corporations** may also desire to elect S corporation status as they are often taxed at a higher rate than a regular C corporation. In addition, corporations that plan to conduct business in more than one state will find it easier to register to do so as an S corporation than as a C corporation. In the case of asset liquidation, S corporation status can also be a benefit because the appreciated value is taxed only on the shareholders' personal income tax. In the case of C corporations, the sale of appreciated assets can result in double taxation because the profit is taxed to the corporation and then to the shareholders to whom it is distributed.

LOSSES AS PERSONAL DEDUCTIONS When an S corporation ends the year with a loss, that loss appears on the shareholders' personal income tax returns, just like profits do. This can mean substantial savings for shareholders, who will end up owing less (or even no) taxes after they deduct their share of the corporation's loss (proportional to their share of stock). In fact, many new small businesses that expect to start off with a loss elect S status so that they will receive this tax credit.

DRAWBACKS OF S CORPORATION STATUS

RECORDKEEPING AND ATTENTION TO DETAIL Because an S corporation is still a corporation, it requires owners to pay careful attention to the details of recordkeeping. In some cases, businesses that did file for S corporation status have not been viewed as such by the courts because they failed to act like corporations. In other words, some small businesses simply apply for the status in hopes of gaining limited liability protection, but they fail to keep separate personal and corporate accounts, for example, or to hold regular director's and shareholders' meetings and take minutes, all of which are requirements for corporations. They may also neglect to change their name to reflect their new corporate status in an effort to avoid the extra cost of ordering new stationary and business cards and changing their sign. As a result, the owners of such companies have been known to be found personally liable just as if their business was a **sole proprietorship** or **partnership**. Simply filing the articles of incorporation does not guarantee limited liability. Moreover, an S corporation may be reverted to C corporation status if it fails to continually meet the eligibility requirements, another factor which requires attention to detail. The sale of stock to one foreign investor, for example, could mean the termination of S corporation status, and once a corporation reverts to C corporation status, it is not eligible to file for S status for another five years. This could be a costly error. Simply filing for S corporation status, therefore, does not guarantee protection from double taxation.

DOUBLE TAXATION FOR COMPANIES SWITCHING FROM C STATUS Businesses that start out as C corporations and change their status to that of S corporations may still be taxed as corporations if certain conditions exist. Corporations switching status from C to S and possessing capital gains, excessive passive investment gains, investment tax credits, or liquidations may be still be subject to double taxation.

FRINGE BENEFITS Unlike C corporations—but like partnerships—S corporations are not allowed to deduct fringe benefits given to shareholders who are employees as a business expense. As a result, shareholder-employees must pay taxes on those benefits. These rules apply to all shareholders who own more than two percent of the corporation's stock and are employees of the corporation. All non-shareholder employees, though, may receive benefits without paying taxes.

STOCK LIMITATIONS To remain eligible for S corporation status, a corporation is only allowed to issue one class of stock, which may be a deterrent to businesses that would like to issue preferred as well as common stock. In addition, a limit of 75 stockholders is placed on the S corporation, and all stockholders must be individuals who reside in or are citizens of the United States. The small business corporation, therefore, is denied the benefit of foreign investors in an increasingly global business world.

TERMINATING S CORPORATION STATUS

It is possible for an S corporation to voluntarily revoke its status if it finds that S status is no longer beneficial, or to lose the status involuntarily. In the first case, a majority of the stockholders is required to make the decision, and a simple notification to the IRS is all that is required. In the second case, any act which disqualifies the corporation's eligibility for S status will result in the termination of that status effective on the date that the infraction occurs. In either case, the corporation becomes a C corporation in the absence of S corporation status.

FURTHER READING:

Cooke, Robert A. *How to Start Your Own (Subchapter) S Corporation.* New York: John Wiley & Sons, 1995.

Goldstein, Arnold S. *Starting Your Subchapter ''S'' Corporation.* New York: John Wiley & Sons, 1988.

Handmaker, Stuart A. *Choosing a Legal Structure for Your Business.* Upper Saddle River, NJ: Prentice Hall, 1997.

J.K Lasser Institute. *How to Run a Small Business.* New York: McGraw-Hill, 1994.

Nichols, Ted. *How to Form Your Own ''S'' Corporation and Avoid Double Taxation.* Chicago, IL: Upstart Publishing, 1995.

Selecting the Legal Structure for Your Business Washington: U.S. Small Business Administration. n.a.

Steingold, Fred S. *The Legal Guide for Starting and Running a Small Business.* 2d ed. Berkeley, CA: Nolo Press, 1995.

SALES COMMISSIONS

The sales commission is a method of compensating members of the **sales force** for the services they provide to their employer. Under so-called ''straight'' commission arrangements, the salesperson receives a previously agreed-upon percentage of the revenue brought in by a sale that he or she makes. Commission arrangements can be used for both service and product sectors. Some employers, however, choose to compensate their salespeople via straight salaries, thus compensating them in the same way as other employees, or via a combination of salary and commission. The chief advantage associated with utilizing a straight commission arrangement is that it gives salespeople a major incentive to work hard on behalf of the company, but detractors contend that the compensation uncertainties associated with such plans sometimes make it difficult to secure good salespeople, and that their complete dependence on commissions may lead them into bad business habits. Even detractors, however, admit that commission set ups do provide salespeople with meaningful incentive to work hard. As a result, the majority of businesses that maintain a sales force use some combination of base salary and commission—also known as incentive pay—to compensate their salespeople. ''Because selling is so difficult, salespeople need to be trained, supported, and, above all, motivated,'' confirmed *The Portable MBA in Entrepreneurship.* ''They need sales literature, administrative support to send out promotional material, and presentation graphics. They also need *incentives* that work—the right combination of commissions, prizes, stock, and whatever else you dream up. What are you doing in these areas and what do you plan for the future to upgrade your selling efforts?''

Some small- and mid-sized businesses have been known to balk at the size of the commissions that they pay to their top-level salespeople. Indeed, businesses that are engaged in industry sectors that are known for the sale and acquisition of so-called "big ticket" items, such as major equipment, or large-volume purchases may distribute commissions of several thousand dollars or more for a single sale. But most business consultants urge employers to remember that if they are doling out large commissions, that also means that those same salespeople are bringing in lots of business for the company. As the editors of *The Portable MBA in Entrepreneurship* indicated, "a good rule to follow is that when you find something that works, stay with it, even if it means paying what seems to be obscene amounts of cash. The best salespeople should earn top dollar.''

BASIC COMPENSATION PLANS FOR SALESPEOPLE

Companies generally compensate their salespeople in one of three ways: straight commission, straight salary, or salary plus additional incentive (often commission).

STRAIGHT COMMISSION Under straight commission compensation arrangements, the salesperson receives a previously agreed-upon percentage of the selling price. The size of the percentage of the commission may vary from product to product. Business experts estimate that fewer than 15 percent of American firms pay their salespeople on a straight commission basis, although the majority of those companies that do choose this method of compensation indicate satisfaction with it. The primary benefit associated with this option, of course, is that it serves as a significant motivator to sales personnel. Moreover, companies that go this route are not forced to pay high salaries to salespeople during periods when sales are slow. But Porter Henry and Joseph Callanan, authors of *Sales Management and Motivation,* indicated that there are potentially significant disadvantages associated with straight commission plans as well. In some cases, salespeople may concentrate on selling those products that are easiest to sell, paying comparatively little attention to high-profit specialty items or new products that are unfamiliar to prospective buyers. One solution to this problem is to pay higher commissions on those new or high-profit goods. Another problem associated with straight commissions is that salespeople may not put forth as much efforts after they reach a certain level of income. In such instances, Henry and Callanan recommended that businesses "adopt a slid-

ing scale, with commissions increasing after a certain volume has been reached.'' Other potential disadvantages associated with straight commission compensation, said Henry and Callanan, include:

1) Problems hiring new sales personnel— "Candidates for sales jobs are more security-conscious than they were in the past. Some quite desirable applicants may be unwilling or unable to face a few months of inadequate income before building up a satisfactory volume.''

2) High turnover—Another employee retention issue. Many good salespeople will choose to go to some other company that features a more secure employee compensation program, unless they are performing quite well under your arrangement. And even then, salespeople with families are may well decide that long-term security— embodied in a steady salary—is preferable to high levels of compensation that could dwindle away with the next industry downturn.

3) Execution of nonselling tasks—Straight commission arrangements often encourage an environment wherein salespeople ignore non-sales related tasks that nonetheless need to be addressed. "You can't blame them,'' wrote Henry and Callanan. "Commission reps are in effect in business for themselves; they get paid for selling, and only for selling. Unless the nonselling jobs (such as taking inventory, setting up displays, collecting back debts) directly contribute to future sales, you're taking money right out of their pockets by asking reps to perform them. Some companies have found it advisable to pay salespeople a nominal fee for handling such duties.''

STRAIGHT SALARY The most frequent criticism of compensation plans that pay sales representatives a straight salary is that they eliminate the employees' incentive to perform. As one sales executive told *Sales and Marketing Management,* companies that offer aggressive incentive structures create hunger among their salespeople, while those that offer comfortable base salaries foster an environment of complacency. Other analysts contend, however, that this admitted drawback can be neutralized to some degree by creating a company culture that rewards top-notch sales performances with prompt salary increases and/or promotions.

SALARY PLUS COMMISSION OR OTHER INCENTIVES This arrangement is by far the most common one employed by organizations that use salespeople. Proponents tout several meaningful advantages associated with compensation plans that combine base salaries with commissions:

- Motivates sales force to expend greater effort.

- Provides company with a way to extend additional rewards to its best sales performers.

- Closely ties compensation to performance (though not to the same degree as straight commission arrangements).

- Generally easy to administer.

- Depending on the arrangement, the bestowal of increased security to employees may allow the company to take a greater percentage of sales profits.

Criticisms of compensation plans that combine salary with commissions or other incentives are usually framed not as rebukes of its philosophical underpinnings, but rather as laments concerning its execution. For example, some companies may offer only token commissions, which do little to foster aggressive salesmanship.

In addition to commissions, some companies choose to provide non-salary compensation to their sales force through **expense accounts, leasing automobiles**, advances against future earnings (usually commission), or sales contests.

Expense accounts are common features in many industries. Indeed, salespeople in a wide range of industry sectors depend a great deal on business lunches, etc. to close deals. Moreover, salespeople often are responsible for large territories, which makes long hours of travel a fundamental element of their job description. Organizations that do not compensate such individuals with expense accounts—or free use of leased automobiles—are likely to have considerable difficulty finding and retaining gifted salespeople. Indeed, most prospective hires will view refusal to take care of expenses as a sure sign of company stinginess and an indication that the company's ownership may not be cognizant of basic business realities.

Sales contests are another popular tool used by business owners to encourage sales activities. Under these programs, sales personnel who meet certain sales goals are rewarded with cash bonuses, paid vacations, etc. But business experts contend that sales contests can have unintended consequences for organizations if they are poorly defined or structured so that only a small segment of the sales force is rewarded. Indeed, some organizations provide incentives only to a certain percentage of top-level performers. Such programs—whether commissions or sales contests—are usually implemented in hopes of creating a competitive environment, but all too often they

have the opposite effect. "Sure, your top salespeople are thrilled about the program—for them, it most likely means another trip to Hawaii or Europe," wrote Melanie Berger in *Sales and Marketing Management*. "But for the vast majority of your sales force, the incentive is yet another opportunity to do one thing: lose. And nobody feels good about losing. All too often, executives planning incentive programs for their sales forces assume they need to motive and reward their top performers—the ones who already generate the bulk of their business. Less successful— shall we say, average—players are ignored, left to remain, well, average."

In order to counteract the negative characteristics associated with traditional sales contests, many business consultants recommend that businesses instead institute so-called "open-ended" incentive programs. These programs are designed so that participants compete against their own past performances rather than their fellow salespeople. As one sales manager told Berger, "very often with closed-ended programs [traditional programs in which salespeople compete against one another for a limited number of rewards], people use the excuse, 'Her territory is better than mine' or, 'They were lucky and closed a big sale; it was the right place at the right time.' The incentive programs that work the best are the ones that are considered fair. What's fair is to have people competing against themselves—that way you're being compared to what you've done in the past, not what the guy next to you is doing." In addition, Berger noted that open-ended programs can be shaped in two-tiered fashion so that a business's very best sales performers receive some extra recognition. For example, salespeople that increase their sales by 10 percent might receive a nice prize, while those that increase their sales by 20 percent would receive an even better one. Open programs, said Berger, can be used in place of closed programs so that "rather than getting better results from just a small number of salespeople, companies can potentially inspire improved performance from all of them. And that translates into increased sales and a stronger bottom line."

Berger did note, however, that there are two objections that are commonly raised to open-ended sales incentives. The first is that such initiatives cast greater uncertainty on sales budgeting efforts. After all, companies that offer an open program "don't know in advance how many winners they'll have or how many prizes they'll need to award." In addition, some observers contend that open programs actually can detract from the performance of a business's top salespeople. "If all reps have to do to win is increase sales by 15 percent, the top producers in an open-ended program could hit that mark well before the year is over, and coast the rest of the way," said Berger. But the impact of both of these negative attributes can be largely neutralized through careful planning (such as studying multi-tiered programs) and continuous monitoring.

FUTURE CHALLENGES

Business researchers believe that companies will have to continually adjust their sales commission/incentives packages in the coming years in order to remain competitive since the overall business environment is changing so rapidly. For example, salespeople are now seen as more likely to move not only from business to business but also from industry to industry. "Salespeople, despite their market specialization, have one thing in common: They want to make lots of money," observed Michele Marchetti in *Sales and Marketing Management*. "And these high-performing people will seek out companies with competitive pay plans—regardless of the industry." In addition, increased emphasis on customer satisfaction and increasing market share with current customers is likely to broaden the responsibilities of salespeople, who will in turn expect to be compensated appropriately. "Today's selling environment is frustrating and fascinating," said Marchetti. "Technology is propelling us into a new way of thinking about business strategy and the way we define success. As always, though, salespeople will do what they're rewarded for doing. That's why compensation plans have to keep up with the changing selling methods. Sales managers must motivate their reps to build real relationships between customers and company, in order to increase the share of each customer's business and to increase the value of each customer to the company."

FURTHER READING:

Berger, Melanie. "When Their Ship Comes In: How to Create an Incentive Program that Motivates All of Your Salespeople—and Sends More Happy Winners on that Coveted Trip." *Sales and Marketing Management*. April 1997.

Bygrave, William D., ed. *The Portable MBA in Entrepreneurship*. 2d ed. New York: John Wiley & Sons, 1997.

Henry, Porter, and Joseph Callanan. *Sales Management and Motivation*. New York: Franklin Watts, 1987.

Marchetti, Michele. "Developing a Competitive Pay Plan: the Key—Benchmarking Your Reps' Compensation Against Other Industries." *Sales and Marketing Management*. April 1997.

Marchetti, Michele. "Rewarding Team Players." *Sales and Marketing Management*. April 1996.

Meyer, Harvey R. "Linking Payday to Cash in Hand." *Nation's Business*. May 1996.

Peppers, Don, and Martha Rogers. "The Money Trap." *Sales and Marketing Management*. May 1997.

"Rethinking the Salesforce." *Management Today*. July 1995.

SEE ALSO: Employee Compensation; Employee Motivation; Sales Management

SALES CONTRACTS

A sales contract is an agreement between a buyer and seller covering the sale and delivery of goods, securities, and personal property other than goods or securities. In the United States, domestic sales contracts are governed by the **Uniform Commercial Code**. International sales contracts fall under the United Nations Convention on Contracts for the International Sale of Goods (CISG), also known as the Vienna Sale Convention.

Under Article 2 of the UCC, which has been adopted by every state except Louisiana, the District of Columbia, and the Virgin Islands, a contract for the sale of goods for more than $500 must be in writing in order to be enforceable (UCC 2-201). The sale of securities is a special case covered in Article 8 (UCC 8-319); to be enforceable a contract for the sale of securities must be in writing regardless of the amount involved. For the sale of other kinds of personal property, a minimum of $5,000 must be involved before an enforceable contract must be in writing. Otherwise, an oral agreement is enforceable as a binding contract.

Contracts that must be in writing to be enforceable are said to be within the Statute of Frauds. The Statute of Frauds dates back to 1677, when the English Parliament decreed that certain types of contracts must be in writing. The applicable parts of the UCC effectively define the types of sales contracts that must be in writing. In addition, every state has its own version of the Statute of Frauds.

Under the UCC a written sales contract should specify the parties involved, the subject matter to be sold, and any material or special terms or conditions. Some states also require that the consideration—the amount and type of payment—be specified. The UCC does not require a formal sales contract, though. In many cases a memorandum or collection of papers is sufficient compliance. The courts have held that a written check can be considered a written memorandum of a sales agreement. The UCC allows a written sales contract to be enforced even if it leaves out material terms and is not signed by both parties. However, one party may not create a sales contract on its own that is binding against another party, and an enforceable contract must be signed by the defendant or the one against whom the contract is sought to be enforced.

In many cases a purchase order, pro forma invoice, or order acknowledgment may serve in place of a formal sales contract. A purchase order is issued by the buyer and sent to the seller, stating the type and amount of goods to be purchased, the price, and any other material terms such as a time limit on filling the order. A pro forma invoice is issued by the seller and sent to the buyer, often in response to a purchase order or oral agreement. In international transactions, the pro forma invoice may enable the buyer to open a line of credit with which to pay for the goods ordered. The pro forma invoice typically includes relevant terms and conditions that apply to the sale.

A formal order acknowledgment is useful for establishing the seller's position in case a dispute should arise. The order acknowledgment is drawn up by the seller in response to a received purchase order. It does not necessarily repeat the details of the purchase order, but it may clarify details such as delivery schedules. When a formal order acknowledgment is countersigned by the buyer, it becomes a type of sales contract.

For international transactions, the Vienna Sale Convention is binding on signatory countries, of which the United States is one. Each of the nations that has signed the convention may state up to five reservations. For example, the United States has stipulated that it shall apply to U.S. companies only when the transaction involves another signatory country. Much of the convention parallels the UCC, with these notable exceptions:

- Acceptance of an offer that includes a request for additions or modifications constitutes a counteroffer.

- There is no provision requiring a contract be written in order to be enforceable.

- The period for discovering defective merchandise may be as long as two years.

Sales contracts are useful in providing for a common understanding between buyer and seller, thus minimizing disputes. When a dispute does occur, the sales contract can help provide for a fair settlement.

FURTHER READING:

Lane, Marc J. *Legal Handbook for Small Business.* AMACOM, 1989.

Lickson, Charles P. *A Legal Guide for Small Business.* Crisp Publications, 1994.

SALES FORCE

A company's sales force consists of its staff of salespeople. The role of the sales force depends to a large extent on whether a company is selling directly to consumers or to other businesses. In consumer sales, the sales force is typically concerned simply with taking and closing orders. These salespeople are not responsible for creating demand for the product,

since demand for the product has already been created by advertising and promotion. They may provide the consumer with some product information, but individuals involved in consumer sales are often not concerned with maintaining long-term customer relationships. Examples of consumer sales forces include automobile salespersons and the sales staffs found in a variety of retail stores.

The sales force takes on a completely different role in business-to-business sales. Industrial sales forces, for example, may be required to perform a variety of functions. These may include prospecting for new customers and qualifying leads, explaining who the company is and what its products can do, closing orders, negotiating prices, servicing accounts, gathering competitive and market information, and allocating products during times of shortages.

Within the business-to-business market, a distinction can be made between selling to retailers, industrial sales, and other types of business-to-business sales and marketing. The concerns and activities of the sales force tend to vary in each type of business market. What they have in common, however, is the desire of the sales force to establish a long-term relationship with each of its customers and to provide service in a variety of ways.

In selling to retailers, for example, the sales force is not concerned with creating demand. Since consumer demand is more a function of advertising and promotion, the sales force is more concerned with obtaining shelf space in the retailer's store. The sales force may also attempt to obtain more promotion support from the retailer. The sales force relies on sophisticated marketing data to make a convincing presentation to the retailer in order to achieve its sales and marketing objectives.

The largest sales forces are involved in industrial selling. An average industrial field sales force ranges in size from 20 to 60 people and is responsible for selling throughout the United States. The sales force may be organized around traditional geographic territories or around specific customers, markets, and products. An effective sales force consists of individuals who can relate well to decision makers and help them solve their problems. A sales manager or supervisor typically provides the sales force with guidance and discipline. Within the company the sales force may receive support in the form of specialized training, technical backup, inside sales staff, and product literature. Direct mail and other types of marketing efforts can be employed to provide the sales force with qualified leads.

In recent years, costs associated with making single business-to-business industrial sales calls have risen dramatically. As a consequence, many businesses have redoubled their efforts to make sure that they get the most possible efficiency out of their sales force, for example, by expanding their territories and increasing their duties.

Sales managers and supervisors can measure the efficiency of their sales force using several criteria. These include the average number of sales calls per salesperson per day, the average sales-call time per contact, the average revenue and cost per sales call, the entertainment cost per sales call, and the percentage of orders per 100 sales calls. The sales force can also be evaluated in terms of how many new customers were acquired and how many customers were lost during a specific period. The expense of a sales force can be measured by monitoring the sales-force-to-sales ratio, or sales force cost as a percentage of total sales.

Using such criteria to evaluate the effectiveness of the sales force allows companies to make adjustments to improve its efficiency. If the sales force is calling on customers too often, for example, it may be possible to reduce the size of the sales force. If the sales force is servicing customers as well as selling to them, it may be possible to shift the service function to lower-paid personnel.

In industrial and other business-to-business sales, the sales force represents a key link between the manufacturer and the buyer. The sales force is often involved in selling technical applications and must work with several different contacts within a customer's organization. Industrial salespeople tend, on average, to be better educated than their consumer counterparts, and to be better paid. However, their cost as a percentage of sales is lower than in consumer sales, because industrial and business-to-business sales generally involve higher-ticket items or a larger volume of goods and services.

The sales force may be compensated in one of three ways: straight salary, straight commission, or a combination of salary plus commission. The majority of today's businesses utilize a combination of salary plus commission to compensate their sales forces, and fewer companies based their sales force compensation on straight commission. It appears that, as a percentage of all sales forces, the use of straight salaries remains constant. Whatever type of compensation system is used for the sales force, the important consideration is that the compensation adequately motivates the sales force to perform its best.

FURTHER READING:

Churchill, Gilbert A., Jr., Neil M. Ford, and Orville C. Walker, Jr. *Sales Force Management: Planning, Implementation, and Control.* 3rd ed. Boston, MA: Irwin, 1990.

Henry, Porter, and Joseph Callanan. *Sales Management and Motivation.* New York: Franklin Watts, 1987.

Newton, Derek A. *Sales Force Management: Text and Cases.* 2d ed. Boston, MA: Irwin, 1990.

Stanton, William J., and Richard H. Buskirk. *Management of the Sales Force.* 7th ed. Boston, MA: Irwin, 1987.

SEE ALSO: Employee Compensation; Sales Commissions; Sales Management; Sales Promotion

SALES FORECASTS

The sales forecast is a prognostication of a business's unit and dollars sales for some future period of time, up to several years or more. These forecasts are generally based primarily on recent sales trends, competitive developments, and economic trends in the industry, region, and/or nation in which the organization conducts business. Sales forecasting is management's primary tool for predicting the volume of attainable sales. Therefore, the whole budget process hinges on an accurate, timely sales forecast.

These technical projections of likely customer demand for specific products, goods, or services for a specific company within a specific time horizon are made in conjunction with basic marketing principles. For example, sales forecasts are often viewed within the context of total market potential, which can be understood as a projection of total potential sales for all companies. Market potential relates to the total capacity of the market to absorb the entire output of a specific industry. On the other hand, sales potential is the ability of the market to absorb or purchase the output from a single firm.

MARKET POTENTIAL The methodology of assessing market potential consists of developing relationships among the dynamic factors of the market served. Analysts on the industry level look for causal factors that, when linked together, demonstrate which economic, demographic, social, and political variables connect to support a market for various products. Analysts for a company must derive their own market potential for specific products based on which variables they believe are most important.

Many agencies and organizations publish indexes of market potential. They base their findings on extensive research and analysis of certain relationships that exist among basic economic data—for example, the location of potential consumers by age, education, and income for products that demonstrate a high correlation between those variables and the purchase of specific products. This information allows analysts to calculate the market potential for consumer or industrial goods. *Sales and Marketing Magazine* publishes buying power indexes. Its commercial indexes combine estimates of population, income, and retail sales to derive composite indicators of consumer demand according to U.S. Census Bureau regions, by state, or by the bureau's organized system of metropolitan areas. The buying-power index (BPI) provides only a relative value which analysts adjust to determine the market potential for local areas.

SALES POTENTIAL AND FORECASTING Forecasting methods and levels of sophistication vary greatly. Each portends to assess future events or situations which will impact either positively or negatively on a business's efforts. Managers prepare forecasts to determine the type and level of demand for both current and potential new products. They consider a broad spectrum of data for indications of growing and profitable markets. Forecasting, however, involves not only the collection and analysis of hard data, but also the application of business judgment in their interpretation and application. For example, forecasting requires business owners and managers to not only estimate expected units sold, but also to determine what the business's production (materials, labor, equipment) costs will be to produce those items.

Computer-aided sales forecasting has revolutionized this process. Advances in computer technology, information highways, and statistical and mathematical models provide almost every business with the ability to execute complex data analyses, thus reducing the risks and pitfalls prevalent in the past. These advances have made the process and costs of forecasting practical and affordable for small- and mid-sized businesses.

FACTORS IN SALES FORECASTING

Sales forecasts are conditional in that a company prepares the forecast prior to developing strategic and tactical plans. The forecast of sales potential may cause management to adjust some of its assumptions about production and marketing if the forecast indicates that: 1) current production capacity is inadequate or excessive, and 2) sales and marketing efforts need revisions. Management, therefore, has the opportunity to examine a series of alternate plans that propose changes in resource commitments (such as plant capacity, promotional programs, and market activities), changes in prices and/or changes in production scheduling.

Through forecasting the company determines markets for products, plans corporate **strategy**, develops sales quotas, determines the number and allocation of salespeople, decides on distribution channels, prices products or services, analyzes products and product potential in different markets, decides on product features, determines profit and sales potential for different products, constructs **advertising budgets**, determines the potential benefits of **sales promotion** programs, decides on the use of various elements of the marketing mix, sets production volume and standards, chooses **suppliers**, defines **financing** needs, and determines **inventory** standards. For the

forecasting to be accurate, managers need to consider all of these factors.

HISTORICAL PERSPECTIVE As a starting point, management analyzes previous sales experience by product lines, territories, classes of customers, and other relevant details. Management needs to consider a time line long enough to detect trends and patterns in the growth and the decline of dollar sales volume. This period is generally five to ten years. If the company's experience with a particular product class is shorter, management will include discernible experience of like companies.

The longer the view, the better management is able to detect patterns which follow cycles. Patterns which repeat themselves, no matter how erratically, are considered to be "normal," while variations from these patterns are "deviant." Some of these deviations may have resulted from significant societal developments that carried an impact that filtered all the way down to your business's sales performance. Management may compensate for these abnormalities by adjusting the figures to reflect normal trends under normal conditions.

BUSINESS COMPETENCE The ability of a company to respond to the results of a sales forecast depends on its production capacity, marketing methods, financing, and leadership, and its ability to change each of these to maximize its profit potential.

MARKET POSITION Forecasting also considers the competitive position of the company with respect to its market share; research and development; quality of service, **pricing** and financing policies; and **corporate image**. In addition, forecasters also evaluate the quality and quantity of the customer base to determine brand loyalty, response to promotional efforts, economic viability, and credit worthiness.

GENERAL ECONOMIC CONDITIONS Although consumer markets are often characterized as being increasingly susceptible to segmentation in recent years, the condition of the overall economy is still a primary determinant of general sales volume, even in many niche markets. Forecasters incorporate relevant data that correlate well or demonstrate a causal relationship with sales volume.

PRICE INDEX If the prices for products have changed over the years, changes in dollar volume of sales may not correlate well with volume of units. At one point in time when demand is strong, a company raises its prices. At another time, a company may launch **discount sales** to draw down inventories. Therefore, accountants devise a price index for each year which compensates for price increases. By dividing the dollar volume by the price indexes, a company can track its "true" volume growth. This process is similar to an inflation index, which provides prices in constant dollars. As a result, management is able to compare the price-adjusted dollar sales volumes.

SECULAR TRENDS The secular trend depicts: 1) general economic performance, or 2) the performance of the specific product for all companies. If a company's trend line rises more rapidly than the secular trend line, a company would be experiencing a more rapid growth in the rate of sales. Conversely, if a company's trend line is below the secular trend line, its performance is below the market's average. Management also uses this type of comparison to evaluate and control annual performance.

TREND VARIATIONS Although the secular trend represents the average for the industry, it may not be "normal" for a particular company. The comparison of company trends to secular trends may indicate that the company is serving a specialized market, or that the company is not faring well. Forecasters study the underlying assumptions of trend variations to understand the important relationships in determining the volume of sales. Although markets may be strong, the **sales force** might need to be adjusted.

"INTRA-COMPANY" TRENDS By analyzing month-to-month trends and seasonal variations over both the long and short terms, small business owners and managers can adjust the sales forecast to anticipate variations that historically repeat themselves during budget periods. Management may then construct a budget reflecting these variations, perhaps increasing volume discounts during traditionally slow periods, exploring new territories, or having sales representatives solicit product and service ideas from current customers.

PRODUCT TRENDS Forecasters also trend individual products, using indexes to adjust for seasonal fluctuations and price changes. Product trends are important for understanding the life cycle of a product.

SOURCES AND MAGNITUDE OF PRODUCT DEMAND In past eras, the introduction of new and improved products drove much of the demand. Currently, consumer attitudes and lifestyles anticipate product introductions and technological changes. Individual consumers are pushing technology to anticipate the needs of an increasingly segmented market. Demand based on anticipation is becoming the dominant feature of the technological age. The rapid pace of technological development and new product introduction have shortened product life-cycles. The combination of demographic considerations and technological change dominate consumer trends to a greater degree than in the past.

FORECASTING TECHNIQUES

There are a variety of forecasting techniques and methods from which the small business owner may choose. Not all of them are applicable in every situation. To allow for adequate forecasting, a business must choose those methods which best serve their purposes, utilize accurate and relevant data, and formulate honest assumptions appropriate to the market and product.

Sales forecasts may be general if they calculate aggregate sales attainable in an industry. Conversely, forecasts may be very specific, detailing data by individual products, sales territories, types of customers, and so forth. In recent decades market analysts have increased their use of focus groups, individual surveys, interviews, and sophisticated analytical techniques aimed at identifying specific markets.

APPROACHES TO FORECASTING In the causal approach forecasters identify the underlying variables that have a causal influence on future sales. The company has no influence over causal variables in the general society, such as population, gross national product, and general economic conditions. A company does, however, maintain control over its production lines, prices, advertising and marketing, and the size of its sales force. After studying the underlying causes and variables in depth, the analysts use a variety of mathematical techniques to project future trends. On the basis of these projections, management derives its sales forecast.

The non-causal approach involves an in-depth analysis of historical sales patterns. Analysts plot these patterns in graphs in order to project future sales. Because no attempt is made to identify and evaluate the underlying causal variables, the analysts assume that the underlying causes will continue to influence the future sales in the same manner as in the past. Although analysts may apply certain statistical techniques to extrapolate past sales into the future, this approach is sometimes criticized as simplistic or naive, especially since most business experts believe that rapid changes in technology are driving fundamental changes in many business operations.

Analysts employ the indirect method by first projecting industry sales. From this data they project the company's share of the industry total. The direct approach, however, skips the industry projection with a straightforward estimate of sales for the company. Either of these methods are applicable to the causal and non-causal approaches.

FORECASTING METHODOLOGIES

A variety of sales forecasting methodologies can be used by small and large businesses alike:

BOTTOM-UP FORECASTING Analysts using this methodology divide the market into segments, and then separately calculate the demand in each segment. Typically, analysts use sales force composites, industry surveys, and intention-to-buy surveys to collect data. They aggregate the segments to arrive at a total sales forecast. Bottom-up forecasting may not be simple because of complications with the accuracy of the data submitted. The usefulness of the data is contingent upon honest and complete answers from customers, and on the importance and priority given to a survey by the sales staff.

TOP-DOWN FORECASTING This is the method most widely used for industrial applications. Management first estimates the sales potential, then develops sales quotas, and finally constructs a sales forecast. Problems arise with the top-down forecasting method, however, when the underlying assumptions of the past are no longer applicable. The correlation between economic variables and quantity demanded may change or weaken over time.

These two forecasting methods encompass a number of methodologies which can be divided into three general categories: qualitative, times-series analysis and regression, and causal.

QUALITATIVE METHODS Qualitative methods rely on non-statistical methods of deriving a sales forecast. A company solicits the opinion or judgment of sales executives, a panel of experts, the sales force, the sales division supervisors, and/or outside expert consultants. Qualitative methods are judgmental composites of expected sales. These methods are often preferred in the following instances: 1) when the variables which influence consumer buying habits have changed; 2) when current data is not available; 3) when none of the qualitative methods work well in a specific situation; 4) when the planning horizon is too far for the standard quantitative methods; and 5) when the data has not yet factored in technological breakthroughs taking place or forthcoming.

The Probability Assessment Method (PAM) forecasts sales volume by utilizing in-house expert opinion that provides probabilities between one and 99 percent, plus and minus, on certain target volumes. Analysts translate these estimates into a cumulative probability curve by plotting the volumes by the probability assigned to them. They use this curve to aid in forecasting.

The Program Evaluation and Review Technique (PERT) requires estimates of ''optimistic,'' ''pessimistic,'' and ''most likely'' future circumstances. Analysts weigh these three estimates to form an expected value from which they compute a standard deviation. In this way analysts convert the estimates of the small business owner and/or staff into measures of central tendency and dispersion. The standard deviation enables the forecaster to estimate a confidence interval around the expected value. While PERT is only an approximation, it is quick and easy to use. The forecaster can take into account the owner's opinion as a check on estimates produced by other methods.

The Delphi Technique relies on the assumption that several experts can arrive at a better forecast than one. Users of this method solicit a panel consensus and reprocess the results through the panel until a very narrow, firm median is agreed upon. By keeping the panel participants isolated, the Delphi excludes many aspects of group behavior, such as social pressure, argumentation, and domination by a few members, from causing undue influence. The expense associated with this method, however, precludes most small business enterprises from pursuing it.

A visionary forecast relies on the personal insights and judgment of a respected individual. Although often supplemented by data and facts about different scenarios of the future, the visionary forecast is characterized by subjective guesswork and imagination and is highly nonscientific. But while such forecasts are not based on reams of scientific information, many small business owners have achieved success by relying on such subjective data.

Historical analogy methodologies, meanwhile, attempt to determine future sales through an in-depth analysis of the introduction and sales growth of a similar product. Historical analogy seeks patterns applicable to the product considered for current introduction. This method requires several years' history for one or more products, and—when used—is generally applied to new product introductions.

The sales force composite gathers forecasts from each individual salesperson for a particular territory. The sales forecast is the aggregate of the individual forecasts. The usefulness of this method is dependent on the accuracy of the data submitted.

An intention-to-buy survey measures a target market's intention to buy within a specified future time period. Market analysts conduct such surveys prior to the introduction of a product or service. Analysts provide consumers with a description or explanation of the product or service with the hope that respondents will provide honest answers. If respondents tell analysts ''what they want to hear,'' the survey will not be accurate. In addition, certain environmental factors, such as a competing technological breakthrough or a recession, may influence respondent buying habits between the time of the survey and the product introduction.

TIME-SERIES ANALYSIS AND PROJECTION Trend projection techniques may be most appropriate in situations where the forecaster is able to infer, from the past behavior of a variable, something about its future impact on sales. Forecasters look for trends that form identifiable patterns which recur with predictive frequency. Seasonal variations and cyclical patterns form more obvious trends, while random variables make projection more complex.

While time-series methods do not explicitly account for causal relationships between a variable and other factors, analysts find the emergent historical patterns useful in making forecasts. Analysts typically use time series for new product forecasts, particularly in the intermediate and long-term. The data required varies with each technique. A good rule of thumb is a minimum of five years' annual data. A complete history is very helpful.

Market research involves a systematic, formal, and conscious procedure for evoking and testing hypotheses about real markets. Analysts need at least two market research reports based on time series analyses of market variables, and a considerable collection of market data from questionnaires and surveys.

In its simplest form, trend projection analysis involves the examination of what has happened in the past. Analysts develop a specific linear percentage trend with the expectation that the trend will continue. The problem with the simple trend projection is the fact of randomness—that is, the random event or element that has a major impact on the forecast.

The moving average is a more sophisticated type of trend projection. It assumes the future will be an average of the past performance rather than following a specific linear percentage trend. The moving average minimizes the impact of randomness on individual forecasts since it is an average of several values rather than a simple linear projection. The moving average equation basically sums up the sales in a number of past periods and divides by the number of periods.

Industry surveys involve surveying the various companies that make up the industry for a particular item. They may include users or manufacturers. The industry survey method that uses a top-down approach of forecasting has some of the same advantages and disadvantages as the executive opinion and sales force composites.

A regression analysis may be linear or multiple. With linear regression, analysts develop a relationship between sales and a single independent variable and use this relationship to forecast sales. With multiple regression, analysts examine relationships between sales and a number of independent variables. Usually the latter is accomplished with the help of a computer that helps analysts to estimate the values of the independent variables and to incorporate them into a multi-regression equation. If analysts find a relationship among various independent variables, they can develop a multiple regression equation for predicting sales for the coming year.

Exponential smoothing is a time-series approach similar to the moving average. Instead of using a constant set of weights for the observation made, analysts employ an exponentially increasing set of weights so that more recent values receive more weight than do older values. More sophisticated models incorporate various adjustments for such factors as trends and seasonal patterns.

Analysts look at the leading indicators because the National Bureau of Economic Research has clearly demonstrated their value in forecasting. These indicators include prices of 500 common stocks, new orders for durable goods, an index of net business formation, corporate profits after taxes, industrial materials prices, and the change in consumer installment debt. Despite their widespread use, the leading indicators do not relate well with specific products. Nevertheless, when such relationships can be established, analysts construct multiple regression models with which to forecast sales.

CAUSAL METHODS When analysts find a cause-effect relationship between a variable and sales, a causal model may provide better forecasts than those generated by other techniques. Life-cycle analysis forecasts new product growth rates based on analysts' projections of the phases of product acceptance by various groups—innovators, early adapters, early majority, late majority, and laggards. Typically, this method is used to forecast new product sales. Analysts' minimum data requirements are the annual sales of the product being considered or of a similar product. It is often necessary to do market surveys to establish the cause-effect relationships.

THE SALES BUDGET

The sales forecast provides the framework for the detailed planning presented in the master budget. Based on planned strategies and its best business judgment, management converts a sales forecast into a sales plan through the commitment of resources and the establishment of control mechanisms. The sales budget provides an evaluative tool by presenting monthly indexes of volume of units and dollars as hard targets for the sales team. Deviations from these indexes indicate to small business owners and managers where they need to adjust their efforts to take advantage of hot products or to remedy difficult situations.

Management determines its sales policies and strategies within its ability to respond to customer needs, technological changes, and the financial prerequisites of marketing. The sales budget projects that portion of potential sales the sales team believes it can achieve. The forecast, then, sets the parameters on the top side while the production capacity and sales acumen of the team sets the floor.

Although sales forecasts may accurately project significant changes in market conditions, a company needs to thoroughly examine its own resources to determine its ability to respond to these changes. A huge drop in demand may decrease the strain on the production process to where a company regains cost efficiencies, or a large increase in demand might be required by a company that needs cash for other projects. The sales budget, therefore, is predicated on a company's ability to meet expected demand at or near its maximum profit potential.

THE PRODUCTION BUDGET Both small and large businesses construct their production budgets within limitations of production, warehousing, delivery, and service capabilities. Subsequently, a company attempts to schedule production at maximum efficiency. By anticipating the variations in monthly sales, management can keep production at levels sufficient to provide adequate supply. Labor costs generally comprise the greatest single production cost. Therefore, management may adjust labor hours to production schedules.

Production levels remain rather constant if current inventory is sufficient to meet increases in sales. If management expects an increase, it may build inventories during the first quarter of the budget, and sell them down to planned levels during the remaining three quarters. From the production budget, a company estimates the mix of materials, labor, and production overhead needed to meet planned production levels.

DEVELOPING A SALES FORECAST

Forecasting sales is inherently more difficult than the construction of the subsequent sales budget. Although management exerts some degree of control over expenditures, it has little ability to direct the buying habits of individuals. The level of sales depends of the vagaries of the marketplace. Nonetheless, a sales forecast must attain a reasonable degree of reliability to be useful.

Fundamentally, sales forecasters follows steps similar to these in developing a forecast of sales potential:

- Determine the purposes for using the forecasts.

- Divide the company's products into homogeneous groups.

- Determine those factors affecting the sales of each product group and their relative importance.

- Choose a forecasting method or methods best suited for the job.

- Gather all necessary and available data.

- Analyze the data.

- Check and cross-check deductions resulting from the analyses.

- Make assumptions regarding effects of the various factors that cannot be measured or forecast.

- Convert deductions and assumptions into specific product and territorial forecasts and quotas.

- Apply forecasts to company operations.

- Periodically review performance and revise forecasts.

FURTHER READING:

Bolt, Gordon J. *Market and Sales Forecasting.* New York: Franklin Watts, 1988.

Cohen, William A. *The Practice of Marketing Management.* New York: Macmillan Publishing, 1988.

Gruenwald, George. *New Product Development.* NTC Business Books, 1985.

Henry, Porter, and Joseph A. Callanan. *Sales Management and Motivation.* New York: Franklin Watts, 1987.

McCarthy, E. Jerome, and William D. Perreault, Jr. *Basic Marketing: A Managerial Approach.* 10th ed. Boston, MA: Irwin, 1990.

Welsch, Glenn A. *Budgeting: Profit Planning and Control.* 4th ed. Prentice-Hall, 1976.

SEE ALSO: Budgets and Budgeting; Competitive Analysis; Operations Management; Product Life Cycle

SALES MANAGEMENT

Sales management refers to the administration of the **personal selling** component of a company's marketing program. It includes the planning, implementation, and control of sales programs, as well as recruiting, training, motivating, and evaluating members of the **sales force**. In a small business, these various functions may be performed by the owner or by a specialist called a sales manager. The fundamental role of the sales manager is to develop and administer a selling program that effectively contributes to the organization's goals. The sales manager for a small business would likely decide how many salespeople to employ, how best to select and train them, what sort of compensation and incentives to use to motivate them, what type of presentation they should make, and how the sales function should be structured for maximum contact with customers.

Sales management is just one facet of a company's overall marketing mix, which encompasses strategies related to the ''four Ps'': products, pricing, promotion, and place (distribution). Objectives related to promotion are achieved through three supporting functions: 1) advertising, which includes **direct mail**, radio, television, and print advertisements, among other media; 2) **sales promotion**, which includes tools such as **coupons**, **rebates**, contests, and samples; and (3) personal selling, which is the domain of the sales manager.

Although the role of sales managers is multidisciplinary in scope, their primary responsibilities are: 1) setting goals for a sales force; 2) planning, budgeting, and organizing a program to achieve those goals; 3) implementing the program; and 4) controlling and evaluating the results. Even when a sales force is already in place, the sales manager will likely view these responsibilities as an ongoing process necessary to adapt to both internal and external changes.

GOAL SETTING

The overall goals of the sales force manager are essentially mandated by the marketing mix. The company coordinates objectives between the major components of the mix within the context of internal constraints, such as available capital and production capacity. The sales force manager, however, may play an important role in developing the overall marketing mix strategies. For example, the sales manager may be in the best position to determine the specific needs of customers and to discern the potential of new and existing markets.

One of the most critical duties of the sales manager is to estimate the market potential and sales potential of the company's offerings, and then to make realistic forecasts of sales. Market potential is the total expected sales of a given product or service for the entire industry in a specific market over a stated period of time. Sales potential refers to the share of a market potential that an individual company can reasonably expect to achieve. A **sales forecast** is an estimate of sales (in dollars or product units) that an individual firm expects to make during a specified time period, in a stated market, and under a proposed marketing plan.

Estimations of sales and market potential are often used to set major organizational objectives related to production, marketing, distribution, and other corporate functions, as well as to assist the sales manager in planning and implementing the overall sales strategy. Numerous sales forecasting tools and techniques, many of which are quite advanced, are available to help the sales manager determine potential and make forecasts. Major external factors influencing sales and market potential include: industry conditions, such as stage of maturity; market conditions and expectations; general business and economic conditions; and regulatory environment.

PLANNING, BUDGETING, AND ORGANIZING

After determining goals, the sales manager of a small business must develop a strategy to attain them. A very basic decision is whether to hire a sales force or contract with independent selling agents or manufacturers' representatives outside of the organization. The latter strategy eliminates costs associated with hiring, training, and supervising workers, and it takes advantage of sales channels that have already been established by the independent representatives. On the other hand, maintaining an internal sales force allows the manager to exert more control over the salespeople and to ensure that they are trained properly. Furthermore, establishing an internal sale force provides the opportunity to hire inexperienced representatives at a very low cost.

The type of sales force developed depends on the financial priorities and constraints of the organization. If a manager decides to hire salespeople, the next step is to determine the optimal size of the force. This determination typically entails a compromise between the number of people needed to adequately service all potential customers and the resources available to the company. One technique sometimes used to determine sales force size is the ''work load'' strategy, whereby the sum of existing and potential customers is multiplied by the ideal number of calls per customer. That sum is then multiplied by the preferred length of a sales call (in hours). Next, that figure is divided by the selling time available from one salesperson. The final sum is theoretically the ideal sales force size. A second technique is the ''incremental'' strategy, which recognizes that the incremental increase in sales that results from each additional hire continually decreases. In other words, salespeople are gradually added until the cost of a new hire exceeds the benefit.

A sales manager who is in the process of hiring an internal sales force also has to decide the degree of experience to seek and determine how to balance quality and quantity. Basically, the manager can either ''make'' or ''buy'' his force. ''Green'' hires, or those without previous experience whom the company must ''make'' into salespeople, cost less over the long term and do not bring any bad sales habits with them that were learned in other companies. On the other hand, the initial cost associated with experienced salespeople is usually lower, and experienced employees can start producing results much more quickly. But as Irving Burstiner noted in *The Small Business Handbook*, few star salespeople are ever unemployed, and a small business probably lacks the resources to find and hire those who are. Furthermore, if the manager elects to hire only the most qualified people, budgetary constraints may force him to leave some territories only partially covered, resulting in customer dissatisfaction and lost sales. Therefore, it usually makes more sense for small businesses to hire green troops and train them well.

After determining the composition of the sales force, the sales manager creates a budget, or a record of planned expenses that is (usually) prepared annually. The budget helps the manager decide how much money will be spent on personal selling and how that money will be allocated within the sales force. Major budgetary items include: sales force salaries, commissions, and bonuses; travel expenses; sales materials; training; clerical services; and office rent and utilities. Many budgets are prepared by simply reviewing the previous year's budget and then making adjustments. A more advanced technique, however, is the percentage of sales method, which allocates funds based on a percentage of expected revenues. Typical percentages range from about two percent for heavy industries to as much as eight percent or more for consumer goods and computers.

After a sales force strategy has been devised and a budget has been adopted, the sales manager should ideally have the opportunity to organize, or structure, the sales force. The structure of the sales force allows each salesperson to specialize in a certain sales task or type of customer or market, so that they will be more likely to establish productive, long-term relationships with their customers. Small businesses may choose to structure their sales forces by product line, customer type, geography, or a combination of these factors.

IMPLEMENTING

After setting goals and establishing a plan for sales activities, the next step for the sales manager is to implement the strategy. Implementation requires the sales manager to make decisions related to staffing, designing territories, and allocating sales efforts. Staffing—the most significant of these three responsibilities—encompasses **recruiting**, training, compensating, and motivating salespeople.

RECRUITING The first step in recruiting salespeople involves analyzing the positions to be filled. This is often accomplished by sending an observer into the field, who records the amount of time a salesperson must spend talking to customers, traveling, attending meetings, and doing paperwork. The observer then reports the findings to the sales manager, who uses the information to draft a detailed job description. The observer might also report on the characteristics and needs of the buyers, since it can be important for salespeople to share these characteristics.

The manager may seek candidates through advertising, college recruiting, company sources, and employment agencies. Candidates are typically evaluated through personality tests, interviews, written applications, and background checks. Research has shown that the two most important personality traits that salespeople can possess are empathy, which helps them relate to customers, and drive, which motivates them to satisfy personal needs for accomplishment. Other important traits include maturity, appearance, communication skills, and technical knowledge related to the product or industry. Negative traits include fear of rejection, distaste for travel, self-consciousness, and interest in artistic or creative originality.

TRAINING After recruiting a suitable sales force, the manager must determine how much and what type of training to provide. Most sales training emphasizes product, company, and industry knowledge. Only about 25 percent of the average company training program, in fact, addresses personal selling techniques. Because of the high cost, many small businesses try to limit the amount of training they provide. The average cost of training a person to sell industrial products, for example, commonly exceeds $30,000. Sales managers can achieve many benefits with competent training programs, however. For instance, research indicates that training reduces employee turnover, thereby lowering the effective cost of hiring new workers. Good training can also improve customer relations, increase employee morale, and boost sales. Common training methods include lectures, cases studies, role playing, demonstrations, on-the-job training, and self-study courses. Ideally, training should be an ongoing process that continually reinforces the company's goals.

COMPENSATION After the sales force is in place, the manager must devise a means of compensating individuals. The ideal system of compensation reaches a balance between the needs of the person (income, recognition, prestige, etc.) and the goals of the company (controlling costs, boosting market share, increasing cash flow, etc.), so that a salesperson may achieve both through the same means. Most approaches to sales force compensation utilize a combination of salary and commission or salary and bonus. Salary gives a sales manager added control over the salesperson's activities, while commission provides the salesperson with greater motivation to sell.

Although financial rewards are the primary means of motivating workers, most sales organizations also employ other motivational techniques. Good sales managers recognize that salespeople have needs other than the basic ones satisfied by money. For example, they want to feel like they are part of a winning team, that their jobs are secure, and that their efforts and contributions to the organization are recognized. Methods of meeting those needs include contests, vacations, and other performance-based prizes, in addition to self-improvement benefits such as tuition for graduate school. Another tool managers commonly use to stimulate their salespeople is quotas. Quotas, which can be set for factors such as the number of calls made per day, expenses consumed per month, or the number of new customers added annually, give salespeople a standard against which they can measure success.

DESIGNING TERRITORIES AND ALLOCATING SALES EFFORTS In addition to recruiting, training, and motivating a sales force to achieve the company's goals, sales managers at most small businesses must decide how to designate sales territories and allocate the efforts of the sales team. Territories are geographic areas assigned to individual salespeople. The advantages of establishing territories are that they improve coverage of the market, reduce wasteful overlap of sales efforts, and allow each salesperson to define personal responsibility and judge individual success. However, many types of businesses, such as real estate and insurance companies, do not use territories.

Allocating people to different territories is an important sales management task. Typically, the top few territories produce a disproportionately high sales volume. This occurs because managers usually create smaller areas for trainees, medium-sized territories for more experienced team members, and larger areas for senior sellers. A drawback of that strategy, however, is that it becomes difficult to compare performance across territories. An alternate approach is to divide regions by existing and potential customer base. A number of computer programs exist to help sales managers effectively create territories according to their goals. Good scheduling and routing of sales calls can reduce waiting and travel time. Other common methods of reducing the costs associated with sales calls include contacting numerous customers at once during trade shows, and using **telemarketing** to qualify prospects before sending a salesperson to make a personal call.

CONTROLLING AND EVALUATING

After the sales plan has been implemented, the sales manager's responsibility becomes controlling and evaluating the program. During this stage, the sales manager compares the original goals and objectives with the actual accomplishments of the sales force. The performance of each individual is compared with goals or quotas, looking at elements such as expenses, sales volume, customer satisfaction, and cash flow. According to Burstiner, each salesperson should be evaluated using both subjective (i.e., product knowledge, familiarity with competition, work habits) and objective (i.e., number of orders compared to number of calls, number of new accounts landed) criteria.

An important consideration for the sales manager is profitability. Indeed, simple sales figures may not reflect an accurate image of the performance of the sales force. The manager must dig deeper by analyzing expenses, price-cutting initiatives, and long-term contracts with customers that will impact future income. An in-depth analysis of these and related influences will help the manager to determine true performance based on profits. For use in future goal-setting and planning efforts, the manager may also evaluate sales trends by different factors, such as product line, volume, territory, and market. After the manager analyzes and evaluates the achievements of the sales force, that information is used to make corrections to the current strategy and sales program. In other words, the sales manager returns to the initial goal-setting stage.

ENVIRONMENTS AND STRATEGIES

The goals and plans adopted by the sales manager will be greatly influenced by the company's industry orientation, competitive position, and market strategy. The basic industry orientations available to a firm include industrial goods, consumer durables, consumer nondurables, and services. Companies that manufacture industrial goods or sell highly technical services tend to be heavily dependent on personal selling as a marketing tool. Sales managers in those organizations characteristically focus on customer service and education, and employ and train a relatively high-level sales force. In contrast, sales managers that sell consumer durables will likely integrate the efforts of their sales force into related advertising and promotional initiatives. Sales management efforts related to consumer nondurables and consumer services will generally emphasize volume sales, a comparatively low-caliber sales force, and an emphasis on high-volume customers.

In his book *Competitive Strategy,* Michael Porter lists three common market strategies adopted by firms—low-cost supplier, differentiation, and niche. Companies that adopt a low-cost supplier strategy are usually characterized by a vigorous pursuit of efficiency and cost controls. Sales management efforts in this type of organization should generally stress minimizing expenses—by having salespeople stay at budget hotels, for example—and appealing to customers on the basis of price. Salespeople should be given an incentive to chase large, high-volume customers, and the sales force infrastructure should be designed to efficiently accommodate large order-taking activities.

Companies that adhere to a differentiation strategy achieve market success by offering a unique product or service. They often rely on brand loyalty or patent protection to insulate them from competitors, and thus are able to achieve higher-than-average profit margins. In this environment, selling techniques should stress benefits, rather than price. Firms that pursue a niche market strategy succeed by targeting a very narrow segment of a market and then dominating that segment. The company is able to overcome competitors by aggressively protecting its niche and orienting every action and decision toward the service of its select group. Sales managers in this type of organization would tend to emphasize employee training or to hire industry experts. The overall sales program would be centered around customer service and benefits other than price.

REGULATION

Besides markets and industries, another chief environmental influence on the sales management process is government regulation. Indeed, selling activities at companies are regulated by a multitude of state and federal laws designed to protect consumers, foster competitive markets, and discourage unfair business practices.

Chief among anti-trust provisions affecting sales managers is the Robinson-Patman Act, which prohibits companies from engaging in price or service discrimination. In other words, a firm cannot offer special incentives to large customers based solely on volume, because such practices tend to hurt smaller customers. Companies can give discounts to buyers, but only if those incentives are based on real savings gleaned from manufacturing and distribution processes.

Similarly, the Sherman Act makes it illegal for a seller to force a buyer to purchase one product (or service) in order to get the opportunity to purchase another product—a practice referred to as a "tying agreement." A long-distance telephone company, for instance, cannot require its customers to purchase its telephone equipment as a prerequisite to buying its long-distance service. The Sherman Act also regulates reciprocal dealing arrangements, whereby companies agree to buy products from each other. Reciprocal dealing is considered anticompetitive because large buyers and sellers tend to have an unfair advantage over their smaller competitors.

Several consumer protection regulations also impact sales managers. The Fair Packaging and Labeling Act of 1966, for example, restricts deceptive labeling, and the Truth in Lending Act requires sellers to fully disclose all finance charges incorporated into consumer credit agreements. Cooling-off laws, which commonly exist at the state level, allow buyers to cancel contracts made with door-to-door sellers within a certain time frame. Additionally, the **Federal Trade Commission (FTC)** requires door-to-door sellers who work for companies engaged in interstate trade to clearly announce their purpose when calling on prospects.

FURTHER READING:

Burstiner, Irving. *The Small Business Handbook.* Upper Saddle River, NJ: Prentice-Hall, 1989.

Churchill, Gilbert A., Jr., Neil M. Ford, and Orville C. Walker, Jr. *Sales Force Management: Planning, Implementation, and Control.* 3rd ed. Irwin, 1990.

Newton, Derek A. *Sales Force Management: Text and Cases.* 2nd ed. Irwin, 1990.

Porter, Michael E. *Competitive Strategy.* Free Press, 1980.

Stafford, John, and Colin Grant. *Effective Sales Management.* East Brunswick, NJ: Nichols Publishing Co., 1986.

Stanton, William J., and Richard H. Buskirk. *Management of the Sales Force.* 7th ed. Irwin, 1987.

SEE ALSO: Employee Motivation; Sales Commissions; Training and Development

SALES PROMOTION

Sales promotion is an important component of a small business's overall **marketing** strategy, along with advertising, **public relations**, and **personal selling**. The American Marketing Association (AMA) defines sales promotion as "media and nonmedia marketing pressure applied for a predetermined, limited period of time in order to stimulate trial, increase consumer demand, or improve product quality." But this definition does not capture all the elements of modern sales promotion. One should add that effective sales promotion increases the basic value of a product for a limited time and directly stimulates consumer purchasing, selling effectiveness, or the effort of the sales force. It can be used to inform, persuade, and remind target customers about the business and its marketing mix. Some common types of sales promotion include samples, **coupons**, sweepstakes, contests, in-store displays, **trade shows**, price-off deals, premiums, and **rebates**.

Businesses can target sales promotions at three different audiences: consumers, resellers, and the company's own **sales force**. Sales promotion acts as a competitive weapon by providing an extra incentive for the target audience to purchase or support one brand over another. It is particularly effective in spurring product trial and unplanned purchases. Most marketers believe that a given product or service has an established perceived price or value, and they use sales promotion to change this price-value relationship by increasing the value and/or lowering the price. Compared to the other components of the marketing mix (advertising, publicity, and personal selling), sales promotion usually operates on a shorter time line, uses a more rational appeal, returns a tangible or real value, fosters an immediate sale, and contributes highly to profitability.

In determining the relative importance to place on sales promotion in the overall marketing mix, a small business should consider its marketing budget, the stage of the product in its life cycle, the nature of competition in the market, the target of the promotion, and the nature of the product. For example, sales promotion and **direct mail** are particularly attractive alternatives when the marketing budget is limited, as it is for many small businesses. In addition, sales promotion can be an effective tool in a highly competitive market, when the objective is to convince retailers to carry a product or influence consumers to select it over those of competitors. Similarly, sales promotion is often used in the growth and maturity stages of the **product life cycle** to stimulate consumers and resellers to choose that product over the competition—rather than in the introduction stage, when mass advertising to build awareness might be more important. Finally, sales promotion tends to work best when it is applied to impulse items whose features can be judged at the point of purchase, rather than more complex, expensive items that might require hands-on demonstration.

GROWTH OF SALES PROMOTION

Sales promotion has grown substantially in recent years. In fact, Donnelley Marketing estimates that expenditures on sales promotion hit $150 billion in 1993. That means more marketing dollars were spent on sales promotion than on advertising (roughly 65 percent to 35 percent). There are several reasons for this dramatic growth in sales promotion.

First, consumers have accepted sales promotion as part of their buying decision criteria. It provides reluctant decision makers with an incentive to make choices by increasing the value offered by a particular brand. Second, the increasing tendency of businesses to focus on short-term results has helped spur growth in sales promotion, which can provide an immediate boost in sales. Product managers also tend to view sales promotion as a way to differentiate their brand from that of competitors in the short term. Third, the emergence of computer technology has enabled manufacturers to get rapid feedback on the results of promotions. Redemption rates for coupons or figures on sales volume can be obtained within days. Finally, an increase in the size and power of retailers has also boosted the use of sales promotion. Historically, the manufacturer held the power in the channel of distribution. Mass marketers utilized national advertising to get directly to consumers, creating a demand for the heavily advertised brands that stores could not afford to ignore. With consolidation and the growth of major retail chains, however, retailers have gained the power to demand incentives from manufacturers to carry their products. Many sales promotions are designed to provide benefits to the retailers.

LIMITATIONS OF SALES PROMOTION

Although sales promotion is an important strategy for producing quick, short-term, positive results, it is not a cure for a bad product, poor advertising, or an inferior sales team. After consumers use a coupon for the initial purchase of a product, the product must then take over and convince them to become repeat buyers. In addition, sales promotion activities may bring several negative consequences, including ''clutter'' due to the number of competitive promotions. New approaches are promptly cloned by competitors, as each marketer tries to be more creative or to be more effective in attracting the attention of consumers and the trade. Finally, consumers and resellers have learned how to milk the sales promotion game. Consumers may wait to buy certain items knowing that prices will eventually be reduced, for example, while resellers have become experts at negotiating deals and manipulating competitors against one another.

CONSUMER PROMOTIONS

Consumer sales promotions are steered toward the ultimate product users—typically individual shoppers in the local market—but the same techniques can be used to promote products sold by one business to another, such as computer systems, cleaning supplies, and machinery. In contrast, trade sales promotions target resellers—wholesalers and retailers—who carry the marketer's product. Following are some of the key techniques used in consumer-oriented sales promotions.

PRICE DEALS A consumer price deal saves the buyer money when a product is purchased. The main types of price deals include discounts, bonus pack deals, refunds or rebates, and coupons. Price deals are usually intended to encourage trial use of a new product or line extension, to recruit new buyers for a mature product, or to convince existing customers to increase their purchases, accelerate their use, or purchase multiple units. Price deals work most effectively when price is the consumer's foremost criterion or when brand loyalty is low.

Buyers may learn about price discounts either at the point of sale or through advertising. At the point of sale, price reductions may be posted on the package, on signs near the product, or in storefront windows. Many types of advertisements can be used to notify consumers of upcoming discounts, including fliers and newspaper and television ads. Price discounts are especially common in the food industry, where local supermarkets run weekly specials. Price discounts may be initiated by the manufacturer, the retailer, or the distributor. For instance, a manufacturer may ''pre-price'' a product and then convince the retailer to participate in this short-term discount through extra incentives. For price reduction strategies to be effective, they must have the support of all distributors in the channel. Existing customers perceive **discount sales** as rewards and often respond by buying in larger quantities. Price discounts alone, however, usually do not induce first time buyers.

Another type of price deal is the bonus pack or banded pack. When a bonus pack is offered, an extra amount of the product is free when a standard size of the product is bought at the regular price. This technique is routinely used in the marketing of cleaning products, food, and health and beauty aids to introduce a new or larger size. A bonus pack rewards present users but may have little appeal to users of competitive brands. A banded pack offer is when two or more units of a product are sold at a reduction of the regular single-unit price. Sometimes the products are physically banded together, such as in toothbrush and toothpaste offers.

A refund or rebate promotion is an offer by a marketer to return a certain amount of money when the product is purchased alone or in combination with other products. Refunds aim to increase the quantity or frequency of purchase, to encourage customers to "load up" on the product. This strategy dampens competition by temporarily taking consumers out of the market, stimulates the purchase of postponable goods such as major appliances, and creates on-shelf excitement by encouraging special displays. Refunds and rebates are generally viewed as a reward for purchase, and they appear to build brand loyalty rather than diminish it.

Coupons are legal certificates offered by manufacturers and retailers. They grant specified savings on selected products when presented for redemption at the point of purchase. Manufacturers sustain the cost of advertising and distributing their coupons, redeeming their face values, and paying retailers a handling fee. Retailers who offer double or triple the amount of the coupon shoulder the extra cost. Retailers who offer their own coupons incur the total cost, including paying the face value. In this way, retail coupons are equivalent to a cents-off deal.

Manufacturers disseminate coupons in many ways. They may be delivered directly by mail, dropped door to door, or distributed through a central location such as a shopping mall. Coupons may also be distributed through the media—magazines, newspapers, Sunday supplements, or free-standing inserts (FSI) in newspapers. Coupons can be inserted into, attached to, or printed on a package, or they may be distributed by a retailer who uses them to generate store traffic or to tie in with a manufacturer's promotional tactic. Retailer-sponsored coupons are typically distributed through print advertising or at the point of sale. Sometimes, though, specialty retailers or newly opened retailers will distribute coupons door to door or through direct mail.

CONTESTS/SWEEPSTAKES The main difference between contests and sweepstakes is that contests require entrants to perform a task or demonstrate a skill that is judged in order to be deemed a winner, while sweepstakes involve a random drawing or chance contest that may or may not have an entry requirement. At one time, contests were more commonly used as sales promotions, mostly due to legal restrictions on gambling that many marketers feared might apply to sweepstakes. But the use of sweepstakes as a promotional tactic has grown dramatically in recent decades, partly because of legal changes and partly because of their lower cost. Administering a contest once cost about $350 per thousand entries, compared to just $2.75 to $3.75 per thousand entries in a sweepstake. Furthermore, participation in contests is very low compared to sweepstakes, since they require some sort of skill or ability.

SPECIAL EVENTS According to the consulting firm International Events Group (IEG), businesses spend over $2 billion annually to link their products with everything from jazz festivals to golf tournaments to stock car races. In fact, large companies like RJR Nabisco and Anheuser-Busch have special divisions that handle nothing but special events. Special events marketing offers a number of advantages. First, events tend to attract a homogeneous audience that is very appreciative of the sponsors. Therefore, if a product fits well with the event and its audience, the impact of the sales promotion will be high. Second, event sponsorship often builds support among employees—who may receive acknowledgment for their participation—and within the trade. Finally, compared to producing a series of ads, event management is relatively simple. Many elements of event sponsorship are prepackaged and reusable, such as booths, displays, and ads.

PREMIUMS A premium is tangible compensation that is given as incentive for performing a particular act—usually buying a product. The premium may be given for free, or may be offered to consumers for a significantly reduced price. Some examples of premiums include receiving a prize in a cereal box or a free garden tool for visiting the grand opening of a hardware store. Incentives that are given for free at the time of purchase are called direct premiums. These offers provide instant gratification, plus there is no confusion about returning coupons or box tops, or saving bar codes or proofs of purchase.

Other types of direct premiums include traffic builders, door openers, and referral premiums. The garden tool is an example of a traffic-builder premium—an incentive to lure a prospective buyer to a store. A door-opener premium is directed to customers at home or to business people in their offices.

For example, a homeowner may receive a free clock radio for allowing an insurance agent to enter their home and listening to his sales pitch. Similarly, an electronics manufacturer might offer free software to an office manager who agrees to an on-site demonstration. The final category of direct premiums, referral premiums, reward the purchaser for referring the seller to other possible customers.

Mail premiums, unlike direct premiums, require the customer to perform some act in order to obtain a premium through return mail. An example might be a limited edition toy car offered by a marketer in exchange for one or more proofs-of-purchase and a payment covering the cost of the item plus handling. The premium is still valuable to the consumer because they cannot readily buy the item for the same amount.

CONTINUITY PROGRAMS Continuity programs retain brand users over a long time period by offering ongoing motivation or incentives. Continuity programs demand that consumers keep buying the product in order to get the premium in the future. Trading stamps, popularized in the 1950s and 1960s, are prime examples. Consumers usually received one stamp for every dime spent at a participating store. The stamp company provided redemption centers where the stamps were traded for merchandise. A catalog listing the quantity of stamps required for each item was available at the participating stores. Today, airlines' frequent-flyer clubs, hotels' frequent-traveler plans, retailers' frequent-shopper programs, and bonus-paying credit cards are common continuity programs. When competing brands have reached parity in terms of price and service, continuity programs sometimes prove a deciding factor among those competitors. By rewarding long-standing customers for their loyalty, continuity programs also reduce the threat of new competitors entering a market.

SAMPLING A sign of a successful marketer is getting the product into the hands of the consumer. Sometimes, particularly when a product is new or is not a market leader, an effective strategy is giving a sample product to the consumer, either free or for a small fee. But in order for sampling to change people's future purchase decisions, the product must have benefits or features that will be obvious during the trial.

There are several means of disseminating samples to consumers. The most popular has been through the mail, but increases in postage costs and packaging requirements have made this method less attractive. An alternative is door-to-door distribution, particularly when the items are bulky and when reputable distribution organizations exist. This method permits selective sampling of neighborhoods, dwellings, or even people. Another method is distributing samples in conjunction with advertising. An ad may include a coupon that the consumer can mail in for the product,

or it may include an address or phone number for ordering. Direct sampling can be achieved through prime media using scratch-and-sniff cards and slim foil pouches, or through retailers using special displays or a person hired to hand out samples to passing customers. Though this last technique may build goodwill for the retailer, some retailers resent the inconvenience and require high payments for their cooperation.

A final form of sample distribution deals with specialty types of sampling. For instance, some companies specialize in packing samples together for delivery to homogeneous consumer groups, such as newlyweds, new parents, students, or tourists. Such packages may be delivered at hospitals, hotels, or dormitories and include a number of different types of products.

TRADE PROMOTIONS

A trade sales promotion is targeted at resellers—wholesalers and retailers—who distribute manufacturers' products to the ultimate consumers. The objectives of sales promotions aimed at the trade are different from those directed at consumers. In general, trade sales promotions hope to accomplish four goals: 1) Develop in-store merchandising support, as strong support at the retail store level is the key to closing the loop between the customer and the sale. 2) Control inventory by increasing or depleting inventory levels, thus helping to eliminate seasonal peaks and valleys. 3) Expand or improve distribution by opening up new sales areas (trade promotions are also sometimes used to distribute a new size of the product). 4) Generate excitement about the product among those responsible for selling it. Some of the most common forms of trade promotions—profiled below—include point-of-purchase displays, trade shows, sales meetings, sales contests, push money, deal loaders, and promotional allowances.

TYPES OF TRADE PROMOTIONS

Manufacturers provide point-of-purchase (POP) display units free to retailers in order to promote a particular brand or group of products. The forms of POP displays include special racks, display cartons, banners, signs, price cards, and mechanical product dispensers. Probably the most effective way to ensure that a reseller will use a POP display is to design it so that it will generate sales for the retailer. High product visibility is the basic goal of POP displays. In industries such as the grocery field where a shopper spends about three-tenths of a second viewing a product, anything increasing product visibility is valuable. POP displays also provide or remind consumers about important decision information, such as the product's name, appearance, and sizes. The theme of the POP display should coordinate with the theme used in ads and by salespeople.

Thousands of manufacturers display their wares and take orders at trade shows. In fact, companies spend over $9 billion yearly on these shows. Trade shows provide a major opportunity to write orders for products. They also provide a chance to demonstrate products, disseminate information, answer questions, and be compared directly to competitors. Related to trade shows, but on a smaller scale, are sales meetings sponsored by manufacturers or wholesalers. Whereas trade shows are open to all potential customers, sales meetings are targeted toward the company's sales force and/or independent sales agents. These meetings are usually conducted regionally and directed by sales managers. The meetings may be used to motivate sales agents, to explain the product or the promotional campaign, or simply to answer questions. For resellers and salespeople, sales contests can also be an effective motivation. Typically, a prize is awarded to the organization or person who exceeds a quota by the largest percentage.

Similarly, push money (PM)—also known as spiffs—is an extra payment given to salespeople for meeting a specified sales goal. For example, a manufacturer of refrigerators might pay a $30 bonus for each unit of model A, and a $20 bonus for each unit of model B, sold between March 1 and September 1. At the end of that period, the salesperson would send evidence of these sales to the manufacturer and receive a check in return. Although some people see push money as akin to bribery, many manufacturers offer it.

A deal loader is a premium given by a manufacturer to a retailer for ordering a certain quantity of product. Two types of deal loaders are most typical. The first is a buying loader, which is a gift given for making a specified order size. The second is a display loader, which means the display is given to the retailer after the campaign. For instance, General Electric may have a display containing appliances as part of a special program. When the program is over, the retailer receives all the appliances on the display if a specified order size was achieved.

Trade deals are special price concessions superseding, for a limited time, the normal purchasing discounts given to the trade. Trade deals include a group of tactics having a common theme—to encourage sellers to specially promote a product. The marketer might receive special displays, larger-than-usual orders, superior in-store locations, or greater advertising effort. In exchange, the retailer might receive special allowances, discounts, goods, or money. In many industries, trade deals are the primary expectation for retail support, and the marketing funds spent in this area are considerable. There are two main types of trade deals: buying allowances and advertising/display allowances.

A buying allowance is a bonus paid by a manufacturer to a reseller when a certain amount of product is purchased during a specific time period. For example, a reseller who purchases at least 15 cases of product might receive a buying allowance of $6.00 off per case, while a purchase of at least 20 cases would result in $7.00 off per case, and so forth. The payment may take the form of a check or a reduction in the face value of an invoice. In order to take advantage of a buying allowance, some retailers engage in "forward buying." In essence, they order more merchandise than is needed during the deal period, then store the extra merchandise to sell later at regular prices. This assumes that the savings gained through the buying allowance is greater than the cost of warehousing and transporting the extra merchandise. Some marketers try to discourage forward buying, since it reduces profit margins and tends to create cyclical peaks and troughs in demand for the product.

The slotting allowance is a controversial form of buying allowance. Slotting allowances are fees retailers charge manufacturers for each space or slot on the shelf or in the warehouse that new products will occupy. The controversy stems from the fact that in many instances this allowance amounts to little more than paying a bribe to the retailer to convince them to carry your company's products. But many marketers are willing to pay extra to bring their products to the attention of consumers who are pressed for time in the store. Slotting allowances sometimes buy marketers prime spaces on retail shelves, at eye level or near the end of aisles.

The final type of buying allowance is a free goods allowance. In this case, the manufacturer offers a certain amount of product to wholesalers or retailers at no cost if they purchase a stated amount of the same or a different product. The allowance takes the form of free merchandise rather than money.

An advertising allowance is a dividend paid by a marketer to a reseller for advertising their product. The money can only be used to purchase advertising—for example, to print flyers or run ads in a local newspaper. But some resellers take advantage of the system, so many manufacturers require verification. A display allowance is the final form of trade promotional allowance. Some manufacturers pay retailers extra to highlight their display from the many available every week. The payment can take the form of cash or goods. Retailers must furnish written certification of compliance with the terms of the contract before they are paid. Retailers are most likely to select displays that yield high volume and are easy to assemble.

FURTHER READING:

Blattberg, Robert C., and Scott A. Neslin. *Sales Promotion: Concepts, Methods, and Strategies*. Upper Saddle River, NJ: Prentice Hall, 1990.

Lodish, Leonard M. *The Advertising and Promotion Challenge.* New York: Oxford University Press, 1986.

Quelch, John A. *Sales Promotion Management.* Upper Saddle River, NJ: Prentice Hall, 1989.

SEE ALSO: Corporate Sponsorship

SECURITIES AND EXCHANGE COMMISSION (SEC)

The U.S. Securities and Exchange Commission (SEC) is a federal agency responsible for administering federal securities laws written to provide protection for investors. The SEC also ensures that securities markets are fair and honest and, if necessary, enforces securities laws through the appropriate sanctions. Basically, the SEC oversees the activities of all participants in the securities markets—including publicly held corporations, public utilities, investment companies and advisers, and securities brokers and dealers—to ensure that investors are adequately informed and their interests are protected. Small businesses are most likely to come into contact with the SEC when they decide to make a public offering of debt or securities. Any business wishing to issue stock must first file a registration statement with the SEC. Another role of the SEC is to serve as adviser to the federal courts in Chapter 11 bankruptcy cases (corporate reorganization proceedings under Chapter 11 of the Bankruptcy Reform Act of 1978).

ORGANIZATION OF THE SEC

The SEC was created by Congress in 1934, under the Securities Exchange Act, as an independent, nonpartisan, quasi-judicial regulatory agency. The commission is made up of five members: one chairman and four commissioners. Each member is appointed by the president to a five-year term. The five-year terms are staggered, so that one appointed member's term expires June 5 of each year. No more than three of the commissioners may be of the same political party.

The commission's staff is made up of lawyers, accountants, financial analysts, engineers, investigators, economists, and other professionals. The SEC staff is divided into divisions and offices, which includes 12 regional and branch offices, each directed by officials appointed by the SEC chairman.

LAWS ADMINISTERED BY THE SEC

The chairman and commissioners of the SEC are responsible for ensuring that publicly held corporations, brokers or dealers in securities, investment companies and advisers, and other participants in the securities markets comply with federal securities law.

These laws were designed to help public investors make informed investment analysis and decisions—principally by ensuring adequate disclosure of material information. There are six major laws that the SEC is responsible for administering:

- Securities Act of 1933
- Securities Exchange Act of 1934
- Public Utility Holding Company Act of 1935
- Trust Indenture Act of 1939
- Investment Company Act of 1940
- Investment Advisers Act of 1940

The Securities Act of 1933, also known as the "truth in securities" law has two primary objectives: 1) to require that investors be provided with material information concerning securities offered for public sale; and 2) to prevent misrepresentation, deceit, and other fraud in the sale of securities. The SEC ensures that both of these objectives are met.

The Securities Exchange Act of 1934 extended the "disclosure" doctrine (from the Securities Act of 1933) to securities listed and registered for public trading on the U.S. securities exchanges. In 1964, the Securities Act Amendments extended disclosure and reporting provisions to equity securities in the over-the-counter market. The act seeks to ensure (through the SEC) fair and orderly securities markets by prohibiting certain types of activities and by setting forth rules regarding the operation of the markets and participants.

The SEC also administers the Public Utility Holding Company Act of 1935. Subject to regulation under this act are interstate holding companies engaged in the electric utility business or in the retail distribution of natural or manufactured gas. Reports to be filed with the SEC by these holding companies include detailed information concerning the organization, financial structure, and operations of the holding company and its subsidiaries. Holding companies are subject to SEC regulation in areas such as structure of the system, acquisitions, combinations, and issue and sales of securities.

The Trust Indenture Act of 1939 applies to bonds, debentures, notes, and similar debt securities offered for public sale and issued under trust indentures with more than $7.5 million of securities outstanding at any one time. Other provisions of the act prohibit the indenture trustee from having conflicts of interest; require the trustee to be a corporation with minimal combined capital and surplus; and impose high standards of conduct and responsibility on the trustee.

The SEC also ensures compliance with the Investment Company Act of 1940. This act seeks to regulate the activities of companies engaged primarily in investing, reinvesting, and trading in securities, and whose own securities are publicly offered. It is important for potential investors to understand that although the SEC serves as a regulatory agency in these cases, the SEC does not supervise a company's investment activities, and the mere presence of the SEC as a regulatory agency does not guarantee a safe investment.

The Investment Advisers Act of 1940—also overseen by the SEC—establishes a style, or a system, of regulating investment advisers. The main thrust of this act requires all persons, or firms, that are compensated for advising anyone about securities investment opportunities to be registered with the SEC and conform to the established standards of investor protection. The SEC has the power and ability to strip an investment adviser of his or her registration if a statutory violation has occurred.

Finally, the SEC is given some responsibility connected with corporate bankruptcy reorganizations, commonly referred to as Chapter 11 proceedings. Chapter 11 of the Bankruptcy Code grants the SEC permission to become involved in any proceedings, but the SEC is primarily concerned with proceedings directly involving significant public investor interest.

FURTHER READING:

Skousen, K. Fred. *An Introduction to the SEC.* 5th ed. Cincinnati: SouthWestern Publishing, 1991.

SEE ALSO: Initial Public Offering; Stocks

SEED MONEY

Seed money, or seed capital, is the financing an entrepreneur needs in the very early stages of launching a new business. It gets its name from the idea that early stage financing plants the seed that enables a small business to grow. Obtaining funding is one of the most critical aspects of starting a small business. In fact, many businesses fail or are prevented from even starting due to a lack of **capital**. Although obtaining financing can be difficult for any small business, it is particularly hard for new ventures; because new ventures lack a track record, potential lenders and investors are likely to be quite negative about their prospects for success. Still, the American economy depends upon small businesses to create jobs and provide needed products or services within their communities. As a result, seed money is usually available from some source for capable and persistent entrepreneurs with solid business ideas.

Many entrepreneurs approach their family, friends, and colleagues for seed money after exhausting their own finances. Because these investors know the entrepreneur, they are more likely to take a risk on funding a new venture than are traditional financing sources—such as banks or venture capital firms. "An entrepreneur needs vast quantities of commitment and enthusiasm in the seed-capital stage, since the venture has little else with which to entice investors," Reed Phillips III wrote in an article for *Folio.* "Because it is almost impossible to predict how successful the project might eventually become, the only outsiders likely to invest are those who respect the entrepreneur's judgment and abilities. And those are the people with whom the entrepreneur has had the longest relationships." By "getting in on the ground floor," the providers of seed money hope to participate in the entrepreneur's success and realize a healthy return as their investment appreciates over time. Still, Phillips noted, "Risking money in the early stages of a start-up is more like buying a lottery ticket than making an investment. Investors know the odds are against them and realize they may lose their entire investment."

In most cases, seed money takes the form of equity financing, so investors receive partial ownership of the fledgling company in exchange for their funds. As a result, it is important for the entrepreneur to take potential investors' personalities and business reputations into consideration when seeking seed money. Since these people will be part owners of the company—and may insist upon having some control over decision making—it is vital to ascertain whether their interests are compatible with those of the entrepreneur. Once compatible investors have been located, the entrepreneur must convince them that the new business venture has a good chance of success. The first step in this process is creating a formal, written business plan, including plausible projections of income and expenses.

The entrepreneur should also have a specific purpose in mind for the seed money. The purpose of seed capital usually involves moving the business out of the idea stage—by building a prototype product or conducting market research, for example—and gathering concrete evidence that it can succeed. In this way, seed money helps the entrepreneur to prove the merit of his or her idea in order to attract the interest of formal investment sources.

As far as the amount of seed money the entrepreneur should try to obtain, Phillips recommended raising only what was needed to accomplish the business's initial objectives. Given its risk, seed capital is usually more expensive for the firm than later stage financing. Thus, raising a small amount at a time helps the entrepreneur to preserve equity for later financing rounds. Ideally, an arrangement can be made that links seed money to launch financing, so the entrepreneur can go back to the same investors for future funding needs. For example, the entrepreneur might set goals for a successful market test of a new product. If the goals are met, then the original investors agree to provide additional funds for a product launch. This approach protects the entrepreneur against the possibility of having a successful test and then running out of money before being able to launch the product. Even if the original investors cannot provide additional funds directly, their vested interest may encourage them to help the venture succeed in other ways.

There are other sources of seed money available to entrepreneurs besides friends and family members. For example, some **venture capital** firms reserve a limited amount of funds to finance new ventures or business ideas. Since start-ups involve greater risks than established businesses, however, the venture capital investors generally require a larger equity position in exchange. In his book *The Entrepreneur's Guide to Preparing a Winning Business Plan and Raising Venture Capital,* W. Keith Schilit estimated that venture capitalists providing seed money would expect a 50 to 100 percent higher return than in a standard venture capital arrangement. There are also nonprofit organizations dedicated to providing seed capital for new businesses. In many cases, these organizations will also assist the entrepreneur in creating a business plan or marketing materials, and establishing cash flow controls or other systems.

FURTHER READING:

Fraser, Jill Andresky. "Seeking Seed Money." *Inc.* December 1995.

J.K. Lasser Institute. *How to Run a Small Business.* New York: McGraw-Hill, 1989.

Phillips, Reed, III. "Raising Seed Money Is a Critical First Step." *Folio: The Magazine for Magazine Management.* February 15, 1995.

Schilit, W. Keith. *The Entrepreneur's Guide to Preparing a Winning Business Plan and Raising Venture Capital.* Englewood Cliffs, NJ: Prentice Hall, 1990.

Silver, A. David. *Up Front Financing: The Entrepreneur's Guide.* New York: Wiley, 1982.

SEE ALSO: Loans

SELF-ASSESSMENT

Self-assessment is a tool that involves performing a critical analysis of one's own goals, interests, skills, and experience. Among its many applications in the business world are employee **training and development**, team performance, and organizational change efforts. But self-assessment is perhaps most valuable for would-be entrepreneurs considering starting a new business. "A business is merely an extension of the people managing it and mirrors their abilities," according to the *Entrepreneur Magazine*

Small Business Advisor. "As an entrepreneur, you have to know your strengths and weaknesses so you can compensate in some way for the areas where you will not be proficient. You can determine your strengths and weaknesses by evaluating the major accomplishments in your personal and professional life and the skills required to complete these tasks." In other words, entrepreneurs may be able to improve their chances of success in business by completing a self-assessment.

By evaluating such personal traits as business skills, experience, and knowledge, financial goals, likes and dislikes, willingness to expend effort, and ability to meet challenges, entrepreneurs may be able to identify the business opportunities for which they are best suited. In some cases, self-assessment may even lead to innovative new business ideas. In addition, completing a self-assessment can help entrepreneurs recognize areas where they will need assistance or training. By increasing self-knowledge, it may also help entrepreneurs to attract investors and impress lenders.

A good place to start in performing a self-assessment is to prepare a detailed resume. This document should list the entrepreneur's educational background and professional experience—describing the requirements and responsibilities of each job in detail—along with hobbies and outside interests. Using the resume as a guide, it may then be helpful for the entrepreneur to separate his or her professional attributes by functional area—such as marketing, accounting, or human resource management—and assign a competency level to each one. Finally, the entrepreneur may wish to create a list of personal attributes—such as ability with numbers, common sense, communication skills, organization skills, people skills, etc.—that may be useful in starting and running a small business. The mere process of thinking about and categorizing one's skills and experience can be informative.

Not surprisingly, the tool of self-assessment can be applied to a wide variety of other business situations as well. For example, it can be used as an aid in employee development as part of a company's performance evaluation and training efforts. A common application is "360-degree feedback" systems—in addition to being evaluated by supervisors, peers, and subordinates, employees evaluate their own performance and participate in setting goals. Self-assessment can also be applied to teams of workers or even overall organizations to help identify strengths and weaknesses and improve performance. Teams might evaluate such elements of team performance as goal setting, communication, decision making, problem solving, and conflict management. At the organizational level, self-assessment performed with the participation of employees can help clarify a company's mission and goals, identify shortcomings, and generate ideas to increase competitiveness.

FURTHER READING:

Caravatta, Michael. "Conducting an Organizational Self-Assessment Using the 1997 Baldrige Award Criteria." *Quality Progress*. October 1997.

The Entrepreneur Magazine Small Business Advisor. New York: Wiley, 1991.

Maron, Rebecca M. "Self-Assessment: A Remedy for Dysfunctional Board Behaviors." *Association Management*. January 1997.

SEE ALSO: Business Planning; Managing Organizational Change

SELF-EMPLOYMENT

Self-employment refers to the status of an individual who—rather than accepting a position as an employee of another person or organization—chooses to go into business for him or herself. Self-employment offers individuals a number of advantages, from the freedom to work without supervision to the ability to deduct the costs of doing business for tax purposes. But it also has some potential drawbacks, including uncertain levels of income, long working hours, isolation, and the need to fund one's own health insurance and retirement plans. People choose self-employment for a wide variety of reasons. Some desire a change in life-style, some are unable to find other employment, some want to work at home in order to care for small children, and some are retirees seeking additional income. Regardless of the underlying motivation, there are ways for self-employed persons to overcome the potential drawbacks and increase their chances for success.

Individuals who choose self-employment must be aware of the rules governing the treatment of independent contractors (also known as freelance employees or self-employees). Classification of someone as an employee or a self-employee is somewhat ambiguous and depends on several factors, including the degree of independence, the freedom to hire others to do the work taken on, the freedom to work for others, and the assumption of risks. Independent contractors typically accept no fringe benefits and pay Social Security, Medicare, and income tax installments directly. Employees have more statutory rights, benefits, and protections than subcontractors, who must generally provide these for themselves. But independent contractors have advantages in terms of freedom, flexibility, and tax deductions.

The **IRS** applies a 20-part test to determine whether a certain worker should be classified as an

employee or an independent contractor. The main issue underpinning the test is who sets the work rules: employees must follow rules set by their bosses, while independent contractors set their own rules. For example, an individual who sets his or her own hours, receives payment by the job, and divides his or her time between work for several different employers would probably be classified as an independent contractor. Other criteria involve who provides the tools and materials needed to complete the work. For example, an individual who works at an employer's facility and uses the employer's equipment would be considered an employee, while one who works at a separate location and provides his or her own equipment would be classified as an independent contractor. Finally, an independent contractor usually pays his or her own expenses of doing business and takes the risk of not receiving payment when work is not completed in accordance with a contract, while an employee is usually reimbursed for business-related expenses by the employer and receives a paycheck whether or not his or her work is completed.

An individual's status as a self-employed, independent contractor can be reinforced by having multiple clients, being paid by the amount of work done rather than by the hour, or obtaining an **employer identification number** from the IRS. Working under a **business name** also helps reinforce this status. Printing invoices, business cards, and stationery can help identify someone as a self-employed person. In general, the person must demonstrate that he or she is in business for the purpose of making a profit.

THE GROWTH OF SELF-EMPLOYMENT

The concept of self-employment received increased attention in the 1980s and 1990s as many large firms responded to increased competition and a lingering recession by "downsizing," or reducing the size of their permanent staffs and hiring temporary employees and independent contractors to reduce overhead. The financial impact of workers' compensation, Social Security, and job protection laws also made employers more cautious about hiring full-time employees. While at one time a large company using freelancers seemed to imply a crisis, it became a commonplace way to control costs and try out new talent in the 1990s. At the same time, many employees who were laid off chose to go into business for themselves rather than reenter an increasingly unstable work force. The growth of self-employed professionals, in turn, enabled smaller companies to enlist the services of people who have had experience at larger, more sophisticated companies, without the cost of hiring them full-time.

Another factor influencing the growth of self-employment was that personal computer and communications technology made working at home (rather than at an office) more feasible throughout the 1980s and 1990s. Through cellular telephones and pagers, the self-employed professional can stay in touch with clients throughout the day. Fax machines and modems make business over a large geographic area feasible and help the one-person office get work out quickly. In addition, on-line services and electronic bulletin boards make instantaneous local, cross-country, and international networking and research feasible. The relatively low price of personal computers, peripherals, and communications equipment have enabled many more people to conduct business independently.

By the early 1990s, one-fifth of all new jobs in the United States were created by self-employment, and self-employed persons accounted for 7.6 percent of the work force. In fact, job growth in this category increased almost twice as fast as overall job growth. The highest growth came in the finance, insurance, property, and business services industries—areas where professionals could expect to earn more by becoming independent.

CHARACTERISTICS OF THE SELF-EMPLOYED

There are many different types of independent contractors, from professionals leaving corporate life to youngsters delivering newspapers and single parents stuffing envelopes at home. Generally, professionals who have built up their skills and their reputations working for large employers. The burden of managing others is often cited as a motivator for starting a business. Some individuals begin their own enterprises to work fewer hours, as 80-hour weeks are not unheard of in corporate life. For women, being able to take time off to raise their children can be priceless perquisite, as can the freedom to bring the children into the workplace. Another factor leading workers to consider self-employment is the downsizing trend itself, which has done much to erode the belief that salaried jobs are more secure. It is also very difficult for older workers to secure permanent jobs after they have been dismissed. Freedom from the necessity of commuting is another factor in the increase in number of home-based businesses in the United States.

Various personal characteristics seem to steer people into self-employment, such as being the oldest child or having parents who were self-employed. In addition, individuals are more likely to become self-employed if they have been fired from more than one job, have been previously employed in small businesses, are college graduates, are realistic risk takers, and are well-organized and good at organizing others. Many entrepreneurs are immigrants or children of immigrants. Some personality requirements for suc-

cess as an independent contractor include confidence, a positive outlook, friendliness, and the determination to succeed.

BENEFITS AND DRAWBACKS OF SELF-EMPLOYMENT

Self-employed individuals as a whole tend to work longer (an additional 17.5 hours per week, according to one study) and harder than their colleagues who are organizationally employed, and they do it for irregular pay and, frequently, fewer tangible benefits. In addition, their salaries and assets are dependent on their work contributions in a more intimate way than are those of their colleagues. Not surprisingly, a study of certified public accountants found self-employed CPAs to have higher levels of organizational commitment.

The self-employed have been found to report lower absences, which has been attributed not to superior health but to the feeling of being indispensable. In fact, their jobs tend to be more physically and psychologically stressful due to the investments in energy the jobs demand. Certain stress factors are generally absent from self-employment—such as corporate meetings and employee discipline problems. However, dealing with clients presents its own stress, such as rush orders and negotiations, and there is also added uncertainty.

Professionals can often expect to earn more after establishing themselves as independent contractors, but the pay differential has been shrinking. According to 1992 Census Bureau statistics, self-employed men earned slightly more (a median of $31,812 per year gross income) than their organizationally employed counterparts in private industry ($30,087), while self-employed women earned much less ($15,032 versus $20,644). Many self-employed women held very low-paying positions, such as child care. Intermittent income is one of the most significant difficulties the newly independent businessperson must face. Downtime can be avoided by overscheduling or moonlighting—working a salaried job on the side. Experts advise new business owners not to rely on their enterprises for income for at least the first six months; comfortable returns may not follow for months afterward.

The self-employed often undercharge for their services or products at the beginning of their enterprises, at times even doing work for free with the hope of impressing new clients. This is partly due to a lack of confidence and partly because of their justified concerns about competing in the marketplace. But underpricing may not necessarily lead to more contracts; in fact, it can connote a lack of quality. Despite this, freelancers starting out are advised to take all the work they need in order to survive—including low-paying projects. Market values for their work can be determined through colleagues or contacts in the business.

ISOLATION AND NETWORKING A significant source of psychological strain for self-employed individuals is isolation. The environment of the typical self-employed individual is quite different from the corporate environment where many professionals gain their experience. This is one reason contact with supportive colleagues becomes crucial. Mentors can provide advice regarding business aspects of a new business owner's operation. Trade and professional organizations can be an excellent way to establish contacts with peers.

Tenacity in **networking** has been cited as a key to survival for business owners, some of whom maintain databases of thousands of contacts. These contacts are also vital in referring clients and providing market information. The role of the contact is made more important as the self-employed individual typically has no staff for marketing support.

It is difficult to exaggerate the importance of referrals to the typical independent professional. Since relationships are so vital, one must exercise the utmost delicacy in terminating employment with one's former employer or turning down a job. One's former employer can even become a good client, besides providing valuable referrals. When turning down clients, the self-employed person can protect those relationships by making referrals or even subcontracting to other colleagues in their network. Provided the work done is of quality, this can strengthen one's reputation. When the client calls back with a more appropriate assignment, the contractor has the choice of the business.

As they begin their enterprises, many self-employed individuals feel compelled to accept a variety of assignments due to sheer scarcity of work. However, specialization can help ensure their long-term survival. For one thing, corporate clients can often find a generalist's abilities in-house. Also, specialization may allow professionals to broaden their client base geographically, thus freeing their fortunes from fluctuations in the local economy. These factors can enable the specialist to earn higher fees and work more consistently. Paradoxically, one's work as a specialist can garner referrals outside one's specialty, so specialization might not be as limiting as a strict definition would imply. The self-employed should be cautioned against changing their specialties too often, as this can confuse clients and make their own operations inefficient.

TAX IMPLICATIONS Self-employment entails both tax advantages and disadvantages. In terms of advantages, individuals who are classified as independent contractors can deduct work-related expenses for tax purposes. In addition, independent contractors often qualify for tax deductions for using part of their home as an office and for salaries paid to other people, while employees usually do not. Independent contractors also have the benefit of sheltering 15 percent of their annual income, or up to $30,000, for retirement, while employees are limited to $9,500 annually. A standard deduction, 30 cents per mile in 1995, may be used by self-employed persons for business-related transportation costs, or actual fuel and maintenance costs. Also, up to 50 percent of medical insurance premiums may be deducted for sole proprietors, partners, and S Corporation shareholders.

The main tax disadvantage for self-employed persons is that they must pay the full amount of Social Security and Medicare taxes themselves and make quarterly estimated tax payments to the federal government. For those who are organizationally employed, the employer withholds income taxes and pays half of their Social Security and Medicare taxes. Although the payment of Social Security and Medicare increases the tax burden of self-employed individuals, these amounts are based on net, rather than gross, earnings. For this reason, it is essential for small business owners to keep an accurate record of expenses.

HEALTH INSURANCE The expense and the limited tax deduction for premiums discourages many self-employed persons from getting health insurance for themselves and their employees. One option for newly self-employed persons is to obtain insurance through a prior employer. The Consolidated Omnibus Budget Reconciliation Act (COBRA) requires companies with more than 50 employees to offer health care coverage up to 18 months after an employee leaves; this may be the only option for people with preexisting conditions that preclude new insurance coverage. Under this plan, however, employees must pay 102 percent of their insurance premiums themselves. Other options include a spouse's company plan, a trade organization plan, or individual coverage.

INCREASING THE CHANCE OF SUCCESS IN SELF-EMPLOYMENT

Self-employment, whether by choice or necessity, does not include any guarantees of success. In fact, nearly two out of every three new businesses fail within five years. But the chances of success can be greatly improved with careful planning, prior savings, and a marketing strategy. Ideally, an individual should implement these steps before taking the plunge to full-time self-employment. As Karen Gutloff noted in an article for *Black Enterprise,* aspiring freelancers should accumulate savings ahead of time, as well as reduce their personal debt. It may also be helpful to make the transition to full-time self-employment gradually, while maintaining at least part-time employment on the side. Although some employers frown on this arrangement, it can provide an individual with time and money to develop a client base and a business plan. Those planning home-based businesses should also take time to prepare family members for the changes that will take place.

Gutloff also recommended that new business owners try to establish one stable client relationship that will provide steady income during the search for additional clients. A particularly attractive option may be an individual's former employer, which will already be familiar with the entrepreneur's reputation and abilities. For this relationship to succeed, however, it is important that the individual use an honest and professional approach when severing ties with their employer. Although one stable client relationship can help establish a new business, it is also important that the self-employed person develop a marketing strategy to find new clients and grow. Many new business owners become so busy serving their existing clients that they do not devote sufficient time to marketing. Sending out brochures, networking, and joining professional organizations are a few possible marketing strategies.

Finally, self-employed individuals should take an organized approach to all business activities in order to increase their chances of success. It may be helpful to draw up a business plan to follow when starting and growing a new business. This plan can help a self-employed person evaluate strategies, plan expenditures, and motivate him or herself. It is also important to keep careful records of income and expenses, set aside money for taxes, and insist upon contracts for all work performed.

FURTHER READING:

Bianchi, Alessandra. "New Businesses." *Inc.* May 1993.

Edwards, Colin C. "A Career in Contracting . . . Is It a Viable Alternative?" *Management Services.* March 1992.

Eliason, Carol. *The Business Plan for Homebased Business.* Denver: U.S. Small Business Administration, 1991.

Elliott, Susan. *Becoming Self-Employed.* Blue Ridge Summit, PA: Liberty, 1987.

Ellis, Barbara. "Tips for the Self-Employed Professional." *Accountancy.* January 1994.

Gutloff, Karen. "Freelance!" *Black Enterprise.* June 1997.

Hand, Larry E. *Freelancing Made Simple.* New York: Doubleday, 1995.

Laurance, Robert. *Going Freelance: A Guide for Professionals.* New York: Wiley, 1988.

Lohse, Deborah. "The Greenest Tax Breaks of All Go to the Self-Employed." *Money.* August 1992.

McCarroll, Thomas. "Starting Over." *Time.* January 6, 1992.

Monheit, Alan C., and P. Holly Harvey. "Sources of Health Insurance for the Self-Employed: Does Differential Taxation Make a Difference?" *Inquiry.* Fall 1993.

Murphy, Anne. "Do-It-Yourself Job Creation." *Inc.* January 1994.

Nelton, Sharon. "Putting Women into Business." *Nation's Business.* October 1992.

Oliver, Suzanne. "Moonlighter's Delight." *Forbes.* June 21, 1993.

Pridna, John P., and Charles J. DeLanoy. "Maximizing Deductions for Self-Employed Persons' Medical Expenses." *Tax Adviser.* May 1993.

Robinson, Peter B., and Edwin A. Sexton. "The Effect of Education and Experience on Self-Employment Success." *Journal of Business Venturing.* March 1994.

Watson, Mark, and Ian Hunter. "Employment Law." *Director.* March 1994.

Wells, Melanie. "Big Shops Put Faith in Free-Lancers." *Advertising Age.* May 31, 1993.

"Working for Yourself." *The Economist.* August 29, 1992.

SEE ALSO: Entrepreneurship; Free-lance Employment/Independent Contractors; Health Insurance Options; Tax Deductible Business Expenses; Tax Planning

SELF-EMPLOYMENT CONTRIBUTIONS ACT

The Self-Employment Contributions Act (SECA) of 1954 is a tax law that requires the owners of small businesses—such as **S corporations**, **partnerships**, and **sole proprietorships**—to pay a tax of 15.3 percent of their net income from **self-employment** to cover their own Social Security, Medicare, and Old Age Survivors and Disability Insurance (OASDI) costs. Workers who are employed by a company or another person (rather than being self-employed) only have to pay half this amount, which is withheld from their paychecks. Their employer pays the other half. In effect, SECA requires self-employed persons to pay both the employer and employee portions of the **Federal Insurance Contributions Act (FICA) tax** (a combination of Social Security and Medicare). To make this situation more equitable, small business owners subject to SECA are allowed to deduct half of their SECA tax amount on their personal federal **tax returns**.

SECA taxes are computed on the basis of net earnings from self-employment. Net earnings are defined as the gross income derived from business activities, less the expenses incurred in the course of doing business. In this way, ordinary business expenses reduce the SECA tax paid by individuals. But some other expenses, such as the cost of contributions to Keogh or Simplified Employee Pension (SEP) retirement plans, are not deductible for the purposes of SECA taxes. As a result, SECA makes it more expensive for the owner of a business to fund his or her own retirement plan than to fund the same plan for employees, because a larger percentage of employee contributions are tax deductible. After computing net earnings from self-employment, the business owner then applies a 15.3 percent rate (based on two separate rates for Social Security and Medicare) on income up to $60,600. A lower rate is applied to higher income amounts.

In general, SECA is believed to adversely affect the small business sector of the American economy. Many political leaders have indicated that they feel small businesses hold the key to employment and economic growth. But legislation increased the SECA rate significantly during the 1980s. Prior to 1984, the SECA rate was set at 50 percent of the regular FICA rate and 75 percent of the regular OASDI rate, giving self-employed individuals tax advantages similar to those enjoyed by individuals employed by others. But between 1984 and 1990, the SECA rate was increased to 100 percent of FICA. Since FICA rates were already increasing due to double-digit inflation at that time, SECA rates had to rise even more quickly to catch up. This increase reduced the after-tax earnings of small firms and thus the availability of capital for small business expansion. As John Brozovsky and A. J. Cataldo II wrote in *Management Accounting,*

"the small firm is taxed at higher rates on larger amounts, further hindering its efforts to expand facilities, increase employment, and provide economic stimulus."

FURTHER READING:

Brozovsky, John, and A. J. Cataldo II. "Inflation Indexing and Small Business." *Management Accounting.* November 1993.

Evanson, David R. "Spare No Expense." *Entrepreneur.* August 1996.

Nadel, Alan A. "Self-Employment Tax Treatment of Keogh and SEP Contributions and Unreimbursed Business Expenses." *The Tax Adviser.* November 1995.

SEE ALSO: Tax Planning

SELLING A BUSINESS

Many small business owners eventually decide to sell their companies, though the reasons for such divestments vary widely from individual to individual. Some owners may simply wish to retire, while others are impatient to investigate new challenges—whether in business or some other area—or tired of the frustrations of the business in which they find themselves. Others decide to sell for reasons more closely associated with the health of the business itself; disputes with partners, incapacitation or death or principals, or downturns in the company's financial performance can all spur business owners to ponder putting their business on the block. Whatever their ultimate reason for selling, though, business owners can get the most

out of their company by carefully considering a number of factors.

TIMING THE SALE OF A BUSINESS

"External economic forces, together with internal financial performance, will dictate when you should put your company on the market so as to achieve the maximum results," wrote Lawrence W. Tuller in his book *Getting Out: A Step-by-Step Guide to Selling a Business or Professional Practice.* "If the timing isn't right, it will take much longer to sell the business, and the price you negotiate will inevitably be less than you should get."

The financial performance and history of the company in question is often the most important factor in determining price at the time of sale. A business owner who chooses to sell after posting several years of steady growth will naturally command a higher price than will the business owner who decides to sell only a year or two into that growth trend—even if the environment continues to appear friendly to the business for the foreseeable future.

The business environment in which the company operates is also an important factor in determining the asking price that the market will bear. If the company in question operates in an industry that is suffering through a downturn, the owner should delay selling the business if at all possible. Few companies are able to buck the tide when the industry in which they operate is stuck in a sluggish cycle, and even attractive businesses will not shine as brightly during such periods. For most business owners looking to sell their company, it is usually wise to ride out the trough and put the company up for sale after the industry enters a more robust cycle. Of course, some industries never post a recovery; business owners engaged in under-performing industries need to determine whether the downturns they experience are simply an inevitable part of the business cycle within a basically healthy industry, or whether changes in the marketplace are fundamentally altering the strength of the industry (establishments as varied as roller rinks and men's hats manufacturers have been relegated to the fringes of the American economy by the ever-changing tastes of U.S. consumers).

The stock market is a third factor that should be analyzed when pondering whether to put a company up for sale. "Stock market averages and trends reflect not only the current health of the national economy, but the projected conditions for the near future," pointed out Tuller. "Major corporate decisions for capital appropriations, expansion or contraction moves, and new product and service introductions are strongly influenced by the perceived well being of the economy. In turn, the magnitude of these corporate decisions affect investor confidence in the stock market. . . . The price an entrepreneur can get for his company will be heavily influenced by public investor attitudes.''

STOCK SALES AND ASSET SALES

Another decision that some business owners need to make early in the selling process is whether to hand over the company through a stock sale or an asset sale. If a business has been incorporated, the owner has the option of making a stock sale or an asset sale. Under the terms of a stock sale, the seller receives an agreed-upon price for his or her shares in the company, and after ownership of those stocks has been transferred, the buyer steps in and operates the still-running business. Typically, such a purchase means that the buyer receives not only all company assets, but all company liabilities as well. This arrangement is often appealing to the seller because of its tax advantages. The sale of stock qualifies as a capital gain, and it enables the seller to avoid **double taxation**, since sale proceeds flow directly to the seller without passing through the corporation. In addition, a stock sale frees the seller from any future legal action that might be leveled against the company. Lawsuits and claims against the company become the sole responsibility of the new stock owner(s).

Partnerships and **sole proprietorships**, meanwhile, must change hands via asset sale arrangements, since stocks are not a part of the picture. Under asset sale agreements, the seller hands over business equipment, inventory, trademarks and patents, trade names, **goodwill**, and other assets for an agreed-upon price. The seller then uses the money to pay off any debts; the remainder is his or her profit. Changes in ownership accomplished through asset transactions are generally favored by buyers for two reasons. First, the transaction sometimes allows the buyer to claim larger **depreciation** deductions on his or her taxes. Second, an asset sale provides the buyer with greater protection from unknown or undisclosed liabilities—such as lawsuits or problems with income taxes or payroll withholding taxes—incurred by the previous owner.

PREPARING TO SELL

When preparing to sell a business, owners need to gather a wide variety of information for potential buyers to review. Financial, legal, marketing, and operations information all need to be prepared for examination.

FINANCIAL INFORMATION Most privately held businesses are operated in ways that serve to minimize the seller's tax liability. As John A. Johansen observed in the SBA brochure *How to Buy or Sell a Business,* however, ''the same operating techniques and ac- counting practices that minimize tax liability also minimize the value of a business. . . . It is possible to reconstruct financial statements to reflect the actual operating performance of the business, [but] this process may also put the owner in a position of having to pay back income taxes and penalties. Therefore, plans to sell a business should be made years in advance of the actual sale.'' Such a period of time allows the owner to make the accounting changes that will put his or her business in the best financial light. Certainly, a business venture that can point to several years of optimum fiscal success is apt to receive more inquiries than a business whose accounting practices—while quite sensible in terms of creating a favorable tax environment for the owner—blunt those bottom line financial numbers.

Would-be business sellers also need to prepare **financial statements** and other documents for potential buyers to review. These include a complete **balance sheet** (with detailed information on accounts receivable and payable, inventory, real estate, machinery and other equipment, liabilities, marketable securities, and schedules of notes payable and mortgages payable), an **income statement**, and a **valuation** report. The latter is an appraisal of the business's market value.

LEGAL INFORMATION The seller should also prepare the necessary information on legal issues pertaining to the company. These range from such basic operating documents as **articles of incorporation**, bylaws, **partnership agreements**, supplier agreements, and franchise agreements to data on regulatory requirements (and whether they are being adhered to), current or pending legal actions against the company, zoning requirements, lease terms, and stock status.

MARKETING INFORMATION Intelligent buyers will want detailed marketing information on the company as well, including data on the business's chief market area, its market share, and marketing expenditures (on advertising, consultants, etc.). In addition, product line information will also be expected. Buyers, for instance, will want to know whether any of the company's products are proprietary, or whether there are potentially valuable new goods in the production pipeline. Descriptions of pricing strategies, customer **demographics**, and competition should also be available for potential buyers to review.

OPERATIONS INFORMATION Finally, business owners looking to sell their company should be prepared to provide detailed information on various aspects of the business's day-to-day operations. The ''operations'' umbrella encompasses everything from company policies to historical hours of operation to personnel listings (including organizational chart (if applicable), **job descriptions**, rates of pay, and **employee benefits**). Other factors that can potentially impact one or more aspects of the company's operations, such as the presence or absence of an employee union, will also have to be detailed.

Once information on all facets of the business has been gathered, it should be organized into a comprehensive business presentation package. A complete business presentation package, remarked Johansen, should include the following:

- History of the business;
- Description of business operations;
- Description of physical facilities;
- Discussion of suppliers (if any) and agreements with those suppliers;
- Review of current and historical marketing practices;
- Description of competition;
- Coverage of personnel and employee issues;
- Identification of owners;
- Description of insurance coverage for business;
- Discussion of pending legal issues or contingent liabilities;
- Financial statements for the past three to five years.

LOCATING PROSPECTIVE BUYERS

EXTERNAL BUYERS Most business owners sell their companies to external buyers—buyers who are not current partners or employees in the organization. There are three primary routes that sellers can take to notify these buyers of the availability of their companies: print advertising, industry sources, and intermediaries.

Many people hoping to sell their businesses make arrangements for advertisements in the Thursday edition of the *Wall Street Journal,* which produces several regional versions of its paper around the country. The *Journal* is a particularly popular option for owners of large, privately held businesses. Owners of smaller businesses, meanwhile, often turn to the classified sections of their own local newspapers to advertise the availability of their company for acquisition. When submitting a ''business opportunity'' advertisement for publication in the newspaper, however, sellers need to take a sensible approach. ''There is a delicate balance to be struck in any kind of advertising between the need for confidentiality and giving enough information to attract potential buyers,'' wrote Michael K. Semanik and John H. Wade in *The Complete Guide to Selling a Business.* ''When your ads describe too much, competitors and others can deduce who you are and find out information you

don't want them to know. Give too little information and you won't attract any interest.'' Advertisements should provide a brief description of the type of business for sale, its primary assets (location, popularity, profitability, etc.), and a way for interested buyers to make contact. Sellers who wish to maintain some degree of anonymity while looking for a buyer may wish to arrange for a post office box rather than include their telephone number.

Industry sources also can be valuable when a business owner decides to sell his or her business. Suppliers, for instance, may know of potential buyers lurking elsewhere in the industry or community. In addition, trade associations and trade journals can be used to get the word out about a company's availability.

A third option that many sellers use is to secure the services of a **business broker** or merger and acquisition consultant to sell their business. Business brokers, who generally handle the sale of smaller companies (though this is by no means an absolute rule), typically charge the seller a fee of about 10 percent of the final purchase price. ''Business brokers are exactly what the name implies,'' wrote Tuller, ''firms that list businesses for sale, then advertise them for sale to the public. They are very similar to real estate brokers but not licensed. . . . A business broker will not usually investigate the businesses he lists but will rely entirely on data given to him by you, the Seller. Valuation of the business is usually left completely up to you, and although a reputable broker will make suggestions, he is generally either not qualified or not interested in spending much time analyzing the business to determine marketability.'' Merger and acquisition consultants, on the other hand, typically specialize in handling larger middle-market companies. ''Their coverage of the entrepreneurial market is usually very broad and they generally know, within specialized industries or regions, which larger companies are actively searching for additions to their product lines or industry groupings,'' said Tuller. Payments to ''M&A'' consultants are usually less than 10 percent but this is in part because of the larger scale of the deals in which they are typically involved. In addition, many consultants ask for a monthly retainer fee. One of the benefits of securing the services of a merger and acquisition consultant is that he or she will typically provide help in preparing presentation packages, valuing businesses, and negotiating with prospective buyers.

A well chosen business broker or merger and acquisition consultant can save the seller of a business a considerable amount of time and effort. However, both groups include hucksters who prey on unwary business owners, so it is important for sellers to conduct the appropriate background research before soliciting services in these areas.

INTERNAL BUYERS Another option sometimes available to business owners is to sell their company to "internal" buyers—employees or business partners. Selling to employees through **employee stock ownership plans (ESOPs)** or other arrangements are particularly attractive for business owners because they accrue significant tax advantages through such sales. Employees interested in assuming ownership of the company via a "management buyout (MBO)" could range from a single key employee, such as a general manager who already has a good grasp on many aspects of the enterprise, to a group of employees (or even all of the company's employees). "This is fertile territory," claimed Tuller. "Most employees yearn to have their own business. All employees are concerned about someone else buying the company and either being fired, or not being able to work for the new boss." Employee convictions that they could improve on the owner's performance often play a part as well. Finally, noted Tuller, "when it comes time to finance the sale, bankers will bend over backwards to assist a [management buyout], although they might not be interested at all in an outside buyer." MBOs that rely on external financing, however, typically require that one or members of the purchasing group have management training in all aspects of the business; if such expertise is lacking, the seller will need to implement a training schedule for one or more employees to fulfill this requirement.

Business partners, meanwhile, are often ideal business buyers when an owner is ready to get out. Indeed, many business owners—especially in professional practices—bring in partners for this express purpose. The advantages of selling to a partner are numerous: the need to search for a buyer—or to use an intermediary—is obviated; terms of payment are often easier to arrange; and the business transition is eased because of the familiarity that already exists between the partner and the enterprise's suppliers, clients, and customers. Small business owners looking to hand over the reins of a company to a partner, however, need to adequately prepare for such a step. Locating a suitable partner, structuring a partnership buyout, and financing a partnership buyout are all important and complex issues that require care and attention.

Finally, business owners also groom people within their organization to take over the business upon their retirement (or death or disability). **Family-owned businesses** often hand over the reins from generation to generation in this fashion. In many cases this transfer of ownership is made as a gift or included as part of the owner's estate.

MAKING THE SALE

Once the seller has found a buyer for his or her company, the next step is to arrange the structure of the transaction. In addition to determining whether to make a stock or asset sale (in the case of corporations), the seller and the buyer need to reach agreement on other terms of the sale as well.

EARN-OUTS An earn out is an agreement wherein the seller takes a portion of the selling price each year for a fixed period of time out of the earnings of the company under its new ownership. These agreements are sometimes employed when a seller cannot get his or her full asking price because of buyer concerns about some aspect of the business. "Most earn out plans are contingent on the level of profits a company earns," wrote Tuller. "No profits, no payments." As a result, some sellers insist on minimum payment amounts. In addition, since the seller's total compensation under this arrangement depends on the company's performance during the specified earn-out period, sellers often "insist on participation in some manner in the policy and/or management decisions during this period," Tuller added. Earn-outs can be calculated as a percentage of gross profit, net profit, sales, or some other mutually agreed-upon figure. Sellers, however, need to make sure that the measurement used is fair and easily verifiable. As Semanik and Wade noted, "profit is a very difficult word to define. A shrewd purchaser could allocate costs in such a way that profit expectations are repeatedly dashed."

INSTALLMENT SALES Under this common arrangement, the seller of the business receives some cash, but the majority of the purchase price is received over a period of years. The down payment for small businesses may range from as little as 10 percent to as much as 40 percent or more, with the rest paid out—with interest—over a period of 3-15 years.

LEVERAGED BUYOUT A **leveraged buyout** or LBO is the purchase of a company through a loan secured by using the assets of the business as collateral. Johansen noted, however, that "because leveraged buyouts place a greater debt burden on the company than do other types of financing, buyer and seller must take a close look at the business's ability to service the debt.

STOCK EXCHANGES In instances where a large, publicly held company is the purchaser, business owners sometimes ask to be compensated with stock in the purchasing corporation. In such cases, the seller is usually required to hold on to the stock for a certain period of time—usually two years—before he or she has the option to resell it.

Buyers sometimes insist on a **noncompetition agreement** as well. "The noncompete agreement is a fair clause in any sales contract," wrote Semanik and Wade, "because it prevents a seller from opening across the street (or town) and winning back the customers." This covenant not to compete with the buyer, which can be incorporated into the purchase and sale agreement or created as a separate document, usually stipulates a market area and/or a period of time (three to five years is common) in which the seller may not open a business that would compete with the enterprise that he or she previously sold.

CLOSING THE DEAL

Once a deal has been struck between the seller and the buyer of the business, various conditions of sale often have to be addressed before the deal is closed. These include verification of financial statements, transfer of licenses, obtaining financing, and other conditions. Most contracts call for these conditions of sale to be addressed by a specified date; if one or more of these conditions is not taken care of by that time, the agreement is no longer valid.

Provided that these conditions have been attended to, however, the parties can move on to the closing. Closings are generally done either via an escrow settlement or via an attorney performs settlement. In an escrow settlement, the money to be deposited, the bill of sale, and other relevant documents are placed with a neutral third party known as an escrow agent until all conditions of sale have been met. After that, the escrow agent disburses the held documents and funds in accordance with the terms of the contract.

If an attorney performs settlement, meanwhile, an attorney—acting on behalf of both buyer or seller, or for the buyer—draws up a contract and acts as an escrow agent until all stipulated conditions of sale have been met. Whereas escrow settlements do not require the buyer and the seller to get together to sign the final documents, attorney performs settlements do include this step.

CLOSING DOCUMENTS

Several documents are required to complete the transaction between business seller and business buyer. The purchase and sale agreement is the most important of these, but other documents often used in closings include the escrow agreement; bill of sale; promissory note; security agreement; settlement sheet; financing statement; and employment agreement.

FURTHER READING:

Johansen, John A. *How to Buy or Sell a Business.* Washington: U.S. Small Business Administration, n.a.

Semanik, Michael K., and John H. Wade. *The Complete Guide to Selling a Business.* New York: Amacom, 1994.

Tuller, Lawrence W. *Getting Out: A Step-by-Step Guide to Selling a Business or Professional Practice.* Liberty Hall Press, 1990.

Yegge, Wilbur M. *A Basic Guide to Buying and Selling a Company.* New York: John Wiley & Sons, 1996.

SERVICE BUSINESSES

Service businesses are enterprises that are established and maintained for the purpose of providing services (rather than or in addition to products) to private and/or commercial customers. The American Marketing Association defined services as "activities, benefits, or satisfactions which are offered for sale or are provided in connection with the sale of goods."

The overall service industry is regarded as an already robust one that should enjoy considerable healthy growth rates in the future as the United States and other nations continue to move from manufacturing-based economies to technologically advanced service economies. "The service sector is a most attractive arena for the aspiring entrepreneur," confirmed Irving Burstiner in *Start & Run Your Own Profitable Service Business.* "Many service enterprises can be launched with far less money than the amount of capital typically needed to open a manufacturing, wholesale, or retail business. Many new service operators are able to begin at home, thus avoiding the expense of renting, buying, or constructing business premises. Moreover, end-of-year earnings in the service sector compare favorably with the profit margins enjoyed by most other types of enterprise." In addition, service businesses enjoy several other advantages over their brethren in other business areas. For one thing, they tend to be local, and they often do not have to contend with the national or international corporate giants that roam across the plains of the manufacturing, retail, and wholesale industries. Moreover, they generally do not have to make the same levels of investment in **inventory**, raw materials, finished goods, operations, or production management as do firms engaged in manufacturing, wholesaling, or retailing.

Of course, initial investment requirements can vary significantly from sector to sector. While some service businesses, like bookkeeping, house painting, child care, lawn care, housekeeping, and tutoring, can all be launched with a modest investment by individuals with special skills or knowledge in those areas, other service businesses require a far greater investment of money. Attorneys, doctors, and other professionals who make their living by providing their services to clients make heavy up-front expenditures (tuition), while entrepreneurs interested in launching service businesses that require extensive investments in facilities and/or equipment (hotels, laundromats, car rental agencies, nursing care facilities, etc.) have to make big up-front expenditures of their own, albeit in different form.

CAUSES OF SERVICE INDUSTRY GROWTH Researchers point to a number of factors that have accounted for the surge in service business start-ups over the last few decades. Many of these factors reflect fundamental changes in societal structure and character. W. F. Schoell and J. T. Ivy, authors of *Marketing: Contemporary Concepts and Practices,* cited the following as major reasons for service industry expansion in North America:

1) Increased affluence—As consumers have raised their standard of living, they have increasingly chosen to purchase services such as lawn maintenance and carpet cleaning that they previously took care of themselves.

2) Increased leisure time—Some segments of the population have been able to garner larger chunks of free time; this trend, coupled with increased wealth, has spurred a higher demand for certain service businesses such as travel agencies and resorts, adult education courses, guide services, golf courses, and health clubs.

3) Changing work force **demographics**— Over the past few decades, increasing numbers of women have entered the work force. This has spurred greater demand for services in realms such as child care, housekeeping, and drycleaning.

4) Greater life expectancy—Another development that has had a particular impact on certain service sectors, particularly in the health care industries.

5) Increased complexity of products/technological advancement—High-tech products have created a corresponding increase in demand for specialists who can fix and maintain those products (computers, cars, and electronic equipment, for example).

6) Increased complexity of life—Many service sectors have enjoyed tremendous growth because of their orientation toward helping individuals and businesses stay on top of the many facets of today's fast-paced society. Tax preparers, psychiatrists and counselors, legal advisors, and other segments are good examples.

7) Increased environmental awareness—General trends toward increased ecological sensitivity and enlightened natural resource management practices have spurred growth in environmental service sectors (waste management, recycling, and environmental advocacy).

8) Increased number of available products— Technological advances have spurred development of service industries in areas such as programming.

TYPES OF SERVICE INDUSTRIES

Following is a representative listing of service businesses in a range of commercial sectors that could conceivably be launched by an enterprising entrepreneur:

- Professional services (physicians, pharmacists, dentists, attorneys, architects, and civil engineers).
- Business services (advertising, financial planning, mailing services, computer and data processing, consulting, training, and recruiting).
- Counseling services (marriage, weight loss, career planning, pastoral, and psychiatric).
- Transportation services (trucking, busing, taxicab service, limousine service, and car rental).
- Personal services (pet grooming, health clubs, catering, beauticians, barbers, hairdressers, tailors and seamstresses, photography studios, realtors, funeral parlors, and wedding planning).
- Restaurants and lodging (diners, family restaurants, taverns, hotels, and cottages).
- Social services (individual and family services, child day care, and residential care).
- Maintenance services (landscaping, plumbing and electrical, appliance, equipment, automobile, and bicycle).

In addition, many service-oriented businesses are, by their very nature, slanted toward meeting the needs of one of two markets: individual consumers or other businesses/organizations. Of course, some service establishments, like carpet cleaning companies, can market their services to both client categories. But the majority of service businesses place their emphasis on meeting the needs of one market segment or the other. For example, a pet grooming establishment will not waste its advertising dollars trying to reach other businesses; its primary clients are going to be individual consumers simply because of the nature of the services they offer. Conversely, the primary clientele of a company that provides security personnel are going to be commercial establishments. Entrepreneurs that hope to market their services primarily to organizations rather than individuals should note that, on the whole, such businesses require greater capital investment at the outset.

KEYS TO SERVICE BUSINESS SUCCESS

"Service supplier skill should be distinguished on at least two levels," wrote Glenn Bassett, author of *Operations Management for Service Industries.* "The first is the technical product/service knowledge level. The service giver is expected to know the offering in depth and detail so that information about its utility and application can be provided on demand. He or she must also be technically competent to deliver the service expected, adapting as needed to varied or changing customer need. The second level of skill pertains to customer relationship. Here it is often as simple as whether the service-giver treats the customer as an object to be controlled and used, or as a unique, important individual to be served.''

Entrepreneurs engaged in service businesses also need to recognize how service marketing differs from product marketing. ''Service marketing,'' said Burstiner, ''can be far more challenging than the marketing of products because of these three distinctive characteristics of service offerings: 1) Services are intangible; 2) Services are perishable; 3) Services cannot be separated from the service providers.''

SERVICES ARE INTANGIBLE Products are concrete objects that can be touched, tasted, or otherwise tangibly examined before the purchase takes place, but services are abstract concepts that cannot be evaluated until the service has been rendered.

SERVICES ARE PERISHABLE ''Unlike products, services cannot be fabricated in advance and then warehoused while awaiting future orders,'' said Burstiner. ''No inventory buildup is possible. The production, delivery, and consumption of a service all occur simultaneously. Services that, for whatever reason, are not consumed at the time of production represent lost income to the service provider.''

SERVICES CANNOT BE DISASSOCIATED FROM THE SERVICE PROVIDER To customers seeking to purchase a service, the service and the service provider are basically one and the same. Burstiner explained that this inseparability is far greater in service sectors than it is in manufacturing segments. ''The inseparability factor is the root cause of variability in service quality, something we see only occasionally in product manufacturing,'' he noted. Whereas quality control methods are routinely applied to manufacturing processes, ''services resist attempts at standardization. Variations in service quality are often noted when the same service is delivered by different providers,'' or even when the same service is delivered on several different occasions to the same customer.

Finally, service businesses need to consider the way in which they distribute their services. Most service businesses can be grouped according to the methodology with which they deliver their services. In other words, does the company bring its service to the customer, or does the customer go to the firm to receive the service? ''In some cases,'' wrote Bateman and Zeithaml in *Management: Function and Strategy,*

''there is no choice. The plumber or house painter has to go to the work. Conversely, the customer goes to the restaurant, and the patient has to go to the hospital for the operation. Some services have options. Either the TV repairperson can go to the customer or the customer delivers the TV to the back room (the repair shop). A service that has traditionally required the customer to come to its facility has a strategic advantage in changing that tradition.'' Indeed, owners of service businesses should examine this facet of their business closely to look for ways of realizing an advantage over competitors. In fact, customer convenience is—next to quality of service rendered— perhaps the single most important factor in securing and retaining new customers.

FURTHER READING:

Adams, Bob. *Adams Streetwise Small Business Start-Up: Your Comprehensive Guide to Starting and Managing a Business.* Holbrook, MA: Adams Media, 1996.

Bassett, Glenn. *Operations Management for Service Industries: Competing in the Service Era.* Westport, CT: Quorum Books, 1992.

Bateman, Thomas S., and Carl P. Zeithaml. *Management: Function and Strategy.* Boston, MA: Richard D. Irwin, 1990.

Burstiner, Irving. *Start & Run Your Own Profitable Service Business.* Englewood Cliffs, NJ: Prentice Hall, 1993.

Crandall, Rick. *Marketing Your Services: For People Who Hate to Sell.* Chicago, IL: Contemporary Books, 1996.

Gronroos, Christian. *Service Management and Marketing: Managing the Moments of Truth in Service Competition.* Lexington, MA: D.C. Heath, 1990.

Schoell, W. F., and J. T. Ivy. *Marketing: Contemporary Concepts and Practices.* Boston, MA: Allyn and Bacon, 1981.

Wheatley, Edward W. *Marketing Professional Services.* Englewood Cliffs, NJ: Prentice Hall, 1983.

SEE ALSO: Customer Service

SERVICE CORPS OF RETIRED EXECUTIVES

The Service Corps of Retired Executives (SCORE) is a national non-profit organization that counsels business owners and aspiring entrepreneurs. There are 389 SCORE chapters throughout the United States offering counseling services to small businesses in all areas at no charge to the client. There is no membership requirement to receive SCORE counseling—a phone call to make an appointment with a local SCORE chapter is sufficient to put the small business owner in touch with this valuable organization.

HISTORY SCORE was founded in 1964 specifically to provide business counseling to entrepreneurs. A national non-profit organization, SCORE is funded primarily by the **U.S. Small Business Administra-**

tion (founded in 1953). The group is made up of retired business executives familiar with all areas of business management. This group donates their services, conducting one-to-one counseling and team counseling and training sessions. Over 3.5 million people have used the services of SCORE volunteers since the organization's inception, or about 250,000 people annually.

MISSION AND PROGRAMS According to SCORE, volunteers ''serve as 'Counselors to America's Small Business.' '' The volunteer members of the organization are ''dedicated to entrepreneur education and the formation, growth and success of small business nationwide.'' In 1996, more than one million volunteer hours were donated to help small business owners.

SCORE counselors provide general business advice on all aspects of business formation and management. This service is provided free of charge and in confidential fashion. Counselors may assist in anything from investigating market potential for a product or service to providing guidance on cash flow management. They may provide insight into how to start or operate a business, how to buy a business or franchise, or how to sell a business. Volunteers also review **business plans**, often offering suggestions before the plans are submitted to a bank for financing consideration. SCORE also holds workshops throughout the country. Workshops on specialized areas of business training such as writing business plans, inventory control, advertising, financing and international trade are available at reduced cost.

SCORE is not, however, an employment service. Members may give advice, but may not accept positions with client companies, nor may they direct a business owner to individuals or firms which may provide employees. SCORE's main function is to provide free advice to small businesses.

SCORE VOLUNTEERS SCORE volunteers (more than 12,000 in the mid-1990s) are usually between the ages of 60 and 70, but there is no age limit for a volunteer. Retired executives interested in joining SCORE fill out a formal application and usually supply a resume for consideration by their local chapter. There is a 90-day probation period during which performance is monitored. To insure quality, SCORE counselors are matched to cases according to the type of business or client seeking advice and the counselor's area of specialty.

FURTHER READING:

Campanelli, Melissa. ''Getting Good Advice.'' *Sales and Marketing Management*. March 1995.

Hamilton, Patricia W. ''Help Wanted: Retirement Options.'' *D&B Reports*. March/April 1991.

Hulpke, John F., and Tom Byrnes. ''SBDC, SBI and SCORE in the Emerald Isle: Management Assistance Programs in Ireland.'' *Journal of Small Business Management*. October 1994.

Lindo, David K. ''Help Wanted: Part-time Manager.'' *Office Systems*. December 1994.

Tarras, John. ''The Search for Financing.'' *Restaurant Hospitality*. December 1991.

Watts, Christina F. ''SCORE Points to Success.'' *Black Enterprise*. January 1995.

SEXUAL HARASSMENT

Sexual harassment is a term used to describe a variety of illegal, discriminatory actions—from unwelcome sexual advances to verbal conduct of a sexual nature—that create a hostile or abusive work environment. The **Equal Employment Opportunity Commission (EEOC)** defines sexual harassment as follows: ''Unwelcome sexual advances, requests for sexual favors, and other verbal or physical contact of a sexual nature constitute sexual harassment when: 1) Submission to such conduct is made either explicitly or implicitly a term or condition of an individual's employment. 2) Submission to or rejection of such conduct by an individual is used as the basis for employment decisions affecting such individuals. 3) Such conduct has the purpose or effect of unreasonably interfering with an individual's work performance or creating an intimidating, hostile, or offensive working environment.'' But legal experts warn managers and business owners that definitions of sexual harassment extend beyond the above borders. ''Most people think that sexual harassment necessarily involves conduct of a sexual nature,'' wrote Theresa Donahue Egler in *HRMagazine*. ''But, sexual harassment includes conduct that is not overtly sexual but is directed at an individual based on his or her gender. Thus, conduct such as profanity and other rude behavior . . . may give rise to liability so long as it is based on gender.''

Savvy small business owners will adopt a proactive stance to make certain that his or her employees know that inappropriate behavior—whether taking the form of displaying sexually explicit photographs, using offensive language, making suggestive or otherwise inappropriate comments, badgering an employee for dates or other interactions outside the workplace, or suggesting that one gender is inferior to another—will not be tolerated in their company. Indeed, firms that do not do so leave themselves open to financial loss via lawsuits as well as other problems (low morale, employee turnover, absenteeism, etc.) that can ultimately impact on financial performance. As EEOC guidelines state, ''with respect to conduct between fellow employees, an employer is responsible for acts of sexual harassment in the workplace where the employer (or its agents or supervisory employees) knows or should have known of the conduct, unless it can show that it took immediate and appropriate corrective action.''

Some observers believe that small businesses are particularly susceptible to sexual harassment problems. ''Small businesses are especially vulnerable because the informal office atmosphere may seem to allow sexual banter and innuendos, and a small business is less likely to have an official sexual harassment policy and training program,'' wrote Steven C. Bahls and Jane Easter Bahls.

''The stakes are high and getting higher,'' concluded Ellen J. Wagner in *Sexual Harassment in the Workplace.* ''In an increasingly litigious society and in an era of ever-increasing employee rights and employer responsibilities, sexual harassment allegations are particularly hazardous.'' *Nation's Business* contributors Robert T. Gray and Donald H. Weiss agreed. ''All the signs point to sexual harassment become a more complex issue in the courts as well as in the workplace, and employers must be ready to respond accordingly,'' they wrote. ''While that response can be prolonged and even difficult, the experts say that the depth of a company's commitment to preventing such conduct can be determined by one step at the moment of the filing of a complaint. That step: Take it seriously.''

HARASSMENT AND EMPLOYEE RIGHTS

Over the past several years, sexual harassment has become a subject of considerable discussion. Previous generations of business owners and managers rarely had to address the issue. Business historians and social observers point to several possible factors for this. Some note that women used to comprise a much smaller component of the workforce, and that various societal pressures may have made them less likely to come forward with complaints. Others point out that many of the legal protections that are now in place against harassment have only developed over the last 30 years. Still other observers contend that the rise in sexual harassment claims simply reflects a general decline in civility in American society. Whatever the reasons, sexual harassment complaints have risen steadily in recent years. In fact, the EEOC reported that from 1990 to 1994, the number of sexual harassment cases that were filed in the United States more than doubled. ''Because an agency complaint is a prerequisite to suit under federal and many state laws, these numbers forecast a corresponding increase in sexual harassment lawsuits in the coming years,'' wrote Egler. ''When it is considered that many more potentially explosive situations are quietly resolves (some at substantial cost) before reaching the complaint stage, it is readily apparent that sexual harassment is a risk that requires proactive management.''

But small business owners and corporate executives alike need to make sure that in their zeal to protect the legitimate rights of employees not to be harassed in the workplace, they do not trample on the rights of those accused of misbehavior. ''While sexual harassment is clearly a pervasive reality, every case needs to be reviewed on its own merit,'' said Wagner. ''Just because harassment is a significant social and corporate problem does not mean it has in fact occurred in a particular instance.'' Indeed, an employee who is punished or dismissed on the basis of a frivolous sexual harassment claim has the same recourse to the law as the victim of sexual harassment who is left unprotected by indifferent managers/owners. Business owners and managers thus need to consider the rights of all parties involved when investigating sexual harassment complaints.

CHANGING DEMOGRAPHICS OF SEXUAL HARASSMENT VICTIMS

Over the past several years, human resource professionals and business consultants alike have pointed to some fundamental changes in sexual harassment **demographics**. The overwhelming number of employees who are victims of sexual harassment continue to be women, but increasing numbers of men have found themselves targeted as well. From 1990 to 1994, for instance, the number of men who filed sexual harassment complaints with the EEOC tripled. Same-sex harassment charges have been on the rise as well. Observers note that some companies have been slow to treat such complaints as seriously as the more prevalent woman-as-victim, man-as-harasser complaints, with sometimes disastrous financial consequences for the businesses.

Some analysts expect women-as-harasser complaints to continue to rise, as the number of women business owners and executives grows. ''Many would say that sexual harassment is nothing but an issue of power—that is, one person exercising power over another and using sex as the tool of power,'' attorney Gary Oberstein told *Industry Week*'s Michael Verespej. ''[Women are now] in a position to see this as a tool, just as men have seen it as a tool for years.'' Verespej points out, however, that the nature of sexual harassment does seem to vary with the gender of the harasser. ''When a male is the victim of harassment by a female, more than 50% of the cases allege a demand for sex—quid pro quo—in order to retain a job or receive a promotion,'' he reported. ''By contrast, less than 15% of the cases in which a female is the victim of harassment by a male is there a demand for sex; the majority allege a hostile work environment.''

DEVELOPING AND MAINTAINING SEXUAL HARASSMENT POLICIES

Ellen Wagner points out in *Sexual Harassment in the Workplace* that "a well-drafted, carefully thought-out policy statement on sexual harassment can be valuable to an organization in at least three major ways: 1) as an employee relations tool, 2) as basic education for both managers and employees on the subject of sexual harassment, and 3) as a way of minimizing legal liability to the organization in hostile-environment sexual harassment cases. . . . Not only is such a policy statement evidence of an organization's good-faith effort to provide a work environment free of harassment but, coupled with a proper investigation that successfully ends illegal or inappropriate conduct, it provides a major offensive weapon in employer efforts to demonstrate that all reasonable steps were taken and that they were effective."

Indeed, business consultants universally counsel both small businesses and multinational corporations to establish formal written policies that make it explicitly clear that no forms of sexual harassment will be tolerated. Some companies prefer to disseminate this information as part of their larger general policy statements because of their sensitivity to giving extra attention to a sometimes awkward subject. But others reason that doing so can effectively bury the company's sexual harassment policies under the weight of all its other statements; these latter business owners and managers claim that dissemination of a separate policy statement not only better informs employees of the policy itself, but also underlines the company's serious approach to the subject.

Whether a business chooses to distribute its policies on sexual harassment via general information sources (**employee manuals**) or separate statements, its policies should list all the various forms that sexual harassment can take (sexually loaded "compliments," sexual advances, denigration of a person's gender, etc.) and explain how the company proceeds when confronted with a sexual harassment complaint. The policy statement should also discuss possible disciplinary consequences for workers who are found guilty of engaging in harassment.

Finally, lawyers and consultants alike counsel their small business clients to make sure that their policy statement is distributed to all employees. As Wagner noted, "the most carefully drafted, best-written policy on sexual harassment is useless if it is not communicated throughout the organization."

Other steps that businesses can take to establish an harassment-free workplace include: establishing internal procedures that address complaints promptly and thoroughly; establishing training programs that educate workers—and especially managers, supervisors, and other people wielding power—about components of sexual harassment and their responsibilities when exposed to such behavior; establishing alternative routes for workers to lodge complaints (in instances where his or her supervisor is the alleged harasser, for instance).

BUILDING A COMPREHENSIVE POLICY Legal experts warn businesses that they need to make certain that their policies reflect a true understanding of the legal responsibilities of the employer, and a full recognition of the multitude of forms that sexual harassment can take. They point out that some companies have put together policies that, while sensible and effective in some or even most areas, are flawed in other areas, either because their policies did not adequately cover all the ways in which sexual harassment can occur, or because their understanding of sexual harassment was incomplete from the outset. For example, many people have long operated under the misconception that for sexual harassment to occur, the harasser must have a bad intent. The reality, however, is that "what may be viewed as perfectly harmless by most men, may be viewed as offensive by most women," wrote Egler. "In recognition of gender differences in perception, the courts have developed a new standard for analyzing claims of sexual harassment. In lieu of the traditional gender-neutral reasonable person standard, which is thought to be biased toward the male viewpoint, sexual harassment claims are analyzed in many jurisdictions from the perspective of a reasonable person of the same sex."

Another important factor that is not always sufficiently appreciated by employers is that they can be held liable for harassing conduct by a third party such as a customer or vendor. Egler explained that "even though these people are not employed by, and thus, not under the direction and control of the employer, the employer can be held responsible for harassment of its employees by such third parties." This mostly occurs in instances where the employer does not respond to such situations. Finally, Egler pointed out that some companies have been slow to recognize that "what appears to be a consensual relationship by both parties may be regarded by the subordinate as an unwelcome obligation necessary for the protection of his or her job, whether or not this is actually the case."

INVESTIGATING SEXUAL HARASSMENT COMPLAINTS

As one business attorney told *Industry Week*, companies "must take every complaint seriously, treat every complaint confidentially, investigate every complaint thoroughly, and take appropriate and immediate disciplinary action [as quickly as possible]." Indeed, employers have a legal duty to investigate such complaints. "The objective of that review is simple," wrote Wagner. "To determine to the extent possible what happened, resolve the situation appropriately, and bring any illegal conduct to an end so that the workplace is once again free of any form of harassment.''

Businesses need to make certain that the person who will investigate the complaint has credibility with the workforce. Ideally, the individual will be knowledgeable about the legal dimensions of sexual harassments, experienced in handling employee issues, familiar with the organization's policies, and socially and organizationally distant from both the alleged victim and the alleged harasser (the investigator should not be friends with the alleged victim, nor directly report to the alleged harasser, or vice versa). With smaller companies, however, it can be more difficult to adhere to such guidelines. If a small business owner has only four employees, and two of them become embroiled in an harassment case, finding an investigator with the above qualities is next to impossible. The owner may be tempted to look into the complaint him or herself in such instances, but business advisors often counsel against this. Instead, they recommend that the owner turn to an outside counsel or external consultant to pursue the complaint.

Whether the person doing the investigating is a third party, an employee, or the owner of the business, he or she should have a focused, carefully thought out investigation plan designed to settle the issue in as timely a fashion as possible. This typically includes a review of relevant organizational records, including complainant's personnel file, alleged harasser's personnel file, performance reviews, and promotional and salary records. Such reviews can turn up everything from prior disciplinary warnings aimed at the accused to possibly relevant indications that the involved parties had previously competed against one another for promotions or other job opportunities. Such data may well be completely irrelevant to the legitimacy of the complaint, but it is the investigator's duty to check into all possible aspects of the complaint.

Every claim should be treated seriously, no matter how unusual or seemingly frivolous it might first appear, until an informed decision can be made. Conversely, an investigator should also suspend judgment on complaints that seem obviously legitimate until a thorough investigation has been completed. As Wagner remarked, ''when sexual harassment is alleged, defamation is never very far away. . . . Since sexual harassment investigations almost always involve matters that might go to the heart of a person's reputation and good name, attention must be paid to minimizing the risks of defamation throughout the investigation and once it is concluded.''

The first step in an investigation usually involves an in-depth interview of the complainant. Areas that

should be pursued during this interview include the cultural background of the complainant (if dramatically different from that of the accused), a detailed reconstruction of the incident(s) that prompted the complaint, the context and circumstances in which it occurred, the involved parties' prior relationship (if any), the nature of the allegations against each individual in instances where incidents involved the participation of more than one person (common in hostile workplace complaints), and the complainant's expectations regarding how the alleged offender should be disciplined.

The investigation then turns to getting the accused's account of events. This step has different nuances, depending on whether the alleged harasser is a supervisor, a coworker, or a third party such as a customer, but basically this part of the investigation aims to secure the accused's perspective. In some instances, the accused may appear angry or shocked when confronted with a sexual harassment charge, so the investigator needs to allow time for the return of some measure of emotional equilibrium. When the initial reaction has subsided, wrote Wagner, the investigator should ask the worker to relate ''what he believed happened during the incidents the complainant has cited. Allow him to relate his understanding of the situation through once, then return to it for specific, step-by-step review. As with the complainant, make sure the discussion is specific and detailed enough to provide the information you need to make an informed judgment later on. Note dates, times, places, circumstances, dress, words exchanged, as well as the specifics of the alleged acts.'' Again, issues such as prevailing work environment, prior relationships, etc. should be discussed.

Once the investigator has finished gathering information from the principal parties, he or she should then turn to possible witnesses. These could range from coworkers who were present when the alleged incident took place to those who have relevant information on either or both of the parties involved. The investigator should not be concerned with unsubstantiated rumors at this juncture; rather, he or she should concentrate on gathering factual data. This can be a very important part of the investigation, for accusations that turn into basic ''he said, she said'' disputes can be profoundly difficult for employers to resolve. ''Immediate action may be difficult when an employer is faced with unsubstantiated accusation on one side and a categorical denial on the other,'' wrote Gray and Weiss. ''In such cases, [attorney Stephen] Bokat says, it is important to realize that 'these things tend not to occur in isolation. If there has been harassment, often someone else has seen or heard the conduct or speech involved or there will be repetitions that will indicate a pattern.' ''

But employers need to interview these witnesses carefully, however. "You must assess the credibility and believability of all persons corroborating some aspect of the complainant's or accused's contention," confirmed Wagner. "Consider the issue of witness motivation and the relationship between each witness and the individual whose word is being corroborated. Make sure you understand what each witness might stand to gain from the situation, as well as what genuine feelings are at work here." Witnesses also need to understand that the subject should not be discussed with coworkers or other individuals; sexual harassment charges are both serious and sensitive, and they should be regarded as such.

Human resources experts also recommend that investigators not really wholly on interviews. Ideally, the investigator should secure written statements from all parties—complainant, accused, and witnesses—as part of this information-gathering process.

Once the investigation into the sexual harassment complaint has been completed, corrective action (if any) needs to be implemented. When corrective action is warranted, it can range from counseling to transfer to dismissal. The key factors that usually determine the severity of the corrective action are: 1) the nature of the offense, 2) the desires of the complainant, and 3) the impact that the incident had on the workplace as a whole.

HARASSMENT OF THE SELF-EMPLOYED

Self-employed individuals who work as independent contractors enjoy fewer legal protections from sexual harassment at the hands of clients. Experts recommend that self-employed people confronted with such unpleasantness react strongly and decisively. They should make it immediately clear that the harassment (which in these situations typically takes the form of unwanted sexual advances) is unwelcome, and that they would prefer to keep their association with their client a professional one. If this line of defense does not work, the self-employed worker may wish to consult an attorney about their state's tort law, which regulates conduct between people and provides monetary damages. In addition, national women's organizations can often provide guidance and legal assistance in these matters. Finally, some observers believe that additional legal protections in this area may be on the way. They point out, for instance, that a bill has been introduced in California that would expressly prohibit sexual harassment against self-employed individuals providing contracted-for services. Violators of this proposed bill would be subject to considerable damages.

FURTHER READING:

Bahls, Steven C., and Jane Easter Bahls. "Hands-Off Policy." *Entrepreneur.* July 1997.

Egler, Theresa Donahue. "Five Myths About Sexual Harassment." *HRMagazine.* January 1995.

"Facts About Sexual Harassment." Washington: U.S. Equal Employment Opportunity Commission, 1997.

Gray, Robert T., and Donald H. Weiss. "How to Deal with Sexual Harassment." *Nation's Business.* December 1991.

Lawlor, Julie. "Stepping Over the Line." *Sales and Marketing Management.* October 1995.

Petrocelli, William, and Barbara Kate Repa. *Sexual Harassment on the Job: What It Is and How to Stop It.* Berkeley, CA: Nolo Press.

Verespej, Michael J. "New Age Sexual Harassment: An Increasing Number of Victims are Men or Same-Gender Workers." *Industry Week.* May 15, 1995.

Wagner, Ellen J. *Sexual Harassment in the Workplace: How to Prevent, Investigate, and Resolve Problems in Your Organization.* New York: AMACOM, 1992.

SEE ALSO: Employment Practices Liability Insurance; Labor Unions and Small Business

SIMPLIFIED EMPLOYEE PENSION PLANS

Simplified employee pension (SEP) plans—also known as SEP/IRAs since they make use of **individual retirement accounts**—are pension plans intended specifically for self-employed persons and small businesses. Created by Congress and monitored by the **Internal Revenue Service**, SEPs are designed to give small business owners and employees the same ability to set aside money for retirement as traditional large corporate **pension plans**. SEP plans are available to all types of business entities, including proprietorships, partnerships, and corporations.

As employer-funded retirement plans, SEPs allow small businesses to direct at least 3 percent and up to 15 percent of each employee's annual salary into tax-deferred IRAs on a discretionary basis. SEP plans are easy to set up and inexpensive to administer, as the employer simply makes contributions to IRAs that are established by employees. The employees then take responsibility for making investment decisions regarding their own IRAs. Employers thus avoid the risk and cost involved in accounting for employee retirement funds. In addition, employers have the flexibility to make large percentage contributions during good financial years, and to reduce contributions during hard times. Like other tax-deferred retirement plans, SEPs provide a tax break for employers and a valuable benefit for employees.

In many ways, SEPs can be more flexible and attractive than corporate pensions. They can even be used to supplement corporate pensions and **401(k) plans**. Many people who are employed full-time use SEPs as a way to save and invest more money for retirement than they might normally be able to put away under IRS rules. In fact, a 1993 *Forbes* magazine article called SEPs a "moonlighter's delight," in that they enable full-time employees to contribute a portion of their self-employment income from consulting or free-lancing outside of their regular jobs.

RULES GOVERNING SEPS

The rules governing SEPs are fairly simple but are subject to frequent changes, so annual reviews of IRS publications 560 (retirement plans for the self-employed) and 590 (IRAs) are recommended. As of 1996, SEPs could be set up using a simple form and—unlike larger, more complicated pension plans—did not require a separate trustee. The maximum allowable tax-deductible SEP contribution per employee is 15 percent of net compensation (up to $150,000), or a total of $22,500. In general, eligibility is limited to employees 21 or older with at least three years of service to the company and a minimum level of compensation.

A similar program is the Savings Incentive Match Plan for Employees (SIMPLE) IRA. SIMPLE plans became available in January 1997 to businesses with less than 100 employees, replacing the discontinued Salary Reduction Simplified Employee Pension (SARSEP) plans. They are intended to provide an easy, low-cost way for small businesses and their employees to contribute jointly to tax-deferred retirement accounts. An IRA set up as a SIMPLE account requires the employer to match up to 3 percent of an employee's annual salary, up to $6,000 per year. Employees are also allowed to contribute up to $6,000 annually to their own accounts. In this way, a SIMPLE IRA is similar to a 401(k), but it is generally less complex and has fewer administrative requirements.

Companies that establish SIMPLEs are not allowed to offer any other type of retirement plan. The main problem with the plans, according to Stephen Blakely in *Nation's Business,* was that "Congress is already drafting legislation that would make SIMPLE less simple and more costly for the very businesses the plans were created to serve."

OWNERS BENEFIT LESS THAN NONOWNER EMPLOYEES

A note of caution is in order. A small business owner who wants to establish a SEP—or any other qualified retirement plan—for him or herself must also include all other company employees who meet minimum participation standards. As an employer, the small business owner can establish retirement plans like any other business. As an employee, the small business owner can then make contributions to the plan he or she has established in order to set aside tax-deferred funds for retirement, like any other employee. The difference is that a small business owner must include all nonowner employees in any company-sponsored retirement plans and make equivalent contributions to their accounts. Unfortunately, this requirement has the effect of reducing the allowable contributions that the owner of a proprietorship or partnership can make on his or her own behalf.

For self-employed individuals, contributions to a retirement plan are based upon the net earnings of their business. The net earnings consist of the company's gross income less deductions for business expenses, salaries paid to nonowner employees, the employer's 50 percent of the Social Security tax, and—significantly—the employer's contribution to retirement plans on behalf of employees. Therefore, rather than receiving pre-tax contributions to the retirement account as a percentage of gross salary, like nonowner employees, the small business owner receives contributions as a smaller percentage of net earnings. Employing other people thus detracts from the owner's ability to build up a sizeable before-tax retirement account of his or her own. In the case of a SEP plan, the business owner's maximum annual contribution is reduced to 13.04 percent of income (compared to the 15 percent maximum that applies to nonowner employees).

Still, a SEP plan offers significant advantages for self-employed persons and small business owners. It allows a much greater annual pre-tax contribution than a standard IRA (at $2,000 or less, depending on the individual's financial status and participation in other retirement plans). In addition, individuals can contribute to their existing IRAs and 401(k)s, and still participate in a SEP plan.

FURTHER READING:

Blakely, Stephen. "Pension Power." *Nation's Business.* July 1997.

Crouch, Holmes F. *Decisions When Retiring.* Allyear Tax Guides, 1995.

Rowland, Mary. "Pension Options for Small Firms." *Nation's Business.* March 1994.

SEE ALSO: Retirement Planning

SMALL BUSINESS CONSORTIA

Business consortia are alliances of individual business enterprises. These firms are often in the same broad field of commerce, though they are rarely in direct competition with one another. Instead, members usually offer products or services that are complementary to those available through other consortium members. Unlike associations and other similar organizations, which engage in efforts to shape legislation and present a unified industry front, business consortia ally themselves for basic business functions, such as marketing. These alliances are not commonplace, but some analysts indicate that in the future, increasing numbers of small business owners may investigate consortiums as a way of sharing common costs, increasing purchasing power, and competing with larger companies.

Business consortia that do form usually come into being for specific reasons, such as competitive threats from a common enemy (whether another business or an unwelcome economic trend), changes in competitive structures, or deregulation. Writing in *Acquisitions Monthly,* John Eric Bigbie observed that by forming a consortium, the companies that are involved are usually admitting that—for the time being, at least—competitive pressures are so great that the business's ability to survive as a completely independent entity is in question.

Participants in business consortia admit that striking such alliances can sometimes curb a firm's ability to act independently, since it's words and actions will reflect on other consortia members. This can be difficult for some entrepreneurs to handle. Moreover, consortia can become crippled if their membership grows too large and unwieldy to make quick decisions, or if individual members fall victim to squabbling or worse as a result of personality conflicts, similar customer bases, or other business disputes. But proponents point out that a business consortium can provide several meaningful advantages to members as well. These include:

1) Increased clout—Whereas individual small businesses sometimes do not enjoy the same name recognition or respect as do larger companies, the collective bargaining and purchasing power of a consortium as well as the individual marketing efforts of members can provide individual businesses with increased recognition and stature in the community.

2) Savings of time and money—Joint marketing and advertising efforts save members money because they can pool their resources for better rates; they also save member businesses time because they do not have to undertake as much work themselves.

3) Expanded customer base—Writing in the *Business Journal,* Jerd Smith noted that since the memberships of business consortia tend to have the same target audience, "word of contracts spreads quickly, allow-

ing the different companies involved to move equally fast to chase the business."

FURTHER READING:

Bigbie, John Eric. "Consortia Back in Business." *Acquisitions Monthly.* April 1994.

Smith, Jerd. "Strength in Their Number." *Denver Business Journal.* March 3, 1995.

SMALL BUSINESS DEVELOPMENT CENTERS

One of many programs administered by the **U.S. Small Business Administration (SBA)**, the Small Business Development Center (SBDC) program is intended to provide management assistance to both established and prospective small business owners. The SBA characterizes the program, which was established in 1976, as a "cooperative effort of the private sector, the educational community, and federal, state, and local governments. It enhances economic development by providing small businesses with management and technical assistance."

The SBA maintained 56 small business development centers in the United States in the mid-1990s. Centers existed in all 50 states—with Texas holding four centers—as well as Puerto Rico, Guam, the U.S. Virgin Islands, and the District of Columbia. Many of these centers have satellite service locations to aid small businesses as well. These satellite locations— nearly 1,000 in all in 1996—are housed primarily at colleges, universities, and community colleges, but they are also maintained at vocational schools, **chambers of commerce**, and economic development corporations.

SBDCs are typically headed up by a director and include paid staff members, but the services of volunteers—qualified individuals from professional and trade associations, members of the legal, banking, and academic community, chambers of commerce representatives, and members of the Service Corps of Retired Executives—are integral to most SBDCs. In addition, SBDCs commonly compensate consultants, consulting engineers, and testing laboratories for services rendered on behalf of SBDC clients.

While Small Business Development Centers are administered by the SBA, that organization is prevented by law from providing more than 50 percent of the operating funds for each state SBDC. The centers turn to state legislatures, private sector foundations and grants, state and local chambers of commerce, economic development corporations, public and private universities, vocational and technical schools, and community colleges for the remainder of their operating funds. In recent years, non-SBA sponsors have accounted for more than 50 percent of their required matching share at a number of centers.

THE SBDC PROGRAM

According to the SBA, Small Business Development Centers are designed to deliver timely and accurate counseling, training, and technical assistance in all aspects of small business management, including financial management, marketing, production and operations, organization, engineering and technical issues, personnel management, and feasibility studies. Some centers also offer assistance in such areas as venture capital formation, rural development, exporting and importing, and procurement of funding (including **Small Business Innovation and Research** grants), depending on the needs of their business clients and the communities in which the centers operate.

SBDC assistance to small business owners takes many forms, from counseling on legal issues to seminars on business finance to aid in putting together a business plan. Many centers also maintain extensive business libraries that contain a great deal of information of value to entrepreneurs and small business owners.

Anyone interested in starting a small business or making improvements to an existing small business is free to make use of the SBDC program, provided that they do not have the financial resources to secure the services of a private consultant. Indeed, the SBDC centers regard their primary clientele to be businesspeople from disadvantaged socioeconomic backgrounds. The SBDC program also makes special efforts to provide assistance to women, the disabled, and military veterans.

FURTHER READING:

SBA Profile: Who We Are and What We Do. Washington: U.S. Small Business Administration, 1996.

SMALL BUSINESS-DOMINATED INDUSTRIES

The United States supports many industries that are dominated by or heavily populated with small firms. The majority of these are in service industries, a fact that reflects the growing dominance of the service sector in the overall American economy. According to the U.S. Small Business Administration, the fastest-growing small business-oriented industries in the country in the mid-1990s were as follows:

1) Employment Agencies

2) Real Estate

3) Automotive Dealers and Service Stations

4) Building Materials and Garden Supplies

5) Automotive Services, Except Repair

6) Millwork, Veneer, and Plywood Manufacturing

7) Paint, Paper Hanging, and Decorating

8) Meat Markets and Freezer Provisioners

9) Retail Stores

10) Agricultural Services

These industries are expected to see continued growth over the coming years, as increasing numbers of small businesses enter the marketplace. But many analysts, citing studies conducted by the SBA's Small Business Advocate office, believe that some other industries currently dominated by small business enterprises are poised for even greater growth. Indeed, statistics compiled by the SBA, the Department of Labor, the Bureau of Labor Statistics, and *Monthly Labor Review* indicated that the greatest rate of growth in employment in small business-dominated industries between 1992 and 2005 would be in the following areas:

1) Residential Care

2) Medical and Dental Laboratories

3) Child Day Care Services

4) Credit Reporting and Collections

5) Public Relations Services

6) Individual and Family Services

7) Travel Arrangement Services

8) Miscellaneous Equipment Rental

9) Accounting, Auditing, and Bookkeeping

10) Job Training and Related Services

RESIDENTIAL CARE Residential care encompasses a variety of facilities, including those devoted to caring for emotionally disturbed adolescents and mentally retarded individuals, but government data indicates that the area in which residential care will see its greatest growth is in the realm of elder care. Analysts expect growth in assisted-living facilities—which range from domiciliary care homes and personal care homes to adult congregate living facilities—to serve as the engine that drives this industry forward over the next number of years, as the American population ages and workers explore various **elder care** options. "These facilities," wrote Jenny McCune in *Journal of Business Strategy,* "are a bridge between traditional nursing homes, which offer round-the-clock, skilled medical care in an institutional setting, and independent retirement housing, in which residents receive no outside help. In assisted living, the elderly live as independently as possible—usually in suites or cottages—but also have access to meal and laundry facilities and get assistance with daily chores such as bathing and dressing.'' Business consultants and current participants in the industry warn, however, that while demand for these services will continue to grow in the coming years, entrance into this business area is costly.

CHILD CARE The **child care** services industry has enjoyed steady growth for a number of years, due to population increases and the growing presence of women in the business world. And as McCune noted, the popularity of child care facilities in recent years has also been driven by the increased professionalism of the industry, as evidenced by the development of accreditation standards. The sheer demand for child care services is expected to insure the continued health of many businesses engaged in this area for years to come, but entrepreneurs should be aware of the hazards that lurk here as well. Business experts note that concerns about child welfare have sparked increased calls for regulation of the industry by OSHA and other government agencies, and that participants face a host of competitors. ''A for-profit center may be competing with non-profit centers sponsored by religious organizations, the local Head Start program, family members who baby-sit for little or no cost, caregivers who work in the home, and even after-hours programs run by local elementary schools.'' Finally, professional day care centers have to grapple with liability issues, encroaching involvement of larger firms, and historically high levels of turnover both among clients and employees.

COLLECTION AGENCIES The surge in credit availability in American households has sparked a corresponding increase in demand for businesses willing to pursue **collections** for clients. As one industry participant told *Journal of Business Strategy,* establishing a business in this area is attractive to some entrepreneurs ''because the cost of entry is low—someone can start out with a phone and a personal computer in a spare bedroom—and clients generally accept smaller vendors.'' Another business owner in the industry observed that effective collection agencies will particularly benefit from increasing demands from clients such as credit card companies; doctors, lawyers, and other professionals; and health care firms. Moreover, many observers believe that privatization initiatives by local, state, and federal government agencies will provide collection agencies with additional business.

TRAVEL AGENCIES Travel and tourism is a huge business area both in the United States and around the world, and independent travel agencies have benefited accordingly. Both business and recreational travel continue to rise in all geographic regions of America, but the hectic pace of modern life has made many of these travelers look to agencies to take care of the specifics of their journeys, from itinerary planning to plane reservations. McCune noted that travel agents do face some challenges today, including slimmer profit margins (because of competitive fares, etc.) and what amounts to a mandate to provide top-level service (since travelers can either go to competitors or make travel arrangements themselves). But she added that travel agencies that are able to improve productivity through available technology can dramatically increase their prospects for success, and noted that ''becoming a specialist in a particular type of travel also gives agencies an edge. [In the mid-1990s], cruises, adventure travel, and eco-tours are what's hot. In addition to being in demand by consumers, such packaged tours also offer better margins. Of course, the key to succeeding in the long run is an ability to uncover the next trendy market in travel. That requires a study of demographics—like the aging of the population and the rise of dual-income families—to identify up-and-coming niches.''

FURTHER READING:

Bregger, John. ''Measuring Self-Employment in the United States.'' *Monthly Labor Review.* January-February 1996.

Goff, Lisa. ''They're In the Money.'' *Crain's New York Business.* September 23, 1996.

McCune, Jenny. ''The Face of Tomorrow.'' *Journal of Business Strategy.* May-June 1995.

''Top 10 Small-Business-Dominated Industries.'' *Journal of Accountancy.* January 1995.

SMALL BUSINESS INNOVATION RESEARCH PROGRAM

The Small Business Innovation Research Program (SBIR) was established by the passage of the Small Business Innovation Development Act of 1982. SBIR, at the time of its passage, required by law that any federal government agency with an extramural research and development budget of more than $100 million set aside 1.25 percent of those funds for the development of high tech small businesses. When the original law expired after ten years, Congress reauthorized SBIR and increased the agencies' contributions to 2.5 percent in 1992. By the latter part of the 1990s, total SBIR funding had reached some $1.2 billion.

Agencies that participate in the Small Business Innovation Research Program include the Departments of Agriculture, Commerce, Defense, Education, Energy, Health and Human Services, and Transportation, as well as the Environmental Protection Agency, the National Aeronautics and Space Administration and the National Science Foundation. According to *Science* magazine, 96 percent of the total

SBIR budget from all agencies comes from the Departments of Defense and Energy, the National Institutes of Health, National Aeronautics and Space Administration, and the National Science Foundation.

These agencies set aside seed funds to help small businesses develop innovative high-tech ideas whose commercial appeal may by some time in coming. Each year the agencies release for consideration more than 3,000 technology topics under which businesses may apply. The topics speak to specific program problems or needs and may be found in the quarterly *Pre-Solicitation Announcement (PSA),* which is only provided online.

Minnesota Project Innovation, Inc., a firm providing assistance to businesses wishing to apply for SBIR funding, says that technical ideas often take many years to go from conception to commercialization. This makes traditional debt financing untenable due to relatively short repayment schedules. Alternatively, venture capital funding is more often available to companies whose products are much closer to market. SBIR funding removes the burden of repayment and the risk of any venture partners' loss of investment.

The SBIR program comprises three phases. This approach allows the government agency to invest a small amount in the beginning and then increase their financial support later should the idea show promise. Once the project nears completion, funding drops off and the business must solicit capital from other sources.

PHASE ONE - THE CONCEPT STAGE *Corporate Report-Minnesota* states that Phase I ''provides up to $100,000 for six months of research and development'' to investigate the feasibility of the project. At this point, business owners must have a well-formed idea for an innovative product and a specific plan for how to transform it into a commercially viable form.

PHASE TWO - THE PROTOTYPE DEVELOPMENT PHASE This phase, for which only Phase One entrepreneurs are eligible, provides up to $750,000 over 24 months, if needed. Funds are to be used to develop a prototype. From here, determinations are made about whether the product is a success or a failure and whether or not it is commercially viable. About 40 percent of Phase One ideas reach this second stage.

PHASE THREE - THE COMMERCIALIZATION STAGE In this stage, funding comes from either the agency's non-SBIR budget or private sources, such as companies, venture capital firms, traditional lenders, and/or universities. These funds are used to bring the product to market. It was estimated by the Government Accounting Office (GAO) in a 1992 survey that 27 percent of the completed projects resulted in commercially available products based on the SBIR-developed technology. These products then generated some $1 billion

in new commercial activity between 1984 and 1987 and were expected to generate more that $2 billion by 1993.

SMALL BUSINESS TECHNOLOGY TRANSFER PILOT PROGRAM (STTR) The Small Business Technology Transfer Pilot Program (STTR) is a parallel program to the SBIR and was created by Congress when it reauthorized SBIR in 1992. This program is a cooperative research partnership between small business concerns and research institutions. It differs from SBIR in two ways. First, it places a greater emphasis on the potential for commercial success. This has spurred participating agencies to be more stringent in their evaluations of Phase I applicants. Secondly, it now requires that universities, federal laboratories, or nonprofit research centers team with businesses to get product into the marketplace. According to *Entrepreneur Magazine*, during the first two years of the STTR program 436 Phase One awards were given, valued at $40.5 million dollars, while 22 Phase II awards worth nearly $11 million dollars were also bestowed.

According to the SBA, to be eligible for SBIR funding, a small business concern must be independently owned and operated; have as its principal place of business the United States; be at least 51 percent owned—or in the case of a publicly owned business, have at least 51 percent of its voting stock owned—by United States citizens or lawfully admitted permanent resident aliens; and employ fewer than 500 people. Nonprofit organizations are not eligible for SBIR awards.

FURTHER READING:

Barlas, Stephen. ''Teaming Up: Universities and Businesses Come Together in a Pilot Program to Fund Innovation.'' *Entrepreneur*, August 1996.

Ross, Duncan M., and Andrew Godley. *Banks, Networks, and Small Firm Finance.* Frank Cass & Co., 1996.

Gillis, Tom S. *Guts & Borrowed Money: Straight Talk for Starting & Growing Your Small Business.* Bard Press, 1997.

Mervis, Jeffrey. ''A $1 Billion 'Tax' on R&D Funds.'' *Science*, May 17, 1996.

Rushmeyer, Sheila. ''SBIR Grants Technical Projects.'' *Corporate Report-Minnesota*, March 1995.

''What Do You Call a Federal Program that Requires No Additional Federal Spending, Costs Virtually Nothing to Administer, and Yields Venture Capital-Like Returns?'' *Inc.*, January 1993.

SEE ALSO: Loans

SMALL BUSINESS INVESTMENT COMPANIES

The Small Business Investment Company (SBIC) program was created in 1958 with the passage of the Small Business Investment Act of 1958.

Licensed by the **U.S. Small Business Administration (SBA)**, SBICs are privately organized and privately managed investment firms that provide **venture capital** to small independent businesses. These loans, which are available both to new and established business establishments, consist of funds borrowed (at favorable rates) from the U.S. government or their own capital.

Two different kinds of Small Business Investment Companies are operated in the United States. In addition to regular SBICs, investment firms known as Specialized Small Business Investment Companies (SSBICs) also exist; this latter type of firm emphasizes service to entrepreneurs who "have been denied the opportunity to own and operate a business because of social or economic disadvantage," according to the SBA. Formerly known as Minority Enterprise Small Business Investment Companies (MESBICs), SSBICs are now officially called Section 301(d) SBICs. Since the differences between SSBICs and regular SBICs are minor, though, they are generally lumped together under the SBIC heading.

THE SBIC ORGANIZATION

Ownership of SBICs generally takes two different forms. The majority of SBICs are relatively small, privately owned and operated firms, but many others are firms owned by commercial banks or insurance companies. For banks, establishment of an SBIC subsidiary is often an attractive proposition, because it enables them to make small business investments that would otherwise be closed to them because of U.S. banking laws and requirements. United States law places few restrictions on SBIC ownership. As the SBA itself said, "almost any person or organization with a minimum initial private capitalization of $5 million and an SBA-approved full time manager who will be in charge of the licensee's operations and who is able to serve the licensee's small business concerns, may be approved for ownership." Indeed, the SBA's interest in encouraging SBICs is evident in the relatively hands-off regulatory environment that they have established for such enterprises. Those regulations that the SBA does enforce are concerned with ensuring the continued financial and ethical health of the SBIC program. SBICs, then, range from limited partnerships to subsidiaries of multinational corporations. Whatever their ownership situation, however, their ultimate goal is to realize a profit from their various business transactions. Some SBICs make most of their revenue from straight debt financing, with their profit coming from the differential between its borrowing costs from the Small Business Administration and the interest rate they charge its small business clients. Other SBICs take a more aggressive tack in seeking profits by making equity-participation loans.

According to the SBA, prospective SBICs (and SSBICs) must have a minimum private capital investment of $5 million to form (the minimum requirement for those firms wishing to utilize participating securities is $10 million). The amount of private capital that an SBIC has at its disposal is important, for the SBA limits its loan guarantees to SBICs to 300 percent of its private capital. The SBA notes, however, that an SBIC "with at least 50 percent of its 'total funds available for investment' invested or committed in 'venture capital' may receive an additional tier of leverage per dollar of private capital for total leverage of 400 percent of private capital. However, in no event may any SBIC or SSBIC draw down leverage in excess of $90 million." An SBIC that engages in leveraging is in essence borrowing additional investment funds from the U.S. Treasury. Only those SBICs that have invested the bulk of its initial private capital and are in full compliance with state and federal regulations are eligible to do this.

Small Business Investment Companies have several different options to choose from in providing financing to small businesses. Most SBICs provide long-term loans to qualified small businesses that need funding for needs that range from expansion of existing facilities to modernization of operation. Sometimes this loan will take the form of equity or debt securities.

OPERATING RESTRICTIONS FOR SBICS

While the SBA provides SBICs with considerable freedom to operate, they do require that these organizations adhere to certain rules. For example, SBICs are not permitted to invest in the following entities: companies with less than one-half of their assets and operations in America; unimproved real estate; finance and investment companies; or companies seeking to purchase or improve farmland, cemeteries, or most other enterprises that would be classified under Major Group 65 (Real Estate) of the U.S. SIC (Standard Industrial Classification) code (exceptions are made for subdividers and developers, title abstract companies, and real estate agents and brokers. Small Business Investment Companies also are forbidden from investing in other SBICs, or in business enterprises that do not fit federal definitions of a "small business."

The SBA also has established regulations in the following areas:

- Conflict of Interest—SBICs are not allowed to make business transactions with any of its associates, which are defined as officers, directors, employees, key "control persons," and certain shareholders.

- Control—the SBA has stipulated that no SBIC may exercise either direct or indirect control over the operations of any small business on a permanent basis. The SBA has, under some circumstances, permitted SBICs to assume temporary control of a business enterprise in order to protect its investment. Before doing so, however, the SBIC and the small business must submit a plan of divestiture for SBA approval.

- Overline Limitations—The SBA has established investment ceilings for both SBICs and SSBICs in their dealings with individual small businesses. SBICs are not allowed to invest more than 20 percent of its private capital with any one small business, while the limit for SSBICs is 30 percent. The SBA does, however, occasionally grant waivers to this rule.

- Cost of Money—The SBA regulates the cost of money on SBIC loans and debt securities issued by SBIC clients.

- Financing Proceeds—The SBA has established regulations designed to ensure that investment funds that are used to purchase securities go directly to the small business that has offered those securities.

- Length of Financing Agreements—SBA rules stipulate (in most cases) that SBIC loan agreements with small business enterprises be made for at least five years, and that the small business taking the loan be given adequate opportunity to fulfill its obligations ahead of schedule if it is able to do so. According to the SBA, loan and debt securities of less than five years' duration are permissible only on those occasions when they are necessary to protect existing financing agreements, are made in contemplation of long-term financing, or are made to finance a change in ownership.

BORROWING FROM AN SBIC

"As is true with venture capitalists in general, SBICs have divergent philosophies and operating policies," wrote Art DeThomas in *Financing Your Small Business*. "Some specialize in equity financing while other provide debt financing in several different forms. This latter group of SBICs is the richest source of debt financing for small businesses outside commercial banks." Small business owners, however, need to weigh several factors before making a loan arrangement with an SBIC.

Entrepreneurs and small business owners seeking financing from SBICs first need to determine how many options they have. Regional SBA offices maintain information on SBICs that operate in their areas, and while they do not provide guidance in directing businesses to particular SBICs, they can give information on the industries and types of investments in which area SBICs have historically shown interest. In addition, a free directory of SBICs is available through the National Association of SBICs.

As many experts note, small businesses should narrow their search for a suitable SBIC by eliminating those that do not provide the business's desired financing route or display adequate management experience in the industry in which the business is involved. Analysts also caution small business owners not to rush through the decision making process. Given the latitude that SBICs have in shaping their loan policies, individual SBICs often maintain dramatically varied lending policies. Entrepreneurs and small business owners should thus take the time to find the program that best meets their needs.

Business consultants also encourage prospective borrowers to negotiate the best possible loan agreement for themselves when talking with SBICs. "Aside from the specifics of SBIC lending that are mandated by existing law or regulation," noted DeThomas, "particulars such as interest rate, maturity, equity participation, and collateral requirements can be negotiated. In general, the more attractive your firm as a financing opportunity—that is, the stronger the business plan—the more negotiating leverage you possess."

SBIC LENDING TO INDIVIDUAL INDUSTRIES

In Fiscal Year (FY) 1996, Small Business Investment Company financing to small businesses reached $1.499 billion. Of this total, nearly two-thirds ($936 million) served as business launch financing for new businesses, while the rest ($563 million) went to already established business enterprises. Only ten years earlier, total SBIC financing had reached just $440 million, so it is evident that SBICs have thrived in the intervening years.

Equity-only financing accounted for the bulk of SBIC loans in FY 1996, reaching $883 million. Another $514 million was classified under combination equity/debt loan packages, while straight debt financing accounted for the final $102 million.

Manufacturing companies accounted for more than 44 percent of SBIC financing in FY 1996, while service establishments pulled in about 25 percent of SBIC financing. Other companies that received meaningful SBIC financial assistance included transportation, communication, and utility companies (8.1 percent); wholesale trade establishments (7.8 percent);

retail trade establishments (7.1 percent); and eligible financial, insurance, and real estate concerns (2.2 percent). The remainder of SBIC financing agreements were made with businesses engaged in mining, construction, forestry, fishing, and other industries.

FURTHER READING:

DeThomas, Art. *Financing Your Small Business: Techniques for Planning, Acquiring & Managing Debt.* Grants Pass, OR: Oasis Press, 1992.

SBA Overview of SBIC Program. Washington: U.S. Small Business Administration, n.a.

SBA Profile: Who We Are and What We Do. Washington: U.S. Small Business Administration, 1996.

Timmons, Jeffrey A. *Planning and Financing the New Venture.* Amherst, NH: Brick House, 1990.

SMALL BUSINESS JOB PROTECTION ACT

On August 20, 1996, President Clinton signed the Small Business Job Protection Act (SBJPA) into law. This law contained a number of provisions impacting various aspects of small business operations, from retirement plans to changes in **S Corporation** structures. The small business community greeted many of the changes contained in SBJPA with considerable enthusiasm, since it was widely interpreted as an act that eliminated a number of unnecessarily burdensome provisions. The act touched on a wide variety of areas relevant to small businesses, especially in the area of **pension plans**. Changes made by the law can be found in such areas as the definition of highly compensated employees, deferred compensation arrangements, family aggregation rules, minimum pension participation rules, "safe harbor" rules for qualified cash or deferred arrangements (CODAs), notice requirements, limits on matching contributions, distributions of excess contributions, elective deferrals includible as compensation, early participation nondiscrimination rules, plan distributions and QJSA waivers, **employee leasing program** provisions, and modification of GATT interest and mortality rate rules. Small business consultants strongly advise business owners who wish to take full advantage of the myriad changes included within SBJPA to consult with a tax advisor or other accounting professional.

IMPACT ON SUBCHAPTER S CORPORATIONS Some observers estimate that the Small Business Job Protection Act will have an effect on approximately two million small businesses that are currently structured as Subchapter S corporations. They note that since the new law allows S corporations to increase its shareholders from 35 to 75, the businesses may be able to attract additional numbers of investors (and capital).

Some analysts question how great an impact this will have, since many S corporations are utilized by family-owned businesses and closely held companies, but others maintain that any expansion is welcome news for S corporations. Another change that is expected to be beneficial for small business owners concerns an expansion in the kinds of organizations that can be shareholders. Under the SBJPA, qualified pension plans will be able to be shareholders in S corporations, beginning in January 1998. Since many pension plans are willing to invest in promising young businesses, S corporation owners will be able to turn to these entities as a source of significant capital.

The Small Business Job Protection Act also provides S corporation owners with greater flexibility in structuring their businesses. Prior to the passage of the SBJPA, S corporations could not own more than 79 percent of another company, but with the new law, they may now own 100 percent of affiliated companies. Finally, business experts note that the SBJPA expands the number of allowable beneficiaries when an S corporation puts together a small business trust.

CHANGES TO RETIREMENT PLANS The SBJPA established a simplified retirement plan for small businesses that is known as the A SIMPLE retirement plan. Under these plans, which are designed for employers with 100 or fewer employees who do not maintain another employer-sponsored plan, employers and employees work together to help ensure that workers have adequate financial security when they reach retirement age. Under the law, employees may make elective contributions of up to $6,000 annually. The employer is required to make matching contributions and do so every year. The SBJPA also requires that businesses contribute at least 1 percent of all employees' compensation or be subject to significant penalties.

The law also impacts other elements of pension plans. For example, for the years 1997, 1998, and 1999, the 15 percent excise tax on excess distributions from pension plans has been suspended. In addition, under the SBJPA, distributions from a qualified plan must begin by April of the calendar year following the later of: 1) the calendar year in which the employee reaches $70\frac{1}{2}$ years of age, or 2) the calendar year in which the worker retires.

FURTHER READING:

Mulleneaux, Natasha M. "Retirement Plan Reform: The Aftermath of the Small Business Job Protection Act of 1996." *Taxes: The Tax Magazine.* August 1997.

Schneider, Mark N., and Marilyn C. Doolittle. "Small Business Job Protection Act Adds Simplicity (and Complexity)." *The Tax Advisor.* June 1997.

Sharp, Joel, Jr., and Hewitt D. Shaw Jr. "Subchapter S Reform: The Small Business Job Protection Act of 1996." *Journal of Corporate Taxation.* Spring 1997.

West, Diane. "401(K)s Catch on at Small Companies." *National Underwriter Life & Health.* June 9, 1997.

SEE ALSO: Retirement Planning

SMALL BUSINESS/LARGE BUSINESS RELATIONSHIPS

Many small business owners see large businesses exclusively in competitive terms. And for some small enterprises, that characterization is an accurate one. An independent record store owner, for example, will undoubtedly—and legitimately—regard the arrival of a new record store operating under the banner of a national chain as a threat. Similarly, a small plastics manufacturer will view larger firms engaged in the same industry sector as competition. But small businesses should recognize that large regional, national, or even international companies can take on other, decidedly more attractive, identities as well. Larger companies also may assume roles as business partners, product distributors, or customers. Indeed, large enterprises wear different hats to different observers. One small business's aggressive competitor may be another small firm's business ally, distributor, or client.

LARGE BUSINESSES AS PARTNERS

The 1990s has seen a general increase in business partnerships between small and large companies. Alliances between large companies are still more prevalent, and many large firms continue to prefer to simply swallow up smaller enterprises via acquisition, but analysts and consultants alike contend that growing numbers of large companies are recognizing the benefits that can accrue from establishing partnerships with nimble, entrepreneurial firms. Small but growing companies can offer mature partners access to new customers, innovative products and management practices, and opportunities to bask in the glow of the small business's innovative, contemporary image. This is especially true in biotechnology sectors and other industries characterized by rapid change and innovation. But as Myron Gould noted in *Direct Marketing,* "Partnerships can be formed in the profit and nonprofit sectors, in the same or different industries, within different divisions of the same company, and in similar market segments/demographics in non-competitive industries."

Indeed, many observers believe that in recent years, festering suspicions and stereotypes in both the large- and small-business camps about the motivations and abilities of the other have begun to give way to an increasing recognition of the positives that they can bring to the table. James W. Botkin and Jana B. Matthews, authors of *Winning Combinations: The Coming Wave of Entrepreneurial Partnerships Between Large and Small Companies,* stated that "entrepreneurs and corporate executives now need each other more than ever. Their needs and their strengths are often opposite and complementary. Both large corporations and small companies can brighten their global prospects by forming collaborative partnerships that capitalize on their complementary strengths while respecting the independence of each party."

Over the past number of years, well-managed smaller companies have proven themselves to be very adept at anticipating market trends, capitalizing on new technologies, and using their lean structures to outpace larger companies. But while their small size enables them to evade the bureaucratic syrup that slows the actions of all but the most progressive larger companies, small companies are also hampered by certain realities that can be easily addressed by big firms, and these impediments are often emphasized if the small firm hopes to establish a presence beyond its domestic borders. "Increasing globalization . . . makes it difficult for small entrepreneurial companies to act alone effectively," wrote Botkin and Matthews. "Their **marketing** and **distribution channels** are frequently inadequate for getting their innovative products and services to an international marketplace. The continual need of small companies for capital also limits their maneuverability. The time and attention of their entrepreneurial management is often diverted to finding and negotiating financing instead of developing markets and distribution systems. . . . Though their innovations may be exactly what the marketplace needs and wants, they are likely to be handicapped in reaching it."

Large firms are an obvious source of assistance in many of the above areas—distribution, financing, marketing, etc.—but small businesspeople have a tendency to regard large corporations with suspicion. After all, many entrepreneurs come from corporate environments that were not necessarily characterized by adherence to any code of **business ethics**, and American corporations have historically shown little respect for small business autonomy (hence the so-called "urge to merge." "Given the 'big fish eats little fish' history of large-to-small encounters, founders of small companies may understandably be leery of forming partnerships that they fear will destroy their company's autonomy and identity," admitted Botkin and Matthews. "But this need not be the case. We suggest that any partnership offer be examined critically and carefully. Entrepreneurs must learn to discriminate between corporate sharks with a bite and swallow mentality and those suitors who have a mutually beneficial arrangement in mind. It's natural to be suspicious. However, many founders of small businesses write off strategic alliances altogether, closing off what might be an increasingly important avenue of rapid growth.''

KEYS TO SUCCESSFUL PARTNERSHIPS WITH LARGER COMPANIES Following are several tips that entrepreneurs should consider when negotiating and maintaining a partnership with a larger company:

1) Research. Some partnership offers sound great on the surface, but are fraught with unpleasantness under the surface. Entrepreneurs should make sure that they undertake diligent research so that they can best assure themselves of finding the right partner, for as Botkin and Matthews admitted, ''not every partnership yields happy results; ill-conceived partnerships can leave your company in worse shape than before. Bad partnerships, like bad marriages, can drain resources, end up in costly litigation, and sour both partners on future relationships.'' Typically, however, warning signs will be there for the small business owner who takes the time to look.

2) Fundamentally sound business practices. Entrepreneurs hoping to secure a partner to bankroll their R&D efforts or market their products are wasting their time if they do not have a viable business already in place. If the small company's business practices are shoddy, disorganized, or incomplete, large companies will be sure to notice.

3) Recognition that the entrepreneur has responsibilities as well. Entrepreneurial companies can reap many benefits from partnering with large firms, but they need to recognize that those big companies are for-profit enterprises; they expect something in return for their financial, marketing, and/or management help. As one executive told G. Steven Burrill and Kenneth B. Lee, authors of *Biotech 91: A Changing Environment,* ''if the arrangement is not good for both parties, it will not be good for either party for long.''

4) Making sure that demands of the partnership do not unduly impact your reasons for launching a small business in the first place. Many partnerships with larger companies require entrepreneurs to make a greater commitment to their business in order to meet the obligations and conditions explicated in the partnership agreement. If the entrepreneur in question launched his or her business for the express purpose of realizing greater personal wealth or establishing a significant presence in a given industry, finding the desire to meet those partnership obligations should not be a problem. If, however, the

entrepreneur launched his or her venture in order to stake out a lifestyle of independence and travel, that person may want to weigh the sort of impact that the partnership could have on those aspects of his or her life.

5) Do not be intimidated. The trappings of the corporate world (high-rise buildings, cavernous conference rooms, legions of blue suits, etc.) can be intimidating, but small business owners have to remember that they run viable businesses of value themselves, and they should negotiate accordingly.

6) Do not sacrifice too much of your independence. Autonomy is assured if you maintain ownership, so be leery of turning over too much equity in the business in exchange for financial help.

7) Communication. Good communication practices are essential to all business relationships, both internal and external, and alliances with large companies are no exception.

LARGE BUSINESSES AS PRODUCT DISTRIBUTORS

Myriad small manufacturers rely on major mass merchandisers (regional, national, or international) to sell their goods. Indeed, these distributors can dramatically heighten a small business's fortunes in a matter of weeks or months. But entrepreneurs seeking to establish such relationships will find that: 1) competition to secure a place on the shelves of major retail outlets is fierce, and 2) some mass merchandisers will be better suited for the small business's product than others.

COMPETITION The single most important factor in securing a distribution agreement with a major retailer is, of course, having a quality product that will sell. But small business owners seeking to establish themselves with a major mass merchandiser also need to make sure that they attend to myriad other business matters every step of the way. After all, the mass merchandiser in question has plenty of product options from which to choose; if your company stumbles at any point, there are plenty of other competitors waiting to take your place on the merchandiser's shelf. Given that reality, entrepreneurs have to make sure that they have a dependable production/delivery operation in place. In addition, small business owners should be prepared to provide prospective distributors with information on the firm's management and financial situation. As one small business owner told *Entrepreneur*'s Karen Axelton, companies like Wal-Mart want to be reassured about your company's capabilities before committing to you. ''They wanted to know about certain aspects of our business—our facility, our financials. At the same time, they were open with us as to what they expect from a vendor.''

COMPATIBILITY Moreover, entrepreneurs need to make sure that they concentrate their efforts on finding mass merchandisers that already sell products to the new product's probable demographic audience. For example, an expensive, ''high-end'' home furnishing product is more likely to be compatible with the existing product lines of an upscale retailer than one of the major discount retailers. Conversely, an inexpensive but functional item that would be commonly used might be better suited to discount outlets rather than a high-end retailer.

LARGE BUSINESSES AS CUSTOMERS

Many small businesses, whether involved in retail, wholesale, manufacturing, or service sectors, count fellow businesses as significant or primary customers. Pleasing corporate clients is in many fundamental respects no different than pleasing individual customers. As Richard Gerson observed in *Great Customer Service for Your Small Business,* ''much of **customer service** comes down to plain old common sense. Simply put, customer service involves everything you and your employees do to satisfy customers. That means you give them what they want and make sure they are happy when they leave. If you just manage complaints, offer refunds or exchanges on returns, and smile at customers, you only provide a small part of excellent customer service. Customer service also means going out of your way for the customer, doing everything possible to satisfy the customer, and making decisions that benefit the customer—sometimes even at the expense of the business [depending on the customer's future potential].''

However, corporate customers sometimes have different needs and priorities than do private individuals, and small businesses that do not recognize these differences are unlikely to provide service that will be acceptable in the long term. For example, delivery deadlines are often far more important for businesses than they are for regular customers. Late delivery of a service or product may constitute no more than a minor convenience to a private-sector customer, but it might mean significant monetary loss for a corporate customer that was depending on that delivery to meet deadlines imposed by its own customers.

Small business owners servicing fellow businesses also need to recognize that the loss of a single corporate customer often constitutes a much more severe blow to a business's health than does the loss of a single retail consumer. Whereas businesses that provide goods or services to the general public will have many customers, establishments that provide their goods or services to corporate clients will in all likelihood have far fewer customers. The loss of even

one such client, then, can have a significant impact because of the percentage of total business that the customer represents. Finally, businesses that rely on corporate clients are more likely to encounter higher levels of paperwork and bureaucracy to satisfy the recordkeeping apparatus of their clients.

FURTHER READING:

Axelton, Karen. ''Scaling the Wal: Is Wal-Mart on Your Wish List? Here's How to do Business with the Nation's Largest Retailer.'' *Entrepreneur.* January 1998.

Botkin, James W., and Jana B. Matthews. *Winning Combinations: The Coming Wave of Entrepreneurial Partnerships Between Large and Small Companies.* New York: John Wiley & Sons, 1992.

Bricklin, Dan. ''My Company, My Self.'' *Inc.* July 1990.

Burrill, G. Steven, and Kenneth B. Lee Jr. *Biotech 91: A Changing Environment.* San Francisco, CA: Ernst & Young, 1990.

''Gathering of the Entrepreneurs.'' *Inc.* November 1989.

Gerson, Richard F. *Great Customer Service for Your Small Business.* Crisp Publications, 1996.

Gould, Myron. ''Partnering for Profit—How to Achieve Impressive Cost-Benefit Results.'' *Direct Marketing.* February 1997.

Lancaster, Hal, and Marj Charlier. ''Bigger Partners Can Cause Problems for Small Firms.'' *Wall Street Journal,* March 4, 1991.

Paajanen, George. ''Customer Service: Training, Sound Practices, and the Right Employee.'' *Discount Store News.* September 15, 1997.

Weinstein, Steve. ''Rethinking Customer Service.'' *Progressive Grocer.* May 1995.

Wilhelm, Wayne, and Bill Rossello. ''The Care and Feeding of Customers.'' *Management Review.* March 1997.

SEE ALSO: Innovation

SMALL CLAIMS COURT

Small claims court is a legal court of law designed to resolve disputes involving small amounts of money in an expeditious manner. Unlike other legal courts, small claims court does not operate by formal rules of evidence, and attorneys are (generally) not utilized. Instead, plaintiffs and defendants simply go before the court and present their respective perspectives on the dispute, and the court makes a judgement based on the evidence presented. Claims made in small claims court, noted writer Sandra R. Bell, typically ''involve purchases made by consumers, disputes over shared property, failure to honor contracts or invoices involving small business, investments that have gone under, and expenses that employees accrued from employers.'' Given the parameters of small claims court, then, it is little wonder that many small business owners sooner or later find themselves involved in a proceeding there, either as a defendant or plaintiff.

APPEARING AS A PLAINTIFF Most small business owners that appear in small claims court as plaintiffs do so because they are having difficulty securing payment for some product or service that they have provided to the defendant. To file a small claims action, the owner needs to first find out if he or she has a case that can even be heard in the court. State limits vary considerably in this regard; some states place a ceiling of several hundred dollars, while others will hear claims for as much as $5,000.

If the plaintiff has a complaint that can be legitimately heard in small claims court, he or she should then check with the local county clerk's office for information on procedures for bringing suit (again, guidelines vary from state to state, although the basic set-up is consistent). The plaintiff also needs to file the claim in the jurisdiction where the defendant resides.

Once the business owner has familiarized him or herself with the basic procedures, he/she should proceed with the filing. This is a fairly basic document, usually only one page in length, that briefly delineates the main reasons for the suit. The document, known as a summons or complaint, should describe the dispute; the time, date, and location that it took place; names of witnesses (if any); and desired compensation. The plaintiff should also try to name the defendant as accurately as possible when filing. "It's very important to have the exact legal listing for a business (named as a defendant)," said one county clerk in an interview with *Business First of Buffalo* contributor Jane Schmitt. "If it's a DBA (doing business as), you want to list them as a DBA. . . . If it's a corporation, make sure you have the exact corporate name. Because while it is not going to make a difference to us, it is going to make a difference to the claimant. . . . If they are successful and want to collect their money, they could hit a snag if they have sued them under an improper legal listing." When the complaint has been filed, the court clerk will inform the plaintiff when the case will be tried. The cost of filing a complaint ranges from about $5 to $25.

In the weeks leading up to the court date, the plaintiff should gather whatever evidence is available to bolster his or her claims. "Bring to court anything that will help prove facts in dispute," wrote Schmitt, "including photographs, written agreements, itemized bills or invoices, written cost estimates for service or repairs, receipts, canceled checks, and other correspondence. If possible, merchandise that is in dispute should be brought to court."

APPEARING AS A DEFENDANT When a small business owner receives notice of claim (this is usually sent via both certified mail and first-class mail), he or she should study the summary of the plaintiff's claims, the amount that is being sought, and begin preparing for the trial date (which is also included in the notification). If the copy of the claim that is sent via regular mail is not returned to the court as undeliverable within 21 days, then it is assumed that the defendant has received notice of the claim.

Once the defendant receives the claim, he or she can either try to reach a mutually satisfactory agreement with the plaintiff prior to the trial date or begin preparing for the case by gathering all favorable evidence available (itemized bills or invoices, written agreements, etc.). "If the claim is not true, you must deny it in no uncertain terms," wrote Bell. "If the basic facts are true, explain why you haven't made restitution. If you are counter-claiming for damages, this must generally be done when you answer the suit. Do not ignore a complaint, and be sure to file your response or counterclaim within the allowable time frame." This time frame, it should be noted, varies from state to state.

RESOLVING SMALL CLAIMS COURT CASES

Small claims court cases are resolved in one of four ways: trial, arbitration, settlement, or default judgement.

TRIAL This is the method that is most familiar to most Americans. Under this arrangement, the plaintiff makes his case, the defendant offers a rebuttal, and the presiding judge makes a judgement based on the evidence presented by both sides. If either the plaintiff or the defendant is unhappy with the judge's verdict, he or she can file an appeal. This step is rarely taken, however, because of the added expense involved (filing an appeal is more expensive than filing an initial claim, and it sometimes requires soliciting the services of an attorney).

ARBITRATION If both sides agree, the dispute can be resolved via arbitration rather than by going to trial. "The advantage of arbitration is that it occurs the same night and is less formal than a trial," said Carol J. Steinberg in *Back Stage*. "The disadvantage is that you cannot appeal the arbitrator's decision so that if you are unhappy with the result, you have no recourse."

SETTLEMENT Plaintiffs and defendants also have the option of settling the case out of court prior to the trial. But as Steinberg indicated, small business owners who consent to a settlement need to be very careful about the various provisions of the agreement, especially if you are owed money: "Your opponent may agree to pay you $150 a month for a year, but if the payments are not made, you have no recourse. If you want to settle the case, make sure that the settlement amount is paid in one lump sum on a certain date. Ask the court to adjourn your case for some time after that. If at that point you have not been paid, you will go forward either with a trial or with arbitration. Be sure that your settlement agreement is in writing and is signed off by a judge.''

DEFAULT JUDGEMENT A default judgement—also sometimes referred to as a liquidated complaint—can be handed down in the event that one of the sides involved in the dispute does not appear at the scheduled trial time (which, say business consultants, is a good reason for people involved in small claims actions to make sure that they leave plenty of time to beat traffic, etc.). In such instances, the judge is presented with the evidence provided by whichever side is present. If the person adequately proves his or her case, a default judgement for the amount claimed is entered, or (in instances wherein the plaintiff does not show up) the case may be dismissed.

COLLECTING MONEY THAT IS OWED

Consultants to small business enterprises warn that winning a small claims case does not necessarily mean that the dispute has been wholly settled. Certainly, if the small business owner mounts a successful defense of a claim, then he or she can return to his business secure in the knowledge that the affair is over. But if the small business owner was a successful plaintiff, he or she still needs to make sure that the amount owed is turned over. There are a variety of enforcement techniques available to successful plaintiffs, but most people owed money can follow basic steps that are generally effective. "The first thing that you do after you win is send a demand letter to your opponent, advising that you will begin judgment enforcement techniques immediately if the full amount of the judgment is not sent to you within 20 days of the date of the letter,'' wrote Steinberg. "You will have an easier time collecting if while you were in court you asked the judge to order the defendant to disclose the assets that would cover the judgment and not to dispose of them until the judgment is paid. The most effective enforcement technique, guaranteed to get the defendant's attention, is to restrain his or her bank account.'' Plaintiffs can do this, stated Steinberg, by locating the defendant's bank and account number on a canceled check (if available). The court then can then impose a restraining order upon the bank, which serves to freeze the account in the amount of the judgement. "If you do not know where the assets are,'' added Steinberg, "the court can help you serve information subpoenas upon banks and any institutions or persons who may have knowledge of your opponent's assets.''

FURTHER READING:

Bell, Sandra R. "Represent Yourself: Here's How You Can Stay One Step Ahead in Small Claims Court.'' *Black Enterprise.* October 1997.

Everybody's Guide to Small Claims Court. Nolo Press.

Schmitt, Jane. "Small Claims Need Not be Big Headache.'' *Business First of Buffalo.* January 17, 1994.

Steinberg, Carol J. "The Performing Artist's Guide to Small Claims Court.'' *Back Stage.* April 28, 1995.

SOLE PROPRIETORSHIP

The sole proprietorship is both the simplest and most common type of business operating in the United States today. Most businesses that are owned and operated by one person take this form; in fact, small business owners who have sole ownership of their enterprises are automatically categorized under this business type if they do not take steps to establish themselves as some other business type.

ADVANTAGES OF SOLE PROPRIETORSHIP

Many aspects of sole proprietorship are attractive to entrepreneurs. Primary reasons why small business owners choose to operate in this fashion include:

- As the only owner, sole proprietors enjoy a great deal of independence and autonomy. As Janet Attard remarked in *The Home Office and Small Business Answer Book,* the sole proprietor makes all the decisions: "You alone can decide what to sell and how to sell it, when to expand the business and when to pull back, when to look for financing, when to buy new equipment, when and how long to work, and when to take the day off—without having to justify your decision to anyone.'' In some instances, sole proprietorships can benefit enormously as a result of this streamlined management structure. An entrepreneur who keeps abreast of business trends, community events, and other factors that can impact on a company's fortunes may, in some cases, be able to adjust to changing business realities far more quickly than a partnership or corporation, where multiple owners and/or managers need to reach agreement on appropriate responses to changes in their business environment.

- Figuring taxes is fairly straightforward. Unlike other business types, sole proprietorships do not have to file separate income **tax returns**. In addition, FICA (Federal Insurance Contributions Act) taxes for such businesses are less than they are for partnerships or other legal operating forms.

- **Accounting** is a relatively simple affair, although small business experts encourage the owners of even the most modest business ventures to establish separate bank accounts and record keeping practices for their enterprise.

- Business operations, too, are generally simpler in a sole proprietorship. Other forms of business often have to contend with more cumbersome or time-consuming regulatory requirements in conducting or reporting on their operations.

- Start-up costs are often modest. This is due in part to the fact that entrepreneurs who intend to establish sole proprietorships do not need to secure the services of an attorney to prepare documents required by state or federal agencies, since none are needed.

- Business losses can be used to offset other income on personal tax returns. Conversely, business profits do not have to be shared with any other owners.

- Sole proprietors are not forbidden from securing and building a work force. Indeed, many businesses that qualify as sole proprietorships have employees, whether it is a delicatessen or a house painting venture.

DISADVANTAGES OF SOLE PROPRIETORSHIP

While business owners who choose sole proprietorship understandably enjoy their autonomy and their freedom from the paperwork that can be a larger factor in other, more complicated, business types, they still need to consider the following drawbacks in the areas of liability and business financing.

"In a sole proprietorship," warned Jocelyn West Brittin in *Selecting the Legal Structure for Your Business,* "the business and the owner are one and the same. There is no separate legal entity and thus no separate legal 'person.' This means that as a sole proprietor you will have unlimited personal responsibility for your business's liabilities. For example, if your business cannot pay for its supplies, the suppliers can sue you individually. The business creditors can go against both the business's assets, including your bank account, car or house. . . . The reverse is also true; i.e., your personal creditors can make claims against your business's assets." She does note that some states offer sole proprietors protection of their personal assets from business risks through legal designations that involve the owner's spouse and/or children, but such arrangements are complex, and should not be entered into without first consulting with an attorney. Business owners can also elected to purchase liability insurance for protection from lawsuits and other threats. In addition to general liability insurance, producers or sellers of goods may also want to

consider securing product liability insurance. The cost of such insurance varies considerably depending on the type of business under consideration.

Raising **capital** for a sole proprietorship can be quite difficult as well (though many businesses that operate as sole proprietorships are of modest size and thus not impacted by this reality). Many lenders are reluctant to provide financing to owners of sole proprietorships—in large part because of fears about their ability to recover the funds should the owner die or become disabled—and even those who make such **loans** require borrowers to provide personal guaranties on the loan. Sole proprietors who consent to such arrangements are in effect pledging their personal assets as **collateral** on the loan. Small business advisors counsel clients who are weighing such stipulations to be cautious before making such an agreement. If a potential lender is taking extra measures to protect itself from default, it may be an indication that the prospective borrower's business plan is viewed—legitimately, perhaps—as flawed or risky. In addition, even well-conceived businesses sometimes fail as a result of circumstances beyond the owner's control. An entrepreneur might, for example, establish a store that is enormously successful for its first few years of operation, only to see it suffer a dramatic downturn in performance with the arrival in town of a much larger store that provides its customers with a wider variety of services and goods. Banks and other lending institutions are aware that such instances occur, and they plan accordingly.

CONTINUITY AND TRANSFERABILITY

Unlike other businesses that can be passed down from generation to generation or continue to exist long after the passage of its original board of directors, sole proprietorships have a limited life. As Brittin wrote, "a sole proprietorship can exist as long as its owner is alive and desires to continue the business. When the owner dies, the sole proprietorship no longer exists. The assets and liabilities of the business become part of the owner's estate."

A sole proprietor is free to sell all or a portion of his or her business to a buyer, but any transaction that transfers ownership or turns the business into one with two or more owners puts an end to the sole proprietorship that had been in existence.

STARTING A SOLE PROPRIETORSHIP

Sole proprietorships often operate under the name of the owner of the business, but this is not a requirement. If the owner decides to select a fictitious name, however, he or she may be required to file a certificate—known as a "doing business as" form or DBA—explaining the arrangement in the region in which he or she is operating the business in question (this requirement also gives the sole proprietor legal protection, for it serves to protect them from other persons who might otherwise use the name for their own business enterprises). In addition, many states forbid business establishments from using words like "incorporated," "Co.," or "Inc." unless they actually qualify as corporations. Some cities and counties also require sole proprietorships to secure a business license before launching their business. Owners who subsequently change their business location or add new locations to their operation are often required to obtain new business licenses for those sites as well.

Many sole proprietorships also will need to obtain federal and state **employer identification numbers (EINs)** for tax purposes. These numbers are required for any businesses that will have employees or will do business with establishments that have employees. Finally, owners of sole proprietorships will, like all other business owners, have to obtain the appropriate operating licenses and certificates, if any, for the area in which they will be conducting business or the goods and services they will offer. Business licenses and zoning permits are among the types of licenses that are sometimes required. Once these few minor licensing issues have been addressed, the sole proprietor is free to conduct business.

Once a sole proprietorship has been established and proven viable, many business owners choose to incorporate eventually. **Incorporation** is both more expensive and more time-consuming than sole proprietorship, but it also affords the business owner considerably more legal protection from lawsuits and other liabilities than does sole proprietorship, and it also makes it easier to secure financing for business expansion.

FURTHER READING:

Attard, Janet. *The Home Office and Small Business Answer Book.* New York: Henry Holt, 1993.

Brittin, Jocelyn West. *Selecting the Legal Structure for Your Business.* Washington: U.S. Small Business Administration, n.a.

The Entrepreneur Magazine Small Business Advisor. Wiley, 1995.

How to Set Up Your Own Small Business. Minneapolis, MN: American Institute of Small Business, 1990.

Kuriloff, Arthur H., John M. Hemphill, Jr., and Douglas Cloud. *How to Start Your Own Business . . . and Succeed.* New York: McGraw-Hill, 1993.

Seglin, Jeffrey L. *Financing Your Small Business.* New York: McGraw-Hill, 1990.

SEE ALSO: Partnerships

STANDARD INDUSTRIAL CLASSIFICATION SYSTEM

The Standard Industrial Classification (SIC) system is a set of hierarchical numeric codes used to identify all industries in the United States. Each SIC code classifies what the government calls "establishments" by the type of economic activities in which they are primarily engaged. The classification system was created by the U.S. government in 1937 for use by various government agencies in formulating economic statistics. It has also been adopted by nongovernmental organizations and private businesses for their own research.

According to the *Standard Industrial Classification Manual,* an establishment is defined as an "economic unit that produces goods or services . . . at a single physical location and is engaged in one, or predominantly one, type of economic activity." Thus an establishment may be a company, but often is only part of a company. To be recognized as a separate industry within the SIC system, a set of establishments must be statistically significant according to criteria such as the number of persons employed and the volume of business conducted. Federal statisticians are interested not in individual companies but in aggregate figures, such as sales and employment, for a specific product or service.

The Federal Office of Management and Budget heads the interdepartmental committee overseeing the SIC system and accepts proposals for changes, such as the addition or deletion of an industry. These changes must conform to the existing structure, reflect historical continuity, and represent industries of sufficient specialization, scope, and economic significance. The system has been revised periodically since its inception to reflect the economy's changing industrial organization. The last revision took place in 1987, as the system was scheduled to be overhauled in 1997.

The SIC system consists of codes of one to four digits. The first digit represents the broadest category and subsequent digits represent subcategories within the broader groupings. For example, the numerical classification 3000 represents the division of manufacturing, 3700 is for manufacturing of transportation equipment, 3710 is for motor vehicles and parts, and 3716 is for motor homes. The major divisions, as designated by the first digit, are as follows:

0—agriculture, forestry, and fishing;

1—mining and construction;

2 and 3—manufacturing;

4—transportation, communications, and utilities;

5—wholesale and retail trade;

6—finance, insurance, and real estate;

7 and 8—services; and

9—public administration.

Various government departments and agencies, such as the Department of Agriculture, the **Federal Trade Commission**, and the Bureau of Labor Statistics, use the SIC system in preparing statistical studies of economic activity under their purview. The U.S. Bureau of Census prepares a Census of Manufacturers and a Census of Service Industries every five years, which together cover every SIC classification. These statistical surveys and censuses are available to the public and are a valuable source for economic and business researchers.

Outside of government, business research and publishing firms have applied the SIC system to their collected company data to facilitate their own research or that of their clients. For example, investment analysis firms use SIC codes when preparing financial analyses of industries. Company directories publishers—such as Standard & Poor's, Dun & Bradstreet, and Gale Research—assign SIC codes to each company they list. Firms that produce on-line and CD-ROM bibliographic databases of articles on companies or industries also assign SIC codes to citation entries as a search field.

In this way, researchers can obtain information by looking up the desired SIC codes; market researchers can create lists of potential client companies or survey market conditions within a given industry; small businesses can learn about their competition by searching for information limited to their own industry; and investors can track the economic trends within given industries.

Despite the heavy reliance on the SIC system for all kinds of business research, the system is not without drawbacks. For example, some within private industry claim that the SIC system goes out of date too quickly. The government, however, tries to maintain the same SIC version as long as possible in order to keep the meaning of the statistics consistent. The basic structure of the SIC system has also been challenged. There are problems classifying traditionally different industries which have begun offering the same services, or new types of establishments that offer a combination of products or services previously considered unrelated.

Furthermore, the SIC system was not designed for company classification, but this is a major use outside government. When a company engages in more than one activity and is assigned more than one code, the relevance of each of the codes may be unclear. Finally, this SIC system is used only in the United States, while other countries have their own systems. As business and industry become increasingly global, there is a greater need for adopting an international standard classification system. In response to this need, the U.S. Bureau of Economic Analysis introduced the North American Industry Classification (NAIC) system in 1997. Covering Canada and Mexico in addition to the United States, NAIC codes were scheduled to replace SIC codes beginning in 1997.

FURTHER READING:

Duncan, Joseph W. "Statistics Corner: Revising Classifications of Economic Activity." *Business Economics*. January 1992.

Norwood, Janet L., and Deborah P. Klein. "Developing Statistics to Meet Society's Needs." *Monthly Labor Review*. October 1989.

Ojala, Marydee. "Industry Searching by the Codes." *Online*. May 1993.

Standard Industrial Classification Manual. Washington: Executive Office of the President, Office of Management and Budget, 1987.

SEE ALSO: Gross Product Originating

STOCKS

Securities issued by a corporation are classified as debt, equity, or some hybrid of these two forms. Debt usually takes the form of a loan and must be repaid, while equity usually takes the form of an ownership claim upon the corporation. The two main types of equity claims are common stock and preferred stock, although there are also related claims, such as rights, warrants, and convertible securities. Growing companies, which tend to lack the **assets** necessary to secure debt, often decide to issue equity securities. Although issuing common stock can be traumatic for a small business—because it can be costly, and because it causes a dramatic redistribution of ownership and control—it can also provide a solid foundation upon which to build a company. Preferred stock offers holders priority in receiving **dividends** and in claiming assets in the event of business liquidation, but it also lacks the voting rights afforded to common stockholders. Many venture capitalists require convertible preferred stock—which can be converted to common stock at some time in the future at a favorable price—as incentive to invest in start-up ventures. The sections below describe the characteristics of common and preferred stock in more detail.

COMMON STOCK

A share of common stock is quite literally a share in the business, a partial claim to ownership of the firm. Owning a share of common stock provides a number of rights and privileges. These include sharing in the income of the firm, exercising a voice in the management of the firm, and holding a claim on the assets of the firm.

DIVIDENDS Sharing in the income of the firm is generally in the form of a cash dividend. The firm is not obligated to pay dividends, which must be declared by the board of directors. The size and timing of the dividends is uncertain. In a strictly rational economic environment, dividends would be considered as a "residual." In this view, the firm would weigh payment of dividends against other uses for the funds. Dividends would be paid only if the firm had no better use for the funds. In this case, declaring or increasing dividends would be a negative signal, since the firm would be admitting that it lacked possibilities for growth.

For widely held, publicly traded firms there are a number of indications that this is not the case, and that shareholders and investors like dividends and dividend increases. The reason is that dividends are taken as a signal that the firm is healthy, and can afford to pay dividends. A decrease in dividends would indicate inability to maintain the level of dividends, signaling a decline in prospects. An increase would signal an improvement in prospects. The signal from a dividend decrease is strong because management will wish to give only positive signals by at least maintaining the dividend, making cuts only when absolutely necessary. The signal from a dividend increase is also strong because management would be hesitant to increase dividends unless they could be maintained. The signaling nature of dividends is supported by cases in which the dividend is maintained in the face of declining earnings, sometimes even using borrowed funds. It is also supported by the occurrence of "extraordinary" or one-time-only dividends, a label by which management attempts to avoid increasing expectations.

This signaling approach is not applicable to closely held firms. In this situation, communication between management and shareholders is more direct and signals are not required. When owners are also the managers, sharing in earnings may take the indirect form of salaries and fringe benefits. In fact, shareholders in closely held firms may prefer that dividends be reinvested, even in relatively low return projects as a form of tax protection. The investment is on a pretax (before personal tax) basis for the investor, avoiding immediate double taxation and converting the income to capital gains that will be paid at a later date.

Dividends are declared for stockholders at a particular date, called the date of record. Since stock transactions ordinarily take five business days for completion, the stock goes "ex-dividend" four days before the date of record, unless special arrangement is made for immediate delivery. Since the dividend removes funds from the firm, it can be expected that the per share price will decrease by the amount of the dividend on the ex-dividend date.

Stock dividends are quite different in form and nature from cash dividends. In a stock dividend, the investor is given more shares in proportion to the number already held. A stock split is similar, with a difference in accounting treatment and a greater increase in the number of shares. The use of the word "dividends" in stock dividends is actually a misuse of the word, since there is no flow of cash, and the proportional and absolute ownership of the investor is unchanged. The stockholder receives nothing more than a repackaging of ownership: the number of shares increases, but the price per share will drop. There are, however, some arguments in favor of stock dividends. One of these is the argument that investors will avoid stocks of unusually high price, possibly due to required size of investment and round lot (100 share) trading. On the other hand, stocks with unusually low price are also avoided, perhaps because they are perceived as "cheap." The price drop accompanying stock dividends can be used to adjust price. Stock dividends have also been suggested as a way to make cash dividends elective while also providing tax-advantaged reinvestment.

With a cash dividend, an investor who wishes to reinvest must pay taxes and then reinvest the reduced amount. With a stock dividend, the entire amount is reinvested. Although taxes will ultimately be paid, in the interim a return is earned on the entire pretax amount. This is the same argument as that for low dividends in a closely held firm. Investors who wish cash dividends can simply sell the stock. Using stock dividends in this way faces restriction from the Internal Revenue Service.

CONTROL The corporate form allows the separation of management and ownership, with the manager serving as the agent of the owner. Separation raises the problem of control, or what is termed the agency problem. Stockholders have only indirect control by voting for the directors. The directors in turn choose management and are responsible for monitoring and controlling management's conduct. In fact, the stockholders' ability to influence the conduct of the firm may be quite small, and management may have virtually total control within very broad limits.

Voting for the directors takes either of two forms. The first form is majority voting. In this form, each stockholder receives votes for each open position according to the number of shares held, and may cast those votes only for candidates for that position. The winning candidate is the candidate winning a majority of the votes cast. The second form is called cumulative voting. In this form, stockholders again receive votes for each open position according to the number of shares held, but may apportion the votes among the positions and candidates as desired. The candidates receiving the most votes are elected.

Excluding minority stockholders from representation on the board is more difficult under cumulative voting. For example, if there are four directors to be elected and one million shares eligible to vote at one vote per share, a stockholder with 500,001 shares would control the election. Under majority voting a dissident stockholder with 200,001 shares could cast only 200,001 votes apiece for candidates for each of the four positions, which would not be sufficient to ensure representation on the board. Under cumulative voting, a dissident stockholder with a minimum of 200,001 shares could be sure of representation by electing one candidate of choice, casting a cumulative 800,004 votes for that candidate. The remaining 799,999 shares could be sure of electing three chosen candidates, but could not command sufficient votes to exceed the cumulative dissident vote four times.

Although the board of directors is supposedly independent of management, the degree of independence is sometimes small. Typically, some members of the board are ''insiders'' drawn from management, while others are ''outside'' directors. Even the outside directors may not be completely independent of management for several reasons. One reason is that few shareholders can afford the time and expense to attend the annual meetings, so that voting is done through the mail. This usually takes the form of a ''proxy'' giving management the power to vote for the shareholder, as instructed. While the shareholder may instruct management on how to vote, the choices may be few and are controlled by management. Management will tend to nominate safe candidates for directorship, who will not be likely to challenge the status quo. As a result, directorship is at times an honor or sinecure, treated as having few real obligations.

Dissidents may mount opposition and seek the proxy votes, but such opposition is liable to face legal challenges and must overcome both psychological barriers and shareholder apathy. Many shareholders do not vote or routinely vote for management. Further, dissidents must spend their own money, while management has the resources of the firm at its disposal. Another reason for a lack of independence on the part of directors is the practice of interlocking boards of directors, who are likely to reach a tacit agreement. Conventional wisdom on Wall Street has long been to sell the stock rather than oppose an entrenched management.

In addition to controlling the proxy system, managements have instituted a number of other defensive mechanisms in the face of takeover threats. It is not unusual to find several ''classes'' of stock with different voting power, some classes having no voting power at all. A number of firms have changed from cumulative to majority voting. Staggered boards, with only a portion of the board terms expiring in a given year, and supermajority voting for some questions have also been used. Takeover defenses include the golden parachute, or extremely generous severance compensation in the face of a takeover, and the poison pill, an action that is triggered by a takeover and has the effect of reducing the value of the firm. All of these measures act to make stockholder power appear more tenuous.

There has been some recent movement towards greater stockholder power. One factor in this movement is the increasing size of institutional investors such as pensions and mutual funds. This has led to a more activist stance, and a willingness to use the power of large stock positions to influence management. Another factor is a renewed emphasis on the duties of the directors, who may be personally liable for management's misconduct. At least part of this movement may be the result of the takeover activities of the 1980s. The takeover and breakup or consolidation of firms, with accompanying job loss, has been much criticized. This activity showed that challenging management was possible, however, and encouraged dissident groups. It also sent a message to management that mediocre performance might not be tolerated. It has been suggested that the threat of takeover may have done much to reinforce the rights of stockholders. The use of defense mechanisms detrimental to the stockholder has called attention to potential managerial abuses. The appropriate level of salary and of management perks, such as use of a corporate jet, has come under scrutiny in the financial and popular press.

RESIDUAL OWNERSHIP The common stockholder has a claim on the assets of the firm. This is an undifferentiated or general claim which does not apply to any specific asset. The claim cannot be exercised except at the breakup of the firm. The firm may be dissolved by a vote of the stockholders, or by bankruptcy. In either case, there is a well-defined priority in which the liabilities of the firm will be met. The common stockholders have the lowest priority, and receive a distribution only if prior claims are paid in full. For this reason the common stockholder is referred to as the residual owner of the firm.

PREEMPTIVE RIGHT The corporate charter will often provide common stockholders with the right to maintain their proportional ownership in the firm, called the preemptive right. For example, if a stockholder owns ten percent the stock outstanding and 100,000 new shares are to be issued, the stockholder has the right to purchase 10,000 shares (ten percent) of the new issue. This preemptive right can be honored in a rights offering. In a rights offering, each stockholder receives one right for each share held. Buying shares or subscribing to the issue then requires the surrender of a set number of rights, as well as payment of the offering price. The offering is often underpriced in order to assure its success. The rights are then valuable because possession of the rights allows subscription to the underpriced issue. The rights can be transferred, and are often traded.

A rights offering may be attractive to management because the stockholders, who thought enough of the firm to buy its stock, are a pre-sold group. The value of the preemptive right to the common stockholders, however, is questionable. The preemptive right of proportional ownership is important only if proportional control is important to the stockholder. The stockholder may be quite willing to waive the preemptive right. If the funds are used properly, the price of the stock will increase, and all stockholders will benefit. Without buying part of the new issue, the stockholder may have a smaller proportional share, but the share will be worth more. While rights are usually valuable, this value arises from underpricing of the issue rather than from an inherent value of rights. The value of the rights ultimately depends on the use of the funds and whether or not the market views that use as valuable.

VALUATION In investment practice, decisions are more often expressed and made in terms of the comparative expected rates of return, rather than on price. A number of models and techniques are used for valuation. A common approach to valuation of common stock is present value. This approach is based on an estimate of the future cash dividends. The present value is then the amount which, if invested at the required rate of return on the stock, could exactly recreate the estimated dividends. This required rate of return can be estimated from models such as the capital asset pricing model (CAPM), using the systematic risk of the stock, or from the estimated rate of return on stocks of similar risk. Another common approach is based on the **price-earnings ratio**, or P/E. In this approach, the estimated earnings of the firm are multiplied by the appropriate P/E to obtain the estimated price. This approach can be shown to be a special case of present value analysis, with restrictive assumptions. Since various models and minor differences in assumptions can produce widely different results, valuation is best applied as a comparative analysis.

In some cases, such as estate valuation, the dollar value of the stock must be estimated for legal purposes. For assets that are widely publicly traded, the market price is generally taken as an objective estimate of asset value for legal purposes, since this is sale value of the stock. For stock that is not widely traded, valuation is based on models such as present value, combined with a comparison with similar publicly traded stock. Often, however, a number of discounts are applied for various reasons. It is widely accepted that, compared to publicly traded stock, stock that is not publicly traded should be valued at a discount because of a lack of liquidity. This discount may be 60 percent or more. Another discount is applied for a minority position in a closely held stock or

a family firm, since the minority position would have no control This discount does not apply if the value is estimated from the value of publicly traded stock, because the market price of a stock is traded already the price of a minority position. There is an inverse effect for publicly traded stock in the form of a control premium. A large block of stock which would give control of the firm might be priced above market.

Finally, it should be noted that the accounting book value is only rarely more than tangentially relevant to market value. This is due to the use of accounting assumptions such as historic cost. While accounting information may be useful in a careful valuation study, accounting definitions of value differ sharply from economic value.

PREFERRED STOCK

Preferred stock is sometimes called a hybrid, since it has some of the properties of equity and some of the properties of debt. Like debt, the cash flows to be received are specified in advance. Unlike debt, these specified flows are in the form of promises rather than of legal obligations. It is not unusual for firms to have several issues of preferred stock outstanding, with differing characteristics. Other differences arise in the areas of control and claims on assets.

DIVIDENDS Because the specified payments on preferred stock are not obligations, they are referred to as dividends. Preferred dividends are not tax-deductible expenses for the firm, and consequently the cost to the firm of raising capital from this source is higher than for debt. The firm is unlikely to skip or fail to declare the dividend, however, for several reasons. One of the reasons is that the dividends are typically (but not always) cumulative. Any skipped dividend remains due and payable by the firm, although no interest is due. One source of the preferred designation is that all preferred dividends in arrears must be paid before any dividend can be paid to common stockholders (although bond payments have priority over all dividends). Failure to declare preferred dividends may also trigger restrictive conditions of the issue. A very important consideration is that, just as for common dividends, preferred dividends are a signal to stockholders, both actual and potential. A skipped preferred dividend would indicate that common dividends will also be skipped, and would be a very negative signal that the firm was encountering problems. This would also close off access to the capital markets, and lenders would be wary.

There is also a form of preferred stock, called participating preferred stock, in which there may be a share in earnings above the specified dividends. Such participation would typically only occur if earnings or common dividends rose over some threshold, and might be limited in other ways. A more recent innova-

STOCKS

ENCYCLOPEDIA OF SMALL BUSINESS

923

tion is adjustable-rate preferred stock, with a variable dividend based on prevailing interest rates.

CONTROL Under normal circumstances preferred stockholders do not have any voting power, resulting in little control over or direct influence on the conduct of the firm. Some minimal control would be provided by the indenture under which the stock was issued, and would be exercised passively—i.e., the trustees for the issue would be responsible for assuring that all conditions were observed. In some circumstances, the conditions of the issue could result in increased control on the part of the preferred stockholders. For instance, it is not unusual for the preferred stockholders to be given voting rights if more than a specified number of preferred dividends are skipped. Other provisions may restrict the payment of common dividends if certain conditions are not met. Preferred stockholders also may have a preemptive right.

CLAIM ON ASSETS AND OTHER FEATURES Another source of the preferred designation is that preferred stock has a prior claim on assets over that of common stock. The claim of bondholders is prior to that of the preferred stockholders. Although preferred stock typically has no maturity date, there is often some provision for retirement. One such provision is the call provision, under which the firm may buy back or recall the stock at a stated price. This price may vary over time, normally dropping as time passes. Another provision is the sinking fund, under which the firm will recall and retire a set number of shares each year. Alternately, the firm may repurchase the shares for retirement on the open market, and would prefer to do so if the market price of the preferred is below the call price. Preferred stock is sometimes convertible, i.e., it can be exchanged for common stock at the discretion of the holder. The conversion takes place at a set rate, but this rate may vary over time.

VALUATION The par value of a preferred stock is not related to market value, except that it is often used to define the dividend. Since the cash flow of dividends to preferred stockholders is specified, valuation of preferred is much simpler than for common stock. The valuation techniques are actually more similar to those used for bonds, drawing heavily on the present value concept. The required rate of return on preferred stock is closely correlated with interest rates, but is above that of bonds because the bond payments are contractual obligations. As a result, preferred stock prices fluctuate with interest rates. The introduction of adjustable-rate preferred stock is an attempt to reduce this price sensitivity to interest rates.

FOREIGN STOCK

Purchases of foreign stock have greatly increased in recent years. One motivation behind this increase is that national economies are not perfectly correlated, so that greater diversification is possible than with a purely domestic portfolio. Another reason is that a number of foreign economies are growing, or are expected to grow, rapidly. Additionally, a number of developing countries have consciously promoted the development of secondary markets as an aid to economic development. Finally, developments in communications and an increasing familiarity with international affairs and opportunities has reduced the hesitance of investors to venture into what once was unfamiliar territory.

Foreign investment is not without problems. International communication is still more expensive and sometimes slower than domestic communication. Social and business customs often vary greatly between countries. Trading practices on some foreign exchanges are different than in the United States. Accounting differs not only in procedures, but often in degree of information disclosed. Although double taxation is generally avoided by international treaties, procedures are cumbersome. Political instability can be a consideration, particularly in developing countries. Finally, the investor faces exchange rate risk. A handsome gain in a foreign currency can be diminished, or even turned into a loss, by shifting exchange rates. These difficulties are felt less by professional managers of large institutions, and much of the foreign investment is through this channel.

An alternative vehicle for foreign investing is the American Depositary Receipt (ADR). This is simply a certificate of ownership of foreign stock that is deposited with a U.S. trustee. The depository institution also exchanges and distributes any dividends, and provides other administrative chores. ADRs are appealing to individual investors. It has also been suggested that the benefits of international investing can be obtained by investing in international firms.

INVESTMENT CHARACTERISTICS

Stocks are diverse in nature and can be classified many ways for investment purposes. For example, stocks can be classified according to the level of risk. Risky stocks are sometimes referred to as aggressive or speculative. They may also be growth stocks, which are expected to experience high rates of growth in size and earnings. If risk is measured by the beta (systematic or nondiversifiable risk), then the term applies to a stock with a beta greater than one. These stocks are quite sensitive to economic cycles, and are also called cyclical. Contrasted are the blue-chip stocks—high-quality stocks of major firms that have long and stable records of earnings and dividends. Stocks with low risk, or a beta of less than one, are referred to as defensive. One form of investment strategy, called timing, is to switch among cyclical and defensive stocks according to expected evolution of the economic cycle. This strategy is sometimes refined to movement among various types of stock or sectors of the economy. Another stock category is income stocks—stocks that have a long and stable record of comparatively high dividends.

Common stock has been suggested as a hedge against inflation. This suggestion arises from two lines of thought. The first is that stocks ultimately are claims to real assets and productivity, and the prices of such claims should rise with inflation. The second line of thought is that the total returns to common stock are high enough to overcome inflation. While this is apparently true over longer periods, it has not held true over shorter periods.

Preferred stock is generally not considered a desirable investment for individuals. While the junior position of preferred stockholders as compared to bondholders indicates that the required rate of return on preferred will be above that of bonds, observation indicates that the yield on bonds has generally been above that of preferred stock of similar quality. The reason for this is a provision of the tax codes that 70 percent of the preferred dividends received by a corporation are tax exempt. This provision is intended to avoid double taxation. Because of the tax exemption, the effective after-tax yield on preferred stock is higher for corporations, and buying of preferred stock by corporations drives the yields down. The resulting realized return for individuals, who cannot take advantage of this tax treatment, would generally be below acceptable levels.

FURTHER READING:

Bodie, Zvi, Alex Kane, and Alan J. Marcus. *Investments.* 2nd ed. Homewood, IL: Irwin, 1993.

Cottle, Sidney, Roger F. Murray, and Frank E. Block. *Graham and Dodd's Security Analysis.* 5th ed. New York: McGraw-Hill, 1988.

Gitman, Lawrence J., and Michael D. Joehnk. *Fundamentals of Investing.* 5th ed. New York: HarperCollins, 1993.

Petty, J. William, Arthur J. Keown, David F Scott, Jr., and John D. Martin. *Basic Financial Management.* Englewood Cliffs, NJ: Prentice Hall, 1993.

Pinches, George E. *Essentials of Financial Management.* 4th ed. New York: HarperCollins, 1992.

SEE ALSO: Debt Financing; Direct Public Offering; Equity Financing; Initial Public Offering; Investor Relations and Reporting

STRATEGY

As James Brian Quinn indicated in *The Strategy Process: Concepts and Contexts,* "a strategy is the pattern or plan that integrates an organization's major goals, policies, and action sequences into a cohesive whole. A well-formulated strategy helps to marshal and allocate an organization's resources into a unique and viable posture based on its relative internal competencies and shortcomings, anticipated changes in the environment, and contingent moves by intelligent opponents." All types of businesses require some sort of strategy in order to be successful; otherwise their efforts and resources will be spent haphazardly and likely wasted. Although strategy formulation tends to be handled more formally in large organizations, small businesses too need to develop strategies in order to use their limited resources to compete effectively against larger firms.

Formulation of an effective business strategy requires managers to consider three main players—the company, its customers, and the competition—according to Kenichi Ohmae in his book *The Mind of the Strategist.* These three players are collectively referred to as the strategic triangle. "In terms of these three key players, strategy is defined as the way in which a corporation endeavors to differentiate itself positively from its competitors, using its relative corporate strengths and weaknesses to better satisfy customer needs," Ohmae explained.

Quinn noted that an effective business strategy should include three elements: 1) a clear and decisive statement of the primary goals or objectives to be achieved; 2) an analysis of the main policies guiding or limiting the company's actions; and 3) a description of the major programs that will be used to accomplish the goals within the limits. In addition, it is important that strategies include only a few main concepts or thrusts in order to maintain their focus. They should also be related to other strategies in a hierarchical fashion, with each level supporting those above and below. Finally, strategies should attempt to build a strong yet flexible position for the company so that it may achieve its goals whatever the reaction of external forces. "Strategic decisions are those that determine the overall direction of an enterprise and its ultimate viability in light of the predictable, the unpredictable, and the unknowable changes that may occur in its most important surrounding environments," Quinn stated.

LIMITS ON STRATEGIC CHOICES

The strategic choices available to a company are not unlimited; rather, they depend upon the company's capabilities and its position in the marketplace. "At the broadest level formulating competitive strategy involves the consideration of four key factors that determine the limits of what a company can successfully accomplish," Michael E. Porter wrote in his classic book *Competitive Strategy.* Two of these limiting factors are internal, and the other two are external. The internal limits are the company's overall strengths and weaknesses and the personal values of its leaders. ''The company's strengths and weaknesses are its profile of **assets** and skills relative to competitors, including financial resources, technological posture, brand identification, and so on,'' Porter stated. ''The personal values of an organization are the motivations and needs of the key executives and other personnel who must implement the chosen strategy.''

The external factors limiting the range of a company's strategic decisions are the competitive environment and societal expectations under which it operates. ''Industry opportunities and threats define the competitive environment, with its attendant risks and potential rewards,'' Porter noted. ''Societal expectations reflect the impact on the company of such things as government policy, social concerns, evolving mores, and many others. These four factors must be considered before a business can develop a realistic and implementable set of goals and policies.''

Once a company has analyzed the four factors, it may then begin developing a strategy to compete under or attempt to change the situation it faces. The approach to strategy development recommended by Porter involves identifying the company's current strategy; revealing underlying assumptions about the company's position, its competitors, or industry trends affecting it; analyzing the threats and opportunities present in the external environment; determining the company's own strengths and weaknesses given the realities of its environment; proposing feasible alternatives; and choosing the one that best relates the company's situation to its environment.

GENERIC STRATEGIES

The number of potential business strategies are probably as great as the number of different businesses. Each distinct organization must develop a strategy that best matches its internal capabilities and its situation with regard to the external environment. Still, many of the numerous strategies pursued by businesses can be loosely grouped under three main categories—cost leadership, differentiation, and focus. Porter termed these categories ''generic strategies,'' and claimed that most companies use variations of them, either singly or in combination, to create a defensible position in their industry. On the other hand, companies that fail to target their efforts toward any of the generic strategies risk becoming ''stuck in the middle,'' which leads to low profitability and a lack of competitiveness.

COST LEADERSHIP The first generic strategy, overall cost leadership, can enable a company to earn above average profits despite the presence of strong competitive pressures. But it can also be difficult to imple-

ment. In a company pursuing a low-cost strategy, every activity of the organization must be examined with respect to cost. For example, favorable access to raw materials must be arranged, products must be designed for ease of manufacturing, manufacturing facilities and equipment must continually be upgraded, and production must take advantage of **economies of scale**. In addition, a low-cost strategy requires a company to implement tight controls across its operations, avoid marginal customer accounts, and minimize spending on **advertising** and **customer service**. Implemented successfully in a price-sensitive market, however, a low-cost strategy can lead to strong market share and profit margins.

Of course, a low-cost strategy—like any other strategy—also involves risks. For example, technological changes may make the company's investments in facilities and equipment obsolete. There is also the chance that other competitors will learn to match the cost advantages offered by the company, particularly if inflation helps narrow the gap. Finally, low-cost producers risk focusing on cost to such an extent that they are unable to anticipate necessary product or marketing changes.

DIFFERENTIATION Companies that pursue a strategy of differentiation try to create a product or service that is considered unique within their industry. They may attempt to differentiate themselves on the basis of product design or features, brand image, technology, customer service, **distribution channels**, or several of these dimensions. The idea behind a differentiation strategy is to attract customers with a unique offering that meets their needs better than the competition, and for which they will be willing to pay a premium price. This strategy is intended to create brand loyalty among customers and thus provide solid profit margins for the company. Although the company may not be able to achieve a high market share using a differentiation strategy—because successful differentiation requires a perception of exclusivity, and because not all customers will be willing or able to pay the higher prices—the increased profit margins should compensate. Naturally, there are risks associated with committing to a differentiation strategy. For example, competitors may be able to imitate the unique features, customers may lose interest in the unique features, or low-cost competitors may be able to undercut prices far enough to erode brand loyalty.

FOCUS Companies undertaking a focus strategy direct their full attention toward serving a particular market, whether it is a specific customer group, product segment, or geographic region. The idea behind the focus strategy is to serve that particular market more effectively than competitors on the basis of product differentiation, low cost, or both. Since focusing on a small segment of the overall market limits the

market share a company can command, it must be able to make up for the lost sales volume with increased profitability. The focus strategy, too, entails risks. For example, there is always a possibility that competitors will be able to exploit submarkets within the strategic target market, that the differences between the **target market** and the overall market will narrow, or that the high costs associated with serving the target market will eliminate any advantage gained through differentiation.

"STUCK IN THE MIDDLE" Each of the three generic strategies identified by Porter requires a company to accumulate a different set of skills and resources. For example, a company pursuing a low-cost strategy would likely have a much different organizational structure, incentive system, and corporate culture than one pursuing a differentiation strategy. The key to successful implementation of one of the three generic strategies is to commit to it fully. As Porter explained, "The firm failing to develop its strategy in at least one of the three directions—a firm that is 'stuck in the middle'—is in an extremely poor strategic situation. This firm lacks the market share, **capital** investment, and resolve to play the low-cost game, the industry-wide differentiation necessary to obviate the need for a low-cost position, or the focus to create differentiation or a low-cost position in a more limited sphere. The firm stuck in the middle is almost guaranteed low profitability."

NEW APPROACHES TO STRATEGY DEVELOPMENT

In the past, the formulation of strategy—at least in large corporations—was the domain of upper-level management. The traditional approach involved top managers coming up with a strategic direction for the company, setting it forth in an annual written strategic plan, and then disseminating the plan to various departments and employees, who were expected to contribute only within their own spheres of influence. This approach seemed to work fairly well for slow-moving companies in a stable external environment. In recent years, however, the process of developing strategy has changed dramatically in response to changes in the overall business world. "There is little question that the traditional approach to strategic planning, formulated in a different era, is often inadequate to deal with the rapid and continuous changes taking place in today's marketplace; it also fails to take into account the increased demand for autonomy in today's work force," Stephen J. Wall and Shannon Rye Wall wrote in an article for *Organizational Dynamics.*

Traditional approaches to strategy development have been criticized for being too rigid, inflexible, and authoritative. Experts claim that these approaches were too concerned with analysis and quantification to

be able to predict and adapt to market changes. As a result, new approaches have emerged that no longer relegate strategy to top management; instead, the strategy formulation process involves all individuals in an organization, particularly those who are in direct contact with customers. "A new approach to the strategic planning process, one that involves managers at all levels, can result in a dynamic process that increases competitive advantage," Wall and Wall wrote. "Strategic planning is evolving due to the increasingly urgent need for responsiveness to market changes."

In large measure, the changes that have taken place in business strategy have come as a result of changes in the environment. As the global marketplace has become increasingly volatile and competitive, companies have had to adjust by reducing their time frames for responding to changing customer needs. In addition, the changes in business strategy have come in part because today's workers tend to want and even demand more control over their work lives. The combination of these two factors has resulted in a new value being placed on employee participation in the strategy process. "In an environment in which change is the norm, the insights of those on the front lines take on a new importance, since those close to the action—salespeople and others who deal directly with outside clients—are first to get wind of changes in customer needs," according to Wall and Wall. "Instead of being a structured, time-bound activity undertaken by a single group of senior managers and professionals, it is evolving into an iterative, ongoing process that involves the entire organization."

Many companies are now choosing to develop strategy through the creation of **cross-functional teams.** Combining employees from various functional areas in this way tends to promote strategic thinking, because the groups are able to focus on broad company goals rather than on more limited functional, department, or individual goals. In addition to establishing cross-functional teams within the organization, some companies are beginning to solicit strategic input from their external customers and suppliers as well.

BENEFITS FROM THE NEW APPROACHES

Employee participation in the strategy process not only helps the company to develop a more responsive strategy, but also improves employee morale and commitment to the organization. Companies that encourage such participation are creating a more knowledgeable workforce, which is particularly important for small businesses since intellectual capital is often one of their most valuable assets.

The new, participative approaches to strategy formulation can also enable companies to improve their focus on customer needs by increasing the access of line employees to top management. "Because of intensifying competition, information about customers' needs, competitors' abilities, and the strength of the company's own products and services is critical," Wall and Wall explained. "Also critical is the path such information takes through the organization. In many organizations, relevant data never makes it to the strategists at the top." In fact, hierarchies are designed to filter the information that goes to upper-level managers. But this lack of information can lead to overconfidence and myopic decision making. Similarly, the new approaches can also help companies to remain flexible and responsive to market changes. The greater amount of information that managers receive about the market enables them to adapt the company's strategic direction to take advantage of new circumstances.

Participative strategic development also may help companies to retain key employees, because employees gain satisfaction by being able to direct and see the results of their efforts. "Retaining these highly skilled and trained professionals will become increasingly important as knowledge has more and more to do with the company's ability to build and maintain a competitive advantage," Wall and Wall noted. Finally, participating in strategy formulation may enable managers to make better use of their time. This benefit is particularly helpful because time is always limited as companies try to do more with less people.

Overall, as Wall and Wall stated, "Organizations are looking to the benefits of a more evolutionary, participatory approach to strategy making to help them achieve a flexible and renewable source of competitive advantage. Competitors who fail to do so will find themselves left behind."

FURTHER READING:

Eccles, Robert, and Nitin Nohria. *Beyond the Hype: Rediscovering the Essence of Management.* Boston, MA: Harvard Business School Press, 1992.

Eisenhardt, Kathleen M. "Strategic Decisions and All That Jazz." *Business Strategy Review.* Autumn 1997.

Hamel, Gary, and C. K. Prahalad. *Competing for the Future.* Boston, MA: Harvard Business School Press, 1994.

Mintzberg, Henry. *The Rise and Fall of Strategic Planning.* New York: Free Press, 1994.

Mintzberg, Henry, and James Brian Quinn. *The Strategy Process: Concepts and Contexts.* Englewood Cliffs, NJ: Prentice-Hall, 1992.

Ohmae, Kenichi. *The Mind of the Strategist: Business Planning for Competitive Advantage.* New York: Penguin, 1982.

Porter, Michael E. *Competitive Strategy: Techniques for Analyzing Industries and Competitors.* New York: Free Press, 1980.

Wall, Stephen J., and Shannon Rye Wall. "The Evolution (Not the Death) of Strategy." *Organizational Dynamics.* Autumn 1995.

SEE ALSO: Competitive Analysis; Industry Analysis; Product Development

SUBCONTRACTING

Subcontracting refers to the process of entering a contractual agreement with an outside person or company to perform a certain amount of work. The outside person or company in this arrangement is known as a subcontractor, but may also be called a freelance employee, independent contractor, or vendor. Many small businesses hire subcontractors to assist with a wide variety of functions. For example, a small business might use an outside firm to prepare its payroll, an accountant to help with its record keeping and tax compliance, or a free-lance worker to handle a special project. Subcontracting is probably most prevalent in the construction industry, where builders might subcontract plumbing, electrical work, drywall, painting, and a number of other tasks to specialists.

Hiring subcontractors offers a number of advantages for small businesses. For example, subcontracting mundane but necessary tasks can free up time and resources to enable the small business owner to concentrate on making money and growing the business. In addition, hiring a subcontractor is usually less expensive than hiring a full-time employee, because the small business is not required to pay Social Security taxes, workers' compensation benefits, or health insurance for independent contractors. Subcontracting does pose some potential pitfalls, however, such as a loss of control over the quality and timeliness of work. But there are steps small business owners can take to help ensure that their relationships with subcontractors are productive and beneficial for all concerned.

SUBCONTRACTORS VS. EMPLOYEES

Although hiring an independent contractor to handle a special project or help out during a busy season may be cheaper than hiring a full-time employee, a small business cannot simply call someone an independent contractor in order to avoid paying Social Security taxes and benefits. The U.S. **Internal Revenue Service (IRS)** scrutinizes employer-subcontractor relationships carefully, and any misrepresentation may be subject to severe financial penalties. To avoid confusion, small business owners should be aware of the distinctions between independent contractors and employees and consider the IRS guidelines when making subcontracting decisions. Most importantly, all subcontractors hired by a small business should present themselves as being in business for the purpose of making a profit. In addition, all work and pay arrangements should be spelled out in a contract that specifically mentions that the work is being performed by an independent contractor.

The IRS applies a 20-part test in order to determine whether a certain worker should be classified as an employee or an independent contractor. The main issue underpinning the test is who sets the work rules: employees must follow rules set by their bosses, while independent contractors set their own rules. For example, an individual who sets his or her own hours, receives payment by the job, and divides his time between work for several different employers would probably be classified as an independent contractor. Other criteria involve who provides the tools and materials needed to complete the work. For example, an individual who works at an employer's facility and uses the employer's equipment would be considered an employee, while one who works at a separate location and provides his or her own equipment would be classified as an independent contractor. Finally, an independent contractor usually pays his or her own expenses of doing business and takes the risk of not receiving payment when work is not completed in accordance with a contract, while an employee is usually reimbursed for business-related expenses by the employer and receives a paycheck whether or not his or her work is completed.

To be safe, a small business may wish to include some of these factors in the contract provided to subcontractors. For example, the contract should specify a certain amount of work to be performed by a given deadline, but should not specify how that work should be performed in terms of working hours or tools and materials used. In addition, payment should be made by the job rather than by the hour, and the subcontractor should not be prohibited from working simultaneously with other clients.

WORKING WITH SUBCONTRACTORS

Small business owners can take a series of steps to help ensure that the subcontracting process provides the desired benefits. First, it is important to assess the needs of the small business to make sure that outside help is needed, decide which specific tasks or projects to subcontract, and determine what sort of subcontractor could best perform the work. The small business owner should also give some thought to the type of relationship he or she wants to have with the subcontractor. Some businesses choose to share control of the project or process with a trusted subcontractor, even including the vendor in strategic decision-making. On the other hand, some companies choose to maintain a high degree of control internally, only subcontracting minor projects on a limited, as-needed basis.

The next step in the subcontracting process involves preparing in-house staff and obtaining the support of key personnel for the decision. Many companies encounter resistance from employees who feel that their jobs are threatened by subcontracting. Other companies may even find that turnover increases when the most interesting or fulfilling jobs are outsourced, leaving employees to perform less attractive tasks. To avoid these problems, in-house employees should be informed of the plans to subcontract work and told the rationale behind the decision. The small business owner may also wish to get employee input about what work will be subcontracted. In an article for *National Underwriter*, Ethel Scully suggested forming a team consisting of an outsourcing expert, representatives from management and human resources, and the leaders of all affected areas of the company to help address employee concerns about the decision.

The next step is to begin contacting potential subcontractors, either formally or informally, and asking specific questions about the services provided and the terms of the contract. The questions should also seek to assess the subcontractor's intentions, or what they hope to gain from the relationship. Some subcontractors may be seeking a long-term business relationship, while others may simply wish to gather information in order to compete in the same field. Overall, the questions should establish whether the subcontractor will provide a good fit with the small business client. Ideally, the subcontractor will have experience in handling similar business and will be able to give the small business's needs the priority they deserve. ''Consider the service company's knowledge of the entirety of your business, its willingness to customize service, and its compatibility with your firm's business culture, as well as the long-run cost of its services and its financial strength,'' recommended service provider Carl Schwenker in *Money*.

Once a subcontractor has been selected, the small business owner should then negotiate a contract in order to help ensure a mutually beneficial relationship. This document should include tangible measures of job performance, as well as financial incentives to encourage the subcontractor to meet deadlines and control costs. The contract should also clearly define responsibilities and performance criteria, so that no questions arise later about whether the subcontractor or the client was supposed to handle a certain task or pay any extra charges incurred. The contract should also outline the procedures for changing the subcontractor relationship, including the means for renewal, cancellation, or termination. Finally, the contract should set strict rules of confidentiality if needed and specify who owns the rights to any new ideas or inventions that may arise from the partnership. Since the subcontractor is likely to have more experience in preparing agreements than a small contracting business company, it may also be helpful to consult with an attorney during contract negotiations.

The next step is to prepare the subcontractor to interact efficiently with the client company during performance of the contract. The small business owner may wish to introduce the subcontractor to key employees, for example, and establish reporting relationships. It is also important to arrange to receive periodic progress reports from the subcontractor, as well as feedback about both the project at hand and the overall relationship. At the conclusion of the project, the small business owner should conduct a post-mortem and provide the subcontractor with an evaluation of the work.

FURTHER READING:

Evans, David, Judy Feldman, and Anne Root. ''Smart New Ways to Manage Subcontractors.'' *Money.* March 15, 1994.

Foxman, Noah. ''Succeeding in Outsourcing.'' *Information Systems Management.* Winter 1994.

Hammond, Keith H. ''The New World of Work.'' *Business Week.* October 17, 1994.

King, William R. ''Strategic Outsourcing Decisions.'' *Information Systems Management.* Fall 1994.

Lacity, Mary, Rudy Hirschheim, and Leslie Willcocks. ''Realizing Outsourcing Expectations: Incredible Expectations, Credible Outcomes.'' *Information Systems Management.* Fall 1994.

Scully, Ethel. ''Many Factors to Weigh in Decision to Outsource.'' *National Underwriter.* January 16, 1995.

Springsteel, Ian. ''Outsourcing Is Everywhere.'' *CFO: The Magazine for Senior Financial Executives.* December 1994.

''Working with Temps, Part-Timers, and Free-lancers.'' *Supervisory Management.* February 1995.

SEE ALSO: Free-lance Employment/Independent Contractors

SUBSTANCE ABUSE

Substance abuse in the workplace is a subject of concern to many small business owners, to one degree or another. Oftentimes the issue is a sensitive one to confront, but business owners and researchers alike agree that if left unchecked, substance abuse has the capacity to cripple or destroy a company.

IMPACT IN THE WORKPLACE

Substance abuse is a hard problem to eradicate in any business setting, but it can be particularly difficult to address in small business settings. After all, many small business owners develop close—or at least friendly—relationships with their employees because they often work together on projects and share smaller work areas. ''Because many small business owners have one-on-one relationships with each employee, dealing with an employee who is addicted to alcohol or drugs is a personal as well as a personnel prob-

lem,'' wrote Barbara Mooney in *Crain's Cleveland Business.*

But substance abuse experts and business researchers alike warn that substance abuse problems are not the sort of problems that tend to go away by themselves. Rather, they often continue to grow and fester, further strangulating the business's productivity and profitability. Indeed, substance abuse often ends up being a tremendous drain on a company's fiscal well-being. This drain takes many forms, including decreased productivity, increased absences, rising numbers of accidents, use of sick leave, and jumps in **workers' compensation** claims. Indeed, *HR Focus* reported in 1997 that ''alcohol and drug abusers are absent from work two-and-a-half times more frequently than nonusers; they use three times the amount of sick leave as nonusers; their worker's compensation claims are five times higher; and they are generally less productive.'' This latter factor—what *HR Focus* termed ''the less dramatic, day-to-day financial losses that accrue in a company when its workers are impaired and performing below potential''—can be particularly deadly to a business precisely because its impact is so hard to detect and quantify. Finally, substance abusers often compromise the efficiency of other workers within the business. Co-workers are often hampered by the substandard work of the abuser, and in many cases their effectiveness may be further curtailed by a sense of obligation to cover for their co-workers—who, after all, are often their friends as well.

Substance abuse problems also open companies up to greater legal liability. According to *Occupational Medicine,* Studies indicate that 1) alcohol and drug abusers are two to four times as likely to have an accident as people who do not use drugs and alcohol, and 2) substance abusers can be linked to approximately 40 percent of American industrial fatalities. Moreover, business consultant Tim Plant indicated to *HR Focus* that drug- or alcohol-addled employees can also wreak harm on people and places outside the company: ''When drivers come to work under the influence of drugs or alcohol,'' he said, ''accidents could happen, causing the disruption of deliveries or other activities. Vehicles could be damaged; people could be hurt or killed. These have an immediate impact on the bottom line for a small- or medium-sized company.''

Finally, in situations where a partner or owner of the business is the one with the substance abuse problem, the very life of the company is often jeopardized. Such people obviously wield a tremendous amount of influence over a company, and if their ability to make reasonable, intelligent decisions in a timely manner is compromised, the financial health of the company will likely deteriorate as well.

CHARACTERISTICS OF SUBSTANCE ABUSERS

Substance abuse experts and business owners who have been forced to deal with drug and/or alcohol abusers in their workplace cited a variety of warning signs that owners and managers should look for if they suspect a problem:

- Increased **absenteeism** and tardiness, especially immediately before and after weekends and holidays.

- Deteriorating work performance, as manifested in big changes in work quality and/or productivity.

- Frequent colds, flus, headaches, and other ailments.

- High rates of mishaps, both on and off the job.

- Unusually high medical claims.

- Excessive mood swings, which may manifest themselves in immoderate levels of talking, anxiety, or moodiness.

- Overreactions to criticism, both real or imagined.

- Avoidance of supervisors.

- Deterioration in physical appearance or grooming.

- Financial problems.

Researchers also note that certain industries and business dynamics seem especially prone to substance abuse problems. One substance abuse counselor flatly told Barbara Mooney of *Crain's Cleveland Business* that the extent of substance abuse problems in small businesses often depends on the makeup of its work force: "It's a problem prevalent among employers who hire a lot of entry-level people in industries with high turnover rates and high stress levels." Such conditions can be found in some retail establishments and especially in the restaurant industry, where late working hours, proximity to liquor, and demographic characteristics (prevalently young and single) provide a fertile atmosphere for substance abuse. **Family-owned businesses** are also cited as being particularly vulnerable to substance abuse problems, in part because family members may have a more difficult time being objective about a relative's work performance.

POLICIES AND STRATEGIES TO CURB SUBSTANCE ABUSE

Although tackling the problem of substance abuse can be a daunting one for small business enterprises, substance abuse experts and business researchers note that affected businesses can utilize a variety of steps that have a track record of effectiveness in curbing workplace drug and alcohol abuse.

One of the most commonly practiced policies employed by businesses of all sizes is random **drug testing**, wherein employees (and prospective employees) are required to submit to scientific tests to determine whether they have been using illegal drugs. Many experts cite the growing popularity of such policies for the apparent downturn in workplace substance abuse incidents in recent years. Drug testing remains controversial, however, as opponents argue that it violates individual privacy rights and sometimes hurts employee morale.

Another option for small business owners is to actively utilize the hiring/interviewing process to screen for substance abusers. "You get what you ask for," contended Gregory Lousig-Nont and Paul Leckinger in *Security Management.* "If you want people who are free from substance abuse problems—just ask for them in your ad." They point out that studies and anecdotal evidence suggests that want ads that include phrases like "Applicant must have a clean drug history" effectively dissuade many applicants with substance abuse problems from submitting an application. "Another commonsense approach to screening applicants," say Lousig-Nont and Leckinger, "is to broach the subject on the application form" by bluntly inquiring whether the applicant has used illicit drugs in the past. "Surprisingly, many people will actually list the drugs they have used. People who use drugs but do not want to tell you about it will leave the answer blank or put a dash on the answer line. People who have not used drugs will usually write a bold 'NONE' in the space provided." They note, however, that even though federal laws do not restrict asking questions about drug abuse, companies should check with their state employment commission to see if any state laws might apply in this area.

With current employees, business owners are encouraged to establish clear, written guidelines that explicitly detail the company's stance on substance abuse. "The policy should take a clear stand against the use, possession, sale or distribution (particularly on company time) of any mood altering substances," stated *HR Focus.* "It should also outline a very clear sequence of events that will ensue if the rules are broken." Small business owners need to make sure that their substance abuse policies abide by various state and federal laws.

Small business owners should also make an effort to enlist the support of employees in establishing a drug-free workplace. "Everyone . . . has an interest in securing a safe workplace and making sure that colleagues pull their loads," commented *HR Focus.* "One of the most effective ways to fight substance abuse is for employees to unite against it," concurred

W.H. Weiss in *Supervisor's Standard Reference Handbook*. "Supervisors can spur such a move by making it clear to their people that alcohol or drug use on the job is absolutely unacceptable."

Business owners should also consider providing an **employee assistance program (EAP)** for its workers. "Adopting an employee assistance program is viewed favorably by both management and employees," wrote Lousig-Nont and Leckinger. "Under such a policy, the company agrees to assist employees who have a substance abuse problem. Assistance generally comes in the form of granting the employee sick leave and paying for a rehabilitation program, and a promise by the company that there will be no retribution against the employee." The responsibility for initiating enrollment in such programs, however, rests with the employee. If management discovers that a worker who has not pursued help through an EAP has a substance abuse problem, he or she may face termination. Employee assistance programs have been hailed by substance abuse experts and businesspeople alike as an effective tool in curbing workplace drug and alcohol abuse, and proponents point out that the cost of such programs is usually far less than the costs that often accrue when management does not deal with a substance-abusing employee.

Finally, when confronted with evidence of workplace substance abuse, managers and owners of small companies are urged to intervene immediately and determine whether a problem exists. If a problem is found, then the business needs to document the performance of the employee. This will offer the company a greater measure of legal protection in case they need to fire the employee or the employee's performance spurs legal claims from outside parties.

FURTHER READING:

"Drug Trends: A Shot in the Arm?" *Security Management*. August 1996.

Gray, George R., and Darrel R. Brown. "Issues in Drug Testing for the Private Sector." *HR Focus*. November 1992.

Humphreys, Richard M. "Substance Abuse: The Employer's Perspective." *Employment Relations Today*. Spring 1990.

Lousig-Nont, Gregory M., and Paul M. Leckinger. "Alternatives to Drug Testing." *Security Management*. May 1990.

Martin, Lynn. "Drug Free Policy: Key to Success for Small Businesses." *HR Focus*. September 1992.

Mooney, Barbara. "Addiction: A Downer for All; Substance Abuse can be an Owner's Toughest Problem." *Crain's Cleveland Business*. August 8, 1994.

"Substance Abuse in the Workplace." *HR Focus*. February 1997.

Weiss, W.H. *Supervisor's Standard Reference Handbook*. 2d ed. Upper Saddle River, NJ: Prentice Hall, 1988.

SEE ALSO: Employee Screening; Human Resource Policies

A succession plan is a written document that provides for the continued operation of a business in the event that the owner—or a key member of the management team—leaves the company, is terminated, retires, or dies. It details the changes that will take place as leadership is transferred from one generation to the next. In the case of small businesses, succession plans are often known as continuity plans, since without them the businesses may cease to exist. Succession plans can provide a number of important benefits for companies that develop them. For example, a succession plan may help a business retain key employees, reduce its tax burden, and maintain the value of its stock and assets during a management or ownership transition. Succession plans may also prove valuable in allowing a business owner to retire in comfort and continue to provide for family members who may be involved with the company.

Despite the many benefits of having a succession plan in place, many companies neglect to develop one. This oversight may occur because the business owner does not want to confront his or her own mortality, is reluctant to choose a successor, or does not have many interests beyond the business. Although less than one-third of family businesses survive the transition from the first generation to the second—and only 13 percent remain in the family for more than 60 years—just 45 to 50 percent of business owners establish a formal succession plan. "Succession and the planning it entails is equivalent to planning one's own wake and funeral," as Ernesto J. Poza, president of an Ohio-based family business consulting firm, remarked in *Industrial Distribution*. "But the fact is that the transfer of power from the first to the second generation seldom happens while the founder is alive and on the scene. The succession transition is the most agonizing change I have ever seen CEOs and top management teams confront." Up to 40 percent of American businesses may be facing the management succession issue at any given point in time.

PREPARING FOR SUCCESSION

Experts claim that the succession planning process should ideally begin when the business owner is between the ages of 45 and 50 if he or she plans to retire at 65. Since succession can be an emotionally charged issue, sometimes the assistance of outsider advisors and mediators is required. Developing a succession plan can take more than two years, and implementing it can take up to ten years. The plan must be carefully structured to fit the company's specific situation and goals. When completed, the plan should be reviewed by the company's lawyer, accountant, and bank.

"One of the main reasons business owners should take the time to create a successful continuity plan is that they should want to get out of the business alive, with as much money as possible," Joanna R. Turpin noted in *Air Conditioning, Heating, and Refrigeration News.* To do this, the business owner has three basic options: sell the company to employees, family members, or an outsider; retain ownership of the company but hire new management; or liquidate the business. An **Employee Stock Ownership Plan (ESOP)** can be a useful tool for the owner of a corporation who is nearing retirement age. The owner can sell his or her stake in the company to the ESOP in order to gain tax advantages and provide for the continuation of the business. If, after the stock purchase, the ESOP holds over 30 percent of the company's shares, then the owner can defer capital-gains taxes by investing the proceeds in a Qualified Replacement Property (QRP). QRPs can include stocks, bonds, and certain retirement accounts. The income stream generated by the QRP can help provide the business owner with income during retirement.

FOUR STAGES OF SUCCESSION

In the Small Business Administration publication *Transferring Management in the Family-Owned Business,* Nancy Bowman-Upton emphasizes that succession should be viewed as a process rather than as an event. She describes four main stages in the succession process: initiation, selection, education, and transition. In the initiation phase, possible successors learn about the family business. It is important for the business owners to speak openly about the business, in a positive but realistic manner, in order to transmit information about the company's values, culture, and future direction to the next generation.

The selection phase involves actually designating a successor among the candidates for the job. Because rivalry often develops between possible successors—who, in the case of a family business, are likely to be siblings—this can be the most difficult stage of the process. For this reason, many business owners either avoid the issue or make the selection on the basis of age, gender, or other factors besides merit. Instead, Bowman-Upton recommends that the business owners develop specific objectives and goals for the next generation of management, including a detailed job description for the successor. Then a candidate can be chosen who best meets the qualifications. This strategy helps remove the emotional aspect from the selection process and also may help the business owners feel more comfortable with their selection. The decision about when to announce the successor and the schedule for succession depends upon the business, but an early announcement can help reassure employees and customers and enable other key employees to make alternative career plans as needed.

Once a potential successor has been selected, the company then enters the training phase. Ideally, a program is developed through which the successor can meet goals and gradually increase his or her level of responsibility. The owner may want to take a number of planned absences so that the successor has a chance to actually run the business for limited periods of time. The training phase also provides the business owner with an opportunity to evaluate the successor's decision-making processes, leadership abilities, interpersonal skills, and performance under pressure. It is also important for the successor to be introduced to the business owner's outside network during this time, including customers, bankers, and business associates.

The final stage in the process occurs when the business owner retires and the successor formally makes the transition to his or her new leadership role. Bowman-Upton stresses that the business owner can make the transition smoother for the company by publicly committing to the succession plan, leaving in a timely manner, and eliminating his or her involvement in the company's daily activities completely. In order to make the transition as painless as possible for himself or herself, the business owner should also be sure to have a sound financial plan for retirement and to engage in relationships and activities outside of the business.

ALTERNATIVE SUCCESSION MODELS

In their book *Family Business Succession: The Final Test of Greatness,* Craig E. Aronoff and John L. Ward outline a number of steps companies should follow in preparing for succession. These steps include: 1) Establishing a formal policy regarding family participation in the business; 2) Providing solid work experience for all employees, to ensure that succession is based on performance rather than heredity; 3) Creating a family mission statement based on the members' beliefs and goals for the business; 4) Designing a leadership development plan with specific job requirements for the successor; 5) Developing a strategic plan for the business; 6) Making plans for the preceding generation's financial security; 7) Identifying a successor or determining the selection process; 8) Setting up a succession transition team to keep decision-makers informed about their role in the changes; and 9) Completing the transfer of ownership and control. Throughout all these stages of preparation, Aronoff and Ward note, communication is key.

Turpin described several steps involved in developing a written succession document. These steps include: 1) Gathering information, on both the personnel involved and the company itself; 2) Choosing advisors, including continuity specialists and people who will be involved internally; 3) Deciding upon the company's objectives, including financial and personal goals, as well as those related to ownership and control; 4) Laying out the components of the plan; 5) Preparing the formal documents and obtaining funding as needed; and 6) Reviewing the plan every one to three years or whenever the company's personnel or structure changes.

A final consideration in succession planning is for the owner to decide what he or she will do after concluding involvement in the business. This step, which is something like a personal succession plan, is important in helping the owner make a successful transition. "It's so much easier to let go of something when you have a new direction in which to move," psychiatrist Barrie Greiff explained in *Industrial Distribution.*

FURTHER READING:

Aronoff, Craig E., and John L. Ward. *Family Business Succession: The Final Test of Greatness.* Marietta, GA: Business Owner Resources, 1992.

Aronoff and Ward. "Rules for Nepotism." *Nation's Business.* January 1993.

Bowman-Upton, Nancy. *Transferring Management in the Family-Owned Business.* Washington: U.S. Small Business Administration, 1991.

Ford, Robert, and Frank McLaughlin. "Nepotism." *Personnel Journal.* September 1985.

Frieswick, Kris. "Successful Succession." *Industrial Distribution.* April 1996.

Shanney-Saborsky, Regina. "Why It Pays to Use an ESOP in a Business Succession Plan." *The Practical Accountant.* September 1996.

Turpin, Joanna R. "Succession Planning Requires Long-Term Strategy, Implementation." *Air Conditioning, Heating, and Refrigeration News.* April 28, 1997.

SEE ALSO: Family-Owned Businesses; Retirement Planning; Selling a Business

SUPPLIERS

Good purchasing practices are integral to small business success, and few factors are as vital in ensuring sound purchasing methodologies as the selection of quality suppliers. Indeed, finding good suppliers and maintaining solid relations with them can be an invaluable tool in the quest for business success and expansion. As James Morgan observed in *Purchasing,* "for a surprisingly large number of procurement organizations, suppliers have become an important factor in their planning. In fact, for many procurement organizations, suppliers have become their secret competitive weapon, their hidden resource, their competitive edge."

"For many companies, suppliers provide an uncommon opportunity to enhance performance,"

agreed management consultant Paul Inglis in an interview with *Purchasing.* "Companies that take time to improve supplier relationships can also negotiate better prices and delivery times. Better supplier relationships create opportunities for both sides to innovate, leading to improved performance." But Inglis added that such improvements will not be realized without meaningful leadership from business owners and executives who recognize the importance of supplier relations. "Leading companies develop tailored supply strategies that are directly linked to their corporate strategies," he said. According to Ingles, these leaders emphasize shareholder-value creation, revenue growth, and cost competitiveness, and establish specific programs with their key suppliers in order to ensure that these priorities are addressed. Smart business leaders, he added, "use suppliers to maximize their own product competitiveness, going beyond the narrow focus of cost reduction. Leaders exceed traditional sourcing practices, adopt new models to fully leverage supplier capabilities, and further their own position in the marketplace."

SUPPLY CHAINS AND PARTNERSHIPS

In recent years, countless management experts and analysts have touted the benefits that businesses of all sizes can realize by establishing "partnerships" with their suppliers. Under such a plan, which is also sometimes referred to as "supply chain management," **distribution channels** are set up across organizations so that all the members of the channel, from suppliers to end users, coordinate their business activities and processes to minimize their total costs and maximize their effectiveness in the marketplace. While this trend has become more prevalent in today's business environment, it is still practiced in only spotty fashion in many industries. According to a 1997 A.T. Kearney survey of business executives, common impediments to establishing true business partnerships with suppliers include: attachment of greater importance to other initiatives; comfortable relationships with existing suppliers; dearth of cross-business unit cooperation; doubts about the benefits of instituting such practices; lack of cross-functional cooperation; poor monitoring and control systems; inexperience at managing improvement programs; and distrust of suppliers. Companies that feature many of these characteristics typically cling to old **competitive bidding** practices that center on perfectly legitimate concerns about price, but at the exclusion of all else. "For a sizable number of companies, supplier partnering still falls into the 'flavor of the month category,'" observed Morgan. "It figures in speech—even in official pronouncements—but not in their planning."

As a result, these businesses miss out on the many benefits that can accrue when effective partnering initiatives are established with suppliers. As Morgan indicated, suppliers can be an important source of information on ways in which both small and large businesses can improve performance and productivity. After studying a major mid-1990s buyer survey, he cited five general categories in which supplier involvement can help buyers compete in the marketplace:

1) Improvement of products through contributions to product design, technology, or ideas for producing new products. In most such instances, suppliers help buyers by point out ways in which designs can be improved or more desirable materials can be used. "In one case the supplier's contribution improved the efficiency of a motor," explained Morgan. "In another, the supplier was instrumental in redesigning a package that allowed for post-consumer recycling. . . . On the materials side, one supplier suggestion resulted in the manufacture of a paper with an acid-free chemistry."

2) Improvements in product quality. In addition to providing design recommendations that result in improved products, suppliers are often sources of suggestions that allow buyers to hold consistent tolerances in production.

3) Improvements in " speed to market." "Some of the most significant contributions in this area came from suppliers to OEM [original equipment manufacturer] manufacturers," said Morgan. "Typical is the instance of an equipment maker whose supplier helped cut 30 months from the design to market schedule."

4) Reductions in total product cost. "Most of the suggestions in this area fell into two main areas," explained Morgan. "Reductions through work simplification and by replacing costly components with less costly ones. Among buyers in the process industries, transportation suppliers (primarily railroads and motor carriers) are a popular source of cost savings ideas. Many of the savings . . . are the result of reduced inventories and better scheduling practices."

5) Improvements in customer satisfaction.

Analysts indicate that suppliers receive some benefits in the emerging purchasing dynamic as well. Reduced paperwork, lower overhead, faster payment, long-term agreements that lead to more accurate business forecasts, access to new designs, and input into future materials and product needs have all been cited as gains. Other observers, meanwhile, point out that some buyer-supplier relationships have become so close that suppliers have opened offices on the site of the buyer, an arrangement that can conceivably result in even greater improvements in productivity and savings. Of course, companies are not going to form such "partnerships" with all of their suppliers. Some form of the traditional purchasing process involving bidding and standard purchase orders and invoices will continue to exist at almost every company, and especially at smaller companies that do not have the financial weight to make large demands on their suppliers.

But many management consultants and business experts contend that even those businesses that are not ideally positioned to create partnerships with suppliers can benefit from the establishment of effective supply chain management practices. Management theorist Jordan Lewis, for example, told *The Economist* that buyer-seller alliances unleash a capacity for innovation that far outweighs the short-term cost savings offered by arm's-length competitive bidding. He added that businesses should explain their overarching needs to several dedicated suppliers and open lines of communication with them rather than simply defining their requirements and waiting for a flurry of bids that are primarily—or exclusively—concerned with submitting the lowest bid.

POTENTIAL DRAWBACKS OF SUPPLIER PARTNER-SHIPS Establishing close relationships with suppliers, though, means that buyers have to conduct the necessary research to make sure that they select the right companies. "Purchasing needs to know a great deal more about supplier capabilities than it did when everything depended on a bid/buy relationship," confirmed *Purchasing*'s Ernest L. Anderson. "Today's emphasis on partnership requires suppliers who can become part of a whole supply system. In fact, major suppliers need to be critically screened and evaluated before they are brought into any new system." Thriving small- and mid-sized businesses that are already well-established will be better able to take on such tasks than will fledgling businesses, but even start ups should take the time to learn more about their suppliers than their prices.

Of course, desired supplier traits vary somewhat depending on which part of the company is being asked (a factor that business owners have to weigh when choosing their suppliers). For example, design engineers tend to place the most weight on product quality when analyzing suppliers, while purchasing professionals place greater importance on cost considerations in conjunction with product quality. Anderson noted that criteria to be evaluated will also vary depending on product category. "There's a difference, for instance, between how you evaluate suppliers for MRO and how you evaluate raw materials suppliers," he said. "Whether an item is proprietary or generic will make a difference in what gets stressed in selection of significant suppliers. Still, the objective of all evaluations is the same: To compare all potential suppliers in a market segment to determine the one best qualified to be your partner. It's important to evaluate strengths and weaknesses of potential suppliers in terms of which one can best help purchasing meet prime objectives. Typical objectives include inventory reduction, quality improvement, elimination of paperwork, and improved handling of incoming goods.''

Companies that do not do the necessary legwork, on the other hand, may find themselves linked to a poor or untrustworthy supplier that will end up hurting the business. ''Poor supplier performance is not the only risk a purchaser faces'' in situations where it has linked with a bad supplier, noted *The Economist*. ''It must also worry about the possibility of a supplier passing trade secrets to competitors, or, with its newfound abilities, venturing out on its own. A company that abdicates too many things [to suppliers] may 'hollow' itself out. All of these risks are especially great in fast-moving, knowledge-intensive industries, which are precisely those for which integrated supply chains otherwise make the most sense.'' Given these potential pitfalls, businesses seeking to establish partnerships with suppliers are urged to proceed with caution.

EVALUATING SUPPLIERS

Whether searching out new suppliers or **benchmarking** the performance of current suppliers, businesses are urged to consider the following when evaluating their options:

- Commitment to quality—Not surprisingly, product quality is regarded as an essential factor in selecting a supplier. Specifics in this realm include the suppliers' statistical process control methods, its QS-9000 registration, its approaches to problem solution and preventive maintenance, and its methods of equipment calibration. ''What gets looked at varies by whether the supplier is a distributor or manufacturer,'' pointed out Anderson. ''With a distributor, the team wants to determine whether it carries mainly Grade A lines or B lines in a particular group. With a manufacturer it's important to have QC people on the team to realistically appraise the supplier's control standards and methods of measuring quality.''

- Cost-competitive—Competitive pricing is another huge factor, especially for businesses that are smaller or experiencing financial difficulties.

- Communication—Suppliers that do not nourish a policy of open communication— or even worse, actively practice deception— should be avoided at all costs. The frustrations of dealing with such companies can sometimes assume debilitating dimensions. Moreover, constant exposure to such tactics can instill a general feeling of unease throughout your entire staff, as they ''wait for the other shoe to drop.''

- Timely service—Businesses strategies are predicated on schedules, which in turn are based on receiving shipments at agreed-upon times. When those shipments slip, business strategies suffer. The blow can be particularly severe if the supplier is negligent or late in reporting the problem. ''Reliable delivery is first among the basics of what we expect [from suppliers],'' one executive told *Industrial Distribution*. ''It doesn't have to be instantaneous—it just needs to get there when they promised it would.''

- Flexibility and Special Services—Many purchasers express appreciation for suppliers that take extra measures to satisfy their customers. These ''perks'' can range from after-hours accessability to training or inventory support.

- Progressiveness—''This tends to be subjective,'' admitted Anderson, ''but probe for knowledge of market, selling techniques, methods, policies. Do managers really understand the business? Also, there are some objective things to look at such as output per employee, total sales per employee, percent of orders shipped from stock.''

- Production Capabilities—The supplier's capacity for program management and production should be considered, including its ability to integrate design and manufacturing functions, its approach to design changes, and its program measurement features.

- Financially Stable—Understandably, businesses heavily involved in purchasing often prefer to make long-term deals with suppliers that are financially stable. Such arrangements allow companies to learn about one another and gain a fuller understanding of each business's needs, desires, operating practices, and future objectives. Moreover, *The Economist* noted that ''being in a meaningful relationship instead of a one-part stand encourages suppliers to make investments that are tailored to the purchasing firm's needs—and to be more thrifty. . . . A trusted supplier is more likely to think about the purchasing firm's own customers.''

- Logistics/Location—Supplier capabilities in this area include transportation capacity, sourcing capabilities, and 'just-in-time' performance. According to Anderson, location can be of critical importance where a system contract is concerned; "the farther away the supplier, the bigger the safety stock the customer will need."

- **Inventory**—According to *Purchasing,* evaluation of this consideration is dependent somewhat on the supplier's business. "If the supplier is a distributor, the emphasis will be on how well his inventory is set up to avoid stockouts. With a manufacturer, emphasis has to be on inventory accessability. If the supplier has a [just in time] program with 24-hour assured delivery, it's in better condition than the manufacturer with a lot of raw material inventory and an eight-week leadtime for raw material."

- Ability to provide technical assistance—Suppliers with top research and development capacities can be quite valuable to buyers, providing them with significant savings in both price and quality.

OTHER KEYS TO SUCCESSFUL SUPPLIER RELATIONSHIPS

A common lament of suppliers is that buyer organizations all too often have unrealistic expectations about the supplier's ability to anticipate buyer needs. As one purchasing executive admitted to *Purchasing,* "In new technology areas we have great difficulty getting the users in our own company to define what they want. Most have an attitude of 'I'll know it when I see it.' And many of these users keep changing their minds."

Honesty on both sides is another important quality in effective buyer-supplier relations. Small business owners hate being misled by their suppliers, yet they are often less than above-board in their own communications with suppliers. This is most common when the business is grappling with past-due payments, but entrepreneurs and analysts alike agree that in most cases, honesty remains the best policy. "Instead of lying and saying the check's in the mail, tell suppliers what's happening and what you propose to do about it," one small business owner told *Nation's Business.* "If you have a note that's due, you call them, instead of waiting for them to call you. They appreciate that. Business people are afraid to make that phone call; they want to make it all sound rosy. But . . . if you owe them, suppliers are eager to find a way to work with you."

FURTHER READING:

Anderson, Ernest L. "Evaluate Critical Suppliers." *Purchasing.* July 14, 1994.

Beard, Tom. "The Art of Cooperation." *Modern Machine Shop.* September 1996.

Fitzgerald, Kevin R. "Key to Donnelly Strategy—Supplier Benchmarking." *Purchasing.* June 5, 1997.

Fitzgerald, Kevin R. "What OEM Engineers Want from Suppliers." *Purchasing.* August 14, 1997.

Forbes, Christine. "Creating the Super Supplier." *Industrial Distribution.* September 1993.

Harrington, Lisa H. "Buying Better: Strategic Sourcing Can Improve Suppliers' Productivity, Component and Product Quality—and Improve the Bottom Line." *Industry Week.* July 21, 1997.

"Holding the Hand that Feeds." *The Economist.* September 9, 1995.

McIvor, Ronan, Paul Humphreys, and Eddie McAleer. "Implications of Partnership Sourcing on Buyer-Supplier Relations." *Journal of General Management.* Autumn 1997.

Morgan, James. "Five Areas Where Suppliers Can Be Your Competitive Edge." *Purchasing.* November 25, 1993.

Mulcahy, David. *Warehouse Distribution and Operations Handbook.* New York: McGraw-Hill, 1994.

"The Nuts and Bolts of Supplier Relations." *Nation's Business.* August 1997.

Porter, Anne Millen. "Purchasing Pros Insist They Buy On Far More than Price." *Purchasing.* May 1, 1997.

Provan, Keith G. "Embeddedness, Interdependence, and Opportunism in Organizational Supplier-Buyer Networks." *Journal of Management.* Winter 1993.

"A Review of Recent Changes in Buyer-Supplier Relations." *Omega.* September-November 1992.

"Strong Supply Relationships Reduce Cost, Spark Innovation." *Purchasing.* January 15, 1998.

SUPPLY AND DEMAND

Supply and demand is a fundamental factor in shaping the character of the marketplace, for it is understood as the principal determinant in establishing the cost of goods and services. The availability, or "supply," of goods or services is a key factor in determining the price at which those goods or services can be obtained. For example, a landscaping company with little competition that operates in an area of high demand for such services will in all likelihood be able to command a higher price than will a business operating in a highly competitive environment. But availability is only one-half of the equation that determines pricing structures in the marketplace. The other half is "demand." A company may be able to produce huge quantities of a product at low cost, but if there is little or no demand for that product in the marketplace, the company will be forced to sell units at a very low price. Conversely, if the marketplace proves receptive to the product that is being sold, the company can establish a higher unit price. "Supply" and "demand,'' then, are closely intertwined economic concepts; indeed, the law of supply and demand is often cited as among the most fundamental in all of economics.

FACTORS IMPACTING SUPPLY AND DEMAND

''When we speak about demand,'' wrote Robert Heilbroner and Lester Thurow in *Economics Explained,* ''most people think the word just means a certain volume of spending, as when we say that the demand for automobiles has fallen off or the demand for gold is high. But that is not what the economist has in mind when he defines demand as part of his explanation of markets. Demand means not just how much we are spending for a given item, but how much we are spending for that item *at its price,* and how much we would spend *if its price changed.*''

The demand for products and services is predicated on a number of factors. The most important of these are the tastes, customs, and preferences of the target market, the consumer's income level, the quality of the goods or services being offered, and the availability of competitors' goods or services. All of the above elements are vital in determining the price that a business can command for its products or services, whether the business in question is a hair salon, a freelance writer, or a cabinet manufacturer.

The supply of goods and services in the marketplace is predicated on several factors as well, including production capacity, production **costs** (including wages, interest charges, and raw materials costs), and the number of other businesses engaged in providing the goods or services in question. Of course, some factors that are integral in determining supply in one area may be inconsequential in another. Weather, for example, is an important factor in determining the supplies of wheat, oranges, cherries, and myriad other agricultural products. But weather rarely impacts on the operations of businesses such as bookstores except under the most exceptional of circumstances.

''When we are willing and able to buy more, we say that demand rises, and everyone knows that the effect of rising demand is to lift prices,'' summarized Heilbroner and Thurow. ''Of course the mechanism works in reverse. If incomes fall, so does demand, and so does price.'' They point out that supply can also dwindle as a result of other business conditions, such as a rise in production costs for the producer or changes in regulatory or tax policies. ''And of course both supply and demand can change at the same time, and often do,'' added Heilbroner and Thurow. ''The outcome can be higher or lower prices, or even unchanged prices, depending on how the new balance of market forces works out.''

SUPPLY AND DEMAND ELASTICITY

Robert Pindyck and Daniel Rubinfeld observed in their book *Microeconomics* that ''the demand for a good depends on its price, as well as on consumer income and on the prices of other goods. Similarly, supply depends on price, as well as on variables that affect production cost. . . . Often, however, we want to know *how much* supply or demand will rise or fall.'' This measurement of a product or service's responsiveness to market changes is known as elasticity. Todd G. Buchholz, writing in his book *From Here to Economy: A Shortcut to Economic Literacy,* used an example from the world of sports business to provide an example of economic elasticity: ''Will football fans buy the same number of tickets if the team jacks up the prices? If they do, then demand is *inelastic.* If higher prices lead the fans to cut back their attendance, then demand is *elastic,* or sensitive to change.''

The quality and degree of marketplace reaction to price changes depends on several factors. These include: 1) the presence or absence of alternative sources for the product or service in question; 2) the time available to customers to investigate alternatives; 3) the size of the investment made by the purchaser. Elasticity, then, is an important factor for small business owners to consider when entertaining thoughts about changing the prices of the goods or services that they offer.

FURTHER READING:

Buchholz, Todd G. *From Here to Economy: A Shortcut to Economic Literacy.* Dutton, 1995.

Heilbroner, Robert, and Lester Thurow. *Economics Explained: Everything You Need to Know About How the Economy Works and Where It's Going.* Revised ed. Touchstone, 1994.

Pindyck, Robert S., and Daniel L. Rubinfeld. *Microeconomics.* 2d ed. Macmillan, 1992.

SEE ALSO: Pricing

SUSTAINABLE GROWTH

The sustainable growth rate (SGR) of a firm is the maximum rate of growth in sales that can be achieved, given the firm's profitability, asset utilization, and desired dividend payout and debt (financial leverage) ratios. Variables typically include the net profit margin on new and existing revenues; the asset turnover ratio, which is the ratio of sales revenues to total assets; the assets to beginning of period equity ratio; and the retention rate, which is defined as the fraction of earnings retained in the business.

Sustainable growth models assume that the business wants to: 1) maintain a target **capital** structure without issuing new equity; 2) maintain a target dividend payment ratio; and 3) increase sales as rapidly as market conditions allow. Since the asset to beginning of period equity ratio is constant and the firm's only source of new equity is retained earnings, sales and assets cannot grow any faster than the retained earnings plus the additional debt that the retained earnings can support. The sustainable growth rate is consistent with the observed evidence that most corporations are reluctant to issue new equity. If, however, the firm is willing to issue additional equity, there is in principle no financial constraint on its growth rate. Indeed, the sustainable growth rate formula is directly predicated on return on equity. "Assuming asset growth broadly parallels sales growth, the SGR is calculated as the retained [return on equity], i.e. your company's [return on equity] minus the dividend payout percentage," wrote John Costa in *Outlook*. "Just as the break-even point is the 'floor' for minimum sales required to cover operating expenses, so the SGR is an estimate of the 'ceiling' for maximum sales growth that can be achieved without exhausting operating cash flows. Think of it as a growth break-even point."

THE CHALLENGE OF ATTAINING SUSTAINABLE GROWTH

Creation of sustainable growth is a prime concern of small business owners and big corporate executives alike. Obviously, however, achieving this goal is no easy task, given rapidly changing political, economic, competitive, and consumer trends. Jayne Buxton and Mike Davidson pointed out in *Strategy and Leadership* that each of these trends present unique challenges to business leaders searching for the elusive grail of sustainable growth. Customer expectations, for example, have changed considerably over the last few generations. Modern consumers have less disposable wealth than their parents, which makes them "more reluctant and discerning buyers," said Buxton and Davidson. "This fact, coupled with the legacy of a decade of quality and cost reduction programs, means that companies will have to attract customers by redefining value based on unique customer insights and keep customers by beating their competitors in enhancing value." Similarly, competition is keen in nearly all industries, which have seen unprecedented breakdowns in the barriers that formerly separated them. "Companies now must look widely afield to identify their competitors and their available option in the search for creating sustainable competitive advantage," they said.

In addition, Buxton and Davidson noted that "the growth challenge is articulated differently by different leaders. For some, developing and launching new products and services to meet the evolving needs of their customers is the issue; for others, capitalizing on global opportunities is key; for still others, the challenge is identifying the one new business that will represent the next major thrust for the company. And for a few, all of these strategic challenges are simultaneously top-of-mind, along with the enormous task of rebuilding organizational capabilities."

Economists and business researchers contend that achieving sustainable growth is not possible without paying heed to twin cornerstones: growth strategy and growth capability. Companies that pay inadequate attention to one aspect or the other are doomed to failure in their efforts to establish practices of *sustainable* growth (though short-term gains may be realized). After all, if a company has an excellent growth strategy in place, but has not put the necessary infrastructure in place to execute that strategy, long-term growth is impossible. The reverse is true as well. "Understanding and distinguishing between growth strategy and growth capability is the first and fundamental step in addressing the growth challenge facing many organizations," observed Buxton and Davidson. "Although they are not entirely separate—capability, in particular, contains the ability to develop and renew strategy—these two ideas do represent different approaches to the growth challenge. . . . Most companies facing a growth challenge do so because they have historically relied solely on strategy to meet their growth ambitions.

At its simplest, growth strategy aims at the creation of competitive advantage by delivering a specific product for which there is increasing demand in the marketplace. When market growth begins to slow, the competitive advantage is still there, but the growth it provides has slowed with the market." But economists and leaders of businesses that have achieved a level of sustainable growth contend that this is insufficient. "The new growth challenge requires leaders to make growth capability their number one priority," wrote Davidson and Buxton. "They often do not recognize that their day-to-day activities are the key processes that need changing if the new capability is to be built." They argue that if business leaders can successfully implement such changes, their firms "will truly be in control of their own destinies through their ability to build and rebuild competitive advantage by developing and delivering attractive, new value propositions—a powerful growth strategy within a strong growth capability."

USING THE SUSTAINABLE GROWTH RATE

The concept of sustainable growth can be helpful for planning healthy corporate growth. This concept forces managers to consider the financial consequences of sales increases and to set sales growth goals that are consistent with the operating and financial policies of the firm. Often, a conflict can arise if growth objectives are not consistent with the value of the organization's sustainable growth.

According to economists, if a company's sales expand at any rate other than the sustainable rate, one or more of the above-mentioned ratios must change. If a company's actual growth rate temporarily exceeds its sustainable rate, the required cash can likely be borrowed. When actual growth exceeds sustainable growth for longer periods, management must formulate a financial strategy from among the following options: 1) sell new equity; 2) permanently increase financial leverage (i.e, the use of debt); 3) reduce dividends; 4) increase the profit margin; or 5) decrease the percentage of total assets to sales.

In practice, companies are often reluctant to undertake these measures. Firms are reluctant to issue equity because of high issue costs, possible dilution of earnings per share, and the unreliable nature of equity funding on terms favorable to the issuer. A firm can only increase financial leverage if there are **assets** that can be pledged and if its debt/equity ratio is reasonable in relation to its industry. The reduction of dividends typically has a negative impact on the company's stock price. Companies can attempt to liquidate marginal operations, increase prices, or enhance manufacturing and distribution efficiencies to improve the profit margin. In addition, firms can source more activities from outside vendors or rent production facilities and equipment, which has the effect of improving the asset turnover ratio. Increasing the profit margin is difficult, however, and large sustainable increases may not be possible. Therefore, it is possible for a firm to grow too rapidly, which in turn can result in reduced liquidity and the unwanted depletion of financial resources.

The sustainable growth model is particularly helpful in situations in which a borrower requests additional financing. The need for additional loans creates a potentially risky situation of too much debt and too little equity. Either additional equity must be raised or the borrower will have to reduce the rate of expansion to a level that can be sustained without an increase in financial leverage.

Mature firms often have actual growth rates that are less than the sustainable growth rate. In these cases, management's principal objective is finding productive uses for the cash flows that exist in excess of their needs. Options available to business owners and executives in such cases including returning the money to shareholders through increased dividends or common stock repurchases, reducing the firm's debt-load, or increasing possession of lower earning liquid assets. Note that these actions serve to decrease the sustainable growth rate. Alternatively, these firms can attempt to enhance their actual growth rates through the acquisition of rapidly growing companies.

Growth can come from two sources: increased volume and **inflation**. The inflationary increase in assets must be financed as though it were real growth. Inflation increases the amount of external financing required and increases the debt-to-equity ratio when this ratio is measured on a historical cost basis. Thus, if creditors require that a firm's historical cost debt-to-equity ratio stay constant, inflation lowers the firm's sustainable growth rate.

FURTHER READING:

Buxton, Jayne, and Mike Davidson. ''Building a Sustainable Growth Capability.'' *Strategy and Leadership*. November-December 1996.

Costa, John. ''Challenging Growth: How to Keep Your Company's Rapid Expansion on Track.'' *Outlook*. Summer 1997.

Higgins, Robert C. ''How Much Growth Can the Firm Afford?'' Financial Management. Fall, 1977, pp. 7-16.

Moore, Darrell M. ''Growing Broke: Sustainable Growth as a Factor in Financial Analysis.'' Business Credit. September, 1988, pp. 49-51.

SEE ALSO: Business Expansion

SYNDICATED LOANS

Syndicated loans are **loans** made by two or more lenders and administered by a common agent using similar terms and conditions and common documentation. According to *Business Credit,* most loan syndications take the form of a direct-lender relationship where the lead lender is the agent for the other lenders in the origination and administration of the loan, and the other lending banks are signatories to the loan agreement. In the last several years the popularity of this type of loan has exploded. Indeed, in the mid-1990s syndicated loans amounted to more than $800 billion annually, according to *Bank Loan Report* and other sources. The businesses that are choosing this option to finance their growth have expanded beyond the Fortune 500 companies that were its first users. Initially developed to address the needs of huge, acquisition-hungry companies, they have now become a flexible funding source for both mid-sized companies and smaller companies that are on the cusp of moving into mid-sized status. In fact, syndicated loans for as little as $10 million have become commonplace.

Most successful small companies that have evolved to the point where they are straining at the boundaries of that ''small'' designation have always dealt with one or a few individual banks, negotiating individual loans and lines of credit separately with each institution. The next financing step, however, may be to consolidate banking activity through one syndicated facility. *Corporate Cashflow Magazine*'s Thomas Bunn noted that while business owners and executives are sometimes loathe to run the risk of alienating banks with which they have long done business, the simple reality is that "companies can outgrow their traditional banks and need new capabilities or an expanded bank group to fund their continued growth."

Of course, businesses can always choose to simply increase their stable of lending institutions, but this has several drawbacks. "Managing multiple bank relationships is no small feat," said Michael Fidler and Patricia Neumeyer in *Business Credit.* "Each bank needs to come to an understanding of your business and how its financial activities are conducted. A comfort level must be established on both sides of the transaction, which requires time and effort. . . . Negotiating a document with one bank can take days. To negotiate documents with four to five banks separately is a time-consuming, inefficient task. Staggered maturities must be monitored and orchestrated. Moreover, multiple lines require an intercreditor agreement among the banks, which takes additional time to negotiate."

Given these obstacles, business owners and executives often express interest in syndicated loans, which offer consolidation of effort and the possibility of making new banking contacts. Lenders support their use as well. "Lenders like syndications because they permit them to make more loans, while limiting individual exposures and spreading their risk within portfolios more widely," explained Fidler and Neymeyer. "Moreover, administration of the loan is extremely efficient, with the agent managing much of the process on behalf of the participants."

Syndicated loans hinge on the creation of an alliance of smaller banking institutions who, by joining forces, are able to meet the credit needs of the borrower. This creation is spurred by selection of an agent who manages the account. "In consultation with the borrower, the arranger will assemble a group of banks to form a syndicate, with each bank lending portions of the required amount," explained John Tsui in *Lodging Hospitality.* "The loan normally is signed six to eight weeks after the mandate has been awarded, and after signing, the borrower can draw down funds."

Borrowers taking out syndicated loans pay upfront fees and annual charges to the participating banks, with interest accruing (on a quarterly, monthly, or semiannual basis) from the initial draw-down date. "One advantage of syndication loans is that this market allows the borrower to access from a diverse group of financial institutions," said Tsui. "In general, borrowers can raise funds more cheaply in the syndicated loan market than they can borrowing the same amount of money through a series of bilateral loans. This cost saving increases as the amount required rises."

OTHER ADVANTAGES OF SYNDICATED LOANS

In addition, economists and syndicate executives contend that there are other, less obvious advantages to going with a syndicated loan. Bunn pointed out that "syndicate banks often will express concerns to the agent that they would not share directly with the borrower," which can provide businesses with additional—and potentially valuable—feedback, since those agents will share legitimate concerns. Other advantages cited include:

- Syndicated loan facilities can increase competition for your business, prompting other banks to increase their efforts to put market information in front of you in hopes of being recognized.

- Flexibility in structure and pricing. As Tsui observed, borrowers have a variety of options in shaping their syndicated loan, including multicurrency options, risk management techniques, and prepayment rights without penalty.

- Syndicated facilities bring businesses the best prices in aggregate, "sparing you the need to go to negotiate individually with each bank," said Bunn.

- Loan terms can be abbreviated.

- Tsui pointed out that "unlike a securitized transaction, a syndicated loan can be handled in a very confidential manner. A firm arranging a loan for an impending takeover bid would invariably insist on such confidentiality to avoid alerting the bid target." (This benefit applies primarily to larger companies with the financial wherewithal to make such bids.)

- Syndicated loans bring the borrower greater visibility in the open market. Bunn noted that "For commercial paper issuers, rating agencies view a multi-year syndicated facility as stronger support than several bilateral one-year lines of credit."

SYNDICATE FORMATION

A borrower's ability to secure a syndicated loan, though, is predicated on its ability to spur the creation of a syndicate in the first place. "No two syndications are identical," wrote Bunn. "The market changes every day. Many intangibles influence the structure and pricing of a credit, including the experience and depth of a company's management team; trends in the industry and market; and financial trends within a company."

The first thing the company has to do is select an agent to facilitate communications and transactions between the borrower and the banking institutions that will form the syndicate. "The first place to look for an agent is among your existing relationships," said Fidler and Neumeyer. "Certainly you will want a bank that has the necessary syndication capability and experience to obtain market credibility. Although the agent need not always be the largest participant in the syndication, the agent should have sufficient capital strength to be the anchor for the credit. Most important, however, is that you are comfortable with the bank. Because the agent is acting on your behalf, they must fully understand your business and share your attitudes and priorities."

"Expect an agent to add value with good ideas and to provide a constant flow of useful information from the bank group and broader marketplace," added Bunn. "Also, expect the agent to recommend and attract a sophisticated, supportive bank group that understands your company and your industry. In turn, the borrower should support the agent with up-to-date information about developments within the company. Few surprises and constant communication build the best relationships."

Once an agent has been selected, the process of finding willing banks is undertaken. This phase of the process can vary considerably in terms of complexity. Some agents gauge the interest level of other lenders by simply sending them necessary financial information on the borrower and the intended shape and size of the syndicate group, as well as data on borrower operations, background, management, and marketing. Bunn noted that in other cases, however, this process can be more complex, "involving extensive due diligence, the preparation of a complete syndication offering memorandum (including financial projections), and a formal bank presentation."

By and large, the length of time necessary to form a bank group is roughly equivalent to the complexity of the proposed deal. Creation of a syndicate can take place over the course of a few weeks or a few months. Analysts note, however, that the length of time necessary to conclude the deal is usually less if the banks are already familiar with the borrower's operations. Once the membership of the group has been determined, "the role of the borrower virtually reverts to that in a single bank relationship," said Fidler and Neumeyer. "This is not to say that the borrower relinquishes control over the process and the participants will still actively call on the borrower. It is merely the interaction between the participating banks that should diminish—to your benefit. The agent should educate you about the market and help you navigate the specifics of pricing and structuring the transaction."

Indeed, the agent's responsibilities are many and varied. The agent is charged with administering the syndicated facility itself, as well as all borrowings, repayments, interest settlements, and fee payments. A chief component of the administration function is to make sure that communications between the lending institutions and the borrower remain open so that both sides remain informed about changing business and market realities. In return for providing these services, the agent is compensated with an annual fee.

FURTHER READING:

Bunn, Thomas. "What Borrowers Need to Know About Loan Syndication." *Corporate Cashflow Magazine.* October 1995.

Fidler, Michael, and Patricia Neumeyer. "Vindication of Syndication—Why Borrowers Should Consider Agented Transactions." *Business Credit.* May 1996.

Tsui, John F. "The Appeal of Syndicated Loans." *Lodging Hospitality.* February 1992.

Wienke, Robert O. "Loan Syndications and Participations: Trends and Tactics." *Commercial Lending Review.* Spring 1994.

SEE ALSO: Banks and Banking

T

TARGET MARKETS

A target market is a group of customers with similar needs that forms the focus of a company's marketing efforts. Similarly, target marketing involves tailoring the company's **marketing** efforts to appeal to a specific group of customers. Selecting target markets is part of the process of market segmentation—dividing an overall market into key customer subsets, or segments, whose members share similar characteristics and needs. The company then selects from among these segments the particular markets it wishes to target. "Small businesses that identify the needs of specific target markets—existing and potential customers who are the focus of marketing efforts—and work to satisfy those needs, are more effective marketers," according to Gloria Green and Jeffrey Williams in *Marketing: Mastering Your Small Business.*

Target marketing is particularly important for small businesses, which often lack the resources to appeal to large aggregate markets or to maintain a wide range of differentiated products for varied markets. Target marketing allows a small business to develop a product and a marketing mix that fit a relatively homogenous part of the total market. By focusing its resources on a specific customer base in this way, a small business may be able to carve out a market niche that it can serve better than its larger competitors.

Identifying specific target markets, and then delivering products and promotions that ultimately maximize the profit potential of those targeted markets, are the primary functions of marketing managers. For instance, a manufacturer of fishing equipment would not randomly market its product to the entire U.S. population. Instead, it would conduct market research—using such tools as demographic reports, market surveys, or focus groups—to determine which customers would be most likely to purchase its products. It could then more efficiently spend its limited resources in an effort to persuade members of its target group(s) to buy. Perhaps it would target males in the Midwest between the ages of 18 and 35. The company may even strive to further maximize the profitability of its target market by breaking it down by age, income, zip code, or other factors indicative of buying patterns. Advertisements and promotions could then be tailored for each segment of the target market.

There are infinite ways to address the wants and needs of a target market. For example, product **packaging** can be designed in different sizes and colors, or the product itself can be altered to appeal to different personality types or age groups. Producers can also change the warranty or durability of the good or provide different levels of follow-up service. Other influences, such as distribution and sales methods, licensing strategies, and **advertising media**, also play an important role. It is the responsibility of the marketing manager to take all of these factors into account and to devise a cohesive marketing program that will appeal to the target customer.

A recent trend in target marketing is the use of database marketing systems. These computerized systems can be used to collect and store huge amounts of data about customers and their purchasing habits. Analyzing this information can enable a company to better identify customer needs and interests and tailor marketing campaigns to appeal to them. "Through their highly sophisticated use of database marketing, big companies have come close to eliminating their small competitors' main advantage: a close, informed, flexible relationship with customers. Yet despite the ominous signs, until recently most small companies did not use database marketing,'' Anne Field commented in an article for *Inc.* ''Now, however, small companies are finally starting to get religion, thanks to the falling costs of hardware and software and to more user-friendly applications.''

FURTHER READING:

Durden, Jonathan. ''Questioning the Term 'Targeting' Is Fundamental.'' *Marketing.* November 3, 1994.

Field, Anne. ''Precision Marketing.'' *Inc.* June 18, 1996.

Green, Gloria, and Jeffrey Williams. *Marketing: Mastering Your Small Business.* Chicago, IL: Upstart Publishing, 1996.

McCarthy, E. Jerome, and William D. Perreault, Jr. *Basic Marketing.* 10th ed. Homewood, IL: Irwin, 1990.

Stevens, Mark. *The Macmillan Small Business Handbook.* Macmillan, 1988.

Weinstein, Art. *Market Segmentation: Using Niche Marketing to Exploit New Markets.* Chicago, IL: Probus, 1989.

SEE ALSO: Demographics

TARGETED JOBS TAX CREDIT

The Targeted Jobs Tax Credit (TJTC), sometimes called the Employment Tax Credit, was a program that provided an incentive for companies to hire unskilled workers from nine targeted groups that have special employment needs or tend to experience a high rate of unemployment. It was first enacted by the U.S. Congress in 1978, then was extended under Tax Reform Act of 1986, and was replaced with the Work Opportunity Credit (WOC) in 1996. The TJTC, like the WOC, applied to people who receive general assistance, Aid to Families with Dependent Children, or Supplemental Security Income, as well as to handicapped persons referred from state rehabilitation or Veterans Administration programs. It also applied to economically disadvantaged Vietnam veterans, ex-convicts, and self-supporting youths between the ages of 18 and 24, as well as youths between 16 and 19 working through cooperative education programs or in summer jobs. The income level required to qualify as ''economically disadvantaged'' varied by county.

Companies that hired a qualified employee under the TJTC program received a tax credit equal to 40 percent of the first $6,000 in wages paid to that employee during their first year of employment, provided the employee worked for more than 90 days or 120 hours. The net savings a company received for hiring a qualified employee was reduced slightly, however, because the company also must reduce the amount of the tax deduction taken for wages paid to that employee. The net savings could still be substantial, however.

The total amount of the credit taken by a company could not exceed the amount of tax owed, but unused credits could be carried back for up to three years or carried forward for up to 15 years. In addition, some states allowed companies to claim an additional employment tax credit on their state returns. It is important to note that the TJTC program required qualified persons to be employed in a trade or business, so the credit did not apply to household employees. Small business owners also could not claim the credit for their relatives. The TJTC proved equally beneficial for small companies and large companies. **Subchapter S** corporations, which can pass tax credits on to their shareholders, found it particularly attractive. The TJTC program also helped companies with high employee turnover to recover some of their hiring costs. Some of the biggest beneficiaries of the program were retail stores, hotels, and fast-food franchises.

Along with its benefits, there were some problems with the TJTC program. In fact, not many companies took advantage of it at first because of the perceived drawbacks. For example, some business owners feared that only undesirable workers would qualify for the TJTC. But many companies found that people they had already hired would have qualified. In addition, some business owners worried that taking advantage of the program would prompt an **IRS audit**. However, there appeared to be no greater likelihood of an audit for companies that took advantage of the program. Other business owners assumed that the program would only be worthwhile for fast-food restaurants and other business that tended to hire large numbers of young people. In reality, people who qualified for the TJTC work in jobs ranging from window washer, parking lot attendant, or assembly worker to grocery store clerk, secretary, or bank teller. Finally, some business owners worried that the questions they had to ask to assess a job applicant's eligibility for the TJTC might expose the company to charges of discrimination.

The most commonly cited problem with the TJTC program involved the paperwork. In order for an employer to receive the tax credit, the potential employee first obtained a voucher from the state employment office. The employer then filled out the voucher and returned it before the person began work. If the person qualified, then the employer received certification of the tax credit that could be retained for year-end accounting. At tax time, the employer filed Form 5884—General Business Credit to claim the tax credit. The new Work Opportunity Credit operated in a similar manner and applied to qualified employees who started work between September 30, 1996, and October 1, 1997. The TJTC program seemed certain to spur other employment incentives for economically disadvantaged people in the near future.

FURTHER READING:

Bishop, John H., and Mark Montgomery. "Does the Targeted Jobs Tax Credit Create Jobs at Subsidized Firms?" *Industrial Relations.* Fall 1993.

Carpenter, Donna Sammons. "Taking Credit." *Inc.* September 1984.

Harris, Yvonne L. "Bulls-Eye for Employers." *Nation's Business.* March 1984.

J. K. Lasser Institute. *Tax Guide for Small Business.* New York: Simon and Schuster, 1988.

Levitan, Sar A., and Frank Gallo. "The Little Tax Credit That Could, But Hasn't." *Across the Board.* July-August 1987.

SEE ALSO: Empowerment Zones and Enterprise Communities; Tax Planning

TARIFFS

A tariff is a tax or duty imposed by one nation on the imported goods or services of another nation. Tariffs have been used throughout history to control the amount of imports that flow into a country and to determine which nations will be granted the most favorable trading conditions. High tariffs create protectionism, shielding a domestic industry's products against foreign competition. High tariffs usually ensure that a given product will not be imported into a country because the high tariff would lead to a high price for the customers of that product, be they other businesses or consumers.

Throughout the 1990s, the trend has been decreased tariffs on a global scale, as evidenced by the passage of well-known treaties such as the **General Agreement on Tariffs and Trade (GATT)** and the **North American Free Trade Agreement (NAFTA)**, as well as the lowering of trade barriers in the European Economic Community, reducing or even abolishing tariffs. There is a growing belief among politicians and economists around the globe that lower tariffs spur growth and reduce prices.

For the most part, the issue of tariffs is of greater concern to businesses in the United States. Generally, the United States imposes lower tariffs on imports than other countries do. According to Albert Holzinger in *Nation's Business,* before NAFTA, for example, Mexican tariffs on U.S. goods entering that country were, on average, 250 percent higher than U.S. duties on Mexican goods.

The Far East has even tighter restrictions than Mexico. Until very recently, tariffs on U.S. goods in Eastern countries made it essentially impossible for U.S. companies to compete. However, things are changing. The *Puget Sound Business Journal* reported that in 1996, the U.S. signed an agreement with the Asian-Pacific Economic Community (APEC) that will largely eliminate tariffs on computers, semiconductors, and computer parts by the year 2000. Negotiations are under way to sign other "sectoral agreements" that would reduce or eliminate tariffs on a business-sector-by-business sector basis.

Lower tariffs especially benefit small businesses because they level the playing field and make it easier for them to compete with larger companies. The majority of small business owners, then, tend to lobby hard for them. As one small manufacturer told *Nation's Business:* "Anytime you make a movement toward more free trade, I know we're going to benefit from it." Conversely, large corporations are in the best position to absorb higher tariffs for the sake of gaining market share—they have the cash to spend up front, even if it means initially taking a loss. Small companies cannot afford making such large initial investment in the hopes that their product will eventually prove successful.

TARIFFS UNDER GATT AND NAFTA GATT is especially beneficial to the small businessman. The 2000-page treaty, which the majority of nations have signed, is expected to drop tariffs worldwide by nearly 40 percent by the start of the next century. Not only does it mean that U.S. companies should find it easier to sell their products abroad, but they should also have more options when purchasing products or materials here in the United States. Auto companies, for example, should be able to buy cheaper, imported steel. Even if a small business does not export itself, it should benefit if the larger companies it supplies increase their exports, essentially "piggybacking" on the success of the larger firm.

NAFTA will also have benefits for small business owners. One direct effect that will be seen almost immediately is that Canadian and Mexican government procurement contracts will now be open to American firms. That should open up a new market for small businesses.

It is important to note that the current move towards lower tariffs is a gradual one. While NAFTA and GATT did eliminate some tariffs immediately, most are designed to be phased out over a period of years, even decades. Every small businessperson should study the provisions of major trade agreements that pertain specifically to their industry before moving ahead with plans to increase exports.

One key area in development in the international arena is Internet tariffs. The United States is pushing hard for international agreements that will ensure that there are no tariffs on equipment used to build the Internet nor on products or services sold over it. This would make the Internet a duty-free zone, which has huge implications, as businesses, especially small businesses, continue to expand their presence on the Internet.

FURTHER READING:

DeMott, John S. "What GATT Means to Small Business." *Nation's Business.* March 1995.

Edmond, Alfred Jr. "Making the Most of NAFTA: Here's What to Do when the Barriers to Mexico's Markets Come Down." *Black Enterprise.* February 1994.

Holzinger, Albert G. "Why Small Firms Back NAFTA." *Nation's Business.* November 1993.

Jacobson, Ken. "U.S. Pushing for Accord Heading Off Internet Tariffs." *New Technology Week.* August 4, 1997.

Wilhelm, Steve. "Banning Tariffs Sector-by-Sector." *Puget Sound Business Journal.* November 7, 1997.

SEE ALSO: Exporting; Exporting—Financing and Pricing Issues; International Law

TAX DEDUCTIBLE BUSINESS EXPENSES

Tax deductible business expenses include a variety of costs that can be subtracted from a company's income before it is subject to taxation. By reducing taxable income, these deductions reduce a company's tax liability and thus improve its bottom line. The standard business deductions—which include general and administrative expenses, business-related travel and entertainment, automobile expenses, and **employee benefits**—are outlined in Section 162 of the Internal Revenue Code. Although the tax law is complex, virtually any expense that is considered ordinary, reasonable, and necessary to the business can be tax deductible. Some expenses are considered "current" and are deducted in the year that they are paid, while others are considered "capitalized" and must be spread out or depreciated over time.

The significant tax deductions available to self-employed persons and small business owners often provide one of the main sources of motivation for going into business. However, it is important for small business owners to maintain a personal awareness of tax-related issues in order to save money. Even if they employ a professional bookkeeper or accountant, small business owners should keep careful tabs on their own tax preparation in order to take advantage of all possible opportunities for deductions and tax savings. "Whether or not you enlist the aid of an outsider, you should understand the basic provisions of the tax code," Albert B. Ellentuck wrote in the *Laventhol and Horwath Small Business Tax Planning Guide.* "Just as you would not turn over the management of your money to another person, you should not blindly allow someone else to take complete charge of your taxpaying responsibilities." In addition, as Frederick W. Dailey wrote in his book *Tax Savvy for Small Business,* "Tax knowledge has powerful profit potential. Knowing what the tax law has to offer can give you a far better bottom line than your competitors who don't bother to learn."

Taking advantage of allowable tax deductions can also offer other benefits to small business owners. "Knowing how to maximize your deductible business expenses lowers your taxable profit," Dailey noted. "To boot, you may enjoy a personal benefit from a business expenditure—a nice car to drive, a combination business trip/vacation and a retirement savings plan—if you follow the myriad of tax rules." Solid record-keeping is vital for small businesses that hope to claim their allowable tax credits and deductions. After all, deductions can be disallowed for even legitimate business expenditures if those expenditures are not adequately supported by business records.

Some of the major categories of tax deductible business expenses are described below:

GENERAL AND ADMINISTRATIVE EXPENSES

All of the basic expenses necessary to run a business are generally tax-deductible, including office rent, salaries, equipment and supplies, telephone and utility costs, legal and accounting services, professional dues, and subscriptions to business publications. Education expenses are deductible if they are necessary to improve or maintain the skills involved in one's present employment or are required by an employer. However, education costs cannot be deducted when they are incurred in order to qualify for a different job. Some other miscellaneous expenses that may be deductible in this category include computer software, charitable contributions, repairs and improvements to business property, bank service charges, consultant fees, postage, and online services.

In most cases, general and administrative business expenses are deductible in the year in which they were incurred. An exception applies to the costs of starting a business that are incurred prior to beginning operations. These expenses must be capitalized over five years, which may seem strange since they are deductible immediately once the business is open. Depreciating the costs of starting a business might be preferable if the business is expected to show a loss for the first year or two. Otherwise, it may be possible to avoid the need to capitalize these expenses by delaying payment on invoices until the business opens or by doing a small amount of business during the startup period.

HOME OFFICE DEDUCTION The use of part of a home as a business office may enable an individual to qualify for significant tax deductions. The home office deduction allows individuals who meet certain criteria to deduct a portion of mortgage interest or rent, depreciation of the space used as an office, utility bills, home insurance costs, and cleaning, repairs, and security costs from their federal income taxes. Although the **Internal Revenue Service (IRS)** has set strict regulations about who qualifies for the deduction, about 1.6 million people claim the deduction each year. According to Gloria Gibbs Marullo in an article for *Nation's Business,* the savings can be considerable: a sole proprietor living in a $150,000 home stands to save about $2,500 in actual taxes annually.

Home office operators may claim a deduction for those offices on IRS Form 8829 (Expenses for Business Use of Your Home), which is filed along with Schedule C (Profit or Loss From Your Business). There are restrictions, however, which are covered in IRS Publication 587 (*Business Use of Your Home*). Failing to abide by these restrictions may put a red flag on a home office user's federal income tax return, which could result in an audit.

In general, a home office deduction is allowed if the home office meets at least one of three criteria: 1) the home office is the principal place of business; 2) the home office is the place where the business owner meets with clients and customers as part of the normal business day; or 3) the place of business is a separate structure on the property, but is not attached to the house or residence. The deduction is figured on the size of the home office as a percentage of the total house or residence. For example, if the total house size is 2,400 square feet and the home office is 240 square feet, 10 percent of the total house is considered used for business. That would allow the business owner to deduct 10 percent of the household's costs for electricity, real estate taxes, mortgage interest, insurance, repairs, etc. as business expenses. The total amount of the deduction is limited to the gross income derived from the business activity, less other business expenses. In other words, the home office deduction cannot be used to make an otherwise profitable business show a loss.

AUTOMOBILE EXPENSES

Most people have occasion to drive a car while conducting business. Business-related automobile mileage is tax deductible, with the exception of commuting to and from work. Any other mileage from the place of business to another location can be considered a business expense as long as the travel was made for business purposes. The IRS allows the mileage deduction to be calculated using two different approaches. The straight-mileage approach multiplies

the cents-per-mile allowed by the IRS (31.5 cents in 1997) by the number of miles attributable to business use of the automobile. For example, a small business owner who drove 1,000 miles at .315 per mile would gain a deduction of $315.

In contrast, the actual-expense approach adds up all the costs of operating the car for a year—such as gasoline, insurance, maintenance, and depreciation—and multiplies that total by the percentage of the annual mileage that was attributable to business purposes. For example, a small business owner who paid a total of $3,000 in operating costs and drove a total of 15,000 miles, only 1,500 of which were business-related, would gain a deduction of $3,000 × .10 or $300. Businesses are required to use the actual-expense approach under certain circumstances—if the vehicle is leased, if more than one vehicle is used for the business, or if the approach was used for that vehicle during its first year of service—but otherwise can choose the approach that yields the larger deduction. In either case, it is necessary to maintain an accurate log of business mileage and associated automobile expenses.

ENTERTAINMENT AND TRAVEL

Reasonable travel and entertainment costs are tax deductible if they are: 1) directly related to business, meaning that business took place or was discussed during the entertainment; or 2) associated with business, meaning that business took place or was discussed immediately before or after the entertainment (i.e., a small business owner took a client out to dinner or to a sporting event following a meeting). Because they include a personal element, only 50 percent of meals and entertainment expenses are deductible as business expenses. Business-related travel, however, is fully deductible.

Careful records are necessary to substantiate the deductions. For business-related meals and entertainment, these records should include the amount, place, date, reason for entertainment, nature of business discussion, and name and occupation of the person being entertained. It is not necessary to retain receipts for expenditures less than $75. Entertainment that is done within the home is also deductible in some cases. Company parties that involve all employees are 100 percent deductible, although they must be infrequent and not overly extravagant. In addition, gifts to clients and customers are deductible to maximum of $25 per year, or $400 if the business name is imprinted on them.

The costs of reasonable and necessary business travel—including meetings with clients and suppliers as well as conferences and seminars intended to expand a business person's expertise—are fully deductible as business expenses. The costs that can be deducted include airfare, bus or train fare, car rental, and taxi fare, hotels and meals, and incidentals such as tips and dry cleaning expenses. Restrictions apply to travel in foreign countries or on cruise ships. In addition, travel to investment-related seminars are not deductible, though the cost of the seminars may be. A variety of rules apply to deducting business travel expenses, so it is necessary to review them in detail or enlist the help of a tax professional.

DEPRECIATION

According to Section 179 of the Internal Revenue Code, small business owners can write off the first $18,000 of equipment purchased for business use each year during the year in which it was purchased. In many cases, it makes sense to take advantage of this tax break immediately, particularly if purchases will be fairly regular from year to year. If the item is a one-time purchase or if the total amount spent is greater than the limit, however, the business owner may wish to depreciate the cost over future time periods. **Depreciation** is a tax-deductible business expense.

Depreciation for tax purposes is determined by an IRS formula and has nothing to do with the actual value of equipment at year end. Instead, the amount claimed as depreciation is designed to spread the cost of the equipment over time and maximize the annual tax deductions associated with it. Most companies use a straight-line depreciation method for their financial statements, because the even amounts approximate the rate at which the equipment is used up and will need to be replaced. However, they tend to use accelerated depreciation methods for tax purposes in order to deduct a larger portion of the equipment's cost sooner. The IRS applies different ''life spans'' to different types of equipment for the purposes of depreciation. For example, it applies a five-year life to telecommunications equipment and automobiles, and a seven-year life to computers and office equipment like desks, chairs, and fixtures.

EMPLOYEE BENEFITS

The cost of providing employees with a wide variety of fringe benefits is considered a tax deductible business expense for employers. Most of these benefits are not considered income for employees, so they receive a tax break as well. Certain types of benefits—particularly retirement and **pension plans**—are also deductible for self-employed persons and small business owners. However, it is important to keep up with the rapidly changing tax laws regarding these matters. Some of the types of employee benefits that may be considered tax deductible business expenses include: retirement plans, health insurance, disability and **life insurance**, company cars, membership in clubs and athletic facilities, dependent care assistance, education assistance, employee discounts, and business meals, travel, and lodging.

RETIREMENT AND PENSION PLANS Small business owners can set up a wide variety of retirement plans in order to gain tax advantages. In most cases, employer contributions are tax-deductible business expenses, and the money is allowed to grow tax-deferred until employees reach retirement age, at which point they will likely be in a lower tax bracket than during their working years. The most important thing to remember is that a small business owner who wants to establish a qualified plan for him or herself must also include all other company employees who meet minimum participation standards. As an employer, the small business owner can establish retirement plans like any other business. As an employee, the small business owner can then make contributions to the plan he or she has established in order to set aside tax-deferred funds for retirement, like any other employee. The difference is that a small business owner must include all nonowner employees in any company-sponsored retirement plans and make equivalent contributions to their accounts. Unfortunately, this requirement has the effect of reducing the allowable contributions that the owner of a proprietorship or partnership can make on his or her own behalf.

For self-employed individuals, contributions to a retirement plan are based upon the net earnings of their business. The net earnings consist of the company's gross income less deductions for business expenses, salaries paid to nonowner employees, the employer's 50 percent of the Social Security tax, and—significantly—the employer's contribution to retirement plans on behalf of employees. Therefore, rather than receiving pre-tax contributions to the retirement account as a percentage of gross salary, like nonowner employees, the small business owner receives contributions as a smaller percentage of net earnings. Employing other people thus detracts from the owner's ability to build up a sizeable before-tax retirement account of his or her own. For this reason, some experts recommend that the owners of proprietorships and partnerships who sponsor plans for their employees supplement their own retirement funds through a personal after-tax savings plan.

Nevertheless, many small businesses sponsor retirement plans in order to gain tax advantages and increase the loyalty of employees. A number of different types of plans are available. In nearly every case, withdrawals made before the age of 59 ½ are subject to an IRS penalty in addition to ordinary income tax. The plans differ in terms of administrative costs, eligibility requirements, employee participation, degree of discretion in making contributions, and amount of allowable contributions.

HEALTH INSURANCE Health insurance benefits provided to employees are also tax deductible. However, self-employed persons are only able to deduct a portion of their own payments for health insurance (40 percent in 1997, gradually increasing to 80 percent in 2006). An exception to this rule is included under Section 105 of the Internal Revenue Code. This loophole allows a small business owner whose spouse works in the business to fully deduct his or her health insurance and unreimbursed medical expenses by creating a medical reimbursement plan for employees. The spouse is then covered under the plan, the small business owner is covered under his or her spouse's insurance, and the entire bill is a tax-deductible business expense. Many tax professionals and insurance providers offer this sort of plan to their clients. It is important to note, however, that the same plan must be available to all of the business's employees.

FURTHER READING:

Dailey, Frederick W. *Tax Savvy for Small Business.* 2nd ed. Berkeley, CA: Nolo Press, 1997.

DeJong, David S., and Ann Gray Jakabcin. *J.K. Lasser's Year-Round Tax Strategies.* New York: Macmillan, 1997.

Ellentuck, Albert B. *Laventhol and Horwath Small Business Tax Planning Guide.* New York: Avon Books, 1988.

The Entrepreneur Magazine Small Business Advisor. New York: Wiley, 1995.

Harrington, Phillip. "Small Firms Get Help from Section 105." *National Underwriter and Health.* July 7, 1997.

Keating, Peter. "Can I Deduct That?" *Money.* March 1997.

Korn, Donald J. "Deducting Home Office Expenses." *Black Enterprise.* September 1996.

Marullo, Gloria Gibbs. "Redefining the Home-Office Deduction." *Nation's Business.* September 1997.

Robertson, Cliff. *The Small Business Tax Advisor: Understanding the New Tax Law.* Blue Ridge Summit, PA: Liberty House, 1987.

Szabo, Joan. "Found Money: Capture Increased Tax Savings with These Ten Business Deductions." *Entrepreneur.* June 1997.

SEE ALSO: Health Insurance Options; Home-based Businesses; Leasing Automobiles; Retirement Planning; Tax Planning

TAX PLANNING

Tax planning involves conceiving of and implementing various strategies in order to minimize the amount of taxes paid for a given period. For a small business, minimizing the tax liability can provide more money for expenses, investment, or growth. In this way, tax planning can be a source of working capital. According to *The Entrepreneur Magazine Small Business Advisor,* two basic rules apply to tax planning. First, a small business should never incur additional expenses only to gain a tax deduction. While purchasing necessary equipment prior to the end of the tax year can be a valuable tax planning

strategy, making unnecessary purchases is not recommended. Second, a small business should always attempt to defer taxes when possible. Deferring taxes enables the business to use that money interest-free, and sometimes even earn interest on it, until the next time taxes are due.

Experts recommend that entrepreneurs and small business owners conduct formal tax planning sessions in the middle of each tax year. This approach will give them time to apply their strategies to the current year as well as allow them to get a jump on the following year. It is important for small business owners to maintain a personal awareness of tax planning issues in order to save money. Even if they employ a professional bookkeeper or accountant, small business owners should keep careful tabs on their own tax preparation in order to take advantage of all possible opportunities for deductions and tax savings. "Whether or not you enlist the aid of an outsider, you should understand the basic provisions of the tax code," Albert B. Ellentuck wrote in the *Laventhol and Horwath Small Business Tax Planning Guide.* "Just as you would not turn over the management of your money to another person, you should not blindly allow someone else to take complete charge of your taxpaying responsibilities." In addition, as Frederick W. Dailey wrote in his book *Tax Savvy for Small Business,* "Tax knowledge has powerful profit potential. Knowing what the tax law has to offer can give you a far better bottom line than your competitors who don't bother to learn."

GENERAL AREAS OF TAX PLANNING

There are several general areas of tax planning that apply to all sorts of small businesses. These areas include the choice of accounting and inventory-valuation methods, the timing of equipment purchases, the spreading of business income among family members, and the selection of tax-favored benefit plans and investments. There are also some areas of tax planning that are specific to certain business forms—i.e., sole proprietorships, partnerships, C corporations, and S corporations. Some of the general tax planning strategies are described below:

ACCOUNTING METHODS **Accounting methods** refer to the basic rules and guidelines under which businesses keep their financial records and prepare their financial reports. There are two main accounting methods used for record-keeping: the cash basis and the accrual basis. Small business owners must decide which method to use depending on the legal form of the business, its sales volume, whether it extends credit to customers, and the tax requirements set forth by the **Internal Revenue Service.** The choice of accounting method is an issue in tax planning, as it can affect the amount of taxes owed by a small business in a given year.

Accounting records that are prepared using the cash basis recognize income and expenses according to real-time cash flow. Income is recorded upon receipt of funds, rather than based upon when it is actually earned, and expenses are recorded as they are paid, rather than as they are actually incurred. Under this accounting method, therefore, it is possible to defer taxable income by delaying billing so that payment is not received in the current year. Likewise, it is possible to accelerate expenses by paying them as soon as the bills are received, in advance of the due date. The cash method is simpler than the accrual method, it provides a more accurate picture of cash flow, and income is not subject to taxation until the money is actually received.

In contrast, the accrual basis makes a greater effort to recognize income and expenses in the period to which they apply, regardless of whether or not money has changed hands. Under this system, revenue is recorded when it is earned, rather than when payment is received, and expenses recorded when they are incurred, rather than when payment is made. The main advantage of the accrual method is that it provides a more accurate picture of how a business is performing over the long-term than the cash method. The main disadvantages are that it is more complex than the cash basis, and that income taxes may be owed on revenue before payment is actually received. However, the accrual basis may yield favorable tax results for companies that have few receivables and large current liabilities.

Under generally accepted accounting principles (GAAP), the accrual basis of accounting is required for all businesses that handle inventory, from small retailers to large manufacturers. It is also required for corporations and partnerships that have gross sales over $5 million per year, though there are exceptions for farming businesses and qualified personal service corporations—such as doctors, lawyers, accountants, and consultants. Other businesses generally can decide which accounting method to use based on the relative tax savings it provides.

INVENTORY VALUATION METHODS The method a small business chooses for **inventory** valuation can also lead to substantial tax savings. Inventory valuation is important because businesses are required to reduce the amount they deduct for inventory purchases over the course of a year by the amount remaining in inventory at the end of the year. For example, a business that purchased $10,000 in inventory during the year but had $6,000 remaining in inventory at the end of the year could only count $4,000 as an expense for inventory purchases, even though the actual cash outlay was much larger.

Valuing the remaining inventory differently could increase the amount deducted from income and thus reduce the amount of tax owed by the business.

The tax law provides two possible methods for inventory valuation: the first-in, first-out method (FIFO); and the last-in, first-out method (LIFO). As the names suggest, these inventory methods differ in the assumption they make about the way items are sold from inventory. FIFO assumes that the items purchased the earliest are the first to be removed from inventory, while LIFO assumes that the items purchased most recently are the first to be removed from inventory. In this way, FIFO values the remaining inventory at the most current cost, while LIFO values the remaining inventory at the earliest cost paid that year.

LIFO is generally the preferred inventory valuation method during times of rising costs. It places a lower value on the remaining inventory and a higher value on the cost of goods sold, thus reducing income and taxes. On the other hand, FIFO is generally preferred during periods of deflation or in industries where inventory can tend to lose its value rapidly, such as high technology. Companies are allowed to file Form 970 and switch from FIFO to LIFO at any time to take advantage of tax savings. However, they must then either wait ten years or get permission from the IRS to switch back to FIFO.

EQUIPMENT PURCHASES Under Section 179 of the Internal Revenue Code, businesses are allowed to deduct a total of $18,000 in equipment purchases during the year in which the purchases are made. Any purchases above this amount must be depreciated over several future tax periods. It is often advantageous for small businesses to use this tax incentive to increase their deductions for business expenses, thus reducing their taxable income and their tax liability. Necessary equipment purchases up to the limit can be timed at year end and still be fully deductible for the year. This tax incentive also applies to personal property put into service for business use, with the exception of automobiles and real estate.

WAGES PAID TO FAMILY MEMBERS Self-employed persons can also reduce their tax burden by paying wages to a spouse or to dependent children. Wages paid to children under the age of 18 are not subject to FICA (Social Security and Medicare) taxes. Under normal circumstances, employers are required to withhold 7.65 percent of the first $62,700 of an employee's income for **FICA taxes**. Employers are also required to match the 7.65 percent contributed by every employee, so that the total FICA contribution is 15.3 percent. Self-employed persons are required to pay both the employer and employee portions of the FICA tax.

But the FICA taxes are waived when the employee is a dependent child of the small business owner, saving the child and the parent 7.65 percent each. In addition, the child's wages are still considered a tax deductible business expense for the parent—thus reducing the parent's taxable income. Although the child must pay normal income taxes on the wages he or she receives, it is likely to be at a lower tax rate than the parent pays. Some business owners are able to further reduce their tax burden by paying wages to their spouse. If these wages bring the business owner's net income below $62,700—the threshold for FICA taxes—then they may reduce the self-employment tax owed by business owner. It is important to note, however, that the child or spouse must actually work for the business and that the wages must be reasonable for the work performed.

BENEFITS PLANS AND INVESTMENTS Tax planning also applies to various types of employee benefits that can provide a business with tax deductions, such as contributions to life insurance, health insurance, or retirement plans. As an added bonus, many such benefit programs are not considered taxable income for employees. Finally, tax planning applies to various types of investments that can shift tax liability to future periods, such as treasury bills, bank certificates, savings bonds, and deferred annuities. Companies can avoid paying taxes during the current period for income that is reinvested in such tax-deferred instruments.

TAX PLANNING FOR DIFFERENT BUSINESS FORMS

"The first step in tax planning—for small business owners and professionals, at least—is to select the right form of organization for your enterprise," according to Albert B. Ellentuck in the *Laventhol and Horwath Small Business Tax Planning Guide.* "You'll end up paying radically different amounts of income tax depending on the form you select. And your odds of being audited by the IRS will change, too." Many aspects of tax planning are specific to certain business forms; some of these are discussed below:

SOLE PROPRIETORSHIPS AND PARTNERSHIPS Tax planning for **sole proprietorships** and **partnerships** is in many ways similar to tax planning for individuals. This is because the owners of businesses organized as sole proprietors and partnerships pay personal income tax rather than business income tax. These small business owners file an informational return for their business with the IRS, and then report any income taken from the business for personal use on their own personal tax return. No special taxes are imposed except for the self-employment tax (SECA), which requires all self-employed persons to pay both the employer and employee portions of the FICA tax, for a total of 15.3 percent.

Since they do not receive an ordinary salary, the owners of sole proprietorships and partnerships are not required to withhold income taxes for themselves. Instead, they are required to estimate their total tax liability and remit it to the IRS in quarterly installments, using Form 1040 ES. It is important that the amount of tax paid in quarterly installments equal either the total amount owed during the previous year or 90 percent of their total current tax liability. Otherwise, the IRS may charge interest and impose a stiff penalty for underpayment of estimated taxes.

Since the IRS calculates the amount owed quarterly, a large lump-sum payment in the fourth quarter will not enable a taxpayer to escape penalties. On the other hand, a significant increase in withholding in the fourth quarter may help, because tax that is withheld by an employer is considered to be paid evenly throughout the year no matter when it was withheld. This leads to a possible tax planning strategy for a self-employed person who falls behind in his or her estimated tax payments. By having an employed spouse increase his or her withholding, the self-employed person can make up for the deficiency and avoid a penalty.

Another possible tax planning strategy applies to partnerships that anticipate a loss. At the end of each tax year, partnerships file the informational Form 1065 (Partnership Statement of Income) with the IRS, and then report the amount of income that accrued to each partner on Schedule K1. This income can be divided in any number of ways, depending on the nature of the partnership agreement. In this way, it is possible to pass all of a partnership's early losses to one partner in order to maximize his or her tax advantages.

C CORPORATIONS Tax planning for **C corporations** is very different than that for sole proprietorships and partnerships. This is because profits earned by C corporations accrue to the corporation rather than to the individual owners, or shareholders. A corporation is a separate, taxable entity under the law, and different corporate tax rates apply based on the amount of net income received. As of 1997, the corporate tax rates were 15 percent on income up to $50,000, 25 percent on income between $50,000 and $75,000, 34 percent on income between $75,000 and $100,000, 39 percent on income between $100,000 and $335,000, and 34 percent on income between $335,000 and $10 million. Personal service corporations, like medical and law practices, pay a flat rate of 35 percent. In addition to the basic corporate tax, corporations may be subject to several special taxes.

Corporations must prepare an annual corporate tax return on either a calendar-year basis (the tax year ends December 31, and taxes must be filed by March 15) or a fiscal-year basis (the tax year ends whenever the officers determine). Most Subchapter **S corporations**, as well as C corporations that derive most of their income from the personal services of shareholders, are required to use the calendar-year basis for tax purposes. Most other corporations can choose whichever basis provides them with the most tax benefits. Using a fiscal-year basis to stagger the corporate tax year and the personal one can provide several advantages. For example, many corporations choose to end their fiscal year on January 31 and give their shareholder/employees bonuses at that time. The bonuses are still tax deductible for the corporation, while the individual shareholders enjoy use of that money without owing taxes on it until April 15 of the following year.

Both the owners and employees of C corporations receive salaries for their work, and the corporation must withhold taxes on the wages paid. All such salaries are tax deductible for the corporations, as are fringe benefits supplied to employees. Many smaller corporations can arrange to pay out all corporate income in salaries and benefits, leaving no income subject to the corporate income tax. Of course, the individual shareholder/employees are required to pay personal income taxes. Still, corporations can use tax planning strategies to defer or accrue income between the corporation and individuals in order to pay taxes in the lowest possible tax bracket. The one major disadvantage to corporate taxation is that corporate income is subject to corporate taxes, and then income distributions to shareholders in the form of dividends are also taxable for the shareholders. This situation is known as "**double taxation**."

S CORPORATIONS Subchapter S corporations avoid the problem of double taxation by passing their earnings (or losses) directly to shareholders, without having to pay dividends. Experts note that it is often preferable for tax planning purposes to begin a new business as an S corporation rather than a C corporation. Many businesses show a loss for a year or more when they first begin operations. At the same time, individual owners often cash out investments and sell assets in order to accumulate the funds needed to start the business. The owners would have to pay tax on this income unless the corporate losses were passed through to offset it.

Another tax planning strategy available to shareholder/employees of S corporations involves keeping FICA taxes low by setting modest salaries for themselves, below the Social Security base. S corporation shareholder/employees are only required to pay FICA taxes on the income that they receive as salaries, not on income that they receive as dividends or on earnings that are retained in the corporation. It is important to note, however, that unreasonably low salaries may be challenged by the IRS.

FURTHER READING:

Dailey, Frederick W. *Tax Savvy for Small Business.* 2nd ed. Berkeley, CA: Nolo Press, 1997.

DeJong, David S., and Ann Gray Jakabcin. *J.K. Lasser's Year-Round Tax Strategies.* New York: Macmillan, 1997.

Ellentuck, Albert B. *Laventhol and Horwath Small Business Tax Planning Guide.* New York: Avon Books, 1988.

The Entrepreneur Magazine Small Business Advisor. New York: Wiley, 1995.

Marullo, Gloria Gibbs. "Hiring Your Child: Tax Breaks and Trade-Offs." *Nation's Business.* June 1997.

Robertson, Cliff. *The Small Business Tax Advisor: Understanding the New Tax Law.* Blue Ridge Summit, PA: Liberty House, 1987.

Wiener, Leonard. "Squaring Your Account with the IRS." *U.S. News and World Report.* August 29, 1988.

SEE ALSO: Employing Minors; Tax Returns; Tax Withholding; Tax Deductible Business Expenses

TAX PREPARATION SOFTWARE

Faced with a tax code which inevitably changes from year to year, many small business owners choose to use one of the many tax preparation software packages which are now widely available in spreadsheet format.

Using tax preparation software will almost certainly result in a more complete and more correct **tax return**. These packages may also steer the taxpayer toward greater savings or little-known deductions, paying for themselves with the returns that they yield. Even if no direct tax savings are realized through the use of the software, many analysts believe that business owners can save themselves a considerable amount of time by using the packages, thus freeing them to use their talents in other business areas.

Purchasing the software to prepare tax returns, no matter which package is purchased, will undoubtedly be less expensive than hiring an accountant. Of course, a CPA can be creative and intuitive about individual circumstances in a way that a computer program can never be, but unless the finances for the year are extremely complicated, the best of these software programs should be sufficient to meet the requirements of most small enterprises. A major drawback associated with using one of the available packages, however, is that in the event of an audit, the small business owner will have to face the IRS without the expert knowledge of the CPA who originally prepared the tax return.

COMPONENTS OF THE PACKAGES Data Entry—All of the software packages have more than one option for entering data into the IRS-accepted forms. The user can always opt for the simple method of entering figures into the forms without assistance from the program, using the software mainly to double-check figures and calculate final amounts. All of the software packages also have an interview function, which asks easily understandable questions to which the user responds by clicking yes or no boxes. This function specifies which schedules are required by the IRS, and which sections of the basic 1040 and schedules can be bypassed. Depending on the program, there may be a third route—a ''fast track'' interview, through which the user can select specific parts of the interview to fill out, speeding up the process and avoiding the sections which are not pertinent to the case at hand.

Many of the programs also have importing features, which allow the user to pull data from other programs directly into the tax preparation spreadsheet. Generally, these work primarily with Quicken and QuickBooks. If the small business owner already uses one of these applications to calculate tax-related expenses, it is relatively quick and easy to transfer information, cutting down on duplicated work. Almost all of the packages also allow the user to import last year's tax information, provided it was prepared with the same package.

Filing—When it comes to methods of filing, most of the packages provide several options for the user to choose between. The forms can be filled out electronically and then printed and mailed to the IRS to be processed in a paper version. Some of the packages offer the abbreviated Form 1040PC, which is also submitted as a hard copy. And some of the packages allow the user to file electronically, although some charge an additional fee for this option (about ten dollars).

Features and Help—All of the software packages automatically check for mathematical mistakes and warn of possible errors when questionable data is entered into a field. Most of the programs can offer advice—some from specific tax experts—about how to maximize the return and minimize taxes paid. Some of the programs offer complete IRS tax guides which can be directly accessed, and some offer only abbreviated versions of this information. Some of the programs even alert the user to potential audit flags resulting from data entered. Several packages offer a review option after the forms are completed; this option can provide advice on what to do differently to pay less taxes the next time around.

Most of the packages offer state tax preparation in addition to the federal forms. Some offer only a few states, while others offer all the states which provide electronic forms. These supplements may be included in the price, or may be priced separately. Prices for the packages range from $20 to more than $50, plus state supplements and filing fees.

DECIDING WHICH PACKAGE TO BUY Choosing a package will depend on how involved the tax return is. A few of the products can manage even very complicated scenarios, while the few at the bottom of the price range tend to be better for simple personal tax returns. For the small business owner who may be dealing with self-employment, home-work environments, and partnerships, it is probably worthwhile to purchase one of the more detailed programs.

The Internet is an excellent resource for information and reviews of tax preparation software; both *CNET.COM* and *PC Magazine Online* periodically have articles on the subject. In addition, business magazines that tailor their material toward small business owners include many informative reviews on such products.

FURTHER READING:

Dailey, Frederick W. *Tax Savvy for Small Business.* 2nd ed. Berkeley, CA: Nolo Press, 1997.

DeJong, David S., and Ann Gray Jakabcin. *J.K. Lasser's Year-Round Tax Strategies.* New York: Macmillan, 1997.

SEE ALSO: Tax Planning

TAX RETURNS

Tax returns include all the required paperwork that accompanies the remittance of taxes to the appropriate government agency, usually the **Internal Revenue Service**. The IRS issues more than 650 different forms for taxpayers to use in calculating and paying their taxes (the complete list is available through IRS publication 676, *Catalog of Federal Tax Forms*). Each form applies to a different situation or purpose. For example, Form 1065 details the income received by a business operating as a partnership, and Form 8826 relates to expenses claimed for business use of a home. Perhaps the most familiar type of tax form is the annual personal tax return, Form 1040, that must be completed by millions of taxpayers each year.

Considering that the tax laws have undergone no fewer than seven major revisions in the past two decades, as well as numerous minor changes, it can be exceedingly difficult for small business owners to prepare their own tax returns. But, as Frederick W. Dailey noted in his book *Tax Savvy for Small Business,* ''The average small business person can't afford to call a tax pro with every question.'' Fortunately, a great deal of information is available through other sources, such as IRS publications and help lines, self-help tax preparation guides and software, trade associations, periodicals, and online services.

It is important for small business owners to maintain a personal awareness of tax-related issues in order to save money. Even if they employ a professional bookkeeper or accountant, small business owners should keep careful tabs on their own tax preparation in order to take advantage of all possible opportunities for deductions and tax savings. "Whether or not you enlist the aid of an outsider, you should understand the basic provisions of the tax code," Albert B. Ellentuck wrote in the *Laventhol and Horwath Small Business Tax Planning Guide*. "Just as you would not turn over the management of your money to another person, you should not blindly allow someone else to take complete charge of your taxpaying responsibilities." In addition, as Dailey noted, "Tax knowledge has powerful profit potential. Knowing what the tax law has to offer can give you a far better bottom line than your competitors who don't bother to learn."

COMMON BUSINESS TAX FORMS AND FILING DEADLINES

Small businesses that employ persons other than the owner or partners are required to withhold payroll taxes from the wages paid to employees, remit these taxes to the Internal Revenue Service (IRS), and make regularly scheduled reports to the IRS about the amount of payroll taxes owed and paid. Payroll taxes include regular income taxes, FICA (Social Security and Medicare) taxes, and FUTA (federal unemployment) taxes. In addition to withholding payroll taxes for employees, employers must remit these taxes to the IRS in a timely manner. The regular income taxes and the portion of the **FICA taxes** that are withheld from employees' wages each pay period must be remitted to the IRS monthly, along with a Federal Tax Deposit Coupon (Form 8109-B). If the total withheld is less than $500, however, the business is allowed to make the payments quarterly.

Employers must also file four different reports regarding payroll taxes. The first report, Form 941, is the Employer's Quarterly Federal Tax Return. This report details the number of employees the business had, the amount of wages they were paid, and the amount of taxes that were withheld for the quarter. The other three reports are filed annually. Form W-2—the Annual Statement of Taxes Withheld—must be sent to all employees before January 31 of the following year. It details how much each employee received in wages and how much was withheld for taxes over the course of the year. Copies of the W-2 forms for all employees also must be sent to the Social Security Administration. The third report, Form W-3, must be sent to the IRS by February 28 of the following year. It provides a formal reconciliation of the quarterly tax payments made on Form 941 and the annual totals reported on Form W-2 for all employees. The final report is the Federal Unemployment Tax Return, Form 940, which outlines the total FUTA taxes owed and paid for the year.

Since they do not receive an ordinary salary, the owners of **sole proprietorships** and **partnerships** are not required to withhold income taxes for themselves. Instead, they are required to estimate their total tax liability and remit it to the IRS in quarterly installments, using Form 1040 ES. It is important that the amount of tax paid in quarterly installments equal either the total amount owed during the previous year or 90 percent of their total current tax liability. Otherwise, the IRS may charge interest and impose a stiff penalty for underpayment of estimated taxes. At the end of the tax year, the income for sole proprietorships is simply reported on the personal tax return of the business owner. Partnerships must file the informational Form 1065 (Partnership Statement of Income) with the IRS, and then report the amount of income that accrued to each partner on Schedule K1.

Corporations must prepare an annual corporate tax return on either a calendar-year basis (the tax year ends December 31, and taxes must be filed by March 15) or a fiscal-year basis (the tax year ends whenever the officers determine). Most Subchapter **S corporations**, as well as **C corporations** that derive most of their income from the personal services of shareholders, are required to use the calendar-year basis for tax purposes. Most other corporations can choose whichever basis provides them with the most tax benefits. At the end of their tax year, corporations file either Form 1120, the U.S. Corporate Income Tax Return, or the shorter Form 1120A. If they expect to owe taxes, corporations are required to make quarterly estimated payments, like other businesses.

FURTHER READING:

Dailey, Frederick W. *Tax Savvy for Small Business*. 2nd ed. Berkeley, CA: Nolo Press, 1997.

DeJong, David S., and Ann Gray Jakabcin. *J.K. Lasser's Year-Round Tax Strategies*. New York: Macmillan, 1997.

Ellentuck, Albert B. *Laventhol and Horwath Small Business Tax Planning Guide*. New York: Avon Books, 1988.

The Entrepreneur Magazine Small Business Advisor. New York: Wiley, 1995.

Guttman, George. "How Simple Can a Simple Form Be?" *Tax Notes*. November 6, 1995.

McTague, Jim. "Tax Man or Father Time: The New Forms Are Supposed to Be Friendlier, and You Get to Stay with Them Longer." *Barron's*. January 2, 1995.

Rieschick, Jacqueline. "Taxpayers Will Spend Less Time on 1997 Form 1040, IRS Predicts." *Tax Notes*. September 22, 1997.

Robertson, Cliff. *The Small Business Tax Advisor: Understanding the New Tax Law*. Blue Ridge Summit, PA: Liberty House, 1987.

"Some Steps You Can Take When the IRS Fouls Up." *Profit-Building Strategies for Business Owners*. April 1990.

SEE ALSO: Electronic Tax Filing; Tax Planning; Tax Preparation Software; Tax Withholding

TAX WITHHOLDING

Tax withholding refers to the portion of an employee's wages that are retained by an employer for remittance to the **Internal Revenue Service (IRS)**. Two main types of taxes are typically withheld—regular income taxes and Federal Insurance Contribution Act (FICA) taxes, which include contributions to federal Social Security and Medicare programs—although most states and some cities apply their own taxes as well.

Employers are required to withhold 7.65 percent of the first $62,700 of an employee's income for **FICA taxes**. Employers are also required to match that amount for every employee, so that the total FICA contribution is 15.3 percent. Self-employed persons are required to pay both the employer and employee portions of the FICA tax. The amount of regular income tax that must be withheld from an employee's paycheck depends on the individual's tax status. Ideally, the total income tax withheld should come close to equaling the employee's overall tax liability at the end of the year. Employees can adjust their income tax withholding by filing Form W-4 with their employer and designating the number of withholding allowances they wish to claim.

Tax withholding can affect entrepreneurs and small business owners in two ways. First, small business owners who have employees other than themselves and their partners must withhold payroll taxes for those employees. Second, entrepreneurs who are employees of a company and also have income from self-employment must designate the amount of wages that are withheld from their paychecks.

Withholding is usually done in standard amounts based on formulas provided by the IRS. Employees designate the number of withholding allowances they wish to claim based on their expected tax liability, which depends on their filing status, family circumstances, other sources of income, and available deductions or tax credits. It is not advisable to overpay taxes—even though the extra amount is eventually refunded to the taxpayer—because it is like giving the government an interest-free loan. At the same time, it is not advisable to underpay taxes because it may be difficult to come up with a lump-sum payment when it is due on April 15. In addition, a taxpayer who underpays his or her income taxes by more than 10 percent may face a penalty and have to pay the government interest on the funds owed.

Unfortunately, the IRS guidelines for withholding can cause problems with overpayment or underpayment of taxes even in simple cases, as Michael M. Watts and James E. Gauntt explained in an article for *National Public Accountant.* For example, a single taxpayer with no dependents and only one source of income would be instructed to claim two withholding allowances to best approximate the total tax owed. But Watts and Gauntt found that this strategy would cause the taxpayer in question to owe between $180 and $190 on April 15. Similarly, a married couple with one income would be instructed to claim three withholding allowances, but this would cause a balance due for the year of $370. The situation was even worse for married couples who both work outside the home.

In addition, many people supplement their regular employment income with interest, dividends, capital gains, rental property, or self-employment income. In many cases, this means that regular withholding from employment income—based on the IRS formulas—is not enough to cover the taxes owed. Instead, these taxpayers should try to estimate their total tax liability and adjust their withholding accordingly. ''Wage earners should monitor their expected tax liability versus withholding throughout the year and make adjustments as needed,'' David S. DeJong and Ann Gray Jakabcin wrote in *J.K. Lasser's Year Round Tax Strategies.*

Taxpayers are required to pay at least 90 percent of their total tax liability in installments prior to April 15, or they may be subject to a penalty. However, the penalty is waived for taxpayers who pay at least as much in total taxes as they had owed the previous year, or for whom the amount underpaid is less than $500. Since the IRS calculates the amount owed quarterly, a large lump-sum payment in the fourth quarter will not enable a taxpayer to escape penalties. On the other hand, a significant increase in withholding in the fourth quarter may help, because tax that is withheld by an employer is considered to be paid evenly throughout the year no matter when it was withheld. For this reason, taxpayers who see a significant underpayment problem looming should have additional taxes withheld by their employers. ''Many people don't realize that they may have as much withheld from their pay as they want, up to the full amount of their salary,'' according to DeJong and Jakabcin. To avoid a penalty, the total tax withheld must reach 90 percent of what will be owed in the current year or 100 percent of what was owed in the previous year.

This strategy can also work for a self-employed person who falls behind in his or her estimated tax payments. By having an employed spouse increase his or her withholding, the self-employed person can make up for the deficiency and avoid a penalty. The IRS has also been known to waive underpayment penalties for people in special circumstances. For example, the IRS might waive the penalty for newly self-employed taxpayers who underpay their income taxes because they are making estimated tax payments for the first time.

FURTHER READING:

Dailey, Frederick W. *Tax Savvy for Small Business*. 2nd ed. Berkeley, CA: Nolo Press, 1997.

DeJong, David S., and Ann Gray Jakabcin. *J.K. Lasser's Year-Round Tax Strategies*. New York: Macmillan, 1997.

Ellentuck, Albert B. *Laventhol and Horwath Small Business Tax Planning Guide*. New York: Avon Books, 1988.

The Entrepreneur Magazine Small Business Advisor. New York: Wiley, 1995.

Robertson, Cliff. *The Small Business Tax Advisor: Understanding the New Tax Law*. Blue Ridge Summit, PA: Liberty House, 1987.

Watts, Michael M., and James E. Gauntt. ''Beware the Withholding Tax Trap.'' *National Public Accountant*. September 1994.

''When and How to Change Withholding on Wages.'' *Taxes: The Tax Magazine*. May 1996.

Wiener, Leonard. ''Squaring Your Account with the IRS.'' *U.S. News and World Report*. August 29, 1988.

SEE ALSO: Self-Employment Contributions Act; Tax Planning; Tax Returns

TELECOMMUNICATIONS

Telecommunications describes all the various technologies that work to connect individuals and businesses with one another through the electronic transmission of impulses. As a business tool, telecommunications is every bit as essential to an enterprise as personnel, capital, and marketing. Telecommunications provides business managers with access to capital, markets, and information, enabling them to act as immediately as possible in making a decision. Telecommunications is nearly universal, allowing communication to occur instantaneously with nearly three billion people—almost half the world's population—virtually anywhere in the world.

The applications of telecommunications go far beyond mere phone conversations, as important as those may be. Various forms of data are transmitted by means of telecommunication, from simple facsimiles, to on-line computer messages, to massive information downloads that might include financial, medical, or scientific data. The proliferation of ever more efficient networks, banded together to form one gigantic network, provides users as well as service providers with tremendous economies of scale. The result is a business resource that can establish agreements and contracts, maintain good relationships, and even provide products. As a result, good management of the telecommunications system is essential.

TELECOMMUNICATIONS SYSTEMS AND COMPONENTS

In its simplest form, the telecommunications system is a network of terminal devices that are connected to switches by countless miles of wire. The terminal devices include telephones, fax machines, modems, computers, and other equipment. The switches are actually integrated systems that direct calls to another location and condition the signals for transmission. The connections between the caller, the switches, and the party called consist of copper wire, coaxial cable, fiber optic cable, and even radio waves. Each piece of terminal equipment is connected to the network with inside wire or building cable. This wire is connected to the public network at a terminal box, or ''point of presence,'' where it meets telephone company wires that lead it to a central office or end office.

Each of these connections is called a local loop, because it consists of a single pair of wires. One sends current from the central office to the terminal equipment, and the other carries it back to the central office. The circuit is broken until a telephone is lifted off its switch hook. This allows current to flow through the circuit, signaling the central office switch that a request for service has been made. The switch then provides dial tone, indicating that it is ready to receive instructions from the caller. These instructions are an address, or telephone number, which tell the switch where to send the call. If the call is to another number served by the same central office, the switch simply sets up a connection between the caller and the person being called. If the call is to a number served by another central office, the switch sends the call over an interoffice trunk to the central office serving that number, and the switch at that location makes the final connection.

If the call is going a great distance, say to another state, the central office will direct the call over another type of trunk to a tandem toll office, which will send the call over long distance lines to a counterpart, and direct the call to another local office serving the party being called. This hierarchy of switching systems is necessary to support the immense number of telephone numbers that have been assigned.

Calls fall into roughly four billing categories, based on the mileage involved. Local calls generally run up to 8 miles, while zone calls cover distances up to 15 miles. Local long distance runs up to 40 miles or so, and distances beyond that are long distance calls. All but local calls are billed according to the duration of the call.

With the divestiture of the Bell System, the Federal Communications Commission established local access transport areas, or LATAs. These LATAs comprise the areas in which the Bell companies may complete calls alone. A call to someone in another

LATA must be carried by a long distance company, or interexchange carrier (sometimes called an IXC). LATAs were created to ensure that local Bell companies do not compete in the long distance market. But in addition to the Bell companies, several hundred independent telephone companies exist that are not bound by LATA restrictions because their presence is not nearly as ubiquitous. In most cases, they have no choice but to hand the call off to an IXC or another local telephone company.

The basic telephone circuit is engineered to carry a voice grade level of bandwidth, comprising 300 to 3300 Hertz. Several conversations may be carried over the same pair of wires through various forms of multiplexing. Frequency division multiplexing literally stacks different conversations by changing their frequency, much like an FM radio signal. Filtering equipment can "tune in" to whichever conversation it is supposed to hear. Time division multiplexing gives each conversation one twenty-fourth of a given transmission period to pass over the wires. Sampling equipment can reconstruct all 24 conversations with completely adequate quality.

The wires used to transmit the calls are called facilities. An ordinary twisted wire pair can support several dozen voice grade conversations. Coaxial cable has greater bandwidth capacity, and can carry up to 10,800 different conversations. Fiber optic cable, which operates on the concept of digital light pulses rather than analog waveforms, has an even greater capacity, handling millions of signals simultaneously.

By and large, digital systems are more accurate than analog because they allow error correction. Over great distances, analog signals must be amplified. But in amplifying the conversation, intermediate transmission equipment also amplifies electrical "noise" that enters the circuit. By contrast, digital signals are regenerated, meaning that transmission equipment hears the message being sent, but rather than amplifying it, it repeats what it has heard. Included in the stream of information are signals that ensure the transmission equipment has heard correctly. If it has not, the system will ask to hear it again and make adjustments, such as changing its timing, to correct the error. The result is a transmission of nearly perfect quality. This is why a long distance call from Hong Kong to Chicago can sound as clear as a call from next door.

Digital signals also are the common language of computer equipment. As a result, in order to be carried over the telephone network, digital computer signals do not have to be translated into analog signals and then turned back into digital signals to be understood. However, most fax machines do work this way. In reading a piece of paper, the scanner in a fax machine signals where it sees black and where it does not. But in transmitting, the information is translated into a series of changes in an analog waveform. This complex signal can be sent over a voice grade line and give accurate instructions to another fax machine where to print black and where to print nothing. Newer generation fax machines use digital technology.

In handling a call, telephone switching equipment determines billing information by reading the identity of the line in use. As it switches the call to interoffice trunks, it provides that identity along with the number being dialed. This information is called automatic number identification, or ANI. ANI allows every carrier associated in completing the call to properly assign charges. Recently, telephone companies have allowed consumers to use ANI by providing a service called Caller ID, that reveals the billing number on a small display device. Caller ID enables the called party to see the number, and in some cases the billing name, of the person calling even before he or she answers.

A more ominous use of ANI is made by inbound telemarketing organizations. By calling the telemarketer's 800 number, customers can reveal their ANI code. The company's computer can be instructed to match a customer record with the incoming call so that when an attendant answers, he or she already has the customer's purchasing and credit history on a computer screen.

These types of business systems are highly complex and always involve the use of private branch exchanges (PBXs). The PBX is a miniature telephone switch owned and operated by a company for its own use. It allows calls to be completed between offices without using telephone company facilities. PBXs can span several buildings and, with connections provided by telephone companies, can even link sites in different states or countries. In some instances, a PBX will connect two different sites with a point-to-point connection that is not switched, called a dedicated circuit. These lines are constantly connected between the two points to ensure that access between the sites is always available. Dedicated circuits use telephone company facilities and are billed at a special rate. Another type of service is the T-1, a collection of 24 circuits that are dedicated for special uses, such as connecting two PBXs in different locations. The T-1 also has special cost advantages, depending on how it is used.

Integrated services digital network, or ISDN, is an application of wire facilities that uses two wire pairs to handle broadband applications, including the simultaneous transmission of voice, computer data, and visual images. Telephone companies have been slow to provide ISDN because the development of applications for the service has been slow, which in turn has been due to the limited availability of ISDN services. But ISDN is gaining acceptance and should become a popular business service early in the 21st century. New generations of digital PBXs are being designed to handle ISDN applications, such as video-conferencing and on-line computer modeling.

For all practical purposes, PBXs, like telephone switches, are computers. Their job is to administer and complete requests for connections and monitor the system for trouble. They can assign billing to specific users—ending unauthorized use of the telephone for personal calls—and can be made to restrict certain types of calls, such as long distance or 900 numbers. PBXs can also be programmed to know which long distance company offers the lowest rate for a given destination and time, and automatically switch outgoing calls to that carrier.

But despite its cost-containment features, the PBX is primarily a tool for maximizing efficiency. An office of 100 people does not need 100 telephone lines, but perhaps the 24 offered by a T-1. This is because, depending on the employees' calling characteristics, no more than 15 or 20 people will be using a phone at any one time. The PBX can be used to match requests for service with available resources, with a minimum of waste. In addition, most PBXs are endowed with diagnostic features that allow the system operator to locate wiring faults and determine the nature of terminal equipment failures.

PBXs with an automated attendant feature can handle call answering tasks, greeting the caller and requesting an extension number to complete the call. If the called party does not answer, the PBX will switch the caller to a voice mail system to leave a message for that party. Automated attendant systems also handle routine menial tasks, such as providing hours of operation, a mailing address, fax number, or other frequently requested information.

For offices with a high amount of inbound calling, such as an order processing center, the PBX may be matched with an automatic call distributor, or ACD. These devices distribute incoming sales calls among a pool of operators, and may even direct calls to those who it knows are least busy. This ensures that operators share the workload evenly.

PBXs range in size from as few as 5 lines to as many as 10,000. Usually, the larger the system, the more sophisticated its capabilities. Many offices today consist of multiple forms of terminal equipment at different workstations. The PBX is designed to handle voice communications and faxes, and in some cases data transfers between computer modems. But with the rapid decline in the cost of computers, PCs have become standard equipment on employees' desks.

Offices with as few as two or as many as several hundred computers may be networked so that each of these computers can communicate with any of the others. This allows all the computers to share processing power and storage capacity, in effect making each

another type of terminal equipment. Networks that connect these computers, called **local area networks (LANs)**, are designed to handle computerized communication functions such as electronic mail and shared databases. LANs are software-driven applications that use building wire—including twisted wire pair, coaxial, and even fiber optic lines—to connect computers on the network.

Separate LANs in different locations may be connected to each other to form wide area networks (WANs). While newer PBXs can support these connections, most systems currently in place use bridge/routers to perform switching functions, linking LANS with dedicated circuits or dialing up a connection over the public switched network.

Other types of terminal equipment, specifically designed for the mobile market, are pagers and cellular phones. Pagers are radio receivers that are programmed to display simple messages, such as the telephone number of someone trying to reach them. Cellular phones are actual telephones, connected to the network not by wires but by a radio signal. Each cellular phone operates off a host antenna located nearest to it. As the caller moves from one area, or "cell," to another, the system hands the call over to another antenna in an adjacent cell. This allows a caller to roam anywhere within a service area without losing the connection.

TELECOMMUNICATIONS TRENDS

The market for long-distance service has been highly competitive for some time now. A business may choose to route all its calls through a single long distance carrier, called a primary interexchange carrier, or PIC. All long distance calls originated by the business are automatically switched by the local telephone company to that long distance company. When AT&T divested its Bell companies in 1984, all local telephone companies were ordered to provide equal access to any long distance company registered to do business. As a result, a company could choose any PIC it wanted, be it AT&T, MCI, Sprint, WilTel, LDDS, or any of the hundreds of others that have sprung up.

That competition is now spreading to the local markets. Until the passage of the Telecommunications Act of 1996, businesses were served by a single local telephone company that was authorized to provide service in a given area. All calls between the business and other parties on the network had to be switched through this local exchange carrier, or LEC. The Telecommunications Act opened local markets to competition, although changes have taken place more slowly than experts anticipated. Local telephone companies face the loss of significant portions of market share to competing cellular telephone companies, digital wireless radio, bypass operators, and even cable television companies.

Bypass operators are the most ominous threat in the business market. They offer to establish alternate connections between a company's PBX and its long distance carrier, completely bypassing the local telephone company. In practice, companies do not transfer all their communications traffic to a bypass operator, but choose to split it between them and the local telephone company to leverage each on price and service reliability.

In the consumer market, cable companies are best poised to provide competition. They have hundreds of miles of cable running through neighborhoods, are connected to millions of households, and have armies of repair and installation workers. Perhaps most importantly, their wiring consists of coaxial cable, which can provide high-speed data and computer networking as well as television programs and telephone calls. The manner in which competition will come to the local market, and how this might affect long distance and other services, has not yet been entirely determined, pending settlement of numerous regulatory and legal questions.

Many changes are already beginning to take place, however, and some of them are expected to have positive implications for small businesses. "Already, start-up and large telecommunications carriers have emerged nationwide to challenge established phone companies," Heather Page wrote in *Entrepreneur.* "Offering all kinds of new and competitively priced services, these vendors are bringing an unprecedented array of choices to small business." For example, many carriers are creating specialized products for the small business market. "Realizing that small business is among the fastest-growing and most profitable markets, carriers large and small are designing competitively priced packages with small-business budgets, preferences, and lifestyles in mind," Page explained. For example, some service providers are bundling all of a small business's telecommunications needs in one package, while others are offering specialized plans for home-based businesses. Many telecommunications companies are also creating specialized customer service departments to assist small business customers.

It is important to note, however, that working with some upstart telecommunications companies may entail risk. If a company proves to be financially unstable, the results could be damaging to small business customers who depend on that company for a wide variety of services. In addition, many carriers are venturing into services they have never offered before, so there is a chance they might abandon these services if they are found to be unprofitable. With all the rapid changes taking place, experts recommend

that small business owners shop around for good deals on telecommunications services and avoid signing long-term contracts. "With so many new services and changes going on, it may be foolish to commit to 1998 prices for the long haul," Page noted. "What's more, with the abundance of new technologies being developed . . . you don't want to get stuck with something that might become outdated."

FURTHER READING:

Green, Harry James. *The Business One Irwin Handbook of Telecommunications.* 2nd ed. Homewood, IL: Business One Irwin, 1991.

Page, Heather. "You Make the Call: Telecommunications Deregulation Has Spawned a Host of New Companies and Services—Just Don't Get Stuck Doing a High-Wire Act." *Entrepreneur.* February 1998.

SEE ALSO: Electronic Mail; Facsimile Transmission; Wide Area Networks (WANs)

TELECOMMUTING

Telecommuting is generally defined as using technology to travel to one's job, rather than physically commuting to it. For instance, a telecommuter might log onto a home computer and dial in to his company's computer system to perform the normal tasks of his job. Telecommuting may also include those who simply work from home for a company they do not own, either on selected days or full time. Those who work from home running their own business are not telecommuters; they are more appropriately referred to as home-based business owners. Telecommuters and home-based business owners share may of the same needs, however, such as ready access to customers and reliable connectivity to the outside world. The trend toward telecommuting is expected to continue to grow in the coming years. This expectation, coupled with widespread predictions that ever greater numbers of Americans will work for companies with 200 or fewer employees, makes a telecommuting staff a distinct possibility for small business owners starting today.

According to *Nation's Business,* the number of telecommuters who will spend at least part of their week working from home will reach 11 million by the year 2000. This trend is driven by several factors. Bill Johnston of the Hudson Institute told *Success* magazine that "the skill requirements of jobs are growing far faster that the skill level of labor, so employers will be hungry for talent." This thinking is corroborated by Linda Shaw, author of *Telecommute! Go to Work without Leaving Home,* who wrote that "the labor pool of employees with specific talents will shrink, making employers more willing to make concessions to keep valued employees happy. A smaller labor pool combined with an increasing demand for highly skilled laborers has fueled employee-driven change in working environments. Scarce, highly skilled workers have begun to demand more flexible work arrangements, especially as they choose to live farther and farther from their employers.'' Shaw and other observers also note demographic changes within the American work force are a factor in the growth of telecommuting. These critics contend that new generations of workers are less willing to sacrifice time with family than their counterparts of previous eras. This desire to spend more time at home and avoid long commutes has helped telecommuting become attractive.

Secondly, and perhaps more importantly, technology has finally made working from home viable. With the advent of high speed modems, fax machines, voice mail, powerful personal computers, electronic mail and the like, workers can now perform their jobs without losing touch with employers and customers. Indeed, Link Resources indicated in 1995 that technology that makes '' virtual offices'' feasible has helped create an industry of about 31 million entrepreneurs, and that about nine million American workers (approximately 6.1 percent of the total work force) telecommuted at least one day per week that year.

ADVANTAGES OF TELECOMMUTING Both employers and employees have found telecommuting beneficial, often mutually so. Among the advantages cited by workers is the ability to avoid long, stressful commutes. Staying at home to work means the telecommuter's work day is shorter, leaving more time for pleasurable activities and more flexibility for changeable tasks like **child care** and **elder care**. Additionally, the sheer convenience of commuting across the hall rather than across town is compelling reason enough for some. Employers find these advantages work for them, too, by making it easier to keep valuable employees.

According to *Nation's Business*, other advantages include increased employee effectiveness. Initially, employers feared **productivity** downturns with home-based workers, but actually the opposite has been true (although there are exceptions, of course). This improvement in morale translates to fewer sick days and lower turnover rates for employers as well.

Another quantifiable benefit for employers is the reduced need for space. Office space and parking space requirements can be curtailed if a portion of one's staff telecommutes. Jack Nilles, president of JALA International, a Los Angeles-based management consulting firm, estimates that companies can save $11,000 per year per twice weekly telecommuter. Compared to the average cost of providing

employees with a personal computer, the investment can easily pay for itself.

Telecommuting will have far-reaching implications for all business owners in the future. As the labor pool shrinks, businesses large and small will compete for workers, many of whom will ask for the telecommuting option. Fortunately, telecommuting has advantages for everyone involved. It saves businesses money by reducing space needs, turnover, and sick time and improves employee morale by increasing personal time and flexibility.

FURTHER READING:

Ditlea, Steve. ''Home is Where the Office Is: Technology Improvements Have Made the Home Office an Effective Workplace Alternative.'' *Nation's Business*, November 1995.

Griffin, Cynthia, and Heather Page, ''Home Improvement: Savvy Strategies for Building Your Home-Based Business.'' *Entrepreneur*, September 1996.

Kugelmass, John. *Telecommuting: A Manager's Guide to Flexible Work Arrangements.* Lexington Books. 1995.

Schepp, Brad. *The Telecommuter's Handbook: How to Work for a Salary Without Ever Leaving the House.* Pharos Books, 1990.

''Seize the Future; Making Top Trends Pay Off Now.'' *Success.* March 1990.

Seymour, Jim. ''Small Office Power.'' *PC Magazine*, June 13, 1995.

Shaw, Linda. *Telecommute! Go to Work Without Leaving Home!.* John Wiley & Sons, 1996.

TELEMARKETING

Telemarketing is the process of using the telephone to generate leads, make sales, or gather marketing information. Telemarketing can be a particularly valuable tool for small businesses, in that it saves time and money as compared to **personal selling**, but offers many of the same benefits in terms of direct contact with customers. In fact, experts have estimated that closing a sale through telemarketing usually costs less than one-fifth of what it would cost to send a salesperson to make a sale in person. Though telemarketing is more expensive than **direct mail**, it tends to be more efficient in closing sales and thus provides a greater yield on the marketing dollar.

Telemarketing is especially useful when the customers for a small business's products or services are located in hard-to-reach places, or when many prospects must be contacted in order to find one interested in buying. Although some small businesses operate exclusively by telephone, telemarketing is most often used as part of an overall marketing program to tie together advertising and personal selling efforts. For example, a company might send introductory information through the mail, then follow-up with a telemarketing call to assess the prospect's interest, and finally send a salesperson to visit.

Telemarketing can be either inbound or outbound in scope. Inbound telemarketing consists of handling incoming telephone calls—often generated by broadcast advertising, direct mail, or catalogs—and taking orders for a wide range of products. Representatives working in this type of telemarketing program normally do not need as much training as outbound reps because the customer already has shown an interest by calling in.

Outbound telemarketing can be aimed directly at the end consumer—for example, a home repair business may call people in its community to search for prospects—or can be part of a business-to-business marketing program. Representatives working on this side of the industry generally require more training and product knowledge, as more actual selling is involved than with inbound operations.

Major applications of business-to-business telemarketing include selling to existing accounts, outbound new account development, inbound order processing and inquiry handling, customer service, and supporting the existing field **sales force**. With the cost of a field sales call continuing to escalate—from an average of $250 a call up to as much as $500 in high-technology fields—businesses are using telemarketing as a way to reduce the cost of selling and give more attention to marginal accounts. Telemarketing programs can be either handled in-house by a company or farmed out to service bureaus. Operations range in size from a one-person in-house staff member at a small business to a major corporation or service center that may have as many as 1,000 telephone stations.

One of the advantages telemarketing has over other direct marketing methods is that it involves human interaction. According to Robert J. McHatton in *Total Telemarketing,* ''Used correctly and by professionals, the telephone is the most cost-efficient, flexible and statistically accountable medium available. At the same time, the telephone is still very intimate and personal. It is individual to individual.''

Although telemarketing has been the center of some controversies—ranging from scams run over the phone to a number of legal issues that have been the center of debate at both the state and national levels—the industry continues to grow. In fact, the American Telemarketing Association found that spending on telemarketing activities increased from $1 billion to $60 billion between 1981 and 1991. In the early 1990s, telemarketing accounted for an estimated $435 billion in sales, and an estimated 481,000 companies sold by phone in the United States. One study projected that the telemarketing industry would account for eight million new jobs in the 1990s, al-

though some in the industry viewed that figure as optimistic.

TYPICAL TELEMARKETING USES

Although telemarketing can be used as a stand-alone operation, it often works best as part of an overall marketing effort. Companies considering the use of telemarketing have to look at such factors as: which products and services are candidates to be sold by phone; whether telemarketing can be used to increase volume through upgrading the sale; how the process can help qualify prospects, define the market, and service existing accounts; and whether telemarketing can help generate new business. Some of the roles telemarketing can be used to fulfill include: selling, generating leads, gathering information, and improving customer service.

SELLING Telemarketing can either supplement or replace face-to-face selling to existing accounts. It can complement the field sales effort by reaching new customer bases or geographic markets at relatively low cost. It can also be used to sell goods and services independently, with no field sales force in place. This method often is used for repetitive supply purchases or readily identifiable products, though it can be effectively applied to other products as well.

The inside sales force can be used to replace direct contact for marginally profitable customers. A general rule of thumb in business says that 20 percent of customers account for 80 percent of sales, so conversely the remaining 80 percent of customers generate just 20 percent of sales. But businesses must keep in mind that marginal does not necessarily mean unprofitable. And the existing customer base is perhaps the most important asset in any business, as sales increases most often come from current accounts and it generally is less costly to maintain current customers than to gain new business. Telemarketers can give these customers the attention they deserve. The reps can phone as often as needed, determine the customers' purchasing cycles, and contact them at appropriate reorder times.

In making such a consolidation between a direct and inside sales force, the company must be careful in determining which accounts should stay with field sales and which should be handled by telemarketing. Some businesses start their telemarketing operations with just small or inactive accounts, gradually increasing the size of accounts handled.

LEAD GENERATION Through telemarketing, a company can compile and update lists of customer prospect leads and then go through these lists searching for sales leads. Telemarketing can screen the leads and qualify them according to priority, passing the best leads to the field sales force for immediate action. The inside sales force also can identify the decision maker with the buying power and set up appointments for the outside sales force.

GATHERING INFORMATION Telemarketing can provide accurate information on advertising effectiveness, what customers are buying, from whom they're buying, and when they will buy again. It is also commonly used in conducting surveys.

IMPROVING CUSTOMER SERVICE Studies show it costs five times more to win over a new customer than to keep an existing one. By using telemarketing as a main facet of **customer service**, companies can go a long way toward keeping customers happy.

SOME ADVANTAGES

Telemarketing offers the quickest and most direct method of reaching customers and prospects. It also provides immediate feedback and a chance to overcome any objections as they occur. Many businesses also see it as a way to help keep costs down in an age where all companies, even the most successful, have to keep a close eye on the budget.

For example, businesses generally acknowledge that field sales calls cost at least $250 each and that outside salespeople make an average of four to six on-premise contacts a day. With time for travel and handling clerical work, one study claimed an average salesperson spends just 40 percent of his or her time selling. An outbound telemarketer, however, should make between 90 and 100 calls a day, resulting in between 35 and 50 complete product presentations—more than a traveling salesperson could make in a week. In addition, when used in conjunction with current computer technology, a telemarketing program can be analyzed in terms of costs and benefits, using quantitative data on the number of contacts, number of presentations, total sales, cost per sale, and income per sale.

ESTABLISHING A SUCCESSFUL PROGRAM

Not all telemarketing programs are successful. Improper execution, unrealistic goals over a short time period, oversimplification, and lack of top management support have caused the ultimate failure of more telephone sales programs than can be imagined. According to an article in *Sales & Marketing Management,* one of the biggest ''myths'' about telemarketing is that to get started, all you have to do is make a few calls and see how it goes. Like any marketing strategy, telemarketing takes time to plan and develop. It takes time to gain confidence in the message, to identify weak areas, and to predict bottom-line results.

Experts agree that companies must be careful in forming telemarketing goals and objectives. Some of the most important factors for success include: developing a complete marketing plan with built-in criteria for accounting and analysis; writing scripts, sales outlines, and presentations to be performed; establishing training and hiring procedures for both supervisors and sales personnel; analyzing and evaluating campaigns, personnel, and cost effectiveness; having support and commitment from management for the telemarketing's role in the overall marketing effort; establishing reachable goals; and placing a continuous emphasis on follow-up.

Some of the most common telemarketing mistakes include: not considering telemarketing as an option; not giving it a total commitment; not utilizing the proper expertise; failing to develop a proper database; improper human resource planning; lack of proper scripts and call guides; lack of quality control; and failing to understand the synergy with other **direct marketing** disciplines. As Richard L. Bencin wrote in *Strategic Telemarketing:* ''Management must understand and agree to the necessary personnel and financial resources, as well as the time required for program development and testing. Telemarketing and related direct marketing techniques can work astoundingly well. But they need a real chance to demonstrate that success. It doesn't happen over a couple of weekends.''

IN-HOUSE VS. OUTSIDE SERVICE BUREAU

When establishing a telemarketing program, a company has the option of setting up the operation in-house, or subcontracting it to an outside service bureau. Both have advantages and disadvantages. In-house programs usually are better if products require extensive technical expertise. They also can be better for firms making a long-term commitment to telemarketing. In contrast, service bureaus can help firms that need around-the-clock coverage for inbound programs, are supporting television ad campaigns, or are running a seasonal marketing program.

SERVICE BUREAUS One of the main advantages of service bureaus is that they can likely offer lower costs. By grouping programs from several different companies, service bureaus can generate sufficient volume to reduce labor and telephone costs, which make up a majority of total costs. They can also get a program started more quickly because they have experienced telephone reps on staff, along with necessary equipment.

When 24-hour coverage is needed on an inbound telemarketing program, it probably is more cost effective to go with a bureau. When setting up an outbound program, the experienced managers at a bureau can help a company avoid making mistakes and often can accurately project call volumes and sales per hour. Service bureaus also can help with testing new programs and have a greater ability to handle demand peaks.

On the downside, several client companies often must compete for a service bureau's attention, and for firms that share service with a broadcast advertiser whose response rates are underestimated, that can be a decided drawback. Stability of service bureaus has also been a problem at times.

IN-HOUSE OPERATIONS The main reason companies decide to run their own telemarketing campaign is that they can maintain total control over all facets, including hiring and firing, scripts and presentations, budgets, advertising, and compensation and incentive policies. When telemarketing programs are kept in-house, phone reps have ready access to company information, so they can confirm delivery, authorize **credit**, and suggest alternatives to out-of-stock items.

Since in-house reps are trained on individual product lines, they can handle highly technical calls no service bureau likely would attempt. Such technical expertise also helps companies maintain effective customer service programs. In addition, it is easier to gain company loyalty from actual employees than from people employed by an outside bureau, as well as to observe the program, monitor calls, and oversee the overall effort. The biggest drawback to taking a program in-house is the large capital investment needed to get a telemarketing program started. It involves hiring and training new personnel, and dealing with a process that is unfamiliar to many in business.

TECHNOLOGICAL AND HUMAN ELEMENTS

Computers have played an important role in the growth of telemarketing. Access to databases provides phone reps with account histories, stock status, order-taking formats, and other vital information. Besides analyzing data, computers are used for scheduling, scripting, and follow-ups. Computers also can be programmed to automatically dial phone numbers and connect the calls to telemarketers only if they are answered, screen out answering machines, and guide the phone rep through the telemarketing presentation.

While technology plays a vital role in keeping telemarketing cost-effective, the human element is critical in making the effort successful. Unfortunately, many firms still view telemarketing positions as clerical-level jobs staffed by people with few skills, no training, and little understanding of the product or service being sold. Often, the manager of a telemarketing operation is the only person in an organization familiar with the discipline. Some firms, though, have come to realize the importance of the telemarketers, as

the firm's image is on the line with every call. They realize the position needs skilled, trained professionals who must be fairly compensated.

For compensation, most companies use a combination of salary, commission, and/or bonuses. Studies indicate that incentives generally aid in sales success, but it is important to link the inducements to the performance desired, be it total sales, calls completed, or presentations given. Some form of quotas also are common so sales reps know what is expected of them. Firms should be cautious in ensuring quotas are reasonable and achievable. If the goals are too high, the reps will become frustrated, and conversely, if they are too low, the reps may become overconfident and complacent about growth.

Due to the stress of facing frequent rejection, telemarketing positions typically show high levels of turnover. Working shorter shifts or using computers to prescreen customers can help reduce the amount of rejection telemarketers experience. While speaking with a potential customer on the telephone, a telemarketer may benefit from the following sales techniques: be specific; control the time and pace of conversation; ask questions and listen without interrupting or rushing the customer's response; meet objections positively; and assess the sales call after closing the deal.

CONTROVERSIES AND FUTURE OUTLOOK

Unfortunately, telemarketing has been the basis for numerous scams over the years. Federal authorities estimate that con artists using the phone bilk people out of at least $1 billion annually. Yet some analysts contend that the figure may be closer to $10 billion, as many embarrassed victims shy away from filing complaints. These frauds have given the telemarketing industry much bad press.

Legislators, on both the state and federal levels, have debated a number of proposed laws that could affect telemarketing in the future. For example, some proposed laws would require registration of telephone solicitors in a state. Registration often includes bonding requirements, submission of scripts and/or names of employees, and other administrative devices designed to create a paper trail to track fraudulent marketers. Another type of proposed legislation, known as ''asterisk bills,'' would require the telephone company or state government to keep a list of people who object to receiving unsolicited phone sales calls. Marketers would be required to obtain the list and not call these people. A similar law passed in 1996 mandated that marketers remove from their calling lists the name of anyone who requests that the marketer not contact him or her again.

A number of other proposed bills seek to restrict the hours available to telemarketers, generally limiting calls to no later than nine o'clock in the evening, local time. Still other laws under discussion would prohibit the completion of some types of phone sales unless a written contract is signed and returned by the consumer. Telemarketers generally favor an alternative allowing firms that offer consumers a right of examination and promise a refund to be exempt from such legislation. Finally, many states have considered enacting legislation that would prohibit or restrict the practice of monitoring customer service employees who work over the phone. The telemarketing industry considers monitoring vital to maintaining quality control and protecting consumers, so many firms ask employees to sign a release allowing such monitoring.

Despite the potential impact of such legislation, the future continues to look bright for telemarketing, particularly in the business-to-business arena. An ongoing study by the consulting firm Arthur Andersen showed that contact with a field salesperson had dropped from the top thing companies expected from their vendors in 1970, to third by 1980, and to eighth by 1990. Conversely, contact with an inside sales person, or telemarketer, ranked fifth in 1970, fourth in 1980, and then jumped to first in 1990. The same study also projected that inside sales reps eventually would account for two-thirds of all sales representatives.

FURTHER READING:

Bencin, Richard L. *Strategic Telemarketing: How to Fit This New Medium into Your Marketing Plans.* Philadelphia, PA: Swansea Press, 1987.

Chesters, Sara. "Defusing the Demographic Time Bomb." *Direct Marketing.* May 1991, p. 35.

Eisenhart, Tom. "Telemarketing Takes Quantum Leap." *Business Marketing.* September 1993, p. 75.

Everett, Martin. "It's Jerry Hale on the Line." *Sales & Marketing Management.* December 1993, p. 75.

Gottlieb, Mag. "Telemarketing and The Law." *Direct Marketing.* February 1994, p. 22.

McHatton, Robert J. *Total Telemarketing.* Wiley, 1988.

Moretti, Peggy. "Telemarketers Serve Clients." *Business Marketing.* April 1994, p. 27.

Neff, Linda J. "Six Myths About Telemarketing." *Sales & Marketing Management.* p. 108.

Oetting, Rudy. "Telephone Marketing: Where We've Been and Where We Should Be Going." *Direct Marketing.* February 1987, p. 86.

Stern, Aimee L. "Telemarketing Polished Its Image." *Sales & Marketing Management.* June 1991, p. 107.

"Telefraud: They've Got Your Number." *Consumer Reports.* May 1987, p. 289.

SEE ALSO: Market Research; Telecommunications

TEMPORARY EMPLOYMENT SERVICES

Temporary employment services (often referred to as temporary employment agencies or firms) provide employees who possess specific skills to client companies for brief and often fixed periods of time. This arrangement can provide a client company with needed help during peak demand periods, staffing shortages, or vacations of regular employees, without requiring the time, expense, and long-term commitment of hiring a new employee. Temporary employment firms typically undertake hiring and firing decisions, issue paychecks, withhold payroll taxes, and make contributions for unemployment insurance, **workers' compensation**, and Social Security for their own employees. Client companies simply describe their staffing needs and time frame, then pay a set hourly rate to the temporary employment agency for the services of a "temp."

The use of temporary employment grew rapidly in the 1980s and 1990s during the trend toward business **downsizing** and restructuring, in which many companies reduced the size of their core work forces. Companies began to substitute temporary for permanent employees because temps receive hourly wages that average 75 percent of those paid to permanent employees, and generally receive fewer benefits. This offered businesses advantages in terms of cost savings, as well as flexibility in the face of changing business conditions. Entering the 1990s, 90 percent of U.S. businesses used some form of temporary employment. Among the areas of most rapid growth are the use of temps in the manufacturing sector—coinciding with the advent of "just-in-time" production systems—and in professional occupations, such as executives, lawyers, and engineers.

Some changes in the nature of the **work force**—such as an increase in the number of working mothers—have contributed to the popularity of temporary employment arrangements. Part-time workers who are employed as "temps" enjoy a great deal of flexibility in setting schedules and choosing assignments. For example, a mother with young children in school might opt to work fairly consistently during the school year, but not at all during the summer months. Some professional workers use temporary assignments as a way to add variety to their jobs, while recent college graduates might view temp work as a stepping stone to permanent employment. But even though temporary employment offers advantages for some workers, many others—who have been laid off or are unable to find permanent positions—work as temps out of necessity rather than preference.

In his book *Alternative Staffing Strategies,* David Nye argued that the expanded use of temporary employment was likely to persist. He wrote: "The forces that gave rise to increased use of temporary workers as an alternative to permanent employment are generally expected to stay with us, if not accelerate. These forces include the shift from production of goods to processing of information and other service industries; employer reluctance to add permanent staff in the face of possible business downturns; increased technology that both requires special expertise and facilitates its deployment; and the availability of capable individuals who either must, or prefer to, enter the temporary labor market."

CHOOSING A TEMPORARY SERVICE

Temporary employment services are a particularly attractive option for small businesses, which often need help on a limited basis but lack the resources to recruit, screen, and pay new, full-time employees. For example, an expanding company could use temporary employees to handle the extra workload until permanent needs can be assessed. Similarly, a company facing a tight deadline could employ temps to help meet it. A temporary employee could also be used as a one-day replacement for a sick regular employee.

A small business that requires the services of a temporary employment agency should consider a number of factors when choosing one. First, it is important to understand the firm's screening process for temporary employees. Though minimal screening is acceptable for low-level jobs, the process should include more sophisticated screening methods—such as personal interviews, computer testing, or psychological evaluations—for mid-level and higher positions. Second, it is helpful to gauge the experience level of the firm's placement coordinator. This person should be able to evaluate the client company's project requirements, time frame, budget, and working environment, and provide a temporary employee with the appropriate skills, availability, and personality.

Third, the small business should consider how easy and convenient it is to work with a particular temporary employment firm. Ideally, the firm should be flexible in accepting last-minute requests for temps or in changing temps in the middle of a project if the first one does not work out. Payment rates should be negotiable, based on the skill level required and the quantity of work. It is also helpful to check whether the temporary employment firm offers a guarantee, whether it is bonded for theft, and how it handles cases where the small business wishes to hire a certain temp on a permanent basis.

FURTHER READING:

"All about Temporary Workers: Filling the Gaps in the Post-Recession Workforce." *New York Times.* April 26, 1992.

Belous, Richard. *The Contingent Economy: The Growth of the Temporary, Part-Time and Subcontracted Workforce.* Washington: National Planning Association, 1989.

"Business and the Temp Temptation: A Permanent Situation." *Washington Post.* October 20, 1993.

"Business Gives in to Temptation." *U.S. News and World Report.* July 4, 1994.

Lee, Mie-Yun. "Temp Choices Put Longtime Mark on Firms." *Crain's Cleveland Business.* September 9, 1996.

Rowland, Mary. "Your Own Account; Temporary Work: The New Career." *New York Times.* September 12, 1993.

Uchitelle, Louis. "Temporary Workers Are on the Increase in Nation's Factories." *New York Times.* July 6, 1993.

SEE ALSO: Employee Hiring; Employee Screening; Flexible Work Programs

TESTING LABORATORIES

Testing laboratories are utilized by all manner of businesses to provide objective analytical data on the quality of a product or process. Some companies look to testing labs for product certification, which can be a significant marketing tool, while others use testing labs to analyze the results of employee **drug testing** procedures. Still others, meanwhile, secure the services of environmental testing laboratories to check on water and soil quality before making a major land and/or facility purchase. Whatever the reason, the services offered by testing laboratories are often of great usefulness to businesses in a wide range of industry sectors.

The number and size of testing laboratories operating in the United States and many other industrialized nations has increased significantly over the last number of years. There are myriad reasons for this growth, but observers generally point to the rise in product testing for the bulk of the increase. "It's the significant diversity in products, growth in consumer demand, and the globalization of sourcing that are providing the major thrust behind testing and certification," claimed a testing industry executive in *Appliance Manufacturer.* Experts agree that these product analysis factors have had a significant impact, but several other trends have also been cited as key to the increased reliance on external testing labs. The rising expense of product liability insurance, for instance, has led many companies to utilize testing labs to check out new or "improved" products prior to general release. "Small to mid-sized companies," wrote *Food Processing* contributor Robert Morgan, "often are looking for a lab to serve as what amounts to their quality control department." Testing laboratories have assumed this role with smaller companies in large measure because of the expense of maintaining comparable facilities in-house. Still, many big firms use them as well in order to secure independent results in areas of quality control and failure analysis.

It should be noted, however, that testing laboratories generally limit themselves to one specific testing area. For example, a company that conducts analysis of employee drug tests will rarely offer services in the realm of environmental analysis; similarly, a company that conducts tests on soil or water may not be of use to a small business owner who is seeking product quality testing services.

ADVANTAGES OF USING A TESTING LABORATORY

Business analysts, laboratory managers, and business owners—both large and small—agree that there are several significant advantages associated with utilizing the services of an independent testing lab. Morgan cited three primary reasons why businesses choose off-site independent labs: objectivity, economic considerations, and safety.

OBJECTIVITY ''The independent off-site testing laboratory focuses on its testing procedures to ensure accurate results,'' stated Morgan. '' 'Third-party testing' or 'tested by an independent laboratory' is a common advertising claim that guarantees the test results are objective and free from the influence, guidance or control of interested parties. The independent laboratory exists for only one purpose: to provide objective analytical data on the quality of a product or process. The laboratory management invests considerable time, money and effort to ensure this objectivity.'' In keeping with this agenda, testing labs usually keep copious documentation on the internal processes that they follow to ensure objectivity and accuracy. Such information, said Morgan, usually includes requirements for: training of personnel, especially analysts; maintenance and calibration of equipment; standardization and adoption of analytical methods; verification of results; sample recovery and handling procedures; quality control measurement procedures; internal and external proficiency programs and certifications; and accreditations.

ECONOMIC CONSIDERATIONS Economics play a central role in the decision of many firms—especially smaller businesses—to utilize an outside lab to conduct quality and safety tests. Indeed, small business owners engaged in establishing or fortifying their enterprises will likely have a host of things on which they will want to spend their money, from new equipment to new advertising campaigns to work force or facility expansion. These businesses may well be better off financially by securing the services of an outside entity, despite the expense involved there, rather than setting up internal testing facilities. ''Commercial independent laboratories have from hundreds of thousands to millions of dollars invested in equipment, facilities, and trained personnel,'' pointed out Morgan. Moreover, many businesses that decide to establish internal testing facilities do so without fully factoring in the ancillary **costs** associated with such activity. Morgan noted that laboratory activities are rife with such ''hidden costs,'' including corporate or upper management salaries and benefits; liability insurance; additional professional services (legal or accounting); **office supplies**, **accounts payable** salaries, **depreciation** and interest expense, and ''last but not least, lost opportunity for profits had the money been invested in profit-making activities.''

SAFETY For companies engaged in producing potentially hazardous materials, they may prefer to utilize an outside firm in testing. Morgan pointed out that in the food processing industry, for example, ''laboratories are enriching and culturing products for organisms that can cause an illness when only a very few are present.'' Since this culturing process increases the risk that the larger facility could be contaminated from testing, ''using an off-site laboratory for detection of pathogenic organisms helps eliminate the possibility of laboratory activities contaminating or adding to the bacterial load of the plant.''

CHOOSING A TESTING LABORATORY

There are many criteria to consider when selecting a testing laboratory. These criteria will be shaped to some degree by the situation of the company making the selection; for example, a smaller company that needs only limited testing done may well make its selection exclusively on the basis of price and quality. But for many companies of varying sizes, several other factors are usually considered as well.

Amazingly, some business owners show a fairly casual attitude in selecting testing laboratories, apparently reasoning that no meaningful differences exist among them. But as Raymond Luce wrote in *Business First of Buffalo*, ''it's important to take as much care in selecting a lab as you would a financial advisor—the accuracy of the results may affect decisions worth thousands or even millions of dollars.''

According to Luce, there are several basic criteria upon which testing laboratories should be selected:

- Quality and accuracy of testing
- Turnaround time
- Nature of analysis services provided
- Additional services
- Cost
- Certification/accreditation

QUALITY This is the most vital consideration in judging any testing lab. Small business owners should look for labs that maintain and adhere to documented quality control programs. "A good laboratory should be eager to discuss its quality control program and have a quality assurance manager whose sole responsibility is to implement and monitor proper use of the program," said Luce, who added that quality control programs should also: perform multi-point calibrations; analyze control standards; use analytical methods in testing; test for inadvertent skewing of results; and test for reproducible results.

TURNAROUND The amount of time necessary to get results on tests from independent labs depends to a large extent on the area in which the labs are involved. Product testing labs, for example, typically take months to complete their tests, and environmental analyses take longer than do medical or clinical tests. Still, most environmental tests can be completed in one or two weeks, and some environmental, clinical, or medical labs are able to speed up analyses in exchange for additional compensation.

NATURE OF SERVICES "A laboratory is a service business, and the level of service varies with each, so find the one that is right for your needs," stated Luce. He noted, for example, that businesses requiring environmental, clinical, or medical tests should find out about the following before committing to a testing laboratory:

- Can the laboratory supply the necessary sample collection equipment and/or guidance?

- Can the laboratory take the sample itself?

- Do the samples have to be delivered or will the lab pick them up?

- Are you given the opportunity to communicate with personnel directly involved in the testing process?

- If the laboratory can not offer a certain kind of test, will it provide good referrals to other facilities that can do so?

EXPENSE Cost is always a concern, especially for smaller businesses with more modest financial resources. But small business owners should make sure that they fully understand the extent of the testing and other services that they are receiving before signing an agreement.

CERTIFICATION "You should ask what certifications or accreditations a laboratory has," said Luce. "Certification differs from state to state. The consequences of a poor choice range from worthless data to the potential staggering costs associated with correction actions based on incorrect data."

Companies preparing a product for testing and certification should make arrangements with a reliable testing laboratory early in the process, so that all pro-cedural issues can be addressed in advance and so both sides are on the same page regarding such issues as timeline and necessary information exchange. "Communication is probably the most important aspect of dealing with an outside certification agency," stated one executive in *Appliance Manufacturer*.

FUTURE CHALLENGES

Several challenges loom for both the testing industry and those companies that utilize its services in the next few years. Likely issues that will assume increased importance include global harmonization and increased regulation.

GLOBAL HARMONIZATION IN TESTING AND CERTIFICATION The rapid expansion of the global marketplace has brought with it a corresponding expansion in the testing and certification offerings of laboratories. Most observers believe that American firms' ability to make inroads into international markets will partially depend on the pace at which the international business community is able to settle on common testing and certification standards. "In the quest to go global, harmonization of testing and certification is critical," contended *Appliance Manufacturer*. Observers point to the European Community's CE Mark as a key component of any harmonization. "[Harmonization is] becoming a major thrust mainly because testing and certification are built into the CE-Marking approach created by the Europeans," one American executive told *Appliance Manufacturer*. "The CE Mark is the EU-required safety mark that must be affixed in order for products to travel freely throughout the EU."

Most experts agree that the development of one globally accepted mark of certification will not happen anytime soon because of a significant obstacle. "Lots of people wish for [global harmonization of testing and certification], but there's a problem," said a testing industry executive in an interview with *Appliance Manufacturer*. "Marks only have significance when constructed and enforced with some legal system as designating compliance to a particular set of standards. That's why almost all marks in the world today essentially have meaning only within some 'national' boundaries, because those are the governing legal systems and still the basis of most standards. Technically, to have meaning a global mark needs a global standard and a global system for enforcement. That's why North American manufacturers and trade associations simply must become integrally involved in the harmonization process."

REGULATORY CHANGES "The product testing industry is complex," wrote Robert C. Cook in *Security Management*. "The picture will become even more complicated as additional government agencies, such as OSHA, get involved. Manufacturers must be prepared to meet these evolving standards to remain competitive and retain customer confidence in their products' performance capabilities.''

FURTHER READING:

"Circling the Globe." *Appliance Manufacturer.* August 1997.

Cook, Robert C. "A Tale of UL Testing." *Security Management.* July 1995.

Crowe, Michelle. "Testing Lab Provides Other Firms With a Competitive Edge." *The Business Journal.* February 9, 1998.

Litsikas, Mary. "Put Products Through Their Environmental Paces." *Quality.* February 1997.

Luce, Raymond. "Selecting a Testing Lab: Questions You Should Ask." *Business First of Buffalo.* April 1, 1991.

Morgan, Robert. "Off-Site Labs Right on Target: An Independent Lab May Be Better than Doing Your Own Testing." *Food Processing.* August 1995.

Munzer, Michael. "Research: Outsourcing of R&D, Testing Seen Increasing in Popularity." *American Metal Market.* May 14, 1996.

Wingo, Walter S. "A Boom Time for Product Testing." *Design News.* March 9, 1992.

Winter, Drew. "Tough Quality Demands Spur Testing Business." *Ward's Auto World.* April 1992.

SEE ALSO: Operations Management; Workplace Safety

TOLL-FREE TELEPHONE CALLS

Toll-free telephone numbers are a staple of business efforts to garner new customers and retain existing ones. By utilizing toll-free phone numbers, businesses provide clients and others with a means of communicating with them at no charge; instead, the business that maintains the toll-free line pays all costs associated with the line.

At one time in the not too distant past, toll-free telephone numbers were a novelty. Since their inception in 1967, however, our economy has become increasingly service-based, so toll-free numbers have come to be expected by customers seeking to make purchases of all kinds of goods and services. But the popularity of toll-free numbers has created a growing shortage of the numbers in recent years. Recent phenomena such as the rise in pager, modem, and cellular phone usage (many of which have 800 numbers), coupled with the ease in obtaining toll-free telephone numbers through promotional packages, 800 number portability from carrier to carrier, and the growth in use of ''vanity'' numbers (i.e., 800-FLOWERS, 800-HOLIDAY) have all drained the unassigned toll-free number pool by 40 percent over the last few years. Indeed, reports indicate that the mid-1990s saw the same number of new toll-free numbers introduced as were assigned during the first two and a half decades of toll-free usage.

In fact, *Telecommunications* reported that by the mid-1990s, Americans were making some 10 billion toll-free calls each year. Toll-free telephone numbers have become so popular that the Federal Communications Commission (FCC) was forced to issue a new prefix in anticipation of the exhaustion of all possible 800 numbers, and analysts expect that the FCC will have to introduce new toll-free prefixes over the coming years.

ADVANTAGES OF TOLL-FREE NUMBERS

Toll-free service offers several advantages to small business owners that traditional toll phone service cannot provide. First and foremost, a toll-free telephone number makes your company more accessible to employees, business associates, and customers. It enhances a business's image as a successful, professional company, and many experts contend that it shows clients that customer service is an important component of the business's operating philosophy. Additionally, toll-free service can help lower business costs if you are currently accepting collect calls or are finding it expensive to keep in touch with the home office while on the road. Lastly, toll-free service usually details incoming calls on your statement, with names and numbers allowing easier customer tracking.

GETTING A TOLL-FREE NUMBER Obtaining a toll-free number is a relatively simple process. Consumers can simply request one from their local or long-distance phone company. The cost of securing and maintaining a toll-free line will vary depending on geographic region and the amount of calls that are transmitted through the line. Some small business owners who request vanity toll-free numbers have reported tremendous success with them, but other experts counsel small business owners to avoid vanity numbers altogether, saying that customers may become frustrated by being forced to hunt and peck their way through an alphabetic toll-free number. Firms that do choose to secure a vanity number can eliminate much of this frustration by advertising both the spelled-out and numeric versions of the number.

FURTHER READING:

Gable, Robert A. "Establishing a Corporate Toll-Free Strategy." *Telecommunications.* October 1996.

Harder, Jerry. "The Brave New World of Toll-Free Service." *Business Communications Review.* February 1996.

Kirvan, Paul. "800 vs.888: Next Generation Toll-Free Service." *Communications News.* November 1995.

Toth, Victor J. "Preparing for a New Universe of Toll-Free Numbers." *Business Communications Review.* November 1995.

Turner, Dan. "Telemarketers Contend with New Number Woes." *Los Angeles Business Journal.* April 15, 1996.

Whitefield, Mimi. ''New Toll-Free Prefixes.'' *Knight-Ridder/ Tribune Business News*, March 1, 1996.

SEE ALSO: Corporate Image; Customer Retention; Customer Service

TOTAL QUALITY MANAGEMENT

Total Quality Management (TQM) refers to management methods used to enhance quality and **productivity** in organizations, particularly businesses. TQM is a comprehensive system approach that works horizontally across an organization, involving all departments and employees and extending backward and forward to include both suppliers and clients/customers.

TQM is only one of many acronyms used to label management systems that focus on quality. Other acronyms that have been used to describe similar quality management philosophies and programs include CQI (continuous quality improvement), SQC (statistical quality control), QFD (quality function deployment), QIDW (quality in daily work), TQC (total quality control), etc. Despite the ambiguity of the popularized term, ''TQM,'' that acronym is less important than the substance of the management ideology that underlies it. TQM provides a framework for implementing effective quality and productivity initiatives that can increase the profitability and competitiveness of organizations.

ORIGINS OF TQM

Although TQM techniques were adopted prior to World War II by a number of organizations, the creation of the Total Quality Management philosophy is generally attributed to Dr. W. Edwards Deming. In the late 1920s while working as a summer employee at Western Electric Company in Chicago, he found worker motivation systems to be degrading and economically unproductive; incentives were tied directly to quantity of output, and inefficient post-production inspection systems were used to find flawed goods.

Deming teamed up in the 1930s with Walter A. Shewhart, a Bell Telephone Company statistician whose work convinced Deming that statistical control techniques could be used to supplant traditional management methods. Using Shewhart's theories, Deming devised a statistically controlled management process that provided managers with a means of determining when to intervene in an industrial process and when to leave it alone. Deming got a chance to put Shewhart's statistical-quality-control techniques, as well as his own management philosophies, to the test during World War II. Government managers found that his techniques could be easily taught to engineers and workers, and then quickly implemented in overburdened war production plants. One of Deming's clients, the U.S. State Department, sent him to Japan in 1947 as part of a national effort to revitalize the war-devastated Japanese economy. It was in Japan that Deming found an enthusiastic reception for his management ideas. Deming introduced his statistical process control, or statistical quality control, programs into Japan's ailing manufacturing sector. Those techniques are credited with instilling a dedication to quality and productivity in the Japanese industrial and service sectors that allowed the country to become a dominant force in the global economy by the 1980s.

While Japan's industrial sector embarked on a quality initiative during the middle 1900s, most American companies continued to produce mass quantities of goods using traditional management techniques. America prospered as war-ravaged European countries looked to the United States for manufactured goods. In addition, a domestic population boom resulted in surging U.S. markets. But by the 1970s some American industries had come to be regarded as inferior to their Asian and European competitors. As a result of increasing economic globalization during the 1980s, made possible in part by advanced information technologies, the U.S. manufacturing sector fell prey to more competitive producers, particularly in Japan.

In response to massive market share gains achieved by Japanese companies during the late 1970s and 1980s, U.S. producers scrambled to adopt quality and productivity techniques that might restore their competitiveness. Indeed, Deming's philosophies and systems were finally recognized in the United States, and Deming himself became a highly-sought-after lecturer and author. The ''Deming Management Method'' became the model for many American corporations eager to improve. And Total Quality Management, the phrase applied to quality initiatives proffered by Deming and other management gurus, became a staple of American enterprise by the late 1980s. By the early 1990s, the U.S. manufacturing sector had achieved marked gains in quality and productivity.

TQM PRINCIPLES

Specifics related to the framework and implementation of TQM vary between different management professionals and TQM program facilitators, and the passage of time has inevitably brought changes in TQM emphases and language. But all TQM philosophies share common threads that emphasize quality, teamwork, and proactive philosophies of management and process improvement. As Howard Weiss and Mark Gershon observed in *Production and Operations Man-*

agement, "the terms quality management, **quality control**, and quality assurance often are used interchangeably. Regardless of the term used within any business, this function is directly responsible for the continual evaluation of the effectiveness of the total quality system." They go on to delineate the basic elements of total quality management as expounded by the American Society for Quality Control: 1) policy, planning, and administration; 2) product design and design change control; 3) control of purchased material; 4) production quality control; 5) user contact and field performance; 6) corrective action; 7) employee selection, training, and motivation.

For his part, Deming pointed to all of these factors as cornerstones of his total quality philosophies in his book *Out of the Crisis.* He contended that companies needed to create an overarching business environment that emphasized improvement of products and services over short-term financial goals. He argued that if such a philosophy was adhered to, various aspects of business—ranging from training to system improvement to manager-worker relationships—would become far more healthy and, ultimately, profitable. But while Deming was contemptuous of companies that based their business decisions on statistics that emphasized quantity over quality, he firmly believed that a well-conceived system of statistical process control could be an invaluable TQM tool. Only through the use of statistics, Deming argued, can managers know exactly what their problems are, learn how to fix them, and gauge the company's progress in achieving quality and organizational objectives.

MAKING TQM WORK

Joseph Jablonski, author of *Implementing TQM,* identified three characteristics necessary for TQM to succeed within an organization: participative management; continuous process improvement; and the utilization of teams. Participative management refers to the intimate involvement of all members of a company in the management process, thus de-emphasizing traditional top-down management methods. In other words, managers set policies and make key decisions only with the input and guidance of the subordinates that will have to implement and adhere to the directives. This technique improves upper management's grasp of operations and, more importantly, is an important motivator for workers who begin to feel like they have control and ownership of the process in which they participate.

Continuous process improvement, the second characteristic, entails the recognition of small, incremental gains toward the goal of total quality. Large gains are accomplished by small, sustainable improvements over a long term. This concept necessitates a long-term approach by managers and the willingness to invest in the present for benefits that manifest themselves in the future. A corollary of continuous improvement is that workers and management develop an appreciation for, and confidence in, TQM over a period of time.

Teamwork, the third necessary ingredient for the success of TQM, involves the organization of cross-functional teams within the company. This multidisciplinary team approach helps workers to share knowledge, identify problems and opportunities, derive a comprehensive understanding of their role in the overall process, and align their work goals with those of the organization.

Jablonski also identified six attributes of successful TQM programs:

- Customer focus (includes internal customers such as other departments and coworkers as well as external customers).

- Process focus.

- Prevention versus inspection (development of a process that incorporates quality during production, rather than a process that attempts to achieve quality through inspection after resources have already been consumed to produce the good or service).

- Employee empowerment and compensation.

- Fact-based decision making.

- Receptiveness to feedback.

In addition to identifying three characteristics that need to be present in an organization and six attributes of successful TQM programs, Jablonski offers a five-phase guideline for implementing total quality management: preparation, planning, assessment, implementation, and diversification. Each phase is designed to be executed as part of a long-term goal of continually increasing quality and productivity. Jablonski's approach is one of many that has been applied to achieve TQM, but contains the key elements commonly associated with other popular total quality systems.

PREPARATION During preparation, management decides whether or not to pursue a TQM program. They undergo initial training, identify needs for outside consultants, develop a specific vision and goals, draft a corporate policy, commit the necessary resources, and communicate the goals throughout the organization.

PLANNING In the planning stage, a detailed plan of implementation is drafted (including budget and schedule), the infrastructure that will support the program is established, and the resources necessary to begin the plan are earmarked and secured.

ASSESSMENT This stage emphasizes a thorough self-assessment—with input from customers/clients—of the qualities and characteristics of individuals in the company, as well as the company as a whole.

IMPLEMENTATION At this point, the organization can already begin to determine its return on its investment in TQM. It is during this phase that support personnel are chosen and trained, and managers and the work force are trained. Training entails raising workers' awareness of exactly what TQM involves and how it can help them and the company. It also explains each worker's role in the program and explains what is expected of all the workers.

DIVERSIFICATION In this stage, managers utilize their TQM experiences and successes to bring groups outside the organization (suppliers, distributors, and other companies have impact the business's overall health) into the quality process. Diversification activities include training, rewarding, supporting, and partnering with groups that are embraced by the organization's TQM initiatives.

FURTHER READING:

Deming, W. Edwards. *Out of the Crisis*. MIT Center for Advanced Engineering Study, 1982.

Hiam, Alexander. *Closing the Quality Gap: Lessons from America's Leading Companies*. Upper Saddle River, NJ: Prentice Hall, Inc., 1992.

Hunt, V. Daniel. *Quality in America: How to Implement a Competitive Quality Program*. Business One Irwin, 1992.

Jablonski, Joseph R. *Implementing TQM*. 2nd ed. Technical Management Consortium, Inc., 1992.

Roberts, Harry V., and Bernard F. Sergesketter. *Quality is Personal: A Foundation for Total Quality Management*. The Free Press, 1993.

Weiss, Howard J., and Mark E. Gershon. *Production and Operations Management* .Needham, MA: Allyn and Bacon, 1989.

SEE ALSO: Quality Circles

TRADE SHOWS

A trade show is an event where companies that are involved in a certain industry gather to exhibit their products, learn about current trends in their industry, and gain knowledge about their competitors. Trade shows provide opportunities for selling, reinforcing relationships, and launching new products. They can range in size from a small regional show with fewer than two dozen companies participating, to giant shows like the National Sporting Goods Association World Sports Expo, which draws hundreds of companies and tens of thousands of visitors.

For small companies with limited marketing budgets, trade shows can be an excellent way to attract new clients and demonstrate the qualities of your company's products. By setting specific goals, targeting clients, and establishing a sound trade show strategy, small business owners can make the most out of trade shows.

Even small businesses that do not have the cash to exhibit at a trade show can still benefit from attending shows as a visitor. By walking the floor and gathering information, a business owner can learn important new information about his or her industry and make initial contacts with key industry personnel. This can make trade shows invaluable.

EXHIBITING AT A TRADE SHOW

The first step in establishing a presence at a trade show is choosing the right show. Finding the show that best meets your needs is crucial, since exhibiting is a costly proposition. Attending the wrong show is a frustrating waste of time and money. To make sure you have the right show, ask a few questions:

- What was last year's attendance? Do not get totally caught up in how many people attended, but do get the numbers. "How many" is important, but even more important is the quality of the people who attended. Is the show visited most by serious buyers or by browsers?

- Is there demographic data available on attendees? For example, how old is the average attendee? Male or female? What is his or her income?

- Who else will be exhibiting? Will your competitors be there?

- How stable and successful is the show promoter? Are they experienced in managing a show and delivering an audience, or are they new to the game?

- What will the cost be? Expect to pay anywhere from $5 to $50 per square foot for booth space, which will probably be about 25 percent of your expenses. Other expenses include 30-35 percent for furnishings, equipment, and other exhibit expenses; 20 percent for show expenses such as utilities; 10-15 percent for transportation to the show; and about 10 percent for promotion and personnel at the booth. The typical staff at a show is four people, and their typical stay is four and a half days. If you only plan to exhibit at one show a year, renting a display is about 20 percent cheaper than buying a display. Smaller companies are having success with portable booths that come in easy-to-assemble kits.

If you have answered all of the above questions and are still not sure about a certain show, test it out first. Volunteer to lead a seminar or sponsor a show-related event without exhibiting at the show. This is an excellent way to gauge interest and the quality of the attendees.

Your should determine what type of show you should attend based on your business's needs. For instance, if you need venture capital or start up funds, then target elite executive conferences instead of huge trade shows. You are far more likely to make key industry contacts there. Or, if you have an established product with low margins, attend large national and regional shows to gain exposure to as large an audience as possible.

Finally, seriously consider whether or not you should even be exhibiting at trade shows. If you are a very small business with limited funds and a clear business model, then perhaps the best route to go is direct mail and promotions to a well-defined target audience. Or, consider open-to-the-public expos for consumers instead of industry trade shows. If you have a consumer product, this allows you to talk directly to customers and gauge their response to products and services.

STEPS TO PLANNING A SUCCESSFUL SHOW

Once a small business owner has decided to attend a show, there are steps that he or she can take to ensure that it is a successful and profitable endeavor. Of course, shows will vary a little from industry to industry, but for the most part, these guidelines can be followed no matter what field your small business is in.

SETTING TRADE SHOW GOALS First, set specific and measurable goals. Perhaps the most important first step to take is to approach the show with enthusiasm and treat it as a sales opportunity and not a money drain. To take advantage of the opportunity, set specific goals. If the purpose of the show is to gather leads, then set a number in advance that would make the show, in your mind, a success. Compare actual leads gathered to that target number to gauge whether or not the show was worthwhile.

Have a preshow meeting with all key personnel who will be a part of the show, from employees who will spend their time at the booth to the shipper who will send your products to the show and be responsible for set-up. Let each person know what is expected of them at the show, and make sure that they are up to speed on various facets of the effort, from the location of promotional brochures to products that should be highlighted. Other assignments, like observation of competitor's booths and materials or breaking down the booth at the end of the show, may be assigned to specific people.

The type of company you are operating and the financial goals you have set for the company will undoubtedly affect the goals you set for trade shows. If you are a small vendor with a new and exciting product seeking national distributors, then the goal would be to attend a national show with high visibility and attendance by all key players. If, on the other hand, you have an existing product that you want to expose to new markets, the goal would not be to attend industry shows, but instead would be to attend shows intended for people active in the new market into which you hope to break. For example, say you produce a software package that was originally designed for the publishing industry. Based on feedback, you think the software also would be useful to teachers and educators, so you would like to expand into that market. To do this, attend trade shows aimed at teachers instead of computer software industry shows. The computer show may be a waste of time unless you were looking for new investors—computer software personnel are not your new audience, teachers are.

TRADE SHOW STRATEGY The next step is to develop a unique show strategy. The worst thing you can do is copy other exhibitors. To gain attention, be different. Attend shows outside your industry to see what innovative approaches other people are taking that no one in your industry has picked up on yet. This can give you a definite edge that will bring in new customers.

Create printed materials for the show; those materials should include a product one-sheet, which is a one-page summary describing a product or service. Present your product as the solution to a problem, something the customer just has to have. In addition to printed materials, prepare a 30-second verbal presentation of the product or service. People have limited time, so this "commercial" should sell them on the product.

When setting up your booth, consider the customer first. Do not have a table, counter, or other obstruction at the front of the booth. Decorate the booth so that people must enter it to see the product or service, gather brochures, or view or participate in a demonstration. It sounds simple, but be sure to have a sign with your company's name and colors on it, and be sure your signage also indicates what you are selling. Be sure to customize the signs for each show to target the right audience. Some companies prefer to use gimmicks and games to draw people to the booth, but most often, decision-makers do not have time for this approach.

In the booth itself, try to have at least two people on duty at all times. However, do not overcrowd the booth with your personnel. This is a turn-off and will drive people away because they think the booth is too crowded already or that they will be cornered by a salesman looking for a hard sell. Do not sit in the booth. Call your visitors guests, make them feel welcome. Avoid the temptation to read their badge, which makes them feel as if you are deciding if they are worthy of attention. Do not hover over visitors. Let them browse, but be ready to answer questions. Above all else, smile.

PRESHOW MARKETING The third important step is to use preshow marketing. According to the Trade Show Bureau, 45 percent of trade show attendees are drawn to a company's exhibit as the direct result of a personal invitation, trade journal publicity, or preshow advertising. A trade show is worthless unless prospective customers visit the booth, and the best way to ensure that is by making them aware of your location on the floor.

Form a database of all past, present, and future clients. Send a letter to all of them letting them know where you will be at and tell them what products you will be exhibiting. Even if they cannot attend, it lets them know your company is active. Ask for a list of registered attendees before the show. If you get it early enough, target hot prospects and write to them in advance. Also take advantage of technology by sending faxes and/or electronic mail whenever possible. Finally, include a show announcement with every piece of mail your company sends out, such as invoices or bills.

Another important preshow step is to use press releases to alert the media about your company and its products. This can include the general media in the city where the show is being held, if your product is unique and newsworthy, or the more specialized media who specifically cover your industry. This can generate interest and excitement about your product or service.

The fourth step in preparation of a show is to train your salespeople. Trade show selling is much different than field sales. The average trade show encounter lasts only 10 or 15 minutes, so the seller must be trained to take advantage of that small window of opportunity. Treat all visitors to the booth as hot prospects until you learn otherwise. Stand in front of the booth, and be helpful and friendly. Have salespeople practice addressing questions and requests. Try to limit people to four-hour shifts in the booth to keep them fresh.

There are two types of booths you can set up at a show, with different sales techniques needed for each. One is designed to make sales at the show, so salespeople should be trained in "one interview selling"—quickly identifying a customer's needs and selling him or her your product to meet that need. At such a booth, it is common to have smaller and less expensive items on display and for sale at the show.

Larger and more expensive items can be sold at show and delivered later. All sales at the show should be at a discount over the regular list price, at least 20 percent. If sales are your goal, be prepared to deal with cash, credit cards, and checks.

The other kind of booth is more informational and less sales-oriented. It is primarily designed to meet people, to demonstrate a presence in the industry, to promote customer relations, or to generate new business leads. It can also serve as an excellent meeting point for people you are hoping will invest in your company or join you in a partnership. Since the focus of this type of booth is not sales, the booth personnel should approach their role differently than that of pure salesperson.

Make sure everyone who will be manning the booth understands the rules of etiquette at trade shows. There should be no eating or drinking in the booth, and no smoking. Do not spend time talking to the other salespeople in the booth. Assume friendly body posture and look receptive to questions. Perhaps most importantly, do not be in a hurry to get out of the show, since many people wait until the end of the show to make their purchases.

The final planning step is to make arrangements to follow up on leads after the show. According to the Trade Show Bureau, as many as 83 percent of exhibitors never follow up after a show, essentially wasting the time spent at the show. Before the show, prepare general thank-you letters and literature packets that will be sent out immediately after the show closes.

TAKING ADVANTAGE OF LEADS Small businesses that maintain a quality presence at a trade show are likely to obtain a number of business leads during the show's duration. Business experts offer a variety of tips to make sure that small business owners make the most of these opportunities:

1) Separate hot leads from those that seemed lukewarm or ambivalent and concentrate on those leads that have a better chance of a sale.

2) Use a lead sheet to collect information on prospective customers who visit the booth.

3) If applicable, send new leads back to the home office every night.

4) Make sure that salespeople follow up on a lead within two to three weeks after the show; time is often of the essence in these cases.

5) Do not gather more leads than you can follow up on. Analysts contend that many businesses owners or representatives that gather a surplus of leads at trade shows are likely to break promises made (sending literature, following up with an answer to a question,

etc.) at the show, which will reflect badly on the company.

6) Do not let new leads keep you from servicing existing customers. If you cannot handle new leads without neglecting the existing customer base, then maybe you should not be at the trade show.

ATTENDING A SHOW

Even if a small business owner considers trade shows to be an important part of his or her marketing strategy, there will be some trade shows that are not worth exhibiting at but that would still be useful to attend. For those shows, there are tips to follow to make the most out of the show.

The first step is to find a good show that is worth the time and trouble it takes to attend. Watch the local papers or industry journals for leads. The biggest shows are typically held in major metropolitan areas, so concentrate on the largest cities in your region. Once you have identified a list of potential shows, contact each and ask for information.

Once you have identified a show to attend, good planning is the key to a successful trip. Make your travel arrangements and submit the show registration far in advance. Allow at least 90 days to avoid snags and delays. Decide in advance what you are hoping to get out of the show—if it is a buying trip, know in advance what you hope to purchase.

Once you arrive at the show, obtain the list of exhibitors and sit down with it to see which companies interest you the most. Highlight those companies and check them off as you visit each one. Some people like to make one general trip around the entire exhibit floor, highlighting interesting exhibits as they go and making a second, more serious trip to those booths. Be forewarned that this approach may not be practical for the largest national trade shows, which are often spread over several floors of a huge convention center. Also, do not ignore the seminars that are offered as part of most trade shows. These may be just as useful as the booths in the exhibit hall. The seminars are educational and are also a great way to meet people.

Prepare to spend the entire day at the show. It is often helpful to take a tote bag along with supplies you might need—a notepad and pens, a personal tape recorder to record notes along the way, traveler's checks and credit cards, business credentials (a list of creditors, for example, if this is a buying trip), business cards, and personal identification. The tote bag will also hold all the product literature you gather at the show.

The final thing to remember is to wear comfortable walking shoes. This sounds like a little thing, but after eight hours on your feet walking the floor, it will seem like a very important item after all.

FURTHER READING:

Braziller, Clay. "Trade Show Tactics." *Computing Canada.* March 15, 1993.

Caffey, Andrew A. "It's Showtime." *Entrepreneur.* February 1996.

Dennis, Kathryn. "Alone in the Crowd." *Marketing Computers.* November 1996.

"For Small Firms, a Really Big Show." *Nation's Business.* November 1996.

"How to Plan a Trade Show Booth." *South Florida Business Journal.* June 27, 1997.

"How to Succeed on the Exhibit Floor." *Nation's Business.* December 1995.

Miller, Steve A. "On With the Show." *Small Business Reports.* June 1992.

Test, Alan. "Trade Show Success." *American Salesman.* September 1995.

Whittemore, Meg. "Tips for Becoming a Better Buyer." *Nation's Business.* February 1995.

SEE ALSO: Business Associations; Networking; Personal Selling

TRADEMARKS

A trademark is a word, phrase, symbol or design—or a combination of words, phrases, symbols, or designs—adopted and used by a manufacturer or merchant to identify its goods and distinguish them from those manufactured or sold by its competitors. In recent years, colors (such as John Deere green), sounds (such as the National Broadcasting Company's use of distinctive chimes), and scents have also been registered as trademarks. Service marks, meanwhile, are identical to trademarks except that they identify and distinguish the source of a *service* rather than a product. The term "trademark," however, is commonly utilized to refer to both trademarks and service marks.

Whereas exclusive rights to other items of **intellectual property** such as **copyrights** and patents eventually expire, trademark rights can last indefinitely, provided the owner of the mark continues to use it to identify its goods or services. The initial term for a federal trademark registration is ten years, but the owner has the option to renew for additional ten-year terms. The **Patent and Trademark Office (PTO)**, however, has stipulated that between the fifth and sixth years of the initial registration term, the registrant must file an affidavit confirming the need to keep the registration alive. If no affidavit is filed, the registration is canceled, and other companies can pursue the mark for their own use if they so desire.

OTHER TYPES OF TRADEMARKS

In addition to trademarks and service marks, there are two other kinds of marks that generally fit under the generic "trademark" umbrella: certification marks and collective marks.

CERTIFICATION MARK A certification mark, explained Richard Levy in his *Inventor's Desktop Companion,* "is a mark used upon or in connection with the products or services of one or more persons other than the owner of the mark to certify regional or other origin, material, mode of manufacture, quality, accuracy, or other characteristics of such goods or services, or that the work or labor on the goods or services was performed by members of a union or other organization." Examples of certification marks include the UL symbol of Underwriters Laboratories (for quality), "Made in the U.S.A." designations (for place of origin), and the Motion Picture Association of America's movie ratings (for service).

COLLECTIVE MARK Collective marks are trademarks or service marks used by members of an association, cooperative, or other group. Organizations as diverse as the National Rifle Association, the Big Ten Athletic Conference, and the Sierra Club all utilize collective marks.

TRADEMARK RIGHTS

Trademark rights to an identifying word, phrase, symbol, design, sound, or color can be secured either by actually using the mark in commerce or by registering the mark with the Trademark Office, a division of the Patent and Trademark Office (PTO). "Federal registration [with the PTO] is not required to establish rights in a mark, nor is it required to begin use of a mark," noted the PTO in its booklet, *Basic Facts About Registering a Trademark.* "However, federal registration can secure benefits beyond the rights acquired by merely using a mark. For example, the owner of a federal registration is presumed to be the owner of the mark for the goods and services specified in the registration, and to be entitled to use the mark nationwide." In addition, owners of federal registration for a trademark often enjoy an advantage if legal disputes over use of a trademark arise.

THE "RIGHT TO REGISTER" According to the Patent and Trademark Office, the ultimate right to register a trademark generally belongs to the first party—whether it is a small business or a large corporation—to use a trademark "in commerce" or file a trademark application with the PTO. ("Commerce" in this situation means commerce regulated by the U.S. Congress, i.e., interstate commerce or commerce between Amer-

ica and another nation; use of a trademark in purely local commerce within a state does not qualify as "use in commerce.")

THE "RIGHT TO USE" As the PTO itself admitted in its *Basic Facts About Registering a Trademark,* "the right to use a mark can be more complicated to determine. This is particularly true when two parties have begun use of the same or similar marks without knowledge of one another and neither has a federal registration. Only a court can render a decision about the right to use, such as issuing an injunction or awarding damages for infringement." As indicated above, possession of federal registration can be a valuable weapon if a court fight erupts over use of a disputed trademark.

TRADEMARK SEARCHES

A small business owner who has come up with a trademark that he or she wishes to use may want to conduct a trademark search before going to the trouble and expense of sending an application to the PTO. As Thomas Field remarked in *Avoiding Patent, Trademark and Copyright Problems,* "one can infringe on another's marks without copying them or even being in direct competition with their owner. All that is necessary is to use the same or a similar mark under circumstances in which consumers may be confused as to the source or sponsorship of the goods or services." A trademark search can uncover whether the mark (or a similar one) has already been registered with the PTO. But even if a search turns up nothing, that does not necessarily mean that the business owner is guaranteed untroubled use of the mark. "In the United States, it is unnecessary for a firm to do more than use a good mark to have trademark rights in its market area," explained Field. "Consequently, a search may not locate all such prior users. Second, people may be able to prevent the use of a potential mark without having used it as a mark themselves; for example, when a trademark can be associated with others in such a way that consumers might presume that some kind of relationship might exist."

APPLICATIONS FOR FEDERAL REGISTRATION

There are two primary ways in which a U.S. applicant can apply to register his or her trademark with the PTO, depending on whether or not the mark has already been used in commerce. An applicant who has already begun using the trademark in commerce may file with the PTO based on that use. This is commonly known as a "Use" application. If an applicant has not yet used the trademark in question in commerce, but has an honest intention to do so, he or she may file an "Intent-to-Use" application with the PTO. A third option, which can only be used by applicants from outside the United States, allows the applicant to file in the United States based on an application or registration made in another country.

Applications for federal registration should include the following:

- PTO Form 1478—this application, also known as "Trademark/Service Mark Application, Principal Register, with Declaration," should be carefully completed and fully signed.

- Drawing of the mark—this drawing must be included on a separate piece of paper; the specifications for the drawing—and the paper itself—are quite extensive, so make sure that the drawing adheres to all guidelines. If a separate drawing page is not included, then the application will be returned to the applicant without a filing date.

- Filing fee—For current information on the application filing fee for trademarks, call the Patent and Trademark Office ("Intent-to-Use" applications are more expensive). If the full amount of the fee is not included in the application, then the application will not be considered. Fees are not refundable, even in instances where trademark ownership applications are turned down.

- Specimens—These are actual samples of how the mark is actually used—or will be used—in commerce. "If the mark is used on goods," wrote Levy, "examples of acceptable specimens are tags or labels which are attached to the goods, containers for the goods, displays associated with the goods, or photographs of the goods showing use of the mark on the goods themselves. . . . If the mark is used for services, examples of acceptable specimens are signs, brochures about the services, advertisements for the services, business cards or stationery showing the mark in connection with the services, or photographs which show the mark as it is used either in the rendering or advertising of the services." Each application must include three specimens, but they do not necessarily have to be of three different uses.

PTO ACCEPTANCE AND REJECTION The federal registration of trademarks is governed by the Trademark Act of 1946 (and amendments thereof), the Trademark Rules, 37 C.F.R. Part 2, and the Trademark Manual of Examining Procedure. When the PTO receives an application for trademark registration, it checks the application in accordance with the above-mentioned guidelines. First, the Office reviews it to see if it meets the minimum requirements for receiv-

ing a filing date. If it meets those requirements, the PTO assigns it a serial number and send the applicant a notification of receipt. If the minimum requirements are not met, the entire thing (including the filing fee) is returned to the applicant.

Applications that pass this first stage are then reviewed by an examining attorney at the PTO, who determines if there are any reasons why the mark cannot be registered. Levy noted that a mark may be turned down for any of the following reasons:

- The mark too closely resembles a mark already registered in the PTO.

- The mark's capacity for causing confusion among relevant consumers with goods or services associated with other parties.

- The mark includes a name, portrait, or signature identifying a particular living individual except by his written consent, or the name, signature, or portrait of a deceased president of the United States during the life of his wife, except in instances where the widow has given her written consent to such use.

- The mark includes the flag or coat of arms or other insignia of the United States or any of its states or municipalities, or of any foreign nation, or any simulation thereof.

- The mark has immoral, deceptive, or scandalous connotations.

- The mark disparages or falsely suggests a connection with persons (living or dead), institutions, beliefs, or national symbols.

- The mark brings such persons, institutions, beliefs, or national symbols into contempt or disrepute.

Objections raised during this stage of the review are sent along to the applicant. Remedies that might make the mark acceptable are sometimes suggested in these letters as well. The application will be deemed abandoned if the applicant does not respond within six months of the mailing date of that letter. In cases in which the applicant's response does not sway the PTO examiner to give approval for the mark, the applicant can turn to the PTO's Trademark Trial and Appeal Board.

"If there are no objections, or if you [the applicant] overcome all objections, the examining attorney will approve the mark for publication in the *Official Gazette,* a weekly publication of the PTO," wrote Levy. "Any party who believes it may be damaged by the registration of the mark has 30 days from the date of publication to file an opposition to registration. An opposition is similar to a formal proceeding in the federal courts, but is held before the Trademark Trial and Appeal Board. If no opposition is filed, the application enters the next stage of the registration process.''

If the application is approved and no opposition is filed, applicants may have a little or a lot to do, depending on their situation. For applicants who filed ''Use'' applications, most of the work is over. The PTO will register the trademark and issue a registration certificate a few months after the date the mark was published in the *Gazette*. Applicants who filed based on their intent to use the trademark down the line, though, need to attend to several matters to make sure that their rights do not slip away. In situations where it has approved an ''Intent-to-Use'' application, the PTO issues a Notice of Allowance approximately 12 weeks after the mark was published. After receiving the Notice, the applicant has six months to either use the trademark in commerce and submit documentation of that use or request a six-month extension. If the documentation of use—called the Statement of Use—is filed and approved, then the PTO will issue the registration certificate for the trademark.

Even if the PTO grants an applicant a trademark registration, however, business experts warn that such registration only provides protection to the owner in the United States and its territories. ''If the owner of a mark wishes to protect a mark in other countries, the owner must seek protection in each country separately under the relevant laws,'' warned the PTO in its *Basic Facts About Registering a Trademark*. ''The PTO cannot provide information or advice concerning protection in other countries.''

FURTHER READING:

Basic Facts About Registering a Trademark. Arlington, VA: U.S. Patent and Trademark Office, 1995.

Field, Thomas. *Avoiding Patent, Trademark and Copyright Problems.* Washington: Small Business Administration, 1992.

Levy, Richard C. *The Inventor's Desktop Companion.* Detroit, MI: Visible Ink, 1995.

Schoell, William F., and Joseph P. Guiltinan. *Marketing: Contemporary Concepts and Practices.* 5th ed. Nedham, MA: Allyn and Bacon, 1992.

SEE ALSO: Inventions and Patents

TRAINING AND DEVELOPMENT

Training and development describes the formal, ongoing efforts of organizations to improve the performance and self-fulfillment of their employees through a variety of methods and programs. In the modern workplace, these efforts have taken on a broad range of applications—from instruction in highly specific job skills to long-term professional development. In recent years, training and development has emerged as a formal business function, an integral element of strategy, and a recognized profession with distinct theories and methodologies. More and more companies of all sizes have embraced training and development as a means of promoting employee growth and acquiring a highly skilled work force. In fact, the quality of employees, and the continual improvement of their skills and productivity through training, are vital factors in ensuring the long-term success and profitability of small businesses.

For the most part, the terms ''training'' and ''development'' are used together to describe the overall improvement and education of an organization's employees. However, while closely related, there are important differences between the terms that center around the scope of the application. In general, training programs have very specific and quantifiable goals, like operating a particular piece of machinery, understanding a specific process, or performing certain procedures with great precision. In contrast, developmental programs concentrate on broader skills that are applicable to a wider variety of situations, such as decision making, leadership skills, and goal setting.

TRAINING IN SMALL BUSINESSES

Implementation of formal training and development programs offers several potential advantages to small businesses. For example, training helps companies to create pools of qualified replacements for employees who may leave or be promoted to positions of greater responsibility. It also helps ensure that companies will have the human resources needed to support business growth and expansion. Furthermore, training can enable a small business to make use of advanced technology and to adapt to a rapidly changing competitive environment. Finally, training can improve employees' efficiency and motivation, leading to gains in both productivity and job satisfaction. According to the U.S. Small Business Administration publication *Human Resources Management*, small businesses stand to receive a variety of benefits from effective training and development of employees, including reduced turnover, a decreased need for supervision, increased efficiency, and improved employee morale. All of these benefits are likely to contribute directly to a small business's bottom line.

Effective training and development begins with the overall strategy and objectives of the small business. The entire training process should be planned in advance with specific company goals in mind. In developing a training strategy, it may be helpful to assess the company's customers and competitors, strengths and weaknesses, and any relevant industry or societal trends. The next step is to use this information to identify where training is needed by the organization as a whole or by individual employees. It may also be helpful to conduct an internal audit to find general areas that might benefit from training, or to complete a skills inventory to determine the types of skills employees possess and the types they may need in the future. Each different job within the company should be broken down on a task-by-task basis in order to help determine the content of the training program.

The training program should relate not only to the specific needs identified through the company and individual assessments, but also to the overall goals of the company. The objectives of the training should be clearly outlined, specifying what behaviors or skills will be affected and how they relate to the strategic mission of the company. In addition, the objectives should include several intermediate steps or milestones in order to motivate the trainees and allow the company to evaluate their progress. Since training employees is expensive, a small business needs to give careful consideration to the question of which employees to train. This decision should be based on the ability of the employee to learn the material and the likelihood that they will be motivated by the training experience. If the chosen employees fail to benefit from the training program or leave the company soon after receiving training, the small business has wasted its limited training funds.

The design of training programs is the core activity of the training and development function. In recent years, the development of training programs has evolved into a profession which utilizes systematic models, methods, and processes of instructional systems design (ISD). ISD describes the systematic design and development of instructional methods and materials to facilitate the process of training and development and ensure that training programs are necessary, valid, and effective. The instructional design process includes the collection of data on the tasks or skills to be learned or improved, the analysis of these skills and tasks, the development of methods and materials, delivery of the program, and finally, the evaluation of the training's effectiveness.

Small businesses tend to use two general types of training methods, on-the-job techniques and off-the-job techniques. On-the-job training describes a variety of methods that are applied while employees are actually performing their jobs. These methods might include orientations, coaching, apprenticeships, internships, job instruction training, and job rotation. The main advantages of on-the-job techniques is that they are highly practical, and employees do not lose working time while they are learning. Off-the-job training, on the other hand, describes a number of training methods that are delivered to employees outside of the regular work environment, though often during working hours. These techniques might include lectures, conferences, case studies, role playing, simulations, film or television presentations, programmed instruction, or special study.

On-the-job training tends to be the responsibility of supervisors, human resources professionals, or more experienced co-workers. Consequently, it is important for small businesses to educate their seasoned employees in training techniques. In contrast, off-the-job tends to be handled by outside instructors or sources, such as consultants, chambers of commerce, technical and vocational schools, or continuing education programs. Although outside sources are usually better informed as to effective training techniques than company supervisors, they may have a limited knowledge of the company's products and competitive situation. In addition, the cost of some off-the-job training methods may be too high for many small businesses to afford.

Actual administration of the training program involves choosing an appropriate location, providing necessary equipment, and arranging a convenient time. Such operational details, while seemingly minor components of an overall training effort, can have a significant effect on the success of a program. In addition, the training program should be evaluated at regular intervals while it is going on. Employees' skills should be compared to the predetermined goals or milestones of the training program, and any necessary adjustments should be made immediately. This ongoing evaluation process will help ensure that the training program successfully meets its expectations.

COMMON TRAINING METHODS

While new techniques are always under development, several common training methods have proven highly effective and should be discussed in detail. Each method has both benefits and drawbacks, but it is important to note that a good trainer can combine several different methods to produce one effective training program.

ORIENTATIONS Orientation training is vital in ensuring the success of new employees. Whether the training is conducted through an employee handbook, a lecture, or a one-on-one meeting with a supervisor, newcomers should receive information on the company's history and strategic position, the key people at the company, the structure of their department and how it contributes to the mission of the company, and the company's employment policies, rules, and regulations.

LECTURES A verbal method of presenting information, lectures are particularly useful in situations when the goal is to impart the same information to a large number of people at one time. Since they eliminate the need for individual training, lectures are among the most cost-effective training methods. But the lecture method does have some drawbacks. Since lectures primarily involve one-way communication, they may not provide the most interesting or effective training. In addition, it may be difficult for the trainer to gauge the level of understanding of the material within a large group.

CASE STUDY The case study method is a non-directed method of study whereby students are provided with practical case reports to analyze. The case report includes a thorough description of a simulated or real-life situation. By analyzing the problems presented in the case report and developing possible solutions, students can be encouraged to think independently as opposed to relying upon the direction of an instructor. Independent case analysis can be supplemented with open discussion with a group. The main benefit of the case method is its use of real-life situations. The multiplicity of problems and possible solutions provide the student with a practical learning experience rather than a collection of abstract knowledge and theories that may be difficult to apply to practical situations.

ROLE PLAYING In role playing, students assume a role outside of themselves and play out that role within a group. A facilitator creates a scenario that is to be acted out by the participants under the guidance of the facilitator. While the situation might be contrived, the interpersonal relations are genuine. Furthermore, participants receive immediate feedback from the facilitator and the scenario itself, allowing better understanding of their own behavior. This training method is cost effective and is often applied to marketing and management training.

SIMULATIONS Games and simulations are structured competitions and operational models that emulate real-life scenarios. The benefits of games and simulations include the improvement of problem-solving and decision-making skills, a greater understanding of the organizational whole, the ability to study actual problems, and the power to capture the student's interest.

COMPUTER-BASED TRAINING Computer-based training (CBT) involves the use of computers and computer-based instructional materials as the primary medium of instruction. Computer-based training programs are designed to structure and present instructional materials and to facilitate the learning process for the student. A main benefit of CBT is that it allows employees to learn at their own pace, during convenient times. Primary uses of CBT include instruction in computer hardware, software, and operational equipment. The last is of particular importance because CBT can provide the student with a simulated experience of operating a particular piece of equipment or machinery while eliminating the risk of dam-

age to costly equipment or the trainee. At the same time, the actual equipment's operational use is maximized because it need not be utilized as a training tool. The use of computer-based training enables a small business to reduce training costs while improving the effectiveness of the training. Costs are reduced through a reduction in travel, training time, amount of operational hardware, equipment damage, and instructors. Effectiveness is improved through standardization and individualization. In recent years, videodisc and CD-ROM have been successfully integrated into PC-platforms, increasing the flexibility and possibilities of CBT.

SELF-INSTRUCTION Self-instruction describes a training method in which the students assume primary responsibility for their own learning. Unlike instructor- or facilitator-led instruction, students retain a greater degree of control regarding topics, the sequence of learning, and the pace of learning. Depending on the structure of the instructional materials, students can achieve a higher degree of customized learning. Forms of self-instruction include programmed learning, individualized instruction, personalized systems of instruction, learner-controlled instruction, and correspondence study. Benefits include a strong support system, immediate feedback, and systematization.

AUDIOVISUAL TRAINING Audiovisual training methods include television, films, and videotapes. Like case studies, role playing, and simulations, they can be used to expose employees to ''real world'' situations in a time- and cost-effective manner. The main drawback of audiovisual training methods is that they are costly to customize for a particular audience, and they do not allow participants to ask questions or interact during the presentation.

TEAM-BUILDING EXERCISES Team building is the active creation and maintenance of effective work groups with similar goals and objectives. Not to be confused with the informal, ad-hoc formation and use of teams in the workplace, team building is a formal process of building work teams and formulating their objectives and goals, usually facilitated by a third-party consultant. Team building is commonly initiated to combat ineffectual group functioning, which may negatively affect group dynamics, labor-management relations, quality, or productivity. By recognizing the problems and difficulties associated with the creation and development of work teams, team building provides a structured, guided process whose benefits include a greater ability to manage complex projects and processes, flexibility to respond to changing situations, and greater motivation among team members. Team building exercises may include a broad range of different training methods, from outdoor immersion exercises to brainstorming sessions. The main drawback to formal team building is the cost of using outside experts and taking a group of people away from their day-to-day work during the training program.

APPRENTICESHIPS AND INTERNSHIPS Apprenticeship programs and **internships** are forms of on-the-job training in which the trainee works with a more experienced employee for a period of time, learning a group of related skills that will eventually qualify the trainee to perform a new job or function. Apprenticeships are often used in production-oriented positions. Internships are a form of apprenticeship which combine on-the-job training under a more experienced employee with classroom learning. Internships are most commonly used to train prospective managers.

JOB ROTATION Another type of experience-based training is job rotation, in which employees move through a series of jobs in order to gain a broad understanding of the requirements of each. Job rotation may be particularly useful in small businesses, which generally require employees to perform a variety of jobs on a daily basis.

APPLICATIONS OF TRAINING PROGRAMS

While the applications of training and development are as varied as the functions and skills required by an organization, several common training applications can be distinguished, including technical training, sales training, clerical training, computer training, communications training, organizational development, career development, supervisory development, and management development.

Technical training describes a broad range of training programs varying greatly in application and difficulty. Technical training utilizes common training methods for instruction of technical concepts, factual information, and procedures, as well as technical processes and principles.

Sales training concentrates on the education and training of individuals to communicate with customers in a persuasive manner. Sales training can enhance the employee's knowledge of the organization's products, improve his or her selling skills, instill positive attitudes, and increase the employee's self-confidence. Employees are taught to distinguish the needs and wants of the customer, and to persuasively communicate the message that the company's products or services can effectively satisfy them.

Clerical training concentrates on the training of clerical and administrative support staffs, which have taken on an expanded role in recent years. With the increasing reliance on computers and computer applications, clerical training must be careful to distinguish basic skills from the ever-changing computer applications used to support these skills. To associate basic clerical skills with a particular system may limit the employees' ability to learn new systems. Clerical training increasingly must instill improved decision-making skills in these employees as they take on expanded roles and responsibilities.

Computer training teaches the effective use of the computer and its software applications, and often must address the basic fear of technology that most employees face, and identify and minimize any resistance to change that might emerge. Furthermore, computer training must anticipate and overcome the long and steep learning curves that many employees will experience. To do so, such training is usually offered in longer, uninterrupted modules to allow for greater concentration, and structured training is supplemented by hands-on practice.

Communications training concentrates on the improvement of interpersonal communication skills, including writing, oral presentation, listening, and reading. In order to be successful, any form of communications training should be focused on the basic improvement of skills and not just on stylistic considerations. Furthermore, the training should serve to build on present skills rather than rebuilding from the ground up. Communications training can be taught separately or can be effectively integrated into other types of training, since it is fundamentally related to other disciplines.

Organizational development (OD) refers to the use of knowledge and techniques from the behavioral sciences to analyze an existing organizational structure and implement changes in order to improve organizational effectiveness. OD is useful in such varied areas as the alignment of employee goals with those of the organization, communications, team functioning, and decision making. In short, it is a development process with an organizational focus to achieve the same goals as other training and development activities aimed at individuals. OD practitioners commonly practice what has been termed ''action research'' to effect an orderly change that has been carefully planned to minimize the occurrence of unpredicted or unforeseen events. Action research refers to a systematic analysis of an organization to acquire a better understanding of the nature of problems and forces within it.

Career development refers to the formal progression of an employee's position within an organization by providing a long-term development strategy and designing training programs to achieve this strategy as well as individual goals. Career development represents a growing concern for employee welfare and their long-term needs. For the individual, it involves the description of career goals, the assessment of necessary action, and the choice and implementation of necessary steps. For the organization, career development represents the systematic development and improvement of employees. To remain effective, career development programs must allow individuals to articulate their desires. At the same time, the organization should strive to meet those stated needs by consistently following through on commitments and meeting the employee expectations raised by the program.

Management and supervisory development involves the training of managers and supervisors in basic leadership skills, enabling them to effectively function in their positions. For managers this typically involves the ability to balance the effective management of their employee resources with the strategies and goals of the organization. Managers learn to develop their employees effectively by helping employees learn and change, as well as by identifying and preparing them for future responsibilities. Management development may also include programs to teach decision-making skills, creating and managing successful work teams, allocating resources effectively, budgeting, communication skills, business planning, and goal setting.

Supervisory development addresses the unique situation of the supervisor as a link between the organization's senior management and work force. It must focus on enabling supervisors to deal with their responsibilities to both labor and management, as well as co-workers and staff departments. Important considerations include the development of personal and interpersonal skills, understanding of the management process, and productivity and quality improvement.

THE FUTURE OF TRAINING

Social, political, economic, and demographic conditions have a profound impact on the direction of training and development. The reduced number of youths entering the work force in the late 1990s, for instance, is predicted to decrease the applicant pool for entry-level positions and place heavier demands on training organizations. At the same time, the aging of the work force will require training organizations to ensure that these employees are continually developing new skills to keep up with the ever increasing pace of technology. In addition, the transformation of the American economy from a manufacturing to a service base creates different training needs. The transition to a global economy will also result in an increased need for cross-cultural training. In short, the training and development functions in small businesses will be facing increasing demands that will dramatically affect the type and scope of training needed.

FURTHER READING:

Craig, Robert L., ed. *Training and Development Handbook: A Guide to Human Resource Development*. New York: McGraw-Hill, 1987.

Fallon, William K., ed. *AMA Management Handbook*. New York: Amacom, 1983.

Goldstein, Irwin L., ed. *Training and Development in Organizations*. San Francisco, CA: Jossey-Bass, 1989.

Roberts, Gary, Gary Seldon, and Carlotta Roberts. *Human Resources Management*. Washington: U.S. Small Business Administration.

TRANSPORTATION

Transportation concerns the movement of products from a source—such as a plant, factory, or workshop—to a destination—such as a warehouse, customer, or retail store. Transportation may take place via air, water, rail, road, pipeline, or cable routes, using planes, boats, trains, trucks, and telecommunications equipment as the means of transportation. The goal for any business owner is to minimize transportation costs while also meeting demand for products. Transportation costs generally depend upon the distance between the source and the destination, the means of transportation chosen, and the size and quantity of the product to be shipped. In many cases, there are several sources and many destinations for the same product, which adds a significant level of complexity to the problem of minimizing transportation costs.

The decisions a business owner must make regarding transportation of products are closely related to a number of other distribution issues. For example, the accessibility of suitable means of transportation factors into decisions regarding where best to locate a business or facility. The means of transportation chosen will also affect decisions regarding the form of packing used for products and the size or frequency of shipments made. Although transportation costs may be reduced by sending larger shipments less frequently, it is also necessary to consider the costs of holding extra **inventory**. The interrelationship of these decisions means that successful planning and scheduling can help business owners to save on transportation costs.

BASIC MEANS OF TRANSPORTATION

There are seven basic means of transporting products. Five of these are means of **physical distribution**, meaning that they can be used for items that have bulk or weight. Such materials can be transported via plane, train, truck, boat, or pump. Many **distribution networks** consist of a combination of these means of transportation. For example, oil may be pumped through a pipeline to a waiting ship for transport to a refinery, and from there transferred to trucks that transport gasoline to retailers or heating oil to consumers. There are also two additional means of information distribution, which encompasses the transportation of data via telecommunications or satellites and relays. Though it may seem strange to classify information distribution under the category of transportation, in reality it is accounting for a greater percentage of the value of shipments all the time.

Each of the means of physical distribution has both advantages and disadvantages. For example, air transportation offers the advantage of speed and can be used for long-distance transport. However, air is also the most expensive means of transportation, so it is generally used only for smaller items of relatively high value—such as electronic equipment—and items for which the speed of arrival is important—such as perishable goods. Another disadvantage associated with air transportation is its lack of accessibility; since a plane cannot ordinarily be pulled up to a loading dock, it is necessary to bring products to and from the airport by truck.

Rail transportation is also used for long-distance shipping and is much less expensive than air transportation. It is about the same speed as trucks over long distances and faster than boats. Trains are ideally suited for shipping bulk products, and can be adapted to meet specific product needs through the use of specialized cars—i.e., tankers for liquids, refrigerated cars for perishables, and cars fitted with ramps for automobiles. Although accessibility is limited, it is possible to avoid this problem by ''piggybacking'' loaded trucks onto trains. Road transportation is less costly than air but more costly than rail and water. Because they are the most accessible means of transportation and the fastest over short distances, trucks are the dominant means of shipping in the United States.

Water transportation is the least expensive means, but also the slowest. It is generally used to transport heavy products over long distances when speed is not an issue. Although accessibility is problem with ships—because they are necessarily limited to coastal area or major inland waterways—piggybacking is possible using either trucks or rail cars. The main advantage of water transportation is that it can move products all over the world. Pipeline transportation is even less expensive than water, but it is severely limited as to speed, accessibility, and the types of materials that can be transported. The main advantage of pipelines is that they can provide a continuous flow of needed products, such as oil.

FURTHER READING:

Bates, Steve. ''The Dog Ate My Shipment!'' *Nation's Business.* December 1997.

Weiss, Howard J., and Mark E. Gershon. *Production and Operations Management.* Boston, MA: Allyn and Bacon, 1989.

SEE ALSO: Business Site Selection; Distribution Channels; Transportation of Exports

TRANSPORTATION OF EXPORTS

An important part of the international trade process for exporters of any size is ensuring that the goods that are shipped reach their destination intact and in timely fashion. Appropriate packaging and proper documentation are essential in meeting these goals.

INTERNATIONAL FREIGHT TRANSPORTION OPTIONS

The exporter's options for transporting goods are dictated in large measure by their final destination. American exporters preparing goods for shipment to Mexico or Canada, for instance, will often make arrangements to transport their merchandise over land routes via trucks, while exports that are headed for destinations unreachable via land routes have to be transported by air or water.

Exporters who are faced with the choice of air or water modes of transport need to be cognizant of the advantages and disadvantages of those two options. While shipping by water is generally less expensive than transporting by air, the difference in cost is narrowed somewhat by ancillary costs associated with sea transport, such as the cost of transporting goods to the dock. Merchandise shipped over water also takes longer to reach its ultimate destination, and since some export transactions do not require the importer to pay until they are in possession of the goods, exporters in immediate need of cash infusions will need to weigh this factor carefully.

Of course, the sheer size of some export shipments render air transportation impractical.

EXPORT PACKAGING

Consultants to companies who engage in exporting note that the merchandise they ship will generally be subject to more handling and potentially damaging forces during transport than will goods headed for domestic destinations. Goods shipped over the ocean, for instance, will be far more exposed to moisture than will merchandise that is merely carted into another state via the interstate highway.

Intelligent **packaging**, then, is a key component of the exporting process. Ideally, exporters should use a packaging approach that minimizes the cost of transportation while simultaneously ensuring that the goods reach their destination intact. Many small exporting companies that do not have the financial or operating resources to take care of packaging themselves utilize firms that specialize in providing such services.

LABELING AND MARKING OF EXPORT MERCHANDISE Exporting firms need to keep abreast of labeling and marking requirements on goods intended for international destinations. Pharmaceutical products, for instance, require special labeling that varies from country to country. In addition, many countries enforce regulations requiring that imported goods bear the name of the country of origin on the outside of their packaging. Packaging containing merchandise intended for foreign ports also typically includes markings indicating the height and weight of the packages, as well as any additional handling instructions.

NECESSARY EXPORT DOCUMENTS

The documentation required for international trade is quite extensive (and potentially confusing), but exporters need to make certain that they have their papers in proper order if they wish to avoid potentially damaging delays in shipment. Documents required for the export of goods include the following:

- Export License—While most merchandise can be shipped to overseas customers without benefit of an actual license, some goods are subject to additional regulations and require an Individually Validated Export License (IVL). ''Should your particular export be subject to export controls,'' explained the Small Business Administration, ''then a 'validated' license must be obtained. In general, your export would require a 'validated' license if export of the goods would: threaten United States national security; affect certain foreign policies of the United States; or create short supply in domestic markets.''

- Shipper's Export Declaration (SED)—This important document is required for mail shipments of $500 or more, all shipments of more than $2500 value, and any shipment that is covered by an IVL. SEDs are utilized by the U.S. Bureau of the Census to track export trends in the United States.

- Commercial Invoice—The commercial invoice is used by both exporters and importers. Exporters use the document as proof of ownership and an aid in securing payment for goods delivered, while importers use it to confirm that the merchandise they have received matches what they ordered. Commercial invoices are also used by Customs officers to figure the correct duty on the goods being imported, so U.S. exporters generally provide translated copies of the invoice when shipping goods to destinations for which English is not the primary language spoken.

- Consular Invoice—This kind of invoice serves the same general purpose as the commercial invoice, but it must be worded in the language of the nation for which the goods are intended. Consular invoices are so named because they can be obtained from the destination country's consulate.

- Bill of Lading—This document serves as evidence of ownership of the goods being exported, and also specifies the responsibilities of the transporting company. Two types of ocean bills of lading can be used. The first, known as the straight bill of lading, provides for delivery of merchandise *only* to the person named in the bill of lading. Under the second bill of lading option, called the shipper's order, goods can be delivered not only to the person named in the bill but also to other designated people. Under the latter option, financing institutions are empowered to take possession of the goods being exported if the buyer defaults; they retain title on the merchandise until all payments and conditions of sale have been fulfilled. For exports that are transported by air, documents known as air waybills serve the same general purpose.

- Certificate of Origin—Some countries require shipments of goods from foreign ports to include certificates that indicate where the merchandise originated. In instances wherein the importing country has trade agreements in place with the country that is doing the exporting, lower tariffs on those goods can sometimes be imposed.

- Export Packing List—This highly involved document provides a detailed description of the contents being shipped. According to the SBA, the export packing list items the material in each individual package, providing information such as individual net, legal, tare and gross weights and measurements for each package. This data is typically measured by moth metric and U.S. systems of measurement. Export packing lists are used by the shipper (or the freight forwarder) to confirm the shipment's contents and figure the total weight and volume of the shipment.

- Inspection Certificate—This documentation is bestowed by independent inspection firms, whose services are required when foreign purchasers ask for independent corroboration that the goods meet agreed-upon specifications.

- Insurance Certificate—Some international transactions require the exporting firm to provide insurance on the shipment. The insurance certificate describes the type and amount of merchandise contained in the shipment, and confirms that the shipment has been insured.

- Inland Bill of Lading—These documents—known as "waybills on rail" in the railroad industry and "pro-forma" bills within the trucking industry—provide information on the inland transportation of goods and the port that will eventually send the exporter's goods on their way.

- Dock Receipt—This paper, which in effect is the international carrier's acknowledgement that goods have been received, serves to transfer responsibility for those goods from the domestic to the international carrier.

- Shipper's Instructions—This document serves to provide transporters of exports with any other information necessary to ensure the effective move of goods to their final destination.

THE FREIGHT FORWARDER

International freight forwarders are important figures in the exporting process for American firms. Knowledgeable about all aspects of international trade—including international and U.S. regulations, import and export rules, and shipping options—freight forwarders serve as agents for exporting businesses, overseeing the transportation of their cargo to overseas destinations.

As the Small Business Administration noted in its *Breaking into the Trade Game,* many freight forwarders provide services at the very beginning of the exporting process by advising exporting firms about freight costs, port charges, insurance costs, consular fees, handling fees, and other expenses. They can also advise small exporters about packaging options, and in some cases can make arrangements to have goods containerized or packed at the port. Freight forwarders also have the power to reserve space on freighters and other ocean vessels in accordance with client specifications.

The SBA also notes that, in order to represent their exporter clients as effectively as possible, freight forwarders can review the wide array of documentation necessary for international business transactions, including letters of credit, commercial invoices, and packing lists. Exporters can also ask freight forwarders to prepare necessary documentation for the exporting process, including bills of lading. Once this documentation has been taken care of, they can be forwarded as needed. Finally, the exporter can also ask the freight forwarder to make arrangements with the customs broker to ensure that their merchandise is in compliance with customs export documentation regulations. Given the wide array of services that they provide, and the importance of those services to the exporting process, trade experts view freight forwarders as an extremely valuable resource for small exporting firms. "The cost for their services," contended the Small Business Administration (SBA), "is a legitimate export cost that should be figured into the price charged to the customer."

FURTHER READING:

Branch, Alan E. *Elements of Export Marketing and Management.* 2d ed. London: Chapman and Hall, 1990.

Breaking into the Trade Game: A Small Business Guide. Washington: U.S. Small Business Administration, n.a.

Sandhusen, Richard L. *Global Marketing.* Barron's Educational Series, 1994.

Sletten, Eric. *How to Succeed in Exporting and Doing Business Internationally.* Wiley, 1994.

SEE ALSO: Exporting; Transportation

TUITION ASSISTANCE PROGRAMS

Tuition assistance programs are a type of **employee benefit** in which an employer reimburses employees for the costs associated with continuing education, such as tuition, fees, and books. Some progressive companies pay for an unlimited number of courses that may or may not be directly related to an employee's current job. Such companies reason that today's rapidly changing work environment requires employees to possess a wide variety of skills, and that education provides a way for them to improve their skills and adapt to the new realities of the business world. Other companies adopt tuition assistance programs on a smaller scale, providing partial reimbursement of certain costs associated with job-related courses.

Although tuition assistance programs can be costly for businesses, there are a number of proven strategies that can be applied to help keep costs down. In addition, tuition assistance programs offer companies a number of important benefits. For example, companies that provide their employees with tuition assistance are building a more educated work force by encouraging workers to pursue higher education. Tuition assistance programs can also provide companies with an effective recruiting tool, enabling them to attract highly motivated people. Finally, tuition assistance can lead to reduced employee turnover and increased loyalty to the company.

In the past, companies were allowed to provide employees with a certain amount of monetary tuition assistance as a tax-free benefit, rather than as taxable income. But it is unclear how recent changes in the tax law will affect tuition assistance payments.

COMMON CONCERNS ABOUT TUITION ASSISTANCE

HIGH COSTS Many companies resist instituting tuition assistance programs because of the cost involved. In fact, poorly planned tuition assistance programs do waste money. One expert quoted by Kathryn Tyler in an article for *HR Magazine* called tuition assistance ''the black hole of company budgets'' and estimated that poorly planned programs cost companies $6,000 per employee. But Tyler mentioned a number of different strategies companies can use to help control the cost of tuition assistance programs. The first step is to determine the specific educational goals of employees in order to better focus their course selections. Outside educational advisory services can help employees understand their goals and thus decrease the chance that they will begin one course of study only to quit and start another. Similarly, education specialists within the company can be made available to advise employees about their educational options, rather than simply explaining the features of the tuition assistance program to them.

Tyler also recommended that employers reimburse fees as well as tuition in order to reduce costs. State-supported universities tend to charge lower tuition rates but higher additional fees than private colleges, which might cause some employees to choose to attend the more expensive private colleges in order to save on out-of-pocket expenses. Another way companies can save money in their tuition assistance programs involves negotiating for discounts with the schools. Larger companies or even smaller ones with specific educational needs may be able to save money by providing a certain number of students for a course. If, for example, a dozen employees from one company need to take a basic class, that company may be able to arrange a reduced rate or even a special class just for employees. Employers may also find it beneficial to arrange to pay certain local colleges and universities directly in order to reduce paperwork and other hassles for their employees.

Another way for companies to save money, as well as make the idea of continuing education more attractive to employees, is to provide nontraditional education options, such as correspondence, television, videotape, or Internet classes. Thousands of accredited courses are available through these alternative means, which allow busy employees with family responsibilities to fulfill course requirements on their own time without having to sit in a formal classroom. Collectively known as ''distance learning,'' these options offer employees a great deal of flexibility. However, it is important to make sure that such programs are regionally accredited so any credits earned will transfer to traditional schools if necessary.

Employers can also save money on tuition assistance programs by helping employees to get college credit for skills and knowledge they may already possess. For example, about 600 colleges offer students the opportunity to demonstrate their knowledge of various subjects through a life-experience portfolio. When employees have mastered the content of a course through work experience, they may be able to obtain college credit without actually having to spend time or money on a class. This option might enable a person employed as a bookkeeper to pass out of an intermediate accounting course, for instance.

Assessment tests, offered by college testing services, provide a similar option. These tests are designed to evaluate students' knowledge in a wide variety of subject areas; students who receive a passing grade can receive credit at many universities without taking the course. For example, an employee who is a Civil War buff may be able to pass a test rather than taking a history course. This stands to benefit the employer, because assessment tests cost around $50, as opposed to a cost of $800 or more for a course. Such testing enables some employees to reduce the amount of formal education they need to obtain a degree, which also reduces the time and cost involved in their education. In addition, gaining credit for skills and knowledge can enhance employees' self-esteem and bring them recognition for their skills at work.

EMPLOYEES WILL NOT APPLY THEMSELVES AS STUDENTS ''One of the most common fears related to offering a liberal tuition reimbursement policy is that an employee will enroll in a course, the company will pay for it, and the person won't invest the effort required to earn a passing grade,'' according to Tyler. ''Clear reimbursement guidelines can reduce the likelihood of that happening. For instance, companies can tie reimbursement to grades—a certain percentage for an A, a B, and so on, or 100 percent reimbursement for a passing grade.'' Employers can also avoid this potential problem by requiring students who fail a course to either repeat it or pay back the company for related tuition and fees.

EMPLOYEES MAY TAKE THE EDUCATION AND THEN LEAVE THE COMPANY ''Some companies are concerned about shouldering the financial burden for an employee's education and then taking a loss when the employee resigns,'' Tyler stated. ''Most companies, however, find that investing in their employees' educations actually reduces turnover.'' In order to reduce the likelihood of losing newly educated employees, some companies require participants in their tuition assistance programs to remain at the company for a certain length of time or else reimburse the company for part of the tuition paid on their behalf. Other companies take the more positive step of rewarding employees who earn their degrees with a gift of company stock. The stock can be set up to mature over a few years, thus giving the employee added incentive to remain at the company.

COMPLEX TAX IMPLICATIONS Finally, some companies are reluctant to establish tuition assistance programs for their employees because of the paperwork related to tax compliance. In the past, employers were allowed to provide up to $5,250 per employee annually in non-job-related, tax-free tuition aid under Section 127 of the Internal Revenue Code. This rule stated that most forms of tuition assistance were non-taxable employee benefits rather than a form of taxable income for employees. But the law, which was first introduced in 1978, has been changed frequently since. The most recent extension ended on July 1, 1997—meaning that tuition assistance provided as of this date had to be reported as income—but bills were before Congress to make the tax benefit for tuition assistance a permanent part of the tax code.

Many observers fear that unless the law is extended, it will deter employees from taking classes because they will not be able to afford the extra taxes.

In addition, it will likely deter companies from offering tuition assistance as an employee benefit because of the paperwork involved. When tuition assistance is considered a form of taxable income, employers are required to keep track of payments made on behalf of employees and report the amounts on their W-2 forms. Even if Section 127 is not extended, tuition payments for some types of courses are still excluded from income taxes. Section 162 of the tax code provides an exception for job-related courses that are required for an employee to keep his or her current position, such as classes needed to maintain a professional license.

FURTHER READING:

Jenks, James M., and Brian L.P. Zevnik. *Employee Benefits Plain and Simple*. New York: Collier Books, 1993.

Roberts, Gary, Gary Seldon, and Carlotta Roberts. *Human Resources Management*. Washington: U.S. Small Business Administration, n.d.

Rubis, Leon. "Legislation Echoes in the Workplace." *HR Magazine*. October 1996.

Tyler, Kathryn. "Expanded Tuition Policies Save in the Long Run." *HR Magazine*. September 1997.

SEE ALSO: Tax-deductible Business Expenses; Training and Development

U

UNDERCAPITALIZATION

Undercapitalization is a situation in which a business has insufficient funds, or **capital**, to support its operations. Although undercapitalization can affect any business, it is particularly common and problematic for small businesses. In fact, undercapitalization is one of the warning signs of major financial trouble for small businesses, as well as a significant cause of small business failures. Undercapitalization also acts to limit the growth of many small businesses, because without sufficient capital they cannot afford to make the investments necessary for expansion. In this way, undercapitalization can pose a problem even for profitable small businesses.

''What separates the successful entrepreneur from the unsuccessful? In many cases, it seems to be whether the prospective business owner has access to sufficient funds,'' Brian Hamilton wrote in the U.S. Small Business Administration publication *Financing for the Small Business*. ''Without sufficient capitalization, companies do not have the staying power to withstand intense competition or downturns in the business cycle,'' Richard Hamilton added in an article for *Manitoba Business*.

The amount of capitalization needed by a small business depends upon a number of factors. For example, businesses that offer a service usually require less funds than those that manufacture a product. Similarly, businesses in which the owners perform most of the work tend to need less up-front capital than those that must hire employees. A company's initial capitaliza-tion also depends on the entrepreneur's ability to invest personal funds and to create a sound business plan.

In order to avoid future problems with undercapitalization, entrepreneurs need to perform a realistic assessment of their expenses and financial needs. Some of the major operating expenses facing a new business include facility rental, equipment, supplies, utilities, insurance, advertising, business licenses, and salaries. Based upon this information, the entrepreneur should prepare a cash flow projection on a monthly basis for the first year. The difference between the funds the entrepreneur is able to contribute, the amount of income the business is expected to generate, and the amount of expenses the business is projected to incur provides a rough estimate of the business's financial needs. The entrepreneur must approach various sources for debt or equity financing to make up the difference and provide the business with sufficient capitalization.

Although more than 50 percent of small business failures can be attributed to undercapitalization, it is important for entrepreneurs not only to raise enough money but also to use that money wisely. In an article for *Inc.,* Norm Brodsky noted that many entrepreneurs fall into an ''image trap,'' trying to present an image of success with fancy offices, expensive but unnecessary equipment, and personal perquisites. Spending valuable funds on such luxury items is a sure invitation to business failure. Instead, Brodsky recommends that entrepreneurs put off such expenditures until the business is successful, and instead concentrate on making good decisions to build the business while making their capital last.

UNDERCAPITALIZATION AND CORPORATE LIABILITY

A little-known problem associated with undercapitalization is that it can increase the likelihood of the owners of a corporation being held personally liable for business-related matters. One of the main reasons that entrepreneurs choose the corporate form of business organization is to protect themselves against personal **liabilities** for business debts and court judgments. **Incorporation** does not afford automatic protection, however. Corporate owners can be held personally liable in a number of situations, including cases where personal and corporate assets are commingled, the corporation does not keep adequate records, or corporate owners intentionally defraud their creditors.

But perhaps the most critical factor in determining whether there should be personal liability for corporate debts is whether the owners provided sufficient capitalization for the business. ''This issue is so important that owners risk personal liability even if it is the only factor a court finds,'' according to Anthony J. Mohr in an article for *Nation's Business*. ''The ultimate test is whether there are enough corporate assets to satisfy corporate obligations.'' For example, an entrepreneur could not contribute only $500 to start a new business, knowing that it actually required an initial capital outlay of $10,000, and expect his or her personal assets to be protected in case the business became insolvent. In this instance, a court would be likely to rule that the extreme undercapitalization of the corporation made the owner personally liable for its debts.

FURTHER READING:

Brodsky, Norm. ''Why Start-Ups Fail.'' *Inc.* December 1995.

Corbin, Ken. ''Are You Undercapitalized?'' *Manufactured Home Merchandiser.* May 1992.

Ettore, Barbara. ''Not a Minute Too Soon.'' *Forbes.* December 5, 1983.

Hamilton, Brian. *Financing for the Small Business.* Washington: U.S. Small Business Administration, 1990.

Hamilton, Richard. ''Will Your Company Survive?'' *Manitoba Business.* May 1996.

Mohr, Anthony J. ''Take Care to Avoid Liability Traps.'' *Nation's Business.* November 1997.

SEE ALSO: Debt Financing; Equity Financing; Nontraditional Financing Sources

UNDERWRITERS LABORATORIES

Underwriters Laboratories (UL) is easily the largest and best known independent, not-for-profit testing laboratory in the world. Based in Northwood, Illinois, UL conducts safety and quality tests on a broad range of products, from fire doors to CCTV cameras. The laboratory provides a full spectrum of conformity and quality assessment services to manufacturers and other organizations. It also assists jursidictional and provincial authorities, offers educational materials to consumers, and works to strengthen safety systems around the world.

UL provides tests in the following areas: fire testing; medical device testing; EPH services (food service equipment, drinking water certification, plumbing equipment); audio/video; Source Verification and Inspection Services (SVIS); electric vehicle components and systems; EMC testing and certification; information technology equipment (ITE) industry services; and telecommunication industry services. It conducts tests on products in these areas to see whether they meet standards set by UL engineers in conjunction with input from manufacturers and product users, but it will also test products to see whether they meet standards set by outside entities, such as a city (in the case of building codes, for instance). In addition, Underwriters Laboratories points out that it maintains services for companies looking to test products for international markets: ''UL's International Compliance Services (ICS) helps bridge the gap between you and the countries you want to access. UL's global conformity assessment experts interact daily with product certification organizations worldwide.'' The ICS division assists clients with the application process, helps with correspondence and translation, and can coordinate the exchange and review of test data.

UL DESIGNATIONS ''Underwriters Laboratories, which has been in existence for more than 100 years, is very sensitive to the prevalent but mistaken belief that it approves products,'' wrote Robert C. Cook in *Security Management*. ''The only entity that can actually approve or reject a product is a federal, state, or local government agency—known generally as the 'Authority Having Jurisdiction' or AHJ.'' However, an AHJ—whether it is a local health code inspection department or the federal Occupational Safety and Health Administration—often requires products to be tested by Underwriters Laboratories or another lab before the agency will approve its use.

UL hands out one of three different designations to products that pass its tests: UL listed, UL recognized, or UL certified. Businesses should note that there is no such designation as ''UL approved''; companies that mistakenly tout their products with such a designation will arouse the ire of Underwriters Laboratories, which will insist that the company clarify the matter immediately.

UL Listed—This designation means that the tested product meets the laboratory's standards and can be used by itself.

UL Recognized—This designation, explained Cook, is the one "that UL grants to a component, or a piece of equipment that must be combined with other components to create a finished product. For example, if a transformer is a plug-in model, it can be used by itself and therefore would receive a 'listed' designation if it passes UL's tests. If the transformer has wire leads and is intended for use in a power supply, it is considered a component of a larger system and would receive a 'recognized' designation. The tests for both designations are equally rigorous. The difference is just a question of how the product is used."

UL Certified—This designation is used by UL when it has been successfully tested to the standards of an outside authority, such as a city's building code requirements.

As Cook noted, "products sent to UL must be tested for the specific purpose for which they will be used. There are cases when a product might be given a general listing, but this designation makes them vulnerable to a government inspector who demands proof that the product will perform as intended by the manufacturer. Because of this potential outcome, UL testing continues to evolve and become more comprehensive. New uses are devised for products, raising new safety concerns. New standards are written; old ones are revised."

Businesses considering enlisting the services of Underwriters Laboratories (or similar labs) should be aware that testing can be both expensive and time-consuming. Bills of several thousand dollars per product tested are not unusual in many industry sectors, and the testing procedures usually take about six months to complete, with some tests extending well beyond that time frame. But the importance of UL acknowledgment is very significant to marketplace image in many industries. "Manufacturers can, of course, sell their products without the tests," said Cook, "and many do. But in some industries, an untested product can be a hard sell to skeptical customers."

FURTHER READING:

"Circling the Globe." *Appliance Manufacturer.* August 1997.

Cook, Robert C. "A Tale of UL Testing." *Security Management.* July 1995.

Sweet, John O. "UL Grows Over 90 Years Into Largest Labs of Kind in World." *Air Conditioning, Heating, & Refrigeration News.* August 12, 1985.

"The Underwriters Labs' Faster Seal of Approval." *Business Week.* December 20, 1993.

Wingo, Walter S. "A Boom Time for Product Testing." *Design News.* March 9, 1992.

UNIFORM COMMERCIAL CODE

The Uniform Commercial Code (UCC) is a collection of modernized, codified, and standardized laws that apply to all commercial transactions with the exception of real property. Developed under the direction of the National Conference of Commissioners on Uniform State Laws, the American Law Institute, and the American Bar Association (ABA), it first became U.S. law in 1972. Since that time, it has undergone a process of constant revision.

The Uniform Commercial Code arose out of the need to address two growing problems in American business: 1) the increasingly cumbersome legal and contractual requirements of doing business, and 2) differences in state laws that made it difficult for businesses from different states to do business with one another. Businesspeople and legislators recognized that some measures needed to be taken to ease interstate business transactions and curb the trend toward exhaustively detailed contracts. They subsequently voiced support for the implementation of a set of standardized laws that would serve as the legal cornerstone for all exchanges of goods and services. These laws—the Uniform Commercial Code—could then be referred to when discrepancies in state laws arose, and freed companies from painstakingly including every conceivable business detail in all of their contractual agreements.

DEVELOPMENT OF THE UNIFORM COMMERCIAL CODE

Work on the UCC began in earnest in 1945. Seven years later, a draft of the code was approved by the National Conference of Commissioners on Uniform State Laws, the American Law Institute, and the American Bar Association. Pennsylvania became the first state to enact the UCC, and it became law there on July 1, 1954. The UCC editorial board issued a new code in 1957 in response to comments from various states and a special report by the Law Revision Commission of New York State. Forty-eight states had enacted the code by 1966. Currently, all 50 states, the District of Columbia, and the U.S. Virgin Islands have adopted the UCC as state law, though some have not adopted every single provision contained within the code.

BUSINESS ISSUES ADDRESSED IN THE UCC

Many important aspects of business are covered within the UCC, and several of them are of particular import to entrepreneurs and small business owners. The Code provides detailed information on such diverse business aspects as: breach of contract (and the options of both buyers and sellers when confronted with breach); circumstances under which buyers can reject goods; risk allocation during **transportation** of goods; letters of credit and their importance; legal methods of payment for goods and services; and myriad other subjects.

ARTICLES The UCC consists of ten articles. Article 1, titled General Provisions, details principles of interpretation and general definitions that apply throughout the UCC. Article 2 covers such areas as sales contracts, performance, creditors, good faith purchasers, and legal remedies for breach of contract; given its concern with the always important issue of contracts, small business owners should be thoroughly acquainted with this section. Article 3, which replaced the Uniform Negotiable Instruments Law, covers transfer and negotiation, rights of a holder, and liability of parties, among other areas. Article 4 covers such areas as collections, deposits, and customer relations; it incorporated much of the Bank Collection Code developed by the American Bankers Association.

Article 5 of the Uniform Collection Code is devoted to letters of credit, while Article 6 covers bulk transfers. Article 7 covers warehouse receipts, bills of lading, and other documents of title. Article 8, meanwhile, is concerned with the issuance, purchase, and registration of investment securities; it replaced the Uniform Stock Transfer Act. Article 9 is another provision that is particularly important to small business owners. Devoted to secured transactions, sales of accounts, and chattel paper, Article 9 supplanted a number of earlier laws, including the Uniform Trust Receipts Act, the Uniform Conditional Sales Act, and the Uniform Chattel Mortgage Act.

Finally, Article 10 provides for states to set the effective date of enactment of the code and lists specific state laws should be repealed once the UCC has been enacted (Uniform Negotiable Instruments Act, Uniform Warehouse Receipts Act, Uniform Sales Act, Uniform Bills of Lading Act, Uniform Stock Transfer Act, Uniform Conditional Sales Act, and Uniform Trust Receipts Act). In addition, Article 10 recommends that states repeal any acts regulating bank collections, bulk sales, chattel mortgages, conditional sales, factor's lien acts, farm storage of grain and similar acts, and assignment of accounts receivable, for all of these areas are covered in the UCC. Individual states may also add to the list of repealed acts at their own discretion.

The UCC has a permanent editorial board, and amendments to the UCC are added to cover new developments in commerce, such as electronic funds transfers and the leasing of personal property. Individual states then have the option of adopting the amendments and revisions to the UCC as state law. For current information on changes within and interpreta-tions of the Uniform Commercial Code, consult the *Business Lawyer's* "Uniform Commercial Code Annual Survey."

U.S. DEPARTMENT OF COMMERCE

The U.S. Department of Commerce (DOP), which was established in 1903, is one of the main government agencies intended to assist businesses—large and small—and represent their interests domestically and abroad. The agency states that its broad range of responsibilities include expanding U.S. exports, developing innovative technologies, gathering and disseminating statistical data, measuring economic growth, granting patents, promoting minority entrepreneurship, and providing stewardship. The department promotes these goals by encouraging job creation and economic growth through exports, free and fair trade, technology and innovation, quality, entrepreneurship, deregulation, and sustainable development. Because of the agency's diversity, it purchases a variety of products and services with a special commitment toward buying from the small business community.

One of the key offices within the U.S. Department of Commerce is the Office of Business Liaison. This office serves as the intermediary between the business community and the agency. Its objectives include:

- To be pro-active in its dealings with the business community and to be responsive and effective in its outreach efforts.

- To keep the current administration aware of problems and issues facing the business community.

- To keep the business community abreast of key administration decisions and policies.

- To regularly meet with members of the business community.

- To help businesses navigate their way through all the federal agencies and regulations through its Business Assistance Program. In addition to producing a wide variety of published materials, the Assistance Program also provides specialists who are available to answer specific questions on government policies, programs, and services.

Another office that is of interest to small business owners is the Office of Small and Disadvantaged Utilization. This office is responsible for ensuring that the DOP purchases goods and services from small businesses. It helps small business owners identify which bureaus they should pursue as potential buyers, clarifies who the key individuals at that bureau are, and provides small businesses with basic information on the procurement process and helps entrepreneurs develop marketing strategies.

Some of the other key offices, departments, and programs at the U.S. Department of Commerce that are also of interest to small business owners include:

- Bureau of the Census—Collects a wide variety of information on all people living in the United States every ten years. It makes this information publicly available, and business owners often use the information for demographic or marketing purposes.

- Economic Development Administration—Fosters the creation of new jobs, retention of existing jobs, and the stimulation of industrial and commercial growth in economically challenged areas of the United States.

- International Trade Administration—Helps U.S. businesses compete in the global market by assisting exporters, helping businesses gain equal access to foreign markets, and making it easier to compete against imports. Includes separate units for trade development and import administration.

- **Minority Business Development Agency**—Fosters the creation, growth, and expansion of minority businesses in the United States.

- Office of Consumer Affairs—Exists to bridge the gap between businesses and consumers, to help businesses improve the quality of the services they offer consumers, to educate consumers, and to speak for the consumer in regard to each administration's economic policy development. The office also helps U.S. businesses to become more competitive in the global marketplace.

- **Patent and Trademark Office**—Protects innovation in the marketplace by providing inventors and authors with exclusive rights to their writings and inventions.

- National Institute of Standards and Technology—Promotes economic growth by working with businesses to develop and apply technology, measurements, and standards. The scope of this institute is of growing interest to U.S. businesses because of the increasing influence of the International Standards Organization (ISO) and its ISO 9000 quality standards.

- Information Infrastructure Task Force—Oversees the administration's vision for the ''National Information Infrastructure,'' which primarily refers to the Internet and how its growth will be managed in the United States. The work of this task force is of special interest to small businesses because of the growing use of the Internet for electronic commerce.

- National Trade Data Bank—Provides the public with access (including electronic) to export and international economic information.

- Trade Compliance Center—Monitors foreign compliance with trade agreements and provides businesses with information about their rights and obligations under existing trade agreements with other nations.

Extensive information on the U.S. Department of Commerce and many of its offices and programs is maintained at http://www.doc.gov/ on the World Wide Web.

U.S. SMALL BUSINESS ADMINISTRATION

The U.S. Small Business Administration (SBA), which was created in 1953, is an independent federal agency charged with aiding, counseling, and protecting the interests of American small businesses. The agency maintains a wide range of programs designed to address various aspects of this mandate. These programs, each of which seeks to assist small business owners in one or more areas of their enterprise, are maintained in the following areas: lending and investment; surety bonds; international expansion and development; disaster assistance; federal procurement contracts; minority small business assistance; veterans' assistance; research and development; business and training; and business information and counseling. The SBA also serves as an advocate for American small businesses in government.

STRUCTURE OF THE SBA

Most SBA programs and services are implemented through U.S. Small Business Administration district offices. District offices are maintained in all 50 states, as well as Washington, D.C., and Puerto Rico (some larger states, such as California, New York, and Texas, have as many as half a dozen offices). Personnel in these offices work directly with small business owners and various cooperating institutions to implement SBA programs.

These field offices report to regional offices of the SBA. In addition to their supervisory responsibilities, the regional headquarters are charged with educating small business owners, lending institutions, and others on issues that affect them; fostering regional economic development; and providing the Office of Field Operations (OFO) with information on SBA programs and small business developments at the district level. OFO is responsible for all aspects of the SBA's field operations, including communications, policy formation, and general performance. It reports directly to the SBA's chief administrator.

Collateral offices maintained by the U.S. Small Business Administration include administration; comptroller; personnel; external affairs; marketing and customer service; public communications, congressional and legislative affairs; Hearings and Appeals; Inspector General; Office of Information Resources Management (OIRM); Equal Employment Opportunity and Civil Rights Compliance; and Office of General Counsel.

Finally, the SBA maintains several departments devoted to providing advocacy services on behalf of American small business owners. The Office of Interagency Affairs oversees enforcement of the **Regulatory Flexibility Act**, analyzes small business issues, develops governmental policy options, and prepares testimony for use before various legislative and regulatory bodies. The Office of Economic Research oversees the SBA's research contracting program, and compiles and interprets various economic data on small businesses. The Office of Information publishes books and economic reports on small business issues, and serves as a distributor of advocacy publications and other materials. Finally, the Office of Advocacy attempts to evaluate the effect of proposed legislation and other policy issues on small businesses. The chief counsel for advocacy acts as the primary spokesperson for small business and represents their views before Congress, local governments, and other agencies. The Office of Advocacy also utilizes regional advocates who work directly with local communities and small businesses, gathering information on policies and regulations that are helping and hurting small businesses and the communities in which they operate.

SMALL BUSINESS ADMINISTRATION PROGRAMS

LENDING PROGRAMS The SBA provides a number of lending options to small business owners. The best known of these is the 7(a) Loan Guaranty, but there are many others that are widely used as well. In all of these cases, the loan is actually delivered through commercial lending institutions and other intermediaries. The SBA helps secure the loans, though, by consenting to cover the cost of the loan should the borrower be unable to pay. Lending institutions value this added protection very highly.

The 7(a) loan program, which was authorized by the passage of the Small Business Act, is primarily designed to address the long-term funding needs of small businesses by guaranteeing loans to qualified enterprises. These loans can be used for all sorts of purposes, including inventory, working capital, equipment, and real estate. Maturities are up to 10 years for working capital and up to 25 years for fixed assets. The SBA can guarantee 80 percent of loans of $100,000 or less, and 75 percent of loans between $100,000 and $750,000. There are several other loan programs available through the 7(a) Loan Guaranty plan as well.

The Low Documentation Loan (LowDoc) program is a streamlined version of the 7(a) loan for businesses seeking less than $100,000. Limited to applicants with a strong credit history, LowDoc loans can be secured with a one-page application (in cases where the loan request is for $50,000 or less). The SBA has made a strong effort to improve response time under this plan, in large measure because it had long been criticized for the bureaucratic red tape associated with even the smallest of its loan programs.

The CAPLines program is an option designed to meet the short-term working capital needs of small businesses. There are several different loan options available under this program, which replaced the SBA's earlier GreenLine program. Loans under CAPLines are generally limited to $750,000.

FA$TRAK loans are part of a relatively new program only available through selected lending institutions. This program gives banks greater freedom to make loans to small businesses in their community, but the SBA does not provide the same level of protection to lenders. Under FA$TRAK, only 50 percent of the loan is guaranteed.

SBA MicroLoans, meanwhile, are short-term loans of up to $25,000. Disseminated through nonprofit groups, MicroLoans are intended for the purchase of machinery and other equipment, office furniture, inventory, supplies, and working capital.

The SBA also offers several targeted lending programs for small businesses. These include the Defense Loan and Technical Assistance (DELTA) program, which provides assistance to defense-dependent small businesses impacted by defense cuts; prequalification pilot loan programs for women and minorities; the Export Working Capital Program (EWCP), which guarantees loans for qualified small businesses engaged in export transactions; the International Trade Loan (ITL), which provides long-term financing assistance to small businesses engaged in international trade and/ or hurt by imports; and the Pollution Control Program, which gives loan guarantees to eligible small businesses proposing to design and install pollution control facilities.

The SBA also maintains a loan program known as the 504 CDC (**Certified Development Companies**), which makes available up to $1 million to qualified applicants. Under this system, long-term, fixed-rate financing is made available to small businesses interested in expanding or modernizing their operations through the purchase of new machinery, equipment, and/ or real estate. DELTA loans are available through this program as well.

The Small Business Administration relies on lending institutions and other intermediaries (such as non-profit organizations, in the case of MicroLoans). But the SBA is careful about the banks and savings and loans companies with which it does business. The most reliable of these lending institutions are eventually designated as "preferred lenders." This status gives them increased powers of loan approval and processing (although the SBA still conducts a final review of loan applications). To become a preferred lender, an institution needs to have established a reputation for solid community lending (to small businesses and minority- and women-owned firms) and a strong history of being repaid by loan applicants.

In the past, the SBA has made occasional "direct" loans to qualifying businesses. The SBA Direct Loan Program offered loans of up to $150,000 to businesses owned by handicapped people or Vietnam-era veterans. This money was taken directly out of the SBA's operating budget. The program lost its funding, however, and as of mid-1997, it had not been restored.

INVESTMENT The SBA maintains three investment programs for small businesses. The first of these, called Main Street Investment, is described by the SBA as "a public/private partnership between the SBA and state governments to make capital more available to lenders who, in turn, make loans to small businesses. Participating states invest tax revenues in community banks that agree to make LowDoc loans." **Small Business Investment Companies (SBICs)**, meanwhile, are SBA-licensed investment firms that— armed with U.S. government-guaranteed debentures or participating securities—make investments and loans to small businesses. Indeed, SBICs exist for the express purpose of funding start-up companies. They operate under extremely stringent guidelines, however, and turn down many applicants. Similar to SBICs are Minority Enterprise Small Business Investment Companies (MESBICs), which provide funding to businesses owned or operated by minorities.

SURETY BONDS In recognition of the fact that contractors to construction projects (whether federal, state, county, or private sector) are commonly required to post surety bonds, the SBA established a program wherein they guarantee bid, performance, and payment bonds for contracts up to $1.25 million for eligible small firms unable to secure surety bonds through commercial lenders. Under this program, the SBA's guaranty goes to a surety company; contractors must apply through a surety bonding agent.

INTERNATIONAL TRADE In addition to maintaining loan programs for small businesses engaged in international commerce, the U.S. Small Business Administration provides a number of other services to these enterprises. The Export Legal Assistance Network (ELAN), for instance, is the product of an agreement between the SBA, the Federal Bar Association, and the **U.S. Department of Commerce**. Under this program, trade attorneys provide free legal consultations to small business exporters.

The SBA also operates information centers called U.S. Export Assistance Centers (USEACs). As with ELAN, the USEACs are the product of an alliance between the SBA and other organizations (in USEACs' case, the Department of Commerce and the Export-Import Bank). These centers are designed to disseminate trade promotion and export financing information to small businesses engaged in international trade. In addition, the SBA maintains a computer database known as the Small Business Automated Trade Locator Assistance System (SBAtlas), which includes market data of interest to exporters.

DISASTER ASSISTANCE The SBA's Disaster Assistance Program is one of the most important that it operates. This federally funded disaster relief program actually consists of a number of different programs aimed at helping various classes of victims. Physical Disaster Business Loans are targeted at businesses of any size that need to repair or replace business property to "pre-disaster" conditions. These loans, which can be used for equipment, fixtures, and inventory, are limited to $1.5 million and are not available to businesses that were insured for their losses.

Economic Injury Disaster Loans (EIDLs), meanwhile, are targeted at businesses that have "sustained economic injury as a direct result of a disaster," said the SBA. "These working capital loans are made to help businesses pay ordinary and necessary operating expenses which would have been payable barring disaster." The maximum amount of an EIDL loan is $1.5 million, but small business experts note that businesses can receive no more than $1.5 million in combined EIDL and physical disaster business loans. An exception to this stipulation is made, however, for those places of business that qualify as major sources of employment. Under the SBA's Major Source of Employment (MSE) program, the $1.5 million loan limit is waived for those businesses that employ 250 or more people in an affected area.

FEDERAL PROCUREMENT The U.S. Small Business Administration maintains several programs designed to help small businesses secure government contracts. These include:

- Breakout Procurement Program—promotes the breakout of historically sole-source contracts for open competition with the aim of aiding small businesses and effecting government savings.

- Prime Contracting Program—designed to help small businesses interested in securing federal contracts; services include support for small business set-asides, counseling, identification of new small business sources, and "assessment of compliance with the Small Business Act through surveillance reviews."

- Subcontracting Program—designed to aid small businesses in their efforts to secure federal contracts as suppliers and subcontractors.

- Certificates of Competency—appeal process that can be used by small businesses that have been denied government contracts because of alleged lack of ability to fulfill job requirements.

The SBA also maintains the Procurement Automated Source System (PASS), a database of U.S. businesses interested in federal procurement opportunities.

MINORITY ASSISTANCE The SBA has several programs intended to provide support to small businesses owned and operated by minorities. Programs maintained by the SBA's Minority Enterprise Development office include 8(a) Small Disadvantaged Business Development, which arranges federal procurement opportunities for minority- and disadvantaged-owned firms, and initiatives which provide management and technical assistance to those firms. The SBA also operates an Office of Native American Affairs (ONAA), which works to provide Native American communities with business development and job creation opportunities.

BUSINESS TRAINING AND COUNSELING SBA-sponsored training and counseling services are available through the following programs:

- **Small Business Development Centers (SBDCs)**—provides management and technical assistance to both current and prospective small business owners through an alliance of educators, the private sector, and federal, state, and local governments. All areas of business are covered, from market research and accounting systems to inventory control and cost-benefit analysis.

- Business Information Centers (BICs)—specializes in providing technology information to small businesses. Subjects covered include advances in telecommunications, software, and computers.

- **Service Corps of Retired Executives (SCORE)**—matches retired business executives with small businesses seeking advice on business issues. SCORE includes more than 12,300 members in hundreds of chapters around the country.

WOMEN'S BUSINESS OWNERSHIP SBA programs specifically directed at women small business owners include the Women's Demonstration Program, which provides women with training and advice on all aspects of business ownership and management, and the Women's Network for Entrepreneurial Training (WNET), wherein established women business owners serve as mentors to other women entrepreneurs.

VETERANS' AFFAIRS The SBA maintains several programs intended to provide information and training to veterans. These include the VET (Veterans' Entrepreneurial Training) Program, the Transition Assistance Program (TAP), and "business opportunity conferences," which helps veteran-owned companies previously reliant on the defense industry to secure other clients.

RESEARCH AND DEVELOPMENT The two principal programs administered by the SBA in this area are the **Small Business Innovation Research (SBIR)** Program and the Small Business Technology Transfer (STTR) Program. STTR is a pilot program that seeks to form research and development partnerships between small firms and nonprofit research institutions. It provides up to $100,000 to companies for the first phase of research, though there are stipulations attached to that figure. SBIR, meanwhile, provides financial rewards to small businesses who propose innovative ideas to problems faced by participating federal agencies. Initially established in the early 1980s, as a result of the 1982 Small Business Innovation Development Act, SBIR has been warmly received by many small companies with expertise in science and high-technology areas.

ONE-STOP CAPITAL SHOP The SBA expects to contribute to the **Empowerment Zones and Enterprise Communities** Program initiative headed by the Department of Housing and Urban Development and the Department of Agriculture through its "One-Stop Capital Shops" (OSCS). These centers, located in designated empowerment zones and enterprise communities, are expected to be headed up by local nonprofit organizations, but they are intended to include access to complete information on various SBA programs and offerings. "Business information centers, located within the OSCSs, will offer the latest high-tech hardware, software, interactive videos and tele-communications to access market research databases, individual planning and spreadsheets, and other tools for the small business owner,'' promised the SBA. ''Individual counseling will be offered in all aspects of starting, running or growing a small business.''

BUSINESS INFORMATION SERVICES A comprehensive range of business development booklets is published by and made available from the SBA. A diverse range of topics are covered in these brochures; sample titles include *Strategic Planning for Growing Businesses, Budgeting in a Small Service Firm, Inventory Management,* and *Evaluating Franchise Opportunities.* SBA also maintains SBA Online, a computer-based electronic bulletin board of small business information, and a toll-free answer desk for small business owners with questions about aspects of their operation. The answer desk is open 24 hours a day, seven days a week, but counselors are only available Monday through Friday, 9 a.m. to 5 p.m. Eastern Time. The toll-free number is (800) 8-ASK-SBA. Finally, the Small Business Administration maintains a page on the World Wide Web at http://www.sba.gov.

FURTHER READING:

Barlas, Stephen. ''Looking Ahead: Three SBA Programs Face Closer Scrutiny.'' *Entrepreneur.* January 1997.

Emrich, Amy., ed. *Small Business Sourcebook.* Detroit, MI: Gale, 1996.

SBA Profile: Who We Are and What We Do. Third ed. Washington: U.S. Small Business Administration, fiscal year 1996.

SEE ALSO: Disaster Assistance Loans; U.S. Small Business Administration Guaranteed Loans

U.S. SMALL BUSINESS ADMINISTRATION GUARANTEED LOANS

The **U.S. Small Business Administration (SBA)** is a major source of financing for small businesses in the United States. The SBA's various loan programs have provided needed funding for thousands of small enterprises who were unable to secure loans from lending institutions on their own; indeed, businesses cannot solicit **loans** from the SBA unless they are unable to get funding independently.

Some of today's most successful businesses, including Intel, Apple, and Federal Express, were given much needed boosts in their early days by SBA loans. This record of success, coupled with the trend toward small-business start-ups and entrepreneurship in America, has encouraged both the SBA and its lending partners to continue to expand its loan programs. The SBA has subsequently set new records in various loan guar-

antee categories in the mid-1990s. In fiscal year (FY) 1996, for example, it made $10.2 billion in loan guarantees through its primary commercial lending programs, and a year later it made a record $10.9 billion in loan guarantees. The two main components of the SBA loan system—its 7(a) programs and its 504 CDC program—accounted for nearly all of this amount. Loan guarantees made through the 7(a) programs totaled $9.46 billion in FY 1997 (a 23 percent increase over FY 1996), while the 504 program delivered $1.44 billion to small businesses during FY 1997.

TYPES OF SBA GUARANTEED LOANS

The SBA's 7(a) Loan Program is the most popular of the agency's programs (46,000 of these loans were bestowed upon small businesses in FY 1996). Under this program, the SBA does not actually make direct loans to small businesses. Instead, it assures the institution that is making the business loan—usually a bank—that it will make payment on the loan if the business defaults on it. Since the SBA is taking responsibility for the loan, it is usually the final arbiter of whether a loan application will be approved or not.

The 7(a) Loan Program was formed to meet the long-term financing needs of small businesses. The primary advantage of 7(a) loans is that business enterprises are able to repay the loan over a very long period of time. Ten-year maturities are available for loans for equipment and working capital (though seven-year terms are more commonplace), and loans for real estate and major equipment purchases can be paid back over as long as 25 years. The SBA can guarantee 75 percent of loans up to $750,000, and 80 percent of loans of less than $100,000. The interest rate of 7(a) loans does not exceed 2.75 over the prime lending rate.

The SBA maintains several individual loan programs under the 7(a) umbrella. These include CAPLines, LowDoc, FA$TRAK, EWCP, DELTA, and an assortment of other lending initiatives targeted at specific sectors of the small business world.

CAPLINES Limited to $750,000, CAPLines loans are given to small businesses with short-term working capital needs. ''Under CAPLines,'' notes the SBA, ''there are five distinct short-term working capital loans: the Seasonal, Contract, Builder's, Standard Asset-Based, and Small Asset-Based lines. For the most part, the SBA regulations governing the 7(a) Program also govern this program.''

LOWDOC The Low Documentation Loan (LowDoc) Program is a simplified version of the 7(a) loan for businesses seeking less than $100,000. It combines a streamlined application process (for many loan requests, the application is only one page long) with the elimination of several bureaucratic steps to improve response time to requests. Any small business that posted average annual sales over the previous three years of $5 million or less and employs 100 or few individuals (including all owners, partners, and principals) is eligible to apply for a Low Documentation Loan. Since its inception, the LowDoc Program has proven enormously popular with small business owners and entrepreneurs. In 1996 it accounted for approximately 45 percent of total 7(a) loans awarded, and accounted for one out of every five SBA dollars that were lent out to small businesses. In late 1996, however, Congress passed legislation that narrowed the number of banks permitted to make LowDoc loans to those with significant experience in making loans to small businesses.

FA$TRAK This relatively new program is only available through selected lending institutions. With FA$TRAK loans, participating banks are allowed to use their own documentation and procedures to approve, service and liquidate loans of up to $100,000. The SBA notes, however, that under FA$TRAK, only 50 percent of the loan is guaranteed.

EWCP The Export Working Capital Program (EWCP) guarantees loans for qualified small businesses engaged in export transactions. It replaced another SBA program known as the Export Revolving Line of Credit Program. Most of the SBA regulations governing the 7(a) Program also govern this program. Loan maturities, however, may be for up to three years, with an option for annual renewals. EWCP loans can be extended for either single or multiple export sales.

DELTA The Defense Loan and Technical Assistance (DELTA) Program was implemented to help ease the impact of national defense cuts on defense-dependent small businesses. According to the SBA, DELTA loans must be used to retain jobs of defense workers, create new jobs in impacted communities, or to make operating changes with the aim of remaining in the "national technical and industrial base." While listed under the 7(a) umbrella of loan programs, DELTA actually uses the 504 CDC program as well.

WOMEN AND MINORITY PREQUALIFICATION LOANS These pilot programs are aimed at providing financial assistance to specific small business segments. Applicants for Women's Prequalification Pilot Loans, which are limited to $250,000, are judged on character, credit history, experience, and reliability rather than assets. The Minority Prequalification Loan Program is constructed in similar fashion.

MICROLOANS SBA MicroLoans are short-term loans of up to $25,000. Disseminated through non-profit groups, MicroLoans are intended for the purchase of machinery and other equipment, office furniture, inventory, supplies, and working capital.

INTERNATIONAL TRADE LOAN (ITL) The ITL provides long-term financing assistance to small businesses who are involved in international trade or who have been hurt by imports. Under this program, the SBA guarantees loans for up to $1.25 million for a combination of fixed-asset financing and working capital needs (though the working capital portion of the guarantee is limited to $750,000).

POLLUTION CONTROL PROGRAM This program extends loans to small businesses engaged in the planning, design, or installation of pollution control facilities.

The Small Business Administration's other major loan program is the 504 CDC (**Certified Development Companies**) Program. CDCs are nonprofit corporations established to aid communities in their economic development efforts; there are nearly 300 CDCs in existence across the country. The 504 CDC Program is designed to provide growing businesses with long-range, fixed-rate financing for major expansion expenditures in the realm of fixed-asset projects. These include: real estate purchases and improvements, including existing buildings, grading, street improvements, parking lots and landscaping, and utilities; long-term machinery and equipment; renovation of existing facilities; and building construction. Monies from the 504 CDC Program cannot be used for refinancing, working capital or inventory, or consolidating or repaying debt.

The SBA describes the program thusly: "Typically, a 504 project includes a loan secured with a senior lien from a private-sector lender covering up to 50 percent of the project cost, a loan secured with a junior lien from the CDC (a 100 percent SBA-guaranteed debenture) covering up to 40 percent of the cost, and a contribution of at least 10 percent equity from the small business being helped. The maximum SBA debenture generally is $750,000 (up to $1 million in some cases). . . . The CDC's portfolio must create or retain one job from every $35,000 provided by the SBA." Small business owners should note, however, that in late 1996 Congress approved changes to the 504 Program that would require companies that have been in existence for less than two years to put up an addition 5 percent equity. Stephen Barlas noted in the January 1997 *Entrepreneur* that the legislation also "increases the guarantee fee paid by 504 borrowers from one-eighth of 1 percent of the principal to seven-eighths of 1 percent. For a $1 million loan, that means instead of paying $1,125 on the $900,000 principal, the business pays $7,875." Barlas pointed out that Congress also added a new one-half of 1 percent onetime fee that will be paid by either the bank, the borrower, or the CDC. These changes—as well as some adjustments in the 7(a) Program—are attributed to concerns about the SBA's ability to liquidate delinquent loans. Proponents of the changes contended that the popularity of the SBA's various loan programs, coupled with cuts in its staffing levels, had stretched the agency's personnel and budget too thin.

The SBA also offers **disaster assistance loans** to businesses that have been victimized by various natural disasters (fires, floods, hurricanes, earthquakes, etc.). The SBA formerly offered direct loans to companies owned by Vietnam-era veterans and handicapped businesspeople as well, but this program—which provided up to $150,000 to qualified applicants out of the SBA's funding—has been discontinued. It remained inoperational in mid-1997.

INTEREST RATES ON SBA LOANS

The **interest rates** on SBA-guaranteed loans are negotiated between the borrowing business and the lending institution, but they are subject to SBA-imposed rate ceilings, which are linked to the prime rate. Interest rates on SBA loans can be either fixed or variable.

According to the SBA, fixed rate loans are not allowed to exceed the prime rate plus 2.25 percent if the loan matures in less than seven years. If the maturity of the loan is seven years or more, however, the rate can be boosted to the prime rate plus 2.75 percent. For SBA loans totaling less than $25,000, the maximum interest rate cannot exceed the prime rate plus 4.25 percent for loans with a maturity of less than seven years (for loans that mature after seven years, the interest rate can be as much as the prime rate plus 4.75 percent). For SBA loans between $25,000 and $50,000, maximum rates are not permitted to exceed 3.25 percent (for loans that mature in less than seven years) and 3.75 percent (for loans with longer terms of maturity).

Variable rate loans, notes the SBA, may be pegged to either the SBA optional peg rate or the lowest prime rate (the optional peg rate is a weighed average of rates that the federal government pays for loans with maturities similar to the average SBA loan). Under variable rate loan plans, the lender and borrower negotiate the amount of the spread to be added to the base interest rate. Such agreements also provide for regular adjustment periods wherein the note rate can be changed as needed. Some agreements call for monthly adjustment periods, while others provide for quarterly, semiannual, or annual adjustments.

ELIGIBILITY ISSUES

The Small Business Administration defines businesses eligible for SBA loans as those that: operate for profit; are engaged in, or propose to do business in, the United States or its possessions; have reasonable owner equity to invest; and use alternative financial resources (such as personal assets) first. In addition, to secure SBA assistance, a company must qualify as a "small business" under the terms of the Small Business Act. That legislation defined an eligible small business as one that is independently owned and operated and not dominant in its industry.

Since the passage of the Small Business Act, the SBA has developed size standards for every industry to gauge whether a company qualifies as a "small business" or not. Size standards are arranged by Standard Industrial Classification (SIC) code, but in general, the following guidelines apply for major industry groups:

- Manufacturing—A key criteria for manufacturing establishments is the size of their work force. Generally, 1,500 employees is the cut-off point for SBA consideration, but even establishments that have between 500 and 1,500 employees may not qualify as small businesses; in such instances the SBA bases its determination on a size standard for the specific industry in which the business under consideration operates.

- Wholesaling—Generally, wholesale establishments seeking SBA financial assistance should not have more than 100 employees.

- Retail and Service—Financial information is the key consideration here; ideally, retail and service industry businesses seeking SBA assistance should not have more than $3.5 million in annual receipts, although the requests of establishments that report up to $13.5 million are considered (depending on the industry). Establishments engaged in construction or agriculture industries are also evaluated on the basis of their financial reports.

The Small Business Administration also considers other factors in determining whether an establishment qualifies as a small business. For example, if a business is affiliated with another company, the owners must determine the primary business activity of both the affiliated group and the applicant business before submitting a request for SBA assistance. If the applicant business and the affiliated group do not both meet the SBA's size standards for their primary business activities, then the loan request will not be considered.

The SBA also has a number of eligibility rules that apply to specific kinds of businesses. Franchisees, for example, are often favored by the SBA because their businesses enjoy a higher success rate than do other businesses. Nonetheless, SBA officials will examine a franchisee's franchise agreement closely before extending any loan guarantees to him or her. If the officials decide that the franchisor wields so much control over the franchise's operations that the franchisee is basically an employee, then the SBA will turn down the request. Other types of businesses, such as those in agriculture or the fishing industry, are free to apply for SBA assistance, but they are directed to first look to government agencies that deal directly with their industries. Farmers, for example, are supposed to first explore loan programs available through the Farmers Home Administration (FHA), while some members of the fishing industry—depending on the nature of their need—should first consult with the National Marine Fisheries Service (NMFS). The SBA also notes that some businesses are disqualified from consideration from the outset by the industry in which they operate. Businesses that operate in gambling, investment, or media-related fields, for example, are all ineligible for SBA loans.

Finally, the SBA notes that loans that they guarantee are only to be used for specific business purposes, including "the purchase of real estate to house the business operations; construction, renovation, or leasehold improvements; acquisition of furniture, fixtures, machinery, and equipment; purchase of inventory; and working capital." Using the money for other purposes—payment of delinquent withholding taxes, acquisition of another business, refinancing of debt, and a whole host of other actions—is not allowed.

APPLYING FOR AN SBA LOAN

The chief challenge of any business seeking to secure a loan from the Small Business Administration is to convince the SBA that it has the ability to be successful in its chosen field. To do so, the small business owner should be equipped with a complete understanding of his or her operation (whether existing or proposed) and the benefits that a loan, if granted, will bring to the business. Of course, it is also necessary to effectively articulate this information to the SBA. Business owners disseminate this data through a variety of documents.

Principal documents that should be submitted by the entrepreneur who hopes to start a new business include: **resume** (and resumes of any other key people involved in the proposed enterprise); current **financial statement** of all personal assets and liabilities; summary of **collateral**; proposed operating plan; and statement detailing revenue projections. Perhaps the most important document, however, is the loan request statement itself, for it is this document that should detail all aspects of the proposed business. For established business owners seeking an SBA loan, the most important documents—besides the loan application—are the company balance sheet, personal financial statements, and business income statements. Consultants urge small business owners to be both careful and realistic in preparing these records. They also caution entrepreneurs and small business owners not to distort figures or facts in their presentation. The SBA does not look kindly on misrepresentations in financial statements or any other part of the loan application.

THE LOAN APPLICATION The SBA loan application form serves to summarize much of the information detailed elsewhere in the total application package. Applicants are directed to furnish basic information about themselves and their businesses, including personal information (full legal name, street address); basic business information (employer ID number, type of business, number of employees, banking institution used); names and addresses of management personnel; estimated business expenditures and costs (including details on the SBA loan request); summary of collateral; summary of previous government financing; and listing of debts.

The SBA loan application form also provides a complete listing of the various other items of information that must be provided for a business's application to be considered. These include a personal history statement; personal and business financial statements; business description; listing of management personnel; equipment list; cosigners; summary of bankruptcies, insolvencies, and lawsuits (if any); listing of any familial relationships with SBA employees; subsidiaries, either proposed or in existence; franchise agreements; and statements of financial interest in any establishments with which applicant business does business, if applicable.

FURTHER READING:

Barlas, Stephen. "Looking Ahead: Three SBA Programs Face Closer Scrutiny." *Entrepreneur.* January 1997.

Bowles, Erskine. "Bite-Sized Loans." *Entrepreneur.* December 1993.

Cohen, William. *The Entrepreneur and Small Business Problem Solver.* New York: Wiley, 1990.

SBA Profile: Who We Are and What We Do. Third ed. Washington: Small Business Administration, fiscal year 1996.

V

VALUATION

Valuation is the process of putting a price on a piece of property. The value of businesses, personal property, **intellectual property** (such as patents, **trademarks**, and **copyrights**), and real estate are all commonly determined through the practice of valuation.

KEY VALUATION FACTORS

In the context of a business valuation, the appraiser considers many factors, including financial attributes (sales and profitability trends, noncash expenses, capital expenditures, tangible and intangible assets and liabilities, contracts, contingent liabilities, and others), marketing attributes (location, competition, barriers to entry, distributor and supplier relationships), and larger economic factors (regulatory environment, labor relations, interest rates, consumer confidence, the stock market, etc.).

In his book *Valuing Small Businesses and Professional Practices,* Shannon Pratt listed six particularly important factors in figuring business value:

- Recent profit history
- General condition of the business (including recordkeeping, equipment and facilities, work environment, etc.)
- Market demand for products or services offered by the business
- General economic conditions (with special emphasis on factors such as loan interest rates that directly impact on the business in question)
- Ability to transfer intangible assets to buyers
- Future profit potential of business

APPROACHES TO VALUATION

Several different valuation approaches can be used to determine the value of a business. Some are better suited to certain business types than others, and as Lawrence Tuller noted in *Getting Out: A Step-by-Step Guide to Selling a Business or Professional Practice,* "everyone has his own theory about the most equitable and accurate method [of valuation]." In addition, wrote Tuller, each business interest tends to favor the "method that best suits his own self-interests. Finance companies value a business at what the assets will bring at liquidation auction. Investment bankers and venture capitalists, interested in rapid appreciation and high returns on their investment, value a business at discounted future cash flow. Statisticians have devised complex deviation curves based on historical performance to project future earnings. Corporate America looks to the prevailing P/E ratios, unless the market is depressed, in which case they use book value."

BALANCE SHEET METHODS OF VALUATION These methods of valuation are most often employed when the business under examination generates most of its earnings from its **assets** (rather than the contributions of its employees). It is also used, wrote John A. Johansen in *How to Buy or Sell a Business,* "when the cost of starting a business and getting revenues past the break-even point doesn't greatly exceed the value of the business's assets."

- Liquidation Approach—This method assesses the value of a business by gauging its value if were to cease operations and sell its individual assets. Under this approach, the business owner would receive no compensation for business **goodwill**—nontangible assets such as the company's name, location, customer base, or accumulated experience. This method is further divided into forced liquidations (as in bankruptcies) and orderly liquidations. Values are typically figured higher in the latter instances. Asset-based lenders and banks tend to favor this method, because they view the liquidation value of a company's tangible assets to be the only valuable **collateral** to the loan. But it is unpopular with most business owners because of the lack of consideration given to goodwill and other intangible assets.

- Asset Value Approach—This approach begins by examining the company's book value. Under this method, items listed on a business's balance sheet (at historical cost levels) are adjusted to bring them in line with current market values. In essence, this method calls for the adjustment of an asset's book value to equal the cost of replacing that asset in its current condition. This method is most often used to determine the value of companies which feature a large percentage of commodity-type assets. The net asset value method is one of the most commonly employed of all valuation approaches. "Simply put, net asset value is the recorded book value of the business, with a few adjustments. It is also referred to as net worth or owner's equity," wrote Tuller. While flawed in some respects, the net asset value method is popular because, "with all its faults, this method at least gives some measure of a company's value and can easily be calculated from existing financial statements."

INCOME STATEMENT METHODS OF VALUATION These valuation methods are perhaps the most frequently used of the myriad valuation approaches that exist.

- Historical Cash Flow Approach—This is the most commonly used of all valuation methods. Many buyers view this method as the most relevant of all valuation approaches for it tells them what the business has historically provided to its owners in terms of cash. As Tuller observed, "the value of assets might be interesting to know, but hardly anyone buys a business only for its balance sheet assets. The whole purpose is to make money, and most buyers feel that they should be able to generate at least as much cash in the future as the business yielded in the past." This method typically takes financial data from the company's previous three years in drawing its conclusions.

- Discounted Future Cash Flow (DCF) Approach—This method uses projections of future cash flows from operating the business to determine company value. The DCF approach requires detailed assumptions about future operations, including volumes, pricing, costs, and other factors. DCF usually starts with forecast income, adding back non-cash expenses, deducting capital expenditures, and adjusting for working capital changes to arrive at expected cash flows. The future cash flow method also is notable for its recognition of industry reputation, popularity with customers, and other "goodwill" factors in its assessment of company value. Once the value of the business's assets has been settled upon, the appropriate discount rate must be determined and used to bring the future cash flows back to their present value at the as-of date of the valuation. DCF in its single period form is known as capitalization of earnings, which usually involves "normalizing" a recent measure of income or cash flow to reflect a steady-state or going forward amount that can be capitalized at the appropriate multiple.

MARKET COMPARABLE APPROACH This approach looks to comparable companies—in terms of industry, size, growth rates, capitalization, and other factors—for which a market value is known or observable (e.g., publicly traded companies) to establish a value for the company under examination. This approach, contended Johansen, is inherently flawed since "rarely if ever are two businesses truly comparable. However, businesses in the same industry do have some characteristics in common, and a careful contrasting may allow a conclusion to be drawn about a range of value."

VALUING PERSONAL SERVICE BUSINESSES

Different valuation methods and emphases are required when assessing the value of a personal service business such as a medical practice. While equipment, supplies, real estate and other assets that are typically included in assessing the value of companies are also included in assessing personal service business values, they are often of little consequence to potential buyers of the business in question. After all, a buyer may have an entirely new location in mind for the business, and costs associated with leases, utilities, and taxes often change dramatically with relocation. Instead, wrote Tuller, the most important consideration in valuing any personal service business ''is how much gross billings can be generated from the customer/client base, not what profits have been recorded or how much cash [the owner has] taken out. . . . A key consideration to keep in mind if you are selling a professional practice is that the goodwill you have built up over the years is really what you are selling. Sometimes, it is called customer or client lists, or client files, but it is really just goodwill.''

VALUATION ISSUES AND STANDARDS

It is important to recognize and deal properly with certain subtleties and standards in the field of valuation. Issues and standards to keep in mind include:

TREATMENT OF DEBT If the method used to determine company value uses a pre-debt-service income measure, then debt must usually be subtracted from the resulting figure.

CONTROL PREMIUMS If the valuation methodology used is based on **price-earnings ratios** of comparable public companies and the interest being valued is the entirety of a company, a control premium may be imposed.

DISCOUNT FOR LACK OF MARKETABILITY This discount, also known as the liquidity discount, comes into play in situations where the business owner's ability to readily sell his or her business is questionable. For example, publicly traded companies are highly marketable, and their shares can be quickly turned into cash. Closely held companies, however, are sometimes far more difficult to sell. Depending on the valuation, it may be necessary to subtract a discount for lack of marketability, or add a premium for the presence of marketability.

STANDARD OF VALUE When determining valuation of a company, the standard of value must be clearly defined. That is, it must be clear whether the valuation is based on book value, fair market value, liquidating versus going concern value, investment value, or some other definition of value. Defining the standard of value is important because of adjustments that are necessary under some, but not all, of these standards.

''AS-OF'' DATES Valuation methods determine the value of a company at a given point in time. Thus, businesses that undergo a valuation process are said to be worth X dollars ''as of'' a certain date. Values of businesses inevitably change over time, so it is critical to state the date for any valuation. In addition, the information used by the appraiser should be limited to that which would have been available at the as-of date.

FORM OF ORGANIZATION The legal definition of the organization under examination is an important factor in any valuation. Different legal forms of entity—C corporations, S corporations, partnerships, and sole proprietorships—are all subject to different tax rules which impact the value of the enterprise being appraised.

FOCUS OF VALUATION The focus of the valuation must be clearly identified. The portion of the business enterprise being acquired, the type(s) of securities involved, the nature of the purchase (asset purchase or stock purchase), and possible impact of the transaction on existing relationships (such as related party transfers) can all affect the value of the entity under examination.

FURTHER READING:

Johansen, John A. *How to Buy or Sell a Business.* Washington: Small Business Administration, n.a.

Pratt, Shannon P. *Valuing a Business.* Dow Jones-Irwin, 1989.

Pratt, Shannon P. *Valuing Small Businesses and Professional Practices.* Dow Jones-Irwin, 1986.

Semanik, Michael K., and John H. Wade. *The Complete Guide to Selling a Business.* New York: Amacom, 1994.

Tuller, Lawrence W. *Getting Out: A Step-by-Step Guide to Selling a Business or Professional Practice.* Liberty Hall, 1990.

Yegge, Wilbur M. *A Basic Guide to Buying and Selling a Company.* Wiley, 1996.

SEE ALSO: Buying an Existing Business; Selling a Business

VARIABLE PAY

Variable pay programs are an increasingly popular mode of compensation in today's business world. These programs, which are also sometimes referred to as ''pay-for-performance'' or ''at-risk'' pay plans, provide some or all of a work force's compensation based on employee performance or on the performance of a team. Variable pay proponents contend that it rewards high performance and does not reward mediocre or low performance, and that it is truly predicated on merit. ''Variable pay is hot these days, and companies are going for bonus programs like bass in a feeding frenzy,'' wrote Jack Stack in *Inc.* ''The idea is to give people an incentive to work harder and smarter, while keeping fixed costs low.'' He noted that the central theory of variable pay programs is that ''people will do more when they know they'll get a nice reward if the company has a great year, outperforms its competitors, and increases its value.''

Variable pay programs can take a range of forms, including annual incentives or bonus payments; individual incentive plans; lump-sum payments;

technical achievement awards; cash **profit-sharing** plans; small group incentives; gainsharing; and payments for skill and knowledge. Some analysts disagree about whether some of the above offerings are true variable pay programs, but most agree that all of the above share a common emphasis on recognizing achievement, which is the ultimate goal of variable pay plans. (All agree that standardized merit programs, in which individual performance is a negligible factor in determining compensation changes, do not qualify.) Business experts say that small business owners seeking to increase productivity should consider variable pay as an option, but they are also discouraged from implementing a plan without first engaging in an appropriate examination of current company issues and future company goals. "In establishing merit increase programs or any other cash bonus incentives, companies should keep in mind the type of work force they have, what the competition in their industry is doing, what the company philosophy is—and have a strong plan in place to set company goals and ensure all business units or departments of the organization are clear about the goals," wrote Brenda Paik Sunoo in *Personnel Journal.*

Indeed, businesses that adopt variable pay have to recognize the importance of tailoring the program to account for different circumstances. Factors that have to be considered, said Sunoo, include:

- Achievement of business and personal growth goals

- Compensation packages that are available to employees if they decided to look elsewhere for work

- Current level of pay based on salary range relative to skills and experience

- Eligibility of variable pay as an ingredient in total cash compensation

"In a pay-for-performance environment, we expect true differentiation based on these types of factors," wrote Sunoo. "Managing a performance-based salary program requires a strong commitment to goal setting and measurement."

VARIABLE PAY AND THE MODERN BUSINESS ENVIRONMENT

The growing prevalence of variable pay alternatives in business compensation strategies has been attributed in part to a couple of other business trends. "Employers are facing up to a new reality about the way jobs should be valued and compensated in an age of rapid technological change," wrote Paul J. Williamson in *Small Business Reports.* "Gone are the days when employees' skills lasted a lifetime and companies could predict the future value of jobs— and thus a fixed pay increase—based on past perform-

ance. Today, as customer needs shift rapidly due to advances in technology, the skills you need to make a profit may change almost before the ink is dry on your job descriptions." At the same time, business observers point out that increased emphasis on quick reactions to changing competitive conditions have triggered a growth in movement toward employee empowerment. As employees become more empowered, employers have had to find new ways to compensate them for their contributions to the overall enterprise.

Other analysts of variable pay frame the issue in terms of **return on investment (ROI)**. "To minimize today's heightened business risk, you must reduce your investment in fixed costs and maximize the use of variable costs, which the company incurs only if it achieves certain results," stated Williamson. "Nowhere is this mandate more essential than in the balance between fixed and variable pay, since compensation often is a company's single largest expense."

ADVANTAGES AND DRAWBACKS OF VARIABLE PAY

Most criticisms of variable pay can be traced to concerns about the nature, implementation, and execution of such programs rather than the theories upon which they are based. *Inc.*'s Jack Stack, for instance, argued that many companies fail to make variable pay programs meaningful to individual employees, which in turn robs the program of much of its power to facilitate increased productivity. "Most [variable pay] programs provide no incentive to anyone and never deliver the promised results," he charged. "Why not? Because in 9 cases out of 10, they are not true bonus programs at all. They are simply profit-sharing programs, and there is a world of difference between the two. By profit-sharing, I mean the practice of taking a percentage of a company's profits, putting it into a pool, and disbursing it to the company's employees, usually sometime after the close of the year." Stack contended that such a distribution plan is not likely to encourage employees toward greater productivity. "The recipients seldom know exactly how they helped generate the profits, beyond just doing their jobs. No doubt, they enjoy getting the money. They may even be grateful for it. But they aren't likely to think or act differently because of it or to be greatly motivated by it." Williamson agreed, adding that "many of the failures to date have occurred because companies simply reshuffled the same amount of compensation in a new plan, offering some through fixed pay and some through incentives. But they didn't use the plan to create reach change in the way they organize and value work."

But business consultants agree that variable pay programs that truly reward individual performance can be helpful. The purpose of a good bonus program, Stack said, should be "to make the company stronger, more competitive, able to survive and prosper in the months and years ahead. . . . A good bonus program draws people into that process. It drives the value of the company by educating people, not with formal training programs but through the work they do every day on the job. It gives them the tools they need to make and understand decisions. It provides them with business knowledge they can use to enhance their own standard of living and job security as they're making a measurable difference to the company as a whole."

ESTABLISHING A VARIABLE PAY SYSTEM

Proponents of variable pay programs contend that implementation of such a system is far more likely to be successful if the following conditions are met:

- Employees must have control over their performance. If employees are overly dependent on the actions and output of other employees or processes, they may have little control over their own performance. Variable pay programs that are not based on principles of employee empowerment are almost certainly doomed to fail.

- Differences in performance must mean something to the business. Employees must see that mediocre and high performances are not rewarded equally, and that results count. "When employees achieve better results— by assuming more risk, addressing more variables in their work, and making better judgments—they should get more pay, not the same amount in a different mix," said Williamson.

- Business goals must be clearly defined and adequately disseminated to employees, and they should be arrived at with their assistance.

- Performance must be measured regularly and reliably. A clear system of performance appraisal and feedback must be put in place, with regularly scheduled meetings as one component.

- Employers should use variable pay as a tool in reaching ambitious business goals. "You need targets that require some effort," argued Stack. "I'm not talking about having stretch goals, which are almost always demotivators, but neither should the targets be so easy that people can take them for granted."

- Businesses should make sure that their variable pay plans reward employees for actions or skills that actually further the aims of the company. "If you pay for skills the company does not fully utilize or, worse yet, does not need at all, the plan won't deliver better results," said Williamson.

FURTHER READING:

Beatty, L. Kate. "Pay and Benefits Break Away from Tradition." *HRMagazine*. November 1994.

Belcher, John G., Jr. "Gainsharing and Variable Pay: The State of the Art." *Compensation and Benefits Review*. May-June 1994.

Boyett, Joseph H., and Henry P. Conn. *Workplace 2000: The Revolution Reshaping American Business*. Plume, 1992.

Clark, Amy W. "Aligning Compensation with Business Strategy." *Employment Relations Today*. Winter 1995.

Hay Group. *People, Performance, & Pay: Dynamic Compensation for Changing Organizations*. The Free Press, 1996.

"Linking Quality and Pay." *Personnel Review*. March 1994.

Milkovich, George T., and Alexandra K. Wigdor. *Pay for Performance: Evaluating Performance Appraisal and Merit Pay*. National Academy Press, 1991.

Stack, Jack. "The Problem With Profit Sharing." *Inc*. November 1996.

Sunoo, Brenda Paik. "Tie Merit Increases to Goal-Setting and Employer Objectives." *Personnel Journal*. November 1996.

Williamson, Paul J. "How to Shake Up Your Pay." *Small Business Reports*. August 1994.

SEE ALSO: Employee Compensation; Employee Reward Systems; Sales Commissions

VENTURE CAPITAL

Venture capital refers to funds that are invested in an unproven business venture. Venture capital may be provided by wealthy individual investors, professionally managed investment funds, government-backed **Small Business Investment Corporations (SBICs)**, or subsidiaries of investment banking firms, insurance companies, or corporations. Such venture capital organizations generally invest in private startup companies with a high profit potential. In exchange for their funds, venture capital organizations usually require a percentage of equity ownership of the company, some measure of control over its strategic planning, and payment of assorted fees. Due to the highly speculative nature of their investments, venture capital organizations expect a high rate of return. In addition, they often wish to obtain this return over a relatively short period of time, usually within three to seven years. After this time, the equity is either sold back to the client company or offered on a public stock exchange.

Venture capital is somewhat more difficult for a small business to obtain other sources of financing, such as bank **loans** and supplier credit. Before providing venture capital to a new or growing business, venture capital organizations require a formal proposal and conduct a thorough evaluation. Even then, they tend to approve only a small percentage of the proposals they receive. Perhaps the most important thing an entrepreneur can do to increase his or her chances of obtaining venture capital is to plan ahead.

Venture capital offers several advantages to small businesses, including management assistance and lower costs over the short term. In addition, venture capital is more likely to be available to startup or concept businesses than other forms of financing. The disadvantages associated with venture capital include the possible loss of effective control over the business and relatively high costs over the long term. Overall, experts suggest that entrepreneurs should consider venture capital to be one financing strategy among many, and should seek to combine it with debt financing if possible.

Entrepreneurs can make contact with venture capitalists in a number of different ways. In recent years, venture capital fairs have been conducted throughout the United States in areas showing strong growth in new ventures. Entrepreneurs can meet and make proposals to potential investors at these fairs, although in some cases only pre-qualified candidates are invited to attend. There are also two major venture capital associations that may provide good sources of information and contacts: the Western Association of Venture Capitalists, based in Menlo Park, California; and the National Venture Capital Association, based in Arlington, Virginia.

THE EVALUATION PROCESS

Since it is often difficult to evaluate the earnings potential of new business ideas or very young companies, and investments in such companies are unprotected against business failures, venture capital is a highly risky industry. As a result, venture capital firms set rigorous policies and requirements for the types of proposals they will consider. Some venture capitalists specialize in certain technologies, industries, or geographic areas, for example, while others require a certain size of investment. The maturity of the company may also be a factor. While most venture capital firms require their client companies to have some operating history, a small number handle startup financing for businesses that have a well-considered plan and an experienced management group.

In general, venture capitalists are most interested in supporting companies with low current valuations, but with good opportunities to achieve future profits of about 30 percent annually. Most attractive are innovative companies in rapidly accelerating industries with few competitors. Ideally, the company and its product or service will have some unique, market-

able feature to distinguish it from imitators. Most venture capital firms look for investment opportunities in the $250,000 to $2 million range, although some are willing to consider smaller or larger projects. Since venture capitalists become part owners of the companies in which they invest, they tend to look for businesses that can increase sales and generate strong profits with the help of a capital infusion. Because of the risk involved, they hope to obtain a return of three to five times their initial investment within five years.

According to LaRue T. Hosmer in the U.S. Small Business Administration publication *A Venture Capital Primer for Small Business,* a typical venture capital organization receives in the neighborhood of 1,000 proposals per year and rejects up to 90 percent of them immediately due to a poor fit with the firm's priorities and policies. They then investigate the remaining 10 percent of the proposals very carefully, and at considerable expense. Whereas banks tend to focus on companies' past performance when evaluating them for loans, venture capital firms tend to focus on their future potential. As a result, venture capital organizations will examine the features of a small business's product, the size of its markets, and its earnings projections.

As part of the detailed investigation, a venture capital organization may hire consultants to evaluate highly technical products. They also may contact a company's customers and suppliers in order to obtain information about the market size and the company's competitive position. Many venture capitalists will also hire an auditor to confirm the financial position of the company, and an attorney to check the legal form and registration of the business. Perhaps the most important factor in a venture capital organization's evaluation of a small business as a potential investment is the background and competence of the small business's management. Hosmer noted that "many venture capital firms really invest in management capability" rather than a small business's product or market potential. Since the abilities of management are often difficult to assess, it is likely that a representative of the venture capital organization would spend a week or two at the company. Ideally, venture capitalists like to see a committed management team with experience in the industry. Another plus is a complete management group with clearly defined responsibilities in specific functional areas, such as product design, marketing, and finance.

This initial investigation may cost a venture capital organization $2,000 to $3,000 per proposal, according to Hosmer. Afterward, the venture capital firm may narrow the field of candidates for investment to 10 or 15 proposals. Additional investigations follow until the venture capital organization finally selects one or two small businesses in which to invest.

VENTURE CAPITAL PROPOSALS

In order to ensure that it will be considered by venture capital organizations, an entrepreneur's proposal should include a number of elements. After beginning with a statement of purpose and objectives, the proposal should outline the financing arrangements requested, i.e., how much money the small business needs, how the money will be used, and how the financing will be structured. The next section should feature the small business's marketing plans, from the characteristics of the market and the competition to specific plans for getting and keeping market share.

A good venture capital proposal will also include a history of the company, its major products and services, its banking relationships and financial milestones, and its hiring practices and employee relations. In addition, the proposal should include complete financial statements for the previous few years, as well as pro forma projections for next three to five years. The financial information should detail the small business's capitalization—i.e., provide a list of shareholders and bank loans—and show the effect of the proposed development on its capital structure. The proposal should also include biographies of the key players involved with the small business, as well as contact information for its principal suppliers and customers. Finally, the entrepreneur should outline the advantages of the proposal—including any special and unique features it may offer—as well as any problems that are anticipated.

If, after careful investigation and analysis, a venture capital organization decides to invest in a small business, it then prepares its own proposal. The venture capital firm's proposal should detail how much money it would provide, the amount of stock it would expect the small business to surrender in exchange, and the protective covenants it would require as part of the agreement. The venture capital organization's proposal is presented to the management of the small business, and then a final agreement is negotiated between the two parties. According to Hosmer, compromises usually must be reached in the areas of valuation, ownership, control, annual charges, and final objectives.

The **valuation** of the small business and the entrepreneur's stake in it is very important, as it determines the amount of equity that is required in exchange for the venture capital. In cases where the present financial value of the entrepreneur's contribution is relatively low compared to that made by the venture capitalists—for example, when it consists only of an idea for a new product—then a large percentage of equity is generally required. On the other hand, when the valuation of a small business is relatively high—for example, when it is already a successful company—then a small percentage of equity is generally required. Hosmer warned that entrepreneurs are likely to find that the valuation of their businesses provided by a venture capital organization will not be as high as they would like.

The percentage of equity ownership required by a venture capital firm can range from 10 percent to 80 percent, depending on the amount of capital provided and the anticipated return. But most venture capital organizations want to secure equity in the 30 to 40 percent range so that the small business owners still have an incentive to grow the business. Since venture capital is in effect an investment in a small business's management team, the venture capitalists usually want to leave management with some control. In general, venture capital organizations have little or no interest in assuming day-to-day operational control of the small businesses in which they invest. But venture capitalists usually do want to place a representative on each small business's board of directors in order to participate in strategic decision-making. In her book *The Entrepreneur's Guide to Capital,* Jennifer Lindsey claimed that venture capital firms thus assist their clients' growth through "active guidance."

Many venture capital agreements include an annual charge, typically two percent of the amount of capital provided, although some firms instead opt to take a cut of profits above a certain level. Venture capital organizations also frequently include protective covenants in their agreements. These covenants usually give the venture capitalists the ability to appoint new officers and assume control of the small business in case of severe financial, operating, or marketing problems. Such control is intended to enable the venture capital organization to recover some of its investment if the small business should falter.

The final objectives of a venture capital agreement relate to the means and time frame in which the venture capitalists will earn a return on their investment. In most cases, the return takes the form of capital gains earned when the venture capital organization sells its equity holdings back to the small business or on a public stock exchange. Another option is for the venture capital firm to arrange for the small business to merge with a larger company. The majority of venture capital arrangements include an equity position, along with a final objective that involves the venture capitalist selling that position. For this reason, Lindsey pointed out, entrepreneurs considering using venture capital as a source of financing need to consider the impact a future stock sale will have on their own holdings and their personal ambition to run the company. Ideally, the entrepreneur and the venture capital organization can reach an agreement that will help the small business grow enough to provide the venture capitalists with a good return on their investment as well as to overcome the owner's loss of equity.

THE IMPORTANCE OF PLANNING

Although there is no way for a small business to guarantee that it will be able to obtain venture capital, sound planning can at least improve the chances that its proposal will receive due consideration from a venture capital organization. Such planning should begin at least a year before the entrepreneur first seeks financing. At this point, it is important to do market research to determine the need for the new business concept or product idea and establish patent or trade secret protection, if possible. In addition, the entrepreneur should take steps to form a business around the product or concept, enlisting the assistance of third-party professionals like attorneys, accountants, and financial advisers as needed.

Six months prior to seeking venture capital, the entrepreneur should prepare a detailed **business plan**, complete with financial projections, and begin working on a formal request for funds. Three months in advance, the entrepreneur should investigate **venture capital organizations** to identify those that are most likely to be interested in the proposal and to provide a suitable venture capital agreement. The best investor candidates will compliment the company's development stage, size, industry, and financing needs. It is also important to gather information about a venture capitalist's reputation, track record in the industry, and liquidity to ensure a productive working relationship.

One of the most important steps in the planning process is preparing detailed financial plans. Hosmer claimed that strong financial planning demonstrates managerial competence and suggests an advantage to potential investors. A financial plan should include cash budgets—prepared monthly and projected for a year ahead—that enable the company to anticipate fluctuations in short-term cash levels and the need for short-term borrowing. A financial plan should also include **pro forma statements**—income statements and balance sheets—projected for up to three years. By showing expected sales revenues and expenses, assets and liabilities, these statements help the company anticipate financial results and plan for intermediate-term financing needs. Finally, the financial plan should include an analysis of capital investments made by the company in products, processes, or markets, along with a study of the company's sources of capital. These plans, prepared for five years ahead, assist the company in anticipating the financial consequences of strategic shifts and in planning for long-term financing needs.

Overall, experts warn that it takes time and persistence for entrepreneurs to obtain venture capital. But venture capital is becoming more widely available in the late 1990s, thanks to the strong American economy, the great interest shown in initial public stock offerings, and the rapid emergence of new technology in areas such as the Internet, telecommunica-

tions, and health care. According to David R. Evanson in an article for *Nation's Business,* another factor increasing the availability of venture capital is the recent rise in private investment. Evanson argued that there is a whole generation of wealthy entrepreneurs in America who are investing $10 to $20 billion per year to aid the growth of other small companies. Another trend in the industry involves foreign venture capital, an arrangement in which overseas companies provide financing to small U.S. firms in exchange for royalties, a percentage of profits, a license for technology, or overseas sales agreements. Basically, these foreign companies try to form strategic partnerships with young American companies that are producing things needed in overseas markets.

FURTHER READING:

Evanson, David R. "Venture Capital, Networks Proliferate." *Nation's Business.* September 1996.

Geer, John F., Jr. "The Venture Capital Boom: It's Gold Medal Time for the Venture Capitalists." *Financial World.* November 18, 1996.

Gladstone, David. *Venture Capital Handbook.* Englewood Cliffs, NJ: Prentice Hall, 1988.

Hamilton, Brian. *Financing for the Small Business.* Washington: U.S. Small Business Administration, 1990.

Hosmer, LaRue T. *A Venture Capital Primer for Small Business.* Washington: U.S. Small Business Administration, 1990.

Lindsey, Jennifer. *The Entrepreneur's Guide to Capital.* Chicago: Probus, 1986.

Schilit, W. Keith. *The Entrepreneur's Guide to Preparing a Winning Business Plan and Raising Venture Capital.* Englewood Cliffs, NJ: Prentice Hall, 1990.

Silver, A. David. *Up Front Financing: The Entrepreneur's Guide.* New York: Wiley, 1982.

Timmons, Jeffrey A. *Planning and Financing the New Venture.* Brick House Publishing Company, 1990.

SEE ALSO: Business Proposals; Business Planning; Equity Financing; Risk and Return

VENTURE CAPITAL NETWORKS

Venture capital networks, or clubs, are groups of individual and institutional investors that provide financing to risky, unproven business ventures. Like other providers of **venture capital**—which may include professionally managed investment funds, government-backed **Small Business Investment Corporations (SBICs)**, or subsidiaries of investment banking firms, insurance companies, and corporations—members of these networks generally invest in private startup companies with a high profit potential. In exchange for their funds, the venture capitalists usually require a percentage of equity ownership in the company, some measure of control over its strategic planning, and payment of assorted fees. Due to the highly speculative nature of their investments, venture capitalists hope to achieve a high rate of return over a relatively short period of time.

The main difference between venture capital networks and other venture capital providers is their degree of formality. Venture capital networks are informal organizations that exist to help entrepreneurs and small businesses connect with potential investors. Before the advent of networks, it was extremely difficult for entrepreneurs to gain access to wealthy private investors, also known as ''angels'' or ''adventure capitalists.'' The networks—which may take the form of computer databases or document clearinghouses—basically provide ''matchmaking'' services between people with good business ideas and people with money to invest. In contrast, formal venture capital firms are professionally managed organizations that exist to earn a high return on funds by investing in new and growing companies. These firms are typically highly selective about the companies in which they invest, meaning that venture capital from these sources is not available to the vast majority of startup businesses.

According to David R. Evanson in an article for *Nation's Business,* wealthy private investors provide American small businesses with $10 to $20 billion annually, which ''dwarfs the investment made by traditional venture capital partnerships and offers a viable source of financing for capital hungry entrepreneurs.'' To a great degree, the membership of venture capital networks consists of wealthy entrepreneurs. These individuals want to invest in up-and-coming new companies not only to earn money, Evanson suggested, but also to provide a resource that would have been helpful to them in the early stages of their own businesses. In many cases, the investors sit on the boards of the companies they fund and provide valuable, firsthand management advice.

HOW NETWORKS WORK

In the past, it was extremely difficult for entrepreneurs to find and make contact with private investors. In response to this problem, many business groups and universities have created networks in recent years to help entrepreneurs gain access to interested investors. One of the earliest such efforts was the Venture Capital Network, a computer database that was established by a professor at the University of New Hampshire. This and other computerized networks are similar to computer matchmaking services. Each entrepreneur posts a **business plan** and a set of financial projections on the network, while each investor submits information describing his or her interests and investment criteria. Due to their previous business experience, different investors may be most interested in investing in companies of a certain size, in a certain industry, or with certain capital requirements. The computer then provides participants with a list of possible matches. Interested parties are left to make contact with one another and try to reach an agreement.

Non-computerized venture capital networks operate in basically the same way. A central clearinghouse solicits business plans from companies seeking capital, then distributes profiles of the companies to private investors who belong to the network. If a certain investor wants to know more about a particular company, he or she might arrange for a formal presentation. In many cases, both business and investor profiles are distributed anonymously—without names attached—until both parties express an interest in proceeding further. Another similar type of arrangement can be found in a private investment club, which are community-based organizations in which several individuals pool their resources to invest in new and existing businesses. Such clubs generally solicit business plans and distribute them to members, and then invest as a group.

The financing provided through venture capital networks ranges from $25,000 to $1 million, although the majority of deals are under $100,000. Business owners typically pay a small fee to participate in a network—between $100 and $350 a year—and institutional investors may pay a somewhat higher fee. Although venture capital networks are usually better sources of funding for startup companies than formal venture capital firms, merely joining a network does not guarantee that a small business will obtain financing. There are usually at least two companies for every one investor listed in databases. In addition, even if a match is made, the entrepreneur still must sell the investor on the proposal and negotiate a mutually beneficial agreement.

FURTHER READING:

Brown, Carolyn R. ''Matchmaking for Venture Capital: Database Networks Can Help Your Business Connect with Willing Investors.'' *Black Enterprise.* June 1994.

Evanson, David R. ''Venture Capital, Networks Proliferate.'' *Nation's Business.* September 1996.

Geer, John F., Jr. ''The Venture Capital Boom: It's Gold Medal Time for the Venture Capitalists.'' *Financial World.* November 18, 1996.

Gladstone, David. *Venture Capital Handbook.* Englewood Cliffs, NJ: Prentice Hall, 1988.

Hosmer, LaRue T. *A Venture Capital Primer for Small Business.* Washington: U.S. Small Business Administration, 1990.

Lindsey, Jennifer. *The Entrepreneur's Guide to Capital.* Chicago: Probus, 1986.

Schilit, W. Keith. *The Entrepreneur's Guide to Preparing a Winning Business Plan and Raising Venture Capital.* Englewood Cliffs, NJ: Prentice Hall, 1990.

SEE ALSO: Angel Investors; Equity Financing; Venture Capital Organizations

Venture capital refers to the initial funding and capital for new and emerging business enterprises. Thus, when individual entrepreneurs or very new businesses need funds or equity for growth and expansion, they are said to be searching for venture capital to fuel the organizational activities. Venture capital organizations are the professional organizations and institutions that specialize in backing new ventures or entrepreneurs. These organizations provide the capital needed by new ventures in exchange for partial ownership of the business or interest on the funds lent. Additionally, venture capital organizations often provide the entrepreneur with management assistance and become involved with the strategic planning of the new venture.

While venture capital organizations may be affiliated with banks or other lending institutions, most are independent and privately managed. Their efforts are focused: business activity is limited to working with start-ups or young organizations. Venture capital organizations provide their clients with capital through direct equity investments, loans, or other financial arrangements. Due to the highly speculative nature of their investments, venture capital organizations are taking big risks by working with new ventures. According to John F. Geer, Jr. in an article for *Financial World,* venture capitalists today expect only two of every ten of their investments to be big successes, and hope that no more than two other small businesses they back will fail completely. In exchange for the high level of risk, venture capital organizations expect a high return on their investments.

BACKGROUND

All businesses need some financial resources to begin activity. The exchange between someone with a good idea (an entrepreneur) and someone with the resources to help make a business out of the idea (a banker, a rich uncle, or a venture capitalist) is as old as business itself. However, venture capital as a distinct form of business financing arose only recently. John Wilson, in his book *The New Ventures: Inside the High Stakes World of Venture Capital,* marks 1946 as the year the venture capital industry originated in the United States. J.H. Whitney brought together partners from the East Coast for the first venture capital fund, working with an initial capitalization of approximately $10 million. The structure of the first fund—a partnership between those contributing to the initial capitalization—was the model for a majority of venture capital organizations that followed as the industry grew.

The passage of the Small Business Investment Act of 1958 by the federal government was an important incentive for would-be venture capital organizations. The act provided venture capital firms organized as **Small Business Investment Companies (SBICs)** and Minority Enterprise Small Business Investment Companies (MESBICs) with an opportunity to increase the amount of funds available to entrepreneurs. The privately managed SBICs and MESBICs had access to federal money through the **U.S. Small Business Administration** which could then be leveraged four dollars to one against privately raised funds. The SBICs and MESBICs, in turn, made the financial resources available to new ventures and entrepreneurs in their communities.

In recent decades, the venture capital industry has become big business. According to the *U.S. Industrial Outlook 1994,* organizations engaged in venture capital disbursed approximately $2.55 billion in funds to new ventures and entrepreneurs in that year. However, the industry has changed since its inception. Early venture capitalists primarily provided money to organizations for start-up activities. But one of the characteristics of the industry in the 1990s was a tendency for venture capital organizations to shy away from early stage and start-up financing, preferring to invest in companies that were relatively established. Rather than provide the entrepreneur or new venture with money early on in the growth of the business (in the first year, for instance), venture capital firms in the 1990s more often provided funds for products and services with proven markets and a higher chance of success in the marketplace. Brand new businesses with financing needs were more often passed over in favor of those businesses with track records (albeit short) and a relatively clear path to profitability.

TYPES OF VENTURE CAPITAL FIRMS

What may have started out as a relatively loose partnership of individuals with money to invest has become a set of organizations with formalized structures and business activities. Venture capital firms, or financial firms who disperse venture funds along with other financing options, have become accepted parts of the business world, finding their own niche as providers of capital for higher risk situations.

As the industry matures, two types of organizations predominate among those disbursing venture capital. The structure of the venture organization usually dictates the means through which the organization makes a profit.

Leveraged firms borrow money from other financial institutions, the government, or private sources, and in turn lend the funds to entrepreneurs and new ventures at a higher rate of interest. Leveraged firms make money by charging their clients a higher interest rate than they pay for the use of the funds. Because leveraged firms rely on interest income, they make most of the disbursements in the form of loans to new ventures.

Equity firms sell stock in the venture capital organization to individual or institutional investors and then use the proceeds from the sale to purchase equity in new ventures. Equity venture capital firms build ''portfolios'' of investments in companies. This kind of venture capital company tries to resell the stock of its portfolio businesses at a later date and for a profit. Whereas a leveraged firm can expect a relatively steady stream of interest income, an equity firm may not experience a return on its investment for years. The return usually comes as a result of the sale of equity in the new venture. Venture capital organizations can either sell their equity back to the company itself or on the public stock exchanges (like the New York Stock Exchange) in an **initial public offering (IPO)**.

Even though there are two primary forms of venture capital organizations, there are a variety of ownership schemes. David Gladstone, in his *Venture Capital Handbook,* discussed the most common forms ownership. A few firms are publicly owned and traded. Because of the nature of the ownership, these firms tend to be larger than most other venture capital organizations. Gladstone notes that an overwhelming majority of firms are private companies. The firms may have been formed by families or small groups of investors. More often, they are limited partnerships formed by insurance companies or pension funds. These organizations generally form the venture capital organizations to achieve a greater rate of return than most of their other investments. Other firms are organized as bank subsidiaries as a way for banks to own equity in small businesses. These organizations are independent of other bank activities. Some firms have been set up by corporations, though Gladstone noted these types of organizations are relatively rare. In other cases, corporations looking to gain high returns on their funds invest in existing venture capital limited partnerships where risk can be shared and liabilities are limited.

TYPES OF FINANCING PROVIDED

Regardless of ownership, the professional managers who run the venture capital firms generally operate in the same manner. The strategy laid out by the firm's managers determines when and how much the firm will invest in entrepreneurial ventures. Venture capital organizations invest at different stages in the development of the enterprise. The managers of a venture capital firm may prefer to invest in brand new companies, or their strategy may dictate investment in businesses that are much more developed. Because the business is unproven, early investments are inherently more risky and the investment firm can demand a higher return. Later investments are more stable and bring a more modest return. Most venture capital firms try to diversify their holdings by investing in a variety of enterprises at various stages of development.

When an entrepreneur solicits capital from a venture capital firm, the firm's managers, working with the entrepreneur, determine which stage the new venture is in. ''Seed capital'' or ''seed money'' is given to individuals or groups in the idea stage—the point at which there is a good idea for a business but no formal organization. At this stage, the entrepreneur is likely to use the money provided by a venture capital organization to conduct further market research, assemble a management team, or develop a prototype.

More often than not, those who look for **seed money** are turned down by venture firms and must rely on their own resources to supply the needed capital. However, after they have developed a **prototype** and proven their idea will be viable, new enterprises may approach a venture capital organization in order to gather funds needed to begin operations. In such cases, venture capital organizations provide ''start-up'' or ''first round'' financing that gives the growing business sufficient capital to meet the demands of defining and developing a customer base and creating solid relationships with suppliers. First round financing usually comes in the form of an equity investment. Venture capital firms will expect a higher rate of return for first round investments.

As a new venture prospers, it may require additional financing to meet the capital needs inherent in expansion. Venture firms can provide ''second round'' or ''expansion-round'' financing to clients whose markets or sales are growing at such a rate that potential for profit looks good. At this point, the small business venture is usually heading towards success. Gladstone noted that those seeking expansion financing are in a better bargaining position than those seeking first round financing or seed money. Speaking as if to an entrepreneur or new venture, he commented that you ''will not have to give up as much of the equity in your company if your venture has reached this stage in the life cycle.''

If the expansion stage is successful, the new venture may begin a period of fast growth. At this point, the company may be making money, but not enough to finance the rapid expansion. Additional ''growth stage'' or ''third round'' capital may be solicited from venture capital firms. In other cases, the new venture may consider offering equity on the public stock markets as a means of gaining a cash infusion.

In addition to financing different stages of growth, venture capital firms can be of service to entrepreneurs in other, related situations. Some venture firms will assist management in **leveraged buyouts (LBOs)**, where the stock of a company is purchased by a management team or a group of other entrepreneurs with the help and financial support of the venture capital firm's managers. In such a case, the money used to purchase the business is loaned to the buyout team by the venture capital firm. Another area of activity for some venture capital firms is "turnaround financing" for businesses that have suffered serious setbacks or are nearing bankruptcy. Funds provided by a venture capital firm are used to finance recovery efforts or launch new programs aimed at turning the business around. Although few firms undertake the risk inherent in financing a turnaround situation, most are willing to consider them as part of their business strategy.

REQUIREMENTS FOR INVESTING

Regardless of the amount or type of financing needed by a client, the venture capital firm must be sure the claims made by the entrepreneur are realistic and attainable. The venture capital firm must have confidence the investment will pay out according to the plans offered by the entrepreneur. Before a venture capital firm makes an investment, it thoroughly investigates the client and the client's business in a process called due diligence. Due diligence means extensive research into the industry, the entrepreneur's background and experience, and the accuracy of the financial projections supplied by the client. In addition, the due diligence process may include a visit to the client's place of business or questions about the client's personal history. By conducting research into the client, the venture capital firm tries to maximize its understanding of the investment opportunity and its potential risks and rewards. By accumulating information, the venture capital firm better prepares itself to make the best possible decision about the investment.

The venture capital firm, in addition to being confident in the abilities and claims of the entrepreneur, must understand the market in which the new venture will operate. The experience and specialties of the firm's management will dictate whether or not the firm will narrow the focus of its business. Some venture capital firms specialize in certain industries or specific technologies. There are firms that only invest in, for instance, computer network technology businesses. Other firms only work with businesses in the bio-technology field. Venture firms that have such specialties turn away those businesses that do not fit into their area of expertise.

There are no hard and fast rules about the types of enterprises venture capital firms will invest in. In general, firms are looking for good investments where both they and the entrepreneur can make money. Experience has led firms to look more favorably on some

areas than others. For instance, venture capital firms will not back a retail venture unless the concept is a major innovation. In general, venture firms prefer businesses that sell products rather than those that provide services. Moreover, products that are technically advanced are more attractive than those that can be easily duplicated or improved upon by competitors. Those products that involve new technical advances or are based on proprietary technology have a competitive advantage. They impose a barrier to competitors and ensure the new venture a greater chance of success. Venture capital firms that back companies with innovative products stand to maximize return on their investment.

The venture capital industry is a business like any other, looking for profits and wealth for the lowest price. Yet the business conducted by firms in the industry has a direct, positive affect on the economy. Venture capital is an important fuel for new business. The professional managers that direct the investments of the venture capital firms are major supporters of the new ventures that help drive innovation, technical advances, and exploration. They help to make invention and creativity profitable. By helping entrepreneurs bring their new products and services to the national and international markets, venture firms foster competition within industry, rewarding those with the energy and vision to innovate and improve.

The 1990s has been a time of rapid growth for the venture capital industry. By the mid-1990s, venture capitalists invested a total of $8.2 billion in American business enterprises and this amount was expected to continue to rise. Some of the premier areas of venture capital investment in the late 1990s included the Internet, telecommunications, and health care. Though the industry was dominated by institutions such as university endowments and pension funds, wealthy individual investors were expected to become more involved in the future. In addition, venture capital was predicted to become more available for early stage financing in the future, as competition within the industry bid up the price of later stage transactions.

FURTHER READING:

Burrill, G. Steven and Craig T. Norback. *The Arthur Young Guide to Raising Venture Capital.* Liberty House, 1988.

Geer, John F., Jr. "The Venture Capital Boom: It's Gold Medal Time for the Venture Capitalists." *Financial World.* November 18, 1996.

Gladstone, David. *Venture Capital Handbook.* Englewood Cliffs, NJ: Prentice Hall, 1988.

Hamilton, Brian. *Financing for the Small Business.* Washington: U.S. Small Business Administration, 1990.

Hosmer, LaRue T. *A Venture Capital Primer for Small Business.* Washington.: U.S. Small Business Administration, 1990.

Kosmetsky, George, Michael D. Gill, Jr., and Raymond W. Smilor. *Financing and Managing Fast Growth Companies: The Venture Capital Process.* Lexington Books, 1985.

Lindsey, Jennifer. *The Entrepreneur's Guide to Capital.* Chicago: Probus, 1986.

Schilit, W. Keith. *The Entrepreneur's Guide to Preparing a Winning Business Plan and Raising Venture Capital.* Englewood Cliffs, NJ: Prentice Hall, 1990.

Silver, A. David. *Up Front Financing: The Entrepreneur's Guide.* New York: Wiley, 1982.

Timmons, Jeffrey A. *Planning and Financing the New Venture.* Brick House Publishing Company, 1990.

SEE ALSO: Angel Investors; Venture Capital Networks

VIOLENCE IN THE WORKPLACE

Workplace violence is a subject of considerable interest to both small business owners and their employees, though experts differ on the extent of the problem. Business consultants have noted that small business owners commonly deny that this grim issue is a concern for them, but in reality workplace violence can strike even tiny start-up firms. And as many analysts and business owners have charged, even the threat of violence can have a dreadful impact on small businesses. Whereas employees of larger firms generally have more avoidance options to choose from when forced to share workspace with a volatile employee, the more modest facilities of smaller businesses do not provide the same level of protection. "The best solution to avoiding workplace violence is to discuss it with your employees and have a plan to deal with it—before you need it," stated business writer Jane Applegate.

Statistics indicate that approximately 1,000 workers are killed on the job on an annual basis in the United States. In addition, Charles Labig, author of *Preventing Violence in the Workplace,* estimates that as many as 12,000 workers take their own lives at work on an annual basis. Moreover, each year workplace violence costs American companies about $5 billion in legal settlements, counseling, and medical bills. But perhaps most disquieting is Donald W. Myers' observation in *Business Horizons* that murders and suicides are the only categories of workplace violence that have been documented in any meaningful way: "Similar categories of data on other types of violent acts committed against employees, such as aggravated assaults, simple assaults, and rape, are not available. In addition, data on these acts are not recorded on a consistent basis, so yearly trends cannot be determined. Furthermore, information is not maintained on workplace violence involving property, such as arson or sabotage. In sum, with the exception of workplace fatalities, no one really knows the magnitude of workplace violence. Nor do we know whether it is increasing or not."

ADDRESSING WORKPLACE VIOLENCE BEFORE IT ERUPTS

Small business owners can take several steps to address the spectre of workplace violence. Hiring and interviewing practices should reflect the company's desire to establish and maintain a good workforce, and the owner should do his or her best to establish a company culture that does not tolerate non-violent forms of intimidation. Myers noted that in extreme forms, insulting and intimidating behavior—which may lead to physically violent behavior if left unchecked—can wreak significant mental harm on its victims, and may even provoke a violent response by victims who feel that they have no other recourse. Indeed, some studies have indicated that victims of harassment actually lost more productivity than employees who were physically attacked.

"Business owners should have a written workplace violence-prevention plan to show they are dealing with the problem," wrote Applegate, who also noted that over the past several years, courts across the country have held business owners liable for monetary damages when employees have been injured on the premises as a result of workplace violence or other factors. Another option, albeit unpleasant to contemplate, is to increase security precautions by adding security personnel or installing metal detectors. Employees should also be made aware in explicit terms that their desks and lockers are company property that can be looked through at any time, and they should be encouraged to report all violent acts to legal authorities. Finally, business consultants and security experts counsel small business owners to recognize that workplace violence does not always stem from internal sources. Indeed, the majority of homicides that take place in workplace settings are actually perpetuated by non-employees (angry customers, robbers, irate spouses or romantic partners).

APPROACHES TO DEALING WITH AGITATED EMPLOYEES

Business owners should remember that workplace violence does not erupt for no reason, and that if it takes place within the walls of the company, the chances are pretty good that it was triggered by a workplace issue or event. Owners and managers, then, should keep in mind that while the overwhelming workers who are stressed or angry about their work are able to keep their cool and act professionally, they are also the ones most likely to carry out a violent action. Demotions, critical performance appraisals, layoffs, and other professional disappointments can all trigger violent behavior.

Applegate noted that "when confronted with a volatile employee, the nature tendency is to fire the troublemaker, which often exacerbates the situation and can provoke a violent episode. The better approach is to suggest the troubled employee get professional counseling. Paying for it out of your own pocket, if necessary, is worth it, if it will avert a disaster.''

FURTHER READING:

Applegate, Jane. ''Workplace Violence Threatens Every Firm: Even Small Companies Need a Plan.'' *Detroit Free Press.* August 25, 1997.

Barton, Laurence. *Crisis in Organization: Managing and Communicating in the Heat of Chaos.* Southwestern Publishing, 1993.

Bensimon, Helen Frank. ''Violence in the Workplace.'' *Training and Development.* January 1994.

Labig, Charles. *Preventing Violence in the Workplace.* New York: Amacom.

Lawless, Peggy. *Fear and Violence in the Workplace.* Northwestern National Life Insurance Co., 1994.

Lipman, Ira A. ''Violence at Work.'' *Business Perspectives.* Summer 1994.

Myers, Donald W. ''The Mythical Work of Workplace Violence—Or is it?'' *Business Horizons.* July-August 1996.

Taylor, Robert. ''Firm Response to Violence at Work.'' *Financial Times.* August 28, 1996.

Thornburg, Linda. ''When Violence Hits Business.'' *HR Magazine.* July 1993.

SEE ALSO: Employee Hiring; Employee Termination; Human Resource Policies; Office Security

VIRTUAL REALITY COMPUTER SIMULATIONS

Virtual reality refers to experiences which are computer-generated; they mimic reality and consist of sensory stimuli, including visual displays, audio elements, kinetic experiences, and sometimes even tastes and smells. These stimuli combine to create what is referred to as a ''virtual world''—a complete, three-dimensional space that can be experienced and explored by the user, but which exists only in cyberspace, as the electronic impulses of a computer.

Virtual reality, or VR simulations have been developing over the past 30 years, since NASA began experimenting with flight simulators. Since then, vast improvements have been made in the equipment used and the quality of the experiences produced; visual displays can be extremely detailed and include color, shading, and texture, and the action can come close to occurring in real time, instead of the jerky, delayed animation action of earlier systems. As development continues, and increasing numbers of businesses utilize the technology for design and other applications, the price of virtual reality systems should continue to fall.

COMPONENTS OF A VIRTUAL REALITY SYSTEM

Whether elaborate, expensive systems put to use in scientific laboratories or more modest entertainment systems for home use, virtual reality systems consist of the following components.

COMPUTER The computer used for running virtual reality simulations can range from the supercomputers used for elaborate and intricate flight simulations and molecular manipulations to the small computers involved in game systems for the PC. Because the best virtual reality simulations involve high-speed and high-quality graphics, it has taken reasonably-priced hardware until relatively recently to catch up. Now, it is possible to run good-quality virtual reality programs from standard PCs.

GLOVES The gloves used in virtual reality simulations, often referred to as ''data gloves,'' are devices either slipped over the hand or strapped onto the hand and forearm. They are equipped with electronic sensors which can monitor the movement of the user and feed this information into the computer, and so change what happens in the virtual world. The highest quality devices can also provide stimulation to the user, mimicking experiences in the real world—the resistance of a wall, the weight of a tool, etc. The gloves can also function the way a mouse does with a PC: they can be used to indicate an element in the virtual world, and then manipulate that object, the way a PC user points and clicks using the mouse. Some virtual reality systems, in fact, use a mouse instead of the glove.

HEADSET The headset is usually equipped with monitors which can sense the position of the user's head, both vertically and horizontally. Because the virtual world is three dimensional, no matter how the user moves his or her head, there is visual stimulation, and the computer must have information on exactly where the user is looking. The headsets also usually have earphones or speakers which provide audio stimuli. And the user has virtual reality goggles which provide stereoscopic images, to simulate the way things look in three-dimensional space.

APPLICATIONS FOR VIRTUAL REALITY

ART AND ENTERTAINMENT Visual artists, film makers, and composers are experimenting with virtual reality by writing and using existing programs to create works of art that are interactive, and which exist only in a virtual world. The commercial aspects of these endeavors are as yet largely unexplored.

The entertainment possibilities, however, are growing quickly. Arcades are expanding to include virtual reality systems that function as games, providing players with more intense and exciting experiences than traditional games can. Home virtual reality systems which run virtual games are also available. There is also an emerging market is the fitness industry: virtual reality-enhanced workouts—from treadmills to racquetball—are promising to be extremely popular.

TRAINING AND EDUCATION Virtual reality simulations are used extensively in the medical sciences, for everything from microscopic investigations to virtual surgery. Mathematicians and other scientists can derive great benefit from the imaging aspects of virtual reality; concepts and computations which are difficult to visualize can be turned into detailed, sensory, interactive experiences.

Other educational uses for virtual reality simulations involve training scenarios, particularly those which involve either elements of danger (which can be avoided by training originally with a simulation program) or which would otherwise involve very expensive equipment or procedures. Pilots currently train using forms of virtual reality; driver's training is beginning to be done through virtual reality as well. Safety training is another case for virtual reality simulations—some training is currently offered for oil rig crews on site using the new technology, but there are many other safety training situations which might also be strong candidates for VR simulations.

DESIGN AND MARKETING Perhaps the strongest benefit of virtual reality is its potential for visualization—the capability to translate the two-dimensional plan into a three-dimensional experience. The user of a virtual reality simulator is completely immersed in the virtual world, and nothing needs to be explained because the user can see it all for him- or herself. Difficult concepts and cryptic graphs and blueprints become readable by almost anyone when they are presented as a three-dimensional, sensory experience. Architects and designers use Computer Assisted Design (CAD) and virtual reality simulations to walk through and around creations. Architects, interior designers, carpenters, cabinet makers, and landscape architects can provide customers with a view of the finished product before any expensive renovations or building has begun. Changes can be made at a very early stage, saving in rebuilding or redesigning costs.

For all types of marketing, virtual reality simulations could provide a much-needed glimpse of what is being offered. Travel agents, for example, could walk clients through a simulation of an exotic location or a luxury hotel room. The possibilities are virtually endless with this tool, which promises to be one of the hottest trends in technology.

FURTHER READING:

Holtzman, Steven. *Digital Mosaics*. New York: Simon and Schuster, 1997.

Multi-Media. Dorling Kindersley, 1996.

Pimentel, Ken, and Kevin Teixeira. *Virtual Reality: Through the New Looking Glass*. New York: McGraw Hill, 1993.

Rheingold, Howard. *Virtual Reality*. Summit Books, 1991.

SEE ALSO: Computers and Computer Systems; Product Development

W

A product or service warranty (also known as guarantee) is an assurance of performance and reliability given to the purchaser of a product or service by the company that provides that product or service. Such warranties have become standard practice in most U.S. industries, although opinions vary somewhat regarding their impact on sales. But misleading language in these guarantees has the capacity to spark significant legal troubles for small businesses that run afoul, however inadvertently, of legal guidelines. As the magazine *Profit-Building Strategies for Business Owners* noted, "consumers and business buyers alike can ask the courts to enforce warranties, whether they're express, implied, written, verbal, or given any other way. So be careful not to overstate your case. In addition to a printed warranty, watch your ads and brochures and keep tabs on your salespeople." Most warranties are covered by local, state and federal laws. The **Federal Trade Commission (FTC)** is the ultimate arbiter of warranty law in the United States. The FTC's primary tool in monitoring product and service guarantees is the Magnuson-Moss Consumer Warranty Act.

ELEMENTS OF A WARRANTY

The Federal Trade Commission requires that written warranties bestowed in connection with the sale of a product or service explicitly detail the following information:

- Who is covered by the warranty;

- Length of warranty;

- Description of the products, parts, properties, or characteristics covered by or excluded from the warranty;

- Steps for customer in the event that warranty coverage comes into play;

- Warrantor's response when confronted with product/service malfunctions, defects, or failures;

- Any exclusions of or limitations on relief such as incidental or consequential damages;

- Statement that indicates that some states do not allow such exclusions or limitations;

- Statement of consumer legal rights;

- Any limitations on the length of implied warranties, if possible.

FULL AND LIMITED WARRANTIES

The Magnuson-Moss Act does not require businesses to provide warranties to customers. Indeed, some business owners decide that written warranties are not even necessary to enjoy success in their chosen field of endeavor. "The obvious reason [for a warranty]—to win customers—may not be valid," contended *Profit-Building Strategies for Business Owners.* "Experts are divided on this issue. Some think warranties don't influence sales and cite consumer surveys to back their views. Most surveys show less than 10% of respondents said a warranty had a bearing on their choice of product. But other manufacturers are convinced that warranties help sell their products. Many retailers think so, too, pointing out that consumers are often eager to purchase service contracts. Find out what your own customers expect before you freely hand out warranties. If they don't give you an edge, you may be able to do without them and save yourself trouble.''

Businesses that choose to provide written warranties may choose from two types: full and limited. FTC regulations concerning full warranties are considerably more stringent than those that apply to limited warranties. According to the Magnuson-Moss Act, ''fully guaranteed'' products or services must meet the following five criteria:

- Customer receives full money back or replacement or repair of any defective part of product in the event of a complaint;

- Prompt and free repairs;

- If repairs are not fully satisfactory to the buyer, a prompt refund is available;

- Customer has no responsibility beyond reporting the defect to the company;

- Acknowledgment of all implied warranties.

''If you're ready to stand by those assurances,'' said *Profit-Building Strategies for Business Owners,* '' 'fully guaranteed' accurately describes your conditions of sale. But if your policy falls short in any way, you can be penalized for making that claim when you're really making a 'limited warranty.' '' Limited warranties, which must be prominently labeled as such, limit the liability of the manufacturer or service provider. A limited warranty may offer to replace defective parts free, but only do so for a limited length of time, or require that the consumer ship the product to a manufacturer-approved service center. The distinctions between full and limited warranties and the obligations of manufacturers to honor them vary from state to state, so it is up to the consumer to carefully read the literature and understand what is covered before the purchase.

EXPRESS AND IMPLIED WARRANTIES

''Express warranties arise from statements you make about a product or service, from a picture, sample, or brochure, while implied warranties arise by automatic operation of law,'' wrote Marc J. Lane in the *Legal Handbook for Small Business.* ''Although the Magnuson-Moss Consumer Warranty Act supersedes state laws regarding express warranties in the sale of products, it does not supersede the **Uniform Commercial Code (UCC)** provisions on implied warranties or state laws applicable to express warranties in the sale of services.'' The provisions of the UCC, which cover all products, basically stipulate that products should look like they do in advertisements, and perform as they do in demonstrations, so express warranties vary in accordance with the nature

of the advertising campaign launched on behalf of that product or service.

In addition, states require that the manufacturer or seller of a product offer an implied warranty—some sort of guarantee that the product will work as advertised once it is out of the box and that it will work under ordinary circumstances in the manner that its manufacturer says it will. This implied warranty is known as the ''implied warranty of merchantability.'' A second implied warranty—known as the ''warranty of fitness for a particular purpose''—is described by *Profit-Building Strategies for Business Owners* as a warranty that ''provides assurance that your product will do the job buyers have in mind, assuming they've explained their purposes to you. . . . Your degree of vulnerability to legal claims depends in part on how clearly buyers explain what they want and in part on who they are. If you're a supplier of institutional dinnerware, your customers are expected to have enough knowledge and sophistication to judge fitness of purpose for themselves. They'd need a strong case to prove you sold them the wrong dishes for their needs. But regular customers can't be expected to know much about various kinds of dinnerware, or even the right questions to ask. So with them you're more accountable.'' The length of time that these implied warranties are in effect varies from state to state.

DISCLAIMERS Vulnerability to express and/or implied warranties can be lessened somewhat through the use of disclaimers. ''A disclaimer may wholly deny that you are making one or more express or implied warranties, or it may limit warranty coverages,'' wrote Lane. ''In the absence of a disclaimer, a breach of warranty will usually give a purchaser of the item the right to recover the cost of the item together with any additional damages caused by that breach.''

Small business consultants note that warranties—both express and implied—can be negotiated with buyers, but they urge business owners to use specific language when adding such disclaimers to a **sales contract**. The term ''exclusive remedy,'' for instance, can give a seller of products or services significant legal protection when it is used to explicitly limit a buyer's legal options in the event of complaints about product defects or workmanship. ''But take care also to see that they buyer receives genuine protection,'' noted *Profit-Building Strategies for Business Owners.* ''If your customer is left in the end without a working product, you can be sued no matter what agreement you signed, on the grounds that it's a remedy that 'fails of its essential purpose.' '' Obviously, the obligations imposed by law in the areas of warranty are extensive, so small business owners should make sure that they consult a legal expert so that they can develop the most effective disclaimer possible.

EXTENDED WARRANTIES

Extended warranties are somewhat controversial, but often profitable, warranty packages offered by manufacturers and service providers. Manufacturers sell these warranties, which are basically extensions of basic warranty packages, in hopes that the extended warranty will not be needed or used, thereby resulting in profits. Consumers buy them for peace of mind, reasoning that they are protecting their initial outlay of money. The controversy revolves around what the warranties cover. Some extended warranties are actually service agreements, resulting in higher charges than might be expected under a warranty. In other cases the fine print in the warranties exclude the very things that the consumer assumes would be covered.

FURTHER READING:

Lane, Marc J. *Legal Handbook for Small Business.* Rev. ed. New York: AMACOM, 1989.

''What You Promise the Buyer When You Warranty Your Product.'' *Profit-Building Strategies for Business Owners.* January 1992.

SEE ALSO: Product Liability

WEB PAGE DESIGN

Web page design is the process of creating a site, or homepage, on the World Wide Web, which is one part of the international series of computer networks known as the Internet. Computer users use a software program known as a web browser to visit those homepages, each of which has a unique address and that can consist of text, graphics, audio, video, and animation. Homepages are really virtual ''storefronts'' opening up previously unavailable markets to any business, anywhere.

For small businesses, the Web represents perhaps the most exciting and innovative development in sales and marketing in decades. For a relatively small fee, a business can establish its own homepage and offer customers direct access to its products and services. Business owners may decide to establish a site for a number of reasons, including:

- The Web is the hot new area and they do not want to be left behind

- To teach potential customers about the company and leave them with a favorable impression

- To develop a qualified list of sales prospects

- To conduct market and customer research

- To sell products directly from the web page.

POPULARITY OF THE WEB

Use of the World Wide Web has exploded in recent years. Formerly the domain of computer and high-tech companies, the web is now host to almost every major company in the world, as well as tens of thousands of small companies. Print and television ads often include a company web page address, and often it is the first place that companies recommend that you go to learn more about them. It is *the* place to be from a **marketing** standpoint.

INFORMING CUSTOMERS

The most common way that small companies establish a presence on the Web is by setting up a simple homepage that provides potential customers with information on the company and its products. The essentially limitless storage space of the computer network means that businesses are free to post as much information as they can about themselves—computerized versions of brochures and press releases; product catalogs, complete with photos; a company overview; news and notes related to the industry the company serves; and contact and technical support information. This makes it easy for consumers to locate information about the company 24 hours a day.

FINDING SALES PROSPECTS

Once people find your web site, there are tools you can use to make it easy for them to contact you to learn even more about your company, For instance, a site can be set up so that access can be gained to it only after a user has registered his or her name, address, telephone number, and electronic mail address. This builds an instant contact list of potential customers—casual users would never take the time to log in that information, so a business owner knows that the person who took the time to register is predisposed to deal with the company. Additional tools include direct access to the company via **electronic mail**, discussion boards, or live chat rooms.

CUSTOMER RESEARCH

Customer research is an extension of locating sales prospects. Instead of just finding people who are interested in buying goods or services, the web can be used to gather people's opinions on a new product or service, or to gauge their satisfaction with a company's level of customer service. Information can be gathered in two ways. The first occurs automatically when someone visits your site. There is software available that will tell you certain information about each person that visits your site—what web browser they were using and who their Internet service provider was, for example. In addition, counter programs track the number of visits to the site, which can be important when establishing advertising rates for the site and when gauging its relative success.

Information can also be garnered from use of some of the same tools used for sales prospecting— questionnaires to gather data about customers, feedback forms, electronic mail addresses, discussion boards, and live chat rooms. **Market questionnaires** are easy to include on a web site and can reveal valuable demographic information about a company's customer base. The questionnaires can be included as part of the order form, or can be a part of a separate promotion, such as a contest or giveaway. In addition to questionnaires, simple feedback forms that collect general comments may also be included.

MARKETING AND SALES

Many homepages will also include the capability to order products or services from the company. In some cases, this may mean printing out an order form and mailing it to the company, but most sites now offer at least telephone ordering, and many allow customers to make purchases directly over the Web. With direct Web purchasing, customers identify an item they wish to purchase from the company, fill out an order form and provide their credit card number, and then transmit that information electronically to the company. The product will then be shipped directly to the customer.

The advantages to this method of selling are obvious. Instead of being restricted to a local market, even the smallest company can now reach users around the world. Customers can locate information about the company or order a product 24 hours a day.

HOW TO DESIGN A WEB PAGE

When designing a web page, certain information should always be included:

- Basic Company Information—This can include vision or mission statements, a history of the business, a summary of business philosophy, etc. The key is to sell the customer on the company.

- Product Line Information—Commercial web pages should include photos and text descriptions outlining the benefits of the products. Features, applications, and examples can also be highlighted. Consultants often recommend that businesses establish separate pages or sections for each major product line—connected, of course, to the main company web site.

- Technical support—Frequently asked questions, parts information, product diagrams,

and technical specifications are just some of the ways a company can provide support from its Web site.

- Ordering information—Companies should include an electronic mail or hardcopy form with instructions on how to order a product.

- Service section—Free information that is of interest to potential customers, designed to keep them coming back to the site. Industry news and trends are good examples of this kind of information, which is a feature of increasing numbers of business-oriented sites.

- ''What's New''—This section is essentially intended to inform visitors of new initiatives, products, etc., that are covered on the Web site.

Once you decide what to put on your homepage, it is time to actually create the site. Web pages are written using a language called the Hypertext Markup Language. HTML, as it is more commonly known, is nothing more than a series of tags and codes that instruct a Web browser on how and where the data on that page should be displayed. Once a page has been written using HTML, the page must be placed on the host computer, or server, of an Internet provider. HTML can be created using any common word processing package or via any one of the proliferating HTML editor software packages available in the marketplace.

One of the most important features of HTML is the ''hypertext'' feature. This means that text can be highlighted on a web page so that when a customer clicks on a word or an image, a link to a new location on that site (or even another site altogether) is called up on the computer screen. This allows customers to move freely on a site and allows for design creativity and flexibility.

Learning the basics of HTML coding is not difficult, and an ambitious business owner who has the time and the initiative may create his or her own homepage from scratch. However, as the Web has continued to grow, pages have become far more sophisticated in appearance. Even the simplest page now often includes at least some intricate coding, so in most cases, it is better to hire a consultant to design the page. Freelance design firms have sprung up all over the place as the Web boom continues unabated; simply look in your local yellow pages or visit the Web itself—all Web designers have their own homepages and most will provide links to the companies they have established sites for, thereby letting you see the quality of their work.

Don't make the mistake of thinking that you can put a site up and the orders will start pouring in though. Maintaining a site takes time and effort, another reason to consider outsourcing. "It takes a lot of market support [to maintain a site]," said Dawn Dayton of the Michigan Small Business Development Center in *Entrepreneur* magazine. "If you put up a site and nobody knows [about it], it's not going to do you any good." Web design firms will make sure people know about your site by advertising it in other Internet locations and by registering the site with dozens of Internet directory services.

Once the site is on a host computer, users from around the world can then access the homepage, which is given an address that is unique to the entire Web. That address is one part of naming your site. The name must be registered with the Internet Naming Council (CHEK), which does a check to determine if the address is unique. A registration fee is required. The addresses themselves can often be confusing, as they involve a series of characters together with dots and slashes, but most companies choose a name that is 1) easy to remember and 2) closely associated with the company itself. The second part of naming the site is picking the everyday name of the site that will be displayed throughout the site and in advertisements. The company name alone might not convey all that you are trying to do at the site. In that case, try to pick a name that is descriptive, short, unique, and memorable.

POSITIONING AND MAINTAINING A BUSINESS HOMEPAGE

Sites can be freestanding, or they can be a part of a larger online "mall." Hundreds of retail "malls" have opened on the Web, some more successful than others. Before choosing an Internet provider to store your homepage, do some research on popular online malls and see where your company might best fit in. Visit the sites yourself, and see what you like and do not like. This research step can be an essential component of Internet success for companies, because location can be just as important on the Web as it is in your community.

Even after your Web site has been successfully launched and is up and running, the work does not end. The site needs to be updated on a regular basis to keep customers up-to-date and to give them a reason to come back. Things to remember when updating a site include:

- Price changes
- Product changes
- Adding pages to describe other parts of your business
- Adding new links and eliminating obsolete links
- Updating images
- Overhauling the entire site as necessary.

Once again, you will have to decide if you want to undertake the updating yourself or if you want to hire a firm to handle the work for you.

COSTS

Simple web pages with just a few graphics will cost approximately $100 per page if you hire a design firm to do them for you. Most will offer a quote on a job if you ask, but the quote will probably not be binding, since most jobs have unique elements that might not be obvious at the bidding stage. Small business owners can sometimes cut costs in this area by offering to supply text and other information to the designer in computer-readable format. Prices vary, but generally, small companies should be able to create an attractive, basic site for less than $1500. For large companies with more money to spend, it is not uncommon for them to spend more than $100,000 developing a web site, and then to allocate additional funds to maintain it.

Small business owners should also keep several other cost factors in mind when weighing an entrance to the Web. Additional costs include the monthly charge paid to your Internet provider for hosting your site, a fee that often escalates if the number of visits to the site become excessive. In addition, businesses should budget money for updating the site on a timely basis.

FURTHER READING:

Dickman, Steven. "Catching Customers on the Web." *Inc.* Summer 1995.

Neelakatan, Shailaja. "We Do Web Work." *Forbes.* Jan. 27, 1997.

Page, Heather. "Tech Smarts." *Entrepreneur.* June 1997

Wilson, Dr. Ralph F. "12 Web Page Decisions Your Business or Organization Will Need to Make." *http://www.wilsonweb.com/articles/12design.htm*

SEE ALSO: Advertising Media, World Wide Web; Internet Commerce

WHOLESALING

Wholesaling is the selling of merchandise to anyone—either a person or an organization—other than the end consumer of that merchandise. Wholesalers, who are sometimes referred to as middle agents, represent one of the links in the chain along which most goods pass on their way to the marketplace. As intermediaries between producers and consumers of goods, wholesalers facilitate the transport, preparation of quantity, storage, and sale of articles ultimately destined for customers. Wholesalers are extremely important in a variety of industries, including such diverse product areas as automobiles, grocery products, plumbing supplies, electrical supplies, and raw farm produce. They are particularly vital to the operations of small retailers. Whereas large retail companies buy directly from the manufacturer and often have their own intermediate warehousing operations, the limited resources of independent retail outlets makes alliances with wholesalers a practical necessity.

Strictly speaking, although a wholesaler may own or control retail operations, wholesalers do not sell to end-customers. Indeed, many wholesale operations are themselves owned by retailers or manufacturers. Even in these instances, however, the enterprise's wholesaling branch exists to facilitate the movement of goods from one area to a market demand in another area. Wholesaling provides manufacturers with an expanded consumer market potential in terms of geographical locations and consumer purchasing power while at the same time providing a cash flow for the manufacturer.

Wholesalers are successful only if they are able to serve the needs of their customers, who may be retailers or other wholesalers. Some of the functions provided by wholesalers to their buyers include:

- Provide producer's goods in an appropriate quantity for resale by buyers.

- Provide wider geographical access and diversity in obtaining goods.

- Ensure and maintain a quality dimension with the goods that are being obtained and resold.

- Provide cost-effectiveness by reducing the number of producer contacts needed.

- Provide ready access to a supply of goods.

- Assemble and arrange goods of a compatible nature from a number of producers for resale.

- Minimize buyer transportation costs by buying goods in larger quantities and distributing them in smaller amounts for resale.

- Work with producers to understand and appreciate consumerism in their production process.

TYPES OF WHOLESALERS

Although there are a number of ways to classify wholesalers, the categories used by the Census of Wholesale Trade are employed most often. The three types of wholesalers are 1) merchant wholesalers; 2) agents, brokers, and commission merchants; and 3) manufacturers' sales branches and offices.

MERCHANT WHOLESALERS Merchant wholesalers are firms engaged primarily in buying, taking title to, storing, and physically handling products in relatively large quantities and reselling the products in smaller quantities to retailers; industrial, commercial, or institutional concerns; and other wholesalers. These types of wholesaling agents are known by several different names, including wholesalers, jobbers, distributors, industrial distributors, supply houses, assemblers, importers, and exporters, depending on their services.

According to E. Jerome McCarthy and William D. Perreault Jr., authors of *Basic Marketing*, merchant wholesalers account for the majority of wholesaling establishments and wholesale sales. ''As you might guess based on the large number of merchant wholesalers, they often specialize by certain types of products or customers,'' added McCarthy and Perreault. ''They also tend to service relatively small geographic areas. . . . Merchant wholesalers also differ in how many of the wholesaling functions they provide. There are two basic kinds of merchant wholesalers: 1) service (sometimes called full-service wholesalers) and 2) limited-function or limited-service wholesalers.'' The latter category of wholesalers, which itself is divided into little niches, offers varying levels of service in such areas as product delivery, credit bestowal, inventory storage, provision of market or advisory information, and sales.

AGENTS, BROKERS, AND COMMISSION MERCHANTS Agents, brokers, and commission merchants are also independent middlemen who do not (for the most part) take title to the goods in which they deal, but instead are actively involved in negotiating and other functions of buying and selling while acting on behalf of their clients. They are usually compensated in the form of commissions on sales or purchases. Agents, brokers, and commission merchants usually represent the non-competing products of a number of manufacturers to several retailers; commission merchants typically are limited to agricultural goods. This category of wholesaler is particularly popular with producers with limited capital who can not afford to maintain their own sales forces.

MANUFACTURERS' SALES BRANCHES AND OFFICES Manufacturers' sales branches and offices are owned and operated by manufacturers but are physically separated from manufacturing plants. They are used primarily for the purpose of distributing the manufacturers' own products at the wholesale level. Some have warehousing facilities where inventories are maintained, while others are merely sales offices. Some of them also wholesale allied and supplementary products purchased from other manufacturers.

THE CHANGING LANDSCAPE OF WHOLESALING

The future of wholesaling appears somewhat ambiguous. One major force affecting wholesaler activity is growth in the power of retail chain stores. The continued mergers and acquisitions taking place between similar regional chains since 1970 means that independent retailers will have a decreasing need for wholesalers. Another negative factor has been an increased emphasis, on the part of both manufacturers and end users, on cutting distribution costs. However, there is a countervailing force at work in that retailing is becoming increasingly fragmented as more and more specialized retailers cater to specialized market niches. As this specialization continues, using wholesalers becomes the most cost-efficient way for manufacturers to cover fragmented retailer market segments. The wholesaler is able to bundle several manufacturers' items into combinations that can all be sold through the specialist outlet. In most cases, wholesalers will capitalize on market opportunities among specialized, independent retailers while they lose ground to chains buying directly from manufacturers. Many wholesalers have adapted nicely by becoming efficient importers, upgrading their operations with computers, improving inventory handling, and automating their warehouses.

But industry observers contend that for many wholesalers, the ultimate key to success will be an ability to: 1) establish closer alliances with retail specialists that offer solid, long-term growth prospects; or 2) concentrate on merchandise categories where chains still must use wholesalers because of needed buying efficiencies. "Most wholesalers are busy changing quickly to offer much more to their retailers than the assembly and conveyance of products," wrote David Merrefield in *Supermarket News.* "Most are mobilizing groups of independent retailers into virtual chains of stores that use a common banner and hew to uniform standards. . . . Wholesalers must actively collect sales data from affiliated retailers to aggregate and make it known to manufacturers. Wholesalers must also make known to their retailer affiliates that the retailers are partners with their wholesaler, their vendors, and even their fellow retailers, all of whom must join the quest for overall low-cost operation."

KEYS TO SUCCESSFUL WHOLESALING

In addition to establishing good working relationships with independent retailers, wholesalers can also take several other steps to give them the best chance of surviving—and even thriving—in today's competitive marketplace. "Error-free management of a wholesale operation is impossible," admitted the editors of *How to Run a Small Business,* "due to the wide variety of items that most wholesalers handle, and the many imponderables (such as delays in shipments from vendors, unforeseeable spurts in consumer demands, and even the vagaries of weather) that wholesalers are subject to. But all wholesalers

have the same problems. What distinguishes successful wholesalers is how well they manage the variables under their control."

In *How to Run a Small Business*, the J. K. Lasser Institute cited several keys to successful wholesaling operation in all stages of performance, from securing clients to performing the various duties associated with the industry:

MARKETING According to the Institute, successful **marketing** is a vital component of wholesaling. "Whether you are just starting up in wholesaling or are an established wholesaler, make sure you have marketing policies and programs which provide services which are unique, superior, and money-makers for both your suppliers and customers."

CUSTOMER SERVICE "Price is not the sole factor considered by retailers in choosing suppliers," noted the editors of *How to Run a Small Business.* "They also take into account the services wholesalers perform and are inclined to go to and stick with those who help them prosper in their businesses. It is the wholesalers who do not offer additional services that have the lowest prices and thinnest margins in their markets."

OPERATIONS MANAGEMENT Astute systems management is a necessity for today's wholesaler. Order processing, inventory control, marketing, internal communications, and product delivery are some of the areas in which wholesalers must be proficient.

INTELLIGENT TERRITORY MANAGEMENT According to the J. K. Lasser Institute, wholesalers that extend their territory too widely run the risk of increasing their operating costs out of proportion to the additional volume of business secured through such a step. "You can approximate the boundaries [of acceptable territory size] by determining the acceptable costs of serving customers and expanding it outward," said the Institute. "Since all costs, other than selling and delivery, can be charged to outgoing merchandise on an equal basis regardless of destination, you can determine the profitability of a given area by adding selling and delivery costs. Then compare the result with the gross profit which the area yields."

GOOD COST CONTROL AND ACCOUNTING SYSTEMS Business consultants say that successful wholesalers are adept at keeping operating costs at acceptable levels and attentive to recordkeeping needs. Indeed, analysts indicate that wholesalers who study their financial figures closely can learn many helpful things about their business, ranging from the credit records of clients to unnecessary overlap in operations. Wholesalers, then, should make sure that they keep detailed records and continually track their status through financial analysis.

FURTHER READING:

J.K. Lasser Institute. *How To Run a Small Business.* 7th ed. New York: McGraw-Hill, 1994.

Matthews, Ryan. "Zen and the Art of Wholesaling." *Progressive Grocer.* January 1996.

McCarthy, E. Jerome, and William D. Perreault, Jr. *Basic Marketing: A Managerial Approach.* 10th ed. Homewood, IL: Irwin, 1990.

Merrefield, David. "The Wholesaling Paradox." *Supermarket News.* November 3, 1997.

Merrefield, David. "Wholesaling's Future: Product or Support?" *Supermarket News.* March 10, 1997.

SEE ALSO: Distribution Channels; Distribution Networks; Retail Trade

WIDE AREA NETWORKS

A wide area network (WAN) is a **telecommunications** network, usually used for connecting computers, that spans a wide geographical area. WAN's can by used to connect cities, states, or even countries. WANs are often used by larger corporations or organizations to facilitate the exchange of data, and in a wide variety of industries, corporations with facilities at multiple locations have embraced WANs. Increasingly, however, even small businesses are utilizing WANs as a way of increasing their communications capabilities.

Although WANs serve a purpose similar to that of **local area networks (LANs)**, WANs are structured and operated quite differently. The user of a WAN usually does not own the communications lines that connect the remote computer systems; instead, the user subscribes to a service through a telecommunications provider. Unlike LANs, WANs typically do not link individual computers, but rather are used to link LANs. WANs also transmit data at slower speeds than LANs. WANs are also structurally similar to metropolitan area networks (MANs), but provide communications links for distances greater than 50 kilometers.

WANs have existed for decades, but new technologies, services, and applications have developed over the years. WANs were originally developed for digital leased-line services carrying only voice, rather than data. As such, they connected the private branch exchanges (PBXs) of remote offices of the same company. WANs are still used for voice services, but today they are used more frequently data and image transmission (such as video conferencing). These added applications have spurred significant growth in WAN usage, primarily because of the surge in LAN connections to the wider networks. Most industry observers expect nearly all LANs to establish link ups with WANs over the next several years.

HOW WANS WORK

WANs are either point-to-point, involving a direct connection between two sites, or operate across packet-switched networks, in which data is transmitted in packets over shared circuits. Point-to-point WAN service may involve either analog dial-up lines, in which a modem is used to connect the computer to the telephone line, or dedicated leased digital telephone lines, also known as "private lines." Analog lines, which may be either part of a public-switched telephone network or leased lines, are suitable for batch data transmissions, such as nonurgent order entry and point-of-sale transactions. Dedicated digital phone lines permit uninterrupted, secure data transmission at fixed costs.

A leading type of point-to-point WAN service in North America is T1, which is based on a method of dividing a digital line service with a rate of 1.544 Mbps into 24 channels of 64 kbps each. Other point-to-point services available include fractional T1, T3, dataphone digital services, switched 56 kbps, and integrated services digital network (ISDN). New technologies that promise greater speeds and reliability include asynchronous transfer mode (ATM) and Sonet. Point-to-point WAN service providers include both local telephone companies and long distance carriers. Packet-switched network services are typically chosen by organizations which have low volumes of data or numerous sites, for which multiple dedicated lines would be too expensive.

Depending on the service, WANs can be used for almost any data sharing purpose for which LANs can be used. Slower transmission speeds, however, may make some applications less practical for WANs. The most basic uses of WANs are for **electronic mail** and file transfer, but WANs can also permit users at remote sites to access and enter data on a central site's database, such as instantaneously updating accounting records. New types of network-based software that facilitate productivity and production tracking, such as groupware and work-flow automation software, can also be used over WANs. Using groupware, workers at dispersed locations can more easily collaborate on projects. WANs also give remote offices access to a central office's other data communications services, such as connections to on-line services and the Internet.

FURTHER READING:

Chappell, Laura A., and Roger L. Spicer. *Novell's Guide to Multiprotocol Internetworking.* Novell Press, 1994.

Pecar, Joseph A., Roger J. O'Connor, and David A. Garbin. *The McGraw-Hill Telecommunications Factbook.* New York: McGraw-Hill, 1993.

Smith, Laura B. "Branch Office, Phone Home: Corporations Cast Nets to Remote Sites in an Internetworking Surge." *PC Week.* May 2, 1994.

''Wide Area Networking Puts Remote Offices On-Line.'' *Managing Office Technology.* September 1994.

WOMEN ENTREPRENEURS

According to the **National Association of Women Business Owners**, there were 6.5 million women entrepreneurs in the United States in 1997. In addition, the Small Business Administration estimates that by the year 2000, over one-half of all self-employed people in the United States will be women. Although women have owned and operated businesses for decades, they were rarely recognized or given credit for their efforts. Often women entrepreneurs were ''invisible'' as they worked side by side with their husbands, and many only stepped into leadership positions when their husbands died.

But a variety of factors have combined in recent years to contribute to a rapid increase in the number of women who start their own businesses. As more women joined the work force, for example, they gained the professional and managerial skills and experience they would need as entrepreneurs. In addition, many women felt as if they were discriminated against in large companies, which provided them with an incentive to be their own bosses. Some women have found entrepreneurship to be an ideal way to juggle the competing demands of career and family, while some single mothers have started businesses as a way out of poverty.

Although the small businesses owned by women have traditionally focused on fashion, food, and other service sectors, in recent years women entrepreneurs have been moving rapidly into manufacturing, construction, and other industrial fields. Women business owners still face difficulties in gaining access to commercial credit and bidding on government contracts, but this situation is changing for the better. Studies also suggest that women entrepreneurs could benefit from better technical and managerial training in order to manage growth of their businesses more effectively. But by the mid-1990s, a vast support network had developed to provide women business owners with resources to turn to for help.

REASONS WOMEN BECOME ENTREPRENEURS

Women start businesses for different reasons than their male counterparts. While men start businesses for growth opportunities and profit potential, women most often found businesses for personal goals, such as achievement, accomplishment, or stepping in to help their family. Some women consider financial success as an external confirmation of their ability rather than as a primary goal or motivation to start a business. According to Joline Godfrey, author of *Our Wildest Dreams,* women entrepreneurs gave the following reasons for starting businesses:

- Happiness/Self-Fulfillment, 38 percent;
- Achievement/Challenge, 30 percent;
- Helping Others, 20 percent;
- Sales Growth/Profit, 12 percent.

Women also tend to start businesses about ten years later then men, on average. Motherhood, lack of management experience, and traditional socialization can all be reasons for delayed entry into a career as a small business owner. Most women never plan to own a business or even consider business ownership as a career option. In fact, over 30 percent of women entrepreneurs reported that they started a business due to some traumatic event, such as divorce, discrimination due to pregnancy or the corporate glass ceiling, the health of a family member, or economic reasons such as a layoff. But a new talent pool of women entrepreneurs is forming today, as more women opt to leave corporate America to chart their own destinies. Many of these women have developed financial expertise and bring experience in manufacturing or nontraditional fields.

As a result, the concentration of women business owners in the retail and service sectors—and in traditional industries such as cosmetics, food, fashion, and personal care—is slowly changing. During the decade of the 1980s, for example, the number of women-owned sole proprietorships in mining, construction, manufacturing, and transportation increased by over 175 percent.

PROBLEMS FACED BY WOMEN ENTREPRENEURS

One of the main problems facing women entrepreneurs is obtaining financing. Most women-owned businesses are undercapitalized and have limited access to resources. In fact, three out of four women-owned businesses started out with their own financing of less than $5,000. After being turned down at banks, many women entrepreneurs resorted to **credit card financing** or loans from family members to establish or expand their businesses. In the early 1990s, study after study confirmed that women business owners did not receive equal treatment at financial institutions. Over one half of women business owners believed that they faced gender discrimination when dealing with a loan officer. And 67 percent of women business owners reported difficulty in working with financial institutions. But this figure had declined by 15 percent by 1997, according to a study conducted by the

National Association of Women Business Owners (NAWBO).

"There's been improvement on both sides," said Julie Weeks, research director for NAWBO. "Not only have women business owners become more savvy about these matters and boast businesses that are more stable and mature, but the banking community has experienced an awakening. They've made tremendous efforts to reach out to women business owners and have taken a proactive role in making the relationship better."

Part of the improvement can be attributed to the success of the U.S. Small Business Administration's Women's Prequalification Pilot Loan Program. Introduced in 1994 and expanded nationwide in 1997, the program helps women seeking loans of under $250,000 to complete their loan applications, and also provides an SBA guarantee for repayment of their loans. Women are prequalified based on their character, credit rating, and ability to repay the loan from future business earnings, rather than on collateral. The prequalification statement from the SBA enables the women to obtain funding much more readily.

Another area in which women business owners have been historically shortchanged is **government procurement**, or the selling of their goods and services to city, state, and federal governments. In the past, fewer than 5 percent of the women-owned firms in the United States were certified to do business with their state government and only 1.5 percent of the billions of dollars in federal contracts went to women-owned firms. But this situation has been changing rapidly as well. If a company is 51 percent owned and controlled by a woman, it can obtain certification and bid on government contracts. Many governments have created set-aside programs which specifically help women-owned businesses in the bidding process.

STRENGTHS OF WOMEN BUSINESS OWNERS

The cooperative management style naturally used by many women business owners comes from their early experiences and focuses on the welfare of the group. Participation is shared among the employees with concern given for their ideas and needs. The style often extends to social issues, which are frequently driving forces within a small company. The business strategy is formed through active listening and educational experiences and focuses on issues in addition to just the bottom line. Women business owners' strengths in terms of building relationships are normally an asset when dealing with customers and suppliers, as well as in the international marketplace. In order to overcome the obstacles they face, women entrepreneurs often come up with creative, out of the ordinary methods to help further their goals.

With more and more women opening businesses every day, the future for the next generation of business owners is bright. While the business world is normally slow to change, economic advantages of women-owned firms will help speed the process. As more young women see a wider range of women business owner role models, they will be encouraged to view **entrepreneurship** as a legitimate career option. Furthermore, as more mothers socialize their daughters to the business world, more young women are likely to aspire to start their own businesses.

RESOURCES

A number of resources now exist to support women entrepreneurs. In 1988, Congress authorized the **U.S. Small Business Administration** Office of Women's Business Ownership. This office recently created a "Low-Doc" loan program which makes it easier for women entrepreneurs to obtain SBA financing. The SBA also has established a Women's Network for Entrepreneurial Training (WNET) which links women mentors with protegees. **Small Business Development Centers (SBDC)** are also co-sponsored by the SBA and operate in every state. They offer free and confidential counseling to anyone interested in starting a small business. In addition, many states now have a Women's Business Advocate to promote women entrepreneurs within the state. These advocates are represented by an organization, the National Association of Women Business Advocates.

A number of trade associations also represent women entrepreneurs. The National Association of Women Business Owners is the largest group throughout the country. There are also some smaller regional groups, which can be located through the Yellow Pages or local chambers of commerce. The American Business Women's Association provides leadership, networking, and educational support. The National Association of Female Executives makes women aware of the need to plan for career and financial success. As women-owned businesses continue to create jobs and become an increasingly important factor in the American economy, the resources to support them should continue to grow as well.

FURTHER READING:

Castro, Janice. "She Calls All the Shots." *Time.* July 4, 1988.

Duff, Carolyn. *When Women Work Together.* Emeryville, CA: Conari Press, 1993.

Eckert, Toby. "Female-Owned Firms Growing at Fast Clip." *Indianapolis Business Journal.* September 16, 1996.

Godfrey, Joline. *Our Wildest Dreams.* New York: HarperBusiness, 1992.

Harrison, Patricia. *America's New Women Entrepreneurs.* Lakewood, CO: Acropolis Books 1986.

Hisrich, Robert, and Candida Brush. *The Women Entrepreneur; Starting, Financing and Managing a Successful New Business.* Lexington Books, 1986.

Nelton, Sharon. "A Good Time to Be a Woman." *Nation's Business.* January 1991.

Pinson, Linda, and Jerry Jinnett. *Women Entrepreneurs, 33 Personal Stories of Success.* Chicago, IL: Upstart Publishing, 1992.

Silver, A. David. *Enterprising Women.* New York: Amacom, 1994.

Zuckerman, Laurie. *On Your Own: A Women's Guide to Building a Business.* Chicago, IL: Upstart Publishing, 1990.

WORK FORCE

The term work force describes the overall group of potential employees available to a company, industry, or nation. The characteristics of and trends affecting the work force are of great interest to business managers. In fact, work force issues influence a wide variety of business decisions, from **business site selection** to hiring, training, compensation, and benefit policies.

In mid-1997, the U.S. unemployment rate reached a 23-year low of 4.9 percent, creating tight labor markets in nearly every field and true shortages in workers with computer and technical skills. As a result, many companies experienced delays in hiring skilled workers and managers. The trend toward low unemployment rates also caused increases in starting salaries for in-demand positions, as recent college graduates could take their pick of several lucrative offers. Such competition for skilled workers can be particularly tough on small businesses, which may have to pay higher salaries to attract such workers in the first place, as well as provide more training and benefits in order to retain them.

Some experts claim that continued shortages might force American companies to look overseas for skilled labor, particularly as members of the baby-boom generation begin to leave the work force through retirement. But in an article for *Fortune,* Anne Fisher pointed out a number of factors that might indicate that the shortages will soon abate. For example, Fisher took note of the phenomenon known as "restless retirees"—people who reach retirement age but do not actually retire. As of 1993, 50 percent of men ages 55 to 61 continued to work while receiving a pension income, and that trend was expected to continue.

"As more and more people take better care of themselves and stay healthier longer—and as people begin to discover that their retirement savings won't necessarily carry them through 25 or 30 years of post-career leisure—it's silly to assume that today's forty-somethings to fiftysomethings will bow out of the labor force on the same kind of clockwork schedule that their parents did," Fisher wrote. "Older workers offer a tremendous amount of work experience, and the nature of temporary assignments may fit their schedules better than permanent employment," Samuel R. Sacco added in an interview with Patricia M. Fernberg for *Managing Office Technology.* "It is true that they may be less computer-oriented than younger workers, but they're also very trainable."

Another factor that may help mitigate current skilled labor shortage is an increase in American birth rates that began in 1977 and lasted through the early 1990s. Fisher claimed that this trend meant that "millions more young people—many of them computer literate almost from the cradle—will be looking for work over the next 5 to 15 years." The average education levels of American workers was also on the rise, as more employed people decided to return to school in order to improve their skills, and as more Americans pursued graduate degrees.

Fisher also noted that businesses have begun to respond to the shortage in skilled labor by increasing the amount and kinds of training that they provide. Employers have increasingly realized that the best way to ensure an adequate supply of trained workers is to train them. In fact, some studies suggest that corporate spending on training may have tripled since 1981.

"Over the past five years, businesses have realized that the school systems in this country have failed them. The government and the unions also have failed to develop a means of helping the U.S. work force make the transition from an industrial economy to a service economy. We have known for years that this economic shift was inevitable, but nobody has taken the initiative to retrain workers in the skills they need for a service economy," Sacco stated. "Businesses have to stop resisting involvement in retraining. The perfect employee is not going to walk through your doors, but if you hire and train the person who does, you are making an investment in the future of your company."

Fisher admitted that it was difficult to predict exactly what changes would take place in the composition of the work force. "Nevertheless, a few things seem certain," she wrote. "The labor force will grow in number over the next few years. More people will be more highly educated than ever before. Market forces will kick in—albeit gradually—and guide people toward the growing number of high-skilled jobs that pay above-average wages."

FURTHER READING:

Fernberg, Patricia M. "The Skills Shortage: Who Can Fill These Shoes?" *Managing Office Technology.* June 1995.

Fisher, Anne. "What Labor Shortage?" *Fortune.* June 23, 1997.

Pennington, Audrey. "Help Wanted: Work Force with the Right Stuff." *Site Selection.* June-July 1997.

SEE ALSO: Employee Benefits; Employee Hiring; Training and Development

WORKERS' COMPENSATION

Workers' compensation is a mandatory type of **business insurance** that provides employees who become injured or ill while on the job with medical coverage and income replacement. It also protects companies from being sued by employees for the workplace conditions that caused such an injury or illness. Someone is injured in an on-the-job accident every nineteen seconds in the United States. The workers' compensation system, which is administered independently by each state, provides such employees with benefits regardless of whether they have health or **disability insurance**.

Businesses are required by law in all fifty states to pay for the medical treatment and lost wages of employees who suffer job-related injuries or illnesses. Seven states provide coverage through monopolistic state-run funds, fourteen offer companies a choice between state-run and private funds, and the remainder foster a competitive environment with no state-run workers' compensation fund. Each state determines its own system's payment schedules, employee eligibility requirements, and rehabilitation procedures. Under typical workers' compensation laws, employers are responsible for all of an injured employee's medical costs and two-thirds of his or her wages during a disability caused by a job-related accident.

Given the mandatory nature of workers' compensation coverage, the cost of such policies is a huge concern for small business owners. Workers' compensation insurance rates rose at more than twice the rate of inflation during the 1980s, while the average benefits paid to insured workers tripled due to a higher number of claims and increased medical costs. Another factor in the rapid increase in rates has been an expansion of the definition of work-related injuries to include stress-related illnesses and repetitive motion injuries to office workers.

Small business owners have less control over the cost of workers' compensation coverage than they do over health insurance costs. State legislatures set the level of benefits and employers pay the full cost, so medical cost-containment strategies like co-payments do not apply. Some insurers avoid handling workers' compensation policies for small businesses because they feel that smaller companies lack the funds to provide a safe working environment. In general, the rates depend upon the type of business, number of employees, and company safety record. Workers' compensation coverage can account for 10 percent of payroll in some lines of business. Many businesses are able to reduce their rates by involving employees in safety programs and loss reduction systems.

BACKGROUND

The workers' compensation system developed in the early industrial age. During that period machine industry workers were being injured at a high rate. Their only remedy for medical care and to replace income lost due to days off of work was to sue the employer in court for negligence. For many this was impossible, but when it did happen the cost to employers was very high. Both employers and employees eventually decided that a legal system of compensation—whereby the employee gave up the right to sue, but was guaranteed legal protection and medical coverage for the injuries—was preferable.

In 1916, the U.S. Congress passed the Federal Employees Compensation Act, providing protection to federal workers. The passage of this law, while it had no legal impact on any private, state, or local workers, aided the cause of state workers' compensation laws by providing a national example of caring for employees. By 1949, every state had a workers' compensation law. Today the federal government also administers the provisions of the Longshoremen's and Harbor Workers' Compensation Act, which provides benefits for longshoremen, and the Black Lung Act, which provides benefits for coal mine workers who suffer from Black Lung disease. Aside from these exceptions, the remainder of the American work force is covered under the varying provisions of the 50 state laws and those of the District of Columbia.

Although provisions of each state's laws differ greatly, the underlying principle is the same—that employers should assume the costs of injuries, illnesses, and deaths that occur on the job, without regard to fault, and partially replace wage income lost. While income replacement under workers' compensation is usually a percentage of the actual wage, is it counted as a transfer payment and thus is not subject to federal income tax. Some state laws exempt certain categories of employees from coverage. Those most likely to be excluded are domestics, agricultural workers, and manual laborers.

TYPES OF COVERAGE AVAILABLE

There are three basic methods available for employers to obtain the required workers' compensation protection: state insurance funds, private insurance, and self-insurance. The latter—which involves setting aside funds in anticipation of workers' compensation claims, rather than purchasing insurance—is seen as a cost-saving method for safety-oriented firms. In the twenty-five states that permit it, many large employers now self-insure, and many small businesses form groups to insure themselves and decrease the risks.

In their book *Employee Benefits for Small Business,* Jane White and Bruce Pyenson note that group self-insurance plans can be a good option for small businesses with better-than-average **workplace safety** records. Such plans work best when the companies involved are in the same or similar industries, so that their level of risk is roughly equivalent. The companies can then join together to purchase stop-loss coverage to protect themselves against claims over a certain amount. Though self-insurance can be less expensive than private workers' compensation policies, small businesses should make sure that they have the financial resources to withstand potential losses.

Changes to state workers' compensation laws are made by state legislatures. In 1993, changes mandated by states included measures to implement managed health care as a way to save money for employers, reduce fraud, and improve safety in the workplace. Fraud is a concern with any type of insurance. But under the workers' compensation program there is the question not only of legitimacy of the injury, but also of legitimacy of the place of injury. The system only covers injuries at the workplace or injuries related to workplace activity. If a worker injures his or her back over the weekend while doing yard work he or she is not covered, yet the injury may cost time from the job. The extension of workers' compensation into the full life of the worker and into caring for the family as a whole has been under study. In 1992, four states—Alabama, Georgia, California, and Maine—began to examine ways in which workers' compensation might be added to a health insurance plan for the general population. The federal Office of Workers' Compensation publishes a review of state workers' compensation legislative activity each year in the January issue of the *Monthly Labor Review.*

FURTHER READING:

Blakely, Stephen. "Finding Coverage for Small Offices." *Nation's Business.* June 1997.

Lynn, Jacquelyn. "A Quick Guide to Insurance." *Entrepreneur.* June 1997.

Nelson, William J., Jr. "Workers' Compensation, Coverage, Benefits, Costs, 1989." *Social Security Bulletin.* Spring 1992.

White, Jane, and Bruce Pyenson. *Employee Benefits for Small Business.* Upper Saddle River, NJ: Prentice-Hall, 1991.

SEE ALSO: Employment Practices Liability Insurance

WORKPLACE ANGER/HOSTILITY

Workplace anger and hostility often manifests itself in ways that have received a great deal of attention from business owners, researchers, legislators, and members of the business press in recent years. Workplace violence and **sexual harassment** are probably the two best known examples of workplace anger and hostility. But anger and hostility can manifest themselves in other, less dramatic ways, such as bullying. These too can have a negative impact on a business by producing an environment marked by poor or nonexistent communication, lousy morale, excessive employee **absenteeism** or turnover, and a host of other undesired conditions. Business owners, managers, and employees who are unable to control their own anger or effectively respond to the angry outbursts of others will likely find that their business and/or career suffers as a result. Entrepreneurs who are prone to expressing anger or hostility in the workplace will likely see their business suffer as they alienate employees and/or customers, while employees who lack the discipline or disposition to constructively handle anger frequently find themselves stalled on the lower rungs of professional advancement.

Of course, not all small businesses that utilize employees are confronted with the challenge of addressing—and hopefully defusing—problem workers who behave in an angry or hostile manner toward coworkers or customers. After all, many enterprises feature a positive work environment and employ staff that enjoy their jobs and relate to one another in a professional manner. But most small business owners that have a payroll will eventually encounter someone who exhibits angry or hostile behavior. "One of the more obvious conditions in the workplace is that people, in their roles as employees, are distinguished by their vast differences," wrote Joseph D. Levesque, author of *The Human Resource Problem-Solver's Handbook.* "They come to us in all forms, divergent experiences and backgrounds, and in remarkably unique psychological makeup. Some are quite stable in their values, lifestyles, reasoning, actions, and direction. Others may be self-serving, deceptive, rebellious, or in many other ways problematic," although such characteristics typically do not show themselves until the person's trial employment period has passed.

Entrepreneurs, then, need to prepare themselves for the day when an employee's actions or words seem to be based on feelings of anger or hostility. Some small business owners underestimate the impact that workplace anger and hostility can have on their business and on their staff, and they do so at their peril. "Many employees face hostility in the course of their work. This can take a number of forms, including sexual and racial harassment, physical assault, verbal abuse, threats, intimidation, and bullying,'' said Andrea Adams in *Personnel Management.* ''It can come from various sources both internal (bosses, colleagues) and external (customers, clients, or the public at large). Organizations which fail to recognize and deal effectively with this problem will suffer as a result. They may be in breach of their legal duty to ensure their employees' health, safety and welfare, or guilty of unlawful discrimination, or open to a claim of constructive dismissal. Their costs will rise because of poor morale and productivity, higher absenteeism and staff turnover. They will find it difficult to attract new staff, and in extreme cases the damage to their image or reputation will mean loss of business.''

''One nasty crack that receives minimal attention from management can get half your work force stewing, not only creating low morale and an unpleasant work environment, but also severely cutting **productivity**,'' wrote Robert McGarvey in *Entrepreneur.* Indeed, incidents of workplace anger or hostility can have a ripple effect throughout the business. Oftentimes, these ''secondary victims,'' as Charlene Marmer Solomon called them in *Personnel Journal,* are ''people who share the same background as the victim.''

Small business owners should be aware that failure to address workplace hostilities can also open them up to legal liability. Moreover, the person who engages in hostile workplace behavior does not have to be an owner or supervisor for the business owner to be vulnerable to charges concerning that person's behavior, because in the eyes of the law, business owners have the power to control their employees. ''Employers typically say, 'But I didn't ask or order my employees to do these things, and I personally disagree with what they did,' '' a professor of employment law told *Entrepreneur.* ''But there is no legal protection in that argument. If an event happens in the workplace, it's attributable to management.''

CAUSES OF WORKPLACE ANGER AND HOSTILITY

Workplace hostility can often be traced to attitudes that have little to do with the current employment situation in which workers find themselves. Deep-seated feelings of hostility toward other people because of their gender, skin color, sexual orientation, political beliefs, or other factors are often firmly in place long before the person begins working at your company. Often, the small business owner faced with such an employee will have limited options available to deal with such problems; instead, he or she will concentrate efforts on making sure that those undesired attitudes do not seep into the workplace.

Factors that cause workplace anger, on the other hand, can sometimes be addressed directly. While workplace anger sometimes can be traced back to prejudices that are at the root of deep-seated hostility, on many other occasions, work-oriented factors serve as the primary catalysts. Common causes of workplace anger included:

- General harassment, whether sexual or some other form.
- Favoritism of one employee over another.
- Rejection of proposal or project in which employee has big emotional investment.
- Insensitivity by owners or managers.
- Criticisms of employees in front of staff or clients.
- Depersonalized workplace environment.
- Unfair (or tardy) performance appraisals or criticism.
- Lack of resources.
- Inadequate training.
- Lack of teamwork.
- Withdrawal of earned benefits.
- Betrayal of trust extended to manager or owner.
- Unreasonable demands on employees.
- Unkept promises.
- Lack of flexibility on part of owner or manager.
- Poor communication.
- Feedback is wholly or primarily negative in tone.
- Absentee leadership (such as instances wherein needed disciplinary action is absent).
- Micromanagerial environment in which staff decisionmaking opportunities are limited.

Of course, sometimes a distinction must be made between legitimate and illegitimate catalysts of workplace anger. For example, an employee may express great anger over a negative performance review even though the appraisal was conducted fairly and honestly. Small business owners and supervisors cannot jettison basic principles of management simply to avoid making one of their employees mad.

SIGNS OF HIDDEN ANGER Workplace anger is often sublimated by employees until they reach a point where they suddenly burst. This ''bursting'' point may manifest itself in a variety of ways. One employee may just yell at his manager, while another may impetuously decide to quit. Still others may resort to workplace violence or vandalism. Small business owners and managers should acquaint themselves with the warning signs of hidden anger so that they can address the causes for that anger and hopefully head off an incident before it occurs.

Writing in *Machine Design,* Eugene Raudsepp listed the following as some typical signs of suppressed workplace anger:

- Procrastination in completing a task or project.

- Preference for sarcasm or cynicism in conversation.

- Silent or sulky behavior.

- Over-controlled monotone speaking voice.

- Sleep disorders.

- Apathy.

- Irritability over minor matters.

- Physical signs, such as clenched jaws, grinding teeth, or excessive sighing.

- Refusal to make eye contact.

"BULLYING" Explicit workplace violence, sexual harassment, and episodes of discrimination garner the most headlines and receive the bulk of attention from consultants because of their potential legal impact on business enterprises. But researchers contend that simple bullying behavior may be a greater threat to business health and productivity than any of the above-mentioned problems. Sometimes bullying takes place between employees, but it often is most evident in supervisor-worker relationships, in which one person is perceived to wield greater power. "Bullying is not just the problem of an individual, however, but, where it exists, of the organization and its culture as a whole," stated Andrea Adams in *Personnel Management.* "Whether it is a bully's persistent intimidation or their devious efforts to make a colleague appear professionally incompetent, these menacing tactics can be difficult to identify. In every organization bullying remains well disguised" under a blizzard of euphemisms that avoid calling the behavior what it really is. "In America employee abuse, as it is called, is also referred to as 'workplace trauma,' " wrote Adams. "It has been identified in research carried out by one psychologist in the USA as a more crippling and devastating problem for both staff and employers than all the other work-related stresses put together. There are always those who will put forward the argument that the making of snide remarks or jokes at other people's expense is 'a part of human nature,' but office banter which is not really designed to offend is undoubtedly different to the persistent downgrading of people by any individual in a position of power."

Adams noted that confronting bullies about their behavior is often difficult: "Where bullying exists and someone is willing to tackle it, the bully will have to be addressed in some way and prevailed on to change. The way in which they see themselves will rarely tally with the view of those who are placed under attack." Small business owners and managers, however, should stand fast. Bullying behavior generally does not take place in a vacuum; other employees are usually aware of the situation, and they should be consulted. Finally, owners seeking to eliminate bullying behavior need to make it clear that anyone who is the victim of bullying tactics will receive their full support.

PEER CONFLICT Another common cause of workplace anger and hostility is peer conflict. Unlike instances of bullying, wherein one employee makes a conscious decision to engage in behavior that is hurtful or uncomfortable for another employee, peer conflict is characterized by mutual feelings of animosity toward the other individual. "Peer conflicts are typically caused by personality or perception differences, moodiness, impatience, or sensitive emotional states such as jealousy, annoyance, and embarrassment," wrote Levesque. "When these rivalries evolve into skirmishes or outbursts, the conflict erupts and people are damaged. Since work relies heavily on the ability of people to interact in a cooperative and harmonious fashion, conflict between employees represents a serious breakdown of those two vital ingredients to effective work relationships."

According to management theorist Peter Drucker, managers can pursue one of the following routes when attempting to resolve peer conflicts:

1) Convince both workers to accept a mutually agreeable view or agreement about the issue that was the cause of the conflict.

2) Support the position of one employee and reject the position of the other.

3) Make your own decision about the issue and force both people to comply with your perception.

"What is important for the manager to keep in perspective," wrote Levesque, "is that the problem belongs to those in conflict and only they can resolve it, but they will need someone to help—you."

Small business owners who find themselves mediating a peer conflict should avoid taking sides (especially if both workers' views have merit), provide an objective viewpoint, keep the discussion from bogging down in tangents or name-calling, and help each one to understand the perspective of the other. Finally, the small business owner's overriding concern should be to explicitly restate his or her expectations of staff performance, including the ways in which staff members should behave toward one another.

KEYS TO STOPPING OR PREVENTING EXPRESSIONS OF WORKPLACE HOSTILITY AND ANGER

Levesque observed that "there are several measures that can be taken . . . to control or correct conduct and performance problems among employees [such as various motivational or inspiration techniques, ignoring undesirable behavior, etc.], but when none of these structured behavioral approaches work with some employees we invariably rely on disciplinary measures as the ultimate tool to resolve the problem. Sometimes it works, and happily so when concluded at informal levels, but sometimes it doesn't produce the desired result. When the desired result isn't achieved, both the employee and organization have lost something, but at least the matter reaches conclusions. Regrettably, in many instances of employee conduct and performance the employee will hand you no alternative but to deal with them in a disciplinary fashion." This discipline can take a variety of forms, from suspension to negative comments in the employee's personnel file to yanking the worker off a plum project. Reports on the effectiveness of such steps vary considerably; some firms contend that such measures inform the employee that his or her problematic behavior will not be tolerated, while others insist that such measures—especially if used without first pursuing other options—may only deepen feelings of animosity and hostility. No two small business enterprises or employees are alike.

Researchers agree, however, that there a number of steps that employers can take to address the issues of workplace anger and hostility before they erupt into full-blown crises.

1) Explicitly state your absolute opposition to unwelcome behavior in writing. This can often be included as part of a new hire's employee guidelines package, but small business owners should also consider displaying such "zero tolerance" statements in public areas. Such statements should also clearly delineate which types of comments and actions are regarded as offensive.

2) Encourage an environment that values diversity. "There must be vision and commitment to the ideal of valuing diversity demonstrated by an underlying respect toward everyone in the organization," wrote Solomon.

3) Recognize that incidents of workplace hostility tend to get worse over time if they are not addressed. For example, remarks that might at first seem to be merely in mildly bad taste can eventually blossom into full-fledged racist, sexist, or otherwise mean-spirited jokes. "Learning to deal with [workplace anger] issues is critical to creating a workplace that is comfortable—and therefore productive—for employees," wrote McGarvey. "An all-too-common reaction, and one that often creates bigger problems down the road, is shrugging off such incidents." Instead, business owners should respond to incidents of workplace anger or hostility promptly and decisively. The whole workforce will likely be watching, looking for some signal about whether management takes such transgressions seriously, or whether it implicitly gives the green light to further incidents.

4) Learn to recognize the symptoms of workplace anger, and try to provide employees with constructive avenues to express frustrations and/or concerns.

5) Monitor workplace culture. "In some parts of the workplace," observed Solomon, "fooling around may entail pushing and other forms of physical macho behavior." Such interactions should not be permitted, since they can escalate into undesirable situations.

6) Make sure you have all the facts before confronting an employee with a charge of workplace discrimination or otherwise unprofessional behavior. This is especially true if you are dealing with hostile actions that are taken anonymously.

7) Make sure that your own actions and deeds are a good model for your employees.

8) Recognize that your primary imperative is not to change an employee's mindset about minorities, women, or other co-workers, but rather to ensure that the employee does not engage in offensive behavior in his or her interactions with co-workers or customers. "We won't change what a person says at a bar, after work, but we can impact how he carries out his job in the workplace," one consultant told *Entrepreneur*. "We won't change attitudes, but we can manage behaviors—and that's your responsibility as an employer."

WHEN THE SMALL BUSINESS OWNER IS ANGRY

Small business owners should also be aware of the challenges of managing their own anger in the workplace. Entrepreneurship brings with it a host of responsibilities and pressures that can make it difficult for them to manage strong emotions such as anger. But it is important for small business owners to handle their anger in an effective manner. "Expressing anger can be constructive when your true intent is to maintain, reestablish, or restore a positive relationship with the person who has offended you,'' wrote Raudsepp. ''When done properly, constructive confrontations assure future harmony, better performance, and improved productivity. . . . When confronting the person who sparked your anger, don't underestimate the value of courtesy. Express your feelings in a reasonable, calm and controlled way. Back your statements with specifics. State the problem as you see it and then give the other party a chance to express his or her side. Listen, empathize, and try to understand what caused the conflict. Make it clear it's the behavior, not the person, that caused the problem.''

FURTHER READING:

Levesque, Joseph D. *The Human Resource Problem-Solver's Handbook.* New York: McGraw-Hill, 1992.

McGarvey, Robert. ''Foul Play: Battling Hostilities in the Workplace.'' *Entrepreneur.* October 1997.

McShulskis, Elaine. ''Workplace Anger: A Growing Problem.'' *HRMagazine.* December 1996.

Raudsepp, Eugene. ''Coping with Anger.'' *Machine Design.*

Solomon, Charlene Marmer. ''Keeping Hate Out of the Workplace.'' *Personnel Journal.* July 1992.

SEE ALSO: Corporate Culture; Employee Performance Appraisals; Employee Rights; Employee Termination; Violence in the Workplace

WORKPLACE SAFETY

Workplace safety refers to the working environment at a company and addresses anything that affects the safety and health of employees. This can include environmental hazards, unsafe working conditions or processes, drug and alcohol abuse, and workplace violence. Workplace safety is monitored at the national level by the **Occupational Safety and Health Administration (OSHA)**. Federal guidelines are complemented by state regulations that are often tougher than those proposed by OSHA.

OSHA has three stated goals that should be memorized by every company, large or small, seeking to improve safety. Those goals are:

1) Improve safety and health for all workers, as evidenced by fewer hazards, reduced exposures, and fewer injuries, illnesses, and fatalities.

2) Change workplace culture to increase employer and worker awareness of, commitment to, and involvement in safety and health.

3) Secure public confidence through excellence in the development and delivery of OSHA's programs and services.

Trying to live up to those OSHA ideals should be the goal of every company, but small businesses face some unique challenges when it comes to workplace safety.

SMALL BUSINESSES AND THEIR ATTITUDES TOWARDS SAFETY

A 1995 survey of 3,200 members of the National Federation of Independent Business by the Insurance Research Council showed that 73 percent of small business owners believed that their employees were at least somewhat concerned over workplace safety. Fifty-four percent of respondents indicated that they did not believe that safety was a serious problem, but the majority of those same respondents had taken steps to improve safety in the five years prior to the survey.

An additional 45 percent believed that safety was a significant problem or one of the most serious problems facing management. Finally, business owners approached for the survey also tended to believe that accidents are more likely to be a result of employee behavior rather than management action or inaction.

In the five years prior to the survey, the majority of owners had made, on average, six different actions to improve safety. Those actions were:

- Providing personal safety equipment

- Providing training on safety issues

- Installing controls or other devices on equipment that make the machines safer

- Conducting an inspection of the entire workplace to identify hazards

- Putting safety guidelines in writing

- Purchasing safer equipment.

Other safety steps adopted include no-smoking policies, changing procedures to increase safety, adopting drug and alcohol testing policies, sending employees to off-site training, starting a driver safety program, and diminishing the purchasing and handling of hazardous materials.

TIPS ON IMPROVING SAFETY AT A SMALL BUSINESS

Some owners erroneously believe that the small size of their enterprise makes them immune from following OSHA regulations. In reality, even though there may be different standards for some regulations, small businesses do have to pay attention to safety. Indeed, workplace safety is an important consideration on a number of levels. Attention to safety issues can not only help businesses avoid legal penalties, but also improve employee morale, productivity, and retention. Following are several considerations that a small firm should weigh when implementing or updating a workplace safety program.

SAFETY MANAGERS AND COMMITTEES One method that many firms have had success with is to appoint one person in the organization as the safety coordinator. The ideal candidate would be someone who has a background in safety, but if no one fits that profile, then choose the candidate who best relates to workers and management, has strong communication skills, and has an interest in and commitment to safety. A common title for this person is "safety manager."

For the safety manager to do his or her job, he or she must have direct access to the top manager in the company. Without management buy-in, safety initiatives will not last long. The manager must also have access to every department and work area, and must be able to question people freely for the purpose of gathering information. Regular status reports should be prepared that update management on current safety initiatives and identify areas that still need improvement. Ideally, the safety manager's role will remain an advisory one: responsibility for implementing the manager's suggestions should fall to upper management and the individuals or teams that are singled out by the safety manager. After all, the safety manager's mandate should be to facilitate change, not implement it.

Many analysts believe that businesses should make certain that safety managers are adequately educated on workplace safety issues as well. Business owners are thus often encouraged to send managers to training and education seminars or classes as part of an overall policy of ongoing education. Additionally, management should encourage the manager to seek out safety professionals at other companies to help him or her build a network of contacts and information. Upper management is also responsible for ensuring that safety performance is made a part of every employee's job responsibility and performance reviews. Only when every employee is held accountable for safety will it become a part of a company's culture.

The best starting point for a new safety manager is often to review company records of past safety problems. By drawing up a list of areas that are known problems, the manager can identify the best place to begin implementation of new safety measures. Of course, it is also important that the manager immediately follow up on any disquieting patterns or dangerous situations that are discovered and implement action steps to correct the problems. Unfortunately, in some instances safety managers will find that workplace safety reports are scant or nonexistent. In such instances, the manager should start from ground zero and begin a formal accident/safety reporting system to gather data.

Documentation and record keeping serves two additional purposes—it provides written evidence that the new safety program is providing positive results and it can be used to protect the firm in the event that a lawsuit is filed or safety inquiry launched. Documentation of employee training sessions is especially important, including the topics covered, when the meetings were held, and any test scores earned by employees at the sessions. Consultants cite testing as a potentially valuable way of determining whether employees really paid attention and comprehended the information they just received.

The safety manager should seek to involve all employees and managers in safety initiatives. Inspections should be conducted by the personnel of each department, not the safety manager. In fact, the manager should let each department handle most of its own safety problems—if proper training has been given to all employees, the safety manager should only have to address serious problems that require his or her knowledge and authority.

Writing in *Occupational Hazard,* William H. Kincaid identified 10 characteristics that every safety manager (whether a business owner or a staffer) should have:

1. Praise employees when they choose safe behaviors.

2. Solicit participation from employees.

3. Reward employee participation.

4. Set a good example.

5. Invest in people (i.e., happy, trained workers are apt to work more safely).

6. Continuously improve and simplify workplace safety.

7. Visit all areas of the company regularly.

8. Be open and honest, keeping employees informed of your activities.

9. Show employees you care by taking the time to learn everyone's name.

10. Try to learn something new at least once a day.

While it is important to have one manager who can do all of this while serving as the central clearing point for safety information and training, studies have shown that safety committees are an excellent addition to a safety program. Only 25 to 50 percent of the firms in the Insurance Research Council survey were shown to have implemented a committee, with the others opting to let the safety manager work alone or try to get by with written guidelines. It is worth noting, however, that safety committees have been shown to reduce the injury rate at companies, which in turn can boost morale and efficiency. Companies that use committees have also reported some unexpected benefits, including an increased sense of teamwork, better sharing of information, and a drop in absenteeism, discrimination claims, grievances, and sick days.

Not all small business enterprises reach a size that warrant creation of such committees. But for growing businesses with a significant payroll, safety and health committees can provide important benefits. The committees, which ideally will include a cross-section of employees, should serve as a central gathering and dissemination point for all information related to safety.

OUTSIDE SAFETY ANALYSIS Another potentially useful option for entrepreneurs interested in determining workplace safety is to have an outside firm conduct a safety analysis. These firms specialize in safety and hazardous materials and can offer many good suggestions on how to improve safety. Analysts note that reports submitted by these organizations often range from warnings of regulatory breaches to suggestions on alternative production methods. Not all safety improvement suggestions are implemented, of course. Some courses of action may be deemed excessively expensive, while others are dismissed because of employee resistance or skepticism about their ultimate impact on workplace safety.

SAFETY INCENTIVES Business owners and consultants alike agree that safety managers and consultants will not have a meaningful impact on a company's safety records if the employees are not willing to do their part to help make things better. One of the best ways to ensure employee cooperation is to offer incentives tied to improvements in safety, although observers are quick to add that safety incentives are not an adequate substitute for a strong safety program. In fact, only companies that have a strong program already in place should even think of using incentives. Cash and non-cash awards should only be used to motivate employees to practice what the already-in-place program preaches, which reinforces behavior and encourages participation.

Incentives should reward behaviors that prevent injury by eliminating unsafe work practices. Reward employees who achieve "zero accidents," but be sure to use a broad definition of accident (such as one that would cause an employee to miss time on the job) so that employees do not try to cover up minor injuries in order to keep their zero accident rating. Once the behaviors to be rewarded are identified, then determine how awards will be given—by individual, by department, or by company. Most experts today recommend creating a team atmosphere with safety awards and recognition, which means the latter two methods are preferable.

To make an incentive program really work, several things must be done. First, the safety incentives must be an ongoing element of the workplace. One-time incentive programs tend to get employees interested for a short time, then cause them to lose interest and fall back into bad habits once the period has passed. Second, meaningful incentives should be chosen. Non-cash incentives tend to work best, since employees tend to pocket the cash and forget about the ongoing message. Some companies do believe that cash works best, while others feel using cash sends people the wrong message by paying them extra for practices that they should already be doing. Good examples of non-cash incentives include recognition awards, token gifts that build morale, and customized items (clothing, for example). Finally, goals and results must be clearly communicated to employees at every step of the process.

Small business owners should not be scared of the costs associated with running an incentive program. Even if the program costs several thousand dollars annually, many economists and business experts contend that the expense is insignificant compared to the productivity lost as a result of poor safety practices. Since the average cost of a disabling injury in the mid-1990s was estimated at more than $27,000, it is easy to see how an incentive program could actually save money for employers in the long run.

DRUG AND ALCOHOL ABUSE AND TESTING PROGRAMS

Drug and alcohol testing has been slow to catch on among small firms. Over 85 percent of the nation's major companies have a testing policy in place, but the rate is much lower for small businesses. Despite evidence that employees who abuse drugs and alcohol are three more times likely to be late than the average employee, are in 3.6 times as many accidents, are a third less productive, and have medical insurance costs that are 300 percent higher than nonabusing employees, many small firms have not implemented testing policies because of concerns about expense, employee privacy, etc.

That is beginning to change as new data rolls in. Studies now show that not only do **drug testing** and anti-abuse policies improve safety and production in the workplace, but they also lower medical insurance costs, decrease the number of sick days taken, and lead to fewer worker compensation claims. Some medical insurance companies are offering up to a five percent reduction on premiums if a company is certified drug-free.

Companies must be careful when implementing drug testing to ensure that the programs are fair to all employees and are clearly explained. The best way to implement drug testing is to have a clear written policy, employ trained supervisors to implement and manage the program, and inform all employees of every facet of the new policy, including the penalties for noncompliance. Also, it is important that a policy include not just punishment, but treatment options and assistance in overcoming drug abuse. Offering to pay for treatment with the promise that the abuser's job will be there when he or she comes back clean is a common provision of drug testing programs.

WORKPLACE VIOLENCE AS A SAFETY ISSUE

Unfortunately, everyone is familiar with the image of a disgruntled employee taking out his displeasure with his employer by resorting to violence. Indeed, the problem of workplace violence has become so widespread in America that the Centers for Disease Control recently declared workplace homicide to be a serious public health epidemic. And with good reason. According to the U.S. Department of Labor, 912 workplace homicides occurred in 1996—an average of 17 per week. It was the number one cause of death for women on the job, and the number three cause for all U.S. workers. Moreover, these statistics do not even take into account the ever-growing number of incidents of physical assaults, threats, verbal abuse, and harassment that take place in some workplace environments.

Every act of workplace violence leaves scars on every person in the organization. Not only is the person who is harmed or killed affected, but so too are those who witness the act or who knew the employee. One act of violence can change an entire company permanently. The working environment can become so toxic that no work gets done—all employees can think about is what happened. From the company perspective, violence also leaves the company exposed to lawsuits and liability that can cost millions of dollars.

There are steps that can be taken to prevent or at least minimize the chances of workplace violence. The most important step is for the company's leadership to communicate a zero-tolerance policy for workplace violence and a corresponding determination to create and maintain a safe workplace for employees. The message that violence will not be tolerated has to come from the top down. Next, businesses study records of incidents that have occurred in the past and study trends and common threads. Pay special attention to causes and precipitating events. Inspect physical work sites and determine if security is stringent enough and if security guards have the resources they need to do their jobs. How easy is it to gain access to your company?

Next, the company should draw up a written workplace violence policy and disseminate it to every employee. Local laws and regulations should be considered when preparing the policy, as should workplace culture and the affect of the plan on employees. If specific hazards have been identified, develop a workplace violence injury and illness prevention plan to meet OSHA guidelines. Finally, provide training and education in workplace violence for all employees, not just managers.

One additional important step that a company can add to its nonviolence policy is to increase the preemployment screening of applicants. Psychological and other tests can identify potential troublemakers in advance, and many tests exist that are completely legal. In the company's physical plant, turn your company into a "fortress" if need be. Add locked access doors as control points, issue badges, or consider "swipe cards" that act as electronic keys.

Small businesses need to be aware that violence can strike them, too. While studies have shown that the larger a business is, the more likely it is to be victimized by acts of violence, it can happen anywhere. Smaller companies have the benefit of knowing every employee and having more control over what type of work environment exists at the company, but the threat is still real and needs to be taken seriously.

FURTHER READING:

Arkin, Alan. "Safer Workplaces Are No Accident." *People Management.* July 25, 1996.

Barrett, Stephen. "Protecting Against Workplace Violence." *Public Management.* August 1997.

Esters, Stephanie D. "Workplace Violence Prompts Policy." *National Underwriter Property & Casualty-Risk & Benefits Management.* February 23, 1997.

Friend, Mark A. "Safety in the Small Business: Getting Started." *Occupational Hazards.* July 1994.

Goldberg, Carol. "Workplace Safety Is a Wise Investment." *LI Business News.* August 19, 1996.

Kincaid, William H. "10 Habits of Effective Safety Managers." *Occupational Hazards.* November 1996.

"New Prevention Program Targets Rise In Workplace Violence." *Business Wire.* October 16, 1997.

O'Donovan, Cheryl. "The Bulletproof Office." *Communication World.* October-November 1997.

Panko, Ron. "Workplace Violence Guidelines Create New Risks." *Best's Review—Property-Casualty Insurance Edition.* July 1996.

Pasher, Victoria S. "Small Businesses Split Over Safety." *National Underwriter Property & Casualty-Risk & Benefits Management.* July 17, 1995.

Quilty, Michelle. "Safety Takes the Prize." *Small Business Reports.* March 1994.

Ronca, Theodore J. "Be On the Safe Side." *Small Business Reports.* September 1994.

Synett, Robert J. "Achieving Safety Excellence: 6 Keys to Success." *Risk Management.* October 1996.

"What Causes Accidents?" *Monthly Labor Review.* December 1996.

Zoeckler, Eric L. "Small Firms Slow at Implementing Detection Strategies." *Puget Sound Business Journal.* October 7, 1994.

SEE ALSO: Corporate Culture; Workplace Anger/Hostility

WRITTEN COMMUNICATION

Written communication involves any type of interaction that makes use of the written word. It is one of the two main types of communication, along with spoken or **oral communication**. Written communication is very common in business situations, so it is important for small business owners and managers to develop effective written communication skills. Some of the various forms of written communication that might be used within a business include memos, reports, bulletins, job descriptions, **employee manuals**, and **electronic mail**. Examples of written communication with others outside of the business include letters, proposals, telegrams, faxes, postcards, contracts, advertisements, brochures, and news releases. In order to understand the principles of effective written communication, it is helpful to look at the basic process of communication.

THE COMMUNICATION PROCESS

The basic process of communication begins when a fact or idea is observed by one person. That person (the sender) may decide to translate the observation into a message, and then transmit the message through some communication medium to another person (the receiver). The receiver then must interpret the message and provide feedback to the sender indicating that the message has been understood and appropriate action taken.

According to Herta A. Murphy and Herbert W. Hildebrandt in their book *Effective Business Communications,* good communication should be complete, concise, clear, concrete, correct, considerate, and courteous. More specifically, this means that communication should: answer basic questions like who, what, when, where; be relevant and not overly wordy; focus on the receiver and his or her interests; use specific facts and figures and active verbs; use a conversational tone for readability; include examples and visual aids when needed; be tactful and good natured; and be accurate and nondiscriminatory. Unclear, inaccurate, or inconsiderate business communication can waste valuable time, alienate employees or customers, and destroy goodwill toward management or the overall business.

Perhaps the most important part of business communication is taking the time to prepare an effective and understandable message. According to Murphy and Hildebrandt, the first step is to know the main purpose of the message. For example, a message to a supplier might have the purpose of obtaining a replacement for a defective part. The next step is to analyze the audience so that the message can be adapted to fit their views and needs. It may be helpful to picture the recipient and think about which areas of the message they might find positive or negative, interesting or boring, pleasing or displeasing. After that, the sender needs to choose the ideas to include and collect all the necessary facts. The next step involves organizing the message, since a poorly organized message will fail to elicit the required response. It may be helpful to prepare an outline beforehand, paying particular attention to the beginning and ending portions. Finally, before transmitting the message it is important to edit and proofread.

ADVANTAGES AND DISADVANTAGES OF WRITTEN COMMUNICATION

In their book *Management: Function and Strategy,* Thomas S. Bateman and Carl P. Zeithaml described several advantages and disadvantages of using written forms of communication. One advantage is that written messages do not have to be delivered on the spur of the moment; instead, they can be edited and revised several times before they are sent. Another advantage is that written communication provides a permanent record of the messages that have been sent and can be saved for later study. Since they are permanent, written forms of communication also enable receivers to take more time in reviewing the message and providing appropriate feedback. For these reasons, written forms of communication are often considered more appropriate for complex business messages that include important facts and figures.

There are also several disadvantages associated with written communication, however. For one thing, the sender is often unable to control when, where, or even if the message is received. In addition, unlike face-to-face communication, the sender does not generally receive immediate feedback to his or her message. The lack of immediate feedback makes it more likely that the receiver may not understand some aspects of the message. Finally, written messages often take more time to compose because they must contain enough information to answer any questions that the receiver might have. For these reasons, written communication is not considered appropriate for simple business messages that depend upon complete understanding or require an immediate answer.

PRINCIPLES OF EFFECTIVE WRITING

The basic principles of written communication are similar to those for overall communication. Since written communication does not usually receive immediate feedback, it is particularly important when using this medium to use simple words and short sentences, and to avoid technical jargon and cliches. Bateman and Zeithaml outlined five traits that characterize good writing: clarity, organization, readability, satisfying readers' needs, and brevity.

"Good writing is more than just correct spelling, punctuation, and grammar; it requires clear, logical thinking," Bateman and Zeithaml explained. Above all, written communication should be clear and never leave the reader confused. Regarding organization, the authors suggested developing an outline before beginning to prepare important letters or reports. If the written communication will be long or complex, it may be helpful to include headings and subheadings, and to indicate in the text where attached charts and tables may provide additional information. Business documents are more readable when they include specific, concrete terms rather than abstract phrases or jargon. Every general statement should be supported by facts and statistics. In order to satisfy readers' needs when writing, it is important to ascertain their level of knowledge about the subject matter, as well as their attitude toward it and toward your organization. Finally, written communication should be as brief as possible in order to hold the reader's interest. It may be helpful to proofread critically before sending any message, deleting any unnecessary words, sentences, or paragraphs.

USES FOR WRITTEN COMMUNICATION

Some of the most important business uses of written communications involve persuading the receiver to take some action, such as invest funds in a small business or agree to purchase a product or service. Persuasive letters have a special organization. According to Murphy and Hildebrandt, they should: 1) attract favorable attention from the reader; 2) arouse interest; 3) convince the reader and create desire; and 4) describe the action the reader should take. When the purpose of the letter is to make a sale, it is also important to include facts about the product and a clear central selling point. Above all, it is important that any type of written communication that originates from a business create or enhance goodwill.

One of the most difficult uses of written communication involves conveying bad news. "Whenever you must send a message that your reader will consider disappointing or unfavorable in some way, the situation requires special planning and careful choice of words," Murphy and Hildebrandt noted. "The underlying purpose of every bad-news message is to present the unpleasant facts . . . in such a way that the reader will consider you fair and reasonable and, preferably, remain a friend of the organization you represent." One of the most important aspects of effectively conveying this type of message is seeing things from the recipient's perspective in order to keep his or her pride intact. The message itself may be organized directly or indirectly.

An indirect organization begins with a "buffer," or a paragraph of pleasant, tactful, neutral information of interest to the reader. It is important that the buffer does not give the impression that the rest of the letter will be favorable, however, or the reader will experience a letdown. The next section should include an honest, convincing explanation of the situation and an analysis of why an unfavorable decision was reached. The next section should state or imply the decision and provide helpful suggestions for alternative action if possible. Finally, the letter should close on a friendly, positive note. The direct organization includes many of the same elements, but is arranged in a different order. The decision is stated first, followed by the explanation and a courteous conclusion. The direct organization is usually used for routine or urgent matters, and the indirect organization is used in most other situations.

FURTHER READING:

Bateman, Thomas S., and Carl P. Zeithaml. *Management: Function and Strategy.* Homewood, IL: Irwin, 1990.

Golen, Steven. *Effective Business Communication.* Washington: U.S. Small Business Administration, 1989.

Murphy, Herta A., and Herbert W. Hildebrandt. *Effective Business Communications.* 6th ed. New York: McGraw-Hill, 1991.

Townsend, Robert. *Up the Organization.* New York: Knopf, 1984.

SEE ALSO: Nonverbal Communication

Y

As the twentieth century draws to a close, the international community has become increasingly concerned about the current inability of many computers and applications to correctly calculate dates once they reach the year 2000. This "Year 2000" computer problem has been the subject of considerable discussion in both the business and general press, with various observers and experts offering widely divergent assessments of the impact that the Y2K issue—as it is commonly referred to in the computer industry—will have on businesses, government agencies, and other organizations. Some people believe that the cost of correcting the problem (or recovering from the havoc that it may cause) will ultimately cost the world community billions of dollars. Others offer far less grim scenarios, although they admit that it will cause problems. "Worst-case scenarios include power outages, ruined financial records, stock market freeze-ups, and air travel problems," summarized *USA Today's* Kevin Maney. "The best case still includes business interruptions and inconveniences ranging from closed ATMs to lost report cards in a school's computer." While analysts disagree on the seriousness of the problem, all concur that the problem is a far-reaching one. "The Year 2000 bug is a small problem on a large scale," wrote Maney. "Fixing the year 2000 problem is simple, but finding it is not. It's scattered through millions of lines of code in each of millions of computers. Programmers have to go over every line of code, then test every bit of software."

ORIGINS OF Y2K PROBLEM Back in the 1960s, when computer technology was in its early stages of devel-opment, programmers made a conscious decision to only include two spaces for registering dates. Tariq K. Muhammad explained in *Black Enterprise* that they did this "in order to conserve, what was then, a very limited (and expensive) supply of internal memory. Thus they incorporated the MM/DD/YY convention for assigning dates—both in computers' basic input/output system (BIOS) and in the coding of applications—limiting the computer to two digits for each field." This worked well for years, but slowly it dawned on programmers, small business owners, and corporate executives that this arrangement would not be able to accommodate dates in the twenty-first century. "The problem is that the computer doesn't inter-pret '00' as the year 2000 but rather 1900, and miscal-culates all computations accordingly," explained National Institute of Standards and Technology (NIST) scientist Gary Fisher in an interview with Muhammad, who noted that the practical impact of this seemingly minor glitch has far-reaching implica-tions. "Accounting, benefits, forecasting, and other date-sensitive applications will potentially malfunc-tion when noncompliant systems try to perform opera-tions that require computations involving 2000 and beyond."

DEBATE OVER "YEAR 2000" REPERCUSSIONS Opinions about the severity of the Y2K problem vary throughout the business, government, and computer communities. The Gartner Group business research firm has estimated that half of all companies will experience computer problems on January 1, 2000. Moreover, analysts note that even if a company ade-quately prepares for the problem, it may still experi-ence interruptions in business operations if any of its customers or vendors are caught in a glitch. Problems with **telecommunications** networks and even basic telephone service could also flare up, according to some experts.

Government agencies in the United States and elsewhere have been heavily criticized for their perceived slow reaction to the threat as well. The General Accounting Office (GAO) of the United States, for example, recently reported that a number of important agencies, including the departments of Defense and Treasury are significantly behind schedule in dealing with the problem. At the same time, other government agencies that thought they had the problem under control have discovered otherwise. The SSA, for instance, has long been touted as one agency that tackled the problem with vigor and skill. Its apparent success in dealing with the problem led to it being held up as a model for other agencies, and SSA administrators held a number of Y2K seminars with personnel from other agencies in which they provided guidance and tips. In 1997, however, the Social Security Administration discovered that millions of lines of code had been overlooked in their efforts. The SSA, it turns out, had done a fine job on correcting its federal system, but it had neglected to carry out the changes in state systems, which are essential for determining eligibility for federal disability payments. Congressional auditors now worry that some of the SSA's systems, which pay out nearly $400 billion in annual benefits, may not be corrected before the Y2K.

Analysts also warn that litigation associated with the Y2K issue could mushroom into a problem of epic dimensions. Maney reported that "litigation resulting from Year 2000 meltdowns will be more costly than asbestos, breast implant, and Superfund cleanup lawsuits combined, several reports say. Total litigation costs could exceed $1 trillion. . . . Litigation could include lawsuits for breach of contract, business interruption or personal injury. There will be shareholder lawsuits if the bug damages the bottom lines and stock prices of companies." In recognition of the possible threat that Y2K poses to the stock market, some members of Congress have even called for legislation that would require publicly traded companies to disclose their degree of Y2K readiness, while large businesses have allocated millions of dollars to addressing the issue.

Other observers, however, are more sanguine about the Y2K problem. They point out that many newer computers and applications will not fall victim to the glitch because of programming changes, and that the usual process of upgrading computer systems has removed many problematic computers from circulation. Other analysts believe that the litigation scenarios are wildly inflated. And others simply do not believe that the glitch itself will be that crippling. "In all but an exceedingly small number of cases, these date bugs will cause little (if any) real damage to corporate networks when the clock strikes midnight

on Dec. 31, 1999," argued Michael Surkan in *PC Week Online*. "Just because a file server has the incorrect date doesn't mean it will cease functioning. The same is true for routers and switches. That's not to say that network date-handling problems won't prove to be a nuisance, but most of them won't shut down your business. . . . When viewed in perspective, many of the year 2000 issues that come up can be calmly dealt with in the new millennium, without the need for crisis management teams today."

ACHIEVING Y2K COMPLIANCE Analysts indicate that single business establishments that need to achieve Y2K compliance can expect to pay about $1 per line of code that was used to create system applications. Jim Keogh, author of *Solving the Year 2000 Problem,* wrote that businesses must take several steps to ensure that they have adequately addressed the issue:

1) Inventory—Programmers (either employees or outside contractors) need to search through the firm for hardware and software that is critical to company operations.

2) Assessment—Each piece of inventory needs to be examined to determine what—if any—impact the year 2000 glitch will have on it.

3) Planning and Repair—This is an evaluation/priority setting step in which the business owner has to determine how and when designated systems will be upgraded.

4) Testing—An important step that is sometimes overlooked by harried businesses, testing is necessary to ensure that no glitches went undetected.

5) Implementation—Completion and installation of the upgrade.

Finally, companies should check with key business partners, vendors, and customers to see if they are making adequate preparations for the Y2K. Some of these establishments will likely be fine, but others may find themselves hamstrung by Y2K. If that is the case, businesses that depend on them are likely to find themselves in trouble as well if they are caught by surprise.

FURTHER READING:

Andrews, Jonathan. "Computer Doomsday." *CA Magazine.* April 1997.

Cane, Alan. "New Computer Timebomb Threatens to Halt Systems." *The Financial Times.* June 17, 1997.

Keogh, Jim. *Solving the Year 2000 Problem.* Boston: AP Professional, 1997.

Khanna, Gopal K. "Gearing Up for the Year 2000." *Journal of Commerce and Commercial.* January 17, 1997.

Maney, Kevin. "Lawyers Circle Over 2000 Time Bomb." *USA Today.* December 2, 1997.

Muhammad, T. K. "The Year 2000 Glitch: Will Your Computer Be Able to Usher in the New Millenium?" *Black Enterprise.* May 1997.

"Save What You Can and Forget the Rest." *Computing.* May 29, 1997.

Surkan, Michael. "What's All the Y2K Panic About?" *PC Week Online.* December 1, 1997.

Yudkowsky, Chaim, and Terry Brock. "Should Your Company Panic about Year 2000?" *Washington Business Journal.* October 18, 1996.

SEE ALSO: Computers and Computer Systems

YOUNG ENTREPRENEURS' ORGANIZATION (YEO)

The Young Entrepreneurs' Organization (YEO) is one of many groups that offer educational opportunities and other kinds of support to young business owners. Membership in such groups has increased dramatically in recent years, as more and more young people have abandoned traditional corporate career paths in favor of the increased autonomy, job security, and financial rewards that are possible through entrepreneuship.

"Times have changed, and today entrepreneurship has become a key career choice for young Americans. Highly publicized corporate downsizings have cast a pall over the traditional path to success, and fueled a general perception that well-paying jobs with room for advancement are scarce," Tariq K. Muhammad wrote in an article for *Black Enterprise.* "The days when professionals could expect to stay with the same company for a lifetime are long gone. Human resources professionals estimate that today's worker will have an average of five to ten career changes in their lifetime. As a result, interest in entrepreneurship has grown."

YEO was founded in 1987 by a group of five successful young entrepreneurs, including the founders of I Can't Believe It's Not Yogurt, the California Closet Company, and Redgate Communications Corporation. The organization grew out of the group's habit of meeting together each year in a tropical locale for vacations. Membership is open to individuals who are under the age of 40 and are the founders, co-founders, or majority shareholders of companies grossing over $1 million annually. According to Barry Henderson in an article for the *Kansas City Business Journal,* YEO grew 40 percent in 1994 and 67 percent in 1995 to exceed 600 members in 40 cities and three countries.

The mission of YEO is to provide its members with **mentoring**, peer **networking**, and educational opportunities. Local chapters hold monthly meetings, as well as sponsor regular educational events or presentations. Many chapters also feature "self-help" forums where groups of about ten entrepreneurs get together to work on common problems faced by small business owners, such as hiring good employees or expanding internationally. "YEO lets me benefit from the experience of my peers, who are also entrepreneurs and have already gone through situations I may be going through," security firm owner Marc Cormier told Muhammad. "When I'm looking to enter new markets, I already have a contact in any part of the world because of my affiliation with YEO."

Another organization that provides support for young entrepreneurs is the National Foundation for Teaching Entrepreneurship (NFTE)—120 Wall Street, 29th Floor, New York, NY 10005, 212-232-3333. NFTE sends successful entrepreneurs into high school classrooms to talk to students about the demands and rewards of starting and running a business. Active in 14 cities, this foundation's programs reach over 4,000 students per year. Many small business owners volunteer their services as teachers out of a desire to pass along advice and information to the next generation of entrepreneurs.

A number of other organizations provide educational programs in entrepreneurship as well. For example, the National Association for the Self-Employed (NASE)—P.O. Box 612067, Dallas, TX 75261, 800-232-NASE—sponsors scholarship programs for young, aspiring entrepreneurs in addition to acting as an advocate for small business owners. The Ewing Marion Kauffman Foundation—4900 Oak Street, Kansas City, MO 64112, 816-932-1000—develops entrepreneurial programs through its Center for Entrepreneurial Leadership. Finally, as many as 800 colleges and universities offer classes or entire programs of study in entrepreneurship.

For more information about YEO and its programs, contact the Young Entrepreneur's Organization at 1010 North Glebe Road, Suite 600, Arlington, VA 22201, 703-527-4500.

FURTHER READING:

Henderson, Barry. "Join the Club." Kansas City Business Journal. May 26, 1995.

Muhammad, Tariq K. "From Buppie to Biz-Wiz: Forget Corporate America—Generation X Is Choosing the Entrepreneurial Path to Success." Black Enterprise. January 1997.

Z

ZONING ORDINANCES

Zoning ordinances are laws that govern activities in townships and other municipalities. These ordinances have to be considered when weighing whether to open a business, whether in a commercial/industrial zone or in your own home.

Most cities and towns are composed of regions that are "zoned" for residential, commercial, or industrial development, and often these zones are subdivided by additional use restrictions (type of business permitted, etc.). Zoning laws and ordinances may affect such varied issues as parking for customers, access for deliveries, the number and types of employees permitted, and the use of signs or other forms of advertising. As a result, people wishing to set up business establishments should check with their city's zoning office and licensing board for restrictions that may apply to the city, or even to their particular neighborhood.

ZONING AND COMMERCIAL BUSINESSES Review of zoning ordinances for areas designated for commercial and/or industrial use is a standard procedure for entrepreneurs seeking to establish a business in such places. In most cases, establishing a business in a building that was previously used for commercial purposes will not run afoul of zoning ordinances for the area. Experts warn, however, that businesses seeking to construct a new facility, acquire an existing building for a new use, or launch extensive remodeling efforts should closely examine local zoning and building codes. In instances where local zoning laws present a problem, the business owner has the option of filing for a zone variance, a conditional-use permit, or a zone change. All three of these options have their drawbacks. A zone change amounts to a permanent change in the zoning of the property; this is obviously desirable, but the procedure to successfully trigger such a change is generally a cumbersome one that goes through City Hall. Variances and conditional-use permits, meanwhile, are in essence requests for special permission to use the property for a purpose other than for which it was zoned. Such permits are often expensive to obtain, and can take two to four months to go through (if they are even approved).

ZONING AND HOME BUSINESSES Checking into local zoning ordinances is a step often overlooked by owners of **home-based businesses** as well. Such neglect can prove troublesome down the line. Janet Attard noted in *The Home Office and Small Business Answer Book,* "zoning laws are established locally, often at the township, city, or village level. Furthermore, each town or village decides for itself what types of home businesses it will allow. Thus in one community you might be able to run a home business that has up to two employees while in another community the same business might be restricted from having any employees. In still another community you might be able to have a homebased business if you are a fisherman or carpenter but not if you are a real estate agent or insurance broker."

Most zoning ordinances restricting home offices in residential neighborhoods were originally designed to protect residential neighborhoods from becoming cluttered with commercial activity and thus maintain the family-friendly flavor and atmosphere of the area. In the past, these laws often were strictly interpreted to keep residents from conducting any sort of business from their home, even if it did not have a visible impact on the rest of the neighborhood. Today, the explosion in home-based business start-ups has sparked a reevaluation of zoning laws in residential areas, but many of the old zoning laws remain on the books.

"The first step to opening a business in your home is to check with the zoning or building codes office in your community," stated Pamala M. Harding in *Black Enterprise.* "Your local city hall or courthouse should be able to provide you with this information. There, you will find out what permits you need to apply for and how much they will cost. Permits range from $25 to more than $100 in some areas of the country." If the community's zoning laws present a problem, home-based business owners have the same options as other business owners—they can apply for a variance or a permanent zoning change.

Observers admit that millions of home-based businesses operate for years in violation of zoning laws, and that many of those businesses prosper without ever running into problems. Indeed, many communities simply ignore violations unless a neighborhood resident or someone else complains. These complaints may be triggered by utterly trivial factors—unhappiness with the frequency with which you mow your lawn, for instance, or anger about some real or imagined social slight—but in the eyes of the law, the motivations behind the complaint will generally be of little consequence. "You cannot assume . . . that it is OK for you to disregard local law because *some* town boards don't enforce regulations and *some* people get away with operating on the sly," said Attard. "If there are laws prohibiting your type of home business, it will only take one complaint to plunge you into a pot of legal hot water."

FURTHER READING:

Attard, Janet. *The Home Office and Small Business Answer Book.* New York: Henry Holt, 1993.

Eliason, Carol. *The Business Plan for Home-Based Business.* Washington, D.C.: Small Business Administration, 1991.

Frank, Michael. "Homework." *Planning.* June 1993.

Hardin, Pamala M. "Keep Your Firm from Zoning Out: Running Your Business from Your Basement May Get You Zapped with Hefty Fines." *Black Enterprise.* March 1996.

SEE ALSO: Business Site Selection; Relocation; Renovation

ENCYCLOPEDIA *of*
Small Business

A

Articles of Incorporation (*See Also* Incorporation) **I: 45–46**, 127, 132, 502, **II:** 865, 894
ASEAN **I:** 455
Assembly Line Methods **I: 46–47**
Assessment tests **II:** 985
Asset **I:** 34
Asset sale **I:** 128, **II:** 894
Asset turnover ratio **I:** 49, **II:** 938
Asset utilization ratio **I:** 49
Assets (*See Also* Liabilities) **I:** 4, **47–49**, 55, 217, 263, 420, **II:** 591, 642, 676, 693, 804, 855, 920, 926, 940, 999
Associations. *See* Business Associations.
Assumptions (*See Also* Accounting Methods) **I: 49–50**
Audiovisual training **II:** 979
Audit report **I:** 395
Audits **I:** 430
Automation (*See Also* Computer-Aided Design; Robotics; Training and Development) **I: 50–52**

B

Balance Sheet (*See Also* Financial Statements; Income Statements) **I:** 4, **55–56**, 126, 134, 419, 423, 426, 497, **II:** 675–76, 784, 894
Bankers' acceptances **II:** 657
Bankruptcy (*See Also* Business Failure and Dissolution) **I:** 8, **56–58**, 97, **II:** 691, 755
Banks and Banking (*See Also* Loans; Venture Capital) **I: 58–60**
Bar Coding **I: 60–63**
Barriers to Market Entry (*See Also* Competitive Analysis; Emerging Markets; Market Research) **I: 63–64**
Bartering (*See Also* Networking) **I: 64–66**
Bartering networks **I:** 64
Behavioral interviewing **I:** 362
Benchmarking **I:** 66, **II:** 822, 936
Better Business Bureaus (*See Also* Business Ethics) **I: 67–68**, 196
Bid pricing **I:** 173
Bilateral contract **I:** 199
Bills of lading **I:** 310
Black Lung Act **II:** 1026
Bonds (*See Also* Debt Financing) **I: 68**, 135, 146, 163, 223, **II:** 835, 857
Bonus payments **II:** 1001
Bonus programs **I:** 343
Bookkeeping **I:** 6, **68–69**, 178
Bottom-up forecasting **II:** 875
Brainstorming (*See Also* Innovation) **I: 69–70**, **II:** 819
Brand franchise extension **I:** 72
Brand identification **II:** 926
Brand image **II:** 926
Brand loyalty **I:** 71, 287, **II:** 632, 873, 926
Brand recognition **II:** 717

Brands and Brand Names (*See Also* Marketing; Trademarks and Copyrights) **I: 70–73**
Breadboard **II:** 809
Break-Even Analysis (*See Also* Budgets and Budgeting) **I: 73–74**, 431
BRTA. *See* Business Responds to AIDS Program.
Budget of cost of goods sold **I:** 79
Budgeted balance sheet **I:** 80
Budgeted income statement **I:** 79
Budgeted statement of cash flows **I:** 80
Budgets and Budgeting (*See Also* Business Planning) **I: 74–80**
Bullying **II:** 1029
Bureau of Labor Statistics **II:** 920
Bureau of the Census **II:** 991
Bureaucracy. *See* Organization Theory.
Business acquisitions **I:** 296
Business Appraisers **I: 80–81**
Business Associations **I: 81–82, II:** 677, 680
Business Brokers (*See Also* Buying an Existing Business; Mergers and Acquisitions; Selling a Business) **I: 82–84, II:** 895
Business Communications (*See Also* Business Literature; Business Press) **I:** 233 .
Business Cycle (*See Also* Government Procurement) **I: 84–87, II:** 828
Business Education (*See Also* Apprenticeship Programs; Training and Development) **I: 87–89**
Business Entertaining. *See* Expense Accounts.
Business Ethics **I: 89–91**, 447, **II:** 913
Business Expansion (*See Also* Buying an Existing Business; Career and Family; Employee Hiring; Entrepreneurship; Work Force) **I: 91–95**, 297
Business Failure and Dissolution (*See Also* Cash Flow Statements; Customer Retention; Strategy; Undercapitalization) **I: 95–97**
Business for Social Responsibility **I:** 91
Business Hours (*See Also* Customer Service; Target Markets) **I: 98–99**
Business Incubators **I: 99–101, II:** 669
Business Information (*See Also* Business Literature; Business Press) **I: 101–03**
Business Insurance (*See Also* Disability Insurance; Employment Practices Insurance; Health Insurance Options) **I: 103–06, II:** 1026
Business Interruption Insurance (*See Also* Business Insurance; Disability Insurance; Risk Management) **I:** 105, **106–07**
Business Literature (*See Also* Business Information) **I: 107–08**
Business Name **I: 108–09, II:** 889
Business Opportunity Plan (BOP) **I:** 105, 364

Business Plan (*See Also* Budgets and Budgeting; Business Planning; Strategy) **I:** 101, **109–13**, 129, 141, 193, 387, 391, 483, **II:** 598, 784, 900, 1006–07
Business Planning (*See Also* Budgets and Budgeting) **I:** 96, **113–18**, 410, **II:** 784
Business Press **I: 118–19**, 512
Business Proposals **I: 119–20**
Business Resource Centers (BRC) **II:** 651
Business Responds to AIDS Program **I:** 30
Business Site Selection (*See Also* Leasing Property; Relocation; Zoning Ordinances) **I: 120–24, II:** 1025
Business Travel (*See Also* Expense Accounts; Tax Deductible Business Expenses) **I:** 64, **124–26**
Buy/sell agreements **I:** 162, **II:** 750
Buyer-supplier relationships **II:** 816
Buying allowance **II:** 885
Buying an Existing Business (*See Also* Business Brokers; Choosing a Small Business; Franchising; Selling a Business; Valuation) **I: 126–29**

C

C Corporation (*See Also* Debt Financing; Equity Financing; Incorporation) **I: 131–33**, 154, 299, 501, **II:** 596, 804, 865, 951, 954
CAD/CAM. *See* Computer-Aided Design and Computer-Aided Manufacturing.
Cafeteria plan **I:** 432
Capital (*See Also* Banks and Banking; Private Placement of Securities; Venture Capital) **I:** 35, 58, 91, **133–35**, 143, 217, 221, 249, 275, 369, 379, 403, 418–19, 512, 555, 557, **II:** 643, 647, 667, 676, 693, 717, 733, 779, 835, 856, 861, 887, 918, 927, 938, 987
Capital asset pricing model (CAPM) **II:** 923
Capital expenditures budget **I:** 79
Capital Gain/Loss (*See Also* Capital; Tax Planning) **I: 135–37**
Capital gains tax **I:** 136
Capital Loss. *See* Capital Gain/Loss.
Capital requirements **I:** 63
Capitalization **II:** 855
CAPLines loans **II:** 995
CAPLines program **II:** 992
Career and Family (*See Also* Child Care; Flexible Work Programs) **I: 137–39**
Career Changing. *See* Career Planning and Changing.
Career development **II:** 980
Career planning **II:** 618
Career Planning and Changing (*See Also* Buying an Existing Business;

ENCYCLOPEDIA OF SMALL BUSINESS

Articles of Incorporation (*See Also* Incorporation) **I: 45–46**, 127, 132, 502, **II:** 865, 894

Employee Performance Appraisals (*See Also* Employee Compensation) **I:** **335–38**

Employee Privacy (*See Also* Human Resource Management) **I:** **338–41**, 494

Employee recognition programs **I:** 342

Employee Registration Procedures (*See Also* Employee Hiring; Tax Withholding) **I:** **341**

Employee relations **II:** 812

Employee retention **I:** 240, 434, **II:** 868

Employee Retirement Income Security Act (ERISA) **I:** 348

Employee Retirement Income Security Act of 1974 (ERISA) **I:** 324, 417, 442, **II:** 807, 852

Employee Reward Systems (*See Also* Employee Compensation; Employee Motivation) **I:** **341–45**, 481

Employee Rights (*See Also* Employee Benefits; Labor Unions and Small Business) **I:** 338, **345–46**, 493

Employee Screening (*See Also* Employee Hiring; Employment Interviewing; Liabilities) **I:** **346–47**

Employee Stock Ownership Plans (*See Also* Buying an Existing Business; Employee Motivation; Equity Financing; Retirement Planning; Succession Plans) **I:** 80, 92, 319, 380, **347–49**, **II:** 592, 896, 933

Employee Strikes (*See Also* Labor Unions) **I:** **349–51**

Employee Termination (*See Also* Constructive Discharge; Employee Manuals; Human Resource Policies) **I:** 300, **351–54**, **II:** 685

Employee Theft (*See Also* Computer Crime; Drug Testing; Employee Screening; Employee Termination; Facility Management; Office Security) **I:** 317, **354–57**, **II:** 711

Employees' morale **I:** 350

Employer Identification Number **I:** **357–58**, **II:** 889, 919

Employing Minors (*See Also* Employee Hiring; Employment Interviewing) **I:** **358–60**

Employment Applications (*See Also* Employee Hiring; Human Resource Policies) **I:** **360–61**, 362

Employment Eligibility Verification Form (I-9) **I:** 341

Employment Interviewing (*See Also* Employee Hiring; Employee Screening; Recruiting) **I:** **361–64**

Employment Practices Liability Insurance **I:** **364**

Employment Tax Credit **II:** 944

Employment visas **I:** 31

Empowerment **II:** 801, 821

Empowerment Zones (*See Also* Community Development Corporations; Targeted Jobs Tax Credit) **I:** **364–66**

Empowerment Zones and Enterprise Communities **II:** 994

Empowerment Zones and Enterprise Communities Act of 1993 **I:** 364

Ending inventory budget **I:** 78

Entrepreneurial Couples (*See Also* Career and Family; Family-owned Business) **I:** **366–68**

Entrepreneurship (*See Also* Business Planning; Choosing a Small Business; Organizational Growth; Organizational Development) **I:** 99, **368–73**, 544, **II:** 1024

Environmental Impact Statement (EIS) **I:** 374, 377

Environmental Law and Business (*See Also* Green Production) **I:** **373–76**

Environmental Marketing. *See* Green Marketing.

Environmental Protection Agency (*See Also* Environmental Law and Business; Green Production) **I:** 373, **376–78**, 462, 490, 506, **II:** 696, 833, 838

Environmental testing laboratories **II:** 965

EPA. *See* Environmental Protection Agency.

Equal Credit Opportunity Act **I:** 227

Equal Employment Act of 1972 **II:** 831

Equal Employment Opportunity Act of 1972 **I:** 26

Equal Employment Opportunity Commission (*See Also* Affirmative Action) **I:** 26, 361, **378–79**, 495, **II:** 900

Equal Pay Act of 1963 **I:** 324, 378, 496

Equipment financing and leasing **I:** 418

Equipment Leasing. *See* Leasing, Equipment.

Equity **II:** 856

Equity Financing (*See Also* Initial Public Offering; Investor Relations and Reporting; Stocks) **I:** 135, 248, 299, **379–81**, **II:** 860

Equity securities **II:** 920

Ergonomics (*See Also* Workplace Safety) **I:** **381–82**

ERISA. *See* Employee Retirement Income Security Act.

ESOP. *See* Employee Stock Ownership Plans.

Estate planning **I:** 405, **II:** 642

Estate Taxes (*See Also* Retirement Planning; Succession Plans; Tax Planning) **I:** **382–83**, 405, 411, **II:** 594

Estate valuation **II:** 923

Estimated tax payments **II:** 955

Estimated taxes **II:** 951

Ethical business practices audit **I:** 525

Ethics. *See* Business Ethics.

Eurodollar deposits **II:** 657

European Article Number **I:** 61

European Union **I:** 455

EWCP. *See* Export Working Capital Program.

Exempt employees **II:** 740

Exit interviews **I:** 190

Expanded Leave **I:** 433

Expansion capital **I:** 92–93

Expense Accounts (*See Also* Record Retention; Tax-Deductible Business Expenses) **I:** **383–84**, 494, **II:** 869

Expenses **I:** 497

Experience and Learning Curves **I:** **384–85**

Exponential smoothing **II:** 876

Export Administration Act **I:** 532

Export-Import Bank (*See Also* Emerging Markets; Exporting; Exporting—Financing and Pricing Issues) **I:** **385–87**

Export-Import Bank of the United States **I:** 392

Export Legal Assistance Network (ELAN) **II:** 993

Export Working Capital Program (EWCP) **I:** 385, **II:** 992, 996

Exporting (*See Also* Exporting—Financing and Pricing Issues; International Marketing) **I:** **387–90**, 534, **II:** 651

Exporting—Financing and Pricing Issues (*See Also* International Exchange Rate; International Marketing; Pricing) **I:** **390–94**

Express contracts **I:** 199

Extended warranties **II:** 1017

External Audits **I:** **394–96**, 523

F

FA$TRAK loans **II:** 992, 996

Facility Layout and Design (*See Also* Construction; Facility Management; Renovation) **I:** **397–99**

Facility maintenance **I:** 64

Facility Management (*See Also* Facility Layout and Design) **I:** 304, **399–402**

Facsimile Transmission (*See Also* Written Communication) **I:** **402–03**, **II:** 704

Factoring **I:** 250, 392, **403–05**, 418

Fair Credit Reporting Act **I:** 227, 414

Fair Debt Collection Practices Act **I:** 227

Fair Labor Standards Act (FLSA) **I:** 170, 323, 358, 496, 542, **II:** 577, 740

Fair Packaging and Labeling Act of 1966 **I:** 24, 414, **II:** 744, 881

Fair use **I:** 203

Family and Medical Leave Act (*See Also* Health Insurance Options) **I:** **407–08**, **II:** 768

Family Friendly Workplace Act **I:** 170

"Family-friendly" policies **I:** 138

Family Limited Partnership (*See Also* Family-owned Business; Partnerships; Succession Plans) **I:** **405–07**

Family-Owned Businesses (*See Also* Career and Family; Family Limited Partnership; Nepotism) **I:** 155, 161, **408–12**, **II:** 638, 674, 896, 931

Farmers Home Administration (FHA) **II:** 998

FASB. *See* Financial Accounting Standards Board).

FASB 95 **I:** 144

Faxes **I:** 178

FCC. *See* Federal Communications Commission.

FCPA. *See* Foreign Corrupt Practices Act.

Feasibility Study (*See Also* Business Planning) **I:** 214, **412–13**

Federal Acquisition Regulation (FAR) **I:** 459

Federal Acquisitions Reform Act **I:** 459

Federal agency notes **II:** 657

Federal Communications Commission **I:** 27, **II:** 956

Federal contracts **I:** 305

Federal Employees Compensation Act **II:** 1026

Federal Insurance Contribution Act **I:** 415

Federal Insurance Contribution Act (FICA) taxes **II:** 754, 892

Federal Mediation Conciliation Service **I:** 44

Federal Procurement Regulation (FPR) **I:** 459

Federal Property and Administrative Services Act of 1949 **I:** 459

Federal Reserve Board **I:** 197, 521, **II:** 581

Federal Reserve System **II:** 659

Federal Tax Withholding Form (W-4) **I:** 341

Federal Trade Commission (*See Also* Consumer Advocacy) **I:** 23, 227, **413–15**, 463, **II:** 610, 881, 920, 1015

Federal Unemployment Tax (FUTA) **II:** 754

FEI. *See* Financial Executives Institute.

FHA. *See* Farmers Home Administration.

FICA Taxes (*See Also* Employing Minors; Medicare and Medicaid; Self-Employment Contributions Act; Tax Withholding) **I:** 415–16, **II:** 950, 954–55

Fictitious name **II:** 918

Fidelity bonds **I:** 357

Fiduciary Duty **I:** 416–17

FIFO. *See* First-in, First-out Method.

FIFO (first-in, first out) **I:** 551

Finance and Financial Management **I:** 418–19

Finance Companies **I:** 250, 417–18

Financial accounting **I:** 3

Financial Accounting Standards Board (FASB) **I:** 3, 144, 285, 497, 523

Financial Analysis (*See Also* Finance and Financial Management) **I:** 419–22

Financial audit **I:** 525

Financial budget **I:** 77, 79

Financial controls **I:** 356

Financial Executives Institute (FEI) **I:** 523

Financial intermediation **I:** 224

Financial modeling **II:** 785

Financial Planners **I:** 422–23

Financial projections **II:** 784

Financial Ratios (*See Also* Financial Analysis) **I:** 49, 127, 421, **423–26**, **II:** 675, 785, 854

Financial Statements (*See Also* Financial Analysis) **I:** 4, 37, 69, 126, 152, 264, 391, 419, **426–30**, **II:** 598, 717, 739, 894, 998

Financial statements audit **I:** 394

Financing **I:** 225, 403, **II:** 647, 653, 733, 809, 873, 887, 913

Firewalls **II:** 712

First-Class mail **II:** 767

First-in, first-out (FIFO) method **II:** 785, 950

Fixed and Variable Expenses **I:** **430–31**, **II:** 774

Fixed annuities **I:** 41

Fixed assets **I:** 48, 55

Fixed budget **I:** 77

Fixed costs **I:** 218, 430

Fixed expenses **I:** 73

Flex-time **I:** 309

Flexible Benefit Plan (*See Also* Employee Benefits) **I:** 431–33

Flexible budget **I:** 77

Flexible manufacturing systems **I:** 50

Flexible spending account **I:** 432

Flexible Work Programs (*See Also* Employee Motivation) **I:** 320, 336, **433–36**, 452

Flexplace **I:** 433

Flextime **I:** 433, 494

Flood insurance **I:** 282

Flow Charts (*See Also* Management Information Systems) **I:** **436–37**

FLSA. *See* Fair Labor Standards Act of 1938.

FMLA. *See* Family and Medical Leave Act.

Focus Groups (*See Also* Marketing; Market Research; Product Positioning) **I:** 437–39, **II:** 621, 626, 631

Focus strategy **II:** 926

Forecasting (*See Also* Strategy; Market Research) **I:** 75, 116, **439–41**

Foreign Corrupt Practices Act (FCPA) **I:** 523, 532

Foreign exchange (FX) rate **I:** 528

Foreign Sovereign Immunities Act of 1976 (FSIA) **I:** 532

Foreign stock **II:** 924

Foreign venture capital **II:** 1006

Found-Space Displays **II:** 640

401(k) Plans (*See Also* Retirement Planning; Employee Benefits; Simplified Employee Pensions) **I:** 41, 320, 343, 432, **441–45**, **II:** 757, 807, 852, 905

Franchising (*See Also* Buying an Existing Business; Choosing a Small

Business) **I:** 92, 141, 161, **445–49**, 534

Franchising and Business Opportunity Ventures Trade Regulation Rules and Subsequent Guidelines **I:** 448

Fraud audit **I:** 525

Freelance Employment/Independent Contractors (*See Also* Employee Hiring; Self-Employment; Tax-Deductible Business Expenses; Work Force) **I:** 449–51

FTC. *See* Federal Trade Commission.

Full costing **I:** 218

Full-Time and Part-Time Employees (*See Also* Employee Benefits; Employee Hiring; Work Force) **I:** 451–53

Fundraising **II:** 681

G

GAAP. *See* Generally accepted accounting principles.

Gainsharing **II:** 801, 1002

GATT. *See* General Agreement on Tariffs and Trade.

GDP. *See* Gross Domestic Product.

General Agreement on Tariffs and Trade (*See Also* International Law; Tariffs) **I:** 376, **455–56**, 517, 531, 536, 548, **II:** 945

General partnership **II:** 746

Generally accepted accounting principles **I:** 3, 264, 498, **II:** 950

Generational marketing **I:** 262

Genetic testing **I:** 339

Global Marketing Strategy (GMS) **I:** 536

Globalization **II:** 913

GNP. *See* Gross National Product.

Good Housekeeping Consumers' Policy **I:** 456

Good Housekeeping magazine **I:** 456

Good Housekeeping Seal (*See Also* Warranties and Guarantees) **I:** **456–57**

Goodwill (*See Also* Buying an Existing Business; Selling a Business) **I:** 34, 145, 162, 211, 230, 240, **457–58**, **II:** 747, 894, 1000

Government bonds **II:** 857

Government contracts **I:** 458

Government Procurement **I:** **458–62**, **II:** 1024

Green Marketing (*See Also* Business Ethics; Corporate Sponsorship; Green Production; Product Life Cycle) **I:** **462–65**

Green Production (*See Also* Business Ethics; Environmental Law and Business; Green Marketing) **I:** **465–67**

Green Seal **I:** 464

Greenmail **II:** 645

Gross Domestic Product (*See Also* Gross National Product; Gross Product Originating) **I:** **467**, 468, 510

Limited partnership **II:** 746
Liquidity **I:** 143, 147, 420
Liquidity ratios **I:** 421, 424
List broker **II:** 612
List compiler **II:** 612
List manager **II:** 612
LLC. *See* Limited Liability Company.
LLP. *See* Limited Liability Partnership.
Loan **I:** 48
Loan Proposals (*See Also* Loans) **I:** 129, **II: 598–99**
Loans (*See Also* Loan Proposals) **I:** 35–36, 135, 151, 226, 248, 417, 521, **II: 599–602**, 667, 693, 918, 940, 995, 1003
Local Area Networks (*See Also* Computers and Computer Systems; Management Information Systems; Telecommunications) **I:** 187, **II: 602–06**, 958, 1022
Logistics Management. *See* Distribution Channels; Physical Distribution; Transportation.
Long-range plans **I:** 114
Long-term debts **I:** 420
Long-Term Disability **I:** 453
Long-term leases **II:** 585
Longshoremen's and Harbor Workers' Compensation Act **II:** 1026
Loss Leader Pricing (*See Also* Pricing; Retail Trade) **II: 606**, 775
Low-cost supplier strategy **II:** 632, 880
Low Documentation Loan (LowDoc) program **II:** 992, 995
Lump-sum payments **II:** 1001

M

Macro-marketing **II:** 630
Magnuson-Moss Consumer Warranty Act **II:** 1015
Magnuson-Moss Warranty-Federal Trade Commission Improvement Act **I:** 414
Mail-Order Business **I:** 272, **II: 607–11**
Mailing Lists (*See Also* Advertising Strategy) **I:** 269, 274, 312, **II:** 609, **611–13**
Main Street Investment **II:** 993
MANA. *See* Manufacturers' Agents National Association.
Managed care plans **I:** 476, 478
Management accounting **I:** 3, 219
Management analysis **I:** 513
Management by Objectives (*See Also* Business Planning; Employee Performance Appraisal) **II: 613–15**
Management Education. *See* Business Education.
Management Information Systems (*See Also* Computers and Computer Systems) **I:** 255, 265, **II: 615–16**
Management rights **I:** 350
Management Team Growth (*See Also* Business Expansion; Employee Hiring; Managing Organizational Change) **II: 616–17**

Managing Organizational Change (*See Also* Business Expansion; Organizational Growth; Organizational Structure; Training and Development) **II: 617–19**
Manuals. *See* Employee Manuals.
Manufacturer brands **I:** 71
Manufacturers' Agents (*See Also* Freelance Employment/Independent Contractors; Sales Commissions) **II: 619–21**, 761
Manufacturers' Agents National Association (MANA) **II:** 619
Manufacturer's suggested retail price **II:** 774
Market Analysis (*See Also* Competitive Analysis; Industry Analysis; Market Research) **I:** 111, **II: 621–22**
Market potential **II:** 872
Market Questionnaire **II: 622–23**, 1018
Market Research (*See Also* Brands and Brand Names; Market Questionnaires; Point-of-Sale Systems) **I:** 439, **II:** 621–22, **623–26**, 626, 630, 793, 800, 876
Market Segment Specialization Program (MSSP) **I:** 527–28
Market Segmentation (*See Also* Marketing; Product Positioning; Target Markets) **II:** 623, 625, **626–28**, 631, 798
Market Share (*See Also* Competitive Analysis) **I:** 12, 14, 74, 91, **II: 628–29**, 717, 797, 927
Marketing (*See Also* Brands and Brand Names; Market Analysis; Product Positioning) **I:** 64, 178, 212, 216, 280, 559, **II:** 617, 621, 623, **630–33**, 640, 643, 778, 798, 811, 827, 881, 913, 943, 1017, 1021
Marketing channels **I:** 293
Markup (*See Also* Costs; Profit Margin) **II: 633–34**
Mass marketing **I:** 261, **II:** 626
Master budget **I:** 77
Master of Business Administration (MBA) **I:** 87
Material Safety Data Sheet (MSDS) **II:** 701
Materials handling **II:** 762
MBA. *See* Master of Business Administration.
MBDC. *See* Minority Business Development Centers.
MBOC. *See* Minority Business Opportunity Committee.
Medical Benefits **I:** 452
Medical savings accounts (MSAs) **I:** 475
Medical/dental benefits **I:** 494
Medicare and Medicaid (*See Also* Self-Employment Contributions Act (SECA)) **II: 634–35**
Medicare Supplemental Insurance **II:** 634
Meetings **I:** 542, **II: 635–39**, 718
Mentoring **II: 639–40**, 1039

Merchandise Displays **II: 640–41**
Merchant wholesalers **II:** 1020
Merger and acquisition consultants **II:** 895
Mergers and Acquisitions (*See Also* Buying an Existing Business; Investor Relations and Reporting; Stocks; Tax Planning) **I:** 110, 458, 512, **II: 641–46**
Merit pay increases **I:** 342
MESBIC. *See* Minority Enterprise Small Business Investment Company.
Metropolitan Statistical Area (*See Also* Business Site Selection; Census Data) **II: 646**
Mezzanine Financing (*See Also* Business Expansion) **II: 647–49**
Micro-marketing **II:** 630
Minimum Wage **I:** 322–23, 542, **II: 649–50**
Minority Business Development Agency **II: 650–51**, 991
Minority Business Development Centers (MBDC) **II:** 651
Minority Business Opportunity Committees (MBOC) **II:** 651
Minority Enterprise Small Business Investment Companies (MESBICs) **II:** 910, 993, 1008
Minority-Owned Businesses (*See Also* Community Relations; Government Procurement) **II:** 650, **651–55**
Minority Prequalification Loan Program **II:** 996
Mission. *See* Mission Statement; Strategy.
Mission Statement **II: 655–56**, 664
Mistake-proofing **II:** 824
Mobile businesses **II:** 656
Mobile Office (*See Also* Business Travel; Communication Systems; Customer Service) **II: 656–57**
Modified accelerated cost recovery system **I:** 264
Modular Assembly **I:** 47
Money Market Instruments **I:** 47, 422, **II: 657–58**
Money purchase pension plans **II:** 854
Money Supply **II: 658–61**
Mortgage bond **I:** 222
Mortgage loans **II:** 601
Mortgage refinancing **II:** 836
Motivation. *See* Employee Motivation.
MSDS. *See* Material Safety Data Sheets.
Multi-buy promotions **I:** 290
Multicultural Work Force (*See Also* Alien Employees; Training and Development) **II: 661–65**
Multiple Employer Trust (*See Also* Employee Benefits) **II: 665–66**
Mutual funds **I:** 41

Term life insurance **II:** 594

Term loans **I:** 223

Testing Laboratories (*See Also* Operations Management; Workplace Safety) **II: 965–68**, 988

360 degree feedback **I:** 337

Time-period assumption **I:** 49

Time value of money **I:** 418, **II:** 770

Toll-Free Telephone Calls (*See Also* Corporate Image; Customer Retention; Customer Service) **II:** 607, **968–69**

Toll-Free Telephone Numbers **I:** 270

Top-down forecasting method **II:** 875

Topologically Integrated Geographic Encoding and Referencing **I:** 149

Tort liability **II:** 680

Total cost of ownership (TCO) **I:** 186, **II:** 815

Total Quality Control (TQC) **II:** 820

Total Quality Management (*See Also* Quality Circles) **I:** 492, **II:** 730, 824, **969–71**

Toxic Substances Control Act (TOSCA) **I:** 377

TQC. *See* Total Quality Control.

TQM. *See* Total quality management.

Trade Compliance Center **II:** 991

Trade credit **I:** 223, 250

Trade journals **I:** 102

Trade secrets **I:** 517, **II:** 678, 808

Trade Shows (*See Also* Business Associations; Networking; Personal Selling) **I:** 124, **II:** 881, **971–74**

Trademarks (*See Also* Inventions and Patents) **I:** 109, 457, 517, **II: 974–77**, 999

Trademarks and Copyrights **I:** 80

Trading with the Enemy Act **I:** 532

Training **II:** 685

Training and Development **I:** 490, **II:** 888, **977–81**

Transaction processing systems **II:** 615

Transactional databases **I:** 246

Transportation (*See Also* Business Site Selection; Distribution Channels; Transportation of Exports) **I:** 295, **II:** 744, 762, 789, **981–82**, 990

Transportation of Exports (*See Also* Exporting; Transportation) **II: 982–84**

Travel. *See* Business Travel.

Travel agent **I:** 125

Travel and tourism **II:** 862, 908

Treasury bills **I:** 223, **II:** 657, 857

Treaty of Rome **I:** 531

Trend projection analysis **II:** 876

Trucking **II:** 763

Trust companies **I:** 58

Trust Fund Recovery Penalty **I:** 416, **II:** 754

Trust Indenture Act of 1939 **II:** 886

Truth in Lending Act **I:** 36, 227, 414, **II:** 881

Tuition Assistance Programs (*See Also* Tax-deductible Business Expenses; Training and Development) **I:** 432, 494, **II: 984–86**

Turnover **I:** 238, **II:** 984, 1027

U

U.S. Agency for International Development **I:** 392

U.S. Bureau of Census **I:** 149, **II:** 920

U.S. Bureau of Labor Statistics **I:** 196

U.S. Chamber of Commerce **II:** 695

U.S. Department of Commerce **I:** 45, 73, 251, 388, **II:** 581, 650, 753, **990–91**, 993

U.S. Department of Labor **I:** 26, 32, 43, 474, **II:** 699

U.S. Department of the Treasury **I:** 526

U.S. Economic Survey **I:** 149

U. S. Environmental Protection Agency. *See* Environmental Protection Agency (EPA).

U.S. Export Assistance Centers (USEACs) **II:** 993

U.S. Hispanic Chamber of Commerce **II:** 654

U.S. Office of Consumer Affairs **I:** 196

U.S. Pan Asian American Chamber of Commerce **II:** 654

U.S. Postal Service **II:** 610, 766

U.S. Public Health Service **I:** 474

U. S. Securities and Exchange Commission. *See* Securities and Exchange Commission.

U.S. Small Business Administration (*See Also* Disaster Assistance Loans; U.S. Small Business Administration Guaranteed Loans) **I:** 5, 101, 141, 151, 250, 281, 305, 366, 385, 388, 391, 459, **II:** 639, 653, 667, 693, 900, 906, 910, **991–95**, 995, 1008, 1024

U.S. Small Business Administration Guaranteed Loans **II: 995–98**

UAW. *See* United Auto Workers.

UCC. *See* Uniform Commercial Code.

UL certified **II:** 988

UL listed **II:** 988

UL recognized **II:** 988

Undercapitalization (*See Also* Debt Financing; Equity Financing; Nontraditional Financing Sources) **II: 987–88**

Underwriters Laboratories **II: 988–89**

Unemployment benefits **I:** 189

Unfair labor practices strikes **I:** 349

UNICITRAL. *See* United Nations Commission on International Trade Law.

Uniform Code Council **I:** 60

Uniform Commercial Code **II:** 870, **989–90**, 1016

Uniform Fiduciary Act **I:** 416

Uniform Franchise Offering Circular **I:** 447

Uniform Partnership Act **II:** 746, 750

Uniform Product Liability Act **II:** 794

Uniform Trustees' Powers Act **I:** 416

Uniformed Services Employment Reemployment Rights Act of 1994 **I:** 363

Unilateral contract **I:** 199

Union organizing **II:** 577

Unions. *See* Labor Unions; Labor Unions and Small Business.

Unit-of-measure assumption **I:** 49

United Automobile Workers (UAW) **II:** 572

United Nations Commission on International Trade Law (UNCITRAL) **I:** 533

United States and Foreign Commercial Service **I:** 388

United States Coast Guard **I:** 377

Unitizing **II:** 765

Universal life insurance **II:** 595

Universal Product Code (UPC) (*See Also* Bar Coding) **I:** 60, **II:** 765, 827

Unsolicited proposals **I:** 119

UPC. *See* Universal Product Code.

Urban Revitalization **II:** 653

USEAC. *See* U.S. Export Assistance Centers.

Utility Patents **I:** 546

V

Valuation (*See Also* Buying an Existing Business; Selling a Business) **I:** 162, 291, **II:** 894, 923, **999–1001**, 1005

Value-added network (VAN) **I:** 311

Variable annuities **I:** 41

Variable costs **I:** 218, 430

Variable expenses **I:** 73

Variable Pay (*See Also* Employee Compensation; Employee Reward Systems; Sales Commissions) **I:** 343, **II: 1001–03**

VEBA. *See* Voluntary Employees' Beneficiary Association.

Venture Capital (*See Also* Business Proposals; Business Planning; Equity Financing; Risk and Return) **I:** 35, 380, **II:** 671, 693, 888, 910, **1003–06**, 1006, 1008

Venture capital fairs **II:** 1004

Venture Capital Networks (*See Also* Angel Investors; Equity Financing; Venture Capital Organizations) **II: 1006–07**

Venture Capital Organizations (*See Also* Angel Investors; Venture Capital Networks) **II:** 1006, **1008–11**

Vertical merger **II:** 642

Video Advertising. *See* Advertising Media—Video.

Vienna Sale Convention **II:** 870

Violence in the Workplace (*See Also* Employee Hiring; Employee Termination; Human Resource Policies; Office Security) **II: 1011–12**

Virtual offices **II:** 960

Virtual Reality Computer Simulations (*See Also* Computers and Computer Systems; Product Development) **II: 1012–13**

Visionary forecast **II:** 875

Visual aids **II:** 719